ACTORS
ON ACTING

Actors on Acting

The Theories,
Techniques, and Practices
of the World's Great Actors,
Told in Their Own Words

EDITED BY Toby Cole AND
Helen Krich Chinoy

CROWN PUBLISHERS, INC.
NEW YORK

Printed in the United States of America

First Edition: Seven Printings

Published simultaneously in Canada
by General Publishing Company Limited

1 0 9 8

ACKNOWLEDGMENTS

We wish to record our gratitude to the following libraries and their staffs who placed within our reach the ramified theatre literature on which this collection is based: The Theatre Collection and Fifty-Eighth Street Branch of the New York Public Library; the Brander Matthews Dramatic Museum and Library of Columbia University; the Yale, Harvard, Toronto and Michigan university libraries; and the libraries of Smith College, the American Russian Institute and the Museum of Modern Art.

We would like to thank here, too, the many publishers who have granted us permission to quote and reprint from their publications.

To Stella Adler, Erwin Piscator, Lynn Fontanne, Eduardo De Filippo, Joseph Chaikin, Judith Malina and Julian Beck, we are indebted for articles which they wrote specifically for this book.

For having made available to us material in their possession we wish to acknowledge our gratitude to the following individuals and institutions: Jean-Louis Barrault, Eric Bentley, Helen Black, Alfred Harbage, Walter Huston, Paul Meyer, Michael Redgrave, Ashton Stevens, Arthur Woehl, Emerson College and the Hispanic Society of America.

We want also to thank Joseph M. Bernstein for his expert translations from several languages; Nora Beeson, Helen Burlin, Bernard L. Koten, David Pressman and Harold J. Salemson for renderings of individual selections; and Elena Balieff, Eric Bentley, Ely Chinoy, Tamara Daykarhanova, Sally Donohue, Rosamund Gilder, Jay Leyda, Kurt Pinthus, Henry Popkin, Lee Strasberg, Carl Weber and Alfred Werner for aid which has benefited this book.

And finally, for giving generously of his discriminating judgments and unsparingly of his time and effort, we are immeasurably indebted to A. M. Krich.

T.C. H.K.C.

TABLE OF CONTENTS

		PAGE
INTRODUCTION	. . . .	xiii

I. GREECE

THE ARTISTS OF DIONYSUS	3
PLATO	6
On Inspiration	6
On Imitation	8
ARISTOTLE	11
Passion, Speech, and Gesture	11
Management of the Voice	12
PLUTARCH	12
Why We Delight in Representation	13
Ancient Actors	14
AULUS GELLIUS	14
The Grief of Polus	14
JULIUS POLLUX	15
Tragic and Comic Masks	15

II. ROME

ACTORS, SLAVES, AND ORATORS	19
CICERO	21
Emotion in the Actor and Orator	21
The Pupils of Roscius	25
QUINTILIAN	26
Action and Delivery	26
LUCIAN	30
Of Pantomime	30

III. THE MIDDLE AGES

THE ANONYMOUS ACTOR	34
ANON. 9TH CENTURY	37
Epitaph for Mime Vitalis	37
ETHELWOLD, BISHOP OF WINCHESTER	37
Instructions for Acting in a Trope	38
ANON. 12TH CENTURY	39
The Representation of Adam	39
ANON. 15TH CENTURY	39
Acting Regulations for the York Plays	40
From Banns of Performance at Chester	40

IV. ITALY

THE COMMEDIA DELL' ARTE	41
LEONE DI SOMI	44
Dialogue on Acting	45
PIETRO MARIA CECCHINI	49
Diverse Advice to Those Who Make a Profession of Playing Improvisations .	50
NICOLO BARBIERI	52
What Is a Buffoon?	53
ANDREA PERRUCCI	55
Introduction to Impromptu Acting	56
EVARISTO GHERARDI	57
On the Art of Italian Comedians	58
LUIGI RICCOBONI	59
Advice to Actors	59

V. SPAIN

PAGE

THE GOLDEN AGE 64
LOPE DE RUEDA 67
   The Strolling Players of Lope de Rueda by Cervantes 67
ALONZO LOPEZ PINCIANO 68
   Of Actors and Playing 68
AGUSTIN DE ROJAS 69
   An Actor's Life 69
TWO CONTEMPORARY ACCOUNTS 72
   At the *Commedia* by Comtesse D'Aulnoy 72
   An Afternoon in the Theatre by Juan De Zabaleta 73

VI. ENGLAND

THE ELIZABETHAN ACTOR 75
WILLIAM SHAKESPEARE 78
   Thoughts on Acting from His Plays 79
BEN JONSON 82
   To Edward Alleyn 83
   An Epitaph on Salathiel Pavy, a Child of Queen Elizabeth's Chapel . . . 83
ANON. c. 1602 84
   A Lesson from Burbage and Kemp 84
THOMAS HEYWOOD 85
   An Apology for Actors 86
JOHN WEBSTER 88
   An Excellent Actor 88
ANON. c. 1633 89
   The Eloquent Actor 89
RICHARD BURBAGE 90
   The Acting of Richard Burbage by Richard Flecknoe 91

VII. ENGLAND

THE GREAT NAMES 92
THOMAS BETTERTON 97
   The Qualifications of a Player 97
COLLEY CIBBER 102
   Apology for His Life 103
ANTHONY ASTON 113
   A Brief Supplement to Colley Cibber 114
AARON HILL 116
   Dramatic Passions 117
CHARLES MACKLIN 120
   The Art and Duty of an Actor 121
JOHN HILL 122
   Understanding, Sensibility, and Fire 123
DAVID GARRICK 131
   An Essay on Acting 133
   Letters on Acting 136
CATHERINE CLIVE 138
   Two Letters to Mr. Garrick 138
SARAH KEMBLE SIDDONS 139
   On the Character of Lady Macbeth 142

VIII. FRANCE

TRADITION AND REVOLT 146
ANON. c. 1610 153
   Three *Farceurs* 153
MOLIÈRE 154
   The Impromptu at Versailles 156
MICHEL BARON 158
   My Opinion of Michel Baron by Elena Riccoboni 159
DENIS DIDEROT 161
   The Paradox of Acting 162
HYPPOLITE CLAIRON 170
   Reflections on Dramatic Art 171

MARIE-FRANÇOISE DUMESNIL 174
   A Reply to "Reflections on Dramatic Art of Clairon" 175
DUMESNIL, CLAIRON AND OTHERS 177
   Fiction and Reality 177
FRANÇOIS JOSEPH TALMA 178
   Grandeur Without Pomp 180
FRANÇOIS DELSARTE 187
   Elements of the Delsarte System 187
BENOIT CONSTANT COQUELIN 190
   The Dual Personality of the Actor 192
SARAH BERNHARDT 202
   The Evolution of the Actor 204
ANDRÉ ANTOINE 209
   The New Acting of the *Théâtre Libre* 211
JACQUES COPEAU 216
   The Manifesto of the *Vieux Colombier* 217
   Notes on the Actor 218
CHARLES DULLIN 225
   The Birth and Life of Characters 226
ANTONIN ARTAUD 234
   Athlete of the Heart 235
LOUIS JOUVET 240
   Comedian and Actor 241
JEAN-LOUIS BARRAULT 245
   Pantomime 246
   Rules of Acting 249

IX. GERMANY

FROM *HAMBURG DRAMATURGY* TO EPIC THEATRE 254
GOTTHOLD EPHRAIM LESSING 261
   The Hamburg Dramaturgy 262
JOHANN WOLFGANG von GOETHE 267
   Rules for Actors 269
FRIEDRICH LUDWIG SCHROEDER 276
   Type and Character 277
AUGUST WILHELM IFFLAND 278
   The Limits of Nature 279
EDUARD DEVRIENT 282
   Simplicity and Convention 282
GEORGE II, DUKE OF SAXE MEININGEN 284
   The Actor in the Ensemble 285
OTTO BRAHM 288
   In Defense of Naturalism 289
MAX REINHARDT 294
   The Enchanted Sense of Play 295
PAUL KORNFELD 299
   Expressionism 299
ERWIN PISCATOR 301
   Objective Acting 301
BERTOLT BRECHT 307
   The Alienation Effect 308
   Letter to an Actor 312
HELENE WEIGEL 314
   Rehearsing the Part 315
THERESE GIEHSE 316
   The Actor's Resources 316
ANGELIKA HURWICZ 319
   Six Parts 319

X. ENGLAND AND IRELAND

THE HERITAGE OF ACTORS 321
EDMUND KEAN 326
   Feeling Without Rhetoric 328
   On Edmund Kean by "Betterton" 329

WILLIAM CHARLES MACREADY 333
   The Audience and the Actor 334
FANNY KEMBLE 337
   Temperament and Talent 338
GEORGE HENRY LEWES 341
   The Actor's Symbols 342
HENRY IRVING 353
   The Importance of By-Play 354
ELLEN TERRY 360
   The Three "I's" 360
WILLIAM ARCHER 363
   Masks or Faces? 363
GEORGE BERNARD SHAW 370
   The Point of View of the Playwright 371
GORDON CRAIG 376
   The Actor and the Ueber-Marionette 377
WILLIAM BUTLER YEATS 385
   The Sovereignty of Words 386
WILLIAM FAY 387
   Advice from an Abbey Theatre Actor 388
HARLEY GRANVILLE-BARKER 390
   The Heritage of the Actor 391
JOHN GIELGUD 397
   Creating my Roles 398
MICHAEL REDGRAVE 402
   The Stanislavsky Myth 403
LAURENCE OLIVIER 408
   The Art of Persuasion 410
PAUL SCOFIELD 417
   The Intuitive Approach 418
PETER BROOK 422
   The Act of Possession 423
CHARLES MAROWITZ 429
   Notes on the Theatre of Cruelty 430

XI. ITALY

STARS AND THE COMMEDIA TRADITION 439
ADELAIDE RISTORI 443
   My Study of Lady Macbeth 444
ERNESTO ROSSI 451
   The Art of Interpretation 451
TOMMASO SALVINI 454
   Impulse and Restraint 454
ERMETE ZACCONI 459
   The Art of Speaking 460
ELEONORA DUSE 465
   On Acting 466
EDUARDO DE FILIPPO 470
   The Intimacy of Actor and Character 471
VITTORIO GASSMAN 472
   Return to Tradition 473

XII. THE SOVIET UNION AND POLAND

THE MOSCOW ART THEATRE AND ITS TRADITION 475
MICHAEL S. SHCHEPKIN 481
   Feeling and Pretense 482
KONSTANTIN S. STANISLAVSKY 484
   The Evolution of My System 485
VLADIMIR I. NEMIROVICH-DANCHENKO 495
   Simplicity in Acting 497
VSEVOLOD MEYERHOLD 501
   A Rehearsal of The Inspector General 502
IGOR ILINSKY 504
   Biomechanics 504
EUGENE VAKHTANGOV 506

PAGE

The School of Intimate Experience 507
RICHARD BOLESLAVSKY 509
Living the Part 510
MICHAEL CHEKHOV 518
The Psychological Gesture 519
VASILI O. TOPORKOV 523
Physical Actions 523
JERZY GROTOWSKI 529
The Actor's Technique 530

XIII. AMERICA

NATIVE PLAYERS AND INNOVATORS 536

EDWIN FORREST 543
Edwin Forrest and the American Style by Walt Whitman 545
DION BOUCICAULT 546
Can Acting Be Taught? 547
JOSEPH JEFFERSON 551
Warm Heart and Cool Head 552
EDWIN BOOTH 557
The Actor's Tradition 559
WILLIAM HOOKER GILLETTE 563
The Illusion of the First Time in Acting 564
RICHARD MANSFIELD 567
Originality 568
EDWARD HUGH SOTHERN 570
I Talk to Myself 571
JULIA MARLOWE 570
The Eloquence of Silence 574
DAVID BELASCO 576
Acting as a Science 577
MINNIE MADDERN FISKE 584
To the Actor in the Making 584
OTIS SKINNER 587
Good Diction 588
ALLA NAZIMOVA 589
The Actor as an Instrument 590
JOHN BARRYMORE 591
Maxims of an Actor 593
LAURETTE TAYLOR 595
The Quality Most Needed 595
WALTER HUSTON 598
The Success and Failure of a Role 599
STELLA ADLER 601
The Actor in the Group Theatre 602
ALFRED LUNT and LYNN FONTANNE 606
Working Together on The Visit 607
Thoughts on Acting 610
MORRIS CARNOVSKY 613
The Quest of Technique 614
LEE STRASBERG 621
The Actor and Himself 623
ROBERT LEWIS 629
Emotional Memory 630
GERALDINE PAGE 635
The Bottomless Cup 635
VIOLA SPOLIN 641
Creative Experience 641
MICHAEL KIRBY 648
Nonmatrixed Performances—Happenings 648
JULIAN BECK AND JUDITH MALINA 652
Messages 654
JOSEPH CHAIKIN 663
The Context of Performance 665

BIBLIOGRAPHY 670

INDEX 695

INTRODUCTION

"We have actors but no art of acting," wrote Lessing of the theatre of his day in the *Hamburg Dramaturgy*. Of our own time it might be said: "We no longer have actors in the traditional sense but we are beginning to make our way toward an art of acting." One of the most striking changes in the twenty years since this book was originally published has been the gradual decline of the featured performer and the decay of the whole structure of conventional show business with its producers, playwrights, and designers that created and lived off the big names. Replacing the old star system are groups of actors working together in studios, ensembles, institutes, and institutional theatres—communities of artists who are turning their backs on Broadway, the West End, and the Boulevards. Highly individual talents are rarely exploited in this alternative theatre (even the more traditional national companies in England, France, East Gemany, and the Soviet Union feature the ensemble rather than the single virtuoso), but the acting process is being explored with an intense and often painful fanaticism. Modern theatre is becoming the collective creation of these actors, whose sounds, patterns, rhythms, confrontations and rituals often provide the playwright with his basic structures. Guided by an all-important director-teacher-guru, who is the star if there is one, these actors are taking upon themselves the rediscovery of theatre in our time.

As we have moved toward what Jerzy Grotowski provocatively calls the "poor theatre" of the actor, the value of the material collected in this volume, especially with its many new additions, becomes increasingly important. How the actor with his human medium reaches out to his fellowmen is the central question of a theatre that is stripping away the expendable trappings of the stage and breaking down the barriers between art and life. Is the actor to draw the audience into his character's truthful emotional life prepared through the Stanislavsky system and related "methods"? Should he distance himself and the audience from the event by Brecht's alienating devices to force a critical, political response? Will his trance dissolve the intellectual and social inhibitions to release the plague of basic human cruelty Artaud prophesied? Can he become Grotowski's holy actor sharing an authentic act of self-penetration with his fellowmen? Is he to be the "living" actor of the Becks who plays himself as each man exteriorizes the interior scream of our age? With everyman a participating actor in the emerging communal rituals, the experience and insight of professional performers over the centuries can provide rich definitions of what it means to act on the stage and in life itself.

The importance of actors' views on acting has long been recognized, but until the first edition of *Actors on Acting,* there seemed to be little available by actors on their art. There was a paradoxical fiction that actors, like magicians, kept secret the intricacies of their craft, or that actors were entranced, intuitive creatures, somnambulists without recollection. In bringing together the literature of the player, *Actors on Acting* replaces that fiction with an important body of histrionic theory, technique, practice and insight.

It has been hard for the actor to take himself seriously as an artist. Some difficulties are inherent in his work. An art that cannot be separated from its artists and examined independently and retrospectively cannot easily elicit from the artist himself or from critics and enthusiasts considered discussion. Actors have been acutely conscious of the evanescence of their art. Shakespeare, an actor turned poet, used this awareness to build the beautiful metaphor, "Life's but a walking shadow, a poor player, That struts and frets his hour upon the stage. And then is heard no more." David Garrick notes in the prologue to *The Clandestine Marriage:* "Nor Pen nor Pencil can the Actor save, The Art and Artist, share one common Grave." Although George Henry Lewes, the distinguished nineteenth-century critic, refused to despair over the brevity of the actor's creation, pointing out that the actor frequently has greater contemporary fame than other artists, the transitory quality of acting is the basic given in any discussion. In the words of Lawrence Barrett, the actor "is forever carving a statue of snow."

The actor's unique relationship to his medium, which is himself, undermines the ideal of artistic objectivity. His creations, the ambitious Macbeth, the jovial Rip Van Winkle, the loquacious Bessie Berger, either seem to wipe out the actor's identity, giving rise to the commonplace that actors acquire personality only on the stage, or else seem to be overbearing displays of self. His relationship to his roles is complex. The dualism that marks most artists sunders the actor, who is both the artist and the work of art. Constant Coquelin offers the view that the actor "has his first self, which is the player, and his second self, which is the instrument." Perhaps the central craft problem mulled over by generations of actors is the manner in which the first self and the second self are related. Does the actor "shed real tears," abandoning himself to the emotion of the character? Or, as in Joseph Jefferson's classic canon "warm heart and cool head," is the duality still sharp and clear at the moment of performance? Can he frankly expose both himself and the character as the often contradictory experiments of the recent avant-garde demand?

Working always with his personal medium, the actor is circumscribed by his humanity. No matter how rigorous his training or how pliable his talents, he can never be mere clay to be molded by the dramatist's imagination. Nor can he be a marionette to be manipulated by the director's touch. In the actor the conflict between verisimilitude and imaginative fiction becomes sharpened. Frankly an impersonator, there is always an aura of illusion and unreality about him. Yet his illusory art must present the likeness to truth which the audience in his particular era demands on the stage. By artifice he must become the "abstract and brief chronicles of the time." "Through the creation of his idea in acting form," as Stark Young points out in his brilliant essay on acting, "the actor achieves a work of art, complete in itself and free of its material."

Historically, the actor has been hampered in developing an aesthetic by the equivocal position of his art and by the vicissitudes of his social status. In ancient Greece, where actors were highly regarded for religious, social and political reasons, Aristotle, our spokesman for this period, does not consider the study of delivery, in which the actor as well as the orator was involved, worthy of serious discussion. When the Romans degraded the acting profession to an occupation for slaves, the luminaries Roscius and Aesop might earn great fame, but on the whole actors had no incentive to analyze their art. The social stigma attached to actors by the Romans became, under the reign of the church, religious and moral cavil. For more than a thousand years, the mimes and jugglers who replaced legitimate actors during the Middle Ages were objects of attack. When the first great modern actors emerged during the Renaissance to be praised like Burbage and Alleyn by both king and cobbler, when acting became a profession, a trade, a "quality," actors and acting troupes still required the protection of noblemen. Even in the eighteenth and nine-teenth centuries, when actors were no longer vagabonds but had become knighted gentlemen, intimations of immorality and vulgarity clung to the profession, and perhaps do so somewhat to this day. Given these circumstances, it is not surprising that apart from anecdotal memoirs, serious expositions of acting by early actors were basically concerned with moral justification of their activities, as was Thomas Hey-wood in his *Apology for Actors*. Later, when that demand was less imperative, the actors began to explore the aesthetics of their art.

Despite these social and artistic limitations, the actor is the best source of insight and analysis of his craft. The extent, variety and excellence of the material in this volume controvert the allegation that the examination of acting begins only in our own era with Stanislavsky and Copeau. The bulk of the selections are discussions of acting theory and accounts of the preparation and interpretation of specific roles by celebrated actors. These reflections and essays increase in number from the six-teenth century on. The palmy days of the eighteenth and nineteenth centuries provide full and rich material. The profound thinking of the actor-directors at the beginning of this century opens the way for the reconsiderations and reevaluations of today, in which directors still play the leading role, but now in creative collabora-tion with their acting group.

Throughout this volume will be found the words of the actors themselves. When a great actor has written nothing that bears directly on his craft, we have occasionally used the comments of eyewitnesses to help us approximate his methods. From the birth of acting in ancient Greece to the Renaissance, actors left no direct written record, but their performances strongly influenced the art of oratory, which up to the eighteenth century was closely related to acting. The earliest codified prin-ciples of public delivery leaned heavily on the art of Thespis. Precepts for orators, thus derived in part from histrionic practice, were later erroneously adopted by actors without modification. Although the rhetoricians' books were later discarded as guides, they reflect the practice of ancient actors and contain the roots of the actor's tradition. Of the many theorists who were not actors, only those of unusual historical importance appear in the following pages. Although dramatic critics from the 1700s on have made significant contributions to the analysis of acting, their work is for the most part outside the limits of this volume.

We have confined ourselves to the Western histrionic tradition, which origi-nated in Greece with Thespis. The expressive and complex art of the Orient is, therefore, not represented. Essays have been selected with an eye to historical value and present-day interest. Over twenty-five appear here for the first time in English, and a number have been especially written for this volume. Most of the players whose greatness has been unchallenged by time will be found here. Some less famous actors who nevertheless contributed important ideas about acting also appear. For the contemporary period we have tried to provide a representative sampling of the varied approaches of actors now working on the stage without either excessively duplicating available material or passing judgment on the actors or the art of our time. This twentieth-anniversary edition includes all the recent innovations and lively controversies—the late work of Stanislavsky, the theories of Brecht, Artaud, Grotowski, Peter Brook, Beck and Malina, Joseph Chaikin, Happenings, Games Theatre, as well as recent debates on the "Method" by Lee Strasberg and Robert Lewis, in addition to comments by leading actors who still speak to us from the stage.

Selections have been arranged in chronological sequence to show the origins and growth of a tradition, and in national groupings to reveal the unique temperament of each country. Although it would be of interest to include actors of all nations, space and the accessibility of material have limited us to those of greatest importance to our theatrical culture. The introductions to each section suggest in outline the historical context of the achievement of the actors represented and the genesis of their practices and ideals. In the biographical sketches the reader may find the more immediate personal background in the light of which the words of the individual actors may be best understood.

From the pages of this volume the cumulative tradition of the art of acting becomes evident. Certain basic preoccupations recur. How does the actor transform himself? Some actors, following the lead of Plato, consign players to intuition and inspiration; others argue for carefully planned artifice. Stanislavsky and his disciples attempt to evolve a method to create by will conditions favorable for the appearance of inspiration. The personality of the actor is repeatedly examined. To some he is a chameleon who assumes different forms; to others he always remains himself, imposing his individual identity on each character. In the repertory systems of the past the actor's performance of many and varied roles brought plaudits for his protean qualities, but the era of stars perpetuated an interest in the unique traits of the individual actor. In the anarchistic "living" theatre of the sixties, everyman is an actor free "to do his thing."

The training prescribed for actors has taken varied forms. When drama was poetry and heroic declamation, study of voice, diction and enunciation was considered primary. For the player of modern realistic drama, characterization and emotion have replaced vocal discipline. For the antiliterary drama of the existentialist-absurdist theatre, the physical presence of an "athlete of the heart" is called for. When asked out of what material they fashion their creations, actors have usually answered that they take from nature the effects used in their art. For each historical period, however, nature has had a different meaning. To the eighteenth century, nature was patterned, lofty and heroic; during the late nineteenth century it was embodied in the petty details of daily existence; in the twentieth century it is a multiform expression of the contending concepts of the modern mind.

Repeatedly the question occurs: Is the actor an original creator or does he merely embody the playwright's text and vivify the director's perceptions? Except for those periods when actors were themselves authors, as in ancient Greece, in the days of the *commedia dell' arte,* or in Spain's Golden Age, there has been a constant struggle between actor and author. In the last century the director has been added to the conflict. Actors have been divided in their allegiance; some advocate the subordination of actor to dramatist; some range themselves with the actors' theatres, where the imagination of the player reigns; others, particularly in recent years, have resigned themselves to be elements in an ensemble shaped by the director. Still others have joined with their innovating directors to rediscover the collective rite of theatre.

Other fundamental problems are raised again and again. What shall the actor study? How shall he create the "illusion of the first time" for each performance? Shall the actor mimic life or transcend it? Is theatrical art fiction or reality?

Votary, clown, apprentice, buffoon, idol, star, guru—these are the guises in which the actor has appeared throughout the ages. His playing has ranged from operatic recitative, verbal pyrotechnics and mimic obscenities to restrained, naturalistic reproduction of reality or absurdist abstractions. "Interpreter of interpreters," he has borne the mark of inspired madness stamped on him by Plato. His intensely personal creations, wrought of the movements of his limbs, the grimace of his face, and the emotions of his heart, have too often been relegated to mystery and magic or reduced to arbitrary schematization. Contrary to the traditional supposition that actors bury their secrets with themselves, here, as Shakespeare said, "they'll tell all."

ACTORS
ON ACTING

I. GREECE

The Artists of Dionysus

The histrionic tradition of the western world originated in Greece during the sixth century B.C. when the first significant step toward dramatic impersonation was taken. Mimetic dance, recitation, and song—component elements of acting—existed in most early civilizations. As far back as 4000 B.C. the Egyptians may have had dramatic religious performances in which actor-priests worshipped the memory of the dead, and the *Osiris Passion Play* of a much later day (c. 1887 B.C.) combined religious celebration and dramatic action. In ancient Greece the basis for the development of both tragic drama and acting lay in the ecstatic dithyrambs, ritual choral dances honoring Dionysus, god of wine and fertility. To the conventional musical narration by a chorus and a leader, Thespis, the first actor, introduced impersonation. From this innovation in Icaria sometime in the first half of the sixth century B.C. emerged both drama and acting.

Thespis, functioning as actor and dramatist, encountered difficulties when he first brought his theatrical invention to Athens (c. 560 B.C.). His impersonations were labeled dangerous deceptions by the Athenian lawgiver Solon. In 535 B.C., however, the tyrant Pisistratus introduced competitive performances of this "deceptive" art at the Dionysian festival in Athens. Thespis, now an old man, was crowned as the first victor. Thereafter each spring at the City Dionysia, great religious festival in Athens, tragedies were acted in honor of Dionysus. With the development and elaboration of these performances, which took the essentially Greek form of contests, the art of acting and the profession of the actor grew.

The contests for tragedy were held on the last three days of the festival, which included athletic competitions and recitations of dithyrambic verse. A civic magistrate, the archon, selected among many applicants the three tragedians whose dramas were to compete for prizes. Each of the chosen dramatists provided three tragedies and a satyr-play, a lighter dramatic performance connected with the worship of Dionysus. The actors and dramatists who participated in this great civic and religious festival were looked upon as honored citizens of Athens.

In the earliest performances there was only one actor, usually the poet himself. He was aided by the chorus and its leader, both of which remained essential elements in tragedy, as they had been in the dithyrambic recitals. Wearing a mask, the actor-poet could impersonate several characters. It was in this manner that Thespis probably performed. When Aeschylus added a second actor, the profession of the actor became distinct from that of the poet. The number of actors in tragedy, apart from the chorus and leader, was set at three when Sophocles added a third actor and diminished the importance of the chorus. Why the number was limited to three and the exact manner in which this limitation affected the plays and the performance of the actors are problems surrounded by doubt and speculation. What seems obvious is that there were no more than three main speaking actors at any one time on the stage, and that the three actors each played more than one role, a practice which the use of the mask permitted.

[3]

The three actors in each tragedy have traditionally been divided into protagonist, deuteragonist, and tritagonist. The protagonist, chosen by the state, played the major roles such as Oedipus or Electra, and probably assigned the remaining parts to the deuteragonist and the tritagonist. In addition it was the protagonists alone who competed for prizes when contests for actors were introduced in 449 B.C. at the City Dionysia. Frequently, too, a protagonist headed the Artists of Dionysus, the actors' guild established in the fourth century. This guild sought to preserve such religious and civic rights of theatre artists as exemption from military service and liberty to travel during time of strife. The deuteragonists probably took minor roles; and the tritagonists, such as Aeschines, acted the parts of tyrants and monarchs in addition to speaking the prologues. Protagonists were extremely jealous of their primary importance. The actor Theodorus, for example, would not allow any other character to precede him on stage.

During the initial period of great dramatic writing in the fifth century, the poets dominated theatrical performances. At first they acted in their own plays. Both Aeschylus and Sophocles followed Thespis in the actor-poet tradition. They chose the other actors, who frequently became associated with their plays. Cleander and Myniscus, for example, were the players for Aeschylus, and Tlepolemus and Cleidemides acted for Sophocles. In addition they trained the chorus. Innovations in gesture and declamation therefore came largely from the poets in their triple role of dramatist, actor, and stage manager.

Gradually, as actors gained skill and prominence, they were distributed among the competing dramatists by the state to prevent a poet from running off with laurels because of the excellence of his protagonist. During the fourth century when literary creativeness in tragedy diminished, the actors replaced the poets in importance. A century of great actors followed the century of great dramatists. Seeking attractive starring roles, the leading actors revived the tragedies of Aeschylus, Sophocles, and Euripides. They were even accused of revising the great dramas in order to carve out meaty parts for themselves. This practice was ended by the orator Lycurgus, who insisted that actors present the dramas in accordance with official texts deposited in the state archives. To the fourth century, the age of Demosthenes, belong the names of the famous Greek tragic actors, Neoptolemus, Thettalus, Athenodorus, Polus, Theodorus, and Aristodemus.

The large stylized mask and the cothurnus, a thick-soled boot, marked the physical appearance of the Greek tragic actor. Although the origin of the mask is probably hidden in ancient religious ritual, it had important practical functions in the Greek theatre. The exaggerated facial expressions of the mask, such as the blood-stained and blinded image of Oedipus, suggested in gross outline the dominant features of the characters to the audience which gathered in the vast circular arena of the Greek theatre. These theatres were huge, seating the many thousands of Greek citizens and foreigners who came yearly to witness the great religious festival. The visual image of the actor and the chorus dominated the performances, for the slightly elevated stage of the amphitheatre possessed no curtain and little by way of scenery. The cothurnus raised the actor to more than normal height, making him seem larger than life. The mask, both through its painted expression and through a mechanism which it probably contained for amplifying the actor's voice, increased the awesomeness of the stage figure. Since all the actors were men, women being unknown on the Greek stage, the mask permitted them to create female characters in an effective manner.

[4]

The stylized appearance of the face and the increased size of the actor were not merely mechanisms for better audience vision, but graphic embodiments of the legendary heroes and mythological characters impersonated in Greek tragedy. In the portrayal of Agamemnon, Oedipus, or Ajax, these devices undoubtedly aided the natural equipment of the actor.

We may well ask what were the natural talents that the Greek actor brought to his art. One quality appears most important—the expressive, well-trained voice. Most of the comments in Greek literature about acting or specific actors stressed the voice as characteristic of the effective actor. Aristotle defined acting as "the right management of the voice to express the various emotions." Demosthenes, who according to Plutarch was trained by the actor Satyrus, indicated that the admirable actor was "splendid in voice and perfect in memory." The catalogue of vocal expression recorded in the *Onomasticon* of Pollux, a Greek grammarian of the second century A.D., further emphasized the primacy of the voice in Greek acting. Poetic and operatic qualities in Greek tragedies demanded that the actor be able to sing as well as recite verse. Not only musical training of the voice in the manner of singers, but detailed study of enunciation, timing, and rhythmic perfection were required. Greek audiences, accustomed to musical and poetic performances in their religious ceremonies, were critical and exacting. Indeed, the very size of the open-air theatres made the "right management" of the voice a basic requisite for good acting.

We know little of the gestures and stage movements used by the Greek actor, but given their rather burdensome costume and mask, we can assume that the expressiveness of the actor depended in part on full body postures and articulate hand movements. The emotional verisimilitude aimed at and attained by the Greek actor is difficult to gauge. The famous incident concerning the actor Polus, who used the ashes of his own dead son to arouse emotion in his portrayal of Electra, provides us with an archetypal story of the actor's personal identification with the character he is presenting.

Several scholars have attempted to divide the history of Greek acting into three periods. The first period, associated with Aeschylus, Sophocles, and their actors in the fifth century, was one of dignified, restrained, and statuesque acting. In the fourth century, a middle period of more natural and human acting was represented by the art of Polus, Aristodemus, Neoptolemus, and Theodorus. The final Hellenistic period was one of decline in which acting was marked by crass imitation of nature and vocal tricks. Although there is little evidence to support these elaborate divisions, apart from a brief comment by Aristotle, it seems likely that the style of acting varied as the tone of tragic dramas changed from the serenity of Aeschylus and the grandeur of Sophocles to the more realistic human emotions presented by Euripides.

We know less of Greek comic actors and their art than of the tragic actors. They too acted at religious festivals, particularly the winter celebration, Lenaea, at which comedies were largely performed. Comedy first came under state control in 486 B.C., and a contest for comic actors was established at the Lenaea around 422 B.C. Early comic performers wore exaggerated grotesque masks, and their padded costumes were marked by the obvious pendant phallus, recalling the origin of comedy in phallic songs chanted to Dionysus. Their art was a popular and frequently vulgar one, utilizing, for example, such tricks as the comic actor Parmenon's imitation of a pig. In the Old Comedy of Aristophanes, during the Greek democracy, their acting was probably lively, bawdy, and unrestrained. Comic acting undoubtedly became more refined and natural in the so-called New Comedy of Menander which dealt with the problems and intrigues of everyday life.

No detailed discussion of the art of acting in ancient Greece remains for us to investigate, no manual of voice and gesture such as we find in later periods. The actors themselves left no record of their approach to their art; and theorists, who were beginning to formulate the principles of dramaturgy, had not yet turned to analyze acting as an independent art. The methods and ideals of the Greek actors must therefore be deduced from such sources as Plato's comments on imitation and inspiration or from Aristotle's remarks on poetry and rhetoric, two arts closely related to acting in ancient times. Plutarch, writing when the great age of Greek theatre was long since over, discussed the relationship of art and nature in theatrical presentations. Still later, in the second century A.D., the Greek grammarian Pollux preserved a listing of masks and of vocal tones which were utilized by the Greek actor. Anecdotes about actors and acting recorded by both Greek and Roman writers shade the dim outline for a picture of the artists of Dionysus.

PLATO

(429-347 B.C.)

The celebrated Athenian philosopher Plato was never directly concerned with acting, but some of his brief comments on this art provided later writers with classical precedent for their opinions. The discourse on imitation in the *Republic,* with its description of superficial realistic imitations, led Plato to condemn pantomimic art along with his general condemnation of poets, who were to be driven from the ideal republic. Renaissance opponents of the theatre frequently utilized Plato's argument against actors and theatre.

The "Ion," a dialogue analyzing the art of the rhapsode, the reciter of poetry, is the source of the recurrent opinion that poets and their interpreters are inspired, mad beings, carried away by the subject of their inspiration. The Socratic questioning in the dialogue draws the conclusion that the rhapsode, like the actor, works only on the basis of inspiration without rules of art. This relegation of acting to divine inspiration has been used both to elevate the position of the actor and at the same time to remove his creations from subjection to artistic rules. The concept of the actor as an inspired, intuitive interpreter appears again and again in the history of acting and accounts in part for the slow development of systematic theories of acting.

On Inspiration

SOCRATES: Welcome, Ion. Are you from your native city of Ephesus?
ION: No, Socrates; but from Epidaurus, where I attended the festival of Asclepius.
SOCRATES: And do the Epidaurians have contests of rhapsodes at the festival?
ION: O yes; and of all sorts of musical performers.
SOCRATES: And were you one of the competitors—and did you succeed?
ION: I obtained the first prize of all, Socrates.

* * * *

Plato: "Ion," *The Dialogues,* translated by Benjamin Jowett. London: Oxford University Press, 1892, Volume I, pp. 497-504.

SOCRATES: I often envy the profession of a rhapsode, Ion; for you have always to wear fine clothes, and to look as beautiful as you can is a part of your art. Then, again, you are obliged to be continually in the company of many good poets; and especially of Homer, who is the best and most divine of them, and to understand him, and not merely learn his words by rote, is a thing greatly to be envied. And no man can be a rhapsode who does not understand the meaning of the poet. For the rhapsode ought to interpret the mind of the poet to his hearers, but how can he interpret him well unless he knows what he means? All this is greatly to be envied.

ION: Very true, Socrates; interpretation has certainly been the most laborious part of my art; and I believe myself able to speak about Homer better than any man....

SOCRATES: Then, my dear friend, can I be mistaken in saying that Ion is equally skilled in Homer and in other poets, since he himself acknowledges that the same person will be a good judge of all those who speak of the same things; and that almost all poets do speak of the same things?

ION: Why then, Socrates, do I lose attention and go to sleep and have absolutely no ideas of the least value, when any one speaks of any other poet; but when Homer is mentioned, I wake up at once and am all attention and have plenty to say?

SOCRATES: The reason, my friend, is obvious. No one can fail to see that you speak of Homer without any art or knowledge. If you were able to speak of him by rules of art, you would have been able to speak of all other poets; for poetry is a whole.

ION: Yes.

SOCRATES: And when any one acquires any other art as a whole, the same may be said of them. Would you like me to explain my meaning, Ion?

ION: Yes, indeed, Socrates; I very much wish that you would; for I love to hear you wise men talk.

SOCRATES: O that we were wise, Ion, and that you could truly call us so; but you rhapsodes and actors, and the poets whose verses you sing, are wise; whereas I am a common man, who only speak the truth. For consider what a very commonplace and trivial thing is this which I have said—a thing which any man might say; that when a man has acquired a knowledge of a whole art, the enquiry into good and bad is one and the same....

ION: I cannot deny what you say, Socrates. Nevertheless I am conscious in my own self, and the world agrees with me in thinking that I do speak better and have more to say about Homer than any other man. But I do not speak equally well about others—tell me the reason of this.

SOCRATES: I perceive, Ion; and I will proceed to explain to you what I imagine to be the reason of this. The gift which you possess of speaking excellently about Homer is not an art, but, as I was just saying, an inspiration; there is a divinity moving you, like that contained in the stone which Euripides calls a magnet, but which is commonly known as the stone of Heraclea. This stone not only attracts iron rings, but also imparts to them a similar power of attracting other rings; and sometimes you may see a number of pieces of iron and rings suspended from one another so as to form quite a long chain; and all of them derive their power of suspension from the original stone. In like manner the Muse first of all inspires men herself; and from these inspired persons a chain of other persons is suspended who take the inspiration. For all good poets, epic as well as lyric, compose their beautiful poems not by art, but because they are inspired and possessed. And as the Corybantian revellers when they dance are not in their right mind, so the lyric poets are not in their right mind when they are composing their beautiful strains; but when falling under the power of music and metre they are inspired and possessed.... For the poet is a light and winged and holy thing, and there is no invention in him until he has been inspired and is out of his senses, and the mind is no longer in him: when he has not attained to this state, he is powerless and is unable to utter his oracles. Many are the noble words in which poets speak concerning the actions of men; but like yourself when speaking about Homer, they do not speak of them by any rules of art: they are simply inspired to utter that to which the Muse impels them.... And you rhapsodists are the interpreters of the poets?

Ion: There again you are right.

Socrates: Then you are the interpreters of interpreters?

Ion: Precisely.

Socrates: I wish you would frankly tell me, Ion, what I am going to ask of you: When you produce the greatest effect upon the audience in the recitation of some striking passage ... are you in your right mind? Are you not carried out of yourself, and does not your soul in an ecstasy seem to be among the persons or the places of which you are speaking....

Ion: That proof strikes home to me, Socrates. For I must frankly confess that at the tale of pity my eyes are filled with tears, and when I speak of horrors, my hair stands on end and my heart throbs.

* * * *

Socrates: And are you aware that you produce similar effects on most of the spectators?

Ion: Only too well; for I look down upon them from the stage, and behold the various emotions of pity, wonder, sternness, stamped upon their countenances when I am speaking....

Socrates: Do you know that the spectator is the last of the rings which, as I am saying, receive the power of the original magnet from one another? The rhapsode like yourself and the actor are intermediate links, and the poet himself is the first of them. Through all these the God sways the souls of men in any direction which he pleases, and makes one man hang down from another.... And every poet has some Muse from whom he is suspended, and by whom he is said to be possessed ... the greater number are possessed and held by Homer. Of whom, Ion, you are one, and are possessed by Homer ... for not by art or knowledge about Homer do you say what you say, but by divine inspiration and by possession....

On Imitation

...we must come to an understanding about the mimetic art—whether the poets, in narrating their stories, are to be allowed by us to imitate, and if so, whether in whole or in part, and if the latter, in what parts; or should all imitation be prohibited?

Plato: *The Republic*, translated by Benjamin Jowett. New York: Modern Library, Random House, Book III, Number 397, pp. 94-99.

You mean, I suspect, to ask whether tragedy and comedy shall be admitted unto our State?

Yes, I said: but there may be more than this in question: I really do not know as yet, but whither the argument may blow, thither we go.

And go we will, he said.

Then, Adeimantus, let me ask you whether our guardians ought to be imitators; or rather, has not this question been decided by the rule already laid down that one man can only do one thing well, and not many; and that if he attempt many, he will altogether fail of gaining much reputation in any?

Certainly.

And this is equally true of imitation; no one man can imitate many things as well as he would imitate a single one?

He cannot.

Then the same person will hardly be able to play a serious part in life, and at the same time to be an imitator and imitate many other parts as well; for even when two species of imitation are nearly allied, the same persons cannot succeed in both, as, for example, the writers of tragedy and comedy—did you not just now call them imitations.

Yes, I did; and you are right in thinking that the same persons cannot succeed in both.

Any more than they can be rhapsodists and actors at once?

True.

Neither are comic and tragic actors the same; yet all these things are but imitations.

They are so.

And human nature, Adeimantus, appears to have been coined into yet smaller pieces, and to be as incapable of imitating many things well, as of performing well the actions of which the imitations are copies.

Quite true, he replied.

If then we adhere to our original notion and bear in mind that our guardians, setting aside every other business, are to dedicate themselves wholly to the maintenance of freedom in the State, making this their craft, and engaging in no work which does not bear on this end, they ought not to practise or imitate anything else; if they imitate at all, they should imitate from youth upward only those characters which are suitable to their profession—the courageous, temperate, holy, free, and the like; but they should not depict or be skilful at imitating any kind of illiberality or baseness, lest from imitation they should come to be what they imitate. Did you never observe how imitations, beginning in early youth and continuing far into life, at length grow into habits and become a second nature, affecting body, voice, and mind?

Yes, certainly, he said.

Then, I said, we will not allow those for whom we profess a care and of whom we say that they ought to be good men, to imitate a woman, whether young or old, quarrelling with her husband, or striving and vaunting against the gods in conceit of her happiness, or when she is in affliction, or sorrow, or weeping; and certainly not one who is in sickness, love, or labor.

Very right, he said.

Neither must they represent slaves, male or female, performing the offices of slaves?

They must not.

And surely not bad men, whether cowards or any others, who do the reverse of what we have just been prescribing, who scold or mock or revile one another in drink or out of drink, or who in any other manner sin against themselves and their neighbors in word or deed, as the manner of such is. Neither should they be trained to imitate the action or speech of men or women who are mad or bad; for madness, like vice, is to be known but not to be practiced or imitated.

Very true, he replied.

Neither may they imitate smiths or other artificers, or oarsmen, or boatswains, or the like?

How can they, he said, when they are not allowed to apply their minds to the callings of any of these?

Nor may they imitate the neighing of horses, the bellowing of bulls, the murmur of rivers and roll of the ocean, thunder, and all that sort of thing?

Nay, he said, if madness be forbidden, neither may they copy the behavior of madmen.

You mean, I said, if I understand you aright, that there is one sort of narrative style which may be employed by a truly good man when he has anything to say, and that another sort will be used by a man of an opposite character and education.

And which are these two sorts? he asked.

Suppose, I answered, that a just and good man in the course of a narration comes on some saying or action of another good man—I should imagine that he would like to personate him, and will not be ashamed of this sort of imitation: he will be most ready to play the part of the good man when he is acting firmly and wisely; in a less degree when he is overtaken by illness or love or drink, or has met with any other disaster. But when he comes to a character which is unworthy of him, he will not make a study of that; he will disdain such a person, and will assume his likeness, if at all, for a moment only when he is performing some good action; at other times he will be ashamed to play a part which he has never practiced, nor will he like to fashion and frame himself after the baser models; he feels the employment of such an art, unless in jest, to be beneath him, and his mind revolts at it.

So I should expect, he replied.

Then he will adopt a mode of narration such as we have illustrated out of Homer, that is to say, his style will be both imitative and narrative; but there will be very little of the former, and a great deal of the latter. Do you agree?

Certainly, he said; that is the model which such a speaker must necessarily take.

But there is another sort of character who will narrate anything, and, the worse he is, the more unscrupulous he will be; nothing will be too bad for him: and he will be ready to imitate anything, not as a joke, but in right good earnest, and before a large company. As I was just now saying, he will attempt to represent the roll of thunder, the noise of wind and hail, or the creaking of wheels, and pulleys, and the various sounds of flutes; pipes, trumpets, and all sorts of instruments: he will bark like a dog, bleat like a sheep, or crow like a cock; his entire art will consist in imitation of voice and gesture, and there will be very little narration.

* * * *

And therefore when any one of these pantomimic gentlemen, who are so clever that they can imitate anything, comes to us, and makes a proposal to exhibit himself and his poetry, we will fall down and worship him as a sweet and holy and wonderful being; but we must also inform him that in our State such as he are not permitted to exist; the law will not allow them. And so when we have anointed him with myrrh, and set a garland of wool upon his head, we shall send him away to another city.

ARISTOTLE

(384-322 B.C.)

Aristotle, who was born at Stagira, is our most important single source of information on the Greek drama of the fourth and fifth centuries B.C. Student of Plato, tutor to the conqueror Alexander the Great, and schoolmaster in Athens, he left encyclopedic writings on politics, logic, and metaphysics, as well as studies of poetry and rhetoric which formed the foundation for investigations in these fields for over a thousand years.

Although Aristotle wrote no treatise dealing with the art of acting, his two classic works on poetry and rhetoric contain the earliest organized comments we possess on drama in ancient Greece. From his *Poetics,* the earliest extant work on dramatic theory, we learn the origin of drama in Greece, the number of players used in performances and, indirectly, we learn some of the qualities attributed to actors and acting. From his *Rhetoric,* we discover that the methods of delivery used by poets, orators, and actors were basically the same, and we also get some indication of what those methods were.

Brief as these comments are, they suggest many of the subjects that reappear in discussions of acting for centuries to come.

Passion, Speech, and Gesture

...In composing, the poet should even, as much as possible, be an actor; for, by natural sympathy, they are most persuasive and affecting who are under the influence of actual passion. We share the agitation of those who appear to be truly agitated—the anger of those who appear to be truly angry.

Hence it is that poetry demands either great natural quickness of parts, or an enthusiasm allied to madness. By the first of these we mould ourselves with facility to the imitation of every form; by the other, transported out of ourselves, we become what we imagine.

* * * *

With respect to diction, one part of its theory is that which treats of the figures of speech, such as commanding, entreating, relating, menacing, interrogating, answering, and the like. But this belongs, properly, to the art of acting, and to the professed masters of that kind.

* * * *

...It [comparison of tragic and epic imitation] may also be compared to what the modern actors are in the estimation of their predecessors; for Myniscus used

Aristotle: *Poetics,* translated by Thomas Twining. London: Everyman's Library, J. M. Dent and Sons, Ltd., 1941, pp. 33, 34, 38, 58, 59.

to call Callipides, on account of his intemperate action, the ape, and Tyndarus was censured on the same account. . . .

But now, in the first place, this censure falls, not upon the poet's art, but upon that of the actor; for the gesticulation may be equally labored in the recitation of an epic poem. . . .

Again, all gesticulation is not to be condemned, since even all dancing is not; but such only as is unbecoming—such as was objected to Callipides, and is objected to others whose gestures resemble those of immodest women.

Management of the Voice

. . . A third [object in the discussion of style] would be the proper method of delivery; that is a thing that affects the success of a speech greatly; but hitherto the subject has been neglected. Indeed, it was long before it found a way into the arts of tragic drama and epic recitation; at first poets acted their tragedies themselves. It is plain that delivery has just as much to do with oratory as with poetry. . . . It is, essentially, a matter of the right management of the voice to express the various emotions—of speaking loudly, softly, or between the two; of high, low or intermediate pitch; of the various rhythms that suit various subjects. These are the three things—volume of sound, modulation of pitch, and rhythm—that a speaker bears in mind. It is those who do bear them in mind who usually win prizes in the dramatic contests; and just as in drama the actors now count for more than the poets, so it is in the contests of public life, owing to the defects of our political institutions. No systematic treatise upon the rules of delivery has yet been composed; indeed, even the study of language made no progress till late in the day. Besides, delivery is—very properly—not regarded as an elevated subject of inquiry. Still, the whole business of rhetoric being concerned with appearances, we must pay attention to the subject of delivery, unworthy though it is, because we cannot do without it. . . . When the principles of delivery have been worked out, they will produce the same effect as on the stage. But only very slight attempts to deal with them have been made and by a few people, as by Thrasymachus in his *Appeals to Pity.* Dramatic ability is a natural gift, and can hardly be taught. The principles of good diction can be so taught, and therefore we have men of ability in this direction too, who win prizes in their turn. . . .

PLUTARCH

(c. 46-120 A.D.)

Plutarch, who is most famous for his biographical study *The Lives of the Noble Grecians and Romans,* was born in Boeotia. He studied philosophy at Athens and for a time lived in Rome, where he lectured on philosophy. Apart from his travels, he spent most of his life in the little Greek town where he was born.

In his *Lives* and in his numerous miscellaneous essays, collected under the title *Opera Moralia,* Plutarch preserved many anecdotes about actors and observations on ancient theatre. These help us to visualize both individual actors and classical act-

Aristotle: *Rhetoric,* translated by W. Rhys Roberts, in *Basic Works of Aristotle,* edited by Richard McKeon. New York: Random House, 1941, Book III, Chapter 1, pp. 1435-1436. Copyright 1941. By permission of The Clarendon Press, Oxford.

ing. The brief essay from the "Symposiacs" of Plutarch, which follows, contains not only the famous story about the comic actor Parmenon, but also a discourse on art and nature in acting that foreshadows many later discussions.

Why We Delight in Representation

Why take we Delight in Hearing those that represent the Passions of Men Angry or Sorrowful, and yet cannot without Concern behold those who are really so Affected?

Of this we discoursed in your company at Athens, when Strato the comedian (for he was a man of great credit) flourished. For being entertained at supper by Boethus the Epicurean, with a great many more of the sect, as it usually happens when learned and inquisitive men meet together, the remembrance of the comedy led us to this enquiry—Why are we disturbed at the real voices of men, either angry, pensive, or afraid, and yet are delighted to hear others represent them, and imitate their gestures, speeches, and exclamations. Every one in the company gave almost the same reason. For they said. he that only represents excels him that really feels, inasmuch as he doth not suffer the misfortunes; which we knowing are pleased and delighted on that account.

But I, though it was not properly my talent, said that we, being by nature rational and lovers of ingenuity, are delighted with and admire every thing that is artificially and ingeniously contrived...for whatever is curious and subtle doth attract and allure human nature, as antecedently to all instruction agreeable and proper to it. And therefore, because he that is really affected with grief or anger presents us with nothing but the common bare passion, but in the imitation some dexterity and persuasiveness appears, we are naturally inclined to be disturbed at the former, whilst the latter delights us.... Thus the continual cackling of a hen or cawing of a crow is very ungrateful and disturbing; yet he that imitates those noises well pleases the hearers. Thus to behold a consumptive man is no delightful spectacle; yet with pleasure we can view the pictures and statues of such persons, because the very imitating hath something in it very agreeable to the mind, which allures and captivates its faculties. For upon what account, for God's sake, from what external impression upon our organ, should man be moved to admire Parmenon's sow so much as to pass it into a proverb? Yet is it reported, that Parmenon being very famous for imitating the grunting of a pig, some endeavored to rival and outdo him. And when the hearers, being prejudiced, cried out, Very well indeed, but nothing comparable to Parmenon's sow; one took a pig under his arm and come upon the stage. And when, though they heard the very pig, they still continued, This is nothing comparable to Parmenon's sow; he threw his pig amongst them, to show that they judged according to opinion and not truth. And hence it is very evident, that like motions of the sense do not always raise like affections in the mind, when there is not an opinion that the thing done was not neatly and ingeniously performed.

Plutarch: "Symposiacs," *Miscellanies and Essays*, edited by William W. Goodwin. Boston: Little, Brown and Company, 1888, Volume III, Book V, Question 1, pp. 314-316.

Ancient Actors

[From the biography of the Greek orator and actor Aeschines]

...he addicted himself to all sorts of bodily exercises; and afterwards, having a very clear voice, he took to playing of tragedies ... and also served Aristodemus as a player of third parts at the Bacchanalian festivals, in his times of leisure rehearsing the ancient tragedies.

[From the biography of the Greek orator Demosthenes]

And being naturally short-winded, he gave Neoptolemus a player ten thousand drachmas to teach him to pronounce long sentences in one breath.... But he was chiefly animated by Andronicus the player, who told him that his orations were excellent, but that he wanted something of action, thereupon rehearsing certain places out of his oration which he had delivered in that same assembly. Unto which Demosthenes gave good ear and credit, and he then betook himself to Andronicus. And therefore, when he was afterwards asked what was the first part of oratory, he answered, "Action"; and which was the second, he replied "Action"; and which was the third, he still answered, "Action.".... One day his [Demosthenes'] voice failing him when he was declaiming publicly, being hissed, he cried out to the people, saying, Ye are to judge of players, indeed, by their voice, but of orators by the gravity of their sentences.[1]

[Concerning the Greek-born Aesop, who became Rome's greatest tragedian]

They tell of this Aesop that whilst he was representing in the theatre Atreus deliberating the revenge of Thyestes, he was so transported beyond himself in the heat of action, that he struck with his sceptre one of the servants who was running across the stage, so violently that he laid him dead upon the place.[2]

AULUS GELLIUS

(c. 123 - c. 165 A.D.)

Gellius was a Latin grammarian and legal practitioner of the second century A.D. His major work, *Attic Nights,* so called because it was composed during long winter nights near Athens, preserved extracts from both Roman and Greek writers. In this elaborate miscellany or scrapbook of information he narrates a famous story concerning the Greek actor Polus.

The Grief of Polus

There was in the land of Greece an actor of wide reputation, who excelled all others in his clear delivery and graceful action. They say that his name was Polus,

---

Aulus Gellius: *Attic Nights,* translated by John C. Rolfe. London: Loeb Classical Library, William Heinemann, Ltd., 1927, Book VI, Chapter 5, pp. 35-37. Copyright 1927. By permission of the Loeb Classical Library, Harvard University Press.

---

[1]Plutarch: "Lives of the Ten Orators," *Miscellanies and Essays,* edited by William W. Goodwin. Boston: Little, Brown and Company, 1888, Volume V, pp. 34, 44, 45, 52.

[2]Plutarch: *The Lives of the Noble Grecians and Romans,* translated by John Dryden and revised by Arthur H. Clough. New York: Modern Library, Random House, p. 1043.

GREECE

and he often acted the tragedies of famous poets with intelligence and dignity. This Polus lost by death a son whom he dearly loved. After he felt that he had indulged his grief sufficiently, he returned to the practice of his profession.

At that time he was to act the Electra of Sophocles at Athens, and it was his part to carry an urn which was supposed to contain the ashes of Orestes. The plot of the play requires that Electra, who is represented as carrying her brother's remains, should lament and bewail the fate she believed had overtaken him. Accordingly Polus, clad in the mourning garb of Electra, took from the tomb the ashes and urn of his son, embraced them as if they were those of Orestes, and filled the whole place, not with the appearance and imitation of sorrow, but with genuine grief and unfeigned lamentation. Therefore, while it seemed that a play was being acted, it was in fact real grief that was enacted.

JULIUS POLLUX

(Second Century A.D.)

The Greek rhetorician Julius Pollux, tutor to the Emperor Commodus and teacher in Athens, compiled a dictionary, the *Onomasticon,* in which he preserved a fund of important knowledge. Confused and uncritical as much of his writing was, he remains an invaluable source of information, especially about the theatre.

Apart from his comments on theatrical architecture, he included in his work a list of vocal expressions which set a precedent for many later codifications by writers on the art of acting. In addition, he recorded a detailed catalogue of Greek tragic and comic masks. This listing enriches our knowledge of Greek actors by revealing the range and variety of stylized expressions of which their masks were capable.

Tragic and Comic Masks

Moreover with respect to masks; the tragic might be a smooth-faced man, a white, grisled, black-haired, flaxen, more flaxen, all of them old: and the smooth faced oldest of these; having very white locks, and the hairs lying upon the prominence. By prominence I mean the upper part of the countenance rising above the forehead.... With respect to beard, the smooth-faced should be very closely shaven, and have thin lantern jaws. The white-haired is all hoary with bushy locks about the head, has an ample beard, jutting eye-brows, and the complexion almost white, but the prominence short. The grisled denotes the hoary hairs to be a mixture of black and grey. But the blair-haired, deriving his name from the color, has a curled beard and hair, rough face, and large prominence. The flaxen has yellowish bushy hair, lesser prominence, and is fresh colored. The more flaxen has a sameness with the other, but is rather more pale to represent sick persons.

The *young men's* masks are the common, curled, more curled, graceful, horrid, second horrid, pale, less pale.

The *common* is eldest of the young men, beardless, fresh-colored, swarthy, having locks clustering, and black. The *curled* is yellow, blustering, with bushy hair

Julius Pollux: "Extracts Concerning the Greek Theatre and Masks," in *Aristotle's Poetics; or, Discourse concerning Tragic and Epic Imitation.* London: J. Dodsley and Messrs. Richardson and Urquhart, 1775, pp. 14-29 (appended).

encompassing a plump face, has arched eye-brows, and a fierce aspect. The *more curled* differs in nothing from the former, but in being a little younger. The *graceful* has Hyacinthian locks, fair skin, is lively, and of a pleasant countenance, fit for a beautiful Apollo. The *horrid* is robust, grim-visaged, sullen, deformed, yellow-haired. The *second horrid* is so much more slender than the former, as he is younger; and an attendant. The *pale* is meagre, with dishevelled hair, and of such a sickly countenance as is suitable for a ghost, or wounded person. The *less pale* is entirely like the common in every other respect except that it is made pale on purpose to express a sick man, or a lover.

The *slaves'* masks are the leathern, peaked beard, flat-nose.

The *leathern* having no prominence, has a fillet, and long white hairs, a pale whitish visage, and rough nostrils, an high crown, stern eyes; the beard a little pale, and looks older than his years. But the peaked-beard is in the vigor of life, has an high and broad prominence dented all round, is yellow haired, rough, ruddy, and suited to a messenger. The flat-nose is bluff, yellow-headed, the locks hang on each side from the forelock; he is beardless, ruddy, and likewise delivers a message.

The *women's* masks are an hoary dishevelled, a freed old woman, an old domestic, a middle aged, a leathern, a pale dishevelled, a pale middle aged, a shaven virgin, second shaven virgin, girl.

The *hoary dishevelled,* surpassing the rest, both in years and dignity, has white locks, a moderate prominence, is inclinable to paleness, and was anciently called, the delicate. The *freed old woman* is of a tawny complexion and hoariness, having a small prominence; the tresses to the shoulders denote misfortune.

The *old domestic,* instead of prominence has a fillet of lamb's wool, and a wrinkled skin.

But the *middle-aged* domestic has a short prominence, and white skin, is grey haired, but not quite hoary.

The *leathern,* younger than her, and has not any prominence.

The *pale dishevelled* has black hair, a dejected countenance, and her name from the color.

But the *pale middle aged* is like the dishevelled, except where she is shaven out of sight.

But the *shaven virgin,* instead of prominence wears a smooth-combed tate, is shaven almost quite round, and of a color inclinable to paleness.

And the other *shaven virgin* is perfectly like her, but without the tate and curls, as if she had been often in misfortunes.

The *girl* is a juvenile mask, such as Danae might have been, or any other virgin.

The *attendant* masks are an horned Actaeon, a blind Phineus or Thamyris, one having a blue eye, the other a black; a many-eyed Argus, or Tyro with lived cheeks, as in Sophocles, which she suffered from the blows of a cruel step-mother; or Euippe, Chiron's daughter, changed into an horse in Euripides; or Achilles dishevelled for Patroclus, an Amymone, a river, mountain, gorgon, justice, death, a fury, madness, guilt, injury, centaur, titan, giant, Indian, Triton; perhaps, also a city, Priam, persuasion, the Muses, hours, Nymphs of Mithaeus, Pleiades, deceit, drunkenness, idleness, envy; which latter might likewise be comic masks.

Satyric Masks

Satyric masks are an hoary satyr, bearded satyr, beardless satyr, Grandfather Silenus. The other masks are all alike, unless where the names themselves show a peculiar distinction, as the Father Silenus has a more savage appearance.

Comic Masks

The comic masks, those especially of the Old Comedy, were as like as possible to the persons they represented, or made to appear more ridiculous. But those of the new were a first grandfather, a second grandfather, governor, long-bearded, or shaking old man, Ermoneus, peaked-beard, Lycomodeus, procurer, second Ermoneus, all of them old. The *first grandfather* oldest, close shaven, having very pleasant eye-brows, an ample beard, lantern jaws, dim sight, white skin, comely face, and forehead. The other *grandfather* is more slender, sharper-sighted, morose, or a pale complexion, has an ample beard, red hair, cropped ears. The *governor,* an old man, with a crown of hairs round his head, stooping, broad-faced, and has his right eye-brow elevated. But the *long-bearded, shaking old man,* has a crown of hairs round his head, an ample beard, no elevation of eye-brows, dimmer sight. *Ermoneus* has a bald crown, ample beard, elevated eyebrows, sharp sight. The *procurer* resembles *Lycomodeus* in other respects, but has distorted lips, and contracted eye-brows; and either a bald crown or pate. The *second Ermoneus* is shaven, and peaked-beard. But peaked-beard has a bald crown, elevated eye-brows, sharp chin, and is morose. *Lycomodeus* has curled beard, long chin, and extends one eye-brow representing curiosity.

The *young men's* masks are a common young man, a black young man, a curled young man, a delicate, rustic, threatening, second flatterer, parasite, a fancied mask, Sicilian. The *common* is ruddy, athletic, swarthy, having few wrinkles upon his forehead, and a crown of hairs, with elevated eye-brows. The *black young man* is younger, with depressed eye-brows, like an educated and accomplished youth. The *curled young man* is handsome, young, ruddy, has his name from his hairs, his eye-brows extended, and one wrinkle on his forehead. But the *delicate young man* is haired like the common and youngest of all, fair, educated in the nursery, showing delicacy. The *rustic* is weather-beaten, broad-lipped, flat-nosed, and has a crown of hairs. But the *threatening young man,* who is a soldier, and braggard, of black complexion, and tresses, his hairs shaking like the other threatener, who is more tender and yellow-haired. The *flatterer* and *parasite* are black, quite unpolished, cringing, sympathizing. The parasite's ears are more bruised, and he is more pleasant; and the flatterer's eye-brows are disagreeably extended.

But the *fancied mask* has cheeks bored, and chin shaven, is superbly dressed, and a foreigner: but the *Sicilian* is a third parasite.

The *slaves'* comic masks are a grandfather, upper slave, thin haired behind, or bristly slave, a curled slave, a middle slave, foppish slave, shaking upper slave. The *grandfather* alone of all the slaves is hoary, and shows the freed-man. But the *upper slave* wears a crown of red hairs, elevates the eye-brows, contracts the forehead, and among slaves is like an aged governor among freed-men. But the *thin,* or *bristly haired behind,* has a bald crown, red hairs, and elevated eyebrows.

The *curled slave* has curled hairs, but they are red, as is likewise his color; he has a bald crown and distorted face, with two or three black curls, and the same on his chin; the *shaking upper slave,* like the upper, except in the hairs.

The *women's* masks are a thin old woman, or prostitute; a fat old woman, a domestic old woman, either sedentary or active.

The *prostitute* is tall, with many small wrinkles, fair, palish, and with rolling eyes. The *fat old woman* has many wrinkles on a plump skin, and a fillet round her hair.

The *domestic old woman* is flat-faced, and in her upper jaw has two axle teeth, on each side one.

The *young women's* masks are a talkative, curled virgin, demi-rep, second demi-rep, hoary-talkative, concubine, common whore, beautiful courtesan, golden harlot, lampadion, virgin slave, slattern.

The *talkative* has full hair smoothed a little, high eye-brows, fair skin.

The *curled virgin* has a distinction of false hair, high eye-brows, and black; and a pale whiteness in her skin.

The *demi-rep* has a whiter skin, and her hair tied behind in a knot, would be thought a bride.

The *second demi-rep* is known by the distinction of her hair only.

The *hoary talkative* indicates her person by the name, she shows the harlot left off trade.

The *concubine* resembles her, but is full haired.

The *common whore* is higher colored than the demi-rep, and has curls round her ears.

The *courtesan* has least finery, and her head bound with a fillet.

The *golden harlot* has much gold upon her hair.

The *mitered harlot* has her head bound with a variegated mitre.

Lampadion has her hair platted in the form of a lamp.

The *virgin slave* wears only a short white frock.

The *slattern* is distinguished by her hair, and is both squat and being dressed in a red gown, waits upon the courtesans.

II. ROME

Actors, Slaves, and Orators

Both drama and acting in ancient Rome were based largely on Greek models. Although there were the germs of a native drama in the rural *Fescennine Verses* and the *saturae,* humorous scenes of daily life, the regular tragedies and comedies which developed in Rome originated in translations of Greek plays introduced by Livius Andronicus, a Greek captive, in 240 B.C. The Roman tragic writers Naevius, Ennius, Pacuvius, and the famous Seneca, as well as the Roman comic writers, Plautus and Terence, all adopted Greek subject matter and style or modified Greek dramatic forms to express Roman stories and ideas.

The Roman dramas were performed at first on temporary stages and in temporary wooden theatres erected in public places during various festival days. Permanent theatres were erected as the number and variety of the plays given and the number of festival days increased. Three such theatres were built in Rome; one by Pompey in 55 B.C.; one by Cornelius Balbus in 13 B.C.; and a third planned by Julius Caesar and built by Augustus in the same year. These three were the only permanent theatre buildings in Rome, but they were huge, seating as many as forty thousand people, and sumptuously adorned. A decorated scene house, a stage, a semicircular orchestra and auditorium were joined together by the exterior walls to form an architectural unity. Upon these stages the plays adapted from the Greek were presented, but the Romans favored spectacular displays that were foreign to the restraint of Greek drama. Cicero, for example, reported the introduction of six hundred mules in a performance of *Clytemnestra.*

Although Roman plays were given on the occasion of various holidays—religious, military and political—they did not have the ritual significance of the Greek contests. Indeed, dramatic performances were forced to share the stage with chariot races and gladiatorial shows, which exceeded the plays in popularity. Terence used the prologue of his play *The Mother-in-Law* to complain that when he first attempted to perform the play, the audience, "rioting, shouting, and fighting for places," ran off after the first act to see a show of gladiators.

In this theatrical atmosphere Roman actors did not enjoy the high social and religious position of their Greek predecessors. Most actors were slaves without legal or religious rights. They were trained by masters or managers who were in charge of acting troupes. The epilogue of Plautus' *The Casket* reports that after the performance "the actor who has made mistakes will get a beating, the one who hasn't will get a drink." The mass of actors were considered mere entertainers whose function it was to gratify the theatrical appetite of the public. But it was frequently an exacting public that demanded excellence in performance and admired expressive gesture and declamation in the players and lavish spectacle in the mounting of the play. An individual player could rise to great renown and wealth as did Quintus Roscius Gallus (d. 62 B.C.). But Roscius and his contemporary, the tragedian Clodius Aesop (d. 54 B.C.), were exceptions whose success and greatness did not raise the status of the actor.

[19]

In appearance and in style of acting such artists as Roscius and Aesop, who performed in the derivative tragedies and comedies, no doubt resembled their Greek predecessors. Tragedians wore the cothurnus (buskin), and comedians a soft slipper, the sock. It is curious, however, that when the attributes of Greek acting were adopted by the Romans, they did not at first copy the mask of the Greek actor. By the first century B.C., however, masks were used. Indeed, it is said that Roscius introduced the mask to hide his squinting eyes. In a comment interesting for the history of acting in this time, Cicero, who was a friend and admirer of Roscius, recorded his objection to the mask even as Roscius used it. The mask, he argued, prevented the dramatic use of the eyes. Roman actors seem to have specialized in particular roles; Roscius, for example, usually played women, youths, and parasites. Having discarded the three-actor limitation of Greek tragedy, the Romans, with their native mimic talent, gave wide range to the development of acting, but placed emphasis on showmanship and virtuosity. The lavish praises given by Lucian to the art of pantomime, as well as the detailed instructions on the use of the hands given by Quintilian, are evidence of the refined, perhaps over-refined, delight in the external nuances of performance.

Despite the great influence of the plays of Terence, Plautus, and Seneca on the drama of the Renaissance, they were never very firmly rooted in the stage of their own time. During the dissolute days of the Empire, regular dramatic performances in the great theatres were largely replaced by solo exhibitions, farcical mimes, and elaborate pantomimic displays. Roman showmanship and histrionic talent excelled in lively, vulgar, and sensuous dramatic forms. The *Atellanae,* popular playlets with masked characters that anticipated the *commedia dell' arte;* the mime, farcical ballet with unmasked male and female actors; and the erotic, aristocratic pantomime were the favorite Roman dramatic entertainments. They were all forms which depended upon the virtuosity of the performer rather than on the literary creator.

The popular mimes were significant for their use of women in an art that since its inception had been confined to men. Many of the female mimes achieved fame for their artistry as did Cytheris, mistress of Mark Antony. Later in the Christian era Pelagia, the "Pearl," was the chief mime of Antioch. In the sixth century A.D. the mime Theodora, known for her wit and her shamelessness, became the mistress and then the wife of the Byzantine Emperor Justinian.

Of the many Roman actors only names and brief anecdotes have been preserved. At the outset there was, of course, Livius Andronicus, popular writer and actor. In addition to his other innovations, he separated gesture and action from speech, preparing the way for the growth of purely pantomimic art. Pellio, one of the first Romans to become famous as a professional actor, was much admired in the plays of Plautus. The greatest actor of the early period was L. Turpio Ambivius, who performed in the plays of Terence.

The glory of Roman acting, however, is linked to the names of Roscius and Aesop, who lived in the first century B.C. The Greek-born Aesop was admired for his powerful tragic impersonations and his emotional fire. According to Plutarch, he was so carried away while performing Atreus that he killed a slave-actor. Roscius earned such wealth and distinction in his profession that he was freed from slavery and became the friend of Cicero. The slaves he trained as actors gained renown from his instruction, and lesser actors sought him out for training and protection. To this very day the appellation "Roscius" signifies histrionic excellence.

Among the mimes the name of Sorex, the archimime, stands out. Another mimic actor Lentulus, mentioned by Juvenal, realistically played the part of a scheming slave who was crucified in the progress of the performance. This role was sometimes taken by a prisoner who was actually crucified before the audience.

The sensuous pantomimic artistry of the Empire is admiringly analyzed and explained by Lucian in the following pages. Bathyllus and Pylades were the greatest practitioners of this subtle, lascivious art. It is said that Pylades wrote a treatise on pantomime and founded a school to promote his methods and theories. His most famous pupil was the pantomime Hylas. Paris, pantomimic dancer and actor, received great renown during the Empire. During these decadent days two regular dramatic actors were lauded. Demetrius, whose gestures were admired by Quintilian, specialized in the portrayal of youths, wives, and old ladies. Stratocles, also mentioned by Quintilian, played old men, parasites, and procurers.

The Roman actors live for us only in the words of poets, orators, and rhetoricians who admired them and studied their art. From the practice of these actors ancient orators borrowed the principles governing voice and gesture in public delivery. Centuries after, actors returned to the pages of Cicero and Quintilian to seek authoritative prescriptions for technique. Many later actors bolstered their belief in emotional identification by citing Horace's lines "If you would have me weep, you must first of all feel grief yourself."

In this circuitous manner, the practice and ideals of Roscius, Aesop, and the slave actors of Rome contributed to the development of histrionic theory.

CICERO

(106-43 B.C.)

In 55 B.C. Marcus Tullius Cicero, the Roman orator, politician, and philosopher, published his observations on the art of oratory. The dialogue as a whole is an exposition of the qualities required by the ideal orator. But in writing a study of public oratory, Cicero indicated throughout those points at which the technique of the orator and the actor coincided. *De Oratore* is therefore valuable to students of acting.

Although Cicero frequently indicated those attributes of the actor which it would be unwise for the orator to imitate, he suggested the close relationship of the two arts when he wrote: "... we take so many points of comparison with the orator from one sort of artist ... Roscius ..." and Roscius, of course, embodied the best qualities of the Roman actor. In addition to recognizing the common elements in these two arts as they were then practiced, Cicero, like Demosthenes before him, belonged to the long line of famous orators who learned effective public delivery by studying actors. If we may take the word of Plutarch, Cicero, in an attempt to improve his oratory, "... paid much attention to the instructions, sometimes of Roscius the comedian, and sometimes of Aesop the tragedian."

The selection "The Pupils of Roscius" from Cicero's defense of Roscius in litigation concerning the slave Panurgus, who was trained by Roscius, clearly indicates the status of most Roman actors and the manner in which they learned their craft.

Emotion in the Actor and Orator

...For who is ignorant that the highest power of an orator consists in exciting the minds of men to anger, or to hatred, or to grief, or in recalling them from
these more violent emotions to gentleness and compassion? Which power will
never be able to effect its object by eloquence, unless in him who has obtained a
thorough insight into the nature of mankind, and all the passions of humanity, and
those causes by which our minds are either impelled or restrained.

...but really, Crassus, when such arts are adopted by you in pleading, I feel
terrified; such power of mind, such impetuosity, such passion, is expressed in your
eyes, your countenance, your gesture, and even in your very finger; such a torrent
is there of the most emphatic and best chosen words, such noble thoughts, so just,
so new, so free from all disguise or puerile embellishment, that you seem not only
to me to fire the judge, but to be yourself on fire. Nor is it possible that the judge
should feel concern, or hate, or envy, or fear in any degree, or that he should be
moved to compassion and tears, unless all those sensations which the orator would
awaken in the judge shall appear to be deeply felt and experienced by the orator
himself.... I never yet, upon my honor, tried to excite sorrow, or compassion, or
envy, or hatred, when speaking before a court of judicature, but I myself, in rousing the judges, was affected with the very same sensations that I wished to produce
in them. For it is not easy to cause the judge to be angry with him with whom you
desire him to be angry, if you yourself appear to take the matter coolly; or to make
him hate him whom you wish him to hate, unless he first see you burning with
hatred; nor will he be moved to pity, unless you give him plain indications of your
own acute feeling, by your expressions, sentiments, tone of voice, look, and finally
by sympathetic tears; for as no fuel is so combustible as to kindle without the application of fire, so no disposition of mind is so susceptible of the impressions of
the orator as to be animated to strong feeling, unless he himself approach it full of
inflammation and ardor.

And that it may not appear to you extraordinary and astonishing, that a man
should so often be angry, so often grieve, and be so often excited by every passion
of the mind, especially in other men's concerns, there is such force, let me assure
you, in those thoughts and sentiments which you apply, handle, and discuss in
speaking, that there is no occasion for simulation or deceit; for the very nature of
the language which is adopted to move the passions of others, moves the orator himself in a greater degree than any one of those who listen to him.... But...that
this may not appear surprising in us, what can be more fictitious than poetry, than
theatrical representations, than the argument of a play? Yet on the stage I myself
have often observed the eyes of the actor through his mask appear inflamed with
fury, while he was repeating these verses....

And if even the player who pronounced these verses every day, could not yet
pronounce them efficiently without a feeling of real grief, can you suppose that
Pacuvius, when he wrote them, was in a cool and tranquil state of mind? Such
could not be the case; for I have often heard that no man can be a good poet (as
they say is left recorded in the writing of both Democritus and Plato) without ardor
of imagination, and the excitement of something similar to frenzy.

* * * *

Cicero on Oratory and Orators, translated by J. S. Watson. London: George Bell and Sons, 1876, selected passages.

...But in an orator, the acuteness of the logicians, the wisdom of the philosophers, the language almost of poetry, the memory of lawyers, the voice of tragedians, the gesture almost of the best actors, is required.

...To judge therefore of the accomplishments of the orator by comparison with this stage player [Roscius], do you not observe how everything is done by him unexceptionably; everything with the utmost grace; everything in such a way as is becoming, and as moves and delights all? He has accordingly long attained such distinction, that in whatever pursuit a man excels, he is called a Roscius in his art.

* * * *

...I would have you first of all...persuade yourself of this, that, when I speak of an orator, I speak not much otherwise than I should do if I had to speak of an actor; for I should say that he could not possibly give satisfaction in his gesture unless he had learned the exercises of the palaestra, and dancing....

* * * *

...Who can deny that the gesture and grace of Roscius are necessary in the orator's action and deportment? Yet nobody would advise youths that are studying oratory to labor in forming their attitudes like players. What is so necessary to an orator as the voice? Yet, by my recommendation, no student in eloquence will be a slave to his voice like the Greeks and tragedians, who pass whole years in sedentary declamation, and daily, before they venture upon delivery, raise their voice by degrees as they sit, and, when they have finished pleading, sit down again, and lower and recover it, as it were, through a scale from the highest to the deepest tone.

* * * *

...Of this species [Cicero is speaking of types of mimicry] is Roscius' imitation of an old man; when he says,
            For you, my Antipho, I plant these trees.
It is old age itself that seems to speak while I listen to him. But all this department of ridicule is of such a nature that it must be attempted with the greatest caution. For if the imitation is too extravagant, it becomes, like indecency, the part of players in pantomime and farce; the orator should be moderate in imitation, that the audience may conceive more than they can see represented by him; he ought also to give proof of ingeniousness and modesty, by avoiding everything offensive or unbecoming in word or act.

* * * *

...But...high excellence and merit in speaking should be attended with some portions of shade and obscurity, that the part on which a stronger light is thrown may seem to stand out, and become more prominent. Roscius never delivers this passage with all the spirit that he can,
            The wise man seeks for honor, not for spoil,
            As the reward of virtue;
but rather in an abject manner, that into the next speech,
            What do I see? the steel-girt soldier holds
            The sacred seats,
he may throw his whole powers, may gaze, may express wonder and astonishment. How does the other great actor utter
            What aid shall I solicit?
How gently, how sedately, how calmly! For he proceeds with
            O father! O my country! House of Priam!

[23]

in which so much action could not be exerted if it had been consumed and exhausted by any preceding emotion. Nor did the actors discover this before the poets themselves, or, indeed, before even those who composed the music, by both of whom their tone is sometimes lowered, sometimes heightened, sometimes made slender, sometimes full, with variation and distinction. Let our orator, then, be thus graceful and delightful ... let him have a severe and solid grace, not a luscious and delicious sweetness....

* * * *

... I dwell the longer on these particulars [the delivery of the orator] because the orators, who are the deliverers of truth itself, have neglected this whole department, and the players, who are only the imitators of truth, have taken possession of it.

In everything, without doubt, truth has the advantage over imitation; and if truth were efficient enough in delivery of itself, we should certainly have no need for the aid of art. But as that emotion of mind, which ought to be chiefly expressed or imitated in delivery, is often so confused as to be obscured and almost overwhelmed, the peculiarities which throw that veil over it are to be set aside, and such as are eminent and conspicuous to be selected. For every emotion of the mind has from nature its own peculiar look, tone, and gesture; and the whole frame of a man, and his whole countenance, and the variation of his voice sound like strings in a musical instrument, just as they are moved by the affections of the mind. For the tones of the voice, like musical chords, are so wound up as to be responsive to every touch, sharp, flat, quick, slow, loud, gentle; and yet, among all these, each in its kind has its own middle tone. From these tones, too, are derived many other sorts, as the rough, the smooth, the contracted, the broad, the protracted, and interrupted; the broken and divided, the attenuated and inflated, with varieties of modulation; for there is none of these, or those that resemble them, which may not be influenced by art and management; and they are presented to the orator, as colors to the painter, to produce variety.

Anger, for instance, assumes a particular tone of voice, acute, vehement, and with frequent breaks.... But lamentation and bewailing assumes another tone, flexible, full, interrupted, in a voice of sorrow.... Fear has another tone, desponding, hesitant, abject.... Violence has another tone, strained, vehement, impetuous, with a kind of forcible excitement.... Pleasure another, unconstrained, mild, tender, cheerful, languid.... Trouble has another tone; a sort of gravity without lamentation; oppressed, as it were, with one heavy uniform sound....

On all these emotions a proper gesture ought to attend; not the gesture of the stage, expressive of mere words, but one showing the whole force and meaning of a passage, not by gesticulation, but by emphatic delivery, by strong and manly exertion of the lungs, not imitated from the theatre and the players, but rather from the camp and the palaestra.... But all depends on the countenance; and even in that the eyes bear sovereign sway; and therefore the oldest of our countrymen showed the more judgment in not applauding even Roscius himself to any great degree when he performed in a mask; for all the powers of action proceed from the mind, and the countenance is the image of the mind, and the eyes are its interpreters. This, indeed, is the only part of the body that can effectually display as infinite a number of significations and changes, as there is of emotions in the soul; nor can any speaker produce the same effects with his eyes shut, as with them open. Theophrastus indeed has told us, that a certain

Tauriscus used to say, that a player who pronounced his part gazing on any particular object was like one who turned his back on the audience....

To the effectiveness and excellence in delivery the voice doubtless contributes most; the voice, I say, which, in its full strength, must be the chief object of our wishes; and next, whatever strength of voice we have, to cherish it.

* * * *

...As to the exertion and exercise of the voice, of the breath, of the whole body, and of the tongue itself, they do not so much require art as labor; but in those matters we ought to be particularly careful whom we imitate and whom we would wish to resemble. Not only orators are to be observed by us, but even actors, lest by vicious habits we contract any awkwardness or ungracefulness. The memory is also to be exercised, by learning accurately by heart as many of our own writing, and those of others, as we can.

The Pupils of Roscius

What was stolen? The advocate, with everyone on the tiptoe of expectation, begins to set forth the history of the partnership in the old actor. Panurgus, says he, was the slave of Fannius, and became the common property of Fannius and Roscius. At this point Saturius first complained bitterly that Roscius had become joint-possessor for nothing of a slave who had been bought by Fannius and was his private property. Of course Fannius, that generous man, careless about money, overflowing with kindness, made a present of him to Roscius. I suppose so!... You assert, Saturius, that Panurgus was the private property of Fannius. But I contend that he belonged entirely to Roscius. For what part of him belonged to Fannius? His body. What part belonged to Roscius? His training. It was not his personal appearance, but his skill as an actor that was valuable... no one judged him by his body, but valued him by his skill as a comedian.... What hopes, what expectations, what enthusiasm, what favor accompanied Panurgus on the stage, because he was the pupil of Roscius. All who were devoted to Roscius and admired him favored and approved of the pupil; in short, all who had heard the name of Roscius thought Panurgus an accomplished and finished comedian. This is the way of the crowd; its judgments are seldom founded on truth, mostly on opinion. Very few appreciated what he knew, everybody wanted to know where he had learnt it. They did not think that anything irregular or wrong could come out of Roscius. If he had come from Statilius [a minor actor] although he might have surpassed Roscius in skill, no one would have looked at him; for no one would think that a good comedian could be made out of a very bad actor....

The same thing also happened recently in the case of the comedian Eros. Driven off the stage, hissed and even insulted, he took refuge as at an altar in the house of Roscius, who gave him instructions, patronage, and his name; and so, in a very short time, he who had not even been considered good enough for the lowest class of actors attained a position among the most distinguished comedians. What was it that raised him so high? Only the recommendation of Roscius, who

Cicero: "For Quintus Roscius Comedian," *The Speeches*, translated by John Henry Freese. London: Loeb Classical Library, William Heinemann, Ltd., 1945, pp. 301, 303. Copyright 1945. By permission of the Loeb Classical Library, Harvard University Press.

after this not only took Panurgus to his house that he might be spoken of as one of his pupils, but taught him with the greatest pains, irritability and discomfort. In fact, the cleverer and more talented a man is, the more ill-tempered and worried he is as a teacher; for when he sees that a pupil is slow at grasping what he himself has mastered so rapidly, he is tormented.

QUINTILIAN

(c. 35-95 A.D.)

Although born in Spain, Marcus Fabius Quintilian became an outstanding Roman instructor in eloquence. For twenty years he headed the foremost school of oratory in Rome, and the Emperor Vespasian created a chair of oratory for him.

In 88 A.D. Quintilian retired from active teaching and pleading at the bar to write his great work, the *Institutio Oratoria,* which, like Cicero's *De Oratore,* out-lined the training and attributes of the accomplished orator. Like the other great studies on oratory in classical times, portions of the *Institutes* earn a place in the history of acting from the close association of the two arts. Quintilian's detailed in-structions on voice and gesture for the orator were probably based on the practice of Roman actors. He recognized the differences between acting and oratory, as did Cicero before him, but this did not prevent later writers on acting from basing their instructions to actors on Quintilian's precepts for orators.

Action and Delivery

Instruction to be received from the actor

Some time is also to be devoted to the actor, but only so far as the future orator requires the art of delivery; for I do not wish the boy, whom I educate for this pursuit, either to be broken to the shrillness of a woman's voice, or to repeat the tremulous tones of an old man's. Neither let him imitate the vices of the drunkard, nor adapt himself to the baseness of the slave, nor let him learn to display the feelings of love, or avarice, or fear; acquirements which are not at all necessary to the orator, and which corrupt the mind, especially while it is yet tender and uninformed in early youth; for frequent imitation settles into habit. It is not even every gesture or motion that is to be adopted from the actor; for though the orator ought to regulate both to a certain degree, yet he will be far from appearing in a theatrical character, and will exhibit nothing ex-travagant either in his looks, or the movements of his hands, or his walk; for if there is any art used by speakers in these points, the first object of it should be that it may not appear to be art.

What is then the duty of the teacher as to these particulars? Let him, in the first place, correct faults of pronunciation, if there are any, so that the words of the learner may be fully expressed, and that every letter may be uttered with its proper sound.

* * * *

The teacher will be cautious, likewise, that concluding syllables be not lost;

Quintilian: *Institutes of Oratory,* translated by Rev. John Selby Watson. London: G. Bell and Sons, Ltd., 1913, selected passages.

that his pupil's speech be all of a similar character; that whenever he has to raise his voice, the effort may be that of his lungs, and not of his head; that his gesture may be suited to his voice, and his looks to his gesture. He will have to take care, also, that the face of his pupil, while speaking, look straight forward; that his lips be not distorted; that no opening of the mouth immoderately distend his jaws; that his face be not turned up, or his eyes cast down too much, or his head inclined to either side. The face offends in various ways; I have seen many speakers, whose eyebrows were raised at every effort of the voice; those of others I have seen contracted; and those of some even disagreeing, as they turned up one towards the top of the head, while with the other the eye itself was almost concealed. To all these matters, as we shall hereafter show, a vast deal of importance is to be attached; for nothing can please which is unbecoming.

The actor will also be required to teach how a narrative should be delivered; with what authority persuasion should be enforced; with what force anger may show itself; and what tone of voice is adapted to excite pity. This instruction he will give with the best effect, if he select particular passages from plays, such as are most adapted for this object, that is such as most resemble pleadings. The repetition of these passages will not only be beneficial to pronunciation, but also highly efficient in fostering eloquence. . . .

Nor do I think that those orators are to be blamed who have devoted some time even to the masters in the palaestra. I do not speak of those by whom part of life is spent among oil, and the rest over wine, and who have oppressed the powers of the mind by excessive attention to the body; (such characters I should wish to be as far off as possible from the pupil that I am training;) but the same name is given to those by whom gesture and motion are formed; so that the arms may be properly extended; that the action of the hands may not be ungraceful or unseemly; that the attitude may not be unbecoming; that there may be no awkwardness in advancing the feet; and that the head and eyes may not be at variance with the turn of the rest of the body. For no one will deny that all such particulars form a part of delivery, or will separate delivery itself from oratory; and assuredly the orator must not disdain to learn what he must practice, especially when this *chironomia,* which is, as is expressed by the word itself, the law of gesture, had its origin even in the heroic ages, and was approved by the most eminent men of Greece, even by Socrates himself; it was also regarded by Plato as a part of the qualifications of a public man. . . .

* * * *

There is great regard paid to character among the tragic and comic poets; for they introduce a variety of persons accurately distinguished. Similiar discrimination used to be observed by those who wrote speeches for others; and it is observed by declaimers, for we do not always declaim as pleaders of a cause, but very frequently as parties concerned in it.

But even in the causes in which we plead as advocates, the same difference should be carefully observed; for we often take upon ourselves the character of others, and speak, as it were, with other persons' mouths; and we must exhibit in those to whom we adapt our voice, their exact peculiarities of manner.

* * * *

Delivery is by most writers called action; but it appears to derive the one name from the voice, and the other from the gesture; for Cicero calls action sometimes the language, as it were, and sometimes the eloquence of the body.

Yet he makes two constituent parts of action, which are the same as those of delivery, voice and motion. We, therefore, make use of either term indiscriminately.

As for the thing itself, it has a wonderful power and efficacy in oratory; for it is not of so much importance what sort of thoughts we conceive within ourselves, as it is in what manner we express them; since those whom we address are moved only as they hear. Accordingly there is no proof, that proceeds in any way from a pleader, of such strength that it may not lose its effect, unless it be supported by a tone of affirmation in the speaker. All attempts at exciting the feelings must prove ineffectual, unless they be enlivened by the voice of the speaker, by his look, and by the action of almost his whole body. For when we have displayed energy in all these respects, we may think ourselves happy, if the judge catches a single spark of our fire; and we surely cannot hope to move him if we are languid and supine, or expect that he will not slumber if we yawn. Even actors on the stage give proof of the power of delivery, since they add so much grace even to the best of our poets, that the same passages delight us infinitely more when they are heard than when they are read; and they gain a favorable hearing for the most contemptible performances, insomuch that pieces which have no place in our libraries are welcomed time after time at the theatre. If, then, in matters which we know to be fictitious and unreal, delivery is of such effect as to excite in us anger, tears, and concern, how much additional weight must it have when we also believe the subjects on which it is bestowed?

For my part, I should be inclined to say that language of but moderate merit, recommended by a forcible delivery, will make more impression than the very best, if it be unattended with that advantage. Accordingly Demosthenes, when he was asked what was the chief excellence in the whole art of oratory, gave the palm to delivery, and assigned to it also the second and third place, until he ceased to be questioned; so that he may be thought to have esteemed it not merely the principal, but the only excellence. It was for this reason that he himself studied it under Andronicus the actor, and with such success that Aeschines, when the Rhodians expressed admiration of his speech, appears to have exclaimed with great justice, What if you had heard him himself deliver it? ... Indeed, as words have much power of themselves, as the voice adds a particular force to thought, and as gesture and motion are not without meaning, some great excellence must necessarily be the result when all these sources of power are combined.

* * * *

Since delivery in general, as I said, depends upon two things, voice and gesture, of which the one affects the eyes and the other the ears, the two senses through which all impressions find their way into the mind, it is natural to speak first of the voice, to which also, the gesture is to be adapted.

In regard to it, then, the first thing to be considered is what sort of voice we have, and the next, how we use it. The natural power of the voice is estimated by its quantity and its quality....

But the good qualities of the voice, like those of all our other faculties, are improved by attention and deteriorated by neglect. The attention to be paid to the voice by orators, however, is not the same as that which is required from singing-masters; though there are many things equally necessary to both....

* * * *

...I may first make some remarks on gesture, which must be in concert with the voice, and must, as well as the voice, obey the mind.

How much power gesture has in a speaker, is sufficiently evident from the consideration that it can signify most things even without the aid of words. Not only a movement of the hand, but even a nod, may express our meaning; and such gestures are to the dumb instead of speech....

In action, as in the whole body, the head holds the chief place, as contributing to produce both the gracefulness which I have just mentioned, and expressiveness.... But the chief part of the head is the face. With the face we show ourselves suppliant, menacing, soothing, sad, cheerful, proud, humble, on the face men hang as it were, and fix their gaze and entire attention on it, even before we begin to speak, by the face we express love and hate; from the face we understand numbers of things, and its expression is often equivalent to all the words that we could use. Accordingly in the pieces composed for the stage, the masters in the art of delivery borrow aid for exciting the feelings even from their masks; so that, in tragedy, the mask for the character of Aërope looks mournful; that for Medea, fierce; that for Ajax, indicates disorder of mind; that for Hercules, boldness; while in comedy, besides other designations by which slaves, procurers, parasites, countrymen, soldiers, courtesans, maidservants, morose or good-natured old men, careful or extravagant youths, are distinguished one from another, the father, who plays the principal part, has, because he is sometimes in passion and sometimes calm, a mask with one of the eyebrows raised, and the other lowered, and it is the practice of the actors to turn that side more frequently to the audience which is more in accordance with the part of the character which they are playing.

[Discussion of the eye, nose, lips, neck, shoulders and arms follows.]

* * * *

As to the hands, without the aid of which all delivery would be deficient and weak, it can scarcely be told of what a variety of motions they are susceptible, since they almost equal in expression the powers of language itself; for other parts of the body assist the speaker, but these, I may almost say, speak themselves. With our hands we ask, promise, call persons to us and send them away, threaten, supplicate, intimate dislike or fear; with our hands we signify joy, grief, doubt, acknowledgement, penitence, and indicate measure, quantity, number, and time. Have not our hands the power of inciting, of restraining, of beseeching, of testifying approbation, admiration, and shame? Do they not, in pointing out places and persons, discharge the duty of adverbs and pronouns? So that amidst the great diversity of tongues pervading all nations and people, the language of the hands appears to be a language common to all men....

...Slowness in delivery is better suited to the pathetic; and hence it was that Roscius was inclined to quickness of manner, Aesop to gravity, the one acting in comedy and the other in tragedy. The same observation is to be made with regard to the motion of the body; and accordingly, on the stage, the walk of men in the prime of life, of old men, of military characters, and of matrons, is slow; while male or female slaves, parasites, and fishermen, move with great agility.

But the masters of the art of gesture will not allow the hand to be raised above the eyes or to fall lower than the breast; and consequently it must be thought in the highest degree objectionable to lift it to the crown of the head, or to bring it down to the bottom of the belly. . . .

In regard to the feet, we observe how we place and how we move them. To stand with the right foot advanced, and to advance at the same time the hand and foot on the same side, is ungraceful. It is sometimes allowable to rest on the right foot, but this must be done without any inclination of the rest of the body; and the attitude is rather that of an actor, than of an orator.

LUCIAN

(c. 120-200 A.D.)

Lucian of Samosata was a Greek writer who lived during the reign of Marcus Aurelius. He was a lawyer for most of his life and also an instructor of rhetoric in Greece. In his old age he became procurator of part of Egypt.

The numerous dialogues which he wrote illustrate life and manners during the second century A.D. Among them are a defense and exposition of the much admired Roman art of pantomime, from which we can form a lively impression of the performance and the performer, both called the pantomime. Professor James Turney Allen (*Stage Antiquities of the Greeks and Romans and Their Influence*) suggests that Lucian's derogatory remarks on tragic actors must not be taken as a portrait of the Greek actor of the fifth and fourth centuries B.C. More likely, Lucian's description represents the decadence of tragic acting, for the exaggeration he depicts is out of keeping with the simplicity of the Greek art in its heyday.

Of Pantomime

In forming our estimate of tragedy, let us first consider its externals — the hideous, appalling spectacle that the actor presents. His high boots raise him up out of all proportion; his head is hidden under an enormous mask; his huge mouth gapes upon the audience as if he would swallow them; to say nothing of the chest-pads and stomach-pads with which he contrives to give himself an artificial corpulence, lest his deficiency in this respect should emphasize his disproportionate height. And in the middle of it all is the actor, shouting away, now high, now low — *chanting* his iambics as often as not; could anything be more revolting than this sing-song recitation of tragic woes? The actor is a mouthpiece: that is his sole responsibility;—the poet has seen to the rest, ages since. From an Andromache or a Hecuba, one can endure recitative: but when Heracles himself comes upon the stage, and so far forgets himself, and the respect due to the lion-skin and club that he carries, as to deliver a solo, no reasonable person can deny that such a performance is in execrable taste. Then again, your objection to dancing — that men act women's parts — is equally applicable to tragedy and comedy, in which indeed there are more women than men.

By comedy, the absurdity of the masks ... is actually claimed as one of its attractions. On the other hand, I need not tell you how decent, how seemly, is the dancer's attire; any one who is not blind can see that for himself. His very mask is elegant, and well adapted to his part; there is no gaping here; the lips

Lucian: "Of Pantomime," *The Works of Lucian of Samosata*, translated by H. W. Fowler and F. G. Fowler. Oxford at the Clarendon Press, 1905, Volume II, pp. 238-263 *passim*. Copyright 1905. By permission of The Clarendon Press, Oxford.

are closed, for the dancer has plenty of other voices at his service. In older days, dancer and singer were one: but the violent exercise caused shortness of breath; the song suffered for it, and it was found advisable to have the singing done independently.

As to the subjects treated, they are the same for both, Pantomime differing from tragedy only in the infinite variety of its plots, and in the superior ingenuity and learning displayed in them.

* * * *

... And now I come to the pantomime. What must be his qualification? what his previous training? What his studies? what his subsidiary accomplishments? You will find that his is no easy profession, nor lightly to be undertaken; requiring as it does the highest standard of culture in all its branches, and involving a knowledge not of music only, but of rhythm and metre, and above all of your beloved philosophy, both natural and moral.... Rhetoric, too, in so far as that art is concerned with the exposition of human character and human passions, claims a share of its attention. Nor can it dispense with the painter's and sculptor's arts; in its close observance of the harmonious proportions that these teach, it is the equal of an Appelles or a Phidias. But above all Mnemosyne, and her daughter Polyhymnia, must be propitiated by an art that will remember all things. Like Calchas in Homer, the pantomime must know all "that is, that was, that shall be"; nothing must escape his ever ready memory. Faithfully to represent his subject, adequately to express his own conceptions, to make plain all that might be obscure;—these are the first essentials for the pantomime, to whom no higher compliment could be paid than Thucydides' tribute to Pericles, who, he says, "could not only conceive a wise policy, but render it intelligible to his hearers"; the intelligibility, in the present case, depending on clearness of gesticulation.

For his materials, he must draw continually, as I have said, upon his unfailing memory of ancient story; and memory must be backed by taste and judgment....

Since it is his profession to imitate, and to show forth his subject by means of gesticulation, he like the orators, must acquire lucidity; every scene must be intelligible without the aid of an interpreter; to borrow the expression of the Pythian oracle,

> Dumb though he be, and speechless, he is heard
> By the spectator.

According to the story, this was precisely the experience of Cynic Demetrius. He had inveighed against Pantomime in just your own terms. The pantomime, he says, was a mere appendage to the flute and pipe and beating feet; he added nothing to the action; his gesticulations were aimless nonsense; there was no meaning in them; people were hoodwinked by the silken robes and handsome mask, by the fluting and piping and the fine voices, which served to set off what in itself was nothing. The leading pantomime of the day—this was in Nero's reign—was apparently a man of no mean intelligence; unsurpassed, in fact, in wideness of range and in grace of execution. Nothing, I think, could be more reasonable than the request he made of Demetrius, which was, to reserve his decision till he had witnessed his performance, which he undertook to go through without the assistance of flute or song. He was as good as his word. The time-beaters, the flutes, even the chorus, were ordered to preserve a strict silence; and the pantomime, left to his own resources, represented the loves of Ares and Aphrodite, the tell-tale Sun, the craft of Hephaestus, his capture of the two lovers in the net, the surrounding Gods, each in his turn, the blushes of Aphrodite, the embarrassment of Ares, his entreaties — in fact the whole story. Demetrius was ravished at the spectacle; nor could there be higher praise than that with which he rewarded the performer. "Man," he shrieked at the top of his voice, "this is not seeing, but hearing and seeing, both: 'tis as if your hands were tongues!"

* * * *

The pantomime is above all things an actor: that is his first aim in the pursuit of which (as I have observed) he resembles the orator, and especially the composer of "declamations" whose success, as the pantomime knows, depends like his own upon verisimilitude, upon the adaptation of language to character: prince or tyrannicide, pauper or farmer, each must be shown with the peculiarities that belong to him. I must give you the comment of another foreigner on this subject. Seeing five masks laid ready—that being the number of parts in the piece—and only one pantomime, he asked who were going to play the other parts. He was informed that the whole piece would be performed by a single actor. "Your humble servant, sir," cries our foreigner to the artist; "I observe that you have but one body: It had escaped me, that you possessed several souls."

The term "pantomime," which was introduced by the Italian Greeks, is an apt one, and scarcely exaggerates the artist's versatility. "Oh boy," cries the poet, in a beautiful passage:

> As that sea-beast, whose hue
> With each new rock doth suffer change,
> So let thy mind free range
> Through ev'ry land, shaping herself anew.

Most necessary advice, this, for the pantomime, whose task it is to identify himself with his subject, and make himself part and parcel of the scene that he enacts. It is his profession to show forth human character and passion in all their variety; to depict love and anger, frenzy and grief, each in its due measure. Wondrous art!—on the same day, he is mad Athamas and shrinking Ino; he is Atreus, and again he is Thyestes, and next Aegisthus or Aërope; all one man's work.

* * * *

I now propose to sketch out the mental and physical qualifications necessary for a first rate pantomime. Most of the former, indeed, I have already mentioned: he must have memory, sensibility, shrewdness, rapidity of conception, tact, and judgment; further, he must be a critic of poetry and song, capable of discerning good music and rejecting bad.... He must be perfectly proportioned; neither immoderately tall nor dwarfishly short; not too fleshy (a most unpromising quality in one of his profession) nor cadaverously thin....

Another essential for the pantomime is ease of movement. His frame must be at once supple and well-knit, to meet the opposite requirements of agility and firmness....

The fact is, the pantomime must be completely armed at every point. His work must be one harmonious whole, perfect in balance and proportion, self-consistent, proof against the most minute criticism; there must be no flaws, everything must be of the best; brilliant conception, profound learning, above all human sympathy. When every one of the spectators identifies himself with the scene

[32]

enacted, when each sees in the pantomime as in a mirror the reflection of his own conduct and feelings, then, and not till then, is his success complete. But let him reach that point, and the enthusiasm of the spectators becomes uncontrollable, every man pouring out of his whole soul in admiration of the portraiture that reveals him to himself....

But in Pantomime, as in rhetoric, there can be (to use a popular phrase) too much of a good thing; a man may exceed the proper bounds of imitation; what should be great may become monstrous, softness may be exaggerated into effeminacy, and the courage of a man into the ferocity of a beast. I remember seeing this exemplified in the case of an actor of repute. In most respects a capable, nay, an admirable performer, some strange fatality ran him a-ground upon this reef of over-enthusiasm. He was acting the madness of Ajax, just after he has been worsted by Odysseus; and so lost control of himself, that one might have been excused for thinking his madness was something more than feigned. He tore the clothes from the back of one of the iron-shod time-beaters, snatched a flute from the player's hands, and brought it down in such trenchant sort upon the head of Odysseus, who was standing by enjoying his triumph, that, had not his cap held good, and borne the weight of the blow, poor Odysseus must have fallen a victim to histrionic frenzy. The whole house ran mad for company, leaping, yelling, tearing their clothes. For the illiterate riff-raff, who knew not good from bad, and had not idea of decency, regarded it as a supreme piece of acting; and the more intelligent part of the audience, realizing how things stood, concealed their disgust, and instead of reproaching the actor's folly by silence, smothered it under their plaudits; they saw only too clearly that it was not Ajax but the pantomime who was mad.... However, it seems that when he came to his senses again he bitterly repented of this exploit, and was quite ill from grief, regarding his conduct as that of a veritable madman.... His mortification was increased by the success of his rival, who, though a similar part had been written for him, played it with admirable judgment and discretion, and was complimented on his observance of decorum, and of the proper bounds of his art.

III. THE MIDDLE AGES

The Anonymous Actor

Dramatic acting degenerated into spectacular exhibitions and solo performances during the decline of the Roman Empire. The political "bread and circuses" of the decaying Roman civilization, the dislocation of theatrical tradition under the impact of the Germanic conquerors, and later the vigorous religious objection of the Christian church virtually destroyed professional theatrical activities. By the fifth and sixth centuries A.D., acting in formal tragedies and comedies had become a lost art.

Although the absence of written drama and regular theatres during the period known as the Dark Ages suggests a world to which the art of acting was utterly unknown, the existence of various semi-dramatic forms of popular entertainment reminds us that the mimetic impulse persisted despite church condemnation of theatrical activity. The folk dances and games performed in feudal villages as well as the recitations before the nobility by the Teutonic scop, the Anglo-Saxon gleeman, or the later French *jongleur* all contained elements of theatre. Although these entertainers cannot legitimately be called actors, since impersonation or the assumption of dramatic personality was absent from their activity, their performances preserved some of the essentials of acting.

It was the wandering mime whose tricks and comic antics kept alive the tradition of professional acting in an age devoid of theatres and plays. The extremely popular mimes were the sole Roman theatre artists to survive during the early part of the Christian era and through the Middle Ages. With jugglers and acrobats they provided entertainment to all classes of people. Like their Roman ancestors they were considered outcasts and vagabonds, beyond the pale of justice and religion. But their tremendous popularity in the village streets and in the courts of the great lords won for them a permanent place in the medieval world.

Some of these mimes narrated heroic deeds, some chanted lusty songs and danced clownish steps, and others engaged in satirical jesting. A few were attached to the courts of noblemen; others in the later part of the era were hired occasionally to enliven the performances given by the amateurs of the religious and craft guilds. Most, however, wandered from town to town providing merriment and living poorly on what they could earn from their sporadic activities. Religious antagonism and social stigma prevented the vagrant players from developing a reputable histrionic art until the early days of the Renaissance.

Paradoxically, it was within the church itself, formidable antagonist of theatrical representation, that both formal drama and acting were reborn in the Middle Ages. Out of the antiphonal singing in the Christian service came the basis for a drama utilizing the Christian epic, life from the Creation to the Judgment Day. Priests, chanting brief Latin dialogues or tropes, were the first medieval actors. The great Easter services provided the framework for the development of liturgical drama, which grew by accretion from the four line *Quem*

[34]

Quaeritis trope announcing the resurrection of Christ to the lengthy series of scenes dramatizing the whole of the Biblical story.

Growing in size and complexity, the liturgical drama was moved from the choir of the church to the nave, and from the nave to the church porch. The intrusion of secular humor and the substitution of vernacular prose for the Latin chant forced the religious drama out of the confines of the church into the village streets. Priests chanting a brief Latin dialogue as part of the church service were replaced by laymen, members of craft guilds, civic organizations, and religious clubs. They breathed local color into the plays and developed incipient comic elements.

Throughout Europe in the fourteenth and fifteenth centuries vast numbers of these amateur actors played serialized dramatizations of the Biblical narrative as well as the lives of the saints and the Passion. In their hands the drama became an expression of the whole community. Each man had his share in the great religious presentations either as actor, scene builder, or spectator. Like the unsung builders of the great medieval cathedrals, the anonymous actors of the Middle Ages were inspired by a communal, religious vision which made this an era of great collective drama.

Based upon a religious impulse centered in an international church, the medieval drama was much the same in each of the countries where it flourished. Universal were the mystery plays, cycles based upon the Bible, which presented the stories and dogma of religion to a public which had no access to the written scriptures. Four such cycles, the *Towneley, Chester, York* and *Coventry,* have survived from England, and three from France, *Le Mystère du Viel Testament, Mystère du Nouveau Testament,* and *Les Actes des Apôtres.* In addition there were plays dramatizing Christ's Passion and the lives and miracles of the saints.

The morality plays, popular in the fifteenth century, were abstract, didactic, and allegorical. In these individual plays the lively pageant of the Bible was abandoned for the presentation of "Everyman" in his struggle between good and evil. Essentially dramatized sermons, the moralities utilized characters that were personifications of human vices and virtues. Good Deeds, World, Lust, and Lechery are among the *dramatis personae.* Simpler and more direct than the unwieldy mystery plays, the moralities were influenced by Renaissance humanism and provided a transition from religious drama to secular national drama. Professional players eventually attached themselves to the morality plays. In the morality *Mankind* we find an early illustration of actors in an inn-yard interrupting a dramatic moment of their performance to collect money from the spectators.

Interspersed throughout the dogmatic, religious moralizing of medieval drama was a spirit of lively comedy and crude realism. If, for example, in a performance of one of the mystery cycles, the scene of Christ in the Temple was full of dry theological discussion, the Harrowing of Hell was vivid and exciting. The antics of the devils, the ranting of Herod, or the domestic difficulties of Noah and his shrewish wife were alive with comedy, satire, and homely realism. Secure in their faith the people could burlesque their religious ceremonies in such raucous celebrations as the Feast of the Ass and the Feast of the Boy Bishop. The comic interlude, the farce, and the antics of mimes and fools were as vital a force in medieval theatre as the religious plays.

In France the mysteries were performed by amateur actors, of whom the most famous were the citizens and craftsmen of the *Confrérie de la Passion,*

organized in the early part of the fifteenth century. Other groups, like the
Basochians, an organization of law clerks, banded together to perform morality
plays and farces, such as the famous *Maître Pierre Pathelin. Sotties* (political
farces), were played by the lively fools' companies like the famous *Enfants
Sans Souci.*

Italy, Spain, and Germany also witnessed a similar development from liturgical
drama to popular religious plays marked by the intrusion of farce and buffoonery.
Italy had the *sacre rappresentazioni,* Spain the *autos sacramentales.* In Germany,
for example, there were amateur performances of Shrovetide farces, of which Hans
Sachs was the greatest writer.

In England the mystery cycles, once they emerged from the church, were
performed by members of the various craft guilds as a civic function. On festival
days, notably the Feast of Corpus Christi, the long cycles were presented on pageant
wagons. Attempts were made to give the individual scenes an air of local perti-
nence; for example, the Shipwrights produced the pageant of *The Building of the
Ark,* the Fishers and Mariners did *Noah and the Flood,* and the Butchers were on
some occasions responsible for *The Crucifixion.* Costumes were not historically
accurate, but vivid and splendid — black jackets with nails on them for the
tormentors of Christ and skins of white leather for God's garments.

The actors were frankly amateur, but the honor of the guild and the pride
of the town demanded that they perform their roles fastidiously. Performers were
provided with food and drink during rehearsals and performances, in addition
to receiving some payment for their work. Shakespeare's amusing portrayal of the
attempted performance of Bottom and his craftsmen in *A Midsummer Night's
Dream* no doubt reflected the professional artist's pleasant scorn of the rustic
amateur. The best evidence, however, of the success of these craftsmen was their
ability to maintain the interest of a rowdy holiday crowd during the long performances. Karl Mantzius (*A History of Theatrical Art*) cites the story of
Lyonard, the young barber's apprentice of Metz who "performed the part of St.
Barbara so thoughtfully and reverently that several persons wept for pity; for
he showed such fluency of elocution and such polite manners, and his countenance
and gestures were so expressive when among his maidens, that it pleased everybody and could not have been better done." Lack of individual characterization
in the mystery plays did not prevent the development of dramatic speaking, such
as Herod's ranting recalled later in Hamlet's advice to the players. Certainly
the morality plays with their emphasis on human foibles gave actors opportunities
to delineate human characteristics. Preoccupation with realism which showed
itself in crude but elaborate scenic effects and costumes probably also affected
the quality of medieval acting. Charles Mills Gayley in *Plays of Our Forefathers*
highlights the realism of the actors by pointing out that "in the Passion play
of Metz, in 1437, both the vicar who was crucified as Christ, and the chaplain
who hanged himself for Judas, came so near dying that they had to be taken
down and rubbed with restoratives."

By the sixteenth and seventeenth centuries these various medieval forms of
drama with their amateur actors were replaced by secular, national dramas written
and acted by professionals. Groups of amateur mystery players may have become
professionalized when they toured the countryside and received payment for their
performances. The growing interest in popular secular drama undoubtedly attracted some of the old mimes and minstrels who became regular strolling players

of moralities and interludes. This growing professionalism, the impact of the Renaissance, and the antagonism of Protestantism eventually destroyed the amateur religious drama. In this transitional period the professional actor emerged once more, leaving behind the mass of anonymous amateur players whose devotion, diligence, and pride in their avocation paved the way for the rebirth of professional acting.

MIME VITALIS

Little is known of the mime named Vitalis whose artistry is celebrated in the following *Epitaph*. The precise period in which he lived has not been determined, but he may belong to the medieval age, perhaps to the ninth century. The *Epitaph,* with its description of the dramatic vigor of the mime, is one of the grains of evidence that documents the persistence of mimic artists. Surviving throughout the Middle Ages and into the Renaissance, the mimes and minstrels formed the nucleus from which the professional players of the mid-sixteenth century developed.

Epitaph for Mime Vitalis

What shall I do to thee, Death, that thou wilt not let us alone?
No jests can gratify thee, no joy can come near thy throne.
Here in this town I won fame; here a rich house I had;
And here applause was showered on me, for I made the people glad.
Always I laughed, for I thought, "If we cannot laugh and sing,
What use is this silly old world, tired with its wondering?"
I calmed every raging hearth that was fiercely burning for wrong;
Grief that was bitter with tears would smile when I sauntered along;
And fear that was pallid and chill would vanish away when I came;
For each hour spent with me was a joy—hearts leaped with delight at my name.
In gesture and word—yea, even when I was talking with serious art,
Joy came on the stage with me, I brightened each weary heart.
When I spoke I so changed my face, my habit so altered, and tone,
Men thought that many were there where I stood all alone.
How oft did they laugh to see, as I mimicked a dainty wife,
My gestures so womanly quaint, the shy blush done to the life!
O Death, thou has slain more than me, for when me you carried away
You carried a thousand off on this bitter predestinate day.
I, to whom life was dear, am mournful now and sad;
O Strangers, who read these lines, pray that my path be glad.
"What joy, Vitalis, you gave!"—this you must utter in prayer—
"Where'er you may go from this earth, may joyousness meet you there!"

REGULARIS CONCORDIA

Ethelwold, Bishop of Winchester, wrote an appendix to the Rule of St. Benedict sometime in the third quarter of the tenth century. Among other religious

"Epitaph for Mime Vitalis," quoted by Allardyce Nicoll: *Masks, Mimes, and Miracles.* London: George C. Harrap and Company, Ltd., 1931, p. 95. Copyright 1931. By permission of Harrap and Co.

regulations, he gave instructions for the proper methods of performing the *Quem Quaeritis,* a segment of the Easter service. The suggestion of chanted dialogue, dramatic action, and imitation in his instructions have caused this brief trope to be called liturgical drama. It was from this type of simple interruption in the regular church service that the vast, popular, amateur medieval drama grew.

Bishop Ethelwold's Instructions for Acting in a *Quem Quaeritis* Trope

While the third lesson is being chanted, let four brethren vest themselves; of whom let one, vested in an alb [a white linen robe], enter as if to take part in the service, and let him without being observed approach the place of the sepulchre, and there, holding a palm in his hand, let him sit down quietly. While the third responsory is being sung, let the remaining three follow, all of them vested in copes [mantles worn over the alb], and carrying in their hands censers filled with incense; and slowly, in the manner of seeking something, let them come before the place of the sepulchre. These things done in imitation of the angel seated in the monument, and of the women coming with spices to anoint the body of Jesus. When therefore that one seated shall see the three, as if straying about and seeking something, approach him, let him begin in a dulcet voice of medium pitch to sing:

> *Quem quaeritis in sepulchro, O Christicolae?*
> Whom seek ye in the sepulchre, O followers of Christ?

When he has sung this to the end, let the three respond in unison:

> *Ihesum Nazarenum, crucifixum, o caelicola.*
> Jesus of Nazareth, which was crucified, O celestial one.

To whom that one:

> *Non est hic; surrexit, sicut praedixerat.*
> *Ite, nuntiate quia surrexit a mortuis.*
> He is not here; he is risen, just as he foretold.
> Go, announce that he is risen from the dead.

At the word of this command, let those three turn themselves to the choir, saying:

> *Alleluia! resurrexit Dominus.*
> Alleluia! The Lord is risen today.

This said, let the former, again seating himself, as if recalling them, sing the anthem:

> *Venite et videte locum.*
> Come and see the place.

And saying this, let him rise, and let him lift the veil and show them the place bare of the cross, but only the cloths laid there with which the cross was wrapped. Seeing which, let them set down the censers which they carried into the same sepulchre, and let them take up the cloth and spread it out before the eyes

---

"Regularis Concordia of St. Ethelwold" in Joseph Quincy Adams: *Chief Pre-Shakespearean Dramas.* Boston: Houghton Mifflin Company, 1924, pp. 9-10. Copyright 1924. By permission of Houghton Mifflin Co.

of the clergy; and, as if making known that the Lord had risen and was not now therein wrapped, let them sing this anthem:

Surrexit Dominus de sepulchro.
The Lord is risen from the sepulchre.

And let them place the cloth upon the altar. The anthem being ended, let the Prior, rejoicing with them at the triumph of our King, in that, having conquered death, he arose, begin the hymn:

Te Deum laudamus.
We praise thee, O God.

This begun, all the bells chime out together.

THE REPRESENTATION OF ADAM

The Representation of Adam is the oldest of the French mystery plays, dating from the twelfth century. The three parts of the play—The Fall of Adam and Eve, The Murder of Abel, and The Prophecies of Christ—were written in Norman dialect. Instructions in Latin indicating the type of scenery, the costumes, and the gestures used accompany the text. In the following selection from the introductory comments we find an early example of medieval histrionic precepts. The stress on appropriate gesticulation suggests medieval antecedents for Hamlet's advice to the players.

The Representation of Adam

[Introductory instructions]

Paradise shall be situated in a rather prominent place, and is to be hung all around with draperies and silk curtains to such a height that the persons who find themselves in Paradise are seen from their shoulders upward. There shall be seen sweet smelling flowers and foliage; there shall be different trees covered with fruit, so that the place may appear very agreeable. Then the Savior shall appear, robed in a *dalmatica* [chasuble of the deacons]; Adam and Eve place themselves in front of him, Adam dressed in a red tunic, Eve in a white garment and white silk veil; both rise before *Figura* [God], Adam nearest, bending his head, Eve lower down. Adam shall be trained well to speak at the right moment, so that he may come neither too soon nor too late. Not only he, but all shall be well practised in speaking calmly, and making gestures appropriate to the things they say; they shall neither add nor omit any syllable of the metre; all shall express themselves in a distinct manner, and say in consecutive order all that is to be said.

PLAYERS AT YORK AND CHESTER

Little is known about the anonymous, untrained amateur players who participated in the great religious drama of the fourteenth and fifteenth centuries. They were ordinary people of the towns and of the craft guilds. Those who had nat-

"The Representation of Adam" quoted by Karl Mantzius: *A History of Theatrical Art in Ancient and Modern Times,* translated by Louise von Cossel. New York: Peter Smith, 1937, Volume II: The Middle Ages and the Renaissance, pp. 9-10.

ural ability were probably chosen to participate in the performances. Civic pride undoubtedly selected the best talent available. The care and interest of the community created among the amateurs a tradition of histrionic excellence that persisted into the early days of the Renaissance.

Acting Regulations for the York Plays

...And all manner of craftsmen bring forth their pageants in order and course by good players, well arrayed and openly speaking.... And that every player that shall play be ready in his pageant at convenient time....[1]

...That yearly in the time of Lent there shall be called before the mayor for the time being four of the most cunning discreet and able players within the city, to search, hear, and examine all the players and plays and pageants throughout all the artificers belonging to the Corpus Christi play. And all such as they shall find sufficient in person and cunning, to the honor of the city and the worship of the said crafts, for to admit and able; and all other insufficient persons, either in cunning, voice or person to discharge, remove or avoid.[2]

From Banns of Performance at Chester

[The plays are not] contrived
In such sort and cunning, and by such players of price
As at this day good players and fine wits could devise,

. . . .

By crafts men and mean men these pageants are played
And to commons and countrymen accustomably before.
If better men and finer heads now come, what can be said?
But of common and country players take thou the story;
And if any disdain, then open is the door
That let him in to hear; pack away at his pleasure;
Our playing is not to get fame or treasure.

Quoted in *York Plays*, edited by Lucy Toulmin Smith. Oxford at the Clarendon Press, 1885, pp. xxxiv, xxxvii.

[1]From a proclamation issued at York in 1415.
[2]From York order of 1476 regulating choice of actors.

Quoted by E. K. Chambers: *The Medieval Stage*. Oxford at the Clarendon Press, 1903, Vol. II, p. 355.

IV. ITALY

The Commedia dell' Arte

During the Renaissance the actor emerged once more as an individual artist. The anonymous players of mysteries and the roving troupes of jugglers and *farceurs* gave way on the whole to professional acting companies and individual great actors, just as the unknown authors of medieval religious plays were replaced by the great names of Ariosto, Lope de Vega, Marlowe, and Shakespeare. In the same manner the unindividualized treatment of the Biblical epic and the abstract allegory of the morality plays were absorbed into the dramatization of individual passion and ambition in the extraordinary flowering of drama during the sixteenth and seventeenth centuries.

The anonymous, religious, and allegorical medieval drama was as international as the church out of which it grew, but the drama of the sixteenth century, despite the common interest in the newly discovered classical dramas, soon became intensely national. We may turn to Italy first as the source of those ideas, interests, and developments which we call the Renaissance.

By a unique combination of circumstances Italy was the first of the European nations in which an awakened interest in the ancient world joined with a new spirit of secularism. Man and his works, desires, and gratifications began to take the place formerly occupied by religion and the church. In this atmosphere grew the artistic creations of Da Vinci, Michelangelo, Petrarch, and Boccaccio. Out of a new academic humanism, too, grew those neo-classical plays which were the source of an interest in drama and theatre that was not Biblical and religious. Of these plays, early tragedies written in Latin — Ugolino Pisani's *Philogenia* and Gregorio Corrado's *Progne* — or those written finally in Italian, such as the *Sofonisba* of Giovanni Giorgio Trissino and Giovanni Rucellai's *Oreste,* were rather close imitations of Seneca. The more successful comedies were on the whole imitative of Terence and Plautus, like the *Calandria* of Cardinal Bibbiena, based on Plautus' *Menaechmi.* The original Italian plays of Ariosto, Machiavelli, and Aretino, satirical descriptions of contemporary society, were marked by a licentiousness, violence, and superficiality which did not lead to great national drama. Italy, torn by internal dissension and foreign intrigues, was probably not yet ready for such a development. Perhaps Italian genius has never excelled in literary drama. These early attempts by the Italians, however, provided the groundwork upon which many of the great Renaissance dramatists in other countries built their art.

The most brilliant aspect of the early Italian Renaissance theatre was the audience for which these plays were performed. The great princes of the Italian cities such as Lorenzo the Magnificent, and the wealthy Cardinals and Popes patronized theatre artists. It was on their private court stages that early Renaissance dramas and great pastoral and operatic spectacles were performed for extravagant, cultured audiences. Painted scenery, perspective, the proscenium arch theatre, elaborate costume, and mechanical contraptions were developed and expanded for their pleasure. Although theatrical designers found a basis for their innovations in classical precedent, in the *De Architecture* of Vitruvius, for example, the lavish theatres and spectacles of the Renaissance mirrored the magnificence of this period in Italian history. Of actors one hears little in these theatres, for it was a stage dominated by inventive stage machinery and design. The players were frequently learned amateurs or professional men of letters, with the usual jugglers and buffoons attached to the courts of the great nobles.

For the true actor we must turn to the unique Italian institution, the *commedia dell' arte*. Although Winifred Smith, in her study *The Commedia dell' Arte*, suggests that in its final form the *commedia* drew much from the courtly theatres of which we have just spoken, it is in the popular sixteenth century theatre, on the street corners, in the squares, at the great festivals with the mountebanks, jugglers, and tumblers that the professional players may be found. Without a theatre, without the aid of elaborate scenery or stage machinery, these actors performed an improvised drama with skill and style which was to make their companies the ideal of the actors' theatre for many years to come.

The term *commedia dell' arte all' improviso*, the professional improvised comedy, best explains the art of these actors. Groups of trained, ingenious actors, each impersonating a stock character, banded together to perform a repertory of conventional dramatic forms with only a skeletal script. One of the earliest of these groups was that of Ruzzante (Angelo Beolco, 1502-1542), who was called the "Plautus and Roscius of his age." They played from a scenario or plot, probably provided by the director of the group. The individual actor supplied his own dialogue upon the theme of the play. Those scenarios which have survived for us to investigate seem dull and lifeless, but the plot or play-script was obviously the least important aspect of these performances.

It was, no doubt, the characters and the *lazzi*, short interpolated comic business, stunts, and witty comments, which gave these performances their life and color. Both the type of comedy and the characters used in the *commedia* seemed to have roots not only in the popular medieval comic characters, but bear traces of the art of the Roman mime, the *Atellanae*, and even of the Greek and Dorian mimes. Allardyce Nicoll, among others, has attempted to trace this continuity of the popular theatre in his volume *Masks, Mimes, and Miracles*. Even without proven ancient sources for the work of the *commedia dell' arte*, it is obvious that they built their art on very popular, traditional elements.

The stock types that peopled every play given in the improvised performances of the *commedia* had sharp, well-defined characteristics. What is unusual is that each actor became identified with one of these characters and spent his professional life perfecting the role. A great actor might even give his own name to a character, as did Isabella Andreini (1562-1604). A full listing of the *commedia* types cannot be given here; the best organized, extensive description is given in Allardyce Nicoll's book. Among the basic stock characters were the following. Usually each play had a pair of young lovers, the *innamorato* and the *innamorata*, fairly "straight" parts, which, however, demanded wit and charm in manner and language. Some of the greatest names of the *commedia* were associated with these roles. Giovan Battista Andreini (1579-c. 1652), writer and theatrical manager, won great fame for his portrayal of Lelio, an *innamorato*. Flaminio Scala (b. 1578), whose collection of scenarii has been preserved, played the young lover called Flavio. Among the women there was, of course, the great Isabella Andreini, mother of Giovan, a beautiful, talented actress and poet, who created an *innamorata* called after her name. Orsola Cecchini, wife of the actor Pietro Maria Cecchini, played as Flaminia.

Typed comic characters were sharply identified with the *commedia*. There was the *Capitano*, a comic, braggart warrior, played by such celebrated actors as Francesco Andreini (1550-1624), husband of Isabella. The foolish old *Dottore*, jurist or medical men, amused the audience with his pedantic manner, windy Latin, and half-digested knowledge. The old man *Pantalone*, who was either mean; greedy, and lascivious, or silly and doting, was a favorite character. Antonio Riccoboni, father of the more famous Luigi, played a Pantalone character.

Of all the *commedia* characters, the *zanni*—masked, madcap comic servants, whose acrobatic antics and tricks provided so much of the verve of these performances—were the most celebrated. *Arlecchino*, wearing a patched motley costume with a half mask and a skullcap, was the most famous of the *zanni*. Among the creators of this role were Tristano Martinelli (1557-1630), author also of a volume called *Compositions de rhetorique*, and Evaristo Gherardi, who left a six-volume collection of scripts in *Le Théâtre Italien de Gherardi*. (A selection from his preface is printed here.) To *Arlecchino* may be added *Brighella* and *Pulcinella*, his boisterous companions, and another comic rogue, *Scapino*. Finally in this tradition appeared *Scaramouche*, the creation of the actor Tiberio Fiorilli (c. 1608-1694), who, in France, shared the *Petit-Bourbon* with Molière, and is said, indeed, to have been Molière's master.

This complex, yet spontaneous art did not belong to the theatre of the streets alone, although it probably had its origin there. These actors found their way into the great courts, where their art replaced in favor the moribund art of the classicists and academicians. The famous companies of these actors, for example, the *Gelosi*, to which Isabella Andreini belonged, were feted in both Italy and France. Part of the *Gelosi* troupe performed in England and Spain. Another famous company was the *Confidenti*, with whose fortunes the names of Flaminio Scala and Nicolo Barbieri were tied for a time. The Cecchinis and Tristano Martinelli were associated with the group known as the *Accesi*, as were Giovan Battista Andreini and his wife, Virginia (d. 1627), who later formed a company known as the *Fedeli*. The life and travels of the companies, who were commanded to perform by great lords in many lands, comprise a picturesque odyssey.

For many years these Italian companies were greatly admired in France. Catherine de Medici invited Alberto Ganassa, of the original *Gelosi* company, to play in France. Later Henry III of France brought some of the *Gelosi* players to his court. Under Henry IV and Louis XIII and his Medici wife the *commedia* performers continued to be popular in France. Marie de Medici wrote to Tristano Martinelli, the famous Arlecchino: "... never has any troupe been so wished for in France as yours, since I hear it is very perfect." The early native French actors were often forced to compete with the favored Italian companies. By 1697, however, the *Théâtre Italien* in Paris was closed. Some time later, in 1716, a new troupe, called the Regent's Company, was established in Paris under the leadership of Luigi Riccoboni. He attempted to elevate the *commedia dell' arte* to literary drama, but unable to compete with the now established French stage, he returned to the traditional entertainment of the *commedia*.

In the middle of the seventeenth century the improvised Italian comedy reached its peak. During the next hundred years its inspiration waned, and by the second half of the eighteenth century the *commedia* disappeared. The influence of this great actors' theatre was, however, significant and enduring. Its companies had traveled to most of the European countries, among them Austria, Spain, and England, where they left the impress of their original art. William Kemp, the famous Elizabethan comedian, may have seen, and then imitated, their style. Molière, in his writing and in his acting, learned from the *commedia* artists. Their spontaneous, improvisational technique has inspired playwrights and actors. Pierrot, Charlie Chaplin, Marcel Marceau, the San Francisco Mime Troupe—all derive from the vivid, brash spirit of the *commedia*.

In the *commedia,* women for the first time in theatrical history assumed an important position. Ornament of the *Gelosi* company, Isabella Andreini, whom poets celebrated in innumerable sonnets, was honored in Italy and in France as actress, dramatist, and poet. Untainted by the immorality and shamelessness of the Roman mimes, Isabella stands as the first great professional actress. The *commedia* boasted other excellent actresses—Orsola Cecchini, known as Flaminia, and Isabella's daughter-in-law, Virginia Andreini, known as Florinda in comedy. The animosity of these two talented actresses, as recorded by Winifred Smith in *Italian Actors of the Renaissance,* forms one of many intriguing sidelights on the life and ways of the *commedia* artists.

Having emerged from insecurity and anonymity, the actors of the *commedia* were the first histrionic artists to record their methods of work and their artistic ideals. Although their unique art has almost completely disappeared as a theatrical form, they have left us evidence of their approach to characterization and their conception of comic art. It is fitting that the creators of the first great actors' theatre, a theatre built almost completely upon the artistry of the professional actor, should be the first to leave a personal, written analysis of their art.

LEONE DI SOMI

(1527-1592)

Leone di Somi, of a distinguished Jewish family in Mantua, was an actor-manager in the second half of the sixteenth century. He directed a company which furnished the nobility of Mantua with most of its entertainment, he became the official author and theatrical manager of the Academy of the Invaghiti, and he proposed the establishment of a permanent public theatre. Di Somi typified the practical theatre artist who directed performances of academic, courtly drama.

A man of literary talent, who found time among his many activities to promote the welfare of the Jews in Mantua and to compose poetry in both Hebrew and Italian, di Somi wrote between 1556 and 1565 a series of *Dialogues on Stage Affairs.* The only extant copy of the *Dialogues* is in the Biblioteca Palatina in Parma. In this early study he described the stage machinery and the costuming of the magnificent court performances. The third dialogue, which follows, is devoted to rules of acting and includes comments on stage truth, speech, appropriate gesture, and movement.

In his preface to the reader of the *Dialogues,* di Somi modestly declares: "I believe that these four Dialogues—which truly were composed more for my own personal convenience than from any desire of securing fame—may be of use to others and to myself as a set of rules, or at least as a record of what must be done in writing or in producing any dramatic poem; otherwise, I have no doubt, they would prove but useless and ill-pleasing. I earnestly beg whoever reads these dialogues for utility to accept whatever is to his purpose (for it is impossible that they can be entirely without service) and pardon me for the rest on account of the difficulty of my theme. I warn any persons who are not seeking for matter of information that they may expect neither usefulness nor pleasure in these writings, since my principal aim in this heavy task has been only to record, rather for myself than for others, in due order those more important rules and more necessary precepts of which I myself have often had to avail myself when obeying the commands of the authorities." In the preface di Somi also justified his serious approach to dramatic production by invoking the analogy of the world as a stage and by pointing, in typical Renaissance manner, to the moral value of theatrical endeavors.

Allardyce Nicoll, the distinguished scholar who has made the *Dialogues* available, deplored their general neglect, asserting that "they constitute an invaluable commentary on stage practice and on histrionic method at the period of their composition, probably about the year 1565, approximately when Shakespeare was born."

Dialogue on Acting

In the Third Dialogue there are treated the rules of acting, the method of costuming, and everything that appertains to the stage, with many valuable comments.

Interlocutors: Santino, Massimiano, and Veridico

SANTINO: We shall be in luck if this excellent fellow gives us as good material on the producing of plays as he has given in his other talks. I like his way of always presenting valid reasons for all his arguments.... Let's start by inquiring how you would set about getting a play ready, supposing, say, the Prince ordered you to start producing one immediately.

VERIDICO: You are presuming, are you, that he has chosen the piece already?

SANTINO: No. I presume that you have the job of finding one.

VERIDICO: Well, first of all I should endeavor to obtain a play that satisfied me, one presenting those qualities which I said specially concern such works of art, above all written in a good prose style and not made tedious by many soliloquies or long-drawn-out episodes or useless dialogue; for I agree with those who declare that a play is perfect when the omitting of the smallest part renders it imperfect. If possible, I should try to get a new play, or at least one little known, avoiding as far as I could those already in print, however masterly they might be; partly because every novelty gives pleasure, and partly because it is certain that those comedies which the audience knows beforehand have little interest. There are many reasons for this, chief among which, I believe, is the fact that, since the actor has to try as hard as he can to cheat the spectator into the belief that what he sees on the stage is true, if the auditor knows already the dialogue and the action of the piece the cheat seems too open and absurd, the plot loses that impression of reality with which it must always be associated, and the spectator, as if he imagined that he had been laughed at, not only condemns the show but chides himself for having childishly gone, as the proverb says, on a wild-goose chase. This does not

---

"The Dialogues of Leone di Somi" (1556 or 1565) in Allardyce Nicoll: *The Development of the Theatre; A Study of Theatrical Art from the Beginnings to the Present Day.* New York: Harcourt, Brace and Company, 1937, Appendix B, pp. 250-253. Copyright 1937. By permission of Harcourt, Brace & Co.

occur in the presentation of new plays, for, however much the spectator realizes from the beginning that he is going to listen to fictional things, yet as he remains intent upon the novelty of the events it seems that little by little he voluntarily permits himself to be cheated until he imagines—if the actors are as accomplished as they ought to be—that he is really looking upon an actual series of real events.

SANTINO: Certainly all you say is true, for I myself have attended good performances of really fine printed plays, and I, in common with others, have found myself dissatisfied. On the other hand, I have derived immense pleasure from seeing other plays which, while they were not nearly so good, were new to me.

MASSIMIANO: Now you have told us about choosing a play would you say a few words about your method of production?

VERIDICO: First I have all the parts carefully copied out and then choose the actors who seem to me fittest for the various roles (taking as much stock as possible of those particular qualities which I shall deal with later). I then gather them all together in one room and give each one that part for which he is most fitted. I get them, after that, to read the whole play in order that they, even the children who take a share in it, may learn the plot, or at least that portion which concerns them, impressing on all their minds the nature of the characters they have to interpret. Then I dismiss them and give them time to learn their parts.

MASSIMIANO: This presents a clear start. Now we come to the question of choosing the actors and distributing the roles—truly a most serious matter.

VERIDICO: You may be surprised to hear me say—indeed, I should set it forth boldly as a fundamental principle—that it is far more essential to get good actors than a good play. To prove the truth of this it is only necessary to call to your minds the number of times we have seen a poor drama succeed and give much pleasure to the audience because it was well acted; and how often a fine play has failed on the stage because of the poor performance. Now, supposing I have a good number of men skilled in acting and ready to follow my directions, first of all I endeavor to select those who speak with a good accent—for that is the primal consideration—then I consider their physical suitability for the part. Thus a lover must be handsome, a soldier stoutly built, a parasite fat, a servant nimble, and so on. I pay also great attention to their voices, for this I find of major importance. I should not give the part of an old man, unless I were positively forced to do so, to an actor with a childlike voice, or a woman's part (particularly the part of a girl) to a deep-voiced actor. So, too, suppose I had to choose some one for a ghost in a tragedy, I should endeavor, in order to produce the impression demanded, to secure an actor with naturally shrill tones or at least one who could counterfeit a trembling falsetto. I should not pay so much attention to the actual facial features, since so much can be done by the aid of make-up in the way of altering the color of a beard, simulating a scar, turning the cheeks pale or yellow, or rendering an appearance of vigor, ruddiness, weakness, or darkness as occasion demands. Masks and false beards I should never employ, since they impede the voice too much. If I were forced to give an old man's part to a beardless actor, I should simply paint his chin to make him appear shaven, with a fringe of hair showing under his cap; I should give him a few touches with the make-up brush on his cheeks and forehead, and by so doing I should make him seem aged, decrepit, and wrinkled. Now, since I can't think of anything else concerning the selection of play or actors, I shall let you ask any questions that occur to you.

SANTINO: I should like to inquire first of all what precepts and methods have to be followed by these actors.

VERIDICO: You set me a very hard task. To give you a general idea of the way I set about this matter, I shall say that in the first place I tell them all to speak firmly without raising their voices to shouting pitch; I instruct them to speak in such a manner as to make their words clearly audible to all the spectators, thus avoiding those uproars which often occur among those in the back seats who cannot hear and which completely disturb the action of a play. The only remedy is having an actor with a naturally fine voice, which, as I said, is the next necessity after a good pronunciation.

MASSIMIANO: That is very true.

VERIDICO: I prohibit entirely as a very serious fault any tendency to haste in utterance: nay, I am always counselling them to go as slowly as possible. For this purpose I make them pronounce their words very deliberately, without letting their voices drop on the last syllables. Through this fault the spectators often lose the ends of sentences.

SANTINO: If, as I think, the actors have to imitate ordinary speech I should have imagined that this slow and deliberate utterance would have seemed unnatural.

VERIDICO: No, it does not in the least, for, apart from the fact that this slow enunciation is no bad thing in itself and is the special feature of dignified persons—those, indeed, who should be imitated by us—the actor must watch to give time to the auditors for appreciating the poet's words and relishing his sentences, which are by no means ordinary and commonplace. I should like you to observe that, while an actor may think he is talking slowly, the spectator does not get that impression, provided that the words are not separated but given continuous delivery without being so mannerized as to raise annoyance. Regarding other rules or methods of acting I do not believe I can say anything precise. In general let us state that, granted the performer has a good accent, good voice, and suitable presence, whether natural or achieved by art, it will be his object to vary his gestures according to the variety of moods and to imitate not only the character he represents but also the stage in which that character is supposed to be at the moment.

MASSIMIANO: Could you make that a trifle clearer, Veridico?

VERIDICO: Well, to take an example. It will not be enough for a person taking, say, the part of a miser to keep his hand always on his purse as if he were constantly in terror lest the key of his desk should be lost; he must learn as occasion demands to imitate the frenzy (for instance) he will experience when he learns that his son has stolen some of his money. If the part is that of a servant, then the actor must learn how, on an occasion of sudden joy, to break into a lively dance; in a moment of grief to tear his handkerchief with his teeth; in a moment of despair to pull his cap to the back of his head, and so on with suitable effects which give life to the performance. And if he has the part of a fool, besides speaking ill to the point as indicated by the author in his dialogue, he must learn on occasion to play the ninny, catching flies, searching for fleas, and suchlike. If he is taking the part of a waiting-maid he must learn to make an exit by tossing up his skirts in a vulgar manner or biting his thumb and so on—actions which the author has not been able explicitly to indicate in his script.

MASSIMIANO: I remember hearing of some actors who were able to make their cheeks go pale on hearing bad news as though in reality they had experienced a great misfortune.

VERIDICO: This is referred to by the immortal Plato in his dialogue on poetic fury. He makes Ion say, "Every time I recite a mournful poem my eyes fill with tears; every time I come on some terrible passages my hair rises on my head," and so on. But in fact these things cannot be displayed very well on the stage, and certainly cannot be learned if they do not come by nature. Although there are references among the ancients to many skilled players, and although one recognizes that theirs was a peculiar art, yet we cannot frame any rules for this profession; truly it must be born in the individual. Among the many gentlemen who take delight in acting today (such as the wonderful Montefalco, the excessively witty Verrato of Ferrara, the piquant Olivo, sharp Zoppino of Mantua, and that other Zoppino of Gazzolo, besides many others we have witnessed) I have always thought and still think that the acting of a young Roman girl called Flaminia is the most extraordinary. Besides being gifted with many beauteous qualities, she is judged so unique in her profession that I do not believe the ancients ever saw or the moderns are likely to see a more brilliant actress. When she is on the stage the audience gets the impression not of a play composed and finished by an author, but rather of a series of real events taking shape before them. She so varies her gestures, tones, and moods in accordance with the diverse nature of her scenes that every one who sees her is moved to wonder and delighted admiration.

SANTINO: I remember hearing her, and I know that many wits, inspired by her rare playing, have written sonnets and epigrams and other poems in her praise.

VERIDICO: ... Now, to get back once more to acting in general, let me say again that the performer must have a natural disposition for his work, otherwise he can never succeed. On the other hand, the man who learns his part well and has the requisite skill finds movements and gestures of an appropriate kind to make his part seem real. For this, as for other things, it is useful to have the author of the play as a director; he generally has the ability to demonstrate some ideas not expressed in the text which improve the play and consequently make the actors seem more lively. I say lively, for above all other things the actor must be vivacious and bright in his diction, except, of course, when he has to express grief, and even on such an occasion he must express it in a vital manner so as not to bore the audience. In fine, just as the poet has to hold the attention of the spectators by a seeming naturalness and a well-planned vivacious dialogue, so the actor has the business of keeping the variety of his actions appropriate to the situations, of maintaining a constant alertness, and of avoiding a tedious dullness; this last simply bores an audience in the theatre and comes from cold interpretation, lacking the necessary fire and fitting power. To remedy this defect the actors (and particularly those who are not very expert in their art) must introduce this vivacity I have spoken of even in their rehearsals; otherwise when they appear before the public they show up but ill.

SANTINO: Assuredly the actor takes a greater place in a play than I imagined. I suppose few realize this.

VERIDICO: I have spoken already to you about actions and words and have indicated that a comedy is built up from them, as our bodies are composed of flesh and spirit; the poet corresponds to one of these parts, the actor to the other. The actor's movements, styled by the father of the Latin tongue the body's eloquence, are of so great importance that perhaps the power of words is not more than the power of gesture. Proof of this is to be found in those silent comedies familiar in certain parts of Europe, wherein the story is so clearly and pleasantly presented by means of action alone that only those who have witnessed this kind of play would credit its force. To this corporal eloquence, although it is of tremendous importance, called by some the soul of rhetoric, and consisting in dignity of movement in head, countenance, eyes, hands, and body, we can apply no laws. I can say only that the actor ought in general to have a lithe body with free-moving limbs, not stiff and awkward. He must place his feet on the ground naturally when he speaks, move them easily when occasion demands, turn his head without artificiality—not as though it were fastened to his neck by rivets. His arms and hands, too, when there is no need to make gestures with them, ought to hang naturally at his sides. The actor should avoid the manner of those many persons who introduce inappropriate gestures and seem to know not what they are doing. To take an example, if a woman playfully puts her hand on her hip or a young man puts his on his sword, neither should remain standing in this position for long; whenever the situation that called for this action is over a change should be made and another gesture should be adopted suitable to the speech that follows. When an appropriate gesture cannot be found or when no movement is called for, then the actor should, as I said, leave his arms and hands in a natural position, loose and easy, without raising or folding them as though they were attached to the body with sticks. He should always employ in his actions just such demeanor as is demanded from the character he represents; and likewise in the tone of his voice, now arrogant, now calm, now timorous, now fervent, with due emphasis on the essential points. In all he has to observe and imitate the natural manner of those persons whom he represents, above all avoiding as a capital crime what I shall call, for want of a better word, a pedantic manner of interpretation, after the style of school-children repeating their lessons before their master. That method of acting, I say, which makes the words seem like a passage learned by rote, must be avoided; and endeavor must be made above all other things to render whatever is spoken thoroughly effective, with suitable alteration of tones and appropriate gestures. The whole dialogue must seem like a familiar talk, wholly improvised. Beyond this I can give you no rules; and since I suppose this subject in general is sufficiently understood, let us dwell on it no longer, but pass on to the question of costume....

PIETRO MARIA CECCHINI

(b. 1563)

As Frittelino, a *zanni*, Pietro Maria Cecchini achieved great fame. Born in Ferrara, he played as an amateur in Mantua when he was about twenty years old, and by 1591 he became a professional actor. He joined the *Accesi* company, which included the celebrated Martinelli brothers, Drusiano and Tristano. With them he traveled to France and Austria. Greatly admired, he was given letters of nobility in Vienna in 1614, and the Vice-Legate at Bologna wrote him: "I am glad when I know that the people are attending your plays and are not wandering about the streets or settled in places of vice; to make my task of governing them easy I should wish you to stay here the whole year round."

Later he and his wife Orsola, known as Flaminia, played with Giovan Battista Andreini and his wife Virginia. The two couples, especially the women, were constantly at each other's throats. Cecchini's life was full of vicissitudes, ups and downs of favor and disfavor. Toward the end of his life he wrote a number of books, among them *Fruits of Modern Comedies and Advice to Those Playing in Them,* published in Padua in 1628. This work, a part of which follows, contains a detailed analysis of the various *commedia* roles.

Diverse Advice to Those Who Make a Profession of
Playing Improvisations

Improvised performances should be given by those who have first given much thought to the qualities referred to above [language, voice, gesture]; and above all, the actor should take care not to speak while another is discoursing, so as to avoid that confusion which is so annoying to the one listening and so disconcerting to the one talking. Before replying, the actor should allow the other player's sentence to come to an end. It is also necessary to point out, however, that long sentences are harmful and displeasing; hence the new speech should have that modulation which is easily learned by listening.

It is also necessary to remind the actor talking alone on the stage that he must suddenly fall silent when he is surprised by another actor who has to speak; and he must pay more attention to this advice than to any part of his own speech that must be left unspoken. Yet it is a prudent thing not to make an exit until the other player has his reply on his lips, which is understood by the one speaking since, as soon as he has finished what he had to say, he makes some kind of a gesture which is very easy to understand. But it is better to plan exits than to disrupt this order.

Concerning the Role of the Young Lover

Those who like to play the difficult role of the young lover should first enrich their minds with a number of noble and charming discourses pertaining to the various themes treated on the stage. But I must warn that the words following the memorized portions should be uniform with the latter, so that the borrowing seems a logical sequence and not a theft. To accomplish this, therefore, it seems to me that the frequent reading of excellent books is most useful, since he who reads absorbs those most tender phrases which deceive the listeners, who think them products of the actor's native wit.

In addition to reading, the actor must see to it that his mind controls his memory (which dispenses the treasure of memorized phrases over the vast field of opportunities constantly offered by comedy), in such a way that he engenders applause and not distaste, as do some who deal with a stupid servant or a base woman with the same methods and ideas as are only to be used with wise men or men of lofty position. So, knowing the differences between human beings and the nature of the themes he is handling, he will certainly understand that he cannot behave similarly toward all people, that their qualities are not all alike and that, as various events transpire, he must trod across the stage in the same way that he walks through life.

Pietro Maria Cecchini: *"Frutti delle moderne comedie et avisi a chi le recita"* (Fruits of Modern Comedies and Advice to Those Playing in Them), Padova, (1628), in *La Commedia dell' arte; storia, tecnica, scenari,* edited by Enzo Petraccone. Naples: Riccardo Ricciardi, 1927, pp. 8-18.

This selection translated by Joseph M. Bernstein.

I know that many teachers of diction will find many places in which I too do not speak well; just as I realize that those who do not know how to speak will not recognize whether I speak well or badly, hence they will go on speaking ill of me. Of these I would desire no other satisfaction than that they admit not understanding what I have said.

Ridiculous Roles

Some ridiculous roles have been invented, so lacking in verisimilitude that I cannot deal with their absurdities save by writing in a similarly absurd vein. At any rate, let us discuss them without suggesting any reforms; for that would necessitate the use of the mind, and such actors, as we see, are convinced that each of them has inherited the mind of Aristotle.

Nevertheless, let us discuss their shortcomings so that they may realize that these, though tolerated, are known.

Doctor Graziano

The role of Doctor Graziano, so entertaining to the audience when played by one who knows how, has today been so altered by those of little understanding that it has preserved scarcely more than the name. Tell me, who can fail to have contempt for an actor who, if you are Pantalone, says to you: *"Piantalimon, Petulon, Pultrunzon,"* and even worse; and then, after a thousand insults, finally asks you to give him your daughter as a wife?

Another variant of the Doctor Graziano role is to be found: this one, thinking to correct the use of insulting language, sets about quoting long and windy Latin phrases. The result is that, by never allowing anyone else to speak, the actor confuses the action of the play and wearies the mind of the audience, since no opportunity is left to understand or even make out the order of business on the stage. And who is to make the pupils of this school perceive that they are acting and speaking badly, if every day a hundred tipplers assure them that they are the most eminent men in the world?

In my opinion, therefore, to play this so attractive role, he who is disposed to act it on the stage should first of all form a good idea of such a man. He should seek to be modern with a contempt for antiquity, and must at the proper moment emit sentences appropriate in content but disjointed in expression. These should be seasoned with the dialect of Bologna as it is used by one who believes there is no finer way of speaking; then, from time to time, he should with some gravity let fall from his lips those words he considers the most elegant but which are in truth the most ridiculous ever heard. Thus, he may say *interpretare* for *impetrare, urore* for *errore, secolari* (believing that he is speaking Tuscan) for *scolari,* and the like, which do not slander either the country or the individual.

Sometimes too the actor should seize upon some silly, trivial, and very well-known fact, and then demonstrate or pretend to believe that it is the newest, most curious, and most mysterious thing in the world. Then, without giving even a hint of a smile, he should behave as if he had caused a sensation.

This character, poorly described by my pen, should be played by one who would light a great torch by the tiny light of this taper which I have illumined merely as a guide, since I am certain that the aim of anyone wishing to play Graziano will be to play the part in his own way.

First and Second Servant

In comedy it is a very fitting and necessary thing that the part of the astute and clever servant, who carries forward the action of the play without clowning, should be followed by that of another and completely different servant. The latter, loutish and ignorant, should also pretend not to know, understand, or be able to repeat what he has been ordered to do. This can give rise to amusing misunderstandings, absurd errors, and other artful blunders which, when performed on the stage by a skillful actor, constitute a most delightful role without blemish.

But nowadays I see many actors so alter this part that, to depict this character in proportions of likeness, they would have to be endowed with sufficient intelligence to understand me adequately. Thus, they change their costume in a way that makes it most inappropriate. Instead of rags and patches (the proper habit of a poor man), they wear an elaborately embroidered costume which portrays them as sullen and lascivious but not ignorant servants; and the confusion in their dress seems to be an index of that in their mind.

These foolish and impetuous madcaps, taking unwarranted liberty with the theme of the comedy, are very often wont to appear on the stage just at a time when two serious actors are conversing and engaged in an animated and difficult affair; and then they say: "Don't make so much noise, the hen is laying an egg," or "The water in the pot cannot boil." With these or similarly mincing phrases, they win merit and applause to the detriment of those who were undoubtedly studying while they were sleeping. Hence, it would be well for that hen and that pot to have enough patience not to lay an egg or to boil until the serious actors have finished talking and settled the rather important business in hand.

Nor are there lacking some headstrong spirits who, as the play unfolds, jump out and with their leap quicken the pace of what has transpired up to then. In order to make a hundred simpletons laugh, they pay no heed to the number of serious-minded and attentive spectators who enjoy a climax, which solves the problem that had hitherto seemed almost insoluble.

I trust that these actors will learn from the unkind things said of them above. For if they refrain from these practices, they will achieve decorum and make fewer errors.

NICOLO BARBIERI

(d. 1640)

Nicolo Barbieri wrote of himself that he left his birthplace, Vercelli, in 1596 to join a mountebank. He created the character Beltrame, the "willfully blind husband." Using the name of Beltrame da Milano, he joined the *Gelosi* troupe. He went to Paris with Isabella Andreini and Flaminio Scala and in 1600 played before Henry IV. After the *Gelosi* was dispersed, he came back to Italy to play with the *Fedeli* company. He returned to France several times with Giovan Battista Andreini, and in 1625 he became the director of his own company.

Barbieri also wrote scenarios, one of which he published with complete dialogue so that it could not be altered by improvisation inferior to that of the *Gelosi* and *Fedeli*. "What is a Buffoon?" is an excerpt from *La Supplica* (1634), which Barbieri wrote in defense, of comedy and *commedia* players.

What is a Buffoon?

Many think that comedians study nothing but clowning. I will neither contest nor defend this slanderous opinion, believing that Hercules had less trouble in
cutting off the Hydra-heads than in wrestling with the perfidy of the malicious.
But I will say to those who do not disdain my arguments that it is stupid to call a
sentinel a spy because he wishes to know what is going on at his post; or to call
a goldsmith vile names because he files off gold and silver dust.

Thus, calling comedians and other performers buffoons because at times they
make people laugh, is an argument either of ingenious sophistry or of genuine stupidity. The aim of the comedian is to entertain by means of his acting, but enjoyment does not always consist of laughter; for sometimes a marvellous thing gives
more delight than any action that produces laughter, and a well-ordered tale is the
real delight of an enlightened mind.

Comedians study and fortify their memory with a wide variety of things such
as sayings, phrases, love-speeches, reprimands, cries of despair, and ravings, in order
to have them ready for the proper occasion. Their studies are suited to the character of the person they portray; and since more actors play serious parts than
ridiculous ones, they devote themselves more to the study of serious matters than
to gay matters. Hence, the majority of them spend more time studying how to
make audiences cry rather than laugh. For laughter can be created more easily by
an exaggerated word or gesture than by a studied and carefully presented one; but
it is a difficult thing to make an audience weep at things that everyone knows not
to be true.

A man may be dying in agony yet no one weeps a single tear. But to cause a
laugh, one sometimes needs only an ugly grimace, a headlong tumble, a monkey-
like gesture, imitating a little puppy-dog or cat, or something similar. There is a
difference between pleasure and laughter: one sometimes laughs in anger or deri-
sion, and one sometimes feels pleasure without moving one's lips, preferring raised
eyebrows to a smile.

Comedy is a thing of pleasure not of clowning, something measured not exaggerated, gay not impudent; and those who give the name of comedy to all sorts
of wantonness, are using a definition of their own fancy. Jests season a work but
not always; for there are serious episodes that are not at all clarified by jests. And
when the latter are inserted, they disrupt the whole tale. But the charm of the study
is the excellence of a well-expounded incident which, though it is not full of absurd
sallies, has unity of action and a logical progression of scenes, as the play demon-
strates. This yields a pleasure which remains a food for noble minds. Hence, those
who consider comedy close to buffoonery are in error.

Gold and lead are both metals, but though of equal weight they are unequal
in value. The stag and the wolf are wild animals; but in hunting-preserves, the
man who kills a wolf expects a reward while the one who fells a stag expects punishment. The same act changes in merit depending on how it is applied, and the

Nicolo Barbieri: *"La Supplica . . ."* Venezia (1634) in *La Commedia dell' arte: storia, tecnica,
scenari,* edited by Enzo Petraccone. Naples: Riccardo Ricciardi, 1927, pp. 25-30.

This selection translated by Joseph M. Bernstein.

aim of the action determines the reward. The laughter of comedy and that of clowning are both laughter, but one arises from pleasing expressions or plays on words, the other from exaggerated quick-wittedness. The aim of the first is to depict virtuous habits, that of the second to ridicule other people. The comedian uses laughter as a seasoning of fine speeches; the buffoon uses it as the basis of his acting. The potter paints his handiwork but is not called a painter, because the basis of his art is to make vases and not pictures. The comedian provokes laughter but is not a buffoon; for the essence of comedy is not to cause laughter but to entertain by means of marvellous imaginings in the realm of history and poetry.

For who is so silly that he does not know the difference between being and pretending? The buffoon is really a buffoon; but the comedian taking a ridiculous part pretends to be a buffoon, and that is why he wears a mask on his face, a beard, and puts on make-up—to show that he is another person. The mask itself is called *persona* in Latin; and a masked person has no right to bear arms during the carnival season because during that period he has assumed another man's person and divested himself of his own. That is why comedians off the stage are different people: they are called by other names, wear different clothes, and have other habits. But the buffoon is always the same in name, traits, and manners, not for two hours of the day but throughout his whole life, and not just in a scene played in a house or on the city-square.

So the comedian is completely different from the buffoon, although each of the two plays the part of a buffoon. And just as the comedian, when he plays a prince, king or emperor, is neither prince nor king nor emperor off the stage, so when he takes the part of a buffoon, he must not be considered a real buffoon. The imaginary stick that beats him on the stage demeans him even as the scepter he holds when playing a king ennobles him. Outside the theatre you do not say *"tu"* to the actor who plays a servant nor do you say "Your Highness" to the one who played the prince.

Comedy is all invention. One actor plays an old man yet has no hair on his chin; an actress playing an *ingénue* role may be the mother of four or six children. These are all tricks of acting. The comedian is one thing and the buffoon another. The buffoon is one who has no virtue in him but who, nimble and impudent by nature, seeks to live for good or for ill by his wits; or if he possesses some little virtue, he exploits it for buffoonery, making the audience hoot at even serious persons by pointing out annoying defects in them. A buffoon is one who stands with his hat on his head in front of his prince; who says insulting things to gentlemen; who assails honor in sharp-tongued phrases; who tells dishonest tales; who for money sometimes allows his entire head to be shaved; who indulges in furtive tricks; who filches whole wax-candles; who eats vile foods; who gambles furiously and behaves cowardly because of his greed for money. A gentleman, however, who has some virtue and is by nature gay and gracious, is never a buffoon but a lively spirit, dear to princes, respected by knights, and desired by women.

This type of person is found among noblemen, writers, and princes; and collections of their fine sayings attest to their wit. How many princes answer ambassadors so cleverly and with such subtle plays on words that the latter find it hard to reply? How many women of wit are there who fill their cavaliers with confusion by addressing them in metaphors, sharp-tongued puns, and reproving jests?

But what happens? Even those who deal with subjects that are not profane feel that this is a good method; and they try to soften their speeches with gay comments and jesting passages. Many do not do this either because they are too austere or not endowed with grace; but of the others, everyone makes an effort to please.

Of what use is a philosopher at court who disdains all charm and flees conversation, remaining constantly with arched eyebrows to inquire into the nature and essence of things, and never finding a way to be merry or to indulge in pleasant banter? Of no use, certainly. But a gentleman who is charming in manner, subtle in rejoinders, elegant in bearing, quick in repartee and pleasing in his turns of phrase, who knows how to converse with everyone and suit his behavior to the ways of others, such a man, even though he makes people smile broadly, will never be a buffoon but a superior mind expending the talents with which heaven and nature have endowed him. Such are meritorious comedians, who know how to make the most of the occasion and of their art.

Cicero praised gaiety even in his serious orations and Plautus tried assiduously to introduce comic interludes into his plays. Hence, he who provokes laughter by using the language of a gentleman is not a buffoon. Some people feel that comedians act out of buffoonery when on their playbills they often write, after the play's title, the words *comedia ridicolosa* [a ridiculous comedy]. But they are wrong because that is said in order to make people come to the theatre and not out of buffoonery. Moreover, all actors use their wits to attract an audience and to get people out of their houses. This invitation to gaiety is like the banners at a tournament, the jewelry of a bride, a musical interlude, or the preparation of a feast. Without this mask, the play would have a small audience and little applause. Yet if things go along smoothly in the world, our affairs as actors must likewise prosper.

Morality in a comedy is like bread at table, and the entertainment is like the other things that adorn the table. No one would ever stir from his house to go to a banquet merely to eat bread; but he would go for the conversation or the variety of tasty foods. Yet no banquet is ever served without bread. The same is true of comedy: no one is invited for the moral or the lesson but for the pleasant things; yet no play is given unless it contains a good lesson. So those hard-hearted or dull-witted ones who assert that the comedian is virtually a buffoon, are wide of the mark.

ANDREA PERRUCCI

(1651-1704)

Andrea Perrucci, born in Palermo, studied law and letters at Naples, where he held a legal post. A prolific writer in Tuscan, Sicilian, Neapolitan, and other dialects, he supplied numerous prologues, *intermezzi,* and plays to the company of the *Armonici di San Bartolomeo.* He also fostered religious representations modeled after the Spanish *comedias.* In 1678 he adapted the legend of Don Juan, which was popular enough to have two printings. His most successful theatrical work, *True Light Among the Shadows, or The Birth of the Human Word,* published under the pseudonym of Casimiro Ruggiero Ugone, was given on Christmas Eve in the popular theatres of Naples throughout the eighteenth century and through part of the nineteenth.

Written in 1699, Perrucci's *Dell' arte rappresentativa, premeditata ed all' improviso* is a collection of scenarii interspersed with comments and playing directions. It is considered a primary source for study of the *commedia dell' arte* technique.

Introduction to Impromptu Acting

The impromptu acting of comedies was not known by the ancients—I have not found one of them who even used the word—but is an invention of our own centuries. Moreover, it seems that up to now only our fair Italy has succeeded in this field. For a famous Spanish comedian named Adriano, who had come with other actors to play their comedies at Naples, could not understand how a comedy could be played by various actors in a single performance with less than an hour's preparation.

It is a most marvelous as well as a most difficult and dangerous undertaking. Only fit and alert people should try their hand at it; and they must know the rules of language, figures of speech, interpolations, and all the arts of rhetoric—for they have to improvise what the poet does premeditatedly.

Hence, although a rehearsed performance seems to be most successful and most highly esteemed, that is because the poet takes pains in composing his play and everything is guided by a single hand. With so much aid, effort, and labor and after so many rehearsals and performances, such plays really should succeed. If they do not, those who after so much work give unfinished and distorted performances, replete with mistakes and shortcomings, rather than play their parts consummately, deserve contempt. That is not the case with improvised comedies, in which the variety of so many characters—including of necessity those who are less consummate and less skillful—gives rise to some unevenness. And there are bound to be some mistakes when the actors speak whatever comes to their lips.

But when an improvised comedy is performed by good actors, it succeeds in a way that bears comparison with a written play. Hence I laugh at those who, accustomed only to performing in written plays, say that those who act impromptu are not good. For whoever knows how to improvise, which is more difficult, will find it easy to act in a written play, which is less difficult. Indeed, the one who improvises will always have a decided advantage: if his memory fails or some mistake occurs, he will be clever enough to save the situation without the audience realizing what is going on. But the one who acts parrot-like, will be found out in every mistake he makes.

The worst of it is that everyone thinks he can play improvised comedies; and the basest, most backward individuals attempt to do so, thinking that it is an easy matter. But their not knowing the dangers involved arises from their ignorance and over-ambition. Thus, the worst rabble and mountebanks get it into their heads that they can charm people and entertain them with words, like so many crowing Hercules in golden chains. They try to act impromptu comedies on the public squares, distorting the themes, talking out of turn, gesturing like madmen, and—what is worse—uttering a thousand ribaldries and obscenities; then they stuff their purses with ill-gotten gains from selling the spectators fake oils, spurious antidotes for poison, and remedies that only bring on the ills they are supposed to cure.

Andrea Perruci: *Dell' arte rappresentativa, premeditata ed all' improviso*, Napoli, (1699), in *La Commedia dell' arte; storia, tecnica, scenari*, edited by Enzo Petraccone. Naples, Riccardo Ricciardi, 1927, pp. 69-72.

This selection translated by Joseph M. Bernstein.

They are like those most ignorant painters who, undertaking to copy the works of the most renowned and illustrious artists, produce scrawls rather than paintings —with this difference, that the good artists copy Apuleius and Titian, while these daubers copy Agatarchi or Zannini da Capugnano.

But let us be done with these vile infamous creatures, deserving of all scorn; and let us say that wherever there is any talent for playing impromptu, something worth while can regularly be given, imitating the best comedians who do this (and who have never failed). And the amateurs can do for pleasure what the best comedians do professionally for a living. There are many schools for this excellent training—in Naples, Bologna, and many other cities of Italy. Even in Palermo some years ago, an academy was founded called the School of Squinternati— and one of its rules was that whoever attended classes had to recite impromptu when called upon. A worthy example of Sicilian wit!

In order to act properly in improvisations, therefore, it is necessary to observe all the rules laid down for written plays. For in this respect neither form of acting is different in the theater—neither in costume, voice, pronunciation, memory, gestures, or action. All that is necessary is that there be some preparations for acting with greater facility and measure, so that the improvisation conform as much as possible to a well-rehearsed performance. If then the impromptu play does not come up to expectations, it will be all the more excusable since sometimes even written plays do not please the public. Examples of this have been known since the time of Terence: his *Hecyra* [*Mother-in-Law*] was given little more than once and then withdrawn, while his *Eunuch* was given so many times and received much great applause. Therefore it is no wonder if an improvisation does not succeed, since it depends so much more on luck than does a written play.

An improvisation has to satisfy the opinions of so many people; and the actor, much more than the orator, has to be the *servant of the people*. I myself have many times experienced what a difficult art it is even for the cleverest. I have tried out poets, scholars, and literary men in impromptu acting. They have been so confused and dismayed that they have not succeeded in uttering a word. Yet they were all gifted men—either in language or with the pen, on the rostrum or on paper.

So, in order to improve this attractive and special mode of entertainment by means of rules, those who practice it should not be ignorant of written plays—they should know beforehand certain general roles which can be adapted to every kind of comedy. Thus, lovers and women should know conceits, soliloquies, and dialogues; old men should know words of advice, discourses, greetings, maxims, and some graciousness. And so that each of these may know some rules, we shall discuss each one of these roles in particular by giving some examples. Everyone may then fashion these examples in his own manner and make use of them as he sees fit.

EVARISTO GHERARDI

(1663 - c. 1701)

Born at Prato, Evaristo Gherardi made his debut in 1689 in France in Jean François Régnard's *Le Divorce*. He acted the role of Arlecchino at the *Comédie Italienne* until its close in 1697. In 1700 he published his collection of scripts in French from the repertory of the Italian troupe at the *Hôtel de Bourgogne*. Passages, which follow—from the introduction to this volume, *Le Théâtre Italien de Gherardi* —add to our knowledge of *commedia* actors and their distinctive technique.

Although a French official once complained of Gherardi's ridicule of officialdom, the comedian was extremely popular. When he died he was widely mourned, and verses were collected in his honor.

On the Art of Italian Comedians

One must not expect to find in this collection[1] finished comedies, because Italian pieces cannot be printed in their entirety. The reason for this is that the Italian comedians learn nothing by heart, and because, in playing comedy, it is enough for them to have seen the subject of it only a moment before going on the stage. Thus the greatest beauty of their comedies is inseparable from their action. The success of these comedies depends absolutely upon the actors who give them more or less point, according as they have more or less spirit, and in accordance with the favorable or unfavorable situation in which they find themselves while acting. It is this necessity of playing on the spur of the moment which makes it so difficult to replace a good Italian comedian, when unfortunately he is missing. . . .

Anyone can learn a part by heart and recite on the stage all that he has learned; but to become an Italian comedian something quite different is necessary. For to speak of a "good Italian comedian" means a man with a foundation, who acts more from imagination than from memory; who, in acting, composes everything that he speaks; who stimulates the players he finds opposite him on the stage; that is to say, who so successfully marries words and action with those of his comrades that he enters immediately into the play and into all the movements that the other demands of him, in a manner to make everyone believe that it has all been prearranged. There is not a single actor who plays *simply from memory;* not one who makes his entrance on the stage merely to unload as soon as possible everything that he has learned, and with which he is so occupied that, without paying attention to the actor or gestures of his comrades, he goes his own way in a furious impatience to be rid of his part as of a burdensome load. One might say that comedians who do that act like school boys who have just tremblingly repeated a lesson they have carefully memorized; or rather they are like echoes, which would never speak had others not spoken before them. They are comedians in name only, but useless and a deadweight on their company. I compare a comedian of this sort to a paralytic arm, which, though useless, is still called an arm. The only difference that I find between a dead arm and the useless member of a company of comedians is that if the first is useless to the body it is likewise certain that it has not received the nourishment from it which has been divided among the members doing their duty; but the second (although entirely useless in the comedy) demands as much nourishment as the most indefatigable actors and those who are indispensable. This is what is said of useless actors, of which nearly every company has its

Evaristo Gherardi: "On the Art of Italian Comedians," translated from the preface of *Le Théâtre Italien de Gherardi.* . . . (1700). New York: *Theatre Arts Monthly,* Volume X, No. 2, February, 1926, pp. 109-111.

[1]*Le Théâtre Italien de Gherardi ou le recueil général de toutes les comédies Italiens du Roi, pendant tout le temps qu'ils ont ete au service.* . . . six tomes. Paris: Jean-Bapt. Cusson et Pierre Witte, 1700.

full share: "People without grace and without art, whom capricious protection or extraordinary luck has elevated to parts of importance, but who therefore look at their calling only from the point of view of the receipts, and not from what it requires of them."

Let us make an entire distinction between these comedians in name only and those comedians in fact, those illustrious ones who learn with a heart for truth, but who, like all excellent painters, know how to conceal art with art, and who charm their spectators with beauty of voice, truth of gesture, precise flexibility of tone, and with a certain gracious, easy, natural air with which they accompany all their movements, and which envelops everything they say....

LUIGI RICCOBONI

(c. 1675-1753)

Luigi Riccoboni, whose career coincides with the last days of the *commedia dell' arte,* was born in Modena, son of Antonio Riccoboni, who was a famous Pantalone at the court of Modena. Luigi followed his father in the profession, acting under the name of Lelio.

One of the most articulate of the *commedia* people, Riccoboni was a transitional figure. He and his wife Elena (Elena Balletti, 1686-1771), who acted under the name of Flaminia, were interested in reviving the classical comedies and tragedies of the Renaissance. Under Luigi's leadership, the Italian company known as the Regent's Company was organized in 1716 to restore Italian acting, which had been defunct in Paris since 1697, when the *Théâtre Italien* had been closed. In Paris, Riccoboni and his actors played a form of comedy that was half French and half Italian, and which eventually led to the demise of Italian comedy.

Luigi Riccoboni's writings on theatre and acting remain among the most important expositions of the style and methods of the *commedia dell' arte.* His *Histoire du Théâtre Italien...,* written in French, contains illustrative and descriptive matter on the *commedia.* He also wrote *Observations sur la comédie et sur la genie de Moliére* (Paris, 1736), *Reflexions historiques et critiques sur les differents théâtres de l'Europe, avec les pensées sur la declamation* (Paris, 1738), and after his retirement from the stage, he wrote *Reformation du théâtre* (Paris, 1767), in which his religious, moralistic, and reformist views led him to the conclusion that the theatre ought to be abolished. It is interesting to note that Riccoboni's son, Antonio Francesco (1707-1772), continued the theatrical tradition of the family, and in the book *L'Art du théâtre* (1750) his views opposed his father's advocacy of emotionalism in acting.

The rather literary "Advice to Actors," which follows in summary, is drawn from Luigi Riccoboni's poetic treatise *Dell' arte rappresentativa* (London, 1728). It presents his attitude toward truth and nature in dramatic art, as well as an analysis of speech, gesture, and emotion.

Advice to Actors

The author [Luigi Riccoboni] gives his advice in metrical form, using the same *Terza Rima* as Dante used for the *Divina Commedia,* and dividing the argument into six cantos.

"Riccoboni's Advice to Actors," translated and paraphrased from *Dell' Arte rappresentativa* (1728) by Pierre Rames. Florence, Italy: *Mask Magazine,* Volume III, April, 1911, pp. 175-180.

In the first Canto he occupies himself chiefly with the necessity for study on the part of the would-be actor, since it is not enough to trust only to natural instinct. He quotes the popular saying that "only to histrions and comedians was no law given" and asks why? Was one perhaps to believe that no rule for the teaching of acting was given because such might be held to be useless, since there is no need to teach men how to stand and walk and turn? Does not every animal, from the time it wakes until it sleeps again, stand, move and walk without instruction, and should not man likewise, without special instruction, be able to express as many passions and emotions as nature prompts? Surely he who sees in those around him the demonstrations of fear, hope, joy, delight and fury has a school in which to study? What can be better than nature itself?

But no, says Riccoboni; this is a mistake. He who has not studied long and closely by rule comports himself, when he comes to act, either too stiffly or in too free-and-easy a manner. Doubtless there are some who say that on the stage one should imitate real life as closely as possible, and that whoever seeks or desires more than this is a fool. But, on the contrary, they are fools who do not so seek and who deny that there is anything further or better to be sought. Nature at times jests, and at times fails, in the shaping of a human being. There are those, for instance, who have one leg shorter than the other, one shoulder higher, or who squint or have some other physical defect, so that one finds nature has its monsters, which are not limited to one country but found among all nationalities alike. Good Mother-Nature endows some with talent and beauty, but to others she acts like a stepmother, distorting their bodies or dulling their minds.

Now, it is obvious that neither a person who is hunchbacked nor one who looks two ways at once is to be imitated by any actor who wishes to make a handsome appearance upon the stage. Nor should all the excesses seen in this one or that one be copied although they should be ceaselessly studied.

The next point enforced is that the actor should be careful not to have a good conceit of himself, nor flatter himself because there flies about a good report of him, always bearing in mind that it is not enough to please the stupid or a few silly women. Undeserved praise is never stable, and, since one person of good sense is enough to enlighten a hundred, the conceited actor should beware of coming across such a one, for his insolent glory, his self-satisfaction and his pride and presumption will then only win for him contempt. It does not need a Solomon to judge him, and he will meet only too many who are very well able to sum him up and value him at his right worth.

The second Canto treats chiefly of physical qualifications.

As a man who is crooked and awkward will only be ridiculous dancing a minuet, so is it foolish for any, unless his figure be adapted, to choose acting as his profession, as how can he hope for success in so gracious and delicate an art? Everyone knows that it is necessary on the stage to have well-formed limbs and to be without physical blemish, and if any should be so unfortunate as to be crooked and ugly and at the same time an actor (a thing to make one's very blood run cold even on an August day!), he should at least have the good sense to select roles fitted to him and beware of choosing parts that demand dignity and gallantry, for in such he will be not only unadmired, but not endured at all.

It is not enough, for instance, for him who plays a king to appear upon the stage amid a noble company and wearing gold and jewelled robes. He must have the fiery eye which menaces death, the bearing at once lofty and courteous, the voice which can both terrify and inspire, and how are such things to be found in one physically deformed?

And so it is in the playing of the lovers' parts. A sigh, a glance, a bow ... these from one so handicapped may be not only unbecoming but positively absurd.

No, the only possible way of escaping the limitations imposed by nature lies in turning defects themselves to advantage by the choice of suitable parts, so that misfortune may itself be made a gain. A fraudulent king or one who falsely feigns himself a knight, such parts as these may yield excellent results when interpreted by one who is deformed since it is ever amusing to see a misshapen person imitating beauty ... and this is advice not to be disdained.

On the other hand, the well-shaped actor is too apt to think that his physical gifts alone are enough to set him above his fellows, but it is useless to be handsome if stupidity lies beneath. The danger of the handsome actor lies in moving too much by rule and compass, calculating every step and acting stiffly as children do when they are set to recite some piece they have learned in school and make five or six set gestures to each word.

Such an actor is too prodigal of gesture, but he should consult reason. What is it which prompts or controls him when he talks with various people in the house or street? So convinced is the author of the importance of this frugality of gesture that he goes on to pray the Muse that each actor may feel as though he were entirely deprived of arms and legs, and so, and so only, he will be unembarrassed and act well and his fame will go from east to west; and he continues praying that he himself, as actor, may understand the true and living sense of what he acts, for he says, "I am the interpreter, I the priest." He declares that in imagination he can hear them all inveighing against the "great reformer" who would thus mutilate the actor of his four principle limbs, leaving him, in moments of the fiercest passion, like a *boccale* [a kind of bottle]; but, let them say what they like; if they can prove him to be wrong he will accept the correction gladly, but he still asserts that "the marking of every comma with a gesture is a trespass against truth" and that nothing is more annoying to the audience.

The principal and necessary thing for the actor is, he asserts, to show clearly that he does not depart from the truth, for so he can almost convince his audience that what is feigned is not false, and unless he attains to this he will not please them. The actor, to give a natural effect, should forget not only his four limbs, but perhaps also the fifth, the head; but he must feel what he acts ... love, anger, jealousy; feel like a king or like Beelzebub, and if he really feels all these emotions, if "with his heart he measures his movements" they will of themselves germinate in him and move him to the right action.

In the third Canto the actor is pictured as objecting that he can't feel like Beelzebub; like Achilles, for instance, he might manage to feel, but not like Beelzebub; no, that is a little too much to expect. The author admits that he has left the actor in a hard position at the end of the last canto, but that he does not really mean to send him to school to Hell. What he means is that when right feeling is master it imparts the right movements to the limbs.

The actor must regard just proportion and not over-pass the truth. He certainly does not want to hear himself called a monkey, and the very characteristic of a monkey is that it imitates the reality of the living man but disfigures it by overstepping truth.

The actor should remember that nature has its limits. He must also avoid

[61]

extremes, bearing in mind that he has to please both the poor man and the prince. But in trying to be human he must be careful not to lower himself. If his imagination sweeps him out of the direct way let him ever keep the helm turned rather towards the higher extreme than the lower. And here the author, to emphasize his meaning, gives an example of the undignified behavior of a king he once saw upon the stage.

This king had assembled before him his royal counsellors to examine and try a serious case. The accused was his own son, and, for the maintenance of the law, there was a universal murmur of "Death." The king, who was seated, rested his elbows on his knees and his chin between his hands, until, says Riccoboni, "he really seemed to me, in all good faith, one of those Pagodas that come from China, the only difference being that he was made of flesh and bone instead of clay." Another example of the unbecoming behavior of such petty kings was in a scene where a monarch, seated opposite his great lords and robed in kingly splendor, received a foreign ambassador and listened to the orator with his legs crossed and nibbling a glove.

Of course all the stupid immediately began to cry out, "how natural, how true to life! why, I did that myself!", "and I, more than once"; which could be well believed, since it was a gesture worthy of base persons, but certainly not of kings. True, a king might have made such gestures, but they should never have been offered as typical "kingly actions" on the stage.

The actor must show nature, yes; but in an elevated and noble form, the trivial (which may be becoming enough to the common people), being reserved for the streets or for the house. "In comedy one smells at every flower, but tragedy is a lady to be respected and full of majesty" and if the actor finds himself applauded for such actions as those cited above he must remember that it is false applause and that the glory bestowed by the base people is of little worth. In comedy it is permissible to show the low and trivial life of the city, but when a king is brought upon the stage (although it may be that in real life there are kings who degrade themselves), he should be shown as noble and with all the dignity and beauty at command.

The actor should be careful to make himself heard to the most distant spectator and also to make all his gestures visible, being heedful at the same time not to appear to those close at hand to be shouting and wildly gesticulating. As for other matters, those must be left to the actor's own good sense until he find the right way.

In the fourth Canto facial expression is principally discussed. The author declares that interest is concentrated upon the actor's face. He cites examples from pictures wherein the impression caused by one central action is differently depicted upon each face in the group, and says that the actor must show feeling or he will not be believed to feel, and in that case all is lost. It is foolish to delude oneself with the idea that the audience note only gesture, form and voice. Why, if a line could be drawn from the eyes of every spectator to the point where his gaze fixes itself where would all the lines terminate and meet? In the actor's face.

This shows the value and importance of facial expression and the actor should practise this in front of a mirror. He should seek after the old mimic art, now unknown to us, remembering that those ancient mimes had only gestures and face by which to express everything, and yet the modern actor, with eyes, hands, ears and mouth at his command, seems often unable to express joy or sorrow or any emotion, giving, by his immobility, the impression that nature sleeps in him.

[62]

In weeping on the stage the actor must be careful not to disfigure his face and so make the people laugh or he will produce the opposite effect from that which he desires. A woman crying in a scene with her lover should, for instance, give the impression that her emotion is real to him, but should make it appear feigned to the audience, so that they may see "the deception joined with the truth and yet distinct." Again, in laughter, that "jewel without which comedy cannot exist," it is important to laugh well and infectiously, for nothing is worse than to see an actor gay and jubilant while his audience is gloomy and bored.

Canto five is chiefly about the cultivation of the voice. It is not enough to be good to look upon, says the author, if you have a voice like a parrot. Also he urges that the actor study the delivery of verse and learn neither to hurry nor to drawl, and that in comedy he be careful to set aside his declamatory manner and use the familiar discourse such as his father Adam used.

The sixth Canto treats principally of the value of silences, and the actor is advised to invoke Arpocrate, "the great ever-silent god." "You think it is so easy to be quiet when you have said your say," says Riccoboni. "I tell you it is the hardest thing there is, and that as a rule to see you at such moments is enough to drive one mad."

V. SPAIN

The Golden Age

The short period of Spain's rise and fall as a great power saw the flowering of the first national theatre in Europe. The abundant output of Spain's dramatists in the sixteenth and seventeenth centuries exceeded that of all other European nations combined. Spain had had a rich medieval drama centered, as in England, around the Corpus Christi Festival. On this holiday *autos sacramentales,* one-act plays dealing with the mystery of the Eucharist, were given. Prior to the growth of secular drama, small bands of professional actors performed these religious plays in villages and towns and animated them with dancing and songs.

Italian neo-classical dramas and *commedia dell' arte* performances were added to the religious drama, which persisted in Spain until the middle of the eighteenth century. As early as 1538, *commedia* actors played at a festival in Seville, and some ten years later the Spanish Court witnessed a performance of a comedy by Ariosto done in the elaborate Italian manner. At the universities, students performed imitations of classical dramas with typical Renaissance enthusiasm and extravagance.

Secular, popular theatre in Spain truly begins with Lope de Rueda. He is the first *autor de comedias* (head of a company of players) whose activities are known to us. The term *autores* was appropriately used for the actor-managers, since many of them, like Rueda, wrote the plays for their troupes. Although Rueda was obviously familiar with Italian Renaissance literature, of which he made use in his plays, he perfected the indigenous, lively *comedias* in prose and originated the *paso,* a gay, comic interlude. With their simple properties packed in a sack, Rueda's company traveled widely, presenting *autos, comedias,* and *pasos* on improvised stages made of boards.

At Madrid, which became the capital city in 1560, the first permanent theatre, the *Corral de la Cruz,* was established in 1579, three years after James Burbage had built The Theatre in England. Just as English playhouses drew on the form of inn-yards, so the Spanish *corrales* were open yards of houses transformed for theatrical purposes. The earliest *corrales* had a simple stage at the rear of the enclosure. Most of the spectators stood in the courtyard around the stage; some, more distinguished, watched the performance from the windows and balconies of the surrounding houses. This crude space open to the sky was improved by Alberto Ganassa, an Italian *commedia* manager, who roofed the stage and erected covered seats around the sides of the *patio.* Like the "groundlings" in England, the *vulgo,* called *mosqueteros* because of their noisy, riotous behavior, stood in the *patio.*

In such *corrales* the various *autores* gave their farces and *comedias.* Performances took place in the afternoon, at first on Sundays and feast-days only; later Tuesdays and Thursdays were added to meet the growing popular requests for *comedias.* The audiences that came to view the plays on the unpretentious stage of the *corrales* were boisterous and noisy. Although there was a special balcony for women spectators, it was usually occupied by those of easy virtue. Respectable ladies came to the theatre masked.

The early career of Lope de Vega (1562-1635), Spain's picturesque, prolific dramatist, coincided with the establishment of the first permanent theatres in Madrid, the *Corral de la Cruz* and the *Corral del Príncipe,* the only public theatres of that city after 1584. At first Lope gave his plays gratis to Jerónimo Velázquez (d. 1613), whose daughter, Elena Osorio, he loved. Later, exiled from Madrid for criminal libel against his former beloved, he went to Valencia. Soon he was fighting on board a ship that formed part of the Armada. He returned to spend his long life shaping the dramatic literature of Spain.

In the fifty years that Lope de Vega wrote for the stage he composed hundreds of plays in varied forms: tragedies, *autos,* farces, and *comedias de capa y espada* (cloak and sword dramas). These latter showed the influence of the *commedia dell' arte,* popular in Spain as it was throughout the rest of Europe. The comic figures, the names of the young lovers, and the amusing situations of the Italian *commedia dell' arte* reappeared in Lope's plays. Popular actresses like Jusepa Vaca, for whom Lope wrote *Las Almenas de toro,* and *autores* like Roque de Figueroa (d. 1651) and Nicolas de los Rios (d. 1610) were colleagues of this fertile poet of Spain's Golden Age.

Although there were many innovations in staging during the half century in which Lope de Vega wrote, scenic effects remained primitive. Like that of his contemporary Shakespeare, Lope de Vega's theatre paid little attention to illusion. There was no curtain in front of the stage, the actors entered before the eyes of the spectators, and change of scene was usually indicated in the dialogue.

There were two types of Spanish theatrical companies. In some the actors were paid a stipend by the *autor;* in others the actors worked on shares. In addition to the *autor,* or manager, a company frequently comprised thirteen or fourteen players. Doubling of parts was common with these troupes, as it was with the Elizabethan companies, since the *dramatis personae* frequently exceeded the number of actors in the company. The agreement forming the company of Andrés de Claramonte (d. 1626) in 1614 preserves a record of the working conditions of these troupes. "That the various roles in the *comedias* shall be assigned among the members of said company in such manner as shall seem most suitable to each in the opinion of said company. During the said time the said members and each of them shall be bound, to attend with all care and punctuality the rehearsals of all the *comedias* to be presented each day, at nine o'clock, at the house of the said Andrés de Claramonte ... and shall not fail to be present ... under penalty of two *reals* to each one who shall not attend them in time and when he is called upon to speak; and if, being present at the said rehearsal, he shall leave it, and another should be obliged to speak for him, he shall pay likewise as a penalty one *real* every time that this happens."

Stringent regulations and constant touring filled the life of Spanish actors with hardships. They were notorious for their careless manner of living, but their never-ending labors were graphically recounted by Agustin de Rojas in the *Entertaining Journey:* "There is no ... slave in Algiers but has a better life than the actor. A slave works all day, but he sleeps at night; he has only one or two masters to please, and when he does what he is commanded, he fulfills his duty. But actors are up at dawn and write and study from five o'clock till nine, and from nine till twelve they are constantly rehearsing. They dine and then go to the *comedia;* leave the theatre at seven, and when they want rest they are called by the President of the Council, or the *alcaldes,* whom they must serve whenever it pleases them. I wonder

[65]

how it is possible for them to study all their lives and be constantly on the road, for there is no labor that can equal theirs." Cervantes, who has left us an account of the strolling players of Lope de Rueda, remarked of actors: "Also I can say of them that in the sweat of their brows they gain their bread by insupportable toil, learning constantly by heart, leading a gypsy life perpetually from place to place, and from inn to tavern, staying awake to please others, for in other men's pleasure lies their profit."

Spain followed Italy in permitting women to appear on the stage. Mariana, first wife of Lope de Rueda, probably acted with his strolling players in the middle of the sixteenth century. In 1587 women were granted freedom to act in Madrid. Young boys still played female roles, but the inclusion of dances like the wild *zarabanda* in the plays made actresses popular. The indecency of the women was curbed and the conflict between women and young boys was settled by a decree in 1615 prohibiting boys from playing women's parts and women from playing in the guise of men.

The rapid and extraordinary growth of national drama, from the primitive beginnings of Lope de Rueda on an improvised outdoor stage to the magnificent court entertainments of Phillip IV in the *Buen Retiro,* called for vast numbers of players. Professor Hugo Albert Rennert's monumental work *The Spanish Stage in the Time of Lope de Vega* lists some 2,000 actors and actresses active from 1560 to 1680. Drawn chiefly from the common people, these hardworking, energetic, colorful actors played throughout Spain.

Of these numerous players, mention should be made of two, an actor and an actress, both praised as the greatest of their day. Damian Arias de Peñafiel acted in many companies up to the time of his death about 1643. He appeared as Don Juan in the first performance of Alarcon's *Las Paredes oyen* in 1617, and in Lope's *El Poder en el discreto* in 1624. In the pages of J. Caramuel's *Rhythmica* (1668) he is described in these words: "Arias possessed a clear, pure voice, a tenacious memory, and vivacious manner, and in whatever he said it seemed that the Graces were revealed in every movement of his tongue and Apollo in every gesture. The most famous orators came to hear him in order to acquire perfection of diction and gesture. At Madrid one day Arias came upon the stage reading a letter; for a long time he held the audience in suspense; he was filled with emotion at every line, and finally, aroused with fury, he tore the letter to shreds and began to declaim his lines with great vehemence, and though he was praised by all, he won greater attention on that day by his action than by his speech."

The famous actress La Calderona (Maria Calderon), like Nell Gwyn, attracted the attention of a king—Phillip IV—became his mistress and mother of his son, Don John of Austria. Even after the birth of Phillip's son, she did not retire from the stage. At the end of her colorful life, she repented her sins and entered a convent, where she was made abbess. It was at the *Corral de la Cruz* that Phillip first saw her. Caramuel writes of her great beauty and imaginative powers. According to him, La Calderona could change the color of her face at will. "At the narration of some happy incident her face was suffused with a rosy tint, but if unfortunate circumstance intervened, she suddenly became deathly pale; and in this she was alone and inimitable." This power seems to have been at the command of a number of players—Virginia Andreini, who was La Calderona's contemporary, Thomas Betterton, Mrs. Sarah Siddons and others.

In the year that Lope de Vega died, Spain's great lyric dramatist Calderón de la Barca (1600-1681) was appointed manager and director of court performances. This philosophical, baroque poet, who was ordained a priest, gave the old medieval *auto* its highest poetic embodiment. With him, Spain's glorious theatre came to an end, for by the mid-seventeenth century, the national inspiration which had made the Spanish theatre illustrious was gone; the old dramatists and their close associates, the *autores,* were dead. No major figures appeared to take the place of the great poets who had written for the members of the companies with intimate and loving knowledge of the stage. Although in the centuries that followed, lively theatrical activity and significant dramatic writing were not absent, Spain never again recaptured the magnificence of her Golden Age.

LOPE DE RUEDA

(d. 1565)

Lope de Rueda, a native of Seville, was trained as a gold-beater. By 1554, however, he presented an *auto* at Benavente. From then on there are records of him and his troupe at Segovia, Seville, Valladolid, and at Madrid. As actor and as playwright Rueda stands at the beginning of modern Spanish theatre.

With Bartolemé de Torres Naharro he shares the distinction of originating the *comedia* in Spain. While Torres Naharro wrote in verse, Rueda wrote his *comedias* in picturesque and seasoned prose. Fitzmaurice-Kelly, in summarizing Rueda's achievement in his book *History of Spanish Literature,* wrote: "...his prose, with its archaic savor, is of great purity and power.... Considerable as were Rueda's positive qualities of gay wit and inventive resource, his highest merit lies in this, that he laid the foundation stone of the actual Spanish theatre, and that his dramatic system became a capital factor in his people's intellectual history."

Typical of all strolling players, Rueda performed wherever and whenever he could gather an audience. At the close of his *comedia Eufemia* he enjoins the audience "only to go and eat their dinners and return to the square, if they wish to see a traitor beheaded, a loyal man freed," etc.

The great Cervantes, born in 1547, is the only eyewitness who has left a record of Lope de Rueda's troupe. As a boy of ten or twelve, Cervantes saw Rueda and his little company of strolling players in the square of Valladolid. Half a century later, Cervantes penned an animated description of the primitive performance of Rueda's little troupe.

The Strolling Players of Lope de Rueda

by MIGUEL DE CERVANTES SAAVEDRA

In the time of this celebrated Spaniard [Lope de Rueda] all the properties of a theatrical manager were contained in a sack, and consisted of four white pelices trimmed with gilded leather, and four beards and wigs, with four staffs, more or less. The plays were colloquies or eclogues between two or three shepherds

---

Cervantes: Preface to *Ocho comedias y ocho entremeses nuevos* (1615) quoted by Hugo Albert Rennert: *The Spanish Stage in the Time of Lope de Vega.* New York: The Hispanic Society of America, 1909, pp. 17-18. Copyright 1909. All Spanish selections appear by permission of The Hispanic Society of America.

and a shepherdess. They were set off by two or three *entremeses* [short farce or interlude], either that of the "Negress," the "Ruffian," the "Fool," or the "Biscayan," for these four characters and many others the said Lope acted with the greatest skill and propriety that one can imagine. At that time there were no *tramoyas* [theatrical machinery] nor challenges of Moors or Christians either afoot or on horse. There were no figures which arose or seemed to arise from the center of the earth through the hollow of the stage, which at that time consisted of four benches arranged in a square, with four or five boards upon them, raised about four spans from the ground, nor did clouds with angels or souls descend from the skies. The furnishings of the stage were an old woolen blanket drawn by two cords from one side to the other, which formed what is called a dressing-room, behind which were the musicians, singing some old ballad without the accompaniment of a guitar. . . . Lope de Rueda was succeeded by Naharro, a native of Toledo, famous as an impersonator of the cowardly ruffian; he improved somewhat the setting of the *comedia,* and instead of a bag for the costumes used chests and trunks. He brought the musicians from behind the curtain, where they formerly sang, out upon the stage, removed the beards of the players, for up to that time no actor appeared upon the stage without a false beard . . . except those who represented old men or other characters which required a facial disguise. He invented stage machinery, thunder and lightning, challenges and battles, but these never reached the excellence which we see now. . . .

ALONZO LOPEZ PINCIANO

(fl. 1596)

These observations of Pinciano, a savant of his day, appear to have been written not later than 1595. The selection given here is from a work, "De los Actores y representantes," written in the form of a conversation between the author and his friends Ugo and Fadrigue. Enthusiasts of the *comedia,* men like these said, "While I am in the theatre I feel neither cold in winter nor the heat in summer."

Of Actors and Playing

So far as the action is concerned, the person, the time, and the place ought to be considered, for it is clear that a different decoration and dress or costume is required for a prince than for a servant, and different ones for youths and old men. Wherefore the second consideration, that of time, is very important, for the Spain of today demands a different decoration and dress from the Spain of a thousand years ago, and hence it behooves to examine carefully histories which throw light upon the costumes of the times, and we should likewise take note of the various countries, for in each they have different kinds of dress. The actor should observe these matters carefully, for the poet rarely pays any attention to them, generally writing the poem to be read rather than to be represented, leaving those matters that refer to the action to the actor, whose business it is to represent. Whence

Alonzo Lopez Pinciano: *Philosophia Antigua* (1595), pp. 522, 533, quoted by Hugo Albert Rennert: *The Spanish Stage in the Time of Lope de Vega.* New York: The Hispanic Society of America, 1909, pp. 82-83 n.

it is to be inferred that the good actor (especially the chief of a company) ought to know much of fiction and of history, so that, in accordance with the difference in time, besides the costumes of the persons in the action, there is required a corresponding decoration for the theatre itself, besides the necessary machinery, which ought to be in conformity with the poem: if it be pastoral, there should be woods; if the action take place in a city, there should be houses; and so in accordance with the other differences, the theatre should have its various decorations. And in the machinery there should be much excellence, for there are some machines which are fitting for a miracle and others for different purposes, and they have their differences according to the persons, for an angel must appear to be flying and a saint going through the air with joined feet, and both must descend from on high, while the demon ascends from below.... In a word, the actor should observe and study the various machinery and artifices, so that suddenly, as if by a miracle, a person be made to appear: by magic art, if terrestrial; without it, if the person be divine.

AGUSTIN DE ROJAS

(b. 1572)

Soldier, actor, and author of *The Entertaining Journey*, Rojas was born in Madrid about 1572. He saw service in the galleons, took part in several actions, and was for a while a prisoner of war in La Rochelle. In 1601 he joined the company of Nicolas de los Rios. In his *Entertaining Journey* the author and three other actors, Rios, Miguel Ramirez, and Agustin Solano, describe the life of roving players. Though Rojas' descriptions of the various bands of actors are perhaps heightened and exaggerated, they are, on the whole, the trustworthy report of one who was himself a strolling player.

An Actor's Life

We left Valencia on account of a misfortune that befell us—Solano and I—one on foot and without a cloak, and the other walking and with only his doublet. We gave them to a boy who got lost in the town, and we were left gentlemen of the road. At night we arrived at a village, worn out and with only eight *quartos* between us. Without supper, we went to an inn to ask for lodging, but they told us that they could not provide for us, nor could a lodging be found anywhere, because a fair was being held. Seeing the little chance there was of our finding a lodging, I resorted to a strategem. I went to another inn and represented myself as a West Indian merchant (for you see I resemble one in the face). The hostess asked whether we had any pack-animals. I replied that we came in a cart and that, while it was coming with our goods, she should prepare two beds for us and some supper. She did so, and I went to the *alcalde* of the village and told him that a company of players had arrived, on their way through, and asked his permission to give a play. He inquired whether it was a religious play, to which I answered

Agustin de Rojas: *Viage Entretenido,* Madrid (1603), pp. 91-101, quoted by Hugo Albert Rennert, *The Spanish Stage in the Time of Lope De Vega.* New York: The Hispanic Society of America, 1909, pp. 166-169.

in the affirmative. Permission was granted, I returned to the inn and advised Solano to review the *auto* of *Cain and Abel,* and then go to a certain place to collect the money, for we were going to play that evening. Meanwhile I went to hunt up a drum, made a beard out of a piece of sheepskin, and went through the whole village proclaiming our *comedia.* As there were many people in the place, we had a large audience. This done, I put by the drum, took off my beard, returned to the hostess, and told her that my goods were coming and asked her for the key of my room, as I wanted to lock them up. To her question what they were I replied spices. She gave me the key, and hastening to the room, I stripped the sheets from the bed, took down some old gilt leather hangings and two or three old cloths, and in order that she might not see me descend the stairs, I made up a bundle, threw it out of the window, and came down the stair like a flash. As I reached the yard, the host called me and said: "Mr. Indian, do you want to see a *comedia* by some strolling players who arrived a short time ago? It is a very good one." I answered, "Yes," and hurried out to hunt up the bundle of clothes with which we were to play the farce, anxious lest the host should see it; but, though I searched everywhere, I could not find it. Seeing the misfortune which faced me, and that my back might suffer for it, I ran to the place where Solano was busy taking the money and told him what had happened. He stopped "gathering," and we left with what he had collected. Consider now the plight of all these people! Some without merchants or bedclothes, the others deceived and without a *comedia!* That night we traveled but little and that on the by-paths. In the morning we took account of our finances and found we had three and half *reals,* all in small coppers. As you see, we were now rich, but not a little timid, when, about a league off, we discovered a hut, and, arriving there we were received with wine in a gourd, milk in a trough, and bread in a saddle-bag. We breakfasted and left that night for another town, where we directly took steps to get something to eat. I requested permission to perform, sought out two bedsheets, proclaimed the eclogue through the streets, procured a guitar, invited the hostess, and told Solano to collect the money. Finally, the house being full, I came out to sing the ballad, *Afuera, afuera, aparta, aparta.* Having finished a couplet, I could go no further, and the audience gazed in astonishment. Then Solano began a *loa* with which he made some amends for the lack of music. I wrapped one of the sheets about me and began my part, but when Solano appeared as God the Father, with a candle in his hand and likewise enveloped in a sheet, open in the middle, and besmeared all around his beard with grape-skins, I thought I should die for laughter, while the poor public wondered what had happened to him. This being over, I appeared as a fool and recited my *entremes,* then continued with the *auto,* and the point arrived when I was to kill the unhappy Abel; but I had forgotten the knife with which I was to cut his throat, so, tearing off my false beard, I cut his throat with it. Hereupon the mob arose and shouted. I begged them to pardon our shortcomings, as the company had not yet arrived. At last, with all the people in an uproar, the host came in and told us that we had better get out, and thus avoid a sound drubbing. Upon this good advice we put distance between us, and that same night we left with more than five *reals* which we had taken in. After we had spent this money and had sold what few effects we had, eating often only the fungi which we gathered on the road, sleeping on the ground, walking barefoot (not on account of the mud, but because we had no shoes), helping the mule-drivers to load their animals or fetching water for them, and living more than four days on turnips, we arrived timidly one night at an inn, where four drivers, who were stopping for the night, gave us twenty *maravedis* and a blood-pudding to play a *comedia* for them. After this hardship and misery we reached the end of our journey, Solano in doublet, without *ropilla* [a close-fitting unbuttoned tunic reaching to the thighs] (which he had pawned at a tavern), and I bare-legged and shirtless, with a large straw hat full of air-holes, dirty linen breeches, and jacket torn and threadbare. Thus ragged, I determined to enter the service of a pastry-cook, but Solano being a shrewd fellow, did not take to any work, and this was the state of things when, one day, we heard a drum beat and a boy announced the excellent *comedia Los Amigos trocados,* to be performed that night in the town hall. When I heard this my eyes began to open. We spoke to the boy, and, recognizing us, he dropped the drum and began to dance for joy. We asked him whether he had any small coin about him, and he took out what he had, which was tied up in the end of his shirt. We bought some bread and cheese and a slice of codfish, and after our repast he took us to the *autor* (who was Martinazos). I don't know whether it grieved him to see us so ragged, but finally he embraced us, and after we had related all our hardships to him, we dined, and he bade us rid ourselves of our fleas, so that they might not cling to the costumes, for we were to act in the *comedia.* That night, in fact, we took part, and the next day he made an agreement with us to act in his company, each one to receive three *quartillos* for each representation. He now gave me a part to study in the *comedia The Resurrection of Lazarus,* and to Solano the role of the resurrected saint. Every time the *comedia* was played the *autor* took off a garment in the dressing-room and loaned it to Solano, charging him especially to let no fleas get into it. When the play was ended he returned to the dressing-room, took off the costume, and donned his old clothes. To me he gave stockings, shoes, a hat with plumes, and a long silk coat, beneath which I wore my linen breeches (which had been washed in the meanwhile), and thus, as I am such a handsome fellow, I came on the stage like a gewgaw (*brinquiño*) with my broad beaming face. We continued this happy life for more than four weeks, eating little, traveling much, with the theatrical baggage on our backs, and without ever making the acquaintance of a bed. Going in this way from one village to another, it happened to rain a good deal one night, so, on the next day, the director told us—as it was only a short league to where we were going—to make a litter of our hands and carry his wife, while he and the other two men would carry the baggage of the company, the boy taking the drum and the other odds and ends. The woman being quite satisfied, we made a litter with our hands, and she wearing a beard,[1] we began our journey. In this way we reached our destination, completely worn out, foot-sore and covered with mud; indeed, we were half dead, for we were serving as pack-mules. Arrived in the village, the director immediately requested permission to play, and we acted the farce of *Lazarus.* My friend and I put on our borrowed clothes, but when we arrived at the passage concerning the sepulchre, the director, who took the part of Christ, said several times to Lazarus, "Arise, Lazarus! *surge! surge!"* and seeing that he did not arise, he approached the sepulchre, believing that he had fallen asleep. He found, however, that Lazarus had arisen, body and soul, without leaving a trace of the clothes behind. Not finding the saint, the people

---

[1]Rojas explains that a beard and sometimes a small mask was worn as protection to the complexion.

were aroused, and it seeming that a miracle had taken place, the director was much astonished. Seeing the fix we were in, and that Solano had left without informing me, I took the road to Zaragoza, without, however, finding any trace of Solano, nor the director of his clothes, nor the spectators of Lazarus, who, they doubtless thought, had ascended to heaven. I then joined a good company and gave up that toilsome life.

TWO CONTEMPORARY ACCOUNTS

Eyewitness accounts of the *comedias* during the lifetime of the great Spanish dramatists are rare, and most of them belong to the middle of the seventeenth century. Today, three hundred years later, these few records still give us a vivid picture of the atmosphere in which the *comedias* were enacted.

In the letter of Comtesse d'Aulnoy, who journeyed through Spain in 1679, the national prejudice of a foreigner with a more or less imperfect knowledge of the language must be taken into account. Hers is the narrative of a curious spectator. The dramatist Juan de Zabaleta, on the other hand, writes with the behind-the-scenes knowledge and insight of a man of the theatre.

At the *Comedia*

by COMTESSE D'AULNOY

After I had rested somewhat from the fatigue of the journey, it was proposed that we go to the *comedia*. . . . When I entered the theatre there was a cry of *mira! mira!* i.e., look! look! The decorations of the theatre were not brilliant. The stage was raised, resting upon barrels, over which were boards, ill arranged. The windows were all open, for they do not use torches, and you can imagine how much this detracts from the spectacle. They represented the *Life of St. Anthony,* and when the players said anything which pleased the audience, everybody cried out victor! victor! I learned that this was the custom in this country. I noticed that the devil was not dressed differently from the other actors, save that his hose were flame-colored and that he wore a pair of horns, to distinguish him from the rest. The *comedia* was in three acts, as they all are. At the end of each serious act they played a farce with some pleasantries, in which the *gracioso* or clown appeared, who, amid a great number of dull jests, occasionally uttered some that were not so bad. These interludes were mingled with dances to the music of harps and guitars. The actresses had castanets and wore little hats. This is the custom when they dance, and when they danced the *Zarabanda,* it seemed that they did not touch the ground, so lightly did they glide. Their manner is quite different from ours; they move their arms too much, and often pass their hands over their hats and faces with a very pleasing grace, and they play the castanets admirably.

Moreover, one must not think that these players—because San Sebastian is a small place—are very different from those of Madrid. I have been told that the King's players are somewhat better, for, after all, they, too, play what they call *Comedias famosas,* that is, the best and most famous comedies, and in truth

---

Comtesse d'Aulnoy: *Relation du Voyage d'Espagne* (1693), Tome Premier, p. 55, quoted by Hugo Albert Rennert: *The Spanish Stage in the Time of Lope de Vega.* New York: The Hispanic Society of America, 1909, pp. 330-332.

the greater part of them are quite ridiculous. For example, when St. Anthony said the *confiteor,* which was quite frequent, everybody kneeled, and each one gave himself such a violent *mea culpa* that one thought they would crush their breasts.

An Afternoon in the Theatre

by JUAN DE ZABALETA

... Our idler moves on into the theatre and approaches the person who assigns the seats and benches, and asks for a place.[1] He is met with the reply that there are none, but that a certain seat which has been engaged has not yet been occupied, and that he should wait until the guitar-players appear, and if it be still vacant, he may occupy it. Our man argues, but to amuse himself, in the meanwhile, he goes to the dressing-room. There he finds women taking off their street clothes and putting on their theatrical costumes. Some are so far disrobed as though they were about to retire to bed. He takes his place in front of a woman who, having come to the theatre on foot, is having her shoes and stockings put on by her maid. This cannot be done without some sacrifice of modesty. The poor actress must suffer this and does not dare to protest, for, as her chief object is to win applause, she is afraid to offend any one. A hiss, no matter how unjust, discredits her, since all believe that the judgment of him who accuses is better than their own. The actress continues to dress, enduring his presence with patience. The most indecorous woman on the stage has some modesty in the green-room, for here her immodesty is a vice, while there it is of her profession.

The fellow never takes his eyes off her.... He approaches the hangings to see whether the doubtful seat is occupied, and finds it vacant. As it appears that the owner will not come, he goes and takes the seat. Scarcely has he been seated when the owner arrives and defends his claim. The one already seated resists, and a quarrel ensues. Did this fellow not come to amuse himself, when he left his home? And what has quarreling to do with amusement?... Finally the quarrel is adjusted, and the one who has paid for the seat yields and takes another place which has been offered him by the peacemakers. The commotion caused by the struggle having subsided, our intruder is also quieted and now turns his eyes to the gallery occupied by the women [*cazuela*], carefully scrutinizing their faces until he finds one who particularly strikes his fancy, and guardedly makes signs to her.

The *cazuela,* my dear sir, is not what you came to see, but the *comedia....* He is looking round in every direction, when he feels some one pull his cloak from behind. He turns and sees a fruit-seller, who, leaning forward between two men, whispers to him that the woman who is tapping her knee with her fan says that she has much admired the spirit which he has shown in the quarrel and asks him to pay for a dozen oranges for her. The fellow looks again at the *cazuela,* sees that the woman is the one that caught his fancy before, pays the money for the fruit, and sends word that she may have anything else she pleases. As the

Juan de Zabaleta: *Dia de fiesta por la tarde,* Madrid (1692), p. 236, quoted by Hugo Albert Rennert: *The Spanish Stage in the Time of Lope de Vega.* New York: The Hispanic Society of America, 1909, pp. 335-336.
[1]The sum paid at the door only entitles the person to admission, not to a seat, for which an extra sum must be paid.

[73]

fruit-seller leaves, the fellow immediately plans that he will wait for the woman at the exit of the theatre, and he begins to think that there is an interminable delay in beginning the play. In a loud and peevish manner he signifies his disapproval, exciting the *mosqueteros,* who are standing below, to break forth with insulting shouts, in order to hasten the players. Why do they do this? ... Not one of those who are shouting would run the risk of saying a word to a player in the street. And besides being foolish and cowardly to treat them thus, it is most ungrateful, for of all people actors are those who strive hardest to please. The rehearsals for a *comedia* are so frequent and so long that it is often a positive torment. And when the time for the first performance arrives, every one of them would willingly give a year's pay to make a good appearance on that day. And when they come upon the stage, what fatigue, what loss would they not willingly undergo to acquit themselves well of their task? If they are to cast themselves from a rock they do it with the fearlessness of despair, yet their bodies are human, and they feel pain like any other. And if in a *comedia* a death-struggle is to be represented, the actor to whose lot it falls writhes upon the dirty stage, which is full of projecting nails and splinters, with no more regard for his costume than if it were the coarsest leather, while often it is very costly.... And I have seen an actress of great repute (who died only a short while ago) representing a passage where, in a rage, she tears a garment to tatters to heighten the effect of her acting, though the article torn may cost twice as much as the money she receives for the performance....

VI. ENGLAND

The Elizabethan Actor

Reputable professional playing emerged during the reign of Queen Elizabeth with the growth of a national, secular drama. Impetus for plays which departed from the medieval religious tradition came at first from the schools, universities, and court circles. Like their Italian predecessors, English Renaissance scholars and courtiers imitated the rediscovered drama of antiquity. To classical models they added native humor in comedies like *Ralph Roister Doister,* written by a schoolmaster for performance by his students. National legendary figures replaced ancient heroes in the first English tragedy *Gorboduc,* written in the manner of Seneca by two young law students and performed before the Queen. In the first flush of Renaissance enthusiasm, schoolboys, university men, and courtiers continued the tradition of amateur acting and writing which had been associated with medieval theatre.

Elizabethan dramatists first gave polished literary form to their imaginative creations for the pleasure of Elizabeth and her noblemen. Under the control of the Master of the Revels, an office which had been created by Henry VIII in 1545 to direct and organize the entertainment of the court, John Lyly and George Peele, among others, presented elaborate, richly worded, allegorical dramas woven around the life of the Queen and her courtiers. Their picturesque plays, given in private halls before royal audiences, were performed by boy actors, who were trained by schoolmasters and choirmasters, sometimes with the liberal use of the rod.

English Renaissance drama might have been mere literary exercise or pretty extravaganza if left in the hands of boy actors and courtly writers. Vigor and maturity were brought to it, however, when the persisting medieval sanctions against masterless men and vagabonds forced the growing bands of strolling players to seek noble patronage. To these players of moralities and interludes, the dramas of the courts and universities unfolded a new world of classical magnificence and humanist ideals. When not needed by their lords, these adult, male, professional actors, now the protected servants of noblemen, performed in and around London in inn-yards and village squares. Drawing sustenance from the plaudits of a lively citizen audience and from the refinements and demands of the court, the professional actors began to flourish.

These new plays and new players built up a background of experience in dramatic practice which prepared the way for the extraordinary effulgence of theatre which followed in the short period from 1580 to 1620. Stimulated by a ferment of new ideas, Englishmen investigated the world around them with fresh vision, retaining in the midst of their strong individuality something of the cohesiveness of medieval society. Not long after Sir Francis Drake and Sir Walter Raleigh had begun to range the distant seas to acquire wealth and fame for themselves, their Queen, and their nation, poets like Christopher Marlowe, William Shakespeare, and Ben Jonson explored the emotions and beliefs of men. In the public theatres, before a variegated audience caught in a national fervor which seemed to cut across social and economic barriers, the poets charted the "brave new world" of their exuberant imaginations. As writers, actors, and directors, the Elizabethan poets charged this brief period with an artistry and vision that created the greatest era in English dramatic history.

Two theatrical companies stood out in the lively theatrical scene of these few decades—the Lord Chamberlain's Company and the Lord Admiral's Company. The Chamberlain's Men (known as the King's Majesty's Servants after the ascension of James I) boasted such players as Richard Burbage and William Kemp (d. 1603), as well as the actor-poet William Shakespeare. The Admiral's Men (later Prince Henry's Men) were controlled by the theatrical financier Philip Henslowe (d. 1616), whose account books provide much of our information about Elizabethan theatrical activities. Their leading player was Henslowe's son-in-law, the mighty Edward Alleyn (1565-1626), who created the heroic figures in the plays of Christopher Marlowe. Although the two companies continued the pattern of noble patronage, they were essentially popular companies acting in the public theatres of London before paying audiences.

Composed of a fairly stable group of leading actors who owned their theatres, the companies commissioned their dramatists and shared the profits of their performances. With them were a number of hired actors, working for wages, and young boy apprentices who played the female roles in a theatre that did not see women actresses until 1656. The poet-dramatists created their plays specifically for these tightly knit groups. Shakespeare, for example, was not only the leading dramatist of the Chamberlain's Men, but also an actor and a sharer of the financial fortunes of the troupe.

The public theatres in which the Elizabethan actors played resembled in part the inn-yards utilized for theatrical performances by earlier groups of players. London's first theatre was built by James Burbage (d. 1597), father of Richard, in 1576. Called simply The Theatre, it was built, as were those that followed it, on the outskirts of the city, since civic magistrates objected to theatres as places of idleness, riot, sedition, and plague. Unroofed and circular, these huge theatres, with an audience capacity of perhaps two or three thousand, contained a simple platform stage, which jutted out into the pit where the "groundlings" stood. Around the sides of the theatre were galleries where the upper class sat, when not displaying themselves on the stage itself. The platform was bare; properties were used but scenery was rudimentary. No curtain or proscenium arch separated the actors from the spectators. The gorgeously clad figure of the actor and the poetry of the playwright dominated the scene at the Fortune, the Swan, or the famous Globe Theatre.

Richard Tarleton (d. 1588), clown, court entertainer, actor and writer, typified the early Elizabethan actor who was part minstrel and part professional actor. His successor in popular favor, William Kemp, was a player in Shakespeare's company. Both were more than mere comic actors; they lived the role of clown or jester. The art of Kemp, who may have traveled in Italy, was like the *lazzi* of the comic *commedia dell' arte* characters. Hamlet's strictures against comedians who speak more than is set down for them may well refer to the improvisational technique that Kemp probably learned from the Italians. So strong was the personality of such comedians as these that the writers fashioned their comic characters to fit their special aptitudes. Shakespeare probably created Costard,

[76]

Bottom, Dogberry, and Launce with the rough antics of Kemp in mind. For Robert Armin (fl. 1590-1610), the witty court jester who replaced Kemp in the company, Shakespeare created more subtle comic roles like Touchstone and Feste.

Among Elizabethan tragedians two men are preeminent—Edward Alleyn of the Admiral's Men and Richard Burbage of the Chamberlain's Men. Alleyn, praised by Thomas Heywood for his impersonation of the titanic heroes of Christopher Marlowe, was much admired for his action on stage. Ben Jonson, who was associated with Alleyn in the Henslowe group, wrote of him: "Only thou dost act," and the playwright Thomas Nashe, extolling English actors above foreign players in *Pierce Penilesse* (1592), gave special distinction to Alleyn, writing: "Not Roscius nor Aesop, those admired tragedians that have lived ever since before Christ was born, could ever perform more in action than famous Ned Alleyn." The rivalry between the Admiral's and the Chamberlain's Men has led to the suggestion that the lines Shakespeare gave Hamlet about the ranting player who "out-herods Herod" were intended to satirize the acting of Alleyn. Ambiguous and general as these comments are, they have marked Alleyn as the player extraordinary in the exaggerated manner.

Of Richard Burbage's art we know little. He acted Hamlet, Lear, Othello, Richard III, and probably other of the great Shakespearean heroes, evidently to the satisfaction of Shakespeare himself. He is regarded as exemplifying the tempered acting recommended in Hamlet's advice to the players. His Protean versatility was admired, but such versatility must have marked most of the Elizabethan actors who were trained in small repertory companies accustomed to doubling of parts and very short runs. Unfortunately we have little precise knowledge of the styles of either of these early great tragic actors of the English stage.

Thomas Heywood, Ben Jonson, and Shakespeare, who achieved their fame primarily as playwrights, must be listed among Elizabethan actors. Just as Shakespeare's plays dominate the drama of the era, so his maxims on acting are primary to discussions of Elizabethan acting. The judicious advice given by Hamlet, stressing moderation, fidelity to nature and devotion to the dramatist's text, has become the acting ideal, but these statements reveal little of the actual style of Shakespeare's company. This is also true of the only other important Elizabethan document on acting, Thomas Heywood's *Apology for Actors,* which is essentially a defense of the dignity of the actor rather than an exposition of his art.

In recent years a number of scholars have attempted to determine whether Elizabethan acting was formalistic or realistic. The information available is meager, but the studies by Harbage, Joseph and others point clearly toward the formalistic. The continuing success of the convention of boys playing female roles supports the thesis of formalistic acting. A contemporary description in *The Rich Cabinet Furnished with Varietie of Excellent Discriptions* (1616) also points to the formalistic quality. The writer says actors were known for "dancing, actiuitie, musicke, song, elloqution, abilitie of body, memory, skill of weapon, pregnancy of wit." Piecing together the brief references in plays and in anecdotes, we may say that the Elizabethan actor was distinguished primarily by his excellent voice. He was expected to base his actions and gestures on the words of the poet and to act with decorum and modesty, keeping in mind the qualities of the character being impersonated. Players were frequently recognized by their elaborate dress, whose lavishness substituted for historical similitude in costuming and provided visual pleasure on a relatively bare stage. They were criticized for strutting and shouting and for directing their attention to the spectators instead of to their fellow players. They were admired for versatility and for maintaining their characterizations consistently throughout the performance.

In the last decades of Elizabeth's reign, acting became a recognized profession, and the personality and art of the actor became subjects of interest. In the plays of Shakespeare, Jonson, Massinger, and others, actors were introduced as characters, and the intricacies of acting provided images for their poetry. While a direct relationship between great drama and great acting is difficult to establish, the integrated theatrical life of these poets, who were actors, dramatists, and probably teachers and directors, would seem to insure a unified, creative theatre.

The audience before which the Elizabethan player performed was probably critically alert. The courtiers and university wits brought their experience in amateur acting and playwriting to the so-called private theatres, indoor houses like the Blackfriars, that attracted upperclass audiences. Even the "groundlings" of the public outdoor theatres had within recent memory participated in the popular religious drama. In this atmosphere Richard Burbage, Edward Alleyn, and later Joseph Taylor (1586-1652) and John Lowin (1576-1658?) perfected histrionic art, won high praise, became wealthy, and raised the position of the actor from disgrace to honor. They heralded the entrance of the great names of the seventeenth and eighteenth centuries.

WILLIAM SHAKESPEARE

(1564-1616)

The ascertainable facts of William Shakespeare's life are few. He was born in Stratford-on-Avon in 1564, the son of a glover. He spent his youth in Stratford; in 1582 he married Anne Hathaway by whom he had three children. By 1592 he was in London, already at work as an actor and a playwright. His subsequent career in London is clouded by doubt and speculation except for the evidence of his magnificent plays. Traditional stories suggest that he began his theatrical career in the lowly position of caretaker of horses at the theatre door or as a prompter's assistant, but these stories are part of a large apocrypha. That he was an actor not only at the beginning of his career but also later when he had already written some great plays is, however, well established. He was with the Chamberlain's Company, headed by Richard Burbage, when it was founded in 1594. He is listed in the cast of Ben Jonson's *Every Man in His Humour* (1598) and in the cast of *Sejanus* (1603). He is said to have played the Ghost in *Hamlet* and Adam in *As You Like It.* In the First Folio of his works, compiled by his two fellow players John Hemminge (d. 1630) and Henry Condell (d. 1627) in 1623, he is also listed as a player.

Of Shakespeare's success as an actor we have no evidence, except for late and contradictory suggestions. But for evidence of his familiarity with the multitude of details that make up the career of an actor we need only turn to his plays. The scenes of Bottom and his fellows in *A Midsummer Night's Dream,* humorous and satirical, suggest some of the characteristics of the age of popular amateur acting. The scene from the Induction to the *Taming of the Shrew* recalls how ancient the tricks of the acting trade are. The soliloquy, "O, what a rogue and peasant slave am I," in *Hamlet* exhibits the power of histrionic art. Hamlet's oft-quoted speech to the players remains the best brief advice to actors and reminds us that according to tradition Shakespeare instructed the players in his company.

Again and again Shakespeare's experiences as an actor shaped the images of his verse. The deposed Richard II is characterized as a minor actor:

> As in a theatre the eyes of men,
> After a well-grac'd actor leaves the stage,
> Are idly bent on him that enters next,
> Thinking his prattle to be tedious,
> Even so, or with much more contempt, men's eyes
> Did scowl on gentle Richard.

In *Troilus and Cressida* he paints Achilles as the bad actor:

> ...a strutting player—whose conceit
> Lies in his hamstring, and doth think it rich
> To hear the wooden dialogue and sound
> 'Twixt his stretch'd footing and the scaffolage....

These and other images of actors and acting, which are woven into the texture of Shakespeare's poetry, reveal how deeply his life had been involved with the art of the actor and the world of the theatre.

Thoughts On Acting From His Plays

THE TAMING OF THE SHREW

Induction
Enter Players.
LORD: Now, fellows, you are welcome.
PLAYERS: We thank your honour.
LORD: Do you intend to stay with me tonight?
PLAYERS: So please your lordship to accept our duty.
LORD: With all my heart. This fellow I remember
> Since once he play'd a farmer's eldest son
> 'Twas where you woo'd the gentlewoman so well.
> I have forgot your name; but sure that part
> Was aptly fitted and naturally perform'd.
PLAYER: I think 'twas Soto that your honour means.
Lord: 'Tis very true.... [he issues instructions for a boy to impersonate a woman]
> And then with kind embracements, tempting kisses,
> And with declining head into his bosom,
> Bid him shed tears, as being overjoy'd
> To see her noble lord restor'd to health,
> Who for this seven years hath esteemed him
> No better than a poor and loathsome beggar.
> And if the boy have not a woman's gift

The Taming of the Shrew (c. 1594-1598) in *The Complete Works of William Shakespeare*, edited by George Lyman Kittredge. Boston: Ginn and Company, 1936, p. 328. Copyright 1936. All Shakespeare selections by permission of Ginn & Co.

To rain a shower of commanded tears,
An onion will do well for such a shift,
Which, in a napkin being close convey'd,
Shall in despite enforce a watery eye.

A MIDSUMMER NIGHT'S DREAM

Act 1, Scene II (Athens. Quince's house.)

QUINCE: Is all our company here?

BOTTOM: You were best to call them generally, man by man, according to the scrip.

QUINCE: Here is the scroll of every man's name which is thought fit, through all Athens, to play in our interlude before the Duke and Duchess on his wedding day at night.

BOTTOM: First, good Peter Quince, say what the play treats on; then read the names of the actors; and so grow to a point.

QUINCE: Marry, our play is "The most Lamentable Comedy and most Cruel Death of Pyramus and Thisby."

BOTTOM: A very good piece of work, I assure you, and a merry. Now, good Peter Quince, call forth your actors by the scroll. Masters, spread yourselves.

QUINCE: Answer as I call you. Nick Bottom the weaver.

BOTTOM: Ready. Name what part I am for, and proceed.

QUINCE: You, Nick Bottom, are set down for Pyramus.

BOTTOM: What is Pyramus? A lover, or a tyrant?

QUINCE: A lover that kills himself, most gallant, for love.

BOTTOM: That will ask some tears in the true performing of it. If I do it, let the audience look to their eyes! I will move storms, I will condole in some measure. To the rest. Yet my chief humour is for a tyrant. I could play Ercles rarely, or a part to tear a cat in, to make all split....

QUINCE: Francis Flute the bellows-mender.

FLUTE: Here, Peter Quince.

QUINCE: Flute, you must take Thisby on you.

FLUTE: What is Thisby? A wand'ring knight?

QUINCE: It is the lady that Pyramus must love.

FLUTE: Nay, faith, let not me play a woman. I have a beard coming.

QUINCE: That's all one. You shall play it in a mask, and you may speak as small as you will.

BOTTOM: And I may hide my face, let me play Thisby too. I'll speak in a monstrous little voice:— "Thisne, Thisne!" "Ah, Pyramus, my lover dear! thy Thisby dear, and lady dear!"

*   *   *   *

QUINCE: ...Snug, the joiner, you the lion's part. And I hope here is a play fitted.

SNUG: Have you the lion's part written, pray you, if it be, give it me, for I am slow of study.

QUINCE: You may do it extempore, for it is nothing but roaring.

BOTTOM: Let me play the lion too....

*   *   *   *

A Midsummer Night's Dream (1595) in *The Complete Works of William Shakespeare,* edited by George Lyman Kittredge. Boston: Ginn and Company, 1936, pp. 234-235.

QUINCE: You can play no part but Pyramus;...
BOTTOM: Well, I will undertake it. What beard were I best to play it in?
QUINCE: Why, what you will.
BOTTOM: I will discharge it in either your straw-colour beard, your orange-tawny beard, your purple-in-grain beard, or your French crown-colour beard, your perfit yellow.

HAMLET

Act II, Scene II

Enter four or five Players.

HAMLET: You are welcome, masters; welcome, all. I am glad to see thee well. Welcome, good friends. O, my old friend? Why, thy face is valanc'd since I saw thee last. Com'st thou to beard me in Denmark? What, my young lady and mistress? By'r Lady, your ladyship is nearer to heaven than when I saw you last by the altitude of a chopine. Pray God your voice like a piece of uncurrent gold, be not crack'd within the ring. Masters, you are all welcome. We'll e'en to't like French falconers, fly at anything we see. We'll have a speech straight. Come, give us a taste of your quality. Come, a passionate speech.

* * * *

POLONIUS: Look, whe'r he has not turn'd his colour, and has tears in's eyes. Prithee no more!
HAMLET: 'Tis well. I'll have thee speak out the rest of this soon. Good my lord, will you see the players well bestow'd? Do you hear? Let them be well us'd; for they are the abstract and brief chronicles of the time. After your death you were better have a bad epitaph than their ill report while you live.

* * * *

HAMLET: Now I am alone.
O, what a rogue and peasant slave am I!
Is it not monstrous that this player here,
But in a fiction, in a dream of passion,
Could force his soul so to his own conceit
That, from her working, all his visage wann'd,
Tears in his eyes, distraction in's aspect,
A broken voice, and his whole function suiting
With forms to his conceit? And all for nothing!
For Hecuba!
What's Hecuba to him, or he to Hecuba,
That he should weep for her? What would he do,
Had he the motive and the cue for passion
That I have? He would drown the stage with tears
And cleave the general ear with horrid speech;
Make mad the guilty and appal the free,
Confound the ignorant, and amaze indeed
The very faculties of eyes and ears.

* * * *

Hamlet (1600) in *The Complete Works of William Shakespeare*, edited by George Lyman Kittredge. Boston: Ginn and Company, 1936, pp. 1164-1165, 1168-1169.

Act III, Scene II.

HAMLET: Speak the speech, I pray you, as I pronounc'd it to you, trippingly on the tongue. But if you mouth it, as many of our players do, I had as live the town crier spoke my lines. Nor do not saw the air too much with your hand, thus, but use all gently; for in the very torrent, tempest, and (as I may say) whirlwind of your passion, you must acquire and beget a temperance that may give it smoothness. O, it offends me to the soul to hear a robustious periwig-pated fellow tear a passion to tatters, to very rags, to split the ears of the ground-lings, who (for the most part) are capable of nothing but inexplicable dumb shows and noise. I would have such a fellow whipp'd for o'er doing Termagant. It out-herods Herod. Pray you avoid it.... Be not too tame neither; but let your own discretion be your tutor. Suit the action to the word, the word to the action; with this special observance, that you o'erstep not the modesty of nature: for anything so overdone is from the purpose of playing whose end, both at the first and now, was and is, to hold, as t'were, the mirror up to nature; to show virtue her own feature, scorn her own image, and the very age and body of the time his form and pressure. Now this overdone, or come tardy off, though it make the unskilful laugh, cannot but make the judicious grieve; the censure of the which one must in your allowance o'erweigh a whole theatre of others. O, there be players that I have seen play, and heard others praise, and that highly (not to speak it profanely), that, neither having the accent of Christians, nor the gait of Christian, pagan, nor man, have so strutted and bellowed that I have thought some of Nature's journeymen had made men, and not made them well, they imitated humanity so abominably.... And let those that play your clowns speak no more than is set down for them. For there be of them that will themselves laugh, to set on some quantity of barren spectators to laugh too, though in the meantime some necessary question of the play be then to be considered. That's villainous and shows a most pitiful ambition in the fool that uses it.

BEN JONSON

(1572-1637)

Ben Jonson, classicist and incisive comic genius of the Elizabethan and Jacobean stage, led an adventurous life. Educated by the scholar William Camden, Jonson worked for a while as a bricklayer, fought against the Spaniards in the Low Countries, and, like Shakespeare, became an actor. Henslowe, the manager, noted a loan made to "Benjemen Johnson player" in 1597. The biographer John Aubrey stated that Jonson "was never a good actor, but an excellent instructor." Thomas Dekker in *Satiromastix*, satirized Jonson as an actor in these words: "...thou putst up a supplication to be a poor journeyman player, and hadst been still so, but that thou couldst not set a good face upon't: thou has forgot how thou amblest (in leather pilch) by a play-wagon, in the highway, and took'st mad Hieronimo's part, to get service among the mimics."

Although Jonson's fame rests on his poetry, plays, and masques, his intimate connection with theatre in an age when writers were also actors and directors makes his words on acting and actors of great interest. From all accounts he was not a successful actor, but he has left us two sensitive poetic appreciations of actors. "An Epitaph on Salathiel Pavy" evokes the unique institution of boy players, who adorned the Elizabethan and Jacobean stage. The success of little Salathiel Pavy in old men's roles, poetically celebrated in the "Epitaph," underscores the excellence of the boy actors. Traditional in its use of the Roscius appellation, the Epigram "To Edward Alleyn" suggests a distinction between the declaimer and the great actor who "acts."

To Edward Alleyn

If Rome so great and in her wisest age,
Fear'd not to boast the glories of her stage,
A skilful Roscius, and grave Aesop, men,
Yet crown'd with honours, as with riches, then,
Who had no less a trumpet of their name,
Than Cicero, whose every breath was fame.
How can so great example die in me
That, Alleyn, I should pause to publish thee
Who both their graces in thyself has more
Outstript, than they did all that went before,
And present worth in all dost so contract
As others speak, but only thou dost act.
Wear this renown. 'Tis just, that who did give
To many poets life, by one should live.

An Epitaph on Salathiel Pavy, a Child of Queen Elizabeth's Chapel

Weep with me, all you that read
    This little story,
And know, for whom a tear you shed
    Death's self is sorry.
'Twas a child that so did thrive
    In grace and feature,
As heaven and nature seemed to strive
    Which owned the creature.
Years he number'd scarce thirteen
    When fates turn'd cruel,
Yet three fill'd zodiacs had he been
    The stage's jewel,
And did act, what now we moan,
    Old man so duly,
As sooth, the Parcae thought him one,
    He played so truly.
So, by error to his fate
    They all consented;

"Epigram 89," *Works of Ben Jonson*, edited by W. Gifford. London: Bickers and Sons, 1875, Vol. VIII, p. 191.

"Epigram 120" (c. 1601), *Works of Ben Jonson*, edited by W. Gifford. London: Bickers and Sons, 1875, Volume VIII, p. 221.

But viewing him since, alas, too late!
They have repented;
And have sought, to give new birth,
In baths to steep him,
But being so much too good for earth,
Heaven vows to keep him.

THE RETURN FROM PARNASSUS, PART II

The Return from Parnassus, Part II, is the third play of a trilogy by an unknown author. The plays were acted at St. John's College, Cambridge, between 1598 and 1603.

The trilogy traces the fortunes of two young college men, Philomusus and Studioso, in search of learning. In the first play, *Pilgrimage to Parnassus,* the two young men pass through the lands of Logic, Rhetoric, and Philosophy on their way to the Muses' spring on Mount Parnassus. In the second play, *The Return from Parnassus,* Part I, the two young men make their way in the world, but do not find satisfactory employment for their talents. In the final play, *Return from Parnassus,* Part II, they turn to baser activities in an effort to find a place for themselves. Like so many of the bright young men in Elizabeth's reign—the University Wits, Marlowe, Greene, Nashe and Peele—the two students of the play turn to the theatre. Richard Burbage and Will Kemp are introduced as characters on the stage to test and instruct them. In this brief scene, these undisputed masters of tragedy and comedy undertake to train the university men in their respective specialties. The play ends, however, with the youths leaving behind them the endeavors of the busy world to seek peace and comfort in the rustic life of shepherds.

Apart from the scene with Burbage and Kemp, given here, which attests to the contemporary fame of these two actors, there is a short amusing passage in the first play, *The Pilgrimage to Parnassus,* descriptive of the tomfoolery of such clowns as Kemp:

Why, what an ass thou! Dost thou not know a play cannot be without a clown? Clowns have been thrust into plays by head and shoulders ever since Kempe could make a scurvey face.... Why, if thou canst but draw thy mouth awrye, laye thy leg over thy staff, saw a piece of cheese asunder with thy dagger, lap up drink on earth, I warrant thee they'll laugh mightily.

A Lesson from Burbage and Kemp

BURBAGE: Now, Will Kemp, if we can entertain these scholars at a low rate, it will be well; they have oftentimes a good conceit in a part.

KEMP: It's true, indeed, honest Dick, but the slaves are somewhat proud; and besides, it's a good sport in a part to see them never speak in their walk, but at the end of the stage; just as though, in walking with a fellow, we should never speak but at a stile, a gate, or a ditch, where a man can go no further. I was once in a comedy in Cambridge, and there I saw a parasite make faces and mouths of all sorts on this fashion.

The Return from Parnassus (c. 1601-1603) in *A Select Collection of Old English Plays,* edited by Robert Dodsley. London: 1874-1876, Volume IX, Act IV, Scene 3, pp. 193-198.

BURBAGE: A little teaching will mend these faults; and it may be, besides, they will be able to pen a part.

KEMP: Few of the university pen play well; they smell too much of that writer Ovid and that writer Metamorphosis, and talk too much of Prosperpina and Jupiter. Why, here's our fellow Shakespeare puts them all down—ay, and Ben Jonson too. O, that Ben Jonson is a pestilent fellow; he brought up Horace, giving the poets a pill; but our fellow Shakespeare hath given him a purge that made him betray his credit.

BURBAGE: It's a shrewd fellow, indeed. I wonder these scholars stay so long; they appointed to be here presently, that we might try them. O, here they come.

STUDIOSO: Take heart, these lets our clouded thoughts refine;
The sun shines brightest when it 'gins decline.

BURBAGE: Master Philomusus and Master Studioso, God save you.

KEMP: Master Philomusus and Master Itioso, well-met.

PHILOMUSUS: The same to you, good Master Burbage. What Master Kemp, how doth the Emperor of Germany?

STUDIOSO: God save you, Master Kemp; welcome, Master Kemp, from dancing the morris over the Alps.

KEMP: Well, you merry knaves, you may come to the honour of it one day. Is it not better to make a fool of the world as I have done, than to be fooled of the world, as you scholars are? But be merry, my lads; you have happened upon the most excellent vocation in the world for money. They come north and south to bring it to our playhouse; and for honours, who of more report than Dick Burbage and Will Kemp? He is not counted a gentleman that knows not Dick Burbage and Will Kemp. There's not a country wench that can dance Sellenger's round, but can talk of Dick Burbage and Will Kemp.

* * * *

BURBAGE: Master Studioso, I pray you, take some part in this book, and act it, that I may see what will fit you best. I think your voice would serve for Hieronimo; observe how I act it, and then imitate me.

* * * *

KEMP: Now for you. Methinks you should belong to my tuition; and your face, methinks, would be good for a foolish mayor or a foolish justice of peace. Mark me:...

* * * *

KEMP: Thou wilt do well in time, if thou wilt be ruled by thy betters, that is, by myself, and such grave aldermen of the playhouse as I am.

BURBAGE: I like your face, and the proportion of your body for Richard the Third. I pray, Master Philomusus, let me see you act a little of it.

* * * *

BUBAGE: Very well, I assure you. Well, Master Philomusus and Master Studioso, we see what ability you are of; I pray, walk with us to our fellows, and we'll agree presently.

THOMAS HEYWOOD

(c. 1570-1641)

Thomas Heywood, prolific writer and actor, was a native of Lincolnshire and a student at Cambridge University. He wrote plays for the Henslowe group, and in

1598 he was hired as a player by Henslowe. In 1602 he was listed as a sharer in the Earl of Worcester's men, another company under Henslowe's management. On the ascension of James, this company became the Queen's Men, and Heywood was associated with it until 1619. From 1619 until his death his exact theatrical affiliations are not clearly known, but he continued to write both theatrical and non-dramatic pieces.

Heywood wrote of himself that he had his hand in some two hundred and twenty plays. In addition to plays, pageants and Lord Mayor's shows, Heywood wrote histories and essays on miscellaneous subjects. His dramatic reputation, however, rests largely on his most remembered play, *A Woman Killed with Kindness.* Charles Lamb called Heywood "a sort of prose Shakespeare."

In 1612 Heywood published *An Apology for Actors,* a defense of both players and plays against the recurrent virulent attacks on the immorality of the theatre and its practitioners. Numerous assaults were leveled against the stage by puritanical critics and civic officers. To read their invective, one would not believe that the plays against which they cried were those of Shakespeare and Jonson and the players whom they flayed were Edward Alleyn, who endowed a college, and Richard Burbage, known for his propriety and good temper. It is against this background that Heywood's *Apology* must be read. He offered a learned answer to the animadversions of the critics. He pointed to the moral edification to be gained from the stage and cited classical authorities to support his statements.

Out of the body of traditional discussion in Heywood can be drawn a composite of the ideals of the Elizabethan actor. Without the magic of Shakespeare's words Heywood reiterates the basic concepts of Hamlet's advice to the actors. He points to the existence of amateur histrionics at the Universities to bolster and add dignity to his defense of the profession. It is interesting to note that for Heywood acting is still intimately associated with the qualities of the orator, but he sounds a fresh note when he stresses the importance of gesture and decorous impersonation in acting.

An Apology for Actors

Do not the Universities, the fountain and well springs of all good arts, learning, and documents, admit the like [the value of plays and performances] in their colleges? and they (I assure myself) are not ignorant of their true use. In the time of my residence in Cambridge, I have seen tragedies, comedies, histories, pastorals and shows, publicly acted, in which the graduate of good place and reputation have been specially parted. This is held necessary for the emboldening of their junior scholars to arm them with audacity again they come to be employed in any public exercise, as in the reading of the dialectic, rhetoric, ethic, mathematic, the physic, or metaphysic lectures. It teaches audacity to the bashful grammarian, being newly admitted into a private college, and, after matriculated and entered as a member of the University, and makes him a bold sophister, to argue *pro et contra* to compose his syllogism, cathegoric, or hypothetic (simple or compound) to reason and frame a sufficient argument to prove his questions or to defend any *axioma,*

Thomas Heywood: *An Apology for Actors* (1612) in *Early Treatises on the Stage.* London: Shakespeare Society, 1853, pp. 28-29, 43-44.

to distinguish any dilemna, and be able to moderate in any argumentation whatsoever.

To come to rhetoric: it not only emboldens a scholar to speak, but instructs him to speak well, and with judgment to observe his commas, colons, and full points; his parentheses, his breathing spaces, and distinctions; to keep a decorum in his countenance, neither to frown when he should smile, nor to make unseemly and disguised faces in the delivery of his words; not to stare with his eyes, draw awry his mouth, confound his voice in the hollow of his throat, or tear his words hastily betwixt his teeth; neither to buffet his chest like a mad man, nor stand in his place like a liveless image, demurely plodding, and without any smooth and formal motion. It instructs him to fit his phrases to his action, and his action to his phrases, and his pronunciation to them both.

Tully in his book *Ad Caium Herennium* requires five things in an orator—invention, disposition, elocution, memory and pronunciation; yet all are imperfect without the sixth, which is action, for be his invention never so fluent and exquisite, his disposition and order never so composed and formal, his eloquence and elaborate phrases never so material and pithy, his memory never so firm and retentive, his pronunciation never so musical and plausive, yet without a comely and elegant gesture, a gracious and a bewitching kind of action, a natural and familiar motion of the head, the hand, the body, and a moderate and fit countenance suitable to all the rest, I hold all the rest as nothing. A delivery and sweet action is the gloss and beauty of any discourse that belongs to a scholar. And this is the action behooveful in any that profess this quality, not to use any impudent or forced motion in any part of the body, no rough or other violent gesture; nor on the contrary to stand like a stiff starched man, but to qualify every thing according to the nature of the person personated: for in overacting tricks, and toiling too much in the antic habits of humors, men of the ripest desert, greatest opinions, and best reputations, may break into the most violent absurdities.

* * * *

... To omit all the doctors, zawnyes, pantaloons, harlakeenes, in which the French, but especially the Italians have been excellent, and according to the occasion offered to do some right to our English actors, as [William] Knell, [John] Bentley, [Tobias] Mils, [Robert] Wilson, [Samuel] Crosse, [John] Lanehan, and others, these, since I never saw them, as being before my time, I cannot (as an eye-witness of their desert) give them that applause, which no doubt, they worthily merit, yet by the report of many judicial auditors, their performance of many parts have been so absolute, that it were a kind of sin to drown their worths in Lethe, and not commit their (almost forgotten) names to eternity. Here I must needs remember Tarleton, in his time gracious with the Queen, his sovereign, and in the peoples' general applause, whom succeeded Will Kemp, as well in the favor of his Majesty, as in the opinion and good thoughts of the general audience. Gabriel, [John] Singer, [Thomas] Pope, [Augustine] Phillips, [William] Sly, all the right I can do them is but this, that, though they be dead, their deserts yet live in the remembrance of many. Among so many dead, let me not forget one yet alive, in his time the most worthy, famous Master Edward Alleyn. To omit these, as also such as for their diverse imperfections may be thought insufficient for the quality, actors should be men pick'd out personable, according to the parts they present; they should be rather scholars, that, though they cannot speak well, know how to speak, or else to have that volubility that they can speak well, though they understand not what, and so both imperfections may by instructions be helped and amended: but where a good tongue and a good conceit both fail; there can never be a good actor. I also could wish, that such as are condemned for their licentiousness, might by a general consent be quite excluded our society; for as we are men that stand in the broad eye of the world, so should our manners, gestures, and behavior, savour of such government and modesty, to deserve the good thoughts and reports of all men, and to abide the sharpest censures even of those that are the greatest opposites to quality.

JOHN WEBSTER

(d. 1634)

Like so many famous writers and actors of the Elizabethan and Jacobean age, John Webster is a shadowy figure. E. K. Chambers (*The Elizabethan Stage*) suggests that John Webster, the author of *The Duchess of Malfi* and *The White Devil*, may have been identical with a John Webster who was one of the English actors who played in Germany in 1596.

This suggestion would accord well with the conjecture that the "Character of An Excellent Actor," which was added to the characters in the sixth edition (1615) of Sir Thomas Overbury's *The Wife,* was written by John Webster. His excellent defense and description of an actor, obliquely indicating the personality of Richard Burbage, who was a painter as well as an actor, was probably provoked by the adverse criticism of players in the essay *A Common Player.* The latter, which appeared in 1615, was typical of the usual objections pressed against actors. The author believes "A common player is a slow payer, seldom a purchaser, never a puritan ... a daily counterfeit ... howsoever he pretends to have a royal Master or Mistress, his wages and dependence prove him to be the servant of the people. When he doth hold conference upon the stage; and should look directly in his fellow's face; he turns about his voice into the assembly for applause-sake...." He also recalls that actors were judged to be rogues in numerous public proclamations. To this attack, Webster replied that the actor has the same qualifications as the honored orator, that he is one with nature, that he makes living personalities of moral precepts, and that he provides good entertainment.

An Excellent Actor

Whatever is commendable in the grave orator, is most exquisitely perfect in him; for by a full and significant action of body, he charms our attention: sit in a full theatre, and you will think you see so many lines drawn from the circumference of so many ears, while the actor is the center. He doth not strive to make nature monstrous, she is often seen in the same scene with him, but neither on stilts nor crutches; and for his voice 'tis not lower than the prompter, nor broader than the foil and target. By his action he fortifies moral precepts with example; for what we see him personate, we think truly done before us; a man of deep

John Webster: "An Excellent Actor" (1615) in *The Miscellaneous Works in Prose and Verse of Sir Thomas Overbury,* edited by Edward F. Rimbault. London: John Russell Smith, 1856, pp. 147-148.

thought might apprehend, the ghosts of our ancient heroes walk'd again, and take him (at several times) for many of them. He is much affected to painting, and 'tis a question whether that make him an excellent player, or his playing an exquisite painter. He adds grace to the poet's labours: for what in the poet is but ditty, in him is both ditty and music. He entertains us in the best leisure of our life, that is between meals, the most unfit time, either for study or bodily exercise: the flight of hawks and chase of wild beasts, either of them are delights noble: but some think this sport of men the worthier, despite all calumny. All men have been of his occupation: and indeed, what he doth feignedly that do others essentially: this day one plays a monarch, the next a private person. Here one acts a tyrant, on the morrow an exile: A parasite the man tonight, tomorrow a precisian, and so of diverse others. I observe, of all men living, a worthy actor in one kind is the strongest motive of affection that can be: for when he dies, we cannot be persuaded any man can do his parts like him.... But to conclude, I value a worthy actor by the corruption of some few of the quality, as I would do gold in the ore; I should not mind the dross, but the purity of the metal.

THE CYPRIAN CONQUEROR
or
The Faithless Relict

The unknown author of *The Cyprian Conqueror* prefaced his play with one of the first schematized analyses of acting in English. Professor Alfred Harbage in his article "Elizabethan Acting" suggests that this play was written not long after Prynne's *Histriomastix* (1633), an intemperate attack on the stage.

The preface relies on classical sources and precedents. Julius Pollux, the Greek grammarian, is represented as the authority on voice, and the standard gestures devised by the author to express various emotions hark back to Cicero and Quintilian. This is the first English illustration of the schematization which characterizes the numerous manuals which followed in the eighteenth and nineteenth centuries.

The Eloquent Actor

... for my part I wish in this play I had done better. Receive then my good will for the deed, since others must act for me, and what is wanting in it, I hope those eloquent tongues of the actors will not be defective in; action being the greatest of winning force, and a greater conqueror than Cytherean. Action is a power of so much efficatiousness that it is the eloquence of the body by which the mind has a generous impression, so that the voice, hands and eyes are made the instruments of eloquence....

Julius Pollux ... [*Onomasticon*] doth report about twenty-five sorts of pronunciation ... a squeaking small voice, such rather seem to pipe than speak ... a narrow voice, which is so that the auditors' ears are filled with it ... a confused voice, so that the articulate sound is not distinct ... a rude, rough or blunt voice

---

Preface to *The Cyprian Conqueror, or The Faithless Relict* (c. 1633), British Museum MS. Sloane 3709-P7320.

...a careless voice...a foolish unapt to persuade...harsh and sharp...sad, amorous and bitter...infirm and weak...loud shrill....

These voices have four attendant virtues: *Purita, Perspicutia, Cultus* and *Habilitas*. Purity is a kind of salubrity in the voice which hath no fault, not effeminate and too womanly, not too rustic and boorish, not absurd or ridiculously affected; this virtue is as well purchased by custom and by nature and is of a great moment. Perspicuity is an articulate light of pronunciation, so that every syllable hath its legitimate stops in speaking; a reverent speech is an ornament, which is a complete composition of the organical part. *Habilitas,* handsome or ableness, is a kind of jocund variety of pronunciation, so that the auditors are refreshed and exhilarated by it, being a variety in equibility, and so that every actor, ought, according to their parts to be endowed with these virtues....

The other parts of action is in the gesture, which must be various as required; as in a sorrowful part the head must hang down, in a proud the head must be lofty; in an amorous, closed eyes, hanging down looks and crossed arms, in a hasty, fuming and scratching the head, etc....

RICHARD BURBAGE

(d. 1619)

Richard Burbage, son of James, the theatre-builder, probably followed in his father's footsteps as a player as early as 1584. He joined the Chamberlain's company at its formation in 1594 and became its great tragedian. He and his brother Cuthbert owned rights in the Globe Theatre and in the Blackfriars Theatre, which the company used as a winter home after 1608.

During his lifetime Burbage was cited in story, anecdote, and plays, as an excellent actor and painter. His name was introduced in the *dramatis personae* of *The Return from Parnassus,* Part II (1602), John Marston's *The Malcontent* (1605), and Ben Jonson's *Bartholomew Fair* (1614).

Shortly after Burbage's death the Earl of Pembroke absented himself from a performance given by the Chamberlain's company for the French Ambassador with the explanation that "I being tender hearted could not endure to see so soon after the loss of my old acquaintance Burbage." The following lines are from an elegy on the death of Burbage:

> Some skillful limner helpe mee, if not soe,
> Some sad tragedian, to express my woe,
> ....
> He's gone and with him what a world are dead,
> Which he revived to be revived soe.
> No more young Hamlett, ould Heironymoe,
> Kind Lear, the greved Moore, and more beside,
> That lived in him, have now for ever dy'de.
> Oft have I seen him leape into a grave
> Suiting ye person (which he seemed to have)
> Of a sad lover, with so true an eye
> That then I would have sworn he meant to die:
> So lively, ye spectators, and the rest

Of his sad crewe, while hee but seemed to bleed
Amazed thought that he had died indeed.
....
England's great Roscius, for what Roscius
Was more to Rome than Burbage was to us:
How to ye person hee did suit his face,
How did his speech become him, and his face
Suit with his speech, whilst not a word did fall
Without just weight to balance it withall
....
Poets! whose glory 'twas of late to heare
Your lines so well exprest: henceforth for beare
And write noe more, of it you doe't, Let't bee
In comic scenes, for tragic parts you see
Die all with him....

Richard Flecknoe (d. 1678?), a poet and playwright, made one brief contribution to the history of English acting. In his play *Love's Kingdom* (1664) is appended a discussion called "Discourse of the English Stage." To his admiration of the Elizabethan poets he added an appreciation of the first great English actors, particularly Richard Burbage. Although it is possible that Flecknoe never saw Burbage on the stage and that he was basing his praise on hearsay and on the example of Thomas Betterton's acting, his account of Burbage sets forth the seventeenth century conception of the ideal actor: transformation, excellent voice and diction, and complete absorption in the performance.

The Acting of Richard Burbage
by RICHARD FLECKNOE

It was the happiness of the actors of those times to have such poets as these to instruct them and write for them; and no less of these poets to have such docile and excellent actors to act their plays, as a [Nathan] Field and Burbage, of whom we may say that he was a delightful Proteus, so wholly transforming himself into his part, and putting off himself with his clothes, as he never (not so much as in the tiring-house) assum'd himself again until the play was done; there being as much difference betwixt him and one of our common actors, as between a ballad-singer who only mouths it, and an excellent singer who knows all his Graces, and can artfully vary and modulate his voice, even to know how much breath he is to give every syllable. He had all the parts of an excellent orator, animating his words with speaking, and speech with acting; his auditors being never more delighted than when he spoke, nor more sorry than when he held his peace; yet even then he was an excellent actor still, never falling in his part when he had done speaking, but with his looks and gestures maintaining it still unto the heighth, he imagining *age quod agis* only spoke to him; so as those who call him player do him wrong, no man being less idle than he was whose whole life is nothing else but action; with only this difference from other men, that as what is but a play to them is his business, so their business is but a play to him.

Richard Flecknoe: "The Acting of Richard Burbage" (1664), quoted by E. K. Chambers: *The Elizabethan Stage.* Oxford at the Clarendon Press, 1923, Volume IV, p. 370.

VII. ENGLAND

The Great Names

Underlying the social cohesiveness which fired Elizabethan dramatic imagination were conflicting forces which were shortly to rend the whole fabric of English society. Since the middle of the sixteenth century English Puritans in a rising middle-class society had been arguing against the immorality and social evil of the theatre. The struggle is highlighted in the numerous vindictive tracts baiting the stage and its players—John Northbrooke's *Treatise wherein Dicing, Dancing, vain Plays . . . (are) reproved,* Stephen Gosson's *The Schoole of Abuse,* and Philip Stubbes' *The Anatomy of Abuses.* Officials of London, representing the stolid property holders and tradesmen, tried to limit or outlaw the activity of the actors. Appealing to the aroused national fervor of the populace and protected by the Court, the players and their dramatists resisted this pressure through the reign of Elizabeth and James.

During the days of Charles I, the great playwriting and acting of the earlier period seemed vitiated. The theatre became more and more a plaything of the Court rather than the oracle of a nation. The indoor private theatres with their fashionable audiences and higher prices usurped the popularity of the old outdoor public theatres. For the elaborate court masques Inigo Jones perfected essentially modern scenic designs. The exuberant "drama-for-acting" of the popular Elizabethan theatres paled as the conflict between the King and the Puritan middle class sharpened. In 1633 when William Prynne launched *Histriomastix,* an attack on play-acting, the officials of the theatre-loving King Charles and Queen Henrietta Maria ordered the author's ears cut off. But the puritanic Prynnes won. When the rising tide of merchants and artisans challenged and overthrew the power of the King and his nobles in the civil war, the theatre was banned.

In 1642 the theatres of London were closed as a war measure. They were kept officially shut by the Puritans who remained in power until 1660 when Charles II was returned to the throne. The closing of the theatres scattered the companies of actors. Some like Michael Mohun (c. 1620-1684) and Charles Hart (d. 1683) acquired military titles, fighting on the side of the King to whom their fortunes had been closely tied. Others attempted to defy official edict by giving surreptitious performances. The authorities retaliated with arrests; they confiscated the actors' costumes and dismantled the old public theatres. Those players who escaped punishment evaded the law by performing "drolls," bits of plays interspersed with music.

Steps toward theatrical revival were taken by Sir William Davenant (1606-1668), playwright before 1642, when he offered in 1656 an "Entertainment . . . by Declamations and Musick . . . after the manner of the Ancients" at Rutland House. In the same year, he followed with an "opera," *The Siege of Rhodes,* initiating the vogue of heroic tragedy popular for the next forty years. This production will also be remembered as the one in which the first English actress, Mrs. Coleman, appeared.

The theatre came to life vigorously as soon as the monarchy was re-established.

In 1660 Davenant and his friend Thomas Killigrew (1612-1683) were granted patents by Charles II to hire or build two playhouses for the presentation of legitimate theatrical performances and to organize two companies of players, the Duke of York's Company and the King's Men. This monopoly of legitimate dramatic performances given the two patent houses remained in effect until 1843. The history of the Restoration and eighteenth century theatre thus mainly revolved around the two patent companies.

Close as the Restoration theatre is in point of time to the triumphs of Shakespeare and Burbage, the twenty-year interruption in theatrical continuity and social life wrought a marked change. Returning after years spent in France during the Commonwealth, the King and his courtiers brought with them a taste for French theatrical décor and French classical drama. The bare platform of the Elizabethans disappeared in a rudimentary, modern picture stage with a proscenium arch, a curtain, and scenery. All that remained of the platform was the large apron on which most of the acting was still done. Here the fops displayed themselves to the annoyance of the players. Costuming which lacked historical accuracy was lavish and extravagant. The outdoor playhouse vanished as new indoor theatres were built to house the primarily upper-class audience. For the first time women graced the English stage.

The Restoration ushered in an era of English theatrical history in which the actor superseded the playwright in importance. Early performances on the Restoration stage were revivals in which the actors of the two patent companies paraded their individual talents. Their personalities influenced writers who again began to write for the stage. Of all the plays produced in the following fifty years, only a handful are still read today. The small, leisure-class audience, aping the theatre-loving Charles II, enjoyed the sententious rhymed couplets of John Dryden and Nathaniel Lee. They probably found pleasure also in the reflection of their manners and gay life mirrored in the comedies of Etherege, Dryden, Wycherley, and Congreve, but only the brilliant, witty talk of the last two is revived on the modern stage.

The Reverend Jeremy Collier's attack, *A Short View of the Immorality and Profaneness of the English Stage* (1698), following the Bloodless Revolution and the victorious emergence of the middle class, introduced a new note of moral reform and sentimentality to the stage. Still, the eighteenth century plays, except for the works of Richard Brinsley Sheridan and Oliver Goldsmith, are little remembered except as vehicles for the great actors of that century.

From Thomas Betterton to Sarah Siddons, the English theatre presents a galaxy of great names in acting. The long span of years from 1660 to the beginning of the nineteenth century saw the evolution of a histrionic tradition to which each of the outstanding actors contributed. For fifty years—1660 to 1710—the genius of Thomas Betterton dominated the stage. As the leading figure in Davenant's Duke's Company, Betterton brought Hamlet to Restoration audiences and created roles in the plays of Dryden, Otway, Congreve and Etherege. He exemplified a style which his contemporaries regarded as restrained and dignified, moving but decorous, maintaining, as Colley Cibber says, "this medium, between mouthing, and meaning too little." His admirers endowed him with the great histrionic virtues: passionate feeling, variety in characterization, and judicious use of the voice instead of exhibitions of lung power for easy applause. Betterton's intelligence and conscious artistry, which are suggested in Anthony Aston's contrast of the actor

"Verbruggen wild and untaught, or Betterton in the trammels of instruction," seemed to differentiate him and his school from the actors who succeeded them.

Dignity in his work and personal life made Betterton and his wife, Mary Saunderson (d. 1712), the first actress to play Shakespeare's heroines, ideal tutors and models for actors. Betterton trained Mrs. Anne Bracegirdle (1663?-1748), heroine in the plays of Congreve, which were written for her, and he tutored Barton Booth (1681-1733), who succeeded him in tragic roles. Mrs. Elizabeth Barry (1658-1713), the finest tragic actress of the day, was his leading lady. Henry Harris, Romeo to Mrs. Betterton's Juliet, was next to Betterton the leading actor of the new Duke's Company.

The rival King's Company had in its troupe Charles Hart and Edward Kynaston (c. 1640-1712), both of whom had been boy actors playing female roles. Pepys wrote of Kynaston that he was "the loveliest lady that I ever saw," but Kynaston was more than a successful female impersonator. As women assumed the female roles, Kynaston, like Hart, became an excellent mature actor. Fascinating Michael Mohun, pretty Nell Gwyn (1650-1687), comic actress more noted for her amours than her art, and the comedian John Lacy (d. 1681) were also in the King's Company.

By 1680 both companies had built new theatres. The Duke's Company was housed in the sumptuously decorated Dorset Gardens and the King's Men played at Drury Lane. The falling off of popular support forced the two groups to unite in 1682 at the smaller Drury Lane theatre, where Betterton became the solitary great figure, since both Hart and Mohun had retired. After thirteen years as a united company, some of the actors led by Betterton revolted against the management of the patentee, Christopher Rich, and opened in 1695 in Lincoln's Inn Fields with a performance of Congreve's *Love for Love*. Sir John Vanbrugh, playwright and architect, built a new theatre in the Haymarket for the company, but vast and gilded as the theatre was, the group had no success there. In the last years of his life Betterton saw struggles and complications in the management of the patent theatres. Finally Drury Lane was taken over by Colley Cibber, Robert Wilks (1665-1732), and Thomas Doggett (d. 1721), who was succeeded by Barton Booth. These men directed it successfully almost to the time of Garrick.

With their lovely leading lady Anne Oldfield (1683-1730) they played popular high comedy and Shakespearean repertory, "improved" according to eighteenth century notions. Many of the new plays, including those of Cibber, Farquhar, Lillo, and Sheridan, were written for specific actors. More than ever it would appear that the actors made dull and unpalatable plays successful.

Acting during this first part of the eighteenth century was marked by emphasis on vocal pyrotechnics and exaggerated action. Musically cadenced speech ("tone"), imported from France, or monotonous declamatory delivery was heard in the theatres. Although James Quin (1693-1766), whom Garrick dethroned, was a popular Falstaff, in tragedy he was described by Richard Cumberland in these words: "With a deep, full tone, accompanied by a sawing kind of gesture, which had more of the senate than of the stage in it, he rolled out his heroics with an air of dignified indifference...." Robert Lloyd, in *The Actor,* one of many critical poems of this period, noted:

> Unskillful Actors, like your mimic Apes
> Will writhe their Bodies in a thousand Shapes,

However foreign from the Poet's Art,
No tragic Hero but admires a Start
What though unfeeling of the nervous Line,
Who but allows his *Attitude* is fine?
While a whole Minute equipoiz'd he stands,
Till Praise dismiss him with her echoing Hands.
Resolv'd, though Nature hate the tedious Pause,
By Perseverence to extort Applause.

Vocal displays, drawn-out pauses, and startling action, which the actors of this period willed to the growing histrionic lore, were never completely discarded by those who followed them.

During the decade before Garrick made his sensational debut in 1741, the old actors Booth, Wilks, and Cibber were making their exit from the stage. At the same time, histrionic art was receiving its first consistent and methodical scrutiny in new periodicals. Aaron Hill, who had done a stint as a theatrical manager in the earlier part of the century, emerged as a significant figure by devoting his semi-weekly publication, the *Prompter,* to discussions of drama and acting. He blamed the plight of the theatre on the absence of training for actors and suggested the establishment of an Academy. Hill undertook the training of actors and formulated a histrionic theory based upon a physiological analysis of the passions.

Thus the startling career of Garrick, in a dramatic era when "declamation roar'd, while passion slept," began in an atmosphere of change. Perhaps it was Garrick's friend and mentor, the irascible Charles Macklin, who broke most completely with the school of the Cibber period. As an actor and a teacher Macklin substituted the quality of common speech for the cadenced tones of tragic grandiloquence. He gave a completely fresh characterization in his portrayal of Shylock and paved the way for authenticity in costuming by dressing his Macbeth in Scottish garb.

David Garrick infused his acting with great native talent, intelligence, and a conscious devotion to his art. He turned to observe the world around him in gathering the insights which made his performances of Lear, Macbeth, and Abel Drugger (*The Alchemist*) notable. As co-patentee at Drury Lane from 1747 to 1776 he finally removed spectators from the stage. Garrick gathered about himself an extremely talented group of actors. Among them were Margaret (Peg) Woffington (c. 1714-1760), Susanna Maria Cibber (1714-1766), Mrs. Hannah Pritchard (1711-1768), Spranger Barry (1719-1777), Mrs. Frances Abington (1737-1815), and Mrs. Catherine (Kitty) Clive (1711-1785). He trained his actors vigorously in his own style of natural characterization, combined with grace in motion and posture.

Contemporary descriptions do not lead us to classify Garrick as a naturalistic actor, in the modern sense, such as Macklin probably was. Garrick, whose acting has been labeled "realistic romanticism," was not above the starts, stops, and drawn-out death scenes which drew applause. Nevertheless, his individual imaginative powers as an actor and his extraordinary ability to inspire his fellow-players elevated English acting to its apex in the Garrick era.

During his last season at Drury Lane, Garrick introduced a young provincial actress of whom he had heard good report. The young Sarah Siddons failed in her London debut as Portia. In June, 1776, Garrick retired, and Sarah Siddons went back to the provinces to perfect her craft. When she returned triumphant in 1782 to Drury Lane, tastes had changed. Her classic simplicity and overpowering emotional depth expressed the qualities which the growing romantic movement extolled. She tempered her statuesqueness and dignity with the natural manner learned from Garrick, perfecting what Lily B. Campbell calls "classical romanticism." Without completely discarding the surprises and "points" of the eighteenth century, she so awed her audiences, particularly in the role of Lady Macbeth, that she has come down to us as "The Tragic Muse."

John Philip Kemble (1757-1823), Sarah's brother, was cold, classical, and correct. He was an actor who took punctilious care in "the disposition of his mantle." His greatest creation was Coriolanus, a role well suited to his mannered, grandiloquent style. As manager first at Drury Lane and then at Covent Garden, Kemble was, however, an innovator. Scholarly and inventive, he was the first to take pains with theatrical production and to introduce historically authentic costuming. With these two great members of the Kemble family, the cumulative histrionic tradition of the eighteenth century came to a close.

This epoch of great names has left us for the first time in English theatrical history voluminous materials on actors and their art. The period abounds with the memorabilia of literary figures, with dramatic criticism in periodicals and books, with anecdotal memoirs and stage histories. The vital documents on acting by Cibber, Macklin, Garrick, Siddons, and others are rich and exciting sources. The age that brought reason and rules to bear on the interpretation of nature, society, and God, also subjected the mysterious art of the actor to "scientific" analysis. According to Charles Harold Gray (*Theatrical Criticism in London to 1795*), early criticism was mainly concerned with the actor's adherence to tradition handed down from Shakespeare's company. The actor was praised for preserving the accents and gestures of his predecessors. To Thomas Betterton, the giant of the Restoration era, is attributed one of the earliest manuals for actors. It emphasized the twin supports of the art—action and speech, and offered a calendar of appropriate gestures that recalls Quintilian and points the way to hundreds of later works. Sharp competition among the leading actors called forth expositions and defenses of particular histrionic styles. Thomas Wilkes, Charles Churchill, Robert Lloyd, Samuel Foote, and others detailed the qualifications of actors, lauded the merits of individual performers, and debated the passions. Aaron Hill sought the source of gesture in ten basic passions and catalogued the methods of histrionic expression. John Hill, adding English examples to his translation of a volume on acting, *Le Comédien*, by Pierre Rémond de Sainte-Albine (1699-1778), provided the first comprehensive analysis of the qualities necessary to the actor. Understanding, Sensibility, and Fire he placed foremost. He added to these basic attributes the need for a close relationship between the appearance and temper of the actor and the character he portrays.

Although "Nature" is given her due in eighteenth century writing on acting, conscious art is most frequently extolled. At the end of the century Romantic critics invoked nature against art which had been codified into the standardized rules of guidebooks. All the commentators utilize the Platonic and Horatian concepts of the actor possessed by and immersed in his role, but stage practice, even that of Garrick, indicates that complete identification of actor and role was an ideal not an accomplishment. Great care was paid to action, gesture, voice, and cadenced recitation. Although study of the passions seemed to point in the direction of modern character dissection, the eighteenth century studied the passions, it would seem, in order to produce the proper stance and gesture on the stage.

THOMAS BETTERTON

(1635? - 1710)

It is proper that the first full-length manual for actors in English should be ascribed to Thomas Betterton. Charles Gildon (1665-1724), who is regarded as the author of the volume called *The Life of Mr. Thomas Betterton the Late Eminent Tragedian, wherein the Action and Utterance of the Stage, Bar, and Pulpit are distinctly Considered* ... (1710), claimed to present Betterton's histrionic ideals. Perhaps that part of the book called "The Art of Playing..." did originate with Betterton, for a later volume *The History of the English Stage* ... also ascribed to Betterton, contains similar material.

Betterton, whose father was under-cook to Charles I, was apprenticed to a bookseller John Rhodes (c. 1606-1710), a theatre enthusiast and manager, from whom he received his first theatrical training. When Sir William Davenant organized The Duke's Men, Betterton became part of the company, and at Davenant's death he aided in the management of the troupe. An original and inventive player, he was greatly admired in his own day by Samuel Pepys and Sir Richard Steele, among others. His performance of Hamlet, for which he was celebrated, supposedly derived its excellence from the fact that Davenant instructed him in the manner inherited from Joseph Taylor (1586? - 1652), who is said to have followed Burbage in the role. Betterton was more than the greatest actor of the age; he was its theatrical leader. King James II, for example, sent him to France to study its theatres.

Betterton's papers on "The Art of Playing and the Duty and Qualifications of Actors," introduced by Gildon in his book, open with a moral defense of players and the stage and an appeal to actors to take "most nice care of their reputation." Although the writer points out that Mrs. Bradshaw "left the figure and action to nature," he recommends rules in the study of acting. His comment that "there seems a necessity of some marks, or rules to fix the standard of what is natural," suggests the interpretation of nature in eighteenth century literature on acting.

Specific principles offered for stage action are schematized instructions similar to those in Quintilian. For the art of speaking, Julius Pollux' old catalogue of voices is utilized, as it was by the anonymous author of *The Cyprian Conqueror*. Study of history, philosophy, rhetoric, painting, and sculpture is recommended to the actor who wants to present characters with decorum.

The Qualifications of a Player

ASCRIBED BY CHARLES GILDON TO BETTERTON

The year before his [Betterton's] death ... my friend and I ... called to see him; and being hospitably received, one day after dinner we retired to his garden, and after a little walk there, we fell into the discourse of acting. Much was said by my friend against the present players, and in praise of those of his younger days, for he was an old man. ... I addressed myself to Mr. Betterton in this manner:

Charles Gildon: *The Life of Mr. Thomas Betterton, the Late Eminent Tragedian. Wherein the Action and Utterance of the Stage, Bar, and Pulpit are distinctly Considered.* . . . London: Printed for Robert Gosling, 1710, pp. 11-12, 14-18, 33-43 *passim*, 54-57 *passim*.

I am sensible, that my friend's taste of these pleasures was stronger in his youth, than at this time, when the moroseness of age rebates the edge of our appetites in more pleasures, than one. He would else allow that no woman of his time excelled Mrs. [Elizabeth] Barry, nor any man yourself. I mean not to flatter you (said I, finding him a little uneasy with my compliment) for it is really my opinion; but I must confess, I see but little prospect, that we have of the stage's long surviving you two, at least, in its most valuable part, tragedy;...I choose...to attribute this decay of tragedy to our want of tragedians, and indeed tragic poets, than to the corruption of the people....

Though I am of opinion (replied Mr. Betterton) that the decay of the stage is in great measure owing to the long continuance of the war; yet, I confess, I am afraid, that too much is derived from the defects of the stage itself. When I was a young player under Sir William Davenant, we were under a much better discipline, we were obliged to make our study our business, which our young men do not think it their duty now to do; for they now scarce ever mind a word of their parts but only at rehearsals, and come thither too often scarce recovered from their last night's debauch; when the mind is not very capable of considering so calmly and judiciously on what they have to study, as to enter thoroughly into the nature of the part, or to consider the variation of the voice, looks, and gestures, which should give them their true beauty, many of them thinking the making a noise renders them agreeable to the audience, because a few of the upper-gallery clap the loud efforts of their lungs, in which their understanding has no share. They think it a superfluous trouble to study real excellence, which might rob them of what they fancy more, midnight, or indeed whole nights debauches, and a lazy remissness in their business.

Another obstacle to the improvement of our young players, is, that when they have not been admitted above a month or two into the company, though their education and former business were never so foreign to acting, they vainly imagine themselves masters of that art, which perfectly to attain, requires a studious application of a man's whole life. They take it therefore amiss to have the author give them any instruction; and though they know nothing of the art of poetry, will give their censure, and neglect or mind a part as they think the author and his part deserves. Though in this they are led by fancy as blind as ignorance can make it; and so wandering without any certain rule of judgment, generally favor the bad, and slight the good. Whereas it has always been mine and Mrs. Barry's practice to consult even the most indifferent poet in any part we have thought fit to accept; and I may say it of her, she has often so exerted herself in an indifferent part, that her acting has given success to such plays, as to read would turn a man's stomach; and though I could never pretend to do so much service that way as she has done, yet I have never been wanting in my endeavors. But while the young gentlemen will think themselves masters before they understand any one point of their art, and not give themselves leisure and time to study the graces of action and utterance, it is impossible that the stage should flourish, and advance in perfection.

I am very sensible (said I, finding that he had done) of the justness of what you have said, Sir, but am apt to believe much of those errors, which you remark proceed from want of judgment in the managers, in admitting people unqualified by nature, and not providing such men to direct them who understand the art they should be improved in. All other arts people are taught by masters skillful in them, but here ignorance teaches itself, or rather confirms itself into the confidence of knowledge, by going on without any rebuke. I have often wished, therefore, that some men of good sense, and acquainted with the graces of action and speaking, would lay down some rules, by which the young beginners might direct themselves to that perfection, which everybody is sensible is extremely (and perhaps always has been) wanted on our stage.... I wish I could prevail with you to deliver your sentiments on this head, so that from them we might form a system of acting, which might be a rule to future players and teach them to excel not only themselves, but those who have gone before them.

Were I, Sir (replied he with a graceful modesty), as capable as you would persuade me that you think me, I should easily be prevailed with to communicate my notions on this head; but being sensible of my incapacity, for the very reasons you have mentioned, of my ignorance of the learned tongues, I must be excused; yet not to disappoint you entirely, I shall fetch you a manuscript on this head, written by a friend of mine, to which I confess I contributed all, that I was able; which if well perused, and thoroughly weighed, I persuade myself our stage would rise and not fall in reputation.

On this he went into his house, and after a little stay returned to us with some loose papers, which I knew to be in his own hand... he thus began.

Being to treat of the Art of Playing, and the Duty and Qualifications of Actors, I think it will be no improper method first to consider, what regard an actor ought to have to his conduct off the stage, before we treat of what he is to do upon it.

I have not found in all the clamors against the stage, any one that denies the usefulness of the drama, if justly managed; nay, Mr. [Jeremy] Collier the most formidable enemy of this diversion... does allow, that the wit of man cannot invent any more efficacious means of encouraging virtue, and depressing of vice.

Hence I believe it is evident, that they suppose the moral lessons, which the stage presents, may make the greatest impressions on the minds of the audience; because the instruction is conveyed with pleasure, and by the ministrations of the passions, which always have a stronger remembrance, than the calmer precepts of reason.

But then I think there is no manner of doubt but that the lives and characters of those persons, who are the vehicles, as I may call them, of these instructions, must contribute very much to the impression the fable and moral will make. For to hear virtue, religion, honor recommended by a prostitute, an atheist, or a rake, makes them a jest to many people, who would hear the same done with awe by persons of known reputation in those particulars...

For this reason, I first recommend to our players, both male and female, the greatest and most nice care of their reputation imaginable....

... To begin... with action, the player is to consider, that it is not every rude and undesigning action, that is his business, for that is what the ignorant as well as skillful may have, nor can indeed want: but the action of a player is that, which is agreeable to personation, or the subject he represents. Now what he represents is man in his various characters, manners, and passions, and to these heads he must adjust every action; he must perfectly express the quality and manners of the man, whose person he assumes, that is, he must know how his manners are compounded, and from thence know the several features, as I may call them, of his passions. A patriot, a prince, a beggar, a clown, etc., must each have their propriety, and distinction in action as well as words and language. An actor therefore must vary with his argument, that is, carry the person in all his manners and qualities with him in every action and passion; he must transform himself into every person he represents, since he is to act all sorts of actions and passions. Sometimes he is to be a lover, and know not only all the soft and tender addresses of one, but what are proper to the character, that is in love, whether he be a prince or a peasant, a hot and fiery man or of more moderate and phlegmatic constitution, and even the degrees of the passions he is possessed with. Sometimes he is to represent a choleric, hot and jealous man, and then he must be thoroughly acquainted with all the motions and sentiments productive of those motions of the feet, hands, and looks of such a person in such circumstances. Sometimes he is a person all dejected and bending under the extremities of grief and sorrow; which changes the whole form and appearance of him in the representation, as it does really in nature. Sometimes he is distracted, and here nature will teach him, that his action has always something wild and irregular, though even that regularly; that his eyes, his looks or countenance, motions of body, hands and feet, be all of a piece, and that he never falls into the indifferent state of calmness and unconcern. As he now represents Achilles, then Aeneas, another time Hamlet, then Alexander the Great and Oedipus, he ought to know perfectly well the characters of all these heroes, the very same passions differing in the different heroes as their characters differ....

To know these different characters of established heroes the actor need only be acquainted with the poets, who write of them; if the poet who introduces them in his play has not sufficiently distinguished them. But to know the different compositions of the manners, and the passions springing from those manners, he ought to have an insight into moral philosophy, for they produce various appearances in the looks and actions, according to their various mixtures. For that the very same passion has various appearances, is plain from the history painters, who have followed nature.... The history painters indeed have observed a decorum in their pieces, which wants to be introduced on our stage; for there is never any person on the cloth, who has not a concern in the action.... This would render the representation extremely solemn and beautiful; but on the stage, not only the supernumeraries, as they call them, or attendants, mind nothing of the great concern of the scene, but even the actors themselves, who are on the stage, and not in the very principal parts, shall be whispering to one another, or bowing to their friends in the pit, or gazing about. But if they made playing their study (or had indeed a genius to their art), as it is their business, they would not only not be guilty of these absurdities, but would ... observe nature wherever they found it offer anything that could contribute to their perfection....

I must say this in the praise of Mr. [Robert] Wilks, he always takes care to give the prompter little trouble, and never wrongs the poet by putting in anything of his own; a fault, which some applaud themselves for, though they deserve a severe punishment for their equal folly and impudence. They forget Hamlet's advice to the players.... This is too frequently done by some of our popular but half comedians. But it is, I think, a greater fault in a tragedian, who through his imperfectness in his part shall speak on any stuff, that comes in his head, which must infallibly prejudice the true expression of the business of the play, let it be passion, description, or narration. But notwithstanding this supinity in general of too many of our modern players, we have sometimes some of them who are in earnest; for I remember I once saw Mr. Benjamin Johnson [d. 1742] (our present Roscius) act ... with such an engagement in the part, that I could not persuade myself, that it was acting but the reality; though this often depends on the poet in his furnishing his characters with matter enough to engage the player to enter entirely into it, but a good player will help out an indifferent poet.

But this address in the performance can never be obtained without the last degree of perfectness, for without that the player can never be free from the apprehension of being out. Among those players, who seem always to be in earnest, I must not omit the principal, the incomparable Mrs. Barry; her action is always just, and produced naturally by the sentiments of the part, which she acts, and she everywhere observes those rules prescribed to the poets by Horace, and which equally reach the actors....

She indeed always enters into her part, and is the person she represents. Thus I have heard her say, that she never said, Ah! Poor Castalio! in the *Orphan,* without weeping. And I have frequently observed her change her countenance several times as the discourse of others on the stage have affected her in the part she acted. This is being thoroughly concerned, this is to know her part, this is to express the passions in the countenance and gesture....

Then that conduct of the other hope of the English stage, Mrs. Bradshaw, (of whom we might say in acting, as one said of Tasso in poetry, that if he was not the best poet, he had hindered Virgil from being the only poet; so that if she be not the best actress the stage has known, she has hindered Mrs. Barry from being the only actress) would certainly be very just; for a friend of mine discoursing with her of the action of the stage, she told him, that she endeavored first to make herself mistress of her part, and left the figure and action to nature.

Though a great genius may do this, yet art must be consulted in the study of the larger share of the professors of this art...and to express nature justly, one must be master of nature in all its appearances, which can only be drawn from observation, which will tell us, that the passions and habits of the mind discover themselves in our looks, actions and gestures.

Thus we find a rolling eye that is quick and inconstant in its motion, argues a quick but light wit; a hot and choleric complexion, with an inconstant and impatient mind; and in a woman it gives a strong proof of wantonness and immodesty. Heavy dull eyes, a dull mind, and a difficulty of conception. For this reason we observe, that all or most people in years, sick men, and persons of a phlegmatic constitution are slow in the turning of their eyes.

That extreme propension to winking in some eyes, proceeds from a soul very subject to fear, arguing a weakness of spirit, and a feeble disposition of the eye-lids.

A bold staring eye, that fixes on a man, proceeds either from a blockish stupidity, as in rustics; impudence, as in malicious persons; prudence, as in those in authority, or incontinence as in lewd women.

Eyes enflamed and fiery are the genuine effect of choler and anger; eyes quiet, and calm with a secret kind of grace and pleasantness are the offspring of love and friendship.

Thus the voice, when loud, discovers wrath and indignation of mind, and a small trembling voice proceeds from fear.

In like manner, to use no actions or gestures in discourse, is a sign of a heavy and slow disposition, as too much gesticulation proceeds from lightness; and a mean betwixt both is the effect of wisdom and gravity; and if it be not too quick, it denotes magnanimity. Some are perpetually fiddling about their clothes, so that they scarce are dressed till they go to bed, which is an argument of a childish and empty mind.

Some cast their heads from one side to the other wantonly and lightly, the true effect of folly and inconstancy. Others think it essential to prayer, to writhe and wrest their necks about, which is a proof of hypocrisy, superstition, or foolishness. Some are wholly taken up in viewing themselves, the proportion of their limbs, features of their faces, and gracefulness of mien; which proceeds from pride, and a vain complaisance in themselves; of this number are coquettes.

In this manner I might run through all the natural actions, that are to be found in men of different tempers.

* * * *

'Tis true, it must be confessed, that the art of gesture seems more difficult to be obtained, than the art of speaking; because a man's own ear may be judge of the voice, and its several variations, but cannot see his face at all, and the motion of the other parts of the body, but very imperfectly. Demosthenes... to make a true judgment how far his face and limbs moved and kept to the rules of good action and gesture, set before him a large looking-glass sufficient to represent the whole body at one view, to direct him in distinguishing betwixt right and wrong, decent and indecent actions; but yet, though this might not be unuseful, it lies under this disadvantage, that it represents on the right what is on the left, and on the contrary, on the left what is on the right hand....

'Tis true, that some have advised the learner to have some excellent pattern always before his eyes, and urge, that Hortensius was so to Roscius and Aesopus, who always made it their business to be present at his pleadings with that attention as to improve themselves so far by what they saw, as to carry away his fine actions and gesture, and practice afterwards on the stage, what they had seen at the bar; yet can I not allow of this imitation in acting; for when a very young player conceives a strong opinion of any one of received authority on the stage, he at best becomes a good copy, which must always fall short of an original. Besides, this instance of the two Roman players will not reach our case, since they were established players, had fixed their characters, and manner of playing; and only did by Hortensius what a player now might do by the fine pieces of history-painting, carry off the beautiful passions and positions of the figures, or the particular appearance of any one passion....

But it may be objected, that what I have delivered all this time seems rather to dwell upon generals, than to come to any particulars. I confess in this art it is much an easier matter to discourse in a general manner, than to deliver particular rules for the direction of our actions. Yet I believe I may venture to say, that as general as my discourse may seem to some, those, who have any true genius to playing, will find such particular instructions, as may be of very great use to them; and this art, as well as most others, but especially poetry, delivers such rules, that are not easily understood without a genius.

COLLEY CIBBER

(1671 - 1757)

Colley Cibber, actor, playwright, manager, teacher, is a good example of the all-around man of the theatre in this period. According to actor Thomas Davies' (1712-1785) *Dramatic Miscellanies,* Cibber, son of a sculptor, pestered John Downes, prompter of Drury Lane, for a job as an actor. Anecdote has it that his first acting chore was to carry a message to Betterton, but Master Colley was so frightened that he disturbed the progress of the scene. He did, however, begin to have success as a comic actor. When the Betterton group left the united theatrical company to form a company of its own, Cibber remained at Drury Lane. From Betterton's death until the emergence of Garrick, he was an important theatrical leader. With Wilks and Booth, he successfully managed Theatre Royal at Drury Lane.

As a playwright Cibber can be credited with initiating the vogue of sentimental comedy in his play *Love's Last Shift*. The success of his writing and acting in this play evoked *The Relapse* by Vanbrugh, in which Cibber created the character of Lord Foppington. His play *The Careless Husband* gave Mrs. Anne Oldfield her first successful role. In addition to writing and managing, Cibber appeared in such roles as Sir Fopling Flutter in Etherege's *The Man of Mode*, as Ben in Congreve's *Love for Love*, and as Iago.

In 1730 Cibber was appointed Poet Laureate, probably as a reward for his political aid to the Hanovers. He was the first actor-writer so honored. Although Cibber seems to have antagonized his associates both as manager and actor and although he earned a place in Pope's *Dunciad*, he did make an important contribution to the theatre. He was a popular author of the new sentimental comic drama, he was an excellent comedian and a competent manager, and in his autobiography, *Apology for his Life*, he emerged as an astute commentator on the art of acting. His statements, some of which follow, are given as descriptions of the famous actors he knew, but as Walter Prichard Eaton has pointed out in *The Actor's Heritage*, their value is greater as an indication of what good acting should be than as pure description.

Himself an actor of the exaggerated school in the early part of the eighteenth century, Cibber nevertheless gives an incisive picture of restraint in his evaluation of Betterton. His discussions of actors in the *Apology* indicate a judicious appreciation of different styles of acting and an understanding of the basic problems in the actor's art.

Apology for His Life

In the year 1690, when I first came into this company, [the united Duke's and King's Companies] the principal actors then at the head of it were:

OF MEN	OF WOMEN
Mr. Betterton	Mrs. Betterton
Mr. Mountfort	Mrs. Barry
Mr. Kynaston	Mrs. Leigh
Mr. Sandford	Mrs. Butler
Mr. Nokes	Mrs. Mountfort
Mr. Underhill	Mrs. Bracegirdle
Mr. Leigh	

These actors, whom I have selected from their contemporaries, were all original masters in their different style, not mere auricular imitators of one another, which commonly is the highest merit of the middle rank; but self-judges

Colley Cibber's Apology for his Life. London: Everyman's Library, J. M. Dent and Sons, Ltd., pp. 56-93 *passim.,* 294-297 *passim.*

of nature, from whose various lights they only took their true instruction. If in the following account of them I may be obliged to hint at the faults of others, I never mean such observations should extend to those who are now in possession of the stage; for as I design not my memoirs shall come down to their time, I would not lie under the imputation of speaking in their disfavor to the public, whose approbation they must depend upon for support. But to my purpose.

Betterton was an actor, as Shakespeare was an author, both without competitors! formed for the mutual assistance and illustration of each other's genius! How Shakespeare wrote, all men who have a taste for nature may read, and know—but with what higher rapture would he still be read, could they conceive how Betterton *played* him. Then might they know, the one was born alone to speak what the other only knew to write! Pity it is, that the momentary beauties flowing from an harmonious elocution, cannot like those of poetry be their own record! That the animated graces of the player can live no longer than the instant breath and motion that presents them; or at best can but faintly glimmer through the memory, or imperfect attestation of a few surviving spectators. Could *how* Betterton spoke be as easily known as *what* he spoke; then might you see the muse of Shakespeare in her triumph, with all her beauties in their best array, rising into real life, and charming her beholders. But alas! since all this is so far out of the reach of description, how shall I show you Betterton? Should I therefore tell you, that all the Othellos, Hamlets, Hotspurs, Macbeths, and Brutus's whom you may have seen since his time, have fallen far short of him; this still should give you no idea of his particular excellence. Let us see then what a particular comparison may do! whether that may yet draw him nearer to you?

You have seen a Hamlet perhaps, who, on the first appearance of his father's spirit, has thrown himself into all the straining vociferation requisite to express rage and fury, and the house has thundered with applause; though the misguided actor was all the while (as Shakespeare terms it) tearing a passion into rags. I am the more bold to offer you this particular instance, because the late Mr. Addison, while I sat by him, to see this scene acted, made the same observation, asking me with some surprise, if I thought Hamlet should be in so violent a passion with the Ghost, which though it might have astonished, it had not provoked him? for you may observe that in this beautiful speech, the passion never rises beyond an almost breathless astonishment, or an impatience, limited by filial reverence, to enquire into the suspected wrongs that may have raised him from his peaceful tomb! and a desire to know what a spirit so seemingly distressed, might wish or enjoin a sorrowful son to execute towards his future quiet in the grave? This was the light into which Betterton threw this scene; which he opened with a pause of mute amazement! then rising slowly to a solemn, trembling voice, he made the Ghost equally terrible to the spectator as to himself! and in the descriptive part of the natural emotions which the ghastly vision gave him, the boldness of his expostulation was still governed by decency, manly, but not braving; his voice never rising into that seeming outrage, or wild defiance of what he naturally revered. But alas! to preserve this medium, between mouthing, and meaning too little, to keep the attention more pleasingly awake, by a tempered spirit, then by mere vehemence of voice, is of all the masterstrokes of an actor the most difficult to teach. In this none yet have equalled Betterton. But I am unwilling to show his superiority only by recounting the errors of those who now cannot answer to them; let their farther failings therefore be forgotten! or rather, shall I in some measure excuse them? for I am not yet sure, that they might not be as much owing to the false judgment of the spectator as the actor. While the million are so apt to be transported, when the drum of their ear is so roundly rattled; while they take the life of elocution to lie in the strength of the lungs, it is no wonder the actor, whose end is applause, should be also tempted, at this easy rate, to excite it. Shall I go a little farther? and allow that this extreme is more pardonable than its opposite error? I mean that dangerous affectation of the monotone, or solemn sameness of pronunciation, which to my ear is insupportable; for of all faults that so frequently pass upon the vulgar, that of flatness will have the fewest admirers.... He that feels not himself the passion he would raise, will talk to a sleeping audience. But this never was the fault of Betterton; and it has often amazed me to see those who soon came after him, throw out in some parts of a character, a just and graceful spirit, which Betterton himself could not but have applauded. And yet in the equally shining passages of the same character, have heavily dragged the sentiment along like a dead weight; with a long-toned voice, and absent eyes, as if they had fairly forgot what they were about. If you have never made this observation, I am contented you should not know where to apply it.

A farther excellence in Betterton, was that he could vary his spirit to the different characters he acted. Those wild impatient starts, that fierce and flashing fire, which he threw into Hotspur, never came from the unruffled temper of Brutus (for I have, more than once, seen a Brutus as warm as Hotspur), when the Betterton Brutus was provoked, in his dispute with Cassius, his spirit flew only to his eyes; his steady look alone supplied that terror, which he disdained an intemperance in his voice should rise to. Thus, with a settled dignity of contempt, like an unheeding rock, he repelled upon himself the foam of Cassius....

But with whatever strength of nature we see the poet show at once the philosopher and the hero, yet the image of the actor's excellence will be still imperfect to you, unless language could put colors in our words to paint the voice with.
... The most that a Vandyke can arrive at, is to make his portraits of great persons seem to *think; a* Shakespeare goes farther yet, and tells you *what* his pictures thought; a Betterton steps beyond them both, and calls them from the grave, to breathe, and be themselves again, in feature, speech, and motion. When the skillful actor shows you all these powers at once united, and he gratifies at once your eye, your ear, your understanding. To conceive the pleasure rising from such harmony, you must have been present at it! 'tis not to be told you!

＊　＊　＊　＊

... Betterton had so just a sense of what was true or false applause, that I have heard him say he never thought any kind of it equal to an attentive silence; that there were many ways of deceiving an audience into a loud one; but to keep them hushed and quiet, was an applause which only truth and merit could arrive at: of which art, there never was an equal master to himself. From these various excellencies he had so full a possession of the esteem and regard of his auditors, that upon his entrance into every scene, he seemed to seize upon the eyes and ears of the giddy and inadvertent. To have talked or looked another way, would have been thought insensibility or ignorance. In all his soliloquies of moment, the strong intelligence of his attitude and aspect, drew you into

such an impatient gaze, and eager expectation, that you almost imbibed the sentiment with your eye, before the ear could reach it.

As Betterton is the center to which all my observations upon action tend,
you will give me leave, under his character, to enlarge upon that head. In the just
delivery of poetical numbers, particularly where the sentiments are pathetic, it
is scarce credible upon how minute an article of sound depends their greatest
beauty or inaffection. The voice of a singer is not more strictly tied to time
and tune, than that of an actor in theatrical elocution: the least syllable too long,
or too slightly dwelt upon in a period, depreciates it to nothing; which very
syllable, if rightly touched, shall, like the heightening stroke of light from a
master's pencil, give life and spirit to the whole. I never heard a line in tragedy
come from Betterton, wherein my judgment, my ear, and my imagination, were
not fully satisfied; which, since his time, I cannot equally say of any one actor
whatsoever: not but it is possible to be much his inferior with great excellencies;
which I shall observe in another place. Had it been practicable to have tied
down the clattering hands of all the ill judges who were commonly the majority
of an audience, to what amazing perfection might the English theatre have
arrived, with so just an actor as Betterton at the head of it! If what was truth
only could have been applauded, how many noisy actors had shook their plumes
with shame, who, from the injudicious approbation of the multitude, have
bawled and strutted in the place of merit? If therefore the bare speaking voice
has such allurement in it, how much less ought we to wonder, however we may
lament, that the sweeter notes of vocal music should so have captivated even the
politer world into an apostacy from sense to an idolatry of sound....

As we have sometimes great composers of music who cannot sing, we
have as frequently great writers that cannot read; and though, without the nicest
ear, no man can be master of poetical numbers, yet the best ear in the world will
not always enable him to pronounce them. Of this truth, Dryden, our first great
master of verse and harmony, was a strong instance. When he brought his
play of *Amphitryon* to the stage, I heard him give it his first reading to the
actors, in which, though it is true he delivered the plain sense of every period,
yet the whole was in so cold, so flat, and unaffecting a manner, that I am afraid
of not being believed when I affirm it.

On the contrary, [Nathaniel] Lee, far his inferior in poetry, was so pathetic
a reader of his own scenes, that I have been informed by an actor, who was
present, that while Lee was reading to Major [Michael] Mohun at a rehearsal,
Mohun, in the warmth of his admiration, threw down his part, and said, "Unless
I were able to play it as well as you read it, to what purpose should I undertake it?" and yet this very author, whose elocution raised such admiration in
so capital an actor, when he attempted to be an actor, himself, soon quitted the
stage, in an honest despair of ever making any profitable figure there. From
all this I would infer, that let our conception of what we are to speak be ever
so just, and the ear ever so true, yet, when we are to deliver it to an audience
(I will leave fear out of the question), there must go along with the whole, a
natural freedom, a becoming grace, which is easier to conceive than describe.
For without this inexpressible somewhat, the performance will come out oddly
disguised, or somewhere defectively, unsurprising to the hearer.... After I have
shown you so many necessary qualifications, not one of which can be spared in
true theatrical elocution, and have at the same time proved that with the assistance

of them all united, the whole may still come forth defective; what talents shall we say will infallibly form an actor? This, I confess, is one of nature's secrets, too deep for me to dive into; let us content ourselves therefore with affirming, that genius, which nature only gives, only can complete him. This genius then was so strong in Betterton, that it shone out in every speech and motion of him. Yet voice, and person, are such necessary supports to it, that, by the multitude, they have been preferred to genius itself, or at least often mistaken for it. Betterton had a voice of that kind which gave more spirit to terror than to the softer passions; of more strength than melody. The rage and jealousy of Othello became him better than the sighs and tenderness of Castalio: for though in Castalio he only excelled others, in Othello he excelled himself; which you will easily believe, when you consider, that...Othello has more natural beauties than the best actor can find in all the magazine of poetry to animate his power and delight his judgment with.

The person of this actor was suitable to his voice, more manly than sweet, nor exceeding the middle stature, inclining to the corpulent; of a serious and penetrating aspect; his limbs near the athletic than the delicate proportion; yet however formed, there arose from the harmony of the whole a commanding mien of majesty which the fairer-faced, or (as Shakespeare calls 'em) the curled darlings of his time, ever wanted something to be equal masters of. There was some years ago, to be had, almost in every printshop, a metzotinto, from Kneller, extremely like him.

In all I have said of Betterton, I confine myself to the time of his strength, and highest power in action, that you may make allowances from what he was able to execute at fifty, to what you might have seen of him at past seventy; for though to the last he was without his equal, he might not then be equal to his former self; yet so far was he from being ever overtaken, that for many years after his decease, I seldom saw any of his parts, in Shakespeare, supplied, by others, but it drew from me the lamentation of Ophelia upon Hamlet's being unlike what she had seen him.

Ah! woe is me!

T' have seen, what I have seen, see what I see!

*   *   *   *

I once thought to have filled up my work with a select dissertation upon theatrical action, but I find, by the digressions I have been tempted to make in this account of Betterton, that all I can say upon that head will naturally fall in, and possibly be less tedious, if dispersed among the various characters of the particular actors I have promised to treat of....

[EDWARD] KYNASTON

Of this real majesty [Henry IV] Kynaston was entirely master; here every sentiment came from him, as if it had been his own, as if he had himself, that instant, conceived it, as if he had lost the player and were the real king he personated! A perfection so rarely found, that very often in actors of good repute, a certain vacancy of look, inanity of voice, or superfluous gesture shall unmask the man, to the judicious spectator; who from the least of those errors plainly sees the whole but a lesson given him, to be got by heart, from some great author, whose sense is deeper than the repeater's understanding. This true majesty

[107]

Kynaston had so entire a command of, that when he whispered the following plain line to Hotspur,

Send us your prisoners, or you'll hear of it!

he conveyed a more terrible menace in it than the loudest intemperance of voice could swell to. But let the bold imitator beware, for without the look, and just elocution that waited on it, an attempt of the same nature may fall to nothing.

But the dignity of this character appeared in Kynaston still more shining, in the private scene between the king and prince his son: there you saw majesty, in that sort of grief which only majesty could feel! there the paternal concern for the errors of the son made the monarch more revered and dreaded. His reproaches so just, yet so unmixed with anger (and therefore the more piercing), opening as it were the arms of nature, with a secret wish, that filial duty and penitence awaked, might fall into them with grace and honor. In this affecting scene I thought Kynaston showed his most masterly strokes of nature; expressing all the various motions of the heart, with the same force, dignity, and feeling they were written; adding to the whole that peculiar and becoming grace which the best writer cannot inspire into any actor that is not born with it. What made the merit of this actor, and that of Betterton more surprising, was, that though they both observed the rules of truth and nature, they were each as different in their manner of acting, as in their personal form and features....

[WILLIAM] MOUNTFORT
[1660-1692]

Mountfort, a younger man by twenty years, and at this time in his highest reputation, was an actor of a very different style. Of person he was tall, well made, fair, and of an agreeable aspect, his voice clear, full and melodious. In tragedy he was the most affecting lover within my memory. His addresses had a resistless recommendation from the very tone of his voice, which gave his words such softness, that as Dryden says,

Like flakes of feather'd snow,
They melted as they fell!

All this he particularly verified in that scene of *Alexander,* where the hero throws himself at the feet of Statira for pardon of his past infidelities. There we saw the great, the tender, the penitent, the despairing, the transported, and the amiable, in the highest perfection. In comedy, he gave the truest life to what we call the fine gentleman; his spirit shone the brighter for being polished with decency. In scenes of gaiety, he never broke into the regard that was due to the presence of equal, or superior characters, though inferior actors played them; he filled the stage, not by elbowing, and crossing it before others, or disconcerting their action, but by surpassing them, in true and masterly touches of nature. He never laughed at his own jest, unless the point of his raillery upon another required it. He had a particular talent, in giving life to *bons mots* and *repartees*: the wit of the poet seemed always to come from him *extempore,* and sharpened into more wit, from his brilliant manner of delivering it; he had himself a good share of it, or what is equal to it, so lively a pleasantness of humor, that when either of these fell into his hands upon the stage, he wantoned with them, to the highest delight of his auditors. The agreeable was so natural to him, that even in that dissolute character of the Rover he seemed to wash off the guilt from vice, and gave it charms and merit....

He had besides all this, a variety in his genius which few capital actors have shown, or perhaps have thought it any addition to their merit to arrive at; he could entirely change himself; could at once throw off the man of sense, for the brisk, vain, rude and lively coxcomb, the false flashy pretender to wit, and the dupe of his own sufficiency. Of this he gave a delightful instance in the character of Sparkish in Wycherley's *Country Wife*. In that of Sir Courtly Nice his excellence was still greater. There his whole man, voice, mien, and gesture, was no longer Mountfort, but another person. There the insipid, soft civility, the elegant, and formal mien; the drawling delicacy of voice, the stately flatness of his address, and the empty eminence of his attitudes were so nicely observed and guarded by him, that had he not been an entire master of nature, had he not kept his judgment, as it were, a sentinel upon himself, not to admit the least likeness of what he used to be to enter into any part of his performance, he could not possibly have so completely finished it....

[SAMUEL] SANDFORD
[— 1700?]

Sandford ... an excellent actor in disagreeable characters ... was not the stage villain by choice, but from necessity; for having a low and crooked person, such bodily defects were too strong to be admitted into great or amiable characters; so that whenever, in any new or revived play, there was a hateful or mischievous person, Sandford was sure to have no competitor for it.... In this disadvantageous light, then, stood Sandford, as an actor; admired by the judicious, while the crowd only praised him by their prejudice. And so unusual had it been to see Sandford an innocent man in a play, that whenever he was so, the spectators would hardly give him credit in so gross an improbability....

For my own part, I profess myself to have been an admirer of Sandford, and have often lamented that his masterly performance could not be rewarded with that applause which I saw much inferior met with, merely because they stood in more laudable characters. For, though it may be a merit in an audience to applaud sentiments of virtue and honor, yet there seems to be an equal justice that no distinction should be made, as to the excellence to an actor, whether in a good or evil character, since neither the vice, nor the virtue of it, is his own, but given him by the poet. Therefore, why is not the actor who shines in either equally commendable? No, sir, this may be reason, but that is not always a rule with us; the spectator will tell you, that when virtue is applauded, he gives part of it to himself; because his applause at the same time lets others about him see that he himself admires it. But when a wicked action is going forward; when an Iago is meditating revenge, and mischief; though art and nature may be equally strong in the actor, the spectator is shy of his applause, lest he should, in some sort, be looked upon as an aider or an abettor of the wickedness in view; and therefore rather chooses to rob the actor of praise he may merit, than give it him in a character which he would have you see his silence modestly discourages. From the same fond principle, many actors have made it a point to be seen in parts sometimes, even flatly written, only because they stood in the favorable light of honor and virtue....

[James] Nokes

[d. 1692?]

I come now to those other men actors who, at this time, were equally famous in the lower life of comedy. But I find myself more at a loss to give you them, in their true and proper light, than those I have already set before you. Why the tragedian warms us into joy, or admiration, or sets our eyes on flow with pity, we can easily explain to another's apprehension; but it may sometimes puzzle the gravest spectator to account for that familiar violence of laughter, that shall seize him, at some particular strokes of a true comedian. How then shall I describe what a better judge might not be able to express? The rules to please the fancy cannot so easily be laid down, as those that ought to govern the judgment. The decency too, that must be observed in tragedy, reduces, by the manner of speaking it, one actor to be much more like another, than they can or need be supposed to be in comedy. There the laws of action give them such free, and almost unlimited liberties, to play and wanton with nature, that the voice, look, and gesture of a comedian may be as various as the manners and faces of the whole mankind are different from one another. These are the difficulties I lie under. Where I want words, therefore, to describe what I may commend, I can only hope you will give credit to my opinion; and credit I shall most stand in need of when I tell you, that Nokes was an actor of a quite different genius from any I have ever read, heard of, or seen, since or before his time; and yet his general excellence may be comprehended in one article, viz. a plain and palpable simplicity of nature, which was so utterly his own, that he was often as unaccountably diverting in his common speech, as on the stage....

He scarce ever made his first entrance in a play but he was received with an involuntary applause, not of hands only, for those may be, and have often been partially prostituted and bespoken, but by a general laughter, which the very sight of him provoked, and nature could not resist; yet the louder the laugh the graver was his look upon it; and sure, the ridiculous solemnity of his features were enough to have set a whole bench of bishops into a titter, could he have been honored (may it be not offense to suppose it) with such grave and right reverend auditors. In the ludicrous distresses, which by the laws of comedy, folly is often involved in; he sunk into such a mixture of piteous pusillanimity, and a consternation so ruefully ridiculous and inconsolable, that when he had shook you, to a fatigue of laughter, it became a moot point whether you ought not to have pitied him. When he debated any matter by himself, he would shut up his mouth with a dumb studious pout, and roll his full eye into such a vacant amazement, such a palpable ignorance of what to think of it, that his silent perplexity (which would sometimes hold him several minutes) gave your imagination as full content as the most absurd thing he could say upon it. In the character of Sir Martin Marr-all, who is always committing blunders to the prejudice of his own interest, when he had brought himself to a dilemma in his affairs, by vainly proceeding upon his own head, and was afterwards afraid to look his governing servant and counsellor in the face; what a copious, and distressful harangue have I seen him make with his looks (while the house has been in one continued roar, for several minutes) before he could prevail his courage to speak a word to him! Then might you have, at once, read in his face vexation—that his own measures, which he had piqued himself upon, had failed. Envy—of his servant's superior wit. Distress—to retrieve, the occasion he had lost. Shame—to confess his folly; and yet a sullen desire, to be reconciled and better advised, for the future! What tragedy ever showed us such a tumult of passions, rising, at once, in one bosom! or what buskined hero standing under the load of them, could have more effectually moved his spectators by the most pathetic speech, than poor miserable Nokes did, by his silent eloquence, and piteous plight of his features? ...

MRS. BARRY

Mrs. Elizabeth Barry was then in possession of almost all the chief parts in tragedy. With what skill she gave life to them, you will judge from the words of Dryden, in his preface to *Cleomenes,* where he says,

"Mrs. Barry, always excellent, has in this tragedy excelled herself, and gained a reputation beyond any woman I have ever seen on the theatre."

I very perfectly remember her acting that part; and however unnecessary it may seem, to give my judgment after Dryden's, I cannot help saying I do not only close with his opinion, but will venture to add that (though Dryden has been dead these thirty-eight years) the same compliment, to this hour, may be due to her excellence. And though she was then, not a little, past her youth, she was not, till that time, fully arrived to her maturity of power and judgment. From when I would observe, that the short life of beauty is not long enough to form a complete actress. In men, the delicacy of person is not so absolutely necessary, nor the decline of it so soon taken notice of. The fame Mrs. Barry arrived to, is a particular proof of the difficulty there is, in judging with certainty, from their first trials, whether young people will ever make any great figure on a theatre. There was, it seems, so little hopes of Mrs. Barry, at her first setting out, that she was, at the end of the first year, discharged from the company, among others, that were thought to be a useless expense to it. I take it for granted that the objection to Mrs. Barry, at that time, must have been a defective ear, or some unskillful dissonance, in her manner of pronouncing. But where there is a proper voice, and person, with the addition of a good understanding, experience tells us that such defect is not always invincible, of which, not only Mrs. Barry, but the late Mrs. [Anne] Oldfield are eminent instances. Mrs. Oldfield had been a year in the Theatre-Royal before she was observed to give any tolerable hope of her being an actress; so unlike to all manner of propriety, was her speaking! How unaccountably then does a genius for the stage make its way toward perfection? For, notwithstanding these equal disadvantages, both these actresses, though of different excellence, made themselves complete mistresses of their art by the prevalence of their understanding. If this observation may be of any use to the masters of future theatres, I shall not then have made it to no purpose.

Mrs. Barry, in characters of greatness, had a presence of elevated dignity, her mien and motion superb, and gracefully majestic; her voice, full, clear, and strong, so that no violence of passion could be too much for her; and when distress, or tenderness possessed her, she subsided into the most affecting melody and softness. In the art of exciting pity, she had a power beyond all the actresses I have yet seen, or what your imagination can conceive. Of the former of these two great excellencies, she gave the most delightful proofs in almost all the heroic plays of Dryden and Lee; and of the latter, in the softer passions of Otway's Monimia and Belvidera....

MRS. BETTERTON

Mrs. Betterton [Mary Saunderson], though far advanced in years, was so great a mistress of nature, that even Mrs. Barry, who acted the Lady Macbeth after her, could not in that part, with all her superior strength and melody of voice, throw out those quick and careless strokes of terror, from the disorder of a guilty mind, which the other gave us with a facility in her manner that rendered them at once tremendous and delightful. Time could not impair her skill, though he had brought her person to decay. She was, to the last, the admiration of all true judges of nature and lovers of Shakespeare, in whose plays she chiefly excelled, and without a rival. When she quitted the stage, several good actresses were the better for her instruction....

MRS. [WILLIAM] MOUNTFORT

Mrs. [William] Mountfort, whose second marriage gave her the name of [Mrs. John] Verbruggen, was mistress of more variety of humor than I ever knew in any one woman actress. This variety, too, was attended with an equal vivacity, which made her excellent in characters extremely different. As she was naturally a pleasant mimic, she had the skill to make that talent useful on the stage, a talent which may be surprising in a conversation, and yet be lost when brought to the theatre.... But where the elocution is round, distinct, voluble, and various as Mrs. Mountfort's was, the mimic, there, is a great assistant to the actor. Nothing though ever so barren, if within the bounds of nature, could be flat in her hands. She gave many heightening touches to characters but coldly written, and often made an author vain of his work that in itself had but little merit. She was so fond of humor, in what low part soever to be found, that she would make no scruple of defacing her fair form, to come heartily into it; for when she was eminent in several desirable characters of wit and humor in higher life, she would be, in as much fancy, when descending to the antiquated Abigail, of Fletcher, as when triumphing in all the airs and vain graces of a fine lady; a merit that few actresses care for. In a play of D'urfey's, now forgotten, called, *The Western Lass,* which part she acted, she transformed her whole being, body, shape, voice, language, look, and features, into almost another animal; with a strong Devonshire dialect, a broad laughing voice, a poking head, round shoulders, an unconceiving eye, and the most bedizening, dowdy dress, that ever covered the untrained limbs of a Joan Trot. To have seen her here, you would have thought it impossible that same creature could ever have been recovered to what was as easy to her, the gay, the lively, and the desirable. Nor was her humor limited to her sex; for, while her shape permitted, she was a more adroit pretty fellow than is usually seen upon the stage. Her easy air, action, mien, and gesture quite changed from the quoif, to the cocked hat and cavalier in fashion. People were so fond of seeing her a man, that when the part of Bayes in the *Rehearsal,* had, for some time, lain dormant, she was desired to take it up, which I have seen her act with all the true coxcombly spirit, and humor, that the sufficiency of the character required....

ENGLAND

Mrs. [Anne] Bracegirdle

Mrs. Bracegirdle was now but just blooming to her maturity; her reputation, as an actress, gradually rising with that of her person; never any woman was in such general favor of her spectators, which, to the last scene of her dramatic life, she maintained, by not being unguarded in her private character. This discretion contributed, not a little, to make her the Cara, the darling of the theatre. For it will be no extravagant thing to say, scarce an audience saw her that were less than half of them lovers, without a suspected favorite among them.... I shall therefore only say of Mrs. Bracegirdle, that the most eminent authors always chose her for their favorite character, and shall leave that uncontestable proof of her merit to its own value....

[Robert] Wilks and [Barton] Booth

Wilks, from his first setting out, certainly formed his manner of acting upon the model of Mountfort; as Booth did his on that of Betterton. But... I cannot say either of them came up to their original. Wilks had not that easy regulated behavior, or the harmonious elocution of the one, nor Booth that conscious aspect of intelligence, nor requisite variation of voice, that made every line the other spoke seem his own, natural, self-delivered sentiment....

When an actor becomes, and naturally looks the character he stands in, I have often observed it to have had as fortunate an effect, and as much recommended him to the approbation of the common auditors, as the most correct or judicious utterance of the sentiments. This was strongly visible in the favorable reception Wilks met with in Hamlet, where I own the half of what he spoke was as painful to my ear, as every line, that came from Betterton was charming; and yet it is not impossible, could they have come to a poll, but Wilks might have had a majority of admirers. However, such a division had been no proof that the preeminence had not still remained in Betterton; and if I should add, that Booth too, was behind Betterton in Othello, it would be saying no more than Booth himself had judgment, and candor enough to know, and confess. And if both he and Wilks are allowed, in the two above-mentioned characters, a second place to so great a master as Betterton, it will be a rank of praise that the best actors, since my time, might have been proud of.

* * * *

How imperfect soever this copious account of them [the actors] may be, I am not without hope, at least, it may in some degree show what talents are requisite to make actors valuable. And if that may any ways inform, or assist the judgment of future spectators, it may, as often, be of service to their public entertainments; for as their hearers are, so will actors be; worse, or better, as the false, or true taste applauds, or discommends them. Hence only can our theatre improve, or must degenerate....

ANTHONY ASTON

(c.1682-1749?)

Anthony Aston, soldier of fortune, was also an actor and dramatist. He is credited with writing an opera and the comedy called *Love in a Hurry*. Aston is said to have played in all the London theatres. It is possible that he was the first professional player to come to the American colonies. He appears to have done some acting first in Charleston in 1703 and later in New York. In his own words: "We arriv'd in Charles-Town, full of Lice, Shame, Poverty, Nakedness and Hunger: —I turned Player and Poet, and wrote one Play on the Subject of the Country."

In his *Brief Supplement to Colley Cibber,* Aston attempted to correct some of Cibber's extravagant praise. "Mr. Cibber," Aston wrote, "is guilty of omission, that he hath not given us any description of the several personages' beauties, or faults— faults (I say) of the several actors.... Or, as the late Duke of Buckingham says of characters, that, to show a man not defective,... were to draw a faultless monster, that the world ne'er saw."

Although some of his objections to Cibber take the form of describing the personal appearances of actors or pointing out very minor faults in the great actors lauded by Cibber, he does provide us with a number of valuable critical insights. In a comment on Betterton acting Hamlet at seventy, he makes a tantalizing parenthetical statement which seems to differentiate impersonating and acting. He is also the source of the suggestion that Betterton, unlike some of the other actors, was a highly conscious artist. His observation about Mrs. Verbruggen that "she was all art, and her acting all acquired, but dressed so nice, it looked like nature" may be a clue to the manner of eighteenth century acting. His frequent comments about "acting strongly with the face" point up the grimacing of the period.

A Brief Supplement to Colley Cibber

Mr. Betterton (although a superlative good actor) labored under ill figure, being clumsily made, having a great head, a short thick neck, stooped in the shoulders, and had fat short arms, which he rarely lifted higher than his stomach. His left hand frequently lodged in his breast, between his coat and waistcoat, while, with his right he prepared his speech. His actions were few, but just. He had little eyes, and a broad face, a little pock-fretten, a corpulent body, and thick legs, with large feet. He was better to meet, than to follow; for his aspect was serious, venerable, and majestic; in his latter time a little paralytic. His voice was low and grumbling; yet he could time it by an artful climax, which enforced universal attention, even from the fops and orange-girls. He was incapable of dancing even in a country dance; as was Mrs. Barry: but their good qualities were more than equal to their deficiencies....

Mr. Betterton was the most extensive actor, from Alexander to Sir John Falstaff; but in that last character, he wanted the waggery of [Richard] Eastcourt [1668-1712], the drollery of [John] Harper, and salaciousness of Jack Evans. But, then, Eastcourt, was too trifling; Harper had too much of the Bartholomew-Fair; and Evans misplaced his humor. Thus, you see what flaws are in bright diamonds. And I have often wished that Mr. Betterton would have resigned the part of Hamlet to some young actor, (who might have personated, though not have acted, it better) for, when he threw himself at Ophelia's

Anthony Aston: *A Brief Supplement to Colley Cibber, Esq.; His Lives of the Late Famous Actors and Actresses* (1747) in Watson Nicholson: *Anthony Aston Stroller and Adventurer.* South Haven, Michigan: Published by the Author, 1920, 75-98 *passim.*

feet, he appeared a little too grave for a young student, lately come from the University of Wittenberg; and his *repartees* seemed rather as apothegms from a sage philosopher, than the sporting flashes of a young Hamlet; and no one else could have pleased his town, he was so rooted in their opinion. His younger contemporary... [George] Powell [1658-1714] attempted several of Betterton's parts, as Alexander, Jaffier, etc., but lost his credit; as in Alexander, he maintained not the dignity of a king, but out-Heroded Herod; and in his poisoned mad scene, out-raved all probability; while Betterton kept his passion under, and showed most (as fume smokes most, when stifled). Betterton, from the time he was dressed, to the end of the play, kept his mind in the same temperament and adaptness, as the present character required. If I was to write of him all day, I should still remember fresh matter in his behalf....

His favorite, Mrs. Barry, claims the next in estimation. They were both never better pleased, than in playing together. Mrs. Barry outshined Mrs. Bracegirdle in the character of Zara in *The Mourning Bride,* although Mr. Congreve designed Almeria for that favor. And yet, this fine creature was not handsome, her mouth opening most on the right side, which she strove to draw the other way, and at times, composing her face, as if sitting to have her picture drawn. Mrs. Barry was middle-sized, and had darkish hair, light eyes, dark eyebrows and was indifferently plump. Her face somewhat preceded her action, as the latter did her words, her face ever expressing the passions; not like the actresses of late times, who are afraid of putting their faces out of the form of non-meaning, lest they should crack the serum, white-wash, or other cosmetic, trowled on. Mrs. Barry had a manner of drawing out her words, which became her, but not Mrs. Bradshaw, and Mrs. [Mary] Porter [d. 1762] (successors).... Neither she, nor any of the actors of those times, had any tone in their speaking, (too much, lately, in use). In tragedy she was solemn and august—in free comedy alert, easy, and genteel—pleasant in her face and action; filling the stage with variety of gesture....

Mr. Sandford, although not usually deemed an actor of the first rank, yet the characters allotted him were such, that none besides, then, or since, ever topped, for his figure, which was diminutive and mean, (being round-shouldered, meagre-faced, spindle-shanked, splay-footed, with a sour countenance, and long lean arms) rendered him a proper person to discharge Iago, Foresight.... But he failed in succeeding in a fine description of a triumphant cavalcade, in Alonzo, in the *Mourning Bride,* because his figure was despicable, (although his energy was, by his voice, and action enforced with great soundness of art, and justice). This person acted strongly with his face, and (as King Charles said) was the best villain in the world.

* * * *

I cannot part with this *non-pareil* [Mr. Thomas Doggett] without saying, that he was the most faithful, pleasant actor that ever was, for he never deceived his audience, because, while they gazed at him, he was working up the joke, which broke out suddenly in involuntary acclamations and laughter. Whereas our modern actors are fumbling the dull minutes, keeping the gaping pit in suspense of something delightful a coming....

He was the best face-player and gesticulator, and a thorough master of the several dialects except the Scots (for he never was in Scotland), but was, for all that, a most excellent Sawney....

Jack Verbruggen, that rough diamond, shone more bright than all the artful, polished brilliants that ever sparkled on our stage.... He had the words perfect at one view, and nature directed them into voice and action, in which last he was always pleasing—his person being tall, well-built, and clean; only he was a little inkneed, which gave him a shambling gait, which was a carelessness, and became him. His chief parts were Bajazet, Oroonoko, Edgar in *King Lear,* Wilmore in *Rover,* and Cassius, when Mr. Betterton played Brutus with him.

Then you might behold the grand contest, viz. whether nature or art excelled. Verbruggen wild and untaught, or Betterton in the trammels of instruction. In Edgar, in *King Lear,* Jack showed his judgment most; for his madness was unlimited. Whereas he sensibly felt a tenderness for Cordelia, in those words, (speaking to her)—"As you did once know Edgar!"... nature was so predominant, that his second thoughts never altered his prime performance.... Verbruggen was nature, without extravagance—freedom, without licentiousness, and vociferous, without bellowing.....

Mrs. Verbruggen claims a place next. She was all art, and her acting all acquired, but dressed so nice, it looked like nature. There was not a look, a motion, but what were all designed; and these at the same word, period, occasion, incident, were every night, in the same character, alike, and yet all sat charmingly easy on her. Her face, motion, etc., changed at once. But the greatest, and usual, position was laughing, flirting her fan, and *je ne sais quois,* with a kind of affected twitter.... Whatever she did was not to be called acting; no, no, it was what she represented. She was neither more nor less, and was the most easy actress in the world.

AARON HILL

(1685-1750)

Aaron Hill, though not an actor himself, was a coach of actors, a theatrical manager, playwright, and poet. He led a varied life, traveled widely, and was involved in a number of unsuccessful commercial schemes. At the end of the first decade of the eighteenth century, during the struggle over the management of the patent theatres, Hill administered Drury Lane for a short time and also produced opera at the Haymarket Theatre.

Later in the thirties he revealed himself an original histrionic theorist; one of his practical suggestions was the proposal to establish a school and academy for actors. Among players whom he coached was Susanna Maria Cibber, one of Garrick's leading ladies.

From 1734 to 1736 Aaron Hill published the *Prompter,* a semi-weekly theatrical periodical in which he proclaimed: "Nor can I think it any Dishonor, since the Stage has so long been transcribing the World, that the World should now make Reprisals, and look as freely into the *Theatres.* ... Let their Managers therefore be upon their Guard; and their Dependents, Tragic or Comic, take good heed to their Parts; since there is, from this Day forward, arisen a PROMPTER, *without Doors,* who hath a *Cat-call,* as well as a *Whistle;* and, whenever the Players grow *flat,* will himself make bold to be *musical*." And he waxed musical unsparingly on the "dependents" in such words as these: "They *relax* themselves, as soon as any Speech in their *own* Part is over, into an absent Unattentivenes to whatever is *replied* by An-

other: looking around and examining the Company of Spectators with an Ear only watchful of the *Cue;* at which, like *Soldiers,* upon the *Word of Command,* they start, suddenly, back to their *Postures,* TONE over the unanimating *Sound* of their Lesson; and, then (like *a Caterpillar, that has erected itself* at the Touch of a *Twig*) *shrink again, to their* CRAWL, *and* their QUIET: and enjoy their full *Ease,* till *next Rowsing."* He proceeded later to dub some of the actors "Mr. Strain-Pipe, Mrs. Ever-Whine, and Mr. All-Weight."

It was in the *Prompter* that the theories of acting which he had been formulating first appeared. Utilizing a rather mechanical approach he evolved a principle by which the imaginative conception of passion would induce the appropriate external expressions. His theory, based on ten primary dramatic passions, sets out with what might be termed a physiological analysis of acting, but soon turns into a short-cut method of projection. Thus the end result of his theorizing was that if actors, viewing themselves in a mirror, could produce the outward gesture, stance, and visage of a particular passion, this muscular configuration would provoke the complete dramatic expression of a corresponding emotion. In this way, Hill tried to put the age-old schematic guides to external expression on a "scientific," reasonable, and natural basis.

Dramatic Passions

The first dramatic principle (and it must be always uppermost, in a good actor's memory, if he hopes to reach perfection in his business) is the following:

To act a passion well, the actor never must attempt its imitation, until his fancy has conceived so strong an image, or idea, of it, as to move the same impressive springs within his mind, which form that passion, when it is undesigned, and natural.

This is absolutely necessary, and the only general rule. And let no actor apprehend it over difficult. The practice of it shall be laid down clearly; and it will be found extremely easy and delightful, both in study, and in execution. And, the truth of its foundation, that it is wholly built on nature, is evident, beyond dispute, upon examining its effects, in this deduction, from their causes.

1st, The imagination must conceive a strong idea of the passion.

2ndly, But that idea cannot strongly be conceived, without impressing its own form upon the muscles of the face.

3rdly, Nor can the look be muscularly stamped, without communicating, instantly, the same impression, to the muscles of the body.

4thly, The muscles of the body (braced, or slack, as the idea was an active or a passive one), must, in their natural, and not to be avoided consequence, by impelling or retarding the flow of the animal spirits, transmit their own conceived sensation, to the sound of the voice, and to the disposition of the gesture.

And this is a short abstract of the art, in its most comprehensive and reduced idea.

"An Essay on the Art of Acting" (1746), *The Works of the late Aaron Hill, esq.; . . . Consisting of letters on various subjects, and of original poems, moral and facetious, with an essay on the art of acting.* London: Printed for the benefit of the family, 1754, Volume 4, pp. 339-346, 352-355.

But there must follow applications of the general rule, by particular references, for the practical use of the actor.

And, first, it should be noted, that there are only ten dramatic passions;—that is, passions, which can be distinguished by their outward marks, in acting; all other being relative to, and but varied degrees of, the foregoing.

These are the ten dramatic passions:

Joy, Grief, Fear, Anger, Pity, Scorn, Hatred, Jealousy, Wonder and Love.

And now, for the application of the rule, to each of these, in its particular distinction:

APPLICATION 1
How an Actor is to express Joy.

DEFINITION
Joy is pride, possessed of triumph.

It is a warm and conscious expansion of the heart, indulging sense of present pleasure, and comparing it with past affliction. It cannot, therefore, be expressed without vivacity, in look, air, and accent.

But it will be proper, for distinguishing the modes of representing this, and every other passion, to consider their effect on speeches, wherein that particular passion governs, which is about to be attempted by the speaker.

And, for ever, let it be the first and chief care of an actor, who aspires to shine, in his profession, to discover where, in all his characters, the writer has intended any change of passions. For, unless the passion is first known, how is it possible it should be painted? ... When the actor has discovered, that the passion ... is joy, he must not, upon any account, attempt the utterance of one single word, until he has, first, compelled his fancy to conceive an idea of joy....

But there is a shorter road, to the same end, and it shall, in due place, be shown him. When he believes himself possessed of the idea of joy, that would not fail to warm a strong conception, let him not imagine the impression rightly hit, until he has examined both his face and air, in a long, upright, looking glass; for there, only, will he meet with a sincere and undeceivable test of his having strongly enough, or too slackly, adapted his fancy to the purpose before him.

If, for example, his brow, in the glass, appears brow-bent, or cloudy, his neck bowing, and relaxed, his breast not thrown gracefully down, and elate; if he sees his arm swing languid, or hang motionless, his back-bone reposed, or unstraightened, and the joints of his hip, knee, and ankle, not strong-braced, by swelling out the sinews to their full extent, all, or any of these spiritless signs, in the glass, may convince him, that he has too faintly conceived the impression; and, at once to prove it, to his own full satisfaction, let him, at that time, endeavor to speak out, with a voice as high raised as he pleases, he will find, that, in that languid state of muscles, he can never bring it to found joy; no, not though the sense of the words were all rapture; but, in spite of the utmost possible strain upon his lungs, his tone will be too sullen, or too mournful, and carry none of the music of sprightliness. But, if on the contrary, he has hit the conception, exactly, he will have the pleasure, in that case, to observe in the glass, that his forehead appears open, and raised, his eye smiling, and sparkling, his neck will be stretched, and erect, without stiffness, as if it would add new height to his stature; his breast will be inflated, and majestically backened; his back-bone erect, and all the joints of his arm, wrist, fingers, hip, knee, and ankle, will be high-strung, and braced boldly. And now, if he attempts to speak joy, all the spirit of the passion will ascend in his accents, and the very tone of his voice will seem to out rapture the meaning.

As to the reason of all this, it is as clear as the conception. For these are nature's own marks, and impressions, on the body, in cases where the passion is produced by involuntary emotions. And when natural impressions are imitated, exactly, by art, the effect of such art must seem natural.

But, because difficulties would arise, in the practice of so strong a conception, before fancy is become ductile enough, to assume such impressions, at will, (as in the instance of joy, now before us) the actor taking the shorter road, above promised him, may help his defective idea, in a moment, by annexing, at once, the look to the idea, in the very instant, while he is bracing his nerves into springiness: for so, the image, the look, and the muscles, all concurring, at once, to the purpose, their effect will be the same, as if each had succeeded another, progressively.

To convince himself of the natural truth of these principles, he has nothing to do but, first, to speak the foregoing example of joy, with his look grave, or idle, and his nerves eased or languid; and immediately afterwards, repeat the same speech, with a smile of delight in his eye, and with his joints all braced high, and his sinews extended—his own ear will become his acknowledged instructor.

* * * *

APPLICATION 4
How Anger ought to be acted.

DEFINITION

Anger is pride provoked beyond regard of caution.

It is a fierce and unrestrained effusion of reproach and insult. It must there-fore be expressed, impatiently, by a fiery propension in the eye, with a disturbed and threatening air, and with a voice strong, swift, and often interrupted by high swells of choking indignation.

To explain this passion, two examples will be necessary: the first, not so much for containing the passion itself, as a great actor's rules, for feeling and expressing it, with nature's spirit and propriety. And I do this right, to Shake-speare, with a double pleasure, as the instance carries with it a clear evidence, how much the play-house old tradition wrongs his memory; for they report him a performer, of no power or compass, and but of a low rate in his profession, as to action.

The second speech shall be, for an example of the passion, with an explanation of two different modes, whereby nature has distinguished its expression.

Shakespeare's comes first; and is, at once, a rule and example:

> Now imitate the action of the tiger;
> Stiffen the sinews, summon up the blood;
> Lend fierce and dreadful aspect to the eye:
> Set the teeth close, and stretch the nostril wide,
> Hold hard the breath, and bend up every Spirit
> To its full height.

It is impossible to draw a picture of anger, more naturally, or an instruction, more complete and clear, for expressing it!

1st, The sinews being braced strong, through all the joints of the body, the look (as a consequence unavoidable) is summoned up, that is, impelled into violent motion.

2ndly, The look becomes adapted, and adds fierceness to the passion, by the fire, that flashes from the eye.

3rdly, The setting of the teeth, and wide expansion of the nostrils, follow naturally—because inseparable from an enraged bent of the eye-brow.

And, 4thly, the breath being held hard, as interrupted or restrained, by the tumultuous precipitation of the spirits, they must necessarily become inflamed, themselves, and will communicate their ardor to the voice, and motion.

And so this passion of anger is bent up to its full height—as Shakespeare, with allusion to the spring upon the sinews, has expressed it.

I explain this passage, to demonstrate his great skill in acting, and in hopes, the player's observation, that this favorite genius of their own profession, had ideas of the art, so plainly founded on the very principles sustained in this essay, will recommend it, with more weight, from the partiality of their affection.

CHARLES MACKLIN

(1697?-1797)

Picturesque and violent in his personal life and in his professional career, Charles Macklin brought natural acting to a theatre accustomed to the declamation and statuesque dignity of Quin and Booth. Born in Dublin, he became a strolling player after being an apprentice and a servant. He had little success in his first trials on the London stage, reminiscing years later that the director of Covent Garden disapproved of him. "I spoke so familiar and so little in the hoity-toity tone of the tragedy of that day, that he told me I had better go to grass for another year or two." Following these failures he returned to the life of a traveling player in the small towns. Finally, in 1733, Macklin came to Drury Lane. The theatre was then under the management of Charles Fleetwood, who was gambling away its profits. It was, according to Thomas Davies, "by the prudent advice of the principal players, more especially, I believe, of Mr. Charles Macklin," that the theatre kept up a respectable level of performance. Macklin's revival of *The Merchant of Venice* in 1741 was the climax of his attempts to put his acting theories into practice. He portrayed Shylock not as the comic figure with which the audience was familiar, but for the first time as a serious character. "This is the Jew, that Shakespeare drew," wrote Pope.

After an unsuccessful revolt of the actors at Drury Lane against Fleetwood, Macklin was not rehired. Embittered at his colleague Garrick's betrayal, for the actors had originally agreed to make terms for return as a group, Macklin turned to giving lessons in acting and formed a company of his own which opened at the Haymarket Theatre in 1744. He continued on the stage until 1789, playing varied roles. Macklin was the first to introduce historical costuming when in 1772 he played Macbeth at Covent Garden in Scottish garb. When he was over eighty, he appeared in his own play *The Man of the World*.

John Hill recorded the following interesting tribute to Macklin:

"We are at present getting more and more nature in playing; and if the violence of gesture be not quite suppressed, we have nothing of the recitative of old tragedy.

"It is to the honor of Mr. Macklin, that he began this great improvement. There was a time when he ... supported himself by a company whom he taught to play, and some of them afterwards made no inconsiderable figure. It was his manner to check all the cant and cadence of tragedy; he would bid his pupil first speak the passage as he would in common life, if he had occasion to pronounce the same words; and then giving them more force, but preserving the same accent, to deliver them on the stage. Where the player was faulty in his stops or accents, he set them right; and with nothing more than this attention to what was natural, he produced out of the most ignorant persons, players that surprised everybody.... People were pleased with a sensible delivery on this little stage, and those that saw that they were, transferred it to the greater where it at this time flourishes, and will flourish, as long as a good sense lives in the audience. Tragedy now has no particular accent or tone, but the most outrageous scenes of it are spoken according to Macklin's plan, as the same words would be pronounced in common speech, only with more energy."

Macklin's biographer, James Thomas Kirkman, is the source of the following verbatim copy from the papers of Macklin. "The Art and Duty of an Actor" indicates Macklin's stress on the unique passion of each dramatic character and strikes a new note in histrionic writing of the time. His efforts to create natural acting in his performances and in his teaching seem to justify the statement of Thomas Davies that "... Charles Macklin ... was the only player I ever heard of that made acting a science."

The Art and Duty of an Actor

It is the duty of an actor always to know the passion and the humor of each character so correctly, so intimately, and (if you will allow me the expression) to feel it so enthusiastically, as to be able to define and describe it as a philosopher; to give its operations on the looks, tones, and gestures of general nature, as it is ranked in classes of character; and to mould all this knowledge, mental and corporeal, to the characteristic that the poet has given to a particular character.

If the actor has not this philosophical knowledge of the passions, it is impossible for him to imitate them with fidelity. It is because Shakespeare knew the passions, their objects, and their operations, that he has drawn them so faithfully. It is manifest, that passions take their habits and characteristics in attorneys, barristers, and judges; subalterns and generals; curates and bishops; clerks and merchants; sailors, midshipmen, captains, and admirals; laborers, farmers, yeoman, and rustic squires; dancing-masters, fiddlers, toothdrawers, music-masters, and hairdressers; they are all to be distinguished into *genus*, *species*, and individual characteristics, like dogs, fowl, apples, plums, and the like *genus*, *species*, and individuals of the creation. Women must be classed in the same manner.

Now, unless the actor knows the *genus*, *species*, and characteristic, that he is about to imitate, he will fall short in his execution. The actor must restrict all his powers, and convert them to the purpose of imitating the *looks*, *tones*, and *gestures*, that can best describe the characteristic that the poet has drawn: for each passion

Charles Macklin: "The Art and Duty of an Actor" in James Thomas Kirkman: *Memoirs of the Life of Charles Macklin, Esq.* .... *principally compiled from his own papers and memorandums.* ... London: Printed for Lockington, Allen and Company, 1799, Volume I, pp. 362-366.

and humor has its *genus* of *looks, tones* and *gestures,* its *species,* and its individual characteristic.

Avarice, for instance, has its *genus, species,* and individual characteristic. Molière has given the *genus.*

As the poet hath drawn an individual characteristic, so ought it to be represented: the actor must take especial care not to mould and suit the character to his looks, tones, gestures and manners; if he does so, it will then become the actor's character, and not the poet's. No; he must suit his looks, tones, gestures, and manners to the character: the suiting the character to the powers of the actor, is imposture. I have seen King Lear, Hamlet, and Richard III, acted without one look, tone, or gesture, or manners of Shakespeare.

On Acting

Acting. A fit subject for a lecture; all people judge of it; some merely for the pleasure they receive from the poet and the actor indiscriminately; others distinguish that portion which they receive from each, but without entering into the science, or the art of acting.

There are various kinds of judges, and of critics; males and females, such as milliners, Mantua-makers, ladies' waiting-maids, and women of fashion, to an infinity.

It would be highly entertaining to give the ridiculous judgments of each.

Truth in art, science, religion, or politics, is known to but very few, and none but those very few will take pains to search for truth; though all delight in truth, except the envious and the ignorant.

What is character? The alphabet will tell you. It is that which is distinguished by its own marks from every other thing of its kind.

The voice of the actor must alter in its intonations, according to the qualities that the words express: from this idea music seems to have taken its birth. The number seven harmonizes in music, and so it does in acting.

JOHN HILL

(1716? - 1775)

John Hill was a man of many parts who devoted some of his life to acting and playwriting. In his youth he was apprenticed to an apothecary and studied botany. He went on the stage in order to earn more money but was unsuccessful at the Haymarket Theatre and at Covent Garden. He wrote *Orpheus,* an opera, and his farce, *The Rout,* was a failure at Drury Lane in 1758. Living by his wits and his pen, he wrote a pamphlet attacking Garrick's pronunciation, was involved in a number of quarrels with literary men, edited a magazine, received a medical diploma, and attacked the Royal Society for refusing to accept him. The King of Sweden honored him for his book *The Vegetable System.*

Among these multifarious activities, Hill published *The Actor: a Treatise on the Art of Playing,* in 1750, which was in large measure a translation of *Le Comédien* (1747) by Pierre Rémond de Sainte-Albine, French journalist. Hill referred to Sainte-Albine in his dedication, saying in typical eighteenth century language that the Frenchmen's rules were "founded on nature and reason." Sainte-Albine's study was an original one which attempted to analyze the essential characteristics of a good actor. By focusing his attention on the personality attributes needed by an actor, Hill (and Sainte-Albine) freed the book from schematized rules for voice and gesture. Excerpts of his analysis of the three qualities of a good actor, Understanding, Sensibility, and Fire, are printed here. The remainder of the book is concerned with such questions as the following, taken from the chapter headings: "A gaiety of temper is absolutely necessary to the players in comedy, whose business it is to make us laugh"; "No man who has not naturally an elevated soul, will ever perform well the part of a hero upon the stage"; "Players who are naturally amorous, are the only ones who should perform the parts of lovers upon the stage"; etc.

This treatise, a more thoroughgoing analysis of the actor and his art than any previous work, had a curious history. First published, as we have indicated, by Sainte-Albine in 1747, it was translated by John Hill in 1750. Hill issued a second edition in 1755 to which he added many illustrations from the work of English actors. In 1769 Antonio Fabio Sticotti, one of the *Comédiens du Roi de la Troupe Italienne,* translated this second edition into French (apparently unaware of its origin) under the title *Garrick ou les acteurs Anglais.* It was this book, with its emotionalist emphasis, that provoked Denis Diderot's *Le Paradoxe sur le comédien* (1773), which denies sensibility as requisite to the actor. In the nineteenth century this quarrel resulted in a war of ideas between Coquelin and Henry Irving and was the subject of William Archer's investigation *Masks or Faces?*

Understanding, Sensibility, and Fire

Of the Principal Advantages which a Player ought to have from Nature

Among the many arts which should never be exercised but by persons who are happy in a variety of natural accomplishments, there are few, to the excelling in which they are more essential, then in performing well in tragedy and comedy. The actor is expected to delude the imagination, and to affect the heart: and in order to his attaining to perfection in this difficult task, nature must have been assistant to him in an uncommon manner.

It is essential to our being rationally pleased with theatrical representations, that the performers to whom the principal parts are allotted, perfectly keep up the illusion we are to be entertained with; as it is peculiarly from them, that we expect what is to move and affect us.

These performers, therefore, more than all the rest, ought to be selected from among persons, whom nature has particularly favored.

In enquiring what are the natural endowments immediately necessary to performers on the stage in general, we shall endeavor to discuss certain preliminary points, which have not hitherto been properly or sufficiently explained; and thence proceed to examine, what are the peculiar qualifications necessary to particular actors. . . .

Can an Actor Excel in his Profession, Without a Good Understanding?

A thing is not always the more true, because it is generally affirmed. We fre-

---

John Hill: *The Actor: A Treatise on the Art of Playing.* London: R. Griffiths, 1750, Chapters 1, 2, 3, *passim.*

quently hear people who pretend to be the best judges of dramatic performances, declare that some of the modern actors, who have a general and not wholly undeserved applause, have mean understandings. But we flatter ourselves, it may be easily proved, that either the actors, whom these severe critics censure, have more sense than they have the discernment to distinguish in them; or that they have less merit, even than they allow them, and have the good fortune to be esteemed much better performers, than they really are.

It is not easy to avoid the allowing a good understanding, even to persons who excel in arts that are merely mechanic; and surely the accomplished actor, if we have no other title to it than that of his being such, ought not to be denied the same concession. Is it possible that a man can, in a series of different parts, continually command our applause, if he have not a just and distinguishing apprehension, to give him at all times, and always with propriety, the necessary admonitions for his just deportment under every circumstance of every one of them? And indeed, if he have not a nice discernment to perceive the affinities of things, and the dependences of the incidents on one another? For this must ever be the directing needle that points out the invariable pole, both to the poet and performer.

It is not enough to entitle a player to our applause, that he remembers every striking incident, every beauty in his part: 'tis equally necessary, that he distinguish the true, the exact manner, under which every single beauty must be represented. It is not sufficient that he knows how to raise his passion, he must know how to raise it by just rules, and to assign it its peculiar bounds and heights, according to the degree the circumstances of his part require, below which it must not sink, and beyond which it must not rise.

It is not sufficient that his figure be in general good and proper for the stage; and that his face can mark the changes of his soul: we shall be dissatisfied with him if his person be not always kept in a proper attitude; and shall quarrel even with the expression of his countenance if it do not regulate itself at every circumstance, not only to the passion, but to the degree of the passion it is to describe to us.

It is not only essential to his success that he never let a passage which he delivers, lose the least part of its force, or of its delicacy, in his speaking it: when he has thus given it all the justice imaginable, he must add to that all the graces that a studied delivery and action can bestow on it. He is not to content himself with following his author strictly and faithfully; but in many places, he must assist and support him; he must even in some instances become a sort of author himself; he must know not only how to give the proper expression to every finesse the poet has thrown into his part, but he must frequently add new ones; and not only execute, but create graces. A start, a gesture, nay, a mere attention, properly employed, are often of as happy effect as a brilliant piece of wit in comedy, or a noble sentiment in tragedy; a peculiar cadence in the actor's voice, or a bare pause artfully thrown in, have frequently produced applause from a sentence, which if it had been delivered by an inferior performer, would not have had any attention paid to it by the hearers.

The art of exciting the passions in an audience by the performer's raising them in himself, with a judgment and exactness proportioned justly to the several circumstances, is at least as difficult to arrive at, as that of giving its due force, or true delicacy, to every passage. The poet who has made himself a master of the power of commanding the passions and throwing the soul into every degree of them that he pleases, exerts his utmost efforts in vain, and uses every art without success, when the actor does not join his skill to the raising the effects he intends by them. When even a good part falls into bad hands, it is no uncommon thing to see the audience laugh, where the author meant to have drawn their tears.

Few people are able to judge of the good understanding that is necessary to the player, in order to his keeping up the sense and spirit of a sentiment; to prevent his exaggerating it to bombast, or weakening and debasing it to nothing in the delivery; and to his distinguishing the different steps through which his author means to lead the passions and the imaginations of his audience; and by which he is to carry himself from opposite to opposite affections.

* * * *

The player has equal necessity for address and for precision, to give the true strength to every passage in his part, and to convey the sentiments delivered to his care, in their proper force and beauty. Nor are these qualifications less useful to him in dictating the necessary gestures which are to accompany the expression; and in the forming not only his countenance, but his whole person, according to the nature of the age, station, and character of the person he represents; and even in the proportioning the tone of his voice and the attitudes of his figure, to the situation in which he is placed.

It is evident then that a good understanding is as necessary to a player, as a pilot is to a vessel at sea. 'Tis the understanding alone that governs the helm, that directs the whole fabric, and calculates and makes out its course.

* * * *

It must be allowed that a long familiarity with the stage will sometimes supply the place of judgment and good sense in the performer. Sometimes also he may have been obliged to nature for peculiar qualifications, and that in so eminent a degree, that often when they are brought into use, though it be merely done by a kind of instinct, not by a judicious adapting of them to the scenes, they shall happen to suit so well with the circumstances of the character he represents, that we cannot deny him a high applause. This however is no more than the deception of the moment; an absurdity that follows immediately after in the voice, the gesture, or the expression of the countenance of this lucky player, lets us into his true character; and we find that it was not the man, but merely his organization that before merited our applause.

How truly pitiable is the condition of that author, who is under a necessity of entrusting his success, his reputation, in a new piece, to these miserable automatons. And on the other side, how happy is the fortune of that writer, who sees his play fall into such hands, that every character of it, not only among the capital but the inferior ones too, is given to a performer who will not only be capable of preserving all the spirit of the most shining parts of it to its utmost height, but of adding graces to those which are less eminent or striking.

The comic writers are above all others happy in falling into such hands, as their pieces are often in a great measure supported by the delicate and judicious address of the performer. How ought the poet in this way to congratulate himself when he finds his principal character in the hands of a player, who knows the nicest rules of joining the delicate to the natural; who knows how to add a graceful and decent dignity to the comic scene; and has even raised more than once the laugh of the pretty gentlemen of the age at their own follies!

The actor who is capable of executing this, surely can never be suspected of wanting understanding. . . .

[125]

Of Sensibility
Whether this Quality of the Heart be More Important to the Performers in Tragedy or in Comedy?

We almost want a word in the English language to express a very essential qualification in an actor, and one which more than any other enables him to affect and please us. The French, who esteem it one of the greatest requisites to every player, of whatever kind, call it *sentiment,* a term that carries much the same meaning with the word sensibility, by which we have chosen to express it; and by which we would be understood to mean, a disposition to be affected by the passions, which are the subjects of dramatic writing.

It is evident that different people have this quality of the heart in a very different degree: if we look round among the audience at a tragedy, we shall find people variously affected by the same words, delivered by the same voice, and under the same circumstances; and in the reading, the same scene in a play shall pass off smoothly from the tongue of one person, while the disturbance of the heart of another, as he goes through it, shall render the organs of his voice incapable of pronouncing the words articulately. The degree of understanding is not concerned in this difference of the effect from the same words; the person who feels least from them often understanding their true meaning, and entering into their beauties perhaps better than the other. 'Tis sensibility, a peculiar quality in the mind, that determines the force of the scene; and 'tis evident that this is a quality of more consequence in playing than in any other profession. In what road of playing it is most important, remains to be enquired into.

... The sense of this term is very extensive; it takes in not only the natural turn of mind in the player, but that pliantness of disposition by means of which the different passions are made easily to succeed to one another in his soul. The heart that enjoys this, in a proper degree, is like soft wax, which, under the hands of a judicious artist, is capable of becoming, in the same minute, a Medea and a Sappho; an easy ductility in the wax is not more requisite to fit it for the purpose of the modeller, than is this sensibility in the heart of the actor, by means of which it is to receive whatever modifications the writer pleases, and that in an easy, an unconstrained succession. Whoever, on a candid examination of himself, finds that he cannot easily submit his mind to all these changes, let him not think of offering himself to the public as a player. The performer, who does not himself feel the several emotions he is to express to the audience, will give but a lifeless and insipid representation of them. All the art in the world can never supply the want of sensibility in the player; if he is defective in this essential quality, all the advantages of nature, all the accomplishments he may have acquired by study, are thrown away upon him; he will never make others feel what he does not feel himself, and will always be as different from the thing he is to represent, as a mask from a face.

The being able to subject the soul to succeeding passions, though they be contrary ones, as is frequently the case, is universally allowed to be necessary, in the highest degree, to the tragedian; the common opinion seems to judge it less essential to the comic performer; but, in reality, it is not only equally necessary to the last, but even more so.

The dignity of tragedy does not permit it to represent to us any other than great and striking incidents. The actions of the persons it represents are all to be of this kind; and it is therefore reduced to a necessity of constantly having recourse to those passions which are the most proper to produce them....

...A few only of the passions, for these reasons, fall to the share of the tragedian; the comic player, on the other hand, has the whole series of them within his province; and he will be esteemed a man of no consequence in his profession, if he cannot, with equal strength and propriety, express the transports of a fond and foolish joy, and those of the most excruciating uneasiness; the ridiculous doting of an old and impotent lover, and the suspicious resentments of a jealous husband, or insulted rival; the noble boldness of a daring, generous mind; and the contemptible timidity of a pusillanimous heart; if he cannot represent to us with the same strength and spirit, a stupid admiration, and an insolent disdain; all the extravagances of the most interested self-love, when flattered with circumstances that favor it, or hurt by contrary accidents. In fine, if he be not able to give a due force to every emotion of the heart; to every species of passion that human nature is capable of being affected by.

It is not sufficient for him that he be able to put on the image of every one of the passions that fall within the reach of his author, if he have not, beside this, the power of throwing himself readily and easily out of one into another of them. The business of comedy is to raise and to keep up a pleasurable sensation, to give joy to an audience; and the powers who excel in this species of writing, well knowing that a dull uniformity in the scene is one of the greatest enemies to this, have ever been atentive to the necessary variety and taken care to make every capital character in the same piece, and not unfrequently in the same scene, the sport of a number of different passions; they have always given it an infinity of contrary impressions, the one of which suddenly drives away another, to be, in its turn, as suddenly banished by a third.

Mr. Garrick, who is as amiable in the character of a player, as censurable in another capacity in which he has too much connection with our theatrical entertainments, gives us an excellent instance of what perfection an actor may arrive at in this way, in his Archer: in this, though not one of the characters in which he makes the greatest figure, how readily does he run through the several artful transitions which the author of the [*Beaux'*] *Stratagem* has thrown into his character, from one passion to another, most foreign, nay, sometimes, most opposite ones! And how wholly does he devote himself to each in its turn, as if no other, of whatever kind, had ever claimed any power over him!...

If in playing comedy it is necessary that the player be able to make the most different impressions succeed one another readily and easily in his heart, it is not less essential to the performer in tragedy that he feel, much more strongly than the other needs to do, every one of those which he is to express to the audience. Sensibility in the comic actor, therefore, must be a more universal agent, and in the tragedian it must be a more powerful one: it must be capable of exerting itself in a stronger manner within its due bounds, and of producing greater effects. The comedian needs only to have a soul equal to that of the generality of man; but the player, who thinks to excel in tragedy, must have one above the common rank.

'Tis from our being in some degree sensible of this, that we are less ready to pardon the comedian, if he does not express, under every circumstance, the just and requisite degree, as well as the just species of passion that he is to describe to us. We are not in a condition to judge, with exactness, of the performance of the tragedian; we want the necessary realities to make the comparison, by which we should be able to determine whether he comes up to his duty in the part; but we are never under this uncertainty in judging of the comedians; we never want the objects of comparison for them; but at any time, if we will only examine what would pass within our own hearts, supposing we were in the same situation in which the author has placed the characters they are presenting, we shall be able to decide whether they are accurate and faithful copies....

Whether an Actor can have too much Fire?

There are some modern performers, who, in scenes where it is required they should be violently affected, are under a necessity of putting off an artificial warmth upon us, in the place of that native fire and spirit, that Promethean heat which they find nature had left them deficient in; and we are unhappy enough to have another set of them, the weakness of those constitutions, the natural imbecility of whose organs will not permit them even to use this resource. We have had many modern instances among these last sort of people, who finding they were not able to cheat our senses, have modestly attempted to impose upon our understandings: they very seriously, and, as they would have it be thought, very wisely tell us, that the fire which the mob is so charmed with, in some of their contemporaries, is much more frequently a fault in players than a perfection.

The first set are a sort of coiners of false money, who would pass copper upon us for gold; the others a set of fools, who attempt to persuade us, that the spangles of hoar frost covering the leafless branches of our trees, are the greatest beauties of nature; because it is their fortune to inhabit a country which is buried in snow the greatest part of the year.

* * * *

Let us not be dupes to the artifices of the first of these sort of players, nor to the sophisms of the latter: let us not always take the exclamations, or the contortions of an actor of the first kind for fire, nor the ice of the latter for prudence. Far from imitating some of the modern frequenters of the theatre, who are continually preaching it up to the young actors, whose success they interest themselves in, that they are of all things to moderate their fire; let us pronounce it as a general rule to every person who attempts to shine upon the stage, that he cannot have too much of this enlivening spirit; that multitudes of players have the ill luck to displease their audiences, only because nature has denied them this great, this interesting requisite; or, which comes to much the same end, because their timidity, or sheepish bashfulness has prevented them from making use of what they have of it; and that, on the other hand, many of our actors, who at present meet with a frequent applause, would establish themselves a reputation much more general, and less liable to be contested, if they were more animated with this invigorating flame, which, as it were, gives life to the representations of the stage.

* * * *

The propositions we have delivered in this chapter will never be called into question by any one who knows how to avoid the common error of confounding the vehemence of declamation with true and genuine spirit, or who will properly reflect on the nature of that quality, and by this means find, that this fire, which we are celebrating in the player, is nothing more than a just rapidity of thought, and vivacity of disposition, in concurrence with which only it is, that all the other qualities that constitute him a good one, are happy in giving the marks of reality to his performance.

When this principle is established, it is easy to conclude from it, that an actor can never have too much fire; since it is impossible that the representation of his character can ever have too much the air of a reality: and, consequently, that the impression on his mind can never be too ready or too lively; nor can the expression of it answer too suddenly, or too faithfully to the impulse he receives from it.

A performer will, indeed, be very severely censured, and very justly too, if his playing be not in all respects consonant with, and perfectly agreeable to the character and circumstances of the person he represents; or, if, under the intent of manifesting his fire, he only exhibits a set of convulsive gestures, or roars out a parcel of inadequate exclamations. But, in this case, the people of taste and judgment will not accuse him of having too much fire, but too little understanding; they will even complain, under these very circumstances, of his wanting fire; and he will find himself under the same sort of censure with certain modern books, which the vulgar accuse of having too much wit in them, but which these sort of judges condemn for having no wit at all!...

We may add that many an actor in performing a favorite part, gives himself up to an extravagance of passion in places where the sense of the author, and circumstances of the character he represents require no such thing; or if his vehemence be not quite out of place, it is often of a very absurd kind. These are faults which a man falls into, not through an excess of fire, as the vulgar suppose, but through a defect of it. He does not perceive that he is exerting his utmost efforts to express a passion which he is not to feel; and in consequence of that blunder he does not feel what he ought; and therefore 'tis impossible he should express it. In this case the actor greatly misinforms himself if he thinks it is fire that he perceives in his temper; it is rather a madness, an absurdity, and as such the more judicious of the audience will be sure to look on it.

Perhaps it will yet remain the opinion of some, that though an extravagant action or a misplaced rant, do not deserve the name of an excess of fire; yet in many characters, even where the player is not blameable in either of these points, he may too freely give himself up to the ardor of his disposition, and be carried away into faults by it.

Under the specious pretense that every actor ought to tie himself down to a certain and regular gradation in his playing, there may be some who will object that the warmth of theatrical action ought only to disclose itself successively; and that if the player, at the first instant of his entering into a passionate part, throws into it all that fire which he ought to have expressed at some period afterwards, it will be just to reproach him with having too much fire, in that first instance.

There is more of show than of solidity in this argument; and it is indeed already answered by the distinction which we have established between the vehemence of action, and the true fire of the actor. The best judges indeed often wish to see the player raising himself into the most violent emotions only by regular degrees, but they would notwithstanding have his fire be always equal. Nature knows no gradations in the rise of this enlivening spirit; nor do they expect to find any on the stage, where every man who knows what he ought to be pleased with, likes to see the readiness of conception and vivacity of expression always at their utmost height.

The actress who has tenderness and sensibility in her nature, and who easily and readily feels every passion that the author intends she should describe, is not for that reason to flatter herself that she may excel in the profession without fire. To feel the passions we are to point out to others, is certainly a necessary first step to perfection in playing; but it is not all that is expected of the performer, they may even be exquisitely felt, and yet for want of this fire they may be but very ill expressed. The feeling them strongly may indeed be alone sufficient for the affecting a few particular persons; but when a numerous audience is to be moved in the strongest and most pathetic manner, much more is required.

In this case there is a necessity not only for a due portion of fire, but even of vehemence. Both these are as requisite here, to the affecting the audience, as agitation of the air is to flame. A fire may be sufficient to warm, nay to burn the neighboring objects, while it smothers within its bounds; but it will never take place upon more distant things, unless it have the assistance of a strong mind to promote and carry on its ravages.

The player, who wants feeling, will never be allowed by those who are judges to be a good one, though he may be acknowledged to have the declamatory talents of some of our best orators; and even he who does not want this great qualification, but who, though he has it, wants fire to give it force and lustre, and who cannot be vehement, when the circumstances of the character he represents require it, will always find his reputation as inferior to that of the performer, who is able to add to the same sensibility, the force of that warmth and energy we have been celebrating, as the success of that orator, whose elocution does not come up to the merits of his reasoning, will be to that of him in whom the auditors find both those advantages united and acting on them together.

* * * *

We would not be understood, even in this eminent view of the superiority on the side of the player, who has both feeling and elocution, to mean that he who has only one of them, is useless in a theatre. We have (thanks to our poets of later times) scenes in which a man who has nothing but a declamatory voice without feeling, nay almost without meaning, may acquit himself well enough....

Vehemence in an actor when ill placed, or when carried beyond the circumstances of the character he represents, or beyond truth or probability, will always be ridiculous. 'Tis only the common herd of an audience who are ready to say, that provided the player affects them strongly, 'tis no matter whether that be done justly or not; but the severest judge will allow that as an absolute perfection is not easy to be arrived at in those parts of a character, where the author means that the performer should exert this quality, it is much better that he should run beyond the goal than fall short of it.

The first intent of all playing is to affect and move the audience, and in all theatrical performances, 'tis an invariable rule that the coldest representation is the most defective. The principal thing the actor has to observe, when the circumstances of his part make it necessary that he should be vehement, is that he does not strain his voice, so as to render it incapable of carrying him through the rest of the piece. We should with great justice laugh at the man engaged in a race, who should throw out his legs to their utmost speed at the setting out, and by that means rendered them incapable of carrying him to the end of the course....

We remember the time when Mr. Garrick ... [ran] himself so out of voice in some of the first scenes in the character of Pierre in *Venice Preserved,* that he could not even be heard when he came afterwards to that great scene in which he reproaches the senate. And when in Richard he cried out to Richmond, "Richard is hoarse with calling thee to battle," the audience was so sensible of the truth of the expression, that they could scarce distinguish the sounds that conveyed it to them.

[130]

But to the honor of this inimitable player, he has now fallen into so happy a method of moderating his fire in the beginnings of these characters, in order to the preserving himself intelligible to their end, that he might be set up as an example.

DAVID GARRICK

(1717-1779)

David Garrick is the first great actor of the English stage about whose life and career we possess not only the gross outlines but also the intimate details. Friend of such celebrated literary figures as Samuel Johnson, Oliver Goldsmith, and Denis Diderot, he appeared as artist and man in their writings. He was vividly pictured in contemporary criticism and in the memoirs of his fellow actors. His letters and diaries throw light upon his personality and his ideas.

Son of a somewhat indigent army captain of Litchfield, Garrick at first went to London to prepare for the bar, but upon inheriting money from an uncle he and his brother became wine merchants. It was in this capacity that Garrick came to know the actors in the coffee-houses around Covent Garden. He met Charles Macklin, and later fell in love with the beautiful actress Peg Woffington. For a time these three set up housekeeping together. Garrick undoubtedly learned something of natural acting from them. Before this time he had participated in amateur plays, took bit parts, and acted for a summer in Suffolk. Unable to make his way in the patent theatres, Garrick won his first success in 1741 by playing *Richard III* in Goodman's Fields, one of the sprouting theatres limited to concerts and general entertainments. Garrick's *Richard III* was sandwiched between two portions of a musical concert. His success was immediate and sensational. It prompted James Quin's remark: "If this young fellow is right, then we have all been wrong." The following day he wrote to his brother Peter: "My mind has been always inclined to the stage. All my illness and lowness of spirits was owing to my want of resolution to tell you my thoughts when here.... Last night I played Richard the Third to the surprise of everybody, and as I shall make very near £300 per annum by it, and as it is really what I dote upon, I am resolved to pursue it.... Though I know you will be much displeased at me, yet I hope when you find that I may have the genius of an actor without the vices, you will think less severe of me, and not be ashamed to own me for a brother."

Garrick came to Drury Lane at a high salary, after a stint at Goodman's Fields and a triumphal tour to Dublin with Peg Woffington. Following an unsuccessful revolt against Fleetwood, manager of Drury Lane, which cost him the friendship of Macklin, Garrick played in Dublin again. Later, back in London, he was at Covent Garden with Quin and Susanna Cibber, and then he became co-patentee at Drury Lane. Here he reigned supreme until his retirement in 1776.

His many activities can only be listed here. He wrote several successful plays, he was a member of the famous group to which Johnson, Burke, and Goldsmith belonged, he was feted and honored in Paris by such people as Diderot and Baron D'Holbach, he made adaptations of Shakespeare and inaugurated a Stratford Jubilee in 1769. All these pursuits were part of his vigorous career, which was untiringly devoted to acting and managing a theatre.

In charge of the artistic problems at Drury Lane, Garrick diligently trained the company that worked with him, as Kitty Clive, one of his leading ladies, noted.

A listing of his roles is a listing of the popular plays of his time and the great plays of the past and attests to Garrick's tremendous versatility. One of his contemporaries wrote to him: "The thing that strikes me above all others is that variety in your acting, and your being so totally a different man in Lear from what you are in Richard. . . ."

Lauded for introducing natural acting on a stage steeped in posturing and sing-song recitative, Garrick borrowed from life the touches that made his character creations great. In preparing his King Lear, one of his greatest roles, Garrick observed an acquaintance who had gone mad after the loss of his child. He is reported to have said, "There it was that I learned to imitate madness; I copied nature, and to that I owed my success in King Lear." Both Garrick and the actors he trained were praised in verse and anecdote for naturalness. Thomas Davies (1712-1785), an actor at Drury Lane and Garrick's first biographer, in a poem called "Nature and Garrick" (1756), has nature cry out that Garrick steals her colors. Dr. Samuel Johnson, the arbiter of literary taste and one time schoolmaster of Garrick, said of him: "Garrick . . . was no declaimer; there was not one of his own scene shifters who could not have spoken 'to be or not to be,' better than he did. True conception of character and natural expression of it, were his distinguished excellencies." The most graphic detailed description of Garrick is preserved in the letters of the German Georg Christoph Lichtenberg who visited London in Garrick's day.

The problem of emotional identification is touched on in these words ascribed to Garrick: ". . . that a man was incapable of becoming an actor who was not absolutely independent of circumstances calculated to excite emotion, adding that, for his own part, he could speak to a post with the same feelings and expression as to the loveliest Juliet under heaven." Anecdotes confirm the fact that he was not completely immersed in his roles. Grimm, who saw him in Paris, reported that Garrick entertained a group of people by letting his face run through the whole gamut of passions without personal emotion. Garrick's cool head recommended itself to Diderot, who used him as an illustration of his thesis that the actor should be devoid of personal emotion.

In all of Garrick's writing there is unfortunately little in the way of a detailed exposition of his methods of artistic creation or his general approach to his art. The major pieces are printed here. An Essay on Acting . . . is the first portion of a humorous pamphlet which Davies says Garrick wrote while he was preparing his performance of Macbeth to "blunt" the remarks he felt critics would make on his original presentation of the character. Apart from the amusing gibes at himself and the humorously brief, traditional definition of acting, this Essay is interesting for its stress on variety in characterization and its emphasis on observation of "nature" in the preparation of a role. The letters of advice to two actors testify to his serious approach to acting.

Although the statement of Davies that "I have never heard him speak warmly in the commendation of any actor, living or dead" may caution the reader against immediate acceptance of Garrick's evaluation of Hyppolite Clairon, the French tragedienne, as inferior because her technique differed from his, the letter about her does suggest Garrick's endorsement of the spontaneous, intuitive approach. We are fortunate in having Clairon's exposition of the same problem in which her words might almost have been written in answer to the very objections raised by Garrick.

Versatile, ingenious, and impassioned as an actor, shrewd and strict as a manager and teacher, and successful as a playwright, Garrick was almost universally admired in his own day and has become the symbol of the great actor. Original as he was, Garrick was nevertheless a child of his own time. He provided Macbeth with a striking death speech and retained the music and dancing introduced in Davenant's version of this play. *King Lear,* one of his triumphs, probably retained a happy ending from earlier versions of the play. His costumes and those of his leading ladies were elaborate contemporary dress, and the scenery that adorned his productions had little relation to his playing. Perhaps Garrick's art is best understood in the light of John Hill's remark that "Natural playing, when it flows from a perfect understanding of the whole art and rules of the profession, is the excellence of theatrical representation; but those who use the term, generally employ it to express that dependence upon nature, which excludes all the assistance of art; and ... such nature will never make a player."

An Essay on Acting

In Which will be Considered the Mimical Behavior of a
Certain Fashionable Faulty Actor ...

As I have a long time (twenty years, or more) made the stage, and acting, my study and entertainment, I look upon myself, and indeed am thought by my intimates, a proper person to animadvert upon, or approve, the errors and the excellencies of the theatre; and as there can be no better opportunity offer itself than now, when the town is running after their little fashionable actor, in a character of which he is, properly speaking, the anti-climax of, or rather the antipode of Shakespeare; I will endeavor in the following dissection of our puppet hero, to convince my dear country men and country women, that they are madly following an *ignis fatuus,* or will of the wisp, which they take for real substantial light, and which I shall prove to be only the rush-light of genius, the idol of fashion, and an air-drawn favorite of the imagination.

How are we degenerated in taste! Oh how chang'd! How fallen! That our theatre shall be crowded with nobility, ladies and gentry, to see *Macbeth* Burlesqued, or Be—g—k'd, which are synonymous, when they might read Mr. Theobald's edition of him, without throwing away their money, mispending their time, ruining their taste, or running the hazard of catching a violent cold, for a mere nonentity. However, that I may not seem to be prejudiced against Mr. G——k, as I really am not, for I admire him, for thus boldly daring to deceive and cheat three parts of the nation; I shall, having now cracked the shell of my spleen against the town, come to the kernel of reason, and present them this little sweet nut of theirs, worm-eaten to the sight, embittered to their taste, and abhorred to their imaginations, as Shakespeare terms it.

In order to do this, I shall present my readers with the following short treatise upon acting, which will show them what acting ought to be, and what the present favorite in question is not.

David Garrick: *An Essay on Acting: In which will be Considered the Mimical Behavior of a Certain fashionable faulty actor . . . to which will be added a short Criticism of His acting Macbeth.* London: Printed for W. Bickerton, 1744, pp. 1-12.

ACTORS ON ACTING

*A Short Treatise upon Acting. By Which the Players May be Instructed,
and the Town Undeceived*

That I may convince the world, that the public good and no private animosity, has extracted the following treatise from its author, I shall first give an ample and clear definition of acting, and make the natural, metaphysical, and consequential deductions, that will immediately elicit the right from the wrong, and show my designs are merely scientifical, and not subservient to pique and partial prejudice.

Acting is an entertainment of the stage, which by calling in the aid and assistance of articulation, corporeal motion, and ocular expression, imitates, assumes, or puts on the various mental and bodily emotions arising from the various humors, virtues and vices, incident to human nature.

There are two different kinds of exhibitions, viz. tragedy and comedy; the first fixes her empire on the passions, and the more exalted contractions and dilations of the heart; the last, though not inferior (*quotidem* science) holds her rule over the less ennobled qualities and districts of human nature, which are called the humors. Now in some cases, passions are humors, and humors passions; for the revenges of an Alexander and a Haberdasher, may have the same fountain, and differ only in their currents, and though the one (Alexander) cannot content himself but with the total subversion of his enemy's kingdom, and the other (the Haberdasher) is satisfied with rolling his antagonist in the kennel; yet, still it is revenge, the mind of one is equally affected in proportion to the other, and all the difference lies in the different ways of satisfying their common passion. But now to the application, and design in hand. If an actor, and a favorite actor, in assuming these different characters with the same passions, shall unskillfully differ only in dress, and not in execution; and supposing him right in one, and of consequence absolutely ridiculous in the other, shall this actor, I say, in spite of reason, physics, and common observations, be caressed, applauded, admired? But to illustrate it more by example. — Suppose the murder of Duncan, and the breaking of a urinal shall affect the player in the same manner, and the only difference is the blue apron and laced coat, shall we be chilled at the murderer, and roar at the tobacconist? Fie for shame! — As the one must be absolutely the reverse of right, I think the public, for so gross an imposition, should drive both off the stage. When Drugger [*The Alchemist*] becomes Macbeth, and Macbeth Drugger, I feel for the names of the immortal Shakespeare, and inimitable Ben; I bemoan the taste of my country, and I would have the buffoon sacrificed to appease the muses, and restore to us a true dramatic taste, by such an exemplary piece of justice. I shall now, as relative to my present subject, describe in what manner the two above-mentioned characters ought to be mentally and corporeally agitated, under the different circumstances of the dagger, and urinal; and by that shall more fully delineate what is meant by passions and humors. When Abel Drugger has broke the urinal, he is mentally absorbed with the different ideas of the invaluable price of the urinal, and the punishment that may be inflicted in consequence of a curiosity, no way appertaining or belonging to the business he came about. Now, if this, as it certainly is, the situation of his mind, how are the different members of the body to be agitated? Why thus — his eyes must be reversed from the object he is most intimidated with, and by dropping his lip at the same time to the object, it throws a trembling languor upon every muscle, and by declining the right part of the head towards the urinal, it casts the most comic terror and shame over all the upper part of the body, that can be imagined; and to make the lower part equally ridiculous, his toes must be inverted from the heel, and by holding his breath, he will unavoidably give himself a tremor in the knees, and if his fingers, at the same time, seem convulsed, it finishes the completest low picture of grotesque terror that can be imagined by a Dutch painter. — Let this be compared with the modern copies, and then let the town judge. — Now to Macbeth. — When the murder of Duncan is committed, from an immediate consciousness of the fact, his ambition is engulfed at that instant, by the horror of the deed; his faculties are intensely riveted to the murder alone, without having the least consolation of the consequential advantages, to comfort him in that exigency. He should at that time, be a moving statue, or indeed a petrified man; his eyes must speak, and his tongue be metaphorically silent; his ears must be sensible of imaginary noises, and deaf to the present and audible voice of his wife; his attitudes must be quick and permanent; his voice articulately trembling, and confusedly intelligible; the murderer should be seen in every limb, and yet every member, at that instant, should seem separated from his body, and his body from his soul. This is the picture of a complete regicide, and as at that time the orb below should be hush as death; I hope I shall not be thought minutely circumstantial, if I should advise a real genius to wear cork heels to his shoes, as in this scene he should seem to tread on air, and I promise him he will soon discover the great benefit of this (however seeming trifling) piece of advice.

The only way to arrive at great excellency in characters of humor, is to be very conversant with human nature, that is the noblest and best study, by this way you will more accurately discover the workings of spirit (or what other physical terms you please to call it) upon the different modifications of matter. Would the painter produce a perfect piece to the world, let him copy from the life, let nature herself sit to the artist: would a player perform equally excellent in his profession, let him be introduced into the world, be conversant with humors of every kind, digest them in his mind, let them be cherished by the genial warmth of his conception, transplanted into the fair garden of his judgment, there let them ripen to perfection, and become his own. *Hic labor! Hoc opus!* The late celebrated Mr. [Thomas] Doggett, before he performed the character of Ben, in *Love for Love,* took lodgings in Wapping, and gathered thence a nosegay for the whole town. Another comedian now living, though not upon the stage (it being so replete with greater geniuses) has been observed constantly to attend the exchange for weeks together, before he exhibited one of Shakespeare's most inimitable and difficult characters, and so far succeeded by his great attention and observation of the manner, dress, and behavior of a particular tribe of people, that the judgment, application, and extraordinary pains he took to divert the public rationally, was amply returned with crowded theatres, and unequalled applause; nay, to so great a degree did they show their approbation to this painstaking genius, that he is at present more known by the name of the character he performed, than by his own.

I shall not enter into the reasons why he is at present excluded from the theatre, but shall only, as an advocate for the public, say that I wish for their sake, that there were many such actors as him upon both theatres.

I have, in as concise a manner as possible, given my sentiments of acting, by example and precept; but there will very soon be published a more complete and expanded treatise upon acting, with an accurate description of each humor and passion, their sources and effects; by which the players may be taught to renounce their errors, and the town its judgment of acting and actors.—

Here ends the essay upon acting.

ACTORS ON ACTING
Letters on Acting

Mr. Garrick to Mr. Powell [1]

Paris, December 12, 1764.

...The news of your great success gave me a most sensible pleasure, the continuance of that success will be in your own power; and if you will give an older soldier leave to hint a little advice to you, I will answer for its being sincere at least, which, from a brother actor, is no small merit. The gratitude you have expressed for what little service I did you the summer before your appearance on the stage, has attached me to you, as a man who shall always have my best wishes for his welfare, and my best endeavors to promote it. I have not always met with gratitude in a playhouse. You have acted a greater variety of characters than I could expect in the first winter, and I have some fears that your good nature to your brother actors (which is commendable when it is not injurious) drove you into parts too precipitately; however, you succeeded, and it is happy that you had the whole summer to correct the errors of haste, which the public will ever excuse in a young performer, on account of his beauties; but now is the time to make sure of your ground in every step you take. You must, therefore, give to study, and an accurate consideration of your characters, those hours which young men too generally give to their friends and flatterers. The common excuse, is they frequent clubs, for the sake of their benefit; but nothing could be more absurd—your benefits will only increase with your fame, and should that ever sink by your idleness, those friends who have made you idle, will be the first to forsake you. When the public has marked you for a favorite (and their favor must be purchased with sweat and labor) you may choose what company you please, and none but the best can be of service to you.

The famous [Michel] Baron of France used to say, that an actor should be "nursed in the lap of Queens"; by which he meant that the best accomplishments were necessary to form a great actor. Study hard, my friend, for seven years, and you may play the rest of your life. I would advise you to read at your leisure other books besides plays in which you are concerned.... But above all, never let your Shakespeare be out of your hands, or your pocket; keep him about you as a charm; the more you read him the more you will like him, and the better you will act him. One thing more, and then I will finish my preaching: Guard against *the splitting the ears of the groundlings, who are capable of nothing but dumb shows and noise* — do not sacrifice your taste and feelings to the applause of the multitude; a true genius will convert an audience to his manner, rather than be converted by them to what is false and unnatural: — *be not too tame neither.* I shall leave the rest to ...your own genius....

Mr. Garrick, as to Madame Clairon

August, 1769.

What shall I say to you, my dear friend [Sturz, Garrick's Danish correspond-

---

The Private Correspondence of David Garrick with the Most Celebrated Persons of his Time ... edited, with a memoir by James Boaden. London: Henry Colburn and Richard Bentley, 1831, Volume I, pp. 177-178, 358, 509.

---

[1]William Powell (d. 1769). Called David Garrick's successor when Garrick engaged him for Drury Lane during his holiday abroad in the years 1763-1765.

[136]

ent], about the "Clairon?" Your dissection of her is as accurate as if you had opened her alive; she has everything that art and good understanding, with great natural spirit, can give her. But then I fear (and I only tell you my fears and open my soul to you) the heart has none of those instantaneous feelings, that life-blood, that keen sensibility, that bursts at once from genius, and like electrical fire, shoots through the veins, marrow, bones and all, of every spectator. Madame Clairon is so conscious and certain of what she can do, that she never, I believe, had the feelings of the instant come upon her unexpectedly; but I pronounce that the greatest strokes of genius have been unknown to the actor himself, till circumstances, and the warmth of the scene, has sprung the mine at it were, as much to his own surprise, as that of the audience. Thus I make a great difference between a great genius and a good actor. The first will always realize the feelings of his character, and be transported beyond himself; while the other, with great powers, and good sense, will give great pleasure to an audience, but never

> *Pectus inaniter angit,*
> *Irritat, mulcet, falsis terroribus implet*
> *Ut magus.* (Horace, Epist., II, i, 211)
> [With airy nothings rings my heart
> In flames, soothes it, fills it with vain alarms
> Like a magician.]

I have with great freedom communicated my ideas of acting, but you must not betray me, my good friend; the Clairon would never forgive me, though I called her an excellent actress, if I did not swear by all the Gods she was the greatest genius too.

Mr. Garrick to Mr. Henderson[1]

Hampton, January 5, 1773.

Sir,

It is with the greatest pleasure I hear of your success: the continuance of it will in great measure depend upon yourself. As the older soldier, I will venture to point out some rocks, which former young men of merit have split upon. Too much intoxication with the applause they have received, and more inclined to be flattered by their inferiors than pursue the means to increase their reputation, they have generally neglected study, to keep indifferent company; by which behavior their little stock of merit has been soon exhausted, and in exchange they have got the habit of idling and drinking, contenting themselves in public with barely getting the words of their parts into their heads, and in private with the poor, unedifying, commonplace gabble of every ignorant pretender who (to the disgrace of it) belongs to a theatre. You must not imagine that I would have a young man always at his book; far from it: it is part of his business to know the world; and conversation, provided it is creditable, will be of the utmost service. I am sorry to say that the conversation I would recommend is not to be found among the *dramatis personae*. Permit me to go a little farther; you have given me a sort of right, by saying that my interest at Bath has served you. I would have you endeavor to read other books besides those of the theatre. Every additional knowledge to

---

[1]John Henderson (1747-1785), called the Bath Roscius.

that of your profession will give you importance; the majority of actors content themselves (like parrots) with delivering words they get from others; repeat them again and again without the least alteration; and confine their notions, talking and acquirements, to the theatre only, as the parrot to his cage. The last and chief matter is your preservation of that character which you set out with, of being an honest man: let no inducements prevail upon you to break your engagements; steadiness and perseverance will, though *slowly,* bring you *surely* to the best end of all our actions; while flights, rambling, and what some call *spirit,* will mislead, distract, and destroy you. So much for preaching.

What I have said, is said to yourself, and meant kindly: if my future advice will be of the least service to you, you shall command it....

CATHERINE CLIVE

(1711-1785)

Catherine (Kitty) Clive, a member of Garrick's company for a time, was one of the liveliest comic artists of the time. Her singing and drollery earned for her the approbation of Dr. Johnson who said, "What Clive did best, she did better than Garrick, but could not do half so many things well." Like many comic artists she aspired to tragic roles but succeeded best in her own domain.

Her letters to Garrick, two of which follow, attest to his role as teacher and director. Clive was only one of a group of excellent actresses in the Garrick company at different times. There was, for a while, his lovely mistress, Peg Woffington. Mrs. Hannah Pritchard was his leading tragic actress, playing Lady Macbeth to his Macbeth, Queen Gertrude to his Hamlet, and Beatrice to his Benedick. She was an actress with strong natural talent, and created excellent effects on stage although it is reported of her that in *Macbeth* she knew only the scenes in which she appeared. George Ann Bellamy (1731-1788), who wrote an extremely picturesque *Apology,* was also one of his leading ladies. Susanna Maria Cibber, wife of Colley Cibber's rather disreputable son, Theophilus, became, next to Mrs. Pritchard, the finest tragedian of Garrick's company.

These women belonged to a developing tradition of English actresses. Unknown on the stage before the Restoration, when all female parts were taken by boys, actresses had emerged in the second half of the seventeenth century to add such great names to the English stage as that of Mrs. Betterton, Mrs. Barry, Mrs. Bracegirdle, Mrs. Oldfield, and later the women of Garrick's hegemony in the theatre.

Two Letters to Mr. Garrick

Mrs. Clive to Mr. Garrick

Twickenham, January 23, 1774.

Wonderful Sir.— Who have been for thirty years contradicting an old established proverb, "you cannot make bricks without straw"; but you have done what is infinitely more difficult, for you have made actors and actresses without genius, that

Quoted by Percy H. Fitzgerald: *The Life of Mrs. Catherine Clive.* . . . London: A. Reader, 1888, pp 93-94, 105-106.

is you have made them pass for such, which has answered your end, though it has given you infinite trouble. You never took much pains for yourself for you could not help acting well, therefore I do not think you have much merit in that, though to be sure it has been very assuaging to yourself, as well as the rest of the world; for while you are laughing at your own conceits, you was [*sic*] at the same time sure they would cram your iron chests....

yours,
C. Pivy

Twickenham, June 23, 1776.

Dear Sir:—Is it really true that you have put an end to the glory of Drury Lane Theatre? If it is so, let me congratulate my dear Mr. and Mrs. Garrick on their approaching happiness: I know what it will be; you cannot yet have an idea of it; but if you should still be so wicked not to be satisfied with that unbounded, un-common degree of fame you have received as an actor, and which no other actor ever did receive—nor no other actor ever can receive;—I say, if you should still long to be dipping your fingers in their theatrical pudding (now without plums), you will be no Garrick for the Pivy. In the height of public admiration for you, when you were never mentioned with any other appellation but Mr. Garrick, the charming man, the fine fellow, the delightful creature, both by men and ladies; when they were admiring everything you did and everything you scribbled, at this very time the Pivy was a living witness that they did not know, nor could they be sensible of half your perfections. I have seen you with your magical hammer in your hand, endeavoring to beat your ideas into the heads of the creatures who had none of their own. I have seen you with lamb-like patience, endeavoring to make them comprehend you, and I have seen you when that could not be done. I have seen your lamb turned into a lion; by this your great labor and pains the public was entertained; they thought they all acted very fine— they did not see you pull the wires.

There are people now on the stage to whom you gave their consequence; they think themselves very great, now let them go on in their new parts without your leading strings, and they will soon convince the world what this genius is. I have always said this to everybody, even when your horses and mine were in their highest prancing. While I was under your control I did not say half the fine things I thought of you, because it looked like flattering, and you know your Pivy was always proud, besides I thought you did not like me then, but now I am sure you do, which made me send this letter.

SARAH KEMBLE SIDDONS

(1755-1831)

The most illustrious member of the Kemble clan, England's distinguished acting family for six generations, was Sarah Kemble Siddons. Contemporary testimony, corroborated by historical authority, has designated her the greatest actress the Eng-lish stage has ever possessed. The tenor of the astounding acclaim which attended her performances and which continued unabated over her two-decade activity on the stage is best expressed in the words of William Hazlitt: "The enthusiasm she excited had something idolatrous about it; we can conceive nothing grander. She embodied to our imaginations the fables of mythology of the heroic and the deified mortals of elder time. She was not less than a goddess or a prophetess inspired by the Gods. Power was seated on her brow; passion radiated from her breast as from a shrine; she was Tragedy personified."

The first child of Roger Kemble, a provincial strolling player and Sarah Ward, daughter of an Irish theatre manager, Sarah was born July 5, 1755, at Brecknock, South Wales. Of the twelve Kemble offspring, half chose to continue in the theatre. Sarah and her brother John Philip succeeded in holding complete sway over the English stage for more than twenty years. As a child, she appeared on the stage with the other members of her family. At eighteen she was married to William Siddons, an indifferent actor in her father's company. Two years later, her success in the provinces came to the attention of David Garrick, through whom she was brought to Drury Lane to make her London debut as Portia on December 29, 1775. This debut marked her first, last, and only failure, accounted for variously by her biographers as due to a decline of her health after the recent birth of her second child; the fact that her voice, tuned to the requirements of the small provincial theatre, could not be projected sufficiently in the two-thousand-seat Drury Lane theatre; and possibly the strangeness of her performance, new to an audience accustomed to the actress-coquette then in vogue. Whatever the reason, she failed to arouse Garrick's interest sufficiently, so that her relationship with Drury Lane was soon terminated.

Mrs. Siddons returned to the provincial circuit, to remain there for the next six years until she was once again called to Drury Lane. Her second London appearance, in the title role of Southerne's *Isabella, or The Fatal Marriage*, on October 10, 1782, so electrified the theatre world that she was immediately recognized as the greatest tragic actress of the period. It was in the midst of her preparations for this performance, in the depth of what she called one of her "desperate tranquilities," that she observed that "the awful consciousness that one is the sole object of attention to that immense space, lined as it were, with human intellect from top to bottom, and all around, may perhaps be imagined, but can never be described; and by me can never be forgotten."

During her second season at Drury Lane Sir Joshua Reynolds immortalized her beauty in his famous portrait *The Tragic Muse*. In this painting, as well as in the numerous others drawn by the greatest artists of her time, one can readily observe the majestic stature, "the human face divine" with its intensely expressive eyes, and the physical qualities which, when put to the service of her fire and profoundly imaginative powers, endowed her with attributes for a tragedian to a point very near perfection.

In the following seasons she graced the stage in unforgettable creations: as Lady Randolph in *Douglas,* Zara in *The Mourning Bride,* Mrs. Haller in Kotzebue's *The Stranger,* Elvira in *Pizarro*—plays, which lacking her presence, have been consigned to oblivion. Her greatest Shakespearean interpretations were considered to be Queen Katherine in *King Henry VIII,* Volumnia in John Philip Kemble's adaptation of *Coriolanus,* and Lady Macbeth, the last acknowledged by all to have embodied the fullest realization of her creative powers.

Mrs. Siddons' biographers are unanimous in their opinion that as an actress, she was not given to dependence on inspiration but achieved her results through painstaking application and a careful and thorough study of every part, with the keenest perception of character delineation. Her touchstone is stated in these words:

[140]

"When a part is first put before me for studying, I look it over in a general way, to see if it is in Nature, and if it is, I am sure it can be played." In keeping with this view she rejected a role in the following manner: "It strikes me that the plot is very lame, and the characters very, very ill-sustained in general, but more so the lady for whom the author has me in his eyes. This woman is one of those monsters of perfection, who is an angel before her time, and is so entirely resigned to the will of Heaven that (to a very mortal like myself) she appears to be the most provoking piece of still life one has ever had the misfortune to meet. Her struggles and conflicts are so worthily expressed, that we conclude they do not cost her much pain, and she is so pious that we are satisfied she looks upon her afflictions as so many convoys to Heaven, and wish her there, or anywhere else but in the tragedy."

Mrs. Clement Parsons, one of her many biographers, finds that "she worked from within outward; first, by yielding herself to the spontaneous flashes of her sensibility, she became the person represented; then, inevitably, brought out the external indications, peculiar and personal."

Her power of concentration and absorption in her characterizations appears to have been so complete that the emotions which possessed her continued for several hours after a performance. Unlike Garrick, who could joke easily between the acts of his most tragic roles, it is said that when she was playing Mrs. Haller in Kotzebue's *The Stranger* she never stopped crying until the time she reached home, and her daughter Sally wrote that "My Mother cries so much at it that she is always ill when she comes home." Mrs. Siddons herself has said: "The quality of abstraction has always appeared to me so necessary in the art of acting, that ...I wish my opinion were of sufficient weight to impress the importance of this power on the minds of all candidates for dramatic fame.... Whenever I was called upon to personate the character of Constance [*King John*] I never, from the beginning of the play to the end of my part in it, once suffered my dressing-room door to be closed, in order that my attention might be constantly fixed on those distressing events, which, by this means, I could plainly hear going on upon the stage, the terrible effects of which progress were to be represented by me.... In short, the spirit of the whole drama took possession of my mind and frame, by my attention being incessantly riveted to the passing scenes." And later she had occasion to remark: "Belvidera [*Venice Preserved*] was hardly acting last night; I felt every word as if I were the real person, and not the representative."

The essay on the character of Lady Macbeth, given here, is one of the two analyses of a role which Mrs. Siddons has left. Karl Mantzius points out that while her conception is interesting to us in that it expresses "the true Kemble attitude towards art, in its striving for the attainment of nobility, beauty, elevation, at any and all cost... it is still more interesting that this reading of the part differs completely from the conception that her impulsive, temperamental genius forced her to carry out on the stage." A record of her performance in this character by an eye-witness, Professor G. J. Bell in H. C. Fleeming Jenkin: *Mrs. Siddons as Lady Macbeth and as Queen Katherine* is available to those who wish to make the comparison.

Charles Lamb has said that "we speak of Lady Macbeth while we are in reality thinking of Mrs. Siddons." She first appeared in this role in 1785 and chose it for her farewell performance in 1812. Campbell, her contemporary biographer, states that "the part accordingly proved, as might have been expected, Mrs. Siddons' masterpiece. It was an era in one's life to have seen her in it."

Remarks on the Character of Lady Macbeth

In this astonishing creature one sees a woman in whose bosom the passion of ambition has almost obliterated all the characteristics of human nature; in whose composition are associated all the subjugating powers of intellect and all the charms and graces of personal beauty. You will probably not agree with me as to the character of that beauty; yet, perhaps, this difference of opinion will be entirely attributable to the difficulty of your imagination disengaging itself from that idea of the person of her representative which you have been so long accustomed to contemplate. According to my notion, it is of that character which I believe is generally allowed to be most captivating to the other sex,—fair, feminine, nay, perhaps, even fragile—

Fair as the forms that, wove in Fancy's loom,
Float in light visions round the poet's head.

Such a combination only, respectable in energy and strength of mind, and captivating in feminine loveliness, could have composed a charm of such potency as to fascinate the mind of a hero so dauntless, a character so amiable, so honorable as Macbeth, to seduce him to brave all the dangers of the present and all the terrors of a future world....

Lady Macbeth, thus adorned with every fascination of mind and person, enters for the first time, reading a part of one of those portentous letters from her husband. "They met me in the day of success; and I have learnt by the perfectest report they have more in them than mortal knowledge...." Now vaulting ambition and intrepid daring rekindle in a moment all the splendors of her dark blue eyes. She fatally resolves that Glamis and Cawdor shall be also that which the mysterious agents of the Evil One have promised. She then proceeds to the investigation of her husband's character....

In this development, we find that, though ambitious, he is yet amiable, conscientious, nay pious; and yet of a temper so irresolute and fluctuating, as to require all the efforts, all the excitement, which her uncontrollable spirit, and her unbounded influence over him, can perform ....

Shortly Macbeth appears. He announces the King's approach; and she, insensible it should seem to all the perils which he has encountered in battle, and to all the happiness of his safe return to her,—for not one kind word of greeting or congratulation does she offer,—is so entirely swallowed up by the horrible design, which has probably been suggested to her by his letters, as to have entirely forgotten both the one and the other. It is very remarkable that Macbeth is frequent in expressions of tenderness to his wife, while she never betrays one symptom of affection towards him, till, in the fiery furnace of affliction, her iron heart is melted down to softness. For the present she flies to welcome the venerable gracious Duncan, with such a show of eargerness, as if allegiance in her bosom sat crowned with devotion and gratitude.

THE SECOND ACT

There can be no doubt that Macbeth, in the first instance, suggested his design of assassinating the King.... Yet, on the arrival of the amiable monarch

---

Sarah Siddons: "Remarks on the Character of Lady Macbeth" in Thomas Campbell: *Life of Mrs. Siddons.* London: Effingham Wilson, 1834, Volume II, pp. 10-34, *passim.*

who had so honored him of late, his naturally benevolent and good feelings resume their wonted power... he relinquishes the atrocious purpose, and wisely determines to proceed no further in the business. But, now, behold his evil genius, his grave-charm, appears, and by the force of her revilings, her contemptuous taunts, and, above all, by her opprobrious aspersion of cowardice, chases the gathering drops of humanity from his eyes, and drives before her impetuous and destructive career all those kindly charities, those impressions of loyalty, and pity, and gratitude, which, but the moment before, had taken full possession of his mind.... Her language to Macbeth is the most potently eloquent that guilt could use. It is only in soliloquy that she invokes the powers of hell to unsex her. To her husband she avows, and the naturalness of her language makes us believe her, that she had felt the instinct of filial as well as maternal love. But she makes her very virtues the means of a taunt to her lord:—"You have the milk of human kindness in your heart...but ambition, which is my ruling passion, would be also yours if you had the courage.... Look to me, and be ashamed of your weakness." Abashed, perhaps, to find his own courage humbled before this unimaginable instance of female fortitude, he at last screws up his courage to the sticking-place, and binds up each corporal agent to this terrible feat.... In the tremendous suspense of these moments, while she recollects her habitual humanity, one trait of tender feeling is expressed, "Had he not resembled my father as he slept, I had done it." Her humanity vanished, however, in the same instant; for when she observes that Macbeth, in the terror and confusion of his faculties, has brought the daggers from the place where they had agreed they should remain for the crimination of the grooms, she exhorts him to return with them to that place.... He, shuddering, exclaims, "I'll go no more! I am affear'd to think of what I have done...."

Then instantaneously the solitary particle of her human feeling is swallowed up in her remorseless ambition, and, wrenching the daggers from the feeble grasp of her husband, she finishes the act which the infirm of purpose had not courage to complete, and calmly and steadily returns to her accomplice.... In a deplorable depravation of all rational knowledge, and lost to every recollection except that of his enormous guilt, she hurries him away to their own chamber.

The Third Act

The golden round of royalty now crowns her brow, and royal robes enfold her form; but the peace that passeth all understanding is lost to her for ever, and the worm that never dies already gnaws her heart....

Under the impression of her present wretchedness, I, from this moment, have always assumed the dejection of countenance and manners which I thought accordant to such a state of mind; and, though the author of this sublime composition has not, it must be acknowledged, given any direction whatever to authorize this assumption, yet I venture to hope that he would not have disapproved of it. It is evident, indeed, by her conduct in the scene which succeeds the mournful soliloquy, that she is no longer the presumptuous, the determined creature, that she was before the assassination of the King: for instance, on the approach of her husband, we behold for the first time striking indications of sensibility, nay, tenderness and sympathy; and I think this conduct is nobly followed up by her during the whole of their subsequent eventful intercourse. It is evident, I think, that the sad and new experience of affliction has subdued the insolence of her pride, and the violence of her will; for she comes now to seek him out, that she may, at least, participate in his misery.... Far from her former habits of reproach and contemptuous taunting, you perceive that she now listens to his complaints with sympathizing feelings; and, so far from adding to the weight of his affliction the burden of her own, she endeavors to conceal it from him with the most delicate and unremitting attention. ... No; all her thoughts are now directed to divert his from those sorriest fancies.... Yes; smothering her sufferings in the deepest recesses of her own wretched bosom, we cannot but perceive that she devotes herself entirely to the effort of supporting him.

Let it be here recollected, as some palliation of her former very different deportment, she had, probably, from childhood commanded all around her with a high hand; had interruptedly, perhaps, in that splendid station, enjoyed all that wealth, all that nature had to bestow; that she had, possibly, no directors, no controllers, and that in womanhood her fascinated lord had never once opposed her inclinations. But now her new-born relentings, under the rod of chastisement, prompt her to make palpable efforts in order to support the spirits of her weaker, and, I must say, more selfish husband. Yes; in gratitude for his unbounded affection, and in commiseration of his sufferings, she suppresses the anguish of her heart, even while that anguish is precipitating her into the grave which at this moment is yawning to receive her.

THE BANQUET

Surrounded by their court, in all the apparent ease and self-complacency of which their wretched souls are destitute, they are now seated at the royal banquet; and although, through the greater part of this scene, Lady Macbeth affects to resume her wonted domination over her husband, yet, notwithstanding all this self-control, her mind must even then be agonized by the complicated pangs of terror and remorse....

Dying with fear, yet assuming the utmost composure, she returns to her stately canopy; and, with trembling nerves, having tottered up the steps to her throne, that bad eminence, she entertains her wondering guests with frightful smiles, with over-acted attention, and with fitful graciousness; painfully, yet incessantly, laboring to divert their attention from her husband. Whilst writhing thus under her internal agonies, her restless and terrifying glances towards Macbeth, in spite of all her efforts to suppress them, have thrown the whole table into amazement; and the murderer then suddenly breaks up the assembly, by the confession of his horrors....

What imitation, in such circumstances as these, would ever satisfy the demands of expectation? The terror, the remorse, the hypocrisy of this astonishing being, flitting in frightful succession over her countenance, and actuating her agitated gestures with her varying emotions, present, perhaps, one of the greatest difficulties of the scenic art, and cause her representative no less to tremble for the suffrage of her private study, than for its public effect.

It is now the time to inform you of an idea which I have conceived of Lady Macbeth's character, which perhaps will appear as fanciful as that which I have adopted respecting the style of her beauty; and, in order to justify this idea, I must carry you back to the scene immediately preceding the banquet, in which you will recollect the dialogue [with Macbeth concerning Banquo and Fleance]....

Now, is it not possible that she should hear all these ambiguous hints about Banquo without being too well aware that a sudden, lamentable fate awaits him. Yet, so far from offering any opposition to Macbeth's murderous designs, she even hints, I think, at the facility, if not the expediency, of destroying both Banquo and his equally unoffending child, when she observes that, "in them Nature's copy is not eterne." Having, therefore, now filled the measure of her crimes, I have imagined that the last appearance of Banquo's ghost became no less visible to her eyes than it became to those of her husband. Yes, the spirit of the noble Banquo has smilingly filled up, even to overflowing, and now commends to her own lips the ingredients of her poisoned chalice.

THE FIFTH ACT

Behold her now, with wasted form, with wan and haggard countenance, her starry eyes glazed with the ever-burning fever of remorse, and on their lids the shadows of death. Her ever-restless spirit wanders in troubled dreams about her dismal apartment; and whether waking or asleep, the smell of innocent blood incessantly haunts her imagination....

During this appalling scene, which, to my sense, is the most so of them all, the wretched creature, in imagination, acts over again the accumulated horrors of her whole conduct. These dreadful images, accompanied with the agitations they have induced, have obviously accelerated her untimely end; for in a few moments the tidings of her death are brought to her unhappy husband. It is conjectured that she died by her own hand. Too certain it is, that she dies, and makes no sign. I have now to account to you for the weakness which I have, a few lines back, ascribed to Macbeth; and I am not quite without hope that the following observations will bear me out in this opinion. Please to observe, that he (I think pusillanimously, when I compare his conduct to her forebearance,) has been continually pouring out his miseries to his wife. His heart has therefore been eased, from time to time, by unloading its weight of woe; while she, on the contrary, has perseveringly endured in silence the uttermost anguish of a wounded spirit.

Her feminine nature, her delicate structure, it is too evident, are soon overwhelmed by the enormous pressure of her crimes. Yet it will be granted, that she gives proofs of a naturally higher toned mind than that of Macbeth. The different physical powers of the two sexes are finely delineated, in the different effects which their mutual crimes produce. Her frailer frame, and keener feelings, have now sunk under the struggle—his robust and less sensitive constitution has not only resisted it, but bears him on to deeper wickedness, and to experience the fatal fecundity of crime.

In one point of view, at least, this guilty pair extort from us, in spite of ourselves, a certain respect and approbation. Their grandeur of character sustains them both above recrimination (the despicable accustomed resort of vulgar minds), in adversity; for the wretched husband, though almost impelled into this gulf of destruction by the instigations of his wife, feels no abatement of his love for her, while she, on her part, appears to have known no tenderness for him, till, with a heart bleeding at every pore, she beholds in him the miserable victim of their mutual ambition. Unlike the first frail pair in Paradise, they spent not the fruitless hours in mutual accusation.

VIII. FRANCE

Tradition and Revolt

In France, as elsewhere, players of religious drama like the *Confrérie de la Passion* disappeared during the early part of the sixteenth century. In an era of religious dissension and national growth only the farces similar to *Maître Pierre Pathelin* survived from an earlier day. The Renaissance influence in France, as in England, was perceptible in the imitations and adaptations of Greek and Roman drama by the *Pléïäde* and other scholarly and literary groups. Etienne Jodelle's *Cléopâtre captive* in 1552 set the pattern for original French plays in the classical manner, a type which reached its apex in the lyrical dramas of Robert Garnier. These classicists laid the groundwork for French drama, but their plays in the mid-sixteenth century had little connection with professional theatre, since they were performed by amateurs for a largely academic and courtly audience.

Professional players who wandered through the provinces and entertained at popular fairs like *La Foire Saint-Germain* were hampered in Paris by the monopolistic control exercised by the *Confrérie de la Passion*. When the decree of 1548 suppressed religious dramas, the *Confrérie* was recompensed for the loss of its repertoire by a renewal of its exclusive right to perform plays in Paris. The *Confrérie* itself ceased to produce plays, but it exercised control by forcing all troupes that wished to play in Paris to pay a tax. In addition, the *Confrérie* imposed a high rental charge for the use of its theatre, the *Hôtel de Bourgogne,* the only theatre in Paris. Through the machinations of the *Confrérie* the *Hôtel de Bourgogne* became the first home of players in Paris.

Italian companies like the *Gelosi,* so popular in France throughout this period, performed at the *Hôtel de Bourgogne.* In this theatre, after competing with the Italians and struggling with the *Confrérie,* the first important native company headed by Valleran Lecomte established itself. Performing the tragi-comedies written especially for them by the prolific Alexandre Hardy and featuring three celebrated comedians, Gros-Guillaume, Gaultier-Garguille, and Turlupin, the King's Men, as the troupe now called itself, prospered. About 1625 a new group called the Players of the Prince of Orange appeared at the *Bourgogne.* France's first famous tragedian, Mondory (Guillaume Desgilberts, 1594-1651), as well as the skillful comedian Jodelet (Julien Geoffrin Bedeau, 1600-1660) belonged to this troupe. Mondory and his fellow actors established themselves at the *Théâtre du Marais* as the second important company in Paris.

During the next years these two troupes entertained Paris. Mondory, who played heroic figures with tremendous vocal and physical exertion, achieved distinction by introducing the plays of Corneille. In the attack inspired by Cardinal Richelieu against Corneille's disregard for the classical unities in the popular *Le Cid,* opponents of the writer credited the success of the play to Mondory's histrionic virtues. Richelieu himself favored Mondory and his troupe, which had employed the parents of the famous Michel Baron. In 1636, however, Mondory's strenuous performance took its toll; while playing the role of Herod, he was struck by an apoplectic fit that paralyzed his tongue.

At the rival *Hôtel de Bourgogne,* which acquired Corneille's plays and the best actors of the *Marais* at Mondory's retirement, Bellerose (Pierre Le Messier, d. 1670) and Montfleury (Zacharie Jacob, 1608-1667) inaugurated an affected, flamboyant, and bombastic style that became the prevailing manner. It was said of Bellerose that he was "an affected actor, who looked where he was putting his hat for fear of spoiling the feathers." The stout Montfleury was heavily satirized by Molière in his *L'Impromptu de Versailles* and ordered from the stage because of his artificiality by the eccentric Cyrano de Bergerac.

While Montfleury was ranting tragic verse at the *Hôtel de Bourgogne* and the comedian Jodelet was providing the city with farce at the *Marais,* Molière was mastering the essentials of acting with the theatrical Béjart family. Years of hard apprenticeship in Paris and in the provinces with this troupe, *L'Illustre Théâtre,* and careful study of Italian comedy perfected Molière's literary and histrionic talents. In 1658 he triumphed before Louis XIV. At the *Petit-Bourbon* and later at Richelieu's old *Palais Royal* his company became the first troupe of France.

Apart from the tremendous interest and controversy aroused by Molière's many plays, people flocked to see the excellent ensemble acting of his group. In addition to the skillful artistry of Molière himself, they could see Charles Varlet La Grange (1639-1692), the invaluable record keeper, playing young lovers; Philbert Gassot Du Croisy (1626-1695) creating Tartuffe; the intelligent Madeleine Béjart (1618-1672); the lovely Armande Béjart (1640-1700), who became Molière's wife; and later the talented young Michel Baron. A contemporary noted of the performance of *L'Ecole des femmes*: "Never was a comedy so well performed or with so much art. Each actor knows how many steps he has to take, and his every glance is counted." *The Impromptu at Versailles,* in which Molière satirized the actors of the competing *Hôtel de Bourgogne,* with the exception of the excellent Floridor (Josias de Soulas, 1608-1671), preserves for us Molière as *régisseur,* instructing his company, warning them against the excessive and unnatural, stressing the ability of the actors to present characters quite opposed to their own personality, and outlining the little details with which they could build their characterizations.

His protégé, the vain, handsome Michel Baron, became France's first great tragedian. After Molière's death he acted at the *Hôtel de Bourgogne* with Mlle. Marie Champsmeslé (1642-1698), who had been trained by Racine. Baron was the first to break the hold of the artificial and unnatural in tragic acting as practiced by Montfleury. At the height of his powers in 1691 Baron retired from the stage to reappear in 1720—still the leading natural actor of the day.

In 1680 Louis XIV created the *Théâtre Français* by ordering the amalgamation of the *Bourgogne* with the old Molière troupe, which had been kept intact by Armande Molière and La Grange. On the foundation of Molière's veteran company the *Théâtre Français* commenced the longest continuous history of any national theatrical institution. France had what no other country had— a permanent company of actors. Despite occasional nepotism or squabbles over position and power, the *Comédie Française* was a house essentially run by actors on a democratic basis, with the major actors, the *sociétaires,* sharing the responsibilities and the fortunes of the theatre.

From 1680 to the French Revolution the story of acting in France is the story of the *Comédie Française*. Every actor of importance made his mark in the *Comédie;* every histrionic contribution could be traced to its portals. Stability and a continuous tradition had disadvantages as well as advantages. A particular style, whether good or bad, could be perpetuated; innovation had to struggle for acceptance. Yet the *Comédie,* mindful of its critical audiences, set a standard that made it the theatre *par excellence.*

Michel Baron's reformation of tragic acting vanished with his retirement in 1691, and Pierre Trochon de Beaubourg (c. 1662-1725), who succeeded to his roles, revived the turgidity of Mondory and Montfleury. Beaubourg's leading lady was Mlle. Duclos (Marie-Anne de Chateauneuf, 1668-1736), who substituted exaggeration for the tragic power of her teacher, Mlle. Champmeslé. Chanting declamation characterized tragic acting in France as it did in England during the eighteenth century. Beaubourg's excesses were eventually replaced by the overrefined manner of Abraham Alexis Quinault-Dufresne (1693-1767), who, Clairon said, succeeded because of the "extreme beauty of his person and his voice."

To the hothouse atmosphere of the *Comédie* with its resplendent, inaccurate costumes and its finely intoned declamations that had little meaning or point beyond their show of skill, Adrienne Lecouvreur (1692-1730) brought in 1717 a personal, brilliant artistry based, in the eyes of contemporaries, on nature. Like Baron, who came out of retirement to act with her, Lecouvreur was eulogized for introducing simple, noble, natural speech and banishing chanting. In one of her rare statements about her art, she wrote a friend: "You say that you would like me to teach you the art of declamation of which you stand in need. You have forgotten that I do not declaim. The simplicity of my acting is my one poor merit; but this simplicity, which chance has turned to my advantage, appears to me indispensable to a man in your profession. The first requisite is intelligence, and that you have; the next, to allow beneficent nature to do her work. To speak with grace, nobility and simplicity, and to reserve all your energies for an argument, are what you will say and do better than any man." Voltaire penned an address spoken at the *Théâtre* on the occasion of her death in which he wrote that she "almost invented the art of speaking to the heart, and of showing feeling and truth where formerly had been shown little but artificiality and declamation." This great actress, like others before her, was buried at night without services.

Contemporary contrasts of Baron and Lecouvreur suggest that Baron was the Macklin of his day and Lecouvreur the Garrick. Baron was the originator who pushed farthest toward natural acting; Lecouvreur tempered style and declamation with human warmth and emotion. It was written of her: "She avoided the swellings, but she never descended below the grandeur of the heroic. She was simple, if you wish, because nature has something easy which approaches simplicity, but not simple like Baron. The basis of her playing was natural, she rejected all that could appear exaggerated, affected, ambitious, but she did not refuse it a certain ornament capable of rendering action more brilliant and more majestic...."

Admiration for Lecouvreur, who acted in Voltaire's (1694-1778) tragedies, may have stimulated him (as did his stay in England) to propel French actors of the mid-eighteenth century toward a more fiery style, one that had "the devil in the flesh" (*le diable au corps*). To his activities the *Théâtre* owed not only its higher standards, the removal of spectators from the stage, and the improved status of actors, but also three brilliant players. Not a little of the impetuosity of Mlle. Marie-Françoise Dumesnil, who played in his tragedies, was the result of his training. Descriptions of her remind one of Kean. "Her play is good only where she had to show passion and fury." Her passionate emotionalism was seen to advantage in the new lachrymose drama (la comédie larmoyante) of La Chaussée and others.

If Dumesnil had Voltaire's "le diable au corps," Mlle. Clairon had the manner and the polish which Voltaire also inculcated. While Dumesnil left all to temperament and to natural inclination, with the cry that dramatic art was reality, Clairon, insisting on the fiction of art, arranged her effects by conscious study and technique. Mlle. Gaussin (1711-1767), an older tragedienne predicted that Clairon "will become a great actress, but she will never make anyone cry."

The third celebrated artist formed under the influence of Voltaire was the great Lekain (Henri Louis Cain, 1728-1778). Tutored by Voltaire from his youth, Lekain labored with tenacious perseverance to master the art of acting. In vocal skill, in judicious silences as well as in reformation of costuming, Lekain presaged the day of Talma, whose tribute to Lekain appears in the following pages. Yet Lekain belonged in his own era—the finest exponent of the Voltaire school.

The middle of the eighteenth century saw the Comédie at its height—Dumesnil, Clairon, and Lekain in tragedy; François René Molé (1734-1802) in pathetic sentimental comedy; Préville (Pierre Louis Dubus), 1721-1799), the original creator of Beaumarchais' Figaro, with his human, witty, comic art; and Mlle. Marie Anne Botot Dangeville (1714-1796) as the charming soubrette. By 1778 when Voltaire was crowned at the Théâtre, the atmosphere was changing; the old actors were retiring; court intrigue and royal censorship were usurping the democratic rights of the Comédie actors and writers. The social corruption which led to the Revolution was felt in the Comédie Française.

François–Joseph Talma, the next great actor to emerge from the historic Théâtre, was a revolutionary in politics and art. Influenced by English acting and Shakespearean romanticism, he came to the theatre with ideals of human characterization. A product of the School of Elocution (later the Conservatoire) established to train the future actors of the Comédie, Talma's first triumph came in Joseph Chénier's republican play Charles IX. After struggling with some of the reactionary sociétaires, Talma led a revolt from the Théâtre Français and established a theatre of his own, where amidst political chaos he carried out his reforms in costuming and staging. In 1799 French theatrical unity was restored by the reunion of the Comédie Française and Talma troupe. Under Napoleon, his friend and admirer, Talma's mature artistry prospered, but the actor who would have been the perfect romantic player died before French romanticism produced a play worthy of him. His theatrical reforms and his intense, truthful acting were wasted on outmoded dramas; he died regretting that he had never had a real human being to portray.

Romanticism in the theatre entered with éclat in 1830 in the production of Victor Hugo's Hernani. Sensational as the first performance was, with its gala, eccentrically clad audience of romantic poets, the play itself was performed somewhat reluctantly by old-line players like Mlle. Mars (Ann Françoise Hyppolite Boutet, 1779-1847), who, until the age of sixty, remained an ingénue. The romantics, despite all the clamor, did not revolutionize the Théâtre Français. It was the pat, well-made prose comedies and dramas of the vaudeville writer Eugène

[149]

Scribe that were played most frequently in the first half of the nineteenth century. In the type of play which Scribe originated, the character actors Joseph Isidore Samson and François Joseph Régnier (1807-1885) perfected a refined manner reflecting middle-class life.

The title role in Scribe's historical drama *Adrienne Lecouvreur* will long be remembered as the creation of the unique Rachel (Eliza Felix, 1821-1858). A street-singer in her impoverished youth, she became the reigning queen at the *Comédie Française* for fifteen years. Trained by Joseph Isidore Samson (1793-1871), an excellent teacher to whom she returned again and again for guidance, Rachel revived the classical repertoire of the *Comédie*. Her eloquent diction, her magnificent grace, and her penetrating interpretations, especially of the heroines of Racine, marked her as the greatest actress of the French stage. George Henry Lewes, the English actor and critic, eulogized her in these words: "Rachel was a panther of the stage; with a panther's terrible beauty and undulating grace she moved, and stood, glared and sprang. There always seemed something not human about her. She seemed made of different clay from her fellows—beautiful but not lovable. Those who never saw Edmund Kean may form a very good conception of him if they have seen Rachel. She was very much as a woman what he was as a man. If he was a lion, she was a panther." Lewes' description is only one of many stirring tributes to Rachel's magnificent subtle artistry. Her contemporaries, the poets and dramatists Alfred de Musset, Théophile Gautier, Gabriel Legouvé, all wrote of her power and brilliance. Rachel herself has left no detailed record of her artistic methods. On her deathbed, however, she summarized her credo in these brief words: "In studying for the stage, take my word for it, declamation and gesture are of little avail. You have to think and weep."

During the nineteenth century new theatres arose to challenge the monolithic *Comédie*. At the *Odéon,* which became the second government theatre, and at the Boulevard theatres, like the *Porte-Saint-Martin,* the romantic and melodramatic plays of Hugo and Dumas *père* were performed by actresses like Mlle. George (Marguerite Joséphine Weimer, 1787-1868) and Mlle. Marie Dorval (Marie-Thomase Amelie Delaunay, 1798-1849). Bocage (Pierre Martinien Tousez, 1801-1862) played the passionate heroes. Eduard Devrient, the German actor, described Bocage's intense naturalness even in the handling of the "furniture of the scene." Frédéric Lemaître (1800-1876) was, however, the romantic actor *par excellence*. Unlike the *Comédie* actors, who limited themselves to particular roles, Lemaître was exceedingly versatile. Having failed the *Conservatoire* examinations, he trained himself with the pantomime players immortalized by Jean-Baptiste Gaspard Deburau (1796-1846), who was the Pierrot at the *Théâtre des Funambules.* At the *Ambigu-Comique,* Lemaître created the famous role of Robert Macaire in the melodrama *L'Auberge des Adrets.* From that time he was the most popular actor in Paris, playing in the dramas of the Romantics. Victor Hugo, in whose plays Lemaître had triumphed, paid tribute to the actor in these words spoken at the death of Lemaître: "There is in the history of the stage a line, a family as it were, of mighty, unique spirits, who follow each other in succession, and whose privilege it is to reveal to the multitude, to bring to life on the stage, the great figures created by the poets. This proud line begins with Thespis, is continued through Roscius, and comes to us in France with Talma. In our century Frédéric

Lemaître has brilliantly carried on the great succession. He is the last of these great actors in point of time, the first in honor. No actor has ever been his peer, because, in the nature of things, none *could* be his peer. Those others, his predecessors, represented . . . what are called Heroes, what are called Gods. He, thanks to the age in which he was born, was *the People* . . . was untameable, robust, pathetic, stormy, fascinating as the people. He was Tragedy and Comedy alike. Hence his universal power. . . ."

The thesis plays of Dumas *fils,* the passionate morality of Emile Augier, and the dramas of intrigue and historical pageantry of Victorien Sardou constituted the theatrical fare in the middle of the nineteenth century. With them are associated the great idols of the French stage. Sarah Bernhardt, from her first successes at the *Odéon* in the romantic dramas of Hugo and Coppée in the 1860's until World War I, was undisputed queen of the French stage. Her personal beauty and magnetism, her magnificent *voix d'or,* and her calculated technique intrigued international audiences. From 1860 to 1909 Coquelin *ainé* breathed life into the great French comic tradition, playing the *valets de Molière,* Beaumarchais' Figaro, and reincarnating Cyrano de Bergerac in Rostand's play. Like Bernhardt he was in and out of the *Comédie Française,* touring widely and directing his own theatres. On Coquelin's death, Lucien Guitry (1860-1925), who played his first successes at the *Théâtre de la Renaissance* and was famed for studied restraint, became France's most versatile actor. The comic brilliance of Gabrielle Réjane (1857-1920) and the tragic nobility of Jean Mounet-Sully (1841-1916), like the artistry of Bernhardt and Coquelin, stemmed from both the traditionalism of the *Comédie Française* and the commercialism of the Boulevard theatres.

These idols had little to offer the followers of Ibsen and Zola who wanted to free the theatre from artificiality, no matter how brilliant, to make it a scientific instrument and a social tribune. How André Antoine, an unknown clerk in a gas company, created a theatre to answer these new revolutionary needs has often been told. Drawing his ideas from the *lambeau d' existence* of Zola, the synthesis of Wagner and the ensemble of the Duke of Saxe-Meiningen, Antoine pioneered the first great experimental theatre at the turn of the century. In addition to giving a home to the naturalistic plays of Zola and Hauptmann, the reformist dramas of Brieux, and the psychological plays of François de Curel, he brought a "slice of life"—real and frequently sordid life—onto the stage. He broke completely with the declamatory tradition of French histrionics; the illusion of the theatre was rejected in favor of absolute fidelity to life—low voices, colloquial tones, turned backs and complete loss of self in the characterization. With Antoine, naturalism found its theatrical expression.

The *Théâtre Libre* inspired movements in France and throughout the world, but some of the groups that took heart from Antoine's success, such as Paul Fort's *Théâtre d'Art,* opposed naturalism with symbolist ideals drawn from Mallarmé and Verlaine. It is curious that almost hand in hand with the triumph of naturalism, in France as elsewhere, went the growth of poetic, formalistic, and obviously "theatrical" theatres. Aurelie François Lugné-Pöe, (1869-1940), an actor from Antoine's company, together with the symbolist dramatist Maeterlinck, took over the work of the *Théâtre d'Art,* when they founded the *Théâtre de l'Oeuvre* to produce those non-naturalistic, symbolic works of such great naturalists as Ibsen and Hauptmann, as well as the plays of Leo Tolstoy, D'Annunzio,

ACTORS ON ACTING

Synge and Kaiser. It was in his theatre that the shocking but seminal *Ubu Roi* of Alfred Jarry was first performed in 1896.

In 1913, Jacques Copeau, dramatist and critic, inculcated his disciples, among them Louis Jouvet and Charles Dullin, with the necessity of restoring beauty to the theatre. In the spirit of Molière, he created the *Théâtre du Vieux Colombier*. In 1921, Dullin organized the *Atelier* devoted to "pure theatre," where his dedication to intensive work on diction, gesture, and basic breathing rhythms became an inspiration to leading actors. Louis Jouvet went from the *Vieux Colombier* to direct, design and act the plays of Jules Romains, Jean Giraudoux, and others at the *Comédie des Champs-Elysées,* and later at his own *Théâtre Athénée.*

Gaston Baty (1885-1952), influenced by the work of Russian and German innovators, created a theatre of devices in which actors and writers were subordinated to the manager's imaginative control. Baty, Jouvet, and Dullin, together with Georges Pitoëff (1886-1939), who produced and acted Pirandello, Shaw, and Andreyev, formed a *Cartel des Quatre* in 1926 to consolidate their common ideals and aspirations in opposition to the commercial theatres.

Out of the nineteen twenties came the playful magician Jean Cocteau, who gave expression to facets of French surrealism in his plays and productions. The "unique phenomenon" of the thirties was Antonin Artaud, stage and screen actor, poet and dreamer. During the decade he published a series of essays on his conception of a "Theatre of Cruelty" in which he rejected western morality and rationalism in favor of primitive magic and a histrionic language, inspired by the East, of gestures, postures, sounds, and breathing rhythms. His redefinition of theatre as a shocking plague intended to reveal to man his metaphysical reality became one of the most dynamic influences in the post-World War II period in France and the other major western theatre centers.

Disciples of these major pre-World War II figures held the important positions in the French theatre of the forties, fifties, and sixties. Jean-Louis Barrault, a student of Dullin and friend of Artaud, sought a "Total Theatre" in which vocal patterns and body rhythms could express the varied images of Claudel, Gide, Ionesco as well as the traditional insights of Racine, Molière and Marivaux. A notable mime, whose work recalls the *commedia dell' arte* influence in France, Barrault has been director of his own *Théâtre Marigny* and of the state *Théâtre de France,* the *Odéon.*

Jean Vilar (b. 1910), also a disciple of Dullin, has been a distinguished actor as well as director. During his reign the *Théâtre National Populaire* in Paris and at its summer home in Avignon celebrated the "collective ceremony" of theatre. Two distinguished actors, Georges Wilson and the late Gérard Philipe, have been associated with Vilar's theatres, Wilson having succeeded him as head of T.N.P.

Tradition and revolt have shaped the life of the French stage. Innovators have broken with the classical *Comédie Française.* They have started theatres of their own; later they have turned to the films. Eventually, however, the fresh spirit of revolt has been absorbed by the traditional *Comédie* and the *Odéon.* For example, Antoine and his disciple, Firmin Gémier, who lead important revolts, were appointed stage directors of the House of Molière. Each generation in the French theatre enriches the present by repossessing the past.

French actors with typical Gallic rationality have been lucid and articulate about their art, although it is also the Frenchman Artaud who has tried to destroy rationality with images of man's inner violence. From Molière's *Impromptu* through the writings of Clairon, Dumesnil, Talma, Coquelin, Jouvet, and Barrault, they have discussed acting with insight and imagination. The classical quality of the spoken word in French dramatic art has undoubtedly sharpened the actors' consciousness of the problem of nature and artifice in acting. The dichotomy between natural emotional expression and controlled artistry and the dualism of the actor as creator and creation have probably been expressed best in the words of the great French actors. It is noteworthy that France is the home of the extreme emotionalist attitude, stated in Sainte-Albine's *Le Comédien,* and of the most absolute statement of the antiemotionalist position, voiced by Denis Diderot in *Le Paradoxe sur le comédien.*

THE COMEDIANS OF THE HOTEL DE BOURGOGNE

The *Hôtel de Bourgogne,* the first theatre in Paris, was the home of the three celebrated *farceurs,* Gros-Guillaume (Robert Guérin, d. 1634), Gaultier-Garguille (Hughes Guéru, 1573-1633) and Turlupin (Henri Lagrand, 1587-1637). In serious plays they were known as Lafleur, Flechelles, and Belleville. Gros-Guillaume had directed a troupe of his own at the *Hôtel de Bourgogne* shortly before the celebrated *Gelosi* company possessed the theatre in 1604. Later these three actors became part of Valleran Lecomte's company, which in 1610 established itself at the *Hôtel de Bourgogne.* They were the major attraction of this first important native company in Paris.

Although the Lecomte group performed the many plays written for them by Alexandre Hardy, they specialized in popular farces. The playing of comedians at the *Hôtel de Bourgogne* and the antics of entertainers and mountebanks at fairs was not clearly differentiated. In their farcical art all of them had clear antecedents in the medieval *sotties.* Their style was coarse, exaggerated, robust and, above all, extremely popular.

Gros-Guillaume, the oldest of the three comedians, was, as his comic name implies, enormously fat. His costume emphasized his girth. A master of grotesque ridicule, he would cover his face with flour which he would blow at his fellow players. Turlupin, red-haired and handsome, wore a mask like the *commedia dell' arte* comedians. He played the comic servant or valet beloved on both the French and Italian stages. Gaultier-Garguille, a thin mimicking player, wore a beard, a mask topped by grey hair, spectacles that had no lenses, and black clothes. These three *farceurs,* who bridged the transition from roving comics and mountebanks to established professional actors, were the most popular French artists in the early part of the seventeenth century.

Three Farceurs

How magnificent is this stage,
How inventive are these actors!
And what preservative against melancholy!

"Inscriptions from Picture Representing Performance at *Hôtel de Bourgogne*" (c. 1610) quoted in Karl Mantzius: *A History of Theatrical Art in Ancient and Modern Times,* translated by Louise von Cossel. New York: Peter Smith, 1937, Volume II, The Middle Ages and the Renaissance, p. 197.

[153]

There they stand in a droll posture
Deriding the bad times,
And charm all the listeners
With a single word.

Here the ingenious Guillaume,
Mimicking a courtier,
Tucked up like a tennis-player,
Amuses himself with abusing love.

Here Turlupin in his awkward way
Tries to pick a pocket,
And the Spaniard, for fear of the shock.
Flies from the Frenchman who is looking at him.

But the true Gaultier surpasses them,
And in spite of the rigor of fate,
He makes us laugh after his death
At the recollection of his grimace.

MOLIÈRE

(1622 - 1673)

It is not mere reverence which has dubbed the *Théâtre Français* the House of Molière. The French theatre owes more of its inspiration and excellence to Molière than to any other single person. Of his literary creativeness which brought to the growing French stage a gallery of magnificent characters, penetrating social insight, and high comic artistry, this is not the place to speak. His contributions to histrionic art and to stage practice alone would earn him an important position in the history of French theatre.

Molière, born Jean Baptiste Poquelin, was the son of an upholsterer attached to the court of Louis XIII. Although he practiced his father's work for a time, Molière received a good education at the College de Clermont, where he was befriended by such people as the Prince de Conti and the poet Cyrano de Bergerac. He studied law, but he had long loved the theatre and eventually became part of an amateur group called *Les Enfants de Famille,* the theatre of the Béjart family. Under Denys Beys and the comedian Du Parc, called Gros-René, the group tried to establish itself professionally using the name *L'Illustre Théâtre.* After vain attempts to capture the theatrical audience of Paris, where Molière (who had now changed his name in order not to disgrace his parents) made his debut in 1644, the group went to the provinces. During twelve years of struggle on the road, Molière played heroic parts which were not his forte. Most important, however, these years brought Molière forth as a comic writer and actor of great originality. In his early work he was strongly influenced by the Italian *commedia dell' arte.* Tiberio Fiorilli, the creater of *Scaramouche,* was said to have been Molière's model and teacher.

By 1658 the Molière group (for he had assumed the artistic leadership of the company) was brought to play before the court of Louis XIV. The actors captivated the brilliant audience with Molière's brief farce *Le Médecin amoureux.* Their performance won them the right to share the use of the theatre in the *Petit-Bourbon* with an Italian company and the privilege of calling themselves the *Troupe de Monsieur* after the King's brother.

Then followed the years of triumph, first at the *Petit-Bourbon,* then at the *Palais Royal,* Richelieu's extravagant theatre which had fallen into disuse. Success was not realized without struggle and controversy. Moliére's marriage to the charming, beautiful young Armande Béjart, who created the delightful young women in his plays, caused him suffering through jealousy and gossip. Armande was the younger sister of Madeleine Béjart, the intelligent actress-manager who had been Molière's mistress in the early days of *L'Illustre Théâtre.* Molière's enemies particularly Montfleury of the *Bourgogne,* circulated stories to the effect that Armande was Madeleine's daughter. Molière's penetrating attacks on the faults of the aristocracy and against hypocrisy earned him much ill will. The prosperity of his company, which in 1665 was under the King's direct protection, aggravated the enmity of the actors of the *Hôtel de Bourgogne.*

A war of the two theatres originated with the tremendous success of Molière's *L'Ecole des femmes* in 1662. The attacks made upon this play caused Molière to strike back in *Critique de l' Ecole des femmes.* But the fight had just begun. The *Hôtel de Bourgogne* retaliated with *The Painter's Portrait* or *Counter-critique of the School of Wives.* At the request of the King, Molière dramatically flayed his critics in *L'Impromptu de Versailles* in 1663.

This little play, seen in its context as part of a battle between the *Hôtel de Bourgogne* and the King's Troupe of Molière, reveals Molière's activities as a director in addition to indicating his criticism of the bombastic style of the *Bourgogne* actors. The *dramatis personae* of the *Impromptu* are the actual members of Molière's company, and the success of the piece depended in part on Molière's wonderful ability to mimic the florid manner of the rival actors. In his earlier play *Les Précieuses ridicules* Molière had indicated the faults of the *Bourgogne* tragedians in these sarcastic lines: "... they alone are capable of doing justice to plays; the rest are ignorant persons who recite their parts just as they talk, and do not know how to make the verses tell, or to pause at a fine passage; how can people know the fine passages if the actor does not emphasize them, and thereby indicate that a burst of applause is expected?" Molière's emphasis on natural delivery led him, Karl Mantzius pointed out, to develop a "system of notation" to train his pupils in proper accentuation. Baron especially is said to have utilized Molière's method in perfecting the natural speech for which he became celebrated.

Although the *Impromptu* was Molière's last blow in the controversy, the *Bourgogne* actors continued their attacks. Their *L'Impromptu de l'Hôtel de Condé,* written by the son of Montfleury, who had been the target of Molière's attack on the *Bourgogne,* caricatured Molière's failure as a tragic actor. The sorties continued, but they did not change the theatrical scene. The *Bourgogne* remained the house of tragedy, Molière's *Palais Royal* the home of comedy, and the old *Marais Théâtre* trailed along as best it could.

Molière went on with the controversial *Tartuffe, Don Juan, Le Misanthrope, L'Avare, Les Femmes savantes,* and *Le Malade imaginaire.* During a performance of the hypochondriac in the latter play, Molière had a seizure and died a few hours later. Victim of the common fate of French actors, this great artist was buried at

ACTORS ON ACTING

night with meager religious service. But thousands walked by torchlight to accompany the beloved comedian to his grave.

The Impromptu at Versailles

MLLE. BEJART: ...since you were ordered to work on the subject of the criticism that is passed on you, why not write that comedy of actors that you have talked about so long?[1] It was a readymade notion, and would have come quite pat; the more so, as, having undertaken to delineate you [in *The Painter's Portrait*] they gave you an opportunity to delineate them; it might have been called their portrait, far more justly than all their productions can be called yours. For, to try to mimic a comedian in a comic part is not to describe himself, but only after him the characters he represents, and making use of the same touches, and the same hues which he is obliged to employ in the various ridiculous characters that he draws from nature. But to mimic an actor in serious parts is to describe him by faults which are entirely his own, since characters of this kind do not carry either the gestures or ridiculous tones by which the actor is recognized.

MOLIÈRE: It is true; but I have my reasons for not doing it; between ourselves, I do not think it would be worth the trouble; and, besides, I should want more time to work out the idea. As their days for acting are the same as our own,[2] I have hardly seen them three or four times since we have been in Paris; I have caught nothing of their style of delivery, but what was at once apparent to the eye; I should have to study them more, to make my portraits very like them.[3]

MLLE. DUPARC: I must say I have recognized some of them in your imitations.

* * * *

MLLE. DEBRIE: Give me a specimen as you have given it to others.

MOLIÈRE: We have no time now.

MLLE. DEBRIE: Just a word or two!

MOLIÈRE: I thought of a comedy in which there should have been a poet, whose part I would have taken myself, coming to offer a piece to a strolling company fresh from the provinces. "Have you actors and actresses," he was to say, "capable of doing justice to a play? For my play is a play...." "Oh sir," the comedians were to answer, "we have ladies and gentlemen who have passed muster wherever we have been." "And who plays the kings amongst you?" "There is an actor who sometimes undertakes it." "Who? That well-made young man? Surely you jest. You want a king who is very fat, and as big

---

The Impromptu at Versailles (1663) in *The Dramatic Works of Molière*, rendered into English by Henri Van Laun. Edinburgh: William Paterson, 1875, Volume II, pp. 300-306.
[1]See *L'Ecole des Femmes* in which the character Dorante suggests: "It would be amusing to put them [the actors] on the stage, with their learned antics and ridiculous refinements . . ."

[2]The comedians of the *Hôtel de Bourgogne* played on the same days as Molière's company, Tuesdays, Fridays, and Sundays.
[3]The *Bourgogne*, which had been satirizing Molière, had had no better opportunity of studying him, than he of studying them.

[156]

as four men. A king, by Jove, well stuffed out. A king of vast circumference, who could fill a throne handsomely.[4] Only fancy a well-made king! There is one great fault to begin with; but let me hear him recite a dozen lines." Then the actor should repeat for example, some lines of the king in *Nicomède* ... in the most natural manner he could. Then the poet:—"What? Call you that reciting? You are joking. You should say things with an emphasis. Listen to me." [He imitates Montfleury] "Do you see this attitude? Observe that well. There, lay the proper stress on the last line; that is what elicits approbation, and makes the public applaud you." "But, sir," the actor was to answer, "methinks a King who is conversing alone with the captain of his guards talks a little more mildly, and hardly uses this demoniacal tone." "You do not understand it. Go and speak in your way, and see if you get an atom of applause." On which an actor and actress should have played a scene together—that of Camilla and Curiatius [Corneille's *Les Horaces*] ... like the other, as naturally as they could. And the poet would break out: "You are joking; that is good for nothing. This is how to recite it".... [Imitating Mme. de Beauchateau, an actress of the *Hôtel de de Bourgogne*] "See how natural and impassioned this is. Admire the smiling face she maintains in the deepest affliction." There, that was my idea; and my poet should have run through all the actors in the same manner.

MLLE. DEBRIE: I like the notion; and I recognized some of them by the very first lines. Do go on.

MOLIÈRE: [Imitating Beauchâteau in some lines from the *Cid*] "Pierced to the center of my heart...." And do you know this man...? [Imitating Hauteroche, a comedian of the *Hôtel de Bourgogne*] ....

MLLE. DEBRIE: I think I know him a little.

MOLIERÈ: And this one? [Imitating de Villiers, another comedian] ....

MLLE. DEBRIE: Yes, I know who he is; but I fancy there are some amongst them whom you would find it hard to mimic.

MOLIÈRE: Good Heavens! there is not one that cannot be had somewhere, if I had studied them well.[5] But you make me lose precious time.... As to you Mademoiselle ...

MLLE. DUPARC: Nay, as to me, I shall act wretchedly; I do not know why you have given me this ceremonious part.

MOLIÈRE: Good Heavens! Mademoiselle, that is what you said when you had your part in *The School for Wives Criticized;* yet you acquitted yourself admirably, and everyone agreed that it could not be better done. Believe me, this will be the same; you will play it better than you think.

MLLE. DUPARC: How can that be? There is no one in the world less ceremonious than I.

MOLIÈRE: True; and that is how you prove yourself to be an excellent actress, representing well a character which is opposed to your mood. Try then, all of you, to catch the spirit of your parts aright, and to imagine that you are

---

[4] An allusion to Montfleury, who was very stout, and of whom one of his contemporaries said: "He is so fat, that it takes several days to give him a sound beating."

---

[5] The only actor of the *Hôtel de Bourgogne* whom Molière does not imitate is Floridor, who was an excellent actor.

what you represent. [To Du Croisy] You play a poet, and you ought to be taken up with your part; to mark the pedantic air which is maintained amidst the converse of the fashionable world; that sententious voice and precision of pronunciation, dwelling on every syllable, and not letting a letter drop from the strictest spelling. [To Brécourt] As for you, you play a courtier, as you have already done in *The School for Wives Criticized;* that is, you must assume a sedate air, and a natural tone of voice, and gesticulate as little as possible. [To La Grange] As for you, I have nothing to say to you. [To Mademoiselle Béjart] You represent one of those women who, provided they are not making love, think everything else is permitted to them; who are always proudly entrenched in their prudery, looking up and down on everyone, holding all the good qualities that others possess as nothing in comparison with a miserable honor which no one cares about. Keep this character always before your eyes, that you may show all its tricks. [To Mademoiselle Debrie] As for you, you play one of those women who think they are the most virtuous persons in the world, so long as they save appearances; who believe that the sin lies only in the scandal; who would quietly carry on their intrigues in the style of an honorable attachment, and call those friends whom others call lovers. [To Mademoiselle Molière] You play the same character as in *The School for Wives Criticized,* and I have nothing more to say to you than to Mademoiselle Duparc. [To Mademoiselle Du Croisy] As for you, you represent one of those people who are sweetly charitable to every one, who always give a passing sting with their tongues, and who would be very sorry if they let their neighbors be well spoken of. I believe you will not acquit yourself badly in this part. [To Mademoiselle Hervé] For you, you are the maid of the *précieuse,* who is always putting her spoke into the conversation, and picks up all her mistress's expressions, as well as she can. I tell you all your characters, that you may impress them strongly on your minds. Let us now begin to rehearse, and see how it will do....

MICHEL BARON

(1653 - 1729)

The most celebrated of Molière's disciples was France's first great tragic artist, Michel Baron. Baron was the child of actors who had been in Mondory's company at the *Marais.* Orphaned at an early age, Baron became a member of a company called Little Actors of the Dauphin, started by Raisin, inventor of the mechanical spinet. Baron became the star of the children's players when the group was continued by the widow Raisin. In 1666 they appeared at Molière's theatre, the *Palais Royal,* where Molière first became interested in the young Baron and trained him in the principles of natural acting which he advocated.

In 1670, after Baron had been in the provinces, Molière invited the young Baron to return to his troupe, and he was soon given a share in the company. Although his forte was tragedy, at Molière's death he studied comic parts in an effort to keep the theatre going. The next season, however, he left the Molière troupe

—then in the hands of La Grange—to join the *Hôtel de Bourgogne,* which was the undisputed house of tragedy.

At the *Bourgogne* he became the greatest actor of the French stage. He succeeded in dislodging the singsong bombast or overly sweet recitative with his natural speech and human emotion, in accordance with the ideals of Molière. At the *Bourgogne* he played opposite the celebrated Mlle. Marie Champmeslé, who was trained by Racine himself.

Baron was an extraordinarily vain and erratic person. At the height of his fame, in 1691, he retired from the stage. His personal triumphs did not influence fellow-actors, for after his departure from the stage, bombast returned with his successor Beaubourg and artificial over-refinement with Quinault-Dufresne. A revival of natural acting came with the first successes of Adrienne Lecouvreur in 1717. Possibly awakened by her example, Baron, after thirty years' retirement, returned to the stage to play opposite her. In spite of his long inactivity, Baron did not appear old-fashioned. He was once again the foremost natural player of his time. Charles Collé, writing of Baron in his *Journal historique* said: "Before he entered the stage he used to work himself up by soliloquizing or whispering to the actor entering with him, and by this means he *was* the character he represented from the very first words he uttered."

The "new style" of acting seen in Baron's performances was the constant talk of the Parisian stage. This is apparent in the following letter of Luigi Riccoboni's wife, Elena, who was called the Isabella Andreini of her time and was also a talented authoress. In speech and gesture, as well as in the portrayal of emotions, Baron was a thoroughgoing reformer. He once declared: "The rules prohibit the lifting of the arms above the head, but if passion carries them there it is right. Passion knows better than the rules."

Contemporary accounts intimate that he sometimes went beyond the decorum deemed necessary in poetic tragedy. One contemporary, quoted by Georges Monval in *Lettres de Adrienne Lecouvreur,* described Baron's art as an attempt to "reduce the gravity of the cothurnus and the majesty of kings, to bring them near the ordinary usage of other men; to render them . . . a little more popular, to remove from voice, gesture, and pronunciation, a certain magnificence that one may suppose in the personage of kings. . . ." In this endeavor to bring high tragedy within the compass of contemporary human emotion, Baron anticipated Talma and the actors of the nineteenth century.

My Opinion of Michel Baron

by Elena Riccoboni

To the honor you have shown me in asking my opinion about the manner of M. Baron, now that he has reappeared on the stage, I reply by letter, first of all

Elena Riccoboni: Letter to Abbé Conti, quoted by Karl Mantzius: *A History of Theatrical Art in Ancient and Modern Times.* New York: Peter Smith, 1937, Volume IV, Molière and his Times; The Theatre in France in the Seventeenth Century, pp. 240-243.

in order to prevent all the concoctions, which in such cases are produced in Paris, and the accusations of saying what I have not said, and secondly in order to be instructed by your profound knowledge in a question in which I might easily be mistaken. I confess that when, before he had appeared on the stage, one part of the Parisian public wanted him to be hissed, the other to be violently applauded, some asserting that he would not please with his old manner, others that he would gain the highest approval, I confess, I say, that I conceived the most ardent desire to hear this excellent man. But when, after the first day of his appearance before the public, I learned that he did not follow the present manner, or resume his earlier manner, but introduced an entirely new one, not hitherto known on your tragic stage, that is to say that he *speaks* and does not *declaim,* then my desire to become acquainted with him increased. At last I found for once an opportunity of leaving my occupations.

In my opinion M. Baron, generally speaking, is an excellent actor. He always listens to his fellow-actors, a thing to which actors, as a rule, pay little heed, and his attention is accompanied by such movements of face and body as are required by the nature of the speeches to which he listens. When speaking, his talk is real conversation. For instance, in *Polyeucte,* where he speaks of the first persecution of the Christians, or in *Les Horaces,* the first scene with Curiatius, which is nothing but a friendly interchange of polite speeches, he conversed with the most delicate naturalness, without falling into any excesses, either of exaggeration to sublimity or of too realistic imitation.

For the rest—be it said with all the respect due to the reputation of so great a man—I certainly always thought the style of M. Baron true and natural; but just as nature is not always beautiful, and every truth is not suitable for the stage, so at times he does not appear to me to be in harmony with the subject. It is indisputable that the tragic hero, in so far as he is a human being must not alienate himself from nature; but certainly it is also true that the great actions and high lineage or position of tragic heroes require a naturally majestic and dignified manner....

I have noticed that M. Baron frequently changes his bearing and allows himself to be carried away by the necessity of laying stress on his verses or the hero's feelings, or of keeping up a situation, and that on these occasions he declaims like the others, and cries out as loud as he can. This necessity makes him appear as an actor with different phases, now sublime and now commonplace, which jars on my ear, as in the same scene and the same actor I seem to hear a tragic Horace and a comic Dorante.

How can it be maintained that Mithridate, in informing his sons of his resolution to go to Rome and make war on its inhabitants, should speak with the same nonchalance and the same cool, everyday tone, as if he were telling them of some entirely indifferent matter? This was how Baron did it....

M. Baron says—and with many of his spectators this is a merit—that he tries by every means to avoid the rhyme. I myself commend him for it, but I cannot admit that a tragic actor, in attempting to disguise the rhyme, ought also to do his best to efface the verse by levelling it to such a degree, and by adopting the tone of the most commonplace talk.

FRANCE

DENIS DIDEROT
(1713 - 1784)

The rising bourgeoisie of France in the eighteenth century found a spokesman in the versatile philosopher Denis Diderot. Son of a tradesman, he received his education at a Jesuit School. He led a bohemian life in Paris, supporting himself by his pen. One of his early writings landed him in prison. In 1748 a bookseller suggested that Diderot elaborate an English encyclopedia into a larger French work, and thus began twenty years in which Diderot labored on the *Encyclopédie* which embodied the most advanced ideas of his day.

Apart from his prodigious work on the *Encyclopédie,* to which Voltaire and Montesquieu contributed, Diderot wrote scientific essays, criticism, philosophy, novels, and dramas. Ideologically, he was a confirmed materialist and naturalist. His original plays, although not very successful, established the *drame bourgeois* which anticipated the reforms of the nineteenth century. In his criticism he advocated that classical tragedy be replaced by a serious drama of everyday bourgeois life written in prose rather than verse.

Diderot's ideas on acting, formulated in his celebrated brochure *Le Paradoxe sur le comédien (The Paradox of Acting),* were part of his broader thinking on the theatre. In a dogmatic manner he insisted that the actor must be devoid of sensibility. The genesis of his brochure is interesting and harks back to the emotionalist work of Pierre Rémond de Sainte-Albine, *Le Comédien* (1747), which advocated sensibility as an essential of the actor's art. *Le Comédien* was translated into English (*The Actor*) by John Hill, whose work was then re-adapted into French by Antonio Fabio Sticotti in 1769 as *Garrick ou les acteurs Anglais.* Sticotti's version provoked Diderot's anti-emotionalist pamphlet written in 1773. It is interesting to note that Luigi Riccoboni's son, Francesco Antonio Riccoboni, anticipated Diderot's stand in his *L'Art du théâtre* (1750). Not without influence on Diderot was his acquaintance with Garrick when the latter visited Paris in the winter of 1764-65. Diderot greatly admired Garrick, as did Grimm, Diderot's literary associate. They were impressed by Garrick's ability to sit in a drawing room and entertain friends by letting his face run through the gamut of emotions without feeling anything himself. Garrick became for Diderot the prime illustration of his principle. The monograph on Declamation in Diderot's *Encyclopédie,* written by Jean-François Marmontel, playwright and lover of Mlle. Clairon, was said to have been based on Garrick's artistry.

Diderot's *Paradoxe* became the source of a long-standing quarrel between the emotionalists and anti-emotionalists. Toward the end of the nineteenth century Henry Irving, representing the emotionalists, and the elder Coquelin, who ranged himself with Diderot, continued the dispute. Their debate precipitated William Archer's *Masks or Faces?,* a study of emotionalism in acting.

Although the *Paradoxe* is extreme, it nevertheless is a suggestive work that raises and discusses a number of important questions concerning histrionic art. In the excerpts which follow, Diderot's position is represented by the First Speaker.

The Paradox of Acting

THE FIRST.

... But the important point on which your author[1] and I are entirely at variance concerns the qualities above all necessary to a great actor. In my view he must have a deal of judgment. He must have in himself an unmoved and disinterested onlooker. He must have, consequently, penetration and no sensibility; the art of mimicking everything, or, which comes to the same thing, the same aptitude for every sort of character and part.

THE SECOND.

No sensibility?

THE FIRST.

None. I have not yet arranged my ideas logically, and you must let me tell them to you as they come to me, with the same want of order that marks your friend's book. If the actor were full, really full, of feeling, how could he play the same part twice running with the same spirit and success? Full of fire at the first performance, he would be worn out and cold as marble at the third. But take it that he is an attentive mimic and thoughtful disciple of nature, then the first time he comes on the stage as Augustus, Cinna, Orosmanes, Agamemnon, or Mahomet, faithful copying of himself and the effects he has arrived at, and constantly observing human nature, will so prevail that his acting, far from losing in force, will gather strength with the new observations he will make from time to time. He will increase or moderate his effects, and you will be more and more pleased with him. If he is himself while he is playing, how is he to stop being himself? If he wants to stop being himself, how is he to catch just the point where he is to stay his hand?

What confirms me in this view is the unequal acting of players who play from the heart. From them you must expect no unity. Their playing is alternately strong and feeble, fiery and cold, dull and sublime. Tomorrow they will miss the point they have excelled in today; and to make up for it will excel in some passage where last time they failed. On the other hand, the actor who plays from thought, from study of human nature, from constant imitation of some ideal type, from imagination, from memory, will be one and the same at all performances, will be always at his best mark; he has considered, combined, learnt and arranged the whole thing in his head; his diction is neither monotonous nor dissonant. His passion has a definite course—it has bursts, and it has reactions; it has a beginning, a middle, and an end. The accents are the same, the positions are the same, the movements are the same; if there is any difference between two performances, the latter is generally the better. He will be invariable; a looking glass, as it were, ready to reflect realities, and to reflect them ever with the same precision, the same strength, and the same truth. Like the poet he will dip for ever into the inexhaustible treasure-house of Nature, instead of coming very soon to an end of his own poor resources.

What acting was ever more perfect than Clairon's? Think over this, study it;

Denis Diderot: *The Paradox of Acting* (c. 1773), translated by Walter Herries Pollock. London: Chatto Windus, 1883, pp. 6-25, *passim.*, 60-65 *passim.*, 108.

---

[1] The first sketch of the *Paradox* was addressed *à propos* of Antonio Fabio Sticotti's *Garrick, ou les acteurs Anglais*.

and you will find that at the sixth performance of a given part she has every detail of her acting by heart, just as much as every word of her part. Doubtless she has imagined a type, and to conform to this type has been her first thought; doubtless she has chosen for her purpose the highest, the greatest, the most perfect type her imagination could compass. This type, however, which she has borrowed from history, or created as who should create some vast spectre in her own mind, is not herself. Were it indeed bounded by her own dimensions, how paltry, how feeble would be her playing! When, by dint of hard work, she has got as near as she can to this idea, the thing is done; to preserve the same nearness is a mere matter of memory and practice. If you were with her while she studied her part how many times you would cry out, That is right! and how many times she would answer You are wrong!...

I have no doubt that Clairon goes through ... struggles ... but once the struggle is over, once she has reached the height she has given to her spectre, she has herself well in hand, she repeats her efforts without emotion. As it will happen in dreams, her head touches the clouds, her hands stretch to grasp the horizon on both sides; she is the informing soul of a huge figure, which is her outward casing, and in which her efforts have enclosed her. As she lies careless and still on a sofa with folded arms and closed eyes she can, following her memory's dream, hear herself, see herself, judge herself, and judge also the effects she will produce. In such a vision she has a double personality; that of the little Clairon and of the great Agrippina.

THE SECOND.

According to you the likest thing to an actor, whether on the boards or at his private studies, is a group of children who play at ghosts in a graveyard at dead of night, armed with a white sheet on the end of a broomstick, and sending forth from its shelter hollow groans to frighten wayfarers.

THE FIRST.

Just so, indeed. Now with Dumesnil it is a different matter: she is not like Clairon. She comes on the stage without knowing what she is going to say; half the time she does not know what she is saying: but she has one sublime moment. And pray, why should the actor be different from the poet, the painter, the orator, the musician? It is not in the stress of the first burst that characteristic traits come out; it is in moments of stillness and self-command; in moments entirely unexpected. Who can tell whence these traits have their being? They are a sort of inspiration. They come when the man of genius is hovering between nature and his sketch of it, and keeping a watchful eye on both. The beauty of inspiration, the chance hits of which his work is full, and of which the sudden appearance startles himself, have an importance, a success, a sureness very different from that belonging to the first fling. Cool reflection must bring the fury of enthusiasm to its bearings.

The extravagant creature who loses his self-control has no hold on us; this is gained by the man who is self-controlled. The great poets, especially the great dramatic poets, keep a keen watch on what is going on, both in the physical and the moral world....

They dart on everything which strikes their imagination; they make, as it were, a collection of such things. And from these collections, made all unconsciously, issue the grandest achievements of their work.

Your fiery, extravagant, sensitive fellow, is for ever on the boards; he acts the play, but he gets nothing out of it. It is in him that the man of genius finds his model. Great poets, great actors, and, I may add, all great copyists of Nature, in whatever art, beings gifted with fine imagination, with broad judgment, with exquisite tact, with a sure touch of taste, are the least sensitive of all creatures. They are too apt for too many things, too busy with observing, considering, and reproducing, to have their inmost hearts affected with any liveliness. To me such an one always has his portfolio spread before him and his pencil in his fingers.

It is we who feel; it is they who watch, study, and give us the result. And then ... well, why should I not say it? Sensibility is by no means the distinguishing mark of a great genius. He will have, let us say, an abstract love of justice, but he will not be moved to temper it with mercy. It is the head, not the heart, which works in and for him. Let some unforeseen opportunity arise, the man of sensibility will lose it; he will never be a great king, a great minister, a great commander, a great advocate, a great physician. Fill the front of a theatre with tearful creatures, but I will none of them on the boards. Think of women, again. They are miles beyond us in sensibility; there is no sort of comparison between their passion and ours. But as much as we are below them in action, so much are they below us in imitation. If a man who is really manly drops a tear, it touches us more nearly than a storm of weeping from a woman. In the great play, the play of the world, the play to which I am constantly recurring, the stage is held by the fiery souls, and the pit is filled with men of genius. The actors are in other words madmen; the spectators, whose business it is to paint their madness, are sages. And it is they who discern with a ready eye the absurdity of the motley crowd, who reproduce it for you, and who make you laugh both at the unhappy models who have bored you to death and at yourself. It is they who watch you, and who give you the mirth-moving picture of the tiresome wretch and of your own anguish in his clutches.

You may prove this to demonstration, and a great actor will decline to acknowledge it; it is his own secret. A middling actor or a novice is sure to contradict you flatly; and of some others it may be said that they believe they feel, just as it has been said of some pious people that they believe they believe; and that without faith in the one case and without sensibility in the other there is no health.

This is all very well, you may reply; but what of these touching and sorrowful accents that are drawn from the very depth of a mother's heart and that shake her whole being? Are these not the result of true feeling? Are these not the very inspiration of despair? Most certainly not. The proof is that they are all planned; that they are part of a system of declamation; that, raised or lowered by the twentieth part of a quarter of a tone, they would ring false; that they are in subjection to a law of unity; that, as in harmony, they are arranged in chords and discords; that laborious study is needed to give them completeness; that they are the elements necessary to the solving of a given problem; that, to hit the right mark once, they have been practiced a hundred times; and that, despite all this practice, they are yet found wanting. Look you, before he cries *"Zaïre vous pleurez,"* or *"Vous y ferez ma fille,"* the actor has listened over and over again to his own voice. At the very moment when he touches your heart he is listening to his own voice; his talent depends not, as you think, upon feeling, but upon rendering so exactly the outward signs of feeling, that you fall into the trap. He has rehearsed to himself every note of his passion. He has learnt before a mirror every particle of his despair. He knows exactly when he must produce his handkerchief and shed tears; and you will see him weep at the word, at the syllable, he has chosen, not a second sooner or later, The broken voice, the half-uttered words, the stifled or prolonged notes of agony, the trembling limbs, the fainting, the bursts of fury—all this is pure mimicry, lessons carefully learned, the grimacing of sorrow, the magnificent aping which the actor remembers long after his first study of it, of which he was perfectly conscious when he first put it before the public, and which leaves him, luckily for the poet, the spectator, and himself, a full freedom of mind. Like other gymnastics, it taxes only his bodily strength. He puts off the sock or the buskin; his voice is gone; he is tired; he changes his dress, or he goes to bed; and he feels neither trouble, nor sorrow, nor depression, nor weariness of soul. All these emotions he has given to you. The actor is tired, you are unhappy; he has had exertion without feeling, you feeling without exertion. Were it otherwise the player's lot would be the most wretched on earth: but he is not the person he represents; he plays it, and plays it so well that you think he is the person; the deception is all on your side; he knows well enough that he is not the person.

For diverse modes of feeling arranged in concert to obtain the greatest effect, scored orchestrally, played *piano* and played *forte,* harmonized to make an individual effect—all that to me is food for laughter. I hold to my point, and I tell you this: Extreme sensibility makes middling actors; middling sensibility makes the ruck of bad actors; in complete absence of sensibility is the possibility of a sublime actor. The player's tears come from his brain, the sensitive being's from his heart; the sensitive being's soul gives unmeasured trouble to his brain; the player's brain gives sometimes a touch of trouble to his soul: he weeps as might weep an unbelieving priest preaching of the Passion; as a seducer might weep at the feet of a woman whom he does not love, but on whom he would impose; like a beggar in the street or at the door of a church—a beggar who substitutes insult for vain appeal; or like a courtesan who has no heart, and who abandons herself in your arms.

Have you ever thought on the difference between the tears raised by a tragedy of real life and those raised by a touching narrative? You hear a fine piece of recitation; by little and little your thoughts are involved, your heart is touched, and your tears flow. With the tragedy of real life the thing, the feeling and the effect, are all one; your heart is reached at once, you utter a cry, your head swims, and the tears flow. These tears come of a sudden, the others by degrees. And here is the superiority of a true effect of nature over a well-planned scene. It does at one stroke what the scene leads up to by degrees, but it is far more difficult to reproduce its effect; one incident ill given would shatter it. Accents are more easily mimicked than actions, but actions go straighter to the mark. This is the basis of a canon to which I believe there is no exception. If you would avoid coldness you must complete your effect by action and not by talk.

So, then, have you no objection to make? Ah! I see! You give a recitation in a drawing room; your feelings are stirred; your voice fails you, you burst into tears. You have, as you say, felt, and felt deeply. Quite so; but had you made up your mind to that? Not at all. Yet you were carried away, you surprised and touched your hearers, you made a great hit. All this is true enough. But now transfer your easy tone, your simple expression, your everyday bearing, to the stage, and, I assure you, you will be paltry and weak. You may cry to your heart's content, and the audience will only laugh. It will be the tragedy outside a booth at a fair. Do you suppose that the dialogue of Corneille, of Racine, of Voltaire, or, let me add, of Shakespeare, can be given with your ordinary voice and with your fireside tone? No; not a bit more than you would tell a fireside story with the open-mouthed emphasis fit for the boards.

THE SECOND.

Perhaps Racine and Corneille, great names as they are, did nothing of account.

THE FIRST.

Oh, blasphemy! Who could dare to say it? Who to endorse it? The merest word Corneille wrote cannot be given in everyday tone.

But, to go back, it must have happened to you a hundred times that at the end of your recitation, in the very midst of the agitation and emotion you have caused in your drawingroom audience, a fresh guest has entered, and wanted to hear you again. You find it impossible, you are weary to the soul. Sensibility, fire, tears, all have left you. Why does not the actor feel the same exhaustion? Because there is a world of difference between the interests excited by a flattering tale and by your fellow-man's misfortune. Are you Cinna? Have you ever been Cleopatra, Mérope, Agrippina? Are these same personages on the stage ever historical per-sonages? Not at all. They are the vain images of poetry. No, not even that. They are the phantoms fashioned from this or that poet's special fantasy. They are well enough on the stage, these hippogriffs, so to call them, with their actions, their bear-ing, their intonations. They would make but a sorry figure in history; they would raise laughter in society. People would whisper to each other, "Is this fellow mad? Where in the world does this Don Quixote come from? Who is the inventor of all this stuff? In what world do people talk like this?"

THE SECOND.

And why are they not intolerable on the stage?

THE FIRST.

Because there is such a thing as stage convention. As old a writer as Aeschylus laid this down as a formula—it is a protocol three thousand years old.

THE SECOND.

And will this protocol go on much longer?

THE FIRST.

That I cannot tell you. All I know is that one gets further away from it as one gets nearer to one's own time and country....

* * * *

...Reflect a little as to what, in the language of the theatre, is being true. Is it showing things as they are in nature? Certainly not. Were it so the true would be the commonplace. What, then, is truth for stage purposes? It is the conforming of action, diction, face, voice, movement, and gesture, to an ideal type invented by the poet, and frequently enhanced by the player. That is the strange part of it. This type not only influences the tone, it alters the actor's very walk and bearing. And hence it is that the player in private and the player on the boards are two personages, so different that one can scarce recognize the player in private. The first time I saw Mlle. Clairon in her own house I exclaimed, by a natural impulse, "Ah, mademoiselle, I thought you were at least a head taller!"

An unhappy, a really unhappy woman, may weep and fail to touch you; worse than that, some trivial disfigurement in her may incline you to laughter; the accent which is apt to her is to your ears dissonant and vexatious; a movement which is habitual to her makes her grief show ignobly and sulkily to you; almost all the vio-lent passions lend themselves to grimaces which a tasteless artist will copy but too faithfully, and which a great actor will avoid. In the very whirlwind of passion we would have a man preserve his manly dignity. And what is the effect of this heroic effort? To give relief and temperance to sorrow. We would have this heroine fall with a becoming grace, that hero die like a gladiator of old in the midst of the arena to the applause of the circus, with a noble grace, with a fine and picturesque attitude. And who will execute this design of ours? The athlete who is mastered by pain, shattered by his own sensibility, or the athlete who is trained, who has self-control, who, as he breathes his last sigh, remembers the lessons of the gymnasium? Neither the gladiator of old nor the great actor dies as people die in their beds; it is for them to show us another sort of death, a death to move us; and the critical spectator will feel that the bare truth, the unadorned fact, would seem despicable and out of harmony with the poetry of the rest.

Not, mark you, that Nature unadorned has not her moments of sublimity; but I fancy that if there is any one sure to give and preserve their sublimity it is the man who can feel it with his passion and his genius, and reproduce it with complete self-possession.

I will not, however, deny that there is a kind of acquired or factitious sensibility; but if you would like to know what I think about it, I hold it to be nearly as dangerous as natural sensibility. By little and little it leads the actor into mannerism and monotony. It is an element opposed to the variety of a great actor's functions. He must often strip it from him; and it is only a head of iron which can make such a self-abnegation. Besides, it is far better for the ease and success of his study, for the catholicity of his talent and the perfection of his playing, that there should be no need of this strange parting of self from self. Its extreme difficulty, confining each actor to one single line, leads perforce to a numerous company, where every part is ill played; unless, indeed, the natural order of things is reversed, and the pieces are made for the actors. To my thinking the actors, on the contrary, ought to be made for the pieces.

THE SECOND.

But if a crowd of people collected in the street by some catastrophe begin of a sudden, and each in his own way, and without any concert, to exhibit a natural sensibility, they will give you a magnificent show, and display you a thousand types, valuable for sculpture, music, and poetry.

THE FIRST.

True enough. But will this show compare with one which is the result of a prearranged plan, with the harmony which the artist will put into it when he transfers it from the public way to his stage or canvas? If you say it will, then I shall make you this answer: What is this boasted magic of art if it only consists in spoiling what both nature and chance have done better than art? Do you deny that one can improve on nature? Have you never, by way of praising a woman, said she is as lovely as one of Raphael's Madonnas? Have you never cried, on seeing a fine landscape, "It's as good as a description in a novel?" Again, you are talking to me of a reality. I am talking to you of an imitation. You are talking to me of a passing moment in Nature. I am talking to you of a work of Art, planned and composed —a work which is built up by degrees, and which lasts. Take now each of these actors; change the scene in the street as you do on the boards, and show me your personages left successively to themselves, two by two or three by three. Leave them to their own swing; make them full masters of their actions; and you will see what a monstrous discord will result. You will get over this by making them rehearse together. Quite so. And then goodbye to their natural sensibility; and so much the better.

* * * *

Garrick will put his head between two folding doors, and in the course of five or six seconds his expression will change successively from wild delight to temperate pleasure, from this to tranquility, from tranquility to surprise, from surprise to blank astonishment, from that to sorrow, from sorrow to the air of one overwhelmed, from that to fright, from fright to horror, from horror to despair, and thence will go up again to the point from which he started. Can his soul have experienced all these feelings, and played this kind of scale in concert with his face? I don't believe it, nor do you. If you ask this famous man, who in himself is as well worth a visit to England as the ruins of Rome are worth a visit to Italy; if you ask him, I say, for the scene of the pastry cook's Boy, he will play it for you; if you ask him directly afterwards for the great scene in *Hamlet* he would play it for you. He was as ready to cry over the tarts in the gutter as to follow the course of the air-drawn dagger.[2] Can one laugh or cry at will? One shall make a show of doing so as well or ill as one can, and the completeness of the illusion varies as one is or is not Garrick.

* * * *

I take thee to witness, Roscius of England, celebrated Garrick; thee, who by the unanimous consent of all existing nations art held for the greatest actor they have known! Now render homage to truth. Hast thou not told me that, despite thy depth of feeling, thy action would be weak if, whatever passion or character thou hadst to render, thou couldst not raise thyself by the power of thought to the grandeur of a Homeric shape with which thou foughtest to identify thyself? When I replied that it was not then from thine own type thou didst play, confess thine answer. Didst not avow avoiding this with care, and say that thy playing was astounding only because thou didst constantly exhibit a creature of the imagination which was not thyself?

THE SECOND.

A great actor's soul is formed of the subtle element with which a certain philosopher filled space, an element neither cold nor hot, heavy nor light, which affects no definite shape, and, capable of assuming all, keeps none.

THE FIRST.

A great actor is neither a pianoforte, nor a harp, nor a spinet, nor a violin, nor a violoncello; he has no key peculiar to him; he takes the key and the tone fit for his part of the score, and he can take up any. I put a high value on the talent of a great actor; he is a rare being—as rare as, and perhaps greater than, a poet.

He who in society makes it his object, and unluckily has the skill, to please every one, is nothing, has nothing that belongs to him, nothing to distinguish him, to delight some and weary others. He is always talking, and always talking well; he is an adulator by profession, he is a great courtier, he is a great actor.

THE SECOND.

A great courtier, accustomed since he first drew breath to play the part of a most ingenious puppet, takes every kind of shape at the pull of the string in his master's hands.

---

[2] Confuses *Hamlet* and *Macbeth*.

FRANCE

THE FIRST.

A great actor is also a most ingenious puppet, and his strings are held by the poet, who at each line indicates the true form he must take.

THE SECOND.

So then a courtier, an actor, who can take only one form, however beautiful, however attractive it may be, are a couple of wretched pasteboard figures?

THE FIRST.

I have no thought of calumniating a profession I like and esteem—I mean, the actor's. I should be in despair if a misunderstanding of my observations cast a shade of contempt on men of a rare talent and a true usefulness, on the scourges of absurdity and vice, on the most eloquent preachers of honesty and virtue, on the rod which the man of genius wields to chastise knaves and fools. But look around you, and you will see that people of never-failing gaiety have neither great faults nor great merits; that as a rule people who lay themselves out to be agreeable are frivolous people, without any sound principle; and that those who, like certain persons who mix in our society, have no character, excel in playing all.

Has not the actor a father, a mother, a wife, children, brothers, sisters, acquaintances, friends, a mistress? If he were endowed with that exquisite sensibility which people regard as the thing principally needed for his profession, harassed and struck like us with an infinity of troubles in quick succession, which sometimes wither and sometimes tear our hearts, how many days would he have left to devote to our amusement? Mighty few. The Groom of the Chambers would vainly interpose his sovereignty, the actor's state would often make him answer, "My lord, I cannot laugh today," or, "It is over cares other than Agamemnon's that I would weep." It is not known, however, that the troubles of life, common to actors as to us, and far more opposed to the free exercise of their calling, often interrupt them.

In society, unless they are buffoons, I find them polished, caustic, and cold; proud, light of behavior, spendthrifts, self-interested; struck rather by our absurdities than touched by our misfortunes; masters of themselves at the spectacle of an untoward incident or the recital of a pathetic story; isolated, vagabonds, at the command of the great; little conduct, no friends, scarce any of those holy and tender ties which associate us in the pains and pleasures of another, who in turn shares our own. I have often seen an actor laugh off the stage; I do not remember to have ever seen one weep. What do they, then, with this sensibility that they arrogate and that people grant them? Do they leave it on the stage at their exit, to take it up again at their next entrance?

What makes them slip on the sock or the buskin? Want of education, poverty, a libertine spirit. The stage is a resource, never a choice. Never did actor become so from love of virtue, from desire to be useful in the world, or to serve his country or family; never from any of the honorable motives which might incline a right mind, a feeling heart, a sensitive soul, to so fine a profession.

*　　*　　*　　*

It has been said that actors have no character, because in playing all characters they lose that which Nature gave them, and they become false just as the doctor, the surgeon, and the butcher, become hardened. I fancy that here cause is confounded with effect, and that they are fit to play all characters because they have none.

But they say an actor is all the better for being excited, for being angry. I deny it. He is best when he imitates anger. Actors impress the public not when they are furious, but when they play fury well. In tribunals, in assemblies, everywhere where a man wishes to make himself master of others' minds, he feigns now anger, now fear, now pity, now love, to bring others into these diverse states of feeling. What passion itself fails to do, passion well imitated accomplishes.

HYPPOLITE CLAIRON

(1723-1803)

Mlle. Clairon (Claire Lérys) was a typical representative of the French stage in the mid-eighteenth century. Poor and unknown in origin, she made her way at the *Comédie Italienne* and then in the provinces. After playing secondary roles at the *Opéra,* she was given an opportunity to make her debut at the *Théâtre Français* through the influence of some of her lovers. Contrary to all expectations this twenty-year-old coquette triumphed in the great tragic role of Phèdre. Through deliberate effort she made herself the great lady of tragedy at the *Comédie Française.* Claire Lérys had become Claire Hyppolite Josèphe Léris de Latude Clairon.

She perfected the grand tragic manner both on and off the stage, preparing her roles with meticulous artistry. Her nobility and grandeur made her a favorite of Voltaire. Later in her career, influenced by her lover, the playwright Jean François Marmontel, and by occasional performances on smaller stages, she tempered her art with a simplicity which made her the delight of theatre connoisseurs. Oliver Goldsmith devoted an article in *The Bee* to her, saying, "Mademoiselle Clairon ... seems to me the most perfect female figure I have ever seen upon any stage."

For twenty-two years Clairon and her rival Mlle. Dumesnil were the leading actresses of the *Comédie Française.* They exemplified opposites—Dumesnil was the natural, erratic performer who could on occasion touch sublimity, and Clairon was the conscious artist, always satisfactory and decorous, but probably never striking the deepest emotional notes.

Clairon retired from the stage in retaliation for indignities she had suffered as a result of outside interference in the affairs of the theatre. Voltaire championed her action by writing, "I cannot blame an actress who prefers giving up her art to practicing it with shame."

During her retirement Clairon undertook to train dramatic aspirants, and in 1798 she wrote the *Memoirs* of her colorful life. In her *Memoirs,* parts of which follow, Clairon tried to provide a system of study for those whose talents were not equal to the creation of original styles. Her remarks are clearly organized, and her approach to acting avoids many of the pitfalls of the usual stylized gesture-books. Her discussion of technique is particularly interesting, for it seems to be a direct answer to the criticism of her made by Garrick. The volume elicited a defense of nature by her rival Dumesnil. We are fortunate in having a record of a discussion of their differences, which took place in 1787 between the two, now aged, actresses.

The exchange between the two actresses as well as Dumesnil's defense follow Clairon's reflections.

FRANCE
Reflections on Dramatic Art

It is the wish of many that I should write my sentiments relative to an art which I have long professed. It is supposed that the reflections I have made, in order to render myself supportable in the eyes of the public, may be of some use to those who are destined to pursue the same career. Perhaps the public, or, at least, the admirers of theatrical representations will contemplate with some degree of pleasure the road I have followed, in order to acquire their favor. But reflection and writing are two such different things: it appears so extraordinary to me to comprehend anything without the aid of physiognomy, gesture and speech; I am so diffident of myself, that I tremble as much in taking up the pen as I once did in appearing before the public.... Without any regular plan, perhaps without system, but certainly without vanity, I am about to trace what I deem necessary to the attainment of this art—an art much more difficult than it is generally supposed to be.

Enunciation: or The Management of the Voice

As it must be the chief object of the actress to be heard distinctly in all parts of the theatre, it is therefore an indispensable requisite that she should be possessed of a strong and sonorous voice.

In order that she may be enabled to give the necessary shade to the picture she means to represent, her voice must be clear, harmonious, flexible, and susceptible of every possible intonation.

A voice which is deficient in point of compass or expression can never be adequate to characters where the stronger passions are displayed....

Strength

A good constitution is a material point: there is no profession more fatiguing. Irritable nerves, weak lungs, or delicate constitutions, cannot long sustain the weight of tragic characters.

I have found, in the course of my time, a number of young authors and fine ladies who have thought that nothing was more easy than to perform Mahomet, Mérope, etc.; that the author had done all that was necessary; that to learn the parts, and to leave the rest to nature was all the actor had to do. Nature! How many use this word without knowing its meaning. The difference of sex, of age, of situation, of time, of countries, of manners and of customs demand different modes of expression. What infinite pains and study must it not require to make an actor forget his own character; to identify himself with every personage he represents; to acquire the faculty of representing love, hatred, ambition, and every passion of which human nature is susceptible,—every shade, every gradation by which these sentiments are depicted with their full extent of coloring and expression.

There are no arts or professions but have certain defined principles. Are there then none required to direct the tragedian? Is it only in the history of mankind he must obtain his information? Reading of itself would be nothing; he must meditate upon and render himself familiar with, what he reads ... he must adapt to every character the genius of the nation to which it belongs; he must reflect

Memoirs of Hyppolite Clairon, the celebrated French Actress: With Reflections Upon the Dramatic Art (1798), translated from the French. London: Printed for O. G. and J. Robinson, 1800, Volume I, pp. 33-36, 40-46, 56, 97-105.

without intermission; repeat a hundred and a hundred times the same thing, in order to surmount the difficulties he meets with at every step. It is not enough to study the character; he must study the history of it, in order to develop the intention of the author, feel the beauties of his composition and adapt his character to the general scope of the work: he must scrutinize the hearts of all connected with the scene, attend the relations they bear towards each other; and finally, he must be able to comprehend why what he hears, and what he sees, is so represented or expressed....

In addition to what I have said, the most arduous test is to be enumerated: it is the indispensable necessity of having one's mind continually impressed with events the most dreadful and terrible and with images of the most horrid nature. The actor who does not identify himself with the character he represents is like a scholar who repeats his lessons; but he who does so identify himself with the personage he is portraying—whose tears seem the effect of nature, who absorbs the idea of his own existence in the miseries of an assumed character; such a person must be wretched: and I maintain it requires a degree of strength almost beyond what human nature is endowed with to perform the characters of tragedy well for more than ten years.

* * * *

In recalling to mind my plan of study, I hope I shall be pardoned for observing that I have often smiled at the folly of those who have upbraided me for having recourse to art. Alas! What should I have been without it? Could I have personated Roxane, Amenaide, or Viriate? Should I be consistent if I was to apply my own feelings and habits to such characters? Doubtless not. How am I enabled to substitute the ideas, sentiments and feelings, which should distinguish those characters in lieu of my own? It is by art alone that it can be done: for if ever I have seemed to personate them in a manner purely natural, is is because my studies, joined to some happy gifts which I may have derived from nature, have conducted me to the perfection of art.

All men are not endowed with creative genius. I will endeavor to direct those who are inadequate to the pursuit of an original system of their own, and for that purpose will resume my examination.

[Memory and Exteriors, figure or appearance, are the two additional major qualities listed as necessary to an actor.]

* * * *

Dancing and Drawing

In order to be able to tread the stage with ease and grace, to give facility to the motions of the body, dignity to the whole appearance, and to prevent the acquirement of habits repugnant to nature, it is indispensably necessary that those who dedicate themselves to a theatrical profession should pay the utmost attention to the art of dancing. They must carefully avoid contracting the airs and manner of a dancing-master; but, in every other respect, a knowledge of the art is requisite.

It were to be wished that every actor should be more or less initiated in the art of drawing: they would thereby become more susceptible of the good effect of preserving proper distances; they would more easily discover the point of perspective, which is so important on the stage, both with respect to their figure and their dress. In pantomimic representations, or pieces calculated for show, the performers

[172]

who are to set off the principal personages are placed more advantageously, and are better adapted to fill up the picture with its proper shade or effect. Such actors as are unacquainted with this art, I advise to study the works of the most eminent painters and sculptors.

Music

Without pretending to acquire a fundamental knowledge of the science of music, it is, nevertheless, necessary for an actor to study its elements, in order to be enabled to form a proper judgment as to the extent of his voice, to render every intonation easy and familiar, to avoid discordance, to regulate his sounds, to preserve and vary them at pleasure, and to impart to every accent, whether vehement or plaintive, that degree of modulation which is necessary.

Without this study, it is almost impossible to play Corneille to advantage. He is either so sublime, or so familiar, that, unless the actor is perfectly sure of his intonation, he runs the risk of appearing bombastical or trivial.

Language, Geography, and Belles Lettres

The study of language is of more importance to an actor than any other. The theatre ought to be the school for foreigners, and of that part of the public who have neither time, nor the means of procuring proper masters, to learn the language of the country in its most perfect purity.

It is almost incredible, that persons who are selected to represent the *chef d'oeuvres* of the most eminent writers of the nation should be unacquainted with the difference between a long and a short syllable, or the distinction between the singular number and the plural; that they should confound the genders of the nouns; that they should scarce know the masculine from the feminine; and that provincial accents should destroy the grandeur and purity of our language. Such, however, is the case with reference to the greater part of our actors. He who is unacquainted with the extent and value of words can never comprehend the meaning of things: if he should stumble upon it, it is only by chance; and I am at a loss to conceive how the public can tolerate those who appear before them with such defects, or who betray such unpardonable ignorance.

It is impossible to read history, with any advantage or improvement, without a knowledge of geography. The right of judging of the merits of such authors as write for the theatre imposes upon an actor the necessity of acquiring every species of knowledge which may enable him to judge with accuracy, and to determine, by a single perusal, the merits of a work which the author has been a year composing. An intimate acquaintance with stage-effect and the rules of the theatre, an accurate ear, a good taste, a sound, discriminating, and attentive judgment, are not all that is required: it is necessary to be acquainted with mythology, history, geography, and language; he must be acquainted with every description of poetry, and the writings of every dramatic author, ancient or modern. He will then be enabled to judge whether an author has made the most of his subject; he will perceive how much has been drawn from the times, places, and characters of which he has written; in short, whether the author has shown a creative fancy, is a servile imitator, or a plagiarist. The approbation of the critic is no ways flattering, nor his censure any disgrace, unless he is known to possess those qualities necessary to enable him to form his judgment with accuracy. It is not enough to approve or reject a work; the man who does either, ought to show himself capable of judging. About two years before my retirement from the theatre, there was a league among certain authors to pay no attention whatever to the judgment of actors. This attempt to invalidate the opinions of a class of men, without whom the authors could be of no use, was as unjust as the pretence for it was false and groundless.

Unless a superior power destroys the right of the actors, it is impossible that any of them should ever consent to such an injustice and degradation. Corneille, Voltaire, and Racine, demanded no other tribunal: their works, however, unlike those of the present day, did not require the illusions of the theatre, or the talents of the actors. It has been said by authors, that the actors robbed them of the reward due to their exertions: the trifling recompense they received was, they said, a proof of it. I can state, in reply to this observation without the least fear of contradiction, that, with respect to the two and tweny years I have been upon the theatre, it is unfounded in truth....

MARIE-FRANCOISE DUMESNIL

(1713 - 1803)

Mlle. Dumesnil (Marie-Françoise Marchand), the rival of Clairon at the *Comédie Française,* like all the actors of the period, worked in the provinces before making her debut in Paris. In 1737 she appeared with great success at the *Théâtre Français* as Clytemnestra in Racine's *Iphigenia in Aulis.*

By 1740 she came under the influence of Voltaire, in many of whose plays she created the leading roles. According to Karl Mantzius, Voltaire trained Dumesnil for her role in his *Mérope.* He drove her to act with greater passion and fire until the actress cried out: "Really, one ought to have *le diable au corps* to strike the note you want." "Just so, mademoiselle," answered Voltaire, *"le diable au corps* in all art, if you want to attain perfection." This guidance, added to Dumesnil's naturally violent temperament, made her the ideal exponent of intuitive acting. Charles Collé said of her: "Mlle. Dumesnil ... in her acting is always good only in the violent parts of her characters, and I confess that in these passages she has more depth and warmth of feeling than Mlle. Lecouvreur. She rises higher than this famous actress. But how different in all the rest! Her play is good only where she has to show passion and fury. Otherwise no dignity, no nobility; love is badly rendered, pride only moderately well; she is often rhetorical.... But where she *is* good she is unsurpassed; she makes you forget all her faults and all her ungracefulness."

Her emotional force and natural insight made her triumphant in the plays of La Chaussée and Marmontel, who created the *comédie larmoyante,* the sentimental domestic plays patterned on English models. Later in her life, it is said, she keyed herself to impulsive, passionate acting by excessive drinking. In 1776 she retired from the stage.

In 1800 after Clairon had published her *Memoirs* in which she attacked the "reality" without "art" of Dumesnil, the latter authorized the publication of her own *Memoirs* as a reply to Clairon. She extolled nature above art and stressed the universality of tragic emotions. Naturalness, pathos, and emotional identification with one's role were the tenets of Dumesnil's art.

FRANCE

A Reply to "Reflections on Dramatic Art" of Clairon

As one may see, Citizeness Clairon begins—in her very title—to substitute pompousness for truth. Your art, Citizeness, is not at all *dramatic art;* it is *theatrical art.* The art of Corneille, Racine, Molière, and Voltaire is dramatic art. The distance between the art of creating and that of reciting is immeasurable. A writer who might publish reflections on the art of great men could only call them *reflections on the dramatic art;* nevertheless, his work would have nothing in common with the one you publish under the same title....

Citizeness Clairon indicates in her article the chief qualities necessary for those who wish to act in the theater: a resonant voice, excellent pronunciation, strength —that is, a good constitution—memory, and an attractive appearance. All writers who have dealt with the theatrical art have demanded the same prerequisites. Rémond de Sainte-Albine has expressed himself admirably in this respect, and everyone feels that these qualities are indispensable in order to follow the career of comedian with some hope of success.

* * * *

Yes, "Nature! How many use this word without knowing its meaning." It seems to me that you do not know its limits, and that you often confuse it with what belongs only to art. Has not every situation a special mode of expression, you ask. Undoubtedly not; but in general every situation has perhaps a different mode of expressing emotions. Yet last year I saw in the grain-market a frantic mother looking for her child who was lost, asking everybody about the child as she burst into tears and showed all the accents of despair. No actress has ever had more expressive, more moving, truer, and nobler gestures than this mother beside herself with grief. I even commented on it to one of my friends. "Have not differences of sex, of age, of situation, of time, of countries, of manners and of customs the greatest influence?" asks Citizeness Clairon. All of them have no more influence on the great traits of nature which feed the fire of tragedy: love, jealousy, revenge, ambition, maternal and filial love, than the various languages in which the tragedies are written. These great emotions are the same from pole to pole, because they enter into the make-up of man who is the handiwork of his Creator. To imbue oneself with great emotions, to feel them immediately and at will, to forget oneself in a twinkling of the eye in order to put oneself in the place of the character one wishes to represent—that is exclusively a gift of nature and beyond all the efforts of art. As for vain conventions, more or less quaint usages, more or less dissimilar customs, more or less foolish prejudices, more or less civil manners—all the handiwork of men and, like them, variable and flexible—rarely does a role demand that an actor accentuate these nuances. And if his role should demand it, this technique, completely within the province of art, is easily acquired provided that one has intelligence and physical advantages. But the sacred fire of great passions—alike in every individual of the human race—can only be lighted by the hands of nature.

Memoires de Marie-Françoise Dumesnil, en réponse anx memoires d'Hyppolite Clairon. . . . Paris, Dentu, 1800, pp. 3-27 *passim.* This selection translated by Joseph M. Bernstein.

[175]

"There are no arts or professions but have certain defined principles. Are there then none required to direct the tragedian?" What a sophism! The basis of theatrical art in tragedy is first of all—and we must insist on this: *"D'avoir reçu du ciel l'influence secrète."* [That one has received from heaven its secret influence.]

That is the source of pathos, of terror, and of one spontaneously forgetting oneself without any effort. It is a divine gift which can almost dispense with the beauties of art, as we have seen in more than one case.... It seems to me that the principles of theatrical art may be completely summed up as follows: Who am I *under all circumstances?* What am I in each scene? Where am I? What have I done, and what am I going to do? And these same questions must be applied to all those who are on the stage with me....

You have never been criticized for *having art*—one would be mad to do so. You have been criticized for not having enough art to make one forget your art—and for being all art. You have been criticized for always allowing the great actress to show through in your so *finished* style of acting. However perfect art may be, it can never absolutely replace nature.... It has been said that, despite all your advantages, you did not receive from nature that degree of feeling which makes art disappear. Indeed, that is something you have never succeeded in achieving, and it is this point of perfection that Dumesnil has always attained without the slightest effort. Nature, so prodigal on your behalf, refused you that deep and inner feeling which, when it explodes, suddenly causes even the outward semblances of acting to disappear and completes the theatrical illusion....

What basically constitutes a tragedian is the sense of pathos. Nature lavishly endowed Dumesnil with this sense, as it endowed Voltaire; but it refused to grant you that sense, even though you were given all the resources of art that come closest to nature. I shall explain what I mean by two examples. Whatever efforts you might have made, you would never have been capable of making audiences sob, of rending their souls, of making them shed torrents of tears, as Dumesnil did in the two scenes of *Iphigenia*—in which she was and always will be inimitable. Nor was she any less striking in her naturalness. Did you ever succeed in questioning little Joash in *Athalie* as did Dumesnil? What a marvel of simplicity, without her yielding one jot of the dignity of her rank! Her splendid naturalness would have seduced any other child but one inspired by God! How moving is the memory of those great scenes! You had too much wit and intelligence to refrain from applauding such perfection. Thus, you did not dare play Mérope, Athalie, Clytemnestra, and Semiramis during Dumesnil's absences. This must be said: Dumesnil disposed of our hearts at will, while you almost always evoked only our admiration. She was the most truly tragic actress who has ever appeared in any ancient or modern theatre; while you have been the finest academic model one could offer to young tragediennes. If nature had ·endowed them with the inestimable gift of pathos (for one does not learn how to feel), they would have found in that model the example of all the beauties of art joined together to the highest degree, and they would then have lacked nothing to aspire to perfection.

FRANCE
Fiction and Reality
Mlle. Dumesnil, Mlle. Clairon, François Joseph Talma, Henri Gourgaud Dugazon and Marie-Joseph Chénier[1]

MLLE. DUMESNIL: [*to Talma*] Of course, one must neither play, nor even represent. You are not to *play* Achilles, but to *create* him. You must not *represent* Montagu [Romeo], you must *be* him.

MLLE. CLAIRON: My dear, you labor under a great delusion. In theatrical art all is conventional, all is fiction. The poet obeys his own rules, so does the actor. Would they be obliged to do so if those rules were in the order of nature? When the gentleman there (pointing to Chénier[2]) makes Charles IX speak, he is neither that king, who did not always talk in verse, though he sometimes wrote poetry, nor is he himself, as he does not think like a feeble monarch, nor like a murderous despot. What is he then? A talented writer whose pliable imagination constructs events that have never taken place, and uses a language which is spoken by nobody. I may say almost the same of an actor. What am I when I act the part of the Queen of Carthage or the mother of Iphigenia? I am neither Clytemnestra nor Dido. I wear their dress in order to delude the senses, and I have the figure and face of a woman, which completes the illusion. But you must remember that what I want to produce is an illusion, and I do produce it, and that, however successful I may be in attaining my end, it can never be anything but play. Don't you hear them exclaim in the midst of their admiration, applause and enthusiasm: "What splendid acting!" So it is Mlle. Clairon, Mlle. Dumesnil, or M. Larive whom they applaud, not Dido or Clytemnestra. These princesses do not care for the bravos, but Racine and M. de Pompignan [author of the tragedy *Dido*] want them. And as for Mlle. Clairon, there was a time when she valued them highly, in the days when they were not wasted on mediocrity.

MLLE. DUMESNIL: It could not be better expressed, my dear friend, but it might be better done. To show intelligence is not all; everything depends on *doing* the right thing. I have a hundred times disproved what you said just now, though without having heard it. You know how—

MLLE. CLAIRON: Yes, you acted from nature. But there was much art in your naturalness.

MLLE. DUMESNIL: Not the least. I was full of my part, I felt it, I yielded myself up to it.

MLLE. CLAIRON: I have never understood how one could do without calculation.

Regnault-Warin: *Memoires historiques et critique sur F. J. Talma* (1827), pp. 240-252, quoted by Karl Mantzius: *A History of Theatrical Art in Ancient and Modern Times*, Volume V: The Great Actors of the Eighteenth Century. New York: Peter Smith, 1937, pp. 276-278.

---

[1]This discussion took place in 1787, when the two aged actresses met in the little theatre *Boule-Rouge*, where Talma was rehearsing his plays.

[2]Marie Joseph Chénier, the dramatist, who was at this time writing his tragedy *Charles IX*, which was to create the first success for both himself and Talma.

ACTORS ON ACTING

I should have been quite out of it if I had yielded myself up.

CHENIER: It seems to me, ladies, that you are both right, because each of you was in harmony with her character, her soul and her gifts.

DUGAZON: It is just like the authors who write poetics for their own works; when you have learned their rules you are not certain if they are right, but you are quite sure of the talent of their authors. The talent of Mlle. Dumesnil and Mlle. Clairon has never been disputed, and it is not the question of the present discussion. Nor is it our object to know whether dramatic art exists, as that is unquestionable, but whether in this art fiction or reality is to dominate.

MLLE. CLAIRON: Fiction.

MLLE. DUMESNIL: Reality....

FRANÇOIS-JOSEPH TALMA

(1763 - 1826)

Talma was a revolutionary in politics and art. He led the revolt against political reaction in the *Théâtre Français* and reformed histrionic art with principles of romanticism. He was the first actor to break completely with the past and pave the way for the triumph of romanticism and realism in the nineteenth century.

His father was a poor man who studied dentistry and then took his family to England, where Talma spent his youth. In London he participated in private theatrical performances given in the French colony. More important, he became acquainted with the English stage and with the work of Shakespeare. The freedom from artificiality of English acting and the robust romanticism of Shakespeare undoubtedly had a strong influence on Talma. When he returned to France, however, the young man followed his father's trade. He soon began his way toward a career on the stage by becoming a pupil at the School of Elocution, recently established as a training place for future *sociétaires* of the *Théâtre Français*. It is interesting to note that the future tragedian became the pupil of the comic artist Henri Gourgaud Dugazon (1746-1809), who taught Talma a good deal but probably allowed him to develop his own style without imposing on him the tragic manner of the *Comédie Française*.

In 1787 Talma made his debut as Seide in Voltaire's *Mahomet* and assumed his position as a minor actor in the celebrated company. He was prevented from playing major tragic roles, since these parts were in the hands of the senior *sociétaires* but even in minor parts Talma began to carry out some of his projected theatrical reforms. As the tribune Proculus in Voltaire's *Brutus* he provided himself with a costume that bore some historical resemblance to Roman dress. This reform in costume was probably influenced by the ideas of his friend, the revolutionary painter David.

Talma's great opportunity came when a leading actor refused to play in Joseph Chénier's revolutionary play *Charles IX*. Talma constructed his role by studying portraits and historical data in order to achieve a truthful picture of his character. His triumph in this role was short-lived, since the play was soon removed from the repertoire because its republican sentiments had caused demonstrations in the theatre. Most of the *sociétaires* of the *Comédie Française,* with the exception of Talma, Dugazon, and few others, were royalists. They refused to revive the play even when Deputy Mirabeau clamored for it. The play was later performed at Talma's insistence, but in turn he was dismissed from the theatre. At the order of the republican government and the populace Talma was reinstated, but several of the conservative members of the company, including Mlle. Raucourt (1756-1815), the leading tragedienne, refused to play with him. Finally Talma, Dugazon, and several of their followers left the *Comédie Française* to start a rival theatre of their own. The long-standing monopoly of the *Comédie Française* had been broken by the National Assembly's decree in 1791 giving every "citizen" the right to erect a theatre and to perform plays.

The new Talma group established itself as *Le Théâtre Français de la Rue de Richelieu* (later the *Thèâtre de la République*) in a theatre more beautiful than that of the *Comédie*. Here Talma embarked on his reforms. The two theatres carried on a bitter struggle, with Talma supporting the republican government and the *Comédie Française* siding with the aristocracy. During the political struggle the leading members of the *Comédie Française* were arrested. Scheduled to be guillotined, they were saved in a melodramatic manner by a theatre-lover employed in the Committee of Public Safety. Both playhouses were subjected to strict censorship. Finally in 1799 they were reunited as the *Comédie Française* in Talma's theatre at the Rue de Richelieu.

Under Napoleon, Talma reaped special honors and was taken by the Emperor to perform before the crowned heads of Europe. It is interesting to note that in 1812, while Napoleon was in the midst of his Russian campaign, he issued the Moscow decree regulating the organization of the *Comédie Française* and its training school, the *Conservatoire*.

In addition to the traditional repertoire, Talma played Jean François Ducis's diluted French versions of Shakespeare. The aged actor once complained to Victor Hugo, who was writing *Cromwell,* which Talma hoped to play, that he had never had a play suited to his abilities. "The actor is nothing without his part, and I have never had a real part . . . a figure that had the movement and variety of life, that was not all of a piece, that was at once tragic and everyday, at once a king, and a human being.—Did you ever see me as Charles IX? I made a great effect in that part with the words: *'Du pain! je veux du pain!'*—because they showed the King suffering, not merely as a King, but as a human being; the effect was tragic and it was true.... Truth! I have been seeking for truth all my life. But what good did it do?—I asked for Shakespeare and they gave me Ducis. Truth in the plays was unobtainable; I had to be content with putting it into the costumes. I played Marius with bare legs! —No one knows what I might have been if I had found the author I was seeking. As it is, I shall die without once having acted."

Talma substituted realistic accuracy and truth to nature for the dignity and repose of classical acting. A contemporary critic noted that his playing of Orestes was like that of a madman in an asylum and that he triumphed in the realistic presentation of passion and horror. He created no school of his own although he trained Mlle. Duchenois (Catherine Josephine Rafuin, c. 1777-1835), a temperamental emotional actress who played opposite him.

Talma's affectionate but incisive tribute to the artistry of his predecessor Lekain follows. It originally appeared as the preface to Lekain's *Memoirs.*

Grandeur Without Pomp

I have no pretension to be an author; all my studies have been directed towards my calling, the object of which is to afford at once pleasure and instruction. Tragedy and comedy, the one by the portraiture of virtue and crime, the other by the exposure of vice or folly, interest us, or make us laugh, while they correct and instruct. Associated with great authors, actors are to them more than translators. A translator adds nothing to the ideas of the author he translates. The actor, putting himself faithfully in the place of the personage he represents, should perfect the idea of the author of whom he is an interpreter. One of the greatest misfortunes of our art is, that it dies, as it were, with us, while all other artists leave behind them monuments of their works. The talent of the actor, when he has quitted the stage, exists no longer, except in the recollection of those who have seen and heard him. This consideration should impart additional weight to the writings, the reflections, and the lessons which great actors have left; and these writings may become still more useful if they are commented upon and discussed by actors who obtain celebrity in our day. Doubtless it is this motive which has induced the editors of the *Memoires Dramatiques* to request me to add to the notice of Lekain some reflections on his talent and on the art which he illustrated.

Lekain had no master. Every actor ought to be his own tutor. If he has not in himself the necessary faculties for expressing the passions, and painting characters, all the lessons in the world cannot give them to him. Genius is not acquired. This faculty of creating is born with us; but if the actor possesses it, the counsel of persons of taste may then guide him; and as there is in the art of reciting verse a part in some degree mechanical the lessons of an actor profoundly versed in his art may save him much study and time.

Lekain, from the commencement of his career, met with great success. His *début* lasted seventeen months. One day, after he had performed at Court, Louis XV said, "This man has made me weep — I, who never weep!" ...

The system of declamation then in vogue was a sort of sing-song psalmody, which had existed from the very birth of the theatre. Lekain—subjected, in spite of himself, to the influence of example—felt the necessity of breaking his shackles and the pedantic rules by which the theatre was bound. He dared to utter for the first time on the stage the true accents of nature. Filled with a strong and profound sensibility, and a burning and communicative energy, his action, at first impassioned and irregular, pleased the young, who were enchanted by the ardor and the warmth of his delivery, and, above all, were moved by the accents of his profoundly tragic voice. His march, his movements, his attitudes, his action had not that liveliness, those graces of our fathers, which then constituted a fine actor, and which the Marcels of the age taught to their pupils in initiating them in the beauties of the minute. Lekain, a plain plebian, a workman in a goldsmith's shop, had not, it is true, been brought up on the laps of queens, as Baron said actors ought to be; but nature, a still more noble instructress, had undertaken the charge of revealing her secrets to him. In time he succeeded in overcoming the bad taste which his inexperience had at first naturally thrown into his acting. He learned to master its vivacity and regulate its movements, yet at first he dared not entirely abandon

François Joseph Talma: *Reflections on the Actor's Art* (1825). New York: Printed for the Dramatic Museum of Columbia University, *Papers on Acting*, Second Series, Number 4, 1915, pp. 7-41. By permission of Columbia University Press.

the cadenced song which was then regarded as the ideal of the art of declamation, and which the actor preserved even in the burst of passion.

Actors ought at all times to take nature for a model, to make it the constant object of their studies. Lekain felt that the brilliant colors of poetry served only to give more grandeur and majesty to the beauties of nature. He was not ignorant that persons deeply affected by the stronger passions, or overwhelmed with great grief, or violently agitated by great political interest, have a more elevated and ideal language—yet this language is still that of nature. It is, therefore, this nature —noble, animated, aggrandized, but at the same time simple—which ought to be the constant object of the studies of the actor, as well as of the poet....

Lekain felt that the art of declamation did not consist in reciting verse with more or less emphasis, but that this art might be made to impart a sort of reality to the fictions of the stage. To attain this end it is necessary that the actor should have received from nature an extreme sensibility and a profound intelligence, and Lekain possessed these qualifications in an eminent degree. Indeed, the strong impressions which actors create on the stage are the result only of the alliance of these two essential faculties. I must explain what I mean by this. To my mind, sensibility is not only that faculty which an actor possesses of being moved himself, and of affecting his being so far as to imprint on his features, and especially on his voice, that expression and those accents of sorrow which awake all the sympathies of the art and extort tears from auditors. I include in it the effect which it produces, the imagination of which it is the source—not that imagination which consists in having reminiscences, so that the object seems actually present (this, properly speaking, is only memory) but that imagination which, creative, active and powerful, consists in collecting in one single fictitious object the qualities of several real objects, which associates the actor with the inspirations of the poet, transports him back to the past, and enables him to look on at the lives of historical personages or the impassioned figures created by genius—which reveals to him, as though by magic, their physiognomy, their heroic stature, their language, their habits, all the shades of their character, all the movements of their soul, and even their singularities. I also call sensibility that faculty of exaltation which agitates an actor, takes possession of his senses, shakes even his very soul, and enables him to enter into the most tragic situations, and the most terrible of the passions, as if they were his own. The intelligence which accompanies sensibility judges the impressions which the latter has made us feel; it selects, arranges them, and subjects them to calculation. If sensibility furnishes the objects, the intelligence brings them into play. It aids us to direct the employment of our physical and intellectual forces—to judge between the relations and connections which connect the poet and the situation or the character of the personages, and sometimes to add the shades that are wanting, or that language cannot express—to complete, in fine, their expression by action and physiognomy.

It may be conceived that such a person must have received from nature a peculiar organization for sensibility, that common property of our being. Every one possesses it in a greater or less degree. But in the man whom nature has destined to paint the passions in their greatest excesses, to give them all their violence, and show them in all their delirium, one may perceive that it must have a much greater energy; and, as all our emotions are intimately connected with our nerves, the nervous system in the actor must be so mobile and plastic as to be moved by the inspirations of the poet as easily as the Aeolian harp sounds with the least breath of air that touches it.

If the actor is not endowed with a sensibility at least equal to that of any of his audience he can move them but very little. It is only by an excess of sensibility that he can succeed in producing deep impressions, and move even the coldest souls. The power that raises must be greater than the power raised. This faculty ought ever to exist in the actor—I will not say greater or stronger than in the poet who conceived the movement of the soul reproduced on the stage—but more lively, more rapid, and more powerful. The poet or the painter can wait for the moment of inspiration to write or to paint. In the actor, on the contrary, it must be commanded at any moment, at his will. That it may be sudden, lively, and prompt, he must possess an excess of sensibility. Nay, more, his intelligence must always be on the watch, and, acting in concert with his sensibility, regulate its movement and effects; for he cannot, like the painter and the poet, efface what he does.

Therefore, between two persons destined for the stage, one possessing the extreme sensibility I have defined, and the other a profound intelligence, I would without question prefer the former. He might fall into some errors, but his sensibility would inspire him with those sublime movements which seize upon the spectator and carry delight to the heart. The superior intelligence of the other would render him cold and regular. The one would go beyond your expectations and your ideas; the other would only accomplish them. Your mind would be deeply stirred by the inspired actor; your judgment alone would be satisfied by the intelligent actor. The inspired actor will so associate you with the emotions he feels that he will not leave you even the liberty of judgment; the other, by his prudent and irreproachable acting, will leave your faculties at liberty to reason on the matter at your ease. The former will be the personage himself, the latter only an actor who represents that personage. Inspiration in the one will frequently supply the place of intelligence; in the other the combinations of intelligence will supply only feebly the absence of inspiration. To form a great actor, like Lekain, the union of sensibility and intelligence is required.

The actor who possesses this double gift adopts a course of study peculiar to himself. In the first place, by repeated exercises, he enters deeply into the emotions, and his speech acquires the accent proper to the situation of the personage he has to represent. This done, he goes to the theatre not only to give theatrical effect to his studies, but also to yield himself to the spontaneous flashes of his sensibility and all the emotions which it involuntarily produces in him. What does he then do? In order that his inspirations may not be lost, his memory, in the silence of repose, recalls the accent of his voice, the expression of his features, his action—in a word, the spontaneous workings of his mind, which he had suffered to have free course, and, in effect, everything which in the moments of his exaltation contributed to the effect he had produced. His intelligence then passes all these means in review, connecting them and fixing them in his memory, to reemploy them at pleasure in succeeding representations. These impressions are often so evanescent that on retiring behind the scenes he must repeat to himself what he had been playing rather than what he had to play. By this kind of labor the intelligence accumulates and preserves all the creations of sensibility. It is by this means that at the end of twenty years (it requires at least this length of time) a person destined to display fine talent may at length present to the public a series of characters acted almost to perfection. Such was the course which Lekain constantly took, and which must be taken by every one who has the ambition to excel on the stage. The whole of his life was devoted to this kind of study, and it was only during the last five or six years of his life, between 1772 or 1773 and 1778, that he reaped his fruit. It was then that his fertile sensibility raised him to the tragic situations he had to paint, and his intelligence enabled him to display all the treasures he had amassed. It was then that his acting was fixed on such bases, and was so subservient to his will, that the same combinations and the same effect presented themselves without study. Accent, inflections, action, attitudes, looks, all were reproduced at every representation with the same exactness, the same vigor; and if there were any differences between one representation and another, it was always in favor of the last. Sensibility and intelligence, therefore, are the principal faculties necessary to an actor. Yet these alone will not suffice. Apart from memory, which is his indispensable instrument, and stature and features adapted to the character he has to play, he must have a voice that can be modulated with ease, and at the same time be powerful and expressive. I need scarcely add that a good education, the study of history—(not so much the events as the manners of the people, and the particular character of historical personages)—and even drawing, ought to add grace and strength to the gifts of nature.

It will be well understood that I here speak only of tragedy. Without entering into the question whether it is more difficult to play tragedy or comedy, I will say that to arrive at perfection in either, the same moral and physical faculties are required, only I think the tragedian ought to possess more power and sensibility. The comedian does not require the same energy; the imagination in him has less scope. He represents beings whom he sees every day—beings of his own class. Indeed, with very few exceptions, his task is confined to the representations of folly and ridicule, and to painting passions in his own sphere of life, and, consequently, more moderate than those which come within the domain of tragedy. It is, if I may so express it, his own nature which, in his imitations, speaks and acts; whereas the tragic actor must quit the circle in which he is accustomed to live, and plunge into the regions where the genius of the poet has placed and clothed in ideal forms the beings conceived by him or furnished by history. He must preserve these personages in their grand proportions, but at the same time he must subject their elevated language to natural accents and true expression; and it is this union of grandeur without pomp, and nature without triviality—this union of the ideal and the true, which is so difficult to attain in tragedy. I shall, perhaps, be told that a tragic actor has a much greater liberty in the choice of his means of offering to the public objects whose types do not exist in society, while the same public can easily decide whether the comedian furnishes an exact copy of his model. I would reply that the passions are of all ages. Society may weaken their energy, but they do not the less exist in the soul, and every spectator is a competent judge from his own feelings. With regard to the great historical characters, the enlightened public can easily judge of the truth of the imitation. It will therefore appear from what I have laid down that the moral faculties ought to have more force and intensity in the tragic than in the comic actor.

As to the physical qualities, it is evident that the pliability of the features and the expression of the physiognomy ought to be stronger, the voice more full, more sonorous, and more profoundly articulate in the tragic actor, who stands in need of certain combinations and more than ordinary powers to perform from the beginning to the end with the same energy a part in which the author has frequently collected in a narrow compass, and in the space of two hours, all the movements, all the agitations, which an impassioned being can feel only in the course of a long life. I repeat, however, that not fewer qualities, though of a different kind, are required in a great comedian than in a great tragic actor; each has need of being initiated into the mysteries of nature, the inclinations, the weaknesses, the extravagances of the human heart.

When we consider all the qualities necessary to form an excellent tragic actor, all the gifts which nature should have bestowed upon him, can we be surprised that they are, so rare? Amongst the majority of those who go on the stage, one has penetration, but his soul is cold as ice. Another possesses sensibility, but intelligence is wanting. One possesses both these requisites, but in so slight a degree, that it is as if he did not possess them at all; his acting is characterized neither by energy, expression, nor confidence, and is without color; sometimes he speaks in a loud and sometimes in a low key, quickly or slowly, as if by chance. Another has received from nature all these gifts, but his voice is harsh, dry and monotonous, and totally incapable of expressing the passions; he weeps without drawing tears from others; he is affected and his audience is unmoved. One has a sonorous and touching voice, but his features are disagreeable; his stature and form have nothing heroic in them. In short, the requisites for a really great actor are so many, and so seldom united in the same person, that we ought not to be surprised at finding them appear at such long intervals.

It must be confessed that Lekain had some faults; but in literature and in the arts of imitation genius is rated in proportion to the beauties it creates. Its imperfections form no part of its fame, and would be forgotten if they were not allied to noble aspirations. Nature had refused to Lekain some of the advantages which the stage demands. His features had nothing noble in them; his physiognomy was common, his figure short. But his exquisite sensibility, the movement of an ardent and impassioned soul, the faculty he possessed of plunging entirely into the situation of the personage he represented, the intelligence, so delicately fine, which enabled him to perceive and produce all the shades of the character he had to paint—these embellished his irregular features and gave him an inexpressible charm. His voice was naturally heavy, and by no means flexible. It was to some extent what is called a veiled voice, but that very veil imparted to it, defective as it was in some respects, vibrations which went to the bottom of the hearer's soul. However, by dint of application, he contrived to overcome its stiffness, to enrich it with all the accents of passion, and to render it amenable to all the delicate inflections of sentiment. He had, in fact, studied his voice as one studies an instrument. He knew all its qualities and all its defects. He passed lightly over the harsh to give fuller effect to the vibrations of the harmonious chords. His voice, on which he essayed every accent, became a rich-keyed instrument, from which he could draw forth at pleasure every sound he stood in need of. And such is the power of a voice thus formed by nature attuned by art, that it affects even the foreigner who does not understand the words. Frenchmen who are totally unacquainted with English have been affected even to tears by the accents of the touching voice of Miss O'Neill.

At the commencement of his career, Lekain, like all young actors, gave way to boisterous cries and violent movement; believing that in this way he triumphed over difficulties. In time, however, he felt that of all monotonies that f the lungs was the most unsupportable; that tragedy must be spoken, not owled; that a continual explosion fatigues without appealing; and that only when it is rare and unexpected can it astonish and move. He felt, in fine, that he auditor, shocked by the ranting on the stage, forgets the personage represented, and pities or condemns the actor. Thus Lekain, often fatigued in long and arduous scenes, took care to conceal from the public the violence of his efforts, and at the very moment when his powers were nearly exhausted they seemed o possess all their strength and vigor.

* * * *

Experience had taught Lekain that all the silly combinations of mediocrity, he contrast of sounds, and ranting and raving might evoke great applause and many bravos; but it conferred no reputation. The lovers of noise and vociferation fancy their souls are wooed, while only their ears are stunned. There is a certain number of artists, connoisseurs, and intelligent persons who are sensible only to what is true and conformable to nature. These persons do not like much noise, and it is upon their opinion that an actor's reputation depends. Lekain despised those plaudits which torment and often distract an actor. He resolved to study only that part of the public which was worth pleasing. He rejected all the charlatanism of his art, and produced a true effect; he always discarded the claptraps which so many others seek to discover. He was, consequently, one of the actors the least appreciated in his day, but he was the most admired by competent judges, and he rendered tragedy more familiar without depriving t of its majestic proportions.

He knew how to regulate all his movements and all his actions. He regarded his as a very essential part of his art. For action is language in another form. If it is violent or hurried, the carriage ceases to be noble. Thus, while other actors were theatrical kings only, in him the dignity did not appear to be the result of effort, but the simple effect of habit. He did not raise his shoulders or swell his voice to give an order. He knew that men in power had no need of such efforts to make themselves obeyed, and that in the sphere they occupy all their words have weight and all their movements authority. Lekain displayed superior intelligence and great ability in the varied styles of his recitation, which was slow or rapid, as circumstances required; and his pauses were always full of deep significance. There are, in fact, certain circumstances in which it is necessary to solicit one's self before we confide to the tongue the emotions of the soul or the calculations of the mind. The actor, therefore, must have the art of thinking before he speaks, and by introducing pauses he appears to meditate upon what he is about to say. But his physiognomy must correspond also with the suspensions of his voice. His attitudes and features must indicate that during these moments of silence his soul is deeply engaged; without this his pauses will seem rather to be the result of defective memory than a secret of his art.

There are also situations in which a person strongly moved feels too acutely to wait the slow combination of words. The sentiment that overpowers him escapes in mute action before the voice is able to give it utterance. The gesture, the attitude, and the look ought, then, to precede the words, as the flash of lightning precedes the thunder. The display adds greatly to the expression, as t discovers a mind so profoundly imbued that, impatient to manifest itself, t has chosen the more rapid signs. These artifices contribute what is properly called by-play, a most essential part of the theatrical art, and most difficult to acquire, retain, and regulate well. It is by this means that the actor gives to his speech an air of truth, and takes from it all appearance of measured speaking.

There are also situations in which a person transported by the violence of feeling finds at once all the expression he wishes. The words come to his lips as rapidly as the thoughts to his mind; they are born with them, and succeed each other without interruption. The mind of the actor, then, ought to be hurried and rapid; he must even conceal from the audience the effort he makes to prolong his breath. This effort he must make, since the slightest interruption or the slightest pause would destroy the illusion, because the mind would seem to participate in this pause. Besides, passion does not follow the rules of grammar; it pays but little respect to colons, and semi-colons, and full stops, which it displaces without ceremony.

* * * *

Lekain was a creature of passion; he never loved but to madness; and, it is said, he hated in the same manner. He whose soul is not susceptible to the extremes of passion will never rise to excellence as an actor. In the expression of the passions there are many shades which cannot be divined and which the actor cannot paint until he has felt them himself. The observations which he made on his own nature serve at once for his study and example; he interrogates himself on the impressions his soul has felt, on the expression they imprinted upon his features, on the accents of his voice in the various states of feeling. He meditates on these, and clothes the fictitious passions with these real forms. I scarcely know how to confess that, in my own person, in any circumstance of my life in which I experienced deep sorrow, the passion of the theatre was so strong in me that, although oppressed with real sorrow, and disregarding the tears I shed, I made, in spite of myself, a rapid and fugitive observation on the alteration of my voice, and on a certain spasmodic vibration which it contracted as I wept; and, I say it, not without some shame, I even thought of making use of this on the stage, and, indeed, this experiment on myself has often been of service to me.

The contrarieties, the sorrow, and melancholy reflections which an actor may apply to the personage he represents, in exciting his sensibility, place him in the degree of agitation necessary for the development of his faculties. Lekain thus found, in his own passions, display for his talents. As to the odious characters and vile passions, of which the type was not in him—for no man was more honorable than Lekain—he painted them by analogy. In fact, amongst the irregular passions which disgrace humanity, there are some which possess points of contact with those which ennoble it. Thus, the sentiment ot a lofty emulation enables us to divine what envy may feel; the just resentment of wrongs shows us in miniature the excess of hatred and vengeance. Reserve and prudence enable us to paint dissimulation. The desires, the torments, and the jealousies of love enable us to conceive all its frenzies and initiate us in the secret of its crimes.

These combinations, these comparisons, are the result of a rapid and imperceptible labor of sensibility, united with intelligence, which secretly operates on the actor as on the poet, and which reveals to them what is foreign to their own nature—the viler passions of guilty and corrupted minds. Thus Milton, a man of austere probity, and so full of the divine power, created the personage of Satan. Corneille, the simplest and worthiest of men, created Phocas and Felix; Racine, Nero and Narcissus. Voltaire has painted the effects of fanaticism with a frightful truth; and Ducis, whose taste was simple, and whose life was religious, painted, in Albufar, in traits of fire, all the transports of incestuous love. These terminate my hasty reflections on Lekain and our art. I have thrown them together without order; but I hope, in the quietude of silence and repose, to resume the subject, and give, for the use of my successors, the result of a long experience in a career devoted entirely to the advancement of the beautiful art I love so deeply.

FRANCOIS DELSARTE

(1811 - 1871)

Delsarte, son of a renowned but impoverished physician, was first apprenticed to a porcelain painter in Paris. A taste and aptitude for music led him in 1825 to seek admission to the *Conservatoire*. Here, by a strange trick of fate, the future master of vocal training and diction lost his voice as a result of faulty instruction. Yielding to the inevitable, Delsarte renounced the stage and assumed the function of professor. Years of diligent study went into Delsarte's attempt to formulate laws of speech and gesture which would be as precise as mathematical principles. In tracing the development of works on acting methods, Lee Strasberg says: "In the nineteenth century the Frenchman Delsarte becomes dissatisfied with the routine acting techniques taught in his time. Aware of its mechanical and stultifying character, he grows to realize that under the stress of natural instinct or emotion the body takes on the appropriate attitude or gesture, and this gesture was not at all what his teachers taught it was. But unable or unwilling to rely on what he had discovered he tried to create a new series of elaborate pictorial descriptions that ended by being just as mechanical as those he originally broke away from. The time was not ready. For the understanding of the conscious and unconscious, the functioning of the senses, the knowledge of the affective behavior, had simply not advanced far enough for it to be utilized in concrete practice."

Delsarte had numerous distinguished pupils—among them the celebrated Rachel—and his influence in the France of his day was widespread. Curiously, Delsarte's ideas, as interpreted by others, had a tremendous vogue in the United States at the end of the nineteenth century. Contemporary advertisements of Delsarte "recitation" books called on "every Delsartean, every elocutionist, every singer, every teacher, and every other cultured person" to use them as texts as well as a "means of acquiring grace, dignity, and a fine bearing for society people."

Delsarte actually left only five chapters of the large work he planned to call *My Revelatory Episodes*. In addition there remain a number of addresses and manuscripts. The material which follows is drawn from these sources.

Elements of the Delsarte System

GESTURE

The artist should have three objects: To *move,* to *interest,* to *persuade.* He interests by *language;* he moves by *thought;* he moves, interests and persuades by *gesture.*

Delsarte System of Oratory: Containing All the Literary Remains of François Delsarte (Given in His Own Words), translated by Abby L. Alger. New York: Edgar S. Werner, 1893, pp. 465-468, 486-487, 522-529.

Language is the weakest of the three agents. In a matter of the feelings language proves nothing. It has no real value, save that which is given to it by the preparation of gesture.

Gesture corresponds to the soul, to the heart; language to the life, to the thought, to the mind. The life and the mind being subordinate to the heart, to the soul, gesture is the chief organic agent. So it has its appropriate character which is persuasion, and it borrows from the other two agents interest and emotion. It prepares the way, in fact, for language and thought; it goes before them and foretells their coming; it accentuates them.

By its silent eloquence it predisposes, guides the listener. It makes him a witness to the secret labor performed by the immanences which are about to burst forth. It flatters him by leading him to feel that he partakes in this preparation by the initiation to which it admits him. It condenses into a single word the powers of the three agents. It represents virtue effective and operative. It assimilates the auxiliaries which surround it, and reflects the immanence proper to its nature, the contemplation of its subject deeply seen, deeply felt. It possesses them synthetically, fully, absolutely.

Artistic gesture is the expression of the physiognomy; it is transluminous action; it is the mirror of lasting things. Lacordaire, that spoiled child of the intellect, spoke magnificently. He interested, he aroused admiration, but he did not persuade. His organism was rebellious to gesture. He was the artist of language. Ravignan, inferior intellectually, prepared his audience by his attitude, touched them by the general expression of his face, fascinated them by his gaze. He was the artist of gesture....

DEFINITION OF GESTURE

Gesture is the direct agent of the heart. It is the fit manifestation of feeling. It is the revealer of thought and the commentator upon speech. It is the elliptical expression of language; it is the justification of the additional meanings of speech. In a word, it is the spirit of which speech is merely the letter. Gesture is parallel to the impression received; it is, therefore, always anterior to speech, which is but a reflected and subordinate expression.

Gesture is founded on three bases which give rise to three orders of studies; that is, to three sciences, namely: The *static,* the *dynamic* and the *semeiotic.*

What are these three sciences, and first of all, what are they in relation to gesture? The *semeiotic* is its mind; the *dynamic* is its soul; the *static* is founded on the mutual equilibrium or equipoise of the agents....

The most powerful of all gestures is that which affects the spectator without his knowing it.

From this statement may be deduced the principle that: Outward gesture, being only the echo of the inward gesture which gave birth to it and rules it, should be inferior to it in development and should be in some sort diaphanous.

SPEECH

Speech is an act posterior to will, itself posterior to love; this again posterior to judgment, posterior in its turn to memory, which, finally, is posterior to the impression.

Every impression, to became a sensation, must first be perceived by the intelligence, and thus we may say of the sensation that it is a definite impression. But, to be definite, it must pass into the domain of memory and there solicit the reappearance of its congeners with which it may identify itself. It is in this apparatus and surrounded by this throng of homogeneous impressions which gather round it, as if by magic, or rather which it draws about it as the magnet draws the iron, it is, I say, in this complex state that it appears before the intelligence to receive from the latter a fitting name. For the intelligence could not give it a name if the homogeneous impressions in which it has, so to speak, arrayed itself, did not serve to point it out.

Now, by this distinction, established by the double operation of the memory and the intelligence, a movement takes place in the soul, of attraction, if the intelligence approve; or of repulsion, if it disapprove. This movement is called the will. The will, therefore, becomes the active principle in virtue of which speech is expressed; thus speech is the express agent of the will. It is speech, in fact, which, under the incubation of this mysterious power, rules, groups and moves bodies with the aid of memory.

Inflection is the life of speech; the mind lies in the articulative values, in the distribution of these articulations and their progressions. The soul of speech is in gesture.

RANDOM NOTES

The Senses

 Taste and smell say: It is *Good.*

 Sight and touch say: It is *Beautiful.*

 Hearing and speech say: It is *True.*

Every agreeable or disagreeable sight makes the body react backward. The degree of reaction should be in proportion to the degree of interest caused by the sight of the object presented to our sight.

The more lofty the intellect, the more simple the speech (So in art).

Accent is the modulaton of the soul.

Routine is the most formidable thing I know.

If you would move others, put your heart in the place of your larynx; let your voice become a mysterious hand to caress the hearer.

Nothing is more deplorable than a gesture without a motive. Perhaps the best gesture is that which is least apparent.

Persuade yourself that there are blind men and deaf men in your audience whom you must *move, interest and persuade!* Your inflection must become pantomime to the blind, and your pantomime, inflection to the deaf.

The mouth plays a part in everything evil which we would express, by a grimace which consists of protruding the lips and lowering the corners. If the grimace translates a concentric sentiment, it should be made by compressing the lips.

Conscious menace—that of a master to his subordinate—is expressed by a movement of the head carried from above downward. Impotent menace requires the head to be moved from below upward.

Any interrogation made with crossed arms must partake of the character of a threat.

There are three great articular centres; the *shoulder, elbow* and *wrist.* Passional expression passes from the shoulder, where it is in the emotional state, to the elbow, where it is presented in the affectional state, then to the wrist and the thumb, where it is presented in the susceptive and volitional state.

Bad actors exert themselves in vain to be moved and to afford a spectacle to themselves. On the other hand, true artists never let their gestures reveal more than a tenth part of the secret emotion that they apparently feel and would hide from the audience to spare their sensibility. Thus they succeed in stirring all spectators.

No, art is not an imitation of nature; art is better than nature. It is nature illuminated.

There are two kinds of loud voices; the vocally loud, which is the vulgar voice; and the dynamically loud, which is the powerful voice. A voice, however powerful it may be, should be inferior to the power which animates it.

Without abnegation, no truth for the artist. We should not preoccupy the audience with our own personality. There is no true, simple or expressive singing without self-denial. We must often leave people in ignorance of our own good qualities.

To use expression at random on our own authority, expression *at all hazards* is absurd.

The mouth is a vital thermometer, the nose a moral thermometer.

An abstract having been made of the modes of execution which the artist should learn before handling a subject, two things are first of all requisite:

1. To know what he is to seek in that subject itself;
2. To know how to find what he seeks.

Speech is external, and visible thought is the ambassadress of the intellect.

How should the invisible be visible when the visible is so little so!

One cannot be too careful of his articulation. The initial consonant should be articulated distinctly; the spirit of the word is contained in it.

Rhythm is that which asserts; it is the form of movement.

Melody is that which distinguishes.

Harmony is that which conjoins.

Let your attitude, gesture and face foretell what you would make felt.

If you cannot conquer your defect, make it beloved.

A movement should never be mixed with a facial twist.

Things that are said quietly should sing themselves in the utterance.

BENOIT CONSTANT COQUELIN

(1841 - 1909)

The name of Coquelin is pre-eminent among the actors of the French theatre in the second half of the nineteenth century. Son of a baker, he entered the *Conservatoire* in 1859 and was in the comedian Régnier's class. Here he won the first prize in comedy and in 1860 made his debut at the *Comédie Française* as Gros-René in Molière's *Le Dépit amoureux*. In the following year he achieved great success in the role of Figaro in Beaumarchais' play.

In 1864 he became a *sociétaire* at the *Comédie,* and during the next twenty-two years he created the leading parts in forty-four new plays, among them those of Augier, Dumas *fils,* and Pailleron. At the *Comédie,* he was later joined by his brother, Ernest Alexandre Honoré Coquelin (1848-1909), who became a *sociétaire* in 1879. In 1886 Constant Coquelin resigned from the *Théâtre Français* after a dispute with the company and went on a profitable tour of Europe and America. He returned three years later but resigned again in 1892 to travel with a company of his own. One of his greatest triumphs was Cyrano de Bergerac in Rostand's play at the *Porte-Saint-Martin,* of which he became the director in 1897. His name will always be associated with that of Sarah Bernhardt with whom he frequently starred. In 1900 they went to the United States together, and on their return he played Rostand's *L'Aiglon* at her theatre. Just before his death he was rehearsing the leading role in Rostand's *Chantecler.*

Coquelin belonged to a line of actors who were uniquely French—the low comedian specializing in the *valets de Molière.* These comic servant characters of Molière, Régnard, and later Beaumarchais had provided excellent roles for many fine actors from Molière himself to Régnier, Samson, and Edmond Got (1822-1901). Coquelin was at his best in those parts, although he also played serious roles in contemporary plays. Rostand created Cyrano with the acting abilities of Coquelin in mind.

Henry James wrote of Coquelin: "But to enjoy the refinement of M. Coquelin's acting the ear must be as open as the eye, must even be beforehand with it; and if that of the American public learns, or even shows an aptitude for learning, the lesson conveyed in his finest creations, the lesson that acting is an art and that art is style, the gain will have been something more than the sensation of the moment—it will have been an added perception...."

Perhaps more than any other actor of his era Coquelin was the exacting artist, working with cold intellectual persistence to create dramatic characters and poetry on the stage. He reported his method of building a new part in the following words: "When I have to create a new role, I begin by reading the play with the greatest attention, five or six times. First, I consider what position my character should occupy, on what plane in the picture I must put him. Then I study his psychology, knowing what he thinks and what he is morally. I deduce what he ought to be physically, what will be his carriage, his manner of speaking, his gesture. These characteristics once decided, I learn the part without thinking about it further. Then, when I know it, I take up my man again, and closing my eyes I say to him, 'Recite this for me.' Then I see him delivering the speech, the sentence I asked him for; he lives, he speaks, he gesticulates before me, and then I have only to imitate him."

In the last decade of the nineteenth century Coquelin and Henry Irving engaged in a paper battle over their respective approaches to the art of acting. Part of their controversy involved the long-standing quarrel of the Diderot *Paradoxe* and led William Archer to his investigation *Masks or Faces?* Without attempting to decide which was the superior actor or which the victor in the literary argument, it is enough to say that Coquelin's varied writings on the art of acting are among the finest attempts to dissect the basic principles of the art. George Jean Nathan said of him: "Coquelin is the only actor who ever lived who proved that he had a critical mind in the appraisal of acting."

The Dual Personality of the Actor

I.

Art, I define as a whole, wherein a large element of beauty clothes and makes acceptable a still larger element of truth.

Thus in the execution of a work of art the painter has his colors, his canvas, and his brushes; the sculptor has his clay, his chisel, and his modeling tools; the poet has his words, rhythm, harmony, and rhyme. Every art has its different instruments; but the instrument of the actor is himself.

The *matter* of his art, that which he has to work upon and mold for the creation of his idea, is his own face, his own body, his own life. Hence it follows that the actor must have a double personality. He has his first self, which is the player, and his second self, which is the instrument. The first self conceives the person to be created, or rather—for the conception belongs to the author— he sees him such as he was formed by the author, whether he be Tartuffe, Hamlet, Arnolphe, or Romeo, and the being that he sees is represented by his second self. This dual personality is the characteristic of the actor.

Not that the double nature is the exclusive property of actors alone; it undoubtedly exists among others. For example, my friend Alphonse Daudet takes delight in distinguishing this double element in the personality of the storyteller, and even the very expressions I am now using are borrowed from him. He confesses that he also has his first self and his second self—the one a man made like other men, who loves or hates, suffers or is happy; the other a being belonging to a higher sphere, whose balance nothing can disturb, and who in the midst of tumultuous emotions can observe, study, and take notes for the future creation of his characters.

But this double nature of the writer is neither so essential nor so conspicuous as that of the actor. The first self of the author watches the second self, but they never mingle. In the actor, on the contrary, the first self works upon the second till it is transfigured, and thence an ideal personage is evolved—in short, until from himself he has made his work of art.

When a painter is about to execute a portrait he first poses his model, and then, concentrating, as it were, in his brush all the striking features that his trained eye can seize, he transfers them to the canvas by the magic of his art, and when he has done this, his work is finished. The actor, however, has still something to do—he must himself enter into the picture. For *his* portrait must speak, act, walk in its frame, which is the stage, and it must convey the illusion of life to the spectator.

Therefore when the actor has a portrait to execute, that is, a part to create, he must first read the play carefully over many times, until he has grasped

---

Benoit Constant Coquelin: "Acting and Actors." *Harper's New Monthly Magazine*, May, 1887, pp. 891-909.

the intention of the author and the meaning of the character he is to represent, until he has a clear understanding of his personage, and *sees* him as he ought to be. When he attains to this, he has his model. Then, like the painter, he seizes each salient feature and transfers it, not to his canvas, but to himself. He adapts each element of this personality to his second self. He sees Tartuffe in a certain costume, he wears it; he feels he has a certain face, he assumes it. He forces, if one may say so, his own face and figure into this imaginary mold, he recasts his own individuality, till the critic which is his first self declares he is satisfied, and finds that the result is really Tartuffe.

But this is by no means all, otherwise the resemblance would be only external; it would merely convey the outward form of the personage, not the personage himself. Tartuffe must be made to speak with the voice that he hears Tartuffe using, and in order consistently to represent the part the actor must learn to move, talk, gesticulate, listen, and also think, with the mind which he divines in Tartuffe.

Now, and not till now, is the picture completed; it is ready to be framed—I mean put on the stage—and instead of exclaiming, "Look at Geoffroy!"[1] "Here comes Bressant!"[2] or whoever it may be, the audience will cry, "Ah, this is Tartuffe!" if otherwise, your labor is lost.

To sum up, the first thing necessary must be a deep and careful study of the *character;* then there must be the conception by the first self, and the reproduction by the second, of the person such as his character inevitably makes him. This is the work of the actor.

Like Molière, he takes his own wherever he may find it; that is, to complete the resemblance he may add to his portrait any striking traits which he himself has observed in nature; thus Harpagon was composed of a thousand misers melted and cast in the mold of a masterly unity.

II.

The two natures which coexist in the actor are inseparable, but it is the first self, the one which *sees,* which should be the master. This is the soul, the other is the body. It is the reason—the same reason that our friends the Chinese call the *Supreme Ruler;* and the second self is to the first what rhyme is to reason—a slave whose only duty is obedience.

The more absolute the subjection of this mistress, the greater the artist.

The ideal would be that the second self, the body, should be a soft mass of sculptor's clay, capable of assuming at will any form, who would become a charming *jeune premier* for Romeo, a diabolical and intellectually fascinating humpback for Richard III, for Figaro a ferret-faced valet with an expression of audacious impertinence. Then the actor would be all-accomplished, and granted he also had equivalent talents, he could undertake every part. Alas! nature forbids this; he would be too forunate. However supple may be the body, however mobile may be the face, neither one nor the other can be changed indefinitely at the will of the artist.

Sometimes it happens that a man's exterior will prevent him from acting

---

[1] Jean-Marie-Joseph Geoffroy (1813-1883).
[2] Jean Baptiste Prospère Bressant (1815-1886).

certain parts which he is, notwithstanding, well able both to grasp and expound. Sometimes nature relentlessly confines an actor to certain kinds of parts; but this touches the question of physique, of which I will speak later.

There are some in whom the *second self,* or the *ego,* rebels, on whom their own individuality exerts so much influence that they can never put it aside, and instead of their going to their role and clothing themselves in its semblance, they make the role come to them and clothe itself in theirs.

This becomes another way of conceiving art, and I do not hesitate to pronounce it inferior to the first, although I am well aware how much can be done in this direction by a highly gifted artist.

The first drawback is that a man becomes, in a measure, the man of a single part; it also leads to the neglect of the study and digestion of the character—to me the only important thing—for the quest of that of the exterior, and of picturesque detail.

Of course picturesque detail is not to be despised, but it should never become the object of exclusive attention, and above all no picturesque trait, however natural, should ever be taken as the starting-point of a role.

It is the *character* that is the starting-point for everything.

If you have assimilated the essence of your personage, his exterior will follow quite naturally, and if there is any picturesqueness, it will come of itself. It is the mind which constructs the body.

If Mephistopheles is ugly, it is because his soul is hideous. I have seen him admirably played in Vienna by Lewinsky, who represents him lame and hump-backed, which is quite appropriate to the character.

But Irving, who has also made a name for himself in this role—Irving, who is a kind of methodical Mounet-Sully, setting great store by the exterior of his parts—Irving cannot avoid seeking after the picturesque even in his slightest movement. If he wishes to touch his chin, he raises his arm and encircles it, his hand makes the tour of his head, striking the audience as it does so with a sense of its leanness, and never seizes the point of his beard till after it has described a complete circle.

The love of dramatic effect, and a very praiseworthy dislike of the hackneyed and commonplace, often induce very intelligent actors to err on this side. They choose first the aspects which they suppose to be characteristic of the person they can represent; then they allow themselves to be tempted by others which are purely picturesque, without considering, or perhaps without caring, if they belong really to the part; and the end is a caricature, not a portrait; a monster or a puppet, never a human being.

Even from the point of view of immediate success, this method of proceeding has one great drawback. The public tires of nothing so quickly as mere picturesqueness of effect. Your entrance once over, they pay no further heed to you; you have missed fire if you have not style, delivery, and the development of the character to fall back on. The style is the man, said M. de Buffon.

More than this: if by a misplaced anxiety to individualize your part you end by catching up a trick, oh, then beware! Instead of amusing your audience, you will prejudice them against you. The public, though it may laugh the first time, will soon become bored, and will not fail to convey its feelings to you by coldness and reserve, or by something more disagreeable still.

FRANCE

III.

Do not misunderstand me. I forbid no one to borrow from observation of a model the peculiarities which betray the inner man. As I have said above, it is one of the necessary qualities of the actor to be able to seize and note at once anything that is capable of reproduction on the stage; but these traits must be adopted with discretion. For example, those must be avoided which are purely individual; the actor must take care not to adopt the characteristics of some special miser whom he may know but whom the public does not know, but instead he should give, as Harpagon, the concentrated essence of *all misers,* which his audience would recognize instantly.

There was one actor, Lesueur[3], who was pre-eminent in this art of true portraiture. No one has ever done more with his second self, or created out of his own personality characters more different in themselves, or with more intense expression. It was really astonishing. But then he studied with the fury of enthusiasm. In his house there was a sort of dark room, with closed windows and locked doors, where he used to shut himself in with his costumes, his wigs, and all his paraphernalia. There, alone before his mirror, he would sit trying experiments with his face by the light of the lamps. He would make up twenty, he would make up a hundred times, before he would succeed in producing the ideal which he felt to be the true one, and of which he could say, "Yes, that is he."

And when he had put the finishing touch to the likeness, he would work for hours at one wrinkle. The result was so extraordinary that judges of acting will never forget his absinthe-drinker, his madmen, nor his old gentleman playing piquet. He was one day Monsieur Poirier, that incarnation of the middle classes, and the next he would be Don Quixote, the type of starving knight-errantry. When he entered the stage in this last part, although he was really a small man, it seemed as if there were no end to his stature, he seemed to draw himself out, like a telescope, till he was as long as his lance. It was indeed the hero of Cervantes in all the melancholy of his interminable leanness.

But in spite of this wonderful talent, fortified by a close study of his parts, he lacked one element necessary to make the illusion complete—command of his voice. He never could manage to train his, and it remained to the last, in all his parts, the voice of Lesueur—very comic, but always comic in the same way, and with a terribly ponderous articulation....

Now articulation is to speech what drawing is to painting.

A single sentence of Samson's, articulated as he knew how to articulate, was as good as a portrait by M. Ingres for enabling you to grasp the character of the person he was representing....

The power of a true inflection of the voice is incalculable, and all the picturesque exteriors in the world will not move an audience like one cry given with the right intonation. Articulation should be therefore the first study of the actor

The public *must* understand every word he says, however quickly he may say it. A word must be able to draw tears or laughter from the mere manner of its articulation.

The voice should not be less finely trained than the exterior. It belongs to

---

[3]François-Louis Lesueur (1820-1876).

the second self, and should be specially supple, expressive, and rich in modifications of tone. According to the part, the voice should be caressing, smooth, insinuating, mocking, bold, eager, tender, despairing. You should be able to ring the changes from the clarinet to the bugle.

The lover's voice is not like the lawyer's voice. Iago has not the voice of Figaro, nor Figaro the voice of Tartuffe. Intonation, key, and note all differ with the role. As Madelon says: "It contains the chromatic scale." In a word, your character should be drawn and portrayed so that even the blind may see him by your articulation, your delivery, and your intonation.

All this should be added to the care that you bestow on your exterior; with the same minuteness as Lesueur, if you will, provided it be also with the same truth to nature. I mean always keeping in mind the character of which the exterior is only the illustration—the person who must be set before men's very eyes without the deformity which comes from exaggeration.

Physiognomy, gesture, and voice should all make one whole. It often happens that characters which are apparently quite insignificant need the greatest efforts of metamorphosis on the part of the actor. For instance, look at Thouvenin in *Denise.* One would think I could not have a more easy role than this extremely simple one. I am not speaking now of my success, but only of my struggles to attain it, of my long hours of study of the character. Thouvenin takes no part in the action; he talks and argues as any honest man would, as I might do myself any day. That is the very rock on which I might wreck myself. In virtue of the relationship between this personage and the man that is in me, the man such as I am in common life, I may be tempted to endow him with my gestures, to make him speak with my voice—to be, in fact, Monsieur Coquelin; and if I did this, I should have betrayed the author, who required that I should be Thouvenin. So it was necessary to watch more carefully than usual to restrain myself, to correct my ordinary ways, to modify my walk to tone down the eagerness of my voice, to keep only the exact vibration that is required for the great speech at the end; to mold my physiognomy in such a manner as to give to Thouvenin his appropriate exterior as an ex-working man who has educated himself and fills creditably his place in the world, but who brings to bear on the usages and conventions of society a liberty of judgment and an originality of language which reveal at once his origin and his character.

The special advantage of a serious study of the parts is to facilitate these transformations. Samson and Régnier hardly ever painted their faces; they contrived to change their expressions solely from within. In this art, as in so many others, Frédéric Lemaître was the greatest master. The word *transfiguration* was applied for the first time, as far as I know, to an actor when he appeared in *Ruy Blas* with such splendid success. Transfiguration will hardly be thought too strong a word to describe the successive representations of Robert Macaire and Ruy Blas. His personifications of the scoundrel, with his shabby hideousness, and of the servant and lover of the Queen, with the tragic splendor of his face, were alike the work of a master; for he was beautiful in *Ruy Blas.* He contrived to throw a shadow of passionate melancholy over everything that was irregular, sharp, and severe in his countenance, till nothing was left but the light of genius, and he seemed to put on beauty like a mask. As no one ever had more accentuated features than he, he deserved all the more credit for his extraordinary transformations. This power is not given to all. Not even the hardest work will enable us always to grasp it; and this brings us back to the question of *physique,* so important on the stage.

IV.

As I have said before, the exterior of an actor, certain details of his physical conformation, of his "architecture," may confine him exclusively to one special kind of part.

There are men whom nature has made *lovers* to the end of time, like Delaunay;[4] there are *duennas* from the cradle, like Madame Jouassain. This indication of a special line often arises from some very slight peculiarity—from the angle made by the nose with the horizon, for example. But on the subject of the influence of the nose, every one should read what Pascal says of Cleopatra: "The destinies of the world would have been different had Cleopatra's nose been shorter." One sort of face suits tragedy, or, at most, serious comedy. Another face, bristling with queer irregularities, is out of place save in farce.

Happy indeed are these actors if their physique which forces them into a certain line allows them to add to it by the help of their talent an amount of universal truth and humanity sufficient to constitute a type. They will leave their image and an undying recollection behind them. This was the case with Henry Monnier[5] in M. Prudhomme. He was never anything but M. Prudhomme; he could not be anything else; but he created in the person of M. Prudhomme a face which has become traditional, a type, a representation of an epoch and of a class. He and his creation will live forever.

But do not misunderstand me. The actor of one part, however fine a study it may be, is inferior to the actor who has the command of many.

It is also an error to hold that the only really admirable creations are those in which the outward conformity of the actor with his role is absolute and entire.

Frédéric created a type which is, in its way, quite as immortal as M. Prudhomme. This was Robert Macaire, to which I have already alluded, and to which I shall have occasion again to refer. To Frédéric alone the creation is due, but this did not prevent him from also creating Ruy Blas.

Notwithstanding, he resembled in himself neither the one nor the other of these two persons, whom he may be said to have almost amalgamated in Don César, and he would be a bold man who would dare to affirm that he was better as an artist in one than in the other. He was, in truth, wonderful in comedy, and sublime in tragedy. He had great powers, and his face was not of a kind to interfere with their outward expression.

The truth is that as long as an actor is free from any natural defects of structure, as long as his countenance is not more laughable nor more unpleasing than the countenances of the generality of men, and the face is sufficiently mobile, even though it may lack beauty, to be able to assume at will a dramatic expression—given all these things, there is no reason why he should not distinguish himself both in comedy and tragedy.

---

[4]Louis-Arsène Delaunay (1826-1903).   [5]Henry Monnier (1799-1877).

It is all a question of degree, and of course a question of talent. It is hardly necessary to quote instances; they abound everywhere, and it is impossible it should be otherwise.

Tragedy and comedy are so closely blended in the contemporary stage that the capacity for the double impersonation is demanded of nearly all. Look at Régnier, my dear master. What admirable creations we owe to him!

Physical beauty, or charm, is indispensable to *jeunes premiers*. In order to make and to receive gracefully declarations of love before an audience, it is necessary to possess no peculiarity which can excite a smile. The actor must either be handsome or able to appear so.

For there is a difference. It is possible to appear handsome, and to have the power of attracting all hearts, without being in the least a model of beauty. I am sure I shall not wound the feelings of my friend Delaunay if I say that his nose is not exactly Grecian in its outline; and yet no one more fascinating ever appeared on the stage. He had so much charm, something so ineffably young and tender and airy, something which I do not hesitate to say has left the stage with him....

To take myself as an example, if I may be allowed to do such a thing, the audience would never for a moment suffer that on my entrance on the stage in the first act, I should receive a declaration of love from a beautiful woman.

I have, however, acted Jean Dacier, where I ended by being loved by a girl of noble birth. But I did not receive her confession till the last act, and then only because I was at the point of death. But it was love that gave the piece its success, and the public accepted it, and watched its progress with interest, because, plough-boy as I was in the first act, then soldier, and finally officer, I raised myself from one height of devotion to another, till I merited the supreme honor of being loved by my wife, for the lady was my wife.

I have been bitterly reproached by many critics for wishing to play serious parts. On this point my artistic conscience is perfectly easy. I have never played parts which were beyond me. No one ever saw me act a lover. Jean Dacier is a character. Who could call Le Luthier de Crémone a lover? He is a hump-back whom nobody loves. And Chamillac? He is an eccentric person, a sort of mustached apostle, who atones for a moment of madness, and who wins love indeed, but only in the end. It is a part full of reserve and capable of expression, but without the excitement of passion. And Gringoire, the unlucky poet condemned to the gallows, can *he* be called a lover? The very first *word* he hears from the girl when her eyes are directed to him is, *"Il n'est pas beau"* (he is not handsome). This is the position, and if I succeed in the end in winning love, it is with the help of poetry and of pity, it is that I am transformed by the aid of song, at any rate in the fancy of the maiden.

There is a race of actors who cannot get outside the limits of prose, others who are bound to be lyrical. I have done my best to belong to the latter class, and it is partly owing to my friends among the poets who have so often intrusted their verses to me.

V.

It is obvious that this essay rests on the theory with which I started, that in the actor the first self should be the master of the second; that the part of us which *sees* should rule as absolutely as possible the part of us which *executes*. Though this is always true, it is specially true of the moment of representation. In other words, the actor should remain master of himself. Even when the public, carried away by his action, conceives him to be abandoned to his passion, he should be able to *see* what he is doing, to judge of his effects, and to control himself—in short, he should never feel the shadow of the sentiments to which he is giving expression at the very instant that he is representing them with the utmost power and truth.

I will not return to what I have already said on this subject in *L'Art et le comédien* [1880], but I emphatically repeat it. Study your part, make yourself one with your character, but in doing this never set aside your own individuality. Keep the control of yourself. Whether your second self weeps or laughs, whether you become frenzied to madness or suffer the pains of death, it must always be under the watchful eye of your ever-impassive first self, and within certain fixed and prescribed bounds.

The best mode of representing a part once decided on, it should henceforth never vary. You must grasp your conception in such a manner as to be able to recall the image you have created, identical down to the minutest particular, when and where you please.

The actor ought never to let his part "run away" with him. It is false and ridiculous to think that it is a proof of the highest art for the actor to forget that he is before the public. If you identify yourself with your part to the point of asking yourself, as you look at the audience, "What are all those people doing here?"— if you have no more consciousness where you are and what you are doing—you have ceased to be an actor: you are a madman. Conceive Harpagon climbing the balustrade and seizing the orchestra by the throats, loudly demanding the restoration of his casket!

Art is, I repeat, not identification, but representation.

The famous maxim, if you wish to make me cry, you must cry yourself, is therefore not applicable to the actor. If he has really to cry, he would, more likely than not, make his audience laugh; for tragedy often becomes comedy to the spectators, and sorrow frequently expresses itself in a grimace.

I can quite well understand how a young man on his first appearance should lose himself in a part, and get *run away* with. Uneasy as to his reception by the public, the emotions which he has to represent become confounded with his personal feelings. This has occurred to me as well as to every one else, and I can recall it without shame, for I was then only seventeen years old. I was acting in public for the first time, and my part was Pauvre Jacques. Pauvre Jacques is an unhappy musician who goes mad from being crossed in love (another proof that I was early corrupted by my preference for tragic parts). I was suffocated with emotion; still I managed somehow to act, and perhaps some of the audience were moved to tears, but when I went behind the scenes I know I felt quite ill. This is the way with all raw recruits. But if it were to happen to me today, I should consider myself dishonored. A practised actor should be beyond the reach of such accidents.

I am aware that this theory has been questioned by many great artists. I remember an intelligent and appropriate remark made on the subject to Madame Adelaide Ristori by a young English lady full of artistic instincts. Madame Ristori was arguing that the actor could only represent truly what he was really feeling. "But, Madame," said Miss T——, "what happens when you have to die?" Plainly Madame Ristori had no intention of really dying. She acted as if she was dying, and acted extremely well, for she had previously studied, considered, and determined the manner of her death, and when the moment of representation came, she rendered her fixed impressions with all her wonderful intelligence, with the full force of her vigor and of her self-possession.

Occasionally an actor who is completely master of himself may indulge in experiments before the public, for he knows that he has himself in hand, and can always pull up. Those who have not their faculties perfectly under control run a great risk of losing their heads, and not being able to regain their self-possession for the rest of the evening. And the worst of it is that it is invariably those actors who are always trying new tricks. As they never have a firm grip of their character, they are incessantly experimenting on it. They even go the length of glorying in the fact. I once overheard some one say of Worms, "I don't care to see him act; I know exactly what he is going to do." At any rate, the speaker might have known that everything Worms did would be done well, and, after all, is not that the chief thing? Is it more satisfactory to watch an actor who, for all we know, will be perpetrating some folly the next minute? It reminds one of the Englishman who followed Batty, the lion-tamer, from place to place in the hope of one day seeing him torn in pieces by his own lions. The interest of the theatre appears to me to be of quite another kind.

VI.

There still remains the delicate question, how far great intelligence is necessary to the actor. There is much to be said on both sides. Examples are by no means rare of actors and actresses who have varied talents. Many are distinguished in literature, in painting, and in both, not to mention in ballooning.

But, after all, this intelligence is a superfluous luxury; the only intelligence indispensable to the actor is *that which belongs to his art.*

Some one, I forget who, once told me that the only French poetry Corot knew was *Polyeucte* and he never read all of that. But this did not prevent him from being a wonderful landscape-painter, and a poet down to the tip of his brush.

In the same way an actor may be totally ignorant of painting, of music, of poetry even, and yet be a good actor, and a poetical actor. It is enough for him to be steeped in his own art, which is different from these others.

And though it is different, it is equally important, and it is unfair to scoff at the special intelligence of the actor. The faculties which can touch and move men are by no means to be despised. And it is not the case that it is the author alone who gives rise to those emotions. To those who hold this I would instance Talma, Frédéric, and multitudes of others who created their own parts out of what was originally absolutely insignificant. It was to their skill and genius alone that the public owed that profound, almost divine, trouble which seizes all of us when we contemplate beauty which rends for the moment the veil of our egotism, and which is the sensation that approaches most nearly to love.

It has been said of endless pieces, "What an absurd play, but wasn't Frédéric magnificent!" Take Robert Macaire, to which I have already alluded—was not the creation of this character a prodigy, showing to what heights an actor's special intelligence can rise? The very authors were the first to be struck dumb at this astonishing conception, which substituted for their solemn puppet an imperishable comic figure.

The dramatic art is, above all, the art of humanity, and this is what makes a play the highest of pleasures, the pleasure which moves the people most powerfully, while it offers to the refined the most exquisite enjoyments.

[200]

In my opinion, therefore, it should always remain an *art;* that is, it should add the sweetness of poetry and the representation of the ideal to the expression of truth. "Naturalism" on the stage is a mistake. In the first place the public won't have it. It always resents the exhibition of revolting hideousness, of pitiless and naked realities. People do not come to the theatre for that sort of thing. Even in arts that are vile and degraded they demand a gleam of ideality....

Just as I would not allow any departure from truth on the plea of picturesque effects, so I would not permit a representation of commonplace or horrible things on the pretext of reality.

I am always on the side of nature, and against naturalism.

Nature in art! How much there is to say about it!

It is a subject that is understood differently according to the country and the century.

When Garrick came over to France he admired our actors greatly, but thought they were hardly natural enough. Perhaps some will say the reason was because they were acting tragedies. But when Talma appeared he introduced into tragedy a natural manner of speaking and moving, and it was to this that he owed his influence and his success. Was his idea of what was natural the same as Garrick's? I do not know; for the genius of the two races is very different, and the love of originality is too deep-seated in our neighbors to allow them always to use a due measure of self-restraint; and anyway today it is we who find fault with Irving for not being sufficiently natural.

The English idea of "nature" does not correspond with ours: that is the whole truth of the matter. We must also make reserves as to the German conception of nature, unnaturally tearful, resembling in its philosophic affectations the "nature" of Diderot and the susceptible school at the end of the eighteenth century.

It was they who, we must remind our readers, were really the innovators. The style which to our ears rings so false was introduced by them to the stage in the name of "nature." And it was likewise in the name of nature that the standard of the romanticists was raised—a standard which today is thrown aside and trampled in the dust by those who are weary of grandiloquence and of posing. They desired to substitute for conventional tragedy a drama which is really human, in which smiles and tears are mingled, and gave us *Anthony, La Tour de Nesle, Lucrèce Borgia.* With the same object in view, Baron Taylor collaborated with the well-known and delightful Nodier, and put on the stage *Melmouth, ou l'Homme errant* (*The Wanderer*), *Les Vampires, Honte et remords* (*Shame and Remorse*), *Amour et étourderie* (*Love and Carelessness*), etc. These were obviously "natural" in quite another sense from that of Voltaire; and the actors, making common cause with the authors, declared Talma to be unnatural. They took it into their heads to speak as people "really speak," in such a way that no one could hear them, and to sit with their backs to the audience. They recited the poetry of *Athalie* precisely as they would have said, "Good morning, how are you?" "Good heavens, yes," said Abner, "I have come to worship the Almighty in His temple. I have come just as I am, cane in hand, to celebrate with my friends the famous occasion on Mount Sinai, where, if I am not vastly mistaken, the law was given to us. *Sapristi!* how times have changed!" They flattered themselves that in this manner they were introducing "nature" into Racine. On the other hand, when they were on their own ground, that is, in the melodramas, the emphasis of the metre once more reasserted itself. It was not indeed the sepulchral and montonous singsong of yore; it was a halting kind of sublimity—wild bursts of verse, and a sudden alacrity in singing. They no longer said, "How are you?" but "Let me grasp that manly hand." There were hidden meanings everywhere. They wore an air of doom from head to foot. It was an era of hat and feather. But is there no feather on the hat of M. Zola? Were he to have his way we should be threatened with a new madness of extremes, but this time it would be the extreme of the trivial and commonplace. What I mean by art that is natural in the modern sense is equally remote from both these extremes. It is classic rather than romantic, for everywhere it regards limit, everywhere it shuns violent antithesis.

The actor with this ideal does not give an exaggerated importance to different aspects of his part. He does not try to play three or four different characters at once; he aims, on the other hand, at unity and a broad general representation of humanity. He sees things as they are, but he conforms to the general rules of theatrical conventions, and to the particular necessities of the part he is interpreting. The "nature" of the tragedy differs from that of the melodrama, and that again from the comedy, and it is impossible to render it in the same way. Hence Frédéric ought never to be reproached for not acting always naturally. The kind of parts he undertook demanded certain exaggerations. He would, after the manner of his school, speak ten lines in a conventional fashion, in order to be able to give to the eleventh a truer and more natural ring. He was forced to say the verses as they were written, and when he at last made his point with the true intonation, it left behind it a deeper impression of naturalness than the foregoing lines had done of unreality.

And here I must close, for this is not a formal treatise on acting, still less an apology. Every artist in speaking of his art seems in some degree a special pleader. Of course he only wishes to preach what he believes to be true, and that which he believes to be true is what he tries to do himself. I have said what the comedian should be, but I am far from flattering myself that I realize my ideal, and if I have alluded to myself, it is only for the sake of illustrating more clearly my arguments. I should have preferred to erase any personal note from these pages, as I have always tried to do from my parts, where my wish is to be, to enter into, nothing but the characters I play. For, after all, that is the essential point, and it is with that I must end. Is not the greatest poet he who has managed to efface himself the most entirely, in whose pages you find every kind of man, but never himself?

It was thus with the father of poetry, Homer; it was thus with Shakespeare and with Molière: all are absent from their works, where humanity in its thousand varied aspects lives eternally.

Herein standeth our honor, the honor of all us players, namely, in this, that these two men, its chief creators after God, were players like ourselves. Therefore should we study their works religiously and without ceasing, nor ever turn from them, save it be to peruse that eternal Comedy of Human Nature.

SARAH BERNHARDT

(1844-1923)

"The Divine Sarah" was born in Paris of French and Dutch-Jewish stock. Her real name was Rosine Bernard. Of her French father hardly anything can be learned. Her mother is described as "a wandering beauty," forever traveling. Sarah's

FRANCE

lonely childhood was spent at a boarding school and later at the Augustinian convent at Versailles. When she was fifteen, a family council voted down Sarah's ambition to be a nun. Instead, she went to the *Conservatoire,* France's famous school for actors of the government theatres. Her intelligence, coupled with extraordinary nervous energy, won her two second prizes, one for tragedy in 1861, and one for comedy in 1862. She never won a first prize, but the discernment of the judges led to a contract with the *Comédie Française.*

Her debut in 1862 in Racine's *Iphigenie* is described by the critic Sarcey, later one of her great admirers: "Mlle. Bernhardt ... is a tall, pretty girl with a slender figure and a very pleasing expression. The upper part of her face is remarkably beautiful. She holds herself well, and her enunciation is perfectly clear. This is all that can be said for her at present."

Bernhardt's career falls into three periods: six years (1866-1872) at the *Odéon,* a playhouse of the Latin Quarter—"the theatre," Bernhardt says, "that I loved the most"; a second term (1872-1880) at the *Comédie Française;* and her long career as her own mistress, accepting engagements where it pleased her, managing her own theatres, and traveling over all the world. In addition to most of the European countries, the United States, and Canada, her tours took her to Mexico, Brazil, Argentina, Egypt, and even as far afield as Australia.

Her first big success came at the *Odéon* at twenty-two, when she recited the choruses in *Athalie* in her celebrated "voice of gold." From then on, for almost fifty years, she worked, and worked hard, molding a fabulous career out of an impetuous feminine personality of amazing vitality. In 1895 George Bernard Shaw, then the dramatic critic of the *Saturday Review,* observed Sarah with shrewd insight which goes to the heart of Bernhardt's fascination for the public: "She is beautiful with the beauty of her school, and entirely inhuman and incredible. But the incredibility is pardonable, because, though it is all the greatest nonsense, nobody believing in it, the actress herself least of all, it is so artful, so clever, so well recognized a part of the business, and carried off with such a genial air, that it is impossible not to accept it with good-humor." Bernhardt's acting, Shaw pointed out, was "not the art of making you think more highly or feel more deeply, but the art of making you admire her...." Every character she created was compounded of her electric personal charm. "She does not enter into the leading character," wrote Shaw, "she substitutes herself for it."

Bernhardt's emotional power and magnetism were at their best in classic roles such as *Phèdre* (1874) and Doña Sol in *Hernani* (1877). In 1899 she attempted Hamlet, to the satisfaction of the French, at least. "She never did anything finer," said Rostand. Other notable Bernhardt productions were *Jeanne d'Arc* by Jules Barbier (1890), Moreau's *Cléopâtre* (1890), Lemaître's *Les Rois* (1893), Sudermann's *Heimat*(1895), and Rostand's *L'Aiglon,* written for her in 1901.

Duse was Bernhardt's only rival and was for many years considered to be her inferior. This opinion has been modified in more recent years. Certainly Duse never captured the public imagination to the extent that Bernhardt at the height of her powers did.

The Bernhardt legend, compounded of a flair for off-stage dramatics which included sleeping in a coffin, horse-whipping a rival, and collecting a menagerie of a cheetah, a wolf, and a half-dozen chameleons, is capped by Sarah's reappearance on the stage following the amputation of her leg in her seventy-first year. Even in the midst of the horrors of the First World War her ordeal gained world-

ACTORS ON ACTING

wide sympathy. From her bedside Sarah issued a characteristic statement: "Work is my life. So soon I shall be fitted with an artificial leg, I shall resume the stage and all my good spirits shall be restored. I hope again to be able to use all that force of art which now upholds me and which will sustain me until beyond the grave." Following numerous "farewell tours," her last appearances on the stage were for the benefit of French war charities. Her death in 1923 was mourned in the hundreds of cities where audiences had idolized her.

Among her many writings on her life and art we find the volume *The Art of the Theatre* from which the following selection is drawn. It presents Bernhardt's evaluation of the art for which she was celebrated.

The Evolution of the Actor

The role of the actor has become increasingly important throughout the transformations of dramatic art. The theatre of antiquity, like modern opera, relied on mass movement; crowds lent it a sustained movement; consequently personal qualities only assumed secondary importance. It will be remembered that in the first Greek dramas the individuals were almost drowned in the chorus. But, as by degrees dramatists applied themselves to the analysis of sentiments, the study of the human soul, and the portrayal of passions, love, hate, vengeance, cupidity, etc., the actor's art developed, exacting greater study, and becoming more complex and less easily acquired. The more tragedy or comedy evolved, and tragedy and comedy remained separate until Shakespeare's time (as far as Europe was concerned this lasted until the advent of Romanticism)—the greater was the stress put upon the personal value of the interpreters. The actor's profession became specialized: in antiquity any citizen of Athens or of Corinth might have been called upon to impersonate Prometheus, Xerxes, or Jupiter. Nearer to our own time, Shakespeare and Molière, who performed in their own plays, appear already as glorious exceptions. The actor of our time remains simply an actor, and his task is big enough and toilsome enough to absorb all his energy.

It is true that there has been a recent tendency for crowds to be put on the stage again; the intention being to depict social evils, and give utterance to collective sentiments—and it might be supposed that in these circumstances the actor would lack an incentive to display his special abilities. One example of these new works is *The Weavers* of Gerhart Hauptmann; but the contemporary author—as Ibsen in *An Enemy of the People* or Björnson in *Beyond Human Power*—takes care to leave each man his special features, and the role of the actor, instead of being facilitated, is rendered more onerous, for he must express his own emotions and form part of the collective soul at the same time. It is therefore permissible to conclude that as the dramatist's art moves towards perfection, more and more work will be imposed upon the actor who intends to keep pace with its progress.

It might be a matter for surprise that so many comedians and tragedians of the first rank can be quoted in modern times, while so few persons of exceptional talent can be placed to the credit of past ages. But the simple reason is that these persons of exceptional gifts either did not exist or found no scope for their abilities.

Sarah Bernhardt: *The Art of the Theatre*. Translated by H. J. Stenning. London: G. Bles, 1924, pp. 83-93, 95-101, 103-106. Copyright 1924. By permission of Geoffrey Bles, Ltd.

In our day, the intrinsic value of a play assuredly counts for much in the reception it will meet with from the public;—but the part of the actor is hardly less great than that of the scenario or the mode of treatment.

If first-rate parts are entrusted to bad actors, it is most likely that the comedy, in spite of all its merits, will be hissed off the stage or withdrawn from the theatre. Works that have moved, roused, and astonished successive generations will leave the public cold and even hostile if they do not find proper interpreters. Le Cid, Polyeucte, Tartuffe, Andromaque, would only be ridiculous, despite their literary beauties and their powerful portrayals of passions, if the parts were entrusted to incapable actors. But the contrary is not quite accurate: a very bad tragedy or a deplorable drama entrusted to actors of the first class never remains a long time on the bills; but a mediocre work—instances are numerous—will last to the hundredth performance or longer, if it be assisted by interpreters of ample powers. In this actors resemble those musical virtuosi whose prodigious talents bestow fame upon pieces of music that are scarcely worth hearing. We cannot therefore overestimate the value of those who play in modern drama. And it is not enough for an author to have composed a comedy of high literary merit or of subtle psychology: he must also discover suitable interpreters, and the latter must combine the rare and manifold qualities that make up a great actor. To be quite truthful, it must be confessed that actors of the first water are not more plentiful than playwrights of genius.

Instruction

If we consider the matter carefully, it will be plain that the actor's most important quality—or better, his primary duty—is comprehensive study. To be sure, it is good for him to possess imagination, even a strong inventive capacity; his imagination must play freely, and he must not feel hampered in the expansion of his nature. Art excludes of necessity everything that is stiff and rigid. But nothing can take the place of the study of men and of periods. The character of Caesar, or of Hamlet, or of Augustus cannot be improvised. If the actor is totally ignorant of history, if he cannot fit characters into their environment, if he is incapable of investing them with the sentiments that were common to their epoch, their generation, their class, even their party, he will never be anything but a second-rate actor. Doubtless this was a matter of less importance in the grand siècle, when local color was systematically banished, and the selection of costumes was held to be secondary. The slight regard paid to historic truth is revealed for example in the language attributed to the characters, and Racine's Mussulmen, in Bajazet, or the Jews in Athalie, or the Greeks in Iphigenie could quite conveniently be taken for courtiers. The knowledge that our actors are required to possess today seemed at that time out of place or useless. And it is precisely because our age and our public show themselves to be more exacting and more ready to ridicule an actor who is feebly endowed with the historic sense that the professional making of the actor requires infinitely more labor.

Consequently the actor must become familiar with the entire past of humanity —and be it said that these researches must not be superficial. What is expected of him is not only a clear conception of the facts and of the men, it is the spiritual content of the manners, the customs, and the passions of different peoples and of different times. It is certain that love does not reveal itself in every age in the same forms, and that the expressions of hate vary from century to century, and from people to people. Moreover, different social groups have their proper characteristics, and just as Molière did not ascribe the same language to Alceste as to Mascarille, to Elvire as to Dorine, so the attitudes, the gestures, and all the mannerisms of the actor must reflect with exactitude the sentiments of the characers. Now how can these sentiments be embodied without dipping into books—for the past—and into the great current of life—for the present, in order to gather the data, which are to be coordinated and systematized, and harmoniously fused in mimicry, in delivery, and in the general representation of character?

Thus from the outset nothing seems more difficult or more laborious than the creation of a part. It is not given to everybody to play the part of an emperor, or a workman, a great lady of the *ancien régime* or of the fashionable world, and no doubt a hasty preparation, immediately before the first performance, would only have an absurdly precarious value. Nothing short of a thorough grounding in his subjects, such as will enable him to draw upon all his resources at a specified moment, and will plunge him in the full personality of the character he is impersonating, of the times through which he moves, will enable the interpreter to rise to the height of all his obligations.

The actor must be—if not a scholar or a learned man—at least what used to be called "an all-round man," that is, he should not be inferior in the matter of acquired knowledge to the average of mankind. It should be noted that each person belongs to a social stratum, from which he cannot emerge save for an extraordinary mishap or exceptional good fortune; that he is as it were chained there for life. It is only the actor who passes from extreme abjection to extreme splendor, from the direst poverty to the most sumptuous opulence, from the age of the Greeks to that of the Inquisition or our own. He expresses in turn the superstition of an Agamemnon, the fantacism of a Duke of Alba, or the social anger of a workman on strike. But in addition to the information derived from books, he is constrained to exercise ceaseless vigilance, and the famous chair of Molière remains the best of symbols. Let the actor be inquisitive about all professions and all strata of society; let him strive to educate himself concerning all the customs of exotic peoples; in a word, let him concentrate in his work the whole of present and the whole of future humanity: the labor is arduous, but its importance cannot be overestimated.

The Choice of a Part

When the parts of a play are being allotted, the actor is not always free to choose his part, to adapt himself to the character that best suits him. Unless he is peerless and his genius has endowed him with exceptional prerogatives, he is bound to accept the part assigned to him. But so far as his abilities permit, he must try to give an impersonation that is consonant with his resources. If it be true that there are no such things as small parts, that an actor can produce good effects from an ephemeral creation—and that the hierarchy that prevails in life does not obtain on the stage—it behooves each person to study his capabilities, and become acquainted with his strong points and his weak points. He who excels in *Othello* will be deplorable in the *Bourgeois Gentilhomme*. This does not mean that distinction of classes must be maintained intact, that comedy must be separated from tragedy or from drama by an insurmountable barrier, and that one should be a slave to literary categories.

But *Othello* and the *Bourgeois Gentilhomme* require the exertion of different qualities that might very well not be combined in the same man. If the sage's motto "Know thyself" is valuable in all the conjunctures of life, it has special application to the case of the actor....

The Will

In every other profession, once a certain position has been acquired, once a certain routine has been organized, a man may rest a little on his oars. In the theatre, the nervous tension never ceases, physical effort is added to and fused with intellectual effort. To be a good actor, to pursue the career of a Talma, of a Kean, of a Rachel, it is necessary to have a firmly tempered soul, to be surprised at nothing, to resume each minute the laborious task that has barely just been finished.

To pass in this way from one part to another, to stride across the centuries, to play Brutus after having impersonated Caesar, or Juliet after having represented Lady Macbeth, to have the thoughts and feelings of numberless individuals and to express them alternately: all this is a weariness likely to break the strongest. No doubt they are sustained by the enchanting joy of creation; they come to earth again when impersonating a fresh character; they live in a world of passions that stimulate their vital force and lift them out of themselves;—but if will power be not invoked, if in their creation of this or that character, they were not sustained at once by their high artistic conscience and a determination that is proof against everything, they would very often be tempted to stick to the parts already mastered.

Now the actor who lacks the versatility enabling him to adapt himself to every exigency, who does not keep abreast of dramatic literature itself, the man who would restrict himself to the Greek poets, or to Molière, or to Shakespeare—such an one falls short in the performance of his duty. He should be prepared to throw himself into the most modern fictions and serve them with the fullness of his talent. Unlike those scholars who always pursue their investigations into the same subject, and whose activities become almost automatic, he must be prepared to sacrifice at any moment the acquired routine, the repose to which he considers himself entitled, in order to plunge into fresh studies. Art is ageless, and the artist must not know age. Not by indolence or by self-indulgence, but by the absolute possession and mastery of his personality will the artist be able to raise himself to the supreme glory of men whose lives are all creation, all labor, and all enthusiasm.

Naturalism

Great actors have always been judged by the naturalism they exhibit in their acting. Fidelity to the truth does not always distinguish in our present-day art, and the public will not tolerate a glossing over of reality. The conventions and affected behavior that might have been admissable at certain periods would certainly not be acceptable at the present time. In this respect dramatic art has made remarkable progress in the course of the last century. But what do we mean by naturalism? Just as literary or pictorial art will suppress certain objects which could not be exhibited to the eyes of the reader or visitor, so the actor must not shock the modesty of those who listen to him. All art whatsoever presupposes enlightened selection, and no purpose is served by being brutally natural. What it behooves the artist to do, and what is expected of him, is that, in observing the minimum of propriety, he should exhibit the feelings that are supposed to animate him, in the manner they are exhibited in real life by average men amongst his contemporaries. And here must be emphasized once again the necessity of profound study. To be natural does not mean that an actor should exhibit the passions in the manner they are exhibited by everybody and under all circumstances in his epoch. Just as the actor is bound, in order to perfect his acting, to be thoroughly acquainted with the character, so he must realize that the degree of sensibility is not invariable in all centuries and in all places. The sorrow of old Horace may not be expressed in the same way as that of the Miser whose cash-box has been stolen. The fury of vengeance does not assume the same aspect with Othello as with a husband in modern comedy who has discovered the treachery of his wife. Thus naturalism is inseparable from study. But what is indisputable is that naturalism involves qualities that are anterior to all study, innate qualities of various kinds. He who is incapable of feeling strong passions, of being shaken by anger, of living in every sense of the word will never be a good actor. . . .

If you would be natural, you must avoid the persistent mannerisms that actors frequently adopt, believing they please the public. In the end these become merely bad habits. You must avoid stiff and chronic poses in order to fit into the innumerable vicissitudes of existence; you must grasp the social position of each character so as to place it in the proper setting. Each class or category of men is different from the next class or category. The spectator must discover his typical manners on the stage and be able to recognize them at first glance. But the true actor specially distinguishes himself in the great crises of passion. There is no one way of representing affliction, or expressing the extremity of anger. Nothing is more distasteful than to act according to a formula that is constantly repeated; to have a laugh ready to be adapted to all characters or a manner of dying which will persist in every dramatic fiction. Nature which has not made two beings alike requires incessant diversity. It is true that the more one attempts to define what is natural, the more one perceives the difficulty of squeezing it into a brief and simple formula. For centuries and centuries artists of every class have discussed this serious problem. But in any case, it is possible and permissable to set up a criterion, which may be arbitrary, but is none the less valuable. When a popular audience is moved to tears by the anguish of the actor, when forgetting theatrical convention it imagines that it is present at a real drama, the actor will know that he has achieved the object of his art: he may pride himself on having been natural, for it is never by employing mannerisms that he can plunge an audience into emotion.

Sensibility

An actor cannot be natural unless he really has power to project his personality. He must in a way forget himself, and divest himself of his proper attributes in order to assume those of his part. He must forget the emotion of the moment, the joy or the sorrow born of the events of the day. . . .

If the actor retains his mode of living, of thinking and of behaving throughout the manifold characters that he successively impersonates, he cannot feel the passions of these characters; and, unless he can enter into the feelings of his heroes, however violent they may be, however cruel and vindictive they may seem, he will never be anything but a bad actor. Coldness will be his portion, and not the impetuous ardor which carries away an audience and which is the hallmark of genius. If he does not really feel the anguish of the betrayed lover or of the dishonored father, if he does not temporarily escape from the dullness of his existence in order to throw himself wholeheartedly into the most acute crises, he will move nobody. How can he convince another of his emotion, of the sincerity of his passions, if he is

[208]

unable to convince himself to the point of actually becoming the character that he has to impersonate?

I cannot forbear repeating here the example of Coquelin, who was insensible to the passions of the dramatic characters that he impersonated. The public itself remained unmoved, at which Coquelin was most illogically surprised. But he never managed to acquire sensibility.

The artist must be like one of those sounding discs which vibrate to every wind, and are agitated by the slightest breeze. If he is not shaken by anger, and if pity does not move him profoundly, he will appear insipid. The public will remember that it is at the play, that an artificial hero is in front of it, that within an hour or two the play will be over, and that, after quitting the sumptuous decorations, it will be back at its dull fireside. The emotion sought after will not have been captured; the anticipated resurrection will not have taken place; the audience that has remained unmoved by the performance of the actor, who can give no artistic pleasure, will rightly complain that it has been cheated.

To be worthy of the name an actor must be capable of a continuous dissection of his personality. Great artists have wept like Juliet or like Andromaque, felt the transports of savage love like Phèdre or Hermione, or suffered the pangs of remorse like Macbeth. Hamlet's frenzy will make the spectators shudder if the actor really feels he is Hamlet. Do not let us delude ourselves that we can wear the vesture of another's soul while preserving our own; do not let us imagine for a moment that we can create an artificial exterior while maintaining our ordinary feelings intact. The actor cannot divide his personality between himself and his part; he loses his ego during the time he remains on the stage, and thus his consciousness skips from age to age, from one people to another, from one social stratum to another, from one hero to another. What he undertakes is a crushing burden; the task he essays is almost super-human if he resolves to accomplish it in all its fullness, and intends to be worthy of his art. He must vivify the thought of the poet or of the dramatist, who also deserts his age and his *milieu* for the age and the *milieu* of his creations. When Shakespeare wrote *Othello* or *The Merchant of Venice,* he ceased to be an Englishman of his generation, he had temporarily sloughed off the real man, in order to be imbued with all the passion of a jealous Moor, or all the cupidity of a fanatical miser. He did not merely forget the material or moral preoccupations which worried him a few minutes previously, but he was transported by thought, on the wings of imagination, towards other skies. The quality of imagination, which is the master faculty of the poet, must be assimilated by the actor, through whose mind the most diverse ideas must pass at will, and these ideas must be vivid enough to efface the preceding thoughts, and to summon to their aid all the effective and intellectual resources of the actor. By virtue of this quality the actor equals the poet in creative power.

ANDRE ANTOINE

(1858 - 1943)

To answer Emile Zola's cry for naturalism in the theatre which would put "a man of flesh and bones on the stage, taken from reality, scientifically analyzed, without one lie," came André Antoine. Born in Limoges, but living most of his life in Paris, Antoine went to work at the age of twelve. He educated himself by reading

[209]

avidly and taking courses whenever and wherever he could. He had always been fond of the theatre, and became a member of the *Comédie Française* claque, that unique French institution of hired applauders. Next he became a supernumerary at the *Théâtre* where he could watch closely the great stars whom he admired. He took lessons in diction and recitation at the *Gymnase de la Parole,* where he tried his youthful hand at directing classical plays. Later he attempted to get into the famed *Conservatoire,* but being without influential friends, he failed.

After five years in the army he became a clerk in a gas company in Paris. Joining the amateur group, *Cercle Gaulois,* he urged them to present original plays instead of those in the archaic repertoire and projected a program of new plays, which included an adaptation of one of Zola's stories. Some of the members refused to participate and denied Antoine the use of their club for rehearsal. Antoine persisted, and with a small group he founded the *Théâtre Libre.* Zola came to the rehearsals and brought along Daudet; both praised the work of the amateurs. The first performance in 1887 succeeded largely through Antoine's acting and directing of the Zola story *Jacques Damour.* The celebrated Free Theatre had begun.

For eight years, struggling with inadequate finances and opposition to their largely naturalistic program, the *Théâtre Libre* produced the plays of Curel and Brieux and provided a theatre for productions of the plays of Tolstoy, Ibsen, and Hauptmann. Antoine's integrity is attested to by the fact that when his talents as an actor brought him an offer from the *Odéon* theatre, at the close of the first season of the *Théâtre Libre,* he refused. Apart from his creative inspiration as a director and producer of important modern French and foreign plays, Antoine was an ex-cellent naturalistic actor. One critic wrote: "He never plays Antoine, he always plays his character and, penetrating the soul of his character, he presents him in an unforgettable manner. It is singular, but it seems that there is no stage, and that the raised curtain of the *Théâtre Libre* discloses people in their houses going about their affairs unconsciously and without knowing that they are being watched." In an effort to create reality on the stage, he often turned his back to the audience, and it became a joke to call the *Théâtre Libre* "Antoine's Back."

He criticized the teaching at the *Conservatoire,* and urged that the art of acting be founded on truth, observation, and the study of nature. Together with these innovations in acting, Antoine also made reforms in staging, influenced heavily by the German Meininger Company, and revolutionized stage settings by introducing the vivid "slice of life."

In 1894 fatigued by years of struggle he turned the theatre over to others. After playing and directing at several theatres he opened the *Théâtre Antoine* in 1897 where he repeated some of his earlier successes. From 1906 to 1914 he was the director of the *Odéon,* the second greatest theatre in Paris. After World War I he became a drama critic and the dean of French theatrical writers, directors, and actors.

Antoine's diaries for the years 1887 to 1929 detail a running account of his life in the theatre. In May, 1890, during the second season of the *Théâtre Libre,* he formulated an artistic program to acquaint the public with his theatrical ideals. The following selection, dealing with the actor in the *Théâtre Libre,* is drawn from this manifesto and is being made available in translation for the first time.

The New Acting of the *Théâtre Libre*

THE ACTORS

I.

It is not too much to assert that, with but a few exceptions, all the works presented by the *Théâtre Libre* have been played by amateurs, that is, by volunteer actors who do not at present follow the acting profession and have never appeared in a public theatre.

The core of the company of the *Théâtre Libre* has been composed, for these three past winters, of young people who have come from various private organizations where they put on plays for their personal pleasure.

This does not, of. course, mean that we consider these performers on the same level as professional actors.

If the monthly performances of the *Théâtre Libre* have at times been judged adequate from the point of view of interpretation, we must not forget how tolerant the audiences have been of our presentations. They were not unaware of the fact these actors-by-night were simple workers or employees who worked hard because of their love of the theatre and who, because of their daily occupations, did the best they could.

As a basis for the comments we are about to make, we should like to choose deliberately, among the various pieces of the *Théâtre Libre,* the cast of the *Power of Darkness.* Whether the audience was unusually indulgent that evening, or whether the masterpiece which our improvised actors had the rare honor of interpreting stimulated the critics, their notices were unanimous in pointing out the irreproachable and adequate (we do not say perfect) performances of the various characters in the play.

Casting a glance at the program for the evening of February 10, 1888, we see that the various roles in Tolstoy's drama were created by an employee of the Ministry of Finances, a secretary in a precinct police-station, an architect, a chemist, a traveling salesman, a wine-merchant, a bronze-manufacturer, etc....

Moreover, the important feminine roles were played by a dressmaker, a bookbinder, a post-office worker, etc. All these young people only rehearsed evenings— as is the custom of the *Théâtre Libre*—and after their day's work.

It is easy to quote here the name of one of the most eminent French critics who, watching the ensemble and following the spirit of their interpretation, stated that he had never seen a theatre piece better acted. M. de Vogüé, an expert in things Russian, openly expressed his amazement in a scholarly study in the *Revue des Deux-Mondes* at the striking truthfulness with which the principal characters in the play were portrayed.

Since then, almost all of these apprentice actors have played to different audiences—at London, at Brussels—and everywhere they have been received as professional actors. Nor have they ever been found wanting in their efforts.

Finally, about a dozen actors of the *Théâtre Libre* have gone in the past three years to other theatres in Paris. Five of them are at present members of the *Odéon*

André Antoine: *Le Théâtre Libre*. Paris: May, 1890, pp. 72-90. This selection translated by Joseph M. Bernstein.

company, where unfortunately the directors either could not or would not utilize the qualities which the critics had discovered in them.

This revealing example leads us to ask if it is not possible to organize a special and unique company for a true theatre, a company which, disregarding personalities and outstanding talents, would give especially interesting productions.

We must ask ourselves if we cannot draw some conclusions from the work of these inexperienced actors, possessing only their natural gifts, their good will and their intelligence, lacking all traditional theatrical training and yet for three years successfully carrying out the difficult task of interpreting the plays of widely assorted dramatists. May we not simply conclude that the traditional training they lacked is perhaps dangerous—and at the very least useless and above all badly organized?

Since we are careful here not to make empty statements and feel duty-bound not to make frivolous accusations but always to test theories by the facts, it becomes necessary—however lacking in interest these digressions may be—to examine in passing this traditional schooling against which we cannot protest strongly enough.

* * * *

III.

We have an outstanding school of acting, one which is strangely diluted in and almost absorbed by a music school which is far more important and more privileged than our theatrical schools. Naturally, the State subsidizes, supports, administers, and watches over this dual institution.

At the school on the Rue Bergère there are four classes in acting, each taught by an eminent actor. Certainly one could choose no better persons than Messrs. Got, Delaunay, Maubant, and Worms. Each one of these teachers, two of whom are very busy at the *Comédie-Française,* devote a two-hour class twice a week to the subject they teach. Since the school year extends over some eight months, the yearly amount of time spent may be estimated at from *a hundred to a hundred and twenty-five hours.* Each instructor teaches a dozen students of both sexes. *Hence it follows that a young man taking a course receives at most ten hours of direct teaching per year.*

What can such a system produce? At the very best, the teacher will have had the time at the end of the school year to give a dozen lessons to a student. Thus, the teaching is limited to a small number of classical scenes given irrespective of the natures and temperaments of the students.

We might easily cite the example of a *jeune premier* admitted to the *Conservatoire* after auditioning a scene of a hundred lines of poetry, who studied three years in the same role, won first prize, and then one fine evening made his debut at the *Comédie-Française* in this self-same passage. How can this prize-winning artist be capable of composing or creating anything whatever when, once he has made his debut, he finds himself called upon to portray another character?

Everyone protests against the deplorable results of these competitions at the end of the school year; everyone demands reforms, which in the present state of affairs are impossible and useless. The source itself is corrupted.

The recruitment of students is not the product of entrance examinations but of recommendations, "pull," and the intervention of influential individuals. It is impossible for a young man endowed with a passion for the theatre, even if he has the finest talent, to get into a class if he is not lucky enough to have influence.

The result is that at the present time some of the prize-winners are not even utilized. Walking the streets of Paris are ten first prize-winners (whom I could name) who are not wanted by any director and who are absolutely unable to exercise an art they have studied for four years under the conditions we have jut outlined.

Why not say so? The instructors at the *Conservatoire* themselves do not believe in the merits of the system; and one of them eagerly sends his pupils to the *Théâtre Libre* where they can learn their profession at the best and the only great school: *the audience.*

IV.

In view of the hoped-for development of a new generation of writers and dramatic works, we are on good grounds if we affirm that this rebirth will demand new means of expression. Plays based on keen study and observation will require interpreters, lively and genuine actors imbued with reality.

These future works, based on a broader and more flexible aesthetic, in which the characters are no longer typed; this new theatre, no longer based—as was the theatre before it—on five or six conventional types, always the same and constantly reappearing under different names and in different plots and settings; this multiplicity and complexity of characters brought to the stage will, I have no doubt, bring forth a new generation of actors apt for all kinds of roles. *Jeunes premiers,* for example, will no longer be just a single type but will become in turn good, evil, stupid, witty, elegant, vulgar, strong, weak, courageous, and cowardly. In short, they will be living beings—complex and variable.

Thus the actor's art will no longer be based, as was that of the acting companies in the past, on physical qualities and natural gifts: it will thrive on truth, observation, *direct* study of nature.

We will achieve in the theatre what has occurred in the other interpretative arts, in painting, for example, where the landscape-artist no longer works in his studio but in the open air and in the midst of life. The theatre will no longer produce dramatic artists repeating the same roles over and over again, roles which have been created and established for centuries by several generations of famous actors. The actor's intellectual talent will again be directed toward truth and exactness.

Since the theatrical style in the new works tends more toward the use of everyday conversation, the performer will no longer have to *declaim* in the narrow and classical sense of the term but will have to *talk,* a feat which will be found to be as difficult.

V.

What at the present time is meant by the term, *the art of elocution,* consists solely of endowing the student with exaggerated enunciation, of developing his voice as a *special* organ quite different from the voice he really possesses. For sixty years now, all the actors have spoken only through their *nose,* simply because that kind of elocution is necessary to be heard by the audience in our *too large halls with their poor acoustics,* and also because speaking through the nose prevents the voice from aging and wearing out with the years.

All of the characters in the present-day theatre have the same gestures and express themselves technically in the same manner, whether they be old or young, ill or in good health. All the *fine-speaking* artists forego those infinitely numerous nuances which could illuminate a character and give it a more intense life....

In most of our theatres, either too huge or badly built, not only do the players not speak, they *yell;* and the unfortunate actors are forced to do this so much that even when they play on the boulevard theatres they retain these excesses and exaggerations which cause an actor to stand out among ten people chatting.

VI.

The same transformation will have to take place in the other spheres of dramatic art: with stage-sets brought back to the actual dimensions of scenes of contemporary life, the actors will play in true-to-life settings, without the constant need to *strike poses* in the customary sense of the term. The audience will enjoy in an intimate play, developing simply and naturally, the simple gestures and natural movements of a modern man living our everyday life.

The actual movements on the stage will be modified: the actor will no longer step out of the setting in which he has been playing and pose before the audience. He will fit in with the furniture and the stage-props; and his performance will be broadened to include those thousands of nuances and details which have become indispensable in capturing the spirit of a character and building it logically.

Purely mechanical movement, voice effects, empirical and redundant gestures will disappear with the simplification of theatrical action and its return to reality. The actor will come back to natural gestures and will substitute *composition for effects achieved solely by means of the voice.* Expressions will be based on familiar and real props: a returned pencil or an overturned cup will be as significant and will have as profound an effect on the minds of the audience as the grandiloquent exaggerations of the romantic theatre.

VII.

Need we add, moreover, that this apparent revolution is nothing but a return to the greatest examples of tradition and that the most illustrious actors who have graced the French stage have owed their magnificent effects to simple means?

Do we not have behind us the lesson of Hippolyte Clairon, playing Racine with more naturalness than her predecessors and rivals had found in him?

What about Tommaso Salvini, the Italian tragedian we admired when he was in Paris? Did he not move us profoundly by the soberness of the methods he used?

Furthermore, has not Got, the present-day dean of our great theatre, in a long series of truly modern creations, proved the power of his admirable art by the simplicity and genuine originality of his portrayals?

Has not Mounet-Sully, in his *Hamlet,* aimed at and achieved the loftiest and most original conceptions of his career by his simple and almost trivial contrasts (2nd and 4th scenes of *Hamlet*)?

Finally, are not the élite of our reigning artists, Réjane, Fèbvre, Dupuis, and St.-Germain actors who aim above all at nature and who attempt to embrace truth?

Did not Molière himself assert on several occasions that it was necessary to "act as one speaks." And does not his Mascarille make fun of the actors who cannot or will not bring out *"the high points"?*

[214]

VIII.

Although it may sound a little paradoxical, one may almost lay down the proposition that: *In an actor, the profession is the enemy of art.*

We mean the professional skill that is abnormally developed, that invades everything; we mean too frequent tricks and cleverness which stifle personality and dominate the supreme quality of the dramatic performer: *emotion,* that kind of special and double senstivity which imbues the actor who is a true artist.

Here, moreover, as in all the arts, sincerity, *élan,* a kind of conviction, and the special fever that grips the interpreter are the most precious gifts.

The teaching of drama, as it is applied, snuffs out this special kind of nervousness and levels all temperaments. Individuality becomes rarer and rarer, and we find that our greatest actors were mediocre students precisely because their artistic temperament resisted traditions and narrow, over-specialized training. How many of the ten noted actors of Paris distinguished themselves in competitions at the *Conservatoire?*

Once someone asked Stendhal if he had ever seen a play perfectly rendered. He replied: "Yes, some time ago in Italy, by mediocre actors in a barn."

Obviously, he was referring to the way in which these obscure and unknown actors had acted as an *ensemble.* And he was certainly right, for is not *ensemble* playing the most complete and the most exquisite joy in the theatre? We must admit that such a treat is almost impossible today; even the *Théâtre-Française,* which nevertheless has in its company the most remarkable actors in Europe, is no longer able to give us such a treat. We have to go back several years and recall the opening performances of *L'Ami Fritz,* for example, to remind ourselves what *true ensemble acting* is like.

The *Comédie-Française* finds itself today in the same situation as the other Paris theatres in which the *star* system has done so much harm to the dramatic art (and to the manager's box-office receipts!). Everywhere, when we spend an evening at the theatre, we are fascinated by one or two first-rate artists around whom everything gravitates and for whom everything is arranged. But in such a state of affairs, what—from the strictly artistic point of view—becomes of the measure, the balance, and the harmony of a dramatic work? Develop this theory before any present-day actor, and he will only be concerned in his performance with the part assigned to him: he will think only of amplifying and developing his own role and its effect, even at the expense of throwing the whole work out of balance.

A very young artist at the *Comédie-Française,* already crowned with success and endowed with a keen intelligence, had to carry in a lamp and a letter in the third act of one of the masterpieces of the contemporary theatre. He was very astonished to hear the following said to him: "But, my dear sir, even though you have shown so much talent, subtlety, and finesse in the modest part you played this evening, you forget one of the basic principles of the art of the actor: *keep the character you portray on his own level.* When you carry the lamp and the letter, you are nothing but a slight incident imagined by the author in order to hasten the course of his action. As you hand over the letter to Mlle. Bartet, one of the protagonists in the play, on whom all the attention and interest of the audience are concentrated at that precise moment by the express will of the author, if you find a way of putting on the entire *Fourberies de Scapin, Les Précieuses ridicules,* and the five acts of *L'Etourdi,* you will win applause from the indulgent playgoers, but you will introduce an extraneous element into the drama, you will harm the skillful ordering of the work you are interpreting." .

This young man certainly did not understand what the other person meant, yet he is one of the outstanding talents in the current theatre.

So the model for an ensemble company would be a group of about thirty actors of moderate talent, all equally gifted. They would be simple people who *always—no matter what happened*—followed this basic law of ensemble acting.

JACQUES COPEAU

(1878 - 1949)

Jacques Copeau was a native of Ile-de-France. Schooled at a *lyceé* in Paris and then the Sorbonne, he wanted to be an actor, but the drama of the boulevards repelled him. He admired the perfection of the symbolists, but believed that it was a perfection realized at the expense of excluding vast areas of human experience. The naturalists, he felt, rejected spiritual content.

Copeau went abroad, married, and then for two years managed a factory left to him by his family. In 1905 he returned to Paris and made friends among the younger men of letters who, a few years later, would form the supporters of the new drama. The life work of Copeau began in 1907 when he was made the dramatic critic of the *Grande Revue*. Of these criticisms, Waldo Frank has written, "they have all the simplicity, and violence, of prophecy.... In all of modern dramatic criticism I know of no work more salient, more honest and irresistible, than these papers which Copeau flung against the contemporary Parisian theatre. One thinks at once of the early fulminations of Bernard Shaw." Those early essays helped greatly toward an understanding of the theatre which was to follow after Copeau's dramatization *Les Frères Karamazov* came to the stage of the *Théâtre des Arts*. Charles Dullin astounded Paris in the role of Smerdiakov, "the deepest incarnation of the blood of Dostoyevsky."

By the spring of 1913, Copeau had his little theatre of five hundred seats in the Rue du Vieux Colombier. With Dullin and Louis Jouvet as the mainstays of his troupe of eleven, the company retired to the country to prepare a repertoire. But they did far more. They did exercises in physical culture and dance; they improvised dramatic scenes; they read aloud, worked on their bodies, their voices, and their minds. The guiding principle of the group was that originality of interpretation grew from a profound knowledge of the text of the play. They learned that the effectiveness of a role depended upon a harmony of the entire mental and physical state of the actor.

During their one season in Paris before the war disrupted their activities, the *Théâtre du Vieux Colombier* presented fourteen dramatic creations including contemporary works like Paul Claudel's *L'Echange,* Jean Schlumberger's *Les Fils Louverné,* classics of Molière, Shakespeare, and modern works like Dostoyevsky's *Brothers Karamazov*. In one year Copeau had created a community of actors and dramatic workers which laid the basis of a modern theatre. During the third year of the war Copeau received a mandate from the French Government to gather the group together and come to the safety of the United States. After the war Copeau returned to Paris, where he produced the work of the moderns—Duhamel,

Gide, Vildrac—and developed his simple architectural stage which is a model of flexibility and economy.

Copeau is represented in this volume by an extract from *Un Essai de réno-vation dramatique,* the manifesto with which he warned Paris of the intentions of his theatre, and by notes on the total process by which the actor learns to give himself by first possessing himself. Both appear here for the first time in English.

The Manifesto of the *Vieux Colombier*

The *Théâtre du Vieux Colombier* is open to all efforts, provided that they reach a certain level and are of a certain quality. We mean: *dramatic* quality. Whatever may be our avowed preferences as critics and men of the theatre or our personal bent as writers, we do not represent a school, whose entire prestige risks being called into question when the first blush of its novelty wears off. We do not bring a formula, nor are we convinced that the theatre of tomorrow will arise and develop from these beginnings. In this respect we differ from undertakings which have preceded us. All of them—we say this without deprecating the contribution of the most famous among them, the *Théâtre Libre,* and without minimizing the high merit of its director, André Antoine—were unconsciously rash enough to limit their field of activity within the narrow confines of a revolutionary program. We do not feel the need of a revolution. Our eyes are concentrated on too great models to feel such a need. We do not believe in the effectiveness of aesthetic formulas which are born and die every month among little groups, whose boldness is for the most part made up of ignorance. We do not know what the theatre of tomorrow will be. We proclaim nothing. But we pledge ourselves to react against all the worst features of the contemporary theatre. In founding the *Théâtre du Vieux Colombier,* we are preparing a place of refuge for future talents.

The Company

Even theatrical companies subsidized by the State are today suffering from a lack of guidance and discipline, from greediness for profit, and the absence of a common ideal. As for the Boulevard theatres, they belong to the great "stars" who force their directors to make ruinous expenditures, throw stage-productions out of balance, attract the audience's attention to themselves rather than to the play, and cheapen the playwright's talent by using their plays only as vehicles for their own stardom.

The last integrated company we saw in France was that of the *Théâtre Libre.* The members had a faith they all shared. And the director brilliantly exploited their common sentiments.

The *Théâtre du Vieux Colombier* in its turn brings together, under the direction of one man, a troupe of young, disinterested, and enthusiastic players whose ambition is to *serve* the art to which they have devoted themselves. To put an end to "ham-acting," to create for the actor a better atmosphere for his development as man and artist, to educate him, to inspire him with a sense of conscience, and to

---

Jacques Copeau: "Un Essai de rénovation dramatique," *Etudes d'art dramatique, critiques d'un autre temps.* Paris: Editions de la Nouvelle Revue Française, 1923, pp. 243-246. Copyright 1923. By permission of Librairie Gallimard. This selection translated by Joseph M. Bernstein.

initiate him into the morality of his art—to that end our efforts will be stubbornly bent. We will always have in mind the perfecting of individual talents and their subordination to the group. We will fight against routine procedures, against all professional distortions, against paralyzing over-specialization. Finally, we will do our best to re-normalize these men and women whose calling it is to represent all human emotions and gestures. As much as we possibly can, we will bring them in contact with nature and life outside the theatre!

For two months now, the full company of the *Théâtre du Vieux Colombier* has been together and its work has begun. On July 1, it moved into its summer headquarters: in a tiny village in the Seine-et-Marne district, way out in the country. There, every day for five hours it is studying the plays in its repertory under the eye of its director. Two further hours are spent in the open, devoted to sight readings as exercises in mental alertness and voice training, to analyses of literary texts (plays, poems, fragments of classic prose), and to physical exercises. The advantages of this kind of training will not be fully appreciated until several years have past. But already they are beginning to be felt.

Today, September 1, already knit together by two months of work in common and in command of a part of its repertory, the company is returning to Paris to rehearse for a month and a half more—on the stage, with costumes and stage-sets.

The Student-Actors

Since our method bears on the very nature and character of individuals who have already been molded by previous influences, we do not doubt that it will encounter strong resistance. Hence, in this respect, we should like to go much further in our reforms. This involves creating not only the theatre but—side by side with it and in the same framework—a real *school for actors*. Admission would be free and we would enroll, on the one hand, very young people and even children, and on the other hand men and women who have a love and instinct for the theatre but who have not yet compromised this instinct by defective methods or professional routine. Such a group of new talents would later constitute the greatness of our undertaking. From among them we would get, in the very first years, actors capable of playing bit-parts and a number of trained walk-ons who felt at home on the stage —far superior to those who are generally used.

We fear that the tremendous burden of work will not permit us to carry out this project for a school right at the outset of our undertaking. But as soon as we are able to do so, we will bend every effort to that end. Then, in a new article, we will outline our organizational scheme.

Notes on the Actor

The actor, onstage, never really does anything. Vaguely, without being aware of it, he imitates certain activities, with a more or less adept grasp of the effect to be produced. In rehearsals, for a multitude of reasons (in particular, the absurd

Jacques Copeau: *Notes sur le métier de comédien: notes recueillies dans le journal et les écrits de Jacques Copeau par Marie-Hélène Dasté*. Paris: Michel Brient, 1955, pp. 27-31, 45-53. Selection translated by Harold J. Salemson.

habit of doing without the props to be used), you never see him doing what he will have to do during the performance, you never see him do anything, even the most elementary things, authentically. He thinks he will do it during the performance, which is to say that during the performance he will instinctively go back to the stage substitute that habit has put in place of the real thing and that always remains the same. But actors like Bouquet, who are conscientious and like things to be well ordered, never get completely through to the end of a new stage instruction. They distort it as they translate it. It would appear that they do not dare, or simply that they do not let themselves go, as if their bodies, onstage, were suddenly exempted from the laws of gravity and duration.

It must be added that modern comedy, being literary, intellectual, indulging in conversation or discussion, has strangely reduced the physical resources of actors.

We are going to try to give our pupils *awareness and experience of the human body*. But this does not mean that, by appropriate methods, we are going to train athletes. Anyway, that would be impossible for us. Our aim is not to develop a bodily attitude or affectation of any kind, to create aesthetic habits that will take the place of unaesthetic habits.

What is needed is to make normally developed bodies capable of adjusting themselves, giving themselves over to any action they may undertake. What is needed is that within them every movement be accompanied by an internal state of awareness peculiar to the movement being done.

Knowledge and mastery of the movements of the body must not, any more than those of the movements of the face, grow out of imitation of oneself, or of others, or of painted or sculpted images. Without banishing human observation or aesthetic knowledge from the training of the actor, it can be said that it is not in trying to reproduce the external signs of passion observed on a face, nor in observing the changes in his own face in the mirror, that the actor will learn to modulate the intensity of his dramatic expression. He will have to have an internal knowledge of the passions he expresses, whether through personal experience or through that kind of divination that is peculiar to the artist. And he will have to acquire the anatomical knowledge, the muscular mastery of his instrument, which is his own face. Likewise, it is not by studying, in order to imitate them, the masterpieces of painting or statuary that the actor will be able to achieve plastic beauty in his own body, if his body, through the natural play of the elements of its muscles and joints, does not give him an awareness of such beauty. It is not enough to have observed, from the outside, the attitudes and movements of craftsmen or workmen plying their trades. One has to have experienced them oneself. The dramatic artist at rest and in action always has an internal awareness of the show he is putting on. At the moment when he expresses it, the passion or the dramatic movement he is interpreting has ceased to be an object of study to him, but it has not ceased to be an object of awareness. He directs them, but he is possessed by them.

No affectation of any kind whatsoever, whether of the body, the mind, or the voice. What we are seeking is headlong harmony.

No deliberate, archaic, so to speak literary, athleticism. It may be that "the compleat athlete" was perfectly in his place on the Grecian stage. He was the product of a social, artistic, and religious upbringing that was harmonious and complete. Today, the athlete is a specialist. When Gémier calls him up onto the stage, among his fat or skinny actors, it takes a very jaded eye not to see that the effect produced is ridiculous.

An actor who is physically overdeveloped is a ham of muscle-building, a virtuoso of artistic nude poses, as despicable onstage as any other kind of virtuoso, as out of place as the conventional operatic ballet dancer or the Dalcroze rhythmicist, or the trained singer in a comic interlude.

Diary, 1919

* * * *

... I am concerned here only with the body and bodily faculties of expression. Some of the remarks that I make on the subject might just as well be applied to facial expressions. But I am deliberately, for the moment, leaving that aspect of it aside.

The starting-point of expression. The state of repose, calm, relaxation, *détente,* silence, or simplicity. This lesson simultaneously touches upon all aspects of interpretation. In reading aloud as well as in his spoken interpretation and in his physical playing or action or business, the actor always starts from an artificial *attitude,* a bodily, mental, or vocal *grimace.* His attack is both too deliberate and insufficiently premeditated, or, what is even simpler and more serious, insufficiently felt. He is not doing what he is doing with simplicity and good faith. Some actors can be seen, backstage, making faces in order to get themselves into the mood, others showing off by doing a somersault before going onstage into a serious situation. There are some actors who can be seen, at rehearsals, doing something over a dozen times to try to carry out a stage instruction that they perhaps understand but which has not really gotten through to them, which they have not yet made part of themselves; or else they keep trying out an intonation a dozen times over, while listening to themselves, as they would tune up an instrument, which is equivalent to looking at oneself in the mirror *to see* whether one is properly expressing a feeling. We know from experience that, onstage, if our initial attack has been wrong, if we got off on the wrong foot, passing alongside the character or the situation, however carefully we may after that watch out for our intonations and gestures, however conscientiously and deliberately we may try to regain control of ourselves, we do not succeed in it. And the more nervously we try, the worse we derail. Never do we hear ourselves or see ourselves more pitilessly than in such cases. It is perfectly clear that the worst actors are those who watch and listen to themselves the most. On the other hand, an actor who is very tired, nervously worn down, may quite naturally enter into his part and never get out of it during the entire performance, without having to make any effort whatsoever, and on that day he may, unconsciously, refresh all of his intonations and his pantomime, because everything comes naturally to him. It will be felt that he has entered into the role, into the situation. He thinks little under such conditions—not much more than he would in everyday life to carry out certain accustomed movements or to obey natural reactions. The question of *sincerity* is too complex to be gone into here. But, without analyzing it in its various elements, without specifying how much artistic sincerity may be made up of elements of insincerity, it can be said that, in the case of dramatic portrayal, nothing can take the place of sincerity, of what we choose to call sincerity, which is no doubt not merely true emotion or gaiety, in their raw state, but a feeling of calm and power, of identity, that allows the artist, as I have already said, at the same time to be possessed by what he is expressing and to direct its expression. This feeling in itself is at least something true, something natural, something certain. I believe that its starting point is a kind of purity, a kind of integrity of the individual, a state of calm, naturalness, relaxation.

[220]

FRANCE

As early as 1915, writing about the exercise of reading aloud, I said:

"Reading aloud a text that has not been worked over is to try for a modest and sincere expression, to which no artificial trick will bring any false appearance. It is to resume a bit of naïveté. It is to learn, in brief, to accost an author's thought in complete good faith, in full humility, to subject oneself to its meaning, to pluck the words in their freshness and as closely as possible to what they are saying of themselves, without adding anything at all to them, except the involuntary emotion of discovering them.

"A good reading, free of any affectation—that is the open ground upon which one can construct a wholesome portrayal."

I do not know how to describe, much less to obtain in someone else, that state of good faith, submission, humility, which, I would like to believe, to a certain extent, from all the viewpoints that concern us here, depends upon culture (physical or intellectual) and, to sum it up in two words, *proper training*. It is not entirely dissimilar to that condition of serenity, calm, and unaffected assurance that can be seen in well-constituted, healthy, and properly experienced human beings. At present, I can use only metaphors that my students will not understand, that do not get through to them. I say to them: "Take the text from the ground up . . . ," "No intonation . . . ," "Exhale . . . ," etc.

In any actor's voice, we always find ourselves up against a drone, a preestablished singsong, some special habit or attitude, which they call their personality. The same goes for the face, the gestures, or the attitudes. I could easily prove that most actors, though they be excellent, have at their disposal only two or three facial expressions, and I am not talking about the cases in which those gestures or expressions are mere *tics* or reflexes.

An actor does not listen. When playing, he does not listen to his partner. Which accounts for the fact that his "side" is never an answer. At rehearsals, he does not listen to the director. He gives no question or instruction the time to get through to him. Or else he lets it get through to his mind only and he believes too readily that he has understood it. What would be needed would be for a designated gesture to get through to him in the limb or the muscle that has to carry it out, so that in order to do it he would not need first to form a visual or intellectual picture of it for himself.

It may be, however, that the visual picture of a gesture or a motion may have its importance in bringing the student around to an awareness of it. That is why it is suggested that students observe what their fellows do, criticize it, try to correct it themselves. I have often observed that what was lacking for actors to be able to understand the importance or necessity of what I was trying to get them to do, was the act of being able to watch it. Presently, we succeed in disciplining actors, in bending them to certain requirements, in getting them to do what we want them to. But they do not see the beauty of this, they do not understand its ineluctable and irreplaceable imperativeness, they do not appreciate that such and such interpretation, though being only slightly different from the one indicated to them, would be false and inharmonious. Which accounts for the fact that, unconsciously, during performances, they undo the direction.

When, several times in a row, I have repeated the same bit of advice, the same instruction to an actor and he has several times tried in vain to carry it out, I can tell from the contractions of his face and voice, the incoherence of his pantomime, that he is trying to accomplish something through a network of influences that paralyze him. What he is groping for in the dark and the void is *a starting point.* What he is not succeeding in doing, I think, is *to establish silence and calm within himself.*

To start from silence and calm. That is the very first point. An actor must know how to be silent, to listen, to answer, to remain motionless, to start a gesture, follow through with it, come back to motionlessness and silence, with all the shadings and half-tones that these actions imply.

Motionlessness. Mastery of motionlessness. To maintain an attitude. An actor always tends to believe that the time he remains motionless is too long, just as, when there is silence, he thinks he has to indulge in facial expressions and, if he is in the background, pretend to be carrying on a conversation in whispers, which is simply grotesque.

An actor always makes many too many gestures, and many too many unintentional ones, on the pretext of being natural. And always many too many facial expressions.

He does not know that motionlessness, like silence, is expressive. He tries to make his silence or his motionlessness expressive by a succession of little interrupted displays that aim at bringing out the slightest shadings of impression created on him by the words of whoever is speaking.

Silence is expressive through the contained sincerity of the person who is listening, through the simple internal preparation of the answer. An actor who thinks and feels impresses the audience through the very quality of his presence, without having to externalize his thought by any grimace whatever. When a man listens to someone talking to him, with his head down and his face hidden from the audience, he will reveal the expressive quality of his silence at the very moment when he raises his head to reply.

Motionlessness, if it is made up of a correct attitude and a proper meaning, is expressive to the extent that it paves the way for the gesture that will follow. In point of fact, except in certain deliberate cases, there is no true motionlessness of the actor onstage. Because that would be the same as not being there. Expressive motionlessness, meaning that which already contains the seed of the action that is to follow, gets across to the audience, without requiring any external manifestation or half-manifestation. The motionlessness that follows a mild gesture is not the same as the motionlessness that follow a violent gesture, that which paves the way for a rapid gesture is not the same as that which paves the way for a slow gesture. (And note that I am saying "paves the way," not *"foreshadows."*)

It will be good to give the student appropriate exercises so that he may learn these differences, as well as the one that separates neutral motionlessness from expressive motionlessness. He will be made to experiment so that he can learn how, in the various cases, *the internal attitude,* the physiological state (of circulation, muscles, joints) will be different. But this whole lesson will be translated into the terms of our art, and not only expressed in scientific terms. Always and at all times, examples will be used. The student will always be made to experience what it is that is being explained to him.

To obtain motionlessness. Then to demonstrate that, from the moment one enters into the dramatic order, there is no longer any such thing as absolute motionlessness. From paving the way for the gesture, to go on to the carrying out of the gesture, the continuity of the gesture in the same direction, with awareness of its progression, its various successive states and their values. To develop the faculty of *holding* a gesture, an attitude. An actor always makes too many gestures, makes them much too fast (as the experience of moving pictures has taught us), makes them incompletely, without continuity, without coordination. To study the reciprocal continuity and coordination of the gestures of different limbs (both in relation to facial expressions and in relation to spoken words) within the action of one individual, then within the simultaneous action of two or more individuals. It is not enough for gestures to contain truth and logic, in order for them to contain expressiveness and beauty. . . .

Diary, 1919

On Diderot's Paradox

I am supposing an actor confronted with the text of a role that he likes and understands, the character of which suits his nature, the style of which is fitted to his capabilities. He smiles with satisfaction. He can sight-read this role without even trying. The first reading that he gives of it is surprising in its correctness. Everything in it is masterfully indicated, not only the overall intention, but already even the shadings. And the author is delighted to have found the ideal interpreter who will carry his work to the heights. "But wait," the actor says to him. "I haven't got it yet." Because he himself has not been fooled by this first grasping of the role which has been effected by his mind alone.

Now he gets down to work. He rehearses, in a hushed tone, cautiously, as if he were afraid of upsetting something within himself. These private rehearsals still retain something of the quality of readings. The shadings of emotion are still perceptible in them for a few privileged listeners. The actor now has the role committed to memory. This is the moment when he begins to be a bit less in possession of the character. He can see what he is trying to do. He is composing and developing. He is setting in place the sequences, the transitions. He reasons out his movements, classifies his gestures, corrects his intonations. He watches himself and listens to himself. He detaches himself from himself. He judges himself. He seems no longer to be giving anything of himself. Sometimes he breaks off his work to say to himself, "I don't feel that." Often correctly, he suggests a change in the wording, the inversion of a phrase, some alteration in the direction that would allow him, he believes, better to feel it. He is trying to find the means to put himself in a proper position, a proper state for feeling: a starting point, which sometimes may be located in pantomime, or in the tone of the voice, in a special relaxation, a simple breath . . . He tries to tune himself up. He sets out his nets. He is organizing to capture something he has understood and foreseen for a long time, but which has remained alien to him, which has not yet entered into him, taken up its abode in him . . . He listens without great attention to the basic instructions that are given to him from the stage box, about the feelings of his character, his motivations, his whole psychological mechanism. And all this time his attention seems totally absorbed by ridiculous details.

That is when the author, with excessive politeness, takes his illustrious interpreter by the arm and whispers to him, "But, my dear friend, why don't you stick to what you did the first day? That was perfect. Just be yourself."

The actor is no longer himself. And he is not yet "the other one." What he was doing the first day escapes him to the very extent that he gets into position to play the part. He has had to renounce the freshness, the naturalness, the shadings, and all the pleasure that he got from his animation, to accomplish the difficult, thankless, painstaking work that consists of turning what is literally and psychologically true into what is theatrically true. He has had to put into place, master, assimilate all the processes of metamorphosis, the very things that simultaneously separate him from his role and lead him toward it. It will only be when he has completed this study of himself in relation to a given character, articulated all of his capabilities, exerted all of his being in the effort to serve the ideas he has conceived and the feelings for which he is paving the way within his body, his nerves, his mind, into the very depths of his heart, only then that he will be able to get a new grip on himself, now transformed, and try to give himself.

At last the actor is fulfilling his role. He now finds nothing empty, nothing artificial in it. He could live it without speaking any words. He has set his sincerity up in a great confrontation with that wonderful "interior silence" that Eleonora Duse used to talk about.

Here now is this man displayed on stage, offered as a spectacle, exposed to judgment. He enters into a different world. He assumes responsibility for it. He sacrifices an entire real world to it, all the real world's worries, discomforts, unhappinesses, sufferings—or rather by it he is freed from them.

But now there is something else: the way his partners handle themselves onstage, a movement in the audience, a disorder backstage, the breaking of a lamp, the folding of a rug, a mistake in stage business, a forgotten property, a tear in a costume, a failing of memory, a slip of the tongue, a temporary weakening of his vital energy—all of these now threaten him, all are arrayed against him, him who, all by himself, is faced with having to maintain a grip over everything. Any little thing can at any moment come between his sincerity, which nothing can force to return if it decides to slip away, and the acting that willy-nilly he has to do; any little thing can deprive him of what he thought he had mastered through his long travail, separate him from the character he had composed out of his own substance but which, like it, can undergo deep, sudden changes.

The rise of the curtain has taken him by surprise . . . His first attack went off somewhat in spite of himself . . . Now he is disconcerted. I can see him twisting the end of his necktie. For a moment he stops feeling. He beats a retreat. He is looking for a point of support. He breathes deeply. I expect that he will get hold of himself again, because he knows his craft. You will tell me that the upset caused him by these futile incidents proves that he did not feel what he was doing. I rather believe that, the more sensitive the actor, the more subject he is to such confusions. But he will get back to feeling it—because he knows his craft.

Let us suppose that he did not cease feeling. He is then reaching fulfillment. But this fulfillment itself would have to be measured. There is a measure of sincerity, as there is a measure of technique. Will it be claimed that the actor feels nothing because he knows how to make use of his feelings? That the tears that flow and the sobs that rack are faked, because they cut off the player's voice only for a moment and scarcely alter his diction? Should we not, on the contrary, even though not even trying completely to understand it, rather admire the admirable instinct, the gift of nature and of reason which, a little while ago, put the disconcerted actor back on the track of feeling, and now prevents his emotion from undoing his dramatic performance? Such acting requires a head "made of iron," as Diderot says, but not "made of ice," as he had originally written. It also requires flexible, resilient nerves, and very quick, very delicate internal operations.

To deny that an actor has sensitivity, on account of his presence of mind, is to discount it in any artist who observes the laws of his art and refuses to allow the tumult of emotions to paralyze his soul. The artist, with a serene heart, rules over the disorder in his workshop and his materials. The more emotion rises within him and exalts him, the more lucid his brain becomes. This coldness and this trembling are compatible, as they are in fever or in drunkenness.

". . . To embrace the full sweep of a great role, work out the lights and darks in it, the soft spots and the weak ones, to appear on an even keel whether in the quiet places or the excited places, to be varied in details, harmonious and unified in the ensemble, and to form for oneself a sustained declamation system . . . this is the work of a cool head, profound judgment, exquisite taste, painful study, long experience, and uncommon tenacity of memory." Diderot is right: Within the actor's mind, "everything has been measured, worked out, learned, organized." But if his playing is nothing but the expression of his mastery and as it were the presentation of an excellent method, he will either fall asleep in its routine performance or dissipate himself in the fireworks of virtuosity. The absurdity of the "paradox" is that it sets the processes of the craft against the freedom of feeling and it denies, in the artist, the possibility of their coexistence and simultaneity.

For the actor, the whole thing is to give himself. In order to give himself, he must first possess himself. Our craft, with the discipline it presupposes, the reflexes it has mastered and holds at its command, is the very warp and woof of our art, with the freedom it demands and the illuminations it encounters. Emotive expression grows out of correct expression. Not only does technique not exclude sensitivity: it authenticates it and liberates it. It upholds and protects it. It is thanks to our craft that we are able to let ourselves go, because it is thanks to it that we will be able to find ourselves again. The study and observation of principles, an infallible mechanism, a dependable memory, obedient diction, regular breathing and relaxed nerves, clearness of the head and the stomach, all of these give us the security that inspires us with durability. Constancy in our accents, our positions, our movements, maintains freshness, clarity, diversity, invention, evenness, renewal; it allows us to improvise.

CHARLES DULLIN

(1885-1949)

Born the last of nineteen children, Dullin made his way in Paris reciting the poems of Villon at the famous Montmartre café Au Lapin Agile. Soon he became an actor in those theatres that specialized in melodrama, where, he later recalled, he learned a great deal about theatrical technique. At Jacques Rouche's *Théâtre des Arts* he had his first success as Smerdiakov in Jacques Copeau's adaptation of Dostoyevsky's *The Brothers Karamazov*. His experience preparing this role was instructive. He began by writing a long analysis of the character, but during rehearsals he realized that such effort was useless. He felt that one should never let the critical or intellectual sense take the place of instinct. "From this moment I felt the needed reform: throw off the yoke of naturalism, take from melodrama that which is authentically theatrical, place the poet at the source of all inspiration, and give to instinct, which is by far the most marvelous gift of the actor, its true place." Dullin was engaged by Copeau in the original company of *Le Vieux-Colombier*, where he became an outstanding actor, whose interpretation of Molière's *L'Avare* was one of his triumphs. After brief service in World War I, he joined Copeau's company in New York.

[225]

In 1921 he founded his own theatre, *L'Atelier,* which he ran until 1938. Much like Copeau's *Vieux-Colombier* in emphasis, it was conceived by Dullin not as a theatrical enterprise but as a laboratory for dramatic studies where the regeneration of the actor was the primary objective. He was a severe master, but not a rigid one bound by useless rules. He devoted himself to teaching his students basic principles in diction, breathing exercises to free the actor, as well as gymnastic, rhythmic, and pantomimic studies. Above all he gave primary importance to studies of improvisation in the style of the *commedia dell' arte.* Dullin also admired the art of the Japanese actor and the innovations of Meyerhold, whom he met in 1930 in Paris. It is interesting to point out that Antonin Artaud was one of Dullin's students at the *Atelier.*

As a director he renounced the excessive elaboration of the naturalistic theatre and all mechanical tricks. What he aimed for in the productions on the small circular stage of his *Atelier* was a poetic, mysterious synthesis of the arts. He made great use of music by such composers as Darius Milhaud and Georges Auric in his stagings. He staged Pirandello, and was responsible for the first productions of the playwrights Salacrou, Achard, Anouilh, and Sartre. But Dullin remained essentially the actor, remembered for the roles he played—for his Harpagon, on which he worked until the end of his career, for his Volpone, his Richard III in André Obey's adaptation, and for his *Atelier* committed to the exploration of the actor's art.

The Birth and Life of Characters

I once asked a producer whether he received many scripts.

"Plenty of scripts," he replied, "but very few plays."

The same applies to characters in the theatre; there are an endless number of parts, but real characters are few and far between. Yet, great characters outlive their authors; they go on doing battle in his name, receiving the pinpricks of critics, arousing enthusiasm in some, lack of understanding in others. They are demigods; they have all eternity before them, yet they never settle comfortably on Olympus.

Hamlet will forever drag his dark cloak across the dusty boards of the stage; Richard III will go limping off, rehashing his old hatreds and fears, and forever die the same violent death only forever to be reborn and die again.

Trygaeus will appeal in vain to the people to pull *Peace* out of the well in which the god of war periodically imprisons her.

Sorry Antiochus wandering in Caesarea, Don Juan possessed of demons, Lear the old fool, thoughtful Brutus, all will continue to go around in the circles within which fate has placed them.

Others will bring about revolutions; one may even be the torchbearer of a whole generation. He will influence the young and call forth the bitter sarcasm of the aging.

But all of them, whoever they may be, if they are to come alive again, need an accomplice to give them flesh for a time on the stage of the world. And just as they overwhelmed their creators, they will do everything they can to overwhelm their portrayers. They will lead them a hard life until they have extracted their *pound of*

Dullin, Charles: *Souvenirs et notes, travail d'un acteur.* Paris: Odette Lieutier, 1946, pp. 33-53 *passim.* By permission of Pierre Demagny. This excerpt translated from the French by Harold J. Salemson.

flesh, more pitilessly than Shylock. Try as one may to bend the stubborn will of these characters to the temporary conformity of a given period, they will always find the way to reappear in their own true guise before the footlights.

In our time, great characters are rare. By depriving the theatre of its sacred aspect, its ceremonial spectacle, by requiring the actor to be like the man in the street, we have succeeded in inverting the roles; there is a better chance to meet a hero now in the audience than on the stage.

If an author, after having conceived his character, suddenly sees him standing before him, in tangible bodily form, with his clothes, sometimes even his mannerisms, he knows he can go ahead with his creative work, without fear of being wrong; for the character will then take him by the hand and lead him; he will not be the one to find the words: the character will do it for him. Perhaps that is why real authors always feel their latest loves are their best and defend them so eloquently, even when they bring them nothing but torment and disappointment; they remain faithful to them until some new character comes discreetly or imperatively knocking at their door.

Quite different the gait when an actor starts to approach his character. Contact is made very slowly between them. The adage "What is well understood will be clearly expressed" is wrong when dealing with the actor. He will often proceed much more *by intuition* than by deduction. However much the author and director may explain the psychology of the character to him, the whys and wherefores of the play, he will for a long time remain deaf to all external appeals. If author and director are not old pros who know how an actor operates, they will often be tempted to think, "What an idiot! He does not understand a thing of what we are telling him!" But if they know the secret gestation that goes on inside the good actor during the rehearsal period, often unbeknownst to him, they will be on the lookout for the appropriate time when they can assist in the delivery.

During this period, the actor is often like a sleepwalker: he mumbles, murders his lines, mispronounces to his heart's content, and seems awkward in his execution of the simplest of movements. From time to time, with an inquiring eye he seeks the approval of the director, who by a motion of the head says to him, "No, that's not quite it yet!"

Sometimes this can degenerate into sulking, or break out in arguments leading to threats of walking out. . . . "I knew this part was never meant for me," the actor snaps. I am naturally speaking here only of actors who are talented and creative; the others experience no such worries; they are neither especially awkward nor awfully bad, but just themselves, nicely or fatuously. They never wait for you to finish stating your comment; the minute you open your mouth, they cut in with, "Yes . . . yes . . . absolutely . . . I understand!" and then do again exactly what they were doing a minute before, or else they see red, become angry, and fume, "Well, sir, you're certainly not going to try to teach me my craft, are you?"

But *the real one, the talented one* goes through agonies. Any little thing is enough to throw him, until he finally feels that he has in a way been taken over by his character. Then he says, "This is it. I've got it!" I've got it: when what he really means is that it's the character that has got him, which is as it should be.

All of this is what I have been able to observe as a director; now I will tell with sincerity what I felt or thought I felt as an actor, using as examples some of the characters I have played.

I will go back to the one that brought me out of obscurity, quite a few years ago, Smerdiakov in *The Brothers Karamazov*. That was in 1911. For the previous five years, after coming to Paris, I had played in a considerable number of melo-dramas, spent nearly two years at Antoine's *Odéon,* toured the provinces, founded a *Théâtre de la Foire* at the Neuilly Fair, and periodically reverted to the Lapin Agile, that refuge for those who were involuntarily "at liberty."

I had just created the role of Pierrot in Saint-Georges de Bouhélier's *Carnaval des Enfants* at the *Théâtre des Arts,* which Jacques Rouché was managing. In the afternoon, I had attended a reading of the adaptation of Dostoyevsky's *Brothers Karamazov,* which Jacques Copeau had just completed, in collaboration with Croué. Copeau had read the play. Among those present were Henry Krauss, who was to play Father Karamazov, Van Doren for Katerina, Margel for Grushenka, and Gary for the role of Ivan. The actor who was being considered for Smerdiakov was not there. I was in a corner of the foyer with my friends Blondeau and Millet and was keeping the turbulent feelings within me quiet. "Damn it," I was thinking, "here's another part that's going to slip right through my fingers . . . and yet I'm convinced that I'm really the one who should be playing it."

Sure enough, the casting sheet posted on the bulletin board a few hours later had me down for an incidental character with very little to say or do. That evening, after our performance, I had gone to meet a few of my friends in a bar on the avenue de Clichy, where we spent part of the night. Around two in the morning, the theatre doorman came panting into the bar, and told me, "Hurry back to the theatre. Durec and the author want to see you right away." I quickly followed him, trying to construct in my mind this interview, which could only be about the casting of Smerdiakov. And it was true: Durec had prevailed upon Copeau to take a look at me before deciding on anyone else. Copeau eyed me curiously for quite a while and then it was agreed that I would be given a tryout the very next day.

With my part in my pocket, I went back to my friends to announce the news to them, but I did not stay long because I was in a hurry to be alone so as the better to enjoy my good fortune. At moments like those, the intoxication we can get from art is very close to the kind of intoxication we get from love.

I spent the rest of the night working; my experience as an actor in melodramas had made me quick at entering into a part and I therefore hoped to be able at the very first rehearsal to show mettle enough so the tryout might turn into a final casting.

Early in the morning I went out to buy a copy of Dostoyevsky's novel, which I wanted to reread without delay. The first rehearsal gave me neither disappoint-ment nor encouragement; Copeau and Rouché watched me with a rather favorable eye, Durec was busy blocking and paid no attention to lines. From the second rehearsal on, I began to gain some confidence. The actor who played Ivan, accus-tomed to doing *boulevard* comedy, became more incensed at each line with Ivan's involuted character, and finally threw the part over. This kind of incident always makes for a certain amount of confusion. For a few days, Copeau himself had to read the part, which put us on a more equal footing and made my position stronger; after that Durec took over, and he finally created the role himself.

Despite the encouraging words I heard, I was not satisfied with myself. I could see my character all right, but I felt that I was playing him too much from the out-side; the little quirks of my own nature, my physical appearance might fool others, but they didn't fool me.

I wrote a long essay about Smerdiakov, dense and crammed with generalities, in which I minutely analyzed the character; everything I had to do was covered in it, from his walk to the trembling of his lips as the epileptic fit came on, all of which only confused me all the more, and for a while even cancelled out my spontaneity and naturalness. As I rehearsed with a great deal of sincerity and gusto, the director and playwrights themselves tended to want to take advantage of this vehemence. Yet I felt that it was getting me away from my model. Fortunately, a few impressions that I experienced very deeply brought home to me what I had sought in vain through extended analysis. At one point, it was a bit of stage business that the director suggested to me that suddenly forced me on into that second state, so necessary to the actor; another time, the natural tone in which I said a single speech reoriented my whole approach and got me beyond ordinary theatrical convention. My character was beginning to speak; what I had so meticulously tried to lay out in that great study of mine was little by little unconsciously translating itself in a living manner. Copeau's intelligent criticism admirably helped along the effort I was making. Day by day I felt myself more possessed by my character. Yet there still remained quite a few dark corners that clashed with the overall effect.

On April 5, 1911, the day of the dress rehearsal, I was completely thrown: the day before, Durec had said to me, "When you face an audience it will be just fine." Those words *just fine* knocked the pins out from under me. If it was only just fine, I might as well go jump into the Seine right away. A few hours before show time, I was wandering around near the Parc Monceau, in a feverish state; I felt that the way I did my final scene was pitiful; I kept going over it inside myself without speaking the words. All of a sudden, when I got to the spot where I ask Ivan to show me the *famous rubles* one last time, and then cry out, "Farewell, Ivan Fyodorovich!," I felt an irresistible urge to run.

At that moment I was alongside the Parc Monceau fence and in spite of myself started to run along it, as if I were chasing after my character, whom I could see on the other side of the fence, climbing the stair to go hang himself. That evening, during the performance, I stumbled over the first step of that tragic stairway precisely where I had had the talk with Ivan just before the crime and as if in a nightmare I climbed those stairs in just the manner of that phantom I had glimpsed in my flash of strange lucidity.

This phenomenon that is both animal and spiritual, in which soul and body feel the need in a way to merge into each other so as to externalize the character, allowed me to take hold of the character and at the same time dictated to me in a more general way one of the great laws of the art of acting. Until then, I had had an unfortunate tendency to repress my instincts while consciously composing my character; I gave to the logic of the lines, their verbal strength, their literary shadings, an importance that detracted from the truthfulness and life of my acting. This was true in spite of my schooling in playing melodramas, perhaps even in reaction against it; despite my time with Antoine, which had had the opposite effect on me, by bringing everything down to everyday truth, to a pitiless rationalism that was just as false as the romantic rigmarole I had encountered among the melodrama players. The need that I felt to cleanse my mind by relying on the poetry of the lines, the genius of the poet, carried me toward a kind of poetical declamation. In my novice's ardor, I put the question from the outside; I felt people would justifiably say, "Dullin . . . yes . . . he's an intelligent actor," and that this would reveal a serious flaw under its rather flattering appearance. Smerdiakov taught me to make use of my true abilities. I can honestly say that since that time, both as actor and as director, I have tried never to allow critical sense and intelligence to gain the upper hand over instinct, which does not mean that I have always succeeded.

This experience had allowed me at a relatively early age to find my bearings. From that moment forward, I became aware also of the reform that was needed: to throw off the yoke of naturalism, to borrow from melodrama what was authentic about it from a theatrical viewpoint, to place the poet at the very inception of all inspiration, and to return its proper importance to instinct, which is the actor's most wondrous gift. I certainly had all of this within me, since only a few years before I had tried at the Neuilly Fair to revive Italian Comedy, an attempt that had been short-lived and more picturesque in its pretensions than significant in its artistic results, and important only because of the tendency it indicated, as it gave a foretaste of my "improvisational" method of teaching young students; a tendency toward a people's theatre, yet not a "populist" one; a tendency to introduce plastic elements into the performance; a tendency to seek after a new kind of ordering of the spectacle.

Copeau had befriended me, and helped me make rapid strides along these lines; we got along together admirably; I never had a single work disagreement with him; his critical sense, which was so correct, and his imagination had the most felicitous influence on me. The founding of the *Vieux-Colombier,* preparing its first presentations, and the 1913 season are unforgettable memories to me. My departure for the war in 1914 was to interrupt and break off this happy period of my adolescence.

Since that time, I have met a lot of such character roles. Almost all of these characters sneaked up on me in the same accidental manner when I no longer expected them.... Very often they would not consent to speak until they were fully costumed and made up. The stage entrance of Baldovino in Pirandello's *The Pleasure of Honesty,* with his suit that was too tight and his straw boater, immediately gave me the feel and tone of the character, his deportment for all the rest of the play. Auguste, in Armand Salacrou's *Atlas-Hôtel,* also came on at the very last minute, as I was adjusting my collar, before a mirror in the green room. Suddenly seeing him in a certain new light, I rushed up the stairs two at a time to get to my dressing-room and make a few key changes in my makeup, which in turn determined the way I would speak and act.

There is another category of characters: those are the ones that reveal themselves enough so that you feel you have grasped them, but which, in reality, you never fully possess. They are the truly great characters, like Harpagon, or Richard III. I have the feeling that I could play them thousands of times and at each performance they would reveal another unexpected peculiarity of their nature or character. It was through old prints that I discovered a certain acting aspect of Harpagon. This aspect helped me avoid the danger of turning him into an abstract figure by driving me to seek out in him the egotist, the penny-pinching bourgeois, the ludicrous lover, and leading me to find the difficult synthesis which is so necessary to the comprehension of the play. As for Richard III, it is rare for me to feel I have held on to him from one end of the play to the other; there are always moments when he tries to get away; I sometimes have the feeling that he is holding out on me during a whole scene. This is because he takes shape in successive appearances at different ages, at different degrees of inurement to evil, without any preparatory transition; his plots, his hatreds, his remorse, his forebodings, his death: so many quick images, without the usual links that simplify the composition of a character. Playing him is never a picnic; it is always a fight.

To say where I discovered Volpone is even more difficult. He appeared to me for the first time in the dense underbrush of the Elizabethan earth. I could see him looming up in the dark prestigious jungle alongside Hamlet, Macbeth, King Richard, but since then I have come across him again during my life and travels, sneaking out of some palace; I caught a glimpse of him in a movie travelogue riding in a rickshaw in a Far Eastern metropolis, magnificently dressed and smothered in jewels. Another time, he was the principal figure in a sensational criminal trial: when he was freed, he walked out through the gate, cheerful as could be, skipping along, and repeating, "Pure as the driven snow!"

This elusive Volpone kept changing his features, too: sometimes he was clean-shaven, sometimes he had a little scraggly drooping moustache, most often a thin Oriental beard standing out against his skinny face—slightly bilious, perhaps, arrogant or servile, magnificent and yet of questionable cleanliness—but always with his sharp soul-voyeur's eye and his fur-lined greatcoat making him look like a silver fox. . . .

Now I want to talk directly to the young fellow-actor whom I have been thinking about as I write this book, for these notes are not intended to be merely a last will and testament. If their only purpose were to recall how picturesque my career has been, I would destroy them immediately, but I believe that in our art it is difficult to describe the technique of an actor without taking into account his nature, his temperament, and for that reason to bring to light certain intimate details, even certain weaknesses which we might prefer to leave in the dark. But the anecdote serves only to underline what is essential: the passionate search for the laws of creativity in the player. I would not make the stupid claim to being the one who discovered them, but rather the more modest wish to contribute to making easier for a few their apprenticeship in an art that is difficult precisely because it ever wends its way through dark paths between instinct and intelligence, intuition and deduction, and in which our emotional moods, our physical makeups, our wills play almost equal parts; the head alone is not enough; *it suggests and controls:* that is a great deal, to be sure, but it is not all.

I believe the problem of personal technique will come up for each actor in a new generation. Aesthetics may vary, fashions may influence the theatre even more than they do the other arts, yet at a given moment all the variations come together in a sort of synthesis. So that the actor who may have played melodrama in neighborhood theatres, gone through the naturalist phase of Antoine's time, undergone the influence of the movement started by Jacques Rouché at the *Théâtre des Arts,* decanted himself so to speak through that *dramatic distillation* which was the experience of Jacques Copeau's *Vieux-Colombier,* from which the *Théâtre du Cartel* grew like natural outcroppings, must be able to do a certain number of things that were never asked of the actor who played Buridan or the Postman in Brieux's *Blanchette.* And yet he must know how to appropriate to himself the tricks that were useful to one group or the other. I fought Antoine's aesthetics yet remain immensely grateful to him for having taught me anew to reconsider my work from within, to start off by basing myself on the truth, to speak a part, and it was in attempting to enrich the much more external, but much more theatrical, technique of melodrama that I discovered what another in turn may find interesting in my own work.

Here then is the ideal way in which I would like to be able to work at a role, if in my own case the job of producer did not too often interfere with my concerns as an actor.

[231]

A first period of incubation is required; I read and reread the play several times; I try to *hear* the author. I no longer write dense essays as I once did about Smerdiakov, and I avoid any kind of theory; *I listen* and I store away. I try to picture to myself each situation in the most realistic, I might even say the most everyday, fashion. I need this solid, human background so as not to lose my way. At early rehearsals, I no longer try, as I used to, to skip some of the steps; I let my character develop at its own pace; I try to find the simplest, most direct way to reply to my partner. In the evening, I come back to this job of prospecting through the text; before chewing on the words, I devour the ideas. It is within such calm that in my head I situate once for all the breathing in the lines, the rhythm of the scenes, the lyrical scope of the internal movements, the variety of situations, and the shadings of emotion.

I commit my lines to memory, *chewing on the words,* sharply enunciating all the consonants, arranging to take breaths *before* the vowels; in this way, I save a lot of time, for I rid myself of the concern of both memory and diction. I cannot really begin to act until I am freed of one and the other.

When I am lucky enough to be able to have someone I trust sitting in the audience, I make every effort to take advantage of the suggestions he makes to me. It is quite difficult to know how to make the most of a suggestion, just as it is for a director to know how to give one clearly. The point is to catch the spirit of it and not be slave to its letter. If a director has to indicate an *intonation,* the actor should avoid imitating it, for that is always insipid. Personal interpretation is indispensable. As early as possible, I see to my wig, my wardrobe, the little details of dress that may be able to give some shading to my character. I know that a successful character is made up of a thousand little details of this sort, much more than of transcendental ideas. When I find myself facing a shrewd actor, the work is made easier by the contributions of his own personality: *it is always better to have a partner who is trying to steal the scene from you, for there is no better way to bring out the best in you.*

There is almost always one very difficult period to go through. It starts as soon as the formative work is done: during a period of days, one's creation has been carried to a certain degree of completion; then, all at once, one stitch snaps and the whole work starts to unravel; you have a feeling of emptiness, powerlessness. The play itself, at the same time, is going through the same kind of crisis: it does not help to know that this is only temporary, that you have already been through such a period, and that you pulled out of it with good effect; you are none the less upset by it, and with good reason, for if this stage continues very long you may well lose your character along the way, although on the contrary this is more likely to be the moment when, as I have illustrated with a few personal anecdotes, he is getting ready furtively to slip into your skin.

I am not an actor particularly subject to stage fright; dress rehearsals have quite the opposite effect on me, they leave me cold, even freeze me. I do not really warm up until there have been a few performances before a real audience. Nevertheless, every time I feel my heart beating too fast and a general uneasiness invading me, I calmly and with all unhurried leisure start doing some breathing exercises; it is very rare for the stage fright not to start dissipating. I urgently advise my young colleague to use this method, as it has a pacifying power one does not suspect.

He must also know how to learn the shortcomings and advantages of a given theatre, quickly, the very first time he appears there.

I consider that after his first few speeches a good actor should be able to regulate the volume and level of his acting. The microphone and the growing use of small theatres have tended to spoil this instinct, which used to be much more highly developed. If the theatre has several galleries, one's tone must be determined in relation to the highest of them. Likewise, for the direction of one's eyes: they should be aimed at the edge of the balcony; nothing is more irritating than eyes that remain always aimed at the orchestra, as if trying to pick out a friend there. When you have thus learned quickly to sense the acoustics of a theatre, you will instinctively be able to tell whether the audience is good or bad, immediately after you make your entrance. An old pro does not even have to wait for that; from backstage, like a hunting dog, he gets the scent of his audience, the slightest clearing of a throat, a single uncalled-for giggle, a planned *effect* that works or does not work, being enough to tip him off.

All of this familiarity with the instrument one will daily be using contributes in large part to constituting the actor's techniques. So it can be seen that, while technique may encompass the highest concerns of our art, I nevertheless do not neglect the petty details of its practice. One must never play to the audience, but rather force it spontaneously to play along with you. Which is to say that what is required is to establish between you and it the kind of communication without which there can be no successful dramatic moments. In order to bring the audience into the game, the best thing to do is to give a maximum of credibility to everything one does. Yet, in spite of this, there are some good actors who do not emit the kind of magnetism that little by little succeeds in electrifying an entire audience; they simply have not been so gifted by nature; they do their best to make their bits of business work, yet they often miss just precisely because they are working so hard at them. The minute the audience can see how the trick is done, it shies away like a mouse from a trap—and the character with it. The actor finds himself left all alone on stage.

One must be able to make a line stand out, without appearing to, while remaining in character, when that line brings some new twist to the plot or dynamic quality to the dialogue, without purely and simply going after an *effect.* This is where the actor needs to call upon that looking-down-from-above with which he always keeps a wary eye on what is going on inside of him; for an actor must remain sufficiently in control of himself so that he can if necessary correct a mistake even in the most highly emotional moments. It is either a mistake or a deception to say that true sincerity is incompatible with the personality-splitting that in essence is the problem posed by Diderot in his *Paradox of Acting,* and one I can illustrate with many examples observed during the course of my own career. The actress who, as she is about to faint, her face torn with grief, running with tears, discreetly arranges the folds of her dress, so that she will look graceful when she falls; the actor who, at the last minute, realizes that a prop indispensable to a certain bit of stage business is missing and who, while continuing the development of his emotion, tries to think of a dodge for overcoming the omission, without allowing the audience to suspect the least distress in his performance, even his partner sensing nothing until the final payoff which he has had to change to fit the circumstance—these are the kinds of incidents that have occurred and continue to occur in various forms. Naturally, such anecdotes do not prove a thing unless the actor involved changes nothing in his performance, and himself remains perfectly sincere.

If, in an emotional scene, one suddenly feels himself not getting into it, he should have the courage not to compensate by overemoting; in a comical scene, if all at once the humor sounds hollow, one's playing should not as a result be grossly broadened; if an audience on a given night appears cold or uncomprehending, one has to play even better than usual for the few among them who do respond, for there are always some; if the theatre is largely empty, do not follow the example of those actors who feel that on such an occasion there is no reason to put out for so small an audience: this is dishonest and beyond that ill-advised, for in that auditorium there may be fifty people whose opinions mean something and who the next day can give you the worst kind of word-of-mouth.

During the course of a performance, one should as much as possible avoid allowing himself to be diverted by the gossip and extraneous activities that are engendered backstage by idleness and lack of involvement. Of course, it is easy, without having to be a virtuoso, to interrupt one's telling of dirty jokes to turn to the audience with a face racked by deep emotion, but doing that is to lie and to play a con game, and the actor turns into a mere facemaker, a vile mummer. Respect for one's art and respect for one's audience in themselves endow the player with a kind of aristocracy.

All of which becomes easy if throughout all the eventualities of a performance we succeed in not departing from the character whom we are entrusted with impersonating. His presence will dictate our behavior to us. He is neither an outside entity nor an abstract personage, but a living being. I call to witness all of those I have known in this motley world of the theatre, in which, after a certain time, the living more easily than one imagines become indistinguishable from the beings of fiction: so that some character that I played in a melodrama at the Montparnasse or the Gobelins now seems to belong to the group of "so nicely spoken, so nicely mannered" friends I used to frequent in those days in the little bars of the Rue Biot or at the Lapin Agile. And I would not swear that Milady de Winter, of the appealing melodrama *The Three Musketeers*, has not remained more alive in my memory than the countess who, at the same period, was offering me the hospitality of her two-horse carriage with all its amenities after the performance.

ANTONIN ARTAUD

(1896-1948)

At the end of his troubled life, not long after his release from an insane asylum in which he had spent almost a decade, Antonin Artaud must have felt that he had failed in his mission "to do what I have dreamed." But the decades that followed have proved him one of the most penetrating and influential theorists of the modern theatre. Wherever one turns to see experiment and innovation currently, one finds the realization of the dreams, the images, the visions of this poet, "actor, director, prophet, blasphemer, saint, madman."

Born in Marseille, he became an actor in the theatres of Lugné-Pöe, Dullin, and Pitoëff and also in the movies; in 1922 he played a monk in Carl Dreyer's *Passion de Jeanne d'Arc*. He was active as a poet in the surrealist movement of the twenties, which he turned from when he founded the *Théâtre Alfred Jarry* in 1927 with the playwright Roger Vitrac. He dedicated his short-lived venture "to return to the theatre that total liberty which exists in music, poetry, or painting, and of which it has been curiously bereft up to now." Drawing inspiration from Jarry's *Ubu Roi*, that first of the avant-garde experiments, he worked out theatrical means for the "ruin of the theatre as it exists today in France." Here he staged his own

[234]

short play *Jet of Blood,* Strindberg's *Dream Play,* and Vitrac's *The Mysteries of Love,* a surrealist drama in which a spectator was to be shot at from the stage in wild dreams of audience involvement.

At the Colonial Exposition of 1931, Artaud saw performances of the Balinese Theatre that profoundly influenced his ideals, which were expressed in the next few years in his First and Second Manifestos of the Theatre of Cruelty. The Balinese performances provided him with a vision of theatre as initiation, trance, frenzy that would "bring the demons to the surface." He declared: "The theatre will never find itself again . . . except by furnishing the spectator with the truthful precipitate of dreams, in which his taste for crime, his erotic obsessions, his savagery, his chimeras, his utopian sense of life and matter, even his cannibalism pour out on a level not counterfeit and illusory, but interior." He renounced the civilized, verbal, ethical western theatre tradition in favor of a sensuous, subconscious, mysterious primitive ritual.

These revolutionary objectives led him to project new stage practices. To satisfy his concept that "the stage is a concrete physical place that asks to be filled, and to be given its own concrete language to speak," he planned and executed for his production of *Les Cenci,* his one experiment in the Theatre of Cruelty in 1935, a violent staging that used many mechanical devices to make the stage whirl, the lights flash, and masses of people move before an involved audience in a theatre in the round. He turned theatre over to the *metteur en scène,* who would not only weld together all aspects of production, but be "magician, priest, maker of myths, and manipulator of signs and hieroglyphs." Because he believed that "the domain of the theatre is not psychological but plastic and physical," he thought of the actor as an "athlete of the heart" who "had to make use of his emotions as a wrestler makes use of his muscles" and by controlling the tempos of his breath can "tap and radiate certain powers." He offered the actor Cabalistic exercises in which he announced: "Through the hieroglyph of a breath I am able to recover an idea of the sacred theatre."

Notable experiments using Artaud's theories have been made by Jerzy Grotowski, by Peter Brook and Charles Marowitz in the Theatre of Cruelty experiment in London in 1963, by Julian Beck and Judith Malina in their Living Theatre productions during the 1960s, when they transformed facets of his vision into dynamic and provocative theatre practice, and in the U.S. by Richard Schechner in the Performance Group's *Dionysus '69,* and by Joseph Chaikin in his productions with the Open Theatre.

Athlete of the Heart

One must grant the actor a kind of affective musculature which corresponds to the physical localizations of feelings.

The actor is like the physical athlete, but with this surprising difference: his affective organism is analogous to the organism of the athlete, is parallel to it, as if it were its double, although not acting upon the same plane.

The actor is an athlete of the heart.

The division of the total person into three worlds obtains also for him; and his is the affective sphere.

Antonin Artaud: *The Theatre and Its Double.* Translated from the French by Mary Caroline Richards. New York: Grove Press, 1958, pp. 133-141. © 1958 by Grove Press. Reprinted by permission of Grove Press.

It belongs to him organically.

The muscular movements of physical effort comprise an effigy of another effort, their double, and in the movements of dramatic action are localized at the same points.

What the athlete depends upon in running is what the actor depends upon in shouting a passionate curse, but the actor's course is altogether interior.

All the tricks of wrestling, boxing, the hundred-yard dash, high-jumping, etc., find analogous organic bases in the movement of the passions; they have the same physical points of support.

With, however, this additional correction, that the movement is reversed: in breathing, for example, the actor's body is supported by his breath whereas the physical athlete's breath is supported by his body.

This question of breath is in fact primary; it is in inverse proportion to the strength of the external expression.

The more sober and restrained the expression, the deeper and heavier the breathing, the more substantial and full of resonances.

Similarly an expression that is broad and full and externalized has a corresponding breath in short and broken waves.

It is certain that for every feeling, every mental action, every leap of human emotion there is a corresponding breath which is appropriate to it.

The tempos of the breath have a name taught us by the Cabala; it is these tempos which give the human heart its shape, and the movements of the passions their sex.

The actor is merely a crude empiricist, a practitioner guided by vague instinct.

However, it is not a matter, whatever one may think, of teaching him to be incoherent.

It is a matter of remedying this wild ignorance in which the whole contemporary theatre moves as if in a fog, ceaselessly stumbling. The gifted actor finds by instinct how to tap and radiate certain powers; but he would be astonished indeed if it were revealed to him that these powers, which have their material trajectory by and *in the organs,* actually exist, for he has never realized they could actually exist.

To make use of his emotions as a wrestler makes use of his muscles, he has to see the human being as a Double, like the Ka of the Egyptian mummies, like a perpetual specter from which the affective powers radiate: the plastic and never completed specter, whose forms the true actor apes, on which he imposes the forms and image of his own sensibility.

It is this double which the theatre influences, this spectral effigy which it shapes, and like all specters, this double has a long memory. The heart's memory endures and it is certainly with his heart that the actor thinks; here the heart holds sway.

This means that in the theatre more than anywhere else it is the affective world of which the actor must be aware, ascribing to it virtues which are not those of an image but carry a material sense.

Whether the hypothesis is exact or not, the important thing is that it is verifiable.

The soul can be physiologically reduced to a skein of vibrations.

This soul-specter can be regarded as intoxicated with its own screams, something like the Hindu *mantras*—those consonances, those mysterious accents, in which the material secrets of the soul, tracked down to their lairs, speak out in broad daylight.

The belief in a fluid materiality of the soul is indispensable to the actor's craft. To know that a passion is material, that it is subject to the plastic fluctuations of material, makes accessible an empire of passions that extends our sovereignty.

To join with the passions by means of their forces, instead of regarding them as pure abstractions, confers a mastery upon the actor which makes him equal to a true healer.

To know that the soul has a corporeal expression permits the actor to unite with his soul from the other side, and to rediscover its being by mathematical analogies.

To understand the secret of the passional time—a kind of musical *tempo* that regulates their harmonic beat—is an aspect of theatre long undreamed of by our modern psychological theatre.

This *tempo* can be discovered by analogy; and it is found in the six ways of apportioning and conserving the breath as if it were a precious element.

Every breath has three kinds of time, just as there are three principles at the root of all creation which find a corresponding pattern even in the breath.

The Cabala apportions the human breath into six principal arcana, the first of which, called the Great Arcanum, is that of creation:

ANDROGYNOUS	MALE	FEMALE
BALANCED	EXPANDING	ATTRACTING
NEUTRAL	POSITIVE	NEGATIVE

I have had the idea of employing this knowledge of the kinds of breathing not only in the actor's work but in the actor's preparation for his craft. For if knowledge of breathing makes clear the soul's color, it can with all the more reason stimulate the soul and encourage its blossoming.

It is certain that since breathing accompanies effort, the mechanical production of breath will engender in the working organism a quality corresponding to effort. The effort will have the color and rhythm of the artificially produced breath.

Effort sympathetically accompanies breathing and, according to the quality of the effort to be produced, a preparatory emission of breath will make this effort easy and spontaneous. I insist on the word spontaneous, for breath rekindles life, sets it afire in its own substance.

What voluntary breathing provokes is a spontaneous reappearance of life, like a voice, in infinite colors on the edges of which warriors lie sleeping. The morning reveille sends them by ranks into the thick of the fight. But let a child suddenly cry "Wolf!" and see how these same warriors leap up. They wake in the middle of the night. False alarm: the soldiers are beginning to return. But no: they run into hostile camps, they have fallen into a regular hornet's nest. It is in a dream that the child has cried out. Its more sensitive, fluctuating unconscious has tumbled into a troop of enemies. Thus by indirect means, the fiction provoked by the theatre falls upon a reality much more forbidding than the other, a reality never suspected by life.

Thus with the whetted edge of breath the actor carves out his character.

For breath, which nourishes life, allows its stages to be ascended rung by rung. And an actor can arrive by means of breath at a feeling which he does not have, provided its effects are judiciously combined and its sex not mistaken. For breath is either male or female; and less often it is androgynous. However, one may have rare undeveloped states to depict.

Breath accompanies feeling, and the actor can penetrate into this feeling by means of breath provided he knows how to select among the different kinds the one appropriate to the feeling.

There are, as we have said, six principal combinations of breaths.

NEUTER	MASCULINE	FEMININE
NEUTER	FEMININE	MASCULINE
MASCULINE	NEUTER	FEMININE
FEMININE	NEUTER	MASCULINE
MASCULINE	FEMININE	NEUTER
FEMININE	MASCULINE	NEUTER

And a seventh state which is beyond breath and which, through the door of the highest Guna, the state of Sattva, joins the manifest to the nonmanifest.

If it is claimed that the actor should not be preoccupied with this seventh state since he is not essentially a metaphysician, we shall reply that even though the theatre may be the perfect and most complete symbol of universal manifestation, the actor carries in himself the principle of that seventh state, of that blood-route by which he penetrates into all the others each time his organs in full power awaken from their sleep.

Indeed most of the time instinct is there to compensate for the absence of an idea that cannot be defined; and there is no need to fall so high to emerge among median passions like those that stuff the contemporary theatre. Moreover, the system of breaths has not been invented to produce median passions. And our repeated exercises in breathing, developing its procedures by intense practice, are not cultivated merely to prepare us for a declaration of adulterous love.

But for a subtle quality of outcry, for the soul's desperate claims—it is for these that an emission of breath seven or twelve times repeated prepares us.

And we localize this breath, we apportion it out in states of contraction and release combined. We use our body like a screen through which pass the will and the relaxation of will.

The tempo of voluntary thought we project by a forcefully male beat, followed without too apparent a transition by a prolonged feminine beat.

The tempo of involuntary thought or even of no thought at all is expressed by a weary feminine breath that makes us inhale a stifling cellar heat, the moist wind of a forest; and on the same prolonged beat we exhale heavily; however, the muscles of our whole body, vibrating by areas, have not ceased to function.

The important thing is to become aware of the localization of emotive thought. One means of recognition is effort or tension; and the same points which support physical effort are those which also support the emanation of emotive thought: they serve as a springboard for the emanation of a feeling.

It is to be noted that everything feminine—that which is surrender, anguish, plea, invocation—everything that stretches toward something in a gesture of supplication—is supported also upon the points where effort is localized, but like a diver pressing against the bottom of the sea in order to rise to the surface: it is as if emptiness gushes from the spot where the tension was.

But in this case the masculine returns to haunt the place of the feminine like a shadow; while, when the affective state is male, the interior body consists of a sort of inverse geometry, an image of the state reversed.

To become conscious of physical obsession of muscles quivering with affectivity is equivalent, as in the play of breaths, to unleashing this affectivity in full force, giving it a mute but profound range of extraordinary violence.

Thus it appears that any actor whatsoever, even the least gifted, can by means of this physical knowledge increase the internal density and volume of his feeling, and a full-bodied expression follows upon this organic taking-hold.

It does no harm to our purposes to know certain points of localization. The man who lifts weights lifts them with his back; it is by a contortion of his back that he supports the fortified strength of his arms; and curiously enough he claims that, inversely, when any feminine feeling hollows him out—sobbing, despair, spasmodic panting, dread—he realizes his emptiness in the small of his back, at the very place where Chinese acupuncture relieves congestion of the kidney. For Chinese medicine proceeds only by concepts of empty and full. Convex and concave. Tense and relaxed. *Yin* and *Yang.* Masculine and feminine.

Another radiating point: the location of anger, attack, biting is the center of the solar plexus. It is there that the head supports itself in order to cast its venom, morally speaking.

The location of heroism and sublimity is also that of guilt—where one strikes one's breast—the spot where anger boils, the anger that rages and does not advance.

But where anger advances, guilt retreats; that is the secret of the empty and the full.

A high-pitched, self-mutilating anger begins with a clacking neuter and is localized in the plexus by a rapid feminine emptying; then, obstructed by the two shoulder blades, turns like a boomerang and erupts in male sparks, which consume themselves without going further. In order to lose their aggressive quality they preserve the correlation of male breath: they expire fiercely.

I have wanted to give only a few examples bearing on a few fertile principles which comprise the material of this technical essay. Others, if they have time, will prepare the complete anatomy of the system. There are 380 points in Chinese acupuncture, with 73 principal ones which are used in current therapy. There are many fewer crude outlets for human affectivity.

Many fewer supports which can be indicated and on which to base the soul's athleticism.

The secret is to exacerbate these supports as if one were flaying the muscles.

The rest is done by outcry.

In order to reforge the chain, the chain of a rhythm in which the spectator used to see his own reality in the spectacle, the spectator must be allowed to identify himself with the spectacle, breath by breath and beat by beat.

It is not sufficient for this spectator to be enchained by the magic of the play; it will not enchain him if we do not know *where to take hold of him.* There is enough chance magic, enough poetry which has no science to back it up.

In the theatre, poetry and science must henceforth be identical.

Every emotion has organic bases. It is by cultivating his emotion in his body that the actor recharges his voltage.

To know in advance what points of the body to touch is the key to throwing the spectator into magical trances. And it is this invaluable kind of science that poetry in the theatre has been without for a long time.

To know the points of localization in the body is thus to reforge the magical chain.

And through the hieroglyph of a breath I am able to recover an idea of the sacred theatre.

N.B.—No one in Europe knows how to scream anymore, and particularly actors in trance no longer know how to cry out. Since they do nothing but talk and have forgotten they ever had a body in the theatre, they have naturally also forgotten the use of their windpipes. Abnormally shrunk, the windpipe is not even an organ but a monstrous abstraction that talks: actors in France no longer know how to do anything but talk.

LOUIS JOUVET
(1891 - 1951)

Louis Jouvet, whose saturnine characterizations have been seen in numerous French films, began as a druggist "with a diploma but with no stomach for his work." The young man did not look for an apothecary, but established himself in a tiny theatre in Montmartre. Waldo Frank, in his little volume on the *Vieux Colombier*, described the importance of these *salles de quartier* in his account of the union between Jouvet and Jacques Copeau. "Copeau recognized in Jouvet, not alone an actor of genius, but as well a craftsman for whom the stage had remained a temple to humble, human effort.... Drama had retreated from the Boulevards: it was beaten and lowly. It was by no means dead. In the cheap *quartier* theatres to which the workman brings his wife and children, in the drenched smoke of the *taverne,* among the *bistros* and improvisations of barrack and provincial fair, it had entrenched itself. It had fled back to the people who had once supported its high ancestry—the *commedia dell' arte*. And here in its last hiding place, Copeau sought it out, and mustered his practical collaborators."

With Charles Dullin, Jouvet became one of Copeau's disciples, studying and acting with the *Vieux Colombier*. During World War I, Jouvet and Dullin were released from service to come to New York and act with Copeau in behalf of the French Government. In 1922 Jouvet was asked to take charge of Jacques Hebertot's *Comédie des Champs-Elysées*. He and Georges Pitoëff alternated in directing the theatre. One of Jouvet's popular productions here was Jules Romains' *Dr. Knock,* played in a stylized setting. In 1934 he came to the *Athénée,* where he employed simple imaginative settings to stage the intellectual dramas of Romains and Giraudoux, whom he admired. In his production of Giraudoux' *Madwoman of Chaillot* Jouvet chose the role of the rag-picker, which John Carradine played in the New York version. The Madwoman, so brilliantly played here by the British actress Martita Hunt, was done by Marguerite Moreno.

The season of 1948 was made memorable at the *Athénée* by Jouvet's production of *Don Juan* after years of preparation and nearly a year of rehearsal.

Jouvet's concern with the deepest implications of the actor's art is borne out in the selection from his book *Réflexions du comédien* which follows.

Comedian and Actor

We must first of all make a technical distinction between actor and comedian, terms that are used interchangeably in common parlance. The actor can only play certain roles; he distorts the others in line with his personality. The comedian, however, can play all roles. The actor takes a part, the comedian is taken by it. Garrick was a comedian: he was able to interpret tragic and comic roles with the same power and the same truthfulness. The confusion in everyday speech may be explained by the fact that the line of demarcation between comedian and actor is never strictly defined. We call attention to this difference from the very outset so that we may explain the workings of the acting profession; but there are actors who are comedians and comedians who are actors.

A tragedian is always an actor, that is, an interpreter whose personality is so strong and so unmistakable that pantomime—even when it plays a large part in his role—always leaves him in possession of his personality.

Pantomime is a human instinct present from the earliest childhood. Hence, the perfect comedian would be one who developed this instinct to its maximum. In any event, we must study the calling and profession of comedian from the human point of view. The qualities of adaptation in a human being, oriented and directed toward a definite goal, make the professional comedian.

The chief difference between the comedian and the actor lies in this pantomime, which is not so extensively developed in the actor as in the comedian. The way in which an artist interprets a role—the process by which he succeeds in building up his characterization—determines how much of an actor or comedian he is. The actor substitutes himself for the character, the comedian operates by means of penetration and insinuation.

When to the instinct for pantomime is added a persistent need for escape and incarnation, there is a calling. This calling usually reveals itself very early and authoritatively; and it must overcome the idea that the comedian's profession is a shameful one. But we may also discern in this calling a very intense desire to please —in a sense, a mania for sociability. A true comedian practices a manner of living. The theatre is more than a profession—it is a passion.

It is hard to formulate rules for the profession, except for several laws of technique. There are several reasons for this: 1. It is an empirical profession. 2. The comedian is an instrumentalist who is his own instrument. Only one other kind of artist, the singer, is virtually in the same position. 3. The study of the theatre is a comparative science which proceeds from the notion of collectivity. There are three kinds of actors, all tightly interdependent: the actor-*author,* the actor-*comedian,* and the *audience* actor. We must always bear in mind the process of osmosis that goes on among these three elements. 4. Exercising the comedian's profession is a perpetual adaptation. Theatrical art, more of an improvisation than any other art, reflects the atmosphere of a period and is subject to the laws of fashion. Hence whatever indications we may give have only a relative value.

Louis Jouvet: "Comedien et acteur," *Reflexions du comédien.* Paris: Editions de la Nouvelle Revue Critique, 1938, pp. 141-153. Copyright 1938. By permission of Editions de la Nouvelle Revue Critique. This selection translated by Joseph M. Bernstein.

A Comedian is Commissioned by the Audience

The mechanism of the comedian's calling is explained by the origins of drama, which is a collective manifestation. Among primitive peoples, for example, a whole tribe begins to dance spontaneously in order to express its sentiments. Then there comes a moment in which one dancer takes precedence over the others and performs more remarkably because he is endowed with more powerful magnetism than his fellows. Gradually the others drop out; and he dances alone in their midst. In a sense he is inspired and sustained by all his companions who have become the audience. He is the soloist, commissioned by the mass.

Similarly in ancient days, an inspired individual got up on a cask or some boards; the jokester of his group, he began to talk or sing. The others did not listen to him right away, but then they encouraged him. The audience sat down and waited, and the "commissioned" individual found out how to respond to them. A dramatic theme was created and the profession of comedian was born. We see this same phenomenon in children's games. At first all the youngsters participate, then one child draws apart. He becomes the protagonist. The others group themselves around him, listen, and spontaneously recapture the state of mind of the first audiences in the ancient world—the circle and the circus.

There are no rules in the theatre when there is a personality. Nevertheless, this "sustaining" of the actor indicates that the play exists and develops to the extent that the audience collaborates with it. When those who serve the theatre are no longer "delegated" or "commissioned," the play has no meaning.

Physical Gifts

Beauty, power, nobility, resonant voice, gestures, and bearing are the first gifts of the comedian. He must acquire flawless articulation, dramatic sensibility, the understanding of a script, and the ability to project it on the stage; he must know how to dress and make himself up, and he must learn how to combine these qualities in a harmonious way. In France, we have had comedians who fulfilled these requirements: Lekain and Mounet-Sully.

One may arrive at a certain degree of excellence in the profession without possessing all the foregoing qualities. Personal gifts must, from the very beginning of one's studies, be confirmed by signs of progress and by medical check-up (physical resistance, the state of the lungs and throat, etc.).

The comedian must train his physique by means of sports. Although he need not indulge in acrobatics as the Romans did or the modern Russian comedians do, yet he must render his body flexible enough for every kind of movement called for in the script.

In training his voice, the comedian must first *pitch* it as singers do; then he must get to know its exact register. Once he has acquired a good diction, he must study elocution. In the seventeenth century, that constituted almost the entire art of the comedian. For a long time acting, properly speaking, was reserved to pantomimists and actors of the *commedia dell' arte*. Once when he was asked his advice, Henry Irving said: "Speak clearly!" He answered all such questions with this motto: "Speak clearly!" and added: "Be human."

Elocution demands perfect enunciation, clear pronunciation, and correct speech. Then comes the correcting of accents and the work of intonation. But the basis of

[242]

this art, like that of dancing and singing, is *breathing*. Only long, painstaking, and regular work will give the perfect diction that is the first quality of a comedian.

Gesture is another language—a universal language. The comedian must strive to be as accurate in gestures as he is in intonation. A Greek proverb speaks of "talking improperly with one's hands." Walking across the stage is one of the first and most important difficulties. During rehearsals of each new play, the comedian must work hard to get "in the swing" of the piece, to become part of the stage-setting and atmosphere. And "knowing a part to one's fingertips" often demands long study.

It goes without saying that a comedian must know how to dress and move about in costumes of the most varied types and periods. Knowing his facial traits and the effects he can achieve by them, he must learn how to alter them by the art of make-up, in which he must have some notions of painting, lighting, and even physiology.

The Script

Emotion must create and guide gesture. Emotion is the share of sensibility contributed by an actor in reciting a script and in bringing it to the stage. The comedian must know how to think through a script—that is, how to visualize it in dramatic terms after receiving definite impressions from his reading of it. As Paul Claudel says: "The script has a savor and substance; it is a source of nourishment." One must be able to size up the plot and the dramatic situation of a play. "A role is a blank page on which one writes first of all one's emotions," says Stanislavsky. Then, depending on whether the interpreter is an actor or a comedian, he tries out the part during rehearsals and finds the proper harmony with his cast.

There are scripts that are hard to play by speaking them—which is the whole art of the modern comedian. The value of our classical plays lies in the fact that they can be both spoken and played. A fine text constantly stimulates the performer and bears repeating. The actor who depends on the script must similarly be able to stimulate the audience. The script engenders emotion, dramatic sensibility, and also a way of listening (a very important quality to which attention is rarely paid). Scripts are of necessity composed with an eye to the dramatic qualities of the performer: either the author in writing his play had a definite actor in mind or the actor naturally corresponds to a part—that is, what is called in the language of the theatre a *type*.

The list of these types has changed with changing periods of the drama. The types in the mystery-plays of the Middle Ages were very different from those in the classical Greek theatre. Later, in the *commedia dell' arte*, one finds the most complete list of these types. In Shakespeare's theatre they were individualized, with women's parts taken by men. In Molière's theatre the types were better defined. Eighteenth-century tragedy marked a further evolution and melodrama required a series of special types.

These were the types in tragedy: first roles, princes, second roles, kings, third roles, confidants. The women included queens, princesses old and young, confidants. In comedy: the outstanding first role, *jeune premier,* third roles and *raisonneurs,* noble fathers, judges, old men, valets; first comic, second comic, servants, walk-ons. The women: heroines, *ingénues,* coquettes, *jeunes premières,* character-parts, *soubrettes,* peasants, servants.

A comedian can play several types. An actor usually sticks to a single kind of role.

In our own day the list of types is quite eclectic and it is difficult to classify them accurately. Authors' creations give rise to types; but actors with strong personalities, reacting in turn on literature, create secondary types.

Harmony with the Audience

After finding the proper harmony with his cast, the actor must achieve harmony with the audience. To attain this is a difficult matter for, as instrument and instrumentalist, he cannot see himself, judge himself, or hear himself, and he is playing in an ensemble. Before going out on the stage, the actor must cultivate an "inner silence" and at the same time bring about a physical deconcentration. But once on the stage, the comedian must be able to put himself in the second state and control himself.

Control of the Emotions

Control of the emotions is a delicate problem which, despite numerous controversies, has not yet been settled. Must the comedian who moves the audience be himself moved? As a matter of fact, the question is badly put. There are only individual cases. Got used to say: "The actor must be dual...that is, as the performer plays and feels, a kind of reasoning being must remain vigilantly within him, by his side...a regulator, as they say in mechanics."

This statement, which sums up the sentiments of all experienced actors, seems to disprove Diderot's famous *Paradoxe*. Works on the acting profession are so infrequent that as soon as a genuine writer composes one, it becomes a kind of document to which everyone refers—even the comedians. Diderot was not himself a comedian; he could not experience and understand the mysterious process of the movements that quicken the actor on the stage. Diderot the writer knew a great deal about performances and back-stage incidents and wrote some splendid comments on life in the theatre. But in reading him we must never forget the title of his work: it is a *paradox*.

Does not this dualism, which Diderot considered paradoxical, exist in every man who, even as he speaks with one of his fellow-men, retains his free powers of reasoning? This dualism also concerns the audience. Someone should also write a *Paradox of the Spectator*. Like all paradoxes, Diderot's is a preconceived state of mind. It is neither a criticism nor a theory, but an enigmatic way of discoursing.

The actor's fear of "stage fright" (which some actors have never been able to overcome) is an added ingredient, a kind of preparation for anaesthesia on the stage and for the grace of inspiration without which there is no great comedian. Mounet-Sully alluded to this grace when, leaving the stage one evening, he said: "Tonight the god did not come."

On the stage and in the presence of an audience, the comedian must remember that he must not only portray a character, he must also be that character and feel his feelings. He must acquire a safety mechanism which then arouses emotions. Thus he will retain the original rhythm of the work; and his personal magnetism will get across the footlights, where it will be felt by the expectant audience.

The Magnetic Field

By virtue of the fact that it has entered a theatre and gathered to wait for the curtain to rise, the audience has already created a magnetic field. If its expectations are disappointed or if, in the course of the performance, the actor's personal magnetism disappears, the audience gets a sense of alienation. It is enough for one actor to be "out of tune" for the play to be ruined or to stop dead.

Every human being has a specific gravity. Before an audience one may say that the comedian has a density—the quality of his presence. The comedian must learn to make use of this dynamism, this kind of *aura* that surrounds him. This presence is of course greater in an actor than in a comedian. The impression of self-sufficiency which certain actors sometimes give is an excess of personality. The same is true of the sense of authority on the stage. Other things being equal, this authority is much greater in an actor than in a comedian; or at least it is not achieved by the comedian except at specific moments when he is in perfect possession of his role.

The shyness and timidity felt by many performers, far from harming them, may be useful and even necessary. Human beings may be divided into inhibitionists and exhibitionists, according to the way in which they externalize their sentiments. An inhibitionist actor is not on the same level as the character he has to interpret. In order to raise himself to the level of his role, he must exploit this "insecurity," which will tend to diminish as he goes on. One cannot become a true professional unless one learns how to utilize this feeling of shyness and fearfulness. As the actor plays a piece, his insecurity disappears, his self-consciousness decreases. His sensibility lessens, but his power of execution gains.

"The actor enters into the work of art with his entire being, his face, his features, his voice, etc., and his task is to identify himself completely with the role he represents. In this connection the poet has the right to demand of the actor that he really put himself completely into the role given him, without adding anything on his own, and that he behave as the creative writer conceived and developed the part. The actor must be in a sense the instrument on which the author plays, a sponge which is soaked in all the colors and makes them unalterable....

"The tone of his voice, his manner of reciting, his gestures and physiognomy —all his outer and inner manifestations—demand an originality in conformity with the specific role.

"Indeed, the actor as a living human being has his innate originality with regard to his voice, his external appearance, and the expression on his face—he is forced either to suppress this originality in order to express a universal passion or a known type, or to harmonize the various facets of his role with the traits that have been strongly individualized by the writer." —(Hegel.)

JEAN-LOUIS BARRAULT

(b. 1911)

Jean-Louis Barrault, familiar to audiences for both his stage and screen work, was the dominant personality of the French theatre during the 1940's and 1950's. A student of art history and an instructor at French College, Chaptel, a secondary school, Barrault began his theatre work in 1930 with Charles Dullin. Five years later, under Dullin's supervision, he directed his first play, an adaptation of William Faulkner's novel *As I Lay Dying*. His first film role was in *Les Beaux Jours,* and he has since made numerous motion pictures. In 1940 he entered the *Comédie Française* and became a *sociétaire,* playing many classical roles.

After World War II Barrault founded with his wife the company Madeleine Renaud-Jean-Louis Barrault. At their *Théâtre Marigny,* he produced revivals and new plays including Paul Claudel's *Partage de Midi* and Albert Camus' *The State of Siege (The Plague).* As guest director for the *Comédie Française,* he staged Claudel's *Satin Slipper* and Mauriac's *The Badly Loved.* It was Barrault who created Hamlet in Gide's translation. In the words of Eric Bentley, who translated the following essay on pantomime by the actor: "Barrault is the only actor I have known who, when he reads *Hamlet,* can believe his own eyes and ears, and consequently can stand by Shakespeare, however extravagant, irrelevantly funny or obscene the poet may seem to be."

Barrault is devoted to the ancient art of pantomime, and uses a technique inspired by Etienne Decroux and the *commedia dell' arte* in mime plays. One of these, *Baptiste,* provided the acclaimed pantomime in the film *Children of Paradise,* in which he reincarnated the figure of the great Pierrot Deburau. But Barrault is more than a mime, he acts with voice as well as with body. He wrote: "Mime and diction are the two sides of an actor's art, and the visual and auditory sensations must crystallize into a unity for the actor as well as for the audience." Barrault's acting ideals derive from Stanislavsky, Pitoëff, and Gordon Craig, whose concept of the superpuppet is a factor in Barrault's opinion that the good actor must have something of the robot in him.

In 1959 Barrault became director of the *Théâtre de France* at the *Odéon,* where he reigned until he was deposed during the student rebellion of 1968. Yet the very season that he left his theatre, this many faceted artist triumphed in staging *Rabelais,* his own creation.

His "Rules of Acting" are taken from *The Theatre of Jean-Louis Barrault,* one of several collections of his reflections on the theatre.

Pantomime

We all receive a weird education. We are taught how to write. We are taught, to a lesser degree, how to speak. But we are rarely if ever taught how to move. We know writing, therefore, and can recognize its fine points, can recognize poetry; we have an idea of the word and can usually appreciate eloquence; but, having little notion of the significance of gesture, only with the utmost difficulty can we appreciate any art that proceeds from it.

If we appreciate dance, it is because dance is to gesture what song is to diction. The word and the gesture are the resources of self, the means of expression. Nothing could be more foolish than to neglect one of these two means, yet it has been happening—and for a long time. The word has been kept going thanks to writing, its subtle and passionate derivative; thanks to an idea of genius, that of fixing what the mouth spits out in bubbles with signs executed by the tip of the hand. Writing, a miraculous artifice, partly preserves the word; *nothing helps to preserve gesture.* Dance and sport may help incidentally, but not consciously. To prove this point, it is enough to take a walk in the street. All the people coming and going around

By permission of Jean-Louis Barrault and Eric Bentley, translator of the selection.

you are people who can write, who talk (more or less), who know their native tongue. Watch them move. Follow them a second or two. Observe the way they step off the sidewalk, the way they pass other pedestrians or walk side by side with them. Watch them shift from one foot to the other when they talk with someone they meet. And then ask why these persons, who know their own tongue, don't know their own feet.

We have lost our instinct for gesture. This is very clear when, during the training of a theatrical company, any given series of gestures must be enacted: the result is chaos. Most people refuse even to give their attention to gesture. They at best deem it a language for the dumb, the *primitive* form of action. In our age writing has drawn everything to itself; we live in an age of talkers.

We must re-examine gesture. For the sake of our education, of our "cultivation," we must clear this terrain so long abandoned. Just as the theatre has for its mission the preservation of the so-called spoken language (as against the so-called written language), we must invest this same theatre with another mission: that of preserving gesture. Tragedy and comedy keep language going. Pantomime will preserve gesture.

Pantomime is not simply a child's diversion or an artist's mania; it is the Art of Gesture in the broadest sense of the word. It is not the feeble art of trying to ape the word by a conventional system of gestural language; it is the re-creation of life by gesture. It is a region of artistic creation that has been so long unexplored that it seems to have regained its virginity; a region across which, in the past twenty years, one or two pioneers have advanced, guided solely by the echo of an instinct more or less lost, their sole resource an intellectual intuition. The task is a double one: that of restoring the notion of gesture to those who are going to be mimes and to perform publicly; and to rehabituate the eyes of the public, restoring to them a taste for gesture, covertly guiding them towards the rediscovery of a lost sense.

A certain taste for pantomime already seems to be returning. In a few years this art will have won back its proper place. It will no longer be considered an inferior form of theatre, good only for fair-grounds and half-literate audiences. It will be recognized as a legitimate department of theatre art. When a man has acquired a taste for the right gesture, he will presumably make his own gestures "right"; and if he moves rightly he will have a better chance of living rightly and might even end by reasoning rightly.

Proust once wrote about Sarah Bernhardt in *Phèdre:* The gesture of these artists said to their arms, and to their tunics, "be majestic," but their unsubmissive limbs allowed a biceps that knew nothing of the role to strut between shoulder and elbow. Let us take *Phèdre* as an example of gesture in spoken theatre.

The verbal form of *Phèdre* is the alexandrine. The alexandrine is founded on Number. The way in which the alexandrine is spoken does not correspond to the ordinary way of speaking: it is a diction whose rhythm is dictated by Number. Nor is the way in which the actions of the play succeed one another the ordinary way. They have been filtered and strained off from a narrative which was already abridged. Their form is circular; they come one upon the other in perfect symmetry.

The total action of *Phèdre* is a pure geometric figure. In composing *Phèdre*, Racine obeyed the exigencies of Number and pure geometry. The language is elliptical, the action is crystallized. In order that this purity may be safeguarded throughout, the actor should also *move* in a way that is not ordinary. His gestures, like the alexandrines he speaks and actions he performs, should be regulated, chosen, rhythmic.

If this is not observed it becomes impossible to pass from a gesture to a sound. The required synthesis of the seen and the heard cannot take place. If, in the theatre one thinks oneself in the presence of ordinary life, one asks why the characters talk and act in so unnatural a way. But if one regards the stage as a magic circle, a mysterious box of illusions, one is disappointed to see such ordinary characters on it. Sensing this weakness, this lack of cohesion, many spectators consider theatre an impure art, vulgar or second-rate. An audience that is used to naturalism in the plastic realm is, in general, bored by tragedy. When they ought to be protesting against the false notes struck by actors ignorant of gesture, as they would exclaim against an orchestra playing cacophonies, the rhythm of the alexandrine lulls them to sleep.

To acquire the science of gesture, to learn to create a language of gesture which is regulated, chosen, and rhythmic and which can be "concerted" with the vocal language of the author, the actor must submit himself to a training which will educate him and make him supple. Let us not hesitate to say it: *there should be, deep in every actor, an element of the robot.* The function of art is to lead this robot towards the natural; to proceed by artificial means towards the imitation of nature. It is because the violin is a hollow box, like a dead body, that it is so satisfying to furnish it with a soul. To re-create life is to defy death; creation must start from death. Exactly like the breath and voice, gesture has its language. Exactly as the heart beats in iambs (systole-diastole), exactly as the breath respires in iambs (inhalation-exhalation), gesture too has an iambic rhythm (contraction-relaxation). We walk iambs. Exactly like the spoken language, the language of gesture has its syntax and its metrics.

Every gesture, indeed, is a phrase. The "attitude" one takes up, the "movement" one makes, and the "pointing out" of something into which the movement is decomposed, do these three phases not recall to our minds "subject", "verb", and "object"? It is, moreover, by the respiratory apparatus that gesture is related to breath. Are not our respiratory movements visible? The thoracic cage is the headquarters where "news" converges and whence orders for the smallest actions depart. The chest turns over the smallest communications, like a butter-churn. *Why regulate the word and not the gesture?* Without analyzing our gestures further, let us say that there exists a tonic-sol-fa of gesture, an alchemy which every actor should know. And the "transposed" gesture is just as far from the ordinary gesture as it is from dance, even as the alexandrine is just as far from prose as it is from song. There should be an absolute similarity between gesture regulated, chosen, and given rhythm by the actor, and the vocal form, regulated, chosen and given rhythm by the author. . . .

FRANCE
Rules of Acting

What follows is not a lesson in dramatic art but simply a personal recapitulation of a few rules which are necessary to the actor. Being continually engrossed in the same work leads one not only to grant an excessive importance to secondary details but also to neglect the fundamental laws that govern true acting. Let us therefore try to recall a few of these obvious rules which one tends all too easily to forget.

The first rule which an actor must observe is that of making himself heard and understood. In fact this is not a rule, it is a matter of elementary politeness, and failure to conform to it is an insult to the spectator. Making oneself heard is within everybody's capacity and has nothing to do with special gifts or talents; it is purely a matter of training, barring of course cases of physiological incapacity.

The second rule rests on observation and imitation, and here natural gifts play a part; nevertheless one must bear in mind the fact that the faculty of observation can be developed by practice and training. There are at least two methods of observation: the objective and the subjective method. For instance, take a box of matches and observe it analytically; concentrate your attention on the content, the quality of the wood, the writing, the marks, etc. After a few minutes of this kind of observation, hide the box of matches and describe it objectively. Practice this method of observation on any object that may come under your gaze, and you will soon note that our sight becomes quicker and sharper. After this apply the same method to the observation of your fellow beings; scrutinize them, take them to pieces in the same way and you will find that this kind of observation will supply you with precious data for future characterizations.

Let us now pass to the subjective method of observation. This time you take only one match but you not only look at it, you feel it, and you say to yourself: "I become wood or a memory of wood from a Swedish forest. What remains of this body? I am thin, very thin, and elongated, and the slightest pressure could crush me, break me into pieces; I should crack up, crinkle, but those who use me do not crush me but strike me on the box and my head becomes alight, for all my fire is in my head. I live in a congested state, my forehead burns, my ears are red. I am living under the shadow of cerebral hemorrhage, my fate is to die at the moment when I myself generate life, heat and light. My existence consumes me; I am a symbol of life and of death at the same time. That's perhaps why I am laid out in advance in a grave, side by side with my sisters and without the slightest room to stretch my feet. There is no room in our box, but perhaps those who make them are right, for I have been told that in serious cases of heart illness one must remain motionless, if not the result is a cerebral hemorrhage. That is what lies in store for us, etc., etc." This kind of subjective observation develops the art of imitation. In order to be able to observe and to imitate one must have certain gifts, but in spite of those gifts one might not know how to observe and how to imitate, and that is where practice comes in. To know how to observe and how to imitate is the second rule of the actor; it is the rule of authenticity. The question of producing effects only comes later. Any attempt at producing an effect in the theatre unfailingly

Barrault, Jean-Louis: *The Theatre of Jean-Louis Barrault*. Translated by Joseph Chiari. New York: Hill & Wang, 1962, pp. 32-39. First published 1959 by Flammarion, Paris, under the title *Nouvelles Réflexions sur le Théâtre*. English translation first published and © 1961 by Barrie and Rockliff (Barrie Books Ltd.) 2 Clement's Inn, London W.C. 2. Reprinted by permission of Hill and Wang, Inc.

reminds one of the shopkeeper's last words, "And now, sir or madam, shall I wrap it up for you?" But one must remember that these are not the words with which he greets you, they are his final words, meant to produce the effect he is aiming at, if he is a good salesman.

Once an actor can make himself heard and understood, and once he has so thoroughly observed a chosen character that he is full of him, and can easily imitate him, impersonate him or give him life, he comes up against the rule which can be summed up by the three vital questions "Whence do I come, where am I going and in what state am I?"

There are various opinions as to the way one should answer these questions, but the actor must have a clear-cut opinion about them at any moment of the performance, even when he is in the wings or backstage. Let us take Scapin as an example. We are in Naples; Naples is a hot place; we are in the Mediterranean world, a world where one practices siesta. Scapin must surely practice siesta, he may even be the king of siesta. Scapin, like every other animal, eats, sleeps, makes love and plays. He is either relaxed or he is active. He is a master at relaxing. Where does he come from? The answer is easy; he has just been shaken out of his moist sleep by the lamentation of Octave and Silvester. Where is he going? Nowhere, of course. Why should he go anywhere? He has renounced all things, he says these things come to him by themselves. In what state is he? Sleepy, he will awaken progressively. His first tirade flows forth from the fumes of sleep and wine and is garlic-flavored. He who is generally so talkative lets the others do the talking. No useless efforts (he knows that he will need all his energy later; but this point will be discussed in connection with another subject). When the others have ceased chattering, he yawns, stretches himself and says, "Here you are, quite as big as your father and mother, and you couldn't discover in your brains or contrive with your wits . . . etc." And he stretches himself again, and once he has done so he has a clearer mind. Hyacinthe awakens him completely. Scapin has a heart and he is not insensitive to young women, so he thinks to himself, "she is not bad at all," then he turns a bit of charm on her, and with that he is off. "All right, I want to help you both," he says, so Scapin gets started and will only stop at the end of the famous scene with the "sac."

The third rule, which we have just discovered, is vital; it is called the rule of verisimilitude. The fourth rule could be summed up with the words, "What am I doing here?" It is a rule about environment. The plot is unfolding, the characters play their respective parts. Agrippine nags Nero who listens, gets bored, thinks of Julia, ends by being angry and completely shuts himself off from his mother's presence. The more one progresses in the rules the more complicated they become. The question "What am I doing here?" implies at least two alternatives. One, what am I determined to allow the other to see, and what am I determined to hide? This rule is very complex for a character because although he thinks he knows himself, he may know himself badly and may sometimes confuse good faith with bad faith. He attaches importance to things that have none, and he is suddenly caught up by things from which he felt protected. A character may think that he is walking in the light and be in darkness, and then the passion against which he is struggling may unsettle his equilibrium, distort his reactions and plunge him into errors. He may think he is walking with a steady step and he stumbles; he may think he sees clearly and he is blind. Now blind people find help in walking sticks. A character who is at a loss as to what to do, might be greatly helped if he could find an object to which he could cling. During Agrippine's sermon, Nero plays with his coat, which becomes his help, his refuge and also his means of expression. An actor who finds the object which connects him with the scene he is playing imparts concrete efficiency to his behavior. To find the right object was the golden rule of Stanislavsky; it is a most precious rule which has countless effects and it is one of the most important rules of realistic art.

The fifth rule is the rule of control, and it is also very important; it deals with sincerity and exactness. There is a prevailing belief that sincerity is automatically right; that is not always true. The actor might be sincere while at the same time the character he is portraying is not quite right within the performance. The reason is that the actor never identifies himself absolutely with the character he is playing, and that is normal since we are in the theatre, a place where life is re-created through art. The point is that it is the character who must be sincere, irrespective of the fact that the actor may or may not be so. The acting will be right if the character is constantly sincere. The closer the identification between actor and character the more sincere they will be. But there are situations in which total identification of the two would bring about disasters. The death of a character compels the actor who plays the part to disconnect himself from it and merely to project the picture of death out of himself, with as much sincerity as he can command. Death is an extreme case, yet there never is complete identification between actor and character. The actor must work within the play's setting, keep on remembering his relationship with the other characters of the play, remain aware that he is in a theatre, and that he must be heard, and that he must stick to the plot, keep an eye on the lighting, etc. The superimposition of the actor's person on that of a given character resembles those cheap colored prints in which the colors overflow the contours of the drawing. Exactitude of performance depends on the sincerity of the character and on the power of control of the actor who must constantly ask himself the question: "In spite of my sincerity is my character truly sincere?"

Such are the five main rules for the basic training of an actor. They are the foundations of his studies and art, and his talent can only blossom thanks to them. Just as in the course of primary, secondary and university studies we spend a great deal of time going through the same cycle or unlearning what we learned with so much difficulty, we seem at this point to run the risk of coming up against rules which might seem to contradict the preceding ones. Yet, in fact they don't. In our young days we might have learned that two and two make four, and later we might have been compelled to realize that it is not quite so; yet this rule does not lose its virtue or its efficiency. In fact, superior rules do not abolish efficient rules, they only refine them. In the same way poetic theatre does not nullify realistic theatre; on the contrary, it raises it to a higher level.

After these five elementary rules which are the basis of normal drama which is realistic, there exist more practical preconceptions. First, the rule of transposition. Once one has carefully laid down the foundations of one's work on truth (whether one is an actor, a producer or a stage designer) one can take the liberty of forgetting everything and begin anew. And so it happens that sometimes, guided by inspiration, one discovers a way of doing things which, although it does not at first sight rest on truth, contains nevertheless aspects which are the very essence of truth. That is truly poetic interpretation.

Let us now return to Scapin. We have previously described the way in which, according to logic, he ought to make his first appearance on the stage. The conception outlined previously was also that of Jouvet who produced *Scapin,* yet that is not the way in which he produced me when I played Scapin under his direction. Jouvet was a great producer and he knew how to invent and to transpose, while starting from reality. He thus invented how to make me appear as if from nowhere right in the middle of the reality of the stage. It was something like the appearance of the Prince of Valets. Truth was respected since the internal rhythm of Scapin remained slow, but the fact of turning his entrance into a kind of sudden emergence produced at the very beginning of the play a poetic tone which echoed from scene to scene. Even if *Les Fourberies de Scapin* was a farce, Jouvet was entitled to produce it as a poetic farce, yet in fact Molière did not call it a farce but a comedy and it is a comedy that contains a kind of poetry to which Jouvet was particularly sensitive. His invention about Scapin's first appearance on the stage follows the rule of transposition. In a transposition there is no apparent logic, there is a metamorphosis. Happy those who possess this sixth sense which transposes truth through poetry. There we have all the art and all the difficulty of Giraudoux's theatre!

Let us pass to another rule. I love horse racing but know nothing about it. Yet I feel that it is with the terminology of horse racing that I should discover my next rule. This new rule which concerns those who play big parts deals with the art of running a race. The actor who plays Hamlet, for instance, loses approximately two pounds in weight at each performance. If he starts too fast he will be short of breath in the second half of the third act; in order to avoid that he will increase his efforts, and will probably be flat out for the fifth. One of the great difficulties of Hamlet is its length. Right up to the beginning of the fourth act (the departure for England) the actor is carried forth by his own impetus without any time for cooling off; during the greater part of the fourth act, Hamlet is no longer very active and he cools off during the scene of Ophelia's madness. His head tired by a three-hour performance is bubbling with all the words, curses and sighs which he has just uttered and his will is liable to flag. The last effort of the fifth act, notably the Graveyard scene, is particularly painful. It sometimes takes him a few minutes before he is again in full control of his reflexes. If *Hamlet* is a long-distance race, *Scapin* is the 800 metres, and everybody knows that 800 metres is a very difficult race to run. Once when I was in Buenos Aires I was curious enough to take my blood pressure before the start of the play and immediately after the scene of the "sac." From 7.11 it had gone up to 9.165. Every race must be run in its own particular way. The actor is like a jockey, he rules his character, or, like one of Goya's witches, he gets on his horse and plunges into the night for his infernal race. There are parts that require a fast start, a sustained tempo with some spurts here and there and then a slight slackening off as if one were traveling on one's acquired speed, in order to gather strength for the final speed burst of the end. Other parts require that the actor should keep his strength in reserve as long as possible until a given bend of the race. The actress who plays Phèdre must rein in her mount during the first act; she must in fact hold her back, and she must continue to control her during the second act (Hyppolyte's declaration). She lets her go in the third act—long strides, deep breathing, fluent diction, avoiding tensing up. Thus she will be prepared to give everything in the fourth act—muscular strength, heart, nerves, senses and intellect. In the first two acts the fire is smoldering; it begins to crackle up with Hyppolyte's declaration, but it only catches on under the wind of the third, and it only spreads and brings down the building in the fourth. In the fifth, we have the smoldering ashes. This way of running the race sets out the worth of the part. Just as small unfinished patches in Despiau's busts enhance the beauty of his work, in the same way it is useful to slacken off for certain brief moments during which actor and public gather strength for the best moment when they will get drunk together. The problem of timing belongs to the rule of control. There are very many rules of control for the actor, and there comes to mind one which I find extremely difficult to apply: it is the rule of relaxation. There are so many exercises to bring about relaxation, but they are not easy to carry out and good results are few.

It seems to me that one of the most important causes of tension is timidity. It is possible to crave to get into somebody's else's skin, and to have the gift of changing personality in order to become a character, but only when one is by oneself, and not before spectators. Timidity renders such an operation impossible. In the presence of the public certain actors become nervous and tense and lose the best part of their means. As they cannot relax, they are likely to be unable to infuse the character that they are playing with the sincerity, the authenticity and spontaneity which it requires. In order to avoid these pitfalls, one must concentrate on the most important rule of all, that of concentration and control of the will. This is the foundation of the whole discipline of acting. There are many excellent exercises for the development of the art of concentration and control of the will which are the basic principles of acting. The rest is silence, and that is, I think, true for theatrical performances as well as for musical performances, which only exist in order to cause silence to vibrate.

IX. GERMANY

From *Hamburg Dramaturgy* to Epic Theatre

At the beginning of the eighteenth century when France had her well-established *Comédie Française* and England her two patent theatres, modern German theatre was only beginning to emerge. While these other countries had developed professional theatres during the 1500's, Germany retained the medieval amateur tradition in the performances of religious and neo-classical plays of Hans Sachs (1494-1576), the prolific Nuremburg author, and others. The trend toward the establishment of a national drama acted by professionals was frustrated in Germany by the disastrous Thirty Years' War, which exhausted the resources of the country and prevented it from raising a national capital where theatrical life could take root.

During the seventeenth century, French, English, and Italian players toured the numerous German principalities. From the foreigners, native troupes gradually acquired repertory and technique, adding the indigenous farces in which appeared the slapstick figure of Hanswurst or Pickelherring. To one of the better companies, that of Carl Andreas Paulsen, Johannes Velten (1640-c. 1693) brought his talents. Educated at the university, Velten, animated by higher ideals, raised the standards of repertory and acting. Most actors, still vagabonds living on the periphery of society, continued to enact the stilted serious plays and the Hanswurst comedy. The numerous offshoots of Velten's company served as training schools for Germany's first important actors and became the nucleus from which most of the significant companies grew.

The modern German theatre begins early in the eighteenth century with the career of Carolina Neuber (1697-1760). With her husband, Johann, she joined the company of Christian Spiegelberg (d. 1732) of the Velten group. Soon they became part of the Haak Company (still another branch of the Velten players) where, with Karl Ludwig Hoffmann and Friedrich Kohlhardt, they tried to elevate dramatic and histrionic standards. When the Neubers undertook the management of their old company in 1727, they advanced the ideas of Johann Christoph Gottsched (1700-1766), the Leipzig professor and litterateur who wanted to replace the old *Haupt-und-Staatsaktionen* (serious or principal plays followed by an after-piece) and the improvised Hanswurstiades with adaptations of declamatory French drama.

Although Carolina Neuber seized upon Gottsched's program with great eagerness, she faced many difficulties in putting it into practice. Her audiences disliked the formal French dramas and clamored for the old plays. Her actors had to acquire a new manner of acting for the imported drama. Accustomed to their improvised comedies, they now had to train themselves to memorize long verse scripts and to embody French heroic characters. Under Neuber's tutelage some members of her troupe perfected the new classical style. Among these, Gottfried Heinrich Koch (b. 1703) and Johann Friedrich Schoenemann (b. 1704) were pre-eminent. Carolina herself did the most to cultivate the group; she devoted careful attention to rehearsals; she introduced elaborate, but fussy costuming, and she improved the morals of the company by having the actresses live under her roof.

[254]

From Leipzig the Neubers went to the thriving town of Hamburg, where Carolina berated audiences for failing to appreciate her reforms. The public demanded Hanswurst, and even though the Neubers held a formal ceremony to banish the farcical figure, he did not disappear from their repertory. A disagreement over costuming, which was one of many differences which Gottsched had with the Neubers, turned him against the company, and their fortunes declined.

Since they had erected their histrionic practice on the edifice of the declamatory French style popular in the eighteenth century, the reforms of the Neubers and Gottsched soon went out of fashion. Their positive contribution lay in the attempt to play a literary and artistic German drama. Gotthold Ephraim Lessing, at that time a student at Leipzig University, gained his earliest knowledge of the stage from the Neubers, who produced his first play.

Carolina Neuber's disciples, Schoenemann and Koch, established troupes while their former mentor struggled in wretched poverty. The first great actors of the German stage were in Schoenemann's company—Sophie Schroeder, Konrad Ackermann (1710-1771), and Konrad Ekhof (1720-1778). Ackermann and Schroeder, who later married, went on to form a company of their own, but Ekhof remained with Schoenemann for many years, developing the first semblance of realistic acting in Germany. In 1753 Ekhof initiated a short-lived Academy for Actors and at one of its first meetings he proclaimed: "Dramatic art is copying nature by art and coming so near up to it that semblance is taken for reality, or to represent things of the past as if they were just happening. In order to obtain some mastery of this art the following things are required: a vivid imagination, untiring application, and a never idle practice." In 1764, when Ekhof became a member of Ackermann's company, which now included Frau Schroeder's son, Friedrich Ludwig, the celebrated realistic school of Hamburg was well established.

Ekhof and the members of the Ackermann company, with the support of some local burghers, founded the Hamburg National Theatre, an ambitious project to promote fine drama and acting. From 1767 to 1769 they performed the plays of Lessing, Schlegel, and Weisse as well as those of Molière, Voltaire, Destouches, and La Chaussée. The National Theatre employed Lessing as their salaried critic to raise the artistic tone of their venture. Although internal dissension destroyed the Hamburg experiment, out of it came Lessing's famous critique, *The Hamburg Dramaturgy*, a body of theatrical theory which appeared in a journal sponsored by the theatre. In this work Lessing tried to annihilate the pervasive influence of French classicism and to encourage an interest in the dramas of Shakespeare. Recognizing that "we have actors, but no art of acting," Lessing began a systematic analysis of acting basing his ideals on the natural performances of Ekhof. Frustrated in his attempt to pursue the "path of the actor" because of the sensitivity of various members of the company, Lessing soon abandoned this aspect of his investigations. Consequently only a small part of the *Hamburg Dramaturgy* is devoted to histrionic practice.

The fortunes of the Hamburg National Theatre might have been different if animosity had not ousted young Friedrich Ludwig Schroeder from their ranks. Schroeder was an agile, versatile actor, dancer, and acrobat. He was twenty when Ekhof came to play in the Ackermann company, and although the arrogant young man taunted and criticized the older artist, he learned much from him. When his stepfather Ackermann died in 1771, Schroeder returned to Hamburg to guide the fortunes of his troupe and to initiate a great new period in the German theatre.

Like the young writers of the *Sturm und Drang* movement, Schroeder was inspired by the passionate and the revolutionary. He abandoned French artificiality; he acted in the plays of Lessing and was the first to perform young Goethe's *Goetz von Berlichingen*. Most significant, however, was the fact that from 1776 to 1780 he produced eleven plays by Shakespeare. Despite his use of a rather mutilated version of the play, his interpretation of *King Lear* was considered the apogee of histrionic art. Like his contemporary Garrick, Schroeder influenced the art of his time not only by his own brilliant realistic interpretations, but also by his careful attention to the ensemble. He prepared each production by reading the play to his company and by suggesting to them the various characterizations. Unlike many actor-managers, he was willing to perform minor roles; in 1776 he played the Ghost to the Hamlet of Johann Franz Hieronymus Brockmann (1745-1812), who later became a central figure of the Vienna *Burgtheater*. Schroeder's strict, exacting manner fashioned the finest troupe in Germany. At the Vienna *Burgtheater* and in Hamburg "The Great Schroeder" played his many roles, some seven hundred in all, and although he never again reached the vigorous creativity of his early days in Hamburg, he was, without doubt, the greatest German actor of the century.

At the Mannheim National Theatre, organized in 1778, three actors who had been trained by old Ekhof at the Court Theatre of Gotha made their fame. Heinrich Beck (1760-1803), Johann David Beil (1754-1794), and August Wilhelm Iffland (1759-1803) played there under the supervision of Baron Wolfgang Heribert von Dalberg. Of the three, Iffland was the most significant both as an actor and as a popular playwright. He took roles in the plays of young Schiller, who was associated with the theatre. The realism of Ekhof lived on in Iffland, although the latter employed a good deal of artifice. A high point in his career was his guest appearance at Goethe's Weimar Theatre.

Apart from the regular commercial theatre, Johann Wolfgang von Goethe, the greatest figure of the century, created a theatre devoted to beauty and literature. Young Goethe came to the Duchy of Weimar in 1775 at the invitation of Duke Karl August. There, among many other activities, Goethe wrote, acted, and directed plays for the Ducal amateur theatre. Later, in 1791, the Duke, dissatisfied with the mediocre professional troupe that entertained in his newly built theatre, asked Goethe to undertake its direction. At Weimar Goethe opened his twenty-six year theatrical reign with one of Iffland's plays. In the prologue Goethe wrote to this play he keynoted his theatrical ideals—harmony and beauty.

Aware that there was little creative originality in his company, Goethe projected his famous "Rules for Actors." These rigid, theatrical prescriptions for posture and pronunciation were a retreat from the creative realism of Schroeder, but they served Goethe well in developing a corps of disciplined if uninspired actors. Unfortunately Goethe's personal fame caused these pedantic dicta to be adopted as histrionic ideals. The artificialities of the Weimar School competed with the realism of the Hamburg artists, and these two styles struggled for supremacy throughout the following century.

In 1798 the dramatist Schiller joined Goethe at Weimar. Here the two poets made the insignificant Duchy theatre the home of fine drama. Although their theatrical tastes differed—Goethe favored classical restraint while Schiller admired flamboyance—they both believed in ideal beauty and produced acting characterized by musical declamation and orchestrated effects.

At the Royal Court Theatre in Berlin Schiller's romantic heroes found an ideal interpreter in the erratic Johann Friedrich Ferdinand Fleck (1757-1801). He created the role of Schiller's Wallenstein for which his fiery acting was well suited. Fleck died young, and Iffland, now director of the famed Royal Court Theatre, assumed Fleck's parts. But the mannerisms of Iffland no longer suited the growing romantic demands.

The gloomy, violent romanticism of the early nineteenth century produced a new type of actor—passionate and wildly inspired—a type represented by Edmund Kean in England. Ludwig Devrient embodied German histrionic romanticism. He developed an original, uninhibited style which earned him his first success as Franz Moor in Schiller's *The Robbers*. At twenty-six he played King Lear in Schlegel's translation and created a fresh interpretation of Shylock. Devrient never realized his desire to portray Iago and Mephistopheles, diabolical roles in harmony with his talents, since Count Bruehl, who directed the Royal Court Theatre, preferred the abilities of the Weimar-trained Pius Alexander Wolff (1782-1828) to those of Devrient. Devrient's unrestrained, strenuous performances drained his weak physique. Even in his younger days he could not complete his presentation of King Lear. His demoniac acting, his ailing body, and excessive drinking cut short his career. Although the Devrients never again produced a genius like Ludwig, the family continued to contribute important actors to the German stage.

During the 1830's the Young Germany movement was founded to breathe national, democratic sentiments into literature and the theatre. Some of the members of this group wrote plays and directed theatres. Karl Immermann (1796-1840) managed a theatre in Duesseldorf, where the actor Karl Seydelmann (1795-1843) played in Lessing's *Nathan der Weise*. The dramatist Heinrich Laube, identified with the Young German group for a while, was director of the Vienna *Burgtheater* from 1849-1866. In the nineteenth century the *Burgtheater,* originally founded in 1741, became one of the finest theatres in Europe. Under Joseph Schreyvogel, manager from 1814 to 1832, the repertory and company of the *Burgtheater* were improved. Here Ludwig Loewe (d. 1871) played the young heroes of Schiller and Grillparzer. Laube contributed his directorial skills to the *Burgtheater*. According to Joseph Gregor, Laube was one of the first directors to prepare minute instructions for each production. The importance of the *Burgtheater* and its actors during this period was well summarized by Maida Darnton in her article on the Thimig family in *Theatre Guild Magazine*. Speaking of Hugo Thimig, who became a member of the theatre in 1874 she wrote: "To be a member of the *Burghtheater* was in those days the dream of every German-speaking actor. The fountainhead of histrionic tradition, exigent in technical standards, unrivaled in range and variety of repertory, the names of some of its greatest actors, Sonnenthal, Lewinsky, Charlotte Wolter, have transcended the limits of language and are famous in the roster of the world's great actors."

In the mid-nineteenth century a new realistic spirit revealed itself in the psychological, middle-class problem plays of Christian Friedrich Hebbel and in the folk plays of Ludwig Anzengruber. As elsewhere in the latter part of the nineteenth century fidelity to real life, historical accuracy, and scientific truthfulness became the battle cry.

George II, Duke of Saxe-Meiningen provided Germany and, by his example, most other European countries with a core of the basic principles upon which the modern theatre is built. Director and designer, he established the importance of the *régisseur*, integrated the actor and the *mise-en-scène*, perfected ensemble playing, and related costuming to the actor's movements and to the historical character of the production. Above all he withdrew the focus of attention from the individual star declaiming from the center of the stage. From 1874, when the Duke brought his company from the small town of Meiningen to perform *Julius Caesar* in Berlin, until 1890, when their work ended, the Meiningers toured throughout most of Europe, visiting thirty-eight cities. Inspired by Charles Kean's archeological productions in London during the middle of the century, the Meiningen Company in turn animated Konstantin Stanislavsky and André Antoine.

Theatrical synthesis, the unity of the various theatrical arts—acting, settings, music, dance, poetry—was the ideal of Richard Wagner (1813-1883) and his impassioned interpreter Adolphe Appia (1862-1928), the Swiss theorist of modern *décor* and lighting. With the Duke of Saxe-Meiningen they cleared the way for integrated theatrical art in which actors as well as other scenic elements were subordinated to an overall theatrical image.

The last step in the creation of modern theatre was still to be taken. Reformations in staging when applied to Germanic mythology or historical dramas would not alone answer the demand for living theatre. Theatrical innovations needed to be put to service in dramas expressing in a realistic manner the problems of daily life. Henrik Ibsen's penetrating dramas were the first vehicles to meet the requirements for the creative fusion of the new form and content. Saxe-Meiningen included several of Ibsen's plays in the repertory of his troupe, and young German intellectuals, inspired by socialist zeal, by the naturalism of Zola, and by the probing social and psychological analysis of Tolstoy and Dostoyevsky, rallied to the new realism. Writers and critics of the Youngest Germany movement began to convert the theatre in accordance with naturalistic ideals corresponding to those of the *Théâtre Libre*.

The genuine revolutionary theatre devoted to naturalism was the *Freie Buehne*, founded by Theodor Wolff and Maximilian Harden. They were joined by others, notably the literary critic Otto Brahm, who soon became the prime mover as the original founders dropped out. Brahm's personal integrity and the clarity of his naturalistic theories molded the new German theatre. Unlike its progenitor, the *Théâtre Libre*, with its amateur actors and small quarters, the *Freie Buehne* had professional actors and was allowed to use the Lessing Theatre, one of the finest houses in Berlin. Subscriptions were secured for the Sunday afternoon performances, and a periodical to publish plays and critical articles was founded. Ibsen's *Ghosts*, the hallmark of the independent theatres, was given at the first performance in 1889. The *Freie Buehne* functioned sporadically for only three seasons, but during that time it performed plays by Ibsen, Tolstoy, Zola, Strindberg, Becque, Anzengruber and, most important, introduced the naturalistic plays of Gerhart Hauptmann to the German public.

In acting, the *Freie Buehne* was the heir of the Hamburg realists, Ekhof and Schroeder, and opposed to the artificialities of the old Weimar School. The distinguished actor Emanuel Reicher (1849-1924) came to play with the group, which produced Rudolf Rittner, Else Lehmann, and Oscar Sauer, whose performances were the acme of the naturalistic school. Albert Bassermann (1867-1952), familiar to American audiences, acted with Brahm and went on to play with Reinhardt and others. Naturalism in Germany was transformed from revolutionary experiment to orthodox theatre when, in 1894, Brahm became the director of the *Deutsches Theater*. This theatre had been founded by Adolph L'Arronge in 1883 to carry on the Meininger tradition in historical dramas and to display some of the new plays depicting Berlin life. With him had been associated Agnes Sorma and the fine Austrian actor Josef Kainz (1858-1910), to whom the lyric dramatist Hugo von Hofmannsthal had penned a beautiful poem.

The most significant theatre to pick up the reins of the *Freie Buehne* was the *Freie Volksbuehne*, organized by Bruno Wille to give Berliners a people's theatre devoted to the realistic presentation of life. Drawing artistic ideas from Brahm, and ideological inspiration from the social democratic movement, Wille and his co-workers initiated the first great people's theatre. Vast popular audiences were introduced to the plays of Shakespeare, Anzengruber, Hauptmann, Strindberg, Shaw, Grillparzer, Ibsen, Schiller, Maeterlinck and others. In the center of the workers' district they built an impressive theatre with the penny contributions of their many thousand members. Above its portals were carved the words, "Art for the People."

Max Reinhardt, whose imagination encompassed all theatrical media, was trained first as an actor in the naturalistic school of Otto Brahm. At his numerous theatres Reinhardt created an eclectic repertory with each play mounted in an individual style. Although Reinhardt lacked a comprehensive histrionic theory, except for his determination to free the actor from the inhibitions of bourgeois society, he possessed the extraordinary ability to fire his actors to their finest efforts. Associated with his various ventures were some of the most celebrated German actors. Of Italian parentage, Alexander Moissi (1880-1935), distinguished particularly for his interpretation of Everyman in Reinhardt's open-air production in Salzburg, was one of the greats of the Reinhardt galaxy, which included among others Albert Bassermann, Emil Jannings, Rudolf and Joseph Schildkraut, Ernst Lubitsch, Conrad Veidt, Paul Wegener (seen in the film *The Golem*), Werner Krauss (*Dr. Caligari*), Gertrude Eysoldt, Agnes Sorma, Elisabeth Bergner, Oscar Homolka, Vladimir Sokoloff, and the Thimigs—Helen, Hugo, Hermann, and Hans.

Reinhardt was one of the first to produce the expressionist dramatists who emerged at the end of World War I. Abandoning conventional theatrical forms, especially the naturalistic reproduction of life, the expressionists sought the essence of life, the abstract truth underlying human existence, the deepest recessses of life in the unconscious, the schematized, direct, violent portrayal of ideas. Between 1917 and 1920, Reinhardt produced the expressionist works of Georg Kaiser, Reinhard Sorge, Franz Werfel, Fritz von Unruh, Oscar Kokoschka, Paul Kornfeld, and Walter Hasenclever, who epitomized the expressionist theory in these words: "Reality on the stage is of no account; all the persons in the play have only to reflect the Ego of the poet as set down in the principal character."

Other directors came to the fore to stage expressionist dramas using obviously "theatrical" devices like those of the Russian innovators Meyerhold and Tairov. Leopold Jessner at the State Theatre in Berlin (once the Royal Court Theatre where the great character actor Adalbert Matkowsky had played) created productions of many plays, especially those of Wedekind, on a stage frequently dominated by a flight of steps on which the main action took place. The powerful oratorical actor Fritz Kortner darted up and down the famous *Jessnertreppen* as the central figure in Jessner's productions.

Juergen Fehling, who began as an actor at the Berlin *Volksbuehne* when it was under the direction of the actor Friedrich Kayssler, was associated with Jessner at the Berlin State Theatre. His first great production at the *Volksbuehne* was *Masse Mensch* by the revolutionary expressionist poet-dramatist Ernst Toller.

ACTORS ON ACTING

The German critic and theoretician Julius Bab suggests that expressionism in
the theatre had two branches—one basically artistic represented by the productions
of Jessner and Fehling, and the other basically political with which are associated
the names of the poet Bertolt Brecht and the *régisseur* Erwin Piscator. Fired by
social ideals, Brecht and Piscator sought to use non-naturalistic techniques to create
a didactic, political theatre. It is significant, however, as Eric Bentley points out in
The Playwright as Thinker, that Piscator and more especially Brecht used the nonillusory aspects introduced by the expressionists to approach man's objective reality,
the original aim of the naturalists, rather than to express the individual subjective
spirit of the expressionists. Their ideals were like those of Karlheinz Martin who
organized the theatre *Die Tribuene* in 1919 with the slogan: "We do not ask an
audience, but a community, not a stage, but a pulpit."

In the 1920's Piscator at his own theatre, the *Piscatorbuehne,* with such productions as *The Good Soldier Schweik* and Brecht at the *Theater-am-Schiffbauerdamm*
with his *The Three-Penny Opera* evolved a new dramaturgy and radical methods
of staging using screens, motion pictures, treadmills and signboards to reduce emotional empathy and increase intellectual decisiveness in the audience. Acting in Epic
Theatre, the name used to distinguish the narrative and educational from the
dramatic emotional theatres, was marked by declamation and nonillusory, nonpsychological interpretations. For Epic Theatre the actor was not to become the
character he played, not to live the part, but he was to understand his role, interpret
it, and comment on it.

During this period Werner Krauss and Fritz Kortner, with stylized gesture
and oratorical delivery, approximated an expressionist style of acting. Agnes Straub
and Gerda Müller, Käthe Dorsch and the powerful Eugen Kloepfer were also associated with the new dramas. Max Pallenberg, the great Austrian comic artist in
buffoon tradition, created the figure of Schweik in Piscator's production. The delicate Elisabeth Bergner, much admired for her Rosalind in *As You Like It,* belongs
to this generation of excellent German actors.

The Nazi regime destroyed this vigorous German theatre in the thirties and
sent many fine artists into exile. Brecht and Piscator were in the United States,
where each in his own way eventually influenced American drama and theatre,
while some of the leading performers found a temporary home in Zurich. By the
end of 1947 Brecht made his way to Zurich, then back to East Berlin, and gradually
reassembled some of his former co-workers into the *Berliner Ensemble* in 1949.
Piscator also returned to Europe in 1951, but to West Berlin where he offered
striking productions at his old theatre, the *Freie Volksbuehne.* In 1954 Brecht's
Berliner Ensemble moved into that same *Theater-am-Schiffbauerdamm* where *The
Three-Penny Opera* had been staged twenty-six years earlier.

In the years before his death in 1956 Brecht made his theatre one of the finest
ensemble companies in the world. Outstanding in his productions of his own late
masterpieces was his wife, Helene Weigel, whose Mother Courage was one of the
acting triumphs of the era. The high creative accomplishment of Brecht's company
was less the result of what he called his "dry theories," which were much read and
pondered outside his company, than the product of his pragmatic, patient, skilled
touch as director. He was more concerned that his performer be able "to take the
lines served him like a tennis player taking a ball" than that he know the "alienation effect." The unique combination of theory, practice, and dedicated group spirit
in the work of this "artist of the theatre" made Brecht, in the words of Peter Brook,

"the key figure of our time, and all theatre work today at some point starts or returns to his statements and achievement."

GOTTHOLD EPHRAIM LESSING

(1729-1781)

Gotthold Ephraim Lessing was the first great German dramatic critic and the first German dramatist of importance. His predecessor, the critic and dramatist Johann Christoph Gottsched, had imbued the Neubers with his admiration for neo-classical French drama. Lessing, on the other hand, undermined the throttling French influence in favor of the freer English drama.

Lessing was born at Kamenz, and after his early schooling went to the University of Leipzig to study theology. It was during his student days there in 1746-1748 that he became acquainted with the Neuber group, for whom he made translations. In 1748 his play *Der Junge Gelehrte* was performed by Carolina Neuber. He came to Berlin to pursue his literary work. Later he took a Master of Arts degree from the University of Wittenberg. In 1755 he wrote *Miss Sara Sampson,* a tragedy of middle-class life, and in the following years came some of his most important works: *Laokoon,* his study of aesthetics, and *Minna von Barnhelm,* regarded as the first great German comedy.

In 1767 he began his work as the salaried critic of the newly established Hamburg National Theatre. Lessing had already made his reputation as a dramatic theoretician through his writings in Berlin periodicals and through his own paper *Theatralische Bibliothek.* At Hamburg in the years 1767-1769 he published the dramatic criticisms known as the *Hamburgische Dramaturgie (The Hamburg Dramatury).* Based on Aristotelian principles, these critical essays made Lessing one of the great theorists of the drama. As Lessing says in his preface, the *Dramaturgy* was to "form a critical index of all the plays performed, and...to accompany every step made here by the art of the poet and the actor...." With his epoch-making dramatic criticism we are not here immediately concerned. We are interested in those few notes which represent one of the first German attempts to analyze the actor's art and to expound fresh and animated acting as an ideal. It is interesting to note that Lessing had translated portions of Sainte-Albine's *Le Comédien* and Francesco Riccoboni's *L'Art du théâtre,* taking a stand between the emotionalist emphasis of the former and the anti-emotionalism of the latter.

Although Lessing based some of his precepts on the example of Ekhof, the great actor of the Hamburg National Theatre, he was nevertheless hampered in his analysis of the performances of the troupe by the unwillingness of the actors to accept his criticism. The leading actress, vain Sophie Friedericke Hensel (1738-1789), objected strenuously to his comments, and some of the others, particularly Susanna Mecour (1738-1784) insisted that Lessing omit them from his considerations altogether. He said himself that he soon grew weary of writing about the recalcitrant actors, and after the twenty-fifth issue of his notes he abandoned his criticism of them. As a paid critic he was obviously not in a position to ignore the demands of the sensitive actors. Despite these obstacles, his analysis of them remains a valuable and far-reaching contribution to histrionic theory.

The 104 numbers of the *Dramaturgy* covered only the first fifty-two performances of the theatre. When the theatre closed, Lessing became a librarian at

Wolfenbuettel. In 1772 he published *Emilia Galotti*, which provided Ekhof with yet another successful role. One of Lessing's last significant works was the beautiful plea for religious tolerance, *Nathan der Weise.*

The Hamburg Dramaturgy

[From the Preface]

The great discrimination of a dramatic critic is shown if he knows how to distinguish infallibly, in every case of satisfaction or dissatisfaction, what and how much of tnis is to be placed to the account of the poet or the actor. To blame the actor for what is the fault of the poet is to injure both. The actor loses heart, and the poet is made self-confident.

Above all, it is the actor who may in this particular demand the greatest severity and impartiality. The justification of the poet may be attempted at any time; his work remains, and can be always brought again before our eyes. But the art of the actor is transitory in its expression. His good and bad pass by rapidly, and not seldom the passing mood of the spectator is more accountable than the actor for the more or less vivid impression produced upon him.

A beautiful figure, a fascinating mien, a speaking eye, a charming gait, a sweet intonation, a melodious voice, are things that cannot be expressed in words. Still they are neither the only nor the greatest perfections of the actor. Valuable gifts of nature are very necessary to his calling, but they by no means suffice for it.

He must everywhere think with the poet; he must even think for him in places where the poet has shown himself human.

No. 3

Why is it that we like to hear the commonest maxim spoken by this actor (Herr Ekhof)? What is it that another must learn from him if we are to find him equally entertaining in the same case? All maxims must come from the abundance of the heart with which the mouth overflows. We must appear to have thought of them as little as we intend to boast of them. It therefore follows as a matter of course that all the moral parts must be very well learnt by heart. They must be spoken without hesitation, without the faintest stammer, in an unbroken easy flow of words, so that they may not appear a troublesome unburdening of memory but spontaneous promptings of the actual condition. It must also follow that no false accentuation lead us to suspect that the actor is chattering what he does not understand. He must convince us by a firm assured tone of voice that he is penetrated by the full meaning of his words.

But true accentuation can, if needful, be imparted to a parrot. Yet how far is the actor, who only understands a passage, removed from him who also feels it! Words whose sense we have once grasped, that are once impressed upon our memories, can be very correctly repeated even when the soul is occupied with quite other matters; but then no feeling is possible. The soul must be quite present, must bestow its attention solely and only on its words, and then only—

And yet even then the actor may really feel very much and still appear to have no feeling. Feeling is altogether the most controverted among the talents of an

---

"Dramatic Notes," *Selected Prose Works of G. E. Lessing,* translated by E. C. Beasley and Helen Zimmern, edited by Edward Bell. London: George Bell and Sons, 1879, pp. 240-248, p. 489

actor. It may be present where we do not recognize it, and we can fancy we recognize it where it does not exist. For feeling is something internal of which we can only judge by its external signs. Now it is possible that certain outer things in the build of a body do not permit of these tokens or else weaken them and make them dubious. An actor may have a certain cast of features, certain gestures, a certain intonation, with which we are accustomed to associate quite different sentiments from those which he is to represent and express at that moment. If this is the case, he may feel ever so much, we do not believe him for he is at variance with himself. On the other hand another may be so happily formed, may possess such decisive features, all his muscles may be so easily and quickly at his command, he may have power over such delicate and varied inflections of voice; in short he may be blessed in such a high degree with all the gifts requisite for dramatic gesture, that he may appear animated with the most intense feeling when he is playing parts that he does not represent originally but after some good model, and where everything that he says and does is nothing but mechanical imitation.

Beyond question, this man for all his indifference and coldness is more useful to the theatre than the other. When he has for a long spell done nothing but copy others, he will at last have accumulated a number of little rules according to which he begins to act and through the observance of which (in consequence of the law that the modifications of the soul that induce certain changes of the body, in return are induced by these bodily changes) he arrives at a species of feeling that has not, it is true, the duration or the fire of that which arises in the soul, but is yet powerful enough in the moments of representation to bring about some of the involuntary changes of body whose existence forms almost the only certain clue we have as to the presence of inner feeling. Such an actor is to represent for instance, the extremest fury of anger. I will suppose that he does not even properly understand his part, that he neither comprehends fully the reasons for this anger nor can imagine them vividly enough in order to arouse anger in his soul. And yet I say that if he has only learnt the very commonest expressions of anger from an actor of original feeling and knows how to copy him faithfully—the hasty stride, the stamp of the foot, the voice now harsh, now smothered, the play of the eyebrows, the trembling lip, the gnashing teeth, etc.—I say that if he only imitates well these things that can be imitated, his acting will thus infallibly cast on his mind a dim feeling of anger that will react on his body and will there produce such changes as do not depend solely upon his will. His face will glow, his eyes will sparkle, his muscles will dilate; in short he will seem to be truly furious without being so, without comprehending in the least why he should be so.

From these principles of feeling in general I have endeavored to ascertain what external tokens accompany those feelings with which moral axioms should be spoken, and which of these tokens are within our command, so that every actor, whether he have the feeling himself or not, may represent them. I think they are the following.

Every moral maxim is a general axiom, which as such demands a degree of calm reflection and mental composure. It must therefore be spoken with tranquility and a certain coldness.

But again, this general axiom is also the result of impressions made by individual circumstances on the acting personages. It is no mere symbolical conclusion, it is a generalized sensation and as such it requires to be uttered with a certain fire and enthusiasm.

Consequently with enthusiasm and composure; with coldness and fire?

Not otherwise; with a compound of both, in which however, according to the conditions of the situation, now one and now the other, predominates.

If the situation is a placid one, the soul must desire to gain a sort of elevation by the moral maxim: it must seem to make general observations on its happiness or its duties, in such a manner that by help of this very generalizing it may enjoy the former the more keenly and observe the latter the more willingly and bravely.

If on the other hand the situation is turbulent, the soul must appear to recall itself by means of the moral axiom (under which definition I comprehend every general observation); it must seem to give to its passions the appearance of reason and to stormy outbursts the look of premeditated resolves.

The former requires an elevated and inspired tone; the latter a tempered and solemn one. For in the one reason must fire emotion, while in the other emotion must be cooled by reason.

Most actors exactly reverse this. In their agitated scene they bluster out the general observations as excitedly as the other speeches, and in the quiet scenes repeat them just as calmly as the rest. It therefore follows that moral maxims are not distinguished either in the one or the other, and this is the cause why we find them either unnatural or stupid and chilly. These actors have never reflected that embroidery must contrast with its ground, and that to embroider gold on gold is wretched taste.

Finally they spoil everything by their gestures. They neither know whether they should make any nor of what kind. They usually make too many and too insignificant ones. When in an agitated scene the soul suddenly seems to collect itself to cast a reflective glance upon itself or that which surround it, it is natural that it should command all the movements of the body that depend upon its will. Not only the voice grows more composed, the limbs also fall into a condition of rest, to express the inner rest without which the eye of reason cannot well look about it. The unquiet foot treads more firmly, the arms sink, the whole body draws itself up into a horizontal position; a pause—and then the reflection. The man stands there in solemn silence as if he would not disturb himself from hearing himself. The reflection is ended—again a pause—and then, according to whether the reflection was intended to subdue his passions or to inflame them, he suddenly bursts forth again or gradually resumes the play of his limbs. Only the face during the reflection still retains the traces of agitation; mien and eye are still on fire and moved, for mien and eye are not so quickly within our control as foot and hand. In this therefore, in these expressive looks, in this fiery eye, and in the composure of the rest of the body, consists the mixture of fire and calm with which I believe that moral reflections should be spoken in passionate situations.

No. 4

But of what kind are the movements of the hand, with which in quiet situations, maxims should be spoken?

We know very little concerning the *Chironomia* of the ancients, that is to say, the nature of the rules prescribed by the ancients in the use of the hands. We know this, that they carried gestures to a perfection of which we can scarcely form an idea from what our orators can compass in this respect. Of this whole language we seem to have retained nothing but an inarticulate cry, nothing but the power to make movements without knowing how to give these movements an accurately determined meaning and how to connect them together so that they may be capable of conveying not only one idea, but one connected meaning.

I am quite aware that among the ancients the pantomimist must not be confounded with the actor. The hands of the actor were by no means as talkative as those of the pantomimist. In the one case they supplied the place of speech, while in the other they were only to lend emphasis, and as natural signs of things to lend life and truth to the preconcerted signs of the voice. In pantomimes the movements of the hands were not merely natural signs, many of them had a conventional meaning and from these the actor had to refrain completely. He therefore used his hands less than the pantomimist, but as little in vain as he. He did not move his hand if he could not mean something thereby or emphasize something. He knew nothing of those indifferent movements through whose constant monotonous use a large portion of actors, especially women, give to themselves the appearance of mere marionettes. Now the right hand, now the left, now a swing from the body, now agitating the air with both hands is what they call action, and whoever can practice it with a certain ballet-master's grace deems that he can fascinate us.

I know well that even Hogarth's *Analysis of Beauty* advises actors to learn how to move their hands in beautiful undulatory lines, but in all directions with all the possible variations of which these lines are capable in consideration of their sweep, size and duration. And finally he only advises it as an exercise to make them supple in movement, to make the movements of grace familiar to the arms, but not in the belief that acting itself consists in nothing more than in always describing such beautiful lines in the same direction.

Away therefore with these insignificant *portebras;* especially away with them in reflective scenes. Grace in the wrong place is affectation and grimace, and the very same grace too often repeated, becomes at last cold and then repulsive. I seem to see a schoolboy say his task when the actor tenders to me moral reflections with the same movements with which a hand is given in the minuet, or as if he spun them down from a spindle.

Every movement made by the hand in such passages should be significant. It is possible often to be picturesque if only the pantomimic be avoided. Perhaps another time I may find an occasion to explain by examples these various gradations from significant to picturesque to pantomimic gestures. Just now it would lead me too far and I will only remark that among significant gestures there is one kind that the actor must note above all and with which alone he can impart to the moral life and light. These are in one word the individual gestures. The moral is a general axiom extracted from the particular circumstances of the acting personages; by means of its generality it becomes foreign to the action, it becomes a digression whose connection with the actual present is not comprehended or noticed by the less observant or less acute spectators. If consequently a means exists to make this connection evident, to bring back the symbolical of the moral to the visible, and if this means lies in certain gestures, the actor must on no account omit making them.

No. 5

If Shakespeare was not as great an actor as he was a dramatist, at least he knew as well what was needed for the art of the one as the other. Yes, perhaps he even pondered more about the former because he had the less genius for it. Certainly every word that he puts into Hamlet's mouth when addressing the players should be a golden rule for all actors who care for sensible approbation.

The fire of the actor is often mentioned, discussions are common as to whether the actor can show too much animation. If those who maintain this cite as an instance that an actor may be passionate or at least more passionate than circumstances require; then those who deny it have a right to say that in such cases the actor has not shown too much animation, but too little intelligence. Altogether it depends greatly what we understand under the word fire. If screams and contortions are fire then it is incontestable that the actor can carry these too far. But if fire consists in the rapidity and vivacity with which all those parts that make the actor, bring their properties to bear, to give his acting the semblance of truth, then we should not desire to see this semblance of truth carried to the extremest illusion, if we deemed it possible that the actor could apply too much fire in this sense. It can therefore not be this fire the moderation of which Shakespeare requires even in the torrent, tempest, and whirlwind of passion. He can only mean that violence of voice and movement; and it is easy to discover why, where the poet has not observed the least moderation, the actor must yet moderate himself in both points. There are few voices that do not become displeasing at their utmost pitch, and movements that are too rapid, too agitated will rarely be dignified. Now our eyes and our ears are not to be offended, and only when everything is avoided in the expression of violent passion that can be unpleasant to these, can acting possess that smoothness and polish which Hamlet demands from it even under these circumstances, if it is to make the deepest impression and to rouse the conscience of stiff-necked sinners out of its sleep.

The art of the actor here stands midway between the plastic arts and poetry. As visible painting beauty must be its highest law, but as transitory painting it need not always give to its postures the calm dignity that makes ancient sculpture so imposing. It may, it must at times permit to itself the wildness of a Tempesta, the insolence of a Bernini; and they have in this art all that which is expressive and peculiar without the offensive element that arises in the plastic arts through their permanent posture. Only it must not remain in them too long, it must prepare for them gradually by previous movements, and must resolve them again into the general tone of the conventional. Neither must it ever give to them all the strength which the poet may use in his treatment. For though the art is silent poetry, yet it desires to make itself comprehended immediately to our eyes, and every sense must be gratified if it is to convey unfalsified the proper impressions to the soul.

It might easily come about that the moderation demanded by art, even in the extremes of passion, does not consort well with applause. But what applause? It is true the gallery greatly loves the noisy and boisterous, and it will rarely omit to repay a good lung with loud hand-clappings. The German parterre also shares this taste in part; and there are actors cunning enough to derive advantage from this taste. The most sleepy actor will rouse himself towards the end of the scene, when he is to make his exit, raise his voice and overload the action, without reflecting whether the sense of his speech requires this extra exertion. Not seldom it even contradicts the mood in which he should depart; but what matters that to him? Enough that he has thus reminded the parterre to look at him, and, if it will be so good as to applaud after him. They should hiss after him! But, alas! the spectators are partly not connoisseurs, and in part too good-natured, and they take the desire to please them for the deed.

Nos. 101-104

... We have actors but no art of acting. If in past times there was such an art, we have it no longer; it is lost, it must be discovered anew. There is enough superficial chatter on the subject in many languages, but special rules, known to every one, pronounced with distinctness and precision, according to which the blame or the praise of an actor can be defined in a particular case, of such I scarcely know two or three. Thence it arises that all our reasoning about this subject always seems so vacillating and dubious, and that it is small wonder if the actor who possesses nothing but a happy routine, feels himself offended by it in all ways. He will never think himself praised enough and will always believe himself blamed too much; ay, he will often not even know whether he has been praised or blamed. Indeed the observation was made long ago that the sensitiveness of artists, with regard to criticism, rises just in that ratio in which the certainty, precision, and number of their principles regarding their art decline. This much in my own defense and in defense of those without whom I should not need to excuse myself.

JOHANN WOLFGANG VON GOETHE

(1749-1832)

Born at Frankfurt-am-Main Goethe, who was to become one of the world's greatest literary figures, was from his youth interested in the theatre. As a student at the University in Leipzig he wrote several plays; later when he was studying law at Strasbourg he penned his first significant drama *Goetz von Berlichingen,* which was heavily influenced by Shakespeare. In 1775, a year after Goethe had achieved great fame with *The Sorrows of Young Werther,* he came to the Duchy of Weimar at the invitation of Duke Karl August. Here he became enthusiastically engaged in a round of theatrical activities, directing and writing plays for the Duke's amateur theatricals. He was an inventive director and enacted many roles in the productions which were given in the great halls or on the lovely grounds of the Duke's estate.

Some years later when a new Duchy theatre was constructed, only a mediocre company could be mustered to utilize it. Eventually the Duke asked Goethe to undertake the direction of the theatre. For twenty-six years, from 1791 to 1817, he guided its activities and devoted himself to elevating the intellectual and social status of the actors and instilling them with his beliefs in artificial beauty on the stage. As the company lacked original creative actors, Goethe was forced to train them in the basic proprieties of stage behavior. In order to mold a disciplined corps of actors that would move and speak with grace, he evolved his "Rules for Actors." Although we are now appalled by the mechanical quality of these ninety-one rules, they aided Goethe in establishing an effective company out of lame material. His dicta on speech, for example, now obvious and almost ludicrous, were necessitated by the variety of dialects of the actors and by the emphasis Goethe placed on the verbal aspect of drama. Without a certain unity in the performance of his actors, his ideal would have been doomed. In the "Rules" themselves he insisted on "imitated presentation and not . . . vulgar actuality."

It is interesting to see how these principles guided Goethe. In response to a question by his interviewer Eckermann as to how he chose the members of his troupe, Goethe replied: "I had various modes of proceeding. If a striking reputation preceded the new actor, I let him act, and saw how he suited the others; whether his style and manner disturbed our ensemble, or whether he would supply a deficiency. If, however, he was a young man who had never trodden a stage before, I first considered his personal qualities; whether he had about him anything prepossessing or attractive, and, above all things, whether he had control of himself. For an actor who possesses no self possession, and who cannot appear before a stranger in his most favorable light, has, in any case, little talent. His whole profession requires continual self-concealment, and a continual existence in a foreign mask.

"If his appearance and his deportment pleased me, I made him read, in order to test the power and extent of his voice, as well as the capabilities of his mind. I gave him some sublime passage from a great poet, to see whether he was capable of feeling and expressing what was really great; then something passionate and wild, to prove his power. I then went to something marked by sense and smartness, something ironical and witty, to see how he treated such things, and whether he possessed sufficient versatility. Then I gave him something in which was represented the pain of a wounded heart, the suffering of a great soul, that I might learn whether he had it in his power to express pathos.

"If he satisfied me in all these numerous particulars I had well-grounded hope of making him a very important actor. If he appeared more capable in some particulars than in others, I remarked the line to which he was most adapted. I also now knew his weak points and, above all, endeavored to work upon him so he might strengthen and cultivate himself here. If I remarked faults of dialect, and what are called provincialisms, I urged him to lay them aside, and recommended to him social intercourse and friendly practice with some member of the stage who was entirely free from them. I then asked him whether he could dance and fence; and if this were not the case, I would hand him over for some time to the dancing and fencing masters.

"If he were now sufficiently advanced to make his appearance, I gave him at first such parts as suited his individuality, and I desired nothing but that he should represent himself. If he now appeared to be of too fiery a nature, I gave him phlegmatic characters; if too calm and slow, I gave him fiery and hasty characters, that he might thus learn to lay aside himself and assume a foreign individuality."

In the history of German acting, the Goethe "Rules" are of great importance since they were subsequently transferred to other theatres by his actors and were widely adopted as the correct histrionic principles. Carrying with them the weight of Goethe's fame, these "Rules" thus generated an external, artificial school of acting against which successive generations in the German theatre fought. Even Otto Brahm, at the end of the nineteenth century, was forced to argue against their pervasive influence.

It is ironic to note that Goethe resigned his post in the Ducal theatre in protest against the performance of a trifling play that had a dog as its star. It was the Duke's actress-mistress, Karoline Jagemann, who had insisted that the play be performed in the theatre that had seen the plays of the two great poets Goethe and Schiller.

Rules for Actors

The art of the actor is made up of speech and bodily movement. In the following paragraphs we shall give some rules and suggestions on both of these, beginning with speech.

Dialect

1

When a provincialism creeps into a tragic discourse the most beautiful poetry is disfigured and the ear of the auditor is offended. Therefore, the first and most necessary point in the training of an actor is that he free himself from all errors of dialect and strive to attain a perfectly pure pronunciation. No provincialism will do on the stage! Nothing must be heard there but pure German idiom, which has been cultivated through good taste, art, and science.[1]

2

He who has to struggle with the habits of dialect should adhere to the universal rules of German speech and seek to enunciate quite clearly the new forms he wishes to develop even more distinctly than they really ought to be. Even exaggerations are advisable in this case, without risk of detriment, for it is a peculiarity of human nature always to return willingly to its old customs, and of its own accord to normalize what has been exaggerated.

Pronunciation

3

As in music the correct, precise, and pure striking of each single tone is the foundation of all further artistic execution, so in the art of the actor the clean and perfect pronunciation of each word is the basis of all higher recitation and declamation.

4

Pronunciation is perfect when no letter of a word is suppressed, but when all appear according to their true value.

5

It is clean when all words are so delivered that the thought strikes the hearer easily and distinctly.

Both together make expression complete.

6

The actor should seek to acquire such a diction, realizing clearly how a slurred letter or a word pronounced indistinctly makes a whole sentence ambiguous, with

---

Johann Wolfgang von Goethe: "Rules for Actors" (1803), translated with an introduction by Arthur Woehl. Columbia, Missouri: *Quarterly Journal of Speech Education*, Volume XIII, Number 3, June, 1927, pp. 247-256, 259-264. (Translation from the text of the Weimar (1901) edition of *Goethe's Werke*, Volume 40, and footnote annotations by Professor Arthur Woehl.) By permission of Professor Arthur Woehl.

---

[1]Although we may regard this as more or less of a commonplace, Goethe had every reason for insisting upon a standard of pure High German at Weimar. He himself spoke the language of his native Frankfurt; Schiller's speech was particularly broad Swabian; and the actors, collected from all parts of Germany, represented almost every other dialect.

the result that the audience loses the illusion and is often provoked to laughter, even in the most serious scenes.

* * * *

14

In order to perfect his diction, the beginner should utter everything very slowly, expressing syllables, and particularly final syllables, strongly and clearly, in order that the syllables which must be spoken rapidly be not unintelligible.

15

It is also advisable to speak in as low a pitch as possible at the beginning, and then, modulating, steadily to rise in tone; for by this means the voice attains great range and is trained to the different modulations needed in declamation.

16

For that reason it is also very well at the beginning to utter all syllables, whether long or short, as long, and in as low a tone as the voice allows, since otherwise in rapid speech one usually emphasizes only the verbs.

17

False or incorrect memorization is for many players the cause of false and incorrect pronunciation. Before one entrusts anything to his memory, he should read, slowly and deliberately, the passage to be memorized. In this one must avoid all emotion, all declamation, all play of the imagination; but one must endeavor only to read correctly and then to learn accurately; thus many an error, both of dialect and pronunciation, will be avoided.

Recitation and Declamation

18

By recitation is understood a delivery which, without emotional raising of the tone, yet not quite without modulation, lies midway between cold, quiet speech and highly excited speech.

The auditor must always feel that in this case the speech is objective.

19

Therefore it is necessary to emphasize the passages to be recited and deliver them with the feeling and the sentiment which the content of the poem inspires in the reader; nevertheless this should be done with moderation and without that emotional forgetfulness of self which is required in declamation. The reciter, to be sure, follows with the voice the ideas of the poet and the impression which is made on him by the mild or horrible, pleasing or displeasing subject; on the horrible he places the horrible tone, on the tender, the tender tone, on the solemn, the solemn tone, but these are merely results and effects of the impression which the subject matter makes on the reciter; he does not alter thereby his original character, he does not disown his nature, his individuality, and is to be compared with a piano upon which I play in its natural tone, given by the mode of construction. The passage which I deliver compels me to observe, by its composition, *forte* or *piano, dolce* or *furioso,* but this is done without my using the modulation which the instrument possesses—on the contrary, it is merely the overflowing of the soul into the fingers, which through their compliance, their stronger or weaker impressing and touching of the keys, put into the passage the spirit of the composition, and thereby excite the feelings which can be stirred by its content.

20

But it is quite different with declamation or heightened recitation. Here I must leave my inborn character, disavow my nature, and place myself wholly in the attitude and mood of him whose role I declaim. The words which I utter must be brought out with energy and liveliest expression, so that I seem to experience each emotional impulse as actually present.

Here the player on the piano employs the soft pedal and all modulations which the instrument possesses. If they are used with taste, each in its proper place, and if the player has studied in advance, with spirit and diligence, the application and the effect which can be produced through them, then he can be sure of the most beautiful and completest result.

21

One might call the art of declamation an art of music in prose, since, in general, it has a great deal that is analogous to music. But one must make the distinction that music, answering its own purposes, moves with more freedom; the art of declamation, on the other hand, is much more limited in the range of its tones and is subject to an alien purpose. Of this principle the declaimer must always take the strictest consideration. For if he varies his tones too quickly, if he speaks either too low or too high, or through too many semitones, then he is singing; but in the opposite case he falls into monotony, which even in simple recitation is a mistake— two rocks, one as hazardous as the other, between which still a third lies sunken, to wit, the ministerial cadence. It is easy, while evading the one or the other danger, to run aground on this one.

* * * *

28

The declaimer is free to select his own stops, pauses, and so forth; but he must guard against destroying the true meaning, which he can do by this means just as easily as by an omitted or badly expressed word.[2]

29

One can readily understand from these few observations what unending toil and time it costs to make progress in this difficult art.

30

For the beginning actor it is very beneficial always to speak everything as deeply as possible. For thus he gains a great range in voice and can give perfectly all further shadings. But if he habitually begins too high, he soon loses masculine depth of tone and with it the true expression of the lofty and spiritual. And how can he be assured of success with a shrill and squeaking voice? If he has completely mastered the lower register he will certainly be able to express perfectly all possible shadings.

---

[2]Anton Genast, stage manager at the Weimar Theatre, tells us of the extreme care and attention which Goethe gave to pauses after punctuation marks. At a reading-rehearsal of Calderon's *The Constant Prince* he laid down definite rules. "He was extremely painstaking about this: Commas, semicolons, colons, exclamation and question marks had to be strictly observed in recitation; he demanded a pause for each of these marks and denoted their varying lengths graphically in this fashion; —, ——; ———! ———? ————."

Rhythmical Diction

31

All the rules and observations made under the head of declamation are here presupposed as fundamental. But it is especially the character of rhythmical delivery that the subject must be declaimed with an even more lofty and emotional expression. Each word is to be uttered with a certain impressiveness.

32

The rhythmical structure as well as the end-rhymes must not be indicated too strikingly, but the context must be observed as in prose.

33

If one has iambics to declaim he must be careful to indicate the beginning of each verse by a slight, scarcely perceptible pause, not sufficient, however, to interrupt the flow of the declamation.[3]

Posture and Movement of the Body on the Stage

34

On this part of the player's art some general principles may also be given, to which, of course, there are innumerable exceptions, all of which, however, go back again to the principles. We must strive so vigorously to assimilate these that they become second nature.

35

First, the player must reflect that he must not only imitate Nature, but must also present her ideally, and that therefore his presentation must unite the true with the beautiful.

36

Hence each part of the body must be completely in his control so that he can make use of each member for the desired expression, freely, harmoniously, and gracefully.

37

Let the position of the body be erect, the chest up, the upper half of the arms to the elbows close to the body, the head turned slightly towards the person to whom one is speaking, yet so slightly that three-quarters of the face is always turned towards the audience.

38

For the actor must constantly remember that he is on the stage for the sake of the public.

39

Accordingly, it is mistaken naturalness for the actors to play to each other as if no third person were present; they should never play in profile, nor turn their

---

[3]This practice was especially scored by Tieck. See his essay, *"Ueber das Temps in welchem auf der Buehne gesprochen werden soll"* (On the Time Which Should Be Observed in Stage Delivery), *Dramaturgische Blatter*, Volume II.

backs to the audience. If it is done for the sake of characterization or of necessity, let it be done with judgment and grace.

40

One must also be especially careful never to speak in toward the stage, but always speak out toward the public. For the player must always divide his attention between two objects: that is, between the person to whom he is speaking and his audience. Instead of turning the whole head away, it is better, when necessary, merely to turn the eyes.

41

It is a cardinal point that when two actors are playing together, the speaker always moves back, and the one who has stopped speaking moves down slightly. If one makes use of this advantage with understanding, and through practice can go about it quite without constraint, the best effect arises for the eye as well as for the intelligibility of the speech. A player who masters this will, with others equally skilled, produce a very fine effect and have a great advantage over those who do not observe it.

* * * *

Pantomime

63

To attain a correct pantomime and also to be able to criticize it rightly, one should note the following rules:

Let one place himself before a mirror and speak what he is to declaim, only softly, or rather not at all, let him simply think the words. The advantage of this is that he is not carried along by the declamation but can easily perceive every false move, which does not express what is thought or softly uttered, just as he can also select beautiful and suitable gesture and imprint on the whole pantomime, as a stamp of art, a movement corresponding to the meaning of the words.

64

But this presupposes that the player has previously made fully his own the character and the whole situation of the person he is to represent, and that his imagination works on the material properly; for without this preparation he will be able neither to declaim nor to act correctly.

65

It is of great advantage for the beginner, in order to master pantomime and make his arms pliant and supple, to try to make his role intelligible to another without reciting it, solely by pantomime; for in that case he is forced to select the most suitable gestures.

To be Observed in Rehearsal

66

To acquire an easier and more suitable movement of the feet one must never rehearse in boots.

67

Let the actor, particularly the younger man, who has to play lovers and other light roles, keep a pair of slippers at the theatre in which to rehearse, and he will

[273]

soon notice the good effects of this practice.[4]

68

One should not permit himself to do anything in rehearsal that he cannot do in the play.

69

The women should put aside their small purses.

70

No actor should rehearse in a cloak, but should have the hands and arms free, as in the play. For the cloak not only hinders him from making proper gestures, but forces him to acquire false ones, which he then repeats involuntarily in the presentation.

71

The actor should also make no movement in rehearsal which is unsuitable to the role.

72

He who places his hand in his bosom in rehearsing tragic roles runs the risk, in the actual performance, of fumbling for an opening in his armor.

Bad Habits to be Avoided

73

Among the very clumsy errors to be avoided is this: the actor who is sitting should not, in order to bring his chair farther forward, pass his hands between his legs, seize the chair, then raise himself slightly, and so drag it forward. This is an offense not only against appearance, but still more against comfort.

74

The actor should show no pocket-handkerchief on the stage; even less should he blow his nose, still less should he spit.[5] It is frightful, in the midst of an artistic production, to be reminded of these natural occasions. One may have with him a small handkerchief, as indeed is now the fashion, as a help in case of need.[6]

Bearing of the Actor in Ordinary Life

75

In ordinary life, too, the actor must remember that he is to be part of a public presentation.

---

[4]This same advice is given the players in *Wilhelm Meister's Apprenticeship*, Book V, Chapter VIII, p. 295. Many other suggestions in this chapter parallel closely the advice given here.

[5]Goethe's impression of this may well have been obtained from the actor Konrad Ekhof, who was guest player at Weimar about two years after Goethe's arrival. He appeared in a play with Goethe, the Duke Karl August, and others. Although a famous actor of some attainment, he had a number of crude mannerisms, among which were spitting and coughing on the stage.

[6]The use of the handkerchief on the stage was a French habit. Vanhove, Talma's father-in-law, found two properties indispensable: a handkerchief in tragedy, a snuff-box in domestic drama—and he would willingly have introduced the habit of using the snuff-box in tragedy also. He did do this on one occasion. Moreover, when presented with his first historically correct Roman costume, he called the tailor's attention to the lack of a pocket, asking him whether he was to believe that the Romans did not blow their noses or blew them with their fingers. He got the pocket.

76

Hence he must guard himself against habitual gesture, postures, and positions of the arms and body, for if during the play his attention must be directed to avoiding such habits, it is to be a great extent lost to the play.

77

It is, therefore, absolutely necessary that the actor be completely free from all habits, so that in the presentation he can imagine himself completely in his role and busy his mind with his assumed character.

78

On the contrary, it is an important principle for the actor to take pains in ordinary life to give such a turn to his body, his bearing, indeed to all his actions, that he will be kept in constant practice. This will be of untold advantage for every part of the actor's art.

79

He who has chosen to be a tragic actor will perfect himself if he seeks to bring out everything that he has to say with a certain accuracy of tone as well as of expression, and also to retain in all gestures a certain lofty manner. This of course must not be carried too far, lest he become a laughing-stock for his fellow men, but with this limitation he may let them constantly recognize the artist training himself. This does him no dishonor, indeed, they will endure quite willingly his peculiar bearing when because of this it happens that they are compelled to look on him with astonishment on the stage as a great artist.

80

Inasmuch as we wish to have everything represented on the stage not only truly, but also beautifully, since the eye of the spectator wishes to be charmed by pleasing groupings and positions, the actor must strive to preserve these even when off the stage; he should always imagine before him a roomful of spectators.

81

When he is learning the role by heart he must constantly address himself to an audience; even when he sits at a table, by himself or with others, he should always strive to form a picture, taking up and setting down everything with a certain grace, as if it were on the stage. In such a manner he must always form part of a picture.

Arrangement and Grouping on the Stage

82

The stage and the auditorium, the actors and the audience, constitute essentially a single whole.

83

The theatre is to be regarded much as a figureless tableau to which the actor adds the figures.

84

Therefore one must never play too near the wings.

85

Just as seldom must one step into the proscenium. This is the greatest impropriety; for the figure steps out of the room in which it makes a complete unit with the scene-picture and with the fellow-players.

86

When one stands alone on the stage, let him remember that he is called upon to decorate the stage, and so much the more so since the attention remains directed quite alone on him.

87

As the augurs with their staff divided the heavens into various parts, the actor can mentally divide the stage into various rooms, which for experiment can be represented on paper by rhombic planes. The stage floor is then a kind of drafting-board; for the actor can determine which houses he will set foot in; he can make a memorandum of them on paper and is then certain that he will not rage artlessly to and fro in impassioned speeches, but will join the beautiful to the significant.

88

He who steps out for a monologue from the wings upstage does well to move diagonally, so that he reaches the opposite side of the proscenium; since in general diagonal movements are very pleasing.

89

He who comes out from the farthest wing to another who is already standing on the stage, must not walk out parallel with the wings but must turn slightly towards the prompter.

90

One must make his own the sense of all these technical-grammatical rules, and constantly practice them so that they become habit. Stiffness must disappear and the rule become only the hidden outline of the living action.

91

This takes for granted that these rules will be observed primarily when one has noble, worthy characters to represent.[7] On the other hand, there are characters which are opposite to these noble ones, for example, the boors, the louts, and so forth. These he will represent so much the better if, with art and understanding, he does the opposite, always remembering, however, that it should be an imitated presentation and not a vulgar actuality.

FRIEDRICH LUDWIG SCHROEDER

(1744 - 1816)

"The Great Schroeder" was born in 1744 after a short period of reconciliation between his mother Sophie and her estranged husband, a musician who was given to excessive drinking. Sophie Schroeder had left her husband originally to go on the stage with Konrad Ackermann and Konrad Ekhof. She left Schroeder again and later married her old friend Ackermann.

Undisciplined as a child, Friedrich Ludwig Schroeder grew up to be an arrogant

---

[7]The "Rules" have special reference to the acting of tragedy.

but talented, versatile young man. An excellent acrobat and dancer, he played French valets in Ackermann's Hamburg troupe. He was twenty when the great Ekhof joined the company. Keenly aware of young Schroeder's talents, Ekhof tried to train him, but he was rebuffed with quarrels and taunts. That Schroeder nevertheless learned much from Ekhof is evidenced by the fact that he wrote short critical analyses of many of the 166 parts that Ekhof played with the company.

Schroeder was not part of the Hamburg National Theatre experiment; he wandered about and then joined the troupe of the Viennese Joseph von Kurz that played in the *commedia dell' arte* manner. From them he learned pantomime and improvisation. When he returned to Hamburg he worked again for his step-father and at the latter's death became the manager of the company. He played Lessing's *Emilia Galotti* and Goethe's *Goetz von Berlichingen*. Most notable however was his presentation of eleven plays by Shakespeare over a period of eight years. He is said indeed to have given Shakespeare his "citizenship papers" in Germany. His King Lear is immortalized in the writings of his contemporaries.

Karl Mantzius in his *History of Theatrical Art* records an interesting conversation between the Dane Jens Baggesen and Schroeder. Baggesen queried: "...then you are not King Lear on the stage, while illuding others you are not under the illusion yourself?"

"Do you think [Schroeder replied] that I should succeed in making the spectators forget Schroeder if for one moment I myself were Lear—or make them fancy they were seeing Lear, if for a moment I forget Schroeder?"

"So you remain cold all the time you are acting?"

"So cold that between the scenes and acts I play the part of manager as if I had done nothing but stand in the wings. My warmth is physical, not mental; it is the heat of bodily exertion, not of enthusiasm."

Whether in Hamburg or Vienna, where he spent four years at the famous *Burgtheater*, Schroeder trained his co-actors. He was one of the first actor-managers to have a strong sense of the necessity for unified productions. By his strict and demanding standards he developed the finest troupe in Germany. Indeed his sternness was said to have caused the suicide of his half-sister, the promising young actress Charlotte Ackermann (1757-1774). But out of his personal brilliance and his understanding of the theatrical ensemble came the finest period of realistic playing almost a century before the development of German naturalism.

Some insight into the methods of the greatest German actor of the eighteenth century can be gleaned from his comments on characterization, in which he emphasized the necessity for individual impersonations. The stress on individuality takes on greater meaning when we remember that Schroeder played some seven hundred roles from the plays of such masters as Shakespeare, Lessing, Goethe, and Molière.

Type and Character

I must ascertain where I stand with regard to art. What I have seen and known has strengthened me in my basic principles. It may be that any one of my individual

---

Quoted by F. L. Meyer: *Friedrich Ludwig Schroeder*. Hamburg: 1819, pp. 337-338. This selection translated by Joseph M. Bernstein.

roles will be played better by an actor who is more favored than I am by his personality or by his more intimate knowledge of the matters portrayed. But it is no real art to play oneself. Any discerning non-actor, who knows how to speak well and who behaves reasonably well, can do that. But only he seems to me to have attained the genuine level of art who conceives of every character in such a way that he includes nothing extraneous in his characterization. He not only points to a general type but also distinguishes himself from kindred characters by the individual traits he draws from his own store of knowledge, in order to fit the poet's inspiration. That distinguishes a good actor from a good reader or reciter. The latter may prove very satisfactory to the audience so long as they have not yet compared him with a true actor. But as soon as a spectator sees a genuine actor, he must realize that previously he had only been reminded of the person at whom he is now really gazing. I believe I have succeeded in this. I think I have been able to express everything which the poet, if he remained faithful to nature, wishes to express in the words or actions of the characters he created. And I hope that in no play have I proved unequal to the just demands of the student of human nature; and that I have consulted no other mirror save that of truth. Art cannot wish to do any more, unless it seeks to become artifice. You can see why that son of nature, Shakespeare, makes everything so easy for me and puts me so much in his debt; why many very wonderful and poetically brilliant passages cost me effort and struggle in order to balance them against nature; and why at the same time I must eliminate them so as not to contradict the character. It does not occur to me to stand out and to be dazzling, but to fill out and be the character. I want to give every role what is its due—nothing more and nothing less. Hence every character must become what no other one can be. The correctness of this aim will not make people suspicious of my reasoning. It is a question of finding out whether I have succeeded. And that is not guaranteed me by the opinions of my friends or of the experts alone. My friends are used to me; and the experts can be corrupted because they pay homage to a great truth. They do not like to argue whenever mere intention agrees with their tastes. The real merit consists in destroying prejudices. If I am what I do not despair of being, then every traditional error, everything that thinks it is art, regardless of the fact that it contradicts nature, must yield to the phenomenon of artistically creative nature. Then I am bound to affect the most untutored as well as the most learned spectator; and then every glance into his own heart is bound to convince the onlooker that he is seeing of me what he ought to see.

AUGUST WILHELM IFFLAND

(1759-1814)

August Wilhelm Iffland was the last of the important eighteenth century German actors. With his friends Johann David Beil and Heinrich Beck he started his career at the Gotha Theatre, then under the management of Ekhof. In 1778 the members of this company became part of the *Nationaltheater* at Mannheim where Iffland remained until 1796. At the Mannheim Theatre, where young Schiller was official playwright, the actors had a council that took up the affairs of the theatre and debated artistic questions. Iffland, Beil, Beck, and others under Baron Heribert von Dalberg's direction, engaged in a series of discussions on dramatic art. Karl Mantzius (*A History of Theatrical Art*) says that the Mannheim discussions "serve as an enduring monument of the fact that actors, when allowed to express their opinions, can think and speak about their affairs almost as well as outsiders, who, as a rule, undertake the task for them." Iffland's contribution to the discussion on the limits of nature in theatrical representation is printed here for the first time in English.

From Mannheim Iffland, popular as both an actor and a dramatist, went to the highest position in the German theatre, leading actor at the Royal Court Theatre in Berlin. Here he reigned until his death.

Although Iffland was popular and had been trained in the realistic school of Ekhof, he was characterized by a French witness in these words: *"Point de nature, peu d'art, beaucoup d'artifice."* He carried his realism to such great lengths that a critic said of one of his performances: "His death was appallingly true, so that a physician found it correct in all its symptoms; the reality of the convulsions at the moment of death made the most disgusting impression on me...." Lacking the genius of Schroeder, he was primarily a studied actor. In this regard it was said of him: "His dignity sometimes looks like stiffness, his resignation like insensibility, and when at last an outburst of passion pierces like a flash of lightning through the December sky of his acting, there is too much calculation in its precision and in every movement of his fingers, arms, and feet."

It was Iffland, the last of his era, who gave the great romantic actor Ludwig Devrient his first opportunity in Berlin. Iffland also originated a unique theatrical tradition when, in his will, he bequeathed an emerald ring to be awarded to the greatest living German actor, who would, in turn, hand it on to his chosen successor. In our own century Albert Bassermann possessed this traditional symbol of excellence. Story has it that on leaving Germany, Bassermann gave the ring to the "non-Aryan" Max Pallenberg, in defiance of the Nazis. At Pallenberg's tragic death shortly after, the ring reverted to Bassermann, who assigned it to the Italian-born Alexander Moissi. When Moissi died in 1935 the ill-fated ring went to the Vienna Theatrical Museum, although Bassermann declared at Moissi's grave that the ring was symbolically buried with Moissi. Hitler's conquest of Austria and the subsequent war and destruction have left the whereabouts of Iffland's ring a mystery.

The Limits of Nature

Nature! I wish that an end were put to the crass misuse of this word. Everything that pleases the eye is then praised as natural without any further ado—yet the word is of profound significance.

It is Nature—that is what people say to bring out the excellence of anything whatever. Here the word "nature" is an image, the finest and boldest ever dared —the image of God's creation. In all nature there is nowhere monotony or disproportion. Nothing is inappropriate. One thing requires another. Every small

---

"Die dramaturgischen fragen und ihre beantwortung" in Wilhelm Koffka: *Iffland und Dalberg: Geschichte der Classischen Theaterzeit Mannheims.* Leipzig: F. F. Weber, 1865, pp. 430-438. This selection translated by Joseph M. Bernstein.

part has a definite relationship to the whole. And beauty comes from gazing at the whole.

So, in order to say of a work:

It is Nature!

I must perceive this exact symmetry of all its relationships and this very beauty.

So it is nature if a thing is so created that the onlooker feels:

Here there is nothing too much, nothing too little—here nothing is missing. Nature and perfection are thus synonymous.

A play is a portrait of human beings, their passions and their deeds. The actor brings the portrait to life through the human beings he represents in his roles.

Hence *nature on the stage* means *representation of human beings.* Representation of human beings? The phrase itself seems to require no further explanation! Nevertheless, the various points of view from which it is approached and the ways in which it is practiced makes an explanation necessary.

Those who depict human beings are the great actors.

If naturalness in depicting human beings does not offend the most delicate feeling for the morally beautiful, then certainly the morally beautiful is the limit of nature. For what determines the former is the feeling of naturalness.

That is my answer to the question: "What is Nature, and what are its true limits in theatrical representations?" I believe I am serving truth if I change the question: "What is Nature—how far do its limits go?" into the important question: "To what extent is Nature possible on our stage?" The portrayal of the whole man is not possible without inspiration; hence what qualities are required in the natural actors, the portrayers of human beings? Their creations tell us that nature was doubly considerate of them in their rich endowments. Animate or inanimate, everything in creation speaks a clear language to them; thus, from every object they get material for their spiritual treasury. They have a high feeling for harmony, a penetrating look which reveals all the minutest things to their fiery powers of imagination.

Wit, a subtle feeling of the sensually beautiful, a power to make distinctions —to these, training adds a sharpened sense of criticism, which arranges all these qualities in the way best suited to achieve the goal.

The highest art is inseparable from nature. The highest art—by that I mean the effect of art on works of inspiration, to which one gives no thought before making use of them, just as one gives no thought to the effect of the nerves on the actions of the body.

Art guides Nature, and Nature rectifies art.

The genius never has to study these matters. What is abstracted from the genius is then bound up in rules for the sake of those who have no genius.

The poet's great inspiration quickens his creations with life. A great portrayal by the actor is like the inspiration of a great poet.

Man cannot often endure this greatness; nor are conditions such that he can be rewarded. Hence there arises:

Neglect!

Unfortunately, one must admit that even these fortunate human beings rest on their old laurels whenever the Goddess turns her face away from them; and by cold imitation they commit the most ungrateful treason against the great secret of

Nature. They pay no heed to the public's gaping at their deformity and desecrate the altar at which they once so brilliantly shone. The more deeply a great representation of nature grips the spectator, the colder must he become when he sees all its features lost in feeble outlines, which are all the more blurred the more subtle the artist usually is. In such acting poor poets become poorer; dull roles become duller. So such a portrayer of human beings contributes little that is useful under the present conditions of the German theatre, for if he does not captivate his audience, he is liable to spread coldness over the entire performance.

But the would-be actors shout about genius and nature, which have nothing to do with the case. It is as if they were seeking to put genius and nature to the test by means of neglect.

They are right to complain, so much is certain. But neglect is not really the reason why they are so often cold, why they prefer to act really badly rather than make use of superficial effects. For it is a truism that *the use of superficial effects corrodes nature to such an extent* that at length the actor is scarcely able to say "Good morning" naturally on the stage. Who cannot think of examples bearing on this point? But since the genius cannot free himself from the professional duties he has once undertaken, since the director does not foster the actor's greatness but only rewards routine obligations (namely, an exact memory, eloquent delivery, and an appropriate contribution to rounding out the play), the portrayer of human beings finds himself obliged to work. Of course he must work—and this necessity to work destroys his reputation. That is how it is, and unfortunately the situation will not soon change. The powerful portrayer of human beings must now and then even rub shoulders with parasites of the theatre.

* * * *

The talent for speaking has very great value—and great value on the stage. I make this distinction between "very great" and "great" because public speeches are seldom given in our time. Even the excellently written speeches of great statesmen are seldom spoken well; only in the debates of the English Parliament does the zeal for country and freedom produce masterpieces in the art of speaking. In our country we should look for them most where we find them least—in the pulpit. The talent for speaking may *be pleasing* on the stage but of itself cannot *deceive.* That is why it is only a subdivision of the art of depicting human beings. It presupposes important attainments and demands at least one side of emotion, but shuts out the other. It can move listeners to tears, but not without a previously prepared build-up on the part of the poet. I have never seen it produce *an electric effect, that real test of human representation.*

I think that between the portrayer of human beings and the great orator there is a difference like that between a lightning-flash and summer-lightning. The art of speaking means talking now louder now softer, now higher, now lower; it is a degenerate, disinherited stepchild of nature which, exempt from any effect on the soul, is a trade. One recognizes it, reasons about it, and stamps it with the word "art." At first, the word is in circulation everywhere, then finally it is so distorted that at best it is handed over the counter merely as a favor like a coin.

These practiced orators, or to use the current word, these so-called declaimers, if they have any experience also try to have their system by which to impress the world. They omit on principle what they are incapable of expressing. That is why they make so many pauses, in order to grab truth by the sleeve; so that maintaining their balance at so many minor points, they lose the main point. These self-styled orators should be vigorously assailed because many a good mind has gone astray because of its preoccupation with oratory. When the soul is free, the first glance is generally the right glance to which one should hold fast; for where reason and emotion move forward with equal pace, it seldom happens that the reason can reproach the emotions. A discerning glance at the whole creates masterpieces. But it must be only one glance, preferably a repeated glance, *nevertheless only a single glance.*

With too much thinking, with that wretched accuracy in little things which, if it is the initial aim, has never created anything great, the fine point of emotion is blunted; reasons proceed alone and the whole will never have heartfelt truth—Nature.

EDUARD DEVRIENT

(1801-1877)

Eduard Devrient, manager and historian of German acting, was a nephew of the great romantic actor Ludwig Devrient. Although Ludwig was obviously the genius of the family, as Julius Bab points out in his volume *Die Devrients,* the family contributed important members to the German theatre. Another of Ludwig's nephews, Karl August Devrient (1794-1872), was famous for his interpretations of the roles of Wallenstein and Lear. Gustave Emil Devrient (1803-1872), still another nephew, was tragedian at the Dresden Court Theatre where he was a notable Hamlet. Otto, son of Philipp Eduard, was a translator of some of Shakespeare's plays.

Eduard Devrient was director of the Court Theatre in Dresden from 1844 to 1846 and then director of the *Karlsruhe Theater* (1852-1869). In addition to his activities as *régisseur,* he traveled widely and familiarized himself particularly with French theatre. His *Letters From Paris* contain interesting references and descriptions of the leading French actors of the day. It was during the years 1848 to 1874 that he published his large five-volume work on the history of German acting, *Geschichte der Deutschen Schauspielkunst.*

Devrient's advocacy of natural acting in opposition to the "antiquated frippery" of the Goethe Weimar School is revealed in the following selection drawn from his writings between 1834 and 1850.

Simplicity and Convention

Quiet, simple acting on the stage is getting rarer and rarer. No one wants to depict a character unostentatiously and unpretentiously, although only in that way does the later heightening of passion in the course of the action really become effective. The actor or singer only thinks of how he can do something striking and sensational in the very first scene. The calmest speech is immediately couched in the strongest tones—with only shouts and grimaces ensuing thereafter. Thus, one

---

Eduard Devrient: *Bemerkungen zur Novelle* (1834-1850), quoted by Ferdinand Rein: *Eduard Devrient als Oberregisseur in Dresden von 1844-1846.* Altenburg, Germany: P. H. Stephan Geibel and Company, 1931, pp. 38, 39, 40, 41. This selection translated by Joseph M. Bernstein.

actor forces all the others to play in the same manner, for no one wants to appear modest by contrast.

It is usually called acting with fire and natural inspiration if the actor plays his part without thinking it through, without going into the various subtleties of mood, and in an emphatic tone of declamation. But I call it cold acting, for it shows complete indifference toward the real inner moods of the character to be portrayed. When an actor looks with love and discernment for nature in every nuance of the character; when he builds his part with intelligence and genuine warmth and, out of true love for his work, avoids any thoughtless exaggeration, he is called cold, calculating, and ponderous. Or the naturalness of his performance seems even too natural—hence, not brilliant, striking, or astonishing.

... Virtuosity has decidedly come to the fore in the art of acting. The actor is taking revenge on the arrogant sense of superiority of the writers of the Weimar School. He has made modern playwrights the slaves of his stage business.... How many actors are there nowadays who bring to their art true naturalness—the first principle of all art? Everything has become theatrical: all stage business, all expressions, and all gestures are conceived and adopted with an eye to their effect.

The conventions of the Weimar School greatly encouraged this tendency and gave rise to a specific style of acting. Everything played in lamp-light, breathing a back-stage atmosphere—that is, poetry as mere performance. And the audience has been so spoiled by this antiquated frippery that it grows frightened or startled whenever it sees naturalness, whenever a breath of fresh air from real life is injected. Everything has been reduced to a scramble for advantage and to selfish commercial virtuosity. All love is gone, including self-love. Self-mirroring has taken the place of artistic insight; egotistical isolation has been substituted for whole-hearted devotion to the over-all impact of the dramatic work.

The modern art of acting is based on theatrical conventions and, in its effects, on the weaknesses of the audiences. Pretentiousness is its distinguishing mark.

It has retained all the vices of the old schools and added new ones. Worst of all, its most objectionable features have been accepted as maxims....

The dramatic art means a passion for human nature and it exercises this passion with love.

Let the artists show the god-like humanity in every character; let him show that this humanity can never be completely obliterated even by the worst perversity or the vilest corruption. Thus he will endow his characters with the deepest truth and will everywhere point to catharsis. He must never tolerate distortions—for the honor of humanity whose priest he is. He must soften the author's caricatures and always give us some human side to his creations.

In his relations with the audience, whose participation is vital to him, the actor must consider himself a kind of preacher. He must never accommodate himself to audiences but must resolutely place himself above them. It must be his pride and joy to have an effect on his listeners; but he must be stern toward himself and them, and never do anything merely to please them....

I have always yielded completely to the impression which the nature of the role has evoked in me; I have always tried to give what I have seen and inwardly felt in the part. Never have I thought out or devised particular nuances in order to highlight a specific point. I have often felt a sense of void in one passage or another. I have sought to improve the situation and wracked my brain to bring out a point; but I have never succeeded in finding anything that I did not think was too forced or artificial. This is why I often worried about a performance, thinking it too empty, stale, and uninteresting. And I was frequently very much amazed when people later made so much of it. I had simply let myself go. I had only conscientiously reproduced what I had naturally felt in the carrying out of my task.

It is a particularly delicate matter to take those scenes which in themselves are unimportant and unsensational and, by means of a lively imagination, lend them special lustre. It is just these quiet scenes in a role—these modest and merely transitional moments—which make the more important ones stand out and which give the performance as a whole the stamp of unforced truth.

That is also the way in which one should use costumes and masks: everything should be genuine, unsought for, unforced, and unadorned. The actor and his role should be fused, neither sacrificed to the other. The costume should not be arbitrarily tailored to fit the person, or the person too much distorted for the sake of the mask.

GEORGE II, DUKE OF SAXE-MEININGEN
(1826-1914)

In the minor principality of Saxe-Meiningen the royal scene designer and director George II established a theatrical troupe which was to have world-wide influence. Without first rate actors, the Duke and his director Ludwig Chronegk (1837-1891) created productions marked by excellent ensemble playing, by historical accuracy in costuming, and by an artistic and vital interrelationship between the movements of the actors and the décor. The Duke would make elaborate drawings for various scenes in order to indicate dynamic movement on the stage. Each play was given its individual settings, costumes, and historical mode. Rehearsals were extensive and detailed, with the Duke in charge of the overall production, his wife, the former actress Ellen Franz, responsible for the interpretation of lines, and Chronegk acting as the stage-manager and disciplinarian.

After their initial conquest of Berlin in 1874, the company performed throughout Germany and visited Rotterdam, Stockholm, Copenhagen, Amsterdam, London, Warsaw, St. Petersburg, Moscow, Odessa and many other cities. Wherever they went they became the inspiration for theatrical reform. In 1888 André Antoine went to Brussels to see them and came away fired with new ideas for the French theatre. In a letter to the critic Francisque Sarcey, Antoine voiced his admiration for the Duke's handling of crowds. Stanislavsky took from the Meininger many of the principles for which the Moscow Art Theatre was to become famous; the careful rehearsals, the ensemble playing, the excellent discipline of the company, and the attention to any minute detail that might destroy the consistency of the performance. At first Stanislavsky took the disciplinarian Chronegk as his model. He wrote: "Very soon the majority of Russian stage directors began to imitate me in my despotism as I imitated Chronegk." But Stanislavsky soon parted ways with the concepts of the Meininger in his opposition to the type of director "who made the actor a stage property on the same level with stage furniture, a pawn that was moved about in their *mise-en-scène*...." It was Chronegk who gave the actors "every inflection and gesture and moved them about at rehearsals on a floor marked out with chalk into squares and numbers, like so many chess men," according to Theodore Komisarjevsky.

The great contribution of the Meiningen Company was in their understanding and perfecting of the ensemble, rather than concern for the individual actor's problems. From their belief in the unifying power of the director came the pervasive influence of the *régisseur* in the modern theatre. Their innovations prepared the way for the development of naturalistic acting. In 1890 when the troupe had reached the end of its work, the Duke refused a final season in Berlin on the grounds that "It is not necessary. The German theatre has learned everything it had to learn."

The following article by the Duke of Saxe-Meiningen was written for an issue of *Deutsche Buehne.*

The Actor in the Ensemble

In composing a stage effect, it is important to keep the middle of the picture from being congruent with the middle of the stage.

If one follows the geometric principle of the golden mean, the stage divides into two even parts, which is likely to lead to monotony in the distribution and grouping. Assimilation in the total picture becomes more or less symmetrical, creating a wooden, stiff and boring impression.

(The charm of Japanese art can be largely attributed to their avoidance of symmetry. *"L'ennui naquit un jour de l'uniformité,"* Boileau remarked about art in general. In the graphic arts, the uniformity the French esthetes call "the mother of boredom" is symmetry.)

The exception proves the rule; the grouping of the principal figure—or principal mass of figures—in the center can work out if the neighboring figures or groups are placed on the side at more or less regular intervals. It can create a happy artistic effect, particularly if a powerfully exalted mood is desired. (One is reminded of the Sistine Chapel. There the picture is one of leisurely rest.) But the stage must always depict movement, the continuous unfolding of the story. That is why this method is to be generally avoided, as it creates a lifeless effect and holds up the action.

It rarely works to have a figure dead center. Scenery and other objects are to be placed whenever possible on the sides, of course at a certain distance from the wings, and so as to be visible to the audience.

The actor must never stand dead center, directly in front of the prompter, but always slightly to the left or right of his box.

The middle foreground of the stage, about the width of the prompter's box, from the footlights to the background, should be considered by the actor merely as a passage-way from right to left or vice-versa; otherwise he has no business there.

Likewise, two actors should avoid standing in similar relation to the prompter's box.

One should give special attention, also, to the relative position of the actor and the scenery. That relation must be correct. . . .

Generally, the first rehearsals of a new play with crowd scenes and a large cast make the director's hair stand on end. He almost doubts the possibility of bringing to life and molding this rigid, inflexible mass. It helps him a great deal in this task

---

Quoted by Max Grube: *Geschichte der Meininger.* Berlin: Deutsche Verlags-Anstalt Stuttgart, 1926, pp. 51-58 *passim.* This selection translated by Helen Burlin.

to have the scenery unchanged from the beginning. Changing the sets, rehanging certain parts of the scenery, moving the furniture during the rehearsals slows up everything, gets on the director's nerves, bores his co-workers and puts them to sleep.

In costume plays, weapons, helmets, arms, swords, etc. must be used as soon as possible, so that the actor is not encumbered by the unusual handling of heavy armor during the performance.

With these plays, it is obligatory that the actors rehearse in costume even before the dress rehearsal, which only differs from the opening night by the exclusion of the public. He should wear either his own costume, or if it is not yet ready, or has to be saved, one distinctly similar in cut. The actors must have, for many rehearsals before the dress rehearsal, the same head-wear, coats, trains, etc., or at least costumes like the ones they will wear at the performance. The performance should not present the actor with any unforeseen or surprising situation. The spectator must be given the opportunity of becoming accustomed to the unusual apparel of the past. The actor should not, by his appearance or gestures give the impression of wearing some costume the wardrobe mistress has just handed him; one must not be reminded of a costume ball or a carnival.

Carriage and gestures are influenced by the changing from modern clothes to those of the past. Our perfectly familiar way of standing with heels together, which is the accepted one for the military at a halt, and which civilians also use in greeting superior and notable people, looks out of place in older costumes—from the ancient Greek period to the Renaissance—and is completely wrong. This position, heel to heel, seems to have been introduced along with the step of the minuet. A peasant leader cannot stand like an "Abbé galant" from the time of wigs, or with clicked heels, like a lieutenant in a modern drawing-room.

The natural, correct and visually satisfying posture in costume from the days of pig-tails on, is feet apart and placed one in front of the other.

The general rule is: all parallels on the stage are to be avoided as much as possible. This applies to costume plays in certain ways as well.

Spears, halberds, lances, javelins, etc. should never be carried pointing in the same direction as the modern guns and bayonets of our infantry and cavalry. There should be a certain freedom in the holding of old weapons; they should not be held at even intervals or point in the same direction. Here, they should be made to crowd each other, there be further apart, not perpendicular but at an angle and intersecting.

Any helmet, not antique, worn by an actor must be pulled down over the forehead until only the muscle above the eye-brows is visible. The popular way of wearing it on the back of the head and neck is tenor-style and does not belong in the theatre. Our costumed heroes and lovers are undoubtedly afraid of disturbing their ringlets by pulling a helmet on correctly. But we can't be affected by that!

The use of parallels is particularly bad in relating the position of one actor with another. Since the parallel position of a single person, facing the footlights squarely, is bad; so two or three actors of approximately the same height doing likewise will give a most disagreeable impression.

Nor should an actor move in a parallel line. For example, an actor moving from forward right to left forward should, by imperceptible and subtle means, break the straight line, not the best on the stage, by moving on a diagonal.

If two or more actors play a scene together, they should never be placed in a straight line. They must stand at angles to each other. The space between the individual actors must always be uneven. Regular intervals create a sense of boredom and lifelessness like figures on a chessboard.

It is always an advantage to have an actor touch a piece of furniture or some other nearby object naturally. That enhances the impression of reality.

Should the stage have different levels—steps, an uneven floor strewn with rocks, and the like—the actor must remember to give his posture a rhythmical, living line. He must never stand with both feet on the same step. He should, if there is a stone close by, stand with one foot on it. Should he be walking down stairs and for some reason—such as having to speak a line or notice some object—be obliged to stop, one foot should always be placed lower than the other. By this device, his entire appearance takes on freedom and ease. "One foot off the ground," should be the director's theme song in such cases.

The handling of crowds on the stage requires a special preparation.

Hardly any theatre exists that can afford to use its own personnel as walk-ons. With the exception of the chorus and the so-called supers, among whom there frequently exists some well-trained actors who feel at home on the stage and can act, a considerable crowd has to be used, for whom these rehearsals and performances are only a side-line, and who must be paid each time. Among this fluctuating crowd whom the director does not know, occasionally are found a few usable people who can take direction, understand what is said to them and are not too clumsy in rehearsals. Naturally, one also finds a completely unusable element, with whom nothing can be done, who are awkward and ridiculous and who sometimes even follow their own inspiration, want to act their way and cause great disruption. It is the first job of the director to sort out of this crowd, and as soon as possible, the talented from the untalented, separating the goats from the sheep. The doubtful and naive ones must only serve as padding.

The walk-ons should then be divided into small groups and trained separately.

Each group is then led by an experienced actor or member of the chorus, who acts as "cover" and stands front of them on the stage. It is in a way the responsibility of this leader to see to it that the group entrusted to him follows orders. He is responsible to the director in seeing that the positions, gestures, etc. are taken at the right moment.

The leader is given cues and certain general directions from the script such as "noise, tumult, murmurs, cries, etc." These are then translated into words by the director and must be learned by heart. These interpolations should naturally be dealt with in various ways and should never be handled in unison.

The job of these leaders is not an easy one. It is a pity and sometimes an artistic error that these "actors" of the group consider their responsibility inferior and unworthy of a real artist. They rid themselves of the job wherever possible, or brush it off and at the performance make obvious their lack of enthusiasm.

At Meiningen, various artists without exception are used as leaders of walk-ons. The amazing effectiveness of first-night performances at Meiningen can be largely attributed to the lively participation of the crowds. This is in contrast to the awkward, wooden apathy of the supers to which we had accustomed ourselves and which makes such a disastrous impression.

The ugly and erroneous positions of individual actors in relation to each other are particularly disturbing in crowd scenes. The chief charm of groups is in the line of the heads. Just as a similarity of posture is to be avoided, so a regularity of height in actors standing near each other is, wherever possible, to be shunned. When it can be done, individuals should stand on different levels. Some can kneel, some stand nearby, some bending, some upright. It is effective to have those looking at one person or situation form an uneven semi-circle whenever it can be done.

Care must be taken that the actors nearest to the public and seen most by the spectators stand so that their shoulders are in various relations to the footlights. One should remind a walk-on to change his position as soon as he notices himself standing like his neighbor. In a good picture, one finds few figures in the same position or facing the same way. One has to repeat this order to the actors and supers at nearly every rehearsal, as it is continuously forgotten.

Special reminders must be given the supers not to stare at the audience. They do this naturally, since for many of them acting is a new and unusual experience, and their aroused curiosity makes them look around the dark auditorium.

Disturbing events like the removal of dead or wounded people should be "covered," meaning kept as much as possible from the audience's sight. This must not be done by means of a thick impenetrable wall of people, which looks self-conscious and ridiculous. The "cover" must be rather flexible so that one sees enough and not too much of what is taking place and can understand what it is all about.

When the impression of a great crowd is desired, one should place the groups so that the people on the sides are lost in the shadows of the wings. No one in the audience can be permitted to see where the grouping stops. The grouping must give the illusion that other crowds are also forming behind the scene.

OTTO BRAHM

(1856-1912)

First as critic and then as director-producer Otto Brahm shaped naturalism in Germany. Born in Hamburg, he worked as a bank clerk and then attended universities in Berlin, Heidelberg, Strasbourg, and Jena. In 1879 he received a doctor's degree; the title of his dissertation was "German Knight Plays of the Eighteenth Century." Then followed a decade in Berlin where he became an esteemed dramatic critic. It was Brahm who defended Ibsen in the German literary and theatrical world. He espoused naturalist drama and naturalist acting, developing theories which he was later to put into effect.

With the formation of the *Freie Buehne,* of which he became president and active leader, Brahm dedicated an experimental theatre to the new drama and encouraged a new style of acting. Emanuel Reicher, called the father of modern German acting, gave his services to the *Freie Buehne.* He voiced the new histrionic ideals. "We no longer wish merely to play 'effective scenes' but rather wish to present complete characters with the whole conglomerate of qualities with which they are endowed. We don't want to be anything else but human beings who find the emotions of the character to be represented from within and who express these with a simple, natural voice—regardless of whether that voice is beautiful and resonant, regardless of whether the accompanying gesture is gracious or not, and regardless of whether it fits in with the conception of stock types. Our problem is to adapt the representation to the simplicity of nature and to show the picture of a complete human being to the audience."

[288]

In 1894, hoping to gather about himself a permanent company, Brahm became director of the *Deutsches Theater*. His best productions here were the plays of the new dramatists although he attempted several naturalistic productions of the classics. These failed for lack of unity in the execution of the roles. Rudolf Rittner and Rose Bertens played their parts in the naturalistic "Brahm style," while Josef Kainz, the great actor of the older school associated with L'Arronge, performed in his own flamboyant manner. Brahm admired Kainz and audiences adored him, but his magnificent voice and grand gestures could not be brought within the compass of the naturalistic mode. Kainz wrote in his diary: "The movements of the actor's body are the expression of the *Psyche,* the external signs of what is happening within. As the sea moves slightly even in calm weather and affords us but an inkling of the coming storm, so the actor's body reacts all the time to what is passing in his mind. But as passions have thoughts behind them, and every reaction has its limitations, an actor, during the stress of emotions as well as when calm or ecstatic, must always remain a thinking human being.... His acting must always be music.... He must become neither a restrained God from Olympus nor a mere beast who surrenders himself to his instincts.... He must know the limits of the scale of his instrument.... He must have a light and sensitive touch for every stage of transition from *piano* to *forte*.... His words and movements must appear from the front as if coming instinctively in harmonious accord." The harmony and beauty of Kainz's manner contradicted the psychological realism of Brahm's efforts. Herbert Henze, one of Brahm's biographers, reported that Brahm once said to an actor who had just finished playing a scene: "Do you think this will achieve a grand effect?" "Jawohl, Herr Direktor." "Then leave it out," replied Brahm.

The struggle between these two styles was dramatized in the sub-plot of *The Rats* by Germany's greatest naturalist dramatist, Gerhart Hauptmann. An old actor-manager says to a student imbued with the new ideals: "But, man alive, you want to become an actor—you, with your round shoulders, with your spectacles and above all, with your hoarse and sharp voice. It's impossible." The student replies: "If such fellows as I exist in real life, why shouldn't they exist on the stage too? And I am of the opinion that a smooth, well-sounding voice, probably combined with the Goethe-Schiller-Weimar school of artifice, is harmful rather than helpful...." The ideas which Otto Brahm expounds in the following selection on the old and new style of acting are the same as those used in Act II of the Hauptmann play *The Rats*.

In 1890 when Bruno Wille gathered together two thousand workmen to discuss the formation of the *Freie Volksbuehne,* Brahm was on the platform, lending his name and his artistic ideals to the great people's theatre that was about to come into being. After his days at the *Deutsches Theater* he became director of the Lessing Theatre, founded in 1888 by the dramatist Oscar Blumenthal. Brahm's principled adherence to naturalism and his artistic integrity gave the German realistic movement a great leader.

In Defense of Naturalism

I should like to speak about the art of the actor, its aims and essence. Impressions of the theatre in recent months have brought this theme home to me. And

---

Otto Brahm: "The Old and the New Art of Acting," *Kritische Schriften ueber Drama und Theater;* herausgegeben von Paul Schlenther. Berlin: S. Fischer Verlag, 1913, pp. 420-429.

in order not to lose myself in a sea of abstractions, I shall use as an anchorage a statement by Karl Frenzel, namely that "there is now being preached to the younger actors the wildest theories of a new art of acting, something like the manner of impressionist painting: imitation of nature at any price, and the distorted reproduction—not of human beauty—but of bestial ugliness." Perhaps it is immodest on my part to assume that this comment is also directed at opinions I myself uttered not so long ago. At any rate, I count myself among the "preachers" of a new art of acting which Frenzel assails—even though I do not believe that my theory is the only one that brings salvation. I would much rather leave that to the gentlemen on the other side, who know exactly what "the true tasks of the art of acting" are. Neither in the performing nor in the creative arts do I know of any such "true tasks," eternal and immutable. But I do feel that I know the requirements of art in our time; and I must openly express my opinion.

The wildest theories, says Frenzel, are now being taught. But what if it turned out that the theories "now" being presented were in essence nothing but the traditional demands of the German art of acting, only adapted to the needs of our day? A brief glance at the history of our theatre will prove this forthwith.

Here I must touch upon certain things that are not generally known: how the first great German art of acting arose with Ekhof and Schroeder, those splendid Hamburg realists, out of the affectations and dance-master's mannerisms of the rococo period; how the Low German style was transplanted to the south by Beil and Iffland; how the movement aiming at the truthful and natural portrayal of character won out in Vienna thanks to Schroeder, and reached its high point in Berlin with Fleck and Unzelmann. All these things Frenzel, the author of *Berliner Dramaturgie,* knows even better than I do. Then, at the end of the 18th century, there came the great counter-movement of classicism: Goethe became the founder and theatrical director of the Weimar school; and Schiller, as dramatist, supported it. To overcome that classicism, to break with it, and find the way back to nature —that may not have been the "true task" in the sense of a formal aesthetic, but it has been the instinctive impulse of our great actors down to the present day.

Clearly and vigorously the historian of the German theatre, Eduard Devrient, sounded the opposition which the actor was bound to feel against efforts of the poets of the Weimar tendency to dominate him. One need not subscribe to every one of Devrient's theories; one may well understand the relative historic justification of the classical movement, the poetic transfiguration and spiritual deepening it contributed—yet one will not find in the greatest of our poets, Goethe, the full realization of the one thing the discerning actor needs. Goethe himself once said that the art of characterization was inwardly more congenial to the Northern spirit than the beautiful art of the ancient world. But from the unique qualities of human nature, which the author of *Goetz* and *Werther* was able to portray as no other, he went on to the universally human, to the typical—rejecting the "dross" of individuality. And the German art of acting had to oppose that trend, on penalty of itself ceasing to exist. The portrayal of human beings had to be its first and last duty; and it could only depict the richly developed personality in its subtlest natural distinctions by expressing the physical as well as the spiritual. But Goethe arbitrarily substituted conventional rules for truth, maxims in place of observation. And just as he imprisoned nature on the stage, so he sought to imprison it wherever possible in the life of his actors. Not only in the theatre did his Weimar players have to speak in as deep a voice as possible and "utter every word with a certain emphasis"; off-stage, among people, they also had to maintain a dignified bearing and consciously indulge in stylized pantomime. The display of stiff and pompous gestures, even at the beerhall table, which is today almost a thing of the past, goes back to the Goethe period.

However, the most dangerous aspect of the Weimar style was the means of expression borrowed from allied arts: sculpture and music. Elaborate lingering poses —where nature and the play demand tempo—may even today be seen in the Viennese and Dresden schools, in a Frau Wolter or a Frau Ellmenreich; and the musical element may still be seen at work in the predilection for artificially deep tones and studiously measured effects, as if planned by metronome. There is a story, whether true or not, which aptly describes the Weimar tradition: namely, that Goethe always used a baton while directing. His pupil, P. A. Wolff, the only one whose meager talents really prospered in Goethe's theatre, confesses quite openly that Goethe proceeded very much like an orchestra-conductor. In Wolff's words: "In all the rules he established, Goethe liked to take music as his model and he illustrated all his directions with figures of speech from music. He staged performances in the same way that an opera is rehearsed: he decided the tempi, fortes, pianos, crescendos, diminuendos, etc., and watched over them with the minutest care." Of course, Wolff feels the need of adding something to this description: "And let no one believe that such a method made the performance less true to nature." But there are not many modern readers who will fail to smile at such an assurance.

These then are the principles on which the nineteenth-century German art of acting arose, and which our "wild theories" seek to refute; this is the "human beauty" in the theatre which, in 1800, may have fitted the needs of the time, but which no longer fit our own needs today. Since then, voices have time and again been raised against Goethe, from among the actors themselves. Thus the great Schroeder told how "it required effort and struggle on his part to adapt many an admirable and creatively brilliant passage to nature; and he had to forego it, as it were, in order not to contradict the character he depicted." To "adapt" to nature, to test his art in accordance with nature, to give a new stamp to mere glittering declamation by portraying the human and the palpably individual—that is the task the modern actor must achieve with respect to classical plays, as it was the task of Schroeder and Fleck. For the modern actor cannot seek to preserve within himself the style of the past: he is a living artist, not an art-historian and antiquarian. And whatever cannot be understood with our present means of expression has no right to live on the stage, which belongs to our time and no other. To sacrifice the here and now, the rights of the living, for the ageless—such a price is too high to pay.

Because of the impact of the great poets, the road to this new yet age-old art of acting could only be traversed step by step. And we see clearly how an experienced dramatist like Heinrich Laube stood midway between the two camps. Laube wrote: "Whether and to what extent the Hamburg and Weimar schools can be united is the real theme which, since the beginning of the [nineteenth] century, has concerned every honest and intelligent friend of the theatre." Indeed, he himself seems to have chosen the side of the Hamburg school, for he added significantly: "To me, the portrayal of human beings on the stage is the essential. Hence truthfulness is my fundamental rule. To me, Lessing and Schroeder have formulated the code of laws of our acting art. I consider it our job to introduce and continue this code of laws." Here, as we see, there is no talk of Goethe and the beautiful and universally human. But such clear insight was blurred by the pressure of still extant traditions. Since Laube as a writer remained a staunch disciple of Schiller, his theory overlooked the theatrical element, concentrating one-sidedly on the listening not the seeing audience. In a play, he explained, the ear was "the more important organ" in the theatre; consequently, he installed a "performance-director" along the lines of Goethe's musical analogies, and he prohibited more elaborate scenery. Not until the Meiningers was such a step taken. But they, unfortunately, forgot one thing: to project onto the true-to-life sets of their stage human beings who acted naturally.

To be sure! Frenzel, the admirer of the Meiningers, will retort. They did not want to imitate nature at the price of "distorted, bestial ugliness." I must frankly confess that I cannot conceive how such strong words can be applied to the modern art of acting; and I would find such an ill-tempered judgment incomprehensible, if I did not know from my study of theatrical history that every forward step toward nature has evoked similarly harsh reproaches.

Here I would like to quote from an impartial third person—not the preacher of a new art. The Goethe-scholar, Julius Wahle, in his work *Das Weimarer Hoftheater* (*The Weimar Court Theater*), tells us: "Talma was the first who broke strict conventions in favor of freer movement. He was the creator of period-costume, and his insistence on natural truth met with strong opposition from his narrow-minded colleagues. In truth and power of expression he excelled all his fellow-actors. He took liberties which no one had hitherto dared to take: Talma does not talk with and to the audience, he really talks with and to the people on the stage; he walks toward the backdrop and turns his back on the audience. Above all, he was the first to dare to disregard the tradition of his predecessors in re-creating old roles. In a word, in his striving for natural truth he comes close to the German realistic conception of art. He infused healthy new blood into the emaciated body of French classicism; and he quickened old forms into new life with his modern romantic conception of art." And it is this—just this—that we demand of the present: that the actor speak in the living speech of our time, that he quicken sluggish old forms with powerful modern feeling.

It may seem a trifling detail when we read that Talma also dared to show his back to the audience. But this detail has symbolic meaning: it aptly characterizes the difference between sincerity in acting and acting based on conventions and mere outward show. Goethe hastened to ban all back-turning; but a Strindberg ardently desires "to see a whole scene played while the actor has his back turned." Here again the very newest development finds a precedent in the older tradition: the audience must realize, said Lessing, that it is there because of the actor, and not the other way around. And Schroeder assures us that he never indulged in that blameworthy practice of an actor conversing with the audience; during his entire career, he asserts, he scarcely looked ten times to see if the house was full or empty. In short, the audience was never visible to him. Compare this with Goethe's attitude; for example, with his opinion of the realistic Leipzig Theatre, and you will see the profound gap between the Hamburg and the Weimar schools. "In the Leipzig Theatre," Goethe noted in his diary in 1802, "there is a complete lack of art and dignity—there is naturalism and loose, unrestrained behavior. A Viennese lady was quite right when she told me: it doesn't make the slightest difference if spectators are present or not. The actors keep on turning their backs and talking to the floor."

I must still go into one final complaint by Karl Frenzel: the corrupters of the youth preach theories to the actors that are somewhat in the style of impressionist painting. Yes, that is true! For we believe that the creative arts, which are making such magnificent progress, can give a decided impetus to the performing arts. And if some inner kinship permits one to influence the other, we see in that only the confirmation that both are well on the road to satisfying the needs of the time. In both camps we can find parallel developments, throughout the entire nineteenth century. Carstens and Cornelius belong with the Weimar theatre: painters who cannot paint but who are full of poetic sentiments; actors who cannot act but succumb to the magic of poetic elocution. Then there followed Piloty, who offered real costumes, but no real human beings. Wallenstein and Seni, the triumphal procession of Germanicus: theatrical themes, orchestrated effects and scenes. There developed in the best creative artists a profound distaste for the theatre, which is only now beginning to disappear; and Anselm Feuerbach complained about "theatrical emotions in art." "I hate the modern theatre," he wrote, "I hate all these ornate trappings from the bottom of my soul. It produces barbarism in taste."

But a new sense of art arose with Adolf Menzel: the best of our theatres, the *Frieb-Blumauer* and the *Doering,* may be compared to his in keen and masterful power of observation. Until finally, there came to us from France an intimate study of nature and the impetus to grasp the real in its unadorned simplicity. Forced movements, exaggerated effects—we are as tired of them in painting as we are on the stage; we praise the *paysage intime* and are quite content if the modern art of acting takes as its model Millet's *Angelus,* with its figures of deep inner truth, with their calm gestures, their folded hands, all nature and genuine emotion.

Let the actor study nature, nothing more than that. Let him study nature in all her spiritual fullness: thus will he avoid banality and triviality. Let him study her outside himself and within himself, in the world and within his own breast. Then the more purely and richly he develops his personality, the stronger his temperament through which, in Zola's magic formula, he observes nature, the more deeply too will he grasp life and reproduce life. Like the giant Antaeus who grew strong whenever he touched the earth, the actor, turning from the theatre to nature, from the conventions of the four boards to truth, will ever win new strength; and he will learn to shun all stylizing, all arbitrary mannerisms, all stage affectations. As for the ideal, the truly beautiful, he can only feel that within himself, not outside himself in precepts that have been handed down. Let him find beauty in fidelity to the artistic whole of which he is a part, in the integrated character he portrays, in the play in which he acts. Here he must adapt himself with harmonious "beauty" to the economy of the work of art. But if someone expects him to reproduce human beauty at the expense of his own actor's art, to look beautiful, to move beautifully, and to speak beautifully—let him simply answer with quiet confidence in the words of Schiller to Goethe: "I think that the analysts have almost drained the concept of the beautiful and turned it into an empty shell. Would that someone would dare to take out of circulation the concept and even the word 'beauty,' with which all such false concepts are now indissolubly bound, and modestly substitute for it truth in the full sense of the term."

MAX REINHARDT

(1873 - 1943)

Max Reinhardt was one of the most picturesque actor-directors of the modern theatre. Born near Vienna, Reinhardt left his native city at the age of nineteen to become an actor at the Municipal Theatre in Salzburg. The young man was playing character parts when Otto Brahm, then director of the *Deutsches Theater,* saw him and gave him a two-year contract. He came to Berlin to work under Brahm's direction, learning naturalistic acting as he played such old men's roles as Foldal in Ibsen's *John Gabriel Borkman,* and Baumert in Hauptmann's *The Weavers.* At the same time he created an intimate cabaret, *Schall und Rauch (Sound and Smoke).*

From his first productions on his own stage, the *Kleines Theater,* in 1902 until the end of his life Reinhardt was thoroughly eclectic in the choice of plays, the style of production, acting techniques, and even in the selection of theatres. At the *Kleines Theater* and at the *Neues Theater* he produced almost fifty plays between 1902 and 1905, including in his repertory Ibsen, Maeterlinck, Schiller, Lessing, as well as his young contemporaries Hugo von Hofmannsthal and Richard Beer-Hofmann. His notable production of Gorky's *The Lower Depths* and his staging of *A Midsummer Night's Dream* have become world-famous. In 1905 he became director of the *Deutsches Theater,* following in the footsteps of L'Arronge and Brahm. To his work at the *Deutsches Theater* he added productions at his intimate *Kammerspiele.*

Inspired by the example of social participation in the ancient Greek and in the medieval theatres, Reinhardt created his gigantic festival productions, such as *Oedipus Rex,* the *Oresteia,* and *The Miracle,* in which he tried to bridge the separation between actors and audiences. In 1919 he realized his dream of an enormous theatre where the masses of people could find emotional release from their "wretched existence." The *Grosses Schauspielhaus,* "Theatre of the Five Thousand," abandoned the illusion of the naturalistic theatre for the arena which boasted one of the best equipped mechanical stages in Europe. He opened the theatre with Aeschylus' *Oresteia,* gave the plays of Hauptmann, Shakespeare, Kaiser, and others.

The failure of this titanic theatre, says Julius Bab, turned Reinhardt back to Vienna and then to Salzburg, whose beauty he loved, to work with the poet Hugo von Hofmannsthal and the composer Richard Strauss. Here he staged a number of impressive productions using the beautiful Austrian Alps as background. One of the most famous of his productions here was the morality *Jedermann (Everyman)* with the great Moissi in the title role. Reinhardt turned in 1922 to Maria Theresa's elegant ballroom which had recently been transformed into a theatre—*Theater in dem Redoutensaal.* Here amidst the chandeliers and the gilt he staged delicate productions suited to the baroque atmosphere. Back in Berlin he directed plays at several theatres until 1933 when, along with other anti-Nazis, he left Berlin. In the United States he staged numerous productions, among them Franz Werfel's *The Eternal Road,* and in Hollywood Reinhardt gathered about himself many of his old companions.

Reinhardt's various theatres have been called actors' theatres, like the Moscow Art Theatre, for despite all the devices used by Reinhardt, he seems never to have subordinated his actors to stage machinery. He had an unusual talent for casting, and under his direction many actors did outstanding work, which they never repeated under other directors. The number of truly significant actors associated with him at various times testified to his histrionic perspicuity. Julius Bab calls him a "born actor" and says that his qualities as a director stemmed from the fact that "he is an actor who can transcend his own physical being to communicate the play of his imagination to others."

R. Ben Ari, the celebrated actor of the Habimah Theatre, worked with Reinhardt and has given an interesting description of his methods in his article "Four Directors and an Actor" published in *Theatre Workshop*. He points out that Reinhardt, unlike Stanislavsky and Vakhtangov, had no histrionic principles, but that he spent much time and much effort working with his actors. Reinhardt's own acting ability and his personality were, however, so strong that some of his actors could not avoid imitating him rather than developing their own artistic individuality. On the other hand, such distinctive theatrical personalities as Albert Bassermann, Alexander Moissi, Max Pallenberg, and Elizabeth Bergner, among others, have been part of Reinhardt's acting family.

The Enchanted Sense of Play

It is to the actor and to no one else that the theatre belongs. When I say this, I do not mean, of course, the professional actor alone. I mean, first and foremost, the actor as poet. All the great dramatists have been and are today born actors, whether or not they have formally adopted this calling, and whatever success they have had in it. I mean likewise the actor as director, stage-manager, musician, scene-designer, painter, and certainly not least of all, the actor as spectator. For the contribution of the spectators is almost as important as that of the cast. The audience must take its part in the play if we are ever to see arise a true art of the theatre—the oldest, most powerful, and most immediate of the arts, combining the many in one.

We all bear within us the potentiality for every kind of passion, every fate, every way of life. Nothing human is alien to us. If this were not so, we could not understand other people, either in life or in art. But inheritance and upbringing foster individual experiences and develop only a few of our thousands of possibilities. The others gradually sicken and die.

Bourgeois life today is narrowly circumscribed, and poor in feeling. Out of its poverty it has made merely virtues through which it pushes its way, severe and upright. The normal man generally feels once in his life the whole blessedness of love, and once the joy of freedom. Once in his life he hates bitterly. Once with deep grief he buries a loved one, and once, finally, he dies himself. That gives all too little scope for our innate capacity to love, hate, enjoy, and suffer. We exercise daily to strengthen our muscles and sinews that they may not grow feeble. But our spiritual organs, which were made to act for an entire lifetime, remain unused, undeveloped, and so, with the passing years, they lose their vitality.

Yet our spiritual like our bodily health depends upon the regular functioning of these organs. Unconsciously we feel how a hearty laugh liberates us, how a good

Max Reinhardt: "The Actor." *The Encyclopedia Britannica* (1929) article THEATRE, Volume XXII, pp. 38-39. Copyright 1929. By permission of the Encyclopedia Britannica.

cry or an outbreak of anger relieves us. We have an absolute need of emotion and its expression.

Against this our upbringing constantly works. Its first commandment is—Hide what goes on within you. Never let it be seen that you are stirred up, that you are hungry or thirsty; every grief, every joy, every rage, all that is fundamental and craves utterance, must be repressed.

Hence the well-known sublimations, the hysterical tendencies of the time, and finally that empty play-acting of which modern life is full.

Our general social ideal is stoicism—always to be unmoved or at least to appear so. Passion, bursts of feeling and fancy, are ruled outside the bounds. In their place we have set up in a row common stereotyped forms of expression that are part of our social armor. This armor is so rigid and constricted that there is hardly any room for natural action. Our clothes are cheaply manufactured in quantity for the masses, and we have only a dozen or two cheap phrases for all occasions. We cultivate a few useful expressions of interest, of pleasure, of dignity, and a set grimace of politeness. We ask people how they feel without waiting for an answer or, in any case, without paying attention to it. With a fixed intonation, which could be written down and reproduced wholesale, we say that we are happy to see them, though the encounter may be a matter of complete indifference to us when it is not actually fatal. At weddings, christenings, burials, festivities we make out of hand-shaking and bowing, out of frowns and grins, a ghostly play, in which the absence of feeling is shocking.

One enters a dance hall and exclaims, Here at last is gaiety, exuberance, desire, rousing din! But all this the musicians are providing, to order. They have not only to furnish the music, the rhythm, they have also to conjure up through stamping, dancing, singing, and laughter, the overflowing gusto of life and all its madness. In the midst of this din, the dancers themselves remain silent, seriously matter-of-fact—so long as they are sober. When they are not sober, it is never the music or the dance, but the bootlegger that has stimulated them. It is astonishing how the feet move but the soul does not dance; the heart remains cold. The physical body is fit and well-developed, the spiritual body of a heavy flabbiness. The emotional inflexibility is fearful to see. The spirits have evaporated, leaving only phlegmatic apathy behind. This "Prohibition" of the spiritual life is the most notable sign of our time.

The modern social code has crippled the actor, whose business it is to body forth feeling. When generations have been brought up to repress the emotions, nothing in the end remains either to inhibit or to show. How can the actor, rooted deep in the bourgeois existence of every-day, suddenly in the evening leap into the life of the mad king, whose unrestrained passion sweeps like a storm across the moors? How shall he make it credible that he is killing himself through love, or that he has killed another through jealousy? It is significant that our modern theatre can hardly boast a true lover. When the actor on the stage says "I love you," it is the custom in many theatres to resort to musical accompaniment of the wood instruments, in order to evoke a poetical atmosphere. The soul is set vibrating by a *vibrato* of the violins—otherwise one could scarcely distinguish an I-love-you from a How-do-you-do. Generally, the women are more impulsive because they still live closer to nature than men.

In former times, when actors were excluded from bourgeois society and wandered about like gypsies, they undoubtedly developed stronger, rarer personalities. They were more unbridled in their passions; their outbursts were more powerful, the spirits that possessed them, more masterful. They had no outside interests. They were actors, body and soul. Today the body is willing, but the spirit is weak, and their interests are divided.

Of course, all these observations and all rules fail before the wonder of genius. But there is little genius, and there are many theatres. Now, to every person nature gives a face of his own. There is as small chance of finding two men who exactly resemble each other as of finding two leaves on a tree which are precisely alike. Yet in the narrow course of bourgeois life, driven hither and thither by the current of every-day, they are in time worn down until they become like round pebbles. One individual looks like another. This grinding process also has its effect upon their psychological make-up. But the highest boon of mankind is personality. In the arts, personality is the decisive factor; it is the living kernel which we seek in every artistic work.

Bourgeois standards should not be applied to artists, for what is it that distinguishes the artist? It is that he reacts to whatever he encounters deeply and powerfully; that things hardly visible, hardly audible, stir and move him; that he is driven by an irresistible impulsion to give all that he experiences back again, realized in some form of expression. It would be a gross injustice to wish to profit by these gifts in the arts, and yet in life outside to condemn them.

The nature of genius is mirrored most clearly in children. Their receptiveness is unparalleled, and the urge to mold or fashion, which shows itself in their games, is irrepressible and truly constructive. They want to discover the world again for themselves and to create it themselves. Instinctively they struggle against taking it in doses of instruction—a spoonful every hour. They do not wish to be crammed with experiences of others. They change themselves, quick as a flash, into all that they see, and change all into whatever they desire. Their imaginative energy is compelling. The sofa?—a railway train!—already the engine rattles and steams and whistles; now someone looks with delight out of the car window at the enchanted landscape flying past; now a severe conductor collects the tickets, and now one arrives at one's destination! A porter panting carries a trunk to the hotel; and then the nearest armchair as automobile whisks noiselessly away, and the footstool as airplane soars through all the seven heavens. What is that? Theatre! Model theatre and ideal dramatic art. Thus we have the phenomenon that children are the best actors on the stage and in the film.

In children's play, the laws of the theatre may be studied in their most fundamental forms: the décor, the thing requisite, suggested by what is actually there, transformed through the sovereign power of imagination, and yet with the clear, ever-present realization that it is all only play. The actor is in the same case. It is a fairy story that he can ever forget the audience. Even in the moment of highest excitement the consciousness obtrudes itself upon him that thousands are following him with breathless, tremulous suspense through the last doors opening to his inmost self. With the children, too, it is all play, which is carried on in dead earnest, play that requires an audience who will yield themselves silently and enter attentively into the game. Well, what do we do? We laugh. Laugh scornfully or sympathetically—at best, we enthusiastically embrace the "little rascal." But by our excitement and enthusiasm something is instantly brushed away. We have done what we never do in the theatre, easily as we might. We have violently broken in upon the middle of a performance; a magic spell has been brutally destroyed.

The art of acting originated in the earliest childhood of the race. Man, allotted a brief existence, in a close-pressing crowd of various kinds of individuals, who were so near him and yet so elusively far, had an irresistible desire to throw himself into a fantastic play of changing one form into another, one fate into another, one effect into another. These were the first attempts to fly above his narrow material existence. The possibilities inherent in him but not brought to full growth by his life thus unfolded their shadowy wings and carried him far over his knowledge and away into the heart of a strange experience. He discovered all the delights of transformation, all the ecstasy of passion, all the illusive life of dreams.

Made as we are in God's image, we have in us something of the godlike creative will. Therefore we create the whole world over again in the arts, with all the elements, and on the first day of creation, as the crown of our work, we make men in *our* image.

Shakespeare is the greatest, the one truly incomparable boon that the theatre has had. He was poet, actor, and producer in one. He painted landscapes and fashioned architectural scenes with his words. In his plays everything is bathed in music and flows into the dance. He stands nearest to the Creator. It is a wonderful full-rounded world that he made—the earth with all its flowers, the sea with all its storms, the light of the sun, the moon, the stars; fire with all its terrors and the air with all its spirits—and in between, human beings with all their passions, their humor and tragedy, beings of elemental grandeur and, at the same time, utter truth. His omnipotence is infinite. He was Hamlet, King Claudius, Ophelia, and Polonius in one person. Othello and Iago, Brutus and Cassius, Romeo and Juliet, Falstaff and Prince Henry, Shylock and Antonio, Bottom and Titania, and the whole line of merry and sorrowful fools lived within him. He engendered them and brought them to birth; they were part of his inscrutable being. Over them he hovers like a godhead, invisible and intangible. Nothing of him is there but this great world. Yet in it he is ever present and mighty. He lives eternally.

Only that art is living, in whose inmost chamber the human heart beats.

For the moment the theatre is, I know, threatened; it is in a decline today because in the noise and rush of the great cities, though material means of existence are given it, its peculiar festal beauty, the enchanted sense of play, has been taken from it. It has not yet been organically co-ordinated with the sudden growth of the modern metropolis.

The arts, especially the theatre, forsaken by the good spirits, can be the sorriest business, the poorest prostitution—there is its pale first cousin, the film, which was born in the city and has undoubtedly flourished better there. But the passion to act in the theatre, to go to the theatre, is an elemental desire in mankind. It will always draw actors and spectators together to the play, and out of that Dionysian union in which they rise above the earth, it will produce the highest art that alone brings felicity.

I believe in the deathlessness of the theatre. It is the happiest loophole of escape for those who have secretly put their childhood in their pockets and have gone off with it to play to the end of their days. The art of the stage affords also liberation from the conventional drama of life, for it is not dissimulation that is the business of the play but revelation. Only the actor who cannot lie, who is himself undisguised, and who profoundly unlocks his heart deserves the laurel. The supreme goal of the theatre is truth, not the outward, naturalistic truth of everyday, but the ultimate truth of the soul.

We can telegraph and telephone and wire pictures across the ocean; we can fly over it. But the way to the human being next to us is still as far as to the stars. The actor takes us on this way. With the light of the poet he climbs the unexplored peaks of the human soul, his own soul, in order to transform it secretly there and to return with his hands, eyes, and voice full of wonders.

He is at once sculptor and sculpture; he is man at the farthest borderline between reality and dream, and he stands with both feet in both realms. The actor's power of self-suggestion is so great that he can bring about in his body not only inner and psychological but even outer and physical changes. And when one ponders on the miracle of Konnersreuth, whereby a simple peasant girl experiences every Friday the Passion of Christ, with so strong an imaginative power that her hands and feet show wounds and she actually weeps tears of blood, one may judge to what wonders through what a mysterious world the art of acting may lead; for it is assuredly by the same process that the player, in Shakespeare's words, changes utterly his accustomed visage, his aspect and carriage, his whole being, and can weep for Hecuba and make others weep. Every night the actor bears the stigmata, which his imagination inflicts upon him, and bleeds from a thousand wounds.

PAUL KORNFELD

(1889- ?)

Paul Kornfeld, who was born in Prague, brought at least one genuine expressionistic drama to the theatre. Although he wrote other plays, among them *Himmel und Hoelle* (*Heaven and Hell*, 1919) and *Palme oder der Gekraenkte* (*Palme; or, The Hypochondriac*, 1924), it is his play *Die Verfuehrung* (*The Seduction*) that embodied the spiritual, abstract quality of expressionistic drama. The play was first performed in Frankfurt-am-Main in 1916.

The dramatist equipped his play with a theoretical justification: "Let us leave character to everyday life; in loftier hours let us be nothing but soul. For the soul is of the heavens, character is of the earth." To his five-act tragedy, *Die Verfuehrung,* he appended an epilogue (*Nachwort an den Schauspieler*) in which he suggested to actors the proper histrionic technique for expressionistic drama. It is this statement, with its complete renunciation of all the tenets of naturalistic acting, which is given here.

It has been reported that Kornfeld perished during World War II at the Auschwitz concentration camp.

Expressionism

I do not know whether this play [*Die Verfuehrung*] will ever be presented on a stage. It has been written for the theatre. If it is never produced, I am prepared to accept any reason except one: namely, that its style is not good theatre. If someone were to say that it was not worth while offering it to the theatre-going public,

---

Paul Kornfeld: "Nachwort an den Schauspieler," *Die Verfuehrung*. Berlin: S. Fischer Verlag, 1921, pp. 163-166. This selection translated by Joseph M. Bernstein.

I would neither agree nor disagree. But I would vigorously protest if someone asserted that it was indeed worth while—but not suited to the theatre.

This assumes that the director and actors will not stage it in a way that runs counter to its spirit. But as the art of acting has developed over the past few decades, this danger does lie in a definite direction. And judging from the form and spirit of most of the "modern" plays presented in these last decades, the contemporary playwright (who is also "modern") faces a double danger. Therefore I feel it necessary to address the following words to the actor. Perhaps there are here and there actors who, as they read this tragedy, will retrospectively correct the images inspired in them; or even form images out of what had previously remained mere words.

Let not the actor in this play behave as though the thoughts and words he has to express have only arisen in him at the very moment in which he recites them. If he has to die on the stage, let him not pay a visit to the hospital beforehand in order to learn how to die; or go into a bar to see how people act when they are drunk. Let him dare to stretch his arms out wide and with a sense of soaring speak as he has never spoken in life; let him not be an imitator or seek his models in a world alien to the actor. In short, let him not be ashamed of the fact that he is acting. Let him not deny the theatre or try to feign reality. On the one hand, he can never fully succeed in the attempt; on the other hand, such a counterfeit presentment of reality can only be given in the theatre if the dramatic art has fallen to such a low estate as to be a more or less successful imitation of physical reality and everyday life—whether steeped in emotions, moral precepts, or aphorisms.

If the actor builds his characters from his experience of the emotion or fate he has to portray and with gestures adequate to this experience, and not from his recollections of the human beings he has seen filled with these emotions or victims of this fate; in fact, if he completely banishes these recollections from his memory, he will see that his expression of a feeling which is not genuine and which has really been artificially stimulated is purer, clearer, and stronger than that of any person whose feeling is prompted by a genuine stimulus. For the expression of a human being is never crystal-clear because he himself is never crystal-clear. He is never only *one* feeling—and if he were only *one,* this *one* would always appear in a different light. If he thinks he has immersed himself in but a single experience, there are nevertheless innumerable psychic facts existing within him which falsify many aspects of his behavior. The shadow of his present environment as well as the shadow of his past falls across him. Many people are comedians to themselves; yet the actor, who merely performs, is truer in his expression than many of those who are victims of an actual fate. Concern for many things prevents the real-life person from externalizing himself completely: the memory of many things is rooted in him and the rays of a thousand events criss-cross within him. So at any given moment he can only be a changing complex of behavior. But the actor is free of all that: he is no complex, he is always only *one.* He is not falsified by anything—hence only he can be crystal-clear and rectilinear. And since he is only this *one* embodiment, he can embody it completely and magnificently. By shaping the character he portrays the actor will find his way unerringly to its essence.

Let him therefore pick out the essential attributes of reality and be nothing but a representative of thought, feeling, or fate!

The melody of a great gesture says more than the highest consummation of what is called naturalness.

GERMANY

ERWIN PISCATOR

(1893-1966)

Descendant of a churchman who translated the Bible in the days of the Reformation, Erwin Piscator returned from the First World War with a conviction that theatre must be related to life. After early directorial experiments, he came to the famous *Volksbuehne* where, from 1924 to 1927, Piscator vivified German theatre with his daring productions. His social ideals and his complete espousal of theatre as a tribunal, theatre as a weapon, led to a split with the directors of the *Volksbuehne*. Piscator's production of Schiller's *The Robbers,* when he was guest director at the Berlin State Theatre, caused great excitement. He then established his own theatre on Nollendorfplatz where he gave his startling Epic Theatre productions of *The Good Soldier Schweik* and *Hoppla! Such is Life.*

With Bertolt Brecht, Piscator was the outstanding exponent of Epic Theatre. In *Das Politsche Theater* (1929) he chronicled the early days of the form. Brecht in a piece "On Experimental Theatre" says that in the twenties, "Piscator's experiments broke nearly all conventions. They intervened to transform the playwright's creative methods, the actor's style of representation, and the work of the stage designer. They were striving toward an entirely new social function for the theatre." Brecht spoke of his own experiments in the twenties as a continuation of the work already done, "especially in Piscator's theatre."

The anti-Nazi Piscator left Germany and made his way to the United States. In an effort to transplant epic theatre in foreign soil, he staged many important productions and headed his own school, the Dramatic Workshop. In 1951 he returned to Germany and for the remaining years of his life he offered audiences distinguished productions, Hochhuth's *Deputy,* Kipphardt's *The Case of J. Robert Oppenheimer,* and Peter Weiss's *The Investigation,* which realized his conception of the stage as a moral institution.

In the following essay written specifically for this volume, Piscator suggests an approach to the Epic Theatre style of acting which differs from that of Bertolt Brecht.

Objective Acting

So you want to become an actor? First let me tell you a little story of what happened to a young actor not so long ago. The young actor was no one but myself. I was barely seventeen. It was my first contact with reality: the war.

We had moved out into Ypres. The Germans were beginning their spring offensive of 1915. It was the first time gas was used. The English and the German guns both pounded against the comfortless grey skies. Our company was practically destroyed to the last man. We had to have replacements. We were continually shuttled from the supporting trenches to the front lines. As the first grenades fell the order was given to go over the top, advance, and dig in. While the others succeeded in advancing I did not. The commanding officer ran up to me shouting "For God's sake, get going!" "I can't!" I answered. In a querulous tone he demanded to know what I had been before the war. I replied, "An actor."

Before all those exploding grenades the word "actor" which I had difficulty in uttering—this profession for which I had been fighting—my idea of the theatre, which had been for me the highest and most important goal I could strive for, seemed so stupid, so ridiculous, so false and so inadequate to the situation I was in, that I was less afraid of the grenades coming toward me than I was ashamed of having chosen such a profession.

It was a little episode, but the impact of it has remained with me. From that time I wanted to rid myself of the feeling which I had experienced that art has nothing to do with reality and is not sturdy enough to help us to face up to it. I have tried to find truth everywhere in order not to be ashamed of my profession. I have sought for it behind the fourth wall of the magical theatre of Max Reinhardt, behind the abstractions of the naturalists, in the open fields of the expressionists, and in the romanticism of the literature of pity. I wanted to feel that art is able to deal with every situation and every problem, and that we artists are able to grow through it to such stature that we can deal with life. I tried to create such a theatre and I found that it called for a new view on acting.

Let me take you into this theatre to participate in what I would call introductory lessons in acting. I will sit in the director's seat, which I occupy during rehearsals. It is usually in the center of the audience. Now sit down next to me. Think of me not as a director but as a man sitting in the audience—the man for whom you are going to play. Tell me of your hopes and expectations concerning your play, and what you think the hopes and expectations of the audience should be. Describe the composition of this audience you will play for. Was it the same a hundred years ago? What makes it what it is this year—or as we assume it will be tonight?

When you have explained all this to me, go slowly up to the stage. Look around as you go—feel your way—be aware of your progress going up the stairs. Continue to talk to me as you are walking. Say something—anything. Speak about the evening, about the play, about the weather. Do you feel the gradual lift this little walk up the sairs has given your whole personality? Yes, you have been lifted out of the audience, but you have not been walking away from me. You and I—we are the two poles in the theatre—the two partners, for the moment. Don't lose your relationship with me because soon we will be building a triangle —you and I and an imaginary partner in the center of the stage. Now you have arrived. Approach the strongest point on the stage. Where is it? Is it right, left, or center? Where do you feel yourself dominant? Go to the place where you feel yourself superior to me.

Concentrate your whole attention on me. Don't forget that you have to convince me not only of your presence, but of your existence. Naturally you can turn away from me, but don't forget that I am always there, and that we can succeed only as a unit. *There is no theatre without an audience.* Whoever has told you that you can shut yourself off behind an imaginary "fourth wall" has misinformed you. I am a part of your "case"—the play—which you are going to present to me and actively defend—with the same interest and the same passion with which I take part in it. The more real, the more convincingly you play, the more you will have served your case—the actor convincing the audience—the more you will have rendered service to the cause of acting.

Whatever you do, your attention is and must be directed constantly toward the center of the theatre—toward me. I know that this may sound quite confusing because you have been taught that the center of attention lies in the center of the stage. Do you remember that charming story told by Stanislavsky? His students couldn't free themselves from the fear of the audience so he went up on the stage and pretended that one of them had lost the heel of his shoe. Everyone was immediately occupied with his shoes, and the reality which he introduced helped them to free themselves and forget the audience. This device really helped the students to forget the audience and to lose the fears which every young actor experiences.

Do you think such a device is necessary? I believe that such devices are untheatrical and as is true of every device, not absolutely honest. You will have to make a terrific effort to convince me of the "fourth wall" and the "as if" philosophy, which is supposed to induce the observer to believe completely in your sincerity and to think of you as completely "natural." Are we ever completely natural on the stage? Don't you begin immediately to speak much louder than in real life, even if you are alone in one room on the stage? If you are only an arm's length from your partner why are you screaming at him while confessing your most intimate feelings? Think of all the queer positions you assume. Don't you always strive to prevent yourself from being hidden and not to hide your partner? Do you really believe in the painted tree behind you, or in the deadly charge of the gun which you point at another human being? Why this make-believe, if you really think that you are all alone on the stage, shut up between four walls, and that there is no audience to be convinced? It is not true that your center of attention is in the center of the stage. Since you are playing for an audience the center of your attention must be expanded forward to the center of that audience. You know that and the *audience* knows it too. Recognizing this we can proceed to the next point.

You have a mission. Your mission is to entertain me and while you are entertaining me you also have to be my teacher. My curiosity grows with the interest you awaken in me and deepens my desire to learn with the same intensity not only about you but about the miracle of the world you introduce to me. Don't deceive yourself into thinking that you can exclude me. I can be your friend or your enemy, but I can never be non-existent. In the two hours of performance, if you can make me your student you have succeeded.

With this understanding of the actor's technique in relation to the audience, we can start to think of the actor in his relation to the other actors. You know that even when you find yourself alone on the stage speaking a monologue, you are in reality not alone. You couldn't play your part all by yourself. You are surrounded by the presence of the other actors—your partners—even if they are, at this particular moment, not on the stage. You exist through them as much as through or by yourself. Without their revelations about you—without their relationships to you—the audience would have a very feeble impression of your character. This is logical, but I assume you have very often heard that you must find yourself and your character within yourself, in a sort of splendid isolation. You can never find yourself before you have learned how to re-act to your partner. In order to find yourself you must go out of yourself. You will say that from reacting to acting is only a little step forward. Yes—but a very decisive one. Your re-action is spontaneous. It comes out of your sincerity without which you would not be creative. But this re-action is passive and has to be set in motion to become action, which in turn gives your character the sense of reality.

Now we begin a new attack. You, the actor, in relation to yourself, your body, your voice, your part in the play. I know you will tell me that to have a spontaneous re-action you need your "fourth wall"—you need to forget me, the audience. I don't think you do. To me it is always very embarrassing when I see the eye of the actor gliding over the heads of the audience, as if we weren't there at all. I am even a little ashamed of such behavior because it seems humiliating for the actor.

He loses contact with the audience and places himself in a false and inferior position. See how the situation changes immediately when his eye meets the audience. The whole stage seems to come alive. Through the directness of that glance, a truth establishes itself between the actor and the audience and brings back a vital contact and a greater reality of the action.

A word about reality of action. How different is the reality of a play by Chekhov or Ibsen, and a musical by Gershwin, Weill or Rodgers and Hammerstein! There are different methods to achieve reality in the theatre. Subjective and objective acting are two methods of creating a character from life upon the stage. By objective acting I don't mean the histrionic and self-conscious acting of some fifty years ago which catalogued every emotion. I don't mean, either, the new technique of acting advanced by Brecht, which he calls *"Verfremdung"* ("alienation"). Objective acting grew out of stage experiment.

For example, after the war, without any money, I tried to play before an audience of workers on a very empty stage. What could we do to give that empty stage the background necessary to the play? We put up little projection screens on which to paint a background. Soon we found that the stage was wonderfully suited either to enlarge or diminish the background. We gave the necessary commentaries just by giving the year or the events at the opening of the story. These commentaries created a very direct relationship with the audience. In fact, it pleased the audience to become associated with the people on the stage and thus make the theatre really their own, with a particular style which also was the style of that particular play, and not meant as a new technique for technique's sake. It was a way to express ourselves primitively within the means at our disposal, a way to be understood. That was all we wanted. Curiously enough, this experiment gave the actor a new sort of freedom. Everything which was untrue and which he had acquired during the years he had considered his profession a romantic one, fell off. He threw it off, being aware suddenly of new possibilities, being faced with the fact that he could be himself and at the same time a related part of the whole. These experiments of the post-war years were by no means an attempt to create a new form of art or to declare a revolution against the accepted or existent forms of the theatre. It was as natural as our new reality of life. It wasn't Expressionism—it wasn't a new formal theatre. It was exactly the sort of theatre that came out of the people of that particular time.

Later, with more money, I had greater possibilities and a bigger theatre. I was able to find new stage designers and engineers and to free the theatre technically. (The Arena stage, Gropius, the Total Theatre, the treadmill, and the turntable.) Thus, a new free style for the actor had become a fact. What was an experiment has become a method. I called it the Epic Theatre.

The Epic Theatre, of course, required a new actor. I could no longer use the classic declamatory actor—in love with his voice and uninterested in what he said, but only in how he said it. Neither could I accept the Chekhovian actor, hypnotizing himself behind the "fourth wall." It is Brecht's contention that Stanislavsky has shot his bolt and that we need a new kind of acting which estranges the events being presented on the stage from the spectator and makes the audience assume an inquiring and critical attitude toward the play. Brecht was right when he asked "that the action should be set before us rather than involve us by means of empathy." But Brecht formulated "alienation" on the basis of Oriental classical theatres, thus romanticizing the concept. I agreed that the "alienation" idea would make use of

[304]

our intelligence and bring us into closer contact with the facts. I, however, wanted to get hold of the complete human being. I will only separate intelligence and emotion so that I can unite them again on a higher level. If we want an intelligent audience, for whom the theatre is more than mere entertainment, we have to break down the "fourth wall" on the stage. The film has done it long ago. We don't want the modern actor improvising his emotions behind the "fourth wall," but we want him to give us commentaries on these emotions—playing not only a result but the thought which created the result. We want to see the roots and not the fruit alone, the seed and not the plant alone. To do this, the modern actor needs a superior control so that he will not be overcome by his emotions. He needs what I have called "the new objectivity."

Painters, musicians and writers know about that objectivity without which no real artistic work has been created. They have it much easier, of course, than the actor, who is object and subject at the same time. The actor is the instrument, he is the brush, the paper, the clay. Schopenhauer describes this objectivity very clearly: "Nobody is ever able to look at his own picture in a mirror with the look of 'alienation,' which is the primary requirement of objectivity. The true objective look is, in the last analysis, possible only through the moral egoism of a deeply felt 'non-I' making it possible to see all the shortcomings, without any reservations, the picture as it is, really faithful and true."

The mirror in the case of the actor *is the audience*. But the faithful and real picture can only be created by both actor and audience. You the actor become the mirror in which the audience can see themselves. It will be your duty to help them to come to the right conclusions and to destroy the untrue and flattering picture of the "I". The audience as your mirror, my actor, and you as the mirror of the audience!

The stage itself will be of help to you in creating this new objectivity. For example, when I separated the Globe in *Rasputin*—that is, the stage—into segments, used documentary films, and projected a commentary on the historical events on the side walls, the stage itself helped the actor to achieve a new reality, a new objectivity. All the modern scenic inventions which I used created a new dimension for the actor.

But I see you hesitating, afraid and a little dejected. I think I know why. You want to ask me about the sorcery, the mystery, the atmosphere and the casting of the spell, the illusion and the trance which make the theatre a magic box so delightful to the actor. Should we do away with all this by asking the modern actor to reach out for objectivity? Should he give up his subjective life which makes him an integral emotional part of the events? No, by all means, no! The more objective he becomes, the more he succeeds in reaching the highest personal (subjective) form. The bold and beautiful architecture of a monologue adds to the text. Subjective and objective acting united produce the highest form of acting. You can see it, for instance, in the work of Laurence Olivier. Let me repeat it once more. When I speak about the new objective acting, I don't mean the cold routine of the standard theatre. I don't mean the dreadful result of the commercial theatre which lowers the artist and makes him a poor automaton—makes him an interpreter instead of a creator—at the best a craftsman, not an artist. Only the creator is important in the actor, not the craftsman, not the artisan. Without the creator, these are nothing.

But where is the modern stage where we can use such modern acting? Does it exist? You are right to doubt it. Neither in London, Paris, Moscow nor New York is there a modern theatre which corresponds to our modern life—a modern theatre which uses the means we have developed and is acquainted with the newest inventions of our day. The modern theatres we have are the films, the radio, and television. But there is still hope for the old magic box—the theatre. We can change it. We can open its bolted doors, break with obvious and customary techniques, destroy the one-set theatre. We can bring in everything that science has created from the growth in human productivity. We can stop the little magic lantern for all the grown up children and make a telescope out of it.

That is what I think the Epic Theatre and its actor can do. This new objectivity will not create a new formalism or orthodoxy. On the contrary, it will free the theatre from frozen forms. Primitively seen, the Epic Theatre provides the old-fashioned theatre box with a new vista, a new article—Space—and it provides the actor with a new freedom. He has been tightly imprisoned for three centuries between the wings of the picture frame theatre. Now he can move again on simultaneous stages, as in the Shakespearean theatre; he can use the half and full arena, as the Greeks invented them; he can walk into the audience like a close-up in the films. You cannot ask the modern man who can fly around the world in two days to sit patiently for two hours and look at one set. It is as though we would confine ourselves to a Victorian room and read by candlelight!

This new theatre will give the actor new dimensions—dimensions accentuated by the moving stage, the turning and lowering of whole segments of the stage. (An example of this, primitive as it was, was seen in my production of *The Good Soldier Schweik*.) These dimensions will not be frustrating or mechanical for the actor, but will be as natural and necessary as the ones in real life. Think of all the machinery which modern man uses for his comfort—uses freely and without frustration.

The Epic actor will be a sort of narrator. I don't mean by this the narrator who remains downstage and addresses the audience directly. Even such formal addresses and commentary, if he knows how to lose himself in the character at the same time, are possible. When he strolls over the stage in the most casual way, he will still be acting as a kind of guide, who knows every one of the pictures he is showing. He will be the conductor who, knowing every note of each instrument, will bring out each voice, and, at the same time, bring out the unity of the composition. The clarity with which he approaches his subject and communicates it has to convince his partner on the stage and me, the third partner in the audience. This Epic actor is no longer a copy of a character, but assumes human proportions, becomes three dimensional. He has many partners. He will make the set his partner. He will make it another actor, or a commentator, as he needs it—and he is himself both actor and commentator. The same thing will happen to the prop— the prop, which certainly is no longer mere support, but is a plastic detail of full human utterance.

It is interesting that actors whom I would qualify as great, and who instinctively play Epic Theatre, are also directors. To mention a few: Laurence Olivier, Jean-Louis Barrault, Louis Jouvet. So was Molière and so was Shakespeare. These great actors can comment on important philosophies in a special monologue one moment and in the next relieve the audience from this seriousness with a relaxing smile. A minute later they divert the audience, introducing certain devices necessary to the plot, making them laugh or cry, according to the function of that minute. With one word—they play a human being, alive, and play a situation which is alive—in which they, as well as the audience, are equally interested. They act with the knowledge that life is more important than the play—but that at the same time, it is understood that at the particular moment, there is no more dignified example of life than this particular slice of life in this particular play. It is the finiteness of the theatre versus the infiniteness of life.

In this unity of reason and emotion—of spirituality and affection and sensation—the actor will discover his creative genius for the stage—the art of acting. Through the union of objective acting with the subjective action, he will be not merely an object in the hands of the playwright, but a creator. By objectivizing himself he becomes a subject—and being governed by both, he becomes alive.

BERTOLT BRECHT
(1898-1956)

Bertolt Brecht, born in Bavaria, studied the natural sciences before he turned to literature. After his first play, *Baal,* he became famous with the production in Munich of his second, *Trommeln in der Nacht* (*Drums in the Night*), which won the Kleist prize in 1922. It expressed the anger of a war veteran who returns to find war profiteers in control of society. For a short while Brecht served as dramaturge for the Berlin theatres of Max Reinhardt.

In the years from 1928 to 1933, before Hitler came to power, Brecht began to work out methods and theories that were to make him the most original and important theatre innovator of his time. German theatre was in these years a forerunner in theatrical exploration, and Brecht drew inspiration from Reinhardt, Jessner, Piscator, and the actor Kurt Valentin. In the early successful productions of *The Three-Penny Opera* (1928) and the 1931 *Mann ist Mann* with Helene Weigel and Peter Lorre or his *Lehrstücke,* like *Die Massnahme* (*The Measures Taken*), he brought together the methods being then tried out—nonnaturalistic devices, choruses, songs, dances, soliloquies, projections, caricatures, impersonal acting—to create an objective, didactic Epic Theatre.

Brecht distinguished his epic, or presentational, theatre from the traditional, representational, theatre in the following chart, translated by Eric Bentley:

The "Dramatic" Theatre:	The Epic Theatre:
the stage embodies a sequence of events	the stage narrates the sequence
involves the spectator in an action and	makes him an observer but
uses all his energy, his will to action	awakes his energy
allows him feeling	demands decisions
communicates experiences	communicates pieces of knowledge
spectator is brought into an action	is placed in front of an action
is plied with suggestion	with arguments
sensations are preserved	till they become insights
man is given as a known quantity	man an object of investigation
man unalterable	alterable and altering
tense interest in the outcome	tense interest in what happens
one scene exists for another	each scene exists for itself
. . . .	. . . .
the world is what it is	the world is what it is becoming
what man should	what man must
his instincts	his reasons
thought determines reality	social reality determines thought

[307]

In this scientific, objective, narrative theatre the actor was required to instruct the audience, to "show" him the meaning of the action. He was to present through the *gestus* or "clear and stylized expression of social behavior of human beings toward each other" the significant choices modern man must make.

Brecht's theories offered the major challenge to those of Stanislavsky, whose system Brecht thought "mystical and cultish." Brecht was "for empathy" at a certain stage in rehearsals, but felt it was not "sufficient." At a conference on Stanislavsky held by Brecht's company in 1953, he acknowledged, however, that they had many points in common. Especially related to his own conceptions was Stanislavsky's concern with the "superobjective." It was his opinion that much could be learned from Stanislavsky, who was usually posed as his arch antagonist. Stanislavsky's views, he felt, had been as badly oversimplified and distorted as had his own. Perhaps the main theoretical preoccupation of actors, worldwide in the fifties and sixties, has been the attempt to bridge the gap between these two approaches.

The theory of the "alienation effect," developed and enunciated by voluminous writings over the years, took on practical meaning when in 1949, after Brecht's return from years of exile to East Germany, the *Berliner Ensemble* was founded. As he staged his late masterpieces—*Mother Courage* and *The Caucasian Chalk Circle*—in his own theatre with his own company of actors, theory and practice were linked in the kind of dialectical relationship Brecht always envisioned. The achievement of Brecht as theorist and master artist challenged the theatre world to reassess the basic meaning and technique of the actor.

The Alienation Effect

In this short paper an attempt will be made to describe a technique of acting which has been used in the German theatre to alienate the events being presented on the stage from the spectator. It has been the aim of this technique of alienation [*Verfremdung*] to make the spectator assume an enquiring, critical attitude towards events. The means employed are artistic.

If the A-effect is to achieve its aim, the stage and the auditorium must be cleared of "magic." No "hypnotic fields of action" must be set up. On the Epic stage, no attempt is made to create the atmosphere of a particular place (a room at evening, a street in autumn), or to generate a mood by a broken speech-rhythm. The actor does not warm the audience up by unloosing a flood of temperament, nor cast a spell over them by tightening his muscles. In short, no effort is made to put the audience in a trance and give them the illusion of witnessing natural, unrehearsed events. As will be seen, the audience's tendency to throw itself into such an illusion must be neutralized by definite artistic means.

If he is to bring off the A-effect, the actor must provide what he has to show the audience with clear gestures of "showing" (meaning by gestures our whole apparatus of expression). The idea of a fourth wall which is imagined separating the stage from the audience, an idea that produces the illusion that the stage action is actually taking place without spectators, must of course be abandoned. This being so, it is possible for the actors to turn directly to the audience.

Bertolt Brecht: "A New Technique of Acting," translated by Eric Bentley. New York: *Theatre Arts*, Volume XXXIII, Number 1, January, 1949, pp. 38-40. Copyright 1949. By permission of Eric R. Bentley.

Usually, as is well-known, contact between audience and stage is established by means of empathy. The conventional actor today concentrates so utterly on producing empathy that one can say, "He sees in it the principal goal of his art." As has already been suggested, the technique of the A-effect is diametrically opposed to that by which empathy is produced. The technique of the A-effect actually prevents the actor from producing empathy—at least to the usual extent.

In his efforts to portray people and show how they behave, the actor need not do without empathy altogether. He uses it to the extent that anyone without histrionic talent or ambition would use it to present another man, that is, to show how he behaves. Such "showing how other men behave" happens every day in countless situations (witnesses of an accident report to newcomers how the victim behaved, jokers imitate a friend's comical walk, etc.) without the people concerned trying to give their spectators any sort of illusion. Yet they do "feel themselves into" other people in order to take on their characteristics.

The actor, then, will make *some* use of empathy. But, whereas at present, the act of empathy is not completed till the actual performance, when the spectator is involved in the process, in Epic Theatre it will be completed at an earlier stage—in fact, at some point in the course of rehearsals while the role is still being learned.

Lest the actors interpret the people and events of a play in too impulsive, frictionless, and uncritical a fashion, a larger than usual number of rehearsals must be held around a table. The actor will eschew all premature "living himself into" the role and as long as possible will just *read* it (though not as one reads aloud to an audience). One important procedure is the *memorizing of first impressions*.

In confronting his role, the actor's attitude should be that of someone who is astonished and resistant. He must carefully weigh, and grasp in all their specialness, not only the occurrence of the events in the story, but also the behavior of the person whom he is to represent. He cannot take any of the events as "given," as something that "couldn't be otherwise," that "was to be expected from the nature of the character." Before memorizing the words, he should memorize the things that astonished him and the ways in which he resisted them. He must hold on to these centers of energy. They belong to his interpretation.

In addition to what he does, he will at all essential points seek something to intimate what he is *not* doing. That is to say, he should play his part in such a way that one sees, and with the greatest possible clarity, the alternatives: his playing gives us an intimation of other possibilities, presents but one of the possible variants. He says, for instance: "I'll make you pay for this" and he does *not* say, "I forgive you." He hates his children, and it is not the case that he loves them. He is going down left and not up right. What he does *not* do must be contained in what he does and brought into relief by it. Hence all statements and gestures signify decisions. The character is kept under control and tested. Put it in terms of *not this but that*—such is the formula.

The actor does not let himself be transformed into the man he presents so that nothing of himself is left. He is not Lear, Harpagon, or the good soldier Schweik—he is "showing" them to an audience. He brings their words forward, and that as genuinely as possible. He indicates their way of living as well as his knowledge of men permits. But he does not delude himself (and therewith others) into the belief that he has completely transformed himself. Actors will know what is meant here if one cites as an example of "acting without being completely transformed" what a director does when showing an actor how to perform a certain passage. Such a director does not transform himself—since the role is not his. He underlines the technical side of the business, and preserves the attitude of some one just making a suggestion.

Giving up the idea of complete transformation, the actor brings forward his text, not as an improvisation, but as a *quotation*. At the same time, it is clear that he has to render, in this quotation, all the undertones, all the concrete, plastic detail of full human utterance. His gestures, though they are frankly a *copy* (and not spontaneous), must have the full corporeality of human gestures.

In this sort of acting, where the transformation of the actor is incomplete, three devices can contribute to the alienation of the words and actions of the person presenting them:

1. The adoption of a third person.
2. The adoption of the past tense.
3. The speaking of stage directions and comments.

The adoption of the third person and the past tense enables the actor to attain the correct, distanced attitude. In addition, the actor seeks directions and comments on his text, and in rehearsal he speaks them ("He stood up and said angrily, for he hadn't eaten..." or, "He heard it for the first time, and didn't know whether it was the truth" or, "He smiled and said in all too carefree a manner...") To speak stage directions or commentaries in the third person is to bring two tonalities into collision in such a manner that the second (the text proper) is alienated. The acting, also, is alienated in that it actually happens after being expressed in words, after being announced. The adoption of the past tense places the speaker where he can look back at a statement. The statement is thereby alienated without the speaker's having to assume an unreal standpoint, for, in contrast to the listener, he has read the play through already and (from the end backwards, from the consequences backwards) can better judge a statement than the latter who knows less and is further away from (more "alien" from) the statement.

Through this threefold process the text is alienated in rehearsal and in general will remain so in performance.

As to speaking of the lines, when the speaker addresses himself directly to the audience, he can and must vary his style—in respect to the greater or lesser significance of his various lines. The way witnesses talk in court affords an example; the way they underline, insist on, what they say must be given a special artistic form. If the actor turns to the audience, he must turn the whole way. He must not use the technique of the aside or the old-time soliloquy. To get the full A-effect out of the verse the actor would do well to rehearse the content, for a time, in crude prose, sometimes together with the gestures that belong to the verse. A bold and beautiful verbal architecture itself alienates a text.

Gesture is a subject for further discussion, but it can be said here that feeling, when it is called for, should be *brought out;* that is, it should become gesture. The actor must find a sensuous outward expression for the emotions of his role—*an action,* wherever possible, which reveals what is going on inside. The emotion concerned must *come out,* must be set free, so that it can be given shape and greatness. Special elegance, strength, and charm of gesture have the A-effect. The Chinese actor handles gesture in a masterly fashion. In visibly observing his own movements, he achieves the A-effect.

Whatever the actor renders by way of gesture and verse-speaking must be *ready* and bear the stamp of readiness, finishedness, the stamp of rehearsal. An impression of ease, which means an impression of difficulties overcome, must be given. The actor must permit the audience to take acting—his own art, his mastery of technical problems—lightly. With consummate skill he presents events as in his opinion they may have happened—or may yet happen—in reality. He does not conceal the fact that he has studied all this any more than the acrobat conceals his training. And he underscores the fact that this is his, the actor's account, version, opinion of the events.

Since he does not identify himself with the man he presents, he can see him from a particular, chosen standpoint, can reveal his opinion of him, and bring the spectator, who also was not invited to identify himself with the character, to criticize him.

The standpoint thus assumed is that of social criticism. By his arrangement of events and his interpretation of his role, the actor gradually brings out those things, those traits, that belong to the social realm. His performance thus becomes a colloquy with the audience—to whom he turns—about social conditions. He induces the listener, according to his class, to justify or change these conditions.

It is the aim of the A-effect to alienate that "social gesture" which underlies all events. By "social gesture" is meant the mimetic and gestural expression of social relations between men in a particular epoch.

In recounting events for the benefit of society, in so ordering them that the key is placed in society's hands, a useful device is a written title for each scene. Such titles must have a historical character.

This brings us to a decisive technical feature, of Epic Theatre, the "historification of everyday life."

The actor must play the events of a play as historical events. Historical events happen once for all and are over. They are bound up with particular epochs. People's behavior in these epochs is not merely human and invariable. It has special characteristics. It contains things, as history proceeds, which are repeated, or could be repeated. It is subject to criticism from the standpoint of the following epoch. Constant historical development estranges from us the behavior of those born earlier. Now, the actor has to assume that distance from occurrences and modes of behavior in the present which the historian assumes from occurrences and modes of behavior in the past. He has to alienate these events and people in the same way.

Events and people of the day, of the immediate environment, seem rather natural to us because we are used to them. To alienate them is to make them stand out. The technique of being irritated by customary, obvious, never-questioned events has been carefully built up by science, and there is no reason why art should not take over so infinitely useful an attitude. It is an attitude which, in the realm of science, resulted from a growth in human productivity. In the realm of art, it results from the same source.

As far as emotion is concerned, experiments with the A effect in the German theatre have demonstrated that even this kind of acting arouses emotions, if not the same emotions as those of the conventional theatre. A critical attitude on the part of the spectator is a thoroughly artistic attitude. The A-effect is not as unnatural as it may sound.

Obviously this kind of acting has nothing to do with "stylization" as commonly understood. The leading preference of Epic Theatre, with its A-effect which has the single aim of showing how the world works, to the end that the world may be changed, is precisely for naturalness and earthiness, for humor, and for the renunciation of all the mysticism that still clings to the conventional theatre, a relic of bygone days.

Letter to an Actor

I have been brought to realize that many of my remarks about the theatre are wrongly understood. I realize this above all from those letters and articles which agree with me. I then feel as a mathematician would do if he read: Dear Sir, I am wholly of your opinion that two and two make five. I think that certain remarks are wrongly understood because there were important points which instead of defining I took for granted.

Most of the remarks, if not all, were written as notes to my plays, to allow them to be correctly performed. That gives them a rather dry and practical form, as if a sculptor were writing a matter-of-fact order about the placing of his work: where it should go and on what sort of a base. Those addressed might have expected something about the spirit in which the work was created. They would find it difficult to get that from the order.

For instance the description of virtuosity. Art, of course, cannot survive without artistry, and it becomes important to describe "how it's done." Especially when the arts have undergone a decade and a half of barbarism, as they have here. But it should not for a moment be thought that this is something to be cold-bloodedly practiced and learned. Not even speech training, which is something that the bulk of actors badly need, can be done cold-bloodedly, in a mechanical way.

Thus the actor must be able to speak clearly, and this is not just a matter of vowels and consonants but also (and primarily) a matter of the meaning. Unless he learns at the same time how to bring out the meaning of his lines he will simply be articulating like a machine and destroying the sense with his "beautiful speaking voice." And within clarity there are all kinds of degrees and distinctions. Different social classes have different kinds of clarity: a peasant may speak clearly in comparison with a second peasant, but his clarity will not be the same as that of an engineer. This means that actors learning to speak must always take care to see that their voice is pliant and flexible. They must never lose sight of the way people really talk.

There is also the problem of dialect. Here again technique needs to be linked up with more general considerations. Our theatrical language is based on High German, but over the years it has grown very mannered and stilted, and has developed into a quite special sort of High German which is no longer so flexible as High German everyday speech. There is nothing against the use of "heightened" language on the stage, that is to say against the theatre's evolving its own stage language. But it must always be lively, varied and capable of further evolution. The people speak dialect. Dialect is the medium of their most intimate expression. How can our actors portray the people and address them unless they go back to

Brecht on Theatre: The Development of an Aesthetic. Edited and translated by John Willett. New York: Hill and Wang, 1966, pp. 233-236. Footnote annotation by John Willett. Copyright © 1957, 1963, and 1964 by Suhrkamp Verlag, Frankfurt am Main. This translation and notes © by John Willett. Reprinted with the permission of Hill and Wang, Inc.

Written 1951. The actor addressed has not been identified. This is perhaps the most important of Brecht's modifications of his extreme theoretical position. The doctrine laid down in the "Short Organum" were by all accounts neither discussed nor put into practice in the *Berliner Ensemble.* Regine Lutz, one of its principal actresses from 1949 on, told me in 1957 that she had never read Brecht's theoretical works.

their own dialect, and allow its inflections to permeate the High German of the stage? Another example. The actor must learn how to economize his voice: he must not grow hoarse. But he must also be able to portray a man seized by passion who is speaking or shouting hoarsely. So his exercises have to contain an element of acting. We shall get empty, superficial, formalistic, mechanical acting if in our technical training we forget for a moment that it is the actor's duty to portray living people.

This brings me to your question whether acting is not turned into something purely technical and more or less inhuman by my insistence that the actor oughtn't to be completely transformed into the character portrayed but should, as it were, stand alongside it criticizing and approving. In my view this is not the case. Such an impression must be due to my way of writing, which takes too much for granted. To hell with my way of writing. Of course the stage of a realistic theatre must be peopled by live, three-dimensional, self-contradictory people, with all their passions, unconsidered utterances and actions. The stage is not a hothouse or a zoological museum full of stuffed animals. The actor has to be able to create such people (and if you could attend our productions you would see them; and they succeed in being people because of our principles, not in spite of them!).

There is, however, a complete fusion of the actor with his role which leads to his making the character seem so natural, so impossible to conceive any other way, that the audience has simply to accept it as it stands, with the result that a completely sterile atmosphere of "tout comprendre c'est tout pardonner" is engendered, as happened most notably under Naturalism.

We who are concerned to change human as well as ordinary nature must find means of "shedding light on" the human being at that point where he seems capable of being changed by society's intervention. This means a quite new attitude on the part of the actor, for his art has hitherto been based on the assumption that people are what they are, and will remain so whatever it may cost society or themselves: "indestructibly human," "you can't change human nature," and so on. Both emotionally and intellectually he needs to decide his attitude to his scene and his part. The change demanded of the actor is not a cold and mechanical operation: art has nothing cold or mechanical about it, and this change is an artistic one. It cannot take place unless he has real contact with his new audience and a passionate concern for human progress.

So our theatre's significant stage groupings are not just an effect or a "purely aesthetic" phenomenon, conducive to formal beauty. They are a part of a hugely conceived theatre for the new social order, and they cannot be achieved without deep understanding and passionate support of the new structure of human relations.

I cannot rewrite all the notes to my plays. Please take these lines as a provisional appendix to them, an attempt to catch up on what had been wrongly assumed.

That leaves me with one thing still to explain: the relatively quiet style of acting which sometimes strikes visitors to the *Berliner Ensemble*. This has nothing to do with forced objectivity, for the actors adopt an attitude to their parts; and nothing to do with mock-rationalism, for reason never flings itself cold-bloodedly into the battle; it is simply due to the fact that plays are no longer subjected to red-hot "temperamental" acting. True art is stimulated by its material. On these occasions when the recipient thinks he is observing coldness it is just that he has encountered the mastery without which it would not be art at all.

HELENE WEIGEL

(b. 1900)

The actress who best exemplifies the full artistic possibilities of Bertolt Brecht's theories of acting is his widow, Helene Weigel. Born in Vienna, she began her career in Frankfurt in 1918 as Marie in Büchner's *Woyzek*. In 1924 she appeared in the *Staatstheater* in Berlin in Brecht's *Trommeln in der Nacht* and then subsequently at the *Deutsches Theater* Berlin, where she met Brecht for the first time. In the middle years of the 1920's she was an actress of great promise, playing in the leading Berlin theatres and on radio, where she appeared as Lady Macbeth in 1927. In the same year she was in Brecht's *In the Jungle of Cities* and played Widow Begbick in the highly experimental production of *A Man's a Man* at the *Volks-buehne*. In 1928, she and Brecht were married.

During the following year Weigel appeared as servant-messenger in a striking version of *Oedipus Rex* and *Oedipus at Colonus* played in one evening under the direction of Leopold Jessner with Fritz Kortner as Oedipus. In a dialogue about acting written at this time Brecht described her performance as bearing the "hallmarks of this new way of acting" he was working out with the "most talented of the younger generation of actors . . . Weigel, Peter Lorre, Oscar Homolka, Carola Neher, and Busch." He praised her "wholly unemotional and penetrating voice," "her astonishment," and her ritual gesture of lamentation, but pointed out that only a "few connoisseurs" appreciated her art because most of those in the audience looked upon the actor's contribution as only "an opportunity for new sensations." At the turn of the decade she worked with Brecht on his didactic "learning pieces."

In 1933 she and Brecht went into exile, and for more than a decade there were few performances by this distinguished actress. In a tribute to his wife called "Weigel's descent into fame," Brecht spoke movingly of her skill as an actress and also of her willingness over these years, "to throw up a brilliant career to take part in little-advertised political performances, to team up with mixed companies of amateurs."

When they returned to Germany in the forties and founded the *Berliner Ensemble* in 1949, Helene Weigel resumed her career. With this world-famous company she has appeared in the title roles in *Mother Courage and Her Children, The Mother*, as Teresa in *Senora Carrar's Rifles*, Natella in *The Caucasian Chalk Circle*, Judith Keith in *Fear and Misery of the Third Reich*, Volumnia in *Coriolanus*, and many others. Her Mother Courage, which can be studied in great detail in the *Modelbuch* for the play and in *Theaterarbeit*, conveyed to audiences in Germany and in London what Epic acting could be. "To a perceptible degree," writes Eric Bentley, "Miss Weigel stands outside the role and in a sense does not even look like Mother Courage. She is cool, relaxed, and ironical. Yet with great precision of movement and intonation she intimates exactly what Mother Courage was like. The art and beauty of the performance bring home to us the awful sadness and relevance of Mother Courage's career. . . . At the very least, Helene Weigel's performance is a lesson in the craft of acting. . . ."

Some of her lessons on the craft of acting, especially Epic acting, may be gleaned from the following comments on observation and tone. Represented here along with Helene Weigel are two other actresses, Therese Giehse, whose Mother Courage Brecht directed in Munich, and a younger actress, Angelika Hurwicz, whose Dumb Kattrin in *Mother Courage* he deeply admired. These three communicate what it means to be an actress in the theatre of Bertolt Brecht.

[314]

Rehearsing the Part

QUESTION: How important is observation? When you make certain gestures or movements in playing a part, do you remember where you got them from?

ANSWER: That differs from part to part. Often I notice something and know right off that I'll be able to use it in a specific part. But usually one doesn't know where the inspiration comes from. Observation and imagination frequently complement each other. That was how it was, for instance, in Gorky's *Mother*. The fact that the character Pelagea Vlassova has a drooping left shoulder made me develop a very halting way of walking. A person built that way can't take firm strides. Or take Mother Courage's moneybag: that's a conspicuous prop one can exploit in the part. Since the bag makes a clicking sound when you shut it, you discover a great many ways of doing so. There's a quick, easy way of closing it, or quite a different way, as when the money is returned at Kattrin's burial. Once—in the scene in which Yvette appears with the old colonel—I developed a kind of aria of clicking sounds. Observation also helped me develop Mother Courage's various intonations. In Scene 9, for example—in the bitter mountain cold among the fir trees, after Mother Courage has suffered disastrous business reverses and sees begging as her only way out—her voice grows dull and lifeless. She continues to speak in dialect, but her tone grows more and more monotonous. I built that up from many observations I have made over the years—in people I have seen on the street or under similar circumstances.

QUESTION: How do our younger actors feel about the power of observation?

ANSWER: In general, most of them are afraid to admit that they use it, because unfortunately observation has fallen into disrepute as an ineffective and purely rational method.

Often the young people stand onstage during a rehearsal and wait for a word that will bail them out. Of course a director, with a mere hint, can give a talented person a great deal. Then one's own creativity often deepens this, even if the specific point again fails to come off at later rehearsals. What is important is that the imagination have enough material to begin working on.

QUESTION: Aren't there talented actors who offer insights on their own?

ANSWER: Yes, but when you have had bad luck, no one notices it—either because the director is incompetent, or because he's just too busy noticing other things, while you may be playing a scene in the most diverse ways. Only at later rehearsals is it impossible for the director to overlook the way in which an actor has worked something out. But it often happens, for instance, that in a given scene one doesn't know in which direction to turn. That's where the outsider's—the director's—judgment is needed.

Sometimes, though, one feels at a dead end. For instance, you've worked out a certain amount of stage business for a part, but it only comes to you in a jumbled, chopped-up way. Then at a rehearsal you discover which bits of business are right and which are not. And then—how can I express this in sensible terms?—you simply let yourself go. You "go to town," so to speak. That's how you bring all the many things together under one hat, rejecting some of them or adding new ones. For this process we've introduced special rehearsals—full-company rehearsals as well as run-throughs.

QUESTION: What about picking up intonation?

ANSWER: I have to answer your question in the negative. An actor who fails to pick

Bertolt Brecht and others, Eds.: *Theaterarbeit*. Dresden: VVV Dresdner Verlag, 1952, pp. 349-353. Translated from the German by Joseph M. Bernstein.

up intonations is in real trouble. He can't synchronize with and develop what his partner says. In my own case, I always gauge my intonation from that of my partner. If the latter takes no notice of it, that's his failing, and I can't help him out of his difficulty. How can I answer a question I have never heard? This tends to slow down rehearsals considerably. It then takes quite a while before the actors achieve smooth repartee, which means genuine dialogue. For if the actor playing opposite me doesn't heed my intonations, how can I myself notice whether they are right? And that's why I'm not entirely sure of my lines until later, because I can't learn a part by heart until I know my partner and can gauge my own intonations according to his.

QUESTION: What about the whole question of diction. Does one have to review and improve one's speech technique from time to time, or can one just go on speaking once one has learned the right way?

ANSWER: I would say that one must never stop working at one's diction. As long as I have been in the theatre, I have rarely let a day go by without doing speech exercises. You can always find time for that. I, for instance, often practice speaking while I wash. Diction is a necessity, an absolutely essential tool—without it you simply cannot act. You must deepen your understanding of speech; then you can extend your range. In *Mother Courage,* for instance, in the first song I deliberately added a half-tone.

One thing that gives me a lot of trouble is reciting poetry. This has been sorely neglected in my generation, and now poetry in our country is at a very low point. Verse has been completely "freed"; every effort is made to reduce it to prose so as to analyze its meaning. But no attention has been paid to the reverse process, to making poetry sound poetic again, by capturing the proper rhythms. That's why poetry recitation today is usually nothing but a chopped-up version of speaking prose.

QUESTION: After the fiftieth or hundredth performance of a play, does one's acting really become automatic and unfocused?

ANSWER: When a play has been poorly rehearsed you may get a great many rough spots. And that's when a performance really begins to get boring. But in a good performance, one that has been well rehearsed and in which everyone is on top of his part, something altogether new is added. There are distinct differences in the way one recites a line, even a single word. By reacting to your partner's subtle changes in tone, you may make a sentence come alive again and virtually re-create it without ever blurring or distorting the overall performance. But you can't attain that freedom until you've given a great many performances.

It's bad to work with people who don't concentrate. Most often lack of concentration is found in young people. But concentration too is a matter of learning, of rehearsing. One must make a determined effort to avoid working mechanically or in a bored way; one should give one's lines scrupulously even if one has to rehearse the same sentence over and over again.

THERESE GIEHSE

The Actor's Resources

QUESTION: What about learning how to observe? Do you have to study that or not?
ANSWER: It depends on your talent. If you have to make a study of what is funny,

Bertolt Brecht and others, Eds.: *Theaterarbeit.* Dresden: VVV Dresdner Verlag, 1952, pp. 353-359. Translated from the German by Joseph M. Bernstein.

for instance, and don't see it right away, there's no talent there. Then in the course of rehearsing you sort out your reactions; you know why you do a thing in one way or another.

QUESTION: In the gestures or movements you make while acting, do you remember why you make them? Do you know where they come from?

ANSWER: Let's take an example. When you want to explain something to an actor, you say: "Once in a railway station I recall seeing a man who did this or that in such-and-such a way...." Imagination makes use of things that are "there," plucking them out of the memory. With imagination one can do marvelous things. Chaplin is an example of that.

QUESTION: How do you react when you watch young actors, beginners?

ANSWER: Every older generation really says: We were better; that wouldn't have happened in our day. Today I find that actors come to rehearsals, they've learned their lines, and they simply "let the part take over." It was never that way with me.

QUESTION: Does that mean the actor has to "offer" something?

ANSWER: Definitely! The actor must have something to offer. It must come out of his own critical sense.

QUESTION: When it is said that an actor must be proficient in his craft, what does that cover?

ANSWER: He has to control his body; he has to master time and space. In the latter case it means that it's not the director who has to tell you where to stand. Because then if you make a false step, the whole space is ruined. An actor has to be able to gauge space. He must be able to do all that, but the director has to check him on that.

QUESTION: In our theatre we stress that a scene must be acted out in terms of plot and not just serve as a pretext for a theatrical commentary or illustration. It seems to me that in the past few decades plot—story line—has been acted out less and less. Is that so?

ANSWER: Yes, that's true of bad theatre. Good actors will act out the story if they're not such "solo players" that they're tuned in only to themselves.

QUESTION: Don't many actors rush through the plot itself so as to get to moments in which they can let loose emotionally?

ANSWER: That indicates lack of intelligence, a serious shortcoming for an actor.

QUESTION: In his reminiscences Stanislavsky tells how—when he was around forty —he concentrated so much on stage business that he found it somewhat difficult to get into the spirit of the character he was portraying. Have you ever had any such experiences?

ANSWER: My experience is I rarely falter during the first ten performances; but that isn't so after the hundredth performance, when parts are played automatically and one doesn't have to rehearse them anymore.

QUESTION: If you want to portray a certain character, how do you work yourself into the part? What do you do? Aren't there two things here, and aren't they contra-dictory? First, you make yourself over into a character and identify completely with it. Second, you want to criticize it. But at that moment you no longer fully understand it; you no longer identify with it. Isn't that a contradiction?

ANSWER: I think one needs both processes.

QUESTION: Close together or simultaneously?

ANSWER: On your first reading of the part you identify with it. But then when you learn it you become critical. Take, for instance, the way to learn a part by heart. We've had to discuss this a lot with young actors. Usually they learn the lines by heart first and then create the role. That isn't right. I can learn the lines by heart only if I know what the character is like. Before I do, I can't remember a single line.

QUESTION: You have rightly complained about our young actors' inability to control their voices—to raise or lower them.

ANSWER: The raising or lowering of the voice is the basis of dialogue. Otherwise one might as well give a lecture.

QUESTION: Aren't two things needed in lowering one's voice: first, the meaning must come through; second, the sound must also come through musically?

ANSWER: Yes, but not only the sound; the temperament too. The audience must know why that tone is used. If someone says: "I can't tell you that," the answer, "Why can't you tell me anything?" must consciously include the thought: Why can't she? One can reproduce the same tone or deliberately shift it into a lower key. It's not only tone and diction; it's what the other person wanted, it's the whole human interplay that must be brought out.

QUESTION: A great actor once told me one has to freshen up one's speaking ability from time to time, just as a director freshens up certain scenes. Is there anything to that? Can one speak the way one swims or rides a bicycle, or is speech different?

ANSWER: He's right about that. But it may also be a matter of fatigue. At this moment, for instance, my throat feels tired. It's nothing serious, but it would be a good thing for me if I didn't have to speak for two weeks. If I do, I'll get symptoms of tiredness: I'll stammer and fluff lines.

QUESTION: In reciting poetry—especially classical poetry—do you identify various schools of delivery? Or does it depend purely on the individual?

ANSWER: I think that now it's purely an individual matter. A while back, say, fifteen or twenty years ago, the Krastel school in Vienna (the *Burgtheater*) was very well known. Theirs was an intelligent, attractive way of delivering poetry. It sounded beautiful. Kainz was very good at that sort of thing. I too am a product of that school. I didn't know Krastel personally but I did go to his school.

QUESTION: In reciting classical verse, do you use traditional rhythms or do you have different ways of doing it?

ANSWER: Different ways. If I find that the meter is there for a purpose, I think one has to let it "ring out." Sometimes I feel the meter is there for the meaning; on other occasions I feel one can just recite one line after another in rhythm. For instance, in Goethe's *Faust:* Martha Schwerdtlein's first soliloquy ("May God forgive my dear husband, he gave me no comfort") is not in "ringing verse." Goethe wanted the verse to flow smoothly but he also wanted to bring out the meaning. In a passage like that one shouldn't be led astray by the rhyme; the meaning is vital. But in Schiller there are passages that, in my opinion, are deliberately composed, like a piece of music.

QUESTION: It seems to me that often within the same scene Shakespeare resorts to verse only because it fits his overall pattern and then again the verse is used for a purpose. What do you think?

ANSWER: I think one should use verse for its effect only when it is necessary. Particularly in Shakespeare. Otherwise I feel one can recite it metrically.

QUESTION: Must a good actor be able to play his part under all conditions? Does he need a certain length of time for working into it, or must he be able at any time to play the part he has learned?

ANSWER: If he really plays the part—at any time. It just requires a certain period of concentration.

QUESTION: Does this involve a so-called creative process?
ANSWER: No. One must concentrate. I don't like stage fright. I think genuine stage fright indicates a certain lack of talent. One must have joy in acting; one must *want* to speak his lines. When something is ready, it is bound to come out.

ANGELIKA HURWICZ
Six Parts

When I worked on Dumb Kattrin, in *Mother Courage,* I learned the difference between realism and naturalism. If I had tried to show that my muteness came from a mutilated tongue—one line in Scene 6 of *Mother Courage* refers to this: "A soldier stuck something in her mouth when she was little"—that is, if in uttering sounds I had visibly curled my tongue against my teeth, as deaf-mutes do, my facial expression might have seemed slightly idiotic. But under no circumstances could I give an impression of mental retardation. It was essential for me to show that intelligent people, born to be happy, are crippled by war. So in this case I had to sacrifice accuracy of individual portrayal for the sake of the overall truth.

Besides, this part was good training in going beyond the acting methods that have dominated and still dominate our stage, ever since Goethe's day—methods that stress the spoken word. How often we hear it said: that actor doesn't know how to move. But it's not because of his lack of grace; it's because the actor in question doesn't know that silent gestures and movements can be just as effective as spoken words.

As the [German] term for bit part (*charge*) implies—the word means a burden, load, necessary chore—a bit part fulfills a definite role in a play. It must bind the threads of the action. But a great playwright gives such a part a life or character of its own, even if he originally created it solely because of its function in the play. Gorky's Anna Onoshenkova is such a part. In a few brief appearances she has to convey obsequiousness, her own opinions, love interest, jealousy, greed, and thirteen years of oppression and rebellion. Mind you, all this in addition to her spying and gossiping as well as her dramatic function. But she has very little time at her disposal· to project her personality. Hence playing a bit part presents a problem. Actors have whole acts or scenes in which to play big parts; they have scenes that run for many pages of text in which to bring out a single mood or idea. In playing a bit part one frequently conveys three thoughts in a single sentence and must not allow a single movement to be random—otherwise valuable material is frittered away.

Mother Blitzer (in Lenz's *Der Hofmeister*) is a comic part. In my opinion comedy is the most difficult genre to analyze. When you play a tragic part well, audience participation at various performances remains at a rather constant level; in comedy you can play a part equally well, but on one evening you will get big laughs and at the next performance almost none. In the broadest terms comedy is based on the effect of contrast. Anyone who gets terribly excited over a trifle, as Mother Blitzer does over a broken coffee set, is funny. But to achieve this effect the actress has to play Mother Blitzer's excitement as seriously as any heroine in tragedy. That is, she must sound as if she were genuinely shattered. For the comic figure does not perceive the situation in the same way as the spectator. She is unhappy about a

Bertolt Brecht and others, Eds.: *Theaterarbeit*. Dresden: VVV Dresdner Verlag, 1952, pp. 369-371. Translated from the German by Joseph M. Bernstein.

trivial thing because she is motivated by another set of values. But since one has to portray unhappiness seriously in order to achieve a comic effect, I find comedy roles as interesting as serious ones. They have to cover the same broad range of emotional nuances as serious parts.

As Mother Blitzer I used the Saxon dialect not really for the sake of comedy but to indicate the locale, Halle, and to contrast the uneducated native inhabitants with the "well-born" students.

Here at last as Emma, Eva, and the Prioress (in Brecht's *Herr Puntila and His Man Matti*) I had a chance to play several parts in one play—unfortunately not alongside one another but in succession. But in doing these three parts I got a somewhat better insight into the differences between humor, comedy, and the grotesque. Smuggler Emma had to be played with gentle humor, even though everything she says is a critique of the prevailing social relationships. Eva, the landowner's daughter, is comic because she has fallen in love with a chauffeur yet can never forget her inbred arrogance; besides, she is intellectually inferior to the chauffeur. To bring this out, I had to stress the naïveté of a country girl whose notions of love have come from reading sentimental novels. The Prioress in Scene 8 is grotesque. The play's climax in that scene, in which Puntilla, after a series of tricks, pulls the most shocking surprise of all by betrothing his daughter to the chauffeur in full view of his society guests, seemed to me to justify the grotesque. There is another consideration: in bourgeois comedy, outrage over marriage to one's social inferior was highly comic; in modern comedy, with its critique of society, the comedy must have grotesque traits.

X. ENGLAND AND IRELAND

The Heritage of Actors

Despite changes in style and histrionic theory, acting in England from 1660 to the beginning of the nineteenth century was part of one continuous tradition. The natural acting of Macklin did not precipitate an era of realistic playing, and the modifications introduced by Garrick did not essentially change what we have come to call the "grand manner" in acting. Although the morality and sentimentality of the growing middle-class influenced the content of eighteenth century drama, the basic form of popular plays remained unchanged. As long, therefore, as tragedy remained a poetic presentation of noble, high flown sentiments, and comedy a pattern of upper-class manners, acting rested within the confines of elocution, standardized gesture, and heightened character creation. Only with the upsurge of industrialism and democracy during the nineteenth century did a new dramatic form evolve and a new style of acting gradually replace the traditional one.

Important shifts in the composition of the audience, changes in the architecture of the theatre, and improvements in scene design accelerated the evolution in acting that occurred during the nineteenth century. Gradually the vigorous, colorful, somewhat rowdy audience of the late 1700's was replaced by polite, respectable theatre-goers. Through the efforts of high-minded actors like William Charles Macready, prostitutes and gamblers were expelled from the theatres. Violent democratic struggles, such as the riot for Old Prices at Covent Garden during Kemble's reign, gave way to a propriety which took its cue from Queen Victoria. This politer audience moved to the front of the theatre to sit in stalls which replaced the numerous backless benches of the pit. The actor was now faced by spectators capable of enjoying quieter theatrical effects which would have bored the old "pittites."

Physically the theatre was transformed. Little by little the apron disappeared; the proscenium became a frame within which the scene was played; gas lighting replaced candles and provided the opportunity for more elaborate scenic effects. Realism invaded the scene with the appearance of the boxed set containing sides and ceiling, real doors, and genuine properties. Historical accuracy in costuming and settings became the hallmark of the big gala productions of the era. Scholarly interest in stage production initiated by John Philip Kemble early in the century was carried on by Macready and by Charles Kean (1811-1868), who was almost archeological in his interest, and culminated in the spectacular productions by Henry Irving and Beerbohm Tree (1853-1917) at the end of the century.

Although the great actors still made their mark in Shakespeare and eighteenth century comedy and sentimental drama, the old repertory was diminishing in importance. Contemporary plays, the native and French melodramas so characteristic of the period, and the faded poetic tragedies of Bulwer-Lytton and Sheridan Knowles were popular fare. The first half of the century probably produced the most undistinguished dramatic writing in the history of the English stage. From the mid-sixties on, however, the beginnings of a new direction were felt in the scripts of Thomas William Robertson (1829-1871). Realistic drama was beginning to impose its point of view and style.

Although the nineteenth century witnessed the decay of the old acting tradition and the emergence of a new mode of stage performance, it was, like its predecessor, a century of actors. In many ways it was the era of the "star." The first decades of the 1800's opened with the celebrated members of the Kemble family still dominating the theatrical scene. Sarah Siddons filled audiences with awe at her majestic tragic performances. John Philip Kemble, statuesque and dignified, played and managed the productions at Covent Garden. But Mrs. Siddons retired in 1812, and John Kemble gave his farewell performance in *Coriolanus* in 1817. With their retirement, classic, traditional acting of the so-called "teapot school" began to disappear from the stage. The meteoric appearance of Edmund Kean in 1814, wrote Leigh Hunt, hastened Kemble's resignation from the stage. His day was over, for Kean, the erratic theatrical genius, represented the romantic movement as it found expression in acting. He was hailed by the romantic critics Leigh Hunt and William Hazlitt. Against the style of Kemble, whom Hunt described as "external and artificial," Hazlitt extolled "the stamp and freshness of Nature" in Kean.

The romantic violence, energy, and variety in both speech and action which marked Kean's acting was widely and assiduously imitated. The defects of his style, the excessive energy followed by uncalled-for languor, his hoarse voice and unique vocal interpretations, although criticized even by his admirers, were adopted by many lesser actors. The physically energetic aspects of Kean's style had been anticipated by George Frederick Cooke (1756-1812), who with Kean influenced the American Edwin Forrest. Kean's style was also imitated by Junius Brutus Booth (1796-1852), whose sons achieved both fame and infamy in the United States. Despite the fact that Kean's acting had destroyed "the Kemble religion" for some, there were many followers of the Kemble school throughout the first half of the century. In the lighter roles of Mercutio, Laertes, or Cassio, Charles Kemble (1775-1854) maintained the niceties of his brother. His daughter, the charming Fanny Kemble, indulged in dance postures and imitated unsuccessfully the drawn-out pronunciations of her great aunt, Mrs. Siddons. Charles Mayne Young (1777-1856), a protégé of John Philip Kemble, continued to work in the tradition of his master. Although she had some of the warmth of the new romantic acting, Miss Eliza O'Neill (1791-1872) recalled the Siddons' tradition.

If we may say that the Kembles, especially John Philip, harked back to the acting of Quin and Barton Booth, and Kean perhaps to Macklin and Garrick, William Charles Macready modified these two older traditions and added a new element which became more and more characteristic of acting as the century progressed. In scholarly attitudes and gentlemanly pretensions Macready, the new idol, recalled Kemble, but his violent variations in speech and gesture took something from Kean. His original contribution, however, was the infusion of domestic touches into high tragedy. Hazlitt noted that "Mr. Macready, sometimes, to express uneasiness and agitation, composes his cravat, as he would in a drawing-room. This is, we think, neither graceful nor natural in extraordinary situations." To Hazlitt his playing was "natural, easy, and forcible. Indeed, we suspect some part of it were too natural...." His leveling down of high sentiment to the manner of the Victorian drawing-room presages the direction both drama and acting were to take later in the century.

These developments in acting and drama, which moved toward the increasingly domestic and melodramatic, coincided with changes in theatrical conditions. In 1843 the long standing monopoly of the two patent theatres, Drury Lane and Covent Garden, came to an end. The spirit of freedom of enterprise invaded the theatre. From then on legitimate drama was no longer the sole property of the two patent houses but the stock-in-trade of all the theatres. Although Kemble, Kean, and Macready had done almost all of their London playing at either Drury Lane or Covent Garden, the fortunes of these two houses had been steadily going downhill. Their great size (both had been enlarged at the turn of the century) made them commercially unprofitable and unsuitable for the increasingly intimate acting that was developing. After 1843 Covent Garden became an opera house, and Drury Lane continued a precarious existence occasionally playing Shakespeare but more frequently exhibiting such spectacles as *Uncle Tom's Cabin.*

During the last years of the patent houses important movements toward realism were being made in the so-called illegitimate houses, where one of the early actress-managers, the lovely Madame Vestris (Eliza Lucy Bartalozzi, 1797-1856), later the wife of Charles Mathews, was carrying realism into comic burlesques. After 1843 many of the old minor theatres came to the fore to raise the standard of fine drama. Samuel Phelps (1804-1878), formerly an actor under Macready, mounted a number of notable Shakespearean productions at the Sadler's Wells, a theatre in a bad neighborhood. Edmund Kean's son, Charles, unable to successfully reproduce the impassioned acting of his father, provided the Princess Theatre, which he managed, with excellent, historically accurate Shakespearean productions. The Haymarket Theatre, the best of the older minor houses, became the most fashionable theatre in London. Under the management of Benjamin Webster (1789-1882) and John Baldwin Buckstone (1802-1879), this house became notable for comedy with realistic overtones. It was at the Haymarket that Macready made his round of farewells to the stage in 1850. Here, too, many American artists played: the Cushman sisters, Mrs. Mowatt, E. L. Davenport, James Hackett, and later Edwin Booth. The Haymarket housed the phenomenally successful production of *Our American Cousin,* in which Edward Askew Sothern (1826-1881), as Lord Dundreary, set a new mode of eccentric comedy characterization. The increasing number of legitimate theatrical houses enabled actors to move from one theatre to another, presenting their special roles and interpretations wherever they performed.

The pioneering of Charles Fechter (1824-1879), Dion Boucicault, Mme. Vestris, E. A. Sothern, and Charles Mathews (1803-1878) paved the way for the Bancrofts and Tom Robertson, who together formed the first significant realistic theatre group in London.

From the seeds of realism in burlesques, melodramas, and sentimental comedies, Tom Robertson, as actor, director, and most important as dramatist, produced a native realism. At the Prince of Wales Theatre Robertson did more than provide Marie Wilton Bancroft and Squire Bancroft with plays; he imparted to them as actors the same qualities that he was trying to achieve in his writing. John Hare (1844-1921), one of the actors with the Bancrofts, wrote of Robertson: "As nature was the basis of his own work, so he sought to make actors understand it should be theirs. He thus founded a school of natural acting which completely revolutionized the then existing methods, and by so doing did incalculable good to the stage." Although Robertson was the first to turn to the life around him for his plays, his "cup-and-saucer" comedies, eminently suited to the talents of the Bancroft group, touched only the surface of life with their humorous realism.

[323]

Commercial theatre in the last decades of the nineteenth century focuses chiefly on the figure of Sir Henry Irving, who brought his brilliant individuality to the playing of Shakespeare and melodrama. Under his direction the Lyceum Theatre became the home of productions unsurpassed for excellent acting, staging, scenery, costumes, and music. In addition to the charming Ellen Terry, Irving had in his company at various times Johnston Forbes-Robertson (1853-1937), considered the Hamlet of his day, the romantic William Terriss (d. 1897), John Martin-Harvey (1863-1944) and others.

Sir Herbert Beerbohm Tree, another of the era's actor-managers, staged productions with an extravagant superficial realism that surpassed Irving's efforts. Sir George Alexander (George Samson, 1858-1918), formerly an actor with Irving, but more receptive to contemporary playwrights than Irving, also belonged to this essentially nineteenth century group of actor-managers. These men were the last exponents of lavish, historical spectacles. Their acting was a composite of the main currents of nineteenth century histrionics—the emotionalism of Kean, the domestic refinement of Macready, and the surface realism of the Bancroft school. They applied their art to plays of Shakespeare, now waning in popularity, as well as to the new plays of Sir Arthur Wing Pinero and Henry Arthur Jones. Excellent as these men were, their methods brought the dangers of superficial extravagance, long runs, and actor-manager domination.

Revolt against commercialism and artificiality in England centered largely around the plays of Henrik Ibsen. Shocking and unacceptable to both the respectable theatre public and the big managers, Ibsen's plays, penetrating far beneath the gentlemanly realism of the English stage, were performed by individual crusaders, Janet Achurch (1846-1916), Charles Charington, Elizabeth Robins, and others. With *Ghosts* in 1891, Jacob Thomas Grein (1862-1935) initiated the Independent Theatre, kindred to Antoine's *Théâtre Libre*. George Bernard Shaw, whose first play, *Widowers' Houses,* was produced by Grein, officiated as the high priest of Ibsenism. His comments on the acting in Ibsen's plays at that period suggest that the refined, native realism was inadequate for the interpretation of the dynamic Ibsen.

Although the Independent Theatre expired in 1897, having launched Shaw, produced Zola, and sponsored a visit of Lugné Poë's *Théâtre de l'Oeuvre,* it was the inspiration of the numerous independent, experimental movements that followed. The Incorporated Stage Society, one of the earliest "Sunday Societies," produced the plays of Shaw, Ibsen, and Granville-Barker. Harley Granville-Barker went on to direct his simplified, experimental productions at the Court Theatre and at the Savoy. The older Elizabethan Stage Society, under William Poel (1852-1920), produced Shakespeare under simulated Elizabethan stage conditions. Sir Philip Ben Greet (1856-1936) organized a group to tour in Shakespearean productions, and Sir Frank Benson, rejecting the facsimile scenic presentations of Irving and Tree, re-established the repertory system using modest décor. The Phoenix, The Pioneers, The Play Actors Society, and many other groups continued the experimental tradition of the Independent Theatre.

Following the ideas that inspired the symbolist poets and dramatists and gave rise to the theories of theatrical synthesis advocated by the Wagnerian Adolphe Appia, Edward Gordon Craig, son of Ellen Terry, called for imagination and beauty in the theatre. Although Craig exerted his influence largely on theatrical design and production, he wanted most to release the imagination of the actor. Not unlike Craig was the Irish poet William Butler Yeats, who tried to establish a poetic, symbolist theatre in Ireland. He failed in this aim, but succeeded in aiding the development of the popular realistic Abbey Theatre, which produced a core of fine Irish actors and provided a theatre for the plays of John Millington Synge and Sean O'Casey.

The nineteenth century, thus, found the actor searching for the illusion of reality on the stage. Fidelity to the surface of everyday life became the ideal. Characterization built up with realistic byplay replaced elocution and standardized gestures from the illustrated guidebooks. Although William Archer's important study of the actor's emotion in *Masks or Faces?* was based on an eighteenth-century controversy, the problem assumed new importance for actors devoted to realistic playing. Archer wrote: "Character acting, which may be defined as mimetic realism, the minute and unconventional reproduction of observed idiosyncrasies, is to be regarded as the distinguishing feature of the period."

By the end of the century, acting began to seem too confined by the demands for realistic delineation of individual personalities. Of Henry Irving's Richard III a critic wrote that "nothing offends and all is artistic and as nearly as possible real. Where, however, is tragedy? It is gone. Richard III is not now a tragic role. It is what is conventionally called 'a character part!'" Of Forbes-Robertson's Macbeth, the same critic complained: "Our actors in tragedy now 'speak in a monstrous little voice,' are most courteous and well bred and loath, apparently, to do anything that might not decently be done in a modern drawing-room.... Pleased as we are, we have ceased to be thrilled."

To satisfy the desire for magnificence, poetry, and the terror of deeply felt tragic acting, Craig and Yeats turned to symbolism and verse while others turned to the probing realism associated with the theatre of Ibsen. These innovations, imposed upon nineteenth-century refined realism, provided the basis upon which the twentieth-century British theatre has devised an electic histrionic art.

In the first half of the twentieth-century, theatre and acting in England as elsewhere were part of an elaborate network of numerous commercial theatres, experimental repertory companies, and interesting semiprofessional and amateur groups. Many of England's fine actors received their training with the independent groups begun at the turn of the century. To those already mentioned must be added the phenomenal Old Vic, transformed from an old, vulgar, degraded theatre by Miss Emma Cons and her niece Lilian Baylis into the home of Shakespeare and opera in English. Here Sybil Thorndike, Edith Evans, Flora Robson, John Gielgud, Laurence Olivier, Ralph Richardson, and Maurice Evans achieved their early fame and did notable work in the years before and after World War II. Also with Sir Barry Jackson's Birmingham Repertory Theatre, his Malvern Festival, and at the Shakespeare Memorial Theatre in Stratford, actors of note have learned their art.

When in 1956 the English Stage Company took over the Royal Court Theatre, where Granville-Barker and Shaw had worked early in the century, a veritable renaissance of British playwriting followed. Although primarily thought of as a playwright's theatre by its inspirational director, the late George Devine, who gave their first productions to John Osborne, John Arden, Arnold Wesker, Ann Jellicoe, N. F. Simpson, Edward Bond—it was also a center for a new breed of English actor. Here were heard the young angry voices and "non-u" speech of Kenneth Haigh, Albert Finney, and Nicol Williamson. It was also the theatre where Sir Laurence Olivier linked himself with the new generation in Osborne's *The Entertainer* and Joan Plowright starred in Wesker's *Roots*.

About this time Joan Littlewood's intense exploration of acting in improvisations and vocal and physical exercises and of new writers brought her East End Theatre Workshop an Arts Council grant, appearances at the Paris International Theatre Festival, and even the commercial success she shunned.

Further transformation of the English scene took place in 1960 when Peter Hall, newly appointed director of the Royal Shakespeare Company, opened the Aldwych Theatre as the London experimental branch that would save the Shake- spearean productions at Stratford by "refracting them" through the modern sen- sibility. Out of this contact of old and new came Paul Scofield's notable King Lear in Peter Brook's production as well as later experiments by Brook with the Theatre of Cruelty that led to his triumphant *Marat/Sade* by Peter Weiss.

In 1963 the establishment of the National Theatre at the Old Vic with Sir Laurence Olivier at its head realized a dream of over a century. England was now to have a permanent ensemble of players (or as close to that ideal as circumstances would permit) to match those of the great foreign troupes, and to make, in Olivier's word's "the art of the actor . . . finally regarded as an important part of the life of the people." With Kenneth Tynan as his literary adviser, Olivier gathered for his repertory of world drama Ralph Richardson, Peggy Ashcroft, Michael Redgrave, Paul Scofield, John Gielgud as well as excellent regulars on his staff like Maggie Smith, Joan Plowright, Colin Blakely and Robert Stephens. Olivier, himself, has given the best of his mature, great talent to this national venture. This triumphant guidance of the English theatre by a great actor, it has been pointed out, is characteristic of a country that "has always looked, in spite of grudges, to its great actors for leader- ship and motivation."

EDMUND KEAN

(1787-1833)

With Betterton, Garrick, and Sarah Siddons, Edmund Kean ranks as one of the geniuses of the English stage. During his short period of triumph from 1814, when he made his debut at Drury Lane as Shylock, to the middle of the twenties, when dissipation and ill health hurried his decline, he provided audiences with in- spired performances that made his acting the acme of histrionic art.

The details of his tragic life have been retold many times. Of uncertain pa- rentage, Kean, given the name of Carey, appeared on the stage in the role of Cupid when he was about three years old. He had some schooling, but until his triumph in London his life was one of great poverty and unhappiness, replete with the anxi- eties of the poor strolling player. Acting, reciting, giving imitations and performing feats as a tight-rope walker, he played throughout Great Britain. He was develop- ing his personal, emotional skill despite the disadvantages of a small figure and an inadequate voice when the theatre was dominated by the statuesque dignity of John Philip Kemble, and the furor of "Master Betty" (William Henry West Betty, 1787-1861). Once he performed opposite the great Siddons who thought that he played well, but was too small a man to amount to much. Finally in 1814 he was given his chance at Drury Lane and chose Shylock as his first role. His success was immediate. A new star and a new mode of playing took their place on the London stage.

The freshness of Kean's interpretations, his energy and violence of emotion in contrast to the cold postures and recitations of John Philip Kemble, made him the ideal of the romantic temper. His playing gave expression to ideas harmonious with those of his contemporaries Byron, Shelley, Wordsworth, and Coleridge who said of him: "To see Kean was to read Shakespeare by flashes of lightning." Byron wrote in his diary, "Just returned from seeing Kean in *Richard*. By Jove, he is a soul! Life, nature, truth without exaggeration or diminution."

For the student of histrionic development the comparison of Kemble and Kean made by Leigh Hunt, the romantic critic, is extremely enlightening not only for the contrast of the men but for the explicit recognition that both Kemble and Kean belonged to an era that considered tragedy and common life completely divorced.

"We believe it was the opinion of a great many besides ourselves that Kean did extinguish Kemble: at all events, we hold it for certain that Kean hastened his going out.... Garrick's nature displaced Quin's formalism: and in precisely the same way did Kean displace Kemble.... It was as sure a thing as Nature against Art, or tears against cheeks of stone.

"We do not deny a certain merit of taste and what is called 'classicality' to John Kemble. He had one idea about tragedy, and it was a good one; namely, that a certain elevation of treatment was due to it, that there was a dignity, and a perception of something superior to common life, which should justly be regarded as one of its constituent portions.... Everything with Kemble was literally a *personation*. It was a mask and a sounding-pipe. It was all external and artificial....

"The distinction between Kean and Kemble may be briefly stated to be this: that Kemble knew there was a difference between tragedy and common life, but did not know in what it consisted, except in manner, which he consequently carried to excess, losing sight of the passion. Kean knows the real thing, which is the height of the *passion,* manner following it as a matter of course, *and grace being developed from it in proportion to the truth of the sensation,* as the flower issued from the entireness of the plant, or from all that is necessary to produce it. Kemble began with the flower, and he made it accordingly. He had no notion of so inelegant a thing as a root, or as the common earth, or of all the precious elements that make a heart and a life in a plant, and crown their success with beauty...."

It was in violence, energy, and strain that Kean succeeded. Hazlitt said of him: "Kean is all effort, all violence, all extreme passion; he is possessed with a fury, a demon that leaves him no repose, no time for thought or room for imagination." In another place Hazlitt said, "Mr. Kean's acting is like an anarchy of the passions, in which each upstart humor, or frenzy of the moment is struggling to get violent possession of some bit or corner of his fiery soul and pigmy body...." In physical emotionality Kean was probably not unlike George Frederick Cooke, an actor who had played with Kemble and Siddons but whose style differed from theirs. To this school of physically intense acting Gustavus V. Brooke (d. 1866) and the American Edwin Forrest belonged.

The emotionally intense actor is usually thought to be the spontaneous actor who relies not on artistic, careful preparations but on the inspiration of the moment. On one occasion Kean complained to the widow of David Garrick of the mistaken notions of the critics in their notices, "These people don't understand their business; they give me credit where I don't deserve it, and pass over passages on which I have bestowed the utmost care and attention. Because my style is easy and natural they think I don't study, and talk about the 'sudden impulse of genius.'

There is no such thing as impulsive acting; all is premeditated and studied beforehand. A man may act better or worse on a particular night, from particular circumstances; but although the execution may not be so brilliant, the conception is the same." An impression of the studied manner of Kean during one of his American tours was given by the Philadelphia critic, "Betterton," whose comments on Kean, printed here, indicate some of the weaknesses of the artist's style. Violent variation in voice, pauses, gesture, and grimace became the obvious earmarks of the Kean method. A contemporary criticism, quoted by Alan S. Downer, in his study of 19th century acting, "Players and Painted Stage," noted of Kean: "He raves, he croaks, he storms," and suggested that his action was "but a dancer's feat."

At his height Kean acted with an emotional power that, from all reports, must have been prodigious. When he played Sir Giles Overreach (*A New Way to Pay Old Debts*), one of his best characterizations, both spectators and fellow actors were said to have fainted from the overwhelming power of his acting. A contemporary periodical writer said of his performance in this role that it "is, without doubt, the most terrific exhibition of human passion that has been witnessed on the stage...."

Junius Brutus Booth, who was said to have imitated Kean's style, was brought to play opposite Kean as Iago in *Othello*. Kean's triumph on that night was so complete that Booth refused to play the second evening's engagement with him. It is interesting to note that Kean's success was just as great when he played Iago to Ira Aldridge's *Othello*.

Ill health, dissipation, and scandal finally broke Kean. His performances in the years before his death recaptured the fire in brief passages only and sharpened some of the defects of his style—the excessive contrasts of energy and languor and the lengthy pauses. A broken man when he died, Kean nevertheless had succeeded in freeing the stage from some of the artificialities of the Kemble school.

Kean had little to say about his art. His estimate of acting appears indirectly in an account which follows of an interrogation by philosophers and critics whom he met in Edinburgh. One of his biographers, Harold Newcomb Hillebrand, says "Kean lives not in his own words, but in those of Tieck, 'Betterton' of Philadelphia and William Hazlitt." He cites the reviews of 'Betterton," whose identity is unknown, "as a summary of Kean which is not only the best American criticism I have seen but one of the most valuable descriptions of that actor's method to be found anywhere...."

Feeling Without Rhetoric

It is easy to foresee that such an opportunity [Kean's visit to Edinburgh] would not be permitted to escape such a scholastic board without interrogatories being put to the great dramatic hero on the genius of Shakespeare and on the eloquence which elucidated him.... Kean had little to disclose, yet that little had to suffice. He had no harangue on eloquence to deliver. He maintained that Shakespeare was his own interpreter, by the intensity and wonderful genius of his language. Shakespeare, he continued, was a study, his deep and scrutinizing research into hu-

Quoted in F. W. Hawkins: *The Life of Edmund Kean From Published and Original Sources.* London: Tinsley Brothers, 1869, Volume 1, pp. 96-98.

man nature, and his sublime and pathetic muse, were to be comprehended only by a capacity alive to his mighty purposes. He had no rhetorician's laws to expound. If a higher estimate was at any time placed upon his performances than upon those of some others who fulfilled the severe calling of the actor, he thought it might be due in part to the devotion which he bestowed on the author, and the conceptions engendered by reflection. I have overlooked, said he, the schoolmen, and while I assume no lofty claims, I have thought more of intonation than of gesticulation. It is the utterance of human feelings which rises superior to the rules which the professor of rhetoric enjoins. It is the sympathy of mental impression that acts. I forgot the affectations of the art, and relied upon the emotions of the soul. It is human nature that gives his promptings. Kean rejected the cadence, or very rarely had recourse to it; it was at war with a successful termination of speech. Sententious thought is cut off and too often loses its effective power by that rule. He considered the low modulation at the end too often destructive to a full comprehension of the sentence. Popular oratory seems more and more to regard it as an obsolete law, and I think from daily observation that our living exemplars of oratorical power, as Everett, Hawks, and others, practically carry out Kean's innovation.

On Edmund Kean

by "BETTERTON"

...Nature has endowed Mr. Kean with a vigorous genius, and important physical qualifications, for his pursuit. He possesses a fine physiognomy, a most expressive eye, a muscular frame, well and even elegantly shaped, except in the shoulders, which, being round and heavy in appearance, detract much from the just effect of his other proportions. He has studied the mechanism or art of the profession, with great assiduity and success; he is fully trained in the tricks of the stage. He can penetrate himself thoroughly with his part, and seem engrossed by it, so as to counterfeit a perfect abstraction from the audience. In every character which I have seen him personate, he furnishes at least some specimens of what is called brilliant execution; some felicities of conception and expression; some manifestations of superior power and consummate skill, that have an electric effect, and give universal satisfaction.

He is eminently successful in situations which admit of intense fire and vivacity of action; inarticulate passion, or rapid alternations of countenance and tone. Sudden and strong vicissitudes of feeling are admirably portrayed in the movement of his features. His eye conveys the most opposite meaning and sensation with singular quickness of transition and versatility of eloquence. There was a fine development of this faculty in his dialogue as Shylock, with Tubal, in the third act of the *Merchant of Venice;* and, occasionally, in his performance of Othello, the character in which he appeared to most advantage in my eyes and left the most vivid remembrance, particularly on the second representation. The rage, despair, fell revenge; the wild tumult of the soul and fierce struggle of the affections, of which so much is to be portrayed in the Moor, gave scope for all the energies and significances of look, the mastery and communicativeness of face and the impetuosity of movement, to which I have adverted above....

"Betterton" in the *Philadelphia National Gazette,* February 6, 7, 8, 1821, quoted by Harold Newcomb Hillebrand: *Edmund Kean.* New York: Columbia University Press, 1933, pp. 367-371.

I have so far spoken only of the pantomime or dumb-show and might have included a special tribute to his general firmness of tread and occasional gracefulness of posture: a confident, elastic gait, attitudes bespeaking athletic vigor, with flexibility of limb, and presenting an easy and regular outline, are not to be overlooked in chronicling the deserts of a tragedian. I would emblazon the dying scenes, which are described by both his English and American panegyrists, as wonders of ingenuity and stupendous achievements of mind and body, but I must confess that I cannot distinguish their justness as imitations; being, as I am, under the conviction that no mortal, wounded and moribund, ever fell with the precision of pitch, and nicety of contour and straightness of prostration, which mark Mr. Kean's exits from the world.

Unless the copy be faithful, it resolves itself, in my humble opinion, into a mere feat of agility and posture; what the French call *tour de force,* which they exhibit daily, of the same kind, in equal perfection, at some of the minor theatres of Paris. *Scaramouche* does as much in Italy. Whether it becomes a modern Roscius to play the symmetrist in like manner, and seek distinction by fanciful, and elaborate pictures of that really inimitable extremity—giving up the ghost—I leave to your better judgment. For my part, though there may be transcendent intelligence, beauty, and fitness in the operation, I cannot discover in it a particle of these qualities.

With respect to Mr. Kean's recitation, the combined use of the understanding and the voice, it is susceptible of praise in the enunciation of passages of a solemn, emphatic tenor, which he does not conceive to require vehemence of tone and velocity of utterance. His cadences are distinct and agreeable in measured and deliberate speech; if his voice is rarely musical, it is not always grating; and as there are feelings and language to which guttural notes, sepulchral sounds, even broken, harsh accents, are appropriate, he at times excels in the oratorical department of his profession.

* * * *

I have conceded as much to Mr. Kean, as liberality would grant within the limits of truth and judgment. Having noted his accomplishments and traits of superiority, I have now to remark the objections to which he is liable. As a general stricture, it may be said that his excellencies are perpetually passing into extremes, or degenerating into defects. He is always in his happiest exhibitions of art, and most brilliant flashes of genius, on the verge of extravagance.

His studied play of physiognomy borders on grimace; his animation of manner becomes incoherent bustle; what is spirited savours of turbulence; what is passionate, of frenzy. He obviously relies more on mechanical resources, than on his general mental preparation and powers, or his fervor of feeling and thorough possession of his part. He is called a natural player, but his style of acting is highly artificial and technical; it is uniformly elaborate, systematic, and ambitious. Nothing is left to the inspiration of the moment. I was particularly struck with this circumstance in witnessing his second representation of Othello. During the first two acts of the piece, it was, if I may be allowed the phrase, a facsimile of the first representation. The identity in every particular of look, movement, tone, pace, posture was a phenomenon in respect to steadfastness of method and force of habit. In the remaining acts, his gesticulation was less violent, and his manner in general more subdued; but this was plainly the result of calculation or physical accident, not of diversity in the momentary impulses of sentiment and judgment.

The stature of Mr. Kean is low, and his shoulders, as I have said, are not happily constructed. Garrick labored under the first disadvantage, and Lekain, the Roscius of the French stage, had to contend with both obstacles, and an ungainly visage in addition. These celebrated players counteracted their mishap by professional discipline and the more effectual correctives of an incessant display of genius, and nobleness of elocution. Garrick could be thought tall and majestic—Lekain was believed by those who only saw him in his vocation, to be of lofty size and commanding aspect.

From whatever cause, Mr. Kean is not so fortunate as either. His most enthusiastic partisans and encomiasts in England have been obliged to confess that there is an almost "habitual want of dignity and elegance about him"—a deficiency which, however, they pretend he redeems by masterstrokes of art and nature, and the energies of passion and action. I have not been sensible of these amends but in a very few instances. The general impression produced by his carriage and mien is the reverse of awe or respect. There is, to say no more, not the least elevation in them, nor any gracefulness in his person and movement at large. As Shylock, he needs none, and nothing is missed. But even in Sir Giles Overreach you require more stateliness and a more magisterial feeling than appear; and in Richard and Othello, you find unremittingly an utter want of physical adaptation and patrician demeanor.

* * * *

Mr. Kean would seem to apply literally to his art, the lesson of Demosthenes with regard to oratory—action, action, action. His limbs have no repose or steadiness in scenes of agitated feeling; his hands are kept in unremitting and the most rapid convulsive movement; seeking, as it were, a resting place in some part of his upper dress, and occasionally pressed together on the crown of his head. I have remarked the process to be the same in his personation of different characters, and I think I may assert that there is no eye which a habit of this kind would not strike as untoward and incongruous....

Quick and irregular motion, vehement and perturbed gesture, are occasionally opposite; but there is a discipline and temperament even for disorder, whether as to action or to utterance, on the stage. Hamlet's lecture to the players has passed into proverb, but like much other axiomatic doctrine is oftener repeated than observed. Situations occur for the tragedian, calling for the highest powers of his genius, and the most curious refinements of his art, in which gesticulation is misplaced and detrimental. It has been emphatically said that dignity has no arms, especially where there is great force of expression in the eyes and other features. Dejection, lowly grief, profound reflection, tender sentiment, contempt, solemn or malicious menace, hauteur, rising passion of whatever nature, require but a look, a motion of the head. The energetic use of the limbs spoils the true and effectual expression.

* * * *

The greatest physical blemish to be signalized in this tragedian, is the imperfection of his voice. This is universally admitted to be in general harsh and broken; while sweetness is, by some, ascribed to its lower tones....

It is artificial when not strained, and in the tempest of passion so frequent with the actor, is painfully hoarse and almost altogether inarticulate. I know of no more irksome noises than those which issue from his breast, when he labors to express rage or horror in their utmost intensity. The exhaustion of his lungs has a two-fold inconvenience; for there is always something contemptible in infuriate passion where the physical powers fail. His consciousness of the natural insufficiency of his voice, seems to stimulate him to more violent efforts in action and aspect, and thus carries him further beyond the bounds which he is otherwise prone to transgress.

The same insufficiency has, indeed, as may be at once perceived, a train of the worst consequences. It subjects him to the reproach which Churchill[1] casts upon Macklin, of dealing largely in half-formed sounds; it causes him to play inordinately to the eye, and attach himself much more to the general, than particular sense and expression of his part; it robs his audience of a good portion of the literary beauties and ethical lessons of the poet. He has fallen into peculiarities in the management of his voice, which form an aggravation of the case. The sudden, mechanical depression and quick, violent vicissitude of tones—the precipitate strain and extreme volubility immediately preceding or following long pauses, or slow, repressed enunciation, which he so frequently affects, may be difficult achievements, but they are very foreign to the interests whether of the actor or auditor. The author is more and more suppressed, and a wider departure committed from the rules of reason and taste. I have amused myself with imagining what impression, Mr. Kean, with his system of declamation, and his dissonant, confused accents in his ebullitions of rage, would make upon a blind person critically conversant with the dramatist whose composition he might be reciting. Certainly it would not be one of much admiration. Nor would the result, I think, be very different, as to any auditory at large, if the tragedian wore a mask. We know that the face was entirely concealed on the ancient stage, and that, notwithstanding, even greater effects were produced than any which are recorded of the best representation of any player of modern times.

Hazlitt remarks of Mr. Kean's Richard on one occasion, that "every sentence was an alternation of dead pauses and rapid utterance," and properly adds that "the most common-place, drawling monotony is not more mechanical or offensive." The length of his pauses, with the studied play of the visage as the substitute of the tongue, while they are maintained, has something of the air and more of the effect of the memorable dispute in Rabelais, between Panurge and the English philosopher, "which was performed without a word of speaking," so that one portion of the audience made one inference and another, another; every one interpreted as he liked best. Garrick's contemporary and rival, Quin, was addicted to long pauses....

But Quin, notwithstanding his pauses, was distinguished for giving full sway to the language and sentiment of his principal the poet. Churchill says of him,

> His words bore sterling weight: nervous and strong
> In manly tides of sense they rolled along;
> Happy in art, he chiefly had pretense
> To keep up numbers, yet not forfeit sense.

Mr. Kean has not pretense and indeed, no ability, to keep up numbers. His auditor can have no perception of rhythm or even verse, where a sort of amalgam is made of whole phrases either by hurry or hoarseness of utterance; and where

---

[1]Charles Churchill: *The Rosciad.*

long pauses are arbitrarily introduced not only between words, but between syllables of the same word. I cannot conceive a more fanciful reading of the dramatic poets, or wilder havoc of their lines, than may be alleged against Mr. Kean, as a general charge. There cannot be the least affinity between the style of his recitation and that of Garrick's, whom he is said to follow in the imitation of nature. That master of the histrionic art was, it is true, energetic but without bombast; simple but without vulgarity; lofty and vehement, but not turgid or vociferous. He declaimed with the utmost truth, elegance and precision, and plumed himself upon setting in the strongest relief the merits of his poet in thought and diction; upon marking all the shades of excellence in a dramatic composition. He avoided the stiff and stately, monotonous manner—as well as the incoherent rant, but he loved high and weighty elocution. Heroic verse was, in his theory, to be metrically and majestically pronounced. It may be seen by the verses I have quoted from Churchill, that, when his practice gave the tone to opinion, the preservation of rhythm was considered as a title to distinction and compatible with the full expression and efficiency of sense, passion and nature.

WILLIAM CHARLES MACREADY
(1793-1873)

William Charles Macready was the son of a travelling player and theatrical manager who had once performed with Charles Macklin. Although Macready's childhood was spent in and around various theatres in London and in the provinces with his parents, he was not at first destined for the stage. He was sent to Rugby where he acquired a gentlemanly education upon which he prided himself for the rest of his life. His intention was to prepare himself for the bar, but at the age of sixteen he found himself assisting the management of the theatre in Manchester which had brought his father to the verge of financial ruin. After some study in London and a short stint as sole manager of his father's theatre, young Macready made his debut in 1810 in the role of Romeo. This first performance in Birmingham was favorably greeted. Macready was launched upon his long career as an actor, a profession towards which this aspiring gentleman had extremely ambiguous feelings.

From 1810 to 1816, Macready played many roles throughout England, Scotland, and Ireland, even supporting the great Sarah Siddons in several plays. At the end of this period he was given a five years' engagement at Covent Garden. As Edmund Kean faded from the scene, Macready earned the position of leading tragedian of the English stage. By 1837 he was regarded as the actor under whose management the legitimate, classical stage could be saved from opera and spectacle.

In this year Macready organized a company at Covent Garden which he managed and starred in for two years. His productions were marked by extensive rehearsals and careful attention to scenery and costumes. He also did much to clear the theatres of rowdyism and make them "respectable" places of entertainment. In 1841 he undertook a similar job at Drury Lane where, despite the decline of the traditional repertory of the legitimate houses, he tried to bear high the standard of fine drama.

After his managerial duties, Macready continued on the English stage for almost ten years and extended his performances to the United States and France. The third of his visits to the United States resulted in one of the theatre's most shameful incidents—the 1849 riot at the Astor Place Opera House in New York, brought on by the rivalry between Macready and Edwin Forrest, America's tragic idol.

While Macready's contributions to the English theatre of the first half of the nineteenth century are undisputed, his position as one of the theatrical greats is less secure. Although he gained his prominence in competition with Edmund Kean and the enduring memory of John Philip Kemble's acting, he seemed to mark a breaking point in the old acting tradition. He essayed the great tragic roles of Macbeth, Othello, Richard, and Coriolanus, but his success in these characterizations was limited. Of his Macbeth Leigh Hunt wrote: "It wants the Royal warrant. We do not mean the mouthing and strut of the ordinary stage King; which are things that Mr. Macready is above; but that habitual consciousness of ascendancy and disposition to throw an ideal grace over its reflections...." In speaking of his performance of King John, Hunt said: "He is best as he approaches domestic passion, and has to give way to soft or overwhelming emotions. His greatest deficiency is shown in passages where the ideal is required; where nature puts on the robe of art, and speaks her truths, as it were, in state."

Unable to burn with the fire of Kean or strut with the dignity of Kemble, Macready reduced the high passions of tragedy to the restraint of the drawing-room. He succeeded best in the plays of his own day, *Virginius* and *William Tell* by Sheridan Knowles, and the *Richelieu* of Bulwer-Lytton, plays which infused the tragic with domestic and melodramatic elements. It was in his famed homely touches that Macready pointed the way toward the refined drawing-room realism that developed in the middle of the nineteenth century.

His self-conscious artistry speaks for itself in the voluminous pages of his *Diaries* and *Reminiscences*.

The Audience and the Actor

From circumstances that I do not remember, the season at Bath was a dull one, and the theatre suffered proportionately with the other places of amusement. But this did not prevent me from using as a means of study for my improvement the practice it afforded me. A full attendance is too generally required as a spur to a performer's exertions, and to a beggarly account of empty boxes many have been in the habit of slurring over (or what is known as "walking through") their parts. Indeed, I have been present when, on their benefit nights, performers have not only walked with contemptuous indifference through their parts, but have resented on the auditors present the absence of those who stayed away. It was a rule with me to make what profit I could out of a bad house, and before the most meager audiences ever assembled it has been my invariable practice to strive my best, using the opportunity as a lesson; and I am conscious of having derived great benefit from the rule. I used to call it "acting to myself"; as indeed it was transferring the study of a character from my own apartment to the stage, where it was much less irk-

Macready's Reminiscences, and Selections from his Diaries and Letters, edited by Sir Frederick Pollock. New York: Macmillan and Co., 1875, pp. 77-78, 83-84, 111-112, 141-142.

some; for in the solitude of a lodging to continue over and over again the repetition of passages, with strict attention to one's elocution, deportment, gesture, and countenance, guarding against exaggeration, whilst lashing oneself up to the highest strain of passion, and this without any stimulus or any test, beyond the individual's trust of having struck the chord aright, was a sort of darkling procedure, groping or feeling of one's way, that called upon me often for strong efforts of perseverance, being more trying to the constancy and patience of the student than falls to the lot of any other art: for in others the advances made are visible in the comparison of the works completed; but the player, by dint of repeated efforts, must perfect himself in tones, attitudes, looks, of which he can only learn the effect under the nervous excitement of experimenting their power on the uncertain sympathies of an heterogeneous assembly.

More than once in my life I have heard, in dogmatic tone and with an oracular air, certain *soi-disant* critics bestowing on a player especial praise on the ground that his acting was quite natural, unpremeditated; that he did not require study, and that he never delivered the salient points of a character twice in the same way. What would reflection deduce from this, but that, although the artist may be subject more or less to the accidental variation of his animal spirits, yet, as there must be one form of expression which he finds nearest to the exact truth, in once attaining this, every deviation or declension from it must be more or less a deterioration? Study will bring ease, grace, and self-possession—the indispensable groundwork of the actor's art; but to evoke the various emotions that will give with fidelity Nature's own expression to his look and voice—*"hic labor, hoc opus est."* As Talma used to say, "there was only one best"—to discover that is the labor of the artist; and having once achieved this, is it reconcilable to common sense that he would endanger his credit by tampering with the truth his patient investigation had wrought out? The approach to perfection is indeed usually so gradual, that, in one whose principle it would be to labor in his several performances to improve on what had gone before, whose motto to the very last words he utters on the scene is "Excelsior," the degrees of his toilsome ascent may be sometimes distinguishable, but beyond such shadowy variations his design and its treatment will remain unchanged.

* * * *

One of the disadvantages incident to the pursuit of the theatrical art is the supposed facility of its attainment, nor is it less cheapened in public estimation by the general assumption of the ability to criticize it. How frequent, to questions of opinion on other arts, are the evasive answers, "I am no judge of poetry"; "I have never studied pictures"; "I do not know much about sculpture." Yet the person confessedly ignorant on these subjects, would be at no fault in pronouncing a decisive judgment on

> "The youngest of the sister Arts,
> Where all their beauty blends!"

It is Addison who describes "a picture" as "a poem without words." In illustrating the poet's thought the actor presents in harmonious succession a series of living pictures, in which his intellectual acuteness often throws light on what might otherwise be obscure, whilst his fervid sensibility compels sympathy with the passion he portrays. But Campbell's beautiful lines condense all that more diffuse prose would seek to express on that theme:

[335]

"For ill can Poetry express
    Full many a tone of thought sublime;
And Painting, mute and motionless,
    Steals but a glance of time.
But by the mighty actor brought,
    Illusion's perfect triumphs come;
Verse ceases to be airy thought,
    And sculpture to be dumb."

It surely needs something like an education for such an art, and yet that appearance of mere volition and perfect ease, which cost the accomplished artist so much time and toil to acquire, evidently leads to a different conclusion with many, or amateur acting would be less in vogue.

* * * *

The language of criticism is frequently dogmatic, exacting deference from the authoritative tone it assumes, sometimes without the needful preliminary application to the subject of which it treats. It was said by no incompetent judge, *"De pictore, sculptore, fictore, nisi artifex, judicare non protest."* [1] But this opinion, as applied to the theatrical art, is repudiated by many; and, as I have before observed, it is held by some writers in England (though not in France) that no particular study is requisite to make a critic or connoisseur of "acting." I have been led by observation to think differently; but, although my active life has been chiefly devoted to the study of poetry and playing, I make no pretension to the critic's chair; and in trying to describe with accuracy what was palpable to my senses, advance my opinions no further than in stating the impressions made upon a very excitable temperament and a very sensitive organization.

On the sum of Kemble's merits judgments differed; that he was a great artist all allowed. His person was cast in the heroic mold, and, as may be seen in Lawrence's splendid portraits of him in Coriolanus, Hamlet, and Rolla, reached the most perfect ideal of manly beauty. But he had serious disadvantages to contend with in a very disagreeable voice, husky and untuneable, and in a constitutional asthma that necessitated a prolonged and laborious indraught of his breath, and obliged him for the sake of distinctness to adopt an elaborate mode of utterance, enunciating every letter in every word. His limbs were not supple—indeed his stately bearing verged on stiffness; and his style more suited to the majestic, the lofty, and the stern, than the pathetic, might not inaptly, in respect to his movement on the stage, be termed statuesque. Mrs. Siddons, speaking of him to Reynolds, the painter, said, "My brother John in his most impetuous bursts is always careful to avoid any discomposure of his dress or deportment; but in the whirlwind of passion I lose all thought of such matters": and this forgetfulness of self was one of the elements of her surpassing power. The admission of Mrs. Inchbald, one of Kemble's most ardent worshippers, corroborates the opinion very generally entertained of his phlegmatic temperament. In the part of Oswyn, in Congreve's tragedy of *The Mourning Bride* she says, "Garrick had great spirit and fire in every scene, but not the fire of love. Kemble has not even the sparks."

In all he did the study was apparent. The *ars celare artem* [the art of concealing art], with all his great talent, he did not reach; but he compelled the respect

---

[1] No one but an artist can criticize the work of artists. Pliny, Epist. i, 10.

and admiration where he did not excite the sympathies of his audience. His noble form and stately bearing attracted and fixed observation, and his studious correctness retained attention; but in the torrent and tempest of his passion he had not the sustained power of Talma or Kean, but, like a Rembrandt picture, his performances were remarkable for most brilliant effects, worked out with wonderful skill on a somber ground, which only a great master of his art could have achieved, and of which, I have endeavored to convey some faint idea in my description of scenes of *Cato* and *Macbeth*.

* * * *

... But uppermost in my mind was always the cultivation of my art; and as the aim and object of all true art is the skillful blending of the real and the ideal, it becomes the student's duty to store his mind abundantly with facts, at the same time that he gives free scope to the exercise of his imagination. Whatever, therefore, might extend my experience of the various aspects human nature may put on in the vicissitudes of pain and pleasure, suffering or enjoyment, I regarded as a needful and imperative study. Under this persuasion it was that I braced up my nerves (always acutely sensitive to a sight of suffering) to go through the lunatic asylum. The superintendent was a very intelligent person, whose conduct of the establishment had gained him great credit; he was most courteous; and in directing my attention to the several peculiarities of the hapless inmates, greatly assisted me in the earnest scrutiny with which I watched every movement, every play of feature of those stricken creatures. It was reading one of the most harrowing pages out of Nature's book, and so faithfully conned over that every character was impressed indelibly on my memory. I had gone through two wards, and when my conductor was applying his key to the grated door of the third, I declined, being, indeed, quite unable to extend my observations further. I took from thence lessons, painful ones indeed, that in after-years added to the truth of my representations.

FANNY KEMBLE

(1809-1893)

Frances Anne Kemble was the last significant representative of a great theatrical family. Her father Charles, younger brother of John Philip and Sarah, did not start out as an actor, but like all the other members of this family, he eventually turned to the stage. He followed the style of his brother John in his cold, rather stilted manner. In heavy roles he never achieved his elder brother's success, but his gentlemanly manner and grace made him a successful actor in such roles as Laertes, Mercutio, and Benedick. Macready dubbed him a first rate actor in second rate parts. He was also successful in refined comedy. When he took over John Philip's share in Covent Garden, the patent theatres were in their declining days and his adventure as a manager was financially disastrous. Artistically his reign as manager will be remembered for several attempts, with the aid of the designer-writer James Robinson Planché, to clothe and mount some of the Shakespearean repertory in historically accurate costumes and sets.

On the verge of bankruptcy in 1829 Charles Kemble introduced his daughter Fanny as Juliet in a production in which her mother, a retired actress, played Lady Capulet and Charles himself played Mercutio. Her performances were the great

[337]

sensation of the theatrical season. People flocked to see yet another Kemble on the stage. But when the first flurry of enthusiasm was over and Miss Kemble was subjected to critical scrutiny, she was found wanting.

Leigh Hunt wrote of her Juliet that the opening impression of charm and naturalness which she gave was soon destroyed as the play progressed. "But the moment she gave us the first burst of feeling," wrote Hunt, "our expectations fell many degrees, and they never rose again. The manner was different in an instant, not as showing more feeling, but as showing less: the regular theatrical start and vehemence were substituted for the natural emotion of the artless girl we had been contemplating ... and then commenced the regular conventional tragic style, both in voice and manner, which was maintained with little variation the whole evening, and which has certainly left an impression on our minds that this young lady is entirely an artificial performer, very apt in catching all that may be learnt in tragic acting, but not essentially superior to many that have had but a brief day of repute. She wanted passion throughout, and variety of feeling.... Her emotion was loud, her gravity dignified and queen-like, her flow of utterance breathed with a regular vehemence of solemnity, something between the tones of her great kins-woman, Mrs. Siddons, and the mellow monotony of the late Mrs. Powell."

In 1832 Fanny Kemble played with her father in the United States, where she married. Eventually she abandoned acting, which she had always disliked, and became a reader. A picturesque person, she has set down her life and ideas in a series of autobiographical books. Her comments on the profession which had made the Kembles great originally appeared in the *Cornhill Magazine* of 1863. She suggested in this piece an interesting contrast between dramatic imagination and the theatrical ability to portray dramatic ideas, a contrast perhaps resulting from her own inability to successfully combine the two powers. Her derogatory remarks about the profession, based on traditional Platonic disparagements, were probably due to her own antagonism toward acting. George Arliss says of her essay: "Considering its brevity, it is perhaps the most careful analysis of the actor in juxtaposition with his art that one is likely to find in dramatic literature."

Temperament and Talent

Things dramatic and things theatrical are often confounded together in the minds of English people, who, being for the most part neither the one nor the other, speak and write of them as if they were identical, instead of, as they are, so dissimilar that they are nearly opposite.

That which is dramatic in human nature is the passionate, emotional, humorous element, the simplest portion of our composition, after our mere instincts, to which it is closely allied; and this has no relation whatever, beyond its momentary excitement and gratification, to that which imitates it, and is its theatrical reproduction; the dramatic is the real, of which the theatrical is the false.

Both nations and individuals in whom the dramatic temperament strongly preponderates are rather remarkable for a certain simplicity of nature, which produces

Frances Anne Kemble: *On the Stage* (1863). New York: Printed for the Dramatic Museum of Columbia University, *Papers on Acting*, Fifth Series, Number 3, 1926, pp. 9-21. By permission of Columbia University Press.

sincerity and vehemence of emotion and expression, but is entirely without consciousness, which is never absent from the theatrical element.

Children are always dramatic, but only theatrical when they become aware that they are objects of admiring attention; in which case the assuming and dissembling capacity of acting develops itself comically and sadly enough in them.

* * * *

The combination of the power of representing passion and emotion with that of imagining or conceiving it—that is, of the theatrical talent with the dramatic temperament—is essential to make a good actor; their combination in the highest possible degree alone makes a great one.

There is a specific comprehension of effect and the means of producing it, which, in some persons, is a distinct capacity, and this forms what actors call the study of their profession; and in this, which is the alloy necessary to make theatrical that which is only dramatic, lies the heart of their mystery and the snare of their craft in more ways than one; and this, the actor's business, goes sometimes absolutely against the dramatic temperament, which is nevertheless essential to it.

Every day lessens the frequency of this specific combination among ourselves, for the dramatic temperament, always exceptional in England, is becoming daily more so under the various adverse influences of a state of civilization and society which fosters a genuine dislike to exhibitions of emotion, and a cynical disbelief in the reality of it, both necessarily repressing, first, its expression, and next, its existence. On the other hand, greater intellectual cultivation and a purer and more elevated taste, are unfavorable to the existence of the true theatrical spirit; and English actors of the present day are of the public, by being "nothing if not critical," and are not of their craft, having literally ceased to know "what belongs to a frippery." They have lost for the most part alike the dramatic emotional temperament and the scenic science of mere effect; and our stage is and must be supplied, if supplied at all, by persons less sophisticated and less civilized. The plays brought out and revived at our theatres of late years bear doleful witness to this. We have in them archaeology, ethnology, history, geography, botany (even to the curiosity of ascertaining the Danish wild-flowers that Ophelia might twist with her mad straws), and upholstery; everything, in short, but acting, which it seems we cannot have.

When Mrs. Siddons, in her spectacles and mob-cap, read *Macbeth* or *King John,* it was one of the grandest dramatic achievements that could be imagined, with the least possible admixture of the theatrical element; the representation of the *Duke's Motto,* with all its resources of scenic effect, is a striking and interesting theatrical entertainment, with hardly an admixture of that which is truly dramatic.

Mrs. Siddons could lay no claim to versatility—it was not in her nature; she was without mobility of mind, countenance, or manner; and her dramatic organization was in that respect inferior to Garrick's; but out of a family of twenty-eight persons, all of whom made the stage their vocation, she alone preeminently combined the qualities requisite to make a great theatrical performer in the highest degree.

* * * *

In my father and mother I have had frequent opportunities of observing in most marked contrast the rapid intuitive perception of the dramatic instinct in an organization where it preponderated, and the laborious process of logical argument by which the same result, on a given question, was reached by a mind of a different constitution (my father's), and reached with much doubt and hesitation, caused by the very application of analytical reasoning. The slow mental process might with time have achieved a right result in all such cases; but the dramatic instinct, aided by a fine organization, was unerring; and this leads me to observe, that there is no reason whatever to expect that fine actors shall be necessarily profound commentators on the parts that they sustain most successfully, but rather the contrary.

I trust I shall not be found wanting in due respect for the greatness that is gone from us, if I say that Mrs. Siddons' analysis of the part of Lady Macbeth is to be found alone in her representation of it; of the magnificence of which the "essay" she has left upon the character gives not the faintest idea.

If that great actress had possessed the order of mind capable of conceiving and producing a philosophical analysis of any of the wonderful poetical creations which she so wonderfully embodied, she would surely never have been able to embody them as she did. For to whom are all things given? and to whom were ever given, in such abundant measure, consenting and harmonious endowments of mind and body for the peculiar labor of her life?

The dramatic faculty, as I have said, lies in a power of apprehension quicker than the disintegrating process of critical analysis, and when it is powerful, and the organization fine, as with Mrs. Siddons, perception rather than reflection reaches the aim proposed; and the persons endowed with this specific gift will hardly unite with it the mental qualifications of philosophers and metaphysicians; no better proof of which can be adduced than Mrs. Siddons herself, whose performances were, in the strict sense of the word, excellent, while the two treatises she has left upon the characters of Queen Constance and Lady Macbeth—two of her finest parts—are feeble and superficial. Kean, who possessed, beyond all actors whom I have seen, tragic inspiration, could very hardly, I should think, have given a satisfactory reason for any one of the great effects which he produced. Of Mlle. Rachel, whose impersonations fulfilled to me the idea of perfect works of art of their kind, I have heard, from one who knew her well, that her intellectual processes were limited to the consideration of the most purely mechanical part of her vocation; and Pasta, the great lyric tragedian, who, Mrs. Siddons said, was capable of giving her lessons, replied to the observation, *"Vous avez du beaucoup étudier l'antique,"* *"Je l'ai beaucoup senti."* The reflective and analytical quality has little to do with the complex process of acting, and is alike remote even from what is dramatic and what is theatrical.

There is something anomalous in that which we call the dramatic art that has often arrested my attention and exercised my thought; the special gift and sole industry of so many of my kindred, and the only labor of my own life, it has been a subject of constant and curious speculation with me, combining as it does elements at once so congenial and so antagonistic to my nature.

Its more original process, that is, the conception of the character to be presented, is a mere reception of the creation of another mind; and its mechanical part, that is, the representation of the character thus apprehended, has no reference to the intrinsic, poetical or dramatic merit of the original creation, but merely to the accuracy and power of the actor's perception of it; thus the character of Lady Macbeth is as majestic, awful, and poetical, whether it be worthily filled by its preeminent representative, Mrs. Siddons, or unworthily by the most incompetent of ignorant provincial tragedy-queens.

This same dramatic art has neither fixed rules, specific principles, indispensable rudiments, nor fundamental laws; it has no basis in positive science, as music, painting, sculpture, and architecture have; and differs from them all, in that the mere appearance of spontaneity, which is an acknowledged assumption, is its chief merit. And yet... [it] requires in its professors the imagination of the poet, the ear of the musician, the eye of the painter and sculptor, and over and above these, a faculty peculiar to itself, inasmuch as the actor personally fulfills and embodies his conception; his own voice is his cunningly modulated instrument; his own face the canvas whereon he portrays the various expressions of his passion; his own frame the mold in which he casts the images of beauty and majesty that fill his brain; and whereas the painter and sculptor may select, of all possible attitudes, occupations, and expressions, the most favorable to the beautiful effect they desire to produce and fix, and bid it to remain fixed forever, the actor must live and move through a temporary existence of poetry and passion, and preserve throughout its duration that ideal grace and dignity, of which the canvas and marble give but a silent and motionless image. And yet it is an art that requires no study worthy of the name; it creates nothing; it perpetuates nothing; to its professors, whose personal qualifications form half their merit, is justly given the need of personal admiration; and the reward of contemporaneous popularity is well bestowed on those whose labor consists in exciting momentary emotion. Their most persevering and successful efforts can only benefit, by a passionate pleasure of at most a few years' duration, the play-going public of their own immediate day, and they are fitly recompensed with money and applause, to whom may not justly belong the rapture of creation, the glory of patient and protracted toil, and the love and honor of grateful posterity.

GEORGE HENRY LEWES
(1817-1878)

Of the important drama critics of the nineteenth century, George Henry Lewes was probably the only one who tried to do more than describe the actors he saw at work. He was conscious that acting was an art like others and had rules and standards of its own which needed to be uncovered before a true critical estimate could be made. His collection of essays, *On Actors and the Art of Acting,* made an attempt to establish some of the principles upon which he based his evaluations of such actors as Edmund Kean, Rachel, William Charles Macready, Charles Mathews, and Frédéric Lemaître.

Lewes was well qualified for his task. The grandson of a famous comedian, Charles Lee Lewes (1740-1803), Lewes himself tried his hand at acting several times. Although he was not prepared for the stage from youth, as were so many of the actors of the nineteenth century, he played with Charles Dickens' amateur company in 1848. In 1849 he appeared as Shylock in a company with Barry Sullivan. He also acted in his own play, *The Noble Heart.* When he turned from acting to writing, his interest in theatre determined much that he wrote. An admirer of French drama, he made many translations of French plays. Lewes was literary editor of *The Leader,* and in 1865 became editor of the *Fortnightly Review.* He was also versed in both philosophy and psychology and wrote books and articles on these subjects, as well as a life of Goethe and a volume on Spanish drama.

In 1875 appeared the book *On Actors and the Art of Acting,* from which selections are printed here. Some of his important contributions to histrionic theory in these essays are his analysis of the symbols of the actor's art, the meaning of natural acting, and his recognition that acting is circumscribed by what he called the *optique du théâtre* and the standards of theatrical truth held by the audience.

The Actor's Symbols

[The Intrinsic Value of the Actor]

It is thought a hardship that great actors in quitting the stage can leave no monument more solid than a name. The painter leaves behind him pictures to attest his power; the author leaves behind him books; the actor leaves only a tradition. The curtain falls—the artist is annihilated. Succeeding generations may be told of his genius; none can test it.

All this I take to be a most misplaced sorrow. With the best wishes in the world I cannot bring myself to place the actor on a level with the painter or the author. I cannot concede to the actor such a parity of intellectual greatness; while, at the same time, I am forced to remember that, with inferior abilities, he secures far greater reward, both of pudding and praise. It is not difficult to assign the causes of an actor's superior reward, both in noisy reputation and in solid guineas. He amuses. He amuses more than the most amusing author. And our luxuries always cost us more than our necessities. Taglioni or Carlotta were better paid than Edmund Kean or Macready; Jenny Lind better than both put together.

But while the dramatic artist appeals to a larger audience, and moves them more forcibly than either painter or author, owing to the very nature of his art, a very slight acquaintance with acting and actors will suffice to show that there can be no parity in the rank of a great painter and a great actor. Place Kean beside Caravaggio (and, though I select the greatest actor I have known, I take a third-rate painter, not wishing to overpower the argument with such names as Raphael, Michelangelo, Titian), and ask what comparison can be made of their intellectual qualifications! Or take Macready and weigh him in the scale of Bulwer or Dickens.

The truth is, we exaggerate the talent of an actor because we judge only from the effect he produces, without enquiring too curiously into the means. But, while the painter has nothing but his canvas and the author has nothing but white paper and printer's ink with which to produce his effects, the actor has all other arts as handmaids: the poet labors for him, creates his part, gives him his eloquence, his music, his imagery, his tenderness, his pathos, his sublimity; the scene-painter aids him; the costumes, the lights, the music, all the fascinations of the stage—all subserve the actor's effect: these raise him upon a pedestal; remove them, and what is he? He who can make a stage mob bend and sway with his eloquence, what could he do with a real mob, no poet by to prompt him? He who can charm us with the stateliest imagery of a noble mind, when robed in the sables of Hamlet, or in the toga of Coriolanus, what can he do in coat and trousers on the world's stage? Rub off the paint, and the eyes are no longer brilliant! Reduce the actor to his intrinsic value, and then weigh him with the rivals whom he surpasses in reputation and in fortune.

George Henry Lewes: *On Actors and the Art of Acting.* New York: Smith, Elder and Company, 1875, selected passages.

If my estimate of the intrinsic value of acting is lower than seems generally current, it is from no desire to disparage an art I have always loved; but from a desire to state what seems to me the simple truth on the matter, and to show that the demand for posthumous fame is misplaced. Already the actor gets more fame than he deserves, and we are called upon to weep that he gets no more. During his reign the applause which follows him exceeds in intensity that of all other claimants for public approbation; so long as he lives he is an object of strong sympathy and interest; and when he dies he leaves behind him such influence upon his art as his genius may have effected (true fame!) and a monument to kindle the emulation of successors. Is not that enough? Must he weep because other times will not see his acting? Must we weep because all that energy, labor, genius, if you will, is no more than a tradition? Folly! (The illustrious mathematician, Jacobi, in his old age, was once consoled by a flattering disciple with the remark that all future mathematicians would delight in his work. He drew down the corners of his mouth and said, despairingly, "Yes; but to think that all my predecessors knew nothing of my work!" Here was vanity hungrier than that of the actor.) In this crowded world how few there are who can leave even a name, how rare those who leave more. The author can be read by future ages! Oh! yes, he can be read; the books are preserved; but is he read? Who disturbs them from their repose upon the dusty shelves of silent libraries? What are the great men of former ages, with rare, very rare, exceptions, but names to the world which shelves their well-bound volumes!

Unless some one will tell me in sober gravity (which is sometimes absurdly said in fulsome dinner speeches and foolish dedications) that the actor has a "kindred Genius" with the poet, whose creations he represents, and that in sheer intellectual calibre Kean and Macready were nearly on a par with Shakespeare, I do not see what cause of complaint can exist in the actor's not sharing the posthumous fame of a Shakespeare. His fame while he lives surpasses that of almost all other men. Byron was not so widely worshipped as Kean. Lawrence and Northcote, Wilkie, and Mulready, what space did they fill in the public eye compared with Young, Charles Kemble or Macready? Surely this renown is ample?

If Macready share the regret of his friends, and if he yearn for posthumous fame, there is yet one issue for him to give the world assurance of his powers. Shakespeare is a good raft whereon to float securely down the stream of time; fasten yourself to that and your immortality is safe. Now Shakespeare must have occupied more of Macready's time and thought than any other subject. Let fruits be given. Let us have from him an edition of Shakespeare, bringing all his practical experience as an actor to illustrate this the first of dramatists. We want no more black letter. We want no more hyperboles of admiration. We want the dramatic excellence and defects illustrated and set forth. Will Macready undertake such a task? It would be a delightful object to occupy his leisure; and it would settle the question as to his own intellectual claims.

The foregoing was written in 1851. This year, 1875, the *Reminiscences and Diaries of Macready* have been given to the world by Sir Frederick Pollock, and they strikingly confirm the justice of my estimate, which almost reads like an echo of what Macready himself expressed. In those volumes we see the incessant study which this eminently conscientious man to the last bestowed on every detail connected with his art; we see also how he endeavored by study to make up for natural deficiencies, and how conscious he was of these deficiencies. We see him over-sensitive to the imaginary disrespect in which his profession is held, and throughout his career hating the stage, while devoting himself to the art. But although his sensitiveness suffered from many of the external conditions of the player's life, his own acceptance by the world was a constant rebuke to his exaggerated claims. He was undeniably a cultivated, honorable, and able man, and would have made an excellent clergyman or member of Parliament; but there is absolutely no evidence that he could have made such a figure either in Church or Senate as would compare with that which he made upon the stage.

[Natural Acting]

... The supreme difficulty of an actor is to represent ideal character with such truthfulness that it shall affect us as real, not to drag down ideal character to the vulgar level. His art is one of representation, not of illusion. He has to use natural expressions, but he must sublimate them; the symbols must be such as we can sympathetically interpret, and for this purpose they must be the expressions of real human feeling; but just as the language is poetry, or choice prose, purified from the hesitancies, incoherences, and imperfections of careless daily speech, so must his utterance be measured, musical and incisive—his manner typical and pictorial. If the language depart too widely from the logic of passion and truthfulness, we call it bombast; if the elevation of the actor's style be not sustained by natural feeling, we call it mouthing and rant; and if the language fall below the passion we call it prosaic and flat; as we call the actor tame if he cannot present the character so as to interest us. The most general error of authors, and of actors, is turgidity rather than flatness. The striving to be effective easily leads into the error of exaggeration. But it by no means follows, as some persons seem to imply, that, because exaggeration is a fault, tameness is a merit. Exaggeration is a fault because it is an untruth; but in art it is as easy to be untrue by falling below as by rising above naturalness.

* * * *

... But in art, simplicity is economy, not meagerness: it is the absence of superfluities, not the suppression of essentials; it arises from an ideal generalization of real and essential qualities, guided by an exquisite sense of proportion.

* * * *

... it has been the great mistake of actors that they have too often brought with them into the drama of ordinary life the style they have been accustomed to in the drama of ideal life.

* * * *

... The art of acting is not shown in giving a conversational tone and a drawing-room quietness, but in vividly presenting character, while never violating the proportions demanded on the one hand, by the *optique du théâtre,* and on the other by what the audience will recognize as truth.

* * * *

... I have always emphatically insisted on the necessity of actors being true to nature in the expression of natural emotions, although the technical conditions of art forbid the expressions being exactly those of real life; but a critic, not understanding this, says:

"In justice to L., however, it should be stated that he does not altogether object to natural acting, but only to acting which follows nature very closely. Being a writer who constructs as well as destroys, he explains what real dramatic art is. An actor should impress an idealized image on the spectator's mind; he should 'use natural expressions, but he must sublimate them,' whatever that may mean; his utterance must be 'measured, musical, and incisive; his manner typical and pictorial'."

It is clear not only from this passage, but from the examples afterwards cited, that my critic considers the perfection of art to lie in the closest reproduction of every-day experience. That an actor should raise the natural expressions into ideal expressions—that he should "sublimate" them—is so little understood by my critic, that he professes not to know what sublimating "may mean." I will not insult him by supposing that it is the word which puzzles him, or that he does not understand Dryden's verses:

> As his actions rose, so raise they still their vein
> In words whose weight best suits a sublimated strain.

But I will ask him if he supposes that an actor, having to represent a character in situations altogether exceptional, and speaking a language very widely departing from the language of ordinary life, would be true to the nature of that character and that language, by servilely reproducing the manners, expression, and intonations of ordinary life? The poet is not closely following nature; the poet is ideal in his treatment; is the actor to be less so? I am presumed to have been guilty of talking nonsense in requiring that the musical verse of the poet should be spoken musically, or the elaborate prose of the prose dramatist should be spoken with measured cadence and incisive effect. I cannot be supposed to approve of measured "mouthing," or to wish for turgidity in wishing for music and precision; would the critic have verse declaimed like prose (naturally, as it is falsely called), and prose gabbled with little reference to cadence and emphasis, like ordinary talk? When he objects to the manner being typical, would he have it not to be recognizable? When he objects to the manner being pictorial, would he have it careless, ungraceful, the slouching of club-rooms and London streets carried into Verona or the Ardennes? Obviously, the pictorial manner which would be natural (ideal) to Romeo or Rosalind, would be unnatural in Charles Surface or Lady Teazle.

* * * *

When we are told that [Edmond] Got "merely behaves just as a warm-hearted man would behave on suddenly receiving the news of a dear friend's death," we ask what warm-hearted man? A hundred different men would behave in a hundred different ways on such an occasion, would say different things, would express their emotions with different looks and gestures. The actor has to select. He must be typical. His expressions must be those which, while they belong to the recognized symbols of our common nature, have also the peculiar individual impress of the character represented. It is obvious, to anyone who reflects for a moment, that nature is often so reticent—that men and women express so little in their faces and gestures, or in their tones, of what is tearing their hearts—that a perfect copy of almost any man's expressions would be utterly ineffective on the stage. It is the actor's art to express in well-known symbols what an individual man may be supposed to feel, and we, the spectators, recognizing these expressions, are thrown into a state of sympathy. Unless the actor follows nature sufficiently to select symbols that are recognized as natural, he fails to touch us; but as to any minute fidelity in copying the actual manner of murderers, misers, avengers, broken-hearted fathers, etc., we really have had so little experience of such characters, that we cannot estimate the fidelity; hence the actor is forced to be as typical as the poet is. Neither pretends closely to copy nature, but only to represent nature sublimated into the ideal. The nearer the approach to every-day reality implied by the author in his characters and language—the closer the coat-and-waist-coat realism of the drama —the closer must be the actor's imitation of every-day manner; but even then he must idealize, i.e., select and heighten—and it is for his tact to determine how much.

* * * *

His [Fechter's] Hamlet was "natural"; but this was not owing to the simple fact of its being more conversational and less stilted than usual. If Shakespeare's grandest language seemed to issue naturally from Fechter's lips, and did not strike you as out of place, which it so often does when mouthed on the stage, the reason was that he formed a tolerably true conception of Hamlet's nature, and could represent that conception. It was his personality which enabled him to represent this conception. Many of the spectators had a conception as true, or truer, but they could not have represented it. This is self-evident. Naturalism truly means the reproduction of those details which characterize the nature of the thing represented. Realism means truth, not vulgarity: truth of the higher as of the lower forms; truth of passion, and truth of manners.

The nature of a Macbeth is not the nature of an Othello; the speech of Achilles is not the speech of Thersites. The truth of the *Madonna di San Sito* is not the truth of Murillo's *Beggar Girl*. But artists and critics overlook this. Actors are especially prone to overlook it, and, in trying to be natural, they sink into the familiar; though that is as unnatural as if they were to attempt to heighten the reality of the Apollo by flinging a paletot over his naked shoulders.

* * * *

[Conventional Acting]

Let me explain more particularly what is meant by the term conventional acting. When an actor feels a vivid sympathy with the passion or humor, he is representing, he personates, i.e., speaks through the *persona* or character; and for the moment is what he represents. He can do this only in proportion to the vividness of his sympathy, and the plasticity of his organization, which enables him to give expression to what he feels; there are certain physical limitations in every organization which absolutely prevent adequate expression of what is in the mind; and thus it is that a dramatist can rarely personate one of his own conceptions. But within the limits which are assigned by nature to every artist, the success of the personation will depend upon the vividness of the actor's sympathy, and his honest reliance on the truth of his own individual expression, in preference to the conventional expressions which may be accepted on the stage. This is the great actor, the creative artist. The conventional artist is one who either, because he does not feel the vivid sympathy, or cannot express what he feels, or has not sufficient energy or self-reliance to trust frankly to his own expressions, cannot be the part, but tries to act it, and is thus necessarily driven to adopt those conventional means of expression with which the traditions of the stage abound. Instead of allowing a strong feeling to express itself through its natural signs, he seizes upon the conventional signs, either because in truth there is no strong feeling moving him, or because he is not artist enough to give it genuine expression; his lips will curl, his brow wrinkle, his eyes be thrown up, his forehead be slapped, or he will grimace, rant, and "take the stage," in the style which has become traditional, but which was perhaps never seen off the stage; and thus he runs through the gamut of sounds and signs which bear as remote an affinity to any real expressions as the pantomimic conventions of ballet-dancers....

[Good and Bad Acting]

...Bad acting, like bad writing, has a remarkable uniformity, whether seen on the French, German, Italian, or English stages; it all seems modeled after two or three types, and those the least like types of good acting. The fault generally lies less in the bad imitation of a good model, than in the successful imitation of a bad model. The style of expression is not simply conventional, the conventionality is absurdly removed from truth and grace. The majority have not learned to speak, much less to act; they mouth and gabble, look at the audience instead of their interlocutors, fling emphasis at random, mistake violence for emotion, grimace for humor, and express their feelings by signs as conventional and unlike nature as the gestures of a ballet-dancer. Good acting, on the contrary, like good writing, is remarkable for its individuality. It charms by its truth; and truth is always original. It has certain qualities which, belonging to the fundamental excellences of the art, are common—such as distinctness and quiet power in elocution, gradation in expression, and ruling calmness, which is never felt as coldness, but keeps the artist master of his effects; yet these qualities have in each case the individual stamp of the actor, and seem to belong only to him.

*　*　*　*

Some of the universal errors are irritating because they spring less from inexperience and incompetence than from misguided vanity. Why, for instance, do actors fail to see the absurdity of not looking at the person addressed, as they would look in real life? Why is an impassioned lover, instead of fixing his eyes on the eyes of his mistress, to fix them on the upper boxes, or the side scenes? Such a mistake not only disturbs the illusion of the spectator, but disturbs the artistic imagination of the actor himself by withdrawing it from its direct object. It is because he is thinking of himself and the audience, instead of imaginatively identifying himself with the character he is representing, that his representation is so feeble and confused. If he kept his eyes fixed on the eyes of the person he is addressing, this alone would hinder his thoughts from wandering away from the scene: it would give a poise to his imagination—a poise all the more needful to him because his artistic feeling is feeble; and since spontaneous suggestions fail to sustain his imagination, all external aids become important. It is an invariable characteristic of good actors that they never seem to be conscious of the audience, but always absorbed in the world of which they represent a part; whereas it is the not less invariable characteristic of bad actors that they cannot forget themselves and the audience.

*　*　*　*

[Physical Qualifications of the Actor]

...acting, because it is a representative art, cannot be created by intelligence or sensibility (however necessary these may be for the perfection of the art), but must always depend upon the physical qualifications of the actor, these being the means of representation. It matters little what the actor feels; what he can express gives him his distinctive value.

* * * *

A more complete failure I have seldom seen made by a good actor [Bressant as Tartuffe] but it was a failure from which actors might learn a valuable lesson, were not the lesson so often taught in vain: namely, the necessity of restricting themselves to parts for which they have the physical qualifications. Acting being personation, it is clear that unless the actor has the personal qualifications requisite for the representation of the character, no amount of ability in conceiving the part will avail.

* * * *

Voice, look and gesture are the actor's symbols, through which he makes intelligible the emotions of the character which he is personating. No amount of sensibility will avail unless it can express itself adequately by these symbols. It is not enough for an actor to feel, he must represent. He must express his feelings in symbols universally intelligible and affecting. A harsh, inflexible voice, a rigid or heavy face, would prevent even a Shakespeare from being impressive and affecting on the stage; whereas a man, with little sensibility, but endowed with a sympathetic, penetrating voice, and a flexibile physiognomy, would rouse the pits to transports.

* * * *

[Elocution and Gesture]

Emphasis and pause are indeed the supreme difficulties of elocution. They are rarely managed by those who read blank verse, even in a room, and on the stage the difficulty is greatly enhanced. Nevertheless no one can pretend to be an actor of the poetic drama who has not mastered this art; although at the present day it is, like many other requisites, boldly disregarded, and we hear the noblest verse spouted (not spoken) with the remorseless indifference of that actor who announced himself thus:

'Tis I, my lord, the early village cock.

* * * *

The great difficulty in elocution is *to be* slow, and not to *seem* slow—to speak the phrases with such distinctness, and such management of the breath, that each shall tell, yet due proportion be maintained. Hurry destroys the effect; and actors hurry because they dread, and justly dread, the heaviness of a slow utterance. The art is so to manage the time that it shall not appear slow to the hearer; and this is an art very rarely understood by actors. No sooner have they to express excitement or emotion of any kind than they seem to lose all mastery over the rhythm and cadence of their speech....

Let them study great speakers, and they will find that in passages which seem rapid there is a measured rhythm, and that even in the whirlwind of passion there is as strict a regard to *tempo* as in passionate music. *Resistant flexibility* is the perfection of elocution.

* * * *

...If the prose of daily life is to be represented on the stage, only such an elevation of the style as is demanded by the laws of stage perspective should be adopted; if the scene be poetical a greater elevation is required; but in either case the fundamental condition is that of representing life; and all obvious violations of the truths of life are errors in art. Prose on the stage is not to be spoken exactly as in the street. Verse is not to be spoken as prose. The natural way of speaking prose or verse is that which, while preserving the requisite elevation, never allows us to feel that it is unusual. It is indeed speaking—not mouthing.

* * * *

...Without a sympathetic voice, no declamation can be effective. The tones which stir us need not be musical, need not be pleasant even, but they must have a penetrating, vibrating quality.

* * * *

After the management of the voice, actors most err in the management of the body: they mouth their sentences, and emphasize their gestures, in the effort to be effective, and in ignorance of the psychological conditions on which effects depend. In each case the effort to aggrandize natural expression leads to exaggeration and want of truth. In attempting the ideal they pass into the artificial. The tones and gestures of ordinary unimpassioned moments would not, they feel, be appropriate to ideal characters and impassioned situation; and the difficulty of the art lies precisely in the selection of idealized expressions which shall, to the spectator, be symbols of real emotions. All but very great actors are redundant in gesticulation; not simply overdoing the significant, but unable to repress insignificant movements....

It would be worth the actor's while to borrow a hint from the story of Voltaire's pupil, when, to repress her tendency towards exuberant gesticulation, he ordered her to rehearse with her hands tied to her side. She began her recitation in this enforced quietness, but at last, carried away by the movement of her feelings, she flung up her arms, and snapped the threads. In tremor she began to apologize to the poet; he, smiling, reassured her that the gesticulation was then admirable, because it was irrepressible. If actors will study fine models they will learn that gestures, to be effective, must be significant, and to be significant they must be rare. To stand still on the stage...is one of the elementary difficulties of the art—and one which is rarely mastered.

* * * *

[Acting and Intellect]

...He [William Farren] certainly had a very keen eye for a wide range of characteristics, and presented a greater variety of memorable types than any actor of his time; and if it is true, as many assert, that off the stage he was rather stupid than otherwise, it only shows, what indeed requires no fresh proof, that acting is an art very much more dependent on special aptitudes than on general intellectual vigor. A man may be a magnificent singer with the smallest philosophical endowments, and a marvellous actor with an amount of information which would deeply afflict Mrs. Marcet, or of critical insight which would excite the pity of a quarterly reviewer. We are too apt to generalize from a general term: we call a man clever because he surpasses his rivals: and as the word clever is used to designate any kind of superiority, we rashly conclude that a clever actor ought to be intellectually distinguished, and because he is a good mime he must be an acute thinker.

Farren, undoubtedly, had in a high degree the intelligence necessary for his art, and the physical qualifications which the art demanded; whatever he may have been in private, he was eminently an intellectual actor, meaning by that phrase an

[349]

actor who produced his effects not by the grotesqueness or drollery of his physique, but by the close observation and happy reproduction of characteristics—i.e., not by appealing physically to our mirthful sensibilities, but indirectly through our intellectual recognition of the incongruous.

* * * *

[Truthful Representation or Simulation]

...In how far does the actor feel the emotion he expresses? When we hear of Macready and [John] Liston lashing themselves into a fury behind the scenes in order to come on the stage sufficiently excited to give a truthful representation of the agitations of anger, the natural inference is that these artists recognized the truth of the popular notion which assumes that the actor really feels what he expresses. But this inference seems contradicted by experience. Not only is it notorious that the actor is feigning, and that if he really felt what he feigns he would be unable to withstand the wear and tear of such emotion repeated night after night; but it is indisputable, to those who know anything of art, that the mere presence of genuine emotion would be such a disturbance of the intellectual equilibrium as entirely to frustrate artistic expression. Talma told M. Barrière that he was once carried away by the truth and beauty of the actress playing with him till she recalled him by a whisper: "Take care, Talma, you are moved!" on which he remarked, "It is really from emotion that difficulties spring: the voice balks, the memory fails, and gestures become false; and the effect is destroyed"; and there is an observation of Molé to a similar effect: "I was not satisfied with myself tonight; I allowed myself to be carried away and did not remain master of myself. I felt the situation too strongly. I was the character himself, no longer the actor who played the part. I had become as real as if I were in my own home. To achieve the scenic illusion one must be otherwise."

Everyone initiated into the secrets of the art of acting will seize at once the meaning of this luminous phrase, scenic illusion; and the uninitiated will understand how entirely opposed to all the purposes of the art and all the secrets of effect would be representation of passion in its real rather than in its symbolical expression: the red, swollen, and distorted features of grief, the harsh and screaming intonation of anger, are unsuited to art; the paralysis of all outward expression, and the flurry and agitation of ungraceful gesticulation which belong to certain powerful emotions, may be described by the poet, but cannot be admitted into plastic art. The poet may tell us what is signified by the withdrawal of all life and movement from the face and limbs, describing the internal agitations or the deadly calm which disturb or paralyze the sufferer; but the painter, sculptor, or actor must tell us what the sufferer undergoes, and tell it through the symbols of outward expression—the internal workings must be legible in the external symbols; and these external symbols must also have a certain grace and proportion to affect us esthetically.

All art is symbolical. If it presented emotion in its real expression it would cease to move us as art; sometimes cease to move us at all, or move us only to laughter. There is a departure from reality in all the stage accessories. The situation, the character, the language, all are at variance with daily experience. Emotion does not utter itself in verse nor in carefully chosen sentences. . . .

The reader sees at once that as a matter of fact the emotions represented by the actor are not agitating him as they would agitate him in reality; he is feigning and we know that he is feigning; he is representing a fiction which is to move us as a fiction, and not to lacerate our sympathies as they would be lacerated by the agony of a fellow-creature actually suffering in our presence. The tears we shed are tears welling from a sympathetic source; but their salt bitterness is removed, and their pain is pleasurable.

But now arises the antinomy, as Kant would call it—the contradiction which perplexes the judgment. If the actor lose all power over his art under the disturbing influence of emotion, he also loses all power over his art in proportion to his deadness to emotion. If he really feel, he cannot act; but he cannot act unless he feel. All the absurd efforts of mouthing and grimacing actors to produce an effect, all the wearisomeness of cold conventional representation—mimicry without life— we know to be owing to the unimpassioned talent of the actor. Observe, I do not say to his unimpressed nature. It is quite possible for a man of exquisite sensibility to be ludicrously tame in his acting, if he has not the requisite talent of expression, or has not yet learned how to modulate it so as to give it due effect. . . . But although it is quite possible for an actor to have sensibility without the talent of expression, and therefore to be a tame actor though an impassioned man, it is wholly impossible for him to express what he has never felt, to be an impassioned actor with a cold nature.

And here is the point of intersection of the two lines of argument just followed out. The condition being that a man must feel emotion if he is to express it, for if he does not feel it he will not know how to express it, how can this be reconciled with the impossibility of his affecting us esthetically while he is disturbed by emotion? In other words: how far does he really feel the passion he expressed? It is a question of degree. As in all art, feeling lies at the root, but the foliage and flowers though deriving their sap from emotion, derive their form and structure from the intellect. The poet cannot write while his eyes are full of tears, while his nerves are trembling from the mental shock, and his hurrying thoughts are too agitated to settle into definite tracks. But he must have felt, or his verse will be a mere echo. It is from the memory of past feelings that he draws the beautiful image with which he delights us. He is tremulous again under the remembered agitation, but it is a pleasant tremor, and in no way disturbs the clearness of his intellect. He is a spectator of his own tumult; and though moved by it, can yet so master it as to select from it only these elements which suit his purpose. We are all spectators of ourselves; but it is the peculiarity of the artistic nature to indulge in such introspection even in moments of all but the most disturbing passion, and to draw thence materials for art. This is true also of the fine actor, and many of my readers will recognize the truth of what Talma said of himself: "I have suffered cruel losses, and have often been assailed with profound sorrows; but after the first moment when grief vents itself in cries and tears, I have found myself involuntarily turning my gaze inwards, and found that the actor was unconsciously studying the man, and catching nature in the act." It is only by thus familiarizing oneself with the nature of the various emotions, that one can properly interpret them. But even that is not enough. They must be watched in others, the interpreting key being given in our own consciousness.

Having something like an intellectual appreciation of the sequences of feeling and their modes of manifestation the actor has next to select out of these such as his own physical qualifications enable him to reproduce effectively, and such as will be universally intelligible. To quote Talma once more: "Yes, we must be sensible, we must experience emotion in order to re-create it better, in order to grasp its nature by study and reflection. Our art requires depth. No improvisation is possible on the stage without penalty of failure. All is calculated, all must be foreseen—both the emotion which seems unexpected and the perturbation which seems involuntary. The intonation, the gesture, and the facial expression which seem inspired will have been repeated a hundred times."

All this I may assume the reader to accept without dissent, and yet anticipate his feeling some perplexity in reconciling it with the anecdotes which started this digression. Surely, he may say, neither Macready nor Liston could have been so unfamiliar with rage and its manifestations that any hesitation could paralyze their efforts to express these. Why then this preparation behind the scenes? Simply because it was absolutely necessary that they should be in a state of excitement if they were to represent it with truthfulness; and having temperaments which were not instantaneously excitable by the mere imagination of a scene, they prepared themselves. Actors like Edmund Kean, Rachel, or Lemaître found no difficulty in the most rapid transitions; they could one moment chat calmly and the next explode. The imaginative sympathy instantaneously called up all the accessories of expression; one tone would send vibrations through them powerful enough to excite the nervous discharge.

The answer to the question, How far does the actor feel? is, therefore, something like this: He is in a state of emotional excitement sufficiently strong to furnish him with the elements of expression, but not strong enough to prevent his modulating the one and arranging the other according to a preconceived standard. His passion must be ideal—sympathetic not personal. He may hate with a rival's hate the actress to whom he is manifesting tenderness, or love with a husband's love the actress to whom he is expressing vindictiveness; but for Juliet or Desdemona he must feel love and wrath.

We sometimes hear amateur critics object to fine actors that they are every night the same, never varying their gestures or their tones. This is stigmatized as "mechanical"; and the critics innocently oppose to it some ideal of their own which they call "inspiration." Actors would smile at such nonsense. What is called inspiration is the mere haphazard of carelessness or incompetence; the actor is seeking an expression which he ought to have found when studying his part. What would be thought of a singer who sang his aria differently every night? In the management of his breath, the distribution of light and shade, in his phrasing, the singer who knows how to sing never varies. The timbre of his voice, the energy of his spirit, may vary; but his methods are invariable. Actors learn their parts as singers learn their songs. Every detail is deliberative, or has been deliberated. The very separation of art from nature involves this calculation. The sudden flash of suggestion which is called inspiration may be valuable, it may be worthless; the artistic intellect estimates the value, and adopts or rejects it accordingly.

Trusting to the inspiration of the moment is like trusting to a shipwreck for your first lesson in swimming.

[352]

ENGLAND AND IRELAND
HENRY IRVING
(1838-1905)

Sir Henry Irving (John Henry Brodribb), the first actor in England to be knighted for histrionic achievements, was the logical heir of Charles Kean's productions at the Princess Theatre in the mid-century. His acting was derived from the major figures of the century, especially from Macready's disciple, the actor-manager Samuel Phelps, whom Irving studied. The realistic innovations of Boucicault, Alfred Wigan, the Bancrofts, and Fechter also influenced his craft.

Born in Cornwall, Irving came to London early to attend school and to work. He studied elocution with an actor in the Sadler's Wells company through whom he met Samuel Phelps. Like others in this period Irving turned to the provinces to acquire experience. He made his first appearance in 1856 and followed it by playing for some two years in Edinburgh with older troupers like Helen Faucit and the American Charlotte Cushman. In the mid-sixties he began to perform successfully in London. He joined H. L. Bateman's Lyceum Theatre company where, in November of 1871, he made his first mark as Mathias in *The Bells,* a role which he kept in his repertory for many years. At the Lyceum he performed also in W. G. Wills' *Charles I* and treated London with his unconventional portrayal of Hamlet.

In 1878 he became the manager of the Lyceum Theatre and began his reign as actor-manager. With him was Ellen Terry, the finest actress of her day. Together they acted such standbys as *The Merchant of Venice, Othello, Much Ado About Nothing,* and *Hamlet.* To all these productions Irving brought not only his original qualities as an actor, but also his excellent taste in staging and scenic design. His plays were artistic spectacles. In 1881 the Lyceum housed a gala theatrical event when Edwin Booth joined Irving and Ellen Terry in performances of *Othello.* The two stars alternated in the roles of Iago and Othello. Irving and his company were as well known in America as in England, for at various times they made long visits to the States.

All agreed that Irving's productions were the finest in good taste and realism. His notable staging of group scenes was probably influenced by the London performances of the Saxe-Meiningen ensemble in 1881. Irving's own acting, however, created violent partisanships. A disciple like Gordon Craig, Ellen Terry's son, admired Irving and praised him for the fact that he acted best in second rate melodramas in which his own creativeness did not compete with that of the author. Most of the critics acknowledged that Irving was unsuccessful in the major, traditional tragic roles. It was not merely his inadequate voice and peculiar gait, which all commented upon, that prevented him from achieving success in these roles. As his address printed here suggests, Irving was more interested in by-play and in the creation of the role as an actor than in merely presenting the words and thoughts of the dramatist. He believed that high tragedy should be played in the realistic manner which had heretofore been confined to comedy and melodrama. Descriptions of Irving as Mathias taking off his shoes in the first scene of *The Bells* reveal the fact that he set the tone of his characterization by realistic by-play.

The critic Clement Scott lauded Irving's intellectual conception of Hamlet and the realism of his performance in Boucicault's adaption of the French play *Louis XI,* but then Scott was the critic who carried the English banner against Ibsen. George Bernard Shaw commented adversely upon Irving, and criticized him severely for neglecting contemporary plays. Max Beerbohm, evaluating Irving after the actor's death, wrote: "A more plausible grievance against Irving, as manager, is that in quest of bustling romances or melodramas he seemed generally to alight on hackwork. I think there can be no doubt that he was lacking in literary sense, and was content with any play that gave him scope for a great and central display of his genius in acting. He did not, of course, invent the 'star' system. But he carried it as far as it could be carried."

The heated paper controversy between Irving and Coquelin on the issues of Diderot's *Paradox of Acting* led to William Archer's investigation of emotionalism, *Masks or Faces?*

The following lecture was delivered by Irving at Harvard University on March 30, 1885.

The Importance of By-Play

Now, what is the art of acting? I speak of it in its highest sense, as the art to which Roscius, Betterton, and Garrick owed their fame. It is the art of embodying the poet's creations, of giving them flesh and blood, of making the figures which appeal to your mind's eye in the printed drama live before you on the stage. "To fathom the depths of character, to trace its latent motives, to feel its finest quiverings of emotion, to comprehend the thoughts that are hidden under words, and thus possess one's-self of the actual mind of the individual man"—such was Macready's definition of the player's art; and to this we may add the testimony of Talma. He describes tragic acting as "the union of grandeur without pomp and nature without triviality." It demands, he says, the endowment of high sensibility and intelligence....

You will readily understand from this that to the actor the well-worn maxim that art is long and life is short has a constant significance. The older we grow the more acutely alive we are to the difficulties of our craft. I cannot give you a better illustration of this fact than a story which is told of Macready. A friend of mine, once a dear friend of his, was with him when he played Hamlet for the last time. The curtain had fallen, and the great actor was sadly thinking that the part he loved so much would never be his again. And as he took off his velvet mantle and laid it aside, he muttered almost unconsciously the words of Horatio, "Good-night, sweet Prince"; then turning to his friend, "Ah," said he, "I am just beginning to realize the sweetness, the tenderness, the gentleness of this dear Hamlet!" Believe me the true artist never lingers fondly upon what he has done. He is ever thinking of what remains undone: ever striving toward an ideal it may never be his fortune to attain....

...There are people who fancy they have more music in their souls than was ever translated into harmony by Beethoven or Mozart. There are others who think they could paint pictures, write poetry—in short, do anything, if they only made the effort. To them what is accomplished by the practiced actor seems easy and simple. But as it needs the skill of the musician to draw the full volume of eloquence from the written score, so it needs the skill of the dramatic artist to develop the subtle harmonies of the poetic play. In fact, to do and not to dream, is the

Henry Irving: "The Art of Acting" (1885), *The Drama*. London: William Heinemann, 1893, pp. 40-69 *passim*.

mainspring of success in life. The actor's art is to act, and the true acting of any character is one of the most difficult accomplishments. I challenge the acute student to ponder over Hamlet's renunciation of Ophelia—one of the most complex scenes in all the drama—and say that he has learned more from his meditations than he could be taught by players whose intelligence is equal to his own. To present the man thinking aloud is the most difficult achievement of our art. Here the actor who has no real grip of the character, but simply recites the speeches with a certain grace and intelligence, will be untrue. The more intent he is upon the words, and the less on the ideas that dictated them, the more likely he is to lay himself open to the charge of mechanical interpretation. It is perfectly possible to express to an audience all the involutions of thought, the speculation, doubt, wavering, which reveal the meditative but irresolute mind. As the varying shades of fancy pass and repass the mirror of the face, they may yield more material to the studious play-goer than he is likely to get by a diligent poring over the text. In short, as we understand the people around us much better by personal intercourse than by all the revelations of written words—for words, as Tennyson says, "half reveal and half conceal the soul within," so the drama has, on the whole, infinitely more sug-gestions when it is well acted than when it is interpreted by the unaided judgment of the student. It has been said that acting is an unworthy occupation because it represents feigned emotions, but this censure would apply with equal force to poet or novelist. Do not imagine that I am claiming for the actor sole and undivided authority. He should himself be a student, and it is his business to put into practice the best ideas he can gather from the general current of thought with regard to the highest dramatic literature. But it is he who gives body to those ideas—fire, force, and sensibility, without which they would remain for most people mere airy abstractions.

It is often supposed that great actors trust to the inspiration of the moment. Nothing can be more erroneous. There will, of course, be such moments, when an actor at a white heat illumines some passage with a flash of imagination (and this mental condition, by the way, is impossible to the student sitting in his armchair); but the great actor's surprises are generally well weighed, studied, and balanced. We know that Edmund Kean constantly practiced before a mirror effects which startled his audience by their apparent spontaneity. It is the accumulation of such effects which enables an actor, after many years, to present many great characters with remarkable completeness.

I do not want to overstate the case, or to appeal to anything that is not within common experience, so I can confidently ask you whether a scene in a great play has not been at some time vividly impressed on your minds by the delivery of a single line, or even of one forcible word. Has not this made the passage far more real and human to you than all the thought you have devoted to it? An accom-plished critic has said that Shakespeare himself might have been surprised had he heard the "Fool, fool, fool!" of Edmund Kean. And though all actors are not Keans, they have in varying degree this power of making a dramatic character step out of the page, and come nearer to our hearts and our understandings.

After all, the best and most convincing exposition of the whole art of acting is given by Shakespeare himself: "To hold, as 'twere, the mirror up to nature, to show virtue her own feature, scorn her own image, and the very age and body of the time his form and pressure." Thus the poet recognized the actor's art as a most potent ally in the representation of human life. He believed that to hold the mirror up to nature was one of the worthiest functions in the sphere of labor, and actors are content to point to his definition of their work as the charter of their privileges.

Practice of the Art

The practice of the art of acting is a subject difficult to treat with the necessary brevity. Beginners are naturally anxious to know what course they should pursue. In common with other actors, I receive letters from young people, many of whom are very earnest in their ambition to adopt the dramatic calling, but not sufficiently alive to the fact that success does not depend on a few lessons in declamation. When I was a boy I had a habit which I think would be useful to all young students. Be fore going to see a play of Shakespeare's I used to form—in a very juvenile way— a theory as to the working out of the whole drama, so as to correct my conceptions by those of the actors; and though I was, as a rule, absurdly wrong, there can be no doubt that any method of independent study is of enormous importance, not only to youngsters, but also to students of a larger growth. Without it the mind is apt to take its stamp from the first forcible impression it receives, and to fall into a servile dependence upon traditions, which, robbed of the spirit that created them, are apt to be purely mischievous. What was natural to the creator is often unnatural and lifeless in the imitator. No two people form the same conceptions of character, and therefore it is always advantageous to see an independent and courageous exposition of an original ideal. There can be no objection to the kind of training that imparts a knowledge of manners and customs, and the teaching which pertains to simple deportment on the stage is necessary and most useful; but you cannot possibly be taught any tradition of character, for that has no permanence. Nothing is more fleeting than any traditional method of impersonation. You may learn where a particular personage used to stand on the stage, or down which trap the Ghost of Hamlet's father vanished; but the soul of interpretation is lost, and it is this soul which the actor has to re-create for himself. It is not mere attitude or tone that has to be studied; you must be moved by the impulse of being; you must impersonate and not recite.

There has always been a controversy as to the province of naturalism in dramatic art. In England it has been too much the custom, I believe, while demanding naturalism in comedy, to expect a false inflation in tragedy. But there is no reason why an actor should be less natural in tragic than in lighter moods. Passions vary in expression according to molds of character and manners, but their reality should not be lost even when they are expressed in the heroic forms of the drama. A very simple test is a reference to the records of old actors. What was it in their performances that chiefly impressed their contemporaries? Very rarely the measured recitation of this or that speech, but very often a simple exclamation that deeply moved their auditors, because it was a gleam of nature in the midst of declamation. The "Prithee, undo this button!" of Garrick, was remembered when many stately utterances were forgotten. In our day the contrast between artificial declamation and the accents of nature is less marked, because its delivery is more uniformly simple, and an actor who lapses from a natural into a false tone is sure to find that his hold upon his audience is proportionately weakened....

To be natural on the stage is most difficult, and yet a grain of nature is worth a bushel of artifice. But you may say—what is nature? I quoted just now Shakespeare's definition of the actor's art. After the exhortation to hold the mirror up to nature, he adds the pregnant warning: "This overdone or come tardy off, though it make the unskilful laugh, cannot but make the judicious grieve, the censure of which one must in your allowance o'erweigh a whole theatre of others." Nature may be overdone by triviality in conditions that demand exaltation; for instance, Hamlet's first address to the Ghost lifts his disposition to an altitude far beyond the ordinary reaches of our souls, and his manner of speech should be adapted to this sentiment. But such exaltation of utterance is wholly out of place in the purely colloquial scene with the Gravedigger. . . .

Like the practiced orator, the actor rises and descends with his sentiment, and cannot always be in a fine frenzy. This variety is especially necessary in Shakespeare, whose work is essentially different from the classic drama, because it presents every mood of mind and form of speech, commonplace or exalted, as character and situation dictate: whereas in such a play as Addison's *Cato* everybody is consistently eloquent about everything.

There are many causes for the growth of naturalism in dramatic art, and amongst them we should remember the improvement in the mechanism of the stage. For instance, there has been a remarkable development in stage-lighting. In old pictures you will observe the actors constantly standing in a line, because the oil-lamps of those days gave such an indifferent illumination that everybody tried to get into what was called the focus—the "blaze of publicity" furnished by the "float" or footlights. The importance of this is illustrated by an amusing story of Edmund Kean, who one night played *Othello* with more than his usual intensity. An admirer who met him in the street next day was loud in his congratulations: "I really thought you would have choked Iago, Mr. Kean—you seemed so tremendously in earnest." "In earnest!" said the tragedian, "I should think so! Hang the fellow, he was trying to keep me out of the focus."

I do not recommend actors to allow their feelings to carry them away like this; but it is necessary to warn you against the theory expounded with brilliant ingenuity by Diderot, that the actor never feels. When Macready played Virginius, after burying his beloved daughter, he confessed that his real experience gave a new force to his acting in the most pathetic situations of the play. Are we to suppose that this was a delusion, or that the sensibility of the man was a genuine aid to the actor? [John] Bannister said of John Kemble that he was never pathetic because he had no children. Talma says that when deeply moved he found himself making a rapid and fugitive observation on the alteration of his voice, and on a certain spasmodic vibration which it contracted in tears. Has not the actor who can thus make his feelings a part of his art an advantage over the actor who never feels, but who makes his observations solely from the feelings of others? It is necessary to this art that the mind should have, as it were, a double consciousness, in which all the emotions proper to the occasion may have full swing, while the actor is all the time on the alert for every detail of his method. It may be that his playing will be more spirited one night than another. But the actor who combines the electric force of a strong personality with a mastery of the resources of his art must have a greater power over his audience than the passionless actor who gives a most artistic simulation of the emotions he never experiences.

Now, in the practice of acting, a most important point is the study of elocution; and in elocution one great difficulty is the use of sufficient force to be generally heard without being unnaturally loud, and without acquiring a stilted delivery. The advice of the old actors was that you should always pitch your voice so as to be heard by the back row of the gallery—no easy task to accomplish without offending the ears of the front row of the orchestra. And I should tell you that this exaggeration applies to everything on the stage. To appear to be natural, you must in reality be much broader than nature. To act on the stage as one really would in a room, would be ineffective and colorless. I never knew an actor who brought the art of elocution to greater perfection than the late Charles Mathews, whose utterances on the stage appeared so natural that one was surprised to find when near him that he was really speaking in a very loud key. There is a great actor in your own country to whose elocution one always listens with utmost enjoyment—I mean Edwin Booth. He has inherited this gift, I believe from his famous father, of whom I have heard it said, that he always insisted on a thorough use of the "instruments"—by which he meant the teeth—in the formation of words.

An imperfect elocution is apt to degenerate into a monotonous uniformity of tone. Some wholesome advice on this point we find in the *Life of Betterton*....

Now, on the question of pronunciation there is something to be said, which, I think, in ordinary teaching is not sufficiently considered. Pronunciation on the stage should be simple and unaffected, but not always fashioned rigidly according to a dictionary standard. No less an authority than Cicero points out that pronunciation must vary widely according to the emotions to be expressed; that it may be broken or cut, with a varying or direct sound, and that it serves for the actor the purpose of color to the painter, from which to draw his variations.... Words are intended to express feelings and ideas, not to bind them in rigid fetters. The accents of pleasure are different from the accents of pain, and if a feeling is more accurately expressed, as in nature, by a variation of sound not provided for by the laws of pronunciation, then such imperfect laws must be disregarded and nature vindicated. The word should be the echo of the sense.

The force of an actor depends, of course, upon his physique; and it is necessary, therefore, that a good deal of attention should be given to bodily training. Everything that develops suppleness, elasticity, and grace—that most subtle charm —should be carefully cultivated, and in this regard your admirable gymnasium is worth volumes of advice. Sometimes there is a tendency to train the body at the expense of the mind, and the young actor with striking physical advantages must beware of regarding this fortunate endowment as his entire stock-in-trade. That way folly lies, and the result may be too dearly purchased by the fame of a photographer's window. It is clear that the physique of actors must vary; there can be no military standards of proportions on the stage. Some great actors have had to struggle against physical disabilities of a serious nature. Betterton had an unprepossessing face; so had Lekain. John Kemble was troubled with a weak, asthmatic voice, and yet by his dignity, and the force of his personality, he was able to achieve the greatest effects. In some cases a super-abundant physique has incapacitated actors from playing many parts. The combination in one frame of all the gifts of mind and all the advantages of person is very rare on the stage; but talent will conquer many natural defects when it is sustained by energy and perseverance.

With regard to gesture, Shakespeare's advice is all-embracing. "Suit the action to the word, the word to the action, with this special observance that you over-step not the modesty of nature." And here comes the consideration of a very material part of the actor's business—by-play. This is of the very essence of true art. It is more than anything else significant of the extent to which the actor has identified himself with the character he represents. Recall the scenes between Iago and Othello, and consider how the whole interest of the situation depends on the skill with which the gradual effect of the poisonous suspicion instilled into the Moor's mind is depicted in look and tone, slight of themselves, but all contributing to the intensity of the situation. One of the greatest tests of an actor is his capacity for listening. By-play must be unobtrusive; the student should remember that the most minute expression attracts attention: that nothing is lost, that by-play is as mischievous when it is injudicious as it is effective when rightly conceived, and that while trifles make perfection, perfection is no trifle. This lesson was enjoined on me when I was a very young man by that remarkable actress, Charlotte Cushman. I remember that when she played Meg Merrilies [in *Guy Mannering*] I was cast for Henry Bertram, on the principle, seemingly, that an actor with no singing voice is admiringly fitted for a singing part. It was my duty to give Meg Merrilies a piece of money, and I did it after the traditional fashion by handing her a large purse full of coin of the realm, in the shape of broken crockery, which was generally used in financial transactions on the stage, because when the virtuous maiden rejected with scorn the advances of the lordly libertine, and threw his pernicious bribe upon the ground, the clatter of the broken crockery suggested fabulous wealth. But after the play Miss Cushman, in the course of some kindly advice, said to me: "Instead of giving me that purse don't you think it would have been much more natural if you had taken a number of coins from your pocket, and given me the smallest? That is the way one gives alms to a beggar, and it would have added to the realism of the scene." I have never forgotten that lesson, for simple as it was, it contained many elements of dramatic truth. It is most important that an actor should learn that he is a figure in a picture, and that the least exaggeration destroys the harmony of the composition. All the members of the company should work towards a common end, with the nicest subordination of their individuality to the general purpose. Without this method a play when acted is at best a disjointed and incoherent piece of work, instead of being a harmonious whole like the fine performance of an orchestral symphony.

The root of the matter is that the actor must before all things form a definite conception of what he wishes to convey. It is better to be wrong and be consistent, than to be right, yet hesitating and uncertain. This is why great actors are sometimes very bad or very good. They will do the wrong thing with a courage and thoroughness which makes the error all the more striking; although when they are right they may often be superb. It is necessary that the actor should learn to think before he speaks; a practice which, I believe, is very useful off the stage. Let him remember, first, that every sentence expresses a new thought, and, therefore, frequently demands a change of intonation; secondly, that the thought precedes the word. Of course there are passages in which thought and language are borne along by the streams of emotion and completely intermingled. But more often it will be found that the most natural, the most seemingly accidental effects are obtained when the working of the mind is seen before the tongue gives it words.

You will see that the limits of an actor's studies are very wide. To master the technicalities of his craft, to familiarize his mind with the structure, rhythm, and the soul of poetry, to be constantly cultivating his perceptions of life around him and of all the arts—painting, music, sculpture—for the actor who is devoted to his profession is susceptible to every harmony of color, sound, and form—to do this is to labor in a large field of industry. But all your training, bodily and mental, is subservient to the two great principles in tragedy and comedy—passion and geniality.

Geniality in comedy is one of the rarest gifts. Think of the rich unction of Falstaff, the mercurial fancy of Mercutio, the witty vivacity and manly humor of Benedick —think of the qualities, natural and acquired, that are needed for the complete portrayal of such characters, and you will understand how difficult it is for a comedian to rise to such a sphere. In tragedy, passion or intensity sweeps all before it, and when I say passion, I mean the passion of pathos as well as wrath or revenge. These are the supreme elements of the actor's art, which cannot be taught by any system, however just, and to which all education is but tributary.

ELLEN TERRY
(1848-1928)

A child of actors, Ellen Terry made her first appearance on the stage as the boy Mamillius in Charles Kean's production of *The Winter's Tale* at the Princess Theatre in 1856. In the next few years she acted such parts as that of Puck, Arthur in *King John,* and Fleance in *Macbeth.* After some work at the Theatre Royal in Bristol she came to London again to play at the Haymarket Theatre in 1863, where she took a part in the famous production of Tom Taylor's *Our American Cousin.* At the New Queen's Theatre under Alfred Wigan's (1814-1878) direction, she had occasion to act with Henry Irving. She spent some time working with Charles Reade, from whom she learned much. With the Bancrofts she made her first great success in the role of Portia, and at the Court Theatre, directed by Sir John Hare, she played the title role of Olivia in W. G. Will's adaptation of *The Vicar of Wakefield.*

The important period of her career came after 1878 when she was engaged by Henry Irving to play Ophelia to his Hamlet. From that time until 1896 she enacted all the leading female roles in Irving's productions. It was her beauty and artistry as well as the characterizations of Irving that drew people to the Lyceum Theatre. Although she was not a tragedian or an actress of very wide range, she was greatly admired in such roles as Portia and Olivia.

Parting with Irving in 1902, she played with Frank Benson and Beerbohm Tree for a while. In 1903 she managed the Imperial Theatre in Westminster, where her son Gordon Craig staged some productions for her. After leaving Irving she performed the plays of her contemporaries Shaw and Barrie. During the second decade of the twentieth century she lectured on Shakespeare in England and in the United States. Her last appearance on the stage took place in 1925 at the Lyric Theatre, Hammersmith, where she played in Walter De la Mare's *Crossings.*

The Three "I's"

Imagination! Imagination! I put it first years ago, when I was asked what qualities I thought necessary for success upon the stage. And I am still of the same opinion. Imagination, industry, and intelligence—"the three I's"—are all indispensable to the actress, but of these three the greatest is, without any doubt, imagination.

* * * *

Ellen Terry's Memoirs, with a preface, notes and additional biographical chapters by Edith Craig and Christopher St. John. New York: G. P. Putnam's Sons, 1932, *passim.*

As I read these notes of his [Charles Reade] on anti-climax, monotony of pace, and all the other offenses against scientific principles of acting... I feel more strongly than ever how important it is to master these principles. Until you have learned them and practiced them you cannot afford to discard them. There is all the difference in the world between departure from recognized rules by one who has learned to obey them, and neglect of them through want of training or want of skill or want of understanding. Before you can be eccentric you must know where the circle is.

Nowadays acting is less scientific (except in the matter of voice-production) than it was when I was receiving hints, cautions and advice from my two dramatic friends, Charles Reade and Tom Taylor; and the leading principles to which they attached importance have come to be regarded as old-fashioned and superfluous. This attitude is comparatively harmless in the interpretation of those modern plays in which parts are made to fit the actors and personality is everything. But those who have been led to believe that they can make their own rules find their mistake when they come to tackle Shakespeare or any of the standard dramatists in which the actors have to fit themselves to the parts. Then, if ever, technique is avenged!

All my life the thing which has struck me as wanting on the stage is variety. Some people are "tone-deaf," and they find it physically impossible to observe the law of contrasts. But even a physical deficiency can be overcome by that faculty for taking infinite pains which may not be genius but is certainly a good substitute for it. When it comes to pointing out an example, Henry Irving is the monument, the great mark set up to show the genius of will. For years he worked to overcome the dragging leg, which seemed to attract more attention from some small-minded critics (sharp of eye, yet how dull of vision!) then all the mental splendor of his impersonations. He toiled, and he overcame this defect, just as he overcame his difficulty with vowels, and the self-consciousness which in the early stages of his career used to hamper and incommode him. His self was to him on a first night what the shell is to a lobster on dry land.... He used to discuss with me the secret of my freedom from self-consciousness; and I suggested a more swift entrance on the stage from the dressing room. I told him that, in spite of the advantage in ease which I had gained through having been on the stage when still a mere child, I should be paralyzed with fright from overacute realization of the audience if I stood at the wing for ten minutes, as he was in the habit of doing.

He did not heed me then, nor during the run of our next play, *The Lady of Lyons;* but when it came to Shylock, a quite new part for him, he tried the experiment, and, as he told me, with great comfort to himself and success with the audience.

Only a great actor finds the difficulties of the actor's art infinite. Even up to the last five years of his life, Henry Irving was striving, striving. He never rested on old triumphs, never found a part in which there was no more to do. Once when I was touring with him in America, at the time when he was at the highest point of his fame, I watched him one day in the train—always a delightful occupation, for his face provided many pictures a minute—and being struck by a curious look, half puzzled, half despairing, asked him what he was thinking about.

"I was thinking," he answered slowly, "how strange it is that I should have made the reputation I have as an actor, with nothing to help me—with no equipment. My legs, my voice, everything has been against me. For an actor who can't walk, can't talk, and has no face to speak of, I've done pretty well."

And I, looking at that splendid head, those wonderful hands, the whole strange beauty of him, thought, "Ah, you little know!"

* * * *

My experiences [Ophelia to Irving's Hamlet] convinced me that the actor must imagine first and observe afterwards. It is not good observing life and bringing the result to the stage without selection, without a definite idea. The idea must come first, the realism afterwards.

* * * *

How important it is to be careful about environment and everything else when one is studying. One ought to be in the country, but not all the time.... It is good to go about and see pictures, hear music, and watch everything. One should be very much alone, and should study early and late—all night, if need be, even at the cost of sleep. Everything that one does or thinks or sees will have an effect upon the part, precisely as on an unborn child.

I wish now that instead of reading how this and that actress had played Juliet, and cracking my brain over the different readings of her lines and making myself familiar with the different opinions of philosophers and critics, I had gone to Verona, and just imagined. Perhaps the most wonderful description of Juliet, as she should be acted, occurs in Gabriele D'Annunzio's *Il Fuoco*. In the book an Italian actress tells her friend how she played the part when she was a girl of fourteen in an open-air theatre near Verona. Could a girl of fourteen play such a part? Yes, if she were not youthful, only young with the youth of the poet, tragically old as some youth is.

Now I understand Juliet better. Now I know how she should be played. But time is inexorable. At sixty, know what one may, one cannot play Juliet.

* * * *

Henry used to spend hours and hours teaching people. I used to think impatiently: "Acting can't be taught." Gradually I learned to modify this conviction and to recognize that there are two classes of actors:

1. Those who can only do what they are taught.
2. Those who cannot be taught, but can be helped by suggestion to work out things for themselves.

Henry said to me once: "What makes a popular actor? Physique! What makes a great actor? Imagination and sensibility." I tried to believe it. Then I thought to myself: "Henry himself is not quite what is understood by 'an actor of physique,' and certainly he is popular. And that he is a great actor I know. He certainly has both imagination and 'sense and sensibility.' " After the lapse of years I begin to wonder if Henry was ever really popular. It came naturally to most people to dislike his acting. They found it queer, as some found the art of Whistler queer. But he forced them, almost against their will and nature, out of dislike into admiration. They had to come up to him, for never would he go down to them. This is not popularity.

* * * *

When we act, we must feel, not necessarily with our own personal feelings. Your voice, your movement, your whole body, are only an instrument for this feeling. However perfect you make the instrument, it won't resound, unless you can feel.

* * * *

My memory! Oh, what agony it has always been to me. I knew all about my parts long before I could get the words into my head. The pleasure of acting was spoiled by the terror of forgetting.

WILLIAM ARCHER

(1856-1924)

Born at Perth and educated at the University of Edinburgh, William Archer began his career as a journalist in Australia. He returned to London in 1879 and became an important English critic and author. His melodrama, *The Green Goddess,* 1921, starred George Arliss and was successful on the stage.

Archer will long be remembered as the great defender of Ibsen in England during the last decades of the nineteenth century. With Edmund William Gosse he introduced the works of the great realistic dramatist to the English public, and it was he who edited the works of Ibsen. The first production of an Ibsen play in London was given under Archer's guidance in 1880. Throughout the acrimonious controversy which raged over his plays, Archer defended Ibsen and the realistic drama. His critical volume, *The Old Drama and the New,* reevaluated the whole course of English drama in the light of the new Ibsen dramaturgy.

In the January, February and March, 1888, issues of *Longmans Magazine,* Archer published the results of an extensive inquiry which he had made into the psychology of acting. Through questionnaires and historical research he attempted to make a scientific study of the problem of emotion in acting as it was suggested by Diderot's *Le Paradoxe sur le comédien.* The issue was brought to the fore by the controversy then being carried on between Coquelin and Henry Irving. Feeling the need for a broader investigation of the topic, the editors of *Longmans Magazine* commissioned Archer "to collect and systematize the views on this matter of the leading actors and actresses of the day." Archer drew up an elaborate questionnaire which he circulated among many leading artists. He then collated his answers, adding to them the recorded statements on the subject of emotion by actors of the past. On the basis of this survey he later published his analysis in book form under the title *Masks or Faces? A Study in the Psychology of Acting.* His conclusions are presented in the following article.

Masks or Faces?

In ordering this discussion, I have had a double difficulty to contend with.... In the first place, there were two questions at issue—a question of fact and a question of theory: do actors feel? and ought they to feel? In the second place, I had not the advantage of starting from an unencumbered base and building up my theory in my own way by a straightforward synthesis of evidence. The issue had been obscured (as it seemed to me) by rash overstatements on both

William Archer: *Masks or Faces? A Study in the Psychology of Acting.* London: Longmans, Green and Co., 1880, pp. 195-210.

sides, and by a general failure to recognize and define the comparatively few points on which rational discussion was possible. Thus my exposition was necessarily mingled with controversy, and I fear the mixture has not thoroughly clarified. If exhaustion has not supervened upon the reader's bewilderment, a brief recapitulation may help him to find his bearings.

Acting is of all the arts the most purely imitative. In this respect it stands at the opposite pole from music, with sculpture, painting, poetry, in intermediate positions. Music deals almost entirely in what may be called soundpatterns, which have no prototypes in external nature. Poetry, and indeed all literary art, leans in the same direction. Its matter may or may not be imitative; its medium must be a more or less rhythmic succession of sounds, which does not depend for its attractiveness on its resemblance to anything under the sun. Painting, in these latter days, tends more and more to the condition of colormusic, the very vocabularies of the two arts being, it appears, interchangeable. Even sculpture, without entirely deserting its function, may present a mere arabesque of curves and surfaces. But acting is imitative or it is nothing. It may borrow from all the arts in turn—from the arts of speech, of song, of color, of form; but imitation is its differentia. Acting *is* imitation; when it ceases to be imitation it ceases to be acting and becomes something else—oratory perhaps, perhaps ballet-dancing or posturing. Everyone knows that the actor is not necessarily a copyist of nature; he may sing, for example, or he may talk alexandrines; but he must always preserve a similarity in dissimilarity; he must always imitate; though we may permit him to steep his imitation, so to speak, in a more or less conventional atmosphere. "He plays naturally," or, in other words, "He imitates well," is our highest formula of praise even for the operatic tenor or the French tragedian, who may not deliver a single word or tone exactly as it would be uttered in real life.

The actor, then, is a man who, through the medium of his own body, imitates the manners and passions of other men. We are all actors in rudiment, the tendency to such imitation being part of the mechanism of animated nature. That is why the stage is besieged by incompetent aspirants, the general tendency being easily mistaken for special aptitude. Conversely, I believe, that is why some theorists seek to exclude acting from the dignity of art. They ignore the amount of labor and thought required to transmute, not only the general tendency, but even a very special aptitude, into accomplished mastery.

By far the greater part of the imitation of man by man which takes place off the stage is totally unconcerned with emotion. In real life the emotions of others are precisely what we do *not* imitate. A child learns to speak, to walk, to sing by imitating its elders; it wails before its eyes are fairly opened to the world. We are all conscious of a tendency to mimic the tics and mannerisms of our neighbors—their gait, their voice, their accent; but the mere muscular copying of emotional manifestations never occurs, except for purposes of ridicule. The grief or laughter of another may seize and overmaster us, through the action of sympathy, though we may know nothing of its cause; but this is not imitation; it is infection. It may be said that all imitation which is not absolutely deliberate partakes of the nature of infection. True; but the infection of feeling has this peculiarity, that it is *not imitative*. We weep our own tears, we laugh our own laughter, without the smallest conscious or unconscious tendency to reproduce the particular forms which these paroxysms assume in the person who has "set us off." Therefore I think there is a clear distinction between mimicking tricks or habits and yielding to emotional contagion. Roughly speaking, the one is an affair of the surface, the other of the centers.

The manners and passions of his fellow-men form, as we have seen, the actor's province. Over part of this domain unemotional imitation will carry him safely. The reproduction of manners, in themselves, is effected by a mere extension of that instinct which makes children the "sedulous apes" of their elders, and causes some of us, even in maturity, to stammer after conversing with a stammerer and to wink and twitch after seeing a victim to St. Vitus's dance. In all characters there is a greater or less element of manner, so that in all characters this instinct of mere imitation is brought into play. A large part of every impersonation is, and must be, as mechanical as the putting on of a wig or the painting of crows' feet under the eyes. But comparatively few dramatic characters consist of manners alone. It is passion that interests and moves us; therefore the reproduction of passion is the actor's highest and most essential task. By what methods, then, can this reproduction be most fitly accomplished?

The external manifestations of passion consist, on analysis, of changes in the face, the limbs, or the organs of speech, many of which can be mechanically imitated with more or less precision, just as one can imitate the limp of a cripple or an Irishman's brogue. For example, we can all contort our faces into the semblance of weeping, we can smile and laugh at will (though the voluntary laugh is apt to be a lugubrious effort), we can sob, we can tremble, we can gnash and grind the teeth, not quite convincingly perhaps, but so that an observer can easily guess what emotion we are simulating. On the other hand, some of the symptoms of those passions which tend to express themselves immediately, forcibly, and unmistakably—the passions of grief and joy, terror and fury—cannot be imitated by the mere action of the will upon the muscles and tissues. No one can blush and turn pale at will; some actors, as we have seen reason to believe, can shed tears at a moment's notice and without any real or imaginary cause; but this faculty is not common, and is the result of long practice. These involuntary symptoms, however, are of such a nature as to be almost imperceptible on the stage. If the more obvious traits are vividly reproduced, a theatrical audience is ready enough to take tears, blushes, and pallor upon trust. It is undeniable, then, that for the practical purposes of dramatic presentation, the symptoms of passion can be mechanically mimicked with tolerable precision, and there is no reason to doubt that exceptional artists have attained astonishing skill in such mimicry.

It is certain, however, that the faculty of mechanically mimicking the ebullitions of passion with anything like deceptive precision is a very rare one. We have seen that our innate mimetic tendency does not generally exercise itself upon these phenomena; perhaps for no more recondite reason than that they are of exceptional occurrence and do not force themselves on our observation with the importunacy of habitual actions. Be this as it may, it is clear that the mechanical mimicking of passions on the stage is not, like the mimicking of manners, a mere extension of an inborn instinct. On the other hand, we have also seen that the paroxysms of passion tend to communicate themselves to those not primarily affected, through that subtle contagion which we call sympathy. Little Mabel breaks her favorite doll and howls piteously over the remains. Her elder brother, Jack, though his sex and his years raise him far above the weakness of doll-worship, nay, though he may have a dim sense of Rochefoucauldian satisfaction in Mabel's misfortune, will very probably yell in concert, as lustily as though the sorrow were his own. He certainly does not suffer anything like Mabel's agony of soul; in a sense he cannot properly be said to suffer at all; and still less can it be maintained that he deliberately mimics his sister. All we can say is that by the mysterious action of sympathy Mabel's grief acts upon Jack's nerve-centers and begets in them a condition so analogous to her own that it results in similar outward manifestations. The difference between the two states might be tested by the exhibition of a counter-irritant. A chocolate-cream will probably dry Jack's eyes as if by magic, while a wilderness of lollipops will leave Mabel inconsolable. In this sympathetic contagion we have an instrument provided by nature for supplying the deficiencies of our power of mechanical mimicry in respect to the subtler symptoms of passion. The poet—say Shakespeare—fecundates the imagination of the actor—say Salvini—so that it bodies forth the great passion-quivering phantom of Othello. In the act of representation this phantom is, as it were, superimposed upon the real man. The phantom Othello suffers, and the nerve-centers of the man Salvini thrill in response. The blood courses through his veins, his eyes are clouded with sorrow or blaze with fury, his lips tremble, the muscles of his throat contract, the passion of the moment informs him to the finger-tips, and his portrayal of a human soul in agony is true to the minutest detail. His suffering may stand to Othello's in the quantitative relation of Jack's grief to Mabel's; but, so far as it goes, it cannot be called other than real.

The anti-emotionalists would have the actor abjure, at any rate in the moment of performance, the aid of this sympathetic contagion. It is too dearly bought, they argue. The accomplished player should be able mechanically to mimic all symptoms of emotion which are of any use in creating illusion in the audience, and he must run no risk of becoming extravagant, inarticulate, or feeble, by reason of the too vehement disturbance of his own nerve-centers. The emotionalists, as I understand their position, maintain that the mechanical mimicry of feeling, even at its best, lacks the clear ring of truth, and that in yielding to the sympathetic contagion the accomplished actor does not in reality run any of the risks on which their opponents are so fond of dwelling.

The two questions, then, which we have had to consider in this discussion—do actors feel, and ought they to feel?—may be restated thus: Do actors habitually yield to the sympathetic contagion? and do the greatest actors—those who have most powerfully affected their audiences—admit or reject this method?

My first three chapters were purely preliminary. I described the methods of investigation I had pursued; traced, historically, the genesis of Diderot's *Paradoxe;* and tried to narrow the issue by analyzing the different meanings attributed in the *Paradoxe* to the term "sensibility," and rejecting some of them as unfair or irrelevant. The investigation proper began with the fourth chapter. In it we found that the shedding of tears—one of the most palpable symptoms of pathetic emotion—is common, and even habitual, on the stage. We learned from Cicero and Quintilian that the Roman actors frequently wept; and we ascertained, in most cases on unimpeachable evidence, that tears have been shed on the stage by Garrick, Mrs. Cibber, Barry, Peg Woffington, Mrs. Pritchard, Mrs. Siddons, Miss O'Neill, Miss Fanny Kemble, Mlle. Champmeslé, Mlle. Duclos, Quinault-Dufresne, Mlle. Gaussin, Frédéric Lemaître, Madame Dorval, Miss Neilson, Charlotte Cushman, Samuel Phelps, Benjamin Webster, Salvini, Mr. and Mrs. Bancroft, Mr. and Mrs. Kendal, Mr. Irving, Miss Ellen Terry, Madame Sarah Bernhardt, Miss Mary Anderson, Miss Alma Murray, Miss Janet Achurch, Miss Clara Morris, Mr. Wilson Barrett, Mr. Beerbohm Tree, Mr. John Clayton, Mr. Hermann Vezin, Mr. Howe, Miss Bateman, Mr. Lionel Brough, and several others. It would not have cost much trouble to extend this list almost indefinitely, but it seems to me sufficient as it stands, both in numbers and in authority. The frequency of real weeping on the stage being thus established, I had next to admit that tears can, in certain cases, be mechanically produced, and that they do not, therefore, afford conclusive evidence of any particular emotional state. In order to show that they are not, as a rule, so fallacious as the anti-emotionalists argue, and at the same time to prove that there is a close analogy between personal and mimetic emotion, I collected, in my fifth chapter, numerous instances of the mingling and (in M. Coquelin's phrase) "kneading together" of the two states, which we found to coalesce indistinguishably, sometimes to the advantage, sometimes to the detriment, of the actor's performance. On the other hand, in Chapter Six, we found scanty evidence of any tendency to mimic in cold blood particular ebullitions of emotion, whether observed or experienced, and no proof whatever that unemotional mimicry is more effective than emotional acting. In the following chapter, treating of laughter as the characteristic expression of joyful emotion, and thus the natural antithesis to tears, we found a rather wide divergence of testimony. Some actors declare themselves highly susceptible to the contagion of their character's mirth, others (of no less authority) are equally positive in asserting their laughter to be always a deliberate simulative effort. I confess myself unable to suggest any satisfactory reason why the contagion of merriment should be less potent and universal than the contagion of tears. Can it be that there is a pessimistic bias in human nature, rending men, on the average, less prone to joyous than to mournful emotion?

Here let me interrupt this recapitulation to point out a fact which is apt to be overlooked. In the course of my interviews with the leading artists of today, I have more than once mentioned, say, to X.—an emphatic emotionalist—that a fellow-artist, Z., had declared himself of the same opinion; whereupon X. would shrug his (or her) shoulders skeptically and remark: "Oh, Z.!—I don't believe *he* ever felt anything in his life!" The doubt in these cases sprang from the common error of thinking that sensitiveness to what we have called the imaginative contagion presupposes unusual sensibility in the ordinary affairs of life. A little consideration will show us that the fact is not so. The executioner in Thackeray blubbered over *The Sorrows of Werther;* and no one will deny that this is a touch of nature. To take an example from real life, Macaulay, who met his personal sorrows in no unmanly spirit, could weep by the hour over a trashy novel. We must all have known people, stoical enough in their own troubles, and perhaps even hard-hearted toward the sufferings of others, who would yet become maudlin over the imagined sorrows of a personage in fiction or on the stage. Thus the actor who owns himself affected by the emotions of his character— the superimposed phantom of his imagination—does not thereby lay any claim to exceptional tenderness of heart in the ordinary relations of life. In that respect, I imagine, actors are very much like other men. Diderot, as we have seen, found them "caustic, cold, selfish, alive to our absurdities rather than touched by our misfortunes." This character certainly does not apply to the players of our nation and time, whose large and ready charity proves that "they know what 'tis to pity and be pitied." But even if Diderot were absolutely just in his general assertion of the heartlessness of actors, we should still have no difficulty in believing them susceptible to emotional contagion from the phantoms of their imagination.

Continuing my summary, I pass to Chapter Eight. Here we ascertained that three symptoms of acute feeling, which are utterly beyond the control of the will—blushing, pallor, and perspiration—commonly, and even habitually, accompany the stage-emotion of the greatest artists. In this, it seems to me, we have proof positive that mimetic emotion is not, as some people argue, a state of mere vague unspecialized excitement, but is closely analogous to the emotion of real life. In the next chapter we inquired into the practice, attributed to several great artists, of mechanically mobilizing the nerve-centers by means of that reaction from external manifestations of passion which Hartmann[1] describes as "auto-suggestion." This proceeding, in various forms, we found to be fairly common; while the habit of mental concentration upon a part during, and even for some time before, the period of performance, proved to be still more general. The rationale of these practices is obvious enough. The one assists the actor to clothe himself, as it were, in the phantom of his imagination, and to keep himself thoroughly enveloped in it; the other heightens the sensitiveness of his organism to contagion from the emotions of his personage. The next chapter was devoted to an inquiry into the multiplex action of the mind whereby the accomplished actor is enabled to remain master of himself even in the very paroxysm of passion. I was able to adduce many cases in which double and treble strata of mental activity were clearly distinguishable, but very few examples of that total and somnambulistic absorption in a part which the anti-emotionalists assume to be the normal condition of the emotional actor. The succeeding chapter touched upon the question of long runs. We saw reason, on the one hand, to reject Diderot's opinion that an actor must gain by reiterating a character until his playing becomes entirely automatic, and to believe, on the other hand, that an actor may repeat a character indefinitely without degenerating into automatism, if only he takes care to allow himself proper intervals of rest and change between the performances of any one part. Finally, in Chapter Twelve, we "Reasoned high of fate, free will, foreknowledge absolute"—I trust the reader will not complete the quotation, adding, "and found no end, in wandering mazes lost." We learned that some actors are artistic Calvinists, insisting on rigorous predestination of every detail of position, attitude, gesture, and inflection; while others, the Arminians of the stage, leave a wide margin for impulse, spontaneity, free-will. The latter sect is probably the more numerous and influential; but we also ascertained that the "foreknowledge absolute" of the necessitarians is by no means inconsistent with the keenest susceptibility to the emotional influence of their characters.

At the very outset of this inquiry, I insisted on the distinction between the

---

[1] Edward von Hartmann: *Philosphie des Schoenen*, 1887.

simple and primary emotions—grief, joy, terror, etc.—and the secondary or complex and habitual emotions—love, hatred, jealousy, etc.—which have no immediate and characteristic outward symptoms, and are rather to be called attitudes of the mind. No one denies, I think, that the primary emotions of an imagined character do in fact tend to communicate themselves to the nerve-centers of the actor, and to affect his organs of expression. Let me add, parenthetically, that it is surely illogical to deny the "reality" of this mimetic emotion, since all emotion, except that which arises from instant physical pleasure or pain, is due to the action of the imagination upon the nerve-centers. This, however, is a mere question of nomenclature. Be it real or unreal, this mimetic emotion tends, in the great majority of cases, to come into play; and the actor who avails himself of it clearly works on the line of least resistance. The anti-emotionalists must prove that this straightforward course is beset with the most fatal pitfalls ere they can hope to induce actors to follow the roundabout route, repressing the action of the imagination and cultivating mechanical mimicry. I have tried to show that the pitfalls from which the anti-emotionalists recoil are either quite imaginary or easily to be avoided. On the other hand, the more we look into the matter, the less are we inclined to believe that even the greatest virtuoso of mechanical mimicry can attain to the subtle and absolute truth of imitation which is possible to the actor who combines artistically controlled sensibility with perfect physical means of expression. "Raised or lowered by the twentieth part of the quarter of a tone," says Diderot, the utterances of feeling "ring false." But is it not just the intervention of imaginative sympathy that enables the actor to produce and reproduce this delicately true vibration? There is no doubt that the imagination can easily bring about minute yet expressive changes, muscular and vascular, which the unaided action of the will is powerless to effect. Blushing and pallor are the chief of these, but there must be many others. Darwin[2] notes that when two dogs fight together in play (this is, when they imagine and act the emotion of anger) their hair at once bristles up, just as in actual warfare. This is a type of many similar phenomena in the human economy. And it must not be supposed that these minute changes do not contribute appreciably to the illusion. We may not consciously note a blush, a sudden pallor, a particular quiver of the lip, distension of the nostril, or corrugation of the brow; but they produce their effect nevertheless. Mr. Kendal once suggested to me what I think a luminous illustration of the difference between mechanically simulated and imaginatively experienced emotion. "A sign painter," he said, "takes a pot of crude vermilion, and daubs the red coat of the Duke of Wellington or the Marquis of Granby. It is undeniably red, and yet somehow it is all wrong. But look into a red robe painted by Rossetti or Holman Hunt, and you will find it composed of a hundred different hues, which blend, at the proper distance, into a true and living whole." To translate the illustration into musical terms, a mechanically mimicked utterance of emotion is like a note without its harmonics. The analogy may be fanciful, but I do not think it is wholly misleading.

In the foregoing pages, there are, no doubt, errors of analysis and of inference which have escaped my ken. On the other hand, no one knows better than I that the subject of mimetic emotion is full of subtleties and intricacies into which I have not penetrated. Some day, perhaps, a better-equipped psychologist

---

[2] Charles Darwin: *Expression of the Emotions.*

may tread the maze to its inmost recesses. Meanwhile, in taking leave of what has been to me a fascinating inquiry, I cannot but hope that it may aid the contending forces in a lingering and somewhat futile controversy to arrive at a clearer understanding of the true points at issue than they have hitherto attained. If each party fully realized its own and its adversaries' position, I believe a treaty of peace would very soon be signed. It was drafted by Shakespeare three centuries ago, when, through the mouth of Prince Hamlet, he counselled the players of his day to acquire and beget a temperance even in the very torrent, tempest, and whirlwind of passion.

GEORGE BERNARD SHAW

(1856 - 1951)

George Bernard Shaw, the patriarch of English letters, was born in Dublin. From his mother's interest in singing, he acquired that love and understanding of music which made his later music criticism exciting. An early enthusiasm for opera was replaced by love of the theatre. The magnetic, graceful, old-school actor Barry Sullivan captured his imagination, and the Dublin performance of Henry Irving convinced him that Irving was the actor for modern drama. But before the young Shaw was to make himself famous as a critic and as a dramatist, he went through years of poverty and struggle, working first in Dublin as a clerk in a land agent's office, then in London as a hack writer and unsuccessful novelist. By 1882 reading Karl Marx had turned him into a socialist; he became a propagandist, an agitator, and a prime-mover in the Fabian Society.

William Archer, drama critic and translator of Ibsen, gave Shaw his first opportunity as a critic. For six years he was a music critic, and in 1895 he wrote the first of his pungent dramatic criticisms. With inimitable wit and brilliance Shaw flayed the evils of the London stage. Sir Henry Irving was his most frequent target. Although Shaw recognized Irving's superiority, he called Irving's inventiveness "hackneyed stage tricks." He never allowed Irving or his public to forget that the great actor confined himself to unworthy melodrama or to Shakespeare, whose works, Shaw said, "have been no more to him [Irving] than the word-quarry from which he has hewn and blasted the lines and titles of masterpieces which are really his own." Shaw carried on an epistolary flirtation with Irving's leading lady, Ellen Terry, who tried unsuccessfully to influence Irving to produce Shaw's *The Man of Destiny*.

Apart from his attacks on Irving, who was the cynosure of the London stage, Shaw chronicled in his exciting words the events of the theatrical scene. Although he was often forced to waste his critical insight on inferior plays and players, when the two great actresses Bernhardt and Duse appeared in London, he penned an analysis of the two that has been called "one of the greatest critical essays in the language." Shaw's understanding of Duse's art elicited an accolade from the usually reticent actress. His grasp of the fundamental principles of histrionic art is evident both when he writes of the necessity for a new mode of playing tuned to the realism of Ibsen and his own plays or when he writes of the great artists of his own day, Duse, Bernhardt, Irving, Forbes-Robertson, Mrs. Patrick Campbell, and Beerbohm Tree.

Shaw became a dramatist partly under pressure to give the Independent Theatre of J. T. Grein British drama in the Ibsen style. His play *Widowers' Houses,* written with William Archer, was performed in 1892 by Grein. Shaw's early plays were all written for and produced by the experimental groups at the turn of the century with actresses like Florence Farr and Janet Achurch, the first to publicly play Ibsen's *A Doll's House.* Later Shaw found in the Granville-Barker and J. E. Vedrenne management a group to produce his work under his own direction. His plays demanded a special acting technique, not the intense realism required in the interpretation of the Ibsen plays, but an adaptation of the rhetorical Shakespearean manner to Shaw's modern ideas. Shaw conducted rehearsals with great care, reading the play to the actors in his vivid way, working patiently with them as they learned the lines, showing them with pleasant geniality how to transfer his characters to the stage.

It is not our purpose to detail here Shaw's varied, active life. We have tried only to suggest his multifold contributions to the art of the actor. The following selection was written by Shaw for a volume of tributes compiled by Max Beerbohm in honor of his brother, Sir Herbert Beerbohm Tree, the famous actor-manager.

The Point of View of the Playwright

A tribute to Tree from the playwright's point of view is a duty of such delicacy that it is quite impossible to be delicate about it at all: one must confess bluntly at the outset that Tree was the despair of authors. His attitude towards a play was one of whole-hearted anxiety to solve the problem of how to make it please and interest the audience.

Now this is the author's business, not the actor's. The function of the actor is to make the audience imagine for the moment that real things are happening to real people. It is for the author to make the result interesting. If he fails, the actor cannot save the play unless it is so flimsy a thing that the actor can force upon it some figure of his own fancy and play the author off the stage. This has been done successfully in several well-known, though very uncommon cases. Robert Macaire and Lord Dundreary[1] were imposed by their actors on plays which did not really contain them. Grimaldi's[2] clown was his own invention. These figures died with their creators, though their ghosts still linger on the stage. Irving's Shylock was a creation which he thrust successfully upon Shakespeare's play; indeed, all Irving's impersonations were changelings. His Hamlet and his Lear were to many people more interesting than Shakespeare's

George Bernard Shaw: "From the Point of View of a Playwright" in *Herbert Beerbohm Tree: Some Memories of him and of his Art,* collected by Max Beerbohm. London: Hutchinson and Company, n.d., pp. 240-243, 247-252. By permission of Max Beerbohm and Curtis Brown, Ltd.

[1]The creations of the actors Frédéric Lemaître and Edward Askew Sothern.
[2]Joseph Grimaldi (1779-1837). One of England's greatest mimes.

Hamlet and Lear; but the two pairs were hardly even related. To the author, Irving was not an actor: he was either a rival or a collaborator who did all the real work. Therefore, he was anathema to master authors, and a godsend to journeymen authors, with the result that he had to confine himself to the works of dead authors who could not interfere with him, and, very occasionally, live authors who were under his thumb because they were unable to command production of their works in other quarters.

Into this tradition of creative acting came Tree as Irving's rival and successor; and he also, with his restless imagination, felt that he needed nothing from an author but a literary scaffold on which to exhibit his own creations. He, too, turned to Shakespeare as to a forest out of which such scaffolding could be hewn without remonstrance from the landlord, and to foreign authors who could not interfere with him, their interests being in the hands of adapters who could not stand up against his supremacy in his own theatre. As far as I could discover, the notion that a play could succeed without any further help from the actor than a simple impersonation of his part never occurred to Tree. The author, whether Shakespeare or Shaw, was a lame dog to be helped over the stile by the ingenuity and inventiveness of the actor-producer. How to add and subtract, to interpolate and prune, until an effective result was arrived at, was the problem of production as he saw it. Of living authors of eminence the two he came into personal contact with were Brieux and Henry Arthur Jones; and I have reason to believe that their experience of him in no way contradicts my own. With contemporary masters of the stage like Pinero and Carton, in whose works the stage business is an integral part of the play, and the producer, when he is not the author in person, is an executant and not an inventor, Tree had never worked; and when he at last came upon the species in me, and found that, instead of having to discover how to make an effective histrionic entertainment on the basis of such scraps of my dialogue as might prove useful, he had only to fit himself into a jig-saw puzzle cut out by me, and just to act his part as well as he could, he could neither grasp the situation nor resist the impersonal compulsion of arrangements which he had not made, and was driven to accept only by the fact that they were the only ones which would work. But to the very end they bewildered him; and he had to go to the box office to assure himself that the omission of his customary care had not produced disastrous results.

Just before the production of my play we lunched together at the Royal Automobile Club. I said to him: "Have you noticed during the rehearsals that though you and I are no longer young, and have achieved all the success possible in our respective professions, we have been treating one another throughout as beginners?" To this, on reflection, he had to assent, because we actually were, relatively to one another, beginners. I had never had to deal with him professionally before, nor he with me; and he was quite unaccustomed to double harness, whilst I was so accustomed to every extremity of multiple harness, both in politics and in the theatre, that I had been trained to foresee everything and consider everybody. Now if I were to say that Tree foresaw nothing and considered nobody, I should suggest that he was a much less amiable man than he was. Let me therefore say that he never foresaw anything or considered anybody in cold blood. Of the foresight which foresees and faces entirely uninteresting facts, and the consideration which considers entirely uninteresting persons, he had as little as a man can have without being run over in the street. When

[372]

his feelings were engaged, he was human and even shrewd and tenacious. But you really could not lodge an indifferent fact in his mind. This disability of his was carried to such a degree that he could not remember the passages in a play which did not belong to or bear directly upon his own conception of his own part: even the longest run did not mitigate his surprise when they recurred. Thus he never fell into that commonest fault of the actor: the betrayal to the audience that he knows what his interlocutor is going to say, and is waiting wearily for his cue instead of conversing with him. Tree always seemed to have heard the lines of the other performers for the first time, and even to be a little taken aback by them.

Let me give an extreme instance of this. In *Pygmalion* the heroine, in a rage, throws the hero's slippers in his face. When we rehearsed this for the first time, I had taken care to have a very soft pair of velvet slippers provided; for I knew that Mrs. Patrick Campbell was very dexterous, very strong, and a dead shot. And, sure enough, when we reached this passage, Tree got the slippers well and truly delivered with unerring aim bang in his face. The effect was appalling. He had totally forgotten that there was any such incident in the play; and it seemed to him that Mrs. Campbell, suddenly giving way to an impulse of diabolical wrath and hatred, had committed an unprovoked and brutal assault on him. The physical impact was nothing; but the wound to his feelings was terrible. He collapsed on the nearest chair, and left me staring in amazement, whilst the entire personnel of the theatre crowded solicitously round him, explaining that the incident was part of the play, and even exhibiting the prompt-book to prove their words. But his *morale* was so shattered that it took quite a long time, and a good deal of skillful rallying and coaxing from Mrs. Campbell, before he was in a condition to resume the rehearsal. The worst of it was that as it was quite evident that he would be just as surprised and wounded next time, Mrs. Campbell took care that the slippers should never hit him again, and the incident was consequently one of the least convincing in the performance....

And here I come to a source of friction between authors and actor-managers which is worth explaining with some care, as it bears on the general need in England for a school of physical training for the arts of public life as distinguished from the sports. An author who understands acting, and writes for the actor as a composer writes for an instrument, giving it the material suitable to its range, tone, character, agility and mechanism, necessarily assumes a certain technical accomplishment common to all actors; and this requires the existence of a school of acting, or at least a tradition. Now we had no such provision in the days of Tree's novitiate. He had not inherited the tradition handed down at rehearsal by Phelps to Forbes-Robertson; nor was there any academic institution with authority enough to impress a novice of his calibre. To save others from this disadvantage he later on founded the Academy of Dramatic Art in Gower Street, which now supplies the want as far as an unendowed institution can. But he had to do without teaching himself. Like Irving, he had to make a style and technique out of his own personality: that is, out of his peculiar weaknesses as well as his peculiar powers. And here he sowed dragons' teeth between himself and the authors. For no uncommissioned author can write for an idiosyncratic style and technique: he knows only the classical one. He must, like Shakespeare, assume an executant who can perform and sustain certain physical feats of deportment, and build up vocal climaxes with his voice through a long crescendo of rhetoric. Further, he assumes the possession of an English voice and an English feeling for splendor of language and rhythm of verse. Such professional skill and national gift are not accidents of personality: they are more or less within every Englishman's capacity. By themselves they will no more make an actor than grammar and spelling will make an author, or fingering and blowing a bandsman; but one expects every actor to possess them, just as one expects every author to parse and spell correctly and every bandsman to finger and blow properly.

Tree, like so many of our actors who have picked up their profession on the stage without systematic training, found that he could not produce these stock effects. When they were demanded by the author, he had to find a way round them, and, if possible, an interesting way. Thus he had not only to struggle against his handicap, but to triumph over it by turning it into an advantage. And his handicap was not a light one. Instead of that neutral figure which an actor can turn into anything he pleases, he was tall, and built like nobody else on earth. His Dutch extraction gave him an un-English voice, which, again, was like nobody else's voice and could not be disguised. His feeling for verbal music was entirely non-Miltonic: he had a music of his own; but it was not the music characteristic of English rhetoric; and blank verse, as such, had no charm for him; nor, I suspect, did he credit it with charm for anyone else.

The results were most marked in his Shakespearean work, and would certainly have produced curious scenes at rehearsal had the author been present. No doubt it is an exaggeration to say that the only unforgettable passages in his Shakespearean acting are those of which Tree and not Shakespeare was the author. His Wolsey, which was a "straight" performance of high merit and dignity, could be cited to the contrary. But take, for examples, his Richard II and his Malvolio. One of the most moving points in his Richard was made with the assistance of a dog who does not appear among Shakespeare's *dramatis personae*. When the dog—Richard's pet dog—turned to Bolingbroke and licked his hand, Richard's heart broke; and he left the stage with a sob. Next to this came his treatment of the entry of Bolingbroke and the deposed Richard into London. Shakespeare makes the Duke of York describe it. Nothing could be easier, with a well-trained actor at hand. And nothing could be more difficult and inconvenient than to bring horses on the stage and represent it in action. But this is just what Tree did. One still remembers that great white horse, and the look of hunted terror with which Richard turned his head as the crowd hooted him. It passed in a moment; and it flatly contradicted Shakespeare's description of the saint-like patience of Richard; but the effect was intense: no one but Chaliapin[3] has since done so much by a single look and an appearance for an instant on horseback. Again, one remembers how Richard walked out of Westminster Hall after his abdication.

Turn now to the scenes in which Shakespeare has given the actor a profusion of rhetoric to declaim. Take the famous "For God's sake let us sit upon the ground, and tell sad stories of the death of kings." My sole recollection of that scene is that when I was sitting in the stalls listening to it, a paper was passed to me. I opened

---

[3]Fyodor Chaliapin, the great Russian singer-actor.

it and read: "If you will rise and move a resolution, I will second it.—Murray Carson." The late Murray Carson was, above all things, an elocutionist; and the scene was going for nothing. Tree was giving Shakespeare, at immense trouble and expense, and with extraordinary executive cunning, a great deal that Shakespeare had not asked for, and denying him something much simpler that he did ask for, and set great store by.

As Malvolio, Tree was inspired to provide himself with four smaller Malvolios, who aped the great chamberlain in dress, in manners, in deportment. He had a magnificent flight of stairs on the stage; and when he was descending it majestically, he slipped and fell with a crash sitting. Mere clowning, you will stay; but no: the fall was not the point. Tree, without betraying the smallest discomfiture, raised his eyeglass and surveyed the landscape as if he had sat down on purpose. This, like the four satellite Malvolios, was not only funny but subtle. But when he came to speak those lines with which any old Shakespearean hand can draw a laugh by a simple trick of the voice, Tree made nothing of them, not knowing a game which he had never studied.

Even if our actors came to the stage with complete executive mastery of all the traditions and all the conventions, there would still be a conflict between the actor's tendency to adapt the play to his own personality, and the author's desire to adapt the actor's personality to the play. But this would not make any serious trouble between them; for a good part can be played a dozen different ways by a dozen different actors and be none the worse: no author worth his salt attaches a definite and invariable physiognomy to each variety of human character. Every actor must be allowed to apply his own methods to his own playing. But if, as under our system, an actor, instead of laying the foundation of a general technique of speech and action, is driven, by the absence of any school in which he can acquire such a technique, to develop his own personality, and acquire a technique of exploiting that personality which is not applicable to any other purpose, then there will be friction at rehearsals if the author produces his own play, as all authors should. For the actor will inevitably try to force a changeling on the author. He will say, in effect: "I will not play this part that you have written; but I will substitute one of my own which is ever so much better." And it will be useless for the author to assert himself, and say: "You *shall* play the part as I have written it." If he knows his business, he will see that the "will not" of the actor really means "cannot," because the author has written for a classical technique which the actor does not possess and cannot learn in three weeks, or even three years. It is better to let the actor do what he can: indeed, there is no alternative. . . .

. . . But the heart of the matter (which I have been coming to slowly all this time) is that the cure for the disease of actor-managership (every author must take that pathological view of it) is actor-author-managership; the cure of Molière, who acted his plays as well as wrote them, and managed his theatre into the bargain. And yet he lasted fifty-one years. Richard Wagner was author-composer-conductor-manager at Bayreuth: a much more arduous combination. Tree should have written his own plays. He could have done so. He had actually begun to do it as Shakespeare and Molière began, by tinkering other men's plays. The conflict that raged between him and me at the rehearsals in his theatre would then have taken place in his own bosom. He would have taken a parental pride in other parts beside his own. He would have come to care for a play as a play, and to understand that it has powers over the audience even when it is read by people sitting round a table or performed by wooden marionettes. It would have developed that talent of his that wasted itself in *jeux d'esprit* and epigrams. And it would have given him what he was always craving from authors, and in the nature of the case could never get from them: a perfect projection of the great Tree personality. What did he care for Higgins or Hamlet? His real objective was his amazing self. That also was Shakespeare's objective in Hamlet; but Shakespeare was not Tree, and therefore Hamlet could never be to Tree what Hamlet was to Shakespeare. For with all his cleverness in the disguises of the actor's dressing-room, Tree was no mere character actor. The character actor never dares to appear frankly in his own person; he is the victim of a mortal shyness that agonizes and paralyzes him when his mask is stripped off and his cothurnus snatched from beneath his feet. Tree, on the contrary, broke through all his stage disguises: they were his robes of state; and he was never happier than when he stepped in front of the curtain and spoke in his own immensity to the audience, if not as deep calling unto deep (for the audience could not play up to him as splendidly as that), at least as a monarch to his courtiers.

I trust...he may find his bard, as Elliston[4] found Charles Lamb. It is my misfortune that I cannot do him justice, because, as author and actor, we two were rivals who regarded one another as usurpers. Happily, no bones were broken in the encounter; and if there is any malice in my description of it, I hope I have explained sufficiently to enable the reader to make the necessary allowance and correction.

GORDON CRAIG

(1872-1966)

The name of Gordon Craig signifies innovations in stage production and design. Less successful in his actual practice than in his theories and dreams, Craig nevertheless set forth the ideals which liberated the theatre from the detailed imitation of surface reality prevalent at the end of the nineteenth century. In his writings, especially *The Art of the Theatre,* which was widely translated, he called for a conception of theatre which was to be poetic and beautiful, suggestive and imaginative rather than concrete and realistic—a conception devoted to the art of the theatre rather than to the words and ideas of the playwright. Modern theatrical designers owe much to the stimulus which Craig gave to a fresh vision of theatre at the turn of the century.

Son of the beautiful Ellen Terry, Craig appeared on the stage from his youth. For more than ten years he played varied roles under Henry Irving's management. He even performed Hamlet successfully for a short period at the Olympic Theatre in London. From all reports he was a talented actor whose services were wanted by many managers, but Craig was on fire to revolutionize the stage, and he therefore turned to production and stage design. In 1897 he ceased to act, and in 1900 he made his first mark as a director when he staged Purcell's *Dido and Aeneas* with his own suggestive designs. In 1903 he staged Ibsen's *The Vikings* for his mother

---

[4]Robert William Elliston (1774-1831), a great comic artist of the early nineteenth century, who is eulogized in Lamb's *Dramatic Essays*.

at the Imperial Theatre. He became much admired throughout Europe for his simplified, evocative design and staging. He created productions for Brahm in Germany, for Duse in Italy, for the Moscow Art Theatre, and for the Royal Theatre in Copenhagen. Max Reinhardt and W. B. Yeats adopted many of Craig's ideas. The School for the Art of the Theatre in Florence, Italy, which he opened in 1913, collapsed as the war broke out. His *avant-garde* publication, *Mask Magazine,* emanated from Florence during the years 1909 to 1929.

It is interesting to note that in his little volume on Henry Irving, Craig acknowledges Irving as one of his inspirations in the movement toward spiritual effect and symbolic design. Both were indifferent to the text and emphasized the creativeness of the producer, the designer, and the actor. Craig's comments on acting from the controversial "Actor and the Ueber-Marionette" suggest that the actor can become an original creator when he is unfettered by the words and ideas of writers, perhaps as the *commedia dell' arte* was. His pronunciamentos on acting are illuminated by the final passages in his book on Irving. Here he allows an imaginary figure of the great actor to speak the following words:

"Offer *The School for Scandal* to an actor of genius—to me—and my first words after reading it will be: I can't play Sir Peter and Joseph, and Charles, and Sir Oliver—*there is no part for me in this play.*

"On hearing this you will think it is confounded conceit on my part to speak so—and you are wrong. You ask me what I mean, and I offend you by the next answer, which is that there isn't a big enough part for me.

"That thoroughly enrages you—but give the thing a little quiet thought....

"You see what I mean: when passive, as a good actor should be, I lose all touch—I am no one. That's why I look for a part which is *active*—a part which, like a vivid personality in real life, seems to have the stage to itself—is only sketched in by the playwright—leaves me much to do, to imagine, to invent....

"Now the next point, is, what kind of part is big enough for me. And the reply is: that kind of part which leaves me free—which leaves me plenty of room in which to display my genius...leaves half undone till I do it.

"You ask if Hamlet, Macbeth, Othello, and Lear will serve. I reply that these do offer me plenty of room, but do not leave me free—although I will admit that I and other actors of genius have made free with the roles....

"Hamlet and Lear have suffered at my hands, it is only natural that in my calmer moments I should realize that, for a display of my powers, in place of a great play a dummy is any day better...."

In *Theatre Advancing* Craig wrote: "I ask only for the liberation of the actor that he may develop his own powers and cease from being the marionette of the playwright."

The Actor and the Ueber-Marionette

It has always been a matter for argument whether or no Acting is an art, and therefore whether the actor is an Artist, or something quite different. There is little to show us that this question disturbed the minds of the leaders of thought at any period, though there is much evidence to prove that had they chosen to ap-

Edward Gordon Craig: "The Actor and the Ueber-Marionette," *On the Art of the Theatre.* Chicago: Browne's Bookstore, 1911, pp. 54-94 *passim.*

proach this subject as one for their serious consideration, they would have applied to it the same method of enquiry as used when considering the arts of Music and Poetry, of Architecture, Sculpture and Painting. On the other hand there have been many warm arguments in certain circles on this topic. Those taking part in it have seldom been actors, very rarely men of the theatre at all, and all have displayed any amount of illogical heat, and very little knowledge of the subject. The arguments against acting being an art, and against the actor being an artist, are generally so unreasonable and so personal in their detestation of the actor, that I think it is for this reason the actors have taken no trouble to go into the matter. So now regularly with each season comes the quarterly attack on the actor and on his jolly calling; the attack usually ending in the retirement of the enemy. As a rule it is the literary or private gentlemen who fill the enemy's rank. On the strength of having gone to see plays all their lives, or on the strength of never having gone to see a play in their lives, they attack for some reason best known to themselves. I have followed these regular attacks season by season, and they seem mostly to spring from irritability, personal enmity or conceit.... They are illogical from beginning to end.... There can be no such attack made on the actor or his calling. My intention here is not to join in any such attempt; I would merely place before you what seem to me to be the logical facts of a curious case, and I believe that these admit of no dispute whatever.

Acting is not an art. It is therefore incorrect to speak of the actor as an artist. For accident is an enemy of the artist. Art is the exact antithesis of Pandemonium, and Pandemonium is created by the tumbling together of many accidents; Art arrives only by design. Therefore in order to make any work of art it is clear we may only work in those materials with which we can calculate. Man is not one of these materials.

The whole nature of man tends towards freedom; he therefore carries the proof in his own person, that as material for the theatre he is useless. In the modern theatre, owing to the use of the bodies of men and women *as their material,* all which is presented there is of an accidental nature. The actions of the actor's body, the expression of his face, the sounds of his voice, all are at the mercy of the winds of his emotions; these winds which must blow for ever round the artist, moving without unbalancing him. But with the actor, emotion possesses him; it seizes upon his limbs moving them whither it will. He is at its beck and call, he moves as one in a frantic dream or as one distraught, swaying here and there; his head, his arms, his feet, if not utterly beyond control, are so weak to stand against the torrent of his passions, that they are ready to play him false at any moment. It is useless for him to attempt to reason with himself.... Hamlet's calm directions (the dreamer's not the logician's directions, by the way) are thrown to the winds. His limbs refuse, and refuse again, to obey his mind the instant emotion warms, while the mind is all the time creating the heat which shall set these emotions afire. As with his movement, so is it with the expression of his face. The mind struggling and succeeding for a moment, in moving the eyes, or the muscles of the face whither it will; . . . the mind bringing the face for a few moments into thorough subjection, is suddenly swept aside by the emotion which has grown hot through the action of the mind. Instantly, like lightning, and before the mind has time to cry out and protest, the hot passion has mastered the actor's expression. It shifts and changes, sways and turns, it is chased by emotion from the actor's forehead between his eyes and down to his mouth; now he is entirely at the mercy of emotion, and crying out to it: "Do with me what you will!" his expression runs a mad riot hither and thither, and lo! "nothing is coming of nothing." It is the same with his voice as it is with movements. Emotion cracks the voice of the actor. It sways his voice to join in the conspiracy against his mind. Emotion works upon the voice of the actor, and he produces . . . the impression of discordant emotion. It is of no avail to say that emotion is the spirit of the gods and is precisely what the artist aims to produce; first of all this is not true, and even if it were quite true, every stray emotion, every casual feeling, cannot be of value. Therefore the mind of the actor, we see, is less powerful than his emotion, for emotion is able to win over the mind to assist in the destruction of that which the mind would produce; and as the mind becomes the slave of the emotion it follows that accident upon accident must be continually occurring. So then, we have arrived to this point: . . . that emotion is the cause which first of all creates, and secondly destroys. Art as we have said, can admit of no accidents. That then which the actor gives us, is not a work of art; it is a series of accidental confessions. . . .

* * * *

. . . As I have written elsewhere, the theatre will continue its growth and actors will continue for some years to hinder its development. But I see a loop-hole by which in time the actors can escape from the bondage they are in. They must create for themselves a new form of acting, consisting for the main part of symbolical gesture. Today they *impersonate* and interpret; tomorrow they must *represent* and interpret; and the third day they must create. By this means style may return. Today the actor impersonates a certain being. He cries to the audience "Watch me; I am now pretending to be so and so, and I am now pretending to do so and so"; and then he proceeds to imitate as exactly as possible, that which he has announced he will *indicate*. For instance, he is Romeo. He tells the audience that he is in love, and he proceeds to show it, by kissing Juliet. This, it is claimed is a work of art: it is claimed for this that it is an intelligent way of suggesting thought. Why . . . why, that is just as if a painter were to draw upon the wall a picture of an animal with long ears, and then write under it "This is a donkey." The long ears made it plain enough one would think, without the inscription, and any child of ten does as much. The difference between the child of ten and the artist is, that the artist is he who by drawing certain signs and shapes creates the impression of a donkey: and the greater artist is he who creates the impression of the whole *genus* of donkey, the spirit of the thing.

The actor looks upon life as a photo-machine looks upon life; and he attempts to make a picture to rival a photograph. He never dreams of his art as being an art such for instance as music. He tries to reproduce nature; he seldom thinks to invent with the aid of nature, and he never dreams of *creating*. As I have said, the best he can do when he wants to catch and convey the poetry of a kiss, the heat of a fight, or the calm of death, is to copy slavishly, photographically . . . he kisses . . . he fights . . . he lies back and mimics death . . . and when you think of it, is not all this dreadfully stupid? Is it not a poor art and a poor cleverness, which cannot convey the spirit and essence of an idea to an audience, but can only show an artless copy, a facsimile of the thing itself. This is to be an Imitator not an Artist. This is to claim kinship with the Ventriloquist.[1]

There is a stage expression of the actor "getting under the skin of the part." A better one would be getting "out of the skin of the part altogether." "What then," cries the red-blooded and flashing actor, "is there to be no flesh and blood in this same art of the theatre of yours? ... No life?" It depends what you call life, signor, when you use the word in relation with the idea of art. The painter means something rather different to actuality when he speaks of Life in his art, and the other artists generally mean something essentially spiritual; it is only the actor, the ventriloquist or the animal-stuffer who, when they speak of putting life into their work, mean some actual and lifelike reproduction, something blatant in its appeal, that it is for this reason I say that it would be better if the actor should get out of the skin of the part altogether. If there is any actor who is reading this, is there not some way by which I can make him realize the preposterous absurdity of this delusion of his, this belief that he should aim to make an actual copy, a reproduction? I am going to suppose that such an actor is here with me as I talk; and I invite a musician and a painter to join us. Let them speak. I have had enough of seeming to decry the work of the actor from trivial motives. I have spoken this way because of my love of the theatre, and because of my hopes and belief that before long an extraordinary development is to raise and revive that which is failing in the theatre, and my hope and belief that the actor will bring the force of his courage to assist in this revival. My attitude towards the whole matter is misunderstood by many in the Theatre. It is considered to be my attitude, mine alone; a stray quarreller I seem to be in their eyes, a pessimist, grumbling; one who is tired of a thing and who attempts to break it. Therefore let the other artists speak with the actor, and let the actor support his own case as best he may, and let him listen to their opinion on matters of art. We sit here conversing, the actor, the musician, the painter and myself. I who represent an art distinct from all these, shall remain silent.... "Tell us," asks the painter, "is it true that before you can act a part properly you must feel the emotions of the character you are representing?" "Oh well, yes and no; it depends what you mean," answers the actor. "We have first to be able to feel and sympathize and also criticize the emotions of a character; we look at it from a distance before we close with it: we gather as much as we can from the text and we call to mind all the emotions suitable for this character to exhibit. After having many times rearranged and selected those emotions which we consider of importance we then practice to reproduce them before the audience; and in order to so do we must feel as little as is necessary; in fact the less we feel, the firmer will our hold be upon our facial and bodily expression." With a gesture of genial impatience, the artist rises to his feet and paces to and fro. He had expected his friend to say that it had nothing whatever to do with emotions, and that he could control his face, features, voice and all, just as if his body were an instrument. The musician sinks down deeper into his chair. "But has there never been an actor,"

---

[1] "And therefore when any one of these pantomimic gentlemen, who are so clever that they can imitate anything, comes to us and makes a proposal to exhibit himself and his poetry, we will fall down and worship him as a sweet and holy and wonderful being; but we must also inform him that in our State such as he are not permitted to exist; the law will not allow them. And so, when we have annointed him with myrrh, and set a garland of wool upon his head, we shall lead him away to another city. For we mean to employ for our soul's health the rougher and severer poet or story-teller, who will imitate the style of the virtuous only, and will follow those models which we prescribed at first when we began the education of our soldiers." Plato (The whole passage being too long to print here, we refer the reader to *The Republic*, Book III, 395).

asks the artist, "who has so trained his body from head to foot that it would answer to the workings of his mind without permitting the emotions even so much as to awaken? Surely there must have been one actor, say one out of ten million, who has done this?" "No," says the actor emphatically, "never, never; there never has been an actor who reached such a state of mechanical perfection that his body was *absolutely* the slave of his mind. Edmund Kean of England, Salvini of Italy, Rachel, Eleonora Duse, I call them all to mind and I repeat there never was an actor or actress such as you describe." The artist here asks, "Then you admit that it would be a state of perfection?" "Why of course! But it is impossible; will always be impossible," cries the actor; and he rises...almost with a sense of relief. "That is as much as to say, there never was a perfect actor, there has never been an actor who has not spoiled his performance once, twice, ten times, sometimes a hundred times during the evening? There never has been a piece of acting which could be called even almost perfect and there never will be?" For answer the actor asks quickly, "But has there been ever a painting, or a piece of architecture, or a piece of music which may be called perfect?" "Undoubtedly," they reply, "the laws which control our arts make such a thing possible." "A picture for instance," continues the artist, "may consist of four lines, or four hundred lines, placed in certain positions; it may be as simple as possible; but it is possible to make it perfect. That is to say, I can first choose that which is to make the lines; I can choose that on which I am to place the lines: I can consider this as long as I like; I can alter it; then in a state which is both free from excitement, haste, trouble, nervousness, in fact in any state I choose (and of course I prepare, wait and select that also), I can put these lines together...so...now they are in their place. Having my material nothing except my own will can move or alter these; and as I have said my own will is entirely under my control. The line can be straight or it can wave; it can be round if I choose, and there is no fear that when I wish to make a straight line I shall make a curved one, or that when I wish to make a curved there will be square parts about it. And when it is ready...finished...it undergoes no change but that which time, who finally destroys it, wills." "That is rather an extraordinary thing," replied the actor. "I wish it was possible in my work." "Yes," replies the artist, *"it is a very extraordinary thing,* and it is that which I hold makes the difference between an intelligent statement and a casual or haphazard statement. The most intelligent statement, that is a work of art. The haphazard statement, that is a work of chance. When the intelligent statement reaches its highest possible form it becomes a work of fine art. And therefore I have always held, though I may be mistaken, that your work has not the nature of an art. That is to say (and you have said it yourself) each statement that you make in your work is subject to every conceivable change which emotion chooses to bring about. That which you conceive in your mind, your body is not permitted by nature to complete. In fact, your body, gaining the better of your intelligence, has in many instances on the stage driven out the intelligence altogether. Some actors seem to say, 'What value lies in having beautiful ideas. To what end shall my mind conceive a fine idea, a fine thought, for my body which is so entirely beyond my control to spoil? I will throw my mind overboard, let my body pull me and the play through'; and there seems to be some wisdom in the standpoint of such an actor. He does not dilly dally between the two things which are contending in him, the one against the other. He is not a bit afraid of the result. He goes at it like a man, sometimes like a trifle too like a centaur; he flings away all science...all caution...all reason and the result is good spirits in the audience ... and for that they pay willingly. But we are here talking about other things than excellent spirits, and though we applaud the actor who exhibits such a personality as this, I feel that we must not forget that we are applauding his personality ... *he* it is we applaud, not what he is doing or how he is doing it; nothing to do with art at all, absolutely nothing to do with art, with calculation, or design."

"You're a nice friendly creature," laughs the actor gaily, "telling me my art's no art! But I believe I see what you mean. You mean to say that before I appear on the stage and before my body commences to come into the question, I am an artist." "Well yes, *you* are, you happen to be, because you are a very bad actor; you're abominable on the stage, but you have ideas, you have imagination; you are rather an exception I should say.

"I have heard you tell me how you would play Richard III; what you would do; what strange atmosphere you would spread over the whole thing; and that which you have told me you have seen in the play, and that which you have invented and added to it, is so remarkable, so consecutive in its thought, so distinct and clear in form, that *if* you could make your body into a machine, or into a dead piece of material such as clay, and *if* it could obey you in every movement for the entire space of time it was before the audience, and if you could put aside Shakespeare's poem, you would be able to make a work of an art out of what is in you. For you would not only have dreamt, you would have executed to perfection; and that which you had executed could be repeated time after time without so much difference as between two farthings." "Ah," sighs the actor, "you place a terrible picture before me. You would prove to me that it is impossible for us ever to think of ourselves as artists. You take away our finest dream and you give us nothing in its place."

"No, no, that's not for me to give you. That's for you to find. Surely there must be laws at the roots of the art of the theatre, just as there are laws at the roots of all true arts, which if found and mastered, would bring you all you desire?"

"Yes, the search would bring the actors to a wall."

"Leap it, then!"

"Too high!"

"Scale it, then!"

"How do we know where it would lead?"

"Why, up and over."

"Yes, but that's talking wildly, talking in the air."

"Well, that's the direction you fellows have to go; ... fly in the air, live in the air. Something will follow when some of you begin to. I suppose," continued he, "you will get at the root of the matter in time, and then what a splendid future opens before you! In fact I envy you. I am not sure I do not wish that photography had been discovered before painting, so that we of this generation might have had the intense joy of advancing, showing that photography was pretty well in its way, but there was something better!"

"Do you hold that our work is on a level with photography?"

"No, indeed, it is not half as exact. It is less of an art even than photography. . . .

. . . Yet the aim of the theatre as a whole is to restore its art and it should commence by banishing from the theatre this idea of impersonation, this idea of reproducing nature; for while impersonation is in the Theatre, the Theatre can never become free. The performers should train under the influence of an earlier teaching (if the very earliest and finest principles are too stern to commence with) and they will have to avoid that frantic desire to put *"life"* into their work; for three thousand times against one time, it means the bringing of excessive gesture, swift mimicry, speech which bellows and scene which dazzles, on to the stage, in the wild and vain belief that by such means vitality can be conjured there. And in a few instances, to prove the rule, all this partially succeeds. It succeeds partially with the bubbling personalities of the stage. With them it is a case of sheer triumph *in spite* of the rules, in the very teeth of the rules, and we who look on, throw our hats into the air,... cheer, and cheer again. *We have to;* we don't want to consider or to question; we go with the tide through admiration and suggestion.... That we are hypnotized, our taste cares not a rap.... We are delighted to be so moved, and we literally jump for joy. The great personality has triumphed both over us and the art. But personalities such as these are extremely rare, and if we wish to see a personality assert itself in the theatre and entirely triumph as an actor we must at the same time be quite indifferent about the play, the other actors, and Beauty....

* * * *

..I suppose all the intelligent men and women of Europe (one does not speak of Asia for even the unintelligent in Asia fail to comprehend photographs while understanding art as a simple and clear manifestation) have protested against this reproduction of nature, and with its photographic and weak actuality; they have protested against all this, and the theatrical managers have argued against them energetically, and so we look for the truth to emerge in due time. It is a reasonable conclusion. Do away with the real tree, do away with the reality of delivery, do away with the reality of action, and you tend toward the doing away with the actor. This is what must come to pass in time, and I like to see the managers supporting the idea already. Do away with the actor, and you do away with the means by which a debased stage realism is produced and flourishes. No longer would there be a living figure to confuse us into connecting actuality and art; no longer a living figure in which the weakness and tremors of the flesh were perceptible.

The actor must go, and in his place comes the inanimate figure—the ueber-marionette we may call him, until he has won for himself a better name. Much has been written about the puppet—or marionette. There are some excellent volumes upon him, and he has also inspired several works of art. Today in his least happy period many people have come to regard him as rather a superior doll—and to think he has developed from the doll. This is incorrect. He is a descendant of the stone images of the old Temples—he is today a rather degenerate form of a God. Always the close friend of children he still knows how to select and attract his devotees.

When anyone designs a puppet on paper, he draws a stiff and comic looking thing. Such a one has not even perceived what is contained in the idea which we now call the Marionette. He mistakes gravity of face and calmness of body for blank stupidity and angular deformity. Yet even Modern Puppets are extraordinary things. The applause may thunder or dribble, their hearts beat no faster, no slower, their signals do not grow hurried or confused; and, though drenched in a torrent of bouquets and love, the face of the leading lady remains as solemn, as beautiful and as remote as ever. There is something more than a flash of genius in the marionette, and there is something in him more than the flashiness of displayed personality. The Marionette ... appears to me to be the last echo of some noble and beautiful art of a past civilization. But as with all art which has passed into fat or vulgar hands, the puppet has become a reproach. All puppets are now but low comedians. They imitate the comedians of the larger and fuller-blooded stage. They enter only to fall on their back. They drink only to reel, and make love only to raise a laugh. They have forgotten the counsel of their Mother, the Sphinx. Their bodies have lost their grave grace, they have become stiff. Their eyes have lost that infinite subtlety of seeming to see; now they only stare. They display and jingle their wires and are cock-sure in their wooden wisdom. They have failed to remember that their art should carry on it the same stamp of reserve that we see at times on the work of other artists, and that the highest art is that which conceals the craft and forgets the craftsman....

To speak of a Puppet with most men and women is to cause them to giggle. They think at once of the wires; they think of the stiff hands and the jerky movements; they tell me it is "a funny little doll." But let me tell them a few things about these Puppets. Let me again repeat that they are the descendants of a great and noble family of Images, Images which were made in the likeness of God; and that many centuries ago these figures had a rhythmical movement and not a jerky one; had no need for wires to support them, nor did they speak through the nose of the hidden manipulator. (Poor Punch, I mean no slight to you! You stand alone, dignified in your despair, as you look back across the centuries with painted tears still wet upon your ancient cheeks, and you seem to cry out appealingly to your dog, "Sister Anne, sister Anne, is *nobody* coming?" And then with that superb bravado of yours, you turn the force of our laughter (and my tears) upon yourself with the heart-rending shriek of "Oh my nose! Oh, my nose! Oh my nose!")

Did you think, ladies and gentlemen, that these puppets were always little things of but a foot high? Indeed, no! The puppet had once a more generous form than yourselves.

Do you think that he kicked his feet about on a little platform six foot square, made to resemble a little old-fashioned theatre; so that his head almost touched the top of the proscenium; and do you think that he always lived in a little house where the door and windows were as small as a doll's house, with painted window blinds parted in the center, and where the flowers of his little garden had courageous petals as big as his head? Try to dispel this idea altogether from your minds, and let me tell you something of his habitation.

In Asia lay his first Kingdom. On the banks of the Ganges they built him his home... a vast palace springing from column to column into the air and pouring from column to column down again into the water. ... A few centuries later, and we find his home a little the worse for wear. From a temple it has become, I will not say a theatre, but something between a temple and a theatre, and he is losing his health in it. Something is in the air; his doctors tell him he must be careful. "And what am I to fear the most?" he asks them.

They answer him: "Fear most the vanity of men."

He thinks, "But that is what I myself have always taught; that we who celebrated in joy this our existence, should have this one great fear. Is it possible that I, one who has ever revealed this truth, should be one to lose sight of it and should myself be one of the first to fall? Clearly some subtle attack is to be made on me. I will keep my eyes upon the Heavens." And he dismisses his doctors and ponders upon it.

And now let me tell you who it was that came to disturb the calm air which surrounded this curiously perfect thing. It is on record that somewhat later he took up his abode on the far Eastern Coast, and there came two women to look upon him. And at the ceremony to which they came he glowed with such earthly splendor and yet such unearthly simplicity, that though he proved an inspiration to the thousand nine-hundred and ninety-eight souls who participated in the festival, an inspiration which cleared the mind even as it intoxicated, yet to these two women it proved an intoxication only. He did not see them, his eyes were fixed on the heavens: but he charged them full of a desire too great to be quenched; the desire to stand as the direct symbol of the Divinity in Man. No sooner thought than done; and arraying themselves as best they could in garments ("like his," they thought) moving with gestures ("like him," they said) and being able to cause wonderment in the minds of the beholders ("Even as he does," they cried) they built themselves a temple ("like his," "like his"), and supplied the demand of the vulgar,... the whole thing a poor parody.

This is on record. It is the first record in the east of the actor.... The actor springs from the foolish vanity of two women who are not strong enough to look upon the symbol of godhead without desiring to tamper with it; and the parody proved profitable. In fifty or a hundred years, places for such parodies were to be found in all parts of the land.

Weeds, they say, grow quickly, and that wilderness of weeds, the modern theatre, soon sprang up. The figure of the Divine Puppet, attracted fewer and fewer lovers, and the women were quite the latest thing. With the fading of the Puppet and the advance of these women who exhibited themselves on the stage in his place, came that darker spirit which is called Chaos, and in its wake the triumph of the riotous Personality. Do you see then, what has made me love and learn to value that which today we call the puppet and to detest that which we call life in art?

I pray earnestly for the return of the image . . . the ueber-marionette, to the Theatre; and when he comes again and is but seen, he will be loved so well that once more will it be possible for the people to return to their ancient joy in ceremonies ... once more will Creation be celebrated ... homage rendered to existence ... and divine and happy intercession made to Death.

WILLIAM BUTLER YEATS

(1865-1939)

The great Irish poet W. B. Yeats from his youth had felt the importance of dramatic writing and as an adolescent wrote poetic plays in imitation of Shelley. His actual participation in theatrical activities came through his interest in restoring the ancient glory of spoken verse and through his friendship with Florence Farr, an actress whose magnificent voice Yeats constantly extolled. In the 1890's Yeats, like many others of his generation, became involved in the controversy over Ibsen's plays as they were presented for the first time in England. He was opposed to Ibsen's realistic, middle-class plays and wrote, "... art is art because it is not nature." He also wrote, "... yet neither I nor my generation could not escape him because, though we and he had not the same friends, we had the same enemies." These enemies were the commercial theatre with its lack of interest in artistically spoken verse, in poetic drama, or in ideas.

Yeats felt that Ireland in its struggle for a national culture could establish a great poetic theatre. His country, having no indigenous theatre, was dependent on English touring companies for its dramatic entertainment. Aided by Lady Augusta Gregory, Yeats founded the Irish Literary Theatre in 1898 with the hope of giving Ireland a theatre like those of Antoine and Brahm, with the difference that it would not be devoted to naturalism but to poetry. George Moore and Edward Martyn assisted in the first productions of the Literary Theatre, which gave three series of plays by Irishmen with English actors. With the demise of the Literary Theatre, Yeats' enthusiasm was once again fired when he saw the amateur Irish group headed by William and Frank Fay. To them he gave some of his plays and with them he formed the Irish National Theatre to continue the work of the Irish Literary Theatre on a more permanent basis. In 1903 this group went to London, where they were very successful. Miss A. E. F. Hornimann, a British theatre enthusiast, gave them a theatre in Dublin on Abbey Street, from which they took the name which has become world famous.

With Yeats, Lady Gregory, and its great original dramatist Synge as directors, the Abbey Theatre grew to be one of the finest acting companies in Europe. Yeats gave the group not only his plays, but his guidance in simplifying scenery, in keeping with his admiration for the work of Gordon Craig. He encouraged dramatists to write for the Abbey and handled much of the practical management of the Theatre. Most of all, he guided the Abbey artistically, constantly stressing beauty of speech and poetry on the stage, and simplicity in gesture and action. But the Abbey, despite Yeats' desire for a poetic theatre, became the home of realistic Irish drama.

Yeats turned from the public theatre to create a private theatre devoted to experimental plays written on the model of the Japanese Noh drama. He was a pioneer in drama utilizing masks, stylized dance postures, and simplified, symbolic stage settings.

The Sovereignty of Words

I think the theatre must be reformed in its plays, its speaking, its acting, and its scenery. That is to say, I think there is nothing good about it at present.

First. We have to write or find plays that will make the theatre a place of intellectual excitement—a place where the mind goes to be liberated as it was liberated by the theatres of Greece and England and France at certain great moments of their history, and as it is liberated in Scandinavia today. If we are to do this we must learn that beauty and truth are always justified of themselves, and that their creation is a greater service to our country than writing that compromises either in the seeming service of a cause. We will, doubtless, come more easily to truth and beauty because we love some cause with all but all our heart; but we must remember when truth and beauty open their mouths to speak, that all other mouths should be as silent as Finn bade the Son of Lugaidh be in the houses of the great. Truth and beauty judge and are above judgment. They justify and have no need of justification....

Second. But if we are to restore words to their sovereignty we must make speech even more important than gesture upon the stage.

I have been told that I desire a monotonous chant, but that is not true, for

W. B. Yeats: "The Reform of the Theatre," *Plays and Controversies.* New York: The Macmillan Company, 1924, pp. 45-49. Copyright 1924. By permission of The Macmillan Co.

though a monotonous chant may be a safer beginning for an actor than the broken and prosaic speech of ordinary recitation, it puts me to sleep none the less. The sing-song in which a child says a verse is a right beginning, though the child grows out of it. An actor should understand how so to discriminate cadence from cadence, and so to cherish the musical lineaments of verse or prose that he delights the ear with a continually varied music. Certain passages of lyrical feeling, or where one wishes, as in the Angel's part in *The Hour Glass,* to make a voice sound like the voice of an immortal, may be spoken upon pure notes which are carefully recorded and learned as if they were the notes of a song. Whatever method one adopts, one must always be certain that the work of art, as a whole, is masculine and intellectual, in its sound as in its form.

Third. We must simplify acting, especially in poetical drama, and in prose drama that is remote from real life like my *Hour Glass.* We must get rid of everything that is restless, everything that draws the attention away from the sound of the voice, or from the few moments of intense expression, whether that expression is through the voice or through the hands; we must from time to time substitute for the movements that the eye sees the nobler movements that the heart sees, the rhythmical movements that seem to flow up into the imagination from some deeper life than that of the individual soul.

Fourth. Just as it is necessary to simplify gesture that it may accompany speech without being its rival, it is necessary to simplify both the form and the color of scenery and costume. As a rule the background should be but a single color, so that the persons in the play, wherever they stand, may harmonize with it and preoccupy our attention. In other words, it should be thought out not as one thinks out a landscape, but as if it were the background of a portrait, and this is especially necessary on a small stage where the moment the stage is filled the painted forms of the background are broken up and lost. Even when one has to represent trees or hills they should be treated in most cases decoratively, they should be little more than an unobtrusive pattern. There must be nothing unnecessary, nothing that will distract the attention from speech and movement. An art is always at its greatest when it is most human. Greek acting was great because it did all but everything with the voice, and modern acting may be great when it does everything with voice and movement. But an art which smothers these things with bad painting, with innumerable garish colors, with continual restless mimicries of the surface of life, is an art of fading humanity, a decaying art.

WILLIAM FAY

(1872-1947)

William and Frank Fay were the two actors who contributed most to the formation and the direction of the Abbey Theatre. William followed his elder brother Frank in his theatrical interest. They were both pupils of Maud Randford, who organized a dramatic school in Dublin, and both participated in an amateur dramatic society along with Dudley Digges. William made his debut in 1891 at the Queen's Theatre in Dublin and then toured in Ireland and England.

After the Fays had organized an all-Irish troupe to perform Irish and Gaelic plays, they attracted the attention of the poet A. E. (George Russell) who gave them his *Deirdre* and who introduced their work to W. B. Yeats. With the two poets and

ACTORS ON ACTING

Lady Augusta Gregory, the Fays created the Irish National Theatre Company, which became the famed Abbey Theatre.

The Fay brothers were responsible for the productions of the Abbey. Frank, who believed that "the basis of all good acting was good speaking," trained the troupe and played the major roles in the poetic dramas of Yeats. William created the chief parts in the plays of Synge, notably Bartley in *Riders to the Sea* and Christopher Mahon in the controversial *The Playboy of the Western World*. The Abbey Theatre corps of actors was distinguished. With the Fays were Dudley Digges, Arthur Sinclair, Barry Fitzgerald, J. M. Kerrigan, J. A. O'Rourke, Maire NicShuibhlaigh, and the sisters Maire O'Neill and Sara Allgood.

After numerous excellent productions the Fays broke with Yeats and the Abbey in a dispute over control of the actors. One senses the tension between Fay and Yeats in the following statement by William Fay: "...I find that most people think of the Abbey Theatre as part and parcel of a national, or rather nationalist movement, that found literary expression in the work of men like W. B. Yeats and A. E. and was represented in politics by Sinn Fein. They are apt to confuse it with the Irish Literary Theatre, which was dead and buried before the Abbey Theatre had been conceived, much less born.... *The Abbey Theatre was first and foremost a theatrical, not a literary movement.* It was the creation not of men of letters but of actors. It is true that it discovered many dramatists of ability...but the playwrights were, so to speak, a supervening phenomenon. It was the zeal of the players that provided the conditions in which they were able to emerge.... Ibsen made a theatre to suit his plays. We of the Abbey made our theatre first and then got plays to suit it, which I venture to submit, is the natural order—at any rate it is what the Elizabethans did. We were not literary men. Most of us were humble folk...what bound us together was enthusiasm for the art of acting."

Other directors of the Abbey have been such prominent men as Nugent Monck, later manager of the Maddermarket Theatre; Lennox Robinson, the playwright and actor; Arthur Shields, actor-brother of Barry Fitzgerald; and the playwright St. John Ervine.

The homely, Irish folk impersonations in which the Fays and their immediate associates excelled shaped the peasant dramas popular at the Abbey Theatre. In 1927 Micheál MacLiammoir and Hilton Edwards, revolting against what they called "the outworn English school clothed in the homespun of a brogue," organized the Dublin Gate Theatre to produce international dramatists.

William Fay toured widely after breaking with the Abbey. In 1908 Charles Frohman brought him to the United States to produce Irish plays in New York and Chicago. He directed numerous groups in England, among them Sir Barry Jackson's Birmingham Repertory Theatre. William Fay has written scenarios and played roles on the screen. He is the author of *A Short Glossary of Theatrical Terms*, *The Fays of the Abbey Theatre*, with Katherine Carswell, and *Merely Players*, from which the following selection is taken.

Advice from an Abbey Theatre Actor

Whatever vocation you follow in life, you can only get out of it what you put into it. As Walt Whitman said: "The acting is to the actor and comes back most

W. G. Fay: *Merely Players*. London: Rich and Cowan, 1932, pp. 19-23. Copyright 1932. By permission of Mrs. W. G. Fay and Richard Steele & Son.

to him," for additional power of self-expression is all that comes to a man from the practice of any of the Arts, and the amount of his subjective life he can make objective will depend on the technical skill with which he can use his medium.

The actor must use his own individuality and personality as the mediums through which he displays the various thoughts, emotions, and actions that constitute the character the dramatist has given him to play. The extent to which he can make his audience believe in its reality is the measure of his professional ability. The audience should feel that everything that happens before them on the stage is as natural to the actor as eating his dinner, or brushing his hair. This natural acting can only be acquired by completely mastering technique and then only using as much of that knowledge as is necessary "to put the part over."

In your first attempts to appear natural don't carry it so far that they will need ear-trumpets to hear you in the stalls. Many young actors are "natural" in that way. "It takes too much out of you to make the people in the gallery hear. It is good enough for the public to see you without wanting to hear you as well." But, strange as it may seem, the audience likes to hear at least some of the author's story. Nothing unsettles them so much as to hear an old lady in the second row of the stalls say in a very loud voice to her friend: "What was that he said?" Then her companion in stentorian tones tells her in detail the story of the play up to date.

When Dame Madge Kendal was being taught by her father, one piece of advice he continually impressed on her was to remember the poor man in the back row of the gallery who has spent a six-pence he could not very well spare to hear you. And take care that he does. Don't forget that the audience pay money to hear you, so carry out your side of the bargain by being audible in every part of the theatre. You need not bellow like a bull; you can coo like a dove if you do it distinctly. It is not a big voice that is needed but distinct articulation.

The following advice is "wrote sarcastic"; Never be punctual at rehearsals; if you are, the other actors will think you are a beginner. You don't want that to happen. Dash on to the stage twenty minutes after the time for which the rehearsal was called. Say, in a loud voice: "Oh, have you started? I hope I'm not late. I threw a party last night, lost £8 at bridge and. didn't get to bed till five." Don't apologize to the rest of the cast for keeping them waiting. Don't excuse yourself to the Producer or the Stage Manager; they are engaged solely to wait on your convenience.

The less you know about your part at rehearsal the better. The best place to learn it is on the stage, not at home where it would take up time that might be devoted to more entertaining things. You can be sure the rest of the company will like being delayed by your lack of knowledge. Don't take note of the movements or business the Producer tells you; it gives him pleasure to tell it to you again each time you rehearse, and it prevents him forgetting it which he might if you remembered it. It enhances your importance to keep the stage waiting each time you make an entrance and gives the Stage Manager a lesson in controlling his temper, which in all probability he needs.

If you have to embrace one of the ladies in the play, the more grease paint you leave on her frock the better she will like you. It is easily taken out of a new frock, and there are plenty of theatrical cleaners always advertising for work. The less grease paint you provide the better, for you will then be able to find out how you stand with your fellow artists when you go round the dressing-rooms trying to borrow some. A slavish adherence to the author's words is not necessary: you are sure to think of better ones yourself, and being your own they will come much more "trippingly on the tongue." If by a lucky chance you should think of a funny one, put it in. If the audience does not roar with merriment when they hear it, console yourself with the thought that the fault lies in their want of a sense of humor.

Always stand on the stage with your legs well apart, so that the audience will have no doubt that you are a real he-man from the wide open spaces and not one of the effete people who live amongst the brick and mortar of towns. Walk on the stage as if it were covered four feet deep in snow and you have to pick your steps. This gives a dignified carriage.

To have a red handkerchief gracefully falling out of your pocket, or pouring tea in your saucer, then blowing on it, can be recommended as two of the safest bits of comic business. Plautus used them in his farces, along with pouring water into the other chap's hat when he is not looking.

Avoid trying to occupy the center of the stage all the time, because the other members of the cast like to have a turn there now and again; besides, it belongs by right to the "leading lady." Instead, you can try standing in front of your fellow actors if they happen to be foolish enough to let you. Don't forget they like being kept "up stage" as much as possible: it helps them to learn humility, a useful addition to the many brilliant qualities they already possess.

HARLEY GRANVILLE-BARKER
(1877-1946)

One of the innovators at the turn of the century, Granville-Barker began his career as an actor in and around London. He toured with Sir Philip Ben Greet's Shakespearean company and played with the Elizabethan Stage Society which was attempting to perform Shakespeare in a manner approximating the conditions of the Elizabethan theatre. He appeared in productions of the Incorporated Stage Society which was devoted to the new English and foreign dramas, such as those of Shaw and Ibsen. In 1902 he joined J. E. Vedrenne at the Royal Court Theatre where, from 1904 to 1907, he directed the plays of Ibsen, those of Shaw, and introduced the first play by Galsworthy to London playgoers. His experiments in staging, design, and lighting made his productions noteworthy.

In addition to his practical theatrical work Granville-Barker translated many Spanish plays with his wife. His prefaces to the plays of Shakespeare have made him an important interpreter of the bard. Not the least of his many accomplishments were his original plays, *Madras House* and *The Voysey Inheritance*.

In his lectures on the drama Granville-Barker has paid a good deal of attention to the problems of the actor and the art of acting. "The Heritage of the Actor" deals with some of the difficulties created by changing conditions in the second half of the nineteenth century. Essentially he asks: What is the role of the actor in the modern drama devoted to realistic character portrayal, the drama that does not provide the actor with exciting poetry to recite or impressive deeds to perform? With the emergence of such important prose realists as Shaw and Galsworthy, how, he questions, can the actor continue the type of creative acting that marked Henry Irving's embellishments of the melodrama *The Bells?*

The Heritage of the Actor

A play is material for acting. It may be far more, but it must be that to begin with. The actor brings it to a technical completion. This, no doubt, puts the matter from the actor's point of view, and while the truth is indisputable, the emphasis of the statement may be misleading. Even so, this point of view counts; if only because, when we bring a play to the theatre, the actor's is the last word in the matter—till the public has its say. If it be argued that the play is implicitly complete when it leaves the author's hands, that the actor's business is interpretation merely, that he can, in truth add nothing to and take nothing away from the material a competent playwright has given him—

There was once, in the 17th century, a gentleman, who, coming out of church on a Sunday morning, found a week-day companion sitting in the stocks.

"What have they put you there for?" he asked.

"Getting drunk."

"Nonsense," said the church-goer, who was a legally-minded man; "they can't put you in the stocks for being drunk."

"Zooks!" said the unfortunate reveller. "But they *have!*"

It is useless to argue that actors can add nothing to and take nothing from the material the playwright gives them. The answer is that they do.... Let any one familiar with play production ask himself what the final effect would be if the actors felt called upon to do no more than speak a speech as the author was good enough to pronounce it to them, trippingly upon the tongue. A certain regardless beauty might result. There are plays that, at first thought, would seem to profit by this treatment. Greek tragedy, with its use of mask and cothurnus, asks for its acting a voice and a presence, and little else; though, even so, it may be found that concentration upon this single means of expression rather heightens than diminishes a personality that *can* so express itself. But in a play which pictures human intercourse in accustomed terms, if the actor did not do something more than repeat its words with such understanding and emotion as they immediately suggested to him, pointing them with appropriate gesture, the result would be unbearably flat and quite unconvincing.

What, then, is the "something more" he is expected to contribute? His personality. What, then, is the extension of this in the terms of his art to be? Drama ranges from the austerity of Greek tragedy to the freedom of the *Commedia dell' arte;* and it is not for one manifestation of it, however respectable, however popular, to deny the validity of any other. The antics of Harlequin are not essentially different from the art that shows us Oedipus. But, to bring the question to a practical and a more or less topical issue, let us rule out both drama that is largely ritual and drama that is inchoate. Let us assume a play

Harley Granville-Barker: "The Heritage of the Actor." New York: *The Quarterly Review*, Volume 239, Number 476, July, 1923, pp. 53-73 *passim.*

conceived by an author in essential completeness, and marked down for interpretation as minutely as words will do it....

The dramatist has a right to expect that any actor, of the required sex and of the right age and appearance—picked out of a list, called off the rank as it were —will be able to say and do with perfect efficiency whatever can be set down for him to say and do. This right, like many others, is often in abeyance. But, with the expectation fulfilled, the dramatist will still ask the actor to *be* something besides. At times, no doubt, this "being" is offensive. We have all seen plays swamped by an elaborate exhibition of some one personality. We have, on the other hand, seen plays of the poorest sort enriched beyond recognition by the imposition—as upon one of those vague backgrounds used by Victorian photographers—of vivid characters, springing, if not from the imagination of the actors of them, then from where? Irving's Mathias will certainly not be found in the original manuscript of *The Bells*. And if one is to be told that it was in some mysterious fashion innate in the story and the play as Erckmann-Chatrian and the adapter wrote them, one must ask further: was Coquelin's conception of the innkeeper-murderer innate there too? If so, the authors had an uncommonly accommodating or a somewhat divided mind....

...The work of the modern theatre, however, where authors and actors of average ability are concerned, is done, as a whole, upon the basis of a compromise by which the author provides essentials and the actor incidentals to taste. The modern invention, the producer, is the honest broker brought in to effect it. It answers, doubtless; and the bulk of the work done under it may be pleasing enough. But is there no more to be said? For there is no future in a compromise....

But it will be owned that this latest period of development in drama has been the playwright's period, not the actor's. Has it not often brought actor and playwright to odds, now openly, now—for good reasons of bread-and-butter— as polite as you please? Once, at a public dinner, Ibsen was congratulated upon the magnificent parts his play provided for their interpreters. The old gentleman scowled terrifically. "Parts!" he said, when he rose to speak; "I do not write parts. I create men and women." On the other hand, could the talk of actors gathered together at many a private dinner during the last forty years be recorded, it would rise to Heaven as the discordant wail of a crushed and desolated race.

The quarrel, I repeat, may seldom be particularized. A theatre is the happiest of workshops and its controllers have to learn that happiness is a necessary part of its efficiency. And, as I have suggested, in practice these conflicting interests are accommodated by a compromise. Let there be so much sheer interpretation of the part I have written, so much exploiting, my dear Mr. So-and-so, of your personality. Never, of course, is it put in so many words, or even thought of with so brutal a clarity. And where the domination of either author or producer on the one hand, or of actor on the other, is perfect and unquestioned, no overt difference will be detected. The author murmurs approvingly from the shrouded stalls, or the actors obediently note that they are not only to do but to feel this and that and no more. Five minutes—five seconds!—at a rehearsal or performance will tell the experienced observer which regime is in force. Some rehearsals, doubtless, run their course upon a basis of conflict to a goal of haphazard performance. If the play is a success—and good plays and bad plays, bad performances of them and good ones, succeed and fail equally—no one concerned asks any questions. If it is a failure, the author feels, "Ah, if *my play* had had a chance...!" and the actors either "Ah, if I'd only had something to act...!" or "If they'd only have let me *act* it!" It is a stupid quarrel. And what is its result for the play-goer? That good actors often prefer bad plays; and that good plays are too often deplorably badly acted.

If this is the dramatist's day, he will be wise to consider the actor, not as a mere appendage to his work, but as its very life-giver. Let him realize that the more he can learn to ask of the actor the more will he gain for his play. But asking is giving. He must give opportunity....

...Why do we go to see a play that we really like again and again? (And return visits are the test; in music, in painting, in drama.) Not to have the story re-told us, however ingeniously it may be told. It is the elucidation of character that does not pall; and it is in this—all virtuosity, all that is learn-able allowed for—that the actor's art finds its final task and its true achievement. As with the actor, so with the playwright; construction and the rest of it are as learnable as is good speaking and the tricks of painting the face; but either he can create men and women in terms of dramatic action or he cannot. And nothing else finally counts. He need not, however, with Ibsen, disdain to think of them as parts to be played. That was in its time, perhaps, a wholesome protest against the actor's egoism. But it has become—frankly—a piece of snobbery and no more. For now as always it is the power of the actor, adopting the speech and action of the author's imagining, to elucidate the character in the terms of his own personality that gives the thing that apparent spontaneity of life which is the drama's peculiar virtue....

Modern drama, the actor may tell us, does not give him the chances that the old did. But in much of it there is more for him to do than he is apt to think. For he thinks of great acting too often in terms of the past; his mind stalks that apron-stage of Garrick's. Or, worse, he thinks of it *in vacuo*. His secret heart asks for a play which shall be but a colorable preparation and excuse for his doing something emotionally tremendous. He wants to "capture" his audience, he yearns (quite rightly) after that emotional intimacy with them which will bring them to crying when he gives the cue and laughing when he laughs, without ever asking the reason why. His instinct tells him indeed that the less reason has to do with it the more satisfying his job will be. Set him free, he feels, to appeal to the hearts of the people and all will be well. Again, he is right from his point of view. All *will* be well enough for that moment of triumph; and he is not responsible for the after-questionings of an audience convalescent from their attack of this Dionysiac disease. What was it all about? That has to be the author's concern; and *he* may—or may not—have a reputation for sanity which he cares to preserve.

In the day of the dramatist, therefore, the actor must not seek that sort of emancipation. He must—it is the only way in art—break to new liberty through fulfillment. Modern plays make demands on him that, he may often think, are less in degree than he deserves; but, as he may even oftener omit to notice, these differ almost in kind from the old demands. Until he has exhausted the possibilities there are he cannot justly reproach, well, he will not wisely reproach—the authors of his histrionic being (if now they have the whip hand of him) with not providing more....

The modern dramatist's side of the case begins with a justification, but ends, it may be, with a question. His demands on the actor do differ greatly from the old demands, and the actor has been slow to recognize it. One need not here try to trace the process of change. . . . But the plain fact is that the writer of today, setting himself to mirror some fraction of contemporary life in dramatic form, goes to work under technical obligations that a century ago could have found no application at all, that fifty years back were but emerging from the tangle of an older, a much worn tradition. If they are to be stated in a phrase or in a dozen phrases, they are none the less obvious. One might try, not quite success-fully, to round them in with a paradox by saying that the footlights which symbolize the illusion of the picture stage now destroy the very division between actors and audience that they first made. Drama's aim has not changed. This is still to create an emotional intimacy between these two; only the means to the end have shifted, have indeed finally been reversed. For—paradox apart—by the old method the stage and the actor were brought into the midst of the audience, by the new the audience is lured in imagination on the stage; if it can be hypno-tized, even, into forgetting that such a thing as a stage exists, so much the better. Wherefore the "realistic setting" has been perfected. We have rooms that we may regard as our own, fires that crackle, lights that our fingers twitch to turn up or down, doors that shut and bang with a familiar sound. It is interesting to remember that the end of *The Doll's House* —of the play which began this movement—was the banging of a door.

To such realism naturally belongs realism, or—if one rejects that abused word—verisimilitude of speech and action and of the drawing of character generally. Now, cause and effect in the development of an art are hard to dis-tinguish. Let us only say then, that these things have in turn been the occasion of a great change of content in plays. The actor must follow where the dramatist leads. Here he has hung back, he has protested, and he has had times of real and times of false enthusiasm for the new thing. He has often succeeded in coaxing the dramatist aside for an old-fashioned frolic. But, on the main path, he has had to follow. And the dramatist—this might be his protest—now puts him in a world which is sometimes far too like the real one to be at all amusing. He is expected to know what a bishop, a stockbroker, a politician, a Frenchman, a Lincolnshire farmer, or a Scottish professor really are like. He is asked, more-over, to devote himself, even by the complete suppression of himself, to exhibiting the commonplace and expounding the abstruse, not to murmur if, when the exhibiting and expounding suffices the purpose of the play, *he* is bundled un-ceremoniously out of it, not to complain if he can only find in the paper the next morning that "the performance was adequate." No wonder he thinks enviously of Edmund Kean and of "loud applause" punctuating every few lines of a performance, and of the days when a Mercutio, after departing to die, promptly returned to bow to the cheering, while Romeo and the rest stood around and the play itself waited his triumph's pleasure.

A generation of actors has already grown up, perhaps, that takes its new leading-strings for granted; otherwise the consequent question would be put more insistently than it is. I will try to put it. Has the dramatist, busy reconstituting his own art to gain full advantage from this theatre of the new illusion, given enough thought to all that the art of the actor has to gain from it? Has, in fact, the art of the actor gained in these days of the dramatist's dominance? And, if not, must not any gain to drama itself be but a very partial gain?

There has lately been revolt against verisimilitude. The dramatists themselves look round for ways of emancipations. But the revolt has been led—oddly enough—not by the actor but by designers of scenery. The actor would have been wise to make the quarrel his own and to make it a quarrel of principle. His is the case, but he has let the best of it go to snatch petty advantages here and there. And the scene designer fights, not in his interest at all, but against him....

...Ibsen and Shakespeare in the shades must wonder indeed when it comes echoing to them that, for their work to have full value for the theatre, it must be be made "expressionistic." Actors, remembering their great predecessors, must feel a little bored when they are recommended to be "presentational," or to wear masks, or, on occasion, to abdicate altogether in favor of marionettes....

The beauty of sublimated human emotion; that is the beauty which properly pertains to drama. Without this and its complements of wit and humor, drama will die, and neither brains in the playwright nor the splashing of paint will avail to save it. But there is no need whatever to suppose that the technique of the modern play of verisimilitude is outworn or that its gains to the dramatist must be abandoned in a search for beauty and emotional power. And the gain to drama itself will be entire if the actor can be brought to contribute more largely from his own peculiar resources, the resources of human emotion. Not how to stifle or suppress this in the name of his own new freedom, but how to employ it to new and to subtler purpose should be the dramatist's problem. But—this must be recognized—it is the problem of a partnership. It will not be resolved under the tyranny of dramatist or actor. In the lack of a fruitful recognition of this the scene designer has come thrusting in where really he has no business. His interference has resulted in a most beneficent improvement of bad scenery into good. But, if it is to be a question of the development of drama itself—no, no; let him mind his paint-pots.

We may sense what is wrong, yet wisely be chary of dogmatizing upon its putting right. Certainly it is futile to request dramatists to give actors better chances of acting, to turn out plays containing such and such ingredients in such and such proportion—as if the making of plays were one with the making of puddings or pills. And the actor's practical difficulty—once he forswears the ideal of a tame dramatist who will make him a play as his cook makes him puddings—is that he must act what he finds to act.... He could more often, strangely enough, find the occasion in plays in which the dramatist has himself been impatient of the form chosen and has surcharged it with thought or with feeling. It is, in fact, to the dramatist's experiments in the enlargement of his own art that the actor should look for the development of his....

What, then, is the actor's case; what should he claim from the modern drama; what has he to offer? The dramatist's chief gain from the theatre of the new illusion and the conventions which belong to it, has been—at the price of some limitation of his power to project things in the doing—a great extension of resource in picturing things as they are. There was more need, as well as more scope, for physical action upon the older stage, even as there was for the spellbinding sway of verse. But by the new illusion the attention of an audience can be focused upon the smallest details without either words or action being used to mark them, light, darkness, and silence can be made eloquent in themselves, a whole gamut of effectiveness has been added. It has brought new obligations—

of accuracy, of sincerity, of verisimilitude in general, as we have noted. Then gain and loss both must be reflected in the actor's opportunity. His chances of doing are curtailed; in their stead new obligations of being are laid upon him. Can he not turn them to his profit?

One is tempted to imagine a play—to be written in desperate defiance of Aristotle—from which doing would be eliminated altogether, in which nothing but being would be left. The task set the actors of it would be to interest their audience in what the characters *were,* quite apart from anything they might *do;* to set up, that is to say, the relation by which all important human intimacies exist. If the art of the theatre could achieve this it would stand alone in a great achievement....

...one may hazard an assertion that the modern dramatist's failure to provide due opportunity for his actors is oftenest this: he has discovered no sufficient substitute for the poetry and rhetoric in which lay the acting strength of the old plays. He may write excellent sense, and the audience, hearing it, will yet remain profoundly uninterested. Is the actor to blame? No; dramatic dialogue needs other qualities before it can be made to carry conviction. There is no solution, needless to say, in the dressing up of the play in poetic phrasing or the provision of a purple patch here and there. One must choose a medium and stick to it; only so can illusion be sustained. But the old dramatists did put into the hands—or, rather, into the mouths—of their actors a weapon of great, of magical power, by which, with little else to aid them, they could subdue their hearers to every illusion of a mimic world. Useless today to imitate its form, to fancy the strength lay in that. The essentials of it must be sought and somehow found. When found they are recognizable enough. Take any play and read two pages aloud. There can be no mistake. Tested by the living voice, either the language has life in it or it has not. A difficult medium, no doubt, to master, the prose of common speech which shall yet have the power of poetry. But it is what the actor asks if he is to command belief in his world of make-believe.

To put it in a phrase then; if the actor is to come to his own in the new drama, something the dynamic equivalent of poetry must be given to him as material for his share of the work. Nor is this too hard a saying. The dramatist's task—and the actor's coming after him—is the building up and exhibition of human character, the picture of men's natures in the intimacies of their working. To this extent it is essentially a poet's task and the means to it are essentially those a poet seeks....

And magic is needed; the power of the spoken word is a magic power. But the art of the theatre is not a reasonable art. A play's dialogue is an incantation, and the actors must bewitch us with it. They must seem, now to be the commonest sort of folk, now superhuman, and the form of their talk must fit them. But, for all appearance, it must ever be of a trebly-distilled strength. It must have this power of poetry in it. It must be alive with more than the mere meaning of words. In content and in form the modern dramatist has often advanced his art. But still, too often, the worthiest plays will leave us cold, respectful, when we should be deeply moved, or paying them instead of laughter a tolerant smile. What is wrong? This, for one thing, I suggest. The dramatist of the new dispensation has yet, as a rule, to learn both what to ask of his actors and how best to help them to answer the demand.

ENGLAND AND IRELAND
JOHN GIELGUD

(b. 1904)

Born in London, Gielgud is the last representative on the stage of the Terry family. His maternal grandmother was Kate Terry, whose Juliet is still recalled, his great-aunt the immortal Ellen Terry. Gielgud is said to have inherited the Terry voice "unique in timbre—warm, tender, glowing, expressive." He went on the stage when he was seventeen with the promise to his family that he would give up the pursuit of that career should he fail to make his mark by the age of twenty-five. Precisely at twenty-five Gielgud became the star of the Old Vic company.

At the Old Vic Gielgud played Romeo, Cleante in Molière's *The Imaginary Invalid*, Antonio in *The Merchant of Venice*, Mark Antony in *Julius Caesar*, Richard II, Macbeth and Hamlet. In 1930 at the West End Theatre he played John Worthing in Wilde's *The Importance of Being Earnest* for the first time. In the season of 1935-36 came Gielgud's memorable production of *Romeo and Juliet* in which Laurence Olivier and he alternated the roles of Mercutio and Romeo with Peggy Ashcroft as Juliet and Dame Edith Evans as the Nurse—the longest run (186 performances) the play has ever had.

Gielgud's roles reveal a remarkable range of talent: Lewis Dodd in *The Constant Nymph*, Charley in *Charley's Aunt*, Hotspur in *Henry IV*, Sergius Saranoff in *Arms and the Man*, the title role in *Noah*, Joseph Surface in *The School for Scandal*, Vershinin in *The Three Sisters*, Valentine in *Love for Love*, King Lear, Prospero, Macbeth, Raskolnikoff in *Crime and Punishment*, Jason in Robinson Jeffers's *Medea*, Julian in Edward Albee's *Tiny Alice* and many others. His Hamlet ranks with the great interpretations of the role. He has toured in almost every part of the world in many of these roles. His "Ages of Man" solo recital of many Shakespearean characters and themes, created in 1958, revealed to his wide international audience his special excellence as an actor. Peter Brook, with whom he has worked on many occasions and with whom he has a warm personal relationship, describes his distinctive magic as an actor very precisely. "His art has always been more vocal than physical; at some early stage in his career he decided that for himself the body was a less supple instrument than the head. He thus jettisoned part of an actor's possible equipment but made true alchemy with the rest. It is not just speech, nor melodies, but the continual movement between the word-forming mechanism and his understanding that has made his art so rare, so touching and especially so aware."

He has worked with some of the great directors of our time, Harcourt Williams of the Old Vic, Harley Granville-Barker, who wrote him valuable letters of criticism over the years, Theodore Komisarjevsky, Michel Saint-Denis as well as Peter Brook. He has himself become a notable director of opera, Shakespeare, period comedy as well as modern plays. He has also made many film appearances.

From the early days of their *Romeo and Juliet* joint venture, Gielgud and Olivier have been the subject of many comparisons. He himself recalls feeling jealous of Olivier's "tremendous energy" in that production, and even in a recent BBC interview spoke of not "risking" certain roles he might like to do again like

Othello and Macbeth because Olivier's interpretation of these parts "was too good for me to compete." Yet, as English critic Alan Dent observed, "Must any decision be come to as to which is the better of our two best tragedians? . . . Both have their glories."

Gielgud's autobiography, *Early Stages,* and his *Stage Directions* reveal the devoted professional artist whose desire or "violent and sincere wish" is to be "a good craftsman, and to understand what I try to do in the theatre, so as to be able to convince the people I work with."

Creating My Roles

. . . Of course, all acting should be character-acting, but in those days I did not realize this. When I played a part of my own age I was acutely aware of my own graces and defects. I could not imagine a young man unless he was like myself. My own personality kept interfering, and I began to consider how I was looking, whether my walk was bad, how I was standing; my attention was continually distracted and I could not keep inside the character I was trying to represent. In Trofimov for the first time I looked in the glass and thought, "I know how this man would speak and move and behave", and to my great surprise I found I was able to keep that picture in my mind throughout the action, without my imagination deserting me for a moment, and to lose myself completely as my appearance and the circumstances of the play seemed to demand. I suppose the truth of the matter was that I was relaxed for the first time. The finest producers I have worked with since have told me that this relaxation is the secret of all good acting. But we were never taught it at the dramatic schools. One's instinct in trying to work oneself into an emotional state is to tighten up. When one is young and nervous one tightens the moment one attempts to act at all, and this violent nervous tension, if it is passionately sincere, can sometimes be effective on the stage. But it is utterly exhausting to the actor and only impresses the audience for a very short space of time.

* * * *

In playing Shakespeare one is bound to be conscious of the audience. The compromise between a declamatory and a naturalistic style is extremely subtle, and needs tremendous technical skill in its achievement. In Chekhov, provided one can be heard and seen distinctly, it is possible, even advisable, to ignore the audience altogether, and this was another reason why I suddenly felt so much more at ease in playing Trofimov than I had in Romeo.

I have extremely good eyesight and I am very observant. From the stage, if I am not careful, I can recognize people I know eight or ten rows back in the stalls, even on a first night when I am shaking with nervousness: late-comers—people who whisper or rustle chocolates or fall asleep—I have an eye for every one of them, and my performance suffers accordingly. I once asked Marion Terry about this difficulty and she said, "Hold your eyes level with the front of

---

John Gielgud: *Early Stages.* New York: Macmillan, 1939, *passim.* Copyright 1939. By permission of The Macmillan Co.

the dress-circle when you are looking out into the front." It has taken me years to learn to follow her advice. But in Chekhov, whose plays are written to be acted, as Komisarjevsky[1] used to say, "with the fourth wall down," I have always been able to shut out the faces in the front, even when I look in their direction, and am conscious of no one but the other characters.

* * * *

Komis's [Komisarjevsky] interest and help had encouraged me tremendously, and I began to feel that I could study a part from the inside, as he taught me, not seizing at once on the obvious showy effects and histrionics, but trying to absorb the atmosphere of the play and the background of the character, and then to build it outwards so that it came to life naturally, developing in proper relationship to the other actors, under the control of the producer.

* * * *

The Constant Nymph gave me my first experience of a long run. To play the same part eight times a week for more than a year is a severe test for any actor. The routine is nerve-racking, and it is agonizing work trying to keep one's performance fresh, without either slackening or over-acting. I am usually guilty of the latter fault, and my tendency to exaggerate every effect becomes more and more marked as the weeks go by. After a long run in London, touring is at first a pleasant change, even in the same play, as one is forced to change the tone and breadth of one's performance to suit the different sizes of the provincial theatres; but by the end of a year's run in London with a six weeks tour of the provinces to follow, acting becomes a real nightmare, and it seems hard to believe one is ever going to enjoy it again. . . .

Long runs have their advantages, however. To begin with, they are necessary for an actor if he is to attract the notice of a large public. Many people can only afford to go to the theatre two or three times a year, and naturally they are inclined to choose for their visits the plays which are big hits of several months' standing. Young actors can often make personal successes in a series of short runs or even failures. The critics may indeed notice them with more attention if they distinguish themselves several times running in a series of indifferent plays. But, though they may be well spoken of in the press, and "fancied" in the small world of the theatre, the general public will never have heard of them until their names have once been connected with a big commercial success.

There is also the question of discipline. A long run, with continual good houses, gives the actor confidence and sureness in his technique; he is able to try many different ways of timing, to study the details of tone and inflection, to watch his mannerisms, and to develop his capacity for give-and-take in acting with his partners. He is forced to control his boredom, to discover a means of producing affections of emotion of which the spontaneous feeling has long since deserted him, to resist the temptation to giggle and play the fool, to find a way of rousing a lethargic house, and to remind himself continually that there are many people in every audience who are seeing and judging his acting for the first time.

* * * *

It is always important to me, in a character part, to be able to satisfy myself with my visual appearance. I imagine at rehearsals how I hope to look, but if my

---

[1] Theodore Komisarjevsky.

make-up comes out well at the first dress rehearsal, my confidence is increased a hundred-fold. In the same way, the right clothes—especially in a part where they must be heavy and dignified—help me at once to find the right movements and gestures for the character. One's expression in a character part develops tremendously quickly after the first few times in making up. Photographs taken at a dress rehearsal only show a kind of mask, a sketch of the actor's invention, just like his performance at an early rehearsal. Photograph him again after he has been acting the part for a fortnight, and the whole expression has deepened, and developed into something much more complete, revealing the mental conception of the part in the eyes and mouth, as well as in the lines and shadows that are painted over them.

*　*　*　*

The last production of my first Old Vic season was *Hamlet*. It was exciting to have the chance of playing it after all, but I did not think it likely that I should give an interesting performance. I had not made a success of Romeo, though I had played the part before, and I considered Richard and Macbeth, in which I had done better work, were both character parts. From my childhood I had had some sort of picture in my mind of these two personages. I could imagine myself at once dressed in their clothes and I tried, in rehearsing and acting them, to forget myself completely, to keep the imagined image fresh and vivid, and to some extent I had succeeded. Hamlet was different. How could I seem great enough, simple enough to say those hackneyed, wonderful lines as if I was thinking of them for the first time? How could I avoid certain passages in the manner of other actors I had seen, how could I put into the part my own personal feelings—many of which fitted the feelings of Hamlet—and yet lift them to a high classical style worthy of the character?

We began to rehearse. Some of the scenes came to me more easily than others; the first appearance of Hamlet particularly—one of my favorite scenes of all the plays I have ever read or acted—sincerity, real emotion, and marvellously simple words to express them in. The second scene, when Hamlet first sees the Ghost, difficult, sudden, technically hard to speak, the following Ghost scene terribly difficult, intensely tiring to act, nothing to say, then, after the Ghost disappears, too many words. Impossible to convey, even with Shakespeare's help, the horror and madness of the situation, the changing tenderness and weary resignation.

The mad scenes. How mad should Hamlet be? So easy to score off Polonius, to get laughs, so important not to clown, to keep the story true—then the intricate scene with Rosencrantz and Guildenstern, and my favorite prose speech in the play, "What a piece of work is a man!..." The arrival of the players, easier again, natural, true feeling, but the big soliloquy is coming in a minute, one must concentrate, take care not to anticipate, not begin worrying beforehand how one is going to say it, take time, but don't lose time, don't break the verse up, don't succumb to the temptation of a big melodramatic effect for the sake of gaining applause at the curtain—Nunnery scene. Shall it be a love scene? How much emotion? When should Hamlet see the King? I feel so much that I convey nothing. This scene never ceases to baffle me.

Interval—The Advice to the Players. Dreadful little pill to open the second part, all the people coming back into their seats, slamming them down, somehow try to connect the speech with the rest of the play, not just a set piece—Tender for the tiny scene with Horatio, a moment's relief—then into the Play Scene. Relax if possible, enjoy the scene, watch the Gonzago Play, watch the King, forget that this is the most famous of famous scenes, remember that Hamlet is not yet sure of Claudius, delay the climax, then carry it (and it needs all the control and breath in the world to keep the pitch at the right level). No pause before the Recorders scene begins, and this cannot make the effect it should unless Rosencrantz and Guildenstern pull their weight and share the scene with Hamlet. Half a minute to collect oneself, and on again to the praying King, such a difficult unsatisfactory scene, and how important to the play—but the closest scene is more grateful, and a woman's voice helps to make a contrast in tone and pitch. The scene starts at terrific emotional tension, though, and only slows up for a minute in the middle for the beautiful passage with the Ghost. The "hiding of Polonius's body" scene...and then grab a cloak and hat in the wings and rush on to speak the Fortinbras soliloquy as if it wasn't the last hundred yards in a relay race.

Now the one long interval for Hamlet, while Ophelia is doing her mad scene, and Claudius and Laertes are laying their plot, and the Queen is saying her willow speech. Last lap. Graveyard scene, with the lovely philosophizing, and the lines about Yorick, and that hellish shouting fight and the "Ossa" speech at the end, which takes the last ounce of remaining breath. Now for Osric, and a struggle to hold one's own with the scene-shifters banging about behind the front cloth, and a careful ear for the first coughs and fidgets in the audience, which must somehow be silenced before the "fall of a sparrow" (I remember one night a gentleman in the front row took out a large watch in this scene, and wound it resignedly). And so to the apology to Laertes, with half one's mind occupied trying to remember the fight, which has been so carefully rehearsed but always goes wrong at least once a week, and on to the poisoning of the Queen and Claudius's death, and, if all has gone well, a still, attentive audience to the very end....

...In rehearsing Hamlet I found it at first impossible to characterize. I could not "imagine" the part, and live in it, forgetting myself in the words and adventures of the character, as I had tried to do in other plays. This difficulty surprised and alarmed me. Although I knew the theatrical effect that should be produced by each scene, I could only act the part if I felt that I really experienced every word of it as I spoke. The need to "make an effort" or "force a climax" paralyzed my imagination immediately, and destroyed any reality which I had begun to feel. I knew that I must act in a broad style, that I must be grander, more dignified and noble, more tender and gracious, more bitter and scathing, than was absolutely natural—that I must not be as slow as I should be if I were really thinking aloud, that I must drive the dialogue along at a regular moving pace, and, above all, that every shade of thought must be arranged, behind the lines, so that nothing should be left to chance in presenting them to the audience correctly and clearly in the pattern which I had conceived. All through rehearsals I was dismayed by my utter inability to forget myself while I was acting. It was not until I stood before an audience that I seemed to find the breadth and voice which enabled me suddenly to shake off my self-consciousness and live the part in my imagination, while I executed the technical difficulties with another part of my consciousness at the same time.

* * * *

Of all the arts, I think acting must be the least concrete, the most solitary. One gains experience continually, both at rehearsals and in performance, from the presence of a large assembly of people. These people are essential to the development of one's performance—they are the living canvas upon which one hopes to paint the finished portrait which one has envisaged. These fellow actors, these audiences, with their shifting variations of quality, are the only means by which an actor may gauge the effect of his acting. With their assistance he may hope to improve a performance, keep it flexible and fresh, and develop new subtleties as the days go by. He learns to listen to them, to watch them (without appearing to do so), to respond to them, to guide them in certain passages and be guided by them in others—a never-ending task of secret vigilance.

But the struggles and agonies of the actor, as he winds his way through this labyrinth process every night upon the stage, are of very little account or interest to anyone except himself. No one cares or is aware that he works for many months to correct some physical trick, or fights against his vocal mannerisms, or experiments with pauses, emphases, timing, processes of thought. No one knows if he is suffering in his heart while he plays an emotional scene, or he is merely adding up his household bills, considering what he will order for dinner, or regretting what he ate for lunch. Last night's audience, which he cursed for its unresponsiveness, may have enjoyed his performance every whit as much as tonight's, with which he feels the most cordial and personal sympathy.

Actors talk unceasingly among themselves of all the varying feelings which assail them during the exercise of their craft; but the experience of each one is different, and nothing really matters except the actual momentary contact between actor and audience which draws the play through its appointed action from beginning to end. At the close of each performance the play is set aside, for all the world like a Punch and Judy show, or the toy theatre of one's childhood; and each time it is taken up again at another performance it seems, even in a long run, comparatively fresh, waiting to be fashioned anew before every different audience. This continual destruction and repetition make the actor's work fascinating, though it must always be ephemeral and sometimes monotonous. The unending conflict in the player's mind as he tries to judge the standard of his work, wondering whether to trust in himself, in critics, in friends or in strangers, makes it often a disheartening and unsatisfactory business.

I have frequently envied painters, writers, critics. I have thought how happy they must be to do their work in private, at home, unkempt and unobserved, able to destroy or renew or improve their creations at will, to judge them in their unfinished state, to watch their gradual development, and to admire the final achievements ranged round them on their bookshelves or hung upon their walls. I have often wondered how these artists would face the routine of the actor which demands not only that he shall create a fine piece of work, but that he shall repeat it with unfaltering love and care for perhaps three hundred performances on end. In my envy I have often wished that I were able to rise in the middle of the night, switch on the light, and examine some performance of mine calmly and dispassionately as I looked at it standing on the mantelpiece.

MICHAEL REDGRAVE
(1908 —)

Michael Redgrave's parents like his offspring, Vanessa, Lynn and Colin, all belonged to the theatre. Born in Bristol, he was educated at Magdalene College, Cambridge, and became a school-master at Cronleigh School. This academic background did not preclude a debut as a baby in arms with his father in an Australian theatre and a chore as a walk-on at the Shakespeare Festival, Stratford-on-Avon, 1921.

As Roy Darwin in *Counsellor-at-Law* he made his first professional appearance in 1934 at the Playhouse, Liverpool, where he spent two years playing repertory. Then, like most of the top English actors, he came to the Old Vic, cradle of stars. Here in 1936 he made his London debut as Ferdinand in *Love's Labour's Lost* and during the season played Orlando in *As You Like It*, Warbeck in *The Witch of Edmonton*, and Laertes in *Hamlet*. Redgrave acquired his early fame as a member of John Gielgud's company at the Queen's Theatre, where he worked with fellow players like Alec Guinness and Peggy Ashcroft. This theatre, destroyed by bombs in 1940, housed Gielgud's excellent productions, in which Redgrave played Bolingbroke in *Richard II*, Charles Surface in *The School for Scandal*, and Baron Tuzenbach in *The Three Sisters*. Under Michael Saint-Denis at the Phoenix Theatre in 1938 Redgrave assumed leading roles. In the years before World War II he performed in *Twelfth Night*, *Springtime for Henry*, *The Beggar's Opera*, and *Thunder Rock*. It was Redgrave who created the leading role in T. S. Eliot's *The Family Reunion*.

Having served in the Royal Navy during the war, Redgrave returned to civilian life to join the ranks of the young actor-directors with *Lifeline*, *The Duke in Darkness*, *Parisienne*, *The Wingless Victory*, *Uncle Harry*, and *Jacobowsky and the Colonel*. During the 1947-48 season Michael Redgrave treated New York audiences with his interpretation of Macbeth, played to Flora Robson's Lady Macbeth.

Some of his important roles in the next years were Rakitin in *A Month in the Country*, the Captain in *The Father*, Hamlet, which was played at Kronberg Castle in Elsinore, Denmark. He joined the Shakespeare Memorial Theatre in 1950 and played Richard II, Hotspur, Prospero, Shylock, Antony, Lear, Hamlet, and others. He also played Hector in Giraudoux's *Tiger at the Gates*.

Olivier invited Redgrave to act in the first season of the National Theatre in *Uncle Vanya, Hobson's Choice* and *The Master Builder*. Long a serious student of acting, Redgrave has recorded his observations on the art in *The Actor's Ways and Means* and *Mask or Face*.

The Stanislavsky Myth

In the theatre even Shakespeare abides our question. At least, some half-dozen of his plays abide unactable, or at any rate unacted. The only actors who escape question are those who escape notice. To find you have a critic who habitually seems to go out of his way to disparage you, or to come to hear now and then of some of the people who cannot bear you, simply cannot bear you, should really be a reassurance to an actor, although to be honest it never is. But here is one figure in the theatrical landscape which is the subject of such violent discussion, mystic adoration, wholly unreasonable dislike, or suspiciously lofty indifference, that it is hard to get people to look at the facts of the case. Stanislavsky is quite high up in the tradition of Russian bogeys.

Opinions about Stanislavsky as an actor are as various as is usual. There are

Michael Redgrave: "The Stanislavsky Myth." London: *New Theatre*, Volume III, Number 1, June, 1946, pp. 16-18. Copyright 1946. By permission of Michael Redgrave.

those who say he mouthed and made faces. Myself, I do not see how anyone with such huge baroque lips could very well help mouthing. But all that is by the way. Whatever his qualities as an actor, he is known chiefly, and did I am sure wish to be known, as a man of the theatre, a director and the creator of an acting method which has exerted incomputable influence throughout the Western Hemisphere. Of his productions those of us who have not seen them must accept the judgment of those who did. Like the Irish Abbey players, many of the actors who worked with him before the revolution are scattered, though one catches occasional glimpses of them (Akim Tamiroff and Michael Chekhov, for example) in certain Hollywood films, where one longs to put them back into the setting to which artistically they belong. But even had not Stanislavsky and Nemirovich-Danchenko's Moscow Art Theatre survived to this day as a living tradition and a contemporary force, we should still receive Stanislavsky's influence through the pages of his book *An Actor Prepares*....

Quite a few actors have, I know, read it and have found it immensely stimulating. Other actors have read it, or partly read it, and find it fairly frustrating. Some others again say they have read it when what they mean is that they have always meant to read it. Some have read some of it and will, frankly have none of it. Some would sooner be seen dead than reading it. For all I know some may even have died reading it. Very few have read it again.

It is because I have read it again several times and because I find myself returning to it that I am writing this. But first let me continue in a personal vein for a little. I have written about it once before, and I find that to become identified with a subject about which there is misunderstanding and prejudice is to invite these things on oneself. I do not mind being greeted with "Hello, Stanislavsky," or "Hi-ya Konstantin," or receiving anxious enquiries as to the state of my "super-objective" or whether "my units" are in order. Only my friends dare do this and in any case it is not unflattering.

What is not so satisfactory is when people suppose that I would mean my own work to be an example of the Stanislavsky method, or assume that I would condemn any style of work which is not based on his method. For of course no single actor could possibly, on his own, give any effective demonstration of the method. This can only be done by a group, and would take years to perfect. As far as I know, the only English-speaking group which has attempted to absorb and put the method into practice has been the Group Theatre of New York, who were seen here only in *Golden Boy*. (Alas, the Group Theatre is also now disbanded, and the better known members of it are known here only through the screen: Luther Adler, Morris Carnovsky, Clifford Odets, John Garfield.) But I have derived great stimulus from the book, and constant reference to the high standards it demands can help check, to some extent, the varying quality of one's work. When I have directed plays I have tried to apply its first principles; that is to say I have tried to dissuade actors from flying at their parts "like French falconers," hoping to give a performance at the first rehearsal, but instead to encourage them to find their way into a part by degrees, and to try to make sure that they supply themselves with a good imaginative foundation to the part.

For again and again we see actors who start off well but who can never give a full expression of the character because they have not imagined it fully and actively and laid its foundations well; or others who have given a good performance on the opening night, while their imaginative powers were still at work, but who gradually lose life and conviction as the run proceeds, repeating maybe each move and inflection with expert precision but finding that they need the stimulus of a "good house" or "someone in front," or a particular scene in which they know they are especially effective to help them give their best. They are aware that something has gone out of their performance, but they do not know what it is. They know that certain scenes become increasingly difficult to play and they do not know why. At worst, they begin to indulge in private jokes which even the audience can see are not part of the play. Even the actor will have recognized some if not all these symptoms in his own or other actors' work. Nor are these flaws primarily caused by long runs. They are caused, quite simply, by the actors losing sooner or later (some lose quite early) the "offered circumstances," on which their part, not to mention the plot, depend.

Every actor knows how the impact of a first night audience adjusts his sense of the play as a whole. Some less thorough actors are never so good as on opening nights. The audience reactions supply such actors with the impulses which should have come earlier. But although audiences vary they do not vary to the extent of supplying a fresh stimulus every night, and then such actors become morbidly dependent on their audiences and cannot give their best except on rare, and unpredictable occasions. Such actors need to go back to the beginning and start again, trying to revive that imaginative faculty of believing in what they are doing. For that is part of what Stanislavsky taught: belief. No half-belief. Not make-believe. Belief that does not begin and end by an intellectual process, but which is so deep-rooted that it fires each movement, echoes in each silence, and penetrates beyond "the threshold of the subconscious," where it becomes creative. . . .

The best short summary of the Stanislavsky method is to be found in Norris Houghton's admirable *Moscow Rehearsals* which prospective and past students of the method would do well to get from the library. As Houghton says: "The Stanislavsky system is really only a conscious codification of ideas about acting which have always been the property of most good actors of all countries whether they knew it or not. Its basis is the work of the actor *with himself* in order to master 'technical means for the creation of the creative mood, so that inspiration may appear oftener than is its wont'." . . .

It is not my purpose here to re-examine or condense the system. But I would like to sweep away one or two of the prejudices which ignorance and fear have treated round that thunderclap of a name: Stanislavsky.

Fear? Yes, where some actors are concerned. For there are those who feel that the very existence of this book implies some criticism of their own achievements and acting experience. Well, it does and it doesn't. It doesn't, for the reasons Houghton gives above. It does, I think, because there is no actor or actress living or dead who could sincerely read this book and not find some chink for doubt if not despair. Do actors despair? Only actors will understand that use of the word. Some actors even will not, those who sublimate their despair, their essential lack of "actual reality," the substance, the essence, the nature or "the thing" which makes them actors, the hellish, or divine, doubt which drives them to live more thoroughly others' lives than their own, to haunt, as it were, their own existence.

"A job is a job," they say. "Less of this talk about art."

But I digress; the actor's temperament is something which need not be more than hinted at here. If an actor can master the self-criticism which reading *An Actor Prepares* will bring he has gone some way towards the reconciliation of such doubt.

He may go further, he may effect a reconciliation with his own exhibitionism, that quality in every actor which none can lose without losing the desire to act, but with which somehow or other he must come to terms, to the point at least of knowing when he controls it or when it is controlling him.

I have said it is likely he will receive some shocks to his self-esteem but for these he is more than recompensed by the startling corroboration and, be it stressed, simplification of many of his own vague and fluctuating ideas and feelings about his craft. It is a truism to say that acting cannot be taught. Certainly no book can teach anyone to act. But no one would deny for a moment that to come in close contact with a great actor working at his craft must be illuminating, and to read *An Actor Prepares* is to be privileged to be in close contact with a great actor-director not in "a fiction and a dream of passion" but in the great evening of his life, still in active contact with what is probably the greatest of living theatres, telling us again and again, with all the clarity of a great intellect, the simple truths of our art.

Foremost among these is the dictum that our three masters are "feeling, mind and will," that feeling comes first but can never effectively operate without the other two. Many great actors have arrived at much the same verdict; notably Talma, who insisted that "sensibility and intelligence" are the two indispensable qualifications for acting: sensibility, the power to apprehend emotionally the entire content of character and action; and intelligence, the power to reduce that emotional experience to a technical formula which can be repeated at will. Sensibility cannot be consciously acquired, which is why acting cannot be taught. Intelligence, one might say, is the power to see the relationship of things, the power to keep these relationships in perspective. Stanislavsky's book is like some great mirror, wherein a man can see, standing close to the glass, the first mirrors of his soul, his own eyes, and in them, the tiny shape of the surrounding countryside; standing further back, he sees his setting reduced into a frame, and somewhere in that frame, looking curiously impermanent, the figure of himself. But, of course, the mirror can only reflect what the man can see for himself. All it constitutes is a sense of nearness, a sense of distance, a relationship, some proportions. For to read *An Actor Prepares* is like going on a trip abroad: a man can receive from either experience only in proportion to what qualities he brings with him. But to read it at all implies some degree of serious respect for his craft and for whatever else he finds in it, the actor-reader will receive the most sustaining reassurance that has yet been put on record that his work can at its best be creative and achieve not merely réclame, but dignity. It will probably make him profoundly dissatisfied with the conditions of work prevailing in this country. All the better.

And for audiences? I find it hard to imagine that any but the most ardent amateurs of acting will find the patience to read the book. It would be worth their pains. It will perhaps induce them to try to distinguish between the actor and his part, a distinction seldom made by audiences, rarely by critics even. It may help them to realize that the abiding necessity for every actor, as for every artist, is the avoidance of cliché, the easy, effective, conventional mode or trick of self-expression. Cliché is like a weed: no garden is free from it all the time. The greatest performances are those which are most free from it, those in which every detail has been freshly conceived and which retain at each performance enough of that freshness. It is this freshness which contributes whatever is most exciting and at the same time satisfying in the theatre.

To take an extreme example: "He dies," says the stage direction. How every amateur actor loves to find that he is to die on the stage! At once he sees himself as the center of all eyes (correctly, as often as not). And yet, however heavily foreshadowed in the action, death on the stage must come, as it comes in life, as a shock: "Can he be, is he, really, dead?" He is, or he is not, and it is not the inert, still body that proclaims the actor dead; as often as not we do not believe it much, but divert our attention to what follows. If we did not know Olivier to be a great actor by other tests we should know it from the manner of his deaths. Each one is in character. His Macbeth died violently, convulsively, as he had lived, but in spite of his defiant last words we knew that he had lost heart. His Richard III had no heart to lose and fought on and on, his muscles still twitching when all sense had left them. In the death of his Hotspur is all the essential simplicity and wonder of that character, and its rough and ready philosophy; we are made to feel, most poignantly, the surprise and astonishment of a brave, headstrong young man cut off in his prime.

As with death, so with a thousand other commonplaces of life and of the theatre: an embrace; a hasty entrance; the light shock to which we react quickly; the deep shock which our feelings, in order to protect us, at first reject; the manner of starting a quarrel; the manner of saying a long farewell. When these things are well and truly acted they seem simplicity itself. "But," says the reader, like the student in Stanislavsky's book, "all this is obvious!" To which his master retorts: "Did I ever say it was anything else?" Yet how often do we see these simple truths really convincingly performed? Do not a great many audiences prefer, or at least feel more comfortable when witnessing, the artifices and the clichés to which they are accustomed. Many prefer to see the wheels going round. They would often rather see an actor "acting" acting, which I suppose makes them feel they know where they are, than acting the part without concession to convention. I feel this to be so and do not see how it could well be otherwise, since in any art the conventional is the most popular. But just as for an actor to give himself up to conventional acting will in time dry up whatever imaginative powers he may possess, so it is with audiences; they become lazy, bored and only the most violent stimuli will satisfy them. Hence, amongst other things, the appetite for "pace" for its own sake, to which must be sacrificed one of the essentials of any artistic performance, rhythm.

There are in England today, roughly speaking, two styles of acting: the acting in which the effect springs from the cause, and that which begins with effect and which rarely, and only in part, seeks the cause. The latter style is still very much the preponderant. It is very seldom we see a production in which more than a few actors are faithful to the author, the director and their artistic conscience.

"Always he sought," said Nemirovich-Danchenko, "the essence of the play in the times and events described; and this he expected the actor to understand. This is what Stanislavsky called the core, and it is this core which must stir the actor, which must become part of him for the time being." Our most-read dramatic critic holds that great acting is achieved in a "blaze of egotism." I personally doubt if this was ever an accurate description of a style of acting which is going out of fashion, a fact of which he is aware but which he chooses to disregard, holding that this age's failure to produce such performers is due to the decadence of the time rather than, as I believe, an inevitable and healthy change in taste. Nowadays our aim is for a theatre of synthesis, not a synthetic theatre. Some of us think that there are heartening signs that we may one day achieve such a theatre.

If you think all that sounds a dull proposition, then the great Russian actor's methods and books are not for you. There will always be plenty of "egotism" smouldering away somewhere, so you pays your money and you takes your choice. But blazing or smouldering, it is consuming itself, leaving the maybe highly-talented egotist to eke out what remains of his or her power in a succession of similar displays or revivals of former successes, until finally there is no capacity, no urge left to explore; the fire has become a formula. If the talent is a great one it will see them through, but they will have contributed only a token payment of the debt which great talent owes. By loving themselves in art and not the art in themselves they have, paradoxically enough, left much of their art unused. It is one of the virtues of Stanislavsky's method that it encourages actors not to let this happen. It is one of the faults of our system, in which actors are casual laborers, that it happens far too often.

LAURENCE OLIVIER

(b. 1907)

Laurence Olivier, director of the National Theatre of Great Britain, relates his own desires as an actor to his objectives in forming and running this long-dreamed-of company. He recalls that his "earliest feelings about acting were suffused with an intense wish to fascinate the public in the art of acting" and that his present desire is "to make an audience watch an actor as keenly, and with as much interest and enthusiasm and fascination, as they watch a player on the soccer field." For almost fifty years he has provided performances that have aroused in audiences this keen enthusiasm and fascination.

Born in Dorking, the son of an Anglican churchman, Olivier went to All Saints Choir School, where he participated in musical and theatrical performances. Acting, he recalls, was very respectable in social circles in those days early in the century after Henry Irving had been knighted. At sixteen his father told him that he was to go from St. Edwards School in Oxford, where he was then studying, to Elsie Fogerty's school in London "be auditioned, and win a scholarship, and you're going to go on the stage." He studied with Miss Fogerty at the London Central School of Drama and Speech and embarked on his professional career even before he completed his studies.

In 1926 he joined Sir Barry Jackson's Birmingham Repertory Theatre, where actors who were "after higher things," who were "serious" about their art learned their craft. At the end of the decade he became a successful West End actor, playing in *Journey's End, Beau Geste,* and *Private Lives,* in which he established a valuable close association with Noel Coward. He played leads in New York during the early 1930s and tried his hand at management, a job he "loved." He also acted often in films, an aspect of his work not covered here.

A turning point in his career came in 1935 when he gave up a starring role in the West End and shortly thereafter joined John Gielgud in the production of *Romeo and Juliet* in which they alternated the roles of Romeo and Mercutio. Olivier's Romeo, which was all youthful passion and verve, troubled Gielgud, who worried that the values in the verse were being lost, and it did not meet favor with the public, except for a discriminating few. His Mercutio, on the other hand, was much admired. He recalls in his recent interview with Kenneth Tynan that he preferred Romeo and contrasts his approach with that of Gielgud, who also directed the production. "I've admired Gielgud all my life with complete devotion; I've never thought of myself as quite the same actor as he is, not the same sort of actor. I've always thought that we were the reverse of the same coin, perhaps . . . the top half John, all spiritual, all spirituality, all beauty, all abstract things; and myself as all earth, blood, humanity; if you like, the baser part of humanity without that beauty."

In 1937 Olivier was invited by Tyrone Guthrie to join the Old Vic and opened with the full-length *Hamlet* interpreted in the light of Ernest Jones's study of Hamlet and the Oedipus complex. This production was repeated at Kronberg Castle, Elsinore, Denmark. He also played Sir Toby Belch, Henry V, Macbeth, Iago, and Coriolanus with the Old Vic in the years before the War. In 1944 he was made codirector of the Old Vic and played for them in *Peer Gynt, Arms and the Man, Uncle Vanya* and *Richard III*. His rich and unusual characterization of Richard marked another turning point in his career; he felt "for the first time that the critics had approved, that the public had approved," and this gave him a feeling he had never had before of "complete confidence." In 1945 he came to New York with a repertory of great performances, Oedipus and Mr. Puff in Sheridan's *The Critic* on one bill, Hotspur, and Dr. Astrov in *Uncle Vanya*.

In the early 1950's he presented himself and the late Vivien Leigh in a series of outstanding productions at the St. James Theatre: *Antony and Cleopatra, Caesar and Cleopatra, Venus Observed*. Malvolio, Titus Andronicus, Macbeth for the Stratford Theatre followed. In 1957 he played Archie Rice, a role he "adored," in John Osborne's *The Entertainer* and Berenger in Ionesco's *Rhinoceros* at the Royal Court Theatre, a move that brought him in touch with the men and plays that were changing the direction of English theatre. He organized the Chichester Festival Theatre, where he directed and acted in a magnificent *Uncle Vanya* together with his wife, Joan Plowright, as part of an exploration of new staging.

In 1963 he was appointed director of the National Theatre of Great Britain, a position he has filled with great success. "I was very frightened of it when I started it," he has said, "but I looked around as honestly as I could, and I hope without self-deception, and thought perhaps I was the fellow with the best sort of experience to start the thing going. I was determined that there should be a National Theatre in our country. I think that a National Theatre is probably the only way of making the theatre a part of people's lives." With devoted associates, Kenneth Tynan, John Dexter, William Gaskill, Joan Plowright, Maggie Smith, Robert Stephens, and visiting artists like John Gielgud, Peter O'Toole, Albert Finney, and others, he has administered, directed, and acted in an effort to get his great enterprise off to a fine start. Never content as an artist, he set himself new challenges especially in his highly original interpretation of Othello, the most difficult of all Shakespearean roles. Franco Zeffirelli's comment on this performance sums up well Olivier's accomplishment. "I was told that this was the last flourish of the romantic tradition in acting. It is nothing of the sort. It's an anthology of everything that has been discovered about acting in the last three centuries. It's grand and majestic, but it's also modern and realistic. I would call it a lesson for us all."

The Art of Persuasion

If somebody asked me to put in one sentence what acting was, I should say that acting was the art of persuasion. The actor persuades himself, first, and through himself, the audience. In order to achieve that, what you need to make up your make-up is observation and intuition. At the most high-faluting, the actor is as important as the illuminator of the human heart, he is as important as the psychiatrist or the doctor, the minister if you like. That's putting him very high and mightily. At the opposite end of the pole you've got to find, in the actor, a man who will not be too proud to scavenge the tiniest little bit of human circumstance; observe it, find it, use it some time or another. I've frequently observed things, and thank God, if I haven't got a very good memory for anything else, I've got a memory for little details. I've had things in the back of my mind for as long as eighteen years before I've used them. And it works sometimes that, out of one little thing you've seen somebody do, something causes you to store it up. In the years that follow you wonder what it was that made them do it, and, ultimately, you find in that the illuminating key to a whole bit of characterization.

QUESTION: I suppose it was your performance of Richard III at the Old Vic, towards the end of the war, that set you on the summit of our classical drama. Did you know at the time that it was going to be one of the key performances of your career?

ANSWER: No, no. A lot of things contributed to it. One thing that may lead an actor to be successful in a part, not always, but it may, is to try to be unlike somebody else in it. At the time when I first began to think about the part Donald Wolfit had made an enormous success as Richard only eighteen months previously. I didn't want to play the part at all, because I thought it was much too close to this colleague's success. I had seen it, and when I was learning it I could hear nothing but Donald's voice in my mind's ear, and see nothing but him in my mind's eye. And so I thought, "This won't do, I've just got to think of something else." And it was the childishly approached differences, really, that started me on a characterization that, without comparing it with Donald's at all, at least made it different. I think any actor would understand this desire on my part not to look the same as another actor. Now this can get you very wrong sometimes, and land you in very hot water indeed; at other times it may land you on to a nice fertile beach, thank you very much.

First of all I had heard imitations of old actors imitating Henry Irving; and so I did, right away, an imitation of these old actors imitating Henry Irving's voice—that's why I took a rather narrow kind of vocal address. Then I thought about looks. And I thought about the Big Bad Wolf, and I thought about Jed Harris, a director under whom I'd suffered *in extremis* in New York. The physiognomy of Disney's original Big Bad Wolf was said to have been founded upon Jed Harris—hence the nose, which, originally, was very much bigger than it was finally in the film. And so, with one or two extraneous externals, I began to build up a character, a characterization. I'm afraid I do work mostly from the outside in. I

Kenneth Tynan interviews Laurence Olivier in *Great Acting,* edited by Hal Burton. New York: Hill & Wang, 1967, pp. 23-32. Copyright © authors and BBC 1966-1967. First published in the U.S. in *Tulane Drama Review,* Vol. XI, No. 3, Winter, 1966. Reprinted by permission of Sir Laurence Olivier and Kenneth Tynan.

usually collect a lot of details, a lot of characteristics, and find a creature swimming about somewhere in the middle of them.

Perhaps I should mention now what everybody's been talking about for years, and that's the Actors Studio and the Method. What I've just said is absolutely against their beliefs, absolute heresy. And it may be, as long as you achieve the result of, don't let's call it naturalism, don't even let's call it realism, let's call it truthfulness, that it doesn't matter which method you use. But in exercises like Shakespeare or Greek tragedy it is an enormous task, because you've got so many facets, so many angles and so many considerations to contend with, in order to achieve the reality or the truthfulness that is necessary. Some people start from the inside, some people start from the periphery. I would say, at a guess, that Alec Guinness is what we would call a peripheral actor. I think I'm the same. The actor who starts from the inside is more likely to find himself in the parts he plays, than to find the parts in himself; perhaps not necessarily in himself, but simply to find the parts, go out to them and get them, and be somebody else.

QUESTION: Who would you say was a typical example of the interior method?

ANSWER: Well, I think personally that most film actors are interior people. It is necessary for them to be so truthful under the extraordinary microscopic perception of the camera; it's very seldom that you get a film actor who dares to characterize very thickly.

QUESTION: Since we're talking about externals, which do you regard as your most important physical attribute, your voice, your hands, your eyes, which?

ANSWER: Well, once upon a time you asked me that question and I said the eyes. That was some years ago. It depends what you are—really it's a fusion of every single part of you that has to go into it. The mime actor doesn't need the voice; the film actor hardly needs the voice, hardly needs the body, except to use it as a marvellous physical specimen in such roles as demand that attribute. The stage actor certainly needs the voice, certainly needs all the vocal control, all the breath control, all the techniques of the voice, certainly needs all the miming power imaginable, certainly needs the hands, certainly needs the eyes—he needs them all.

QUESTION: When you were playing Richard, was there a moment when you knew you were there, that all was set fair for your future?

ANSWER: Well, I'd been on the stage now for twenty years. I'd just finished making Henry V and, I don't know how, or why, I just went into it with the same distrust of the critics, the same fear of public opinion as I had always experienced. I went on to the stage frightened, heart beating, came on, locked the door behind me, approached the footlights and started. And I—I just simply went through it. I don't think anybody in the company believed in the project at all. I think everybody was rather in despair about the whole production. And nobody particularly believed in my performance, none of us particularly believed in any of our performances; I don't think even our producer, John Burrell, believed in it much. In the first three plays which we presented, Ralph Richardson had brought Peer Gynt off brilliantly, Arms and the Man was a success on its own, and now there was this rather poor relation, with a part that people had seen quite a lot of. And so I didn't know—I didn't know; I was just once more going to have, as we say, a bash. I had developed this characterization, and I had got a lot of things on my side, now I come to think of it, from the point of view of timeliness. One had Hitler over the way, one was playing it definitely as a paranoiac, so that there was a core of something to which the audience would immediately respond. I fancy, I may be quite wrong, but I fancy I possibly filled it out, possibly enriched it a bit with a little more humour than a lot of other people had done, but I'm not sure about that. I only know that I read a few notices, stayed up till three and drank a little bit too much.

My next performance was the next-day matinee, for which I was all too ill-prepared. But there was something in the atmosphere. There is a phrase—the sweet smell of success—and I can only tell you (I've had two experiences of that), it just smells like Brighton and oyster-bars and things like that. And as I went down to the prompt corner, darling Diana Boddington, my stage manager, and still one of our stage managers at the National, sort of held out her hand and said, "It's marvelous, darling," or something like that, and I said, "Oh, is it?" and as I went on to the stage—the house was not even full—I felt this thing. I felt for the first time that the critics had approved, that the public had approved, and they had created a kind of grapevine, and that particular audience had felt impelled to come to see me. It was an overwhelming feeling, a head-reeling feeling, and it went straight to my head. I felt the feeling I'd never felt before, this complete confidence. I felt, if you like, what an actor must finally feel: I felt a little power of hypnotism; I felt that I had them. It went to my head, as I said, to such an extent that I didn't even bother to put on the limp. I thought, I've got them anyway, I needn't bother with all this characterization any more. It's an awful story really.

QUESTION: You said there was another occasion when you felt this whiff in the air. When was that?

ANSWER: That was after *The Entertainer*. It was when we'd finished the run at the Court and we revived it a few months later at the Palace, and my dear old friend George Relph and I went down to the theatre together, walked on to the stage and said together, "Smell it, it's okay."

QUESTION: In the 1945-6 season there was *Oedipus* and I can remember a notice I wrote in which I tried to answer some of your critics who were saying that you had tricks, vocal mannerisms and physical mannerisms. I said that these tricks might exist, but that they were unique and only you could pull them off. Do you think you have mannerisms?

ANSWER: I'd like not to think so, of course. I know I have because I see them, and when they're pointed out I feel them. But what are mannerisms? Mannerisms are cushions of protection which an actor develops against his own self-consciousness. An actor comes on to the stage on a first night and hangs his head, or does something or other, and for that second it's a comfort to him, it gives him a little moment of reality at this terrifying moment; and it goes into the works. In the future, if he's not very careful, he resorts to it on any first night, and those things collect and collect up, and you've got about twenty-four, thirty-seven things that you finally can't do without. Those are mannerisms.

QUESTION: One of them, for instance, is your habit of lilting an upward inflection at the end of a line, like "God for Harry, England and St George" in *Henry V*, when your voice suddenly soars up. It's very exciting.

ANSWER: I don't think that was for any feeling of protection. I thought it was a good thing to do; I probably thought it was exciting. You must remember that parts of that size are not usually parts into which you can segregate any one part of your personality. I did do a very special, rather limited characterization in

Richard III, that thin voice and all that, in order to present myself in an entirely different light from anything else I was doing that season. But Shakespeare, as a rule, does not tolerate a very sharp light thrown across his work. You get into great trouble if you think of a special or topical theme for a Shakespearean production; he just doesn't tolerate it. I remember Michael Redgrave once did a very brave and courageous thing at Stratford: he played Richard II as an out-and-out queer with all the effeminate mannerisms. He simply said, "Richard II was a homosexual, in my opinion, and I'm going to play it like that." Well, it worked, it worked brilliantly; but I don't think, and I've never talked to him about this, that it worked all the way through, because at the end Shakespeare says of Richard III, Richard II, Hotspur and a lot of parts you could have taken a very sharp characteristic slant upon, "I'm not tolerating that, you're now going to become St George." So you can't do it, you have to stop all that characterization.

QUESTION: Did you ever find that you had to change your performances when you translated a Shakespearean character from stage to screen?

ANSWER: Not very much. Only out of respect for the technique of the medium, I think.

QUESTION: Now let's talk about *Othello.* At the beginning you were very reluctant to play the part at all. Why was that?

ANSWER: Well, I knew it was a terror. I knew from past experience that it was almost impossible. When I was on tour in Europe one time doing *Titus Andronicus,* and Anthony Quayle was playing Aaron, we had a little interval together, about five minutes. It was very hot in that part of Europe and we didn't bother to go to our dressing-rooms, with those huge stages, we sat at the back on a sofa and used to talk a little bit, gossip a little bit. One day he said to me, "Is this a very bad one for you, this Titus Andronicus?" and I said, "Yes, awful, awful," and I said, "But you've played Macbeth too. I think you'll agree that Macbeth is the worst." And he said, "You haven't done the black one yet, have you?" And I said, "No—why? Is that terrible?" He said, "Terrible. The worst parts, the most difficult ones to bear, are the ones that are complaining all the time, the ones that moan. Macbeth is all right because he is positive," he said, "but you know what you hate about Titus, he's always going 'oh, oh, oh, look at—fancy them doing that to me, oh, oh, oh.' And how many ways are there of saying 'oh, oh.' It's very tough on your imagination, it's very tough on your resourcefulness of variations of all kinds, and, therefore, it's also a very great strain physically." He said, "Othello is all of that and you have to black up as well."

QUESTION: You'd been involved in the play just before the war when Ralph Richardson played Othello and you played Iago. Was there anything off beat about that production?

ANSWER: Yes, very much indeed. Tony Guthrie and I, as I told you before, had studied the works of Professor Jones. Now Professor Jones was quite sure that it wasn't the Oedipus complex. The trouble was the part of Iago, not the part of Othello. Nobody has ever really disputed what makes up Othello, but they've certainly wondered about Iago, what makes him such a thoroughly beastly fellow as he is; and Jones's theory was that Iago was subconsciously in love with Othello. Well, Tony Guthrie and I were completely sold on this idea. Ralph wouldn't hear of it at all. However, there came one moment in rehearsal, so the story goes, and I don't remember this, but this is the story that is told—that losing all control of myself, I flung my arms round Ralph's neck and kissed him. Whereat Ralph, more in sorrow than in anger, sort of patted me and said, "Dear fellow, dear boy," much more pitying me for having lost control of myself than despising me for being a very bad actor.

QUESTION: When you came to play Othello yourself, did you feel physically equipped for it in every respect?

ANSWER: No, I didn't. That was another thing that had troubled me. I didn't think that I had the voice for it. But I did go through a long period of vocal training especially for it, to increase the depth of my voice, and I actually managed to attain about six more notes in the bass. I never used to be able to sing below D, but now, after a little exercising, I can get down to A, through all the semitones; and that helps at the beginning of the play, it helps the violet velvet that I felt was necessary in the timbre of the voice. And then, from the physical point of view, I went through, and I still do, a very severe physical training course.

QUESTION: What was there in your conception of the part that made it different from the conventional Othellos that we're used to seeing?

ANSWER: Well, you know that very rough estimate of the theme of Shakespearean tragedy. It's constantly said that Shakespearean tragedy is founded by Shakespeare upon the theme of a perfect statue of a man, a perfect statue; and he shows one fissure in the statue, and how that fissure makes the statue crumble and disappear into utter disorder. From that idea you get that Othello is perfect except that he's too easily jealous; that Macbeth is perfect except that he's too ambitious; that Lear is perfect except that he's too bloody-minded, too pigheaded; that Coriolanus is too proud; that Hamlet lacks resolution; and so on. But there seems to me, and there has grown in me a conviction over the last few years, that in most of the characters, not all, but in most of them, that weakness is accompanied by the weakness of self-deception, as a companion fault to whatever fault may be specified by the character in the play. It's quite easy to find in Othello, and once you've found it I think you have to go along with it; that he sees himself as this noble creature. It's so easy in the senate scene for you to present the absolutely cold-blooded man who doesn't even worry about marital relations with his wife on his honeymoon night, to reassure the senate that he's utterly perfect, pure beyond any reproach as to his character, and you can find that, and trace it, constantly throughout. He's constantly wishing to present himself in a certain light, even at the end, which is remarkable. I believe, and I've tried to show, that when he says "Not easily jealous" it's the most appalling bit of self-deception. He's the most easily jealous man that anybody's ever written about. The minute he suspects, or thinks he has the smallest grounds for suspecting Desdemona, he wishes to think her guilty, he wishes to. And the very first thing he does, almost on top of that, is to give way to the passion, perhaps the worst temptation in the world, which is murder. He immediately wants to murder her, immediately. Therefore he's an extremely hot-blooded individual, an extremely savage creature who has kidded himself and managed to kid everybody else, all this time, that he's nothing of the kind. And if you've got that, I think you've really got the basis of the character. Lodovico says it for us: "Is this the noble Moor ... whom passion could not shake. ... I am sorry that I am deceived in him."

QUESTION: There is also a sense of a caged animal in your performance. I remember writing that you communicate more than almost any actor I know a sense of danger, you feel at any moment that the great paw may lash out and someone's going to get hurt. Are you conscious of this power you have over audiences—and over other actors for that matter?

ANSWER: I'm not very conscious of the workings of it. I feel consciousness of the desirability of having that ingredient in my work, very much so. *Othello,* of course, screams for it. It's the only play in the whole of Shakespeare in which a man kills a woman, and if Shakespeare gets an idea he goes all out for it; he knows very well that for a black man to kill a white woman is a very big thrill indeed, to the audience, and he doesn't pull any punches. As an alchemist Shakespeare gets hold of that one all right. Therefore, if you feel that thing in yourself, that sort of easily released or closely guarded animal inside you, you must use it in this part of all parts.

QUESTION: Perhaps we'd better move on to your excursions into contemporary plays. Things like *The Sleeping Prince* by Terence Rattigan, John Osborne's *The Entertainer,* Ionesco's *Rhinoceros,* and *Semi-detached.*

ANSWER: I absolutely adored them all, particularly *The Entertainer.* I think it's the most wonderful part that I've ever played. I loved *Rhinoceros* a little less well. I didn't find it quite such a good work. It was very interesting, very interesting and I was just mad for it because it was another modern part. I adored *Semi-detached.*

QUESTION: Why do you think it wasn't a success?

ANSWER: I like to think it wasn't my fault, but it may well have been. I think it was a very cruel play, and I remember coming moaning to you once and saying, "I don't know why it is they don't like this piece," and you said, "Well, it's extremely cruel and you are making the audience suffer, and that's the idea of the play; but you can't always do that and get away with it."

QUESTION: What I meant was that it was the first time you'd played a complete swine without any redeeming charm or pathos.

Are there any actors who have had a particular influence on you?

ANSWER: Yes, lots of them. I've mentioned Fairbanks and Barrymore whose *Hamlet* I first saw when I was seventeen years old. Noël Coward in his way influenced me a great deal, he taught me a very stern professionalism. Alfred Lunt taught me an enormous amount, by watching him, in the field of really naturalistic acting; he had astonishing gifts, an astonishing virtuosity in overlap, marvellous. That was when I first saw him in 1929 in *Caprice* at the St James's Theatre.

QUESTION: Overlap meaning what?

ANSWER: Oh, overlapped conversations with his wife, Lynn Fontanne. They must have rehearsed it for millions of years, it was delicious, absolutely delicious to watch, and they carried on their own tradition in that way for many, many years. Valentino made me see that narcissism is important. Of all the people I've ever watched with the greatest delight, I think, in another field entirely, was Sid Field. I wouldn't like anybody to think that I was imitating Sid Field when I was doing *The Entertainer.*

QUESTION: Well, there were little things in it.

ANSWER: Little things, but Sid Field was a great comic and Archie Rice was a lousy one. But I know when I imitate Sid Field to this day, I still borrow from him freely and unashamedly. I watch all my colleagues very carefully, admire them all for different qualities. I think the most interesting thing to see is that an actor is most successful when not only all his virtues but all his disadvantages come into useful play in a part. The man who, I think, gave me the best sort of thoughts about acting was my friend Ralph Richardson. I watch Rex Harrison for timing. I watch all my colleagues for different qualities that I admire, and I imitate them and copy them unashamedly.

QUESTION: You talked about actors using their disadvantages. Which of your own qualities, for instance, do you dislike most as a person?

ANSWER: Well, I've got an awful way of flinging my hands about which I detest, and I try to control it. But sometimes, as I say, sometimes a part requires all you've got, weaknesses and all, and I just let myself go; I let it all happen and hope for the best.

QUESTION: Talking about narcissism, are you competitive as an actor?

ANSWER: Not with anybody else on the stage, and not with younger actors or anything like that. No, no, no, I never feel that. I never have been, I'm glad to say; I'm very thankful for it. No, the teamwork on the stage is a great essential to me. The actors must understand each other, know each other, help each other, absolutely love each other: must, absolutely must.

QUESTION: How aware are you of other actors on stage, of what they're doing, where they are, how their performances are going?

ANSWER: Oh, very much, very much. You can upset each other without meaning to very easily. If you suddenly have a mental aberration and forget a line, or forget a word, and you see it's upset the actor, it upsets you too. And, sure enough, if one actor starts drying up, another will and another, it becomes a sort of round the company drying up; it catches on like a terrible disease. I couldn't act competitively with anybody. I couldn't do the thing that Kean did to Macready and act him off the stage. I think it would be terribly wrong and I don't think I would have the power to do it anyway.

QUESTION: In an unguarded moment you once said that you need to be a bit of a bastard to be a star. Is that true?

ANSWER: Well, I think that came out of the fact that, at one time, I may have thought that somebody lacked the necessary *edge* to be a star. I think you've got to have a certain edge, that might be traced to being a bit of a bastard, inside. You've got to be a bit of a bastard to understand bastards, and you've got to understand everybody. I think the most difficult equation to solve is the union of the two things that are absolutely necessary to an actor. One is confidence, absolute confidence, and the other an equal amount of humility towards the work. That's a very hard equation.

QUESTION: Do you think actors ought to be influenced at all by their private convictions and political ideas? For instance, would you accept a really first-rate part in an anti-Negro play?

ANSWER: Only if, in the character concerned, I was able to show something that was true about people, and that's quite possible. I wouldn't like politics to take hold of a play more directly, more obviously, than is done by Anton Chekhov, the great prophet of the revolution. But the way he did it was always an illumination of the human heart, to show the people the knowledge of themselves more clearly, a little sadly, a little despairingly. But he doesn't go out and make red, black, white, or blue win, or anything like that, or say they're right or wrong.

QUESTION: Are there any major parts, Shakespeare or others, that you'd still like to have a crack at?

ANSWER: No, no, there aren't, really. It sounds very self-satisfied. I don't mean to sound like that, but the fact is that, as you said, I have got other work. I think that work gives me enough opportunity to do what I'm able to do. As one gets older, quite naturally, one's range becomes more limited. I mean age does show, we can't help that. If you're a kid of seventeen you can't play King Lear properly —you might make a very good shot at it, but if you're a kid of fifty-eight then I'm afraid you can't play Romeo any more; therefore the field does narrow. It's bound to narrow as the grey hairs creep in or they disappear altogether. Your limitations are bound to show more, therefore you're more inclined not to bother so much about carving yourself up into different facets, to suit different characterizations when different characterizations aren't going to be all that different. I'm afraid, as time goes on, one's ambitions are necessarily narrowed by Dame Nature.

QUESTION: You developed into the kind of actor you are when there were no real permanent ensembles, subsidized ensembles, in this country. Do you think you would have developed in the same way if you had joined a company of that kind when you were beginning?

ANSWER: Well, in a way, from time to time, that has been so with me. I was with the Birmingham Rep. for two seasons. I was at the Old Vic for two years. I was with Ralph Richardson, engaged on work for the Old Vic at the New Theatre, for five years, when we tasted the blessings of a permanent troupe. When a foreign company, such as the Moscow Art Theatre, which is used to the idea of a permanent ensemble, arrives upon our shores, and we see their work, it is that hot breath of unity that always seems to me to be more important than the star system. Ultimately it is more important to an audience than the star system, though goodness knows how many years it's going to take us to make that clear to them. . . .

QUESTION: Our situation now is that we've got plenty of openings for actors in this country. Our subsidized theatre has opened up so much. But if you could look ahead, say five or ten years hence, what changes would you look for in our own company at the Vic? What would you like it to have developed into?

ANSWER: I'd like better conditions first of all: I'd like a better theatre, better conditions in order to increase our activities, so that eventually, perhaps, the art of the actor may finally be regarded as an important part of the life of the people.

PAUL SCOFIELD
(b. 1922)

Paul Scofield was born in Birmingham, but grew up in Sussex, where his father was headmaster of a Church of England school. He played Juliet and Rosalind at the boys school in Brighton and his success determined him to become an actor. Two terms at the Croyden Repertory Theatre School outside of London, and then a period at a school attached to the Westminster Theatre gave him his first formal training. In the summer of 1944 he joined the Birmingham Repertory Theatre of Sir Barry Jackson, who had provided opportunities to several generations of English actors. He was asked to go to Stratford-on-Avon when Sir Barry became administrative director in 1946. With him was Peter Brook with whom he was to work over the years with great success. At Stratford he gained confidence in his craft and was able to explore "aspects of human nature that I wanted to make clear to the audience." He played Cloten in *Cymbeline*, Lucio in *Measure for Measure*, Mercutio in *Romeo and Juliet*, Pericles and Henry V. In his third season he played

Hamlet in a Gothic-style production that "exactly matched Scofield's range of evocation."

After these successes at Stratford he returned to London to play in several notable productions, *The Seagull* and *Ring Round the Moon*, and then joined with John Gielgud for a season at the Hammersmith Lyric Theatre. With Gielgud, whose personal and artistic qualities he greatly admires, he played in *Richard II*, in which his wife Joy Parker also appeared, *The Way of the World*, and *Venice Preserved*, directed by Peter Brook.

In 1955-1956 he played at the Phoenix Theatre under Peter Brook's direction in T. S. Eliot's *The Family Reunion, Hamlet*, which they took to Moscow, and Graham Greene's *The Power and the Glory*. His creation of the priest who has gone to pieces in Greene's play challenged his resources and became one of his most memorable roles. In 1960 he opened in London in Robert Bolt's *A Man for All Seasons*, the role that brought him international fame for his quiet, humorous, sensual, but deeply spiritual martyr Sir Thomas More. In 1962 he and his former co-worker Peter Brook set a whole new approach to Shakespearean production in their *King Lear*. Using Samuel Beckett as his frame of reference, Peter Brook saw the traditional tragedy as a "metaphysical farce which ridicules life, death, sanity and illusion." In the "Lear Log" which Charles Marowitz, the assistant director, kept, he describes Scofield circling the character of King Lear like "a wary challenger measuring out an unbeaten opponent and it was apparent from the start that this challenger was a strategist rather than a slugger." The careful, intelligent, emotionally honest Scofield seemed the perfect modern actor to transform Shakespearean interpretation for the generation of the sixties.

The Intuitive Approach

In 1946, Barry Jackson was asked to be an administrative director for three years at Stratford on Avon, and he asked me and Peter Brook and one or two others to go along with him. It was a very good professional opportunity from a purely practical point of view. I went to Stratford, and stayed for three seasons. My voice developed, and I had a chance to act with known and successful actors. I found Godfrey Tearle particularly helpful; he gave one a feeling of self-confidence, not by specific encouragement but by the way he treated one in general. And I must have been influenced in those days by Richardson, Gielgud, and Olivier, although I had then seen Olivier only in films. I was paid twenty pounds a week at first, which was quite a lot, and I started on a new phase of acting. The first character I played was Cloten in *Cymbeline;* I was able to make this oafish character, who is a little bit stupid, come very much to life. I was finished with the groundwork that I had had to lay and that every actor has to lay, and was able to find the clearest, simplest way of building the structure of the character. Then I played Don Adriano de Armado in *Love's Labour's Lost*, and the title role in *Henry V*, and again I found I didn't have to waste much time on the technical requirements of the part, and was free to create the character. I was now exploring aspects of human nature that I

Lillian Ross and Helen Ross: *The Player*. New York: Simon and Schuster, 1961, pp. 180-187. Copyright © 1961 by Lillian Ross © 1962 by Lillian Ross and Helen Ross. Reprinted by permission of Simon and Schuster.

wanted to make clear to the audience. Shakespeare is particularly well suited to an actor who wants to make his own comment. The lines spoken by Shakespeare's characters mean something different to every actor, just as everybody who reads a book reads it differently. In contemporary plays, the actor is much more interpretive of the author's intention. Stratford was altogether different from Birmingham in many ways. I attracted attention that was national instead of purely local. Most of the critics gave me notices, some bad and some good, the latter more or less to the effect that here was a good new actor who had a faculty for getting under the skin of very different types of characters. The second season, I played Mercutio in *Romeo and Juliet* and the title role in *Pericles,* and I was able to consolidate what I had learned during the first season. Between seasons, I got some London jobs that were good for me professionally—the part of Tegeus-Chromis, the lead, in *A Phoenix Too Frequent,* by Christoper Fry, and the juvenile lead, Young Fashion, in Sir John Vanbrugh's *The Relapse, or Virtue in Danger,* with Cyril Ritchard and Madge Elliott.

In 1948, my third season, I was asked to play Hamlet for the first time. The production was in Victorian dress, and Robert Helpmann and I played the lead on alternate nights. I played Hamlet again in 1955, in a more conventionally costumed production, which we opened in Birmingham, took to Moscow, and then brought to London. Anyone can play Hamlet. Any actor with facility and technical skill can play him, because the character has such universality. Macbeth is rather more specific. When I was first asked to play Hamlet, I was happy, of course, but I was immediately preoccupied with how I was going to play him. We rehearsed for the play off and on over a period of two months that had been allotted us for rehearsals of the three plays of that season; the others were *King John,* in which I played Philip, the King of France, and *The Merchant of Venice,* in which I played Bassanio. In 1948, I was an actor with less developed abilities than in 1955, when I had more to bring to the part, and less. The first time, I was much more vulnerable, because I was younger; I had a less sophisticated approach to the play—I was more naïve. In 1955, I had more knowledge and more control over my abilities, and less frailty. One man can play Hamlet only one way. But the first time I wasn't so capable of analyzing what I was doing as I was later. However, I do know that I was temperamentally suited to the part in 1948, when I was twenty-six, in a way that is difficult to recapture. My Hamlet of 1948 was frail. Claire Bloom played Ophelia, and she was so young then that she had a green ration book, the color of the ones given to children; mine was buff. In 1955, Mary Ure played Ophelia. The second time, my Hamlet had more positive assurance and there was probably less of Hamlet in it. The acting was better, the approach was more assured, but something had been lost. If I were to do it a third time, I might learn from the mistakes of the second. That second Hamlet aroused less sympathy, because I was deliberately trying to play it in a more positive way. . . . Output in the theatre requires greater energy than anything else I know. Doubt of one's energy is the worst of all. One's output in the theatre requires energy of a sort that is never a factor in family life. Family energy generates itself. Social life outside the family can be exhausting. I don't care much for social life with people in the theatre. I'm rather good at being with people when I want to make the effort, but I'm bad at listening to people when I know what they're going to say. It isn't very interesting, and on the whole it's very draining. The interesting thing in the theatre is the work and working with people. I usually like the people in the work, but I can't go on with them outside the work as long as most actors can. And when I'm working on a part I'm thinking about it all the time, going over all the possibilities in my mind. I like to be alone when I'm working.

After the 1948 season at Stratford, I went to London in a big way, playing Alexander, the lead, in Terence Rattigan's play *Adventure Story*. It was a flop, but was artistically successful, and it led to my playing Treplev in a West End production of *The Seagull*, with Mai Zetterling, Isabel Jeans, and Ian Hunter. For two years, from 1950 to 1952, I was in *Ring Round the Moon*, Christopher Fry's adaptation of a Jean Anouilh play, with Claire Bloom and Margaret Rutherford. During the run of *Ring Round the Moon*, I appeared on two Sunday nights in my own production of *Pericles* in London. Then I did a season of plays with John Gielgud at the Hammersmith Lyric Theatre, which is sort of Off Broadway. He and I took the lead parts, and most of the time he directed. We put on *Richard II*, in which I played the lead and my wife played the Queen; Congreve's *The Way of the World*, with Gielgud and Margaret Rutherford, in which I played my first comic role in London—Witwoud—with a lot of splendid ladies; and Thomas Otway's *Venice Preserved*, directed by Peter Brook, with Pamela Brown and Eileen Herlie. Gielgud, of course, was one of the ones we had gone to see and learn from in the early days. He had a tremendous interest in anybody who is new in the theatre, because he cares about new life in the theatre. He is a very considerable person, a genius, who brings life to everything he does. As a director, he never tried to impose his own conception of the role on me, but paradoxically, with an actor as individual and powerful as Gielgud it is impossible not to feel that his way is the way you should follow. He has total mastery of all aspects of the theatre. He participates with tremendous energy in every aspect of a production he is involved in. His knowledge is very stimulating. He has style. Everything he does he informs with a beauty of style, both vocal and physical. But one doesn't model oneself on anyone else. One wants to go one's own way. I'm aware of being referred to by some people as the new Olivier. Every strong new actor is called the new Olivier at some point. How can one be the new anything? I've never worked with Olivier, but I've always admired him.

One of the most important seasons I've ever played in was the one at the Phoenix Theatre in London in 1955-1956, with Peter Brook directing. We put on three plays, in all of which I played the lead; one was T. S. Eliot's *The Family Reunion*, with Sybil Thorndike, and the others were the *Hamlet* we took to Moscow, and Dennis Cannan and Pierre Bost's adaptation of Graham Greene's *The Power and the Glory*. The program of three plays depended mostly on me, and it was the most that had ever been demanded of me. After the overwhelming experience of seeing Sybil Thorndike in *Medea*, I was a bit wary of her, but I found her very down-to-earth and warm and friendly—not the remote type of leading actress at all. One of the most enjoyable plays for me was *The Power and the Glory*, in which I played the priest, because I had to go further in one direction than I'd ever gone before. The play presented me with bigger demands on my abilities and also took me in a new direction. The character of the priest was an extremely intricate one—he was drawn as a mess of a human being—and I had to make a truthful character of him somehow. The man was a priest; he was also a peasant. I didn't know how I should make him sound. It gave me an opportunity to work in a completely nonclassical, realistic style, in which I could still use more of my classical training than ever before. In *Venice Preserved*, I also had to go further, playing an extremely violent revolutionary. This role demanded that I be extroverted and tough. Up to that point, sensitivity was mostly what had been demanded of me. In a sense, I feel that I'm part of no group in the theatre. I come sort of half-way between two schools—one exemplified by John Gielgud, with the classic style of speaking, and the other by the Royal Court Theatre, which puts on the work of so many of the good new playwrights. I'm somewhat detached from both groups, although I do come out of the same sort of stable as most English actors, in a general way. There's something about English actors that makes them depend on themselves. I was brought up in the theatre of articulateness. The plays of Shakespeare and Shaw deal with articulate people—people who can express their thoughts. In the plays of Chekhov, on the other hand, everything the characters say has nuances. I don't have a psychological approach to acting; fundamentally, I have an intuitive approach. For me, the totally intellectual approach is never satisfactory. What matters to me is whether I like the play, for one thing, and, for another, whether I can recognize and identify myself with the character I'm to play. My intuition for a part has failed me only once—for the part of Thomas More in Robert Bolt's *A Man for All Seasons,* which opened in London in July of 1960. I felt a tremendous warmth toward the character. Then I came to play him, and I didn't know how. As the play is written, it gives nothing more than the bare lines of what the man is saying. It's all in the lines. There is no opportunity for embroidery. I had to start from scratch and just work on facts, making myself totally faithful to what was on the page: More was a lawyer, a man of tremendous faith, a complex and subtle character. Everything in him led inevitably toward a kind of forensic point of view. It was a rather cold-blooded way of ordering one's mind. I found that the part had what seemed like dogmatic exposition. Simply saying the lines for what they were worth would make More sound like a very pompous and noisy man. If I said the lines with all the intensity they seemed to require, he would seem an aggressive man. And he was not an aggressive man. So I had to find a way of making the man sound not pompous and not aggressive. And yet he had to sound strong. If you can see it, then you can do it. First, I had to find the way the man would feel; then I was able to find the way he should sound. Eventually, I discovered that if I used a specific range of my voice, and characteristics of my voice that I had never used before, I might make him sound mild, even though what the lines themselves said was not mild. When I played Hamlet, I used a lot of voice. For Thomas More, I used a voice you wouldn't hear at all if I used it for Hamlet. I used an accent for More that was absolutely a bastard thing of my own. My parents are Midland people, with a very regional accent, and I drew somewhat on this accent and mixed it with some others. The way More sounded just came out of my characterization of him as a lawyer. His dryness of mind, I thought, led him to use a sort of dryness of speech. It evolved as I evolved the character. I would flatten or elongate a vowel in a certain way to get a certain effect I wanted. Not too much happened to the voice as a result of More's being a man of faith and spirituality. One of the great traps in playing a man of spiritual depth is that one is given only a certain number of lines, and if they are not made to sound absolutely true they are likely to sound very self-satisfied and sentimental. The false note is so often struck. Next, I discovered More's humor, and knew that that would be the thing to make him not smug. Then, More was a flesh-and-blood man, with strong family affections. His spiritual attitudes did not put him at all in a backwater of life. He was fully alive and sensual, in the true sense of the word.

He used his senses. He enjoyed the things of life—food and wine and the rest. He was reluctant to die. He didn't relish physical discomfort. And he wouldn't want to be hurt. At one point in the play, he says, "This is not the stuff of which martyrs are made." Because you're thinking and feeling all these things, the voice comes out in a certain way. It's constant communication between thinking and feeling. Otherwise, the muscles don't work right, don't take the right shape. One's voice follows the rest. It somehow becomes a willing instrument. I didn't go very far in my idea of how I should look as Thomas More: thin and pale, with a hat on—and a gown on. That's the picture. Actors get into some awful habits through their preoccupation with their faces. You have to look at your face in order to get it looking right, but you get more tired of your face than other people do. As soon as you're in rehearsal, it's necessary to start thinking about what you look like. You're enclosed by the structure of the author's writing. You have to hold back on deciding how you should look until you find what is commensurate with what the lines require. I don't think very often of how I myself look: I've got hair— brown hair with gray in it—and lines in my forehead, lines down past my mouth, and bags under my eyes, and my height is just over six feet. That is the kind of professional knowledge one has.

PETER BROOK

(b. 1925)

Peter Brook's early career in the theatre was that of the "boy genius," the "Wunderkind," as his associate and biographer Charles Marowitz calls him. At five he made his parents sit through his toy theatre production of *Hamlet;* at seventeen he went up to Oxford, determined to make his mark as a film director. As part of his preparation he staged Marlowe's *Dr. Faustus* at a small theatre rented for the occasion, and then went on to make a film of Sterne's *Sentimental Journey.* A London production of *Pygmalion* in 1945 earned him an invitation from Sir Barry Jackson of the Birmingham Repertory Company to stage *Man and Superman.* He cast young Paul Scofield as Jack Tanner, the first of their many important ventures together.

With Sir Barry he went to the Shakespeare Memorial Theatre at Stratford-on-Avon, where his productions of *Love's Labour's Lost, Romeo and Juliet* and *Measure for Measure* were all marked by a special brilliance. He then was director at Covent Garden for two years, at which time he "came to the conclusion that opera as an artistic form was dead."

In the next decade he became a director of international standing as he worked in London, Paris, and New York at almost every variety of theatre, musicals, realistic dramas, poetic dramas, both old and new, and in films, which had been his first love. Some of his notable productions in these years were several in 1956 in which Paul Scofield starred, *Hamlet, The Family Reunion,* and *The Power and the Glory; The Visit* with the Lunts during 1958; *The Balcony* in Paris in 1960, and the Scofield *King Lear* at the Royal Shakespeare Theatre in 1962. From the fascinating "Lear Log" kept by his assistant director, Charles Marowitz, we can learn how he approached this towering tragedy. Marowitz, who in addition to his own books, essays and productions, has done much to make the creative innovations of Brook accessible, tells us that Brook spoke of the play as a mountain whose summit had never been reached. On the way up one found the shattered bodies of other climbers strewn on every side. "Olivier here, Laughton there; it's frightening." At the first readings in the Stratford theatre, he outlined the task ahead: "The work of rehearsals is looking for meaning and then making it meaningful." To him this great play, long deemed unactable, could only be "comprehended existentially—on a stage." Brook's "frame of reference" was the world and work of Samuel Beckett, and he viewed Lear as "a vast, complex, coherent poem designed to study the power and the emptiness of nothing—"

In 1962 he became one of the directors of the Royal Shakespeare Theatre, which had inaugurated its London seasons at the Aldwych Theatre. It was here that Brook staged his extraordinary production of Peter Weiss's Marat/Sade in 1964. The style of Brook's interpretation was heavily indebted to both Bertolt Brecht and Antonin Artaud. Especially important to the final shape of the production were the experiments Brook conducted in the fall of 1963 in his Theatre of Cruelty; these are described in this book by his associate Charles Marowitz, whose collage Hamlet formed part of the program. Committed to this work Brook turned from "star" productions to improvisation, the collective life of an ensemble of players, and "direct theatrical creation" unburdened by a set text. The exploration of the actor and his relationship to the audience now became the center of his creative work. A collective creation by his company about the Vietnam war, US, an experimental staging of The Tempest, in which audiences were free to sit in either "safe" or "dangerous" areas, and a startling rendition of Seneca's Oedipus all reveal the search of this major creative artist for a living, "Immediate Theatre," which, to use the divisions so brilliantly analyzed in his book The Empty Space, may be "Rough Theatre" or "Holy Theatre," but never "Deadly Theatre."

The Act of Possession

Acting begins with a tiny inner movement so slight that it is almost completely invisible. We see this when we compare film and stage acting: a good stage actor can act in films, not necessarily vice versa. What happens? I make a proposition to an actor's imagination such as, "She is leaving you." At this moment deep in him a subtle movement occurs. Not only in actors—the movement occurs in anyone, but in most nonactors the movement is too slight to manifest itself in any way: the actor is a more sensitive instrument and in him the tremor is detected—in the cinema the great magnifier, the lens, describes this to the film that notes it down, so for the cinema the first flicker is all. In early theatre rehearsals, the impulse may get no further than a flicker—even if the actor wishes to amplify it, all sorts of extraneous psychic psychological tensions can intervene—then the current is short-circuited, earthed. For this flicker to pass into the whole organism, a total relaxation must be there, either god-given or brought about by work. This, in short, is what rehearsals are all about. In this way acting is mediumistic—the idea suddenly envelops the whole in an act of possession—in Grotowski's terminology the actors are "penetrated"—penetrated by themselves. In very young actors, the obstacles are sometimes very elastic, penetration can happen with surprising ease, and they can give subtle and complex incarnations that are the despair of those who have evolved their skill over years. Yet later, with success and experience, the same

Peter Brook: The Empty Space. New York: Atheneum, 1969, pp. 109-120. Copyright © 1968 by Peter Brook. Reprinted by permission of Atheneum Publishers.

young actors build up their barriers to themselves. Children can often act with extraordinary natural technique. People from real life are marvelous on screen. But with adult professionals there has to be a two-way process, and the stirring from within has to be aided by the stimulus from outside. Sometimes study and thought can help an actor to eliminate the preconceptions that blind him to deeper meanings, but sometimes it is the reverse. To reach an understanding of a difficult role, an actor must go to the limits of his personality and intelligence—but sometimes great actors go further still if they rehearse the words and at the same time listen acutely to the echoes that arise in them.

John Gielgud is a magician—his form of theatre is one that is known to reach above the ordinary, the common, the banal. His tongue, his vocal chords, his feeling for rhythm compose an instrument that he has consciously developed all through his career in a running analogy with his life. His natural inner aristocracy, his outer social and personal beliefs, have given him a hierarchy of values, an intense discrimination between base and precious, and a conviction that the sifting, the weeding, the selecting, the dividing, the refining and the transmuting are activities that never end. His art has always been more vocal than physical: at some early stage in his career he decided that for himself the body was a less supple instrument than the head. He thus jettisoned part of an actor's possible equipment but made true alchemy with the rest. It is not just speech, not melodies, but the continual movement between the word-forming mechanism and his understanding that has made his art so rare, so touching and especially so aware. With Gielgud, we are conscious both of what is expressed and of the skill of the creator: that a craft can be so deft adds to our admiration. The experience of working with him has been among my most special and my greatest joys.

Paul Scofield talks to his audience in another way. While in Gielgud the instrument stands halfway between the music and the hearer, and so demands a player, trained and skilled—in Scofield, instrument and player are one—an instrument of flesh and blood that opens itself to the unknown. Scofield, when I first knew him as a very young actor, had a strange characteristic: verse hampered him, but he would make unforgettable verse out of lines of prose. It was as though the act of speaking a word sent through him vibrations that echoed back meanings far more complex than his rational thinking could find: he would pronounce a word like "night" and then he would be compelled to pause: listening with all his being to the amazing impulses stirring in some mysterious inner chamber, he would experience the wonder of discovery at the moment when it happened. Those breaks, those sallies in depth, give his acting its absolutely personal structure of rhythms, its own instinctive meanings: to rehearse a part, he lets his whole nature—a milliard of supersensitive scanners—pass to and fro across the words. In performance the same process makes everything that he has apparently fixed come back again each night the same and absolutely different.

I use two well-known names as illustrations, but the phenomenon is there all the time in rehearsal, and continually reopens the problem of innocence and experience, of spontaneity and knowledge. There are also things young actors and unknown actors can do that have passed beyond the reach of fine actors with experience and skill.

There have been times in theatre history when the actor's work has been based on certain accepted gestures and expressions: there have been frozen systems of attitudes that we reject today. It is perhaps less obvious that the opposite pole, the

Method actor's freedom in choosing anything whatsoever from the gestures of everyday life, is equally restricted, for in basing his gestures on his observation or on his own spontaneity the actor is not drawing on any deep creativity. He is reaching inside himself for an alphabet that is also fossilized, for the language of signs from life that he knows is the language not of invention but of his conditioning. His observations of behavior are often observations of projections of himself. What he thinks to be spontaneous is filtered and monitored many times over. Were Pavlov's dog improvising, he would still salivate when the bell rang, but he would feel sure it was all his own doing: "I'm dribbling," he would say, proud of his daring.

Those who work in improvisation have the chance to see with frightening clarity how rapidly the boundaries of so-called freedom are reached. Our exercises in public with the Theatre of Cruelty quickly led the actors to the point where they were nightly ringing variations on their own clichés—like Marcel Marceau's character who breaks out of one prison to find himself within another. We experimented, for instance, with an actor opening a door and finding something unexpected. He had to react to the unexpected sometimes in gesture, sometimes in sound, sometimes with paint. He was encouraged to express the first gesture, cry or splash that came to him. At first, all this showed was the actor's stock of similes. The open mouth of surprise, the step back in horror: where did these so-called spontaneities come from? Clearly the true and instantaneous inner reaction was checked and like lightning the memory substituted some imitation of a form once seen. Dabbing the paint was even more revealing: the hairbreadth of terror before the blankness, and then the reassuring ready-made idea coming to the rescue. This Deadly Theatre lurks inside us all.

The aim of improvisation in training actors in rehearsal, and the aim of exercises, is always the same: it is to get away from Deadly Theatre. It is not just a matter of splashing about in self-indulgent euphoria as outsiders often suspect; for it aims at bringing the actor again and again to his own barriers, to the points where in place of new-found truth he normally substitutes a lie. An actor playing a big scene falsely appears false to the audience because, instant for instant, in his progression from one attitude of the character to another, he is substituting false details for real ones: tiny transitional phony emotions through imitation attitudes. But this cannot be grappled with while rehearsing big scenes—too much is going on, it is far too complicated. The purpose of an exercise is to reduce and return: to narrow the area down and down until the birth of a lie is revealed and caught. If the actor can find and see this moment he can perhaps open himself to a deeper, more creative impulse.

Similarly, when two actors play together. What we know most is external ensemble playing: much of the teamwork of which the English theatre is so proud is based on politeness, courtesy, reasonableness, give-and-take, your turn, after you, and so on—a facsimile that works whenever the actors are in the same range of style—i.e., older actors play beautifully together, and so do very young ones; but when they are mixed up, for all their care and mutual respect, the result is often a mess. For a production I did of Genet's *The Balcony* in Paris it was necessary to mix actors of very different backgrounds—classically trained, film trained, ballet trained and simple amateur. Here, long evenings of very obscene brothel improvisations served only one purpose—they enabled this hybrid group of people to come together and begin to find a way of responding directly to one another.

Some exercises open the actors to one another in a quite different way: for example, several actors may play completely different scenes side by side, but never speaking at the same moment, so that each has to pay close attention to the whole, in order to know just what moments depended on him, or else developing a collective sense of responsibility for the quality of an improvisation, and switching to new situations as soon as the shared invention flags. Many exercises set out first to free the actor, so he may be allowed to discover by himself what exists only in himself: next, to force him to accept blindly external directions, so that by cocking a sensitive enough ear he could hear in himself movements he would never have detected any other way. For instance a valuable exercise is dividing a Shakespeare soliloquy into three voices, like a canon, and then having the three actors recite at breakneck speed over and over again. At first, the technical difficulty absorbs all the actors' attention, then gradually as they master the difficulties they are asked to bring out the meaning of the words, without varying the inflexible form. Because of the speed and the mechanical rhythm this seems impossible: the actor is prevented from using any of his normal expressive equipment. Then suddenly he bursts a barrier and experiences how much freedom there can be within the tightest discipline.

Another variant is to take the two lines "To be or not to be, That is the question" and give them to ten actors, one word each. The actors stand in a closed circle and endeavor to play the words one after the other, trying to produce a living phrase. This is so difficult that it instantly reveals even to the most unconvinced actor how closed and insensitive he is to his neighbor. When after long work the sentence suddenly flows, a thrilling freedom is experienced by everyone. They see in a flash the possibility of group playing, and the obstacles to it. This exercise can be developed by substituting other verbs for "be," with the same effect of affirmation and denial—and eventually it is possible to put sounds or gestures in place of one or all of the words and still maintain a living dramatic flow between the ten participants.

The purpose of such exercises is to lead actors to the point where if one actor does something unexpected but true, the others can take this up and respond on the same level. This is ensemble playing: in acting terms it means ensemble creation, an awesome thought. It is no use thinking that exercises belong to school and only apply to a certain period of the actor's development. An actor like any artist, is like a garden and it is no help to pull out the weeds just once, for all time. The weeds always grow, this is quite natural, and they must be cleaned away, which is natural and necessary too.

Actors must study by varying means: an actor has mainly an act of elimination to make. Stanislavsky's title *Building a Character* is misleading—a character isn't a static thing and it can't be built like a wall. Rehearsals don't lead progressively to a first night. This is something very hard for some actors to understand —especially those who pride themselves most on their skill. For mediocre actors the process of character building is as follows: they have an acute moment of artistic anguish, at the very start—"What will happen this time?"—"I know I've played many successful parts before but, this time, will inspiration come?" This actor comes in terror to the first rehearsal, but gradually his standard practices fill the vacuum of his fear: as he "discovers" a way of doing each section, he battens it down, relieved that once again he has been spared the final catastrophe. So on the first night, although he is nervous, his nerves are those of the marksman who knows he can hit the target but is afraid he won't get a bull's-eye again when his friends are watching.

The really creative actor reaches a different and far worse terror on the first night. All through rehearsals he has been exploring aspects of a character which he senses always to be partial, to be less than the truth—so he is compelled, by the honesty of his search, endlessly to shed and start again. A creative actor will be most ready to discard the hardened shells of his work at the last rehearsal because here, with the first night approaching, a brilliant searchlight is cast on his creation, and he sees its pitiful inadequacy. The creative actor also longs to cling onto all he's found, he too wants at all costs to avoid the trauma of appearing in front of an audience, naked and unprepared—still this is exactly what he must do. He must destroy and abandon his results even if what he picks up seems almost the same. This is easier for French actors than for English ones, because temperamentally they are more open to the idea that nothing is any good. And this is the only way that a part, instead of being built, can be born. The role that has been *built* is the same every night—except that it slowly erodes. For the part that is born to be the same it must always be reborn, which makes it always different. Of course, particularly in a long run, the effort of daily reaction becomes unbearable and unthinkable, and this is where the experienced creative artist is compelled to fall back on a second level called technique to carry him through.

I did a play with that perfectionist Alfred Lunt. In the first act, he had a scene sitting on a bench. In rehearsal, he suggested, as a piece of natural business, taking off his shoe and rubbing his foot. Then he added shaking the shoe to empty it before putting it back on again. One day when we were on tour in Boston, I walked past his dressing room. The door was ajar. He was preparing for the performance, but I could see that he was looking out for me. He beckoned excitedly. I went into the dressing room, he closed the door, asked me to sit down. "There's something I want to try tonight," he said. "But only if you agree. I went for a walk on Boston Common this afternoon and found these." He held out his palm. It contained two tiny pebbles. "That scene where I shake out my shoe," he continued, "it's always worried me that nothing falls out. So I thought I'd try putting the pebbles in. Then when I shake it, you'd see them drop—and you'd hear the sound. What do you think?" I said it was an excellent idea and his face lit up. He looked delightedly at the two little stones, back at me, then suddenly his expression changed. He studied the stones again for a long anxious moment. "You don't think it would be better with one?"

The hardest task of all for an actor is to be sincere yet detached—it is drummed into an actor that sincerity is all he needs. With its moral overtones, the word causes great confusion. In a way, the most powerful feature of the Brecht actors is the degree of their *insincerity*. It is only through detachment that an actor will see his own clichés. There is a dangerous trap in the word sincerity. First of all, a young actor discovers that his job is so exacting that it demands of him certain skills. For instance, he has to be heard: his body has to obey his wishes: he must be a master of his timing, not the slave of haphazard rhythms. So he searches for technique: and soon he acquires a know-how. Easily, know-how can become a pride and an end in itself. It becomes dexterity without any other aim than the display of expertise—in other words, the art becomes insincere. The young actor observes the insincerity of the old-timer and is disgusted. He searches for sincerity. Sincerity is a loaded word: like cleanliness it carries childhood associations of goodness, truth-telling and decency. It seems a good ideal, a better aim than acquiring more and more technique, and as sincerity is a feeling, one can always tell when one's being sincere. So there is a path one can follow; one can find one's way to sincerity by emotional "giving," by being dedicated, by honesty, by taking a no-holds-barred approach and by, as the French say, "plunging into the bath." Unfortunately, the result can easily be the worst kind of acting. With any of the other arts, however deep one plunges into the act of creating, it is always possible to step away and look at the result. As the painter steps back from his canvas other faculties can spring into play and warn him at once of his excesses. The trained pianist's head is physically less involved than his fingers and so however "carried away" he is by the music, his ear carries its own degree of detachment and objective control. Acting is in many ways unique in its difficulties because the artist has to use the treacherous, changeable and mysterious material of himself as his medium. He is called upon to be completely involved while distanced—detached without detachment. He must be sincere, he must be insincere: he must practice how to be insincere with sincerity and how to lie truthfully. This is almost impossible, but it is essential and easily ignored. All too often, actors—and it is not their fault, but that of the deadly schools with which the world is littered—build their work on fag-ends of doctrine. The great system of Stanislavsky, which for the first time approached the whole art of acting from the point of view of science and knowledge, has done as much harm as good to many young actors, who misread it in detail and only take away a good hatred of the shoddy. After Stanislavsky, Artaud's equally significant writings, half-read and a tenth digested, have led to a naïve belief that emotional commitment and unhesitating self-exposure are all that really count. This is now fed further by ill-digested, misunderstood bits of Grotowski. There is now a new form of sincere acting which consists of living everything through the body. It is a kind of naturalism. In naturalism, the actor tries sincerely to imitate the emotions and actions of the everyday world and to live his role. In this other naturalism the actor gives himself over just as completely to living his unrealistic behavior, through and through. This is where he fools himself. Just because the type of theatre he's connected with seems poles removed from old-fashioned naturalism, he believes that he, too, is far from this despised style. In fact, he approaches the landscape of his own emotions with the same belief that every detail must be photographically reproduced. So he is always at full flood. The result is often soft, flabby, excessive and unconvincing.

There are groups of actors, particularly in the United States, nourished on Genet and Artaud, who despise all forms of naturalism. They would be very indignant if they were called naturalistic actors, but this is precisely what limits their art. To commit every fiber of one's being into an action may seem a form of total involvement—but the true artistic demand may be even more stringent than total involvement—and need fewer manifestations or quite different ones. To understand this, we must see that along with the emotion there is always a role for a special intelligence, which is not there at the start, but which has to be developed as a selecting instrument. There is a need for detachment, in particular, there is a need for certain forms: all of which is hard to define, but impossible to ignore. For instance, actors can pretend to fight with total abandon and genuine violence. Every actor is prepared for death scenes—and he throws himself into them with such abandon that he does not realize he knows nothing at all about death.

In France an actor comes to an audition, asks to be shown the most violent scene in the play, and without a qualm plunges into it to demonstrate his paces. The French actor playing a classical part pumps himself up in the wings, then plunges into the scene: he judges the success or failure of the evening by the degree he can surrender to his emotions, whether his inner charge is at its maximum pitch, and from this comes a belief in the Muse, in inspiration and so on. The weakness of his work is that this way he tends to play generalizations. By this I mean that in an angry scene he gets on to his note of anger—or rather he plugs into his anger-point and this force drives him through the scene. This may give him a certain force and even at times a certain hypnotic power over the audience, and this power is falsely considered to be "lyrical" and "transcendental." In fact, such an actor in his passion becomes its slave and is unable to drop out of the passion if a subtle change of text demands something new. In a speech that contains both natural and lyrical elements he declaims everything as though all the words were equally pregnant. It is this clumsiness that makes actors appear stupid and grand acting seem unreal.

Jean Genet wishes the theatre to come out of the banal, and he wrote a series of letters to Roger Blin when Blin was directing *The Screens,* urging him to push the actors toward "lyricism." This sounds well enough in theory but what is lyricism? What is "out of the ordinary" acting? Does it dictate a special voice, a high-flown manner? Old classical actors seem to sing their lines. Is this the relic of some valid old tradition? At what point is a search for form an acceptance of artificiality? This is one of the greatest problems we face today, and so long as we retain any sneaking belief that grotesque masks, heightened makeups, hieratic costumes, declamation, balletic movement are somehow "ritualistic" in their own right and consequently lyrical and profound—we will never get out of a traditional art-theatre rut.

At least one can see that everything is a language for something and nothing is a language for everything. Every action happens in its own right and every action is an analogy of something else. I crumple a piece of paper: this gesture is complete in itself: I can stand on a stage, and what I do need be no more than what appears at the moment of the happening. It can also be a metaphor. Anyone who saw Patrick Magee slowly tearing strips of newspaper precisely as in life and yet utterly ritualistically in Pinter's *The Birthday Party* will know what this means. A metaphor is a sign and is an illustration—so it is a fragment of language. Every tone of speech, every rhythmic pattern is a fragment of language and corresponds to a different experience. Often, nothing is so deadly as a well-schooled actor speaking verse: there are of course academic laws of prosody and they can help to clarify certain things for an actor at a certain stage of his development, but he must eventually discover that the rhythms of each character are as distinctive as thumb-prints: then he must learn that every note in the musical scale corresponds—what to? That also he must find.

CHARLES MAROWITZ

(b. 1934)

A native New Yorker, Charles Marowitz has been living in London since 1956. He has served the theatre in many different capacities—producer, director, adapter, editor, critic-historian. He was editor of *Encore* magazine, the controversial theatre periodical. His interest in new modes of expression, especially for the actor, showed itself in his volume *Stanislavsky and the Method,* originally published in London in 1961.

Marowitz served as assistant director to Peter Brook in 1962 on the important production of *King Lear* with Paul Scofield at the Royal Shakespeare Theatre, Stratford-on-Avon. His "Lear Log" is an invaluable record. In the following year he .worked with Peter Brook to form an experimental group associated with the Royal Shakespeare Company. The group's stated intention was "to explore certain problems of acting and stagecraft in laboratory conditions, without the commercial pressures of public performance." Marowitz's account of the experiment, which follows, is a fascinating record of how he and Brook, inspired by Antonin Artaud, tried to work out in concrete exercises the way to a theatre that is more than literal or literary: that is a poetic, penetrating, "holy theatre." Out of their extensive explorations came a five-week run of "The Theatre of Cruelty" at the LAMDA Theatre Club in London. All their experimentation came to a natural culmination when the script of Peter Weiss's *Marat/Sade* was taken up by the group, which then disappeared as a separate entity and was reabsorbed by the main company of the Royal Shakespeare Theatre.

Marowitz is artistic director of the Open Space in London, and his comments on the contemporary theatre scene appear often in the New York *Village Voice* as well as in many theatre and cultural magazines.

Notes on the Theatre of Cruelty

Introduction to Sounds

On the very first day of work, before the actors had properly met each other, and without Brook or myself delivering any orientation lectures, the actors were handed objects: boxes, bangers, scrapers, vessels, sticks, etc. Each actor had something or other to bang with, and something or other to bang on. They were then asked to explore the range of their *instrument* (the sound the thick end of a ladle made on a tin can; the sound the tin can made against the floor, muted with one palm, held suspended in two hands, tucked inside a sweater, rapped with the knuckle instead of the ladle, with the forehead instead of the knuckle, the elbow instead of the forehead, etc. etc.).

Once the range of the instrument had been explored, a series of rhythms were rapped out. Some of these were then varied while others remained the same; some were accelerated while others were slowed down; there were combinations of twos and threes; dialogues between broom handles and empty crates; scenes from *Romeo and Juliet* played out between metallic tinkles and bass percussions; mob violence with soap crates, and pitched battles with tennis rackets, etc.

Eventually *rhythm,* a generalized and overused word in the theatre, was redefined in exact, physical terms. Not only did actors experience basic changes of rhythm but endless combinations of cross-rhythms, elaborate syncopations, etc.

Charles Marowitz and Simon Trussler, editors: *Theatre at Work.* New York: Hill & Wang, 1968, pp. 164-185 *passim.* Copyright Marowitz and Trussler, 1967. Reprinted by permission of Hill and Wang, Inc. First published in *Tulane Drama Review,* Vol. XI, No. 3, Winter, 1966.

Shortly, the attitude the actors had taken to their objects was applied to their voices and bodies. This was a tortuous adjustment, for always one was fighting that primordial instinct in English actors that believes the voice is the medium for *good speech, projection* and *resonance,* the carrier of the theatrical "message," and the body a useful but secondary adjunct. Little by little, we insinuated the idea that the voice could produce sounds other than grammatical combinations of the alphabet, and that the body, set free, could begin to enunciate a language that went beyond text, beyond subtext, beyond psychological implication and beyond monkey-see-monkey-do facsimiles of social behaviorism. And most important of all, that these sounds and moves could communicate feelings and ideas.

Sound and Movement Similes

Sound Exercise

You come back to your apartment after a hard day's work. Enter, take off your coat, hang it up, pour yourself a drink and sit down at the table. On the table is a letter which you suddenly notice. You put down the drink, open the letter and begin to read. The contents of the letter are entirely up to you; the only condition is that it contains news that puts you into a highly emotional state of one sort or another. Express this state using only a sound and a movement.

The moments in the exercise leading up to the final beat are entirely naturalistic, but the final beat is an externalized expression of the character's inner state and totally nonnaturalistic. At first, all the choices were commonplace. People jumped for joy; fell into weeping; bolted upward with surprise; stamped with rage. . . . When none of these simple expressions were acceptable, the actors began to realize the nature of the exercise. With all their naturalistic choices dismissed out of hand, they had to go in search of a more stylized means of communication. Eventually, the choices became more imaginative. Sounds were created which had the resonance of wounded animals; of prehistoric creatures being slain by atomic weapons. Movements became stark and unpredictable. Actors began to use the chairs and tables as sculptural objects instead of as functional furniture. Facial expressions, under the pressure of extended sounds, began to resemble Javanese masks and Zen sculpture. But once the actors realized what we were after, some of them began to select an arbitrary sound or movement, effective in itself but unrelated to the emotional state growing out of the exercise. Very quickly, frighteningly quickly, actors became as glib with nonnaturalistic sounds and movements as they were with stock dramatic clichés. One wondered if Artaud's idealized theatre ever were established, whether, in five or ten years, it too would not become as practiced and cliché-ridden as the present-day Comédie Française, or commercial West End stage.

Discontinuity

One of the main objects behind the work was to try to create a discontinuous style of acting; that is, a style that corresponded to the broken and fragmentary way in which most people experience contemporary reality. Life today (I am not philosophizing, merely trying to illustrate) is very much like the front page of a daily newspaper. The eye jumps from one story to another; from one geographical location to another; from one mood to another. A fire in Hoboken; an election in Paris; a coronation in Sweden; a rape in London; comedy, passion, ceremony, trivia—all flooding one's consciousness almost simultaneously. The actor, however, through years of training and centuries of tradition, moves stolidly from point A to point B to point C. His character is *established;* his relationships *develop;* his plot thickens and his conflicts resolve. In short, he plods on in his old Aristotelian way, perpetuating the stock jargon of drama, and the completely arbitrary time-system of the conventional theatre.

To break the progressive-logical-beginning-middle-and-end syndrome, one uses improvisation (i.e., personal and organic material rather than theatrical *données*) and uses it simply as rhythmic matter.

Exercise

The life of a character is briefly built up. X is an out-of-work writer.
Scene 1: His landlady asks him for rent which is months in arrears.
Scene 2: His girl-friend wants to know when they're going to get married.
Scene 3: His father urges him to give up writing and take a job with the firm.
Scene 4: His pub crony exhorts him to come out, have a drink, and forget his troubles.
Scene 5: His school friend drops in and wants to relive old times.
Scene 6: An insurance man persistently tries to push an unwanted policy on him.
    Etc. etc. etc.

Each scene is built up independently for five minutes or ten minutes; just long enough for it to have a little meat, but not long enough to develop any real sinew. Then X is placed in the center of the room and each character—on cue—resumes his scene with him. The scenes, all unrelated except that they are all centered around the same main character, follow hard upon one another. With the addition of each new scene, X quickly adapts to the changed situation, the different relationship. Eventually, three and four scenes are being played at once. Soon all are being *played* simultaneously. At a point, the exercise becomes unbearable and impossible, but before that point, X and his fellow actors have experienced a frantic sense of discontinuity that just begins to convey the complexities to which any, even the simplest, sensibility is prone.

A Collage *Hamlet*

A couple of years before the Royal Shakespeare Experimental Group, I had invited Brook along to a play I was doing at the In-Stage studio-theatre in Fitzroy Square. It was a short play by Raymond Abel called *A Little Something for the Maid*. Originally intended for radio, it consisted of a series of short, discontinuous scenes in which the female character became, by turns, everyone in the male character's life: wife, sweetheart, charlady, male employer, secretary, mother, etc. Discussing it afterwards, Brook had said it would be fascinating to see *Hamlet* played that way, reshuffled like a deck of familiar cards. A year and a half later, Brook's idea still knocking around in my head, I tried my hand at restructuring Shakespeare's play.

The idea of the LAMDA (London Academy of Music and Dramatic Art) *Hamlet* was to condense the play into about twenty minutes, without relying on narrative. This was on the assumption that everyone knew *Hamlet*—even those people who hadn't read or seen it—that there was a smear of *Hamlet* in everyone's collective unconscious, and that it was possible to predicate a performance on that mythic memory.

The play was spliced up into a collage with lines juxtaposed, sequences rearranged, characters dropped or blended, and the entire thing played out in short, discontinuous fragments which appeared like subliminal flashes out of Hamlet's life and, in every case, used Shakespeare's words, although radically rearranged.

Of all the discontinuity exercises, this had the firmest foundation, as all the actors knew the original play and therefore had an emotional and narrative frame of reference. The first version was essentially a clever exercise in Burroughs-like cutups. In the later, expanded, 85-minute version, which played in Germany, Italy and later London, the style was better assimilated, the play had more intellectual content and was at the service of a clear-cut interpretation.

Contact

The building of any company sense demands the construction of those delicate vertebrae and interconnecting tissues that transform an aggregation of actors into an ensemble. A protracted period of togetherness (like at a rep, for instance) creates an accidental union between people, but this isn't the same thing as actors coiled and sprung in relation to one another—poised in such a way that a move from one creates a tremor from another, an impulse from a third, an immediate chain reaction. Contact doesn't mean staring in the eyes of your fellow actor for all you're worth. It means being so well tuned in that you can see him without looking. It means, in rare cases, being linked by a group rhythm which is regulated almost physiologically —by blood circulation or heart palpitation. It is the sort of thing that exists between certain kith and kin; certain husbands and wives; certain kinds of lovers or bitter enemies. . . .

Improvs and Essentials

There was a good deal of conventional improvisation (i.e., built up on actions and reducible to beats) but the more useful work came from variations and extensions of the stock Method approach. For instance: after a scene was played, the actor was asked to divide the improv into three units, and to give a Line-Title to each unit. Once this was accomplished and it was generally agreed the Line-Titles were appropriate to the situation just played, the scene was replayed in its entirety with the actors using only their three Line-Titles as dialogue. Then the actor was asked to choose only one word from each of the three Line-Titles and the scene was played a third time with the sound-components of those words serving exclusively as the dialogue. Then (and only then) could the actor choose a sound which accurately reflected the main quality of his scene, and play the scene for a final time, using variations of that sound. The playing in sound invariably prompted a nonnaturalistic use of movement, and it was fascinating to see how, once the situation had been ground down to basic impulses, the movement graphically expressed the true intentions behind the scene.

Example of a Scene

A wants to break off long-standing affair with his girl friend B. He now realizes he does not love her, and it would be lunacy to marry. B, however, has become helplessly attached to A and cannot bear the idea of parting. She tries desperately to maintain the relationship.

Scene Breakdown in Terms of Line Titles: First Replay

BOY: 1—I want to break off this affair.
2—I want to be as kind as possible.
3—I won't be persuaded to change my mind.
GIRL: 1—I want to keep my hold on A.
2—I want to reason with him so as to change his mind.
3—I refuse to be hurt.

Second Replay: Essential Words

BOY: Break.
Kind.
Won't.
GIRL: Keep.
Reason.
Refuse.

Third Replay: Sounds

BOY: Ey-aye-oghn.
GIRL: Eey-zoohz.
(The sounds are fluid and free, merely *based on* the vowels and consonants of the essential words.)

Stanislavsky and Artaud

Having been brought up on Stanislavsky and the ideal of inner truth, it was a major adjustment to discover there was also *surface truth,* and that in certain contexts, the latter was even more persuasive than the former. An even more difficult adjustment was to realize that artifice and downright artistic fraud could create a plenitude of truth for an audience and was, therefore, according to the pragmatic laws that govern acting, legitimate. The Method argument for inner truth holds water only if its main contention is true: that is, that the spectator experiences feeling to the same degree the actor does. But we all know this is not always the case; that there are hundreds of instances of turned-on actors splitting themselves with inner intensity which communicates nothing to an audience but effort and tension. It is equally true that an actor who is almost totally turned off but going through the right motions in the right context, can powerfully affect an audience—almost involuntarily.

The Method actor's test for truthfulness is the authenticity of his personal feeling. The Artaudian actor knows that unless that feeling has been shaped into a communicative image, it is a passionate letter without postage. Whereas pure feeling can be mawkish or leaden, a pertinent stage-image—a gesture, a movement, a sequence of actions—is a statement in itself, which doesn't require the motor power of feeling in order to register, but, when emotionally charged, is twenty times more effective.

There is no fundamental disagreement between the Method actor and the Artaudian actor. Both rely on consciousness to release the unconscious, but whereas the Method actor is chained to rational motivation, the Artaudian actor realizes the highest artistic truth is unprovable. Like certain rare natural phenomena that defy scientific analysis, they *can* exist—and the actor's task is to conjure them into being.

The Artaudian actor needs Stanislavsky in order to verify the nature of the feelings he is releasing—otherwise he becomes a victim of feeling. Even Artaud's celebrated actor-in-trance is responsible to the spirit that is speaking through him. A seance where nothing is communicated but atmosphere is not half as rewarding as one in which messages are received loud and clear. The very state of trance itself is arrived at methodically. The medium's secret is knowing when to let go of the mechanisms that have produced it—in order to transcend. The same is true for the actor—any actor—who uses either intellect or instinct to bring him to the proper jumping-off point.

Changing Gears

Improvisation

Three actors, A, B and C, are given cue sounds (a bell for one, a buzzer for the second, a gong for the third). When Actor A hears his cue he initiates a scene, and B and C, adapting themselves to A's choice, enter into the situation as quickly as possible. After two or three minutes when the scene is either approaching a high point or running down because of lack of invention, B is given his cue. B suddenly leaps into a completely new situation, entirely unrelated to the one preceding; A and C adapt themselves immediately. A short development, then C is cued, another unrelated scene, the others adapt again, etc. etc. etc.

As important as the actual material thrown up by the scene is the moment chosen for breaking it and beginning another. There is a moment in almost every improvisation where things reach a head and are moving quickly toward a resolution. If one can trigger off the new scene just at that moment, the actor's emergency equipment is instinctively brought into play. Improvisations like these feed on (and sometimes are destroyed by) their sense of danger. There is an inescapable imperative on the actors. They must think and act with lightning speed. They know that within a seven- or ten-minute period, they have to devise as many as five or six different situations, and they soon discover they cannot cheat by planning ahead, because a prearranged choice is immediately apparent (as is the instinctively appropriate choice which could not have come from anywhere else but the given circumstances). It brings into play a quality that actors tend to think they do not possess: the ability to associate freely and without regard to fixed character or logical consistency. For me, the great eye-opener in this exercise was how, under the pressure of changing gears, actors who had never heard of surrealism were able to make the most stunning surrealist choices; and actors who claimed to have no sense of humor, suddenly found themselves dipping into deep wells of fantasy and absurdity that lie on the threshold of their consciousness. Choices which, if actors had time to deliberate them, would never be made, or would be doctored or modified, leaped out with astonishing clarity and boldness.

Actors and Actors

The hallmark of a good actor is his attitude toward change. Most actors make their decisions in the first stages of rehearsal, chart the shortest distance between two points and then proceed in a straight line. For these, the rehearsal period is a tunnel with light on one end and light on the other, and a great stretch of darkness in the middle. Another sort of actor retains the ability to re-think and reorganize his role throughout. He follows every lead and yields to every permutation, and isn't put off by detours and secondary routes. He may take longer to arrive but when he does, he brings a better-rounded result.

This attitude toward change almost distinguishes two separate breeds of actor, and in England today, these breeds intermingle in almost every company. It is too sweeping to designate one *traditional* and the other *modern,* but there is a grain of truth in that distinction, as those actors who have passed through the Royal Court, Theatre Workshop and the ferment of the past ten years do tend to have a more open attitude than is to be found among the academy-bred, rep-oriented actors of an older formation. Each of these types almost has a vernacular of its own.

Trads	*Mods*
Let's get it plotted.	Let's get it analyzed.
Fix inflections and "readings."	Play for sense and let inflections take care of themselves.
Plot as soon as possible.	Move freely for as long as possible.
Play for laughs.	Play for contact.
Final decisions as soon as possible.	Final decisions as late as possible and always open to reversal.
It was a bad house.	It was a bad performance.
I take orders.	I give suggestions.
Am I being masked?	Am I important at this moment in the play?
	Are my intentions clear?
Can I be heard?	I'm not getting what I expected, so I
I'm getting nothing from my partner.	shall adjust.
Just as we rehearsed it.	As the immediacy of the performance dictates.
Let's get on with it and stop intellectualizing.	Let's apply what reason we have to problems at hand.
More feeling.	More clarity of intention so as to produce more feeling.
Hold that pause.	Fill that pause.
Everything's in the lines.	Everything's in the subtext.
I'll play this role symbolically.	I can't play concepts, only actions.
I am the villain.	I refuse to pass moral judgments on my character.
My many years of professional experience convince me that . . .	Nothing is ever the same.

Speak with Paints

Exercise

You have just come out of your flat, locked the door, and put the key in your pocket. You walk over to the elevator and ring. Casually, you look through your newspaper as you wait for the elevator to arrive. On a sound cue, the elevator arrives, the doors slide open and in the elevator you discover a completely unexpected person toward whom you have a strong, specific attitude of one sort or another.

[436]

(The actor decides background beforehand.) At that instant, you rush to the easel and immediately express that attitude in paints.

As in the similar exercise with the letter, the most delicate moment in the exercise is the one in which the actor confronts his stranger and moves to express his attitude. If one can organically link one with the other, the result is clear and communicative. If there is even a second's hesitation, the result is self-conscious, unnatural and merely illustrated. A later version of this exercise, which proved more successful, was for the actor to play out an improvisation with the Stranger in which the chosen attitude was actually manifest. Then to have an interim scene inside the flat, followed by the exercise situation. Otherwise the actor is working too exclusively from a mental frame of reference.

At first the paint results were sloppy and crude. On the third and fourth repeat, they were almost artistic, in that they were meaningful, impressionistic blotches which *did* suggest an internal state, interpretable by the other group members. The paint exercise was used directly in Artaud's *Spurt of Blood,* by author's direction in *The Screens,* and, in a more sophisticated version, in the *Marat/Sade.*[1]

Reforms

One must assume that Artaud's "fragile, fluctuating center that forms never reach" refers to states beyond the reach of *linguistic* forms, but accessible by other kinds. Otherwise it is soapy mysticism. The potential superiority of an Artaudian theatre—compared even to an overhauled and much-improved realistic theatre—lies in the fact that its language is not yet discovered, therefore not yet tarnished and empty. The danger is that a backlog of five centuries filled wth verbal debris may never enable us to hit bedrock. Or to put it even more pessimistically: the actor's social and psychological conditioning is both the main obstacle to be removed, and the one factor which is immovable. . . .

The *Marat/Sade* marked the dissolution of the Group, or rather its assimilation into the larger Company—the end for which it was intended. One of Peter Hall's aims had been to use the work of the Group as a kind of healthy antitoxin which, after being injected into the bloodstream of the mother company, would produce a greater robustness. Actually, the arithmetic was all against that, as there were seventeen in the Group and over a hundred in the Company. I expected the LAMDA work would simply disappear. As it turned out, it was the pivotal factor in The *Marat/Sade* rehearsals, and the key by which the overall company developed the style of the new production.

It was unfortunate that the LAMDA program was called Theatre of Cruelty and that serious work should have spawned yet another label for journalists to bandy in their columns. On reflection, I have asked myself: where, in all of this, was Artaud? It was never our intention to create an Artaudian theatre—to do what, in fact, Artaud himself never did. But there were too many provocative insights and tantalizing challenges in *The Theatre and Its Double* not to take him up. What was *Artaudian* in our work was the search for means, other than naturalistic-linguistic means, of communicating experience and insights. Also, our attitude to the classics—

---

[1] Although the progeny of the red and blue paint sequences in The *Marat/Sade* stemmed from a similar effect in Brook's production of *Titus Andronicus,* where Vivien Leigh used an unfurled red ribbon to symbolize the flow of blood.

not as peerless masterworks, but simply as *material* that could be reworked and rethought in very much the same way that Shakespeare reworked and rethought Kyd, Holinshed, Boccaccio and Marlowe. And what was characteristically Artaudian was the shared distaste and impatience the group's directors felt toward prevailing theatre trends; the well-upholstered, self-esteeming cul-de-sac in which the contemporary theatre found itself.

The quest for Artaud, if it's lucky, will not simply discover sounds, cries, groans and gestures, but new areas that never even occurred to Artaud. His value is that of the devastating skeptic whose very posture and tone of voice questions the validity of highly coveted achievements. How important is the accurate reproduction of the trivia in our lives? asks Artaud. How significant is the arbitary social thesis that so elaborates a partial insight that we are persuaded this is the whole story? How valuable, asks Artaud, is a theatre that elegantly, excitingly and wittily reiterates the clichés of our lives—compared to a theatre that suddenly opens up, like a mountain crevice, and sends down a lava that scours the lies, half-truths and embedded deceptions of our civilization? *Metaphysical* has become a pretentious word with highfalutin connotations, but if one defines it as a form of imagery through which we can rediscover the essential links between sky, rock, land, sea, gods and men—that is a lesson worth learning, and one the theatre is not yet able to teach. The cruelty that Artaud referred to (this is a truism worth repeating) did not refer exclusively to torture, blood, violence and plague, but to the cruelest of all practices: the exposure of mind, heart and nerve ends to the grueling truths behind a social reality that deals in psychological crises when it wants to be *honest,* and political evils when it wants to be *responsible,* but rarely if ever confronts the existential horror behind all social and psychological façades. This is where Artaud becomes practical and level-headed because he declares, if we want to have a theatre that isn't trivial or escapist, we have to find a new way of operating such a theatre, a new way of generating the actor into action, the playwright into meaning, and the public into consciousness. An exhortation couched in rhetoric isn't the same as a body of work and achievement, but at certain junctures in history—and I believe we're at one at this moment—it is the healthiest noise we can hear.

XI. ITALY

Stars and the *Commedia* Tradition

The histrionic tradition of the Italian people is a long and glorious one. In the annals of no other people is there a name to equal that of Roscius, who was lauded and honored by his Roman compatriots and who has become the very symbol of perfection in acting. Italy's *commedia dell' arte* remains the only theatre erected solely on the basis of the actor's art, unaided by the imagination and text of playwrights. Three Italian artists, Adelaide Ristori, Tommaso Salvini, and Eleonora Duse, born in one century, became the cynosure of international adulation.

The excellence of Italian acting has not been matched by a vigorous dramatic literature. Few Italian playwrights have won the world-wide reputation achieved by her actors. The neo-classical drama of the Italian Renaissance left no rich heritage except myths and tragic choruses which stimulated the growth of the one scenic art form in which the Italians excelled—opera.

Commedia dell' arte players left a richer heritage. The stock *commedia* figures and the improvisational technique stamped their imprint on Italian theatre. By the middle of the eighteenth century its unique inspiration had begun to wane, but before it disappeared completely the *commedia* had one last period of glory. Carlo Goldoni, the first great Italian playwright, started out as a writer of *commedia dell' arte* scenarii. The desire to create incisive realistic satire in the vein of Molière led this prolific writer to oppose the conventions of the *commedia dell' arte*. With the popular comic art as a base, he constructed literary plays that expressed his ideas rather than bare scripts to be enlivened by the ingenious masked *commedia* actors. Goldoni worked for various theatrical managers, frequently travelling with the companies that gave his numerous popular plays. To him the *commedia* masks seemed restrictive since their stylized quality prevented the individualized emotional expression he was seeking. In his memoirs he wrote: "The mask always interferes immeasurably with the actor's performance, whether he be interpreting joy or sorrow. Whether he be wooing, or ranting, or clowning, he always has the same 'leather' face. He may gesticulate and change his tone as often as he will, he can never communicate by the expression of his face the passions that rend his soul.... The masks of the Greeks and Romans were a kind of megaphone designed to carry the voice throughout the amphitheatre. In those times actors did not interpret the *nuances* of passion and sentiment that are in vogue at present; nowadays the actor is required to have 'soul,'... That is why I propose to reform the masks of the Italian comedy and replace farce by comedies." But the mask was not easily destroyed even in the popular plays of Goldoni. When the Pantalone Darbes tried to play one of Goldoni's comedies without a mask, the play failed miserably. Only when Goldoni supplied Darbes with plays in which he could appear masked was the success of both the actor and the writer assured.

Thus in Goldoni's hands the *commedia* took on literary form to become Italy's comic art, but in turn written comedy eventually sapped the vitality of the improvisational technique of the *commedia dell' arte*. Although "Papa" Goldoni's work,

ACTORS ON ACTING

which included *La Locandiéra* (*The Mistress of the Inn*), was of lasting importance, he was driven from his native Venice by the brief resurgence of *commedia dell' arte* brought about by the down-and-out aristocrat Count Carlo Gozzi. Gozzi's romantic fantasies written for the *commedia* temporarily eclipsed the realistic comedies of Goldoni. Gozzi's brother Gaspare became manager of the *Sant' Angelo* theatre which had produced *La Locandiéra*. Carlo himself worked with the Sacchi company, for which he wrote such fantasies as *Turandot* (revived in the famous production of Eugene Vakhtangov). Gozzi wrote of the Sacchi company: "Never again shall we see a Truffaldino like Sacchi, a Brighella like Zanoni or a Tartaglia like Fiorilli, this Neapolitan full of fire, and so justly famous throughout Italy. Nor shall we see again another Pantaloon as Darbes, this comedian self-contained or impetuous at will, majestic, stupid, and so true to life that the Venetian citizen thinks to see himself mirrored upon the stage when he beholds this perfect model of his absurdities.... With three words these people knew how to play a scene so as to make their audiences die of laughter.... Goldoni placed his trust in imposing and deceptive words; and words are omnipotent with spirits of narrow limitations;..." Despite his love of the traditional *commedia,* Gozzi himself contributed to its demise. His love for the inferior actress Teodora Ricci, whom the aging Sacchi also loved, led Gozzi to write mediocre pieces especially for her and also led to the dissolution of the troupe.

In the eighteenth century, Italy, lacking national unity, had no center for theatrical art. The tragic writer Marchese Francesco Scipione di Maffei tried, with the aid of Luigi Riccoboni, to establish an Italian National Theatre in Verona. Maffei's attempt failed as others did; although Italy had beautiful theatres built by the members of the celebrated Galli-Bibiena family and others, individual stars belonging to no company travelled from city to city with their performances.

The nineteenth century opened with Italy in bondage to Napoleon, deriving her art as well as her rulers from France. The years following the restoration of the Italian nobility in 1814 did not bring peace. Leaders like Cavour, Mazzini, and Garibaldi waged a struggle for freedom and national unity. During this conflict the theatre became a public place of entertainment for the whole populace, whereas in the preceding centuries, with the exception of the *commedia,* the drama belonged to the court and the aristocracy.

The mid-period of the century saw acting refined by the "Italian Kean," Gustavo Modena (1803-1863), a liberal patriot. He discarded the grotesquery of the old *commedia* technique and the stilted chanting and grand manner of classical tragedy in an attempt to establish natural, realistic acting that would yet have beauty and power. Among his reformations was the introduction of accurate period costuming. Dressed as a Hebrew shepherd he played the title role in *Saul,* by the fine eighteenth century dramatist Count Alfieri.

Modena's intuitive desire for greater realism in playing was part of the general international surge towards drama and acting that would reflect real life. While the Italian theatre was still on the whole characterized by stars, touring with a classical repertory, the French, for example, were developing ensemble playing for the realistic dramas of Dumas *fils* and Emile Augier. It was the French company of Meynardier, playing in Italy the dramas of these two writers, that introduced the new realistic style to the Italians. Louis Belloti Bon (1819-1883), an Italian, organized a troupe which copied the innovations of the French. For the virtuosity of the star, Belloti Bon substituted the well-trained corps of actors.

[440]

Adelaide Ristori, the celebrated tragedienne, was trained in the old traditions of the Italian stage. By the time she was fifteen she was appearing in the leading roles of Shakespeare, Schiller, and Hugo. *Figlio d'arte,* child of actors, like most of the other great Italian players, Ristori inherited the passionate, fiery acting of her people, but she tempered the grand manner with realistic touches borrowed from the new French school. Ristori, like Modena, tried to combine truth to life with a certain classical elevation. Henry James, describing her performance of Mary Stuart during her U. S. tour in 1875, wrote: "...The last act is rendered as no one but Madame Ristori could render it. The expression of dignity reaches a great height. No one but Madame Ristori could manage the farewell to her weeping servants, could gather the group about her, and handle it, as one may say, with that picturesque majesty. It is realism, especially in the closing moments, of a downright pattern; but it is realism harmonized by a great artistic instinct."

Ristori's intelligence and her serious belief in the importance of the actor as an artist made her the most honored actress of the Italian stage. When she went to Paris in 1855 and swept even the great Rachel before her triumphant acting, her fame, as the dramatist Roberto Bracco says, became part of Italian national pride.

Ristori's contemporary, Tommaso Salvini, shared many of her noble qualities. He began as a harlequin in a play by Goldoni, but under his friend and teacher Gustavo Modena, he became a great tragedian. Soldier of liberty himself, he acted in the plays of Giovanni Battista Niccolini, who opposed foreign tyranny, and created the role of Corrado, the escaped convict in Paolo Giacometti's drama about prison reform, *La Morta civile.* In 1844 Salvini saw Ristori on the stage and was stimulated by her intelligent, beautiful manner. An actor of tremendous power, Salvini was excellent as King Lear, as Hamlet, and at his best as Othello, a role he played on his many tours.

Another of Modena's pupils was the third of this great early triumvirate. Ernesto Rossi, actor and playwright, played as leading man with La Ristori. Like the French Talma, to whom he has been likened, Rossi presaged the school of realistic acting. Without the overwhelming genius of Ristori or Salvini, Rossi was an influential figure through his pupil, the actor-manager Cesare Rossi (1829-1898). The latter played in Ernesto Rossi's company and also in Louis Belloti Bon's realistic troupe. Cesare Rossi was an excellent teacher, and it was in his company that the greatest of all modern actresses made her official debut.

Eleonora Duse was fourteen when she played Juliet in Verona. The playing of the young girl was sensational. As the actress matured into a sad, expressive, beautiful woman, she revealed an artistry that has been spoken of only in superlatives. The only actress of her era to abandon completely traditional artifice and declamation, she became the ideal interpreter of the modern drama of Dumas *fils,* Sudermann, Ibsen, and D'Annunzio. Without the intensity of Duse, who loved him, D'Annunzio's morbid but passionate plays would probably not have captured the imagination of audiences. She performed his dramas with the belief that she was aiding the cause of poetic beauty and native theatre.

Duse played in Paris against the dazzling Sarah Bernhardt as Ristori had played against Rachel. Comparisons of these two great actresses are an exciting part of theatre lore. To the "supreme feast" offered by Bernhardt was contrasted the soul of Duse. Stark Young wrote of her: "I should not say that she was the greatest actor that I have seen, but that she seemed of them all the greatest artist ... it must be said that she was one of those artists, appearing from time to time in every art, who tend to break down the long and painfully built structure of the art they profess. To them their mere craft is only a clutter of old boards, rags, a necessary but obstructing shell. Their passion is truth, an immediate and urging truth in them. These artists by their labor and gifts master the domain of the art with a security and completeness that few artists professing it can ever hope to approach. But whatever craft one of these artists masters he smashes, restates, forces to vanish, scorns save only as a means to an end. Duse could never be a school or a craft, her method was herself.... She had no tricks, no efforts to attract or pique or impress, but only the desire to exist in the life to which she had given herself for those two hours on the stage, only the desire to convey to us and to confirm for herself the infinity of living within the woman she portrayed there. This detachment and intense absorption with the truth she endured and expressed gave Duse's art its extraordinary purity, free of all exterior considerations and effects."[1]

Stark Young's observations on Duse like those of George Bernard Shaw reveal the impossibility of defining Duse's technique and also perhaps account for her inability to speak of her art. She created out of the depths of her own personal genius as perhaps no other actor has. Even the traditional weakness of Italian actors, their reluctance to hold to the text and to set a role and repeat it without endless variations, became a virtue in Duse who, in the words of Silvio D'Amico, "relived the part evening after evening, always with new and surprising variations, but always with the same essential line."

Duse's leading man in many of her performances was Ermete Zacconi, who with her was the outstanding Italian player of modern drama. A student of Cesare Rossi, he was especially successful as Oswald in Ibsen's *Ghosts,* as Nikita in Tolstoy's *The Power of Darkness,* as well as in leading roles of Hauptmann, de Curel, and the native dramatists Bracco, Rovetta, and D'Annunzio. It has been said that "he is the pathologist and clinical student of modern dramaturgy." His acting embodied the Italian verist (naturalistic) ideals. At the age of eighty Zacconi still performed in King Lear and Othello.

Ermete Novelli, the character actor, played with Belloti Bon. He and Zacconi were the greatest male actors of their day. Novelli was exceedingly versatile, playing comedy, tragedy, and farcical monologues which he himself composed. While Zacconi excelled in modern repertory, Novelli played classical repertory—Molière, Goldoni, and Shakespeare. Silvio D'Amico describes Novelli directing his company in a rehearsal of Oscar Wilde's *Salome,* cutting all the typical verbal flashes of Wilde, yet able in a moment without the aid of words to create the figure of Herod. Novelli, an admirer of the *Comédie Française,* tried to establish an Italian national theatre, which he called *La Casa di Goldoni.* He opened his theatre in 1900, but like earlier attempts, the project failed.

To these internationally famous idols must be added the names of significant but less well-known Italian actors: Giovanni Emanuel, portrayer of Lear, Hamlet, and Othello; Giovanni Grasso, the realistic actor of fierce, brutal, passionate Sicilian life; Angelo Musco, the Sicilian mime; Raffaele Viviani, the Neapolitan comedian; Ruggero Ruggeri, interpreter of D'Annunzio and Pirandello; Flavio Ando and Tina di Lorenzo, who together played the realistic dramas of Roberto Bracco; Irma Gramatica, considered the successor of Duse; Emma Gramatica, her sister, excellent in Anglo-Saxon characters; Ettore Petrolini, heir of the *commedia dell' arte.*

With the beginning of the twentieth century came several attempts to establish

---

[1]Stark Young: *Theatre Practice,* 1926. By permission of Charles Scribner's Sons.

permanent theatrical centers in Italy, but the ancient chaotic system of touring companies persisted. Actor-managers competed against each other with their starring roles and their shabby sets. It was in the little theatres of Italy, as elsewhere, that some of the important theatrical experiments were made. The note sounded by the expressionists throughout Europe was echoed by the futurist Marinetti, who advocated "simultaneity," "illogicality," and "unreality." The Futurists said: "We have a profound disgust for the contemporary theatre (verse, prose, and music) because it wavers stupidly between historic reconstruction (a pastiche or a plagiarism) and photographic reproductions of our daily life." The performances of futurist plays were first-night sensations, but had little lasting influence.

The greatest dramatist of modern Italy, Luigi Pirandello, managed a company with the actress Marta Abba, seen here in *Tovarich*. In 1925 he organized a short-lived theatre in Rome where he introduced foreign authors like Evreinov and Lord Dunsany. It was his hope to establish a permanent theatre and to banish improvisation from regular drama, but his actors deserted him for the traditional touring to which they were accustomed.

Although under Fascism, Italian theatre was organized to provide some spectacular entertainments, everything was subordinated to political propaganda. During World War II and in the liberalized postwar years drama and theatre took on new life with the playwrights Ugo Betti and Eduardo De Filippo, and the new directors Luchino Visconti, Giorgio Strehler of the *Piccolo Teatro* of Milan, Luigi Squarzina of the *Teatro Stabile* of Genoa and the internationally known designer-director, Franco Zeffirelli.

Each of ten major cities is supposed to have its *teatro stabile,* a permanent company with state subsidy, and there are as well several *semistabile,* groups with no permanent home but a regular personnel, the one run by Anna Proclemer and Giorgio Albertazzi, and another in which Giorgi de Lullo, Rossella Falk, Romolo Valli and Elsa Albani work. Whatever their home base, most actors tour widely with the result that except for the few leading companies with a fine director or a local master like Eduardo De Filippo, there is little significant theatre and little theatre training. There are stars like Anna Magnani, Alberto Sordi and Vittorio Gassman, who work on the stage and in the vigorous film industry. But Italian theatre artists lament the absence of a national theatre, the result of regional tongues and regional dramatic traditions. Without a national focus and language, many feel that the lively theatricality of the Italian will continue to remain more forcibly expressed in the streets than on the stage.

ADELAIDE RISTORI

(1822-1906)

Adelaide Ristori, the "Italian Siddons," was born in Venice and like so many children whose parents were actors, she appeared on the stage in infant roles. At thirteen Ristori was already playing "second ladies"; three years later she was offered the opportunity to be leading lady in the Moncalvo Company. The possibility of a short-lived fame as a prodigy was rejected in favor of a post as *ingénue* in the company of the King of Sardinia. For eighteen years Ristori developed her craft in this group, enhancing the talent revealed in her youth. Ristori determined, she tells us in her *Memoirs,* to combine the naturalness of the new French school of acting with the fire and intensity of the Italian tradition.

In 1855 Ristori and her husband the Marquis del Grillo took the Royal Sardinian Company to Paris. Her success there challenged the supremacy of Rachel, and some viewed Rachel's departure for America as a retreat before the triumphs of Ristori. In the spring of 1856, she was offered Legouvé's *Medea*. This was a role which Rachel had refused to accept, and Ristori, too, was at first repelled at the thought of playing a mother who kills her own children. But *Medea* eventually became one of her greatest roles. Ristori excelled in the characterization of noble, tragic women such as Mary Stuart in Schiller's play, Marie Antoinette and Elizabeth of England in plays written by Giacometti.

During her second London engagement in 1857 Ristori appeared in an Italian translation of *Macbeth*. Hers was a basically unscrupulous Lady Macbeth, characterized by ambition to share the throne with Macbeth. Her interpretation of this role is recalled by witnesses as "one of the great pictures of the contemporary stage." Twenty-five years later, following a 'round-the-world tour, the indefatigable Ristori returned to London to play the role in English, which she had learned especially for that performance. During her final American engagement in 1885, Ristori played Lady Macbeth to the Macbeth of Edwin Booth. She also appeared as Mary Stuart, acting in English, with the German company of the Thalia Theatre in New York. This linguistic feat matches the polyglot performances of Tommaso Salvini who used to act in Italian while his American fellow-players replied to him in English.

Throughout Ristori's career there are evidences of the careful study, observation, and thought which she put into every role. In her early years with the Royal Sardinian Company she visited asylums to note the effects of madness; when she went to Athens she stood before the Caryatides so that she might study the folds of Grecian drapery. Observation of the world about her and careful examination of the inner motivation of each character made Ristori a great forerunner of the realists in the theatre.

My Study of Lady Macbeth

The study of this character was for me the source of great difficulties, seeing before me not the ordinary person, filled with perverted passions and frivolous excesses, but a colossal conception of perfidy, of dissimulation, of hypocrisy, which is treated with a masterly grandeur by Shakespeare with so many hyperbolical manifestations as to frighten any dramatic genius.

Some of the critics, going back to the origin of the legend from which Shakespeare gained his inspiration, form the opinion that love for her husband was predominant in Lady Macbeth, and so strong as to induce her to become guilty of many crimes for the sake of seeing him reign.

With me, the close investigation of this character, produced the conviction that with Lady Macbeth affection for her husband was the last factor actuating her deeds —that she was animated only by her excessive ambition to reign with him, and that, knowing his inferiority of mind, his weak nature, which was not able even to move the greed for possession which burned in his veins and in his brain to action —she used her affection for him as a means to satisfy her ambition. Being con-

Memoirs and Artistic Studies of Adelaide Ristori, rendered into English by G. Mantellini. New York: Doubleday, Page and Company, 1907, pp. 161-174. Copyright 1907. By permission of Doubleday & Co., Inc.

scious of the fascination that she exercised over him, she took advantage of it for the purpose of instilling into his mind the virus of crime, putting it in the most natural light and with the most insinuating and persuasive reasonings.

By this I do not mean to say that Macbeth did not possess a nature inclined to do evil. Shakespeare shows us the germ of ambition that was gnawing him, and the kind of chimerical illusions that ran through his mind. He only concealed them from others because it seemed to him impossible to make them realities. I could not better succeed in depicting the nature of this man, than Shakespeare so marvellously does in the lines of the first monologue of Lady Macbeth who, owing to her profound perspicacity, so well understands her husband. This appreciation of mine will appear even more evident in the analysis I make further on of that passage. Perhaps one might admit a similar monstrous tenderness in Lady Macbeth if she had not shared together with her husband the power and the royal greatness; but as they derived from their crime all its advantages, I maintain that it was not solely owing to her ambition and love for her husband that she became its instigator, but also for the sake of obtaining the supreme honors and powers which she so much longed for. Any mother, any woman who pretends to know how great is the love for a son who has been nursed with her own milk, and is able to declare to her husband, without tremor, that if she had sworn to crush the skull of her own child she would not have hesitated a moment (and this to make Macbeth feel ashamed of his pusillanimity in flinching before the only means suitable to his guilty purpose), is not a woman, not a human being, but a creature worse than a wild beast, and as such, it cannot be admitted that there existed in her any sweet affection. Nevertheless, not wishing to proclaim my conception as an infallible one, I made new studies and new investigations of the various judgments of this tragedy and the interpretations that some of the most renowned actors had adopted.

Great was my satisfaction on reading in the magazine *The Nineteenth Century,* of February, 1878, the magnificent study made by Mr. G. J. Bell, Professor of Laws, in the Edinburgh University, of the interpretation which the renowned English actress, Mrs. Siddons, gave to the part of Lady Macbeth. Among the various passages this one is, according to my opinion, most important: "Her troublesome and inhuman nature does everything. She draws Macbeth to gratify her purpose, she uses him as a simple instrument, becoming herself his guide, his leader, insinuating to him all the plot. As the wicked genius of Macbeth, she rushes him along the crazy path of ambition and cruelty, from which he would have liked to withdraw."

Hoping that I have plainly shown, with substantial arguments, that my interpretation of the character of Lady Macbeth, was as Shakespeare had intended and indicated it to be by his own words and the nature of the action, I shall proceed with the analysis of other important points of this difficult part.

Various are the opinions referring to the interpretation of the reading of the message, which Macbeth sends from the field of battle to his wife, and which Shakespeare makes her hold in her hands at her first appearance upon the stage. There are some who maintain that a message coming to her from her husband at such a moment should fill her with so great a desire to know its contents that it would not appear natural for her to wait until she comes before the audience to read it, and hence she should have taken knowledge of it before.

I will say instead, that it was not very natural either that Shakespeare, that great poet, that great philosopher and reader of human nature, should have employed the frivolous expedient of having Lady Macbeth read the letter on the stage with the sole object of making the audience acquainted with its contents, exposing himself to such an obvious criticism. Only an inexperienced and insignificant writer, dull of mind and imagination, would have had recourse to such an expedient, not the great poet of the fervid imagination, who passes from the beautiful to the sublime with the greatest facility.

It must certainly have been purposely devised by the author in order that it should appear that Lady Macbeth has received the message a little before the moment she comes on the stage and her manner is both easy and natural. When she begins to look anxious and agitated, she makes the spectators understand that owing to his message—whose contents she partly knows—some great events are revealed which will change all her existence, and carry her to a supreme height, and all the circumstances of the play indicate the culmination of the projects which are brewing in her mind. Another proof that Lady Macbeth on presenting herself before the audience, has already commenced the reading of the message, is shown by the first verse which she reads:

"They met me in the day of success."

Can this be the beginning of an important message? Macbeth must already have given her the account of the battle, of the victory and of the existence of the witch sisters.

I have resolved to read that missive straight down as if I had already read the first words of it while I was entering the stage, only stopping at the places where the strange knowledge of what has happened is in accord with what the regulating destiny of all the events had long before led her to foresee.

For instance my expression would portray a superstitious wonder on reading that the fatal sisters "made themselves air, into which they vanished," after the prophecy they had cast at him, addressing him: "Hail, king that shalt be!"

Having ended the reading I make a long pause, as if analyzing the fatal content of that missive, which was in accordance with what I had anticipated. Then, for a moment I remain sadly steeped in thought, gloomy, considering and fearing on account of the weak nature of my husband; then reflecting on the most striking passages of the missive, I say:

"Glamis thou art, and Cawdor, and shalt be
What thou art promised."

And to that "shalt be" I would give a supernatural force of expression.

Later on, I was happy to read in the interesting essay of Prof. Bell that Mrs. Siddons, also, with a prophetic and exalted tone, as if all the mysteries of the future were present to her soul, in the lines: "Glamis thou art and Cawdor, and shalt be what thou art promised," accentuated emphatically "shalt be."

This is another convincing proof that Mrs. Siddons also understood the importance of analyzing the missive, of weighing every sentence, in order to transmit to the public the mystic meaning. With her eager ambition, the expression would naturally have been different if Lady Macbeth had had the whole knowledge of the missive....

The frightful soliloquy in the scene which follows the departure of the messenger, reveals all the diabolical perfidy and cruelty of this monster in human likeness, and this inhuman power with which she is armed in order to succeed in leading her husband to become the instrument of her ambition. In a word, she becomes the Satanic spirit of the body of Macbeth. He has a hard struggle between the "wishing and not wishing"; that woman, that serpent, becomes absolute mistress of this man, entwines him in her grasp, and no human power can ever tear him from it. Consequently, the first words of this monologue I pronounced in a cavernous voice, with my eyes bloodshot, with the accent of a spirit which comes from the abyss, and I ended it with a *crescendo* of thundering voice, which changed into an exaggerated expression of joy on beholding my husband enter.

During this first scene with Macbeth I show a cold, reserved and patient demureness, not minding at all the weak denials of my husband in his endeavor not to listen to my criminal insinuations. I make it apparent that he will have to yield to my influence. I therefore imagined a counter-scene at the exit of the *personae,* in order to portray the powerful fascination that this woman exercised upon her husband. I fancy that Macbeth wished to interrogate me again and ask of me further explanations. For the purpose of preventing him, I had the thought of inducing him to pass his left arm around my waist. In that attitude I take his right hand and placing his index finger upon my lips I charge him to be silent, in the meanwhile I am slowly pushing him behind the wings, his back turned to them. All this was executed with a mingling of sentiments and magnetizing glances, which fascinations Macbeth could not very well resist.

The hypocrisy, the false humility of Lady Macbeth must be excessive when she goes to meet King Duncan, and with the most perfidious, simulated sweetness invites the old man to enter the castle.

In the following scene between Lady Macbeth and her husband, it is necessary to delineate clearly and strongly two things: First, her energetic reproof of Macbeth for his pusillanimity in not wanting to do at that moment what he had wished a little before—a sudden change of mind caused by his vacillating conscience; second, in contrast with this energy, the fiendish persuasive art that she brings into play in order to render simple and natural the plan of the proposed crime and the impossibility of its detection....

I jump straight to the second act, there being only some clear situations furthering the procedure of the action which do not offer any difficulty in their interpretation, though they embrace the tremendous impressions which, later on, torment the waking hours and cause the agony of Lady Macbeth. All will easily understand the anxiety that she experienced to discover the result of the attempt against Duncan's life, which she had so well planned; the joy of knowing that it was done, the agitation arising from terror which dominated her, the fear and the exaggerated remorse of her husband. The fright she experiences when she hears knocking at the door of the castle with so much insistence, is not caused by a cowardly fear that the crime may soon be discovered, but by the state of prostration of Macbeth which may betray everything.

In the third act there are situations worthy of special comment, which I am going to analyze in detail showing that I have studied to produce them as they were outlined by the author.

It is in this act that one can plainly see the skill of Shakespeare. Lady Macbeth must—not only with words but with her "stage business"—either diminish or enlarge a great many of the striking episodes of the drama. Such considerations led me to make a logical analytical study of this part. For instance, I did not allow to pass unobserved the entrance of the hired assassin, who comes in to announce to Macbeth the accomplishment of the murder of Banquo, and the failure of the attempt against Fleance's life. This news, which causes two very different forms of emotion, should not escape a watching eye like that of Lady Macbeth. And then again, at the sight of the hired murderer who presents himself in the banquet hall, she must be the only person to see that man speaking in a whisper to her husband, and to notice his excited gestures, never losing sight of him for a moment. She fears some imprudence on his part, remembering that Macbeth has told her shortly before "that a great deed would be accomplished to cause her to wonder."

I have taken into consideration that during this scene Lady Macbeth must show her fear, lest the guests may notice this strange conversation between Macbeth and the murderer, in that place and at that moment, and suspect some wrong-doing against themselves. I found it, therefore, necessary to play a double part, a dramatic one with Macbeth and a graceful one with my guests. While taking part in the conversation and the toasts that the guests are making who remain seated upon their stools, I cast at intervals fearful and investigating glances toward my husband and the hired murderer....

I would show great agitation and great fright at the incomprehensible and furious visions of Macbeth, seeing that he is on the verge of revealing the secret of our guilt. Though the reproach is a bitter one, Lady Macbeth, by speaking to her guests, should keep up her pretended gaiety with her facial expression, and apologize for the eccentricities of her husband by attributing them to an old infirmity of his.

In the end, finding that all her efforts at repressing the strange horrors of Macbeth have proved vain, the noble lady sees herself forced to take leave of the guests in an excited manner, in order to be alone with Macbeth and put an end to a situation which becomes dangerous.

After the guests' departure, I thought it best to begin to indicate the state of prostration of Lady Macbeth by imagining a counter-scene showing distress and failing power, making manifest my painful conviction that it is useless to struggle against the adverse destiny which has suddenly risen before me. I show how remorse begins to torment me, and in showing the beginning of those terrible sufferings I found it necessary for its justification to render realistic the impending end of that great criminal.

At the end of the act, at the moment of leaving, I make it apparent that I am penetrated with a deep sense of pity for Macbeth who for my sake has become the most miserable of men, and tell him:

"You lack the season of all natures, sleep."

I take hold of his left hand with my right and place it over my right shoulder, then painfully bending my head in deep reflection and turning toward my husband with a look filled with remorse which is agitating my mind, I drag him toward our chamber in the same manner that one leads an insane person. When reaching the limit of the stage Macbeth, frightened by the tail of his cloak lining trailing at my feet, again shudders suddenly. Then, with a quick turn, I pass on the other side of him, and try to master the terror with which I am also seized in spite of myself. Using a little violence I succeed in pushing him behind the wings, while quieting him with affectionate gestures.

This mode of acting was not contradictory to the logic and reality of the situation, and always produced a great effect.

In the fifth act Lady Macbeth appears only in a scene of short duration, but which is the most marvellous one among all the philosophical conceptions of the author, and it offers to the actress a very difficult study of interpretation.

This woman, this colossus of both physical and moral force, who with one single word had the faculty of imagining and causing the execution of deeds of hellish character—there she is, now reduced to her own shadow which, like the bony carcass left bare by a vulture, is eaten up by the remorse preying on her mind. In her trouble she becomes so thoroughly unconscious of herself as to reveal in her sleep her tremendous, wicked secret. But what do I say "in her sleep?" It is like a fever which, rising to her brain, softens it. The physical suffering taking hold of her mind with the recollection of the evil of which she has been the cause masters and regulates all her actions, causing her, spasmodically, to give different directions to her thoughts....

The true rendering of this artificial and double manifestation and fusing of these effects without falling either into exaggeration or into the fantastic at every change of countenance, of gesture, of voice, all demanded from me a most exhaustive study. I enter the stage with the looks of an automaton, dragging my feet as if they wore leaden shoes. I mechanically place my lamp upon the table, taking care that all my movements are slow and intercepted by my chilled nerves. With a fixed eye which looks but does not see, my eyelids wide open, a difficult mode of breathing, I constantly show the nervous agitation produced by the derangement of my brain. It was necessary to clearly express that Lady Macbeth was a woman in the grasp of a moral disease whose effects and whose manifestations were moved by a terrible cause.

Having placed the lamp upon the table, I advance as far as the footlights, pretending to see on my hands still some spots of blood, and while rubbing them I make the motion of one who takes in the palms of his hands a certain quantity of water in order to wash them. I am very careful with this motion, which I repeat at various moments. After that I say:

"Yet here's a spot. Out damned spot! out, I say!"

Then listening, I say softly:

"One: two: why, then 'tis time to do't."

Then, as if answering:

"Hell is murky!—Fie, my Lord, fie! a soldier, and afraid? What need you fear? Who knows it, when none can call our power to account."

And at this place, returning to the cause of my delirium:

"Yet who would have thought the old man to have had so much blood in him?"

And I show here that I am struck by the color of blood in which it seems to me as if I had dipped my hands. Returning to my manifestation of delirium, I add:

"The Thane of Fife had a wife: where is she now?"

And looking again at my hands with an expression between rage and sadness:

"What, will these hands ne'er be clean?"

With a convulsive motion I rub them again. Then, always a prey to my delirium, in a bitter tone, and speaking excitedly, I pretend to whisper in Macbeth's ear:

> "No more o' that my lord, no more o' that; you mar all with
> this starting."

Then coming back to my first idea, I smell my hands, pretending they smell of blood, and I break forth with passion:

> "Here's the smell of the blood still: all the perfumes of Arabia
> will not sweeten this little hand. Oh! oh! oh!"

And I make these exclamations as if an internal shudder convulsed my heart and caused me to breathe with difficulty, after which I remain with my head thrown back, breathing slowly, as if in a deep lethargy.

During the short dialogue between the gentlewoman and the doctor, I pretend in my delirium to be taken to the scene of the murder of Duncan, and, as if the object of my regard were the chamber of the king, bending my body, advancing slowly and mysteriously toward my right side where I imagine the murder has taken place, I pretend that I hear the quick step of my husband and anxiously inclining my ear in the posture of one who waits I express how Macbeth is coming to confirm to me the accomplishment of the deed. Then, with an outburst of joy, as if I saw him appear and announce the deed, feeling very much agitated, I say:

> "Wash your hands, put on your nightgown; look not so pale.
> I tell you yet again, Banquo's buried; he cannot come out
> on's grave."

I took much care never to forget that the woman who spoke was in troubled sleep; and during this scene, between one thought and another, I would emit a long, deep and painful sigh.

The following verses:

> "To bed, to bed! there's knocking at the gate:
> Come, come, come, come, give me your hand.
> What's done cannot be undone. To bed, to bed, to bed!"

I speak these words in an insistent tone, as if it were a thing that should be done quickly; then, frightened, fancying that they knock at the door of the castle and come to surprise us, I show great emotion, a greater fear, as if I found it necessary to hide ourselves quickly in our own rooms. I start in that direction, inviting Macbeth to follow me, saying in a very imperative and furious tone: "Come, come, come!..." Then, simulating the act of grasping his hand, I show that I am dragging him with great pain, and disappear from the sight of the audience, saying in a suffocating voice: "To bed, to bed, to bed!..."

With this ends the "compendium" of the manifestations and of the strange sentiment of this character which seems as though it could not have been conceived by a human mind, and the study of which has proved so difficult to me, owing to the singularity of situations which I saw myself induced to portray according to the imagination of the poet.

Though I flatter myself that I entered into the spirit of this character in the best way I could, I trust this analysis of mine—this interpretation of the part of Lady Macbeth—to the appreciation of the critic. From what I have stated it must be clearly evident what an amount of strenuous study, and how much mental labor such an interpretation cost me.

ERNESTO ROSSI

(1829-1896)

Rossi, sometimes known as the "Italian Talma," was both actor and playwright. Born in Leghorn, he was sent by his father to the College of San Sebastian, but the moody young man left school to go on the stage. In 1846 while acting with a group of strolling players, he attracted the attention of Gustavo Modena, and eventually Rossi became Modena's favorite pupil.

In 1852 he joined the Royal Sardinian Company which was headed by Ristori, whom he accompanied to Paris in 1855. By 1857 he was in Vienna with his own troupe. In the following years Rossi mastered the major Shakespearean roles, Hamlet, Othello, Macbeth, Romeo, Shylock, Lear, Richard III, and Coriolanus. He played his Shakespearean repertory throughout Europe and on foreign tours which brought him to America. Finally in 1876 he presented his roles in London, capturing the English audiences with his interpretations. His performances in Russia during 1877-78 created a "Rossi furor." No less an observer than Konstantin Stanislavsky has left the following account of Rossi in one of his best roles, Romeo: "In lyric passages, in love scenes, in poetic descriptions, Rossi was inimitable. He had the right to talk simply, and knew how to do it. This is very rare among actors. He had a fine voice, a wonderful ability to handle it, an unusually clear diction, a correctness of intonation, a plasticity that had reached such perfection that it became second nature with him. And his own nature was created mostly for lyric emotions and experiences."

Among the many anecdotes of extravagant honors heaped upon Rossi by royal houses is the following tribute. The King of Holland after hearing him recite Dante pointed to his throne and said: "Take it, it is yours. I am only the monarch of a small kingdom, but you are the Emperor of all hearts." A Paris correspondent wrote of his Lear: "In the last scene, when he sobs out his life over the corpse of his favorite child, the tears of many present, although the actor was speaking in a language unknown to most of them, came fast and plentiful, and it was almost a relief to the pent up feeling of pain when the old king dropped lifeless into the arms of his attendant and the curtain fell. His death was thrillingly natural, and indeed the whole performance may be considered perfect in this respect, and utterly devoid of exaggeration." The American actress Charlotte Cushman admired his Hamlet, which was said to be the best non-Anglo-Saxon interpretation of the role.

Rossi directed the Fonda Theatre at Naples, and the theatre at Prato was named after him. The following comments are drawn from the actor's memoirs which were published in Russia, revealing again the extent of his influence there.

The Art of Interpretation

I would like to express my views on the artist and the actor. In my opinion, the difference between the qualities of the artist and the actor are very important.

---

50 *let artisticheskoi deiatel'nosti Ernesto Rossi* (50 Years of the Artistic Activity of Ernesto Rossi). Compiled from the memoirs of E. Rossi, by S. I. Lavrenteva. St. Petersburg: A. M. Lesman, 1896, pp. 1–7 *passim*. This selection translated by Bernard L. Koten.

For me, an artist is one who incorporates with his natural wealth—a dignified, beautiful appearance, a fine accent, clear pronunciation—a wide intellectual education, the study of history, the perfection of his own language, a close acquaintance with literature, primarily the dramatic, an ear trained to the melodic harmony of verse and a developed esthetic taste. That sense which the philosophers have called the sixth, should be inherent in everyone: in classicists as well as in romanticists, in tragedians as well as in comedians.

But, more than any other, I call an artist one who is in full possession of that most indispensable quality, namely, the talent to enter bodily, physically and morally, into the image of the character he is portraying on the stage, mastering his thoughts, his feelings, his passions, his defects, his virtues, and making the transfiguration so complete as to make it fully live, in just the way the author thought to present it.

The artist must forget his own personality as completely as the author must forget his. It is in this way that the fullest possible illusion in the portrayal of a character is achieved. And it is only in this way that he can reach the heights of art and truth, be the interpreter of a given production, merit the name of artist.

But whoever possesses all of the above mentioned talents, with the exception of the ability to transform his personality (a talent in my opinion, not to be acquired through study, if it is not a specific gift of nature), cannot merit the name artist. He may be a fine, conscientious, pleasing actor with a resonant voice, clear pronunciation and varied gestures. He can be handsome and may wear rich costumes with dignity, play his parts with feeling and zeal, if the role be a dramatic one, and with witty animation, if he be a comedian, and not only earn the approval of an audience, but captivate it as well. But this fascination will be of a moment's duration, only for the brief time of the performance, while the performer and his endowments are before the eyes of the audience. He will never consolidate his title of interpreter of an author's works. He will remain only an actor.

By virtue of transforming his own personality, an artist becomes the indispensable interpreter of a work, rising to the level of a spiritual dissector. Probing man's heart in all its most minute manifestations, carefully studying all the phases of the development of his intellect, the artist becomes a real partner of the poet.

He possesses the secret of unmasking imitations of characters which are not formed freely from the passions of the personality itself, but are slaves of the ideas, principles and feelings born in the intellect of the poet.

The elegant adornments of harmonious verse, of beautiful ideas, an attractive facade—all of this is not enough. The result will be a piece of work made of good material; but yet a building which does not have a solid foundation.

I admit that theses are always dangerous, and that science narrows the boundaries of limitless nature to too great an extent on the stage. Inspiration should be sovereign there, in an unbroken tie with art, since the one cannot be divided from the other under any condition.

Everyone knows that the poet lives in his works. But he lives too in those characters who appear to proclaim loudly what the poet has whispered into their ears. To merely express the poet's will through movements and actions, is like the maneuvering of little wooden soldiers and turns the theatre, which should be a true mirror reflecting human passions,—into a marionette show-booth.

How can an artist be an unprejudiced critic of a dramatic work at the same time that he himself has an interest in it? He is certain to be generous or severe in his criticism, depending on his sympathy with the author or his own personal interests.

The mediocre actor only runs through a role trying to find places in it in which he may be able to produce an effect. Such an actor concerns himself only with details without first delving into the substance of the entire work. He does not seek the point of origin of the action, which little by little develops into heterogeneous scenes and gives the characters that vitality, that completely natural and gradual development that leads to the denouement. It is by virtue of this superficial analysis and careless study that those sad and strange spectacles take place on our stage, when an excellent but poorly rehearsed artistic producton fails, while a mediocre play artificially inflated is praised to the skies.

Like the sculptor, the author hews out his statue to his own image. Like the musician, it is in his own soul that he seeks for tender notes and harmonious sounds. The sculptor, the musician, the poet—all of them have their statue, their music, their poem before their eyes: they see their growth, closely observe their perfections and shortcomings; they correct some, satisfy themselves on others and having carried their production to completion, present them to the public for judgment. But where will the dramatic artist find the mirror that can reflect his shortcomings and virtues? His one mirror, his one corrector, his true censor—is his intellect and his art.

The drawing, the coloring, the plastic art, the harmony of sounds and feelings are joined in his mind; the statue, the picture, the action—all of these are manifested in his talent and in his art. The work appears in its entirety before an audience. But the curtain has fallen, the statue is broken, the picture has grown dim, the action has frozen and everything is once again locked in the mind of the actor, constrained again to incarnate itself and present itself on the morrow. And will he always be as lucky and successful in the reproduction of his portrayals? If the artist is such as he should be, he will have no doubts. He may, for physical reasons, sometimes be weaker in his portrayal; but we will never retreat from the original ideal, because this ideal has been incarnated in his mind and in his art. The true actor cannot call anything to his aid but his own mind and his art. Once convinced of what he is doing, he will always repeat it.

Studying his hero, he must renounce himself completely. He must set the character up before himself, as a separate personality, and attentively, with his mind's eye, study, so to speak, dissect him through and through, so as to acquaint himself with the virtues and the shortcomings inherent in him, and with those traits which have elevated him or have caused his final destruction. Could the artist who has taken it upon himself to portray a hero out of pagan times, or of the days of Judaism, or of ancient Christianity, (who does not conceive himself a mannequin talking from the stage), appear as a live person of flesh and blood, if he did not transform himself into this person through a profound study of classic forms and characters dealt with by the poet? We have seen artists who have fully attained such results. Talma in *Le Cid*, Rachel in *Phèdre*, Ristori in *Mirra*, Modena in *Saul*, Salvini in *Merope*. These can serve as prime examples in their intellect and in their art.

TOMMASO SALVINI

(1829-1915)

A native of Milan, Salvini was the son of actors. As a boy of fourteen he appeared as Pasquino in Goldoni's *Donne Curiose*. Later he studied with Gustavo Modena and by 1847, he was an important member of Ristori's company, playing the title role in Alfieri's *Oreste* at the Teatro Valle in Rome. In 1849 the tragedian became a soldier in the fight for Italian independence.

Salvini's career was an unbroken series of triumphs. He acted frequently in England, and made five visits to America. In 1866, on his fourth tour, he played Othello to the Iago of Edwin Booth. Salvini retired from the stage in 1890, but in Rome, January, 1902, he took part in the theatrical celebration of Ristori's eightieth birthday.

As an actor Salvini tempered the grand style with intelligence, but his outstanding trait was an inner fire which audiences as well as fellow-players found very moving. Stanislavsky went to see him frequently during his Russian tour and found his technique inspiring. Salvini's great role was Othello, in which he is said to have terrified his Desdemonas with the violence of his attack in the murder scene. Henry James wrote of his Othello: "It may seem to many observers that Salvini's rendering of the part is too simple, too much on two or three notes,—frank tenderness, quick suspicion, passionate rage. Infinite are the variations of human opinion; I have heard this performance called ugly, repulsive, bestial. Waiving these considerations for a moment, what an immense impression—simply as an impression—the actor makes on the spectator who sees him for the first time as the turbaned and deep-voiced Moor! He gives us his measure as a man; he acquaints us with that luxury of perfect confidence in the physical resources of the actor which is not the most frequent satisfaction of the modern playgoer. His powerful, active, manly frame, his noble, serious, vividly expressive face, his splendid smile, his Italian eye, his superb, voluminous voice, his carriage, his tone, his ease, the assurance he instantly gives that he holds the whole part in his hands and can make of it exactly what he chooses—all this descends upon the spectator's mind with a richness which immediately converts attention into faith, and expectation into sympathy. He is a magnificent creature, and you are already on his side. His generous temperament is contagious; you find yourself looking at him, not so much as an actor, but as a hero."

Other outstanding Salvini creations were Corrado in Giacometti's *La Morta civile*, Egisto in Alfieri's *Merope*, Saul in the same playwright's *Saul*, Paolo in Pellico's *Francesca da Rimini* and Oedipus in Niccolini's play of that name. Salvini also essayed Macbeth and King Lear.

Some of Salvini's thoughts on focal histrionic problems from his writings follow.

Impulse and Restraint

By familiarizing myself with great writers, I formed a fund of information which was of the greatest assistance to me in the pursuit of my profession. I made

Leaves from the Autobiography of Tomasso Salvini. New York: The Century Company, 1893, pp. 65-66, 69-71, 76.

comparisons between the heroes of ancient Greece and those of Celtic races; I paralleled the great men of Rome with those of the Middle Ages; and I studied their characters, their passions, their manners, their tendencies, to such purpose that when I had occasion to impersonate one of those types I was able to study it in its native atmosphere. I sought to live with my personage, and then to represent him as my imagination pictured him. The nice decision as to whether I was always right must rest with the public. It is very certain that to accomplish anything in art requires assiduous application, unwearied study, continuous observation, and, in addition to all that, natural aptitude. Many artists who have ability, erudition, and perseverance will nevertheless sometimes fall short of their ideal. It may happen that they lack the physical qualities demanded by the part, or that the voice cannot bend itself to certain modulations, or that the personality is incompatible with the character represented.

*   *   *   *

...I did not reflect, at that time, of how great assistance to me it was to be constantly surrounded by first-rate artists.... I observed frequently in the "scratch" companies which played in the theatres of second rank young men and women who showed very notable artistic aptitude, but who, for lack of cultivation and guidance, ran to extravagance, over-emphasis, and exaggeration. Up to that time, while I had a clear appreciation of the reasons for recognizing defects in others, I did not know how to correct my own; on the other hand, I recognized that the applause accorded me was intended as an encouragement more than as a tribute which I had earned.... By good fortune, I had enough conscience and good sense to receive this homage at its just value. I felt the need of studying, not books alone, but men and things, vice and virtue, love and hate, humility and haughtiness, gentleness and cruelty, folly and wisdom, poverty and opulence, avarice and lavishness, long-suffering and vengeance—in short, all the passions for good and evil which have root in human nature. I needed to study out the manner of rendering these passions in accordance with the race of the men in whom they were exhibited, in accordance with their special customs, principles and education; I needed to form a conception of the movement, the manner, the expressions of face and voice characteristic of all these cases; I must learn by intuition to grasp the characters of fiction, and by study to reproduce those of history with semblance of truth, seeking to give to every one a personality distinct from every other. In fine, I must become capable of identifying myself with one or another personage to such an extent as to lead the audience into the illusion that the real personage, and not a copy, is before them. It would then remain to learn the mechanism of my art; that is, to choose the salient points and to bring them out, to calculate the effects and keep them in proportion with the unfolding of the plot, to avoid monotony in intonation and repetition in accentuation, to insure precision and distinctness in pronunciation, the proper distribution of respiration, and incisiveness of delivery. I must study; study again; study always. It was not an easy thing to put these precepts in practice. Very often I forgot them, carried away by excitement, or by the superabundance of my vocal powers; indeed, until I had reached an age of calmer reflection I was never able to get my artistic chronometer perfectly regulated; it would always gain a few minutes every twenty-four hours.

[From "Some Views on Acting"]

To my quiet country villa among the woods of Vallombrosa echoes reached me of the friendly controversy which seems to have been waged in American and English magazines and newspapers regarding one of the underlying principles of the art to which I have devoted my life; a controversy in which were ranged on opposite sides two such eminent actors as Mr. Henry Irving and M. Constant Coquelin. These echoes have remained ringing in my ears until, despite the fact that I think an actor is as a rule better employed in studying the words of others than in committing phrases of his own to paper, I have ventured to shape, as briefly and simply as possible, my own views on the point in dispute. This point, if I have rightly understood it, resolves itself mainly into the simple question, "Should an actor feel positively and be moved by the emotions he portrays, or should he be entirely negative and keep his own emotions at arm's length, as it were, and merely make his audience believe that he is moved?"

Let me, in the first place, frankly state my own opinion, warning my readers first of all that it is merely an opinion (for questions of art can never be solved definitely, like a mathematical problem) and then I can at greater length strive to show why I hold such view. I believe then, that every great actor ought to be, and is, moved by the emotion he portrays; that not only must he feel this emotion once or twice, or when he is studying the part, but that he must feel it in a greater or less degree—and to just that degree will he move the hearts of his audiences—whenever he plays the part, be it once or a thousand times. This is what I believe and always have believed, and I think it must be acknowledged that my position as to the point at issue is no doubtful one.

M. Coquelin, on the other hand, maintains, if I rightly interpret his extremely well and forcibly put expression of opinion, that an actor should remain perfectly calm and collected, however stormy may be the passion he is portraying, that he should merely make believe, as it were, to feel the emotion he strives to make the audience believe he really feels, and that he should act entirely with his brain and not with his heart, to typify by physiological organs two widely differentiated methods of artistic work. That M. Coquelin really and truly believes this somewhat paradoxical theory and endeavors to put his theory into practice, I do not for a moment doubt. Accomplished and versatile an artist as he is, I have been struck more than once, as I have enjoyed the pleasure of his performance, with the thought that something amid all the brilliancy of execution was lacking; and this want, so apparent, was due, I apprehend, to the fact that one of the most skillful artists in the world was deliberately trying to belittle himself and the art of which it was in his power to raise to such lofty heights. The actor who does not feel the emotion he portrays is but a skillful mechanician, setting in motion certain wheels and springs which may give his lay figure such an appearance of life that the observer is tempted to exclaim, "How marvelous! Were it only alive it would make me laugh or weep." He who feels, on the contrary, and can communicate this feeling to the audience, hears the cry: "That is life! That is reality! See—I laugh! I weep!"

Tommaso Salvini: "*Some Views on Acting.*" New York: *Theatre Workshop*, October, 1936, pp. 73-78.

[456]

It is, in a word, the power of feeling that marks the artist; all else is but the mechanical side which is common to all the arts. There are many born actors who have never faced an audience, as there are many true poets who have never written a verse, and painters who have never taken a palette in hand. To some only is given the power of expression as well as of feeling, and they become artists in the sight of the world as the others are in the sight of our semi-divine mistress, the Art universal.

It is at this point that I approach more closely to M. Coquelin. "The actor," he says in effect, "must carry self-restraint so far that where the creature he simulates would burn, he must be cold as ice. Like a callous scientist, he must dissect each quivering nerve and lay bare each throbbing artery, all the time keeping himself as one of the gods of old Greece, lest a rush of hot heart's blood come and spoil his work." I also say that the actor must have the gift of impassivity, but to a certain point only. He must feel, but he must guide and check his feelings as a skillful rider curbs and guides a fiery horse, for he has a double part to play: merely to feel himself is not enough; he has to make others feel, and this he cannot do without the exercise of restraint. Let me make use of an instance afforded me by M. Coquelin himself. Once, he says, he was tired before he came on the stage, and falling asleep when feigning sleep, he snored real snores instead of feigned ones. The result was, he tells us, that he never snored so badly. Naturally so, since he had lost control of the steed of his feeling, by the fact of his sleeping, and so it ran away and carried him he knew not where; but had M. Coquelin at some time in his experience shed real tears, while at the same time in full possession of his waking facilities, and had he been able to guide these tears into the channel that his artistic sense told him to be the right one, then we should not have heard that the audience found those real tears less effective than tears wholly feigned and the product of intellect rather than of feeling. . . .

It is difficult for me to write on a subject such as this without incurring, or running the risk of incurring, the reproach of being egotistical. I cannot, however, refrain from referring to my own experience and my own methods in some degree, especially as by so doing I can, I doubt not, make more clear the theory I hold than by any other means; for I shall be able, as it were, to show not only how I put my theory into practice, but what the visible results have been. That I am chiefly guided by feeling is probably the reason that I have never been able to play with satisfaction, either to my audience or to myself, any part with which I have not full sympathy, and of late years I have not even attempted such parts. This attitude of mine towards his creations should, I conceive, be assumed in a greater or less degree by every actor who has a part to play, and not be confined simply to those who, like myself, have indentified themselves more closely with what, for want of a better term, I may call "heroic" roles. One may sympathize even with a villain and yet remain an honest man, so that in counseling a student first of all to put himself in sympathy with his character, I am by no means urging on him the acquirement of even the remotest obliquity of moral vision. After having satisfied myself that the character I was about to attempt was one with whom I could put myself in full sympathy, I have next set myself laboriously to study its inner nature, concerning myself not one particle with the outward characteristics or the points wherein the supposititious being might differ in his figure, bearing, or speech from the rest of his fellow-men. These are trifles, the simulation of which is, or ought to be, within the scope of any actor who has learned his trade and is skilled in the mechanics of his art. What is of supreme importance, though, is the mental and spiritual differentiation of the character from those around him. As to how I actually attain this object, I can speak in no way that could be clearly understood by my readers, for I do not clearly understand the process myself. It is perhaps at this point that what we are wont to call inspiration comes to our assistance, and helps to elevate the artist above the artisan. Now, having got in touch with the inner workings of my character's nature, by this process of spiritual dissection, which I find so difficult to classify, I proceed by slow degrees to an understanding of how he would speak and act in the various situations in which he has been placed by the dramatist, and here I am on surer ground, so far as giving some comprehension of the means I adopt towards the end is concerned. I simply try to be the character I am playing; to think with his brain, to feel with his feelings, to cry with him and to laugh with him, to let my breast be anguished by his emotions, to love with his love and to hate with his hate. Then having thus hewn my creation out of the block of marble provided me by the dramatist, I clothe him with his proper clothes and endow him with his proper voice, his tricks of gesture, his walk—in short, his outward and bodily appearance, as distinct from, though doubtless depending upon, his inward and spiritual fashioning. When this is completed to my satisfaction, when I have my man shaped, both in his inner and outer being, as I would have him, I am ready to place him before the public, and they help me to his further completion. M. Coquelin, doubtless, if he adheres with fidelity to his admirably expressed theories, could play a part as successfully and artistically in an empty room as in a crowded theatre. I must confess that I could not. I cannot live my mimic life save in the glare of the footlights; for it is only the sympathy and feeling of my audience which react upon me and allow me, on my part, to cause my audience to sympathize and feel with me. But what I particularly wish to impress upon my readers, is that while I am acting I am living a dual life, crying or laughing on the one hand, and simultaneously so dissecting my tears and laughter that they appeal most forcibly to those whose hearts I wish to reach. And what has been my experience has been the experience of all the greatest artists I have known. Ristori shed actual tears night after night, as she herself has told me; while one of the most gifted comedians it has ever been my pleasure to know has assured me that he entered so fully into the spirit of the character he was playing that he became to all intents and purposes one with him, enjoying his humor as though he himself had fathered it.

That this susceptibility of the emotions tends to uneven or unequal impersonations of the same character by the same actor on different occasions, I absolutely deny. That the jealously conscientious soul of the artist is at times troubled by the consciousness that on some certain occasion he has not equalled his own best work is doubtlessly true; though, as I conceive it, the conscience of the devotee of the mechanical system must be equally touched at times, for even the most skillful woodturner cannot every day turn his rings of exactly equal size and shape. But if this difference is due to the emotional nature gaining too great control and taking the mental bit into its mouth instead of being guided by it, then art is lacking, and knowledge and skill of craft also. There are actors, it is true, who allow themselves to be guided by the emotion of the moment; there is one who by her genius has added lustre to the American stage; but genius notwithstanding, they are not artists in the true sense of the word. This is the Scylla of unrestrained, untrained, and disproportionate emotion, akin almost to hysteria, which we must avoid, while at the same time keeping clear from the Charybdis of cold, deliberate mechanical artificiality, which leads indubitably to monotony of method and treatment, and to consequent lack of the art which conceals the art and its mechanism from the most keen eyes of watchful spectators.

I gather that M. Coquelin deplores the tendency of the day to subordinate the actor to the costumer and scene-painter—a tendency which will, in my judgment, after working an infinity of harm to art, end by being swept away by a reaction which will carry us back to something akin to the archaic simplicity of the days of Shakespeare, Molière, and Alfieri, or, to go even farther along the corridors of time, to those of Sophocles and Euripides. I deplore it, I say, and yet I fail to see that it is more dangerous to the art we both love than would be the general adoption of the views he has so eloquently, and in a manner so much more graceful than my own, espoused; views which would degrade the art of acting to the level of mere mimicry and make of the actor but a cleverly articulated piece of mechanism, informed by no breath of the Promethean fire we call genius; views which would inevitably rob it of all claim to be considered as a channel of as ennobling an art in its highest aspect as can be claimed by the poet, sculptor, or painter.

ERMETE ZACCONI

(1857-1948)

Ermete Zacconi became the leading player of the "verist" school in Italy. After playing with several companies, around 1887 he worked with Cesare Rossi, one of the important actor-manager-teachers, in whose company Eleonora Duse made her debut. He began to reveal the special talent he possessed for bringing to life the new drama of ideas and realism. It was Zacconi who popularized the work of Ibsen, playing *Ghosts, An Enemy of the People* and *John Gabriel Borkman.* The role of Oswald in *Ghosts* was one of the repeated triumphs of his career. The dramatist Roberto Bracco wrote that Zacconi's "representation of the progressive moral and corporeal decay of Oswald contained details so true and so excruciating that the spectators felt unable to bear them, and did not realize that they bore them, because his art nailed them to their seats."

Zacconi was equally successful in his interpretation of Nikita in Tolstoy's *The Power of Darkness.* His playing of this spiritless nonentity diavowed all stage tricks for a searing truthfulness that "brought the ideas of the great Russian thinker down from the pulpit and gave them to the public in an exact vision of the reality that had stirred the author's humanitarian and Christian soul."

In 1899 he joined Eleonora Duse in a tour presenting plays by D'Annunzio and Dumas *fils* and played with her on other occasions over the years as the outstanding male interpreter of modern drama. He offered the public roles in the plays of Turgenev, Hauptmann, de Curel and Molnar. Roberto Bracco wrote especially for him the socialist drama, *The Right to Live,* as well as *The Triumph* about the conflict of "the flesh and the spirit."

Over his long career, however, he brought his deeply psychological and verist interpretations to many of the great roles of the traditional repertory in plays of

Shakespeare, Alfieri, Goldoni and Beaumarchais. Even in his old age he gave spirited performances as Othello and King Lear.

This leading artist of the "verist" school was able to play so well both the classics and the moderns because his interpretations were based upon excellent technique, especially in "The Art of Speaking," about which he writes in the selection below. His "felicitous diction" was widely praised; it was said that "words fell from his lips with the value of notes from a piano or a violin."

The Art of Speaking

To speak simply and naturally is a rare gift, facilitating one's job of talking like a real human being in the ephemeral life of the stage. Actors of genius who do not possess that precious gift study tirelessly and fight hard to acquire it. We have had woefully ignorant actors whom fate endowed with that talent: when one of them was taken in hand by a capable, intelligent director, the talent became priceless. Of course, left to his own devices the same actor would have been incapable of true artistic understanding and insight. He might be termed a "tolerably good speaker" or, as I pefer, "a mere mouther" of the written word (because of his simplemindedness); but he obscured the spirit and ideas the author put into his words.

Actors or actresses who base their art on natural talents, even though they may become well known or attain what seems like fame, find themselves in a state of living death while still alive. Once those talents are gone, all of their charm vanishes. A beautiful face or voice, sincerely felt tears or laughter, fresh and simple diction may easily be taken as artistic miracles by someone who looks solely at the surface of things. But in that kind of "art" nothing remains! What does survive is the memory of those few who had the supreme virtue of artistic creativity; who, with resolute spirit and understanding mind, were able to develop to the utmost the talents with which nature endowed them. Only then did they succeed in acquiring the other talents that seemed to have been denied them. Originally Emanuel did not have a voice suited for tragedy but managed to develop one. Luigi Monti and Benini were not good-looking but made audiences forget that fact. Claudio Leigheb looked like a tough drill sergeant but could assume an expression of gayest comedy. Giacinta Pezzana became beautiful and Adelaide Tessero elegant.

To become a really good speaker as well as interpreter—for good diction cannot be divorced from interpretation, being its suitable outer expression—you must know not only the play in which you are performing but all the works of the playwright in question. You must try to grasp his views on social problems, politics, and religion. You must understand the basic idea that gave rise to the play, study the ideas and concepts flowing from that original thought and the conclusions derived from it. If there are clashes or outbursts of passion in the play, you must determine whether they are the sick products of sick minds or simply aspects of interpersonal relations; then you must try to get a clear picture of every one of the characters involved and of the setting in which the play unfolds. You must probe the way in which these characters and settings confront one another in life; examine on what level and in

Zacconi, Ermete: *Ricordi e battaglie*. Milan: Garzanti, 1946. This excerpt tranlsated from the Italian by Joseph M. Bernstein.

what light the character you have to portray appears vis-à-vis the other characters. When all that is very clear in your mind and you feel sure of every aspect, when with brain and heart you have vibrated to the character and lived it, then you can proceed to study the role. You can learn the words by heart, repeating them over and over again, striving always to give life and context to the thoughts, revealing all the subtle nuances hidden in a sentence that, uttered in Act I, powerfully affects what transpires in the second and third acts. You must be aware of the author's language and bring out its rhythms because this too requires attention and study. You must learn to be, in turn, elegant, superficial, insinuating, incisive, sober in speech, rich in modulations. You must use your voice as an instrument just as the playwright used his mind to elaborate his thoughts, remembering at the same time that every human being has a unique way of expressing himself. Thus Armand Duval's simple, sincere way of speaking cannot be the same as that of Scarli the lawyer. The voice, manner, walk, and gestures of these two men cannot be the same since they differ in nationality, social status, education, habits, in spirit and life style. Had Armand been Scarli, he would have killed his unfaithful wife. In Armand's place, Scarli would not have pursued his runaway wife but would have remained alone with his sorrow, without doing harm to anyone.

It is too easy to appear on stage every evening as oneself, ever the selfsame personality. That is the wrong way, since the character one is portraying is quite different from one's own personality. Remember that a play—comedy or tragedy— has three hours at most in which to present events, characters, physiological and psychological processes, and many other things as well. To explain, clarify, and comment on all this, the playwright has but a few words and a brief span of time. So the content of every sentence must be worth ten or a hundred in real-life conversation. The actor who "babbles" will only confuse rather than clarify the dramatist's ideas.

The art of speaking—how great is its charm! Those who have mastered the art— and they are many—make music out of words from the depths of their own feeling and reveal the profound, sublime thoughts of the poets, philosophers, and humanitarian thinkers. They can move and sway persons even in far-off countries who speak a different language. I remember once hearing the noted Portuguese actor Braccao reciting lines from a play in Portuguese. I did not know a word of the language, and the play was completely unknown to me, yet he gave me the illusion that he was speaking in my own tongue, so clear and expressive yet so simple and natural was his language.

Unfortunately the art of speaking is dying out. Italian actors were once masters of the art because they were always able to express the most rhetorical sentences in a most human way. At one time Italian writers of tragedy helped us perfect our speech: Alfieri, Monti, Pellico, Niccolini, Marenco forced us to sharpen our minds so that we could understand their verses; we had to study long and hard to make the spoken verses intelligible to audiences. This trained us to bring out the true value and meaning of words that in verse form were often out of their usual position and context. So we strove constantly to remain real flesh-and-blood humans in the trappings of ancient heroes and to recite in human tones high-sounding, harsh, abstruse, and excessively convoluted verses. We tried to remain true to life, without losing any of the sweep and dignity of the tragedy. Thus we were so well trained in all our faculties as actors that when we started to act in modern plays we all found it quite easy to convey beauty of style as well as profundity of ideas.

In addition to the difficulties mentioned above, there is the question of fluency in dialogue—the fluency that rounds out speech and prevents it from sounding like something learned by rote, that lends conviction to words and makes them seem to rush spontaneously from the heart and brain of the one uttering them. Moreover, you have to know how to change your own body. Even before you apply makeup, your face has to change; by an act of will you have to bring a different look into your eyes and reshape your very flexible facial muscles. This effort, this patient and painstaking work must begin at rehearsals and go on and on—until finally you have created the character who on opening night enters into us, whom we watch and follow attentively with that well-known phenomenon of dual personality.

At this point I should like to comment on a question raised by my friend Alessandro Varaldo in his Italian translation of Diderot's *The Paradox of Acting*. In his preface Varaldo strongly urges young actors to pay close attention to the Diderot work, in which the great encyclopedist maintains that to be a great actor one must be stripped of all sentiment and sensitivtiy. Let us take a hard look at this curious point of view.

How can we imagine such an absurd contradiction in nature? Perhaps Diderot, so rich in intellect, had no human feelings and so could not accept in art what he ignored in nature? Or, as happens with many of the intellectual élite, the more he tried to approach the theatre and understand it, the more mysterious it remained to him?

Perhaps for Diderot as well as for Varaldo and, alas! too many others, the actor, the performer, is not a true artist. They may consider words learned by heart and human passions rendered mechanically, with a complete lack of feeling, the highest expression of dramatic art. What a mistake! How can one say that the actor is not an artist? How, in view of the state of the actor's profession of his time, could Diderot determine what art is? He wrote his *Paradox* around the middle of the eighteenth century. Varaldo says we must overlook the fact that Diderot wrote it when the actor's art had declined and become bombastic rhetoric. But that is just what we must take into account if we are to analyze his ideas correctly. All the actors and actresses of that period, the whole world over, though they may have been adept enough at playing comedy credibly, struck a disgustingly false note the minute they attempted tragedy. There was a whole "system" for expressing sorrow: the trembling voice, the quivering lips, the narrowed eyes, the thumb and index finger of the right hand shaking wildly on high, then at the proper moment dropped to the base of the nose as a prelude to bitter tears. Equally studied and artificial were expressions of joy, anger, envy, disdain.... What we got in tragedies was a succession of statuesque poses and voices ranging the entire gamut of the musical scale. And all the dramatists in every country followed the rules of this theatrical game. So that whenever, here and there, an artist attempted timidly or furtively to get out of the bind it must have seemed at best a reckless break with the rules of the profession. How could Diderot have felt what an actor's authentic projection of emotion would have produced in him? Did he ever experience what actors of our time achieve when, with deep and poignant sensitivity, they portray human sorrow with such unerring naturalness?

No, my dear Varaldo, Diderot's *Paradox* should remain in the period in which it was written. It is ridiculous for a man like you to recommend it for study to our young actors. In Italy traditional methods of acting continued unchallenged down to Giacomo Modena, father of the great Gustavo. But then a young Lombard, De Marini, an artist to his fingertips with a keen mind and a revolutionary spirit, took the first halting steps toward a more truthful way of acting. Breaking with traditional dogmas, he went from triumph to triumph as he brought truth, logic, and deep human sensitivity to the actor's art. In his wake, suddenly, came Gustavo Modena and a whole series of intelligent and cultured actors: Angelo Vestri, Gaetano Gattinelli, Alemanno Morelli, Achille Maieroni, Tommaso Salvini. . . .

So from generation to generation the young actors drew inspiration from the art of their elders, making in turn their own contributions arising from their native intelligence and genius. What De Marini did for Italy was done in France by the great André Antoine, then by Lucien Guitry and Gabrielle Réjane.

Diderot's encyclopedic mind, my dear Varaldo, understood everything except the theatre. This happens with many others as well. And for that very reason he too, like many others, wrote two works for the stage that are generally ignored. Hence they have had no success, because if two plays from the pen of such a well-known writer have remained obscure it means that they are valueless. Diderot took revenge for his failure as a dramatist by writing *The Paradox of Acting*.

That too is not mentioned in the history of the theatre.

You also assert, my friend, that Diderot had all the qualities requisite for an art critic—including *the spirit of sarcasm*. Does one really need a sarcastic spirit to be a good and honest critic of the arts? Let's examine this point. I'm not talking about written texts against which everyone can test the critic's intelligence and good faith. What I mean is the art of the actor, which unfortunately offers no way of being tested except by the senses and emotions of those who have seen and heard him. To judge a performer the critic must possess, first of all, the God-given gift of a superior mind—a clear and penetrating mind—that no school can give him. If this supreme gift is missing what we get is dull academicism, a most harmful thing for criticism. Together with intelligence the good critic must have integrity and serenity of spirit. The critic must praise what he deems good and criticize what he finds bad, always ready to acknowledge that the error may lie with him as well as in the actor. Who can define the limits of intelligence of the critic and of the performer? And why should a critic need a spirit of sarcasm? Perhaps for the sadistic pleasure of making failure even more bitter by adding derisive irony to his harsh judgment? The artist who sheds his own personality in order to bring to life characters created by another artist operates under the sway of something that is not purely cerebral. His entire mental and physical being is involved. Within him is some kind of mysterious divine essence, the origin and location of which no philosopher has thus far been able to ascertain. The great actor is an artist, master of an art that demands, in addition to talent, unheard-of commitment and sacrifices. Nor does he exert himself solely during his creative moments, when he recites his lines. Equally intense is his devotion during the long hours in which he studies his part, trying to attune his own spirit with that of the faraway playwright who may have died centuries before, and striving to grasp the meaning that may be hidden in a few words. Then the actor's mind quickens and sharpens. A meeting of minds seems to occur. The actor seems to possess a kind of divination: lines from Shakespeare, Ibsen, Tolstoy, which have hitherto escaped everyone's notice, now light up for him.

I maintain that only an artist is in a position to judge an artist. Of course I am speaking here of interpreters, not routine performers. It may be objected that a playwright's work needs performers, not interpreters; that the work interprets itself. No doubt one can decide to stay at home and read the play, thinking about it and understanding it as best one can. But here I am talking about theatre—above all, the theatre of my time, as we Italians understood, loved, and interpreted it. To us theatre meant poverty, passion, faith, study, anxiety, probing. Today the theatre is pursuing other paths about which I shall refrain from passing judgment. I believe nobody expects to hear me express things differently from what I feel. These are things that are very close to me, my souvenirs—and only mine.

Evolution does not have to mean destruction. We must improve on what has been done up to now. But to reject it, root and branch, is a fatal mistake the results of which will soon become apparent. Destroy the interpreter—is that possible? Destroy the actor-interpreter so as to create the director-interpreter? Is that what you want? Will that be a big improvement? I have my doubts. When all is said and done, the dramatist's work will always be presented in terms of individual interpretation. So the audience will applaud the director instead of the actor, because no one is going to tell me that the director isn't looking for applause. He most certainly is; he is delighted when the audience shouts "bravo." Of course a critic may find that the whole production was wrong; the author didn't mean "this," he meant "that." The critic knows for certain because a little angel whispered in his ear, and many angels whispered their truths in the ears of the other critics. So the director will find himself in the same boat as the actor: either he will have to suffer the critics' onslaughts or disregard them. And, naturally, the only irresponsible ones will be the actors. I can imagine how deeply the director must suffer at having to make use of the voice, face, and gestures of so many talented human "instruments" in order to win over the audience. I can understand how the *personality* of a great actor attracts the audience's attention at the expense of the play's content. Why then don't we set up attractive reading rooms in which cultured critics—experts—with good looks and good speaking voices give readings of play scripts and explain them in advance. To *me*—and I must emphasize this so as not to leave a shred of doubt as to how I feel—the theatre is flesh and blood. Living flesh and blood, vibrant, luminous life—real life illuminated by the ideas of the person who has written the words and by the art of the person who speaks these words. When a poet, thinker, or philosopher writes a dramatic work, he knows what he is doing; he wants to write a play, not a piece of rhetoric. If he wanted to write literature he would have written a good book instead of a good play. To understand the theatre you have to have it in your blood. It's not enough to deal with it as a cultural theme; you have to know, feel, live the theatre to understand it. Writing about it in the press or reading about it with enthusiasm is, I am sorry to say, quite another thing. How many cultured and intelligent men and women, capable of writing magnificent books, are incapable of writing even a tenth-rate play!

The art of the theatre—my dearly beloved art! I have always defended it as best I could, I have always respected it, I have always loyally served it. I have been richly rewarded for my efforts in ways that nothing can diminish or disturb. These rewards are all inside me, in my heart; they are my laurel wreath. These are the rewards my audiences have bestowed on me when, by an imperceptible, indefinable thread, their heads and hearts were bound up with my own.

If my road, like that of my father and my grandparents before me, has been a big mistake, I bless that mistake. It has been so bountiful in results, so rich in poetry and beauty. I have lived gloriously for it; gladly would I die for it.

I T A L Y
ELEONORA DUSE
(1858-1924)

For two generations, Eleonora Duse's forbears had been actors. Her grandfather, Luigi Duse, is said to have founded the Garibaldi Theatre at Padua. His five sons were all actors. Like Ristori, Duse literally knew the theatre and its life from her first day. She was born in a third-class railroad carriage while her parents were on their way with the Duse family troupe to an engagement in Milan.

A career as a stage child with its unconsciously absorbed technique has been an advantage enjoyed by many great actresses. To this early experience has been credited much of Duse's ability to go to the heart of an emotion without recourse to traditional histrionic devices. At seven Eleonora was the prompter of the humble family company. By the time she was twelve she was appearing regularly on rural stages, often impersonating characters much older than herself. At fourteen she played Juliet, in Verona, the home of the Capulets. In Naples, in 1879, when she was twenty, her apprenticeship came to an end. Called in an emergency to replace the leading actress on the eve of the presentation of *Thérèse Racquin*, she scored a triumph at the famous Florentine Theatre, the same stage on which Salvini and Ristori had played. Cesare Rossi, one of the distinguished men of the theatre in Italy, was present and immediately placed Duse under his management. In the ensuing decade Duse established herself as the leading Italian actress.

In 1893 her tours brought her to New York. A contemporary critic gives this excellent account of her characterization of Camille: "Her power over an audience was manifested in a very striking manner before she had been on the stage five minutes. The actress had scarcely made her appearance and given her careless nod of recognition to De Varville before everybody was in an attitude of strained attention. Already the old and hackneyed character had been revivified by the power of genius. Signora Duse does not attempt to make a Frenchwoman of Camille, but fills her with the fire and passion of her own Italian temperament. But both the fire and passion, except at very rare intervals, are kept under complete control. Their glow is apparent in all the love scenes, and breaks into flame at one or two critical moments, but it is by the suggestion of force in reserve that she makes her most striking effects. Only an artist of the highest type could create so profound an impression with so little apparent effort or forethought, by some light and seemingly spontaneous gesture, by a sudden change of facial expression, or by some subtle inflection of the voice. The chief beauties of her impersonation are to be found in its lesser and, to the inexperienced eye, insignificant details. All her by-play, although it appears to be due only to the impulse of the moment, is clearly the result of the most deliberate design, and changes with every variety of mood or condition which it is meant to illustrate...."

Inevitably, Duse invaded Paris. Comparison between Duse and Bernhardt, both of whom were in their prime in the 1890's, was a favorite speculation of the day. Duse's few weeks in Paris in the early summer of 1897 mark the climax of her career. Whatever Sarah Bernhardt's motives, she induced La Duse to play in her theatre under her aegis and in *Camille* which was one of Sarah's own greatest triumphs. The story of Duse's initial disappointment in that first performance and her ensuing triumph form a strange chapter in the history of the stage. In that season Paris enjoyed a rare display of acting, culminating in a gala performance as a memorial to Dumas with Bernhardt and Duse both playing.

Comparing the two great tragediennes, George Bernard Shaw gave Duse the foremost place. "I should say without qualification that it is the best modern acting I have ever seen.... Sarah Bernhardt has nothing but her own charm.... Duse's own private charm has not yet been given to the public. She gives you... the charm... belonging to the character she impersonates... behind every stroke of it is a distinctively human idea."

Duse as an actress and as a woman struck her contemporaries as being surrounded by a great sadness. According to one account, her father claimed that she had contracted a disease known as "The Spleen of Venice" in which the victim is "enveloped in a fantastic mist, with the sadness of the past, the bitterness· of the present, and the uncertainty of the future." Her triumph over poverty, her unsuccessful marriage, her turbulent relationship with D'Annunzio, whose plays she introduced, appear to have made her shy, proud, and somewhat detached from the petty ambitions of theatrical life. Never very robust, she succumbed to pneumonia in April, 1924, during an American tour. She died in Pittsburgh, for her, *"la plus hideuse ville du monde."*

Among the many plays in Duse's repertory were Sardou's *Theodora* and his *Divorçons,* Goldoni's *La Locandiéra,* Dumas' *La Dame aux camélias,* D'Annunzio's *La Citta morta,* Pellico's *Francesca da Rimini,* Ibsen's *Ghosts,* and Sudermann's *Magda.* Duse made one rather disastrous movie. At her own request the reels were destroyed. Duse's feeling about the film is worth recording: "If I were twenty or thirty years younger, I would start afresh in this field with the certainty of accomplishing much. But I should have to learn from the bottom up, forgetting the theatre entirely and concentrating on the special medium of this new art. My mistake, and that of many others, lay in employing 'theatrical' techniques despite every effort to avoid them. Here is something quite, quite fresh, a penetrating form of visual poetry, an untried exponent of the human soul. Alas, I am too old for it!"

Retiring in her personal life, Duse was also reluctant to discuss her art. The following statements garnered from diversified sources provide a clue to an intensely personal attitude. Her comments on acting are as rare as they are disturbing in their vehemence.

On Acting

I have read certain letters . . . or studies on our Art that . . . shall I tell you? They brought back my blissful childhood: the time cranky Grandpa gave me the beautiful Pulcinella with the movable arms and legs and the laughing, shriveled-up face that we—restless children that we were—had to break, in order to find out how he was put together. Is it of Art that you wanted me to speak to you? It seems to me that it is . . . unless the successes of Rome have beclouded my brain . . . it seems to me that it is. And does it seem to you that it is possible to speak of Art? It would be the same as explaining love! Along that Way of the Cross we all have

"Lettere di Eleonora Duse," in *Antologia del grande attore,* edited by Vito Pandolfi. Bari: Editori Laterza, 1954, pp. 380-384. Translated by Vivien Leone.

traveled; we all have talked about it, but absolutely no one has defined it *completely*. One loves, or is an artist, according to one's ability. Precepts, customs, conventions, are worthless, especially in art. The ways of love and of art are equally various. There is the love that ennobles and leads to goodness, and there is the love that obliterates all will, all strength, all intelligent channeling. This, as far as I am concerned, is the more true, but there is no doubt that it is fatal.

It is that way in Art . . . which sometimes reveals itself as the *expression* and *expansion* of a soul, with the result that it soars to such heights that it is imprinted with feeling and passion.

He who claims to teach Art understands nothing whatsoever about it.

And since you will lose your way if you keep following me down all these strange passageways, I shall be brief and begin speaking with you by way of a bit of reportage.

Without posing (because it is important to me that you know I am no poser; I am not yet at that stage of imbecility), I tell you that I never dared hoped for a season as successful as this one in Rome has been. It all fills me with a happiness and an optimism that—to put it mildly—do me so much good! And should someone tell you that success ruins the artist, you must respond with a firm contradiction. Success is without doubt a tonic, and it is success that provides the enthusiasm indispensable to the continuance of the daily struggle, that burden of years and years of toil required to achieve *repose,* the repose that lives on memories.

As for me, when that time arrives, and my youth is passed, and I must write *fine* beneath all my successes, both the ones I achieved and the ones I only hoped for, I shall retire from my career in silence, and with a strong and sweet conviction I shall know: that it was in Art—both the inward thought and the outward expression—in Art that I placed all my soul. It shall be a compensation. . . .[1]

* * * *

Act? What a nasty word! If acting were all there was to it; I feel that I have *never known* nor *shall I ever know how to act!* Those poor women in my plays have entered so totally into my heart and head, that while I am striving as best I can to make the audience understand them, I almost feel like comforting them . . . but it is they who, little by little, end up by comforting me!

How—and why, and at what point—this affectionate, inexplicable, and undeniable "exchange" takes place between those women and me . . . it would take too long and be too difficult to relate precisely. The fact remains that, while everybody else is suspicious of the women, I get along beautifully with them! I pay no attention if they have lied, if they have betrayed, if they have sinned, if they were born crooked, as long as I feel that they have wept, that they have suffered as a result of lying or betraying or loving . . . I put myself with them, and I ransack their emotions not out of any mania for suffering, but because the *communal lamentation* among women is greater and more detailed, is sweeter and more complete, than that which is granted to them by men.[2]

* * * *

I have a heart that is moved by things good and bad, a head that is perfectly calm, and a will that is firmly and unshakably *of* and *in* my work.

I have a fine slender sadness for the grief of others, I have a *serenity,* I have a silence in my soul for my own griefs.

---

[1]Letter to Icilio Polese, October 15, 1883.

[2]Letter to D'Arcais (?), 1885.

I have had to keep all this quiet, and I have been obliged—by contract and as an artist—to achieve success, and I have done it . . . I never knew I was so strong! While poor Diotti was sick (he battled five days against that cursed illness), we—without him—(how to replace him, eh? ah, how sad it was)—we went on. The first night, *Fedora*—packed house—and your little Nennella was an utter *fiasco* . . . huge theatre . . . it made me feel weak and tiny . . . my voice . . . it seemed impossible to me that it could reach the back of the pit . . . I would have had to say: "I love you, O Loris" as though I were saying "Get out!" if I wished to be heard . . . A continual murmuring, everlasting, exasperating, from the orchestra and from the boxes, right up to the end of the play . . . My head—like my voice—could hold out no longer . . . I got dressed quickly and went home more rapidly than ever. What despondency. What emptiness that evening! The next day, no performances; here they play only three times a week. The newspaper reports were vague. They remarked only that I had a certain something that had impressed them, but that they had heard scarcely more than a feeble half-measure of my voice. The next day . . . *Denise,* second performance; theatre—that plaza of a space—almost empty. Four or five rows down front and four or five boxes, on the sides, those nearest the stage were occupied by the press . . . Now pay attention to this.

My poor plain Denise, without great robes or a kingdom, who had nothing in common with the feverish Fedora, easily made herself heard in the first and second acts. I wept, and made them weep in the third as much as I could, as much as they let themselves. The boat began to glide a bit . . . a little more . . . yes . . . slowly . . . but at least my sensation of being out of tune with the theatre . . . with its amplitude, began to subside. . . .

Another thing that night was that Cottin stepped in to play Fernando for Diotti, who was still in a critical condition. The substitution estranged me from the detail of the scene. It seemed to me that in order to act one would need to lock the heart and mind into the present, without evoking the past. And yet . . . what was at stake was the life of a poor man . . . young . . . good . . . who had never done me any harm . . . who had never in his life done anyone harm . . . so, there, in front of that curtain—abominable and blessed—I said: "Madonna, grant us the grace of saving this poor creature, do it, do not fail, save him and let *me* be lost as an artist; save that poor man . . . he has a father and mother . . . that are waiting for him *down there . . . down there.*

Two days later all was ended, and we . . . we . . . left on the battlefield, acted, without him; and your little Nennella won . . . she won . . . My third appearance was in *Fernando.* I was never aware of having so much heart, such vitality, intelligence, *will.* I acted well, and, nobly, to you I confess it, you who are good, you who are noble . . . you do not ridicule those who exalt the soul and the intellect . . . you did not tell me that life is trivial, you and only you, have agreed with me that life is serious.[3]

* * * *

To questions that are presented to me regarding the dramatic art I have only one answer to offer. It is this: that all I care to say is said through the medium of my art and in the form of the new plays I am now presenting. In these new plays I have faith. From this statement, one may draw one's own conclusions. I do not like to judge other people's work, either in my native land, or anywhere else. Let every lover of the theatre raise an ideal from his own

---

[3]Letter to Matilde Serao, Rio de Janeiro, August 28, 1885.

soul and follow it faithfully. In this way the artistic evolution will inevitably accomplish itself. To act is the essential thing. To watch a beautiful garden in its blossoming is a great joy, but I am not interested in the way the blossoms are produced. I came from far away and have faith in my star. That is all. I can say no more, nor do I wish to know more.[4]

* * * *

I disdain to be the virtuous person who makes a fuss over her ability; I also disdain to put my personal successes above the play, because the interpreter of a work of art must be merely the faithful attentive collaborator, who forces herself to transmit, without deforming it, the poet's creation to the public. It has been said that in my new repertoire I have not created any new personage. This I consider is my best eulogy.[5]

* * * *

Interpretation is the evidence of growth and knowledge, the latter through sorrow—that great teacher.

If the sight of the blue skies fills you with joy, if a blade of grass springing up in the fields has power to move you, if the simple things of nature have a message that you understand, rejoice, for your soul is alive; and then aspire to learn that other truth, that the least of what you receive can be divided. To help, to continually help and share, that is the sum of all knowledge; that is the meaning of art.

The artist-actor gives the best of himself; through his interpretations, he unveils his inner soul. By these interpretations only should he be accepted and judged. When the final curtain falls between him and his audience, nothing can be said or done, add or detract from his performance. His work is done, his message is delivered.[6]

* * * *

To save the theatre, the theatre must be destroyed, the actors and actresses must all die of the plague. They poison the air, they make art impossible. It is not drama that they play, but pieces for the theatre. We should return to the Greeks, play in the open air: the drama dies of stalls and boxes and evening dress, and people who come to digest their dinner.

The one happiness is to shut one's door upon a little room, with a table before one, and to create; to create life in that isolation from life.

We must bow before the poet, even when it seems to us that he does wrong. He is a poet, he has seen something, he has seen it in that way; we must accept his vision, because it is vision.

Since Shakespeare and the Greeks there has been no great dramatist, and these gathered up into themselves the whole life of the people and the whole work of their contemporaries. When we say Shakespeare we mean all the Elizabethan drama. Ibsen? Ibsen is like this room where we are sitting, with all the tables and chairs. Do I care whether you have twenty or twenty-five links on your

---

[4]Quoted by Gertrude Norman: "An Interview with Eleonora Duse." New York: *Theatre Magazine,* April, 1906, p. 105. By permission of Paul Meyer.
[5]Quoted by Jeanne Bordeaux: *Eleonora Duse: The Story of her Life.* London: Hutchinson and Company, 1924.
[6]Quoted by Sir John Martin-Harvey: *The Book of Martin-Harvey.* London: H. Walker, Ltd., 1930, pp. 54, 55.

ACTORS ON ACTING

chain? Hedda Gabler, Nora and the rest: it is not that I want! I want Rome and the Coliseum, the Acropolis, Athens; I want beauty, and the flame of life. Maeterlinck? I adore Maeterlinck. Maeterlinck is a flower. But he only gives me figures in a mist. Yes, as you say, children and spirits.

I have tried, I have failed, I am condemned to play Sardou and Pinero. Some day another woman will come, young, beautiful, a being all of fire and flame, and will do what I have dreamed; yes, I am sure of it, it will come; but I am tired, at my age I cannot begin over again....

Could I live without the stage? ...I have passed three years without acting. I act because I would rather do other things. If I had my will I would live in a ship on the sea, and never come nearer to humanity than that.[7]

EDUARDO DE FILIPPO

(b. 1900)

Outside of Italy Eduardo De Filippo is best known as a prolific Neopolitan playwright, some of whose work has been translated into successful films. Some of his most popular plays are *Filumena Marturano, Napoli milionaria!* and *Questi fantasmi.* But he is, in fact, one of those rare total theatre artists whose accomplishments as writer and producer-director grow out of his basic creativity as an actor, "perhaps the finest actor in Italy today."

Head of his own theatre in Naples since 1953 where he and his sister Tina and brother Peppino have worked together, he has devoted a major part of his career to the life of a great city and region expressed in performances and plays in Neopolitan dialect. Early in his career he worked with the *Compagnia Vincenzo Scarpetta* and the *Compagnia Teatro Nuovo.* In 1931 he was cofounder with his brother Peppino De Filippo of *Il Teatro Umoristico I De Filippo.* In 1953 he became owner and director of the *Teatro San Ferdinando* in Naples.

De Filippo is usually referred to as a traditionalist who has kept alive the style, themes and characters of the *commedia dell' arte.* As an actor he has given interpretations of the old masks, as in his pathetic versions of Pulchinella in a Neapolitan comedy by Antonio Petito. As a playwright-actor he began his career elaborating scenes for a character he was developing. His relationship to the *commedia,* however, is not that of a self-conscious artist re-creating a style, but of a popular regionalist working in a realistic vein for the people of his own area in their own dialect. Eric Bentley has analyzed those special qualities in Eduardo De Filippo that make him more likely "to be the heir of *commedia dell' arte* than any other important performer now living." His realistic style "makes few large departures from life. No oratory, no stylization. Both in speech and in gesture, rhythm, accent, and tempo are in imitation of life. The 'art' consists in the skill of the imitations, the careful registering of detail and nuance, and a considered underlining of the effects." Bentley attributes much that is distinctive in De Filippo to Naples, "the reservoir on which, consciously and unconsciously, Eduardo draws." His talent and his use of a working, living tradition, about which he writes in the following brief answers in questions put him by the editors, have made him a unique modern artist.

Quoted by Arthur Symons: *Eleonora Duse.* New York: Duffield and Company, 1927, pp. 3-5.

The Intimacy of Actor and Character

I have never wanted to write on the art of acting, because the theatre is evolving continuously, incessantly, like life; the important thing is not to fix on paper a moment of such flux, but to understand that all of us living theatre men are "moments," generated by moments that have preceded us, and that we shall, in turn, generate future moments in the evolution of the theatre which, as I see it, will cease only with the end of man.

I believe that those who theorize, even though they may do so in good faith, create only confusion. For example, actors and directors are still using today certain methods of Stanislavsky and Brecht, although if these two theatre men were alive and working, they would long since have abandoned such methods, passing along to others, and then again to still others. The real "method" of learning to act is to make theatre with those who know how to make theatre. This is how tradition is formed, and tradition renders all theories superfluous.

The actor dies without being able to say he has reached perfection; he gives to the public the results of his continuous artistic experience, but that experience is superseded at the very moment in which it is acquired.

In order to practice what I preach, I shall address myself only to the questions that have been put to me, taking care to point out that, since I am also a playwright, my case is a special one.

The main influences on my work as an actor have been life, humanity, nature, the *commedia dell' arte* tradition.

Although very much admiring the major theorists of the modern theatre, I have always preferred to seek my inspiration from the natural source of art, life.

My work as an actor and as a playwright has been interrelated in the same way in which rapport develops, or ought to, between an author and his interpreter: by means of a certain distance and reciprocal respect. Author and actor ought to complete each other, not compete with each other, and each ought always to respect the limits of his task.

I approach the creation of a role by trying to understand the thinking and the essence of the character, with the help of the author's words. Even though—or perhaps because—I am an author, I know that a real intimacy can exist only between character and actor. The author creates the character, but the actor must give the character life. Besides the word, the actor has at his disposition gestures, glances, movements, and the audience, which by way of its reactions can little by little let him know the true theatrical nature of the character. I am convinced that despite reflections and rehearsals, the real study begins above all on contact with the audience, and, in effect, such a study continues until one is acting the character. Perhaps the study never really ends at all.

My most successful role? When I act I am onstage, not in the gallery, and hence I cannot know which of my roles has come out best. But I can say which has been my favorite: Antonio Barracano, in *Il Sindaco del Rione Sanità,* which seems to me to be one of the most difficult, but also one of the most interesting, parts an actor could wish for.

Well, yes, I guess I did, in a certain sense, train the members of my troupe, since I am the director of the company. I believe that the function of the director,

Translated by Vivien Leone. Reprinted by permission of Eduardo De Filippo.

with regard to the actor, is not to impose his own vision of how the role ought to be acted, but rather to stimulate the actor's creation of the role, and then to help perfect that creation, combining it with that of the others and with the pace of the show. In general, I pay much more attention to a creative actor than to one who awaits orders. The former is a collaborator, the latter a hireling.

The Neapolitan actor who comes from a theatrical family has naturalness, spontaneity, rhythm, creativity; he knows how to improvise (an extremely difficult thing for the Italian actor); he has a traditional sack of scenic conventions, subterfuges, tricks that add up to a useful inheritance if they are accompanied by sensitivity and education. The major defect of the Neapolitan actor is ignorance.

I would say he differs from the Italian actor in that the Italian has neither tradition nor playwrights (Pirandello, Goldoni, Verga, Viviani, etc., are Sicilians, Venetians, Neapolitans): these two gaps make everything more difficult for him since, in the absence of true roots, the Italian actor faces an almost impossible task.

VITTORIO GASSMAN

(b. 1922)

Italy's foremost interpreter of the great dramas of the past did not start out to become an actor. Born in Genoa, he studied law at the University of Rome, and even when he went to Rome's Academy of Dramatic Art, he did not feel a powerful calling to become an actor. Indeed, he thought he might become a journalist. His interest in literature and scholarship has shown itself even during the height of his career as an actor in his translations of important plays and his editions of texts like Seneca's *Thyestes.*

Despite his uncertainty and a weak voice, Gassman's disciplined, intensive work turned him into one of the most popular idols on stage and screen. He worked extensively under the director Luchino Visconti during the 1940's playing such roles as Orlando in *As You Like It,* Stanley Kowalski in *A Streetcar Named Desire,* the title role in Alfieri's *Oreste.* Among the other plays in which he appeared during this decade were *Peer Gynt, Romeo and Juliet, Detective Story.*

In 1952 Gassman organized his own company in which Luigi Squarzina served as director. His intention was to bring the great classical drama to the people of Italy. His production and interpretation of *Hamlet* was both modern and highly romantic. He played *Thyestes* by Seneca, *The Persians* by Aeschylus and the *Bacchae* of Euripides. He appeared with great success in the Greek Theatre of Syracuse. He has played both Iago and Othello in Shakespeare's tragedy, Richard III, and Agamemnon and Prometheus in the tragedies of Aeschylus. His range is very great; it also includes many modern plays by Ibsen, Pirandello, and even the recent *Rosencrantz and Guilderstern Are Dead* by Tom Stoppard.

In the movies, where Gassman has had an outstanding career since 1946, he has appeared as a naturalistic and comic actor; however, his stage style has been characterized as the traditional overplaying of Italian actors. He has observed: "Everyone is an actor in Italy, preferring to play out the drama in their lives than to pay professionals to do it. That's why there are only five hundred Italian working actors against five thousand in France and fourteen thousand in England. If you banished the theatre in Italy, no one would notice." Yet with his commanding presence and prestige as a star, he has tried to keep theatre alive in Italy. He organized a mobile theatre venture in 1960, which, however, did not meet with success.

Despite disappointments, he continues to act on stage and screen, and tours widely since he can play in several languages with equal ease. He believes that "You can't be an actor and be completely normal. . . . As an actor you live your life watching yourself live your life and watching others watch you too. Acting is based on lying, a noble type of lying. . . ." He feels that the theatre is an obsession. "It is the only thing that brings me satisfaction and anguish at the same time. To me, the theatre is slow suicide, a place where every night I leave a piece of my life."

Return to Tradition

I have often asked myself: How should the Italian actor orient his work in order to develop to the utmost the qualities he derives from belonging to a cultural, artistic, and moral tradition as distinctive as is the Italian?

The tradition of Italian drama, especially in the field of tragedy, is a courtly one: from Machiavelli to Alfieri, and from Alfieri to Pirandello, it has been strongly marked by strict formalism. This does not mean that there has not also coexisted a frankly theatrical tradition, endowed with powerful stage vitality. But this vital tradition has been original to the extent that the play text has been imbued with life.

The full theatrical effect of Alfieri's tragedies is brought out when the plays as literary material—without losing their own character, in fact, displaying this character with greater vigor—come alive and acquire inner tension. For this tension to be fully expressed, a stage tradition is absolutely essential. The same is true of the basic elements of theatre in Pirandello's plays. The specific nature of Italian dramatic literature creates a fundamental problem for the Italian actor: to master its form, to overcome inevitable rough spots, to soften its severities with flexible interpretation, to transform material that was originally literary into theatrically sensitive material.

Obviously, such a problem can be solved only if one firmly masters the techniques of speech in its various aspects. This technical underpinning cannot be acquired on a purely individual basis; it requires the constant contributions of innumerable individuals who operate within the framework of a tradition, each helping to improve the others' results.

Between the nineteenth and twentieth centuries this tradition was gradually lost in Italy, especially because the Italian actor was faced with problems that took him farther and farther away from live contact with Italian dramatic literature. Instead, he was impelled toward foreign dramatic literatures, which stressed closer, more immediate adherence to reality and in which the literary element carried less weight in the staging.

In the past few years I have devoted attention to works like Seneca's *Thyestes* and Alfieri's *Oreste* because of the growing desire within me to return to this distinctively Italian tradition of theatre. In so doing, I have tackled all the technical problems involved, problems that are quite special. Above all, there is the question of how the lines should be spoken and, in the case of the Alfieri play, the question of poetry. Alfieri's verse is harsh, involuted, broken up. At first one may even get

---

Calendoli, Giovanni: *L'attore: storia di un'arte.* Rome: Edizione dell Ateneo, 1959, pp. 618-619, translated from the Italian by Joseph M. Bernstein. Reprinted by permission of Vittorio Gassman.

[473]

the impression that it is no longer recitable, that it no longer constitutes an effective means of communication today. Obviously it is not, if we mean the prosody of realism. But seen from another angle, precisely because of its harshness it has rich possibilities for expression and for infinitely varied effects. This harshness must be accepted intact, as a positive factor, and then transformed into an instrument of eloquence by means of a delivery that obeys the law of poetry. This law cannot be evaded; it must be humbly obeyed. But it must be made clear, productive, distinct, illuminating. If we confront this problem boldly, we get decisive results— in the staging as well. We discover that Alfieri's theatre, for example, can move present-day audiences; in fact, sometimes it grips audiences of today more than plays written in simpler language and closer to contemporary problems. The Italian actor has neglected this possibility offered him by our Italian dramatic literature. Yet it is probably the closest to his native talents, his temperament and natural disposition, even though such works may seem difficult to perform.

In this way the Italian actor has become separated from his true historical tradition. To bridge this gap is by no means a simple matter; but an attempt must be made if we want to restore the Italian theatre to its past strength and breathe life again into the far from insignificant heritage of its history.

XII. THE SOVIET UNION AND POLAND

The Moscow Art Theatre and Its Tradition

The modern theatre in Russia began with the same revolutionary ideals that characterized the independent theatre movements throughout Europe. Along with Antoine, Brahm, and Grein, Stanislavsky "protested against the customary manner of acting, against theatricality, against bathos, against declamation, against over acting, against the bad manner of production, against the habitual scenery, against the star system which spoiled the ensemble...." The search for truth, reality, and serious theatrical artistry motivated Konstantin Stanislavsky and Vladimir Nemirovich-Danchenko in their now famous conversation at the restaurant "Slavic Bazaar." Here in the long hours of a summer night in 1897 they agreed upon the ideals and outlined the structure of the Moscow Art Theatre, which became the most enduring, productive, and significant modern theatre.

Although the Art Theatre was part of an international movement for theatrical reform, it had strong native roots. As early as the eighteenth century, when Russian theatre and drama were in their infancy, the brilliant tragic actor Ivan Dmitrevsky (1734-1821) demanded that the actor should not only perform creatively but should also appreciate the ties between his art and the life of his country. Dmitrevsky went abroad to observe French and English theatres, met Garrick, and became the Director of the first Theatrical School in Russia founded by Catherine the Great. The early actor and playwright, Peter Plavilshchikov (1760-1812), also advanced the idea of the uniqueness and national peculiarities of Russian art. "Feeling for one's native land, should, it seems, be the first theme in theatrical composition.... I ask, why not create in the theatre a taste that is acceptable to our kin? And why should it not be perfect of its kind? The Russians demand not words, but deeds; they desire little to be said, but much to be implied; they love the intricate, but cannot endure the excessively sweet; love order and will not suffer pedantry—in a word, Russians desire the perfect, which cannot exist in imitation, for all imitation is far removed from its original." These pleas for native expression were a reaction to the overwhelming foreign influences in the theatre. Even the indigenous masterpieces of Pushkin, Lermontov, Gogol, Ostrovsky, Turgenev, and Tolstoy could not entirely oust foreign fashions from the Russian stage of their time.

Russia had great actors and acting before its national ideals found expression in dramatic literature. The tragedian Pavel Mochalov's (1800-1848) interpretations of Shakespearean heroes, particularly Hamlet, incarnated Russian romanticism of the early nineteenth century. As early as Mochalov, the inward search for outward form, so characteristic of the Moscow Art Theatre, was evident. "Spiritual profundity and a flaming imagination are two qualities which form the main components of talent," he wrote. "Only when an actor has the ability to imagine what he himself is living with the mind and soul of the audience, that is, when he can force the audience to share his joy and tears, force his imagination vividly to conjure up the scene; in a word, only when the actor feels keenly his position,

[475]

then, for a moment, can he force the audience to forget itself. This great gift can be considered the main aspect and embellishment of talent."

Michael Shchepkin (1788-1863) is rightly considered the founder of Russian stage realism. From Shchepkin to the playwright and theatrical director Alexander Nikolayevich Ostrovsky to Stanislavsky there is a straight line of development. Shchepkin, who spoke of acting as the "song of the heart," always fought against outward theatricality and insisted on psychological expressiveness and realistic justification of every detail and every gesture. In 1850 during the Russian tour of the American Negro tragedian Ira Aldridge, a contemporary reported this conversation between Shchepkin and Aldridge. "Tell him," Shchepkin said to the interpreter, "that I disapprove of the entire scene of Desdemona's arrival. After her galley moors, Aldridge moves calmly and majestically to meet her, offers her his arm and leads her to the foreground. Now doesn't this seem to be quite impossible? He forgets absolutely that Othello is a Moor, that hot southern blood seethes in his veins, that he not only loves, but passionately adores.... Why, he ought to rush at her, gather her up, carry her in his arms and only then remember that he is an army commander and that many curious eyes are following his movement...." This heritage of psychological realism left by Shchepkin passed into the hands of the Maly Theatre and later, the Art Theatre actors and directors Maria Yermolova (1853-1928), Glikeria Fedotova (1846-1925), Alexander Pavlovich Lensky (1847-1908), Nemirovich-Danchenko, Ivan Moskvin (1874-1946), Vasily Kachalov (1875-1948), and many others. Stanislavsky called Shchepkin "our great law-giver, our artist" and treasured those fragments of practical stage advice culled from the master's letters which are presented in this collection.

Considered by many to have been the greatest Russian actor of the nineteenth century, Alexander P. Lensky inherited the mantle of Shchepkin at the Maly Theatre. He forms a genealogical link between Shchepkin and the Moscow Art Theatre, which was observing its tenth anniversary on the day of his funeral. Of Lensky, Stanislavsky said, "I imitated to a point of disgust the most talented and attractive actor I had ever seen, A. P. Lensky."

To Alexander Ostrovsky Russian theatre owed not only a repertory of realistic drama, but also the first organization to protect the rights of Russian dramatists, whom the monopolistic Imperial Theatres had refused to pay adequately, although they lavished money on foreign stars. In 1881 he addressed an appeal to Alexander III which called for drama for the people, for inexpensive seats, and overall theatrical reform; to abolish the star system and institute ensemble acting. Through Ostrovsky's efforts the Imperial Theatres were deprived of their monopoly, and in 1882 private theatres were legalized. Ostrovsky was appointed director of the Moscow theatres and established the Russian Academy of Dramatic Art, but he died the following year without carrying out his projected plans. Ostrovsky sounded the note of the Art Theatre when he wrote in one of his plays about the theatre, *The Forest*: "Play actors? No, we are artists, noble artists, and it is you who are the play-actors. If we love, then we love truly; if we hate, we fight; if we help, then we help with our last penny."

The Russian tour of the Duke of Saxe-Meiningen's Company in 1885, by its example of historical exactitude and its ensemble, further spurred native *régisseurs* to seek methods of rehearsal and direction which would weld their many individually talented actors into a cohesive ensemble. All through the nineteenth century there was an intense but frustrated interest in acting which grew out of the urge to express creatively the rich new national literature. Emphasis in Russian drama on characters in their milieu rather than on the individual hero required new acting techniques and new staging. Only two years before the Moscow Art Theatre's historic performance of Chekhov's *The Sea Gull*, that play, as performed in the usual manner by the Imperial Theatre in St. Petersburg, the Alexandrinsky Theatre, had failed miserably. Chekhov declared: "Never will I write these plays or try to produce them, not if I live to be 700 years old." Stanislavsky's assertion that "Chekhov cannot be presented; he can only be experienced," suggests why *The Sea Gull* was the Art Theatre's first great triumph. It was this desire to give truthful representations to new, profound native drama that generated the techniques of the Moscow Art Theatre.

Together, Stanislavsky and Nemirovich-Danchenko, one as actor and director, the other as playwright and literary adviser, created a theatre in 1898 devoted to carefully rehearsed and extraordinarily detailed naturalistic productions of Russian and foreign classics. They might have been no more than an excellent troupe had Nemirovich-Danchenko not urged them to play Anton Chekhov's former failure *The Sea Gull*. Aware that a second failure might be fatal to the ailing and discouraged Chekhov, they sought more than ever for the inner emotion of his tenuous tragedy. Their inner realism in acting and external realism in staging gave life first to Chekhov's plays, then to those of Maxim Gorky. These playwrights in turn provided the theatre with a body of dramatic writing perfectly suited to their histrionic ideals.

The Art Theatre was, and still is, an actors' theatre. Nemirovich-Danchenko wrote: "The director should become lost in the creative process of the actor. Need I say that for this the director must possess the potentialities of the actor? Practically speaking, he himself must be a profound, diverse actor." To achieve a theatre which would go beyond photographic realism, every player individually and in ensemble must follow "the law of inner justification" in order to reveal the deepest intent of the dramatist. No longer would the actor declaim lines to the accompaniment of artificial gestures and postures; he would "incarnate" his role in terms of his own personality. Out of these ideas was born the body of acting theory known as the Stanislavsky system.

The principles Stanislavsky elaborated are fundamentally those which great actors of all times have utilized in their art. They appear again and again in the writings collected in this volume. Mere statements, however, that "the actor should live his role" were not enough. Stanislavsky recognized that what was needed, especially by actors in naturalistic dramas, was a systematic technique that would create "a favorable condition for the appearance of inspiration by means of the will, that condition in the presence of which inspiration was most likely to descend into the actor's soul." He wrote: "All that has been written about the theatre is only philosophizing, very interesting, very deep, it is true, that speaks beautifully of the results desirable to reach in art, or criticism of the success or failure of results already reached. All these works are valuable and necessary, but not for the actual practical work in the theatre, for they are silent on how to reach certain results, on what is necessary to do firstly, secondly, thirdly, and so forth, with a beginner, or what is to be done with an experienced and spoiled actor.

"What exercises resembling solfeggi are needed by him? What scales, what arpeggi for the development of creative feeling and experience are required by the actor? They must be given numbers ... for systematic exercises in the school and at home. All books and works of the theatre are silent on this score. There is no practical textbook."

Stanislavsky perfected a practical, flexible system for the training of the actor, the building of a character and the analysis of the overall action of the play. Over a period of some thirty years he experimented, testing each formulation of his system in production, revising and discarding in his search for stage truth. In all his work he kept alive the spirit of inquiry and change that had led him in the first decade of the century to question his own creativity as an actor and the very nature of theatre.

His system as utilized by the Moscow Art Theatre involved the actor's work on himself and his work on roles in specific productions. The training of the actor centered on perfecting his medium, that is, his own physical and sensory capacity. The actor had to learn to control his nervous system so that he could be relaxed and yet concentrate on his playing. To avoid distractions, he was to put himself within an imaginary "circle" from which he could not step as long as he was acting. He had to develop his imagination and his sense of fantasy and to memorize past emotions with minute detail so that he could re-create them in his role. By improvisations and exercises he was to store up rich, accurate memories of sensory and emotional experience for use on the stage. The actor had to be naïve and to believe in the creative *if*, "the imagined truth which the actor can believe as sincerely and with greater enthusiasm than he believes practical truth."

In each play the actor had to master the "offered circumstances," the situations presented by the author. It was necessary to learn the logic of the contact between the characters onstage and develop with one's fellow actors a rhythm for each piece based on the "offered circumstances" of the author. Finally, the actor had to grasp the "kernel" of the character—his internal and external personality.

Moscow Art Theatre rehearsals began with intensive first readings of the play —"table work." Once the enthusiasm of the actor was stimulated, a long period was spent in analyzing the "sub-text," the meaning that underlies each line. Then the play was examined in its historical context. Detailed study of the lines began again as short segments (*kuskii*) were grouped together into units·like musical measures. The actor had to understand the "aim" that motivated the character so that he could answer the question, "What do I want and why?" After this analysis, the actors "incarnated" their roles.

In the last years of his life, Stanislavsky, always working out new ideas, turned away from this elaborate historical and psychological discussion and emotional probing guided by the director to a "method of physical actions" that allowed the actor to take the lead as he performed acts that would not only arouse his emotional life but would determine the director's production concept. The production of *Tartuffe*, described by V. I. Toporkov in this section, was initiated by Stanislavsky to demonstrate this new method of work which overturned many of his earlier procedures; he died, however, before it was finally offered the public in 1939.

The roster of brilliant players of the Moscow Art Theatre over the years is too long to record here, but brief mention must be made of some of the original members of the company. Olga Knipper-Chekhova, wife of the playwright, played many of the leads in her husband's plays and most of the others, often opposite Stanislavsky himself. Ivan Moskvin, the great high comedian, played Yepikhodov in *The Cherry Orchard,* Luka in *The Lower Depths* and the title role in Alexei Tolstoy's *Tsar Fyodor,* which he created and played for forty-three years. Vasily Kachalov played Hamlet in the experimental Gordon Craig production, Baron in *The Lower Depths* and Ivan Karamazov in *The Brothers Karamazov,* as well as other roles. Among the many other notable performers in this great ensemble theatre were Alla Tarasova, Maria Germanova, Vasily Luzhsky, Alexander Vishnevsky and Maria Petrovna Lilina (wife of Stanislavsky). A role created by one of these actors often took a full year of study and rehearsal and was kept alive in the repertory. In 1918, for example, after two hundred performances, five of the important roles in *The Three Sisters* were still being played by those actors who had created them in 1901.

Just as the theatres of Antoine and Brahm harbored the seeds of revolt against naturalism within their own companies, so from the Moscow Art Theatre came the innovators Vsevelod Meyerhold, Alice Koonen, wife of Alexander Tairov (1885-1950), and Eugene Vakhtangov. Meyerhold led the revolt against naturalism with bold theatrical experiments. It was Meyerhold as Treplev in the original production of *The Sea Gull* who cried: "To my mind the modern theatre is nothing but tradition and conventionality. . . . We need new forms and if we can't have them we had better have nothing." He sought to bridge the gulf that separates actor and spectator through nonillusory theatrical devices. He turned to the theatre of Japan, to medieval spectacles, to the *commedia dell' arte,* to Renaissance platform stages, to the circus and the music hall for rhythmic movements, stylized symbols, poetic gestures and spatial innovations. Head of the avant-garde, he became in the first years after the Russian Revolution leader of the new theatre whose job it was, he said, "to make a Revolution in the theatre and to reflect in each performance the struggle of the working class for emancipation." For more than a decade he experimented brilliantly with constructivist sets, new mass audiences drawn directly into the performance, and actors trained in "biomechanics" to express through their gestures and attitudes the essence of modern man and the new Soviet life. During the thirties his theatre declined and actors left him as he tried to reconcile his views with the new demands for "socialist realism." His theatre was closed in 1938. Called upon to recant his artistic heresy in 1939, he instead rejected the official theatre as "frightful and pitiful" and "without art." Three days after his bitter attack on intolerance and conformity in art, he was arrested and sent into exile, where he died in 1942.

Alexander Tairov, who with his actress-wife Alice Koonen founded the Kamerny (Chamber) Theatre in 1914, also protested against the realistic theatre which in his opinion "neglected the symbolic gesture and rhythm of the complete theatre." Like Meyerhold and the other *régisseurs,* Tairov and his wife completely controlled their theatre. Using intoned speech and stylized gestures, Tairov wanted to create a heroic theatre which, unlike Meyerhold's, preserved some of the emotional intimacy of the Art Theatre. In describing his objectives, Tairov said: "We are aiming at the creation of a great synthetic production, vast in its dimension, classical in its severe simplicity, emotional in its intensity, dynamic in the structure of the stage space, tragic in its action, optimistic in its substance, realistic in its methods and romantic in its experience and exposition of genuine reality." Tairov managed to keep his theatre going during the difficult decade of the thirties and even into the post-World War II years.

Eugene Vakhtangov, a student of Stanislavsky, effected during his brief lifetime a compromise between the extreme theatricality of the *régisseur* Meyerhold and the complete naturalism of the actor Stanislavsky. He wrote: "Meyerhold is the only Russian director who instinctively feels the theatrical. In his general search for truth Stanislavsky brought the truth of life to the stage. But Meyerhold removed

the truth from the stage and in his zeal destroyed all true feeling in the theatre.
. . . The perfect work of art is eternal. But only then does a work of art exist when
content, form and material are in perfect harmony. Stanislavsky could find harmony
only in the moods of the society of the time. Not everything of the times is eternal,
but the eternal is always of the times. Meyerhold cannot feel tomorrow; he can
only feel today. But one should be able to feel today in tomorrow and tomorrow in
today." Vakhtangov's concept of "perfect harmony" was realized in such famous
productions as *The Dybbuk*, performed by the Habimah Theatre, and *Princess
Turandot*, his last production. A profound influence on all who knew him, his
theatre was continued by his close associate, the actor Michael Chekhov, and by his
other disciples after his untimely death in 1922.

In the midst of these movements and countermovements, with emphasis on
"biomechanics" and stylization, the Moscow Art Theatre never abandoned its belief
in the theatre of inner feeling. Relatively static for some years after the Revolution,
it preferred to serve the new society by preserving its link with the best theatrical
tradition of the past until its actors could grasp the inner reality of the new revolutionary man. In the enormous expansion of the Russian theatre from about 250
playhouses in the days of the Tsar to over 900 Soviet professional theatres and
thousands of farms and factory stages in the thirties, the Art Theatre remained the
fountainhead of acting theory and practice. In 1934 Norris Houghton reported
that the Stanislavsky system was the basis for the training of actors in the traditional Maly Theatre as well as in the Kamerny, Revolutionary, Vakhtangov, Second
Moscow Art, Gypsy and Jewish theatres. Even the actors of Meyerhold's Theatre
divided their time between the tumbler's mat and the study of the "system."

To actors throughout the world the Moscow Art Theatre has been an ideal.
In the spirit of Stanislavsky's slogan "The only king and ruler of the stage is the
talented actor," the Art Theatre, by precept and example, raised the artistic stature
of the acting profession. Stanislavsky and his co-workers developed an organized
body of histrionic theory and practice that inspired actors to serious study of their
craft. From the Art Theatre and its several studios came a number of actors and
actresses who began their careers in Russia and then came to the United States
where they had a broad influence both as performers and teachers. Among these are
Richard Boleslavsky, Michael Chekhov, Leo Bulgakov, Alla Nazimova, Tamara
Daykarhanova, Maria Ouspenskaya and Akim Tamiroff.

The Moscow Art Theatre weathered the changes in official attitude toward
theatre and the devastation of World War II, but the cultural "thaw" that set in
after the death of Stalin in 1953 brought new challenges to the Stanislavsky tradition of realism. The innovators of the fifties and sixties felt the old-fashioned but
prestigious museum presentations of the MAT were "a brake upon imaginative techniques." They turned to the heritage of Meyerhold, reviving some of his productions and his methods. The publication in 1968 of a two-volume complete collection of Meyerhold's articles, letters and speeches is evidence of his rehabilitation
and importance.

Nikolai Okhlopkov, a Meyerhold protégé, was one of the first to pick up the
banner of experiment again. In the 1930's as director of the Realistic Theatre he
drew audiences and actors together in intensely emotional mass dramas staged in
novel theatre-in-the-round arrangements. He combined the "inner techniques" of
the actor's theatre with the striking stagings of the director's theatre. He declared:
"Thus we assert the realism of the theatre through theatrical means, appealing to

[480]

the imagination of the spectator and at the same time providing it with a powerful stimulus. Thus the audience cooperates with the actors in every performance, so that the actors applaud the audience as well as the audience the actors." After the repressions of the late thirties and the difficulties of the war, Okhlopkov emerged with bold stagings as soon as he had the opportunity. He produced an exciting *Hamlet,* gave Russia its first taste of Brecht with *Mother Courage,* and offered a version of Euripides' *Medea* with a choir of a hundred voices that commented on the deadly spirit of Russia under Stalin. He projected an experimental playhouse that would seat three thousand under a plexiglass roof that could be open to the skies on summer nights, but he died in 1966 with this dream unfulfilled.

Valentin Pluchek, director of the Moscow Theatre of Satire, revived Meyerhold's stagings of Mayakovsky's satires, *The Bedbug* and the *Bathhouse,* removed from the stage in 1930. Yuri Lyubimov directed spectacular pop versions of John Reed's *Ten Days That Shook the World* and Voznesensky's *Antiworlds* at his Taganka Theatre. Oleg Yefremov provided the first Russian productions of John Osborne's *Look Back in Anger* and Eugène Ionesco's *Rhinoceros.* Georg Tovstanogov gave pointed contemporary relevance to his staging of classics and brought Brecht's *Arturo Ui,* directed by Erwin Axer of Warsaw, to his Gorky Theatre.

These newer leaders as well as the older directors and actors like Yuri Zavadsky of the Mossoviet Theatre and Reuben Simonov of the Vakhtangov Theatre now combine the best of the two traditions of modern Russian theatre. This contemporary view is well expressed by Tovstanogov, whose theatre has been equated with England's Royal Shakespeare and National Theatre or Barrault's *Théâtre de France:* "Everything in the Russian theatre is based on Stanislavsky, . . . But Stanislavsky is a beginning step. After all, he revealed a direction for the theatre of his time, not *this* time. So he must be advanced . . . Meyerhold was form, Stanislavsky content. Like many others, we believe it is a very good combination."

In the other lively theatres of Eastern Europe in the 1960's the pattern is much the same. The most notable student of the actor's art is Jerzy Grotowski of Poland. Although the important experiments at his Institute for Research into Acting are heavily influenced by Meyerhold, Brecht, and Artaud, he holds Stanislavsky, in whose system he was trained, to be the most significant predecessor, for he alone devoted his life to perfecting a method for the complex human art of the actor.

MICHAEL S. SHCHEPKIN

(1788 - 1863)

A serf to the age of thirty-three, Shchepkin began his career in the theatre attached to his master's estate. Already known as an excellent actor, Shchepkin, aided by members of the Moscow intelligentsia, was able to purchase his freedom in 1821. Gogol, one of his staunchest supporters, rejoiced in Shchepkin's freedom. "The time will come when one will go to the theatre anxious not to miss a single word pronounced by Shchepkin. His speech will have the weight of gold."

Two years later Shchepkin joined the Maly Theatre in Moscow and remained there for more than forty years. The great actor refined scenic art by discarding the false pathos and artificial delivery which had been imported from abroad and which dominated the Russian theatre at the end of the eighteenth and beginning of the nineteenth centuries. "Fate," Shchepkin wrote in his *Memoirs of an Actor-Serf,* "has given the Russians the opportunity to elevate the art of acting. We have no ruts of false-classicism in which to bog down."

Shchepkin's brand of realism has been characterized by Theodore Komisarjevsky as follows: "Shchepkin's acting was the condensed *imaginative* acting of life-like characters. Although Shchepkin held that a close observation of people was necessity for an actor, he called imitative acting 'actoring.' To Shchepkin realistic forms and characters served as a means to express his feelings and ideas, and he condensed and adapted them to suit his artistic and philosophic purposes."

Shchepkin has been the teacher and unsurpassed example for Russian actors for many generations. The present Academic Maly Theatre and the Art Theatre preserve Shchepkin's heritage of realism. The Maly, scene of his long creative life, is known as "Shchepkin's House."

Feeling and Pretense

About the Author's Idea[1]

Yes, real life and stirring passions, in all their truth, should be brightly revealed in art and real feeling should be permitted to the extent that the idea of the author demands it. No matter how true the feeling, if it steps beyond the bounds of the general idea, there will be no harmony, which is the general law of all art. Naturalness and true feeling are necessary in art, but only to the extent that the general idea permits of them. That is what all art consists of, to grasp this feature and to be true to it.

To the Actor Shumsky[2]

Take full advantage of all opportunities, work and develop the talents given you by God to their fullest measure. Do not reject criticism, but search for its deeper meaning, and in order to test yourself and the criticism, always keep in mind—nature: crawl under the skin of your character, so to speak, study well his particular ideas, if there are any, and do not even exclude from consideration the social influences of his past. Then, no matter what situations are taken from life, you will always express them truthfully: you may sometimes play poorly, sometimes only satisfactorily (that often depends on your own inner disposition), but you will always play truthfully. Remember that perfection is not given to man; but by applying yourself industriously, you will be approaching it to the extent that nature has given you the means for it. For God's sake, don't be concerned with amusing your audience, for both the ridiculous and the serious derive from a true conception of life, and believe me, in two or three years you will notice that you act your roles differently, with every year you will become more versatile and more natural. Watch yourself ceaselessly, even if the public is satisfied with

---

Lvov, Nikolai I, and I. Maksimov: *Masterstvo Aktiora* (The Actor's Craft). Moscow: Gosizdat, 1935. This selection translated by David Pressman.

[1]Letter to the writer Annenkov, November 12, 1853.

[2]Letter to Shumsky, March 27, 1848. (S. V. Shumsky, 1821-1878, a well-known actor of the Maly Theatre.)

you, you must be your own severest critic. You must believe that inner satisfaction is worth more than applause. Be among people—as much as time will permit, study the human being in the mass, pay attention to all anecdotes, and you will always discover why things have happened one way and not another; this living book will serve you well until we have a body of theory, which unfortunately, our art as yet does not possess. Consequently, study all classes of people without prejudice, and you will see that there is good and evil everywhere. This will give you the ability in acting to give each group its due—that is, if you play a peasant you will not be able to observe the social niceties when expressing extreme joy, and when playing an aristocrat you cannot shout and wave your hands in anger, as a peasant might do. Do not place yourself above hard work on situations and details encountered in life, but remember that they are only an aid, and not a goal—that they are only valuable when you understand your goal in acting.

Wherein Lies the Difference Between Actors?[3]

... One actor does not cry on the stage, but only makes a pretense of crying, yet he makes the audience cry. Another actor is bathed in bitter tears, but the audience does not respond. One may conclude, therefore, that true feeling is not essential in dramatic art, but only cold craft, that is, simply "acting." Perhaps I am wrong, but in my opinion it is not so. How can I express my ideas more clearly? For instance, one person has been endowed with a soul responsive to all beauty, to all good: To him all human interests are dear. No matter on what level of society he finds himself, he is sensitive to its grief and its joy, he responds hotly to everything (as if he himself were touched by it), and that is why he will weep and laugh with society. Another person is more of an egoist. Living in society, encountering at every step both sorrow and laughter, he will participate in both, only to the extent that his own interests are affected. He may feel sorry, for instance, for one who has been robbed of a hundred thousand rubles, but it won't enter his head to consider how terrible it is for a pauper to lose his last ruble. He'll sympathize with some nobleman whose wife has been seduced by so-and-so, but won't wrinkle a brow when told that the same nobleman has taken the footman's wife away. Such people reason coldly. In order not to appear selfish, they demonstrate their sympathy as though it were real sympathy, and, being always inwardly calm, the emotion appears convincing. And so it is on the stage. It is so much easier to play mechanically—for that you need only your reason. Reason will approach sorrow and joy to the same extent that any imitation can approach nature. But an actor of feeling—that's something else again. Indescribable labors await him. He must begin with wiping out his self... and become the character the author intended him to be. He must walk, talk, think, feel, cry, laugh—as the author wants him to. You see how the work of this actor is more meaningful. In the first case you only need to pretend to live—in the second you have to live.... You might say that this is impossible. No, it is only difficult. You may say why struggle with some kind of perfection when there are much simpler means of pleasing the audience? One can only answer to that, why have art? If you should ever have the opportunity of seeing two actors, both working conscientiously, both equally sincere and devoted to their art, one of whom is intelligent, reasoned, who has achieved the art of pretense to a high degree, and the other, with a flaming-soul, with that heavenly

---

[3]Letter to the actress Shubert, March 27, 1848.

[483]

spark—then you will see the immeasurable distance between true feeling and pretense. I saw Plessis and Volkis[4] and would say that I have witnessed both types of performance. The first of these two actresses almost in the prime of life, with a fresh voice, is a master of art, and is perfectly fine, very fine! The second is almost forty years old, with a voice that has suffered, but she feels, feels passionately, and how pale Plessis appears, with all her art! All I heard from Volkis were a few sounds of distress, but I shall remember them all my life.

On the Art of Rachel[5]

Yes, that's art; she is a remarkable woman! I admire her too much to say I love her. And with all that I feel sad. What would be the result, if, with this talent, she were to study art with its modern demands, or, at least, as we Russians look at it! Indeed, that would be a miracle! Strange—throughout all Europe they still content themselves with such declamation, that is, with whining, whereas we cannot get accustomed to that singing; we sang and sang in that style and then we threw it over! How many singing words we have! But with us it is the heart that sings them!

KONSTANTIN S. STANISLAVSKY

(1863-1938)

In the world of the actor few names are more revered than that of Konstantin Sergeyevich Stanislavsky (Alexeyev). Born in Moscow on January 17, 1863, of a wealthy merchant family, his whole life was devoted to the theatre. As a boy he appeared in the amateur theatricals given at the private theatre of the Alexeyev country home. Passionately fond of the stage, he undertook the serious study of acting with such great Russian actors as Sadovsky, Maria Savina (1850-1915), and Yermolova. It was during this period that the Italian actor Ernesto Rossi made the great impression on the formation of Stanislavsky's concepts of acting described by him in *My Life in Art*. Writing about Rossi's performance as Romeo, Stanislavsky says, "he drew its inner image to perfection." "This wonderful idea" that required the actor "to reflect all that is best and most profound in his creative spirit ... to store up within himself this great inner content and identify it with the spiritual life of the part he is playing" became the cornerstone of Stanislavsky's system.

In 1888 Stanislavsky together with other devotees of the vanguard theatre formed the Art and Literary Society. As both actor and producer, Stanislavsky began his search for a theatre which would ban the spurious and artificial from the stage. The Society laid the foundation for the Moscow Art Theatre and prepared the way for the future artistic partnership with Nemirovich-Danchenko. The excerpts from Stanislavsky's *Art Notes* printed here deal with performances given by the Society and are selected to show the early development of Stanislavsky's theories on the art of the actor. The second selection records a later stage in Stanislavsky's thinking when he began to work out in some detail the central concepts of his system.

As producer and artistic director of the Moscow Art Theatre, Stanislavsky staged over fifty different plays by such authors as Ostrovsky, Chekhov, Gorky,

---

[4]Plessis and Volkis were known to the Russian public by their performances at the Mikhailov-sky Theatre in St. Petersburg, where a French company played permanently.

[5]Letter to Annenkov, February 20, 1854, about Rachel who played in Russia in 1850.

Maeterlinck, Goldoni, Ibsen, Alexei Tolstoy and Leo Tolstoy. In the course of twenty-five years Stanislavsky played a number of memorable parts on its stage: Uriel in *Uriel Acosta;* Astrov in *Uncle Vanya;* Stockman in *An Enemy of the People;* Vershinin in *The Three Sisters;* Gayev in *The Cherry Orchard;* Rakitin in *A Month in the Country.* Those significant words, "A man... what a proud ring the word has!" reverberated from the stage for the first time when Stanislavsky played Satin in Gorky's *Lower Depths.* Stanislavsky's career was an embodiment of that belief in mankind.

Stanislavsky was not a systematic theorist but rather a pragmatic questioner whose books, teaching and productions together reveal the full range of his lifelong search for truth in art. The uniqueness of Stanislavsky's approach is clearly stated by Lee Strasberg, the American director and teacher of acting. "The Stanislavsky system ... represents a sharp break with traditional teaching and a return to actual theatre experience. It tries to analyze ... what actually happens when an actor acts. Theatres and actors of great variety and diversified form have created outstanding works on the basis of the training acquired by use of Stanislavsky's principles. The works created are never copies or imitations of one another but are original creative achievements. That is the purpose of the Stanislavsky idea. It teaches not how to play this or that part but how to create organically."

Stanislavsky did not live to complete the comprehensive work he had planned on the art of acting. Rough notes and fragments remained at the time of his death. The Soviet government appointed a special commission to organize the 12,000 manuscripts left by him. Seven volumes of an eight-volume *Complete Works of Stanislavsky* have now appeared in Russian; these provide the full range of his changing ideas. In English the evolution of his system is covered in three main volumes, *An Actor Prepares* (1936), *Building a Character* (1949), and *Creating a Role* (1961), all edited and translated by Elizabeth Reynolds Hapgood. In *Creating a Role,* Stanislavsky's emphasis on "physical actions" has brought about a shift in the interpretation of the method.

The Evolution of My System

[From *Art Notes*]

A dreadful and solemn day.[1] A great many people came. Actors, artists, professors, princes and counts. Imagine having to play a responsible role! I dreaded my appearance in *The Miser-Knight,* and was sure of myself in *Dandin.* But things turned out quite the contrary. *The Miser-Knight* went better and pleased the audience more, though the first act was a failure. The audience did not even applaud. Before I went on, a kind of apathy, the most unpleasant mood an actor can fall into, came over me. At first I could not feel my part, my tone was shaky, and I

Konstantin S. Stanislavsky: Excerpts from *Art* Notes, 1877-1892. Moscow: *International Literature,* Nos. 11-12, November-December, 1940, pp. 170-187 *passim.* By permission of Helen Black.

[1]December 8, 1888, the first program by the amateurs of the Art and Literary Society, which presented Pushkin's tragedy *The Miser-Knight,* Molière's *Georges Dandin,* and scenes from *The Godunovs,* a tragedy by A. F. Fedotov. Stanislavsky had two leading parts—the Baron in *The Miser-Knight* and Satonville in *Georges Dandin.* It was after this first performance that the actors, in cooperation with whom he subsequently entered the Moscow Art Theatre, joined Stanislavsky and formed a group.

dragged out the pauses. Towards the end of the monologue I got worked up and the forceful part went, apparently, very well. Medvedeva[2] the actress praised my *Miser-Knight,* but remarked that I had made the pauses a little too long.

The actor Shilovsky[3] praised me but reproached me for a certain sameness of tone and abrupt transitions of voice from low to high. He interprets this role in a different way, too, much of the surface only, too theatrically. Count Sollogub[4] praised me up to the skies and said that the impression I produce is overwhelming. After the second act the audience called for me three times in an extremely friendly way, and the same after the third act.

It is a queer thing, but when you really feel your role, the impression you make on your audience is poorer; when you have yourself well in hand and do not give your part everything you have in you, it turns out much better. I begin to grasp something of progressiveness in the role. I tested the effect of acting without gestures (there were only two in the last act). I wear the costume well, that I can feel. The plastic side is developing, and I am beginning to understand pauses. Mime is going on well, too. They tell me I died very well, plastically and convincingly. There was quite a lot of talk about me the following day at the Maly Theatre; naturally, only the most flattering opinions reached my ears. Saying goodbye to me, Medvedeva added: "You are a serious actor and you love the stage. I worship you. It is a very rare thing for a young man to give money for a good cause and play well into the bargain." Then she kissed me and assured me that our productions would go well, because they were much better than those at the Korsh Theatre.[5]

There is one thing I should like to say about *Dandin*: we were too sure of ourselves in it, and once the weight of *The Miser-Knight* was off our minds, we ceased to worry and played carelessly. Yuzhin[6] praised me. Shilovsky, who is an expert in the matter of costume and make-up, said that my Satonville was the first genuine Molière he had ever seen.

A certain Ustromskaya[7] told me that she sat through the performance of *The Miser-Knight* with some vexation; the technique was excellent, but there was no truth in the acting. She concluded that I ought not to play old men and dramatic parts. Fedotova said that when I appeared in the vault and spoke in a low voice under the arched ceiling, the illusion was perfect—just what she wanted. Philipov the critic declared that my portrayal in *Dandin* was inimitable and that I might compete with anyone. My recital of my part in *The Miser-Knight* was good, but

---

[2]Nadezhda Medvedeva (1832-1899), a well known actress of the Maly Theatre. In *My Life in Art* Stanislavsky says, "I remember Medvedeva well not only as an actress but as an interesting human being, self taught. To a certain degree she was my teacher and exercised a great influence over me."

[3]K. S. Shilovsky, a Maly Theatre actor.

[4]Count Fyodor Sollogub (1848-1890), a talented poet and artist. He painted the scenery for *The Miser-Knight* and designed the costumes for *Georges Dandin.* He also performed successfully in some of the Society's presentations.

[5]The Korsh Theatre was founded in 1882. The company included many excellent actors, but Korsh was chiefly interested in the commercial side of the undertaking, and practically every week brought the presentation of a new production.

[6]A. I. Yuzhin (Prince Sumbatov), a talented actor, subsequently *régisseur* and director of the Maly Theatre. Author of several plays.

[7]Maria Ustromskaya. Took part, under the stage name of "Mareva" in the performances of the Art and Literary Society.

there was no acting. In his opinion I should go in for ordinary everyday characters, as I am no tragedian.

* * * *

We got tired of *Dandin*.[8] The comical situations are no longer fresh and do not amuse the actors—and that is, probably, why we played so lifelessly.

I begin to understand what precisely it is that is so difficult in acting; the ability to throw one's self into a part no matter what external obstacles may present themselves, the ability to enliven one's self and not allow the part to grow stale. I have no experience in this as yet.... While on the stage, I fancied it was not going so badly, but the audience did not laugh in the first act and said that the tempo was too slow. During the second act people brightened up and to my surprise, called for both Alianchkova and myself after my exit.... The surprising thing was that they called for us again after our exit. What could it have meant?

The Flare-Up went off very pleasantly. Perevoshchikova's[9] acting was wonderfully feminine and simple....

* * * *

I may be mistaken, but I think that in the parts I played at the beginning of the year, I set the tone at the very first rehearsal. Now there is nothing, not a single living note. I am becoming terribly afraid of routine; has it, perhaps, got a firm hold on me already? How can I determine that, if I am not at all certain that I know what this thing called routine is, and where it begins, where it springs from, and where to find a way of preventing its deadly roots from fastening in me. Probably under routine they understand theatricality, that is to say, some peculiar way of walking and talking on the stage. If so, then routine should not be confused with the necessary conditions of the stage, since the latter undoubtedly requires something special, something that is not to be found in life. Then, herein lies the problem; to bring life itself on to the stage, but avoid routine (which kills this life), while transgressing none of the stage rules. This is the chief, and perhaps one of the final difficulties confronting an actor who, at the beginning of his career, has to overcome a number of obstacles and, like a jockey at a race, reaches at last the worst of all, the Irish banquette. If the actor manages to make his way through the narrow and dangerous defile between routine on the one hand and stage-conditions on the other, he comes out at long last to the real road of life.

It is a road that lasts forever, it is fascinating, with plenty of room for variety, in short, there is scope for talent to develop. But if you get caught in the narrow defile, you will be stifled, for there is no fresh air to be got in routine, no space or freedom in it at all. In these conditions talent withers and dies. I fancy I am coming now in this dangerous stage. Why now, of all times? Here are the facts, which will answer this question: to act, one must not only possess talent and other necessary qualifications, but also become accustomed to the stage and the public, acquire a certain power over one's nerves, a self-control to a considerable degree. This ABC and grammar of acting, are, comparatively speaking, not difficult, although in the majority of cases they take years to acquire. Without them, it is im-

---

[8]The Program of the Art and Literary Society given February 2, 1889, included *Georges Dandin*, and two vaudeville sketches: *The Flare-Up On the Heart* and *Woman's Secret*. Stanislavsky played his former part of Satonville in *Georges Dandin* and Megriot the student in *Woman's Secret*.

[9]Maria Petrovna Lilina. Subsequently an outstanding actress in the Moscow Art Theatre, and Stanislavsky's wife. He greatly respected her opinions of his work.

possible to live on the stage, impossible to forget one's self, impossible to throw one's self wholeheartedly into one's part and bring real life on to the boards.

This is a felicitous definition. How can anyone read fluently and feel it, when the letters and commas keep distracting his attention? It seems to me that I have gone through the elementary grammar of dramatic art, mastered it, got used to it, and that now, and only now, my real work—mental and spiritual—begins, only now creation, to which the true path has been opened, can begin. The main thing is to find the true path. Of course, the surest is that which leads nearest to truth, to life. But to reach it, one must know what truth and life are. There it is then,— my task: to get to know the one and the other. In other words, one must train one's self, one must think and develop morally and give one's mind no rest. Can I command sufficient energy and strength and time for this? I do not know, but at any rate I am thankful that I have at least elucidated and motivated the task before me, at least I need not wander any more in darkness, but can settle down to work as far as it is in my power.

...I have come to the most difficult of the obstacles, to the most dangerous period for a young actor. Routine is in me; my performance betrays it in—say— the sameness of the mime, the voice, the tone, which are repeated in several roles, and also in the rehearsals for *A Debt of Honor*. There is also some creative power— or at least faint suggestions of it—in me. They come out, I think, in unexpected, unprepared, spontaneous movements and alterations of tone that I sometimes introduce impromptu into the performance itself. Further proof of them is my correct tone as Obnovlensky, a tone that emerged quite unexpectedly, and this I owe to the illusion and surroundings at the dress-rehearsal of *The Ruble*. In exactly the same way, my mood in the performance of *A Debt of Honor* prompted me to make certain movements of a very vital nature, and they produced an impression on the audience.

I am going over in my own mind, scene by scene, my role as Baron, and trying to remember what was vital and living in each, and what was not. I shall mark the rehearsals, which, not excepting the dress-rehearsal, were all feeble and lifeless. I shall make only a brief explanatory note: the play was produced according to Fedotov's directions. The parts were handed out by him and not chosen by us, so that I had to adapt myself to the feelings of another person and not to my own. This, in my opinion, is the principal reason why I took so long to enter into the mood of my role and did not live it. On the day of the performance itself, thanks to the audience I felt the part and came to life in it.... Komisarjevsky[10] said that we played so well that it was really a pity to see so much effort being wasted on such a trashy play.

＊　　＊　　＊　　＊

During the summer, which I spent abroad, I read up the part of Imshin,[11] thinking that I would master it, but I did not, I had only to take it up to feel disappointed at once in it and in my abilities. I felt it was much too difficult for

---

[10]Fyodor Komisarjevsky (1838-1905), the famous operatic tenor. One of the founders of the Art and Literary Society. Father of Vera and Theodore Komisarjevsky.

[11]The first theatrical performance given by the Art and Literary Society after a long interval was held on November 26, 1889. It was Pisemsky's *Autocrats*, a tragedy in five acts. Stanislavsky took the part of Prince Platon Imshin, a general during the reign of Paul I (1796-1801).

me; I understood how it ought to be played, how Salvini would have played it, but in myself I could discover no sign of those capacities that might create the role. In my search for the right vein I fell into the error of trying to give the part an everyday character. In short, I began to think too much of externals, and endeavor to bring out the autocrat, his arrogance, the outwardly cruel and overbearing appearance of Imshin. And then the photograph I saw of Samarin[12] as Imshin, wearing a sort of morose grimace on his face—further encouraged me in my error. I got into routine, into a banal tone, allowed them to bind me hand and foot, and the role not only refused to become mine, but began to weary me. The end of it all was that I lost its inward meaning, I ceased to feel it. That was the state of things up to the first reading. The first reading with the new *regisseur* (Ryabov)[13]— this has always been an epoch in my life, and this time it was an epoch of a very depressing nature. My spirits sank. Ryabov would stop me, and me alone, after every sentence, and gave the part an entirely different psychological aspect. Naturally, these interruptions made me nervous. I was extremely reluctant to agree to them, particularly as I am very stubborn in matters of this kind. Still, Ryabov was right; I was too harsh to my role, I drove it too hard and brought out only the bad qualities of the autocrat, forgetting that the part contained pleasanter and brighter sides. . . .

* * * *

I am no Don Juan[14] and thank God for that, but it is a pity that I cannot manage the part. Why is it? Can it be that I do not understand it, or that every member of the audience understands it too well for himself? No, the secret lies in neither the one nor the other, but, so far as I can see, in quite the opposite. None of the people in the audience has a clear conception of Don Juan. Why Don Juan is the conqueror of feminine hearts, and they are whimsical! Could anyone name with certainty the weapon that can pierce these hearts the easiest? There are too many weapons of this kind, and they are too diverse. The poetic Romeo, his mildness and youthful passion win the heart of Juliet; on the other hand, the unhandsome Moor wins the heart of Desdemona by his strength and stories of heroism, while Petruchio's manliness and energy are the weapons that tame Katherine, and Benedick's wit and hatred of women wins Beatrice. All these are means that Don Juan might use in his love-affairs. If he were a little bit cloying, and had a poetic exterior reminiscent of a *tenor di grazia,* he would have attained his aim with as much success as another Don Juan with a manly exterior and a powerful, sonorous voice (even if it were a bass). He ought, of course, to be passionate, but that in itself would not be sufficient to distinguish him from thousands of other Spaniards. Don Juan must be original and attract general attention by his personality. Let me illustrate this by the first example that comes into my head. Shumsky had an impediment in his speech—a very serious drawback for an actor. Yet, strange as it may seem, it was so becoming to him that it turned out to be to his advantage, and actually induced others to imitate him. Now, in order to copy Shumsky, actors had to seize on his most striking feature, his greatest shortcoming, and pronounce their words as though they had an impediment in their speech. Nothing came of it, of course. Padilla, the singer, the best Don Juan I have ever seen, possessed—

---

[12]I. V. Samarin, an outstanding artist and pedagogue of the Maly Theatre.

[13]P. Y. Ryabov, an actor of the Maly Theatre and one of the stage-managers in the Society.

[14]Pushkin's *Stone Guest* was presented by the Art and Literary Society on February 4, 1890.

in addition to passion, lordliness and a very handsome appearance—a hoarse voice. This is a tremendous drawback for a singer, yet in his case it became an advantage because it somehow suited him, and a Don Juan with a hoarse voice was highly original, and therefore drew attention. But I have no individual traits and so my Don Juan is simply a *jeune premier* and nothing more. If my rendering is passionate and takes the public by storm, or if it is plastic and beautiful, many will say that it is possible to fall in love with a Don Juan like that. But had I some individual trait—no matter what, as long as it suited me—my Don Juan would have been original, claiming the interest of everyone. The audience would have said then: "It is impossible not to fall in love with his Don Juan." And why? Simply because you will never meet another like him. You may create a better or a worse Don Juan, but of this particular, original one you will never find the double.

[From *My Life in Art*]

The eve of great events surrounded us in its thunder clouds. The death of Chekhov tore out a large part of the heart of our Theatre. The illness, and then the death of Morozov,[15] tore out another part of that heart. Dissatisfaction and anxiety after the failure of the Maeterlinck plays and the catastrophic demise of the Studio on Povarskaya,[16] dissatisfaction with myself as an actor, and the complete darkness of the distances that lay before me, gave me no rest, took away my faith in myself, and made me seem wooden and lifeless in my own eyes.

It was in this condition that I went to spend the summer of 1906 in Finland. After I arrived, I would spend my mornings on a cliff that overlooked the sea, taking stock of all my artistic past. I wanted to find out where all my former joy in creation had vanished. Why was it that in the old days I was bored on the days when I did not act, and that now I was happy on the days I was free from work? It was said that it could not be different with a professional who played every day and who often repeated the same roles, but this explanation did not satisfy me. Apparently the professionals of whom this was said did not love their roles and their art. It would have been better for them to clerk in a bank or in a shop. The explanation would only fit some mechanical trade. But a role and art can never become tiring. Duse, Yermolova, Salvini, had played their great roles many times more than I had played mine, but this did not stand in their way of making those roles more perfect with every repetition. Why was it then that the more I repeated my roles the more I sunk backward into a stage of fossilization? Examining my past step by step, I came to see clearer and clearer that the inner content which was put into a role during its first creation and the inner content that was born in my soul with the passing of time were as far apart as the heaven and the earth. Formerly all issued from a beautiful, exciting, inner truth. Now all that was left of this truth was its wind-swept shell, ashes and dust that stuck in the niches of the soul due to various accidental causes, and that had nothing in common with true art. For instance, there was my role of Doctor Stockman in *An Enemy of the*

Konstantin Stanislavsky: "The Beginnings of My System," *My Life in Art*, translated by J. J. Robbins. New York: Theatre Arts Books, 1948, pp. 458-467. Copyright 1948. By permission of Mrs. Elizabeth Reynolds Hapgood and Robert M. MacGregor, Theatre Arts Books.

[15]Savva Timofeyevich Morozov, the Maecenas of the Art Theatre.

[16]The liquidation of an experimental laboratory in which Meyerhold worked to create impressionistic acting.

People. I remembered that when I played it at first it was easy for me to assume the viewpoint of a man with pure intentions, who sought only for the good in the souls of others, who was blind to all the evil feelings and passions of the little men who surrounded him. The perceptions that I had put into the role of Stockman had been taken by me from living memories. I had seen with my own eyes the destruction of one of my friends, an honest man whose inner conscience would not permit him to do what was demanded of him by the great of this world. On the stage, during the playing of the role, these living memories used to guide me, and always and invariably awoke me to creative work.

But with the passing of time I had forgotten the living memories, I had even forgotten the feeling of truth which is the fundamental element, the awakener, the mover and the lever of the spiritual life of Stockman and the leit-motif of the entire play.

Sitting on a bench in Finland and examining my artistic past, I accidentally struck on the feelings of the Stockman long lost in my soul. How was it that I could have lost them? How could I have gotten along without them? But how well I remembered every movement of every muscle, the mimetics of the face, legs, arms, body, and the slitting of the eyes that belonged to a short-sighted man.

During our last journey abroad, and in Moscow before that journey, I had mechanically repeated these fixed appurtenances of the role and the physical signs of absent emotion. In some places I had tried to be as nervous as possible and even exalted, and for this purpose I had made quick, nervous movements. In other places I had tried to look naive and in order to do so had achieved childlike and innocent eyes by technical means; in still other places I had exaggerated the manner of walking, the gestures typical to the role, and the outer results of an emotion that was long dormant. I copied naivete, but I was not naive; I moved my feet quickly, but I did not perceive any inner hurry that might cause short quick steps. I had played more or less artfully, copying the outer appearances of experiencing my part and of inner action, but I had not experienced the part or any real necessity for action. From performance to performance I had merely made a mechanical habit of going through all these technical gymnastics, and muscular memory, which is so strong among actors, had powerfully fixed my bad theatrical habit.

In the same manner I examined other roles, trying to make head or tail of the living material from which they had been created in their time, that is, in my own memories of the experiences that had been the awakeners of creativeness. I examined in my memory all those places of the role and those moments of creativeness which had come to me with a great deal of pain; I recalled the words of Chekhov and Nemirovich-Danchenko, the advice of stage directors and comrades, my own creative pains, and separate stages in the process of the birth and development of my roles. I reread the notes in my artistic diary which rebuilt in my mind all that I had experienced during the process of creativeness. I compared all this to what remained in my soul, and I was amazed. God, how my soul and my roles were disfigured by bad theatrical habits and tricks, by the desire to please the public, by incorrect methods of approach to creativeness, day after day, at every repeated performance!

What was I to do? How was I to save my roles from bad rebirths, from spiritual petrification, from the autocracy of evil habit and lack of truth? There was the necessity not only of a physical make-up but of a spiritual make-up before every performance. Before creating it was necessary to know how to enter the temple of that spiritual atmosphere in which alone it is possible to create.

With these thoughts and cares in my soul, I returned after a summer's rest to begin the season of 1906-1907 in Moscow.

* * * *

During one performance in which I was repeating a role I had played many times, suddenly, without any apparent cause, I perceived the inner meaning of the truth long known to me that creativeness on the stage demands first of all a special condition, which, for want of a better term, I will call the creative mood. Of course I knew this before, but only intellectually. From that evening on this simple truth entered into all my being, and I grew to perceive it not only with my soul, but with my body also. For an actor, to perceive is to feel. For this reason I can say that it was on that evening that I "first perceived a truth long known to me." I understood that to the genius on the stage this condition almost always comes of itself, in all its fullness and richness. Less talented people receive it less often, on Sundays only, so to say. Those who are even less talented receive it even less often, every twelfth holiday, as it were. Mediocrities are visited by it only on very rare occasions, on leap years, on the twenty-ninth of February. Nevertheless, all men of the stage, from the genius to the mediocrity, are able to receive the creative mood, but it is not given them to control it with their own will. They receive it together with inspiration in the form of a heavenly gift.

Not pretending at all to be a god and to hand out heavenly gifts, I neverthe-less put the following question to myself:

"Are there no technical means for the creation of the creative mood, so that inspiration may appear oftener than is its wont?" This does not mean that I was going to create inspiration by artificial means. That would be impossible. What I wanted to learn was how to create a favorable condition for the appearance of in-spiration by means of the will, that condition in the presence of which inspiration was most likely to descend into the actor's soul. As I learned afterward, this cre-ative mood is that spiritual and physical mood during which it is easiest for inspiration to be born.

"Today I am in good spirits! Today I am at my best!" or "I am acting with pleasure! I am living my part!" means that the actor is accidentally in a creative mood.

But how was one to make this condition no longer a matter of mere accident, to create it at the will and order of the actor?

If it is impossible to own it at once, then one must put it together bit by bit, using various elements for its construction. If it is necessary to develop each of the component elements in one's self separately, systematically, by a series of certain exercises—let it be so! If the ability to receive the creative mood in its full measure is given to the genius by nature, then perhaps ordinary people may reach a like state after a great deal of hard work with themselves,—not in its full measure, but at least in part. Of course the ordinary, simply able man will never become a genius, but it will help him to approach and in time to become like a genius, of one school with the genius, the servant of the same art as the genius. But how was one to reach the nature and the component elements of the creative mood?

The solution of this problem had become the "regular enthusiasm of Stanislavsky," as my friends expressed themselves. There was nothing that I left undone in order to solve the mystery. I watched myself closely, I looked into my soul, so to say, on the stage and off. I watched other men and actors, when I rehearsed my new parts or their new parts with them. I also watched them from the auditorium. I performed all sorts of experiments with them and myself. I tortured them; they grew angry and said that I had turned the rehearsals into an experimental laboratory, and that actors were not guinea pigs to be used for experimentation. And they were right in their protests. But the chief object of my researches remained the great actors, Russian, and foreign. If they, oftener than others, almost always walked the stage in the midst of a creative mood, whom was I to study if not them? And that is what I did. And this is what I learned from what I saw: in Duse, Yermolova, Fedotova, Savina, Salvini, Chaliapin,[17] Rossi, as well as in the actors of our Theatre when they appeared to best advantage in their roles, I felt the presence of something that was common to them all, something by which they reminded me of each other. What was this quality, common to all great talents? It was easiest of all for me to notice this likeness in their physical freedom, in the lack of all strain. Their bodies were at the beck and call of the inner demands of their wills.

The creative mood on the stage is exceptionally pleasant, especially when it is compared with the state of strain to which the actor is subject when the creative mood is absent. It can be compared to the feelings of a prisoner when the chains that had interfered with all his movements for years have at last been removed. I luxuriated in this condition on the stage, sincerely believing that in it lay the whole secret, the whole soul of creativeness on the stage, that all the rest would come from this state and perception of physical freedom. I was only made anxious by the fact that none of the actors who played with me, or the spectators who saw me play, noticed the change which I believed had taken place in me, leaving out of consideration the few compliments I received about one or two poses, movements and gestures that I had stressed.

After the production of *The Drama of Life* I was free of new roles and the work of stage direction until the end of the season of 1906-1907. Playing my old parts, I continued by researches, my experiments, my public exercises and the study of the problems of the theory and the technique of our art. The habit of free physical creative mood on the stage grew stronger little by little, became dynamic, and gradually assumed the character of second nature.

And then, like Doctor Stockman, "I made a new discovery." I began to understand that I felt so pleasantly and comfortably on the stage because my public exercises centered my attention on the perceptions and states of my body, at the same time drawing my attention away from what was happening on the other side of the footlights, in the auditorium beyond the black and terrible hole of the proscenium arch. In what I was doing I ceased to be afraid of the audience, and at times forgot that I was on the stage. I noticed that it was especially at such times that my creative mood was most pleasant.

There was one fact that made me very happy. At one of the performances given by a visiting star in Moscow, I watched his acting very closely. In my capacity

---

[17]Stanislavsky believed that Chaliapin had attained a perfection in operatic diction that was necessary for the actor.

of actor, I felt the presence of the creative mood in his playing, the freedom of his muscles in conjunction with a great general concentration. I felt clearly that his entire attention was on the stage and the stage alone, and this abstracted attention forced me to be interested in his life on the stage, and draw closer to him in spirit in order to find out what it was that held his attention.

At that moment I understood that the more the actor wishes to amuse his audience, the more the audience will sit in comfort waiting to be amused, and not even trying to play its part in the play on the stage before it. But as soon as the actor stops being concerned with his audience, the latter begins to watch the actor. It is especially so when the actor is occupied in something serious and interesting. If nobody amuses the spectator there is nothing left for him to do in the theatre but to seek himself for an object of attention. Where can that object be found? On the stage, of course, in the actor himself. The concentration of the creating actor calls out the concentration of the spectator and in this manner forces him to enter into what is passing on the stage, exciting his attention, his imagination, his thinking processes and his emotion. That evening I discovered the greater value of concentration for the actor. Besides, I noticed at that performance that the concentration of the actor reacts not only on his sight and hearing, but on all the rest of his senses. It embraces his mind, his will, his emotions, his body, his memory and his imagination. The entire physical and spiritual nature of the actor must be concentrated on what is going on in the soul of the person he plays. I perceived that creativeness is first of all the complete concentration of the entire nature of the actor. With this in mind, I began the systematic development of my attention with the help of exercises I invented for that purpose. I hope to dedicate more than one chapter of my next book to these.

I looked at another great visiting star in his great roles. He pronounced the introductory words of his part. But he did not strike directly on true emotion, and yielding to the mechanical habit of the theatre, fell back on false pathos. I looked at him carefully and saw that something was taking place in him. And really, he resembled a singer who used a sounding fork to find the true note. Now it seemed that he had found it. No, it was a trifle too low. He took a higher note. No, it was too high. He took a note a little lower. He recognized the true tone, came to understand it, to feel it, placed it, directed it, believed in it, and began to enjoy the art of his own speech. He *believed!*

The actor must first of all believe in everything that takes place on the stage, and most of all he must believe in what he himself is doing. And one can believe only in the truth. Therefore it is necessary to feel this truth at all times, to know how to find it, and for this it is inescapable to develop one's artistic sensitivity to truth. It will be said, "But what kind of truth can this be, when all on the stage is a lie, an imitation, scenery, cardboard, paint, make-up, properties, wooden goblets, swords and spears. Is all this truth?" But it is not of this truth I speak. I speak of the truth of emotions, of the truth of inner creative urges which strain forward to find expression, of the truth of the memories of bodily and physical perceptions. I am not interested in a truth that is without myself; I am interested in the truth that is within myself, the truth of my relation to this or that event on the stage, to the properties, the scenery, the other actors who play parts in the drama with me, to their thoughts and emotions.

The actor says to himself:

"All these properties, make-ups, costumes, the scenery, the publicness of the performance, are lies. I know they are lies, I know I do not need any of them. But *if* they were true, then I would do this and this, and I would behave in this manner and this way towards this and this event."

I came to understand that creativeness begins from that moment when in the soul and imagination of the actor there appears the magical, creative *if*. While only actual reality exists, only practical truth which a man naturally cannot but believe, creativeness has not yet begun. Then the creative *if* appears, that is, the imagined truth which the actor can believe as sincerely and with greater enthusiasm than he believes practical truth, just as the child believes in the existence of its doll and of all life in it and around it. From the moment of the appearance of *if* the actor passes from the plane of actual reality into the plane of another life, created and imagined by himself. Believing in this life, the actor can begin to create.

Scenic truth is not like truth in life; it is peculiar to itself. I understood that on the stage truth is that in which the actor sincerely believes. I understood that even a palpable lie must become a truth in the theatre so that it may become art. For this it is necessary for the actor to develop to the highest degree his imagination, a childlike naivete and trustfulness, an artistic sensitivity to truth and to the truthful in his soul and body. All these qualities help him to transform a coarse scenic lie into the most delicate truth of his relation to the life imagined. All these qualities, taken together, I shall call the *feeling of truth*. In it there is the play of the imagination and the creation of creative faith; in it there is a barrier against scenic lies; in it is the feeling of true measure; in it is the tree of childlike naivete and the sincerity of artistic emotion. The feeling of truth, as one of the important elements of the creative mood, can be both developed and practised. But this is neither the time nor the place to speak of the methods and means of such work. I will only say now that this ability to feel the truth must be developed to such an extent that absolutely nothing would take place on the stage, that nothing would be said and nothing listened to, without a preparatory cleansing through the filter of the artistic feeling of truth.

If this were true, then all my scenic exercises in loosening the muscles as well as in concentration had been performed incorrectly. I had not cleansed them through the filter of spiritual and physical truth. I took a certain pose on the stage. I did not believe in it physically. Here and there I weakened the strain. It was better. Now I changed the pose somewhat. Ah! I understood. When one stretches himself in order to reach something, this pose is the result of such stretching. And my whole body and after it my soul, began to believe that I was stretching towards an object which I needed very much.

It was only with the help of the feeling of truth, and the inner justification of the pose, that I was able more or less to reach the loosening of the muscles in actual life and on the stage during performances.

From that time on all my scenic exercises in the loosening of muscles and in concentration passed under the strict control of my feeling of truth.

VLADIMIR I. NEMIROVICH-DANCHENKO

(1858-1943)

Nemirovich-Danchenko, born in the Caucasus in 1858, has been called one of the drama's greatest teachers. He is an important contributor to the Stanislavsky system. Many of the great Russian actors of the last half-century were his pupils,

Kachalov, Moskvin, Meyerhold, Nazimova, and Olga Knipper-Chekhova, of whom Stanislavsky said "something seemed to open in her soul" under the guidance of Danchenko. He himself had acted in amateur productions. Though he never attained the stature of Stanislavsky as an actor, he had already written and produced thirteen plays by the time the co-founders of the Moscow Art Theatre held their historic eighteen-hour conversation at the "Slavic Bazaar" in Moscow on June 21, 1897. During the fifteen years preceding the advent of Chekhov, Gorky, and Andreyev at the beginning of the twentieth century, Nemirovich-Danchenko was, as Stanislavsky says, "the most popular and talented playwright in Russia." Some of his plays were forerunners of the later realism of the Art Theatre. In *The Wild Rose*, produced as far back as 1882, Danchenko showed the facade of a two-story house and then raised the wall to reveal the inside of the rooms. This was forty-two years before that "innovation" in O'Neill's *Desire Under the Elms.*

The talents of the two creative personalities—Danchenko and Stanislavsky—complemented each other to form a perfect division of labor. With the exception of the book *My Life in the Russian Theatre,* Danchenko's contribution is little known abroad. Yet the Art Theatre was never a "one man theatre"; it would not have survived as a living theatre without this principle of artistic collaboration. As the record of the famous founding conversation puts it: "The literary veto belongs to Nemirovich-Danchenko: the artistic veto to Stanislavsky." Nemirovich-Danchenko brought to the Moscow Art Theatre an extensive background of world drama. It was he who urged the reluctant actors of the Art Theatre to undertake Chekhov's *The Sea Gull* which made both the playwright and the theatre famous. "He could talk of a play so well," Stanislavsky says, "that one had to like it before he was through." Nemirovich suggested the title *Lower Depths* to Gorky who wrote him: "I am indebted for half the success of this play to your mind and art."

During the experimental period in the theatre following the Revolution, Danchenko innovated new methods of acting in opera. His Musical Studio, founded in 1920, inaugurated the idea of the "singing actor." After the death of Stanislavsky in 1938, Danchenko carried on the tradition of the Moscow Art Theatre. As late as 1941, he produced and directed a new version of *The Three Sisters.* Danchenko died at the age of eighty-five, after devoting almost a century to advancing the art of the theatre.

In his book *My Life in the Russian Theatre* he sets forth briefly his concepts of the ideal relationship between the author, director, and actor, and asks of the actor "that he should not act anything; decidedly not a thing; neither feelings, nor moods, nor situations, nor words, nor styles, nor images. All this should come of itself from the individuality of the actor, an individuality liberated from stereotyped forms...." He further maintains that "in the end, when you watch a performance you must forget not only the *régisseur,* you must forget even the author, you must yield wholly to the actor. He can gratify you, or distress you. The actor speaks, and not the author, and not the *régisseur.* Both one and the other have died in him, even as have died and become resurrected the innumerable observations and impressions experienced by him in the course of his whole life, from childhood to this very evening. All this, as though long since passed away, is resurrected under the pressure of that force which is embodied in a theatrical performance."

The observations which follow were dictated by Danchenko toward the close of his career and are being made available in English for the first time.

Simplicity in Acting

It seems that simplicity is but a partial aspect of the actor's technique. As a matter of fact, if this subject were considered as carefully as it should be, absolutely all aspects of the actor's art would be encompassed. There is simplicity and simplicity. There is the simplicity which passes over into crude simplicity, a simplicity which it is said is worse than theft; there is the simplicity of actors, who, from our point of view, are run-of-the-mill (but who, if we were to tell them they were not simple, would be amazed, would not understand, and would take it as carping criticism); there is simplicity which holds back flight of fancy. There is the simplicity of the theatre, i.e. a communicative, infectious simplicity; and there is simplicity which despite all the nobleness of purpose is tedious, too private; there is the simplicity, which the actor has attained through fine technical and imitative work; there is the simplicity attained by means of complicated, deep, inner examination, searchings, preparation, by work on one's stage qualities, by scrupulously cleansing one's methods of any artificiality. Finally, there is the simplicity in which, from the moment the actor appears on the stage it seems he has never been exposed to temptation, as if he had been born especially for the boards—belonged naturally to the stage....

Aspirations toward simplicity, I think, were engendered in the theatre from the earliest beginnings of the actor's art; and immediately entered into battle with the art of performance. Somehow from the very beginning, the actor, desirous of winning attention, sympathy, applause, handclapping, "bravos" from the public, has sought ways to this end through theatrical means. Enveloped in exalted fancy and in themes on the grand scale—no matter whether they are tragic or comic, creating a play of the passions, of human feelings—in an arena before an audience, the actor involuntarily is carried away by methods divorced from the simple feelings and everyday experiences of life. And at this very moment, or on the next day following the intoxication of success, his sense of truth somehow forces him to catch himself up and to try either to overcome this breaking away from life or to fill in this gap with simple, living content.

When you think of the actors of the earliest periods of the art of the theatre— no matter whether they played the tragedies of Euripides and Aeschylus, or the comedies of Plautus and Aristophanes, or, later, of the *commedia dell' arte,* of Goldoni or of Molière, or of Shakespeare and so on, before our times—you observe mentally, these parallel paths of the aspirations of actors in all epochs and in all periods of the development of the theatre. These paths sometimes diverge sharply. The tragedian is contemptuous of the mode and manner of life, of the petty, from his point of view, everyday subjects of the theatre. The comedian, on the other hand, cannot, and does not want to rise above this life, but, on the contrary, digs into it assiduously. Both seemingly follow sharply inimical lines of art. Still the comedian is right to ridicule the tragedian if, in pomposity and in stiltedness, he loses that most wonderful, most important aroma of the living spirit, which somehow constitutes the very kernel of the actor's art. And the tragedian, at some time,

Vladimir I. Nemirovich-Danchenko: "Simplicity in Acting," in *The Moscow Art Theatre Year-book for 1944 (Ezhegodnik MKHAT 1944).* Moscow: Museum of Moscow Art Theatre, 1946, pp. 19-24. By permission of Helen Black.

Dictated to a stenographer by V. I. Nemirovich-Danchenko (but not edited by him) August 14, 15 and 16, 1940. V. I. Nemirovich-Danchenko called what he had dictated: "For Myself, Various Thoughts."

in the more sober moments of his feelings concerning the theatre, must admit that the comedian is often right. At the same time the tragedian is right when the comedian limits himself to petty, amusing peculiarities of life, dulling his imagination and his human dignity, and repudiating his lofty mission of elevating the feelings of the spectator. The comedian may respond to this task with such inspired, deeply penetrating insight into the comical sides of human existence, that he finds within himself the theatrical means of infecting a large public with the same perception. In this role he becomes great and equal to the tragedian. These are the two parallel paths which at times converge and at other times diverge. The merging of these two paths into a deep synthesis constitutes an ideal; and perhaps hundreds of years ago in the times of Shakespeare, or even earlier—constituted the truest quest of genuine art.

A persistent quest for simplicity which does not burden the actor's imagination with trivia, but preserves the features and forms of the living man, helps the actor elevate his imagination, and in this way lifts the imagination of the spectator to highly generalized images, to all that is called poetry. That is why I say that in the discussion of the subject of simplicity in acting, all fields of the actor's art will be encompassed. . . .

It seems to me at this moment that it is necessary to speak of all the elements of the creative power of the actor, to speak of each separately, basing myself on my practical experience, on my sense of what the actor's art is, and, in particular, on my acquaintance with scores of acting personalities. The summation of all these fragments, opinions, does not yet constitute a science, of course. The science will come from the working-out of the question "how" and not "what" in training the young actor. I shall attempt to sift out these elements. (At present this will be dictated in total discorder, lacking a system, without any manner of tendentious sequence.)

1. Experience. As soon as we begin to talk in this area, we very quickly observe that even the word itself does not express all its connotations. The actor of experience [one who lives the role] and the actor of performance [one who presents role] do not seem to be antipodes, i.e. opposites, to such a degree as was supposed when Stanislavsky first began to direct his pedagogical-theoretical thoughts into a clear, definite channel. The fact that we often see an actor of performance going through a realistic experience or an actor of experience skillfully and ably performing, leads us surely to the conclusion that something else should be substituted for the definition of "experience."

2. Naturalness. This somehow is identified with simplicity—and with sincerity. It is here that the controversies will begin.

What is theatrical truth? Where are the points of organic identity between the natural feelings of the actor and the theatrical? There can be no total identity. The actor and the actress exalt in the experience of deep suffering on the stage, something we cannot say of man when he is suffering: there is no element of joy there. Here you have the very root, the kernel of the difference between the truth of the theatre and the truth of life, of nature.

3. Infectiousness. What is this? In essence, infectiousness is talent. One acting personality possesses the infectiousness, let us say, of tragic experience; another— of comic experience. One actor will hardly have sent out his thoughts to those nerves which participate in a given area of experience, and will forthwith infect

the audience. An actor's voice will barely have quivered, he will just have raised his finger to his eye, seemingly to wipe away a tear,—and the audience is ready to weep. Another personality, more usually a woman, bursts into the most genuine tears on the stage, and the audience sits cold, dry-eyed. One actor will just have uttered half a phrase of comical content, perhaps even, will merely have cast a glance, before uttering this phrase, and the whole hall is smiling. And another will try to make one laugh with all his power—and he will not succeed. About what psychological factors are we talking here? It is here that we can see who has talent—dramatic, lyric, comic.

Here it is that a great, important, awesome question arises for the actor's science: can this be taught or not? Perhaps not teach it, but imbue, train, implant, again perhaps even infect one with all of this? Or must one be born with such a gift?

Stanislavsky maintained that you have to be born a director: you cannot make a director of yourself, but you can make an actor of yourself. Perhaps, if I think this problem out more thoroughly than I have up to now, I will arrive at the same conclusion. But up to now I have thought differently. I have thought that a director should possess all of the powers of an actor. And if you have to be born a director then consequently you have to be born an actor, too.

Briusov[1] has put it well somewhere: "The ability to create—is the same sort of phenomenon as beauty or a magnificent voice, i.e. something you have to be born with, something you cannot attain no matter what the effort." Most likely, it is in this area that considerations of the external gifts of an actor will be encountered: his voice, his face, his eyes, his gestures—everything that helps infectiousness in its power and clarity.

4. Charm. What sort of thing is this? Strange as it may seem, such a great director as Stanislavsky became conscious of the power of charm in none too short a time. And yet, this feature is practically the most decisive in acting, or to put it more correctly, in the field of infectiousness and its influence on the audience. The actor, and especially the actress, never know the extent of their charm, or are even aware of its presence. It would seem that the perception of charm is much too subjective; you cannot make of this quality an object of scientific research. Still, the audience, almost in its entirety, feels the presence or absence of charm. What role does the actor's charm play in the achievement of his creative tasks? An actor of little charm can, with the aid of all of his other qualities, create a true, deep and characteristic image. An actor may display imagination, intelligence and taste, but his influence on audience perception will stop at some point; whereas the actor with charm takes hold of the spectator completely, authoritatively. Can charm be implanted, can charm be acquired through training? ...

5. Sincerity. Perhaps this is the same thing as naturalness, simplicity. When I examine in my mind a group of actors who were extraordinarily, boundlessly sincere, striking in their naturalness and simplicity, in almost all cases I come up against the fact that these actors lacked the least bit of expressed or cultivated technique. I am thinking of Leshkovskaya[2] and Nikulina.[3] Even so it has

---

[1]Valery Y. Briusov (1873-1924), a well-known writer and poet of the Symbolist School.
[2]Elena K. Leshkovskaya (1864-1925), a Maly Theatre actress from 1888 to her death.
[3]Nadezhda A. Nikulina (1845-1929), a Maly Theatre actress from 1863, pupil of Shchepkin and Samarin.

sometimes seemed to me that an actor was sincere only in portions of his role and that it was in just those portions that all his technical work on the role seemed not to be apparent.

6. Is it possible for an actor, who has not attained the great simplicity, aspired to by Russian art, to create a theatrical image? If an actor prepares a role but does not experience it, can you then have such a creation? This question is most intimately tied up with the problem of simplicity, experience and performance. And what is creation? Again reviewing various acting personalities in my experience, I encounter a phenomenon concerning which I have spoken more than once. The fame of an actor, his reputation, results not from the number of roles he has played but rather only from the number of roles he has *created*. Let us take such and such an actor. When he was alive his fame was great and it resounds after his death. Almost his entire career passed before my eyes. But his whole reputation hung on those four or five roles he had created. He played some three to four hundred roles in all. Of them, he created these five. Well, he played some fifty roles well, the rest he played badly (to put it boldly). Nevertheless, he is renowned, and he did contribute something to the history of Russian art. And here is an actor who, too, has played some four hundred roles, perhaps 500-600 roles, and all well, some roles even very well. But he did not create even one role. And his fame will die with him.

The road to the creation of a role is an extraordinarily deep one. And, of course, the whole significance of Stanislavsky's work comes down to the fact that he acknowledged only those roles on the stage which had been created. (I am speaking of the second, the most important, half of his pedagogical activity, and not of his first—his work as a director.)

When I look closely into the elements of an actor's genius, they fall into three large divisions in my mind.

The first is the personality of the actor, his individual qualities, his charm, his fancy, his faculty to inspire the infectiousness of his temperament. All of these amount to one thing—the actor's personality.

The second is naturalness, sincerity of experience.

And the third is technique, proficiency.

Both the elements of the second and the third divisions can be taught. An actor can be trained from youth in naturalness, in great simplicity and to be sincere on the stage; taste can be implanted; his practical work can be guided correctly; he can be prompted in technical methods that are not run-of-the-mill; the acquisition of proficiency can be accelerated. But just as you cannot endow an actor with external characteristics, so you cannot implant charm into his personality. You can struggle with individual shortcomings, with personal peculiarities; you can help in the development of existing qualities; you can develop a talent for fantasy; you can give training in taste; you can teach manner. To a certain extent we can count on the power of Moses' rod, i.e. on the getting of water from a stone. But this will be pure chance, the results will be of only seeming quality and not stable or true.

The Briusov quotation I cited, is concerned, I think, less with the faculty to create than with the charm which comes naturally, just as does personal beauty or a beautiful voice. But these are qualities of an actor's personality and of his individuality which, it seems to me, are not attainable through work, technique, the development of taste, etc. This is a tremendous question for the actor's school.

A long time ago in the Art Theatre, they began to speak of the fact that you could make an actor out of anyone. I will not err if I say that this was all the easier at the time of the establishment of the First Studio since the Studio was always supposed to be in small quarters where the voices of the actors, their art of mimicry, their gait, their figures did not play as decisive a role as they do on a large stage. And what took place in the whole series of studios which were subsequently established only confirmed this. Such a problem seemed to be posed: is it easy to recognize whether a given actor has authentic, profound stage talents? Practice has shown that we can err in one or the other direction not only during the early tests, not only even during the first year, but even after two or three years. The student who seemed to have no talent for the stage, later turned out to be truly talented, except that chance, the situation, the atmosphere during these early years had not offered the opportunities of revealing this talent. And contrariwise, a student with all the wherewithal for stage presence has later proved a dud.

Everyone is acquainted with the case of Knipper, for example, who was not admitted to take the examinations for the Imperial Theatrical School; and I myself for the first half-year considered that Moskvin had little ability. Upon passing over into his second half-year I even warned him it was hardly likely he would be any good for the theatre. And only after I had run across him in some entirely minor role, while he was in his first year class, did I say: "Ah! No, it seems you're a talented young man."

Translated from the Russian by Bernard L. Koten

VSEVOLOD MEYERHOLD

(1874-1942)

While Stanislavsky sought a perfect stage illusion reproducing life itself, so Vsevolod Meyerhold elaborated a "theatrical" theatre. His creative revolt against realistic stage representation opened the revolutionary period of bold and interesting theatrical experiments. Meyerhold sought to synthesize theatrical conventions which would condition an emotional reflex in the spectator. He believed that reality should be created in the minds of the spectator rather than on the stage, and based his work on Pavlov's *Theory of Association*.

In his early experimental days Meyerhold directed plays of the symbolists Maeterlinck, Alexander Blok, and Leonid Andreyev at the theatre of one of the most celebrated Russian actresses, Vera Komisarjevskaya (1864-1910), whose brother Theodore replaced Meyerhold as director. Meyerhold spent four years as an actor with the Moscow Art Theatre. In 1908 he became stage-director of the two St. Petersburg Imperial Theatres. In 1910 he staged his sensational production of Molière's *Don Juan*. After the Revolution Meyerhold came to the forefront with startling staging which dispensed with the curtain, extended the stage into the illuminated auditorium, and employed bare constructivist settings. He was extremely eclectic in his methods, borrowing heavily from primitive and Oriental practice. Frequently he re-wrote or re-organized classic plays to fit the mood of his own theatrical motif.

In the preparation of each theatrical *jeu* Meyerhold reigned supreme, enacting all the roles by creating every gesture, every movement, every nuance of delivery for his actors. The technique of bio-mechanics, so closely identified with the name of Meyerhold, is described by the British observer André Van Gyseghem in these words: "Bio-mechanics are the mechanics of life, and the training of an actor must proceed according to the natural laws of movements.... The whole technique of bio-mechanics lies in the careful study of the time of *preparation* for a certain action: of the emotional and physical state of the moment of *action itself:* and the resulting anti-climax of *reaction.* On this Meyerhold has said that an actor should be trained, and on the conscious use of these three states or conditions he builds up his whole production.... Bio-mechanics teaches the actor to use the space about him on the stage three-dimensionally.... Through exercises he is taught to achieve the feeling of the place of the actor in space, time and rhythm. But more important still, he is taught how to coordinate his own body with other people on the stage, with the properties he handles and the scenery he is acting against so that he becomes a plastic part of a harmonious whole."

Within this concept the player who is most malleable and can be molded by the director as a sculptor models clay becomes the best actor. No individual actor of note was identified with Meyerhold, with the exception of the versatile Igor Ilinsky, (b. 1901), his favorite and most gifted performer.

The amazing control of his medium exercised by Meyerhold is revealed first in the following verbatim transcript of a portion of his work with his actors in his most famous, controversial production, Gogol's *The Inspector General,* and then in Ilinsky's recollections, published in a 1961 autobiography.

A Rehearsal of *The Inspector General*

Meyerhold (to the actor playing the part of the Mayor): The whole entrance is effected before you come to the lines. Once we have agreed to carry the role through at a certain tempo, it is up to me, as a technical expert, to do what I can to lighten the work of the actor and to think of putting him in circumstances that will be easy for him. The actor must be freed from everything that creates weight on him. Forget about talking like an old man. Let the make-up show a man of fifty, but in speech, be young. We shall discuss the reason for this too. It seems to me that among this museum piece collection of idiots—even the superintendent of schools is an idiot, and Luke Lukich, and the judge are idiots, the postmaster is an idiot—among all these completely stick-in-the-mud and the-devil-knows-what kind of creatures, the Mayor stands out in relief. He is more clever and more intelligent and is a man with a certain polish. It is possible that this Mayor was yesterday in some other town. Not in the capital, of course, but if this is a district town, he was in the chief city of a province. He has come here after having been elsewhere. All the directions indicate that he is head and shoulders above all the others. In the Mayor you see traces of some sort of external polish, it would be difficult to call it education. You see it in what he says about teachers, in that he knows something about history, and in his orders—to put up a monument of some sort—in all this there is a quasi-culture; of course, what kind of culture! But when he talks, he controls his tongue, he knows how to form phrases a great

Norris Houghton: *Moscow Rehearsals: An Account of Methods of Production in the Soviet Theatre.* New York: Harcourt, Brace and Company, 1936, pp. 276-279. Copyright 1936. By permission of Harcourt, Brace & Co.

deal better than Bobchinsky or Dobchinsky. Their brains work hard but he has a kind of adaptability which makes it possible for him to find his way around as soon as he is on good terms with people. He is an orator, *sui generis,* he can recite a monologue. It is necessary to give him a youthful aspect. To have a characteristic mode of speech would not be of advantage, it would be difficult. It would be better to forget it. It would be better for him to have a mobile diction. Why is it that up to now he has always been played by old actors with great ponderousness? Maksheyev, for instance, and Vladimir Nikolayevich Davidov played him when they were getting on in years, and when younger actors took the role they played under Davidov and imitated him. I don't know how Vladimir Nikolayevich played the Mayor when he was young, when he was still at the Korsh in Moscow, but it is possible, according to tradition, that even he played him as an old man. That is why all these gestures and intonations have accumulated and waxed strong, because they were used by people who played according to the example of older men with big names.

Inasmuch as you are young—because you must be twenty, or at least fifteen years younger than I am—forget all about talking like an old man. Fire away with completely free, clear-cut diction. Don't try any groans for the present, not until later when we have straightened out things a bit. Perhaps we shall give you, even during rehearsals, a big easy chair—to sit in, to think, to get ready, to begin. Until he puts on his uniform the Mayor is always in his dressing gown. Perhaps he takes a nap after midday dinner, then he receives the letter before he has gotten up and gives orders to send for all the heads of departments, and then is taken ill himself. Give him that easy chair out of *The Forest.* Let him sit there, like an invalid. Give him a glass of boiled water....

Meyerhold (to Hibner): This is what the doctor has to do (Is that clean water? Answer: Yes.) Interfere with him; give him some water from time to time in a teaspoon. You bother him, but he is obliged to take it. He takes it, sometimes he pushes it aside, sometimes he drinks it, then he takes the glass in his hands and takes several swallows, finds it is something one can drink by the tumblerful. You should say your lines in German so that your lines will get mixed up with his. This will help him slightly to get rid of his difficulty. You will set the pace. This will be the first obstacle, and you will help him to increase the pace. In direct proportion to the obstacles will arise the desire and the necessity to get rid of them. You can even speak loudly, never mind if the public hears. Keep talking constantly. He's a kind of *perpetuum mobile....*

All in the foreground—over there. All are seated. The Mayor comes in. But we shall begin quietly, after he has settled himself in his easy chair. He groans. You (Hibner) get ready his glass of medicine and all sorts of things. As soon as he has spoken a few lines, begin to make him drink. When they all say, "What, an Inspector-General?" they must do it all alike. Some must stagger the syllables— In-spec-tor. There should be a variety of logical accents, and also some should pronounce it briefly while others drawl it out.

"Well, for God's sake!" etc., very quick. The reaction must be quick and they do not say this in character. The public won't know anyhow who is saying what. They all sit in a crowd on the sofa, perhaps ten of them. You must soft pedal charactertistics.

ACTORS ON ACTING

IGOR ILINSKY

Biomechanics

Many spectators who saw *The Magnificent Cuckold* (by F. Crommelynck) and the young actors working with Meyerhold, I among them, considered this his most complete and significant production. From the point of view of his credo for actors, of the purity of acting style, this was the most expressive demonstration of the "biomechanical" system. Along with the rehearsals of *The Cuckold*, Meyerhold began his experiments with biomechanics. I also attended these sessions. Inasmuch as biomechanics was at that time a fresh and novel fascination for Meyerhold, he used this system to its fullest extent in the production of *The Cuckold*. I shall try to recall what I remember about biomechanics and how I understood it.

First of all it is necessary to say that Meyerhold "invented" theatrical biomechanics, never formulating or explaining his "method." His theorizing on this subject was quite vague and mainly polemical, directed against the "theories of experienced feelings"—against Stanislavsky chiefly, who insisted that actors must experience and relive feelings onstage as they had experienced them in real life.

Meyerhold demanded that an actor's every movement be suited to the execution of any task. At first he wanted to come to terms with "experiences." He felt that the precise execution of a formal design, precise physical movements and body comportment would in turn produce true content, true intonation and true emotions. The physical position of an actor's body determines his emotions and the expressions in his voice. He wanted actors to have easily excitable reflexes. He called the ability to respond in movement and in words to outside stimuli excitability. Acting consists of coordinating the manifestations of his excitability. Let us take this example: an actor representing fear must not experience fear first and then run, but must first run (reflex) and then take fright from that action. Translated into today's theatrical language this means: "One must not experience fear but express it onstage by a physical action."

Here, it seems to me, lies the junction between Meyerhold's biomechanics and Stanislavsky's method of physical action. I hasten to add that I am not an avid follower of one or the other method. It seems to me that blindly following either path impoverishes an actor, diminishes his power as an artist, and enslaves him to some degree. At the same time I feel that the study and practical knowledge of Meyerhold's biomechanics, especially in its later stage and when understood in its larger sense, as well as Stanislavsky's method, can enormously enrich and round out an actor's technique.

Gradually Meyerhold changed his definition of biomechanics; the polemical ardor and sharpness weakened. With his biomechanical system Meyerhold tried to establish laws for acting movements in regard to the space onstage, experimenting with training exercises that took into account the actor's place on the stage.

What does this mean practically speaking?

An actor does exercises in biomechanics. Here are some of them: in a particular manner he grabs the body of his partner, who is lying on the floor, throws it over his shoulder and carries it off. He lets the body fall to the floor. He throws an imaginary disc and draws an imaginary bow. He slaps his partner (in a certain manner) and gets slapped. He jumps on his partner's chest and gets jumped on in

Igor Ilinsky: *Sam o Sebe* (*I About Myself*). Moscow: VTO, 1961, pp. 154-159. This selection translated by Nora Beeson.

[504]

return. He jumps on his partner's shoulders, and his partner runs around with him, etc. There were simpler exercises: take the partner's hand and pull him to the side, push the partner away, grab him by the throat, etc.

We were not to transfer these "devices" to the stage, although in the beginning we sometimes demonstrated them in performances. These exercises were to train us and give us a state for a specific movement onstage. The exercises, partly gymnastic, partly plastic movement, partly acrobatics, were to teach acting students how to calculate their movements; to develop a keen eye, coordinate movements in reference to their partners, and in general give them flexibility so that in future performances the actor could move more freely and expressively in the scenic space. Similarly a person who has studied and knows many dance steps can more easily improvise and dance to music, endlessly varying these steps, than a person who cannot dance at all.

Meyerhold based his biomechanics on the *rational* and *natural* use of movement. He felt that an excessive use of ballet steps exaggerated the "ballet style"; the same is true about acrobats, even some sportsmen. He wanted biomechanics to be free from any obtrusive style and manner, wanted it to be only *natural* and *efficient*. Unfortunately many ardent "biomechanicians" became extremely mannered since biomechanics became for them an end in itself.

Meyerhold valued highly the expressivity of the body. He often demonstrated with a puppet. With his fingers in the puppet he achieved many different effects: despite the fixed expression of the puppet's mask we could see the expression of joy —widely extended arms, grief—hanging head, and pride—head thrown backward. This masked figure, correctly used, could express everything that the mimic can express. Remember the masked figures in *The Caucasian Chalk Circle* by Brecht. Thus Meyerhold gave great importance to the expressiveness of the body and to the various ways of foreshortening the body on the stage. "You must," he said, "know your body so that in any position you know exactly what effects it produces."

This faculty of the actor he called "self-mirror."

Meyerhold considered the spectator to be an integral part of the performance. He felt that in many ways (with noise, movement, laughter, coughing) the actor could feel the relationship the spectator had to the spectacle.

It is well known that Stanislavsky taught his students not to pay attention to the audience, telling them to fence off the audience with a fourth wall.

But the fourth wall does not exist in reality! And the audience does exist, breaking into the performance with laughter, applause, coughing and rustling. All this at one time disturbs, and another time helps the actor, improves his playing, helps to shorten or lengthen pauses, enlivens or quiets what happens onstage, distracts or inspires the actor. A tragedy can be heightened by the blowing of noses, comedy by laughter.

Recently I asked one of Stanislavsky's students (now a teacher): "Why does Stanislavsky believe in the fourth wall? He knows very well how important the live breathing of an audience is to the rhythm and life of a performance. If a spectator laughs unexpectedly, then the actor should wait for the end of the laughter, changing and finding a new justification for his existence onstage."

"Well, of course he will wait," he answered. "This is only a pedagogic device. Stanislavsky does not want the student actors to play, as it is called, to the audience."

It is not necessary to play "to the audience." But an actor does play for an audience. The spectator is present in the theatre and, in my opinion, one cannot forget about him, cannot put blinkers on the actors' eyes. Such blinkers are necessary only for ignorant actors without taste.

The basic difficulty in acting, according to Meyerhold, is that the actor should be the initiator, leader and organizer of the material. The actor and medium are one and the same thing. This perpetual dichotomy presents great difficulties. Let's take Othello. Othello strangles Desdemona; the skillful actor must convey the utmost of his part, at the same time being in possession of himself so that he does not really strangle his partner. Here lies the difficulty. Biomechanics shows the actor how to control his acting, how to coordinate his acting with his partner and with the audience, how to understand the expressive function of the sets, movements, perspective, etc.

In defending his biomechanical system Meyerhold said: "My concern as director-biomechanician is with the actor's health; I see that his nerves are in good order, that he is in a happy mood. Despite his acting in a sad play, he must be happy, inwardly at peace. The actor-artist must above all think. Thinking makes the actor assume a sad position, and that position in turn helps him feel sad; thinking makes the actor run, and running makes him feel afraid."

The very fact that Meyerhold considers thought to be the most significant part in the creative acting process gives the actor a great importance in every performance. Everyone says that Meyerhold does not need talented and independent actors, that any actor—a puppet or robot who executes his task accurately—satisfies him completely. But in reality it becomes more and more clear that the actor, whose role Meyerhold never minimized, becomes more and more important in the "director's theatre."

And another time Meyerhold said: "Intonation must not be invented or found at home; it must be born in rehearsal."

Later Meyerhold was more circumspect in regard to problems pertaining to the psychology of creation. In his work on later productions he continued to expand and change his biomechanical system, never letting it become dogmatic.

As paradoxical as it may seem, after having become an actor in as realistic a theatre as the Maly, where I encountered Stanislavsky's method of physical action, looking back on the artistic road I have traveled, I realize that I now accept much more from Meyerhold's biomechanical system than when I was a Meyerhold actor. At that time Meyerhold's main value for me was as an artistic director who, in a practical manner, took the actor by the hand, opening for him and showing him plainly the inexhaustible richness of the actor's art.

EUGENE VAKHTANGOV

(1883-1922)

Vakhtangov is considered by many to have been Stanislavsky's most gifted pupil and disciple. Active in the First Studio of the Moscow Art Theatre with Sulerzhitsky and Michael Chekhov, nephew of the playwright, Vakhtangov later founded the Third Studio, which today bears his name. American playgoers have had an opportunity to judge the scope of Vakhtangov's theatrical genius. The Habimah Theatre's production of *The Dybbuk,* shown during the tours of the Hebrew-language troupe in 1926, and again in 1948, is substantially unchanged since it was first mounted for the company by Vakhtangov in Moscow.

Vakhtangov's stage concepts bridge the conflict between the extremes of theatricality and the theatre of "inner feeling." In 1918 he wrote: "Meyerhold calls a performance 'good theatre' when the spectator does not forget for a moment that he is in the theatre. Stanislavsky on the contrary, wants the spectator to forget that

he is in the theatre. We all know that Chekhov's plays cannot be staged successfully without chirping crickets, orchestra music, street alarms, the cry of peddlers,
the chimes of a clock. All these are theatrical means.'"

R. Ben-Ari, a former member of the Habimah Theatre, analyzing the differences
between Stanislavsky and Vakhtangov writes that "Stanislavsky's slogan of complete physical and spiritual submergence of the actor was no longer the question;
now the actor must lead a two-fold life on the stage. It should appear as if the
actor were saying to the spectator: 'Now I am crying, but I, the actor, know
about it. Look, I'm wiping my tears, and look, I'm not only wiping my tears, but
notice how I'm doing it.' The emphasis was placed not on *what* but on *how*....
The actor, according to Vakhtangov, has to become integrated with his interpretation and social approach. One must not only strive to play well, to excel, but
also to *feel one's attitude to the character and to history as a whole*. No role may
be played without a personal approach. No production may be staged without
the personal approach of the director. In this manner Vakhtangov created a theatrical form. The basis of Vakhtangov's interpretation and approach to this or that
play was the modern approach. Any production could be transformed into a modern
production, including all of its social, economic and political problems. Vakhtangov
retained the basic principles of Stanislavsky in spite of the fact that he went his
own way in particular phases of interpretation."

Vakhtangov died in 1922, but his influence on Soviet theatre practice is perhaps second only to that of Stanislavsky. His approach to the problem of combining
the realistic style with theatrical symbolism was ably continued by B. E. Zakhava
and I. Rapoport at the Vakhtangov Theatre. Typical of the forceful productions
of the Vakhtangov Theatre are the following: Maxim Gorky's *Yegor Bulychev*
(1932), Lev Slavin's *Intervention* (1933), and Nikolai Pogodin's *Aristocrats*. In
estimating the stature of Vakhtangov John Gassner wrote: "Vakhtangov has remained a living memory and an invaluable example to Soviet directors. His practice of 'controlled spontaneity', decorativeness, and illuminating fantasy was not
only theatrically beautiful but notably interpretive and creative; his production of
Princess Turandot was acclaimed as one of the loveliest creations of the twentieth
century stage."

The notes which follow are from the diary of Vakhtangov and were originally
translated for the use of the Group Theatre in its acting classes.

The School of Intimate Experience

The Stanislavsky Method aims to develop in the student those abilities and
qualities which give him the opportunity to free his creative individuality—an individuality imprisoned by prejudices and stereotyped patterns. The liberation and
disclosing of the individuality; this must become the principle aim of a theatrical
school. A theatrical school must clear the way for the creative potentialities of the
student—but he must move and proceed along this road by himself; he cannot be

---

Eugene Vakhtangov: "Preparing for the Role; From the Diary of E. Vakhtangov" in *Acting:
A Handbook of the Stanislavsky Method*, compiled by Toby Cole. New York: Lear Publishers,
1947, pp. 116-119. Copyright 1947. By permission of Lear Publishers.

taught. The school must remove all the conventional rubbish which prevents the spontaneous manifestation of the student's deeply hidden potentialities.

Stanislavsky showed the actor how to achieve a creative state, to establish the conditions in which a genuine creation upon the stage becomes possible.

If all the conditions of the creative state are established, but the pupil still shows himself incapable of genuine creative work, if no movement takes place even after the way has been cleared for his creative potentialities—then it is not the fault of the school, but of nature which has deprived the student of the one thing that might have given him the opportunity of expressing himself upon the stage—scenic talent.

If the school attempts a different task, if it does not bring out within the pupil the singular qualities which predetermine the possibility of creative work; but attempts to teach him creativeness itself, then it may ruin a scenic talent given by nature. Instead of freeing the pupil from prejudices and stereotypes, it will impose upon him a set of new prejudices, characteristic of a given school.

It is impossible to teach anybody how to create because the creative process is a subconscious one, while all teaching is a form of conscious activity which can only prepare the actor for creative work.

Consciousness never creates what the subconscious does; for the subconscious has an independent faculty for gathering material without the knowledge of the consciousness.

In this sense each rehearsal of a play is most effective when it serves to evoke the material for the following rehearsal. The creative work of refashioning the newly perceived material takes place in the intervals between rehearsals. Out of nothing, nothing can be created. That is why a role cannot be performed by inspiration only. Inspiration is the moment when the subconscious, without the participation of the conscious, gives form to all the impressions, experience, and work preceding it. The ardor accompanying this moment is a natural state. Whatever is invented consciously does not bear this characteristic. Whatever is created subconsciously is accompanied by a discharge of energy which has an infecting quality. This ability, the subconscious carrying away of the subconscious of the spectator, is a characteristic of talent. Whoever perceives subconsciously and subconsciously expresses it—that one is a genius.

Critics of Stanislavsky's doctrine often overlook the statement which takes first place in the system and methods of Stanislavsky: that the actor should not be concerned about his feeling during a play, it will come of itself. They label as auto-suggestion and narcotic self-intoxication the help which Stanislavsky gives to his students in recalling their intimate experiences. But Stanislavsky maintained the opposite: don't try to experience, don't make feelings to order, forget about them altogether. In life our feelings come to us by themselves against our will. Our willing gives birth to action directed towards the gratification of desire. If we succeed in gratifying it, a positive feeling is born spontaneously. If an obstacle stands in the way of gratifying it, a negative feeling is born—"suffering." An action directed towards the gratification of will is continuously accompanied by a series of spontaneous feelings, the content of which is the anticipation of the coming gratification or the fear of failure.

Thus, every feeling is a gratified or a non-gratified will. At first, a desire arises that becomes the will, then begins to act consciously aiming towards its gratification. Only then, altogether spontaneously, and sometimes against our will, does the feeling come. Thus, feeling is a product of will and the conscious (and sometimes subconscious) actions directed towards its gratification.

Therefore the actor, Stanislavsky taught, must think first of all about what he wants to obtain at a particular moment and what he is to do, but *not* about what he is going to feel. The emotion, as well as the means of its expression, is being generated subconsciously, spontaneously, in the process of executing actions directed towards the gratification of a desire. The actor must, therefore, come on the stage not in order to feel or experience emotions, but in order to act. "Don't wait for emotions—act immediately," Stanislavsky said. An actor must not simply stand upon the stage, but act. Every action differs from feeling by the presence of the will element. To persuade, to comfort, to ask, to reproach, to forgive, to wait, to chase away—these are verbs expressing *will action*. These verbs denote the task which the actor places before himself when working upon a character, while the verbs to become irritated, to pity, to weep, to laugh, to be impatient, to hate, to love—express feeling, and therefore cannot and must not figure as a task in the analysis of a role. Feelings denoted by these verbs must be born spontaneously and subconsciously as a result of the actions executed by the first series of verbs.

Desire is the motive for action. Therefore the fundamental thing which an actor must learn is to wish, to wish by order, to wish whatever is given to the character. An actor who is a mere journeyman does the opposite of what nature demands from him and what the school of Stanislavsky teaches. He grasps with bare hands at feelings and tries to give a definite form to their expression. He always begins from the end; that is, from the final ends of his part, Stanislavsky used to say.

In life a man who weeps is concerned about restraining his tears—but the actor journeyman does just the opposite. Having read the remark of the author (He weeps), he tries with all his might to squeeze out tears, and since nothing comes of it, he is forced to grasp at the straw of the stereotyped theatrical cry. The same is true of laughter. Who does not know the unpleasant, counterfeit laughter of an actor? The same takes place with the expression of other feelings.

Thus we may say that Stanislavsky did not invent anything. He teaches us to follow the road pointed out by nature itself.

RICHARD BOLESLAVSKY

(1889-1937)

Richard Boleslavsky was the first to teach the techniques of Stanislavsky and the Moscow Art Theatre to American actors in a formal way. Few were better qualified than this Polish-born artist to transmit the system as Stanislavsky had evolved it in the first decades of the century.

Boleslavsky became a member of the Moscow Art Theatre in 1906 and attended the Art Theatre school for three years. He participated in some of the first productions in which Stanislavsky tried out his new approach: Turgenev's *A Month in the Country* and Tolstoy's *The Living Corpse*. In 1911 he was one of Gordon Craig's assistants in the famed production of *Hamlet* for the Moscow Art Theatre. In that same year he became part of the First Studio, organized by Stanislavsky to experiment with those new principles that were to become his acting System, and he directed its first production, Hejermans' *The Good Hope*. Of this production Stanislavsky said that it "displayed in all who took part in it a certain special, and until this time unknown, simplicity and depth in the interpretation of the life of the human spirit." Boleslavsky was involved in the work of the First Studio until 1920 at which time he left Russia.

In 1922 Boleslavsky came to the United States and was here to greet Stanislavsky and the members of the Art Theatre when they toured in 1923. With Maria Ouspenskaya, who remained in the United States when the rest of the Art Theatre returned to Russia, he founded the American Lab Theatre. Here American actors and directors had their first opportunity to study the System of Stanislavsky. Boleslavsky gave a series of lectures on acting at the Princess Theatre in New York in 1923, and in that year began to publish in *Theatre Arts Magazine* his lessons on acting through which many first learned of "Concentration," "Memory of Emotion," and other facets of the System. His presentation of these concepts in a series of working lessons made the new approach accessible to beginning students of theatre.

Boleslavsky and his associates planned a curriculum at the American Lab Theatre that would train both what Boleslavsky called the actor's "outer means of expression"—his body and voice—and his "inner means of expression"—his imagination, emotions and his general cultural and intellectual potential. The school had a repertory theatre linked to it after a few years, and Boleslavsky devoted much of his energies to it and to the work of the most advanced students. His Lab attracted many interesting faculty members and students: among the former were John Mason Brown, Mikhail Mordkin, Douglas Moore, the composer, and Francis Fergusson; among the latter were some who were to dominate the teaching of acting for the next forty years—Lee Strasberg, Harold Clurman, and Stella Adler. The "Method" as developed by these teachers is heavily indebted to Boleslavsky, who directly and through his students transformed American acting.

After the 1929 crash Boleslavsky went to live in Hollywood, where he worked as a film writer and director. In 1933 *Theatre Arts* published his articles as *Acting: The First Six Lessons,* the first text on the Stanislavsky system in America. The following selection by this important teacher is drawn from unpublished notes made by Boleslavsky in 1923.

Living the Part

An ideal actor has to combine in himself the following qualities:

1. Talent
2. An apt mind
3. Education
4. Knowledge of life
5. Observation
6. Sensitiveness
7. Artistic taste
8. Temperament
9. Voice

Richard Boleslavsky: Lecture notes of Boleslavsky organized and translated by Michel Barroy. In manuscript, 1923, Theatre Collection, New York Public Library.

10. Good enunciation
11. Expressive face and gestures
12. Well-built body
13. Dexterity
14. Plastique of movements
15. Tenacity in work
16. Imagination
17. Self-control
18. Good health

All these qualities with the exception of talent could and should be developed by the actor. But this development must be done gradually in a definite and logical sequence. To start with, the actor has to realize the three different planes of this development: the *spirit*, the *intellect*, and the *body*.

What must he do for the development of his spirit?

First: He has to train his own willpower to the point of becoming complete master of his soul. This can be achieved by developing a quality known as "Spiritual Concentration."

Second: He has to make his spirit sensitive and flexible. This, again, can be achieved by developing another quality called the "Spiritual" or "Affective Memory."

Third: He has to educate his spirit in order to have it strong and healthy in feelings. This could be accomplished by daily exercises on the *"fulfillment of spiritual problems."*

What must he do to develop his intellect?

He has to educate his artistic taste and sensitiveness by frequent *contact and study of all possible works of art.* He must increase his knowledge of life by constantly training his *observation*. Develop in himself to the greatest extent the faculty of *imagination*.

What must the actor do for the development of his body?

He must train his *voice* by vocal exercises; his *body* by dancing, fencing, different kinds of sports, and by control of his muscles; his *face*—by makeup; his *speech*—by diction and enunciation. Besides the above-mentioned exercises he must develop in himself the *art of inner and outer mimicry and incarnation.*

To get a knowledge, even though an elementary one, of the first principles of the Psychoanalysis of Human Feelings, using any popular manual of Psychology. (Ribot).

What Is the Meaning of "Living" the Part?

All the qualities of the actor, mentioned in my last lecture, are essential for him in order to "live his part." An actor who "lives his part" is a creative actor; the one who simply imitates different human emotions without feeling them each time is a "mechanical" one. The difference between them is the same as between a human being and a mechanical puppet, or as between an artist's painting and a photograph. No matter how fine a photograph may be, it could never be a work of art. It is nothing but a copy, a mechanical repetition of life, a stamp—while a painting is unique, being an individually created bit of "better" life.

An actor who "lives his part" uses a brand-new, fresh feeling each time he plays his role. Sometimes he expresses it in an entirely different manner, merely following the fundamental lines of his main problem, but without adhering to the once-set stage mechanics.

The creative actor, being sensitive and responsive to his surroundings, should be able to find the life's truth in all circumstances and situations. Examples—a scene in Hejermans's *The Good Hope,* when the mother, trying to persuade her son not to be afraid of the sea and sail on the next boat, shows him a couple of beautifully carved coral earrings; promising to give them to him in case he sails, she describes their beauty, pointing to the carved ships. On the opening night the property man forgot to put the earrings in the drawer. The actress playing the mother did not lose her presence of mind and, holding the imaginary earrings, started to describe them so eloquently that the audience actually believed it was seeing them. After the show a couple of people asked Stanislavsky where in the world he had acquired such a remarkable set of earrings.

A creative actor lends his ear exclusively to his soul, and does not try to *invent* new feelings, but merely invests his own in different forms prompted by his imagination. He is never concerned with the external effect of his part but merely in the inner, spiritual side of it. According to Stanislavsky's expression, "He does not love himself in art, but loves the art in himself." He controls his art always and everywhere. He does not look for any artificial excitement furnished by the footlights, the public, the applause, the costume, the sets, a girl friend in a box and so forth—the only thing he needs to have in front of him is a definite problem.

A creative actor is generally inclined toward beautiful literary works with great and eternal themes because those are the only ones that will supply him with spiritual food. Such an actor belongs to the class of "artists-creators" of the living theatre, while the "actor-imitator" of human feelings will always remain among the so-called "utilities" of the theatre.

"Living one's part" means complete spiritual and physical self-abandon for a definite period of time, in order to fulfill a real or fantastical problem of the theatre.

What Is "Spiritual Concentration?"

The main condition for each work is the ability to surrender one's entire being or at least the maximum of one's strength and energy to this particular work or creation. The most valuable quality of a good tradesman is attention. An ordinary actor is usually very attentive towards his lines or his stage business. But this is merely an outer attention. According to our theory, the main attention should be paid to the "life of the human spirit" or the "life of our inner feelings."

I cannot play Hamlet if I have never been afflicted by the loss of anyone dear to me, if I do not know what a deep grief means and have not developed this feeling in my soul. The discovery and the development of such feelings is the main work of a creative actor and demands a great deal of concentration, which in that particular case is called *"Spiritual Concentration."*

"Spiritual Concentration" is the ability to say to any of your feelings: "Stop, and fill my entire being!" This faculty can be developed and trained as much as one can train a human body,— and this training is the main problem of a creative school of acting.

Spiritual concentration is the energy produced by the entire human physiological and psychological apparatus, concentrated on one definite single problem.

A hunting dog, pursuing game, spends all his energy in dashing rapidly back and forth in order to discover his prey. The very moment the hound comes upon the scent he stops as if petrified. He commands all his feelings and energy to stand still and concentrates on one single thought: to trap the animal and to leap upon it at the proper moment. At this moment the entire muscular and spiritual energy of the dog is concentrated on three senses: seeing, hearing, and smelling. All that hinders him in the way of the complete and utmost functioning of these feelings is removed and forgotten. You can see it particularly by his muscles; the tail is dropped, the lifted paw hangs in the air as though broken, all the muscles of his body are relaxed and do not deprive him of even a single particle of his energy that is concentrated on nothing but these three senses.

This is an example of ideal concentration on one's primary feelings. As far as it concerns us—humans—there are two things that stand in the way of our complete abandonment and concentration. They are our muscles and our contemporary spiritual and physical life. We may counteract the opposition of our muscles by certain daily exercises, but the task of conquering the resistance of our modern life is much more complicated.

How are we handicapped by our muscles?

Let us take a look back at our childhood: on the way we were taught to carry ourselves, the conventionality of our clothes and shoes; on the unnatural way of our modern locomotion compared to the one indicated by nature itself. Think of rush hour in streetcars or subways, when we travel for hours suspended like grapes, falling over each other at each jerky movement of the car—and you'll understand how much energy we are wasting and how far we are removed from the free body of an ancient Roman or an animal. Compare the free stride of a savage with the walk of a modern girl.

You will not find much difficulty in conquering the opposition presented by your muscles. The only thing you have to do is to think of them constantly, to relax them as soon as you feel any tension, and to develop them by using some specially devised daily exercises. You must watch yourself all day long, at whatever you do, and be able to relax each superfluous tension of your muscles, letting only those of them work which are indispensable to the performance of a certain physical problem. . . .

Here are some exercises which should be done daily in order to relax your muscles from useless tension.

1. The concentration of your thoughts on each separate group of your muscles, bringing them from the state of tension into one of relaxation.

2. The verifying of your muscles in the sense of supplying them only with the necessary amount of strength during the performance of the following exercises: walking, sitting down, the lifting up of different articles from the floor, taking down of same from a high shelf, pointing at different things, calling, greeting, lighting a cigarette, the handing of a burning match to someone while a third person tries to blow it out, kicking with your foot articles of a different weight, lacing a shoe, any physical exercise, followed by complete rest, the taking of an intricate position followed by an immediate relaxation of all the muscles with its natural result—the fall of the body, the giving of a blow, the defense from a real or imaginary blow.

In doing all these exercises you must follow exclusively the example of nature and perform all of them in a high spirit and in a joyous frame of mind. You must understand as well that the *relaxation* of your muscles does not mean by any means their *weakening*. You must train your muscles every day without making of it a meaningless series of physical exercises. Each of your muscles must understand the reason for its particular training.

Let us see now what the manifestations of our modern life are that stand in the way of our *spiritual concentration*. First, it is the constant struggle for our existence that subordinates us to those on whom our livelihood depends and does not leave us any time for meditation on *our God,* absorbing our whole mind in worries about our next meal. How can we struggle against such a cruel and seemingly inconquerable condition?

Only by a boundless faith in our vocation, and the continual support of our spirit through close communion with the geniuses of humanity who suffered for the triumph of their ideals. Think of Cervantes, . . . of the destitute youth of Dickens; of Savanarola burned at the stake; of Mayor McSweeney of Cork, and hundreds of others whose examples teach us the conquest of life.

No one expects you to retire from life and be sinless, but it is important to be conscious of your own shortcomings and to be able to combat them. . . .

How can we return to the great creative rhythm and spirit of humanity? Only by approaching nature, by loving it, and by constant meditation about it:

Cast your eyes at a piece of blue sky among the skyscrapers of Broadway and you'll understand where the truth lies. Lend your ear to the beat of the surf and you will understand where the real key is for the appreciation of music. Look at a rushing mountain brook or at a falling star and you'll understand the meaning of speed.

I am certain that any architect could create a much more beautiful building if instead of working in the city he secluded himself for a few months in an isolated house somewhere in the mountains surrounded by a rustling forest.

Don't miss any chance you have, to concentrate and to think of nature. Don't cast away a flower or even a tree leaf without entering into communion with it and penetrating into its mystery. Listen to the twittering of each bird, watch the thoughtfulness of each small fish in an aquarium; do not repulse any animal that approaches you to be caressed; gaze as often as you can at the stars—and all this will help you in your struggle for spiritual concentration.

The third opposition in this struggle, and perhaps the most serious one, we find in our own passions, emotions, and desires.

How to withstand our ambitions, our craving for priority? How to resist our personal grief when we have to rush to the theatre to play a merry comedy? How to renounce the petty things of life obstructing our mind—a new hat, a drink of whisky, flirtation, etc.

You must always remember that you actors are the material, the clay of which you yourself have to mold your works of art; well—then consider yourself as such— as the material which must not be spoiled or soiled. And don't forget to invest it, whatever you do, with a colorful—more than that—with a beautiful form!

In other words, if we learn how to control our muscles and to dominate life that surrounds us, we shall develop and begin to get hold of our Spiritual Concentration.

Just as the hand of a pianist or a violinist requires daily exercises, so does our spirit, with the only difference that the exercises of our spirit are much harder than those on a piano or a violin. . . .

Be prepared: the first exercises for the development of your spiritual forces are very tedious and not easy to master just like the playing of scales, which requires long and painstaking practice before it shows us any results.

Be ready for disappointments and ridicule in this abstract and purely spiritual work, and think of Paganini who all of his life exercised seven hours a day, and then perhaps you will not mind spending the miserly half an hour which I ask you to devote to the following exercises:

1. *Bringing yourself into a happy frame of mind and complete spiritual ease, concentrate on your primary feelings: seeing, hearing, feeling, smelling, and taste* (the first three with real objects, the last two with imaginary ones).

2. Remember all the details of the day and mark every one of its sad or happy moments.

3. Remember last New Year's Day, and decide whether during the course of it you experienced more sad or gay moments.

4. Remember the dress you wore on the day you experienced an event of great importance.

5. Say mentally the "Lord's Prayer," realizing the *vital significance of every one of its words.*

6. *Inhale and exhale evenly and deeply several times in succession, trying to feel and to understand the work of your lungs.*

7. *Listen to the beating of your own heart and try to understand its work.*

8. *Transmit mentally to any living person your blessing and wish for complete happiness.*

9. *Recall your last anger or irritation, trying to justify it or to reproach yourself for it.*

10. *Remembering your last strong emotion, try to retain it for a certain period of time.*

11. *Remain in a good or bad mood for a certain definite period of time.* (The time should be gradually increased from a few moments to several hours.)

12. Compare two paintings or two pieces of sculpture to discover the essential difference between them.

13. Try to analyze and to understand the mood of a certain person you have just met.

14. Create in your mind a mental picture of all the sets in full colors and other details of a play you have just read.

15. Recall in your mind any time you wish and try to retain for a certain time the mood that particular memory generally brings to you.

16. As you walk or while you do some physical exercises, keep different moods, beginning with the simplest ones and increasing them gradually up to the most complicated rhythms of your inner feelings.

17. Take a certain pose and keep it for a specified period of time without moving.

18. Transmit mentally an order to someone (don't expect an immediate result).

19. Go over one of the roles you have studied or over a familiar poem without saying the lines aloud but simply using the corresponding moods and emotions.

20. Arouse in yourself according to your own choice a certain feeling, then transmit it to some imaginary being like the spirit of a deceased friend, or a phantom of a forest and get a response from it that will bring to you the state of peace or alarm.

All these exercises should not be performed one after another. Take a good rest after each of them in order to start the new one with a perfectly fresh and relaxed mind. It would be much better to do just a few exercises or even one at a time than many without the required feelings.

It is advisable to perform all this in your usual, distracting surroundings, instead of shutting yourself up in your own room where nothing is in the way of your concentration. Only in the very beginning, while you are groping in the dark, trying to make yourself familiar with that elusive "spiritual concentration," should you perform these exercises in complete solitude.

But as soon as you succeed in finding your way and get hold of that feeling, you must take it out into the open and continue the training of your spirit, exposing it to all kinds of dangers and temptations. Do it wherever you can, during your walks, your meals, and even while resting.

Only after a month of daily persistent work may you expect to feel the first results of that training. In other words only after a month of the most strenuous work will you begin to realize the meaning of "Spiritual Concentration."

What Is Spiritual or Affective Memory?

This condition was mentioned for the first time about forty years ago by the French psychologist Ribot. According to his terminology "affective memory" is the ability of the human organism to retain imperceptibly for man himself different psychological shocks and emotions and to live them all over again in the case of an identical repetition of outer physical occurrences.

For instance, while returning home with a bunch of freshly gathered lilies of the valley, a girl finds out about the tragic death of her beloved fiancé. The very moment she was hearing the news she was inhaling the aroma of these flowers. Many years have passed since then. She was married and has lived in perfect happiness—but each time she smelled the scent of lilies of the valley she would become nervously excited just as she was at the time of the tragedy, without even being conscious of the fact. More than that, unconscious tears were coming to her eyes at the mere sight of these flowers. Later on this became so much of a habit that it remained with her until the end of her days.

How to Use "Affective Memory" in Preparing a Part

After having decided what feeling is necessary for a certain part of his role, the actor tries to find in his "affective memory" a recollection similar to that particular feeling. He may use all kinds of means in order to bring that feeling to life, starting with the actual lines of the author and finishing with experiences from his own life, recollections from books, and finally using his own imagination. Then by a series of gradual exercises and rehearsals he brings himself into a state, enabling him to arouse to the strongest degree the necessary feeling by a mere thought of it and to retain it for the necessary period of time.

For instance, an actor playing Othello comes to the conclusion that a part of his role is filled by the feeling of jealousy. He searches in his so-called "golden casket of feelings" for some recollections having to do with jealousy and discovers several of them having to do directly or indirectly with that feeling: for instance having read in a paper a criticism about a very successful performance of one of his colleagues, he experienced a feeling of acute envy, similar to that of jealousy. This feeling was expressed by excessive irritation and exaggerated amiability toward his colleague. Then, he remembers that his wife once received a letter addressed in a strange handwriting. For some reason she did not tell him its contents while he, on the other hand, did not want to question her about it. This aroused in him quite a number of new feelings: an inner struggle between the desire to find out the contents of the letter by reading it and a feeling of respect toward her that wouldn't allow him to.

Another case—when arriving at the theatre he found his seat occupied by another person and, being certain that it belonged to him, he claimed it and defended his right to it.

Sometimes the mere recollection of a feeling enables the actor to live it all over again and, as in the above-mentioned case, his heart begins to beat faster at the mere recollection of the success of his colleague. In such a case, the only thing he has to do is to develop that feeling by continuous repetition of that recollection, until it becomes near and familiar to the point of getting hold of him at any moment according to his order.

But sometimes the mere recollection would not be sufficient and the actor has to arouse his "affective memory" by purely physical means, as for instance, the sight of his wife reading anything at all would bring to him the feeling he experienced while she was reading that mysterious message.

Sometimes, though, the actor has to use his imagination solely. As in this case— a persistent thought of a lost article he was fond of might supply him with the necessary feeling.

In other words, this work consists in finding and developing necessary feelings, but not in their outer reproduction.

We may call this the actor's "homework"—the preparation of the palette, and supplying it with necessary colors.

He must not think during this work *how* he is going to reproduce a certain feeling—his only concern should be to *find it, to sense it with his entire being, to get used to it, and to let nature itself find forms for its expression.*

The next period of the actor's work is when, having discovered and developed in himself the necessary feelings, he starts to apply them to the lines supplied by the author. This is one of the most beautiful moments of our work.

If until then the actor, who has collected all the familiar colors of jealousy and developed them to the point of making them near and vivid, did not dare to touch the Shakesperean text, he can begin to do it now.

Aroused to the heights of exaltation, in full possession of all the shadings of his new feeling, the actor begins to pronounce in the solitude of his workroom the immortal words of the author.

Timidly to start with, as though not daring to touch them, he begins to invest them with new forms, prompted not by the rules of elocution but by the great creative mind of the author in complete union with his own creative spirit.

By this time the actor knows his part perfectly, and the words come to him easily as though prompted by feelings. He never touches the words without being aroused and moved by feelings. He never reads or repeats his role—*he actually lives it.* . . .

If the author has expressed his feeling in the right way, the actor cannot change or add a single word to it, their feelings have to be in harmony and their hearts must beat in the same tempo. If this does not take place, the director's business is to discover it and to correct either one or the other, according to whose feeling is more valuable.

MICHAEL CHEKHOV

(1891-1955)

Nephew of Anton Chekhov, Michael Chekhov was born in St. Petersburg. After study at a dramatic school, he joined the Moscow Art Theatre and became one of the notable younger actors who first accepted and utilized Stanislavsky's system, but later developed his own, rather different emphasis.

He was one of the original members of the First Studio founded by Stanislavsky in 1911 as a special workshop for experiments on his system. He appeared in the first production of the Studio, directed by Richard Boleslavsky, and in the second, Dickens' *Cricket on the Hearth,* directed by Leopold Sulerzhitsky, a man of great moral and spiritual intensity who helped to make this Studio the creative center for such artists as Eugene Vakhtangov, Richard Boleslavsky, and Chekhov. In 1921 Chekhov revealed some of his unique qualities as an actor in a performance of the title role of Strindberg's tormented and contradictory *Eric IV* at the First Studio. This production was directed by Vakhtangov with whom Chekhov had the closest relationship.. Yuri Zavadsky, the Soviet director, claims that it is impossible to tell whether it was Chekhov who influenced Vakhtangov or Vakhtangov who influenced Chekhov. "It is well known that Vakhtangov worked with Chekhov when the latter prepared his best parts, including that of Khlestakov for the Moscow Art Theatre."

This last role, the leading one in Gogol's *The Inspector General,* was performed by Chekhov in 1921 under the direction of Konstantin Stanislavsky, for whom this was the third production of this great Russian comedy. Chekhov's grotesque, exaggerated interpretation made Khlestakov a "metaphysical image of vulgarity and triviality with strong mystical overtones." In his work on this role he could be seen turning from the naturalism identified with Stanislavsky. He felt that the "creative state was not concentration on emotional authenticity as Stanislavsky contended, but an inspiration stemming from the actor's vision of a dramatic work and of his own role in it." It is reported by his colleague Vera Soloviova that Chekhov disagreed with Stanislavsky about the value of emotional memory work, which he found of little use to him. Stanislavsky is said to have countered that Chekhov did not need the aid of these exercises because of an "overactive imagination" not present in most actors.

In 1923 the Studio became the Second Moscow Art Theatre with Chekhov as its director. His production of *Hamlet* in 1924 was highly stylized and exaggerated in the manner of Vakhtangov and Meyerhold rather than that of Stanislavsky. Interest in symbolism and spiritual purification and views of theatre as religious experience eventually put him at odds with the Communist authorities, although he continued to be highly admired as an actor. He was condemned by some of his associates for stressing idealism and inspiration in his methods, which he taught his students and wrote about. He left the Soviet Union in 1927, and lived the rest of his years on the Continent, in England, and in the United States.

In 1935 Chekhov and his company of actors were brought to the United States by Sol Hurok. His expressive, rhythmic, rich style met with mixed critical response and was much debated among followers of the Stanislavsky system then developing in the Group Theatre. Harold Clurman remembers that "Chekhov was rejected time and time again. He was too mystical and diffuse."

Unable to work as he hoped in the United States, Chekhov went to England at the invitation of Mr. and Mrs. Leonard Elmhurst, founders of Dartington Hall in Devonshire, where he developed the Chekhov Theatre Studio with Beatrice Straight, daughter of Mrs. Elmhurst, as manager. The school moved to Ridgefield, Connecticut, in 1939. Chekhov staged Dostoevsky's *The Possessed* in New York in that year.

The last decade of his life was spent in Hollywood, teaching and acting in films. In 1953 his important record of his method of work, *To the Actor,* was published. He revealed clearly his emphasis on imagination, intuition and the archetypal "psychological gesture," but paid tribute to Stanislavsky as the creator of the one method "expressly postulated for the actor," who had urged him to "organize and write down your thoughts concerning the technique of acting." Some of these thoughts follow.

The Psychological Gesture

> *The soul desires to dwell with the body because without the members of the body it can neither act nor feel.*
>
> —LEONARDO DA VINCI

I [have] said that we cannot directly command our feelings, but that we can entice, provoke and coax them by certain indirect means. The same should be said about our wants, wishes, desires, longings, lusts, yearnings or cravings, all of which, although always mixed with feelings, generate in the sphere of our willpower.

In the qualities and sensations we found the key to the treasury of our feelings. But is there such a key to our willpower? Yes, and we find it in the *movement* (action, gesture). You can easily prove it to yourself by trying to make a *strong,* well-shaped but simple gesture. Repeat it several times and you will see that after a while your willpower grows stronger and stronger under the influence of such a gesture.

Further, you will discover that the *kind* of movement you make will give your willpower a certain direction or inclination; that is, it will awaken and animate in you a *definite* desire, want or wish.

So we may say that the *strength* of the movement stirs our willpower in general; the *kind* of movement awakens in us a definite corresponding *desire,* and the *quality* of the same movement conjures up our *feelings.*

Before we see how these simple principles can be applied to our profession, let us take a few examples of the gesture itself in order to get a broad idea of its connotations.

Imagine that you are going to play a character which, according to your first general impression, has a *strong* and unbending *will,* is possessed by dominating, despotic *desires,* and is filled with *hatred* and *disgust.*

You look for a suitable overall gesture which can express all this in the character, and perhaps after a few attempts you find it.

It is *strong* and well shaped. When repeated several times it will tend to strengthen your *will*. The direction of each limb, the final position of the whole body as well as the inclination of the head are such that they are bound to call up a *definite desire* for *dominating* and *despotic* conduct. The *qualities* that fill and permeate each muscle of the entire body, will provoke within you feelings of *hatred* and *disgust*. Thus, through the gesture, you penetrate and stimulate the depths of your own psychology.

Another example:
This time you define the character as aggressive, perhaps even fanatical, with a rather fiery will. The character is completely open to influences coming from "above," and is obsessed by the desire to receive and even to force "inspirations" from these influences. It is filled with mystical qualities but at the same time stands firmly on the ground and receives equally strong influences from the earthly world. Consequently, it is a character which is able to reconcile within itself influences both from above and below.

For the next example we will choose a character that in a way contrasts with the second. It is entirely introspective, with no desire to come in contact either with the world above or below, but not necessarily weak. Its desire to be isolated might be a very strong one. A brooding quality permeates its whole being. It might enjoy its loneliness.

For the following example, imagine a character entirely attached to an earthly kind of life. Its powerful and egotistical will is constantly drawn downward. All its passionate wishes and lusts are stamped with low and base qualities. It has no sympathy for anyone or anything. Mistrust, suspicion and blame fill its whole limited and introverted inner life. The character denies a straight and honest way of living, always choosing roundabout and crooked paths. It is a self-centered and at times an aggressive type of person.

Still another example. You might see the strength of this particular character in its protesting, negative will. Its main quality may seem to you to be suffering, perhaps with the nuance of anger or indignation. On the other hand, a certain weakness permeates its entire form.

The last example. This time your character is again a weak type, unable to protest and fight his way through life; highly sensitive, inclined to suffering and self-pity, with a strong desire to complain.

Here also, as in the previous cases, by studying and exercising the gesture and its final position, you will experience its threefold influence upon your psychology.

You are strongly urged to bear in mind that all the gestures and their interpretations, as demonstrated, are only examples of possible cases and are in no way obligatory to your individual approach when searching for overall gestures.

Let us call them *Psychological Gestures* (hereinafter referred to as PG's), because their aim is to influence, stir, mold and attune your whole inner life to its artistic aims and purposes.

Now to the problem of applying the PG to professional work.
There is a written play before you with your part in it. It is only an inanimate literary work as yet. It is your task and your partners' to transform it into a living and scenic piece of theatrical art. What are you to do to fulfill this task?
To begin with, you have to make a first attempt to investigate your character,

to penetrate it in order to know whom you are going to perform on the stage. You can do this either by using your analytical mind or by applying the PG. In the former case you choose a long and laborious way because the reasoning mind, generally speaking, is not imaginative enough, is too cold and abstract to be able to fulfill an artistic work. It might easily weaken and for a long time retard your ability to *ict*. You may have noticed that the more your mind "knows" about the character, the less you are able to perform it. This is a psychological law. You might know only too well what the feelings and desires of your character are, but that knowledge alone would not enable you to fulfill the desires truthfully or experience its feelings sincerely on the stage. It is like knowing everything about a science or an art and ignoring the fact that this intelligence per se is far removed from being proficient in it. Of course, your mind can and will be very helpful to you in evaluating, correcting, verifying, making additions and offering suggestions, *but it should not do all these before your creative intuition has asserted itself and spoken fully.* This is by no means an implication that reason or intellect should be done away with in preparing the part, but it is an admonition that you should not appeal to it, should not rest your hopes on it, and that it must at the outset remain in the background so that it will not obtrude and hamper your creative efforts.

But if you choose another and more productive way, if you apply the PG in order to study your character, you appeal to your creative forces directly and do not become a "bookish" or rote actor.

Many an actor has asked, "How can I find the PG without first knowing the character for which the PG should be found, if use of the intellect is not recommended?"

From the results of previous exercises you certainly will have to admit that your sound intuition, your creative imagination and your artistic vision always give you at least *some* idea of what the character is, even upon the very first acquaintance with it. It might be just a guess, but you can rely upon it and use it as a springboard for your first attempt to build the PG. Ask yourself what the *main* desire of the character might be, and when you get an answer, even if it is only a hint, start to build your PG step by step, using at first your *hand* and *arm* only. You might thrust them forward aggressively, clenching your fist, if the desire reminds you of grasping or catching (greed, avarice, cupidity, miserliness); or you might stretch them out slowly and carefully, with reserve and caution, if the character wishes to grope or search in a thoughtful and diffident manner; or you might direct both your hands and arms upward, lightly and easily, with palms open, in case your intuition prompts that the character wants to receive, to implore, to beseech with awe; or maybe you will want to direct them downward, roughly with palms turned earthward, with clawing and crooked fingers, if the character lusts to overpower, to possess. Having once started this way, you will no longer find it difficult (in fact, it will happen by itself) to extend and adjust your particular gesture to your shoulders, your neck, the position of your head and torso, legs and feet, until your *entire* body is thus occupied. Working this way, you will soon discover whether your first guess as to the main desire of the character was correct. The PG itself will lead you to this discovery, without too much interference on the part of the reasoning mind. In some instances you might feel the need to do your PG by starting not from a neutral position but from one that the character suggests to you. Your character might be introspective or introverted and his main desire might be defined as an urge to be open and receptive to the influences coming from above. In that case you might start from a more or less closed instead of neutral position. In choosing a starting position you are, of course, just as free as in creating any PG.

Now you continue developing the PG, correcting and improving it, adding to it all the qualities you find in the character, slowly leading it to the stage of perfection. After a short experience you will be able to find the correct PG practically at once, and will have only to improve it according to your or your director's taste while aiming at its final version.

By using the PG as a means of exploiting the character, you actually do more than that. You prepare yourself for acting it. By elaborating, improving, perfecting and exercising the PG you are, more and more, becoming the very character yourself at the same time. Your will, your feelings are stirred and awakened in you. The more you progress in this work, the more the PG reveals to you the entire character in *condensed* form, making you the possessor and master of its *unchangeable core*.

To assume a PG means, then, to prepare the entire part in its *essence,* after which it will become an easy task to work out all the details in actual rehearsals on the stage. You will not have to flounder and grope aimlessly, as often happens when you start dressing a part with flesh, blood and sinews without first having found its spine. The PG gives you this very spine. It is the shortest, easiest and the most artistic way of transforming a literary creation into a theatrical piece of art.

Until now I have spoken of the PG as applicable to the entire character. But you can use it just as well for any segment of the role, for separate scenes or speeches if you wish, or even separate sentences. The way to find and apply it in these shorter instances is exactly the same as for the entire character.

If you have any doubts about how to reconcile the general, overall PG for the whole part with particular, smaller PGs for separate scenes, the following illustration should serve to clarify the point:

Imagine three different characters—Hamlet, Falstaff and Malvolio. Each of these characters can become angry, grow pensive or start laughing. But they will not do any of these things in the same way because they are *different* characters. Their difference will influence their anger, pensiveness and laughter. The same with different PGs. Being an *essence* of the whole character, the overall PG will of its own accord influence all smaller, particular PGs. Your well-developed sensitivity to the PG will show you intuitively which nuances in all the minor PGs must be elaborated to make them match up with the major PG. The more you work upon PGs, the more you will realize how flexible they are, what unlimited possibilities they offer you in coloring them the way you like. What may seem an insoluble problem for the dry and calculating mind is resolved most simply by creative intuition and imagination, from which the PG springs.

On the other hand, you might use these minor PGs only so long as you need them to study your scene, your speech, etc., and then drop them entirely. But the overall PG for the character will remain with you *always.*

Another question that may arise in your mind is, "Who tells me whether the PG I find for my character is the right one?" The answer: *Nobody but yourself.* It is your own free creation, through which your individuality expresses itself. *It is right if it satisfies you as an artist.* However, the director is entitled to suggest alterations to the PG you have found.

The only question you can permit yourself in this connection is whether you fulfill the PG correctly; that is, whether you observe all the necessary conditions for such a gesture.

There are two kinds of gestures. One we use both while acting on the stage and in everyday life—the natural and usual gesture. The other kind is what might be called the *archetypal* gesture, one which serves as an original model for all possible gestures of the same kind. The PG belongs to the second type. Everyday gestures are unable to stir our will because they are too limited, too weak and particularized. They do not occupy our whole body, psychology and soul, whereas the PG, as an archetype, takes possession of them *entirely.*

VASILI O. TOPORKOV

This distinguished Russian actor and director began his career in St. Petersburg in the early years of this century. From 1919 to 1927 he acted at the Korsh Theatre. His excellence as an actor lay in his character parts and comic creations, such as Truffaldino in Goldoni's *A Servant of Two Masters* and Captain Chris Christopherson in O'Neill's *Anna Christie.*

In 1927 he became a member of the Moscow Art Theatre. Among the roles he played in this period were the Cashier in Katayev's *The Embezzlers,* Chichikov in Gogol's *Dead Souls* and Orgon in Molière's *Tartuffe.* In these latter roles he was directed by Konstantin Stanislavsky, whose work with him is described in detail in the essay that follows. Stanislavsky initiated the production of *Tartuffe* to explore his new concern with "physical actions" or the external means as a way of stimulating the emotional content of the role. In all his performances he realized the finest intentions of the Stanislavsky system, which he followed with great devotion. It was said of his performance of the adventurist Chichikov that it had all the richness Gogol's creation demands. His Orgon was a model of comic form. In 1935 he played the title role of a highly principled surgeon who serves the people in Korneichuk's *Platon Krechet.* In the 1940's one of his triumphs was Yepikhodov in Chekhov's *The Cherry Orchard,* and he continued in leading roles in plays by Korneichuk and others through the 1960's.

Toporkov also served as a director of many productions beginning in the 1940's. But one of the most important contributions of this fine actor has been as popularizer, propagandist and teacher of the Stanislavsky system. Since 1948 he has been a professor at the Moscow Art Theatre and has written many books and articles, given speeches and lectures on Stanislavsky's theory and practice. Some of his writings are *Theatrical Almanac, Improvisation and the Creation of the Actor, Theatrical Life* and *Why Do People Go to the Theatre.* He is People's Artist of the Union of Soviet Socialist Republics and has represented his country and the Moscow Art Theatre at international meetings.

Physical Actions

... If you study Stanislavsky's work, you can see how frequently he tried to get his actors to reveal their feelings, their real humanity, on the stage—in a word, to reveal their creative selves. Every one of his efforts, however important and progres-

Toporkov, V. O.: "Le Rôle de l'improvisation dans l'incarnation du personnage scénique," in *Le Role de l'improvisation dans l'enseignement de l'art dramatique.* Bucharest: Centre Roumain de L'IIT (Inernational Theatre Institute) 1965, pp. 53-65 *passim.* Translated from the French by Joseph M. Bernstein. Reprinted by permission of the Romanian Center, International Theatre Institute, through the courtesy of Rosamund Gilder.

sive for their time, ended in disappointment for the great teacher. This was the story until he came to his final method: *the method of physical actions.* This method consisted of getting into the actor's creative self and molding it by the logic of organic actions that focused on that objective.

Stanislavsky proceeded from the idea that intuition is extremely sensitive to truth and responds readily to it. It is hard to obtain emotional truth consciously, because emotions do not easily yield to the will; it is much easier, however, to find truthful physical actions. Their logic will inevitably provoke logic in emotions. That is the *Law of the Unity of the Physical and Psychical* in man's nervous system. Going through a series of physical actions and thereby obtaining logic in his emotions, an actor has a surer chance of achieving his aim: to create the life of the human spirit in a stage setting. It is worthwhile recalling that Stanislavsky himself considered the expression "method of physical actions" a conventional one. They are psychophysical actions, he used to say, but we call them physical to avoid philosophical debate. Physical actions are concrete and material, they are easier to perceive and define; but they are closely connected with a person's typical attitudes and feelings. When he performs a purely physical act, the actor inevitably introduces elements of the emotional and psychic into the process of creation. . . .

In his work as theatre director and teacher, Stanislavsky paid special attention to an actor's physical behavior in the process of creating a role. Stanislavsky knew that only a well-structured line of physical actions would enable the actor to create the precise outlines of the role. . . .

In the chapter "Physical Action" in the book *Stanislavsky Produces Othello,* he wrote:

"Remember how an airplane rises: for a while it taxis along the ground and acquires momentum. An air movement then surrounds the wings and lifts the plane. The actor too, we may say, takes off by means of physical actions and acquires momentum. At the same time, by means of the given circumstances—the magic 'if'—the actor spreads out his invisible wings of faith that lift him on high, into the realm of the imagination (and, I add, of improvisation) in which he sincerely believes."

The above-mentioned phrases "given circumstances" and "the magic 'if'" have great significance in Stanislavsky's method. By "given circumstances" he means the things he wants actors to take into consideration in the unfolding of the play itself: facts, events, time, place, and length of action, obstacles that may arise, etc. "The magic 'if'" is the springboard of creation. To an actor unable to decide how to play a scene Stanislavsky recommends that he ask himself: "What would *I* do, *if* I found myself, here and now, in the same situation as the character I am supposed to portray?" According to Stanislavsky this question has a "magic" action on the creative process.

Here, for example, is how Stanislavsky counsels his actors to create the chain of physical actions in the scene in *Othello* in which Othello and Desdemona are together the morning after their nuptial night and before any shadow has crossed their love. "How should an actor live that scene?" What line should he follow? What line should he think about as he comes on stage? Is it the line of love, of passion (that is, of feelings), the character line, the literary line, the story line, etc.? No, it is the line of action, the line of truthful actions and of genuine confidence in them.

Here is the line of physical actions: (1) Try to find Desdemona and kiss her as quickly as possible; (2) she is enjoying herself and is coy with Othello; the actor must fall in with her playfulness and joke lightheartedly with her; (3) on the way Othello has met Iago and, in a good mood, has jested with the latter; (4) Desdemona has come back to draw Othello over to the couch and he, again playful with her, follows her; (5) they lie down.—Remain that way; let your wife fondle you and, insofar as possible, respond in the same way. Thus the actor lives through five of the simplest physical tasks.

In other words, if the actor performs his physical tasks by means of the simplest words and deeds but in such a way that he feels their truth and sincerely believes in that simple physical truth, he need not worry: he has prepared the ground for the right emotion and will live his task to the extent that he can live it on that particular day. If you are in a bad mood that day you will probably act less well than at the previous performance. But that is no calamity, for, as the great Russian actor Shchepkin used to say, "Whether you act well or badly is not important—the main thing is for you to act right."

If you follow the pattern of physical actions under the given circumstances and if you believe in them, don't worry: you are acting right.

In Stanislavsky's words: "A few dozen tasks and physical acts, that's how you have to master your part . . . that's my advice to you in preparing a part, especially a part like that of Othello, which requires both tremendous strength and an economy of strength."

I had the good fortune to work on several parts under Stanislavsky's direction during the period in which the new method was initiated and developed. And that is why I feel I had good training under so great a teacher.

One of the most complicated parts I played was that of Chichikov, in the play adaptation of Gogol's *Dead Souls*. It was not a part suited to my style of acting, so I had to "sweat blood" over it.

Let me cite one instance so as to give you an idea of how Stanislavsky worked with actors. First, let me briefly summarize *Dead Souls*. Chichikov, a small landowner, has devised a scheme. He buys serfs—"souls"—with the intention of then leasing them to the government. In reality, however, these are dead serfs, but until the next census they are still kept on the lists as living persons. With this in mind, Chichikov arrives in the provincial capital and immediately pays a visit to the governor. What I am about to talk about refers to this scene, called in the play: "At the governor's."

Stanislavsky asked me to come to a rehearsal alone and we began to discuss the play. First of all, we went into Chichikov's aim in visiting the governor, spelling out how important it was to him. He wanted the governor himself to introduce him to the local bigwigs.

"What does Chichikov have to get during his brief visit?" Stanislavsky asked me. "Say it, define it in a single word that *must* be a verb. Say the word that will throw the clearest light on his line of action."

"I think . . . he has to please the governor," I replied.

"Yes, but more specifically."

"Well, he must flatter him."

"Let's say he has to have him on his side, has to win him over . . . do you understand? How will you begin your action?"

"I will behave very obsequiously . . ."

"Then he'll say to himself: 'What a lickspittle!' and he'll kick you out within a few minutes. You're seeing the governor for the first time and that's why it's essential *for you to know him,* find out what kind of a man he is, know how to get around him.—The first moment of action consists of your *quickly getting your bearings,* of feeling your way. That's what we always do in life and forget to do on the stage. So, how shall we begin?"

"But ... who'll play opposite me?"

"I will. Go out of the room and come in as if you were seeing me for the first time. Behave in such a way ás to produce the best impression on me."

"But ... what about the script?"

"Why do we need a script? Begin by acting. What interests me is the way you behave. What are you thinking about?"

"I ... I really don't quite know where to begin ..."

"Creation begins with the magic 'if.' Put this question to yourself: *if I* were in the character's place, what would I do? Notice what I said: What I would *do,* not what I would feel! How would I behave in order to win over the governor? Have you ever in your life had occasion to be in that kind of a situation?"

"Yes, but nothing came of it."

"Why?"

"Because one wants to do something and then does just the opposite."

"But suppose you did behave the way you wanted to? Think all the time of what you have to do to win me over and then just go and do it. Do the first two or three actions."

"The thing is I'm not used to working like this ... and I don't know how to begin ..."

"What! You don't know what you have to do to enter a room? You've got to knock on the door and, when you're invited in, you open the door and come in. Surely you can do that! But before doing it, think of the magic 'if.' Suppose today, at this very moment, I had to enter Stanislavsky's office and make a good impression on him: *How would I knock on the door? How would I open it? How would I come in? How would I greet him?* Get a clear picture of those things and then begin. Do those four physical actions as you would in real life, without any thought of the stage, in accordance with the truth and until that truth becomes second nature."

For two hours I rehearsed my entrance until Stanislavsky declared himself satisfied. At that time I was over forty and a seasoned veteran of more than twenty years in the theatre.

Next, I worked on the whole scene in the same spirit. To tell the truth, what followed was easier. Gradually I paid more attention to my physical behavior as I got rid of my usual worries about my emotional reactions. Thus, little by little, the uninterrupted line of Chichikov's physical behavior took shape. When I mentioned Chichikov's character traits, Stanislavsky said to me:

"Practice intensively all the required physical actions until you master them; then you'll have the pliability needed to play the smooth-tongued swindler as Gogol characterizes him."

To portray Chichikov's special way of greeting people, so brilliantly described by Gogol, Stanislavsky asked me to keep doing the following exercise:

"Make believe you have a drop of mercury on the top of your head. Then let it fall the whole length of your spine, down to your heel. But fall in such a way that it doesn't reach the ground too soon. Do that exercise every day. Understand?"

One day during a dress rehearsal of *Dead Souls,* during the scene "at Plyushkin's," the chair I was sitting on collapsed under me. I fell on the floor and, interrupting the scene, apologized to Stanislavsky who was sitting in the orchestra.

"Why apologize to me?" Stanislavsky replied sharply. "Is your mind more on your audience than on your fellow actor? That means you didn't enter into your part. You didn't break my chair; you broke Plyushkin's chair. And he, why, he's our Russian Harpagon—the typical miser. Think a little about *whose* chair you have just broken, about *whom* you've made suffer. You've lost an opportunity to improvise a marvelous scene: Chichikov breaks Plyushkin's chair. Because of that clumsy act, Chichikov's whole scheme might have fallen through. Ah! What Varlamov would have done with that!"

Yes, Varlamov would not have been upset if something unforeseen had happened on the stage. But he was Varlamov! A great actor, a master of improvisation.

At the turn of the century Varlamov—Uncle Kostya, the people fondly called him—acted at the Alexandrinsky Theatre in St. Petersburg. Among the many great actors in the realistic theatre of that period his was a position of special eminence. Stanislavsky often said that his method was based on his study of the creations of the great actors—above all, those of Varlamov. He never lacked a special kind of creativity—inspiration, intuition, call it what you will. To him there was no difference between life and the stage; and whenever he walked onstage he behaved as naturally as in real life. He did not have to strain to be creative; he seemed effortless in the way he succeeded in every role he played. The general stage directions of a play were enough for him; he never delved deeply into the text. With the naïveté of a child he entered into a performance as if it were a children's game, and he acted with the seriousness and total absorption that only children have. He was an artist whose physical as well as spiritual qualities were on the grotesque side. In his art he did not have to invent or add a thing—he was unusually gifted, his nature overflowing with talent. Stanislavsky used to say to him:

"When Varlamov comes on stage and merely says: 'Good morning,' his greeting expresses not only Russian heartiness but the heartiness of the whole world."

Brilliant improviser, he never lost his head onstage. When the unexpected occurred, he calmly fitted it into the framework of the character he was portraying with unerring logic. He did not need Stanislavsky's method or any other method—he was a *phenomenon*. With such actors there are no artistic laws; they create the laws.

Michael Chekhov, of the Moscow Art Theatre, was also a fine improviser. But in contrast to Varlamov, his improvisations were the result of much preliminary work under the guidance of directors like Stanislavsky and Vakhtangov. He was a master in molding the contours of a part. During rehearsals he did exercises so as to attain perfection, polishing each link in the chain of the character's behavior. His extraordinary improvisations occurred during actual play productions. Every performance was a new creation. Theatre buffs in Moscow would go time after time to see the famous lying scene in Gogol's *Inspector General;* each time they saw it Michael Chekhov would amaze them with his unexpected improvisations, with the subtle nuances he gave to the typical traits of Gogol's hero. The very way in which Chekhov improvised coincided with the character of Khlestakov—an improviser of fantastic lies in the mayor's house. But I must point out that while he interpreted the part in that way, Chekhov never violated Gogol's text, never added or cut a single line. His improvisations were really brilliant models, illuminating Gogol's literary masterpieces in terms of theatre.

In conclusion I should like to talk about one of my improvisations, a success I achieved when I used Stanislavsky's method to create a part.

The last play the great director of the Moscow Art Theatre worked on was Molière's *Tartuffe*. Undertaken with an actors' group shortly before his death for purely pedagogical purposes, Stanislavsky's direction sought particularly to train the play's cast psychotechnically. Stanislavsky was especially strict and demanding when it came to the purity of his method. In my book *Stanislavsky at Rehearsal*,[1] I have described his work on *Tartuffe* in detail, hence I shall not go into it here. Let me simply say that Stanislavsky tried, by means of the most painstaking theatre technique, to present Molière's immortal comedy as a work of great passion, with sharp clashes, and with a great human theme shining through it. He wanted to avoid the usual Molière production, full of stage effects and a whole bag of tricks and clichés. In a word, Stanislavsky wanted the actors in *Tartuffe* to interpret *the life of the human spirit*.

Let me pause for a moment and dwell on something directly connected with my theme. During one rehearsal, at Stanislavsky's express request *we were not acting out anything on the stage,* simply running through the lines. That day, doing my utmost to pay close heed to the line of action, I managed to approach that creative state in which one feels free, unusually at one's ease in doing things. We were rehearsing a lively scene: Orgon's son Damis is unmasking Tartuffe's hypocrisy in front of his father. Orgon, enraged, brandishes his stick at his son and drives him out of the house, shouting after him:

"Rascal, I'll cut you out of my will
And, what's more, give you my curse."

I have already said that while studying my part of Orgon this scene gripped me so that I felt an amazing rush of creative freedom. So when I seized my stick and rushed at my son, I realized that I was going to improvise. I can't recall what I did then, but the high point of my improvisation has remained in my memory. After driving out my son, I turned toward Tartuffe. Instead of addressing him in tones of sorrow, I suddenly cut capers like a child and exclaimed with glee: "I no longer have a son."

Those present gave me an ovation. It may seem as if Orgon's joy, after he has cursed his son, is out of place and contrary to all logic. But for me it underlined in an unexpected way Orgon's blind faith in Tartuffe. By driving away his son he was removing the reason for which Tartuffe could be forced to leave his house. The words "I no longer have a son" might have had as a subtitle: "Now nothing prevents me any longer from devoting myself to holy things." That is what brings on Orgon's ecstasy of joy. Yet I confess that never before had I thought of playing the scene that way. It came to me by *intuition,* as a result of the creative freedom I had acquired through the right method of work. This improvisation was a bonus given an actor for his strenuous work.

Now let us return to our subject and see how important improvisation is in the actor's art.

It seems to me to be the very essence, the soul of the art of the theatre of life— the high point of the actor's creation on stage. Improvisation is subconscious creation that comes into being by virtue of the actor's conscious work, once he has mastered psychotechnical techniques.

That is why the last method Stanislavsky formulated lies at the basis of our

---

[1] V. O. Toporkov: *K. S. Stanislavski na Repetitzii.* Moscow: Iskustvo, 1950.

theatre teaching. With us, the student's education always begins with a study of the main elements of organic behavior: attention, communication, physical action, logic, and truthfulness.

By means of various exercises we try during the first year to develop in the student a heightened sense of the *truth* of his actions, just as one develops a musician's sense of hearing or a painter's sense of sight. Having developed this quality, we gradually give our students such stage problems as sketches, play fragments, etc. There are probably other ways of training young actors. And Stanislavsky said many times that he was ready to accept any way, any method, provided it did not contradict the organic laws of nature but that in harmony with them it led to our great common aim—the theatre of the human heart, *the theatre of the living man.*

The laws of creation in the theatre have not been invented; they are furnished by nature itself. What we have to know is how to use them. It is wrong to think that inspiration is the basis of work; on the contrary, inspiration results from work. By dint of arduous study the actor, assuming of course that he has talent and that in his art he respects the laws of development of living nature, makes his way toward inspiration—toward creative improvisation.

JERZY GROTOWSKI

(b. 1933)

The most thorough exploration of the methods by which the actor can become a vital creative artist since the researches of Stanislavsky is that of Jerzy Grotowski at his Theatre Laboratory in Wroclaw, Poland. Since 1959 Grotowski and his very select group have worked with religious fervor to find out how the actor can strip away all barriers in order to make "a total gift of himself" in his communion with his audience.

Grotowski, born in Rzeszow in the eastern part of Poland, went to the Cracow Theatre School, where he received a diploma as an actor as well as doing work in production. He became a director at the Teatr Stary in Cracow and at the Teatr Polski in Poznan. Among the plays he prepared at these theatres were *The Chairs* by Ionesco, *Uncle Vanya* by Chekhov, and *Faust I* and *II* by Goethe. In 1959 he headed the Teatr 13 Rzedow in Opole, the youngest director to have such a position. This became the Theatre Laboratory.

In 1965 the Theatre Laboratory moved to Wroclaw, now officially recognized as The Institute for Research into Acting. Supported by the state, Grotowski's theatre does not function in an ordinary way. It is a genuine laboratory in which the productions are, as Grotowski says, "detailed investigations of the actor-audience relationship." In his intimate theatre, with the aide of his architect, Jerzy Gurawski, and his leading actor, Ryszard Cieslak, he directs "two ensembles," the actors and the spectators. The performance results from an integration of these two "ensembles."

Grotowski resents being thought "experimental" in the usual sense of "toying with some 'new' techniques each time." Rather he sees himself evolving from the heritage of the great modern innovators a definition of "what is distinctively theatre." He turned from the notion of theatre as a synthesis of all the arts, which he calls "Rich Theatre," toward a conception of a "Poor Theatre," in which everything that "proved superfluous"—sets, costumes, makeup, theatres—was eliminated. What remained was the "direct-'live' actor-audience relationship," which is for him the essence of theatre. Although this view is not novel, Grotowski's practice is new because he "rigorously tested" the implications in practice of doing away with all but the essential element, the actor, and then to that core he devoted his whole energy and talent.

Brought up in the Stanislavsky tradition, Grotowski still considers the Russian master his personal ideal, for "Stanislavsky asked the key methodological questions." Others he has studied with care are Dullin, Delsarte, Meyerhold, Vakhtangov, Brecht and Artaud, though, he points out in the interview translated below, the last two are aestheticians rather than creators of an acting method since they do not address themselves adequately to the question, "How can this be done?"

His own method involves arduous physical exercise to give the actor complete control over his physical and mental capacity. "Ours is a *via negativa*," he has said, "not a collection of skills but an eradication of blocks that stand between him [the actor] and his creative confession. It is not the instruction of a pupil but an utter opening to another person, in which the phenomenon of a 'shared or double birth' becomes possible. The actor is reborn not only as an actor, but as a man and with him I am reborn. What is achieved is total acceptance of one man by another."

The collection of his statements, interviews, and exercises in the volume *Towards a Poor Theatre* has made the work of this important innovator available to more than the few who have attended his classes in Wroclaw, brief sessions in London for Peter Brook, occasional Continental workshops, New York University for the Theatre Division, and the limited public appearance of his company in New York in the fall of 1969.

The Actor's Technique

D.B.: Jerzy Grotowski, I would like you first to specify for me your position in relation to various acting theories as, for example, those of Stanislavsky, Artaud and Brecht, and to explain how, through reflection on those theories and naturally through your personal experience, you have been led to elaborate your own technique for the actor, defining both its aims and means.

J.G.: I believe it is necessary to distinguish between methods and aesthetics. Brecht, for example, explained many very interesting things about the possibilities of a way of acting that involved the actor's discursive control over his actions, *the Verfremdungseffekt*. But this was not really a method. It was rather a kind of aesthetic duty of the actor, for Brecht did not truly ask himself: "How can this be done?" Although he has provided certain explanations, these remain general . . . Certainly Brecht did study the technique of the actor in great detail, but always from the standpoint of the director observing the actor.

Artaud's case is different. Artaud offers without doubt an indisputable stimulus for research relative to the possibilities of the actor, but what he proposes are in the end only visions, a sort of poem about the actor, and one cannot draw any conclusions from his explanations. Artaud pointed out—as we know from his essay "Un Athlétisme Affectif" in *Le Théâtre et son Double*—that there is an authentic parallelism between the efforts of a man who works with his body (e.g. picking up a heavy object) and the psychic processes (e.g. receiving a blow, react-

Jerzy Grotowski: *Theatre Laboratorie*. Wroclaw, 1967. "The Actor's Technique," translated by Helen Krich Chinoy. Reprinted by permission of the author.

ing to it). He understands very well that the body possesses a center that decides the reactions of the athlete, and those of the actor who wants to reproduce psychic efforts through his body. But if one analyzes his principles in a practical way, one discovers that they lead to stereotypes: a particular type of movement to exteriorize a particular type of emotion. In the end this leads to clichés.

To be sure it was not a cliché when Artaud was doing his research and, as an actor, he observed his own reactions and sought an escape from the exact imitation of human reactions and cold reconstructions. But let us consider his theory. One can see in it a useful stimulus. However, if one treats it as a technique, one ends in clichés. Artaud offers a fruitful starting point for research and an aesthetic point of view. When he asks the actor to study his breathing, to exploit the different elements of respiration in his acting, he is giving him a chance to enlarge his possibilities, not only of acting through words but also through that which is inarticulate (inspiration, expiration, etc.). This is a very fruitful aesthetic proposition, but it is not a technique.

There are, in fact, very few acting methods. The most developed is that of Stanislavsky. Stanislavsky posed the most important questions and he supplied his own answers. During his numerous years of research, his method evolved, but not his disciples. Stanislavsky had disciples for each of his periods, and each disciple is limited to his particular period; from that came discussions like those of theology. He, himself, was always experimenting and he did not suggest recipes, but the means whereby the actor might discover himself, replying in all concrete situations to the question: "How can this be done?" This is essential. All this was naturally in terms of the theatre of his country, his time, of a theatre of realism....

D. B.: ... An interior realism ...

... An existential realism, I think, or rather an existential naturalism.

J. G.: Charles Dullin also devised many good exercises, improvisations, games with masks, or again exercises taking such themes as "man and plants," "man and animals." These are very useful for the preparation of the actor; they stimulate not only his imagination, but also the development of his natural reactions. But this does not really constitute a technique for the formation of the actor.

D. B.: What then is the originality of your position in relation to these diverse conceptions?

J. G.: All conscious systems in the field of acting ask the question: "How can this be done?" This is good. A method is the awareness of this "how to do it." I believe that one must ask oneself this question once in one's life, but when one enters into the details it must no longer be asked, for, at the very moment of formulating it, one already creates stereotypes and clichés. One must then ask the question: "How not to do it?"

Technical examples are always the clearest. Let us take that of respiration. If we ask the question "How should I do it?" we will consider a precise perfect type of breathing, perhaps the abdominal type. We can, in fact, observe that children, animals, people who are closest to nature, breathe principally with the abdomen, the diaphragm. But then we come to the second question: "What sort of abdominal respiration is the best?" And we could try to discover among numerous examples a type of inhalation, a type of expiration, a type of position for the vertebral column. This would be a terrible mistake for there is no perfect type of respiration valid for everyone, nor for all psychical and physical situations. Breathing is a physiological reaction linked with specific characteristics in each of us and which is dependent on situations, types of effort, physical activities.

Most people, when breathing freely, naturally use abdominal respiration, but the number of types of abdominal respiration is unlimited. And, there are also exceptions. For example, I have met actresses who, having thoraxes that were too long, could not naturally use abdominal breathing in their work. For them it was therefore necessary to find another type of breathing controlled by the vertebral column. If the actor tries artificially to recover perfect, objective abdominal respiration, he blocks the natural process of respiration, even if his is naturally of the diaphragmatic type.

When I find myself in the presence of an actor and I begin to work with him, the first question I ask myself is: "Does this actor have any breathing difficulties?" He breathes well; he has enough air to speak, to sing. Why, then, create a problem by imposing on him a different type of respiration? This would be absurd. But, perhaps he does have difficulties. Why? Are there physical problems? . . . Psychical problems? If they are psychical problems, what kinds of problems are they?

For example, an actor is tense. Why is he tense? Each of us is tense in one way or another. One cannot be completely relaxed as is taught in many theatre schools, for he who is totally relaxed is nothing more than a wet handkerchief. Living is not being tense, no more than it is being relaxed; it is a process. But if the actor is always too tense, we must discover the cause blocking the natural respiratory process—almost always of a psychical or psychological nature. We must determine which is his natural type of respiration. I observe the actor; I suggest exercises that compel him into total psychophysical mobilization. I watch him when he is in a moment of conflict, play or flirtation with another actor, in those moments when something changes automatically. Knowing the actor's natural type of respiration, we can more exactly define the factors that act as obstacles to his natural reactions and have as their aim then to eliminate them. Here lies the essential difference between our technique and the other methods: our technique is not positive.

We do not look for recipes, the stereotypes that are the natural accompaniment of professionals. We do not attempt to answer questions such as: "What does one do to show irritation? How should one walk? How should Shakespeare be played?" (For in the end these are the sorts of questions usually asked.) Instead one must ask the actor: "What are the obstacles blocking you on your way toward the total act that must engage all of your psychophysical resources, from the most instinctive to the most rational?" We must find out what it is that blocks him in the way of respiration, movement and—most important of all—human contact. What resistances are there? How can they be eliminated? I want to take away, steal from the actor all that disturbs him. That which is creative will remain within him. It is a liberation. If nothing remains, it is because he is not creative.

One of the greatest dangers that threatens the actor is, obviously, lack of discipline, chaos. One cannot express oneself through anarchy. I believe that spontaneity and discipline are the two sides of the creative process. Meyerhold based his work on discipline, exterior formation, etc.; Stanislavsky on the spontaneity of daily life. These are relatively the two complementary aspects of the creative process.

D. B.: But what do you mean by the "total act" of the actor?

J. G.: It is not only the mobilization of all the resources of which I have spoken.

It is also something far more difficult to define, even if very tangible from the point of view of work. It is the act of laying oneself bare, of tearing off the mask of daily life, of exteriorizing oneself. Not in order to "show oneself off," for that would be exhibitionism. It is a serious and solemn act of revelation. The actor must be ready to be absolutely sincere. It is like a step toward the summit of the actor's organism in which are united consciousness and instinct.

D. B.: In practice the formation of the actor must then be adapted to each case?

J. G.: Yes, I don't believe in recipes.

D. B.: Therefore, there is no such thing as the formation of actors, but the formation of each individual actor. How do you go about this? You observe them? You question them? And then? . . .

J. G.: There are exercises. We speak very little. During the training each actor is asked to search for his own associations, his personal variants (recalling memories, evoking his needs, all that he has not been able to realize).

D. B.: Is the training done collectively?

J. G.: The starting point of the training is the same for everyone, but. . . . Let us take as an example the physical exercises. The elements of the exercises are the same for all, but each one must do them in terms of his own personality. An onlooker can easily see the differences according to the individual personalities. The essential problem is to give the actor the possibility of working "in security." The work of the actor is in danger; it is necessary to create under continuous control and observation. An atmosphere must be created, a working system in which the actor feels that he can do absolutely anything, that nothing he does will be the object of jokes, that all will be understood and accepted. It is often at the moment when the actor understands this that he reveals himself.

D. B.: There is, therefore, total confidence between the different actors and between them and you.

J. G.: There is no question of the actor having to do what the director proposes, but that he must realize that he can do whatever he wishes and that even if in the end his own suggestions are not accepted, they will never be used against him.

D. B.: He will be judged and not condemned . . .

J. G.: He must be accepted as a human being, as he is.

D. B.: Regarding the actor's integration into the performance, you readily use the term "score" and not "role." This nuance is obviously very important in your work. Could you define exactly what you mean by the actor's "score"?

J. G.: What is the role? In fact it is almost always the text of a character, the typed text that is given to the actor. It is also a particular conception of the character, and here again there is a stereotype. Hamlet is an intellectual without greatness, or else a revolutionary who wants to change everything. The actor has his text; next an encounter is necessary. It must not be said that the role is a pretext for the actor, nor the actor a pretext for the role. It is an instrument for making a cross-section of oneself, analyzing oneself and thereby reestablishing contact with others. If he is content with explaining the role, the actor will know that he has to sit down here, cry out there. At the beginning of rehearsals, associations will be produced normally, but after twenty performances there will be nothing left. The acting will be purely mechanical.

To avoid this the actor, like the musician, must have a score. The musician's score is one of notes. Theatre is an encounter. The actor's score is one made up of the elements of human contact: "give and take." Take other people, confront them with oneself, one's own experience, one's thoughts, and give a reply. In these almost intimate human encounters there is always this element of "give and take." The process is repeated, but always *hic et nunc:* that is to say it is never quite the same.

D. B.: For each production this score is gradually established between the actor and you?

J. G.: Yes, in a sort of collaboration.

D. B.: The actor is free. How does he succeed (and this was one of the great problems posed by Stanislavsky) in finding for each performance the creative state that allows him to play the score without it becoming too rigid, without a purely mechanical discipline setting in? How can one preserve at the same time the vital existence of the score and creative liberty of the actor?

J. G.: It is difficult to reply in a few words, but if you will allow me a popularization I shall answer: if during the work of rehearsals the actor has fixed the score as something natural, organic (the pattern of his reactions, "give and take"), and if, before performing, he is prepared to make this confession, hiding nothing, then each performance will attain its fullness.

D. B.: "Give and take" . . . To the spectator too?

J. G.: One must not think of the spectator while acting. Naturally this is a delicate problem. First stage, the actor structures his role; second stage, the score. At that moment he seeks a sort of purity (the elimination of the superfluous) as well as the signs necessary to expression. Then he thinks: "Can one understand what I am doing?" and this question implies the presence of the spectator. I myself am there, guiding the work, and I say to the actor: "I don't understand," "I understand" or "I believe but I do not understand" . . . Psychologists readily ask the question: "What is your religion?"—not your dogmas or philosophy, but your point of orientation. If the actor has the spectator as his point of orientation, he will be in that position. In a sense, he will be offering himself for sale.

D. B.: This will be exhibitionism . . .

J. G.: A sort of prostitution, bad taste, etc. It is inevitable. A great Polish actor from before the war called it "publicotropism." Yet I don't believe the actor should neglect the fact that the spectator is present and say to himself: "There is no one there," for that would be a lie. In a word, the actor must not have the audience as a point of orientation, but at the same time he must not neglect the fact of the public. You know that in each of our productions we set up a different relationship between actors and audience. In *Dr. Faustus,* the spectators are the guests; in *The Constant Prince,* they are the onlookers. But I think the essential thing is that the actor must not act for the audience, he must act *vis-à-vis* with the spectators, in the presence of the spectators he must do an even more authentic act in place of the spectators, do an act of extreme yet disciplined sincerity and authenticity. He must give himself and not hold himself back, open up and not close in on himself in a narcissistic way.

D. B.: Do you think that the actor needs a long preparation before each performance in order to attain what some people call "a state of grace?"

J. G.: The actor must have time to remove himself from all the problems and distractions of daily life. In our theatre we have only thirty minutes of silence— that's all—during which the actor is busy, he prepares his costumes, perhaps goes over certain scenes. These are quite natural things. A pilot about to try out a new plane for the first time also removes himself for a few minutes—fifteen or sixty.

[534]

D. B.: Do you think that your acting technique can be used by other directors than yourself, that it can be adapted to ends other than yours?

J. G.: There again one must distinguish in my work between my aesthetic and the method. Of course in the Theatre Laboratory there are the elements of an aesthetic that is personal to me and which must not be copied by others, for the result would be neither authentic nor natural. But we are, and even officially, an institute for research into the art of the actor. Thanks to this method, the actor can speak and sing in a very wide register; that is an objective result. That he speaks and he has no problems with his breathing is also objective. The fact that he can utilize different types of physical and vocal reactions which are very difficult for many people, that again is objective.

D. B.: At present there are, then, two aspects in your work: on the one hand the conscious aesthetic of a creator, and on the other the search for a technique in acting. Which comes first?

J. G.: The most important thing for me today is to rediscover the elements of the actor's art. I was first trained as an actor, then as a director. In my first productions in Cracow and Poznan I rejected concessions and theatrical conservatism. Little by little I developed and discovered that to fulfill myself was far less fruitful than studying the possibility for self-realization for others. This is not a form of altruism; on the contrary, it is an even greater adventure. In the end the adventures of a producer become easy, but encounters with other human beings are more difficult, more fruitful and more stimulating. If I can attain from the actor —in collaboration with him—a total self-revelation, as with Ryszard Cieslak in *The Constant Prince,* this is for me far more fertile than putting together once again or, that is to say, to create purely in my own name. Little by little, I have, therefore, oriented myself towards a parascientific research in the field of the actor's art. This is the result of a personal evolution and not an initial plan.

XIII. AMERICA

Native Players and Innovators

Actors and acting spell the story of American theatre from its beginning until the First World War. Although there were native dramatists who wrote interesting plays during the nineteenth century, important dramatic literature appeared only with America's national maturity. Nineteenth century theatre is not remembered for the names of even its best playwrights, Augustin Daly, Bronson Howard, or Clyde Fitch, but for the names of its popular actors, Edwin Forrest, Charlotte Cushman, Joseph Jefferson, and Edwin Booth.

Although the first dramatic performances in the New World took place in the Spanish Southwest, American theatrical tradition originated among the English colonists of the East. Amateurs like the Virginia men who performed *Ye Bare and Ye Cubb* in 1665 gave the colonists their first theatrical entertainment, but just as America imported its social and economic institutions from England, so it imported English drama and English professional players. Anthony Aston, ubiquitous English adventurer and player, was one of the first to perform on American shores.

The first significant theatrical company to come to America was that of Lewis Hallam (1712-1758), whose troupe opened in Williamsburg in 1752. Descendant of an English theatrical family, Hallam brought with him the English acting tradition and the mid-eighteenth century English repertory: Shakespeare, Rowe, Farquhar, Cibber, Congreve, Fielding, and Garrick. Hallam's activities and those of David Douglass, who married Hallam's widow, define the theatrical condition of the colonial period. The company was well received by the hospitable, pleasure loving southern gentry, but the frugal and rigid Puritans and Quakers of the northern cities disapproved of them. In Philadelphia and New York, two cities which subsequently became America's theatrical centers, the actors faced strong opposition, and in New England they played *Othello* as a "moral dialogue" to evade censure. Wherever the company performed, they had to build temporary theatres or renovate buildings to suit their purposes. Under the leadership of Douglass the first permanent brick theatre in the colonies was constructed in Philadelphia in 1766. This troupe, known as The American Company, had the distinction of performing Thomas Godfrey's *The Prince of Parthia,* the only native play produced in the colonies before the Revolutionary War.

The war for independence cut short this early growth of professional theatre. In 1774 the Continental Congress, despite its lack of enforcing power, issued a resolution discouraging plays along with other entertainments. During the war itself, however, plays were performed in the camps of both the British and American soldiers.

Peace and independence brought a relaxation of restrictions, and America picked up the threads of theatrical development started in colonial days. Lewis Hallam Jr. (1740?-1808), who had acted in his father's group before the Revolution, reconstituted the American Company with the aid of the actor John Henry (d. 1795). Their troupe produced Royall Tyler's *The Contrast,* the first professionally performed

American comedy. The success of this play inspired William Dunlap, who brought his plays to the American Company. Dunlap, America's first important author-producer, became joint manager with the actor John Hodgkinson, known as "The Provincial Garrick" (1767?-1805), of the new Park Theatre of New York, for half a century the most brilliant American theatre. At the end of his career Dunlap wrote a *History of the American Theatre,* the first of its kind, in which he pointed out the dominance of the actor in this early period of the native theatre. In these first days after the Revolution American theatre began to expand as Thomas Wignell (1753?-1803), George Washington's favorite comedian, left the American Company in 1794 to form a group of his own in Philadelphia.

Both Wignell and Henry, representing the two outstanding companies at the turn of the century, returned frequently to England to find new actors for their respective troupes. Wignell, for example, brought the following actors to the United States: James Fennell (1766-1816), a popular Othello; Mrs. Whitlock (1762-1836), sister of Sarah Siddons; Mrs. Anne Merry (1769-1808), considered another Siddons; Thomas Abthorpe Cooper (1776-1849), whose Hamlet had been applauded by Charles Macklin; and William Warren (1767-1832), father of the famous comedian. Cooper, who later became co-manager of the Park Theatre with Dunlap, invited the great George Frederick Cooke to the States. Cooke's appearance at the Park Theatre in 1810 heralded the age of English stars playing on the boards of this and other theatres. Some like Cooke, Junius Brutus Booth, and James William Wallack (1795-1864) remained to become permanent features of the American theatrical scene; others—Edmund Kean, William Charles Macready, Charles Mathews, Charles and Fanny Kemble, Charles Kean, and Ellen Tree, to mention a few of the huge roster—came on starring tours to play their celebrated roles with the support of indigenous companies.

America's native players came from the local stock companies. The parade of names begins in 1826, the year in which the first two significant American actors made their important debuts in New York. James Henry Hackett (1800-1871), who appeared at the Park Theatre in that year, became a celebrated interpreter of Falstaff, playing the role first to the Hotspur of Charles Kean in 1832. He was the original creator of Rip Van Winkle and played the role of the Yankee Nimrod Wildfire with great success. Edwin Forrest, who appeared as Othello at the Bowery Theatre in 1826, became America's first national idol. In addition to presenting the usual repertory of *Othello, Macbeth, Lear, Virginius,* and *Douglas,* Edwin Forrest acted in native plays especially written for him. This robust American established a style of acting based upon the inheritance of George Frederick Cooke and Edmund Kean. His bow-legged defiant stance and his oratorical delivery won popular approval, although refined taste pointed to his lack of subtlety. Forrest's acting became the criterion by which other American actors were judged.

Power and passion also marked America's first great actress, Charlotte Cushman (1816-1876). Known as well in England as in the United States, Charlotte Cushman, whose acting recalled the art of Siddons, created Lady Macbeth, Meg Merrilies in Scott's *Guy Mannering,* Nancy Sykes in *Oliver Twist,* and Mrs. Haller in *The Stranger.* John Ranken Towse says of her Lady Macbeth: "She was the source and mainspring of the whole tragedy. She was inhuman, terrible, incredible, and horribly fascinating."

In the 1850's when Edwin Forrest was still at his peak, a more natural histrionic manner began to emerge. It was seen in Matilda Heron's (1831-1877)

Camille and it was apparent in the Hamlet of Edwin Booth. Critics were conscious when they watched Booth that they were seeing acting that had few characteristics of the so-called American style of Forrest. In place of the latter's animal strength and power, Booth substituted a quiet refinement which made Hamlet his triumph. According to William Winter the success of Booth's style prepared the way for the superior acting seen in the second half of the nineteenth century.

Joseph Jefferson, like Booth, came of a theatrical family and like Booth, Jefferson acted with restraint and good taste. He brought dignity, tenderness, and pathos to his comic art, especially to his interpretation of the shiftless, lovable Rip Van Winkle. Jefferson's natural ease impressed his audiences, but from his *Autobiography*, we realize that his genuineness was the result of planned, conscious artistry. William Winter eulogized Jefferson as a "poet among actors."

Jefferson's associate from 1880-1892 in performances of *The Rivals* was Louisa Lane Drew (1820-1897), America's revered actress-manager. Extraordinarily versatile, she acted with all the leading figures, Forrest, Macready, Charlotte Cushman, etc. When she took over the management of the Arch Street Theatre, Philadelphia, in 1861, she established an excellent stock company with which the finest actors of the time played. Her children, John Drew (1853-1927) and Georgiana Drew (1856-1893) were members of Augustin Daly's Company, where the latter met the handsome Englishman Maurice Barrymore (1847-1905), whom she married. The Barrymore children, Lionel, Ethel, and John carried on the tradition of this Royal Family.

For these popular actors the American dramatists wrote their plays. John Howard Payne (1791-1852), actor-playwright of the early part of the century and author of *Home, Sweet Home,* attested to the preeminence of the actor when he wrote in the preface to his play *Therese*: "It is necessary in the production of modern drama to consult the peculiarities of leading performers." He himself wrote plays especially for J. W. Wallack and even for Edmund Kean. Hackett and Edwin Forrest played dramas written for them and adapted dramas to accommodate their own best points. The actors stimulated playwriting directly by offering prizes, as did Forrest and Wallack.

The work of a number of actor-playwrights perpetuated the tendency to keep nineteenth century playwriting geared to good acting parts. Anna Cora Mowatt (1819-1870), author of an early social comedy *Fashion,* wrote plays in concert with her talents and those of her leading man, Edward Loomis Davenport (1816-1877), the fine Shakespearean actor. Edward Harrigan (1845-1911), whose work was derived from vaudeville, acted in his own plays of Irish life in American cities. Dion Boucicault, a pioneer in sentimental realism both in England and the United States, wrote and adapted many plays in which he and his wife, Agnes Robertson (1832-1916), starred.

James A. Herne (1839-1901), an American innovator in realistic character dramas, performed in his own plays and created some of his finest characters for his actress wife, Katherine Corcoran. William Gillette, a native realist like Herne, also brought his own creations to the stage.

The theatrical managers of the century, who were frequently writers or actors, also sharpened the interest in histrionic art. Augustin Daly, an original dramatist and an adapter of foreign novels and plays, had the finest troupe in New York in the two decades between 1870 and 1890. Among his actors were some of the brightest stars of the era: Fanny Davenport (1850-1898), Clara Morris (1846-1925),

John Drew, Maurice Barrymore, Adelaide Neilson (1846-1880), Ada Rehan (1860-1916), Otis Skinner, and Maxine Elliott (1871-1940). Steele MacKaye (1844-1894), actor, inventor, writer, and manager, at the Madison Square Theatre and at the Lyceum, established a school of acting which furthered the growing movement toward realism by introducing the Delsarte system of acting. David Belasco, the "psychologist of the switchboard," was another actor-writer-manager who pioneered realistic lighting and stage effects and made stars of Mrs. Leslie Carter (1862-1937), Blanche Bates (1873-1944), David Warfield, and Frances Starr.

Although many nineteenth century American actors made their fame in native plays and adaptations, some written especially for them, they almost all tried their hand at Shakespeare, the touchstone of the actor's quality. Toward the end of the century Lawrence Barrett (1838-1891), who had played with Booth and John Mc-Cullough (1832-1885), became America's leading actor. A scholarly man, noted for his productions of such native plays as George Henry Boker's *Francesca da Rimini* and William Dean Howells' *Yorick*, adapted from the Spanish, Barrett still played the popular roles in *Hamlet, Macbeth, Richard II, Merchant of Venice* and *Julius Caesar*. In 1887-89 he made a very successful tour in traditional repertory with Edwin Booth. Richard Mansfield, who played varied roles in *Doctor Jekyll and Mr. Hyde, Cyrano de Bergerac,* and *Beau Brummel,* nevertheless derived much of his fame from his performance of Richard III. Edward Hugh Sothern, successful as a romantic actor, became a noted Shakespearean interpreter, touring the country with the lovely Julia Marlowe.

Thus it was that although acting during the second half of the nineteenth century in the United States as elsewhere was turning toward realism, histrionic art remained a contest of individual stars pitted against each other in a traditional repertory. An audience that came to see Salvini play Othello in Italian to Edwin Booth's Iago in English or Fanny Janauschek (1830-1904) play Lady Macbeth in German to Booth's Macbeth was obviously mainly interested in the standard "points" of the great roles.

By the end of the nineteenth century dramatic production in America had shifted from stock company repertory to long run plays, cast in New York and sent out to tour the country. In 1896 Charles Frohman, the commercially successful creator of stars like Maude Adams (1872-1953), Henry Miller (1860-1925), and Billie Burke, spearheaded the organization of a syndicate to manipulate the booking of road companies. Theatrical control passed from the hands of the individual actor or independent manager into the hands of businessmen. Theatre became "show business" despite the efforts of Belasco, Mrs. Fiske, Richard Mansfield, and others to hold out against the power of the syndicate. Matters only became worse when the Shubert brothers started an independent movement to compete with the syndicate. The theatre was torn between the competition of these two monopolistic ventures, and acting deteriorated as the long run star system triumphed. The death of "the road" and the concentration of theatre in New York deprived thousands of actors of employment and the opportunity to grow in the theatre, foreshadowing the economic insecurity of today's Actors Equity members.

Twentieth century acting and theatre is a history of the revolts against growing commercialism and the spiritual emptiness of the theatre. New directions were in the wind when Madame Modjeska (1844-1909) introduced Ibsen's *A Doll's House* in 1883. Ibsen's heroines were played by the very popular Minnie Maddern Fiske and by Beatrice Cameron, whose husband, Richard Mansfield, introduced the reformist plays of Shaw to the American public. In the serious theatrical artistry of William Vaughan Moody, the community dramas of Percy MacKaye, the university work of George Pierce Baker, Brander Matthews and others, a new spirit was making itself felt.

Throughout the country small theatrical groups took their stimulus from the innovations now well under way in Europe—the unified ensemble playing of the art and independent theatres and the new stagecraft of Gordon Craig and Adolphe Appia. A large scale attempt to reinstate repertory was made at the sumptuous New Theatre in 1909, but the first productions which "starred" Edward Hugh Sothern and Julia Marlowe in Antony and Cleopatra betrayed the very ideals behind this expensive experiment. The drive for change was propelled by the numerous little theatre movements that mushroomed in the days before the First World War.

The Toy Theatre of Boston, the Chicago Little Theatre, Winthrop Ames' Little Theatre, and The Neighborhood Playhouse in New York were among the avant garde. In 1914 Robert Edmond Jones, Lawrence Langner, Philip Moeller, Helen Westley, and Lee Simonson organized the Washington Square Players which produced one-act plays in the rear of a Greenwich Village store. Dedicated to the principles of "art theatre," they incorporated themselves as the Theatre Guild in 1919. The Guild, with its school, its repertory ideal, and its subscription-audience, effectively combined artistic productions and commercial gain. It produced the important experimental European dramatists Toller, Strindberg, Shaw, Kaiser, and provided a theatre for the new native dramatists, Eugene O'Neill, Sidney Howard, Elmer Rice, Philip Barry, Maxwell Anderson, and others. In the middle years of the twenties the Guild had for a time an acting company headed by Alfred Lunt and Lynn Fontanne; the leading actors and actresses appeared under their auspices: Pauline Lord, Helen Hayes, Helen Westley, Dudley Digges, Claire Eames, Judith Anderson, Alice Brady, Alla Nazimova, Edward G. Robinson, Margalo Gillmore, and others. Although the Guild propounded no new histrionic theories, its dedication to fine theatre encouraged realistic acting and ensemble playing.

There were other important organizations. The Provincetown Playhouse, first in the artists' colony on Cape Cod and then on MacDougal Street in Greenwich Village, made its greatest contribution by kindling the fire of Eugene O'Neill, who became the first internationally significant American dramatist. O'Neill, Robert Edmond Jones, and Kenneth Macgowan carried on the work of the Provincetown group, producing Strindberg, Stark Young, Walter Hasenclever, and others in addition to O'Neill's provocative dramas. Paul Robeson and Walter Huston were among the fine actors who played for them.

During this period of ferment, Negro actors attained for the first time a rightful place as serious artists interpreting American life. The performances of Ridgely Torrence's Three Plays for a Negro Theatre, in April, 1917, marked, in the words of James Weldon Johnson, "an epoch for the Negro on the stage." Torrence's plays, Emilie Hapgood's production, Robert Edmond Jones' direction provided the stimulus for the fine acting of Inez Clough and others. These performances, hailed by the critics, were "a turning point in Negro theatre history," wrote Edith Isaacs in The Negro in the American Theatre. With the exception of the very early African Company of Negro actors, with its leading artist James Hewlett, and the European fame of the great tragedian Ira Aldridge, Negro actors had succeeded only in minstrel shows and musical comedy, where Bert Williams, George Walker, Abbie Mitchell, and others made their success. After 1920 there were increasing opportunities for Negro actors to perform, largely in plays by white dramatists like Eugene O'Neill, Paul Green, Dubose and Dorothy Heywood, Marc Connelly. The creations of Charles Gilpin, Rose McClendon, Paul Robeson, Richard Harrison, Rex Ingram, Leigh Whipper, Ethel Waters and Canada Lee were high points in American performance. Black theatre, however, is a development of the sixties, when for the first time Black writers, actors, and directors, including LeRoi Jones, Ossie Davis, Douglas Turner Ward, Robert Hooks, Robert Macbeth, Lonne Elder, Ed Bullins, Ruby Dee and James Earl Jones started to create a theatre expressive of their own life and culture.

In the years 1926 to 1933 Eva Le Gallienne initiated and guided the destinies of New York's only professional repertory theatre, a cause to which she has given her undiminished efforts over the years. At her Fourteenth Street Civic Repertory Theatre, Miss Le Gallienne schooled a host of young American actors and gave her audiences classical repertory at low prices. Walter Hampden offered himself in a repertory of great roles in *Hamlet, Othello, An Enemy of the People* and the ever-popular *Cyrano de Bergerac*.

In the Twenties the target of revolt had been commercialism and impoverished theatre. Depression and social dislocation in the Thirties generated a new species of revolt. The desire to make "theatre a weapon" in the struggle for economic and political justice motivated such organizations as the Group Theatre, the Theatre Union, the New Theatre League, and Labor Stage, the latter a cultural arm of the International Ladies Garment Workers Union. In these theatres were ably performed the plays of Clifford Odets, Paul Green, Irwin Shaw, William Saroyan, John Howard Lawson, Albert Maltz, George Sklar, Paul Peters, and others. It was these groups with their dedication to social theatre that gave new, serious attention to the art of the actor.

In 1931 Harold Clurman, Lee Strasberg, and Cheryl Crawford, all from the Theatre Guild, founded the Group Theatre. Taking their credo from Vakhtangov's definition of the theatre as "an ideologically cemented collective," the members of the Group worked together as a creative community. Their objective was to do contemporary plays of social significance, to establish a permanent acting company on the model of the Moscow Art Theatre, the *Vieux Colombier,* and the Abbey Theatre, and to develop actor-training on the principles of the Stanislavsky method. More than a producing organization, the Group sought "significant contemporaneity," "inner experience," and "the attainment of truth on the stage." In the decade of its existence its corps of actors included Morris Carnovsky, Franchot Tone, Sanford Meisner, Stella Adler, Phoebe Brand, J. Edward Bromberg, Luther Adler, Alexander Kirkland, John Garfield, Frances Farmer, Clifford Odets, Art Smith, Philip Loeb, Elia Kazan, and Lee J. Cobb. In Clifford Odets the Group brought forth from its own ranks one of the most important American dramatists whose plays were the signature of the Group as Chekhov's had been for the Moscow Art Theatre. Odets' *Golden Boy* sent the troupe to London where James Agate, critic of the *London Times,* said: "The acting attains a level which is something we know nothing at all about."

The New Theatre League's network of non-professional groups utilized mass chants, skits, one-act plays, and songs to dramatize national and local issues. They sought out their audience away from the theatre in labor halls, on picket-lines, and on street corners. Their periodical *Theatre Workshop* was one of the few conscientiously devoted to theatre craft, and their play contests produced *Waiting for Lefty, Bury the Dead,* and *The Cradle Will Rock.* The Theatre Union's provocative productions not only brought new ideas to its audiences but also new concepts in staging and acting.

Out of the unemployment and social ferment of the Thirties came the great experiment—the Federal Theatre. Geared primarily to providing jobs for actors, directors, and designers, the Federal Theatre for the first time gave American audiences artistic, significant entertainment at low prices. To outlying districts this national project brought all types of theatre. Apart from its economic assistance to the profession and its value to national culture, Federal Theatre gave birth to the unconventional productions of Orson Welles, the incisive music-dramas of Marc Blitzstein, and the vital, topical dramaturgy of the Living Newspaper.

The twenties and the thirties initiated new theatrical institutions and released new talents and new conceptions of the actor's art. World War II and the immediate postwar years saw the culmination of the earlier developments. Many who first made their mark in the twenties continued to star—the Lunts, Katharine Cornell, Helen Hayes, but it was the Group Theatre alumni and their progeny who became notable directors, actors and teachers of acting and whose "Method" produced a generation devoted to the "inner approach." The Actors Studio, founded in 1947 by Elia Kazan, Cheryl Crawford and Robert Lewis, and then led by Lee Strasberg from 1951 on, shaped most of the actors who gave life to the plays of Arthur Miller, Tennessee Williams, William Inge and the posthumously produced plays of Eugene O'Neill. For the drama of these authors "that found in the inner struggles of the individual its most compelling subject," Paul Gray has pointed out, "a new, distinctly American, Method has been formed."

But when America entered the second half of the century, it became apparent that as the "nation moved into an age of affluence . . . the theatre skidded downhill." American acting, as Howard Taubman observed, had "not become a rationalized, cultivated craft"; "the young actor has few places where he can learn and grow"; he has no opportunity to "experience the equivalent of the young physician's internship." Even the few highly talented craftsmen carefully honing their art at the various studios, including the famed Actors Studio, had no theatres in which to play the important, varied roles that alone can form an Olivier or a Scofield.

Attempts were made to remedy the limitations of the haphazard, success-oriented commercial theatre with numerous regional companies. American actors, however, turned out to be woefully unprepared to play Shakespeare, Molière, Sophocles and equally ill-equipped for the heightened histrionic style of Brecht, Beckett and Ionesco, who began to be played in this country. It was not talent that was lacking, but opportunities—even for those who had become stars—to learn and grow in a healthy theatrical institution.

The complete failure of the theatrical establishment to satisfy the needs of its actors—as well as its writers, directors, designers and audiences—led in the fifties and sixties to the development of an alternative theatre—first Off- and then alternatively Off-Off-Broadway. Here in coffeehouses, churches, East Village lofts and warehouses, the American theatre is being revolutionized. Far from the Great White Way—geographically, politically and aesthetically—a number of groups are presenting theatrical experiences in which personal commitment, audience participation and political stance are more important than mellifluous voices, neat dramatic construction and box-office appeal. Their work is experimental, improvisational and rhythmical. To the rituals they perform at Judson Poets' Theatre, Cafe LaMama, the Performance Group, they bring a religious intensity. Although there are few notable actors in these theatres, the art of acting is investigated in experimental efforts. The most revolutionary and innovative of these theatres, the Living Theatre of Julian Beck and Judith Malina, in self-imposed exile in Europe since 1964, and the Open Theatre of Joseph Chaikin, are dedicated to exploring the human potential of the actor in visceral, highly physical, vigorous improvisations and exercises. Abandoning traditional refinements of voice, diction, deportment and even psychological nuance, they make the direct confrontations of the actor, who is often literally stripped of his social trappings, and the audience the central political, social, sexual, theatrical act. The theories and practices of this new theatre, heavily influenced by Artaud, Brecht, Grotowski, John Cage and Happenings, among others, are presented here together for the first time in several essays, some written especially for this edition.

No one style characterizes twentieth-century American acting. Those who built upon the foundations of the Stanislavsky system in the thirties reached the highest peaks of American acting in the ensemble of the Group Theatre—an artistic achievement unparalleled in the American theatre. For the most part, however, American actors have been eclectic and have accommodated their talents to the demands of directors. Periodically the theatrical scene has been illuminated by flashes of individual brilliance; John Barrymore in *Hamlet,* Jeanne Eagels in *Rain,* Pauline Lord in *Anna Christie,* Laurette Taylor in *The Glass Menagerie,* Lee J. Cobb in *Death of a Salesman,* Frederic March and Florence Eldridge in *Long Day's Journey Into Night,* Marlon Brando and Jessica Tandy in *A Streetcar Named Desire,* Julie Harris in *A Member of the Wedding,* Kim Stanley in *The Three Sisters,* Geraldine Page in *Sweet Bird of Youth,* Anne Bancroft in *The Miracle Worker,* Uta Hagen in *Who's Afraid of Virginia Woolf.* Lacking a national theatre or genuine repertory companies where they can test their skill in great roles, American actors suffer in hastily prepared and short-lived vehicles or in excessively long runs of "hit" shows, neither of which provide opportunity for artistic growth and development. Repudiating the conventional Broadway scene completely, the younger generation of actors has set about redefining the theatrical experience. At the heart of their redefinition is a new conception of the actor and his art that challenges many of the basic assumptions about the distinctive talent of the imitative artist, whose former glory was to create a gallery of fictional men and women. Their work is fragmented, brutal, vulgar and even dull on occasion, but they have returned theatre to its essential creator, the actor, and beginning once again with his collaboration and his humanity, are renewing the ancient art of theatre.

EDWIN FORREST

(1806-1872)

The first native idol of the American stage was Edwin Forrest, archetype of the vigorous, self-made actor. With little education and no money, he started on his way to success at a very early age. He made an impressive debut as Norval in Home's *Douglas* at the age of fourteen. A native patriot greeted his appearance with these words:

Dear child of genius! round thy youthful brow
Taste, wit, and beauty bind the laurel now.
No foreign praise thy native worth need claim;
No aid extrinsic heralds forth thy name;
No titled patron's power thy merit decked. . . .

The national and democratic pride evidenced in these words animated Forrest
and his admirers throughout the actor's life. As Montrose Moses pointed out in his
biography of Forrest, the actor grew with his nation. Like the other theatrical people
of his time, Forrest was a pioneer, blazing his way across part of the continent, facing uncertainty, deprivation, and the challenges of frontier life. After his schooling
in the rigors of the travelling players, Forrest made his way in the Eastern theatres.
He played second roles to Edmund Kean on the latter's visit to the United States
in 1825 and was praised by the erratic English star. Early in his career Forrest was
pitted against William Charles Macready, who was to be a formidable antagonist in
later years.

When the New York Bowery Theatre opened in 1826 Edwin Forrest became
its major star. This robust, somewhat plebeian theatre, whose popular vigor was celebrated by Walt Whitman, became the competitor of the refined Park Theatre where
celebrated visiting stars played. Once Forrest became established and secure in his
profession, he started a campaign for native plays. His offer of a money prize for a
tragedy "of which the hero or principal character shall be an aboriginal of this
country" elicited several plays, whose artistic merit was secondary to the fact that
they suited the dramatic talents of Forrest. Such plays as *Metamora* or *The Gladiator* gave Forrest a chance to express his patriotic and democratic sentiments in picturesque grand movements and full-voiced speech. A product of the physical acting
of George Frederick Cooke, who spent his dying days in the United States, and of
the emotionalism of Kean, Forrest was vigorous and agile, given to dramatic
stances and sonorous speech. His accents recalled those of the great American orators and were imitated by speakers as well as actors. He carried his audiences by
his physical power and deep-toned voice, not by subtlety or insight.

Forrest's two professional tours in England met with a mixed reaction. Perhaps the most important aspect of these visits was the violent antagonism which developed between him and Macready. Their clash involved great differences in acting techniques (the intellectual finesse of Macready and the physical power of Forrest), in temperament (the simmering jealousy of Macready and the hot-tempered-
ness of Forrest), and perhaps above all differences of class and nation. This antagonism finally ended with the shameful riot at the Astor Place Theatre in New York
in May, 1849. At this point the conflict between Forrest and Macready became an
organized effort against "aristocrats and foreigners." The militia was called out and
lives were lost. What had begun as a struggle of tempers and histrionic style ended
as a political weapon of Tammany Hall.

Montrose Moses tells us that "the American actor has left nothing but a stately
reverence for his models, without comment. In fact, the silence of Forrest regarding the art of the actor, save a casual reference here and there, would indicate that
his own practice was outward rather than inward. In fact, so outward that he
sought to 'fix' the impression in pictures. His acting was himself—depths of voice,
pauses, starts, glances, display of biceps, firmness of leg muscles . . . outward ex-

pression and pose of majesty and power were there, with cavernous depths within, but there seemed to be lacking those qualities of mind and spirit which are a measure of the greatest acting."

Forrest's significance lies in his emergence as "the American actor" in the face of the long-standing English dominance over the American theatrical scene. Walt Whitman, reporting for *The Brooklyn Eagle,* has left us his description of the widely imitated Forrest.

Edwin Forrest and the American Style

by WALT WHITMAN

... Mr. Forrest is a deserved favorite with the public—and has high talent in his profession. But the danger is, that as he has to a measure become identified with a sort of American style of acting, the crowd of vapid imitators may spread quite all the faults of that style, with none of its excellencies. Indeed, too, in candor, all persons of thought will confess to no great fondness for acting which particularly seeks to "tickle the ears of the groundlings." We allude to the loud mouthed ranting style—the tearing of every thing to shivers—which is so much the ambition of some of our players, particularly the younger ones. It does in such cases truly seem as if some of Nature's journeymen had made men, and not made them well—they imitate humanity so abominably. They take every occasion, in season and out of season, to try the extremist strength of their lungs. They never let a part of their dialogue which falls in the imperative mood—the mood for exhorting, commanding, or permitting—pass by without the loudest exhibition of sound, and the most distorted gesture. If they have to enact passion, they do so by all kinds of unnatural and violent jerks, swings, screwing of the nerves of the face, rolling of the eyes, and so on. To men of taste, all this is exceedingly ridiculous. And even among the inferior portion of the audience it does not always pass safely. We have frequently seen rough boys in the pit, with an expression of sovereign contempt at performances of this sort. For there is something in real nature which comes home to the "business and bosoms" of all men. Who ever saw love made as it is generally made upon the stage? How often have we heard spontaneous bursts of approbation from inferior audiences, toward acting of the most unpretending kind, merely because it was simple, truthful, and natural! ... If we thought these remarks would meet the eye of any young theatrical artist, we would like through him to beg all—for we cannot call to mind any who are not more or less tainted with this vice—to take such hints as the foregoing, to their hearts—aye, to their heart of hearts. It is a common fallacy to think that an exaggerated, noisy, and inflated style of acting—and no other—will produce the desired effect upon a promiscuous audience. But those who have observed things, theatres, and human nature, know better. Where is there a good, truthful player that is not appreciated? Who, during the past season, has dared compare the quiet polish of Mrs. Kean [Ellen Tree] with the lofty pretensions of the general run of tragedy queens?

Walt Whitman: "The Gladiator—Mr. Forrest—Acting," *The Brooklyn Eagle,* December 26, 1846, in *The American Theatre as Seen by Its Critics,* 1752-1934, edited by Montrose J. Moses and John Mason Brown. New York: W. W. Norton and Company, 1934, pp. 69-70.

DION BOUCICAULT

(1820?-1890)

Although he was born in Dublin and achieved his first successes on the London stage, Dion Boucicault became an important force in American theatre when he came to this country in 1853. After spending his novitiate in the English provincial theatres, Boucicault gained fame with the production of his play *London Assurance* at Covent Garden in 1841. The play itself was less important than the then revolutionary realistic setting provided for it by Madame Vestris and Charles Mathews, managers of Covent Garden. A set with a ceiling and boxed sides and the use of real stage properties were among the innovations introduced. Shortly thereafter Boucicault spent four years in France where he acquired that knowledge of popular French drama which was to inspire his many adaptations from that language. Back in England in 1848 he became an assistant to Charles Kean at the Princess Theatre.

In the United States Boucicault continued his career as actor and writer. He was a most prolific playwright, although many of his products were adaptations of foreign plays. In his numerous plays he provided excellent acting parts for himself, for his wife, Agnes Robertson, and for many other actors including Joseph Jefferson and Lester Wallack (1820-1888). Boucicault had the dramatic sense to localize even his adaptations. His version of the French play called *Les Pauvres de Paris* was re-christened *The Poor of New York* and used native references. With unfailing theatrical sense he utilized a melodramatic, but terrifyingly realistic fire sequence in several of his plays. In the *Octoroon* he used the American color problem with telling dramatic effect. His Irish plays brought a new note of realistic Irish life to the stage and provided both him and his wife with some of their best parts.

Boucicault was co-director of the New York Winter Garden Theatre where his adaptation of Dickens' *The Cricket on the Hearth* was played with Joseph Jefferson in the role of Caleb Plummer. From 1860 to 1872 the Boucicaults were again in England where they both acted and managed a theatre. While in England Boucicault wrote *Arrah-na-Pogue,* one of his best Irish plays, which was also produced in New York. At this time he wrote a new version of *Rip Van Winkle* for Joseph Jefferson.

Back in New York he wrote and played in *The Shaughraun,* one of his most popular Irish parts. Although he continued his theatrical activities for a long time, his popularity began to wane. Probably his melodramatic, sentimental realism was becoming unpalatable to an audience that was beginning to turn to more serious realistic drama. At the end of his life Boucicault was teaching acting in a school connected with the Madison Square Theatre in New York.

Apart from his acting and his writing Boucicault brought about two important changes in the American theatrical scene. He succeeded, after the vain attempts of other writers, in having the first copyright law in the U.S. passed to protect the work of writers. This action was part of Boucicault's long campaign to raise the financial position of dramatic authors. Another of his innovations revolutionized the system of theatrical production. The long run had already begun to take its place as a successful alternative to the rapidly changing repertory, which up to the middle of the nineteenth century had characterized dramatic productions. Boucicault went a step further by introducing special casting for each production and by organizing road companies to tour various cities with one play cast at some such central place as New York. This change destroyed the base of the old stock company system, which had supported the individual travelling star in a varied repertory. Frequently, of course, these local companies had provided inadequate, careless, and inartistic support to the stars, but the stock system had encouraged the development of local actors and playwrights. With the establishment of the new system the old stock tradition began to die, and thus began an era of theatre dominated by a small well-organized group in New York.

Perhaps the most important of Boucicault's contributions was his continuous effort to accommodate popular taste with sensational realism in plays, in acting, and in staging. He, with the Vestris group and Charles Fechter, were the originating realists in melodrama and sentimental comedy. They set the scene for the growth of realism in England and in the United States.

Boucicault delivered the following lecture to an audience of actors and actresses during one of his visits to England at the Lyceum Theatre, which was lent for the occasion by Henry Irving.

Can Acting Be Taught?

Ladies and gentlemen, I feel very much flattered indeed to see before me such an assembly, and more particularly as I have seen on the plan that it is mainly composed of my fellow members and colleagues of our own profession. I am glad that they have so great an interest in questions that we are about today to discuss. I am not going to give you a lecture in any sense, much less to keep you to hear me speak on every form of acting. Nobody could do that in an hour, or an hour and a quarter. All of you know that perfectly well. All I have to do today is to explain how acting can be taught, and I hope you will agree with me, before I end, that this is the way acting should be taught. There was, you are aware, a few weeks ago, a lively discussion with regard to the establishment of a permanent school. There was one project that was put forward by members of our own profession. I say of our own profession, because I know I am addressing actors and actresses, my colleagues, and my fellow students. That project was dropped, suspended, put aside, because certain good patrons of the drama had organized another project and pushed it forward with a great deal of energy. During this discussion certain influential members of the public press—graciously taking, as they have always done, great interest in the art dramatic—in their editorials pronounced their opinion that acting could not be taught; that it was not an art at all; that it was a gift; that it was the effusion of enthusiasm; that, in point of fact, actors, like poets, were born, not made. Now that appeared to me to place our art below that of a handicraft, for no art becomes respectable or respected until its principles, its tenets, and its precepts are recognized, methodized, and housed in a system. If it be said that we cannot teach a man to be a genius, that we cannot teach him to be talented, that is simply a fact; but I ask you in any art what great men, like, for example, Michelangelo, Landseer, Murillo, would have existed if some kind of art had not preceded them by which they learned the art of, say mixing colors, the principles of proportion, and the principles of perspective. Where would Shakespeare have been if he had acci-

Dion Boucicault: *The Art of Acting.* New York: Printed for the Dramatic Museum of Columbia University, *Papers on Acting*, Fifth Series, Number 1, Columbia University Press, 1926, pp. 19-24, 28-30, 33-35, 41-53. By permission of the Columbia University Press.

dentally and unfortunately been born in some remote region at the plow-tail, where there was not within his reach the drama school of Stratford-on-Avon? He would have perished at the plow-tail and have been buried in a furrow, and we should never have known it. You must absolutely have principles in all arts. You cannot produce your own thoughts, your own feelings, unless you have some principles as some guide, some ground. I am not an eloquent man. I am simply an actor, an author, one who is in the habit of giving speeches to others, and supplying speeches for others, rather than delivering speeches myself.

... Well, this is, as I have said, a large subject. I cannot do more in an hour than just skim the surface. I can, as Newton said, but wander on the shore of the great ocean and pick up the shells. I can but give you enough to make you understand what our art is, its philosophic principles; that a good actor is not due to accident, that a man is not born to be an actor unless he is trained.

You know that in Paris acting is taught. You are aware also that actors and authors are in the habit on the stage of teaching the actors how the characters they have drawn should be played. I allude, for example, to the great Mr. T. W. Robertson, one of the greatest producers of our age, who has revolutionized the drama of his period. That man was in the habit of teaching and conveying his ideas to actors on the stage, and as to how the parts should be rendered. I may also refer to M. Sardou in Paris, who, it is notorious, does the same thing, as well as many of the stage-managers of the present day. Alexandre Dumas is known to be constantly doing the same thing. I may refer also to Mr. Gilbert, the author, who does the same thing, and so stamps the character that that character is entirely new, and one that you have never seen before. You know that all active managers, such as Mr. Irving, Mr. Wilson Barrett, Mr. Bancroft, Mr. Hare, Mr. Kendal, all teach the younger actors and actresses how to play their parts. They are obliged to do so in the present condition of affairs, because there is no school in the provinces to lick the novices into shape and to teach them the ground of their art, how to walk and how to talk—that is, to teach them acting.

Acting is not mere speech! It is not taking the dialogue of the author and giving it artistically, but sometimes not articulately. Acting is to perform, to be the part; to be it in your arms, your legs; to be what you are acting, to be it all over, that is acting. The subject of acting may be divided into the voice for the treatment of the production; the expression of feature or gesture. I call gesture that action of the body above the waist—the arms, the neck, the head, and the bust. The carriage is that action of the body which is below the waist.

* * * *

I must now go to a subject of a rather delicate nature, and that is really the first part of my subject—the voice. You know there are certain voices on the stage —you are perfectly aware of this—that the actor does not use off the stage; that are exclusively confined to tragedy. It is not the actor's ordinary voice. The idea is that the tragedian never has to use his own voice. Why? What is the reason? Before this century the great French tragedians before Talma and the great English tragedians before Kean used their treble voice—the teapot style. They did it as if they played on the flute. Then came the period when the tragedian played his part on the double bass.... There was no reason for it. Now we perform that part in the present age in what is called the medium voice. The reason is this. It is the transcendental drama tragedy. When I call it transcendental I mean unreal, poetic, to distinguish it from the realistic or the drama of ordinary life. The transcendental drama assumes that the dialogues are uttered by beings larger than life, who express ideas that no human being could pour out. The actor has accustomed himself to feel that he is in a different region; and, therefore, he feels if he uses his ordinary voice it might jar on the transcendental effect. I have fought out this very question with the great tragedians in France; and it seemed as if the tragedians were afraid of destroying the delicate illusion of the audience, who are sent about four hundred years back, as if they were living with people whom they had never seen and had no knowledge of. The consequence is those characters are too big for any ordinary human being, and the actor tries to make his manner and his voice correspond.

* * * *

To the young beginner I would say, when you go upon the stage do not be full of yourself, but be full of your part. That is mistaking vanity for genius, and is the fault of many more than perhaps you are aware of. If actors' and actresses' minds be employed upon themselves, and not on the character they wish and aspire to perform, they never really get out of themselves. Many think they are studying their character when they are only studying themselves. They get their costume, they put it on, see how it fits, they cut and contrive it, but all that is not studying their character, but their costume. Actors and actresses frequently come to me and say, "Have you any part that will fit me?" They never dream of saying, "Have you any part that I can fit? that I can expand myself or contract myself into; that I can put myself inside of; that I, as a Protean, can shape myself into, even alter my voice and everything that nature has given to me, and be what you have contrived? I do not want you to contrive like a tailor to fit me." That is what is constantly happening. . . .

It was not so forty years ago. They had their faults many of them, but they did not constitute costume and make-up as the study of character, which it is not. I will tell you what did happen forty years ago. I was producing a comedy in which Mr. Farren, the father of the gentleman who so ably bears the same name (old Farren), played a leading part. He did not ask what he was going to wear, but he came to me, and said, "Who did you draw this party from; had you any type?" I said, "Yes, I had," and mentioned the names of two old fogies, who, at that time, were well known in London society. One he knew, the other he did not. He went and studied Sir Harcourt Courtley, and he studied by the speediest method, for the study was absolutely and literally out of the mouth of the man himself. That will give you an idea how they studied character. . . .

That is the way to study character, to get at the bottom of human nature, and I am happy to say that, amongst some young actors who have come out within the last ten or fifteen years, I have seen a natural instinct for the study of character and for the drawing of character most admirably, and much more faithfully than they drew it twenty or thirty years ago. There is a study of character that we may call good and true that has been accomplished within the last fifteen or sixteen years.

Now, I will say something by way of anecdote to show how utterly unnecessary it is for you to bother your minds so much about your dress. I was producing *The Shaughraun* in New York. I generally had enough to employ my time. I get the actors and actresses to study their characters, and generally leave myself to the last. But the last morning before the play was produced I saw my dresser hobbling about, but afraid to come to the stage. At last he said, "Have you thought of your costume?" I said I had not done any such thing. It was about three o'clock in the afternoon, and I had to play about seven o'clock in the evening. I went upstairs, and said, "Have you got a red coat?" "Yes; we have got a uniform red hunting coat." "Oh, that is of no use!" "We have got one that was used in *She Stoops to Conquer*." That was brought, but it had broad lapels, and looked to belong to about one hundred and fifty years ago. "Oh!" said the man, "there is an old coat that was worn by Mr. Beckett as Goldfinch." When he came to that it reached all down to my feet, and was too long in the sleeves. So I cut them off with a big pair of shears, and by the shears and the scissors I got some sort of a fit. Then I got an old hunting cap, a pair of breeches, and sent for some old boots that cost about 2s 6d, and did not fit me, and that is how I came on the stage. The editor of one of the newspapers said, "Where on earth did you get that extraordinary costume from?"

Believe me, I mention these circumstances simply to show that the study of character should be from the inside; not from the outside! Great painters, I am told, used to draw a human figure in the nude form, and, when they were proposing to finish their pictures, to paint the costumes; then the costumes came right. That is exactly how an actor ought to study his art. He ought to paint his character in the nude form and put the costume on the last thing.

Now, let me give this particular advice to all persons going on the stage. Many of you are already on the stage, but others may be going on. Having arrived at that conclusion as to what your line is going to be, always try to select those kinds of characters and the line that is most suited and more nearly conforms to your own natural gifts. Nature knows best. If you happen to have a short, sharp face, a hard voice, an angular figure, you are suited for the intellectual characters of the drama, such as Hamlet and so forth. If you are of a soft, passionate nature—if you have a soft voice and that sort of sensuous disposition which seems to lubricate your entire form, your limbs, so that your movements are gentle and softer than others, then this character is fitted for a Romeo or an Othello. You will find, if you look back at the records of actors, there are few great actors that have shone in the two different lines, the intellectual and the sensual drama. Kemble could do Hamlet, but he could not do Othello. Kean could do Othello, but he could not do Hamlet. The one was passionate and sensual, the other was an intellectual, a noble, grand actor.

Now, after you have made this preliminary study you will recollect that in every great character, there are three characters really. We are all free men, in one sense, speaking, of course, of our inner life; but we have three characters. First there is the man by himself—as he is to himself—as he is to God. That is one man, the inner man, as he is when alone; the unclothed man. Then there is the native man, the domestic man, as he is to his family. Still there is a certain amount of disguise. He is not as he is to other men. Then there is the man as he stands before the world at large; as he is outside in society. Those are the three characters. They are all in the one man, and the dramatist does not know his business unless he puts them into one character. Look at Hamlet in his soliloquies, he is passionate, he is violent, he is intemperate in himself, he knows his faults and lashes his own weakness. But he has no sooner done that when Horatio comes on the stage with a few friends. Horatio is the mild, soft, gentle companion; with his arm round his neck, Hamlet forgets the other man; he gets a little on, but he is the same man to Horatio as he is to his mother, when he gets her in the closet. But when he encounters the

[550]

world at large, he is the Prince! the condescending man! You have seen Hamlet played, and if you watched closely, you have seen those three phases of his character have been given on this stage! So it is in nearly all characters—comic or otherwise. You will find that the three characters always combine in the man....

Now, ladies and gentlemen, I have kept you a long time. All I say now is that I have to give you most heartily and conscientiously, as an old man, an old dramatist, and an old actor, this advice. Whatever is done by an actor let it be done with circumspection, without anxiety or hurry, remembering that vehemence is not passion, that the public will feel and appreciate when the actor is not full of himself, but when he is full of character, with that deliberation without slowness, that calmness of resolution without coldness, that self-possession without over-weening confidence, which should combine in the actor so as to give grace to comic and importance to tragic presence. The audience are impressed with the unaffected character of one who moves forward with a fixed purpose, full of momentous designs. He expresses a passion with which they will sympathize, and radiates a command which they will obey....

JOSEPH JEFFERSON

(1829-1905)

Joseph Jefferson was one of the best loved figures of the American stage. Grandson and son of actors, Jefferson made his debut at the age of four. Like many nineteenth century American players, he acted in the South and in the West and even followed the American Army into Mexico.

Jefferson had his first important part as Dr. Pangloss in *The Heir-at-Law* when he was a member of Laura Keene's company in New York. With the same group he created the role of the Yankee in *Our American Cousin* in which Edward Askew Sothern played the role of Lord Dundreary. With the Boucicaults at the Winter Garden he appeared as Caleb Plummer in Boucicault's version of *The Cricket on the Hearth* and as Salem Scudder in Boucicault's *The Octoroon*. Bob Acres in *The Rivals* was also one of his popular parts.

But it is for his portrait of Rip Van Winkle that Jefferson will long be honored. The history of the dramatizations of the Irving tale of Dutch life in New York is a curious one. Performances of a play based upon the story were given as early as 1838. James Hackett, who became the American interpreter of Falstaff, played the role in another version. It is interesting to note that in the cast with Hackett were an uncle, an aunt, and a cousin of Jefferson. Charles Burke, a half brother of Jefferson, played the role of Rip in New York and in Philadelphia. When Jefferson first essayed the role he used a version of his own based upon other available dramatizations. Finding it unsatisfactory, however, he asked Boucicault, when they were both in London, to revise the play for him. It was in Boucicault's dramatization, with many modifications Jefferson made as he continued to portray the role, that he became forever identified with the part of the Dutch loafer.

Each of the actors who had played the role made it successful by what they as actors contributed to it. Hackett undoubtedly brought his pathos and skill in dialects to the part. But Jefferson, in the words of a contemporary critic, informed the role with "human tenderness and dignity." Although his performances seemed the essence of natural ease, Jefferson's characterization was built up with the artistic care which he recommends in the chapter of his autobiography printed here. His "impersonation," wrote the critic of the *Atlantic Monthly* in 1867, "is full of what are technically known as *points;* but the genius of Mr. Jefferson divests them of all 'staginess', and they are only such points as the requirements of his art, its passion, humor, or dignity, suggest. From the rising of the curtain on the first scene, until its fall on the last, nothing is forced, sensational, or unseemly. The remarkable beauty of the performance arises from nothing so much as its entire repose and equality."

No slave to realistic detail, Jefferson consciously heightened what he called the "fairy tale" elements of the play. Although Jefferson became indelibly associated with the role, he was a versatile player who while infusing his roles with warm emotion, controlled his performance with conscious artistry. He summed up his position in the heated controversy between emotion and control, which was being waged by Henry Irving and Coquelin, in these judicious words: "For myself, I know that I act best when the heart is warm and the head is cool."

Warm Heart and Cool Head

Acting has been so much a part of my life that my autobiography could scarcely be written without jotting down my reflections upon it, and I merely make this little preparatory explanation to apologize for any dogmatic tone that they may possess, and to say that I present them merely as a seeker after truth in the domain of art.

In admitting the analogy that undoubtedly exists between the arts of painting, poetry, music, and acting, it should be remembered that the three former are opposed to the latter, in at least the one quality of permanence. The picture, oratorio, or book must bear the test of calculating criticism, whereas the work of an actor is fleeting: it not only dies with him, but, through his different moods, may vary from night to night. If the performance be indifferent it is no consolation for the audience to hear that the player acted well last night, or to be told that he will act better tomorrow night; it is *this* night that the public has to deal with, and the impression the actor has made, good or bad, remains as such upon the mind of that particular audience.

The author, painter, or musician, if he be dissatisfied with his work, may alter and perfect it before giving it publicity, but an actor cannot rub out; he ought, therefore, in justice to his audience, to be sure of what he is going to place before it. Should a picture in an art gallery be carelessly painted we can pass on to another, or if a book fails to please us we can put it down. An escape from this kind of dullness is easily made, but in a theatre the auditor is imprisoned. If the acting be indifferent, he must endure it, at least for a time. He cannot withdraw without making himself conspicuous; so he remains, hoping that there may be some improvement as the play proceeds, or perhaps from consideration for the company he is in. It is this helpless condition that renders careless acting so offensive....

* * * *

In the stage-management of a play, or in the acting of a part, nothing should

The Autobiography of Joseph Jefferson. New York: The Century Company, 1889, pp. 428-454 *passim.*

be left to chance, and for the reason that spontaneity, inspiration, or whatever this strange and delightful quality may be called, is not to be commanded, or we should give it some other name. It is, therefore, better that a clear and unmistakable outline of a character should be drawn before an actor undertakes a new part. If he has a well-ordered and an artistic mind it is likely that he will give at least a symmetrical and effective performance; but should he make no definite arrangement, and depend upon our ghostly friends Spontaneity and Inspiration to pay him a visit, and should they decline to call, the actor will be in a maze and his audience in a muddle.

Besides, why not prepare to receive our mysterious friends whether they come or not? If they fail on such an invitation we can at least entertain our other guests without them; and if they do appear, our preconceived arrangements will give them a better welcome and put them more at ease.

Acting under these purely artificial conditions will necessarily be cold, but the care with which the part is given will at least render it inoffensive; they are, therefore, primary considerations, and not to be despised. The exhibition of artistic care, however, does not alone constitute great acting. The inspired warmth of passion in tragedy and the sudden glow of humor in comedy cover the artificial framework with an impenetrable veil: this is the very climax of great art, for which there seems to be no other name but genius. It is then, and then only, that an audience feels that it is in the presence of a reality rather than a fiction. To an audience an ounce of genius has more weight than a ton of talent; for though it respects the latter, it reverences the former. But the creative power, divine as it may be, should in common gratitude pay due regard to the reflective; for Art is the handmaid of Genius, and only asks the modest wages of respectful consideration in payment for her valuable services. A splendid torrent of genius ought never to be checked, but it should be wisely guided into the deep channel of the stream from whose surface it will then reflect Nature without a ripple. Genius dyes the hues that resemble those of the rainbow; Art fixes the colors that they may stand. In the race for fame purely artificial actors cannot hope to win against those whose genius is guided by their art; and, on the other hand, Intuition must not complain if, unbridled or with too loose a rein, it stumbles on the course, and so allows a well-ridden hack to distance it....

* * * *

An audience should understand what the actors are doing if it does not hear all that they are saying. It is eager to do this, and quite competent, if we only give it a fair opportunity; but inarticulate delivery and careless pantomime will not suffice.

We must not mistake vagueness for suggestion, and imagine that because we understand the matter we are necessarily conveying it to others. Sheridan, in his extravaganza of *The Critic; or, a Tragedy Rehearsed,* gives a humorous illustration of this error. During the rehearsal of Mr. Puff's play the character of Lord Burleigh enters walking slowly and majestically down to the footlights. The noble knight folds his arms, shakes his head solemnly, and then makes his exit without saying a word.

"What does he mean by shaking his head in that manner?" asks Mr. Dangle, a theatrical critic.

To which Mr. Puff replies: "Don't you know? Why, by that shake of the head he gave you to understand that even though they had more justice in their cause and more wisdom in their measures, yet, if there was not a greater spirit shown on the part of the people, the country would at last fall a sacrifice to the hostile ambition of the Spanish monarchy."

"Did he mean all that by shaking his head?" asks Mr. Dangle.

To which Mr. Puff replies, "Yes, sir; if he shook it as I told him."

As this satire was written over a hundred years ago, it is quite evident that the vanity of vagueness is not a new histrionic development.

And here the quality of permanence as allied to the other arts and not to acting presents itself. If we do not at first understand a great picture, a fine piece of music, or a poem, each of these, being tangible, still remains; so, should we desire it, we can familiarize ourselves with it, and as we grow older and become more highly cultivated we will understand a school of art that was at first obscure. But there must be no vagueness in acting. The suggestion should be unmistakable; it must be leveled at the whole audience, and reach with unerring aim the boy in the gallery and the statesman in the stalls.

* * * *

Much has been written upon the question as to whether an actor ought to feel the character he acts or be dead to any sensations in this direction. Excellent artists differ in their opinions on this important point. In discussing it I must refer to some words I wrote in one of the early chapters of this book:

The methods by which actors arrive at great effects vary according to their own natures; this renders the teaching of the art by any strictly defined lines a difficult matter.

There has lately been a discussion on the subject, in which many have taken part, and one quite notable debate between two distinguished actors, one of the English and the other of the French stage.[1] These gentlemen, though they differ entirely in their ideas, are, nevertheless, equally right. The method of one, I have no doubt, is the best he could possibly devise for himself; and the same may be said of the rules of the other as applied to himself. But they must work with their own tools; if they had to adopt each other's they would be as much confused as if compelled to exchange languages. One believes that he must feel the character he plays, even to the shedding of real tears, while the other prefers never to lose himself for an instant, and there is no doubt that they both act with more effect by adhering to their own dogmas.

For myself, I know that I act best when the heart is warm and the head is cool. In observing the works of great painters I find that they have no conventionalities except their own; hence they are masters, and each is at the head of his own school. They are original, and could not imitate even if they would.

So with acting, no master-hand can prescribe rules for the head of another school. If, then, I appear bold in putting forth my suggestions, I desire it to be clearly understood that I do not present them to original or experienced artists who have formed their school, but to the student who may have a temperament akin to my own, and who could, therefore, blend my methods with his preconceived ideas.

* * * *

...The great value of art when applied to the stage is that it enables the performer to reproduce the gift [of acting] and so move his audience night after night, even though he has acted the same character a thousand times. In fact, we cannot

---

[1] Sir Henry Irving and Constant Coquelin.

act a character too often, if we do not lose interest in it. But when its constant repetition palls on the actor it will as surely weary his audience. When you lose interest—stop acting.

This loss of interest on the part of the actor may not be visible in the action or pantomime; but unless care and judgment are observed it will assuredly betray itself in the delivery of the language, and more particularly in the long speeches and soliloquies. In dialogue the spirit of the other actors serves to stimulate and keep him up; but when alone, and unaided by the eye and presence of a companion, the old story fails to kindle the fire. An anecdote of [William Charles] Macready that I heard many years ago throws a flood of light upon this subject; and as I think it too important a one to remain in obscurity I will relate it as I got it from Mr. Couldock, and then refer to its influence upon myself and the means I used to profit by it. The incident occurred in Birmingham, England, some forty years ago. The narrator was present and naturally listened with interest to a conversation upon art between two such able exponents of it as Mr. Macready and Mrs. Warner. What they said referred to an important scene in the tragedy of *Werner,* which had been acted the evening before.

Mr. Macready, it seems, had much respect for Mrs. Warner's judgment in matters relating to the stage, and desired to consult her on the merits and demerits of the preceding evening's performance. As nearly as can be remembered, his question and her reply were as follows:

"My dear madam," said Macready, "you have acted with me in the tragedy of *Werner* for many years, and naturally must be very familiar with it and with my manner of acting that character. I have noticed lately, and more particularly last evening, that some of the passages in the play do not produce the effect that they formerly did. There is a certain speech especially that seems to have lost its power. I refer to the one wherein Werner excuses himself to his son for the 'petty plunder' of Stralenheim's gold. In our earlier performances, if you remember, this apology was received with marked favor, and, as you must have observed, last evening it produced no apparent effect; can you form any idea why this should be? Is it that the audience has grown too familiar with the story? I must beg you to be candid with me. I shall not be offended by any adverse criticism you may make, should you say that the fault is with me."

"Well, Mr. Macready, since you desire that I should speak plainly," said Mrs. Warner, "I do not think it is because your audience is too familiar with the story, but because you are too familiar with it yourself."

"I thank you, madam," said Macready; "but how does this mar the effect of the speech?"

"Thus," said Mrs. Warner. "When you spoke that speech ten years ago there was a surprise in your face as though you then only realized what you had done. You looked shocked and bewildered, and in a forlorn way seemed to cast about for words that would excuse the crime; and all this with a depth of feeling and sincerity that would naturally come from an honest man who had been for the first time in his life accused of theft."

"That is as it should be given," said Macready. "And now, madam?"

"You speak it," said his frank critic, "like one who has committed a great many thefts in his life, and whose glib excuses are so pat and frequent that he is neither shocked, surprised, nor abashed at the accusation."

"I thank you, madam," said the old actor. "The distinction may appear at first as a nice one, but there is much in it."

When I heard the story from Mr. Couldock it struck me with much force. I knew then that I had been unconsciously falling into the same error, and I felt that the fault would increase rather than diminish with time if I could not hit upon some method to check it. I began by listening to each important question as though it had been given for the first time, turning the query over in my mind and then answering it, even at times hesitating as if for want of words to frame the reply. I will admit that this is dangerous ground and apt to render one slow and prosy; in fact, I was accused, and I dare say quite justly, of pausing too long. This, of course, was the other extreme and had to be looked to, so that it became necessary that the pauses should, by the manner and pantomime, be made sufficiently interesting not to weary an audience; so I summed it up somewhat after the advice of Mr. [George Henry] Lewes to take time without appearing to take time.

It is the freshness, the spontaneity, of acting that charms. How can a weary brain produce this quality? Show me a tired actor and I will show you a dull audience. They may go in crowds to see him, and sit patiently through his performance. They have heard that he is great, they may even know it from past experience; so they accept the indifferent art, thinking, perhaps, that they are to blame for a lack of enthusiasm.

* * * *

Many instructors in the dramatic art fall into the error of teaching too much. The pupil should first be allowed to exhibit his quality, and so teach the teacher what to teach. This course would answer the double purpose of first revealing how much the pupil is capable of learning, and, what is still more important, of permitting him to display his powers untrammeled. Whereas, if the master begins by pounding his dogmas into the student, the latter becomes environed by a foreign influence which, if repugnant to his nature, may smother his ability.

It is necessary to be cautious in studying elocution and gesticulation, lest they become our masters instead of our servants. These necessary but dangerous ingredients must be administered and taken in homeopathic doses, or the patient may die by being over-stimulated. But even at the risk of being artificial, it is better to have studied these arbitrary rules than to enter a profession with no knowledge whatever of its mechanism. Dramatic instinct is so implanted in humanity that it sometimes misleads us, fostering the idea that because we have the natural talent within, we are equally endowed with the power of bringing it out. This is the common error, the rock on which the histrionic aspirant is oftenest wrecked. Very few actors succeed who crawl into the service through "the cabin windows"; and if they do it is a lifelong regret with them that they did not exert their courage and sail at first "before the mast."

Many of the shining lights who now occupy the highest positions on the stage, and whom the public voice delights to praise, have often appeared in the dreaded character of "omnes," marched in processions, sung out of tune in choruses, and shouted themselves hoarse for Brutus and Mark Antony.

If necessity is the mother of invention, she is the foster-mother of art, for the greatest actors that ever lived have drawn their early nourishment from her breast. We learn our profession by the mortifications we are compelled to go through in order to get a living. The sons and daughters of wealthy parents who have money at their command, and can settle their weekly expenses without the assistance of the box-office, indignantly refuse to lower themselves by assuming some subordinate character for which they are cast, and march home because their fathers and mothers will take care of them. Well, they had better stay there!

* * * *

...I met... [a] lady...who seemed much interested in *Rip Van Winkle*. Among the many questions she asked of me was how I could act the character so often and not tire of it. I told her that I had always been strangely interested in the part, and fearing that I might eventually grow weary of it, I had of late years so arranged my seasons that I played only a few months and took long spells of rest between them, but that my great stimulus, of course, was public approval, and the knowledge that it must cease if I flagged in my interest or neglected to give my entire attention to the work while it was progressing.

"Another question, please. Why don't you have a dog in the play?"

I replied that I disliked realism in art, and realism alive, with a tail to wag at the wrong time, would be abominable.

"But don't you think that the public would like to see Schneider?"

"The public could not pay him a higher compliment, for it shows how great an interest they take in an animal that has never been exhibited. No, no; 'hold the mirror up to nature' if you like, but don't hold nature up—a reflection of the thing, but not the thing itself. How badly would a drunken man give an exhibition of intoxication on the stage! Who shall act a madman but one who is perfectly sane? We must not be natural but appear to be so."

EDWIN BOOTH

(1833-1893)

The quiet, intelligent acting of Edwin Booth captivated New York in 1857. He brought a new personality and a new style to the American stage which was still dominated by the mannerisms of Edwin Forrest. Booth became the American Hamlet, dark, sad, poetic, and melancholy. He played Shakespearean repertory throughout the United States and England and was perhaps the last standard bearer of the traditional drama in this country.

Edwin was the son of Junius Brutus Booth, that strange theatrical figure who had unsuccessfully competed against Edmund Kean. In the United States the elder Booth pursued his career, acting throughout the length and breadth of the country. His intense dramatic personality was dissected by Walt Whitman who wrote that Booth "illustrated Plato's rule that to the forming of an artist of the very highest rank a dash of insanity (or what the world calls insanity) is indispensable. Without question Booth was royal heir and legitimate representative of the Garrick-Kemble-Siddons dramatic traditions but he vitalized and gave an unnameable *race* to those traditions with his own electric personal idiosyncrasy. (As in all art-utterance it was the subtle and powerful something *special to the individual* that really conquered.)"

On Booth's tours went the young Edwin as companion and keeper of his erratic, talented father. On his travels Edwin learned to sing and to play the violin and the banjo, but his father did not want him to become an actor. Nevertheless Edwin Booth was schooled in the theatre and made his first unheralded appearance in 1849 as Tressel to his father's Richard III. The success of the young man made managers eager to bill the two together, but the father refused. Perhaps Edwin's career truly began when he replaced his father as Richard III in New York when the latter suddenly decided that he would not play. But a long period of wide-spread travels followed before Edwin Booth became a star in his own right. He played in California, in Australia, even in the Sandwich Islands. Finally returned to the East, he successfully starred in Boston in the role of Sir Giles Overreach. In 1857 he appeared in New York in *Richard III*.

His success assured, he went to England in 1861 for an engagement. In 1863 while playing in New York his young wife died, and he was driven to seek consolation in increased activities. Booth leased the Winter Garden Theatre, where in 1864, he gave his celebrated one hundred night run of *Hamlet*. At the peak of his success came another tragic event. His brother, John Wilkes, also an actor, assassinated Lincoln, and Edwin retired from the stage. He reappeared, however, in 1866 and made the Winter Garden Theatre the scene of many notable productions, particularly of Shakespearean plays. The Winter Garden was destroyed by fire, and Booth took to the road, all the time planning to erect another theatre. He opened his Booth's Theatre at Sixth Avenue and Twenty-third Street in New York with *Romeo and Juliet* in 1869. Mary McVicker, who became his second wife, played Juliet. At his theatre until 1874, when financial reverses sent him into bankruptcy, Booth gave New York a series of outstanding Shakespearean performances and productions that recalled the days of Charles Kean at the Princess Theatre. Losing his theatre, Booth again went on tour throughout the United States and again visited London where he played with Henry Irving. During the American tours, he played with Salvini and with Ristori. At the end of the Eighties he went on the road with Lawrence Barrett, and also played with Modjeska. He gave his last performance in 1891 as Hamlet at the Brooklyn Academy of Music.

Booth's acting appeared to his contemporaries as something fresh and different, a great contrast with that of Forrest. The partisanship of the followers of the two actors was sharp. Booth felt that his acting was "somewhat quieter" than that of his father, representative of the older generation. At one point Booth commented that he could not "paint with big brushes—the fine touches come in spite of me, and it's all folly to say: 'Don't elaborate, don't refine it'—I can't help it. I'm too damned genteel and exquisite, I s'pose, and some buster with a big voice and a broadaxe gesticulation will oust me one of these fine days."

In 1880 a critic wrote of Booth: "Instead of being the slave of 'tradition,' I found him constantly neglecting old traditional points.... Edwin Booth was eminently natural, and to be looked on as an admirable exponent of the more approved 'new school'." Yet when he appeared in England after the "new school" of the Bancrofts, Fechter, and Irving was well under way, he seemed old fashioned. An early commentator quoted by Richard Lockridge (*Darling of Misfortune*) struck at the heart of Booth's problem: "We regard it as Mr. Booth's misfortune that he is divided between two widely different schools of acting—the romantic and the natural. The tradition of his youth, his early observation and training, compelled him to the romantic or heroic school. His organization, taste, aptitude, perhaps his later study also, inclined him to the side of nature. But he seems never to have made a deliberate choice between the two; his favorite plays are romantic; in his treatment he aims at naturalism. Hence the incongruity." Lockridge points out that by the time audiences realized what Booth was trying to achieve with what his first wife Mary Devlin called "the conversational, colloquial school" of acting, Booth's innovations were no longer new.

Booth's own creative methods and his style are revealed in his brief comments on Edmund Kean and in his excellent footnotes to *Othello* and *The Merchant of Venice* in the Furness Variorum edition of Shakespeare. His constant admonition in these notes to "play down" in "subdued tones," record the subtle artistry of this great actor.

The Actor's Tradition

In my study... I have often sat until dawn, alternately reading memoirs of great actors of the past, and contemplating their portraits and death-masks which hang upon the walls; and somehow I seem to derive a more satisfactory idea of their capabilities from their counterfeit presentments than from the written records of their lives.

What a void in the gallery of old masters of Dramatic Art is made by the absence of any portraits of Thespis, Roscius, or Burbage. We might perhaps get a taste of their quality, could we see some semblance of their features.

My impressions may have no worth. They are offered simply as the mere fancies of one who, while placidly puffing his midnight pipe, holds communion with the departed; not by means of spiritism, but, as I have said, through the medium of their biographies, their pictures, and the plaster casts of their dead faces.

To begin with our earliest tragic actor of whom we have any authentic portrait, I can read no line of tragedy in the face of Thomas Betterton, although Cibber's opinion must be respected; and I doubt if Quin's features, of which I have no likeness worth considering, would convince me of his excellence in the higher range of tragedy. Certainly those of Barton Booth and Spranger Barry do not; yet all of them manifest much dignity. The beautiful features of Garrick evince wonderful mobility, but they suggest more of the comic than of the tragic quality. All his best known portraits depict him as the incomparable comedian; even in Hogarth's *Richard* the expression of horror seems weak; and as his friend and admirer, the great Johnson, declared that his death eclipsed the gaiety of nations, I am inclined to believe that Davy was more favored by Thalia than by Melpomene. Old Macklin and George Frederick Cooke gaze at me with hard immobile features, denoting great force in a limited tragic range, such as hate, revenge and cunning. Nothing poetic or sublime can be found in either countenance, nor anything approaching the humorous, unless it be a leer in the latter's eye which indicates cajolery, or the sardonic mirth of Shylock, Richard or Iago. I cannot imagine either of these famed actors as being satisfactory in Lear, Macbeth, Hamlet or Othello. From them I turn to the noble front of Kemble, whose calm majestic features seem to say, "See what a grace was seated on this brow!" whereon indeed is clearly set the impress of the tragic crown; and then to his sister, Siddons, the unexpressive she, whose lips and eyes made forever eloquent by Reynolds, tell us that her jealous mother, Melpomene, cabin'd, cribb'd, confin'd and bound her in the limitations of the awful circle, although lavish Nature gave her the utmost range of human emotions, whether of

Edwin Booth: "A Few Words about Edmund Kean," in *Actors and Actresses of Great Britain and the United States; From the Days of David Garrick to the Present Time*, edited by Brander Matthews and Laurence Hutton. New York: Cassell and Company, Limited, 1886, Volume III: Kean and Booth; And Their Contemporaries, pp. 4-12.

joy or of grief, anger, remorse, or the very levity of mirth. Neither Kemble nor Siddons was able to doff the buskin for the sock successfully. Their spheres were high, but circumscribed.

The sweet, sad face of the great German, Ludwig Devrient, and that of his nephew, Emil—by many considered the better actor—and the feline loveliness of Rachel, which clearly shows the scope of her ability, must be passed by as foreign to the subject; my object being simply to compare the portraits of some of the most renowned English tragedians, as they affect me, with that of our great Protagonist —Edmund Kean.

There is no art to find the mind's construction in the face, the living face; but Death frequently reveals some long hidden secret, a gleam of goodliness, a touch of tenderness, even a glimpse of humor, which life conceals from us. In the uncanny case of the head of the dead Kean, which hangs above his portrait opposite my desk, I discover the comic as well as the tragic element, and in his ghastly, yet to me, fascinating features, only, do I perceive any trace of the two qualities combined. All this there is to be seen, by my eyes at least, in the distorted face, even in its last agony, wasted by disease and suffering; and more than this, I perceive a smile for the weary-hearted wife who sobbed forgiveness at his deathbed, loving to the last.

Lewes, who certainly knew more of this subject than I do, and who was apparently a careful critic, says that Kean had his limitation in tragedy; and that he was devoid of mirth. Lewes, as a lad, had seen Kean in life. I have seen only his dead, weird beauty; and contemplating this as I have often done, and recalling the words of one who acted with and against him, I can hardly agree with Lewes. Once and only once my father gave me a glimpse of his reminiscences; on that occasion he, who seldom spoke of actors or the theatre, told me that in his opinion no mortal man could equal Kean in the rendering of Othello's despair and rage; and that above all, his not very melodious voice in many passages, notably that ending with "Farewell, Othello's occupation gone," sounded like the moan of ocean or the soughing of wind through cedars. His peculiar lingering on the letter "l" often marred his delivery; but here, in the "Farewell," the tones of cathedral chimes were not more mournful. Now, I believe that he who could, as Kean did, perfectly express Othello's exquisite tenderness, as well as his sombre and fiercer passions, must have been capable of portraying the sublimest, subtlest, and profoundest emotions. The fact that Kean disliked to act Hamlet and failed to satisfy his critics in that character is no proof that his personation was false. If it was consistent with his conception and that conception was intelligible, as it must have been, it was true. What right have I, whose temperament and mode of thinking are dissimilar to yours, to denounce your exposition of such a puzzle as Hamlet? He is the epitome of mankind, not an individual; a sort of magic mirror in which all men and women see the reflex of themselves, and therefore has his story always been, is still, and will ever be the most popular of stage tragedies. As for the absence of mirth in Kean, the same has been said of all actors with features severely molded. Kean played piano accompaniments to the songs he sang; he told quaint stories, and performed mad pranks in the very ecstasy of merriment. Besides, he made a giant stride from Harlequin to Hamlet, a god-like step from the lowest to the highest plane. Still, after treading the boards on the stilts of Tragedy, his descent to the lower walk may not have been graceful. Most players of what is called the old school, which simply means the only school of acting, now closed I fear forever, had similar training; but how many have ascended the frail ladder of Fame so successfully as Kean? In not retaining the lighter parts of his repertory he showed a worthy ambition to be regarded as a tragedian, a denizen only of the highest realm of Art. If he failed to satisfy in the lesser serious roles wherein he was but one of a group, it was because, like a riderless racer, he felt the need of weight. Accustomed to carry alone the burthen of a tragedy, he naturally felt ill at ease when others shared the responsibility with him.

That the son of the only man who shook this monarch on his throne should be so bold in his defense may be considered strange, and indeed it is somewhat out of the way of human dealings; but I know that their rivalry was but the result of managerial trickery, which for a time estranged them. . . .

They were so much alike in feature, in manner and in stature—although my father boasted of an inch above Kean in the latter particular and in that only—that in the scenes where Booth's brown hair and blue eyes were disguised by the traditional black wig of tragedy and by other stage accoutrements, he appeared to be the very counterpart of his black-eyed, swarthy rival. Their voices were unlike—the latter's harsh and usually unpleasing to the ear, the former's musical and resonant. Their reading of the text was not the same. Kean was careless, and gave flashes of light after intervals of gloom. Booth was always even, a careful expounder of the text, a scholar, a student and—but enough of comparisons; they were made, *ad nauseam,* long years ago, and belong to the written history of the London stage; they need have no admission here. Suffice it that the mere similitude stamped the second comer as an imitator, although he had never seen his predecessor. Kean said, and I believe him, that he had never seen Cooke act; nevertheless many critics declared him to have been a copyist of the great George Frederick.

The word imitation seems to be used as a slur upon the actor alone. The painter and the sculptor go to Italy to study the old masters, and are praised for their good copies after this or that one. They are not censured for imitation; and why may not the actor also have his preceptor, his model? Why should he be denounced for following the footsteps of *his* old master? Why should he alone be required to depart from tradition? True, other artists see the works of their predecessors and can retain or reject beauties or blemishes at will; but the actor relies solely on uncertain records of his master's art, and thereby is frequently misled into the imitation of faults, rather than into the emulation of virtues.

In the main, tradition to the actor is as true as that which the sculptor perceives in Angelo, the painter in Raphael, and the musician in Beethoven; all of these artists having sight and sound to guide them. I, as an actor, know that could I sit in front of the stage and see myself at work I would condemn much that has been lauded; and could correct many faults which I feel are mine, and which escape the critic's notice. But I cannot see or hear my mistakes as can the sculptor, the painter, the writer, and the musician. Tradition, if it be traced through pure channels, and to the fountain head, leads one as near to Nature as can be followed by her servant Art. Whatever Betterton, Quin, Barton Booth, Garrick and Cooke gave to stagecraft, or as we now term it, business, they received from their predecessors; from Burbage, and perhaps, from Shakespeare himself, who, though not distinguished as an actor, well knew what acting should be; what they inherited in this way they bequeathed in turn to their art, and we should not despise it. Kean knew without seeing Cooke, who in turn knew from Macklin, and so back to Betterton just what to do and how to do it. Their great mother Nature, who reiterates her teachings and preserves her monotone in motion, form and sound, taught them. There must be some similitude in all things that are True. . . .

As I gaze on the pitiable face of him, the waif, the reputed chick of Mother Carey, a stormy Petrel indeed, but perhaps the first really great tragedian that trod the English stage; and at the same time recall my experiences with one of a similarly erratic brain, I am convinced that Kean's aberrations were constitutional, and beyond his control. The blots in the 'scutcheon of genius, like spots on the sun, are to us dim-eyed gropers in the vast Mystery, incomprehensible, inscrutable! Who shall say that even our very evils, still existing in defiance of man's mightiest efforts to extirpate them, are not a part of the All-wise economy?

[Comments on Shylock][1]

My notion of Shylock is of the traditional type, which I firmly believe to be "the Jew which Shakespeare drew." Not the buffoon that Dogget gave according to Lord Lansdowne's version, but the strongly marked and somewhat grotesque character which Macklin restored to the stage, and in which he was followed by Cooke, by Edmund Kean, and by my Father. 'Tis nonsense to suppose that Shylock was represented in other than a serious vein by Burbage, merely because he "made up," doubtless after some representation of Judas, with red hair to emphasize the vicious expression of his features. Is there any authority for the assertion which some make that he also wore a long nose? What if he did? A clever actor once played the part of Tubal with me, and wore red hair and a hook'd nose. He did not make the audience laugh; 'twas not his purpose; but he looked the very creature that could sympathize with Shylock. His make-up was admirable. He's the son of the famous John Drew, and is an excellent actor, now a leading member of Daly's Company. Let Burbage have the long nose, if you will, but I am sure that he never under Shakespeare's nose made the character ridiculous. No, not till Lansdowne's bastard came did the Jew make the unskilful laugh and the judicious grieve. From that time, perhaps, until Macklin restored the original method of representing the character, it was treated as a "low comedy" part. I doubt if Macklin or Cooke wore red wigs for Shylock—but no matter, Burbage did, and neither was he nor were they funny. If Edmund Kean was the first to wear black hair when red was the usual color worn at that time, 'tis easily accounted for, when you reflect that he was very poor and probably had a very limited stock of stage "props"—he doubtless had no other old man's wig (except a white one for Lear) and the "black bald" did service for Sir Giles Overreach, and several other elderly gentlemen besides Shylock. I believe that Burbage, Macklin, Cooke, and Kean (as did my Father) made Shylock what is technically termed a "character part"—grotesque in "make up," and general treatment, not so pronounced, perhaps, as my personation has been sometimes censured for. I think Macready was the first to lift the uncanny Jew out of the darkness of his native element or revengeful selfishness into the light of the venerable Hebrew, the Martyr, the Avenger. He has had several followers, and I once tried to view him in that light, but he doesn't cast a shadow sufficiently strong to contrast with the sunshine of the comedy—to do which he must, to a certain extent, be repulsive, a sort of party that one doesn't care to see among the dainty revellers of Venice in her prime....

Do not forget, while you read the poet's plays, that he was a player, and, mark you! a theatrical manager with a keen eye to stage-effects; witness the "gag" of Shylock's sharpening the knife—a most dangerous "bit of business," and apt to

---

[1]Quoted in *The Merchant of Venice; A New Variorum Edition of Shakespeare*, edited by Horace Howard Furness. Philadelphia: J. B. Lippincott Company, 1888, Volume VII, pp. 383-384.

cause a laugh; be careful of that "point." Would the heroic Hebrew have stooped to such a paltry action? No, never, in the very white-heat of his pursuit of vengeance! But vengeance is foreign to Shylock's thought; 'tis revenge he seeks, and he gets just what all who seek it get—"sooner or later," as the saying is. Had his motive been the higher one, Shakespeare would have somehow contrived his success without doubt; but Shylock had grown too strong for him. 'Tis said, you know, that he had to kill Mercutio, else the merry fellow would have killed the tragedy; so Shylock would have killed the comedy had he been intended to typify Vengeance. The storm-cloud of his evil passions having burst, he is forgotten in the moonlight of fair Portia's gardens.

WILLIAM HOOKER GILLETTE

(1855-1937)

In the movement toward a more realistic presentation of character and events both by the dramatist and the actor, William Gillette holds an important place. He was the son of a United States Senator, and although he achieved early notice as an actor, he attended classes at several colleges to give himself a wider range of education and experience. His first writing efforts were collaborations and adaptations. His original play, *Held by the Enemy,* is called by Arthur Hobson Quinn (*A History of the American Drama*) the "first important drama of the Civil War." The atmosphere and the characterizations of the play were carried forward with great success in Gillette's most popular play *Secret Service,* the story of a Civil War spy. In the cool-headed yet sympathetic figure of the spy, Captain Thorne, Gillette created one of his best parts. He also adapted and acted the title role in *Sherlock Holmes.*

Gillette's essay "The Illusion of the First Time in Acting" is an excellent analysis of some of the problems that face the actor who plays in realistic drama. Other American actors had discussed this problem, but Gillette tackled two of the crucial difficulties encountered by the actor who wants to create a life-like portrait of a character realistically delineated by the author. When the emphasis in drama shifted from universal truth and poetic utterance to a slice of life presented within the proscenium arch, the actor's art shifted from attention to the broader strokes of character, posture, and recitation to the illusion of reality created by a myriad of realistic details. If life on the stage was to be "simulated life as it is lived," to use Gillette's own words, rather than a transcendence of reality, then the actor faced more than ever the necessity of making each performance seem to present the character going through his realistic actions for the first time.

This emphasis on "simulated life" led Gillette to the position that the Protean versatility, so admired in earlier theatrical days, was not a desirable goal for the actor. In Gillette's opinion the actor was to build his characterizations on the dominant qualities of his own personality. He would succeed in roles where there was a close relation between the fictional attributes of the character and the individuality of the actor. That Gillette took these two problems as the focal point of his discussion of acting is in itself evidence that the realistic drama ushered in a new evaluation of the actor's problems and his goals.

The Illusion of the First Time in Acting

So far as painted, manufactured and mechanical elements [of the play] are concerned, there is comparatively little trouble. To keep these things precisely as much in the background as they would appear were a similar episode in actual life under observation—*and no more*—is the most pronounced difficulty. But when it comes to the Human Beings required to assume the Characters which the Directions indicate, and not only to assume them but to breathe into them the Breath of Life—and not the *Breath* of Life alone but all other elements and details and items of life so far as they can be simulated, many and serious discouragements arise.

For in these latter days life-elements are required. Not long ago they were not. In these latter days the merest slip from true life-simulation is the death or crippling of the character involved, and it has thereafter to be dragged through the course of the play as a disabled or lifeless thing. Not all plays are sufficiently strong in themselves to carry on this sort of morgue or hospital service for any of their important roles.

The perfectly obvious methods of character assassination such as the sing-song or "reading" intonation, the exaggerated and grotesque use of gesture and facial expression, the stilted and unnatural stride and strut, cause little difficulty. These, with many other inherited blessings from the Palmy Days when there was acting that really amounted to something, may easily be recognized and thrown out.

But the closeness to life which now prevails has made audiences sensitive to thousands of minor things that would not formerly have affected them. To illustrate my meaning, I am going to speak of two classes of these defects.... There are plenty more where these two came from. I select these two because they are good full ones, bubbling over with dramatic death and destruction. One I shall call—to distinguish it, the "Neglect of the Illusion of the First Time"; the other, the "Disillusion of Doing it Correctly." There is an interesting lot of them which might be assembled under the heading the "Illusion of Unconsciousness of What Could Not Be Known"—but there will not be time to talk about it. All these groups, however, are closely related, and the First Time one is fairly representative. And of course I need not tell you that we have no names for these things—no groups—no classification; we merely fight them as a whole—as an army or mob of enemies that strives for the downfall of our life-simulation, with poisoned javelins. I have separated a couple of these poisons so that you may see how they work, and incidentally how great little things now are.

Unfortunately for an actor (to save time I mean all known sexes by that), unfortunately for an actor he knows or is supposed to know his part. He is fully aware —especially after several performances—of what he is going to say. The character he is representing, however, does *not* know what he is going to say, but, if he is a human being, various thoughts occur to him one by one, and he puts such of those thoughts as he decides to, into such speech as he happens to be able to command at the time. Now it is a very difficult thing—and even now rather an uncommon thing— for an actor who knows exactly what he is going to say to behave exactly as though he

William Hooker Gillette: *The Illusion of the First Time in Acting.* New York: Printed for the Dramatic Museum of Columbia University, *Papers on Acting*, Second Series, Number 1, 1915, pp. 37-48. By permission of Columbia University Press.

didn't; to let his thought (apparently) occur to him as he goes along, even though they are there in his mind already; and (apparently) to search for and find words by which to express those thoughts, even though these words are at his tongue's very end. That's the terrible thing—at his tongue's very end! Living and breathing creatures do not carry their words in that part of their systems; they have to find them and send them there—with more or less rapidity according to their facility in that respect— as occasion arises. And audiences of today, without knowing the nature of the fatal malady are fully conscious of the untimely demise of the character when the actor portraying it apparently fails to do this.

In matters of speech, of pauses, of giving a character who would think time to think; in behavior of eyes, nose, mouth, teeth, ears, hands, feet, etc., while he does think and while he selects his words to express the thought—this ramifies into a thousand things to be considered in relation to the language or dialogue alone.

This menace or death from Neglect of the Illusion of the First Time is not confined to matters and methods of speech and mentality, but extends to every part of the presentation, from the most climacteric and important action or emotion to the most insignificant item of behavior—a glance of the eye at some unexpected occurrence—the careless picking up of some small object which (supposedly) has not been seen or handled before. Take the simple matter of entering a room to which, according to the plot or story, the character coming in is supposed to be a stranger; unless there is vigilance the actor will waft himself blithely across the threshold, conveying the impression that he has at least been born in the house—finding it quite unnecessary to look where he is going and not in the least worth while to watch out for thoughtless pieces of furniture that may, in their ignorance of his approach, have established themselves in his path. And the different scenes with the different people; and the behavior resulting from *their* behavior; and the love-scenes as they are called—these have a little tragedy all their own for the performers involved; for, if an actor plays his part in one of these with the gentle awkwardness and natural embarrassment of one in love for the first time—as the plot supposes him to be—he will have the delight of reading the most withering and caustic ridicule of himself in the next day's papers, indicating in no polite terms that he is an awkward amateur who does not know his business, and that the country will be greatly relieved if he can see his way clear to quitting the stage at once; whereas if he behaves with the careless ease and grace and fluency of the Palmy Day actor, softly breathing airy and poetic love-messages down the back of the lady's neck as he feelingly stands behind her so that they can both face to the front at the same time, the audience will be perfectly certain that the young man has had at least fifty-seven varieties of love-affairs before and that the plot has been shamelessly lying about him.

The foregoing are a few only of the numberless parts or items in drama-presentation which must conform to the Illusion of the First Time. But this is one of the rather unusual cases in which the sum of all the parts does not equal the whole. For although every single item from the most important to the least important be successfully safe-guarded, there yet remains the spirit of the presentation as a whole. Each successive audience before which it is given must feel—not think or reason about, but *feel*—that it is witnessing, not one of a thousand weary repetitions, but a life episode that is being lived just across the magic barrier of the footlights. That is to say, the whole must have that indescribable life-spirit or effect which produces the Illusion of Happening for the First Time. Worth his weight in something extremely valuable is the stage-director who can conjure up this rare and precious spirit!

The dangers to dramatic life and limb from the "Disillusion of Doing It Correctly" are scarcely less than those in the First Time class, but not so difficult to detect and eliminate. Speaking, breathing, walking, sitting, rising, standing, gesturing—in short behaving correctly, when the character under representation would not naturally or customarily do so, will either kill that character outright or make it very sick indeed. Drama can make its appeal only in the form of simulated life as it is lived—not as various authorities on grammar, pronunciation, etiquette, and elocution happen to announce at that particular time that it ought to be lived.

But we find it well to go much further than the keeping of studied and unusual correctness *out,* and to put common and to-be-expected errors *in,* when they may be employed appropriately and unobtrusively. To use every possible means and device for giving drama that which makes it drama—life-simulation—must be the aim of the modern play-constructor and producer. And not alone ordinary errors but numberless individual habits, traits, peculiarities are of the utmost value for this purpose.

Among these elements of life and vitality but greatly surpassing all others in importance is the human characteristic or essential quality which passes under the execrated name of personality. The very word must send an unpleasant shudder through this highly sensitive assembly; for it is supposed to be quite the proper and highly cultured thing to sneer at personality as an altogether cheap affair and not worthy to be associated for a moment with what is highest in dramatic art. Nevertheless, cheap or otherwise, inartistic or otherwise, and whatever it really is or is not, it is the most singularly important factor for infusing the life-illusion into modern stage creations that is known to man. Indeed, it is something a great deal more than important, for in these days of drama's close approximation to life, it is essential. As no human being exists without personality of one sort or another, an actor who omits it in his impersonation of a human being omits one of the vital elements of existence.

In all the history of the stage no performer has yet been able to simulate or make use of a personality not his own. Individual tricks, mannerisms, peculiarities of speech and action may be easily accomplished. They are the capital and stock in trade of the character comedian and the lightning change artist, and have nothing whatever to do with personality.

The actors of recent times who have been universally acknowledged to be great have invariably been so because of their successful use of their own strong and compelling personalities in the roles which they made famous. And when they undertook parts, as they occasionally did, unsuited to their personalities, they were great no longer and frequently quite the reverse. The elder [Tommaso] Salvini's Othello towered so far above all other renditions of the character known to modern times that they were lost to sight below it. His Gladiator was superb. His Hamlet was an unfortunate occurrence. His personality was marvelous for Othello and the Gladiator, but unsuited to the Dane. Mr. Booth's personality brought him almost adoration in his Hamlet—selections from it served him well in Iago, Richelieu, and one or two other roles, but for Othello it was not all that could be desired. And Henry Irving and Ellen Terry and Modjeska, Janauschek and Joseph Jefferson and Mary Anderson, each and every one of them with marvelous skill transferred their personalities to the appropriate roles. Even now—once in a while—one may see Rip

Van Winkle excellently well played, but without Mr. Jefferson's personality. There it is in simple arithmetic for you—a case of mere subtraction.

As indicated a moment ago I am only too well aware that the foregoing view of the matter is sadly at variance with what we are told is the highest form of the actor's art. According to the deep thinkers and writers on matters of the theatre, the really great actor is not one who represents with marvelous power and truth to life the characters within the limited scope of his personality, but the performer who is able to assume an unlimited number of totally divergent roles. It is not the thing at all to consider a single magnificent performance such as Salvini's Othello, but to discover the highest art we must inquire how many kinds of things a man can do. This, you will observe, brings it down to a question of pure stage gymnastics. Watch the actor who can balance the largest number of roles in the air without allowing any of them to spill over. Doubtless an interesting exhibition if you are looking for that form of sport. In another art it would be: "Do not consider this man's paintings, even though masterpieces, for he is only a landscape artist. Find the chap who can paint forty different kinds." I have an idea the theatre-going public is to be congratulated that none of the great stage performers, at any rate of modern times, has entered for any such competition.

RICHARD MANSFIELD

(1857-1907)

The earliest phases of Mansfield's career saw him as a monologist and then as a singer in the D'Oyly Carte Gilbert and Sullivan Company. Mansfield's mother, the former Erminia Rudersdorff, had been a distinguished Continental operatic soprano. In 1882 Mansfield arrived in New York from England, and after an appearance in the comic opera *Three Black Cloaks* he played small parts at the Union Square Theatre. When Stoddart turned down the part of an old roué, Baron Chevrial in *A Parisian Romance,* Mansfield was offered the role which was to make him famous. Biographers recall that Mansfield used every resource at his command to compose his performance of the old rake. He studied the type in hospitals, in the clubs, and sought the advice of doctors on the physical disorders of this kind of man. It is said that while he was working on the part Mansfield scarcely ate or slept. On the eve of his performance Mansfield told some friends, "Tomorrow night I shall be famous. Come and see the play." On the first night following the scene in which the old hedonist dies, "champagne glass in hand," the audience recalled the actor a dozen times with wild enthusiasm. Mansfield was famous.

Always fortunate in his roles, a series of hits from 1887 to 1893—*Prince Karl, Doctor Jekyll and Mr. Hyde, Richard III, The Merchant of Venice, Cyrano de Bergerac, Beau Brummel* (especially written for him by Clyde Fitch)—established Mansfield as a leading American player. In 1894 his production of *Arms and the Man* introduced Shaw to America. Another Mansfield first was his staging in 1907 of *Peer Gynt.* During this season Mansfield was already suffering from cancer and was soon too ill to perform. He died in August of that year.

Norman Hapgood's contemporary review of Mansfield's *Henry V* in 1900 indicates some of the qualities which made him respected as an actor and manager: "Mr. Mansfield's performance of Henry showed his skill as an actor to a high degree. Many players carefully choose roles that fit their personalities. Not so Mr.

Mansfield. Famous for satire and character parts, he now stood forth as a king who was half-warrior and half-saint, so that every stroke the actor made had to be with his talent against his natural physical characteristics. Nonetheless he gave a performance of the extremely difficult role which was in every way worthy to stand among this able and varied actor's proudest achievements."

Originality

Hans Christian Andersen once attended a performance of Shakespeare's *Tempest* as presented by an actor of great reputation. He stated afterward that in spite of the magnificence of the production, which he described at great length, he would prefer seeing the play in a barn, provided the actors engaged spoke their words clearly, and with sense and feeling. I am quite of Mr. Andersen's opinion. The extravagance of the stage today is alarming. It is not only alarming: it is the ruin of the pure drama. There seems to be a perversion of the advice concerning the mirror and nature entirely in favor of inanimate objects, and we are called upon to admire the ingenuity of the master carpenter and the fidelity of the scene painter, to the almost entire extinction of the art, *pur et simple,* of the actor. What is the art of the actor? It is the expression in voice, in word, in face, and in form of the emotion born of the situation devised by the author. The voice must be the voice of the peculiar individual portrayed by the actor, attuned to the emotion, it must be either harsh or gentle, winsome or repellent, powerful or feeble, but it must never betray the limit of the organ. The words, no matter what the voice may be, must be comprehensible. That is the first duty the actor owes the author, at least. The eye, the mouth, the figure, must be in harmony.

An actor, in portraying various characters diametrically opposite, has no right to offer his own personality in each. That is not the art of acting. The business sense of a man who has learned that the more the public is familiarized with the individuality of an actor the greater his popularity, is a poor excuse for bad acting.

The true student will merge himself in the character he presents, and he will present each creature as he conceives him, or as the author has painted him. A man who cannot so envelope himself in the robe of the part, who cannot be this man today and that man tomorrow, no matter how smart a fellow he may be, cannot be considered an actor.

There are numberless professions open to clever people without voices and without other necessary requirements for the stage. They may be statesmen, and some actors of reputation seem to enjoy an ability in that direction far beyond any qualification for our art; they may be priests and parsons; they may be barristers and lawyers—in all these parts they need never rob the public of a view of their own inestimable personality; upon the stage they must. It is absurd for Fagin to be Romeo, and Romeo, Benedick—you may label them, but there is no deception, and the art of the actor is deception.

Time was when an actor declaimed the lines of Shakespeare, and that was enough. It isn't enough today. The world does not stand still, nor does the art of acting. Declaiming is not acting; the actor must pretend to be what he is not; he

Richard Mansfield: "Concerning Acting." New York: *The North American Review*, September, 1894, pp. 337-340.

must be what he pretends to be. There is a royal road to success—it is humbug. There is no royal road to success on legitimate lines—it means endless labor, heartache, sorrow, and disappointment. If you desire to be an actor, you must choose the latter—you will be welcome. The actor lives for his art; the world may see the pictures he paints, the lessons he inculcates; he breathes life into them for a moment; they fade away and die; he leaves nothing behind him but a memory. The actor has no connection with scenery and mechanism, he does not perceive them— he should not know that they surround him; the picture of the place, be it what it may, is the creation of his fancy, and what he sees there he contrives to communicate to his audience. He can, if he will, bring with him the salt air of the sea, the perfumed atmosphere of the boudoir, the flower-scented zephyr of the grove, or the dank breath of the cloister. His day is study, his evening the result. He should have no opinions to buy, no critics to placate, no axes to grind or wires to pull. You can buy opinions one way or another, you can win hosts of friends, you can grind axes and pull wires, and achieve wealth and fame, but you will not achieve art! And the crowd of sycophants and courtiers cannot still the voice within that tells you every hour, "You're a lie!"

Do not be led away by men who tell you to be original—in other words, to be odd and eccentric and to attract attention to yourself by these means. Do not strive to be original; strive to be true! If you succeed in being true, you will be original. If you go forth to seek originality, you will never find truth. If you go out to seek truth, you may discover originality. Do not be dazzled by the success of chicanery or charlatanism. You will not find it satisfying, for, however much you may impress others, you will never believe in yourself, unless you are insane. The mediocre actor generally enjoys popularity, he offends no one and arouses no jealousies—and mediocrity is easy of comprehension. The merchant will tell you that the rarest products are unsalable.

The actor who plays to the groundlings, who has a good word for everyone, who has never racked his nerves or tortured his soul, who has not earned his bread and salt with *"Kummer und Noth,"* who has not realized the utter impossibility of ever accomplishing his ideal, who is not striving and searching for the better in art, who is content to amass wealth by playing one part only; the actor, in short, who is not unsatisfied, is a poor fool of an actor.

It is impossible for an actor to attempt an arduous role and having done his full duty to be as unruffled and calm and benign as a May morning.

The very center of his soul has been shaken; he has projected himself by force of will into another being, another sphere—he has been living, acting, thinking another man's life, and you cannot expect to find him calm and smiling and tolerant of small troubles, dumped back on a dung heap after a flight to the moon.

If, when the curtain has fallen, you meet this clever calculating and diplomatic personage, know that you are not in the presence of an actor. He is, no doubt, a thousand times more pleasant to encounter, more charming in society, *gratissimus* to the fatigued, harassed, often humiliated and misunderstood newspaper hack— but he is not an actor.

The actor is *sui generis,* and in the theatre not to be judged by the ordinary rules applied to ordinary men. The actor is an extraordinary man, who every evening spends three hours or more in fairyland and transforms himself into all kinds of odd creatures for the benefit of his fellow men; when he returns from fairyland, where he has been a king or a beggar, a criminal doomed to death, a lover in despair, or a haunted man, do you fancy the aspect of the world and its peoples is not tinged with some clinging color of his living dream? ...

The actor's art will be more widely honored by thinking men when they discover in the actor the unostentatious manners of a simple gentleman. Men will not blame the actor for eccentricities or idiosyncrasies which he may have inherited, or for which nature or ill health is responsible; they will accept them as they accept them in other friends, but they will be swift to perceive their assumption for a purpose.

Aside from the personal opinion of individuals the public has no concern whatever in the private life of the actor; it belongs to him as much as it belongs to the lawyer, the painter, the writer, or the architect, or to any other free-born citizen.

The stage is the actor's studio and gallery of exhibition; away from it his deeds are of no moment, and many actors would be less known and others more popular if the world judged the actor only by his work.

Society, as a whole, cares very little for art. True art without the humbug is as little tolerated in society as a nude figure. ...

EDWARD HUGH SOTHERN
(1859-1933)

JULIA MARLOWE
(1870-1950)

Edward Hugh Sothern was the son of a celebrated nineteenth century actor. His father, Edward Askew Sothern, though English born, made his way on the American stage. His great role was that of Lord Dundreary in *Our American Cousin,* a part which he built up with the eccentric touches from his own imagination. Many English actors, such as Squire Bancroft, studied his characterization. The son, Edward Hugh, was educated in England, but joined his father in the United States and made his debut at the Park Theatre in 1879. He failed through terrible stage fright.

Later he acted with various companies in the United States before he achieved success. He was made a leading man by Daniel Frohman when Frohman took over the Lyceum Theatre in 1886. He built up his reputation as a light comedian and as an actor of romantic parts. One of his successes was Rudolf in *The Prisoner of Zenda,* in which he toured the country. His revival of his father's role in *Our American Cousin* was extremely popular. In 1904 he began his association with Julia Marlowe in Shakespearean repertory under the aegis of Daniel Frohman. In 1911 they were married. Sothern and Marlowe from that time on were identified with the roles of Shakespeare. In 1907 and in 1926 they presented their repertory in England. Arthur Symons said of them: "We have actresses who have many kinds of charm, actors who have many kinds of useful talent; but have we in our whole island two actors capable of giving so serious, so intelligent, so carefully finished, so vital an interpretation of Shakespeare, or, indeed, of rendering any form of poetic drama on the stage as the Englishman and Englishwoman who came to us ... in the guise of Americans: Julia Marlowe and Edward Sothern?"

In the lively dialogue from his autobiography Sothern reviews the long arguments concerning the actor as an artist and the study needed by the actor to achieve greatness on the stage.

Julia Marlowe (Sarah Frances Frost) was born in England and brought to America when she was about five years old. When she was thirteen she was engaged to play a small part in one of the juvenile Gilbert and Sullivan companies which were popular in those days. Later using her mother's name, Fanny Brough, she appeared in a *Rip Van Winkle* company and by 1883 had minor roles in *Romeo and Juliet* and *Twelfth Night* in the company of Colonel Miles. After a period of study and training in New York she appeared in a long list of plays, and by 1897, when she came under the management of C. B. Dillingham, her prosperity began. She specialized in dramatized novels and in popular melodramas. Her association in the Shakespearean repertory with Sothern put her talents to work in a long and distinguished career as an interpreter of the Bard.

I Talk to Myself

by Edward Hugh Sothern

"The child is father to the man," said I to myself as I contemplated that picture of "Me".... "And if you could materialize," I continued, "you would no doubt get down from your perch and demand of me, your offspring, how I have realized your hopes and expectations; to what extent, and why I have departed from your ideals; why I have compromised here and retreated there, and generally call upon me to explain why I am what I am, where I am, and who I am."

To my consternation, the large-headed, chubby-legged image climbed down from the chair, emerged from the photograph, fixed his goggle-eyes upon me and spoke: ...

"Acting is not an art!" said "Me."

"Really," said I, "you are a little prig."

"Abuse is no argument," said "Me."

"You repeat the cant of the critics," said I. "Look here—a dictionary—Webster: 'Art. The fine arts are those which have primarily to do with imagination and taste, and are applied to the production of what is beautiful. They include poetry, music, painting, engraving, sculpture, and architecture, but the term is often confined to painting, sculpture, and architecture'."

"Well?" said "Me."

"There you are," said I.

"But it does not mention acting," said "Me."

"No, it doesn't," said I, "but—"

"As I remarked," interrupted "Me," "acting is not an art. Now, poetry—"

"The poet must have an interpreter," said I.

"Pooh!" said "Me," "the actor is merely the instrument, as a fiddle—"

"Precisely," said I, "as a fiddle to the master violinist who interprets the works of the composers, so is the body of the actor to the directing mind of the actor. He executes upon himself as the violinist, the harpist, the pianist executes on his instru-

Edward Hugh Sothern: *Melancholy Tale of "Me"; My Remembrances.* New York: Charles Scribner's Sons, 1916, pp. 375, 381-397 *passim.* Copyright 1916, 1944. By permission of Charles Scribner's Sons.

ment. The difference is this: the musician's instrument is made by the hand of man, the actor's instrument is made by the hand of God. But—and here is the crux— the actor's instrument being himself—his own limbs, eyes, voice—the studied exercise of these members and faculties would seem to the vulgar mind ... that the trained, premeditated, selected, tasteful, inspired use of these faculties requires no art, no method of 'doing well some special work,' to quote from Webster's definition of art again."

Said "Me": "Any one can walk and talk and look and gesticulate."

"True," said I, "any one can do so in nature, but any one cannot do so with premeditated art"....

"Of course," said "Me," "you as an actor desire acting to be looked upon as an art."

"Assuredly I do," said I. "And there is the difficulty. It is hard for the player to speak for himself, a special plea seems a specious plea.... The last person who is permitted to have an opinion concerning the art of acting is the actor. It is admitted that he can know nothing about it....

"I tell you an actor can't speak for himself. I must confound you with authorities. Perception, selection, arrangement, execution: these are the steps of the artist in any art. These are the steps of the actor in the playing of his part. 'All artists have an individual style, a manner,' says Lewes. 'It is a fact, little understood by imitators, that the spots on the sun in no wise warm the world, and that a deficiency in light and heat cannot be replaced by a prodigality of spots.' A certain clever mimic had the good taste to perpetrate a burlesque of Henry Irving at a club supper. Irving complimented him and said: 'Excellent! excellent! Exactly like me. Why don't you play my parts?' Why indeed?"....

I continued: "A theatrical manager once wrote a volume to prove that acting was merely a collection of tricks, and that if one could learn all the tricks of all the celebrated actors one could exhibit or teach the art to the multitude with exactness. This, of course, is as though we should select all the mannerisms of all the distinguished painters, and exhibit them in one painting, or the styles of all the poets and combine them in one poem. 'Not from without *in*, but from within *out*,' speaks the artist. His mind informs and illuminates his medium, not his medium his mind. On the other hand, we should surely study the results achieved by the great actors, the means by which they secured their effects, just as one studies the old masters of painting or the giants of literature. At last one will formulate a style of one's own, as Robert Louis Stevenson relates that by practicing many styles he found himself. The facets of individuality are infinite, but each can reflect nature.

... "Tell me, and speak the truth, why do people go on the stage?"

"Some to make a living, as men preach or write books or sell pickles; some who are drawn to the drama as a means of expression."

"Expression of what?" yawned "Me."

"Of themselves, their conception of beauty, of life, or the ideal, as a vent for the imagination.... The imagination is exercised to an even greater extent in acting than in mere contemplation. I am not speaking of the gratification of the auditor, that is a separate matter. I mean the experience of the player. A man who can act, experiences an added exaltation over and above that of the simple reader. To passively absorb the poet's thought is a small satisfaction compared to the elation of acting greatly a great part, and conducting the emotions of an assembly as one conducts a vast orchestra. Shakespeare's plays were written by an actor for actors to act. They are an inspiration to the player, and, well acted, an inspiration to the auditor. Here is enough reason that a man or woman of intellect should go on the stage....

"...drama depends for success on fine acting. Fine acting is the result of practice and cultivation and ceaseless effort to train and perfect expression of voice, gesture, eye, and mind. All the scenery in the world will not set before you the heroes and heroines of Shakespeare. One great actor is worth all the paraphernalia on earth. Let us have a national theatre to satisfy the hunger of the poor, not to be a toy added to the superfluous playthings of the rich. All the precepts in the world cannot teach the art of acting. One must act to learn to act, as one must dance to learn to dance, or speak to learn to speak. Theory is useless without practice, and practice can only be secured on a stage before an audience. It has been said: 'In the theatre those who can act, act; those who can't act, teach acting.' This may not be entirely just. But it is certain that there is much leading of the blind by those who are in need of spectacles....

"To learn how to think, to avoid tricks, to express from within out, to steadily and patiently labor toward light and understanding and accomplishment—these can be acquired, given opportunity and instruction....

"It is most interesting and romantic to read of the difficulties encountered and overcome by Kean, Irving, and other great actors, also the comment is picturesque that obstacles beget solutions and prove the mettle of a man, but hearts are broken at this game as often as strengthened; great artists are slain as well as evolved by such a struggle. Who would not have had Chatterton and Francis Thompson dealt with more gently by fate? Might not Edmund Kean have been even a greater artist than he was had evil fate not wrung from him the tragic cry: 'If I succeed I shall go mad?' Is it not sad that genius cannot be planted at once in the soil where it may gather to itself all the glory of the earth?...

"The divine fire of genius cannot be ignited at will, but the weapons to be wielded by talent, and which even genius must keep keen and bright, may be sharpened and polished, and handled with skill even by those who are not inspired. Harsh, throaty, or nasal voices can be made musical; vile enunciation can be made perfect; awkward bodies and limbs can be made graceful; restlessness can be trained to repose; even taste and tact and observation of color, form, and sound can be quickened and cultivated. These transformations industry and opportunity may accomplish....

"...actors... must be gifted with imagination, with a high order of intelligence ...they must have sympathies quick and deep, nature capable of the greatest emotion dominated by passion. They must have impressive presence, and all that is manly should meet and unite in the actor; all that is womanly, tender, intense, and admirable should be lavishly bestowed upon the actress. The great actor must be acquainted with the heart, must know the motives, ends, objects, and desires that control the thoughts and acts of men. He must be familiar with many people, including the lowest and the highest, so that he may give to others clothed with flesh and blood the characters born of the poet's brain. The great actor must know the relations that exist between passion and voice, gesture and emphasis, expression and pose. The great actor must be a master of many arts. ...to produce a great play and put it worthily upon the stage involves most arts, many sciences, and nearly all that is artistic, poetic, and dramatic in the mind of man...."

The Eloquence of Silence

by JULIA MARLOWE

A carefully trained voice, able to follow all the "windings of the lengthened *oh*," is, of course, of great importance to the actress; yet it would seem to me, from observing great players, that they achieve their most impressive results through depicting in the countenance "the events of the soul."

Too much importance has been given to the human voice. It is for this reason that many players have given their whole attention to its cultivation, forgetting that in the delineation of character by impersonation, there are other and even more important aids.

It is curiously the case, that very many great actors were woefully deficient in the matter of enunciation. It was said, for example, of the great Colley Cibber that he had a "shrill voice apt to crack"; that Betterton's voice was "low and grumbling, like the notes of a harp played upon with a hammer"; that Garrick's generally failed him in great roles; and that Edmund Kean's was generally hard and husky, not naturally agreeable, and was wont to mount into a squeak.

John Philip Kemble, generally acknowledged during his time as a great actor, was constantly twitted by dramatic writers on account of his painfully singular enunciation. Reviewers of her time generally referred to Peg Woffington's voice as being harsh, and Mrs. Abington's as "not naturally pleasing to the ear." Another case in point is that of the famous French actress, Sophie Arnould. She was a great favorite during the time of Louis XIV and holds a high place among the idols of the French stage. Yet it was said of Sophie that she had "the finest asthma ever heard."

It will be seen, then, that these eminent players were able to achieve distinction in their calling despite the fact that their voices possessed qualities ungrateful to the ear. In other words, they were able to delineate and depict the "deep events of the soul." Great acting then does not depend upon the voice solely. Indeed, some of the most effective pieces of acting are achieved solely through the ability of keeping silent. A poet during Garrick's time hit off this truth in a couplet:

A single look more marks the internal woe
Then all the windings of the lengthened *oh*.

I recall, when a young girl, the first time I saw Edwin Booth. He and Lawrence Barrett were appearing in *Othello*. Barrett impersonated Othello, and Booth, Iago. As I had never seen Booth, I did not know him when he appeared on the scene. Suddenly I discovered a figure at the back of the stage intently watching the Moor. You could see plainly that he contemplated some demoniac act. His eye and manner at once caught the attention of the house long before he had said a word. The look on his face was crafty and devil-like. This one incident proved to me that there was very much more in acting than the polished delivery of lines.

I recall an even more striking example. Years ago, I saw a dramatization of Zola's novel, *Thérèse Racquin*. In this play there was the character of an old woman who became paralyzed through seeing a murder committed. This character during the entire action of the piece uttered not a word, and pretended that she could not

Julia Marlowe: "The Eloquence of Silence." New York: *The Green Book Magazine*, Volume IX, Number 3, March, 1913, pp. 393-401. Copyright 1913. By permission of Mrs. Edward Hugh Sothern.

hear. The audience knew that this was a ruse, yet she sat through the entire action of the play listening to the conversation of the guilty persons. Now this old woman, who did not once use her voice after the paralytic stroke, proved to be the most important figure in the play.

In Gordin's *The Kreutzer Sonata,* there is quite a remarkable example of the eloquence of silence. It will be recalled by those who saw the play that the wife, suspicious of her husband, sits down in silence by the window during an entire evening. The woman's sister and her husband have gone to the opera. She utters not a word, and after some little time, during which there is a most impressive silence, the curtain descends. Three hours are supposed to elapse before the next act, and when the curtain rises, the woman is still in the same attitude, silently meditating. This device pictured better than words her agonizing state of mind.

Another equally effective example is supplied by *Crime and Punishment,* a dramatization of Dostoyevsky's novel, which Paul Orleneff, the famous Russian actor, presented in New York two years ago. A critic described this incident: "The scene is in a little drinking place. A few stolid, roughly dressed men sit around wooden tables, with vodka before them. Among them is an old, broken-down drunkard. Orleneff, as the student Raskolnikoff, enters, seats himself before a glass of vodka, and listens to the old drunkard telling the story of his life.

"For nearly half an hour Orleneff does not say a word, and hardly moves. As the old man tells about his wife and children, how drink has ruined him and his family, how his young daughter has sold her virtue for the sake of the others, how he has learned to adore and worship the abandoned girl, who seems to him almost a saint, Orleneff's face, without the help even of his hands, reflects the drama in the old man's life. It does far more than that. By subtle, perfectly natural pantomime, the actor expresses not only sympathy and growing understanding of the old drunkard's situation, but a solemn, intensely serious criticism of all that poverty means. One feels that the Russian student is in line with the Nihilist tradition of Russia, and that what has been theoretical philosophy with him is taking concrete form as he listens to the old man. It is one of the most dramatic scenes I ever witnessed, and yet nothing happens in the usual sense of the word. But Orleneff's face tells the story of what is happening to him spiritually, and that accounts for the murders he commits in the next act."

A similar case is to be found in Bernstein's play *The Thief.* It will be recalled that the husband, while extracting a confession from his wife, utters not a word— a most effective piece of stage business. . . .

The inability to listen and to depict in the countenance what others have said has spoiled many a good actress. Only last winter I saw a young actress in a comedy who, had she not slighted this necessary requirement, would have been a most effective performer. When called upon to speak a line, or enter actively in a scene, she was excellent; but during intervals in which she was not engaged, she seemed utterly unconscious of what was going on. Her stolid inability to enter into the life of the play greatly marred its effectiveness, and utterly ruined her own part in it.

We have seen that many great actors such as Betterton, Garrick, Kean, Kemble, Woffington, and others, though handicapped by faulty enunciation, yet rose to the highest distinction in their calling. These actors, however, were exceptions to the rule, for we are informed that Barry's voice "could charm the birds off the bushes"; that Mrs. Oldfield's was particularly adapted to the proper interpretation of ripples of daintiness and fascinating fiction, and that Forrest's was like the martial music of a tramping host. But after all, it is the actor with an "eye" speaking like the star of night, who has won the greatest applause. A look often speaks volumes and reveals what the tongue could not—"the silent rhetoric of persuading eyes." The voice is important only when in use; the eye is never at rest. I think it was the late George Meredith who said that the flash of a woman's eye is an idea striking a light inside.

There is grandeur in stillness, and it is the eye that is the mind's signal and the soul's interpreter. It is the actor's chief business to express the emotion of the human heart. The eye discloses the tumult that rages within, and speaks the inner thought even more completely than can the tongue. It has a language of its own —an expression that is as far above any language as the eternal firmament is above the ephemeral butterfly.

Horace Walpole said that the voice of Mrs. Cibber, the soul of Mrs. Pritchard, and the eye of Garrick, formed a combination which in one actor would render him superior to all the actors the world had seen or should see. Walpole does not, however, give his opinion as to which of these—the voice or the eye—is more important. Howbeit, Garrick was the greatest of the trio, and it was his eyes and expression that made him so.

The imperfection of Edmund Kean's voice has been alluded to, yet a writer who had known him said: "He was remarkable for the silence and shyness with which he took his seat in the green room, his eye alone discoursing most eloquent music." His eyes at times "threatened like a loaded and leveled pistol," gleaming with scorching lustre. All who saw him act were struck with their marvelous power, in which might be seen the flash and outbreak of a fiery soul. He was able to still an angry audience with a single look, and in his most tragic flights, the superb play of his eye was said to be magnificent. Beneath the drooping lashes "slept a world of eloquent meaning."

All the mighty histrions of the dead past had singularly beautiful and expressive eyes—the unfailing symbols and insignia of a great soul. Tony Aston, in his *Brief Supplement*, dwells at considerable length on Betterton's wonderful and expressive eyes—eyes that spoke the soul's thoughts before the voice uttered them. He could transfix with a look, and a soft glance melted the hearts of the hardest listeners. In silence they had a speech which all could interpret.

Theatre-goers of today recall Edwin Booth's ever-glowing and radiant eyes, able unfailingly to express melting tenderness or withering scorn; love, anger, and avarice—all visibly moved those beautiful black orbs.

In brief, unless the actor is able to discourse most eloquently without opening his lips, he lacks the prime essential of a finished artist.

DAVID BELASCO

(1859-1931)

Of English-Portugese-Jewish stock, David Belasco was born in San Francisco, to which his actor-father had come during the gold rush. Young Belasco was sent to be educated at a monastery. (Perhaps this explains the semi-clerical garb Belasco wore throughout his life.) He ran away from the sheltered life to join a circus and soon became a barnstormer in rugged camp towns.

At a theatre in Virginia City, a Nevada mining town, Belasco met Dion Boucicault, from whom he acquired playwriting technique and ideals of realistic staging and acting. Under Boucicault the outlying theatre at Virginia City was transformed into a veritable school of acting. Belasco became Boucicault's secretary but did not follow him East. Back in San Francisco Belasco supported Edwin Booth and John McCullough, who performed in the lively western theatres.

By 1882, when he came to New York, he had already played 170 parts and had his hand in a hundred plays. In New York he was hired as stage manager and dramatist of the Madison Square Theatre. Here on the stage improved by the inventive Steele MacKaye, he continued realistic acting and staging in the Boucicault manner. In 1886 he joined Daniel Frohman at the Lyceum Theatre, where the productions, in Belasco's words, "were marked by great simplicity of treatment. There was no attempt to be theatrical. We used to depict life as the men and women who came to see us experienced it."

In 1895 when he starred Mrs. Leslie Carter in *The Heart of Maryland*, he emerged as an independent producer. Despite his difficulties with the Theatrical Syndicate, he persevered, overwhelming audiences with his magnificent productions and his new stars, Blanche Bates, David Warfield, Frances Starr, Lenore Ulric, and others. His plays were vehicles for his actors and for his lavish stagings.

Built in 1907, his Belasco Theatre on Forty-fourth Street housed the picturesque, naturalistic, detailed productions which have made this actor-playwright-producer famous. Although Belasco's facsimile stagings fell before the "new art" of Craig and Appia, his inventiveness especially in the use of stage lighting led Montrose Moses to say that Belasco understood better than anyone else the "response of the electric switchboard to human understanding."

An actor himself and a creator of stars, Belasco trained his performers and devoted much thought to the problems of the actor.

Acting as a Science

It is maintained often and with vigor that the school of acting is not of benefit in preparing for a career upon the stage—that acting cannot be taught. I have always wondered why a doctrine so subversive of reason should be—as it is—of such wide diffusion and enduring vitality; and likewise why discussions of it should be —as usually they are—restricted to proponents of the negative belief. I suppose the explanation is to be found in a general prevalence of what Mephistopheles designates "the spirit that denies." For my part, I believe that in most things the spirit that affirms is of far more service to the world. My views about learning to act are entirely affirmative, and accordingly they may perhaps be found of use by students for the stage.

Both a Science and an Art

When our teeth ache we visit a dentist; when the plumbing breaks we call a plumber. When acting and the teaching and learning of it are to be considered, the views of a veteran teacher of acting—who, as it happens, also is an old actor and an active producing theatrical manager—certainly are pertinent and admissible,

David Belasco: "About Acting." New York: *The Saturday Evening Post*, September 24, 1921, pp. 11, 93-94, 97-98. Copyright 1921. By permission of Edward M. Belasco.

and should be of interest and value. The notion that instruction in acting cannot be given, or rather that it cannot be received, is a mistaken one. . . .

Of course I do not mean to say that a novice can be made a master of stage technique by a few lessons—much less by reading anybody's essay on the subject. But acting is, like music, at once a science and an art—a science in its theory, an art in its practice. Being so, it is regulated upon definite, ascertained, enduring principles, and it is to be practiced according to "those rules of old discovered, not devised." Its grammar or mechanism can accordingly be taught, and must be learned by all histrionic aspirants if ever they are to become true and worthy artists of the stage.

And even within the limits of such an article as this, valuable suggestion can be offered and even practical instruction be imparted.

That which cannot be imparted is, of course, ability to act—which is innate or is not at all. But neither, for example can ability be imparted to paint, to compose music, to sing, to create literature. Yet the arts of painting, of musical and literary composition, of singing, are all taught to those who possess native aptitude for them; and so should acting be taught.

The Actor's Fundamental Attributes

By "the ability to act" I mean that strange natural faculty or gift, possessed by the born actor, whereby he is enabled to enter into, comprehend and interpret to others the experiences of, successively, many persons, often most unlike himself; of seeming to be them, to know all their joys and sorrows, think their thoughts, and veritably to live their lives. The requirement which underlies and conditions the doing of this is possession of extreme sensibility combined with quick and powerful intelligence.

A man may possess these attributes in combination and not be an actor; but he cannot truly be an actor if he does not possess them both; and, lacking them, some profession other than the stage should be selected, because if an actor does not possess sensibility far in excess of his audience he need not expect ever greatly to move it, while if he does not possess quick and powerful intelligence to perceive, control and direct the operations of his sensibility, he cannot become truly an artist, because he cannot ever be sure of his command of the expedients of expression and thus of his effects.

In my long and varied experience as a director I have, in performance or at rehearsal, observed such deplorable and destructive inability or incertitude scores of times. An actor possessed of the highest intellectual capacities but deficient in sensibility will be always cold, barren and ineffective; his performances will impress as, so to speak, lectures upon the characters he attempts—never as impersonations of them.

On the other hand, an actor possessing sensibility but lacking in power of mind and self-control will perhaps be capital in rendition of some scene of special emotional stress; called upon to go back and repeat the same scene his rendition will be puerile. Why? Because at best he possesses but half of the essential requisites for an actor; he cannot, at will, operate the expedients and devices of histrionic art. In a word, he does not know, can never master his business. The method must be mastered just as much in acting as in singing. A complaint which I make against players of the present is that as a class—and not forgetting honorable exceptions—

they are uneducated, or at best are very imperfectly educated, in the technique of their calling, and are indifferent to or unaware of their shortcomings.

Moreover, there are a great number of persons on the stage today who are not properly qualified by Nature for that vocation. But, even so, I venture to assert that the average of acting visible in America at the present time would be far higher if the generality of our actors had received even one year of competent instruction in the rudiments of that art which most of them have come to regard merely as a money-making business and vehicle for self-exploitation. A superfluous and merely mechanical actor, if well trained, is surely preferable to one who is not trained at all!

According to tradition these words in Latin were affixed as a motto to the Globe Theatre, London, in Shakespeare's time: "Everybody follows the trade of acting." In the present day it apparently is true that pretty much everybody feels competent to do so—and that without seeking even the slightest training for the trade. Yet acting is the most exact and exacting of arts. In it nothing can ever be left to chance —to an inspiration of the moment—after the performance has begun.

To wait, in acting, for inspiration to flash upon you is about as sensible as to wait until your house is in flames before looking for a fire escape. Night after night, often for many months, the same words must be spoken, the same actions be performed in the same way, in order to produce the same effects upon audiences which continually vary.

This is the reason why long and careful preparatory rehearsals are essential to all fine acting. And, oddly enough, a spirit of rebellious opposition to adequate rehearsals is daily growing stronger among actors themselves—who are incompetent to render their services without them! Nothing, I think, more impedes the restoration and maintenance of general prosperity in this country than the general greed to get more in return for less labor. Nowhere, I am sure, is that spirit stronger than it is in the theatre.

It is, I believe, safe to say that no actor ever produced a truly great effect in acting except as a result of long study, close thought, deliberate purpose and careful preparation. That is the testimony of all the masters—and to it I humbly add mine.

Salvini gave a year to the construction of his performance of Othello before he ventured to exhibit it in public—and he has testified that he never ceased to work on that part, yet could count upon the fingers of one hand the times when he had satisfied himself in it. Henry Irving studied and fashioned his personation of Becket —the character which, with Hamlet, he loved the best and in which he was perfection—during twenty years before he played it. So it has ever been with all great actors.

In the annals of the theatre the representative type of the impulsive actor, the consummate master of passionate expression, is that fiery genius Edmund Kean. Yet the impulsiveness of Kean—the torrid blaze and torrential flow of feeling in his acting—was all in seeming. So careful an artist was he, while at his best, that when he was rehearsing on a new stage he accurately counted the number of steps required to take him from one station to another, or the number that he should take before beginning a certain speech.

Of course there have been flashes of inspiration or fortunate accidents in acting, but they have been rare, and as far as I know they have affected only details. Thus Edwin Booth once early in his career, when acting Hamlet, in his first scene with the Ghost, accidentally let fall his drawn sword and, snatching it up in haste, held out toward the apparition, not the point of the blade as all actors hitherto had done, but its hilt—the protective symbol of the Holy Cross. And I have Booth's word for it that the expedient was clumsy and ineffective as thus first done naturally by accident, but impressively effective as done thereafter carefully and by design.

To all beginners on the stage, then—aye, and today to most of its veterans likewise—very earnestly do I say this: Remember in speaking that every sentence, sometimes every word, expresses a new thought or elaboration of thought. The thought, of course, precedes the word, and therefore by facial expression and bodily movement you must first make your audience, as it were, see you think, and then hear you think, by precise use of the most minute shadings of intonation required to express and convey the flow of thoughts.

In a discourse on acting by my old friend William Winter, delivered in New York nearly forty years ago, he said: "To convey your author's meaning correctly you must, of course, first correctly grasp it; and then in speaking you must cause it to well up in your mind, as though for the first time." So, too, in the beautiful drama of Deburau, which it was last season my privilege to produce in this country, the famous Pierrot, instructing his son and successor as to method in acting, says "First think it right."

One great aid in acquiring this faculty of thinking it right is scrupulous attention in listening to the speeches of all other characters than your own, receiving and weighing what they say always as though it were heard for the first time—and letting your speeches in reply well up in your consciousness as caused by what has been said to you.

The last time that ever I heard Booth speak Hamlet's immortal soliloquy on life and death was the last time that ever he spoke it in public, at the old Academy of Music, in Brooklyn, April 4, 1891. In the preceding fifteen years I had heard him speak that speech probably forty times; he was then old, worn and frail, yet the familiar words seemed to come from his lips for the first time, to utter thoughts then first formulated. . . .

The Art to Conceal Art

In acting take Nature as your model—but never fall into the error of attempting to present Nature in the stead of art. The speech of the stage should seem to be the speech of Nature. I say "should seem to be" because it is one of the parodoxes of acting that it cannot seem to be and never has seemed to be the speech of Nature when actually it is so.

That great thinker, the poet Goethe—a theatrical manager, by the way, and a successful one!—cogently remarked that "Art is art precisely because it is not Nature." True of all arts, it is most conspicuously true of the art of the theatre. There the incidents, events and emotions of days, months, years, often of a whole long lifetime, are to be epitomized and portrayed in moments. Everything about a stage representation is radically artificial. There with unrealities we work to create the effects of reality. It is easy to picture the consequences of turning loose upon the stage real sunlight, real fire, real rain, real wind, real dust, and so following.

We create the stage effects of real phenomena by mechanical imitations which seem real. So, likewise, is it and ever must it be in acting. That which seems real on the stage always is the illusory product of finished art; it is when the actor lacks art to conceal art that the audience sees him to be artificial.

Upon the stage it never is sufficient merely to indicate a meaning; there meaning must be conveyed. The art of acting is preeminently the art of expression. The casual easy utterance which serves for conversation in an ordinary room will not serve in a stage room, which always is of unnatural size, shape and condition—having canvas walls and being open upon one side—for there the sounds of a conversation must fill not merely a few hundreds but, instead, many thousands of cubic feet of space.

On the stage, accordingly, the play of facial expression must be quickened and intensified; the voice must be strengthened; the sigh which an audience is to hear as such must leave the actor's lips as almost a sob; the step in walking must be lengthened; the gesture broadened; the carriage elevated.

The Great Master has told us that the purpose of playing is "to hold, as 'twere, the mirror up to Nature." No way to failure in acting is so sure and so short as that of attempting to hold up Nature itself instead of the picture or reflection of Nature. The perfection of acting may be summarized in two words—namely, "illusion" and "effect." It is when the would-be realistic actor forgets this primary fact —which customarily he does forget—that he defeats his own purpose and, striving to be what he supposes is natural, seems to be only artificial and commonplace.

Does the Actor Feel His Part?

...It is as impossible for an actor who is incapable of feeling to be great in the representation of anything as it is for a painter to paint without colors. On the other hand, to assert that any actor must or even can really feel, when acting, all that he represents—assuming, of course, that he is representing any vital or even vivid emotional experience—is merely to maintain what is manifestly nonsensical. In acting there never can be, in the very nature of things, any real feeling.

Those dicta, taken together, sound paradoxical: An actor must feel in order to act; but in order to act he must not feel! The contradiction, however, is only apparent.

Let us look into the logic of the matter, and let me point my meaning with an extreme illustration...

An actor is called upon to represent a regicide and a bloody, brutal murderer —Macbeth, let us say. He cannot do so; he cannot portray the emotions of that character unless he really feels them—and he cannot of course really feel them unless he first murders a trusting old king—no very easy person to find these days—and a score or so of other innocent creatures....

The preposterous absurdity of such doctrine is patent, and it is none the less preposterous when applied to lesser experiences and feelings than those just indicated. What, for example, would be the condition of a player who, every night for even one week, should feel all the emotions of Hamlet or Othello or Lear; of Queen Margaret or Lady Macbeth or Juliet?

On the other hand, it is equally preposterous to expect actors to portray and express what they are incapable of feeling. And, parenthetically, it is because they cannot do so, and because as a class they are not notable for profound feeling, that we have so few great actors....

How, then, is the actor to traverse his dilemma if he must be capable of the most intense feeling, yet in acting must not feel at all? Why, by the medium of the imagination.

I have previously said that the fundamental requirement for the making of an actor is possession of extreme sensibility combined with quick and powerful intelligence. Those qualities are fundamental, but to them must be added imagination—and, all operant together, affecting each the others, they make acting possible.

The imagination conceives and evokes all the emotional sensations and reactions of a special character which is to be presented, in the circumstances and situations prescribed; the sensibility—by which I mean the capability of being vividly impressed and the capacity for being profoundly moved—experiences those sensations and reactions to the fullest extreme; the quick and powerful intelligence minutely observes their every effect and manifestation—registering in memory every inflection of voice, every play of feature, every movement of the body, every gesture—applies itself to creation of a perfect mental picture or record of them, and then to the reproduction and delicate exaggeration of them by means of all the artistic mechanism it has mastered and formulated.

This threefold process is repeated over and over again: at first in the lonely hours of study; then at rehearsals, finally during performance after performance in public, till at last the result is a reflection, a portrayal, a picture so vivid and exact in its apparent spontaneity and fidelity to truth that the fortunate spectators are enthralled and pronounce it perfect Nature. It is in fact perfect art.

What actors really mean—those of them who really are actors and not mere mountebanks—when they talk of real feeling is imagined feeling. But, it may be objected—as indeed, it often has been—if the actor must be capable of experiencing the profundity of emotions through the operations of his imagination upon his sensibility, why is he not thus to experience them when actually enacting them?

The answer is decisive: Because if he does so he will inevitably derange his artistic mechanism and, rendering himself incapable of expressing anything, defeat his purpose.

An actor in order to act must at all times be complete master of his resources and implements. Otherwise, though he may perhaps greatly affect himself, he will not at all affect his audience—unless it be to make it uneasy or excite its ridicule. Nowhere are complete self-control, dominion, poise, authority more absolutely essential to success than they are in acting, and they cannot exist where sensibility is permitted to hold sway.

In real life, the operations of elemental passion or profound feeling are never smooth; they never pause and wait their due effects upon dissociated observers. But the actor depicting them must, unperceived and unsuspected, continually do so. "I never saw an actor lose himself," declared Henry Irving, "who did not instantly lose his audience."...

One night, when playing Othello in America, Salvini, as he spoke the final words, "no way but this, killing myself to die upon a kiss," and collapsed in his appalling simulating of death, murmured to Miss Viola Allen, the player of Desdemona: "For the one hundred and third and last time this season!"...

...A great American comedian used to say, "Acting is a game of psychology." It is true. All that the actor does is but to reveal to the minds and souls of obervers the workings and experiences of the mind and soul of an assumed personality. And if you are going to affect and impress an audience you must dominate it—the audience must never dominate you....

...The actor who aims at being, and not seeming to be, real always also aims at being natural; the two things go together in his mind. The result of being natural is that an actor becomes merely commonplace and that most fatal of all things —uninteresting.

Why? Well, let us consider. What is natural—in any given situation? Many different persons would behave in many different ways in the same situation—even assuming that each felt the situation in the same way and to the same degree. Moreover, in many situations it is the disposition of most persons to repress their strong emotions—and as a rule the stronger those emotions are, the stronger will be the effort to control and conceal them.

In acting, however, the object must be expression, not repression. The actor must not attempt to do merely what would be natural for him to do; he must first ascertain what would be the natural reaction to and conduct in a given situation, of the special character he is to represent; and he must then display them by means of symbols common to and recognizable by humanity—for acting, like all arts, is symbolical.

Even when he has to portray a person of resolute, self-contained, reticent character and great self-control, who represses his emotions, the actor must by what one writer has named the device of transparency reveal to the audience that the person enacted feels but will not exhibit the appropriate motions.

The Individual Behind the Artist

The student of stage art will always encounter much decrying of the element of personality in acting—that is, he will hear much belittling of actors who possess vivid, pervasive, dominant personalities. It is detraction both stupid and idle. Personality is the greatest, the decisive element in art; above all, in the art of acting, where not only the art but the artist is on exhibition.

If you do not master the technique of acting, personality will never make you a true actor—though it may make you, as it often has made others, a popular success. But if you have not a personality of vivid, notable quality the most perfect mastery of stage technique will never make you a great actor or even a popular success. If you have not a message to transmit—what signifies it that your method of transmission may be perfect?

One of the wisest of dramatic critics—perhaps the only one who was not only a master of the art of criticism but who also had mastered the mechanism of acting —wrote: "Behind the artist always stands the individual." It is a simple but significant truth. What the artist does—and, ultimately, the manner and effect of its doing—always will be determined by what, essentially, the individual is.

Every character that an actor assumes must, of course, have a separate and distinctive physical investiture. It must be the face, the form, the voice, the gestures, the thought, feeling and experience of the assumed character, which are presented to the public. But as the face, the form, the voice, the mind of the actor are both the basis and the medium of the embodied personality, so, inevitably, the personality of the actor will appear, and should appear, in all the characters he represents.

When it was falsely rumored that Joseph Jefferson's place, as Rip Van Winkle, was being taken by one of his sons, purchasers of tickets requested the return of their money; they wished to see the great actor as Rip—not a substitute. It will always be the same. When you go to the theatre to see David Warfield play Peter Grimm, or Lenore Ulric as Kiki, you wish to see Mr. Warfield or Miss Ulric, and not understudies. It is the same in all arts. Who wants a portrait by Sargent which cannot be recognized as a Sargent?

MINNIE MADDERN FISKE

(1865 - 1932)

Mrs. Fiske (Mary Augusta Davey) was a force in American theatre for half a century. Born in New Orleans, a daughter of Thomas Davey, a pioneer theatre manager of the South and West, and the actress Lizzie Maddern, she was brought up in the theatre. Before she was sixteen she had appeared with Laura Keene, J. K. Emmet, Lucille Western, John McCullough, Joseph Jefferson, E. L. Davenport, and others. By 1880 she had become an *ingénue*. Her singing of "In the Gloaming" in *Caprice* made the song popular.

At twenty-five, following an unsuccessful first marriage, she became the wife of the playwright and dramatic critic Harrison Grey Fiske. Mrs. Fiske returned to the stage in 1894 in her husband's *Hester Crewe*. In the same year she also played *A Doll's House,* one of the first American performances of Ibsen. In 1901 the Fiskes leased the Manhattan Theatre as their headquarters and for eight years waged war against the Theatrical Syndicate, a combination of theatre owners and producers who had been cornering the leases or ownership of the majority of the country's theatres. The resistance of the Fiskes strengthened other independents.

Although as Minnie Maddern she was best known as a comedian, as Mrs. Fiske she was eager to attempt the modern drama—Pinero, Wilde, Shaw, and Ibsen. Seeking plays which would probe more deeply into the realities of human character, she encouraged native dramatists of the newer school. Langdon Mitchell's comedy of divorce, *The New York Idea,* and Edward Sheldon's *Salvation Nell* were two of her big successes. A contemporary observer tells us that in the first act of *Salvation Nell* "Mrs. Fiske, as the scrubwoman in the barroom, sat holding her drunken lover's head in her lap for fully ten minutes without a word, almost without a motion. Gradually one could watch nothing else; one became absorbed in the silent pathos of that dumb, sitting figure. Miss Mary Garden, herself a distinguished actress, said of this 'Ah to be able to do nothing like that!' "

Writing of her last New York appearance in *Ladies of the Jury,* the critic Robert Garland paid tribute to an aging favorite: "That Great Lady of the Theatre, that High Class Low Comedienne, that Grand Old Trouper whose name is Mrs. Fiske has returned once more to town...lending distinction to a shaky little play and acting circles around the younger generation.

"But pay no attention to anything I say in connection with the Great Lady of the Theatre.... Where Mrs. Fiske is concerned, I am in no way responsible. In these prejudiced and unreliable eyes, she can do no wrong."

To the Actor in the Making

...I like to remind myself that there can be, that there is, a complete technique of acting. Great acting, of course, is a thing of the spirit; in its best estate a conveyance of certain abstract spiritual qualities, with the person of the actor as medium. It is with this medium our science deals, with its slow, patient perfection as an in-

---

Mrs. Minnie Maddern Fiske: *Her Views on Actors, Acting and the Problems of Production; as told to Alexander Woollcott.* New York: Century Company, 1917, pp. 76-89 *passim.* Copyright 1917. By permission of the Viking Press, Inc.

strument. The eternal and immeasurable accident of the theatre which you call genius, that is a matter of the soul. But with every genius I have seen—Janauschek, Duse, Irving, Terry—there was always the last word in technical proficiency. The inborn, mysterious something in these players can only inspire. It cannot be imitated. No school can make a Duse. But with such genius as hers has always gone a supreme mastery of the science of acting, a precision of performance so satisfying that it continually renews our hope and belief that acting can be taught.

The science of acting is no term of mine. I first heard it used by the last person in the world you would ever associate with such a thought—Ellen Terry. It may be difficult to think of her indescribable iridescence in terms of exact technique, yet the first would have gone undiscovered without the second.

Undiscovered? Who shall say, then, how many mute and inglorious Duses have passed us in the theatre unobserved for want of this very science?

As soon as I suspect a fine effect is being achieved by accident I lose interest. I am not interested in unskilled labor. An accident—that is it. The scientific worker is an even worker. Any one may achieve on some rare occasion an outburst of genuine feeling, a gesture of imperishable beauty, a ringing accent of truth; but your scientific actor knows how he did it. He can repeat it again and again and again. He can be depended on. Once he has thought out his role and found the means to express his thought, he can always remember the means. And just as Paderewski may play with a different fire on different nights, but always strikes the same keys, so the skilled actor can use himself as a finely keyed instrument and thereon strike what notes he will. With due allowance for the varying mood and interest, the hundredth performance is as good as the first; or, for obvious reasons, far better. Genius is the great unknown quantity. Technique supplies a constant for the problem.

Fluency, flexibility, technique, precision, virtuosity, science—call it what you will. Why call it anything? Watch Pavlova dance, and there you have it. She knows her business. She has carried this mastery to such perfection that there is really no need of watching her at all. You know it will be all right. One glance at her, and you are sure. On most of our players one keeps an apprehensive eye, filled with dark suspicions and forebodings—forebodings based on sad experience. But I told [Gabrielle] Réjane once that a performance of hers would no sooner begin than I would feel perfectly free to go out of the theatre and take a walk. I knew she could be trusted. It would be all right. There was no need to stay and watch.

...Consider your voice; first, last, and always your voice. It is the beginning and the end of acting. Train that till it responds to your thought and purpose with absolute precision. Go at once...to some master of the voice, and, if need be, spend a whole year with him studying the art of speech. Learn it now, and practice it all your days in the theatre.

...One would be tempted to say that with the voice good and perfectly trained, our young actor might forget all the rest. It would take care of itself. And such a nicely calculated science it is! Just let me give you an illustration. You are to utter a cry of despair. You could do that? Are you sure it would sound perceptibly different from the cry of anguish? Do they seem alike? They are utterly different. See, this cry of despair must drop at the end, the inescapable suggestion of finality. The cry of anguish need not. They are entirely different sounds. And so it goes. Does it seem mechanical? Do these careful calculations seem belittling? They are of the science of acting. Only so can you master the instrument. And next your imagination....

Most of us would put the imagination first in the actor's equipment. Miss Terry did, and I suppose I should. Knowledge of life, understanding, vision—these, of course, are his strength. By these is his stature to be measured—by these and his imagination. If I put the voice first, it is a little because that is something the actor can easily develop; because it is, after all, concerned with the science of acting; and because also, he is likely to forget its importance, and if we put it first, he will remember it longer. The all-important thing, then, is the voice.

...and the imagination. And be reflective. Think. Does this seem so obvious as to be scarcely worth saying? Let me tell you... that an appalling proportion of the young players who pass our way cannot have spent one really reflective hour since the stage-door first closed behind them. I am sure they haven't. It would have left some trace. Why, the whole world may be the range of the actor's thoughts. I remember how delighted I was when I saw Duse quoted somewhere as saying that in her own art she had found most helpful and suggestive her studies in Greek architecture. That was so discerning and charming a thing to say that I'm afraid she didn't say it at all. But she should have.

Be reflective, then, and stay away from the theatre as much as you can. Stay out of the theatrical world, out of its petty interests, its inbreeding tendencies, its stifling atmosphere, its corroding influence. Once become "theatricalized," and you are lost, my friend; you are lost.

...Imagine a poet occupying his mind with the manners and customs of other poets, their plans, their methods, their prospects, their personal or professional affairs, their successes, their failures! Dwell in this artificial world, and you will know only the externals of acting. Never once will you have a renewal of inspiration.

The actor who lets the dust accumulate on his Ibsen, his Shakespeare, and his Bible, but pores greedily over every little column of theatrical news, is a lost soul. A club arranged so that actors can get together and talk, talk, talk about themselves might easily be dangerous to the actor in the making. Desert it. Go into the streets, into the slums, into the fashionable quarters. Go into the day courts and the night courts. Become acquainted with sorrow, with many kinds of sorrow. Learn of the wonderful heroism of the poor, of the incredible generosity of the very poor—a generosity of which the rich and the well-to-do have, for the most part, not the faintest conception. Go into the modest homes, into out-of-the-way corners, into the open country. Go where you can find something fresh to bring back to the stage. It is as valuable as youth unspoiled, as much better than the other thing as a lovely complexion is better than anything the rouge-pot can achieve.

There should be, there must be, a window open somewhere, a current of new air ever blowing through the theatre. I remember how earnestly I wanted to play Hedda Gabler, as though she had just driven up to the stage-door and had swept in not from the dressing-room, but out of the frosty night on to the stage. This you cannot do if you are forever jostling in the theatrical crowd. There you lose the blush of youth, the bloom of character. If as author, producer, director, or actor you become theatricalized, you are lost. The chance to do the fine thing may pass your way, but it is not for you. You cannot do it. You have been spoiled. You have spoiled yourself.

It is in the irony of things that the theatre should be the most dangerous place for the actor. But, then, after all, the world is the worst possible place, the most corrupting place, for the human soul. And just as there is no escape from the world, which follows us into the very heart of the desert, so the actor cannot escape the theatre. And the actor who is a dreamer need not. All of us can only strive to remain uncontaminated. In the world we must be unworldly; in the theatre the actor must be untheatrical.

... When a part comes to you, establish your own ideal for it, and, striving for that, let no man born of woman, let nothing under the heavens, come between it and you. Pay no attention to the other actors unless they be real actors. Like Jenny Wren, we know their tricks and their manners. Unless it is a bitter matter of bread and butter, pay no attention, or as little attention as possible, to the director, unless he is a real director. The chances are that he is wrong. The overwhelming chances are that he is "theatricalized," doing more harm than good. Do not let yourself be disturbed by his funny little ideas. Do not be corrupted, then, by the director. And above all—above all, you must ignore the audience's very existence. Above all, ignore the audience ... if you don't, you are lost forever....

OTIS SKINNER

(1858-1942)

One of the richest and most varied careers the American stage has known belonged to Otis Skinner. Born in Cambridge, Massachusetts, he received his first introduction to theatre managers through P. T. Barnum. In 1877 he made his professional debut at the Philadelphia Museum in the role of an aged Negro. In his first year at the Museum he appeared in no less than ninety-two parts. "There was no part I did not play," he wrote. "Even sex was no bar, for I was sometimes clapped into skirts for ... wenches and coarse old hags. I scowled as villains, stormed as heavy fathers, dashed about in light comedy, squirmed in character parts, grimaced in the comics, and tottered as the Pantaloon in the pantomime."

In the ensuing years Skinner acted with Edwin Booth, Mary Anderson, Lawrence Barrett, Madame Modjeska, and Mrs. Fiske. He was a member of the Augustin Daly Company with May Irwin, John Drew, and Ada Rehan. Hamlet, Macbeth, Shylock, and Falstaff were among his Shakespearean roles. Of his Falstaff John Mason Brown wrote: "It was a delight to see an actor unafraid to tackle the comic passages in Shakespeare, and able to keep them comic. His Sir John was no mere funny fat fellow, depending on his padding for his laughs. He was a rotund old devil of the taverns; self-indulgent and gluttonous, and yet possessed of an alchemy of pathos that made him lovable beyond his faults. He was sensed as a character, appraised in the terms of his theatre values, his 'points' ... catapulted across the footlights."

The roster of roles in which this fabulous trouper appeared in fifty years of his stage life is too enormous to list here. Otis Skinner has chronicled his epoch in a number of reminiscences including *Footlights and Spotlights, Mad Folk of the Theatre,* and *The Last Tragedian.* His daughter, Cornelia Otis Skinner, has carried on the family tradition as an actress, *diseuse,* and writer.

In 1929 Otis Skinner was awarded the American Academy of Arts and Letters Gold Medal for good diction on the stage. His speech of acceptance is given here

Good Diction

Since it is diction that has given me the favor of your consideration, perhaps it may not be amiss in me to say a word or two concerning my idea of what diction really is. It is a subtle and elusive thing, and in the maelstrom of confused standards in our polyglot American speech something readily ignored and often utterly lost sight of.

Since the birth of our nation demoralizing vocal seepings from every part of the globe, civilized and savage, have muddied the clear stream of our mother tongue. Even in England it has had to struggle through the handicaps of a dozen different dialects to sustain itself as English pure and undefiled, and by dialects, I am not omitting the London cockney, the gargled and throaty speech of the West End toff, the despairing wail of the Church of England clergyman, or the resigned melancholy in the professorial tones of the Oxford and Cambridge don. The Irishman will tell you that the only pure English is to be heard in Dublin and the Scotchman will insist that there is no true standard but Edinburgh.

In our own country the diversity of vocal tang is perhaps not so noticeable because it is spread over such vast areas, and our ears have grown callous to a universal sloppiness of utterance. We do not forget that we are a democracy and in our great Republic every man has a right—a *constitutional* right—to free speech, and "age cannot wither, nor custom stale, its infinite variety."

In the pot-pourri one hears the Puritanical nasality of New England, the shrill and raucous emphasis of Pennsylvania, the soft Negroid of Virginia, the drone of the mountaineer, the flat tones of Kentucky and Tennessee, the assertive R of the Middle West—that is so cherished in Michigan and Illinois it even attaches itself to the word *idea*—the Scandinavian lilt of Minnesota and Wisconsin and (God save the mark!) *New Yorkese*. Upon the speech of these sections has been superimposed the influence of every known language from Polynesia to Kamchatka. It is shot at our ears from the lips of public servants, saleswomen in department stores and our charming girl graduates; from Rotary and Kiwanis gatherings, from legislative halls and women's luncheon clubs. Its most devastating influence is all too frequently found in the unchastened accents of instructors in our public schools.

In this welter of mispronunciation—this catarrhal Babel—we must seek the material of which the future hope of the American theatre is formed. The first step in the development of our young actors is to rid them of the influence of linguistic neglect and it is astonishing to find how tone deaf most of them have become.

It seems to be a fact that the untrained ear tends to pick up the sins of enunciation sooner than its virtues, just as the immigrant Italian, quite innocently, is wont to babble words of profanity and blasphemy as his first contribution to the language of his adopted country. There is something fascinating in linguistic crime. Its insidious poison is like the one rotten apple in a basket of healthy fruit. Many of our youngsters in cultured families think it a bit unmanly to speak with care and accuracy. Their heroes are those of the movies and cheap fiction.

For some years we have had a menace to the well-being of the theatre in the movies and now a newer one in the radio. The first because it is silent and affords no example of diction to be followed, and the second because it does speak and

Otis Skinner: "Good Diction on the Stage." Boston: *The Emerson Quarterly*, Volume IX, Number 3, March, 1929, pp. 3-4. Copyright 1929. By permission of Emerson College.

with the generally raw voice of the announcer to say nothing of the rank material commonly constituting its amusement program. There was a time when the theatre held up a standard of diction in America. In France, Germany, Scandinavia and, in a large measure, in England, a standard is still maintained. Students are to this day sent to the *Théâtre Français* to listen to the perfect French of the actors.

I say of our stage "there was a time." This was in the days of the popularity of standard and classic plays—before the invasion of the dialect play, and the sports play, the crime play, the argot of the prize ring and the burlesque show—all written and spoken in the vernacular. The stage, however, should not be too severely censured for such vocal and verbal sins. It but reflects the linguistic evils of our time, and we have it on the authority of Shakespeare that the purpose of playing is "to hold as 'twere the mirror up to nature—to show the very age and body of the time his form and pressure."

I am not clamoring for a return of the formal utterance of the stage of our grandsires—its grandiloquence would be laughed at today. I can imagine nothing more uncomfortable than a household whose conversational tones were governed by the examples of Forrest, Macready and Charlotte Cushman, or to find myself at table with a hostess who carried her meticulous diction into daily life as did the celebrated Mrs. Siddons. It is reported of that lady that at dinner she stabbed her potatoes as though she were murdering King Duncan and, when purchasing a length of muslin for a dress, demanded of the mercer's clerk, "In God's name, sirrah, will it wash?"

Diction, then, is the means of clothing our ideas, of sustaining our arguments and sympathies with our daily companions in vocal terms which draw no attention from the subject matter. In its perfect form it is the common currency of our conversational intercourse with our fellowmen and its due reflection in the pulpit, the platform, the forum and the theatre. As with our monetary currency we must beware of its inflation or its debasement. It conserves the music of our mother tongue and keeps it free from corrupting influence.

When we are conscious of a precision in diction, of enunciation for its own sake, we are listening to speech too ornate or meticulous to be of value to human interest. If diction is in any way an art, it is an art that conceals itself. It is no longer an art when it obtrudes. It is a means, not an end; and the means of acquiring it are merely an attentive ear and a little care....

ALLA NAZIMOVA

(1879 - 1945)

Nazimova is the prototype of those cosmopolitan actresses who have enriched the American stage with their contributions of European technique and interpretation. Born in Russia and educated in Switzerland, Nazimova received her theatrical training under Nemirovich-Danchenko at the Philharmonic Society School and later with the Moscow Art Theatre. An obscure performance in Chirikov's *The Chosen People,* played in Russian in a hall on the lower East Side in 1905, marked her American debut. Though generally ignored, this production had the significance of introducing on the American stage a new type of acting and ensemble playing, derived from the work of the Moscow Art Theatre. A year and a half later, Nazimova triumphed in *Hedda Gabler,* this time in English. The next years saw her in a succession of Ibsen plays—*A Doll's House, The Master Builder, Little Eyolf*—which established her as the foremost interpreter of Ibsen characters. Her vivid, somewhat exotic, personality led an early critic to call her "a tigress in the leash of art." Important Nazimova characterizations were seen in O'Neill's *Mourning Becomes Electra* and in the 1936 revival of Ibsen's *Ghosts*.

Nazimova appeared in a number of motion pictures, including *A Doll's House, Salome, Camille,* and *The Madonna of the Streets*. Robert Benchley reviewing O'Neill's *Mourning Becomes Electra* wrote that "Nazimova, in spite of her Russian accent...made so much of the sinning Clytemnestra that the drama lost much when she withdrew into the shades of the House of Mannon never to return."

The following material is excerpted from an interview given by Alla Nazimova to Morton Eustis, who has recorded it in his valuable book *Players at Work*.

The Actor as an Instrument

The actor should not play a part. Like the Aeolian harps that used to be hung in the trees to be played only by the breeze, the actor should be an instrument *played upon* by the character he depicts. All the impulse which sets him free as a technician, or artist, should stem from the creature of the dramatist's imagining. The actor himself should be a creature of clay, of putty, capable of being molded into another form, another shape. The wind had but to ripple through the trees and the harp would play without conscious effort. The actor's assignment is more difficult. The breeze which stirs the player must sift, from the character, through the player's brain, his imagination and his body. And then, by conscious technical effort, the player must create the sound or fury, sense or sensibility, which the characterization demands....

An actor must never see himself in character. I study the woman. I look at her under a magnifying glass and say to myself: "Is she right? Is she logical? Is she true to herself? Can *I* act that woman? Can I make *myself* over into *her?*"

I am nothing. I am nobody. I have to reconstruct my whole self into this woman I am to portray—speak with her voice, laugh with her laughter—move with her motion. But if you can see the person as a living creature, quite removed from yourself, you can work objectively to adapt yourself to the part. Personally, I am no more like Hedda Tesman, Madame Ranevsky in *The Cherry Orchard*, or the brooding Christine in *Mourning Becomes Electra* than I am like the earth-bound O-Lan.[1] But if I can project the character so completely that the audience believes I *am* that character, then I have done my job well.

[Once you know] what she is thinking, what her inner response is, her feeling, when some other character is holding the stage...once you know what she *is*, what she *does* becomes easy to interpret.... You see that she could not possibly wear red, could not tie a pink bow in her hair, that she must wear gray, that she must be a blonde, that she must move in a given way, speak with a certain inflection. Sometimes, even, you may conceive a character as a blonde and play her as a blonde, though you do not wear a blonde wig. Nora in *A Doll's House* will always be a blonde to me, though I have always acted her with brown hair.

Morton Eustis: *Players at Work; Acting According to the Actors*. New York: Theatre Arts, 1937, pp. 51-58 *passim*. Copyright 1937. By permission of Mrs. Eustis and Robert M. MacGregor, Theatre Arts Books.

[1] Nazimova played the role of O-Lan in the Theatre Guild's *The Good Earth*.

Once the actor knows everything there is to know about a character's thoughts —far more, even than the author—he should grasp the vocabulary almost instinctively.

The director ... should tell the actor only what *not* to do. If he attempts to read lines, to show the actor the gesture he should use, he is a murderer—or he realizes, unfortunately, that he has to deal with an actor devoid of brain and imagination, and therefore must drill him as he would a parrot!

Directing is like conducting a symphony. There are musical sentences—*leit motifs* one can trace through the play. They grow and fade. Each act, like a piece of music, is divided into sections and each section has its own inner rhythm.

Sincerity and the correct use of voice are the greatest things in the art of acting. ... If I were to advise any American actors, I would say: "Make gramophone records. One false note or inflection may ruin an entire performance."

A good actor should be able to make an audience, any audience, feel what he wants it to feel. That is his assignment. ... But no losing yourself in the part! No being transported into other worlds by the emotion of the play! ... One watches oneself always. And the inspiration, the emotion, that the actor may feel —and often does feel—depend not so much on himself or on the character as on the interpretation, on the realization that he is projecting the desired illusion. If I thought for one second about *my* emotion while acting, I would be completely side-tracked.

First, last and always, a player must have imagination. Without imagination, he might as well be a shoe-black as an actor. Imagination kindles the feelings, steers the actor through the character into emotion, enables him to reproduce feelings he himself has never experienced.

If any playwright can teach an actor how to play, Ibsen has taught me. The reason is that he is true. There is not one line, one word, whose origin of thought you cannot trace. The same is true of Chekhov. But it is a very rare quality in a playwright.

JOHN BARRYMORE
(1882-1942)

John Barrymore was a scion of a great theatrical family. From his grandmother, Louisa Lane Drew, his uncle, John Drew, his mother, Georgianna, and his father, Maurice Barrymore, he inherited a family histrionic tradition almost a hundred years old.

Although the three Barrymores, John, Lionel, and Ethel, took their place in the American theatrical pantheon, none of them wanted to make theatre his life's work. John, like Lionel, wanted to become a painter. He studied art for a while and did illustrations for newspapers. "Neither Jack nor myself," Lionel Barrymore once said, "preferred the stage. ... Yet it seemed that we had to be actors. It was as if our father had been a street cleaner, and had dropped dead near a fire hydrant, and we went out to pick up the shovel and broom to continue his work."

The ups and downs of John Barrymore's Villonesque career have been chronicled in Gene Fowler's affectionate biography, *Good Night, Sweet Prince.*[1] Fowler tells us that by 1903 John Barrymore had acquired some professional theatrical experience and made his New York debut as Corley in *Glad of It.* During the next

---

[1]All quotations from *Good Night, Sweet Prince* by permission of the Viking Press.

four years he was trained as a comedian by William Collier, with whom he went to England to play in Richard Harding Davis' *The Dictator*. It was thus as a comedian that Barrymore achieved his early stage success. The part of Nat Duncan in *The Fortune Hunter* made him a star in 1909.

The erratic young comedian, influenced by his friend, the dramatist Edward Sheldon, turned to serious drama by 1916. His performances in *Justice* and *Peter Ibbetson* established his popularity and his serious artistry. Constance Collier, his leading lady in *Peter Ibbetson,* said of him, "He was the greatest of all the actors I ever saw, and I knew Irving and Tree and so many of the great ones."

It was with Arthur Hopkins as director that Barrymore created his great roles. Hopkins reports that he and Barrymore "dreamed of a great classical repertoire that would one day tour the world." Their first joint effort was Tolstoy's *Redemption*. During the preparations for this production Hopkins began to understand Barrymore's unique personality and genius. "His rich imagination seemed to find its most arresting conjurings in ribaldry. There was constantly being unrolled before him a series of hilarious pictures, for which he knew the precise and shattering words. One realized that it was no easy task for a mind so engrossingly inhabited to avoid all pleasant wanderings and really confine itself to the painful creation of an entirely new picture, the picture of a proud, human soul in turmoil and death. . . . Rehearsals for him were a ceaseless quest. This was not externalized by a conscious seeking for the impressive pose or the embroidered reading. He weaved himself into the complete texture, leaving no bright threads lying to emphasize his presence. He was the director's dream, an actor who asked no special emphasis." Hopkins and Barrymore cut short the flourishing success of *Redemption* to continue building their projected repertory. Their second venture, *The Jest,* was equally acclaimed, but the performances were terminated to make way for the overwhelming work on *Richard III*.

Hopkins tells us that the production of *Richard III* was planned for a year with the hope that its success would "open the door to Shakespeare." Barrymore gave all he had, hard work, intensity, imagination, to the creation of the deformed Richard. He studied with Margaret Carrington to improve his voice and to gain the control necessary for speaking verse. Even in the matter of costume Barrymore was meticulous. Shabby, rented stage armor was not for him. He had an authentic suit of heavy armor made for him and a sword copied from originals of the period. Every detail of the character, external and internal, was subjected to careful scrutiny. There is little doubt that Barrymore was justified when he said, "I don't know how bad or good I was in Richard. I rather believe it was the first genuine acting I ever managed to achieve, and perhaps my own best. It was the first time I ever actually got *inside* the character I was playing. I thought I *was* the character, and in my dreams I *knew* that I was he."

Again a successful production was abruptly ended; this time the intensity of the role and the "frantic pursuit of a new marriage" brought Barrymore to the verge of collapse. The Hopkins-Barrymore plans for a "great repertoire" faded. Of the remaining plays in their scheme, which included *Liliom, Cyrano de Bergerac,* and *Richard II,* only *Hamlet* was eventually done.

In 1922 the plan for the production of *Hamlet* took shape. Barrymore's greatest performance was the result of long study and careful preparation. All the intricacies of the complex character were explored before the lines were memorized. As director Arthur Hopkins allowed Barrymore to create a Hamlet "unencumbered by traditional barnacles." Robert Edmond Jones provided a subtle set. Unfortunately Barrymore has left no analysis of his method of work and interpretation of his master role. All we know is that he found the part easy and reveled in its theatrical breadth. "You can play it standing, sitting, lying down, or, if you insist, kneeling. . . . It makes no difference as regards your stance or your mood. There are, within the precincts of this great role, a thousand Hamlets, anyone of which will keep in step with your whim of the evening." Audiences and critics alike hailed "the first Hamlet of our generation." Barrymore outdistanced Edwin Booth's celebrated 100 performances by one. "The new prince was entering his kingdom."

Always quixotic, sensitive, moved by strange impulses, Barrymore left the stage at the height of his career following his successful London performances of *Hamlet*. He came to Hollywood to make films on a contract that gave full recognition to his artistic position and his fame. Even before this time John and Lionel had been associated with numerous early films. Between 1925 when the successful actor reigned supreme in the production of *The Sea Beast* and 1936 when he played Mercutio, supporting Norma Shearer and Leslie Howard in *Romeo and Juliet,* Barrymore's comet flared and faded.

In 1938, beset by economic and marital difficulties, Barrymore returned to the stage. Advancing years, bouts with the "barleycorn," and occasional lapses of memory had dimmed the lustre of the star. Barrymore began to play, on stage and off, a "clownish crucifixion" of the great mime. His old friend Ashton Stevens wrote of his final stage vehicle, *My Dear Children*: "His role in the crude comedy practically amounted to an autobiography of the Barrymore of first-page fiction and gossip columny and radio self-caricature. He hammed and hawed the role to their hoarse delight." Amidst this gargantuan grotesque of his life and talent, Barrymore yet fascinated audiences by that very art which he was lampooning.

All those who worked with Barrymore have testified to his serious, personal artistry. He himself treated acting publicly as merely one of many activities in his rollicking life and left only few casual remarks about his work. Arthur Hopkins, the director of his greatest performances, eloquently analyzed Barrymore's art. "At all moments Barrymore was the artist. He created out of his own texture. He borrowed nothing. He copied nothing. His whole search was within himself. His wine was from his own vine. Whatever jewels adorned his final creation were brought from his own inner contact with the deep richness that is hidden in all men but found by so few. It is the finding that makes the true artist brother to all mankind. In revealing himself he reveals others to themselves."

Maxims of an Actor

Acting is the art of saying a thing on the stage as if you believed every word you utter to be as true as the eternal verities of life; it is the art of doing a thing on the stage as if the logic of the event demanded that precise act and no other; and of doing and saying the thing as spontaneously as if you were confronted with the situation in which you were acting, for the first time.

A man isn't an actor until he commands a technique which enables him to get an impression across into the heart of an audience without reference or relation to his own individuality. The better the actor, the more completely is he able to eliminate the personal equation. It is irritating to hear people talk about "David Warfield parts," or "John Drew parts," or "Mrs. Fiske parts," as if such fine and genuine art as theirs were circumscribed to a narrow, personal form of expression.

Take the case of Leo Ditrichstein, for example. Nothing can be less like Leo Ditrichstein than a Leo Ditrichstein part. Mr. Ditrichstein is a serious, scholarly, musical gentleman, and yet because he has no peer .in portraying the philandering dillettante, he is constantly cast for that type of character. And audiences identify him with that kind of role, forgetting or ignoring the fact that the fine technique which enables him to play those gay triflers with brilliant freshness and conviction, would stand him in good stead in widely different roles.

The art of America is poorer today because the will of the public obliged an actor so trenchantly equipped for a wide range of roles as was Joe Jefferson to confine his genius to one line of characterization and to play Rip Van Winkle for a period longer than the lifetime of most actors.[1]

* * * *

... An actor's performance, at best, is the way he happens to feel about a certain character....

I'm a bit of Peter Ibbetson and a bit of Jack Barrymore. At least, I never utterly forget Jack Barrymore—or things he's thought or done—or had done to him. It's a curious mental state. I never can understand the actors who say they lose themselves completely in a part. I don't know what they are talking about. Yet there's a double identity that's very real—to me—and, somehow, never quite the same. I mean the details are not always the same. I'll try to explain:

I leave my dressing room to make Peter's first entrance. I am Jack Barrymore —Jack Barrymore smoking a cigarette. But before I make the entrance I have thrown away the cigarette and become more Ibbetson than Barrymore. By the time I'm visible to the audience I am Ibbetson, quite.

That is, you see—I hope to make this clear—on my way to the entrance I have pased imaginary flunkies and given up my hat and coat. Peter would have had a hat and coat—naturally; and would have given them up. And he's a timid fellow. He gives up his imaginary hat and coat to these imaginary flunkies just as I, Jack Barrymore—and very timid then—once gave up my hat and coat to flunkies at a great ball given by Mrs. Astor.

Of course I don't always make Peter's entrance with the memory of a bashful boy at Mrs. Astor's ball. That would harden the memory—make it useless. You couldn't keep on conjuring up the same thing. You have to have different things to get the same emotion....

At times I think of my own mother (when choking Colonel Ibbetson) putting me to bed—how sweet she was. Then I can put a lot of gusto into choking the old rascal.

One time—when my brother Lionel played him—I had him get some horrible, some cheap and nasty, perfume. A whiff of that and I could feel a fine frenzy. Not that I ever actually whiffed it. But the idea of this old stinker smelling like what he really was—you understand—or maybe you don't at all—I'm afraid I'm a bum psychologist....[2]

---

[1]Helen Ten Broeck: "From Comedy to Tragedy; an interview with John Barrymore." New York, *Theatre Magazine*, July, 1916, pp. 23.

[2]Ashton Stevens: *Actorviews*. Chicago: Covici-McGee Company, 1923, pp. 64, 66-67. Copyright 1923. By permission of Ashton Stevens.

LAURETTE TAYLOR

(1887-1946)

Laurette Taylor served an apprenticeship in vaudeville and the off-Broadway stage before her first New York appearance in 1903 in *From Rags to Riches*. By the winter of 1912 when her name went up on the marquee of the Cort Theatre as the star of *Peg O' My Heart*, she had behind her a long list of successes; *Alias Jimmy Valentine, Girl In Waiting, Seven Sisters, A Bird of Paradise,* and others. Written by her husband J. Hartley Manners, *Peg,* the tale of an Irish-American waif, ran for 604 performances including a special showing at eleven o'clock in the morning for Sarah Bernhardt.

In 1916, after she had returned to New York from London, where *Peg* had been given for five hundred performances, Laurette Taylor played in *The Harp of Life.* Supporting her was an English-born actress whom Miss Taylor had brought from London—Lynn Fontanne. For ten years Laurette Taylor appeared only in plays written by her husband. The only exception was a series of special matinees devoted to scenes from Shakespeare in which she essayed the roles of Juliet, Portia, and Katherine. In addition to supplying Laurette Taylor with good scripts, Hartley Manners had taught her much about acting. "He has given me," she said, "a sense of the fitness of things—a sense of proportion." When he died in 1928, Miss Taylor virtually retired from the stage for ten years until the role of the charwoman mother of a wayward son, Mrs. Midget in *Outward Bound,* challenged her imagination. Interviewed during the run of this play Laurette Taylor gave a newspaper reporter a provocative definition of her art: "Acting is the physical representation of a mental picture and the projection of an emotional concept."

Six years elapsed before Laurette Taylor found the role which would reveal to a new generation of theatre-goers the magic of her playing. As Amanda Wingfield in Tennessee Williams' *The Glass Menagerie,* she gave a completely remarkable performance, modern, fresh, and unmarked by any sign of "return to the stage" by an actress whose last great starring vehicle had been Fannie Hurst's *Humoresque* in 1923. Of her very "personalized" characterization of Amanda Wingfield, Norris Houghton wrote: "The student of acting sits before her performance and marvels at the series of constant surprises with which she rewards him. Her phrasing and accent of a line is so often unexpected, her movement so unanticipated. But each surprise is confirmed and justified by its inevitability.... To traffic in the unexpected for its own sake is dangerous; when Miss Taylor offers the unexpected, you say 'Of course. That is the only way it should have been done.' There is not a single cliche in her performance from beginning to end. That is why you sit so breathless to see what this woman will do next."

For an indication of the well-spring of her amazing artistry we turn to Laurette Taylor's credo written early in her career.

The Quality Most Needed

I have been asked to discuss, for the benefit of those who may go on the stage, the qualities which are most important as elements of success. If merely the finan-

Laurette Taylor: "The Quality You Need Most." New York: *The Green Book Magazine,* April, 1914, pp. 556-562. Copyright 1914.

cial or popular success of a woman star is meant, I should say that beauty is more essential than magnetism. But if by success you mean all that is implied by the magical word *Art*—success in the sense that Bernhardt, Duse and Ellen Terry are successes—I should say most emphatically the reverse. And I should add that imagination is more important than either.

Mere beauty is unimportant; in many cases it proves a genuine handicap. Beautiful women seldom want to act. They are afraid of emotion and they do not try to extract anything from a character that they are portraying, because in expressing emotion they may encourage crow's feet and laughing wrinkles. They avoid anything that will disturb their placidity of countenance, for placidity of countenance insures a smooth skin.

Beauty is not all-important as an asset, even when the star is not anxious to achieve true greatness. Many of our most charming comediennes are not pretty women. Rather, they are women of great charm and personality. I cannot for the moment recall a single great actress who is a beauty. At least not in the popularly accepted idea of what constitutes beauty.

Personality is more important than beauty, but imagination is more important than both of them.

Beauty as I understand it does not mean simple prettiness, but stands for something illusive and subtle. The obvious seldom charms after one has had to live close to it for any length of time. Being all on the surface, there is nothing left to exhilarate, once the surface has been explored. On the other hand, the beauty which emanates from within becomes more enchanting upon close acquaintance. It is constantly revealing itself in some new guise and becomes a continual source of joy to the fortunate persons who have the privilege of meeting it frequently.

That is beauty of the imagination, and that beauty all the really great actresses have.

The case of Bernhardt is as good an example as one would wish. In her youth especially, she was the very apotheosis of ugliness; still, through the power of her rich imagination that glorified her every thought and act, she held her audiences in the hollow of her hand. It is the strength and richness of her wonderful creative mind that makes it possible for her to present the amazing illusion of youth which she does even today.

It isn't beauty or personality or magnetism that makes a really great actress. It is imagination, though these other qualities are useful.

You see a queer little child sitting in the middle of a mud puddle. She attracts you and holds your interest. You even smile in sympathy. Why? Simply because that child is exercising her creative imagination. She is attributing to mud pies the delicious qualities of the pies which mother makes in the kitchen. You may not stop to realize that this is what is going on in the child's mind, but unconsciously it is communicated to you. It is the quality of imagination that has held your attention. . . .

We create in the imagination the character we wish to express. If it is real and vital to us in imagination we will be able to express it with freedom and surety. But we must conceive it as a whole before we begin to express it.

There will be those who will disagree with me and say that magnetism presupposes imagination. This is a mistake. Many magnetic actresses are wholly lacking in imagination, their hold upon the public resting chiefly upon personality and charm and beauty. Have you ever gone to a tea party where you met some very magnetic woman who radiated charm, who not only held your attention but exhilarated you until you became impatient to see this scintillating creature on the stage, where you might realize the fullness of her wonder? And have you not felt, when your opportunity came and you saw her on the stage at last, the disappointment of realizing a wooden lady with a beautiful mask for a face, speaking faultlessly articulated lines—an actress who rose desperately to the big moments of her part, and who never for a moment let you forget that it was she, that actress, whom you saw, not the character whom she was portraying? There may have been splendid acting but you were conscious of the fact that it was *acting*. There was no illusion. She was conscious at the big climax that she was acting this part and that she must reach this climax. She was acting as much to herself as to you. That is not the art of the great actress. The imaginative actress builds a picture, using all her heart and soul and brain. She builds this picture not alone for the people out in front but for herself. She believes in it and she makes the people across the footlights believe in it. Unless she has done this she has failed. She must stimulate the imagination of the audience. An actress should not only be able to play a part; she should be able to play *with* it. Above all, she should not allow anything to stand between her and the thing she is expressing.

How often does an actress play a part so as to leave you with the feeling that you have so intimate a knowledge of the character that you could imagine its conduct in any position, aside from the situations involved in the action of the play? Unless this happens, you feel that after all you have seen a limited portrayal of the character and you realize that though the acting was practically flawless there was something missing. And, in nine cases out of ten, that is because the woman playing the part did not use any imagination. She was entirely bound by the traditions of the theatre. She did everything just as it would have been done by anyone else on the stage. This is fatal.

You feel untouched by the play because it was not made *real* to you.

The artist looks for the unusual. She watches everyone, always searching for the unusual in clothes, in manner, in gesture. The imaginative actress will even remember that the French have characteristics other than the shrug!

Think of the number of times that there have been Irish plays, of the number of times that the Irish character has been used in the working out of a plot. Yet never, to my knowledge, has an Irishman been played on the stage. (This excepts, of course, Lady Gregory's players and Guy Standing's rendition of a current Irish-American role.) Real Irishmen have never been played. The Irish can be the most melancholy people on the face of the earth, yet the traditional stage Irish have been lilting colleens and joking Paddies.

The most interesting thing to me in acting is the working out of the character itself, the finding of that which is uncommon and the small, seemingly insignificant trait which will unconsciously make an appeal to the audience and establish the human appeal. Too much importance is laid on clothes. In the main, I think that all clothes hamper unless they express the character. Personally, I detest "straight" parts for that reason. They necessitate the clothes that make me self-conscious—or, rather, "clothes conscious."

I want to get right inside the character and act from the heart as well as from the head. That is impossible unless one is free from outside interference.

I think actresses pay too much attention to the tradition of acting. That is a great mistake. It cramps creative instinct. I received a good deal of criticism for my walk in *The Bird of Paradise*. Some of the critics said I should be taught how to walk across the stage. Of course I paid no attention to that. My walk was the walk of the barefoot Italians who carry loads on their heads, and I had learned it from them. It certainly was not the traditional stage walk, but we are living in a time when simplicity and truth are the watchwords of the theatre. The traditional stage walk would not have fitted the character I played.

The stage has come to a period of simplicity. A few years ago the direct attitude adopted by the younger actresses of today toward their roles would have been considered ridiculous. The changes have been positive but subtle, and the actress without concentration has been unable to discern them. They are the ones who are still sparring for time in their emotional scenes, using the traditional tricks to express grief, joy, surprise, chagrin; and they wonder why they are sitting at home without engagements. They cannot comprehend that the very little basket of tricks which made them the idols of a few years ago fails utterly to get results today....

The time has come when we may as well realize that we can no longer give a filmy portrayal of emotion and pad it out with stereotyped pieces of "business." The younger actresses of today express the elemental emotions as the elemental person would express them in real life. There is no such thing as a compromise in the logical development of a character in order to make a theatrical effect....

Too few actresses follow their instinct. I think instinct is the direct connection with truth.

It is not enough to know just what you are to do yourself in the action of a piece; you must know also the exact relation you must bear to every other character in the play.

For instance, take the business of dying. You must in your imagination realize not only the fact that you are dying but the effect which your death will have on every character related to your part. You know that you are not dying and the audience knows it, but in your imagination you must really believe you are. The business of dying becomes actual to you; also, you compel the audience to believe in you by the very sincerity of your attitude.

This trait is really remarkable in Maude Adams. Recall her work in *Chantecler*. Without her tremendous imagination to gild her impersonation, this frail little woman would have been hopeless in the part. Yet through her marvelous richness of imagination she produced the illusion of bigness that many women better fitted physically could not have done.

One would never say that Maude Adams is beautiful, in the sense that she is pretty or has a beautiful physique; but she has charm, magnetism and imagination. These three make a beauty that transcends mere beauty.

Beauty, personality and magnetism are not important in the equipment of a star, when compared to the creative faculty of *imagination*. The first three qualities are valuable adjuncts, and no one should sneeze at them. But you might get along without the slightest beauty and little or no personal magnetism if you were generously endowed with the imaginative mind.

WALTER HUSTON

(1884 - 1950)

Walter Huston is representative of the veteran trouper schooled in stock, vaudeville, the stage, and the screen. Born in Toronto, he made his first stage appearance

there in 1902. New York saw him first in 1905 in Hal Reid's drama *In Convict Stripes,*
followed by a minor role in Richard Mansfield's production of *Julius Caesar.* After
touring in *The Sign of the Cross,* Huston left the stage for a number of years. In
1909 he reappeared in vaudeville with his first wife. As Whipple and Huston, they
did sketches on the circuit until 1924. In that year Huston undertook the role of
Ephraim Cabot, the frost-bitten patriarch in O'Neill's *Desire Under the Elms.* This
production in Greenwich Village was sponsored by O'Neill, Kenneth MacGowan,
and Robert Edmond Jones, who directed it with great sensitivity. Although the play
brought down the wrath of the blue-noses it was defended by established, respectable theatrical figures like Brander Matthews, Percy MacKaye, and Edward Sheldon.
Other early roles included Ponce de Leon in *The Fountain,* Flint in *Kongo,* and a
memorable performance as Nifty Miller in *The Barker.*

In 1934 came Huston's Sam Dodsworth in Sidney Howard's stage version of
the Sinclair Lewis novel. Huston and Fay Bainter as Mrs. Dodsworth were the perfect personification of the typical mid-western middle-class couple. Huston created
the role again for the films. At Central City, Colorado, in 1934, Huston first shaped
the role of Othello which he brought to New York in 1937. It is the problems
growing out of this characterization which are analyzed by Mr. Huston in his contribution to this volume.

Walter Huston has had a distinguished film career which began in 1928 with
Gentlemen of the Press and has included *Abraham Lincoln, Rain, The Shanghai
Gesture,* and many others. Huston's portrayal of the toothless prospector in his son
John Huston's *Treasure of the Sierra Madre,* which featured Humphrey Bogart,
won an Academy Award in 1949. John Huston, carrying on the family tradition in
a new medium, took the Academy Award for the best direction.

The Success and Failure of a Role

...We were about to open *Othello* in New York.... We knew we were fairly
intelligent actors. But just so there would be no doubt about it we sailed in and
played *Othello* with a relish and a zest, played it as we would have on a dare—
with all the knowledge we had, with all the verve and understanding we could
bring to it. Our performances were made better by the stimulation of a large New
York first-night audience, which always brings a great excitement to bestow upon
the play if the actors will absorb it.

For my own part, I never felt better on any stage than I did that night. My
performance, it seemed to me, had never been so keen. Between acts I spoke of it,
"I'm really enjoying this," I said. "I've never known it to go like this." And everyone else seemed to feel the same. There was no doubt in our minds that the audience felt it too, for we on stage could sense it. We felt we had it in the palms of our
hands. That we could move it at will ... we were certain we were a success ... we
earnestly believed, as deep down as a man can, that we had given a hell of a performance, as fine a piece of work as our lives ever fashioned....

Certainly I had never had that warm feeling of successful achievement as I had

---

it that night. It occurred to me during the broil and confusion of the aftermath that I had spent too many years of my life outside the magic circle of Shakespeare....

I awoke at seven o'clock ... and, having awakened, I could not resist the disturbing desire to see the morning papers ... I decided to read the *News* first, for I knew that Burns Mantle's star system of rating could be seen at a glance ... the two-and-a-half stars I found above Mr. Mantle's column gave me a shock. That meant he had found little in *Othello* to praise....

Hastily I picked up the *Times*.... Tabloids might be all right for the movies and the modern drama, but for appreciation of the classics, I assured myself, one had to look to the *Times*. Imagine the shock to find that Mr. Atkinson's opinion was no more favorable than Mr. Mantle's! Quickly I snatched up the other papers, as a stunned prize fighter clutches his opponent, but as I read them one by one it slowly dawned on me that the show was a failure. I could hardly believe it. After all those months of work, after all that fond care, after all that had been said, after hundreds of changes and experiments—after we had patted down every minute detail, could it be that we had produced a poor thing?

The brunt of all the criticism fell on me. No matter how I deluded myself, I could not escape the clear cry against my performance. I tried to tell myself that the trouble with the critics was that they did not want me, whom they considered a homespun fellow, to try to put on airs. I refused to see any truth in the adverse criticism I read, but instead turned it around and used it to criticize the critics. Did they not know that I had studied the role longer, had given it more thought than any role I had ever played? Couldn't they accept my conception rather than dictate to me from their own ignorance? But then I knew this argument would not hold water, either. All they knew about my performance, I was slow to admit, was that it did not move them; that it did not grasp and hold their interest; that it did not entertain them, did not ring their approbative bells. On the contrary, their stomachs ached for me. But then I knew that even if I had encompassed the character of the Einstein Theory so that it made plain and good sense to me, it need not necessarily therefore appeal to the public. That was a hard and large lump to swallow.

What made it so hard, I guess, is the fact that *Othello* [was] my first failure in thirteen years—that and the fact that I had bent every effort toward making it as fine a production as the American theatre had ever known....

[Here] it appears, is my principal fault in playing the Moor: I was not ferocious enough; I did not rave and rant. I have no intention of defending myself here, of justifying my performance, my conception of the character of Othello. Either I was convincing in my performance or I was not; and evidently I was not. But after the abundant criticism, when it was obvious we were going to sink, I decided to play the role as my critics thought I should. I went forth with a mighty breath in my lungs and tore through the performance like a madman. I hammed the part within an inch of burlesque; I ate all the scenery I had time and digestion for; I frightened the other actors, none of whom knew I had changed my characterization. And upon my soul, the audience seemed to enjoy it. But please accept it from me—that performance was no good; on the contrary, it was terrible. Any twenty-year-old schoolboy could have played it that way. I was ten-twenty-thirty melodrama of the very lowest sort, so far as my actions were concerned, in beautiful costumes and against magnificent settings. If that is acting then I have spent the last thirty-five years in vain. My subdued conception may not be the right one for

Othello, I will grant, but it is so far superior to giving the role the works that there is no comparison, honestly. If I had the whole thing to do over again...I think I would arrive at the same characterization I gave opening night....

It is good to have a failure every now and then, especially for someone like myself who has had so much good fortune. It balances the books, you might say: it draws you up sharp and makes you take stock. That is not always pleasant. You know, you forget about failures if you have a series of successes. It seems to you odd that men cannot get along in this world. In all probability you begin thinking you are composed of extraordinary ingredients, that you are not like other men. So you feel sorry for the beggars on the streets and give them dimes. Now I'm not trying to be sentimental, and I hope I'm not being too platitudinous when I say what any fool knows—that is, that success breeds success, just as money breeds money, and rabbits breed rabbits. It is true also that the rich man loses heavily. That is good. He should. I'm glad I was a failure or I should have forgotten these simple things, things I learned many years ago when, wandering about the streets of New York looking for a job, I was penniless and hungry. It does you good to quit kidding yourself....

I don't think I'm through playing Shakespeare. There is no desire in me to show anybody, and least of all the dramatic critics of New York newspapers, that I can play it. The hell with such vanity. But the truth is that I have become ensnared by the magic of the guy's web. It is quite clear to me now why so many of the world's great actors (practically all of them) have grown up to play Shakespeare. His work is a challenge to any actor. His work holds a fascination for the actor such as nothing else in the literature of our theatre does. Having played Shakespeare, even in a production which flopped, was an experience by which my life is immensely enriched. I'm tickled pink to have done it. And I'm not picking up any crumbs when I say I am not in the least disheartened that it was not a success.

And yet, just the same, it would have been nice if it had been.

STELLA ADLER

Born in New York City, Stella Adler is the youngest daughter of Jacob and Sarah Adler, progenitors of one of the largest family groups functioning in the contemporary American theatre. In 1939, the date which marked the fiftieth anniversary of Sarah Adler's debut on the American-Jewish stage, it is estimated that there were no less than seventeen members of the family active in the theatre. Jacob Adler, internationally called "the Jewish Henry Irving," as far back as the turn of the century was presenting at the Bowery theatres an unusual repertory of plays with great skill. Norman Hapgood wrote that his visits to Adler's theatre gave him "more to think about and less reason to regret time ill-spent than most of my theatre evenings on Broadway. The acting averages high, and Jacob Adler is one of the most complete and finished actors I have seen. Asked once why he didn't play a certain part, he replied, 'It is a fine role, and I should enjoy it, except that I once played a part much like it.' Such a statement from an American actor would be a surprise, as our players have 'lines.' Mr. Adler plays everything."

Stella Adler acted with her parents both here and abroad in the plays of Tolstoy, Ibsen, Hauptmann, Shakespeare, and other classics. She recalls playing the part of a page-boy in the *Merchant of Venice* at the age of four. After study at New York University she appeared in numerous Broadway productions, including

Karel Capek's *The World We Live In* and Lynn Riggs's *The Big Lake*. She was a student at the American Laboratory Theatre of Richard Boleslavsky and Maria Ouspenskaya. As one of the most accomplished performers in the Group Theatre she played leads in *The House of Connelly, Success Story, Night Over Taos, Gentlewoman, Gold-Eagle Guy, Awake and Sing* and *Paradise Lost*. In 1935 she and Harold Clurman, to whom she was then married, met with Stanislavsky in Paris. She spent six weeks with the master reviewing at first hand the problems of actor training as they revealed themselves in the practice of the Group. Her detailed report brought about modifications in the way the Group Theatre used the Stanislavsky system.

In the forties she played roles on Broadway and in London; directed the California and London productions of *Golden Boy,* made numerous films, and was for a while an associate producer for Metro-Goldwyn-Mayer. She taught acting at the New School for Social Research, and since 1949 has been director of the Stella Adler Theatre School in New York. In 1966 she became a member of the faculty of the Yale Drama School.

"The Actor in the Group Theatre," which was especially written for this volume, describes the creative climate in which the Group Theatre actors matured. Miss Adler has compared her impressions of this period with those of a Group Theatre colleague, Sanford Meisner.

The Actor in the Group Theatre

The actors of the Group Theatre at its inception varied in their social backgrounds, in the level of their craftsmanship, their talent, and their personal aims. Some were idealists, others were dreamers or careerists; there were still a few others who could manage with absolute sincerity to be a combination of all three. This is not unusual or unique in a good actor.

A less homogeneous group of people would have been difficult to find; and once found, to mold them into an ensemble required foresight, courage, and a fanatical will power. Having this will, you soon discovered that they all had many things in common from the very beginning. They had an intense need for continuity of work and for earning a livelihood. On an artistic level, they had a desire and a deep need to develop themselves as actors.

At the earliest stages of the Group's formation, the attention of some of these actors was caught by fiery and enthusiastic talks on the theatre. The theatre was analyzed and dissected and reshaped, and the actors' place in terms of this theatre which was being founded caught their particular interest from the beginning. They listened and tried to understand. From this emerged two ideas which challenged and lured them. These two ideas contained what later became the signature of the Group Theatre. Those actors who stayed on to listen decided to follow and only then gave their allegiance to this theatre.

The first idea asked the actor to become aware of himself. Did he have any problems? Did he understand them in relation to his whole life? To society? Did he have a point of view in relation to these questions?

A point of view was necessary, he was told. The actor should begin to question and learn to understand a great many things. A better understanding of himself would inevitably result. It would be of great artistic use for the actors to have a common point of view which they could share with the other co-workers of the theatre. The actor was told that it was necessary and important to convey this point of view through plays to audiences; that theatrical means and methods had to be found to do this in a truthful and artistic way.

The second idea talked of the actor in relation to his craft. He must develop himself as an actor through his craft. It was necessary for the actors to use the same basic craftsmanship. Only in this way could they achieve a real ensemble and through the ensemble, a creative interpretation of a play.

When these two ideas merged, the actors realized that this theatre demanded a basic understanding of a complex artistic principle; that all people connected with this theatre, the actor, designer, playwright, director, etc., had of necessity to arrive at a single point of view which the theme of the play also expressed. And that each of the above artists would best express that point of view through his individual craftsmanship. This idea was reiterated in a thousand ways; it never changed in its basic philosophy.

The individual actor was supposed to understand this more or less, but it would be difficult to say when the understanding became organic in each one. It was interesting to most actors who listened, but how the idea was helpful to him as an actor varied with each individual. There were those probably who understood. The others tried to be clear and often tried to clarify each other. Most actors are not really ashamed when an intellectual or artistic idea remains outside his understanding. Each knew, however, that it would be of greatest benefit if it could be made to work. Where would this benefit be possible? Most certainly, through his performance.

And so it was. Each actor could see the overall aim being channeled into each individual's craft: the playwright in his rewrite; the scenic artist incorporating it through his sets; the approach of the director to the basic intention of the play; and in the actor himself, the understanding of the character he was to play. It now steered the actor's whole conception and therefore his performance. In this way, slowly, over the years was he able to say that he could understand it organically. It was mostly this practice and new use of himself in relation to the idea of the theatre that made him able to sacrifice many important things for the Group Theatre.

The Group's approach to the actor in accomplishing this aim was unique in this country. The individual actor's total personality was supposed to be dealt with. It was the actor's development which was needed. He had to become a craftsman, to acquire a craft in which he could put experience, talent, intuition, etc. For this, a basic technique had to be found. The actor, like everybody else, had personal problems. These problems had to be understood and respected and to some degree resolved. His economic, personal and artistic problems were of direct concern to the theatre. The actor's growth depended to some degree on his being understood and helped. Also, this theatre, by its very nature, involved him in many problems, economic and artistic, which would have made it impossible for him to function without sympathy and help. If an actor in this theatre was uneven in his performance, it was clear that there was a problem of his discipline which had to be dealt with. If another actor, through intolerance in some form or other, was emotionally limited in his scope, he had to be clarified, sometimes re-educated. Another actor's talent, through shyness or insecurity, was becoming limited. Such a problem affected his performance, the other actors, the play, and, in fact, the whole theatre and the way it functioned. Therefore, this approach was considered necessary so that the actor could bring the maximum of himself to his work and consequently to the whole theatre.

It was not taken for granted by the Group Theatre that because an actor had proven talent or a background of experience that he could necessarily help achieve such a theatre. This puzzled a great many actors who were anxious to work with the Group. The actors who were interested from the beginning in the formation of such a group were those who accepted the theatre's over-all concept—and consequently knew his place in relation to it, especially as it pertained to the actor's ego. The very nature of ensemble demanded this understanding. It was from the first inevitable that many sacrifices had to be made, especially in terms of importance of the parts assigned and the question of salary. The actors of the Group had to be strong to survive the hardships involved. And there were those who survived and those who were destroyed.

Only a very few actors at the beginning had studied the Stanislavsky method. Most of the ensemble had achieved the craftsmanship one gets by acting on any stage under various circumstances; Broadway plays, little theatres, stock, etc. The others had less experience or schooling of one type or another. A new approach to acting had been created by Stanislavsky and practiced in Russia by the Moscow Art Theatre. When that theatre came here, we became aware of a new high standard in ensemble acting. Two of his most important disciples, Mr. Boleslavsky and Madame Ouspenskaya, first taught this method to young American actors. It was considered by far the soundest creative technique for actors and it was used by the Group Theatre from the beginning, although in a very special way.

The Stanislavsky method is complicated and difficult to explain. Stanislavsky himself knew the danger of trying to formulate his theory in this way. One can make an honest but limited attempt by saying that the actor is first trained in a very real use of himself in relation to actions, sense of truth, imagination, the use of justification, and the approach to emotion. The actor discovers many ways to build his craft and release his emotions each time anew rather than imitate or approximate. This is part of the training, however, not an end in itself. The end through this craft permits him truly to interpret a character. For many reasons, it was considered necessary for the Group Theatre, at the beginning, to start with rehearsals of a play. The play was read, analyzed and the author's intention was clarified through analysis. The actor was then faced with the study of his part. These first rehearsals constituted the Group actor's first schooling in the method.

The analytical approach to the play as soon as rehearsals began interested and stimulated many of the actors. There were others, however, who preferred to get close to the play more slowly. They preferred the character to unfold through the process of rehearsal, absorbing the content of the part and play from one rehearsal to another. These actors felt the greater satisfaction of creating the characterization themselves rather than assimilating it through the director's understanding. The analysis of plays to this degree diminished in later years, the director finding that it crowded the actor too much. The system was immediately incorporated stressing the use of actions, a variety of improvisations and exercises called "Affective Memory." The use of actions permitted an actor the immediate understanding of the text as it related to his own part. Through their use, he learned to act what was really going on in the sub-text, that is, behind the words. Through improvisations, these actions became alive in the actors before the words of the text were studied.

They were also used in many ways for development of characterization and to clarify the play's real situation. "Affective Memory" exercises were used mainly to catch a particular emotion needed for mood, for coloring, for characterization.

Some of the actors worked in classes outside rehearsals, on other aspects of the method or their interpretation of it. This was done most generally for the development of imagination and characterization. The Group Theatre used these methods for three years during which it produced six plays. Only in 1934 was the approach to the actor's craft changed very radically. The emphasis which had been put very strongly on the conscious manipulation of the actor's exact emotion was abandoned by most of the actors. The Stanislavsky system was from then on reinterpreted by pressure coming from his own statement. This clarified the area in which the Group had misunderstood his theories. From that time on, the emphasis shifted. Now emphasis was put on the circumstances of the play and a much stronger use of the actor's need to find greater justification in the use of these circumstances and a more *conscious* use of them. There is little room in this article to attempt by illustration further clarification which could be helpful.

The system, mostly through the clarity of actions as they helped both the director and actor, had in it so much strength that even before these important changes were made, it had, from its first production, created the most important ensemble to date developed in this country. And consistently afterwards, during all the years, the ensemble of the Group Theatre never fell below the standard it first established for itself. It was said of this ensemble that it was "skillful and inspired," that the performance was an expression of the ideal, that the Group Theatre method was the only way to prepare a play. It could also be said that the original Group Theatre credo seeped through to the whole theatrical organism from the very first production, rather than to individual actors. From the collective effort, from the entire Group's sincerity, from the fervor and enthusiasm and dedication to an aim, each play was filled with a spirit that gave to the play a greater artistic meaning than any individual's contribution.

Many of the actors from the beginning suffered strain, despite the importance of relaxation in an actor's work. To a large degree, this was because the actor was asked through the use of this "Affective Memory" or emotional substitution to deal consciously with that part of himself which was intended to remain unconscious. The Stanislavsky technique has an over-all aim in relation to the actor. It teaches him what to do consciously so that he can be free and spontaneous emotionally. From the beginning, therefore, the system benefited chiefly the more experienced actors. They knew they could act—had already done it—had fulfilled the requirements needed in the professional theatre. They were able to bring an independence, therefore, which they had achieved through experience. They had the confidence which comes with performance, no matter how self-critical one is. They used the method in this context. They added these new acting elements and were therefore able to feel themselves more alive, more emotionally fluent than before. They became aware of this growth and could now recreate a part with each performance.

The others, less experienced, less hardy, accepted the new approach literally. A great many of these failed in their development as actors and lost confidence in their old techniques. They became confused. Nevertheless, their individual performances were often excellent because of the rehearsal methods; each scene was given an architectural solidity which was difficult for anyone to break down, and no matter what their individual acting problems were, they nevertheless helped enormously to achieve the ensemble excellence. Beginning with the season of 1934, those people who joined the Group as younger actors, or apprentices, or even hangers-on, began to grow as craftsmen in this alive enterprise. These new people were given a chance to work more slowly before they were asked to take over responsible parts. They were able through their crafts to create a conscious structure for the spontaneous opening up of the subconscious. It was only then that the actor as an individual became an independent creator. These years produced some of the best and most typical Group Theatre talents who together with the older actors were able to influence through acting, directing, and teaching, an important part of the American theatre.

LYNN FONTANNE
ALFRED LUNT

Lynn Fontanne and Alfred Lunt, America's greatest acting team for over thirty-five years, started out early in the century, she an English-born protegée of Ellen Terry with whom she studied in 1903, he a character actor in the Castle Square Theatre stock company in Boston. Miss Fontanne was brought to the United States by Laurette Taylor and went on to success in *Dulcy* by Marc Connelly and George S. Kaufman in 1921. Mr. Lunt had his first triumph in *Clarence,* which Booth Tarkington wrote especially for the young actor. During the run of this play he won the applause of Broadway and the heart and hand of Lynn Fontanne.

They were married in 1922, and although they continued their separate careers, they began to shape a new theatrical star, known to vast audiences at home and abroad as The Lunts. Their important appearance together for the Theatre Guild in Molnar's *The Guardsman* in 1924 marked a turning point in the career of these young stars. In becoming part of the Theatre Guild they sacrificed money and billing to work together under a creative director, Philip Moeller, for a producing organization interested as they were more in the art of the theatre than in the usual Broadway successes. Alexander Woollcott's review of *The Guardsman* suggests the sense of the occasion. He wrote: "They have youth and great gifts and the unmistakable attitude of ascent, and those who saw them last night bowing hand in hand, for the first time, may well have been witnessing a moment in theatrical history. It is among the possibilities that we were seeing the first chapter in a partnership destined to be as distinguished as that of Henry Irving and Ellen Terry."

In the next season they played Shaw's *Arms and the Man* with even greater success, and during the run of this play they signed a three-year contract with the Theatre Guild, which then proceeded to recruit a permanent company of outstanding players—Dudley Digges, Margalo Gillmore, Morris Carnovsky, Clare Eames, Edward G. Robinson, Earle Larimore, Claude Rains, Blanche Yurka, Philip Loeb, and others. Until 1930 the Lunts played exclusively for the Guild, together in *The Goat Song, At Mrs. Beam's, The Brothers Karamazov, The Second Man, The Doctor's Dilemma, Caprice, Meteor, Elizabeth the Queen, Reunion in Vienna;* individually, Lunt played in *Juarez and Maximilian, Ned McCobb's Daughter, Marco Millions* and *Volpone;* Lynn Fontanne played in *Pygmalion* and *Strange Interlude.* The range and the variety of their work together and apart in these years were notable as was their interest in plays of every type. Years later they rightly resented being stereotyped by young playgoers as "specialists in comedy." Lunt complained: "Why didn't Elia Kazan give us a crack at *Death of a Salesman?* I would have loved to play Willy Loman. And wouldn't Lynn have made a heartbreaking Mrs. Loman? But nobody ever showed us the script." He reiterated their openness to "anything that's good," and recalled joining the Theatre Guild when it was an "art theatre." They worked with the Guild for "the joy of acting" and "because we believed the theatre has a mission to perform for its audiences."

After a highly successful London season in 1929, they determined never to play separately again, a decision that led them eventually to break with the Theatre Guild. In 1933 they produced with Noel Coward his *Design for Living* and later acted in his *Point Valaine.* Between 1936 and 1940 they did *Taming of the Shrew, Idiot's Delight, Amphitryon 38, The Seagull* and *There Shall Be No Night* in New York and on tour. The next decade they continued their careers with several plays that many felt unworthy of their talents. Lee Strasberg's reputed comment about them seemed to sum up the response of the current generation. "A man like Alfred Lunt has more equipment as an actor and director than Laurence Olivier. But what do the Lunts do? Fool around with tired Noel Coward . . . make nice nostalgic pictures in the Sunday supplement." When in 1958 they were persuaded by Peter Brook to do Duerrenmatt's bitter drama *The Visit,* their usual nostalgic audiences during the pre-London tryouts were shocked and dismayed. The opening in New York at the new Lunt-Fontanne Theatre, however, was one of the true occasions in the American theatre as two great performers brought an important modern drama to life for a new generation of theatregoers. Some observations about their work together on this play and a few general thoughts on acting follow.

ALFRED LUNT

Working Together on *The Visit*

The late Theresa Helburn of the Theatre Guild sent us *The Visit* in April, 1957. We thought it an extraordinary, a fascinating play; original, superb theatre, and important, but we turned it down as we needed a long rest and wished, for that reason, to make no commitments. But we urged Miss Helburn to buy it and by all means to put it on as quickly as possible. Two weeks later Roger Stevens telephoned us, said he had bought the play, and wanted us to do it. Again we declined for the same reason. We went to England in June, where the producer, Hugh Beaumont, offered us the play and this time we agreed, since rehearsals could not begin for five months—because of Peter Brook's busy schedule—and five months was exactly the length of the vacation we wanted.

Miss Fontanne thought, moreover, that the script needed straightening out; she felt that there was something wrong with the translation since it had been done from German into French and then into English. Peter Brook, too, had many reservations about the script. Brook, Valency, and Duerrenmatt met in Paris and the reworking of the play began, to the delight of all.

In rehearsal, we put ourselves in Peter Brook's hands entirely, and tried to do everything he asked. Although I myself have done a great deal of directing, that

Randolph Goodman: *Drama on Stage.* New York: Holt, Rinehart and Winston, 1961, pp. 400-401. Copyright © 1961 by Randolph Goodman. Reprinted by permission of Holt, Rinehart and Winston, Inc.

makes no difference in my relationship with a director. In fact, we both like being directed. We thought we worked slowly but it was Brook's opinion that we worked with "lightning speed." Actors, you see, are not the best judges of how they operate or even of what they do best, any more than an author or, say, a cook is. You may like to do certain parts better than others, because they come easier, just as authors may like to write novels rather than plays or cooks may prefer to prepare a ragout rather than a soufflé but that doesn't mean that the customers will like it better. Playing a part is like baking bread; the best cooks know when the dough has reached the right consistency, no cookbook can teach that. You can't teach timing, and you can't teach a person to be amusing. A young actor I knew who was supposed to get laughs never got them. I asked him, "Are you afraid of criticism? Do you dislike being laughed at?" He said, "That's the one thing that terrifies me." He was afraid to get laughs even for the character he was playing.

In studying a part, the first thing we do is learn our lines, which is agony, and we always perform within the pattern of the play. We try to act with truth, hoping the author and the audience will find our characters *real,* without trace of what some people call "technique." Around the 200th performance, we find we are getting nearer to our "people." We played *There Shall Be No Night* and *O Mistress Mine* sixteen hundred times and still found much to do. Movements and gestures must be in character, not like *us.* I built Anton Schill on a man in Genesee Depot, in looks, in clothes, in gestures. Miss Fontanne had many "Claires" in mind, one in particular. You'd be surprised if you dig into the past what you will find—not always pleasant. We've never played roles like Anton and Claire before. Has anyone? They are not sympathetic parts. They are not really "star" parts; this is an ensemble play from the actors' point of view, but they are fascinating roles to play, difficult as they are short.

Many people find *The Visit* uncomfortable to watch and hear, repellent, unbearable. One lady in Cleveland wrote, "Dear Mr. and Mrs. Lunt: I saw your play. It was well acted, as is always the case with you. But it made me quite ill and I am going straight to bed." "Why do you do it?" they ask us. We do it because of its terrible truth, its seriousness of purpose, its universality. These people make Claire the villain. She is not! I say, "It is the townspeople who are the villains. You!" They say, "No, it's not so; we are innately good, underneath." That's an awful rationalization.

On our cross-country tour, *The Visit* was given a remarkable reception. It may sound vain of me to say so, but when we played in Salt Lake City they stood up and cheered. If we could have stood one-night stands, we could have stayed out for years and years with this play. We were brought up in a theatre where touring was part of your job. If you had a success in New York, you naturally took it out. The road is still very much alive and hungry for plays but the cost of touring— transportation, actors' salaries and so on—makes it prohibitive for a big production. . . .

INTERVIEWER: What is the secret of your teamwork?[1]

LUNT: I don't know. I guess each of us is interested in the other. That's one thing. And, of course, there is our way of speaking together. We started it in *The Guardsman.* We would speak to each other as people do in real life. I would,

[1]Lewis Funke and John E. Booth: *Actors Talk About Acting.* New York: Random House, 1961, pp. 45-47. Copyright © 1961. Reprinted by permission of Random House.

for instance, start a speech, and in the middle, on our own cue, which we would agree on in advance, Lynn would cut in and start talking. I would continue on a bit, you see. You can't do it in Shakespeare, of course. But in drawing-room comedies, in realistic plays, it is most effective. How can I make that clear? We what is known as overlapped . . .

INTERVIEWER: Without waiting . . .

LUNT: Yes, in the middle of a sentence. This is exactly what I mean, what we are doing right now. We are talking together, aren't we? You heard what I said, and I heard what you said. Well, to do that on the stage, you see, you have to work it very, very carefully, because you overlap lines. So that once I say the line, "Come into the next room and I will get ready," your cue really is "the next room," and you say, "All right," and I continue and say, "and I will get ready," underneath, as it were. Of course, I must lower my voice so that she is still heard. Is it clear?

INTERVIEWER: This interaction is presumably what every actor dreams of.

LUNT: They thought it couldn't be done. They said you will never do it. And when we first played *Caprice* in London, they were outraged because we talked together. Really outraged, the press was. But it was a great success. And I think it was the first time it was ever done. I don't know. It just happened because we knew each other so well and trusted each other. Although sometimes I have been accused, and I accuse her, of stepping on a line or a laugh or a bit of business. "Why do you come in so quickly?" "Why don't you . . . ?"

INTERVIEWER: Is this something that is inseparable from your personal lives? You are used to each other, your cadences, your thought processes.

LUNT: No, I don't think so, because the lines are not ours. They belong to somebody else.

INTERVIEWER: How do you study your roles together?

LUNT: Well, when we were doing this, for instance, for the first forest scene in *The Visit,* she learned her lines and I learned mine, and I might say that it was a very difficult scene. It is a very strangely written scene and—well, you stumble along until you know it, and then you begin—when you really know it—you begin playing to each other, into the eyes, as it were, until it has some reality. For instance, there was a line in this play, and for some weeks I could never get it, when Lynn said, "And you married Mathilde Blumhard," and I thought I should say, "Oh, don't be angry with me for marrying Mathilde," in a kind of German sentimental hurt way, you know, it was an awful thing to do—but it wasn't any good because it lacked the intimacy of the old days. Then one day I decided I'd become angry, and that was true. It had the right ring. It had more truth in it. In effect I was saying, "Don't blame me. Just think of what I did for you," because I'm also protecting my home—self, too. I feel like I should protect myself, do you understand? The problem is always to arrive at some truthful—truthful expression, manner—what is the word?—more truthful . . .

INTERVIEWER: Feeling?

LUNT: Yes, a feeling—a true feeling. And that is the way it comes. Does that mean anything?

INTERVIEWER: Yes. You don't adhere to any one method?

LUNT: No, I just try to be as real—say I try to act with as much reality as I can. I once had a class of G.I.'s after the war, and they said, "What is technique?"— you know, acting techniques—and I said, "I haven't the slightest idea, I'll go home and ask my wife." And I did. And she said: "You just read your part with as much reality as you can—truthfulness—a little louder than in an ordinary room and don't bump into each other, that's all." Noel (Coward) has picked that up and uses it. It's true. But there is much more to it than that, I suppose.

INTERVIEWER: In this play—how do you find the truth, the reality of these very vicious people whom you portray?

LUNT: For me, a man I know in Genesee Depot immediately came into my mind. This man in Wisconsin was not quite as bad as Schill, the character I play. But pretty bad, and I tried to look like him and walk like him.

INTERVIEWER: You mean you related your character to that man?

LUNT: Yes, although, mind you, he wasn't as bad as Schill. Schill is an awful man. Yet, you know, there is also a temptation to try to make him something of a hero, but he isn't, and so, maybe, I make the mistake and pull it the other way. I suppose I could look better, but Peter, our director, didn't want me to and I didn't want to, either. I suppose I could be a little more attractive and still give you the idea of what he was and yet . . . I sometimes have to bring out a picture when I am doing this, and look at myself and say, "When I was a young man, I wasn't so bad."

INTERVIEWER: You start off feeling very sympathetic for Schill. As a member of the audience I did and then suddenly you realize that . . .

LUNT: He's forgotten. He's forgotten what he did, it's been fifty years.

INTERVIEWER: How did you develop the scene in the store when your anger and fear begin to overcome you? When you realize you are likely to die—it must be so hard not to overplay it, I should think.

LUNT: Well, originally, in the play, the minute Schill saw the shoes he began to scream; he screamed right on to the end of the play. But Peter [Brook] didn't want it to be done that way. It was, I might add, the way it was written, too. And I said at the beginning, "But I can't do it any other way, Peter, that is the way it will have to be. I'll try it, but we'll never get it the way you want to." It was pulled back all the time, always pulled back for control. And that is due to Peter. Anything you see that is good is due to Peter.

LYNN FONTANNE

Thoughts on Acting

Laurette Taylor had played so many years with stock companies in the West and she was accustomed to handling quickly every unexpected situation that might occur during a performance. She showed me how to exploit my resources and how to work spontaneously and not to be all tensed up inside. You see, what there was about her was that she could be absolutely free from expressing her emotion onstage. She hadn't any fear of doing anything she wanted to do and saying anything she wanted to say. So I saw how you must come to feel completely at home onstage and then you would forget it was a stage.

Lynn Fontanne: "Thoughts on Acting." These observations have been drawn from the following sources: Maurice Zolotow: *Stagestruck.* Harcourt, Brace & World, © 1964, pp. 36, 127; 184; Reprinted by permission of Harcourt, Brace & World, Inc. Lewis Funke and John E. Booth: *Actors Talk About Acting.* Random House, 1961, pp. 72, 75, 63. Copyright © 1961 by Lewis Funke and John E. Booth. Reprinted by permission of Random House. The final item is from a letter to the editors, 1969.

There is a school of actors who play an emotional scene without any—I don't know whether it is without feeling or emotion or without tears. Certainly without tears. They think that—they watch actors, and the more they cry the less effective they are. That is one school of actors. That is the Helen Hayes school of acting. And, of course, God knows, she plays an emotional scene divinely, you see—and is very moving. So, I don't know, but I must, for myself, if I feel a thing, it does something funny to my voice, and I think that is a good thing. I don't know. I let it do it. My judgment on it, my own personal judgment on it, is that it is good to do that. I imagine Helen does that, too, that she lets it come to her voice. She must do it. And it is a real thing, like that curious swelling of the throat. That happens when you cry, when you are going to cry—not when you are crying actually, when you are going to cry, you know. That curious swelling of the throat. And if you forbid it, you get an ache there. But when your voice comes out, when it is swelling like that, it is very good, it is full of hurt and tears and whatever you wish to convey. I said to a doctor once, "Why is it that actors who go through an agonizing scene and convey such agony can come off and throw it instantly—and they are perfectly all right. For an emotional—a screaming, emotional scene they do it eight times a week. Why aren't they ruined by that? If human beings went into such a fit of emotion eight times a week, they'd die. They would not be able to live. They would certainly go mad." And he, this doctor, said, "Well, I think it's because"— and I thought it was a very wise answer—"I think it is because an actor comes off-stage and knows he had done well and that supplants the emotion.... Also his grief doesn't continue, you see, it is not a real grief. It is the grief of an imaginary man. So when he comes off he is himself again."

When I am on a stage, I am the focus of thousands of eyes and it gives me strength. I feel that something, some energy, is flowing from the audience into me. I actually feel stronger because of these waves. Now when the play's done, the eyes taken away, I feel just as if a circuit's been broken. The power is switched off. I feel all gone and empty inside of me—like a balloon that's been pricked and the air's let out.

You could not cut a line without Shaw finding out. The only actor that cut Shaw without being found out was Henry Travers. Henry played the dustman Alfred Doolittle, in *Pygmalion*. Henry had a slight stutter and he had got into a habit of swallowing and twisting sentences and words around so he wouldn't meet his stutter, do you see? I once asked him, "How is it that you sound so natural when you're speaking Shaw's dialogue and the rest of us don't? Because, you see, for an actor, Shaw's dialogue is not how people really talk and it does sound like a book, not stage dialogue. And Henry whispered to me, "M-my d-dear, I gargle all those lu-lines and tu-tu-whist them about." And do you know I went off and did and chewed them about a bit, oh, it was marvelous fun, and, you know, Shaw's spies never found me out and it was mainly because of this that many people said my Liza Doolittle was more natural than Mrs. Campbell's, for whom Shaw had written the part.

I think comedy more difficult to play and I'll tell you why. Because if you are capable of playing tragedy it means that you have a great well of emotion in you— and you just push yourself off and roll downhill. That is what it is, in a scene. But, of course, you have to learn how not to spend it all at the beginning. Nurse it along so you don't wear out or get it in at the end—that you have to learn. Comedy— you really have to have that ear out and that eye on yourself. You really do. You have to be very up and very brilliant and faster, much faster than you are when you play tragedy. And that, of course, is very tiring, very exhausting. Also in comedy, breath control comes in more than it does in the other kind of thing. If you take a deep breath you can play with a sentence. There is no doubt you can get your laugh, you know, if you say it right. But if you don't take your breath—and you have to take a breath during the line—it is as if you'd gagged on something. It isn't as funny and you often miss your laugh. Mysterious, isn't it? Because you would think that the line would be as funny in any way, wouldn't you? All comedians tell you that.

———————

I think that [teamwork] is something that grows with good actors. I think if two good actors play together long enough, it gets that way. When we have finished our rehearsal in the daytime, then Alfred and I always rehearse our particular scenes over again that evening, so that we really, during rehearsals, work at least twelve hours a day. What's Equity going to do about that? Well, there—as I was saying, we work and work at home and slowly you get into the character of the person you are playing—the walk, the gestures. I try not to think too much about my role, that is, my character. But, gradually, I become more and more acquainted with her, and then as the days go by I sink deeper and deeper into her, discovering traits and things about her I did not know existed when I began to rehearse. Inflections, intonations become sharper and truer, and the false notes are corrected. This is a process that continues all during the run of the play, even after it has opened.

———————

There are things that I regard as absolute necessities. Your basic speech should be clear and unaccented. If it isn't already, you had better work on it until it is your natural speech. If you have to play a part from Boston, California, or from England, you can always learn it—and if you are not good at accents, don't play the part. I was fortunate enough to learn my speech from Ellen Terry, but I have played many parts with an accent. When you are beginning, you will find you give better performances in the evening if you stay quiet during the day—no lunches, and certainly no cocktail parties. Remember you are overpaid, so take your money at the end of the week with as clear a conscience as you can.

I have discovered for myself little things that help, such as—when you have been playing a part for a long time and you begin to feel stale and unnatural-sounding, in your imagination pull down that curtain and be in a room, not on the stage, and I found all my readings are entirely different and, I *think*, for the better.

There are a few things that I find young actors are concerned with that I now know are not worth bothering about. When they sign their contract it won't push them on any further in the world if they demand this kind of dressing room or that kind of dressing room, their name in this position and in that size on the billing. The only thing of importance is their performance when they get out on the stage. Some consider the best position is for them to be a little bit upstage from the character they are playing with. That also is a fallacy because it only engenders a dislike between you and the other character. A private battle ensues and in the process both his performance and yours goes "up the spout." It is better to establish as friendly relations as possible both for your own enjoyment and for the sake of the play.

MORRIS CARNOVSKY

(b. 1897)

More than most American actors Morris Carnovsky has linked his destiny with permanent acting companies. Born in St. Louis, Missouri, and a Phi Beta Kappa graduate of Washington University, he started his serious work in the theatre as a member of the Theatre Guild acting company that had at its top the Lunts. He played various character roles in most of the important productions of the Guild between 1924 and 1930—*Saint Joan, Marco Millions, Volpone, Uncle Vanya, Elizabeth the Queen.* He was one of the first people the organizers of the Group Theatre recruited for their project, and he appeared in the initial Group Theatre production, *The House of Connelly,* 1931.

In the years of the Group Theatre's existence, Carnovsky was not only one of the best and most employed actors, but also in some ways the "Dean"—as he was nicknamed—of the acting company and deeply devoted to its ideals. Among the plays he appeared in were *Night Over Taos, Awake and Sing, Waiting for Lefty, Johnny Johnson, Golden Boy, Rocket to the Moon, Thunder Rock, Night Music.* Mr. Bonaparte in *Golden Boy* and Jacob in *Awake and Sing* were outstanding in his gallery of finely etched portraits. No matter how others may have felt when the Group Theatre broke up, he considered it a success during its whole active period. He has said: "The Group Theatre is without question the great unifying experience of my career . . . not only did it prove the value of a permanent relationship between actors working . . . but it gave us an opportunity to be absolutely honest and downto-earth about the rules of the craft that we were pursuing." He also said that the Group was important as "the first theatre in this country to have a philosophy."

During the forties he was a member of the Actors Laboratory Theatre in Hollywood, where he directed a number of plays. On Broadway he appeared in such hits as *My Sister Eileen, Café Crown* and *Counterattack.* During the fifties and sixties he played Mayor Stockman in the Arthur Miller version of *An Enemy of the People* and Priam in Giraudoux's *Tiger at the Gates,* Father in S. N. Behrman's *The Cold Wind and the Warm,* and the Logician in Ionesco's *Rhinoceros.* But during this period he once again associated himself with a permanent theatre by becoming part of the American Shakespeare Festival at Stratford, Connecticut. Many have commented on the success in Shakespearean roles of this actor who is identified with the Stanislavsky Method, naturalized in the country by the Group Theatre. He has explained his work in Shakespearean roles by the combination in himself of romantic and realistic qualities—a combination he finds in most American actors—and which he thinks is suited to developing a unique American approach to Shakespeare. With the Festival theatre he has played many plays from *King John* to *The Taming of the Shrew,* but his outstanding contributions have been Shylock and King Lear. Each of these roles has been informed by his special contributions—his voice, his intelligence, his ease, and his "sense of self," that "acceptance and use of your own individuality, no matter what part you may be playing," which he feels is central to the art of acting.

Mr. Carnovsky has written several important articles on his interpretation of roles and the problems of the actor.

The Quest of Technique

The word "technique" has to be explained, especially in regard to my own craft, since for many it still retains the atmosphere of a bright and glossy competence, something machine-made, inevitable in the way it functions—"you put it in here and it comes out there"—particularly adapted to sparkling dialogue and sophisticated effects, "timing," creased trousers and secure *décolletage,* smart deaths and entrances. Measured sobs and gusts of professional laughter to account for the anguish of loss and the joy of living. An actor of my acquaintance has made a tidy career for himself out of something called "footwork"—this, he solemnly assured me, was the underlying secret of all good acting. Malvolio might have said it: " 'Tis but footwork—all is but footwork." My friend neglected to tell me what happened when he was sitting down! However—

In the twenties, when I first came to New York and to the service of the theatre, the stage was the stamping ground of many an attitude and fixed persuasion such as the above. It was a field day for every sort of exhibitionism, dominated by "stars" who were expected to be the exhibitionists par excellence. It was a competition not so much of living or cultural values as of showmanship. The lily of truth was often unrecognizable for the gilding that weighed it down. Among these stars there were some, of course, that burned with a purer light; it was as if they didn't know how to conceal the thing they *were*. David Warfield, with one shoe on the rich soil of the ghetto, the other getting a shine up in The Lambs Club. Otis Skinner, using every trick in the bag to convey the juiciest romanticism I have ever seen. Mrs. Fiske, Mistress of the Theatrical Inn, barely disguising a warm heart beneath her devastating and witty rhythms. "Whizzing exhalations" like Emily Stevens and Jeanne Eagels burning in their comets' flight with an alcoholic blue flame, giving themselves to the fires with obstinate grandeur—what else was there to do?

If the student of acting took these as his models, he was more likely to absorb their foibles and eccentricities than the magnificence of their *Idea*. To talk and walk brightly with crisp "stylish" diction in the hectic manner of the day, this was what they'd learned in "School"—that is, by observation, by Stock, and the threat of losing their job. They were often pathetically self-conscious about this "technique" of theirs. A very good actor I knew and admired had a singular trick of elongating vowel sounds in the most unlikely places—monosyllables like "if," "as," "but," particularly "but." "Bu-u-ut," he would say, "Bu-u-ut screw your courage to the sticking point a-a-and we'll not fail." Or "I—i-if you be-e-e." Etc. I asked him about it once and he answered promptly and with pride, "Why, that's my sostenuto *but!*"

Now, you must not think because I describe these interesting phenomena as quirks that I dismiss them entirely as unworthy of the craft of acting. Or that I regard a pleasant, fastidious, and crisp manner of speech and presence as a sign of decadence. In our last decade poor Marlon Brando has precipitated upon his head the reputation and credit for having restored the Yahoo to his rightful place in society, but we need not admire him the less for that. All innovators must take

Morris Carnovsky: "Design for Acting: The Quest of Technique." *Tulane Drama Review,* V, Spring, 1961, pp. 68-85 *passim*. Reprinted by permission of Morris Carnovsky and *Tulane Drama Review.*

their chances. And there is generally a deeper reason for odd behavior, stemming from something that is striving to be said.

For myself, I learned as much as I could, largely by imitation, from the "technique" of these older actors. I even think I now understand what they were driving at. For example, my friend of the "footwork." I now believe that he had discovered for himself a useful and comfortable arcanum in the area of physical rhythm, a very important thing for actors. He had found through experience that it was blissfully reassuring to be in the right place at the right time! His dukes and his butlers were never caught flatfooted, as they say in boxing. Out of the balance between his words and his movements he had perfected a kind of personal dance. This pleased him and gave him ultimate confidence. . . . And what of him of the sostenuto "but"? He was a lover of words—*all* words, even those that are customarily neglected. He rescued them from oblivion and gave them dignity. But (bu-u-ut) more importantly, he made them *act!* There was a warning note in that "but" of his, a promise in his "and," a threat in his "if." I find that most interesting, because it betokened an *inner* life and energy that was the mark of this man's talent, his brushstroke, as it were.

The actors of the twenties often seemed to be all dressed up with no place to go. Except into the thirties—which is what they did, eventually. They went pitching down the funnel of the years, practicing all the techniques they knew, believing in their own effectiveness and their own sincerities. And reaching out, too, for a better language of craft, more expanse to their horizons, greater satisfaction for their spirits. They had no leadership. It was each man for himself. The murmurs that reached them from foreign shores, murmurs of vibrant new names—Craig, Appia, Jessner, Reinhardt, Stanislavsky, Copeau—these seemed to promise a new kind of showmanship, but there was no one around—with the exception of a few scene designers who began to sit up and take notice—to interpret the swelling theme of a new *Theatre* to them. Theatre possibly for the first time understood as a profound organic experience shared by *all* its elements, audience, designers, lighting experts, producers, directors—and, of course, actors.

I say there was no one around to utter a warning or to say: "Be of good cheer! At last you are about to receive a vessel for your talents. Not a knighthood nor an empty citation, nor a cigar banded with your name. No champagne banquets with speeches to inflate your vanity and encourage you in your worst professional habits. No fan clubs milling about the stage door and shouting your name in the worn, ironic streets. Not these things, but a place—a place where your actors' nature will be understood and used, through work, through discipline, through struggle, through proper organization, to the end that you will inherit the only thing worth having—namely, your Self.". . .

Certainly in those days I wasn't very articulate about my own notions of craft —I hadn't earned the right to be. It was a case of no foundation all along the line. Tension of the body, mirrored by inner tension, leading inevitably to forced, mechanical, exhibitionistic action (Get that laugh! Nail down that effect!), with here and there a saving grace of truthful feeling that would disentangle itself and float upward like a wisp of smoke into the flies. When it didn't happen, squeeze as I might, I was unhappy. I was considered a good actor, too, and *that* made me ashamed. I was fed up with fumbling. I was undoubtedly learning many valuable lessons along the way, but I didn't know them by name. I see now that the effort to depict the character led me too far from its proper roots in my own individuality. I had misplaced my Self, which was far worse than a hand left dangling in the air. I yearned for my own return and I didn't know how to get it back. I think it could be said of me then, as now, that I was *seeking my Image.* Call it a wholeness, integrity; *my* life in Art, if you will.

I was not alone, as I discovered more and more when the Group Theatre got under way. My fellow workers all aspired to earn the name of Actor. The smell of greasepaint was but one element in the confused aroma that drifted our way from the gardens of this brave new world. We set sail into the thirties on the good ship Nonconformity. The isle as we approached it was full of noises, and we aimed at making sense of it all. We were eager to get down to First Causes, even if it meant making fools of ourselves—which history records we often did. We were at once exploring for the lost Adam and the gold of Peru. If the memory of our endeavors vibrates somewhat with a fuzzy romanticism, I'm not too concerned. Shakespeare may have had his fellow actors in mind when he put it down: We are such stuff as dreams are made on. We *were* romantic, from necessity—and necessity for whatever reason is very real. We needed, as I said, a Place for our exercises; we needed peace, in which to learn the grammar of struggle. . . .

If our sight had remained so fanatically focused only on the dark and private world of our actors' organism, we might really have emerged as "old nosers," with new "footworks" and "sostenuto buts." But—aside from the fact that we were mindful of our bodies and took normal delight in them, the more so as we sensed the organic interflow of mind and body, the sovereignty of will and Imagination to arouse and control them—aside from this fact, the new-found concentration on our functions as actors, forced us also to turn our eyes outward upon the nature of the *objective* world. Our citizenship in this world was acquiring a gravity and an interconnection and even a responsibility that we hadn't dreamed of in that other time before we'd crossed the Jordan. The world of music and plastic movement, the world of painting and photography, of current history and politics, of the many cultures that made our American culture, the consequences of the Depression and the grim incredible prevalence of the shivering breadline and the apple-seller. That new awareness of ours expanded in all directions; according to temperament and capacity, each person drank of the world around him, even though sometimes it ran like a bitter liquor through his veins. Sympathy or repulsion—they were bred of objective circumstances, a look at the world. "Watchman, what of the night!" When we returned to our exercises we had something to say about it.

Plus ça change; but *plus* not altogether *la même chose.* The interpenetration of the two longings I have described—intense consciousness of Self combined with an insatiable thirst to understand our contemporaries and their times—produced a "new" type of actor. Shall we label him actor-philosopher, or actor-citizen? Or, socially conscious actor? One hesitates to encase this fly in amber; better to call him —just—actor. "Abstract and brief chronicle of the time"—that word "abstract," though Shakespeare didn't altogether intend it so, permits me to say this: as one of these creatures, I am not willing to see the wild flutter of its wings nailed down upon a ticketed board. The important point lies in the fact that the amalgamation I speak of provided an enormous quickening of the imagination, and when that happens, laws and labels are apt to fly out of the window. The creative impulse— like Ariel—is essentially wild and homeless, chafing against limitations. Somewhere in the heart of this impatient shimmering movement is a spirit, heedless of normal lots and hindrances. It craves to release itself, in a burst of music. All the more, therefore, unless it is to be allowed to attain freedom beyond all recognition, does it need the bondage imposed upon it by some master-force and will. The name of Setebos will have to yield to Prospero—Prospero Sergeitch.

Stanislavsky . . . Adam in the Garden of Eden apparently had no difficulty at all about the names he chose for all created things. He was divinely inspired! Even in translation from Edenese, they come across magnificently: tiger, lamb, elephant, hyena, cat—most satisfactory. But if you want to know what really was happening, and how the struggle for concrete forms takes place without supernatural prompting—then consider *My Life in Art* by Stanislavsky.

On rereading this book recently, I was struck again and again by the quantity of things that we already take for granted these days about ourselves as actors. "But of course," we say, "how obvious!" It is the case again of Columbus's egg— very clear, once it's been demonstrated. The touching quality in Stanislavsky's book is the first one he confesses in himself, obstinacy. To the very last page, for all his majesty of presence and overwhelming knowledge and sophistication, he remains a child, with the concentrated purposefulness of a child learning to walk. "Strange," he seems always to be muttering to himself, "Strange, very strange. I fall. But— let's try again." Like a good captain, he shares every hardship of his men; he bivouacs on the bare cold ground. He loves them for every glimmer of progress they show; he growls at their laziness, their complacency, their vanities. He presides over his province with farsighted roving eyes, with the look of a skeptical lion. "Know your enemies," he seems to rumble in his throat, "False pathos, cheap tricks, artificiality, disrespect, timidity, tension, fashionableness. And again, laziness!" . . . "*I don't believe you!*"—his actors flinched and quailed before that dreaded battle cry of his, roared out of the depths of the auditorium. And yet, on opening nights, when Stanislavsky, being often ill, was obliged to stay home from the theatre, they would call him on the telephone to be reassured and steadied by the sound of his voice. . . .

Stanislavsky did not dread change. He welcomed it. It was with joy that he saw younger actors and directors, in his lifetime, absorb what he had taught and give it forth in new forms. Michael Chekhov, Vakhtangov, many others. Though he referred to it as "my system," he was never "Sir Oracle" about it. He gloried in the fact that the voices to which he listened were but promptings from the greatest technicians of the past, and confirmed by the most stirring practice of his own youthful observation—Salvini, Rossi, Chaliapin, Yermolova, Duse. The "system" was for those that needed it. To Harold Clurman he once said: "One only asks, is it truthful, is it beautiful? And if I see such beautiful acting anywhere, shall I say, Just a moment there! It's true, you act marvelously, I am deeply moved, nevertheless I must reject it because you've never been to my School!" He may have talked of "mysteries," but he was much more concerned with the "revelation" that might make them clear as day. For the actor there is only one "mystery" and it lies in the interrelationship of the refractory body with the wayward soul. The particular solution may determine *anyone's* life in art. The key that Stanislavsky placed in the hands of the actor was—the actor's own consciousness.

What does this include? Everything. Everything that comes within the grasp of his five senses and is subject to his will. The use of his body, his voice, his inner gifts, sense of rhythm, response to imagery, his sympathies, even his moral point of view. Always, his *conscious recognition* of these things. As he grows in their service, he will grow to love himself, but not with self-love, only as a vessel of craft. If it's Shakespeare he's playing, or Aeschylus, or Molière, or Shaw, he will love their words because they have been chosen and arranged with deep craft, almost with guile—a camouflage to deceive mortality. . . .

Such are the splendors and the miseries of the actor's world. But one thing is certain, mere thinking won't make it come to pass. It's not a general matter of "work to be done," but of concrete tasks, consciously undertaken and mastered by repetition. They are the irreducible minimum of our business. Specific things done, moment to moment. Grasp this, and at once there's a clearing of the decks—all reliance on so-called actors' instinct, inspiration, divine fire, and such-like dangerous fantasies must go. Not that these things don't matter in their place; there will be a time for such a word, to misquote Macbeth. But for the actor they are the consequence, not the shapers of action. One must not be in a hurry to dismiss divine fire when it happens. But it *is* a matter of *when* it occurs. Perhaps this *Gottsach,* as the Germans call it, has to do with our ingrained memories. We are the sum of what we have experienced, yes, but more deeply, we are what we remember in our bones. . . .

Here, at the threshold of the unconscious, as Stanislavsky called it, is the continental divide of our discussion. It is time we climbed down to the flatlands. Since I have hinted at some of the rapt possibilities, I expect you to ask: But how?—just how do you go about achieving them? Even now, I have an impulse to shirk the answer—to say merely: go to the ant, thou sluggard!—in this case, the mighty ant Konstantin Sergeitch. For it is all there, in his books and in the evidence of his practical collected works.

Not always were his followers capable of seizing upon the full meaning of his work, or enlarging upon it. The exception was Eugene Vakhtangov, the brilliant young director, or better still, the partnership of Vakhtangov–Michael Chekhov, since it was the latter who has left us (in a single smallish volume—*To the Actor*) the conclusions that followed from their flint-and-steel collaboration. I knew Chekhov. He was an immensely complicated man, an Ariel, a great teacher. Simplicity is a very complicated thing, and Michael Chekhov set out to simplify the vast implications of his Master's artistic struggles. The basic discoveries having already been made, he took them into his body, so to speak, filtered them through his own powerful individuality and imagination, and gave them an even more elementary character. It is interesting to set some of their terminology side by side. Where Stanislavsky spoke of "Relaxation of Muscles," Chekhov did not hesitate to call it "Feeling of Ease." Where Stanislavsky broke off his brilliant observations on Action and Objective, Chekhov combined them with Character in his marvelous intuition of the Psychological Gesture. Most of all, he understood the harmony of "Body and Psychology," as he put it. "Listen to your bodies," he would say, "and they will interpret the movement of your *inner* impulses." Great intellect though he was, he scorned its usefulness for the actor, preferring to obey what one might call the "muscularity" of the Imagination.

But to return to your question of "How?" . . . Perhaps it will be useful to imagine, to visualize exactly what is happening, in a play we are looking at. Not so much *in,* as *behind* it, *through* it. As an audience, let us say we are fortunate; we are witnessing a realistic play of stature performed by a company of highly trained craftsmen, sensitive and experienced men and women. We are familiar with their work; we like them even before the curtain rises, but this only sharpens our sense of responsibility. It is they who have taught us what to expect of them; it is for us to be alert and fully attentive. In this way we will be able to give the play back to them; by seeing the point, we will confirm them in their power to make us *see* the point. We want them to be what they have always been—the beautiful, expressive voices, the subtle, sinewy bodies, their lightness and resiliency of spirit, their moody transformations, their seeming worship of the ultimate good in life. We want all of these things all over again, yet offered to us somehow in a new light, as these fine technicians know how to turn them.

The curtain rises. Within the music of the playwright's words we begin to perceive an issue that embodies a basic struggle. The decision lies in the hands of a group of characters who battle it out to the final curtain, and even beyond, in the aroused responses of the spectators. That much could be the summary of almost any play in the doing. But we are here for a special pleasure—to observe our actors, to tent them to the quick. The first five or ten minutes seem to pass in a kind of sparring, easy yet tentative, as if they hadn't quite made up their minds. And then, here it comes, as so often before, stealing upon us before we are aware, the realization that these people are in the highest degree in *connection* with each other. And this they are without strain, by no overt means. Not offhand; if these actors *wanted* to be offhand, they would *be* offhand. But as if they were saying with simple deliberation: I am here—you are there—we are here—and we are in this together. We sense again the peculiar and reassuring pleasure there is in watching our actors *look*, simply look; their eyes are full of vision, when they look, they *see*. They see not only what they want to see by an act of special concentration which explores the significance of the moment, they also prepare for future looks, future significances. Already this is life, but it is above life. It is the same with their listening. They not only listen, they hear. And so with their other senses, of which perhaps touching is the most obvious. But one sense cannot be divided from the others. These actors come alive all in one piece; they can touch with their eyes, taste and smell with their ears. And what's more, they *talk*. That is to say, they *truly* communicate by means of words and silences.

The dialogue begins to prepare for a small event—one of the actors has a speech to which the others all listen. You know in advance that he loves this speech, for there's a glow of anticipation in him as it comes near, the mouth of his imagination begins to water—he launches into it, tearing at it with little nips, the speech feeds him with imagery and his eyes light up as he *sees* ever more and more. He enjoys the responses of his fellows—they give him strength and a strange freedom as he goes plunging along to the end. In the chorus of yesses that follows, enters one bearing a gift. He is elderly, self-deprecating, though his heart is full of love. But these qualities are not yet fully established in him; we sense him alternately feeding at some center within himself and reaching out to find some object or person with which or whom he can establish outer connection. Before long he has it; eye meets eye, an intangible circle is defined, he snuggles into his character as into a warm coat; life in the form of the ensuing action radiates from him without effort, with infectious reality. . . . There is another, who has been brooding to one side of the stage. We know him as the Bear. He seems apart from the others, objective, critical. But his inner attitude, not yet revealed, scorns any obvious indications, bodily or facial; it simply radiates out of some energy he has known how to store up in himself. The speech of the previous young actor has apparently stayed with him; now, strolling lazily toward the group, he harks back to it with challenge and contempt. He cuts through the scene like a hot plowshare; challenge and contempt become welded into a private grief—his face becomes ironed out into a moving simplicity, strangely classical. He remains connected with some image within himself, tears stand in his eyes, he distains them with an angry lift of his head, you can see they have come unbidden and we divine in this moment that actor and man have found an intense union. They, too, are connected. . . . A woman has wandered in during this last outburst; she is the one we call Greensleeves. We know about her. Life has dealt her many a hard blow, but she has found in herself the strength to resist bitterness. Now her lovely face is molded into an expression past suffering, compassionate and pure. *There* is one of her characteristic gestures, head on the side, a quizzical fleeting smile, the partly open hand raised and let fall. She hears the man's words, her face becomes grave; she wants to stay out of it, she turns away and describes little circles with her finger on the table; then she hears a strange tone in the man's voice, she turns to see the tears glistening—a flash of sullen resistance crosses her face, "What have I to do with you?" followed by a sigh. She is connected with him through understanding—her face is a mask of compassion. She folds her arms and waits, filled with some special grace for which there is no name but her own, and which is yet not static, but suspended, in conflict. Two powers seem to fill the stage with dramatic potential—the power of masculine integrity and the power of love.

In the performance of these four or five little "pictures" that I have pilfered from various places and strung together at random, I want to point out that there is nothing *calculated*—not the man's tears, nor the woman's sigh, nor the old man's radiations, nor the young man's abandonment. These actors do what they have to do—it is second nature by now—out of obedience to certain fundamental stimulations which make everything else come to pass. They are too wise to fall into the error of copying themselves. Nevertheless, night after night they are capable of conveying the content of the play without superficial indication or studied effectiveness, simply by safeguarding the truth. One notices that 1) they accept themselves; they open themselves, too; they know how to leave themselves free to receive all impressions. 2) They accept and relate to each other. 3) They adapt to the circumstances of the play with intelligence and sensitiveness. 4) They give and take through their senses; also through action and reaction. 5) They have rhythm in speech and action. 6) They are constantly in contact with something, whether it be an inanimate object, their partners, a thought, an image, or a memory. 7) As a result of all these, their emotions simply occur, easily, abundantly.

There are larger vistas beyond—the completion of the Main Action, the grades and climaxes, the whole composition of the play. But I deliberately set these aside in order to examine the intimate condition of the actor at work. One is rightly suspicious of readers' digests as substitutes for a man's lifelong labor. But I think we can agree that the unit of what happens when that curtain goes up is the Moment. The Moment is the responsibility of the actor at work. And if I had to reduce the great gold vein of Stanislavsky's mine to a single practical nugget, I would say—that for the actor there is no moment on the stage that cannot be examined and accounted for in terms of three basic elements—the Self, the Object, and the Action.

The actor, like all craftsmen, brings himSelf to the work. He also finds himSelf *in* the work, and he brings back this perpetually renewed Self time after time, *to* the work. Technically, this is what I understand by Stanislavsky's Relaxation, Chekhov's Feeling of Ease. You may take it as relaxation and leave it at that if you prefer. But for me, it is a more central and intimate way of feeling at home on the stage. More than that, it is a source of power, and inexhaustible. The Self is all we have—it is well to realize it, to accept it, and most importantly, to use it. Does this seem obvious?—then why is our stage still afflicted with tensions of all kinds, tensions of the body and the mind, contortions of the spirit? When the curtain rose on those little "pictures" of ours it was the first thing we sensed—these actors were not self-conscious, they were Self-possessed. We will return, in the end, to Self.

Michael Chekhov prefaces one of his chapters with this remark by Leonardo da Vinci: "The soul desires to dwell with the body because without the members of the body it can neither act nor feel." In much the same way, the Self needs the objective world—otherwise it has no meaning, it is like a motor idling, it is not connected. May we not think of our waking day (and according to the Freudians much more importantly our sleeping time!) as an uninterrupted succession of pictures, ideas, thoughts, fantasies, actualities. We are constantly seeing, even when our eyes are closed. The actor's Self utilizes this fact significantly; collaborating with the Author's lines, and between the lines as well, he weaves a continuous tissue of these Objects, these "lies like truth," amusing fictions, coruscating images, grim deeds and memories. He is on intimate terms with them, unbidden as they frequently are when they come. In return they "give" him something, as we say—a focus of concentration, a storehouse of reassurance. As long as they are alive, he is alive. That actor of ours, brooding off there on the side was drinking deep of this flow of objects; the woman Greensleeves, drawn in almost against her will, the victim of memories and faiths of which she herself has become the sacrifice—then, when they could contain themselves no more, they overflowed in action.

Which is the third of our three ingredients. Action, considered thus, may be thought of as an expression of the *energy* which is set up between the Self and the Object. As such it has an "oscillating" character—back and forth, back and forth. Is this to consider it too curiously? And are we discarding Stanislavsky's orthodox dictum of desire: I want, therefore I act? Well—have we actors not found in practice that often and often even the word, desire, killeth? But isn't desiring the electrical continuum of looking and seeing? "And the eyes of them both were opened, and they knew that they were naked." (Genesis 3 : 7) The Bible comes to the support of Prospero Alexeitch. And once we have set that energy *going,* will it be so difficult to know what we *want?* Again, I must warn you, as I warn myself, that these things must not be taken mechanically, lest we fall again into the error of the "old noser." They are neither a formula nor a recipe. They are the short-hand, as it were, of a long experience. Symbols. All symbols have to be earned, and paid for with the usual legal tender—blood, sweat and tears.

LEE STRASBERG

(b. 1901)

The best-known acting teacher in America, Lee Strasberg is credited with turning Stanislavsky's Russian system of acting into an American "Method." Although his contributions to acting and to theatre in America are the subject of acrimonious debates between disciples and critics, there is little doubt that his early work in the Group Theatre was one of the major avenues through which a new approach to acting reached the American theatre, and he has been one of the most influential figures in acting for almost forty years.

Born in Austria-Hungary, he was in business as a wigmaker when he became interested in acting at the Chrystie Street Settlement House. The visit of the Moscow Art Theatre to New York in 1923 spurred his decision "to take a crack at the theatre," and he found his way to the American Laboratory Theatre recently organized by Richard Boleslavsky and Maria Ouspenskaya, former members of the Moscow Art Theatre. Here Strasberg absorbed the major ideas on which his teaching and practical work have been built. According to one biographical sketch, "he still has the notes taken on his first day in Boleslavsky's class." He pursued his career as an actor by becoming a member of the Theatre Guild corps, where he met Harold Clurman and Cheryl Crawford with whom he was to found the Group Theatre in 1931.

Strasberg not only directed the first production of the Group Theatre, Paul Green's *House of Connelly,* but also undertook the training of the actors based on his interpretation of the Stanislavsky method learned from Boleslavsky, and the writings of Vakhtangov and Michael Chekhov. His main emphasis was on the creation of "true emotion" through improvisation and exercises in "affective memory." It was his concentration on emotional recall and on the actor's use of his personal circumstances rather than the "given circumstances" of the play that was to be a source of theoretical conflict with some of his colleagues in the Group Theatre and at a later date between Strasberg's "Method" and other interpretations of Stanislavsky. Stella Adler's work with Stanislavsky in Paris in 1934 was a turning point for Strasberg's relationship with his co-workers in the Group Theatre, for Miss Adler brought back word from the master that they were overemphasizing the emotional memory exercises. Strasberg at first felt that "Stanislavsky had gone back on himself," but then tried to modify his work, while defending his approach as a peculiarly American version of Stanislavsky, whom it was unwise to follow rigidly. Years later in a letter to Christine Edwards that appears in her study of *The Stanislavsky Heritage,* Strasberg stated: "By saying that the Group Theatre used an adaptation of the Stanislavsky Method, we mean that we emphasized elements that he had not emphasized and disregarded elements which he might have considered of greater importance."

When Strasberg left the Group around 1937, he continued his directing career with *The Fifth Column, The Big Knife, Peer Gynt,* and others, but seemed to find his true role when he returned to teaching in the late 1940s—in private classes, at the American Theatre Wing, and, from 1949 on, at the Actors Studio. Although he was not among the founders of the Studio, he began to train a new generation of actors and prepared them for the private, psychological dramas popular in the 1950s.

For over a decade Strasberg at the Actors Studio provided what professional actors in America seemed to need: a place to extend their skills and technique. For some it served as a home, a school, a casting office, a psychoanalytic couch. The work of the Studio and its Method actors, whose names compose a Who's Who of American theatre in the period—Julie Harris, Montgomery Clift, Marlon Brando, David Wayne, Eli Wallach, Paul Newman, Karl Malden, Kim Stanley, Geraldine Page, James Dean, Ben Gazzara, Anne Bancroft, Shelley Winters, and Marilyn Monroe—made copy not only for theatre pages, where their "fetishes" and stereotypes were debated, but also for news and gossip columns. The directors Elia Kazan, Robert Lewis, and Harold Clurman, all formerly associated with Strasberg, drew heavily on his Studio actors for their important productions. Despite criticism from many quarters of the cultishness of the Studio, Paul Gray points out in his important chronology on the Stanislavsky method in *Tulane Drama Review,* that "Strasberg had obviously found a key—he could bring certain qualities to the surface." Strasberg told Gray, for example, that "Kazan usually casts people who can use the Method because he expects them to get a lot of work done by themselves. But he casts people who he thinks have a certain something deep inside them—which if it could come out would be essential to the role. To succeed, then, he would have to find some way of bringing this something to the surface." Strasberg elaborated his exercises, including the highly controversial one he calls "the private moment," as ways of getting at the "certain something" in the actor and freeing him for revelations onstage. There is ample testimony from leading actors of his capacity, in Kim Stanley's words, of "nurturing" talent and "making it go."

In the decade of the sixties, there developed a strong feeling, however, that without a theatre, without plays and productions, the actors of the Studio tended to reveal only their own personalities. When the Actors Studio reorganized after the departure of Elia Kazan to his post as head of the new Lincoln Center Repertory Theater and tried its hand at production, including Strasberg's *The Three Sisters,* its basic approach was questioned. It was argued that Strasberg's intensive focus on "The Actor and Himself" did not prepare Studio members for the new demands of contemporary theatre, but many actors and directors continued to acknowledge his profound influence on their development.

Strasberg's extensive, detailed, highly personal comments on actors' work in the Studio has been edited from tapes in *Strasberg at the Studio,* from which the following selection is drawn.

The Actor and Himself

The extraordinary thing about acting is that life itself is actually used to create artistic results. In every other art the means only pretend to deal with reality. Music can often capture something more deeply than any other way, but it only tells you something about reality. Painting tells something *about* the painter, *about* the thing painted, and *about* the combination of the two. But since the actor is also a human being, he does not pretend to use reality. He can literally use everything that exists. The actor uses thought—not thought transcribed into color and line as the painter does, but actual, real thought. The actor uses real sensation and real behavior. That actual reality is the material of our craft.

The things that fed the great actors of the past as human beings were of such strength and sensitivity that when these things were added to conscious effort, they unconsciously and subconsciously led to the results in all great acting, the great performances accomplished by people who would say if asked, "I don't know how I do it." In themselves as human beings were certain sensitivities and capacities which made it possible for them to create these great performances even though they were unaware of the process.

The actor's human nature not only makes possible his greatness, but also is the source of his problems. Here in the Studio we have become aware that the opposite is also true, that an individual can possess the technical ability to do certain things and yet may have difficulty in expressing them because of his emotional life, because of the problems of his human existence. The approach to this actor's prob-

Lee Strasberg: *Strasberg at the Actors Studio,* edited by Robert H. Hethmon. New York: Viking Press, 1965, pp. 74-87, *passim.*

lem must therefore deal first with relieving whatever difficulties are inherent in himself that negate his freedom of expression and block the capacities he possesses.

All actors who have worked at their craft have found it hard to describe what they have done. Stanislavsky had difficulty because he didn't think abstractly. But this was wonderful because it kept him from arriving at the abstract conclusions with which most people had previously satisfied their minds. Most people suppose they have really solved something when in fact they have only made an impressive formula. It means something to them but is not cogent enough to mean anything to anybody else.

The clearest and most precise statement about acting to be found is a fifteen-page essay written by the great French actor Talma—one of the greatest actors of all time. In it he states everything you need to know about acting. For example, sensibility without control or intelligence is wrong; there must be a unification of inner and outer resources; intelligence and intellectual control must be involved to ensure a proper use of all elements. Talma's essay is the best ever written about acting, but nobody can understand it who has not already found out what it means. It has made no impression on the theatre because it is abstract.

One of the most brilliant descriptions of the actor's problem comes from Jacques Copeau. He describes the difficulties the actor has with his "blood," as he calls it. The actor tells his arm, "Come on now, arm, go out and make the gesture," but the arm remains wooden. The "blood" doesn't flow; the muscles don't move; the body fights within itself; it's a terrifying thing. To someone on the outside this sounds like verbalization or poetry. But we know, because we have often felt what it means to stand on the stage and know that what you are doing is not what you mean to do, that you meant to move your arm differently and you meant to come over to the audience with ease and warmth, and instead you're standing there like a stick. Copeau calls it "the battle with the blood of the actor."

Copeau was also the first to bring to my attention the marvelous phrase Shakespeare used about acting. Remember where Hamlet says, "Is it not monstrous that this player here, but in a fiction, in a dream of passion, could force his soul so to his own conceit . . . ?" Isn't it monstrous that someone should have this capacity? The profession of acting, the basic art of acting, is a monstrous thing because it is done with the same flesh-and-blood muscles with which you perform ordinary deeds, real deeds. The body with which you make real love is the same body with which you make fictitious love with someone whom you don't like, whom you fight with, whom you hate, by whom you hate to be touched. And yet you throw yourself into his arms with the same kind of aliveness and zest and passion as with your real lover—not only with your real lover, with your realest lover. In no other art do you have this monstrous thing.

The basic thing in acting is what William Gillette calls "the illusion of the first time." It must seem that this has never taken place before, that no one has seen it before, that this actress has never done this before, and that in fact she's not an actress. Even in stylized forms of theatre, unless you feel that what you are seeing is somehow at that moment being creatively inspired, you say, "Well, he's repeating," or, "It's very good, but seems mechanical; it seems imitative," or "It seems as if he's getting tired of it." The conditions of acting demand that you know in advance what you are going to do while the art of acting demands that you should seem not to know. This would appear to make acting impossible, but that is not so in practice. It is just that there is a slight confusion about the problem.

A piano is a precise instrument. It exists outside of yourself. When we say that the pianist is doing something real, we mean that he knows the music, that with a definite finger of a particular hand he will hit a certain note, and that he knows he means to hit it with a certain amount of energy and a certain amount of feeling, and therefore not only of physical pressure but also of rhythmic and mood pressure. However—and this is what preserves the illusion of the first time—when his hand comes down on the piano, because it is a real instrument and cannot be misled by the pianist's intention, the sound that comes out is the precise result of the amount of energy that he employed. But the actor has no piano. In the actor pianist and piano are the same. When the actor attempts to hit on some key of himself, on some mood, thought, feeling, or sensation, what comes out is not necessarily what he thinks he should have hit, but what he actually hits. He may consciously follow the same procedure which he employed on a previous occasion to evoke the desired response, but instead some unconscious pattern may well trigger an entirely different and unwanted response. There is no such situation in any other art. . . .

Edwin Booth was an intelligent actor though never an actor of passion. One day he was playing Hamlet. His daughter was sitting in a box, and as he started to speak about Ophelia, thoughts of his daughter's being trapped in Ophelia's situation came to his mind, and he was very moved. He became emotional. Tears flowed. And he was shocked and surprised when people at the end told him, "It was a very bad performance you gave today. What happened?" He assumed that it should have been a good performance.

The human being who acts is the human being who lives. That is a terrifying circumstance. Essentially the actor acts a fiction, a dream; in life the stimuli to which we respond are always real. The actor must constantly respond to stimuli that are imaginary. And yet this must happen not only just as it happens in life, but actually more fully and more expressively. Although the actor can do things in life quite easily, when he has to do the same things on the stage under fictitious conditions he has difficulty because he is not equipped as a human being merely to playact at imitating life. He must somehow believe. He must somehow be able to convince himself of the rightness of what he is doing in order to do things fully on the stage.

When the actor comes off the stage, he often knows that something went wrong, but because of the ego that is involved in acting he is usually ashamed and afraid to ask what people are referring to when they say, "What the hell happened today?" It is not merely that the actor fears he was bad. He is much more afraid that he will find out he was fooling himself by thinking that what was bad was really good. That would mean that he literally doesn't know what is happening on the stage, that he goes on without knowing what is going to happen. He is then in a desperate situation. To go on then, he must have either an absence of ego—which is impossible—or a degree of faith that is equally impossible.

In the modern theatre we have begun to be aware of the intrinsic relation between the capacity of the human being and what happens to that capacity when he starts to act. The things that affect the actor as a human being condition his behavior and his achievement on the stage to a much greater extent than is commonly recognized. . . .

In life, life itself is a sure standard, because if you deal with life unreally, it reacts in such a way that it forces you to correct. On the stage, and in art generally, mistakes are never noticed unless somebody is sensitive enough, willing enough to think. The audience comes into the theatre inactive and becomes active only as a result of what the actors do. Therefore, the basic problem for the actor is not how he deals with his material in terms of his audience, but how he begins to make his material alive to himself. Once he has carried his understanding of the play beyond conventionally conceived textures and experiences, he must then meet the problem of how to evoke and create these fuller and more real textures and experiences on the stage.

In regard to this problem there are two schools. One solves the problem by very good observation; this is the French school, which was dominant in the training of the actor until modern times. The actor of the French school at its best recognizes what is going on in the scene and then tries to find out how he should behave accordingly. He asks himself, "What must I choose to do?" The best French acting and the best German acting are quite superb. The details are finely arrived at. They can differentiate between a girl's being half excited and her half not knowing what she's excited about and her being half frightened. They are able on each line to do something—a flicker of the eye, a movement of the hand, some little look, some breathless little heaving—which manages to capture the image of what they are trying to create.

The other school, our school, starts basically the same way. In all good acting the actors perceive the reality of what is to be acted, but the ways of arriving at it differ. When it is a matter of suggesting and demonstrating, we can do that as well as anyone else, because that is easy. But we believe that the actor need not imitate a human being. The actor is himself a human being and can create out of himself. The actor is the only art material capable of being both the material and the reality so that you almost cannot tell the two things apart. Only in theatre do we have the emotions, soul, spirit, mind, and muscles of the artist as the material of art. We believe that a greater fusion of all these elements with the reality of what is to be acted can take place than is accomplished by the French school. We therefore have ways in which we advise you to work. Basic to these is a recognition of the great difference between conventional reality, which most good actors settle for, and the kind of reality envisioned by our school.

Conventional reality makes no sense. It does not excite the audience. It does not tell the audience what the scene is really about. It is willing to be effective, but nothing beyond effectiveness emerges. We believe that art has the function of giving the audience something without which it would be less—less human, less alive, less amused and entertained, not on a light level but on the topmost level of which theatre is capable.

Once when two people worked here on a scene from *Macbeth*, an observer from abroad came over following the session and with great sympathy said, "Now if you really want to work on *Macbeth*, I can recommend some books for you to read." And I said, "The books should have been sent to Shakespeare; obviously they would have helped him a great deal." The actor is constantly being interfered with by the idea that if you send him a couple of books and give him the right ideas and explain the scene to him he will be a great actor. Whereas, what we try to come to grips with here is the basic process of creation, which exists in all the arts, which is the same in all the arts, and which has always been the same.

Mrs. Siddons, who was probably the greatest Lady Macbeth of all time, has told how, when she had to play certain parts, she would stand backstage and watch the entire play before she made her entrance; otherwise she could not act the scene. She didn't know about getting into the scene the way that we pretend to know. She didn't know about the psychology of imagination. She didn't know about concentration as a definable element of consciousness. She didn't know any of the things that Stanislavsky and others have brought to our attention. She knew only the actor's problem of appealing to his imagination. She, one of the greatest actresses of all time, had the same difficulty of whipping herself into a scene, of getting herself in the mood, of starting herself in the play that we do. Yet she understood what the play was about as well as anyone.

The appeal to the imagination, to the unconscious and the subconscious, is the strongest lever in artistic work. The essentials of the creative mood or moment, when something begins to happen, when the actor unconsciously begins to work, are relaxation and the presence of something that stirs the actor subconsciously. This something is not the kind of mental knowledge that gives the actor answers that have no meaning for him. This something is not the kind of subconscious answer that brings him alive, feeds him, makes his imagination work, makes him feel, "I can now get up and act. I would like to act. Things are working for me now."

I am not talking about not knowing what one is doing. I do not mean hysteria or hypnosis or anything like that. I mean employing the unconscious or subconscious knowledge that we have, the experiences that we have stored away but which we cannot easily or quickly put our hand on by means of the conscious mind. I mean employing in acting the knowledge that functions in dreams, where we often come up with things that seem to make no sense, with things that happened many, many years ago but which we have long supposed to be forgotten. . . .

If there is not the willingness to conceive, to go, to take the imaginary thing and see what can happen, all the actor's work, no matter how good it may be, will stop short at a certain point.

The essential thing for the actor is to use himself, to be willing to trust and to go with the scene, himself, and the audience. On the stage the actor cannot be one-third actor, one-third critic, and one-third audience. He must be 99 percent actor and a little bit critic and a little bit audience. If he is 100 percent actor, that is no good. He does not know what he is doing. There has to be one little bit left that makes him aware of what he is doing. The actor never permits himself to go out of control—though the point at which the actor goes out of control is usually much beyond the point where he begins to fear he will go out of control.

The actor must guard against a search for perfect solutions. Neither on the stage nor in life do we find perfect solutions. However, often when you know that something has to be there to move you and you are still willing to go on the stage without having found that something, although you say to yourself, "Isn't that funny? I can't find an experience that really moves me that strongly," the audience will often see you creating exactly the right kind of degree of experience. An actor need not do a thing 100 percent in order to do it. A little coffee is coffee. A little of anything always contains the ingredients of the whole. A drop of blood contains all the elements of blood. On the stage, if we are willing to concentrate on and give ourselves to a problem, we are already dealing with that problem. The willingness to go step by step without worry about whether you have the 100 percent is the big secret in acting.

In the human being there is expression when he is least concerned about it. The actor is an instrument that pays attention. Something happens to him as a result of paying attention which is pure expression. It is happening even when he thinks nothing is being expressed. I'm not talking about energy. I'm not talking about loudness. I'm not talking about *strength* of expression. I'm talking about the expressiveness which is part of the fundamental equipment of the human being—and therefore of the actor.

Acting exists in every human being. Its extent differs with different human beings; that makes for the degrees of talent. Inspiration is within the actor; something starts it off. If you push a button and no electricity is attached, nothing happens. Electricity comes only from where electricity is, not from where the button is. In the actor both electricity and button are usually unconscious. Often the button seems to be external to the actor, but it is not. When a lot of people are watching the same thing, and only one is inspired, the inspiration is not in the thing being watched; otherwise all the watchers would be inspired. Inspiration—the appeal to and functioning of the actor's imagination—is within the actor. The problem of creation for the actor is the problem of starting the inspiration. How does the actor make himself inspired?

Other artists are free as to when they create. In them inspiration can take place spontaneously, even accidentally. They can wait for it. They can recapture it by correcting what they have already done. We can't. Fortunately, the human being is built with a natural need to repeat. He wants to repeat, and he sets himself to repeat, but unfortunately the second time he repeats coldly what he did the first time out of impulse. So in acting we not only need to repeat, but we have to watch that the impulse stays fresh. If the impulse does stay fresh, the response and expression that it gives rise to will invariably tend to repeat. Little by little the repetition conditions the actor, so that whenever this particular impulse comes, the need for the associated expression comes.

ACTRESS G: Can you contrive an impulse?

STRASBERG: That's what we constantly do. The central thing that Stanislavsky discovered and to a certain extent defined and set exercises for was that the actor can be helped really to think on the stage, instead of thinking only in make-believe fashion. Once the actor begins to think, life starts, and then there cannot be imitation. "Make-believe thinking" is a mental idea of thought, a paraphrasing of the character's lines rather than the kind of thought a human being really thinks. Before Stanislavsky, actors were criticized as conventional or mechanical or imitative, but no one had ever set himself the problem of defining exactly what that means. The actor obviously wants to be good, original, and striking. Stanislavsky was the first to realize that the cliché, the conventional idea of what is to be accomplished in a scene, satisfies a very strong need both in the human being and in the actor; that the cliché functions as a habitual response; that it is at best a caricature of what really happens in life; and that once the habitual response is interrupted by something the actor does not expect, the cliché vanishes because the actor then really has to think on the stage.

When Actress H was doing *The Millionairess* here, and she stopped and I said, "Don't throw her the line. No line. Go on," at that moment something happened. Earlier she had forgotten a line and had asked for it and had gotten it, and nothing had happened. She walked around. She was just acting, but the next time, when she was forced to stop, and thus something in her had to take hold and think, with that real thought something then began really to happen. Wonderful things came from her, a freeness, a looseness, real laughter. A whole new range of colors was released in her and therefore in the play.

The actor must have full belief in whatever he thinks and says on the stage. A good deal of routine acting work merely consists of finding substitutes for that faith and belief. But when the actor can really believe, when he allows himself really to think, when his imagination really functions, he does not need clichés and preconceptions, because this natural process of acting makes him feel, "I'm working," and something begins to happen in him, and from that he gets the certainty and security to go head.

Stanislavsky's basic point is that his training work is not intended directly for production on the stage. The training work teaches the means by which the actor incites this imagination, this thing that takes place and makes him feel, "I think I know what it is. I can't quite put it into words. Let me do it." Then the actor wants to act. He does not quite know what he wants to do, yet he's impelled to go ahead. He is creative. Stanislavsky's entire search, the entire purpose of the "Method" or our technique or whatever you want to call it, is to find a way to start in each of us this creative process so that a good deal of the things we know but are not aware of will be used on the stage to create what the author sets for us to do.

ROBERT LEWIS

(b. 1909)

A distinguished director, acting teacher, and author, Mr. Lewis represents what he calls "a third force" in the training of actors. In his classes and his discussions he stresses the need for an approach that combines the "truthful feeling" associated with Stanislavsky and the sense of style, form, or poetry, which he feels is essential to the expressiveness of all art.

Born in New York City, he attended City College and the Juilliard School of Music, since his first ambition was to become a musician. His sense of form and his conception of careful training derive in part from his musical orientation. His first experience as an actor came in 1929 when he joined the Civic Repertory of Miss Eva Le Gallienne, an actress who offered many their start. His first exposure to the Stanislavsky method came at this time too, when he overheard a conversation between Miss Le Gallienne and Jacob Ben-Ami, whom he greatly admired, about "emotional memory," the difficult topic which he discusses in the following essay written many years after his introduction to the Method.

During the 1930's he was part of the Group Theatre working as an actor, teacher, and, at the end of the decade, as a director, the field in which he has won his greatest distinction. His first Broadway production, William Saroyan's surrealist and episodic *My Heart's in the Highland,* in 1939, revealed his unique ability to fuse "the usual work on the psychological meaning" with "poetic expression of the content" in order to create a unified, poetic stage image. Many of his later successes as a director were marked by this special sensibility and skill—*Brigadoon* in 1947, *The Happy Time* and Arthur Miller's version of *An Enemy of the People* in 1950, *The Grass Harp* in 1952, *Teahouse of the August Moon,* for which he won the Critics' Circle Award in 1954, *Witness for the Prosecution* in 1954, *Candide* in 1959 and many others.

Like other Group Theatre alumni, Robert Lewis has not been content simply to work at his profession, but has been involved in several studios and workshops devoted to creative and technical enrichment for the theatre. In 1947 he, along with Elia Kazan and Cheryl Crawford, founded the Actors Studio. Although he left after that first year to found his own workshop, which still functions, his students in that short period included Marlon Brando, Montgomery Clift, Eli Wallach, Karl Malden, Jerome Robbins, Herbert Berghof, Mildred Dunnock, and Maureen Stapleton. In 1962 he was called upon once again for a training program with his Group Theatre associate Elia Kazan, this time for the newly organized Lincoln Center Repertory Theatre. He did not continue with the company beyond his initial commitment for eight months because he felt little use was being made of the discoveries by him and the actors prior to the initial productions of the company.

His clear, witty "no-nonsense" approach to acting and the whole art of the theatre was made available to students and teachers outside of the profession in New York when his series of lectures given at the Playhouse Theatre in 1957 was published as *Method—or Madness?* The book spelled out the distortions Lewis saw in the application of the Stanislavsky Method in America and called for art that "must have form," for a theatricality that grows out of "real substance," and for "truth that need not be drab or limiting if it is clothed with a sense of form and nurtured by our imagination."

Emotional Memory

In the second chapter of my book *Method—or Madness?,* the lecture analyzing the chart of the Stanislavsky system, I skipped somewhat cautiously over Item Number 17: "Emotional Memory." Rather than take the risk, in a public talk, of adding to the dangerous nonsense that has been spread around over the years on this subject, I contented myself with a definition and let it go at that. I also felt that this was one of the most involved elements of technique in the Method and could ultimately be made clear to the actor only through actual classroom work. However, because this subject is one of the most fundamental problems of acting: namely, how to generate real, and at the same time appropriate, emotion, I would now like to expand a bit on this point.

Ordinarily, if all other elements in the scene are being properly taken care of, if his "intention," or inner "action" as it is called on that chart of the Method— the reason why he is on stage, what he is there to accomplish, and by what means he is accomplishing it—is completely fulfilled, then the actor's emotion should automatically be correct. To make up a situation: if the actor has to say a line like "Don't do that," WHAT he might be doing is "to warn the girl," WHY he is doing it is "because he loves her and wants to protect her," and how he is doing it is "furtively," because he doesn't want to be overheard. If all these circumstances of the situation, plus his relationship with the other character, are understood and believed in, then, quite likely, there will result within the actor the correct emotion for that moment, as well as the proper amount of feeling. In other words, he may have a built-in emotional reference for what is required.

But suppose more emotion is required for a scene than has been achieved from doing all those usual things in working out the part. This contingency might arise, for example, by a sudden switch in feeling from gaiety to agony through the receipt of terrible news by the character. Or, the actor may have to enter the scene in a high state of emotion. On such occasions, unless he is the kind of performer who

---

Robert Lewis: "Emotional Memory." *Tulane Drama Review,* VI, Summer, 1962, pp. 54-60. Reprinted by permission of Robert Lewis.

is content to "fake" or "indicate" the required emotion, he then searches around for a way to summon up some more real feeling.

It is here that Stanislavsky turns to what he calls "Emotional Memory." Richard Boleslavsky, an actor of the Moscow Art Theatre, in lecturing at the American Laboratory Theatre in 1925, and in 1933 in his book, *Acting: The First Six Lessons,* called it "Memory of Emotion." During the Group Theatre days in the thirties, we called it "Affective Memory." . . . But, by whatever name, it was accomplished, roughly, as follows:

The first thing to achieve in performing an Emotional Memory exercise is complete physical relaxation. In order for feelings to flow properly it is important to be muscularly free. First, it is advisable to sit in a comfortable position. Then, aided by your willpower, relax your muscles until all tensions disappear. Now start to concentrate on an incident chosen from your life that you feel will summon up an emotion similar to what is required in the scene. The incident should be one that made a real impression on you emotionally. Preferably, it should have taken place some time ago rather than recently. An emotion achieved by summoning up the not-too-near past is apt to be more artistically usable. Be careful you do not try to remember how you *felt* at that time. Rather, recall and re-create all the physical circumstances of the occasion. Remember all the details of the place where the event occurred, the time of day, how everything looked, who was there and how they appeared. The ability to recall and, more importantly, to reexperience the sensory impressions of the incident is of primary concern. Our sensory re-creations are closely related to the problem of conjuring up emotional memory. Now, in detail, go over in your mind exactly what transpired. If it is a properly chosen strong situation from your life, you should soon start to experience emotion resulting from the recall. You can then use this emotion as you step into the scene you are to play.

At this point it is important that you concentrate on the situation and events of the scene and not try to "hang on" to the feeling aroused by the exercise. The emotion is there and acts as fuel for you. But if it is to seem appropriate to the moment, to be deriving from the situation in the play, you must "forget" the exercise and act out the objective of your scene. You must allow your emotion the freedom to feed the scene as you act. Indulging the feeling derived from the affective memory exercise and disregarding the specifics of the scene, the behavior of your partner, etc., is a malpractice of certain misguided actors who claim to be using "The Method." It leads to that mysterious look that comes over the player and that makes the audience feel something interesting is happening but is hard put to say just what. There has not been nearly enough emphasis placed on this important moment when the actor who has done a personal emotional memory exercise "releases" himself from the exercise and lets the *scene* take over.

Now, if the exercise has worked for you and you have successfully achieved an emotion, you should, at two other times, do the exercise again. If it works three times in a row, you can be fairly certain you have an emotional source that you can tap when needed for some time to come. After awhile, if it is a good exercise for you, it may only be necessary to do a part of it to get your desired result. In other words, it may be possible for you to concentrate on a certain crucial portion of the exercise—without doing the whole thing—and the emotion will still come. This crucial portion I speak of may be, as I've indicated, the recalling of some sensory aspect of the exercise. We know that certain tastes, smells, etc., often bring back feelings experienced at some specific time when that same gustatory or olfactory sensation was present. Incidentally, sometimes an emotional memory exercise wears thin after repeated usage and a new one has to be found for that particular moment in the part.

The application of this exercise in emotional memory as a means of preparation before going on the stage to start a scene has probably been responsible for all the jokes about "getting in the mood." Yet we've all heard the story of Macready who, not wishing to come on cold for an emotional scene in *Othello,* stood in the wings and shook a heavy ladder until his "emotional motor" was revved up enough to plunge him into the scene. Well, this attempt I have just described—that is, to recall, in an affective memory exercise, the events of a strong incident in our experience and so summon up an emotion to be used in a scene—was Stanislavsky's modern (*vide* Pavlov's canine experiments, etc.) counterpart of Macready's more primitive preparation for this need. Those who have actually seen this exercise properly employed will know how effectively this emotional fuel can feed a scene. Naturally, one then has to *play the scene,* not indulge the emotion for its own sake. The trick is to be sure that the feeling your exercise summons up bears a direct relation to what is needed in the playing out of the scene. You may have to try several different incidents from your memory before you find the one that will work for you in a particular case.

It does not follow that the incidents of your exercise have to be the same as the ones in the actual scene. For example, if, as a wife in a play, you have to enter your lover's apartment frightened because you think you saw your husband following you down the street, it is quite possible for you to summon up the desired feeling of fright by doing an exercise based on a time when a door sprang open and you were discovered in some other compromising situation by someone (not necessarily your husband). In addition to the feeling of fright, the attendant element of shame that might be evoked from such an exercise could also serve you in good stead for that particular scene in the play and thus the exercise would have been a good choice. This finding of the right exercise and the correct application of it to the scene must be more thoroughly understood either by witnessing it operate in actual rehearsal or studio work, or performing it oneself. No proper evaluation of the efficacy of this work can be safely made until one has had real experience with it.

It is said that Stanislavsky himself, toward the end of his life, worried about this particular method of using "emotional memory" as a means of stimulating the actor's feeling. In any event, it is something to be used sparingly, in cases where a special, strong emotion is required that does not arise from the natural playing out of the scene, or is needed *before* the actor comes on the stage.

However, there is another application of this principle of "emotional memory" that, although perhaps a partial one, I feel might constitute a more fundamental, more generally useful and more normal approach. I speak of a sort of "continuous affective memory": a process that is ever-present, that is operating all the time you are on the stage. After all, a performing musician who is a true artist "senses" or "feels" the music in his being, so to say, and then executes that feeling with his technique: his fingers, his bow, or whatever. And when we are expressing ourselves in life aren't we often "referring" to some feeling from real or imagined experience in the past? For instance, if we want to let someone know that he is backward in his thinking and we say, "Don't be a dinosaur," we must be referring to some aspect of that prehistoric animal that we now understand and have a feeling about (even though we never have seen one). We are referring to something about a dinosaur that impressed us from hearing or reading about it or from seeing a drawing of it. Also, in using emotional responses artistically there is such a thing as SUBSTITUTION. In other words, if you have to re-create the feeling of killing someone, you don't really need to have had that actual experience! And yet you do know *something* about killing. Have you not at one time or other been so tortured by a mosquito that in a fine rage you slapped your hand down and squashed the bloody life out of the pest? Even on that low level you can begin to understand the wish, the need, the desire, the compulsion, to kill and the sensation experienced from carrying out that wish. Now, with the aid of the actor's all-important ingredient, IMAGINATION, it is only a step to the understanding of the sensation of murdering a human being. Artistic creation of emotion is always some combination of a real source plus the imagination.

Now suppose a man in a play, wishing only to help his family, does something that has a disastrous result. Let's say the wife then has to say to him, "I knew what you were doing, dear." It may be that the actress desires in that speech "to let him know she understands and forgives him." After deciding that that is the intention, it behooves the actress to make her feeling for the husband theatrically true for herself by being sure the desired emotion emerges from some source in her understanding of that particular kind of moment. This will give it artistic validity because, in point of fact, it will be coming from a real source of truth in herself. In thinking about this moment while studying her role at home she might recall that her own father was that sort of man, that he performed a certain, sweet, but ineffectual rite: in order to protect his family in case of a burglar he never slept without a hammer under his pillow (I am now drawing on my own particular knowledge of someone in my experience). The actress now truly understands something deeper in that moment in the play by having experienced through simple memory recall an example like it from her own emotional life. She understands the *nature* of the moment from having thoroughly examined this similar personal experience. Now when she looks at her husband (in the play) and says, "I knew what you were doing, dear" and wishes "to let him know she understands and forgives him" her intention is bolstered by the feeling gleaned from this homework she did: namely, finding a source of emotional truth from her own experience.

To recapitulate: In the work on the role, you, the actor, when studying your part, should first (if the director has not formulated it for you already) understand what your *intention* is in a scene (example: to refuse to believe she can be lying, to realize for the first time she could leave you, etc.). If the desired emotion results from the proper playing out of this "objective" and your understanding of all the attendant circumstances, plus your relationship with your partner, etc., very well and good. But if you find more feeling is required for the moment than so far has been aroused, you should then ask yourself, "What is this moment really like?" "What is the nature of it?" "What do *I* understand in it?" This exploration of what the emotional truth of the situation is to you will lead you to recall some specific, comparable experience that will stimulate your emotional juices when you come to play that moment on the stage. The feeling you have stirred up through this private work comes through as you speak your line (with its fully experienced intention). The more work of this kind you do at home, or in your training studio, the fuller your emotional "storehouse" will become for future use in roles. You won't need to imitate the feelings of others because you will have your own supply. The source is in you; it is in all the large and small emotional experiences recalled from your own life. It seems to me that this is a more professional and less chancy approach to one of the most important ingredients of acting.

That, then, is a practical application of this process of attempting to achieve the desired feeling in the part at all times. It is a most important aspect of the actor's private work. After all, the director may only say, indeed, should only be required to say, "This character should feel so and so here." The actor, in turn, with his technique, should be able to guarantee that that feeling will be there, will always be there, and that it will emerge from his real experience and so convince the audience of its validity. I am not going to take the time now to answer those who will say that I am speaking only of "serious" plays, not comedy; or of a certain style of acting, or "Method acting," or what have you, other than to say this: There has never been a good actor playing Odets, Shakespeare, Molière, or anything else, who has not faced this problem of truthfully feeling whatever situation he was going through in any part in any play, from the most realistic to the most fantastic. For example, I recently saw the Berliner Ensemble in four of its most famous productions. Now when one discusses the Brechtian principles of alienation (*"Verfremdungkeit"*) the discussion had better center around the director's production schemes, for in that company, as well as any other, the acting itself seemed to me to be just good or bad. When it was great, as in the cases of Brecht's widow, Helene Weigel, and Ernst Busch, in *Mother Courage,* whether in some instances the actor's "partner" may have been the audience instead of another character, all the processes of great acting that we associate with Duse or Chaliapin, to take two quite different examples, were present. They "connected" with each other, or with the audience, when it was right to do so; they "talked" and "listened," they experienced very real and often very deep emotions themselves in accordance with the requirements of the scenes, and this emotion transmitted itself to the audience—the choice of the feeling being all-important. It amused me that, after the performance of *Mother Courage,* in a discussion with some theatre people, a theatrical journalist who was present said of the one performer some of us felt was the least adequate because she was "indicating" her feelings instead of experiencing them, "Ah, but she was the one who was doing the alienation business."

The emotion that we observe in some acting on the stage today seems more often like an *illustration* of feeling than the real McCoy. It is as if the actors are describing some feelings that are happening, or have happened, to someone else. What is wanted is the true emotion that is the direct and natural result of the particular experience of the moment. It seems to me that the trick is to be able to summon up those feelings that will be true to us because they are arrived at from experiences of which we have some real personal knowledge. This knowledge can come from many sources: from having, in life, participated in something more or less similar to what is transpiring in the part, from sensitive observation of someone else having done that, from reading, from imagination; in fact, from anything that has strongly impressed us emotionally. This is why it is so important for the actor in his daily living continuously to store up emotional fuel for subsequent use in the performance of his parts. He should observe and savor all aspects of life, his own as well as the life around him. Only in this way can he become an instrument that can easily be tapped for those needed emotional responses. Wasn't it Copeau who said that, being an artist, he wanted to experience all the possible emotions in life so that he would die exhausted?

GERALDINE PAGE

(b. 1924)

Geraldine Page says of herself that she "always wanted to be good at something, to be somebody," and when at the age of seventeen she played her role in a church group production, she knew that acting was what she had been looking for. She went to the Goodman Theatre, acted in summer stock in the Middle West, then came to New York in 1950 to try her luck on Broadway. She studied with Uta Hagen whom she regards as a teacher of very great value.

Miss Page's first break came in the Circle-in-the-Square production of Tennessee Williams' *Summer and Smoke:* she played the part of Alma for eight months in 1952. Roles on Broadway and on tour followed, and in 1955 Miss Page became an observer, and subsequently a member, of the Actors Studio. It was there that Elia Kazan saw her working on a scene from *Mourning Becomes Electra.* He sent her Williams' *Sweet Bird of Youth* with an offer to play the lead, Princess Pazmezoglu, a role she played for a year and a half beginning in 1959. When the Actors Studio developed a producing unit in 1963, Miss Page was not only one of the members of the "directorate" of the organization, but also starred in several of the productions. She played Nina Leeds in their revival of *Strange Interlude,* directed by Jose Quintero, and Olga in *The Three Sisters,* directed by Lee Strasberg. Her development as an actress and her work with various teachers and directors is described in the following interview with Richard Schechner, then editor of the *Tulane Drama Review.*

The Bottomless Cup

QUESTION: When do you feel you hit your stride as an actress?

PAGE, *laughing:* In the first play I was in. I always thought I was good.

QUESTION: Do you use your role in costume to get the life of your character, or do you use your own personal experience?

PAGE: That's changed over the years. Back when I worked stock, and at school, I depended on the costume and the look of the character. Then, when I started studying with Uta [Hagen], I did more conscious work on relating my own experience to the role.

QUESTION: How did you build the role of Princess in Williams' *Sweet Bird of Youth?*

PAGE: That was a funny thing. [Elia] Kazan saw me do a scene at the Studio. Lee [Strasberg] had been lecturing me not to "interpret" things—just see how high, wide, and handsome I could go. I was doing a scene from *Mourning Becomes Electra:* chewing up the scenery and shaking the walls. Kazan sent me Williams' script and I was as shocked as anybody that he offered it to me.

When I read it, I thought a few things: "The woman's vain about her legs."

Geraldine Page: "The Bottomless Cup," interview by Richard Schechner, edited by Charles Mee, Jr. *Tulane Drama Review,* IX, Winter, 1964, pp. 114-130 passim. Reprinted by permission of *Tulane Drama Review.*

Now Kazan's vision of things is very strong and forceful. He communicates them that way and he got hold of me right from the start. He told me how he wanted Princess to look, and every time I'd get shy, he'd push me. For example, I didn't want to go downstage and talk right at the audience. During rehearsals I'd get frightened and Kazan would say, "What's the matter?" and I'd say, "They'll hate me." And he'd say, "Every time you go down there and you get scared, get louder and nastier." Even in performance, I used to frighten myself; but every time I did what he said, the audience loved it.

QUESTION: How did you begin work on *Three Sisters?*

PAGE: I saw the Cornell, Gordon, Anderson productions and David Ross's production. I've always wanted to play in it. The play cooked inside me a long time, so I did a dangerous thing: I didn't do any work. I went to rehearsal to see what would happen.

QUESTION: What happened?

PAGE: I learned a lot of things about Olga. I also learned interesting things about quiet, sweet characters. I found out how strong their emotions are. I found out how murderous Olga feels when Natasha starts messing around.

QUESTION: You found this out in rehearsals?

PAGE: Yes, by doing it, by the repetition of it, especially in a production where we were left alone as much as we were. Lee left us alone when we didn't expect it and he told us to do things when we didn't expect him to.

QUESTION: Examples?

PAGE: He visualized certain moments very strongly. Masha [Kim Stanley] kept wanting to get up off the couch in the beginning of the fire scene. Lee wouldn't let her. And once, before rehearsals began, I was talking to Lee about something else and he brought out a Japanese print and said, "This is how I see the fire scene." The print showed two women—one sitting on something draped and the other coming out from behind a screen with a candle, sort of listening, caught in some kind of horror. This visualization stuck like a nail in his head, and he tried to have me hold a candle when I came around the corner. That didn't work out, but I do enjoy having the screen there.

QUESTION: Why?

PAGE: It's the sort of thing you never do—act behind a screen. I don't know how it looks from the house, but I like being in unusual and interesting places. In stock there was an actor who used to force everyone away so that he could have upstage center. I used to think, "Let him stand there. Look at all the wonderful nooks and crannies in this set."

Sometimes Lee would not say anything in a place where I thought I needed help. But he was right, because I figured it out for myself—and that's better than being told. In the fire scene, the more we rehearsed it, the more I wanted to kill Natasha. I had trouble with this reaction. Olga has a line, "Oh, it's getting all black before my eyes." I thought I'd never be able to say a line like that without breaking up. But the more I worked, the more clearly I saw that she doesn't do anything because she's incapacitated by her titanic rage. One time, during rehearsals, when Fyodor Ilyich said, "Olga, if it hadn't been for Masha, I'd have married you—you have such a generous nature," I felt so guilty. I was murderous, and he thought I was generous! I'd just been thinking, "If I could kill Natasha I would put an ax right through her; I'd slice her in half and pull the pieces apart and throw them to the dogs."

QUESTION: Did you draw on your own experience in preparing the role?

PAGE: Of course. There's that silly little thing where we talk about what it was like "in Moscow." I was there, thank God, for a week. That comes into it. Then when we talk about the bridge and the water under it—I grew up in Chicago with all those funny bridges there. That made me a little homesick during rehearsals.

A line can go by me for weeks on end and then, suddenly, the association will pop into my mind. I hopefully assume that the associations are there unconsciously; otherwise, I wouldn't be able to understand my own reactions. Sometimes when things hit me I don't know what they are, but as long as they go well I don't worry. It's only when I have a patch in the play where nothing's happening that I consciously try to dig something up.

QUESTION: Do you work for objectives?

PAGE: I always thought I ought to, but I don't. In class I do the conscious work—set objectives and work for them. And the reason I keep studying is so that class will be class and work will be work. Then all the study is in my mind and I don't have to say, "Aha! Here we do this and here we do that." If I work that overtly on roles, I get too self-conscious.

QUESTION: How did you get the feeling of a family, the four of you?

PAGE: We all know each other—we've worked at the Studio, watched each other struggle with problems. The kind of work we do there is so agonizing and soul-baring, it welds a family feeling. . . .

QUESTION: In *Three Sisters,* how do you relate to the other actors, how do you get into their lives?

PAGE: There's a conscious effort made to interrelate. I had fun seeing how Olga felt about all the different people. And it changes. For instance, we never know how the whole conglomeration up at the table at the end of the first act will turn out.

QUESTION: But you didn't improvise during rehearsals?

PAGE: We did in a way; all the ad-libbing is improvised.

QUESTION: What's the value of improvisation?

PAGE: Oh, I think it's marvelous! I love it. As a matter of fact, I adore it in performance. . . . If you just say the lines as written, you often have to leap from mountain crag to mountain crag in your own thinking. But if you can improvise and stretch the fabric and poke around in it for a while, then you find the links that aren't immediately observable.

QUESTION: Have you done Private Moments at the Studio?

PAGE: I have the illusion that I do them all the time. But never as an exercise. Lee's never given one to me. That's the least of my troubles.

QUESTION: What kind of work do you do at the Studio?

PAGE: . . . Well, the first thing Lee said was, "I want you to do a scene—pick anything, it doesn't matter—and I want you to stand still and talk loud. No gestures, no line readings." I thought, "How dare he? What am I, a sack of potatoes?" They were doing a scene from Giraudoux' *Electra* and they asked me to play Clytemnestra. That part just pulls at you to do all sorts of marvelous things. And I had to stand still and talk loud. "It'll kill me," I thought, and I couldn't sleep for a week. But I did it. And it was very good for me because the complaints about my mannerisms quieted down. Lee kept after me. I found out how much less I had to do to make a scene come across.

[637]

QUESTION: What kind of work are you doing now?

PAGE: I'm exploring difficult characters. At first Lee wouldn't let me work on interpretation because I had other things to master. But recently I worked on Lady Macbeth and Lady Capulet and found out fantastic things about them. Lee promised me that if we ever do *Romeo and Juliet* I can play Lady Capulet.

I started reading *Macbeth,* the letter scene. Associations jumped into my mind; I started reading the letter to myself and I got furious. I thought, "Look at him, that so-and-so, he gets all excited because those damn witches out there told him what I've been telling him for years! They tell him and he gets excited and thinks it's going to happen because they said so." I get mad at Rip [Rip Torn, Miss Page's husband] sometimes because he does something on television that gasses me and I say, "It's so great, what you did," and he says, "yeah, yeah." Then some guy on the street says, "I saw you on television and you were fabulous," and he says, "Guess what? So-and-so said I was—" and I get mad. That's probably why that thought occurred to me about Macbeth's letter.

The way Lady Macbeth is usually played in the letter scene is for her to get elated and say, "Aha! Now's the time we're going to do it." And I thought, "She's not happy at all. She's furious." Then I started looking around, saying, "Well, we'll redecorate." I was already thinking of the practical things that would happen after we got rid of Duncan. Then there's the thing about the child. At that point I thought, "Duncan killed my father." . . .

QUESTION: Did you work out such an inner life for Olga?

PAGE: Not as much. I'd lived with the play a long time. Nothing was so near to the surface. A lot of the inner life was shaped by Lee so early that I didn't have a chance to see what I would have thought otherwise. But I did ask him—before rehearsals began—for a breeze in the window at the beginning. So he arranged for the curtains to move.

I'm correcting the papers, but the day—the unusually delicious weather—puts me in that kind of mood people in California don't know about because they have eternal spring. I feel vaguely delicious with spring fever and warmth and the work's not so bad because we're going to Moscow. Then, as I get back to work, it doesn't make sense, so I check back a couple of pages and I say, "Oh, yes," and I grade the paper. Then my eye falls on the little plant that's on my desk. A year before . . . it's so vague, it's not specific. I think, "The plant was smaller. Oh, that was a year ago." And then I tell them about father dying, how unreal it seems to me.

Isn't it funny? I can't talk about it much.

I want to go to Moscow and I hate the house. But I've taken care of it all these years. It's my house. That's one of the wonderful contrasting things about the play. I'm very possessive about the house, even though I, as Olga, don't know that I am. . . .

QUESTION: Can you work in such intense detail with actors who don't have Method training?

PAGE: Usually, when there are problems, if they've trained the way you've been trained there is at least the hope of communication. But wonderful actors are wonderful to act with—it doesn't matter how they've been trained.

QUESTION: But you feel it's essential to relate to the other actor, to let him bring the impulses out of you, make the connection?

PAGE: Sure. When I was in *The Rainmaker* everybody was from the Studio. It was the first time I'd been in a play where everybody had the same training. I never had such a good time in my life. That's one of the reasons we've gone through all the trouble of starting a theatre—so we can work together.

QUESTION: What do you share?

PAGE: The freedom to be improvisational, for one thing. Changing a thing doesn't outrage us. This doesn't always depend on Method training. Eric Portman is anti-Method, at least that's what he says, but I never knew where he was going to be onstage. He had the greatest freedom of movement.

QUESTION: Do you ever get so involved in a performance that you forget the audience?

PAGE: No. I can't believe that people are unaware of the audience. You can ignore them, but that's different.

QUESTION: In what roles do you think you've accomplished the most?

PAGE: I suppose *Summer and Smoke* and *Sweet Bird*. *Summer and Smoke* was the first time I consciously worked on revealing my own self on stage. I worked with a psychoanalyst on that. I had always been more comfortable playing character parts, but if they were close to my own age they were very difficult. Alma was awfully close to me and I worked very hard. I got a new freedom from that work.

QUESTION: How did you work with the analyst?

PAGE: I talked about all the aspects of the play that related to me, and about the parts I didn't want to act in front of an audience. For instance, the struggle with the mother. I found out that part of the inhibiting factor preventing me from relaxing and giving myself to the part (not acting "her" but mixing more of "me" in it) was that I didn't want people to know I fought with my mother.

QUESTION: You were in analysis at the time?

PAGE: I'd just started.

QUESTION: And *Sweet Bird* is at the other end of the pendulum?

PAGE: The Princess is a wider part. It had been so long since I'd played such an overt type of woman. I had been typecast by then as a retiring, quiet person, so it took a lot of technical voice work—plain hard work—to do that part. Her behavior is very unnatural to me: that loud and shoving kind of person. In life, I'd be terrified to treat people the way she does.

QUESTION: Did Quintero work much differently than Kazan or Strasberg?

PAGE: He worked *Summer and Smoke* in a way I haven't encountered since, even from him. We had no pressure. We weren't paid anything; nobody came to see our plays. We didn't have to please anybody but ourselves. The freedom was fantastic. We started rehearsals and he'd talk for a while about the town and the people—he has a marvelous imagination and understanding. Then he'd say, "Now, what do you think about it?" And we'd talk. And he'd say, "Don't you think such-and-such?" He used to set props around while we were rehearsing. One day I found a fan and once a little basket full of ribbons.

QUESTION: Do you use emotional recall?

PAGE: I would never shut it out. But I don't try to get one. My whole effort is to relax and keep the doors open so that there's room if one should pop up.

There was one in *Summer and Smoke*, in the scene where we're all in the house together—Mama, Papa, and me. The doctor's son has come back to town and the parade is going by and we go to the window and look out. One time I was trying to envision the parade and see him, and I looked out through the empty space and saw someone I'd known from Goodman; I saw it as you see a movie: I imagined he'd come to New York and was in a big Broadway play.

The vision was so startling that it shocked me as if I'd been hit in the stomach. I catapulted back and hit the father and nearly knocked him down. It was marvelous! The whole thing went much better after that.

QUESTION: When performing, how much do you relate to these inner states you've described, and how much do you project onto objects and people?

PAGE: I try to do both. Lee cut me down on the props. I was working a scene from *Mourning Becomes Electra* and I came in carrying a tray with a glass of milk, a piece of fruit, and a knife. Lee said, "Do it again with no props." But I adore props. I love to use them to invent messages for the audience.

QUESTION: Why did Strasberg deprive you of props?

PAGE: It's related to something Uta told me. When she saw *Summer and Smoke* she said, "Some day you're going to have the courage to do the big moment. You build so carefully, you weave the little moments marvelously, and when the big moment comes you stand back and let all the work you've done take care of it. Then you pick up again afterwards. It's great—it doesn't take anything out of you and it works. The audience does your job. But you'll never do what you're capable of until you do the great moments." Lee's discipline is related to that. It's harder for me to skip the big moments without props.

Every actor has a different group of gifts he brings to his work. You get better the more you bring. And I agree that good as my work is, it would be better if, along with all the little work, I would bring my whole emotional life to the role. I look askance at the people who look down on all the helps and only come out with their great emotional thing. Those performances are like bullfights. You've got to wait a lifetime and maybe once you'll see them when it's really there. Otherwise you see someone pumping up tears and writhing around, and you couldn't care less.

Nobody can, eight times a week, lay his whole soul on the stage and have it fully express the play. You cannot do it, no matter what kind of nut you are. Therefore, I think it's best to know how to do it the other way. But at the same time, don't paint yourself into a corner; leave enough space so that when the things come to take you, you're free to let all the props fall on the floor and go. And then, when the spirit's left you, keep the technical stuff there and make it send the messages to the audience. . . .

QUESTION: I'm a Uta Hagen fan, and I notice that you refer to her almost as often as to Strasberg.

PAGE: I studied with Uta first, for seven years. She covers the ground. Lee's very Zen in the way he teaches. With Uta you get things you can retain and repeat. But Lee always equivocates. He teaches people opposite things; he's a postgraduate course.

QUESTION: I have just one more word: Stanislavsky.

PAGE: Ah, Stan the Man. I'm so fond of him.

QUESTION: Why?

PAGE: He wrote all the stuff down. He tried to systematize it so that you can keep working at it and not just sit and wait for the angel to visit you. After I graduated from Goodman, I assumed—like my fellow students—that I knew all about it. And then to find out that if I studied for the next ninety years I'd just be scratching the surface was divine. It's like suddenly being handed a bottomless cup.

VIOLA SPOLIN

The inspiration for a new approach to acting worked out by Viola Spolin in her book *Improvisation for the Theatre* goes back to youthful "spontaneous operas" performed at family gatherings in Chicago. From 1924 to 1927 she worked with Neva Boyd, who founded the Recreational Training School at Hull House in Chicago and was a sociologist at Northwestern University. She acknowledges her substantial debt to Miss Boyd's original use of games as ways of "stimulating creative expression in both children and adults through self-discovery and personal experiences."

During the 1930s Miss Spolin spent several years as teacher and supervisor of creative dramatics for the WPA Recreational Project in Chicago. Here, working with students with little theatre background, she experimented with "nonverbal, nonpsychological" approaches to help them carry on as teacher-directors in the local neighborhood settlement houses. Her game improvisations freed children and adults alike from the rigid, mechanical qualities of the usual amateur performance.

In 1942 she established the Young Actors Company in Hollywood, where she continued to refine and develop her games and creative group approach. For the young actors she perfected an uncomplicated structure that would give them rich, original, spontaneous creativity.

To her son Paul Sills, one of the founders of the first professional improvisational theatres in the country, The Compass—and codirector of the highly successful Second City Theatre in Chicago, Miss Spolin gives credit for use of her material and assistance in shaping the first manuscript of her book. In her workshops at the Second City Theatre, where she taught such actors as Alan Arkin and Barbara Harris, and with her son's further development of her ideas, she revised and elaborated them. In 1963 she published the results of long years of experimentation.

Her detailed handbook with its more than two hundred theatre games, anti-authoritarian techniques and emphasis on interpersonal relations have made her book and her popular workshop demonstrations important to new movements in both the theatre and in educational and community groups. The Becks acknowledge that one of Miss Spolin's eye exercises became the basis of a scene in one of the Living Theatre productions, and *Film Quarterly* called her book "an important document in practice and theory . . . full of insights into the manifold problems of performance. But the book can also be read as a problem in freedom . . . a system of instruction technical on one level, but on another a demonstration of world view: 'Improvisation is openness of contact with the environment and each other and willingness to play.' "

Creative Experience

Everyone can act. Everyone can improvise. Anyone who wishes to can play in the theatre and learn to become "stageworthy."

We learn through experience and experiencing, and no one teaches anyone anything. This is as true for the infant moving from kicking to crawling to walking as it is for the scientist with his equations.

Viola Spolin: *Improvisation for the Theatre.* Northwestern University Press, 1963, pp. 3-17 *passim.* © 1963. Reprinted by permission of Viola Spolin, and Northwestern University Press.

If the environment permits it, anyone can learn whatever he chooses to learn; and if the individual permits it, the environment will teach him everything it has to teach. "Talent" or "lack of talent" has little to do with it.

We must reconsider what is meant by "talent." It is highly possible that what is called talented behavior is simply a greater individual capacity for experiencing. From this point of view, it is in the increasing of the individual capacity for experiencing that the untold potentiality of a personality can be evoked.

Experiencing is penetration into the environment, total organic involvement with it. This means involvement on all levels: intellectual, physical, and intuitive. Of the three, the intuitive, most vital to the learning situation, is neglected.

Intuition is often thought to be an endowment or a mystical force enjoyed by the gifted alone. Yet all of us have known moments when the right answer "just came" or we did "exactly the right thing without thinking." Sometimes at such moments, usually precipitated by crises, danger, or shock, the "average" person has been known to transcend the limitation of the familiar, courageously enter the area of the unknown, and release momentary genius within himself. When response to experience takes place at this intuitive level, when a person functions beyond a constricted intellectual plane, he is truly open for learning. . . .

Acting can be taught to the "average" as well as the "talented" if the teaching process is oriented toward making the theatre techniques so intuitive that they become the students' own. A way is needed to get to intuitive knowledge. It requires an environment in which experiencing can take place, a person free to experience, and an activity that brings about spontaneity.

Seven Aspects of Spontaneity

Games

The game is a natural group form providing the involvement and personal freedom necessary for experiencing. Games develop personal techniques and skills necessary for the game itself, through playing. Skills are developed at the very moment a person is having all the fun and excitement playing a game has to offer—this is the exact time he is truly open to receive them.

Ingenuity and inventiveness appear to meet any crises the game presents, for it is understood during playing that a player is free to reach the game's objective in any style he chooses. As long as he abides by the rules of the game, he may swing, stand on his head, or fly through the air. In fact, any unusual or extraordinary way of playing is loved and applauded by his fellow players. . . .

Playing a game is psychologically different in degree but not in kind from dramatic acting. The ability to create a situation imaginatively and to play a role in it is a tremendous experience, a sort of vacation from one's everyday self and the routine of everyday living. We observe that this psychological freedom creates a condition in which *strain* and *conflict* are dissolved and potentialities are released in the spontaneous effort to meet the demands of the situation.[1]

Any game worth playing is highly social and has a problem that needs solving within it—an objective point in which each individual must become involved, whether it be to reach a goal or to flip a chip into a glass. There must be group

---

[1] Neva L. Boyd: *Play: A Unique Discipline.*

agreement on the rules of the game and individual interaction moving toward the objective if the game is to be played.

Players grow agile and alert, ready and eager for any unusual play as they respond to the many random happenings simultaneously. The personal capacity to involve one's self in the problem of the game and the effort put forth to handle the multiple stimuli the game provokes determine the extent of this growth.

Growth will occur without difficulty in the student-actor because the very game he plays will aid him. The objective upon which the player must constantly focus and toward which every action must be directed provokes spontaneity. In this spontaneity, personal freedom is released, and the total person, physically, intellectually, and intuitively, is awakened. This causes enough excitation for the student to transcend himself—he is freed to go out into the environment, to explore, adventure, and face all dangers he meets unafraid.

The energy released to solve the problem, being restricted by the rules of the game and bound by group decision, creates an explosion—or spontaneity—and as is the nature of explosions, everything is torn apart, rearranged, unblocked. The ear alerts the feet, and the eye throws the ball. . . .

With no outside authority imposing itself upon the players, telling them what to do, when to do it, and how to do it, each player freely chooses self-discipline by accepting the *rules of the game* ("it's more fun that way") and enters into the group decisions with enthusiasm and trust. With no one to please or appease, the player can then focus full energy directly on the problem and learn what he has come to learn.

Approval/Disapproval

The first step towards playing is feeling personal freedom. Before we can play (experience), we must be free to do so. It is necessary to become part of the world around us and make it real by touching it, seeing it, feeling it, tasting it, and smelling it—direct contact with the environment is what we seek. It must be investigated, questioned, accepted or rejected. The personal freedom to do so leads us to experiencing and thus to self-awareness (self-identity) and self-expression. The hunger for self-identity and self-expression, while basic to all of us, is also necessary for the theatre expression.

Very few of us are able to make this direct contact with ourselves. Our simplest move out into the environment is interrupted by our need for favorable comment or interpretation by established authority. We either fear that we will not get approval, or we accept outside comment and interpretation unquestionably. In a culture where approval/disapproval has become the predominant regulator of effort and position, and often the substitute for love, our personal freedoms are dissipated. . . .

Trying to save ourselves from attack, we build a mighty fortress and are timid, or we fight each time we venture forth. Some, in striving with approval/disapproval, develop egocentricity and exhibitionism; some give up and simply go along. Others, like Elsa in the fairy tale, are forever knocking on windows, jingling their chain of bells, and wailing, "Who am I?" In all cases, contact with the environment is distorted. Self-discovery and other exploratory traits tend to become atrophied. Trying to be "good" and avoiding "bad" or being "bad" because one can't be "good" develops into a way of life for those needing approval/disapproval from authority—and the investigation and solving of problems becomes of secondary importance.

Approval/disapproval grows out of authoritarianism that has changed its face over the years from that of the parent to the teacher and ultimately the whole social structure (mate, employer, family, neighbors, etc.). . . .

The expectancy of judgment prevents free relationships within the acting workshops. Moreover, the teacher cannot truly judge good or bad for another, for *there is no absolutely right or wrong way to solve a problem:* a teacher of wide past experience may know a hundred ways to solve a particular problem, and a student may turn up with the hundred and first! This is particularly true in the arts. . . .

True personal freedom and self-expression can flower only in an atmosphere where attitudes permit equality between student and teacher, and the dependencies of teacher for student and student for teacher are done away with. The problems within the *subject matter* will teach both of them. . . .

The shift away from the teacher as absolute authority does not always take place immediately. Attitudes are years in building, and all of us are afraid to let go of them. Never losing sight of the fact that *the needs of the theatre are the real master,* the teacher will find his cue, for the teacher too should accept the *rules of the game.* Then he will easily find his role as guide; for after all, the teacher-director knows the theatre technically and artistically, and his experiences are needed in leading the group.

Group Expression

A healthy group relationship demands a number of individuals working inter-dependently to complete a given project with full individual participation and personal contribution. If one person dominates, the other members have little growth or pleasure in the activity; a true group relationship does not exist.

Theatre is an artistic group relationship demanding the talents and energy of many people—from the first thought of a play or scene to the last echo of applause. Without this interaction there is no place for the single actor, for without group functioning, who would he play for, what materials would he use, and what effects could he produce? A student-actor must learn that "how to act," like the game, is inextricably bound up with every other person in the complexity of the art form. Improvisational theatre requires very close group relationships because it is from group agreement and group playing that material evolves for scenes and plays.

For the student first entering the theatre experience, working closely with a group gives him a great security on one hand and becomes a threat on the other. Since participation in a theatre activity is confused by many with exhibitionism (and therefore with the fear of exposure), the individual fancies himself one against many. He must single-handedly brave a large number of "malevolent-eyed" people sitting in judgment. The student, then, bent on proving himself, is constantly watching and judging himself, and moves nowhere.

When working with a group, however, playing and experiencing things together, the student-actor integrates and finds himself within the whole activity. The differences as well as the similarities within the group are accepted. A group should never be used to induce conformity but, as in a game, should be a spur to action.

The cue for the teacher-director is basically simple: he must see that each student is participating freely at every moment. The challenge to the teacher or leader is to activize each student in the group while respecting each one's immediate capacity for participation. . . .

When competition and comparisons run high within an activity, there is an immediate effect on the student which is patent in his behavior. He fights for status by tearing another person down, develops defensive attitudes (giving detailed "reasons" for the simplest action, bragging, or blaming others for what he does) by aggressively taking over, or by signs of restlessness. Those who find it impossible to cope with imposed tension turn to apathy and boredom for release. Almost all show signs of fatigue.

Natural competition, contest extension, on the other hand, is an organic part of every group activity and gives both tension and release in such a way as to keep the player intact while playing. It is the growing excitement as each problem is solved and more challenging ones appear. Fellow players are needed and welcomed. It can become a process for greater penetration into the environment. . . .

Therefore, in diverting competitiveness to group endeavor, remembering that process comes before end result, we free the student-actor to trust the scheme, and help him to solve the problems of the activity. Both the gifted student who would have success even under high tensions and the student who has little chance to succeed under pressure show a great creative release, and the artistic standards within the workshop rise higher when free, healthy energy moves unfettered into the theatre activity. Since the acting problems are cumulative, all are deepened and enriched by each successive experience.

Audience

The role of the audience must become a concrete part of theatre training. For the most part, it is sadly ignored. Time and thought are given to the place of the actor, set designer, director, technician, house manager, etc., but the large group without whom their efforts would be for nothing is rarely given the least consideration. The audience is regarded either as a cluster of Peeping Toms to be tolerated by actors and directors or as a many-headed monster sitting in judgment.

The phrase "forget the audience" is a mechanism used by many directors as a means of helping the student-actor to relax onstage. But this attitude probably created the fourth wall. The actor must no more forget his audience than his lines, his props, or his fellow actors!

The audience is the most revered member of the theatre. Without an audience there is no theatre. Every technique learned by the actor, every curtain and flat on the stage, every careful analysis by the director, every coordinated scene, is for the enjoyment of the audience. They are our guests, our evaluators, and the last spoke in the wheel which can then begin to roll. They make the performance meaningful.

When there is understanding of the role of the audience, complete release and freedom come to the player. Exhibitionism withers away when the student-actor begins to see members of the audience not as judges or censors or even as delighted friends but as a group with whom he is sharing an experience. When the audience is understood to be an organic part of the theatre experience, the student-actor is immediately given a host's sense of responsibility toward them which has in it no nervous tension. The fourth wall disappears, and the lonely looker-in becomes part of the game, part of the experience, and is welcome! This relationship cannot be instilled at dress rehearsal or in a last-minute lecture but must, like all other workshop problems, be handled from the very first acting workshop.

If there is agreement that all those involved in the theatre should have personal freedom to experience, this must include the audience—each member of the audience must have a personal experience, not artificial stimulation, while viewing a play.

If they are to be part of this group agreement, they cannot be thought of as a single mass to be pulled hither and yon by the nose, nor should they have to live someone else's life story (even for one hour) nor identify with the actors and play out tired, handed-down emotions through them. They are separate individuals watching the skills of players (and playwrights), and it is for each and every one of them that the players (and playwrights) must use these skills to create the magical world of a theatre reality. This should be a world where every human predicament, riddle, or vision can be explored, a world of magic where rabbits can be pulled out of a hat when needed and the devil himself can be conjured up and talked to.

The problems of present-day theatre are only now being formulated into questions. When our theatre training can enable the future playwrights, directors, and actors to think through the role of the audience as individuals and as part of the process called theatre, each one with a right to a thoughtful and personal experience, is it not possible that a whole new form of theatre presentation will emerge? . . .

Theatre Techniques

Theatre techniques are far from sacred. Styles in theatre change radically with the passing of years, for *the techniques of the theatre are the techniques of communicating.* The actuality of the communication is far more important than the method used. Methods alter to meet the needs of time and place.

When a theatre technique or stage convention is regarded as a ritual and the reason for its inclusion in the list of actors' skills is lost, it is useless. An artificial barrier is set up when techniques are separated from direct experiencing. No one separates batting a ball from the game itself.

Techniques are not mechanical devices—a neat little bag of tricks, each neatly labeled, to be pulled out by the actor when necessary. . . .

When the actor knows "in his bones" there are many ways to do and say one thing, techniques will come (as they must) from his total self. For it is by direct, dynamic awareness of an acting experience that experiencing and techniques are spontaneously wedded, freeing the student for the flowing, endless pattern of stage behavior. Theatre games do this.

Carrying the Learning Process into Daily Life

The artist must always know where he is, perceive and open himself to receive the phenomenal world if he is to create reality onstage. Since theatre training does not have its practice hours in the home (it is strongly recommended that no scripts be taken home to memorize, even when rehearsing a formal play), what we seek must be brought to the student-actor within the workshop. This must be done in such a way that he absorbs it, and carries it out again (inside himself) to his daily living.

Because of the nature of the acting problems in [my] book, it is imperative to sharpen one's whole sensory equipment, shake loose and free one's self of all preconceptions, interpretations, and assumptions (if one is to solve the problem) so as to be able to make direct and fresh contact with the created environment and the objects and the people within it. When this is learned inside the theatre world, it simultaneously produces recognition, direct and fresh contact with the outside world as well. This, then, broadens the student-actor's ability to involve himself with his own phenomenal world and more personally to experience it. Thus *experiencing* is the only actual homework and, once begun, like ripples on water is endless and penetrating in its variations. . . .

The world provides the material for the theatre, and artistic growth develops hand in hand with one's recognition of it and himself within it.

Physicalization

The term "physicalization" as used in [my] book describes the means by which material is presented to the student on a physical, nonverbal level as opposed to an intellectual or psychological approach. "Physicalization" provides the student with a personal concrete experience (that he can grasp) on which his further development depends; and it gives the teacher and student a working vocabulary necessary to an objective relationship.

Our first concern with students is to encourage freedom of physical expression, because the physical and sensory relationship with the art form opens the door for insight. Why this is so is hard to say, but be certain that it is so. It keeps the actor in an evolving world of direct perception—an open self in relation to the world around him.

Reality as far as we know can only be physical, in that it is received and communicated through the sensory equipment. Through physical relationships all life springs, whether it be a spark of fire from a flint, the roar of the surf hitting the beach, or a child born of man and woman. The physical is the known, and through it we may find our way to the unknown, the intuitive, and perhaps beyond to man's spirit itself.

In any art form we seek the experience of going beyond what we already know. Many of us hear the stirring of the new, and it is the artist who must midwife the new reality that we (the audience) eagerly await. It is sight into this reality that inspires and regenerates us. This is the role of the artist, to give sight. What he believes cannot be our concern, for these matters are of intimate nature, private to the actor and not for public viewing. Nor need we be concerned with the feelings of the actor, for use in the theatre. We should be interested only in his direct physical communication; his feelings are personal to him. When energy is absorbed in the physical object, there is no time for "feeling" any more than a quarterback running down the field can be concerned with his clothes or whether he is universally admired. If this seems harsh, be assured that insisting upon this objective (physical) relationship with the art form brings clearer sight and greater vitality to the student-actors. For the energy bound up in the fear of exposure is freed (and no more secretive) as the student intuitively comes to realize no one is peeping at his private life and no one cares where he buried the body.

A player can dissect, analyze, intellectualize, or develop a valuable case history for this part, but if he is unable to assimilate it and communicate it physically, it is useless within the theatre form. It neither frees his feet nor brings the fire of inspiration to the eyes of those in the audience. The theatre is not a clinic, nor should it be a place to gather statistics. The artist must draw upon and express a world that is physical but that transcends objects—more than accurate observation and information, more than the physical object itself, more than the eye can see. We must all find the tools for this expression. "Physicalization" is such a tool.

When a player learns he can communicate directly to the audience only through the physical language of the stage, it alerts his whole organism. He lends himself to the scheme and lets this physical expression carry him wherever it will. For the kind of improvisational theatre the author proposes few or no props, costumes, or set pieces are used, the player learns that stage objects must have space, texture, depth, and substance—in short, physical reality. It is his creating this reality out of nothing, so to speak, that makes it possible for him to take his first step into the beyond. For the formal theatre where sets and props are used, dungeon walls are but painted canvas and treasure chests empty boxes. Here, too, the player can create the theatre reality only by making it physical. Whether with prop, costume, or strong emotion the actor can only *show* us.

MICHAEL KIRBY

(b. 1931)

Michael Kirby has directed theatre productions off-Broadway and in stock and was director of the Actors Playhouse. He is also a sculptor who has exhibited in several New York galleries. This combination of interests in theatre and the arts is apparent in his important analysis of the new theatre form, "Happenings."

In his view theatre, which lagged behind the other arts that have "vastly expanded their materials and scope" since the turn of the century, has begun to move into the main stream of modern experimentation in the last few years. One of the major features of the new theatre is that it exists "not as an entity but as a continuum blending into the other arts." Inspired in large measure by the work of John Cage, a number of artists and dancers began to shape performances that were "nonmatrixed" and not based on the "information structure" of literary dramas. Many names were given to these experiments—Action Theatre, Kinetic Theatre, Ray Gun Theatre, Theatre Piece, etc. The name that has been used most frequently, however, for these events is "Happenings," taken originally from *18 Happenings in 6 Parts* by Allan Kaprow. The kind of acting called for in these performances, in which chance, indeterminacy, and alogical patterns replace the time-space, information matrix of traditional drama, is the subject of the following excerpt from the Introduction to an anthology on Happenings edited by Michael Kirby. Mr. Kirby has worked with many of the artists who have produced Happenings, and has himself produced them in New York and elsewhere.

Nonmatrixed Performances—Happenings

In traditional theatre, the performer always functions within (and creates) a matrix of time, place and character. Indeed, a brief definition of acting as we have traditionally known it might be the creation of, and operation within, this artificial, imaginary, interlocking structure. When an actor steps onstage, he brings with him an intentionally created and consciously possessed world, or matrix, and it is precisely the disparities between this manufactured reality and the spectators' reality that make the play potentially significant to the audience. This is not a question of

Happenings. Written and edited by Michael Kirby. New York: E. P. Dutton, 1966, pp. 14-19. Copyright © 1965 by Michael Kirby. Reprinted by permission of E. P. Dutton & Co., Inc.

style. Time-place-character matrices exist equally in Shakespeare, Molière and Chekhov. Nor is it equivalent to the classic "suspension of disbelief," although the matrix becomes obvious when pressure is applied to it. (This pressure can be intentional, as in *Six Characters in Search of an Author,* where we seem to be asked to *believe* that these new people onstage are not actors inside of characters but characters without actors; or unintentional, as when Bert Lahr loses his place in the confusingly similar lines of *Waiting for Godot* and, starkly out of character, confides to the audience, "I said that before.") Presentational acting and devices designed to establish the reality of the stage-as-a-stage and the play-as-a-play do not eliminate matrix. Nor do certain characters who function in the same time and place as the audience rather than that of the other roles: the Stage Manager in *Our Town,* Tom in *The Glass Menagerie,* Quentin in *After the Fall.* Even in musical comedies, which interrupt the story line with little logical justification for a song or dance in which the personality of the performer himself predominates, the relationship of mood and atmosphere to situation and plot is retained, and the emotions and ideas expressed are obviously not those of the singer or dancer himself.

Time-place matrices are frequently external to the performer. They are given tangible representation by the sets and lighting. They are described to the audience in words. Character matrices can also be external. For example, the stagehands rearranging the set of *Six Characters in Search of an Author* may be dressed like real stagehands and function like real stagehands (they may even *be* real stagehands), and yet, because of the nature of the play that provides their context, they are seen as "characters." As part of the place-time continuum of the play, which happens to include a stage and the actual time, they "play roles" without needing to "act." They cannot escape the matrix provided by the work. Even when one of the actors in *The Connection* approaches you during the intermission to ask for a handout (as he has promised to do from the stage during the first act), he is still matrixed by character. He is no longer in the physical setting of the play, and he is wearing ordinary clothes that seem disreputable but not unreal in the lobby, but neither these facts nor any amount of improvised conversation will remove him from the character-matrix that has been produced.

Since time and place may be ambiguous or eliminated completely without eliminating character (i.e., time and place both as external, physical, "environmental" factors and as elements that may be subjectively acted by a performer), role-playing becomes primary in determining matrix. By returning from the lobby too soon or sitting through the intermission of a production performed on a platform stage with no curtain to conceal the set changes, one can see the stagehands rearranging props and furniture. Although some productions might rehearse mimes or costumed bit players for these changes, most would just expect you to realize that this was not part of the play. The matrices are neither acted nor imposed by the context: the stagehands are "nonmatrixed." This is exactly what much of the "acting" in Happenings is like. It is *nonmatrixed* performing.

A great variety of nonmatrixed performances take place outside of theatre. In the classroom, at sporting events, at any number of private gatherings and public presentations there is a "performer-audience" relationship. The public speaker can function in front of an audience without creating and projecting an artificial context of personality. The athlete is functioning as himself in the same time-place as the spectators. Obviously, meaning and significance are not absent from these situations, and even symbolism can exist without a matrix—as exemplified in religious or traditional ritual or a "ceremony" such as a bullfight. In circuses and rodeos, however, the picture becomes more complex. Here clowns who are strongly matrixed by character and situation function alternately with the nonmatrixed performances of the acrobat and the broncobuster. The distinction between matrixed and non-matrixed behavior becomes blurred in nightclubs, among other places. The stand-up comedian, for example, may briefly assume a character for a short monologue and at other times present his real offstage personality. From the clearly nonmatrixed public speaker to the absolutely matrixed performer delivering a "routine," there is a complete continuum. Yet the concept of the nonmatrixed performer is still valid, as in the case of the football player making a tackle, the train conductor calling out stops, even the construction worker with his audience of sidewalk supervisors. A difference of opinion has traditionally existed between the "monists" such as Stanislavsky, who felt that the performer should be unseen within his character, and "dualists" such as Vakhtanghov and Brecht, who felt that the performer should be perceived simultaneously with the character so that the one could comment on the other. Now a new category exists in drama, making no use of time, place, or character and no use of the performer's comments.

Let us compare a performer sweeping in a Happening and a performer sweeping in traditional theatre. The performer in the Happening merely carries out a task. The actor in the traditional play or musical might add character detail: lethargy, vigor, precision, carelessness. He might act "place": a freezing garret, the deck of a rolling ship, a windy patio. He might convey aspects of the imaginary time situation: how long the character has been sweeping, whether it is early or late. (Even if the traditional performer had only a bit part and was not required to be concerned with these things, he would be externally matrixed by the set and lights and by the information structure.)

If a nonmatrixed performer in a Happening does not have to function in an imaginary time and place created primarily in his own mind, if he does not have to respond to often-imaginary stimuli in terms of an alien and artificial personality, if he is not expected either to project the subrational or unconscious elements in the character he is playing or to inflect and color the ideas implicit in his words and actions, what is required of him? Only the execution of a generally simple and undemanding act. He walks with boxes on his feet, rides a bicycle, empties a suspended bucket of milk on his head. If the action is to sweep, it does not matter whether the performer begins over there and sweeps around here or begins here and works over there. Variations and differences simply do not matter—within, of course, the limits of the particular action and omitting additional action. The choices are up to him, but he does not work to create anything. The creation was done by the artist when he formulated the idea of the action. The performer embodies and makes concrete the idea.

Nonmatrixed performing does not eliminate the factor of ability, however. Although the walking section of *Autobodys,* for example, could be performed by almost anyone, the prone hopping of *The American Moon* would be difficult or impossible for many people to do well.

Nor is all performing in Happenings nonmatrixed. Character and interpretation have sometimes been important, and traditional acting ability has been required. This was especially true in Oldenburg's productions at his store when he employed a "stock company" of himself, his wife Pat, and Lucas Samaras in every performance. On the other hand, Whitman, in an attempt to prevent "interpretation," prefers not to explain "meanings" to his performers.

Although entrances and exits may occasionally be closely cued, the performer's activities are very seldom controlled as precisely as they are in the traditional theatre, and he generally has a comparatively high degree of freedom. It is this freedom that has given Happenings the reputation of being improvised. "Improvised" means "composed or performed on the spur of the moment without preparation," and it should be obvious that this definition would not fit the Happening as an artistic whole. Its composition and performance are always prepared. The few Happenings that had no rehearsal were intentionally composed of such simple elements that individual performers would have no difficulty in carrying them out, and in many of the works the creators themselves took the major roles.

Nor would it be accurate or precise to say that even the small units or details of Happenings are improvised. For one thing, the word already has specific references—primarily to the *commedia dell' arte,* various actor-training techniques connected with the Stanislavsky method, and certain "improvisational theatres" (such as Second City and The Premise)—which have no significant relationship to the freedom of the performer in Happenings. All of these uses of improvisation are concerned with accurate and successful functioning within the traditional matrices. In both *commedia dell' arte* and improvisational theatre, character, time and place are given: details within, and in terms of, the matrix are invented. Although Stanislavsky's techniques are diverse enough to find use in ordinary nonmatrixed behavior, the actual application in countless acting classes and study groups is on the specific control of various aspects of personality and of imaginary time-place orientation. Secondly, in improvisational theatre and in jazz improvisation, one performer reacts to and adjusts his own work to that of another. There is a constant qualitative crisis of choice. But in Happenings, there is no momentary challenge. One performer reacts only functionally, and not esthetically or creatively, to the actions of another. If involved in a movement pattern, for example, he may get out of another's way or fall down if bumped by him, but he does not consciously adjust the qualities of his movement in order to fuse it visually with that of the other performers. The action in Happenings is often *indeterminate* but not improvised.

Even the most rigid acting technique will show variation from performance to performance if measured carefully, but these small differences are overlooked as presenting no artistic problem. Because of indeterminacy, the differences in detail are greater between two successive performances of a Happening than between two successive performances of a traditional play, but, again, these variations are not significant. (This does not mean that one performance of a Happening cannot be much better than another, but, just as in traditional theatre, this entails discussion of essential performance qualities rather than technique and method.)

Thus in many Happenings the "acting" tends to exist on the same level as the physical aspects of the production. While allowing for his unique qualities, the performer frequently is treated in the same fashion as a prop or a stage effect. When there is no need for continuity of character or statement of personality, the same performer will appear many times, carrying out a variety of tasks. As the individual creativity and technical subtlety of the human operation decreases, the importance of the inanimate "actor" increases. Occasional compartments in Happenings contain nothing but performers; more frequently they work with props, and the balance between the human and the mechanical varies with each work and each artist. But there are numerous examples of entire compartments dominated by physical effects: the balloon in *The American Moon,* the sound passages in *A Spring Happening,* the cars and concrete mixer in *Autobodys.* Performers become things and things become performers. The frequently used shadow sequence perfectly symbolizes this blending of person into thing, this animation and vitalization of the object. From this point of view, Happenings might simply be called a "theatre of effect."

[651]

JULIAN BECK
(b. 1925)
JUDITH MALINA
(b. 1926)

For over twenty years Julian Beck and his wife, Judith Malina, have worked together to fashion a theatre that would unify art and politics into a meaningful life style. Although each started out in a somewhat conventional way, he with a year at Yale and she with studies at Erwin Piscator's Dramatic Workshop of the New School for Social Research, they have never become part of the theatrical establishment. In a way they have been "doing their own thing" since 1947 when they founded their Living Theatre, but what that "thing" has been has changed over these two decades.

When they started producing plays, which meant designing, directing and acting in them with a small troupe, they were an avant-garde poets' theatre experimenting with plays by Picasso, Gertrude Stein, William Carlos Williams, Pirandello, Racine. In a recent interview, Beck explained that in the period around 1950, they were "very much conditioned by the art of that time, and we felt that what was necessary was some kind of breakthrough in the area of form, both in language and in theatre production. So all of our early efforts were very much concerned with poetry of the theatre verbally and with poetry of the theatre plastically." Politics in the period of the fifties had to be kept out of art.

But in a subtle way, in those days when they played in their own living room or later at their own theatres on upper Broadway and on Sixth Avenue, they were working toward theatrical goals that are now part of their political theatre. They were breaking down the barrier between public and performer, actions that keep their productions probing, provocative ones. Jack Gelber's *The Connection* with the actor-junkies panhandling during the intermissions and Pirandello's *Tonight We Improvise* with Julian Beck directing a play with Julian Beck were notable experiments in seasons that featured Yeats's *Purgatory* and Brecht's *In the Jungle of Cities* and *Man is Man*.

The production of Kenneth Brown's *The Brig*, in 1963, moved them more directly into the political arena expressed through highly charged choreographed movement. "In it," Beck wrote in the preface to the play, "are all the things which constitute the history of The Living Theatre's direction . . . the search for exactness . . . the search for strict formalism in the very nature of the action, the elements of choreography and of music, of rhythm . . . in all the improvisations, the indeterminate scenes . . . the search for a Theatre of Chance. . . . In its vehement exposure of the human attrition wrought by authority was a complete critique of the damaging force of our society. In the reverence for truly spoken speech . . . thick hints of the new poetry we were seeking."

The Brig "politicized the cast," says Judith Malina, and their new conception of themselves as more than performers in a fiction was dramatically shown when the cast refused to leave the theatre as the Internal Revenue agents arrived to seize it and dispossess the troupe. The three-day sit-in at the theatre became known as "*The*

Brig epilogue," but these events were really prologue to the new life of the Becks and their Living Theatre. With a completely committed company of twenty-six, they went into exile to Europe in 1963 to live a new life as an anarchist commune out of whose total common experience a new conception of theatre was to emerge.

In various European countries and on their return to the United States in 1968, they offered audiences, who were encouraged to be participants, rituals in which traditional narrative, language, and even action had been replaced by frenzied choreography, yoga trances, grunts, groans, howls and screams, all intended to allow "the exteriorization of the interior scream." Free bodily expression, indeed bodies naked to the limit of the law, sexual expression, free political statement, and communal action all combined in works at once highly controlled and yet open to the actors' and audiences' free improvisations. From *Mysteries,* their first collective creation, through *Antigone, Frankenstein* and *Paradise Now,* their work has moved more and more out of theatre toward an ecstatic, real experience for participants onstage and in the audience.

Discussions of the Becks and their latest innovations have ranged from the political implications, the psychosexual benefits or evils, the aesthetic heritage from Artaud, Brecht, Piscator, Cage, to the aesthetic future. For this volume, their view of the actor is the central issue. They have written especially for this collection an exploration of their theory and of their method of work. What is the actor and what is his activity—when instead of imitating, playing, the actor is living? "We don't want to do a play in which we are enacting, pretending," Beck said in an interview. "We create a work where we go into a state of being; therefore, actors play themselves, personally." Their concern is not with skilled performance of set roles, but with "actuality and truth," and with participation. The key concepts are "going through a very real experience," "not creating a role," "becoming a part of ourselves," "presenting your real self, as real as you can get, as close as you can get to your authentic self." The "actuality of the theatre" in the streets of Paris during the May Revolution was the performance that was to them true theatre of our time. Real people "were playing the heroic play, 'The People Against the Repressive Forces.' They were playing it quite magnificently, and to put any kind of artificial play there was pure *ancien régime.*" When the students lowered the curtain in the *Théâtre de l'Odéon* and opened a twenty-four-hour confrontation, Beck felt it was the greatest theatre he had ever seen. When he was accused of trying to put himself as an actor out of a job, the response was, "Of course, put me out of power." Judith Malina rejects the "power" of her own talent as an actress and asks if this power, too, corrupts if it is not used to serve the revolution. Robert Brustein, critic and dean of the Yale Drama School, in a fascinating interview, suggested that the Becks were caught in a fatal contradiction. "What attracts people to your theatre is your technique, the fact that you are superior. You are trying to introduce a democratic procedure into a process which . . . has always been a process created by people who are better at what they do than the people who watch them." The Becks acknowledge this traditional theatre, but have "made a kind of decision that for the moment in history, at this particular time, some other emphasis is needed. There is a fine art of acting as we know it in the theatre, of interpreting, of fine language. But there are other areas that are unexplored, or not really explored enough. And those are the things we have chosen to investigate."

Messages

The Theatre of Changes

Change the world. Marx. Change life. Rimbaud.
How to be what we are and not what we seem to be.

Toilet Paper

Rufus Collins, an actor of physical and psychological intensity, ended an impassioned improvisation by throwing a wad of toilet paper at the audience.
Bill Shari, who is quite a scrupulous pacifist, said that he couldn't play the breathing scene that precedes this improvisation if Rufus persisted in that kind of insult to the spectator. Rufus said: "I'm not only playing Rufus Collins, I'm playing the Black Man crying out, rising up, anguished and angry."
Bill Shari shook his head.
That night after the breathing, Rufus gave an incredible outcry and afterwards swiftly threw the toilet paper on the stage floor.

The Theatre of Pain

The child feels pain, the child cries, the elders find ways to suppress the crying. What does this mean to the actor?
The crying that represents the pain is hard for the elders to take. It reminds them of their own. And so we suppress it, but we do not eliminate it, and we go on to our eternal ruin with music and fatal pomp of flowers, with toys, distractions and coffee breaks to ease, for instance, the pain and boredom of hated labor. But the pain remains.
When the spectator begins to feel the pain, then the actor begins to accomplish a vivid purpose: to heighten awareness.

Acting Lesson

Acting Lesson: Open your ears. Do you hear the screaming? You don't? Why? Are they too far away, the ones dying because we haven't saved them? The hungry, because we haven't found a way to feed them? Don't you hear the people ripped apart by wars we haven't found a way to stop? The choking miners? The slaves to hated toil? Listen to them. Then, when you hear them, open your mouth. And let their needs speak through it. Move. Toward them, toward yourself-in-them.
Now, anytime you don't hear them, stop and listen. If you don't hear them you've shut your inner ear to the sound of your brother's blood crying out from the earth. Don't act when you don't hear them. Stop and listen till you do. Then act.
Now be joyous.

Awareness

Intellectual Awareness is not enough. We have been intellectually aware for

---

"Messages" was written jointly, especially for this volume. Alternate paragraphs in roman type are by Julian Beck; the italics, by Judith Malina.

thousands of years. We have to be physically aware. If we could feel the pain, we could not tolerate it and would find the means to eliminate it. Artaud.

Passion, Anger, Sadness, Weeping

When the actors cry out against the pain, our detractors say: "They are filled with hate." Imagine! They can't tell the difference between passion and anger.
It is better to rage against the preventable suffering
/because it leads to the
suggestion of gorgeous alternatives/
than to express our sadness. We could do a whole evening (maybe a lifetime) of just weeping, and say (as we always do anyway): "This is a play about the human condition."

Why do we go to the theatre?

To crack your head open and let in the oxygen. To revivify the brain, inform the senses, awaken the body, consciousness physical and mental, to what's happening to you, to you, the person watching. To go beyond watching into action. To find the keys to salvation (a ceremony in which the actor serves as guide). To find out how to enter The Theatre of Life. To enter The Theatre of Daily Life.

How the Acting Exercise leads to the playing of the scene

Acting exercises: We develop an exercise to create a scene that needs such an exercise. Sometimes we do some breathing work. A Yogin from the circus in Perugia teaches some of the actors his breathing. Allen Ginsberg does Mantras with us in Brooklyn. Things like that.
But our major exercise is in practicing an increasing, an uncanny, an extraordinary sensitivity to one another. And this we do in our everyday lives which include rehearsal and performance, but no less our packing the cars, or our meals, or our teaching of our children:
Gene Gordon says he feels vibrations in his heart when Jenny coughs. Luke Theodore knows when to console me with jokes and when to be silent. Rufus is always visibly shaken when any of the children are sick. We sense each others' details like lovers. We know when Mary Mary wears pale colors. . . . And onstage we are beginning to deal with each other in a language we can only call magic because it has no other category.
That's the exercise.
To include the audience in this sensitivity and this language and to let the audience include the world in this sensitivity and this language is playing the scene for which this exercise is created.

The Theatre of Fiction

At this stage of our development the portrayal of character is not sufficient work for a man. An actor is a man, he has to do more than span experience by being a fictitious character. For 2,500 years we have had this great form of acting to illustrate how man can extend his consciousness to include consciousness of characters other than his own. We have reached that stage in our development at which The

Theatre of Fictional Character thus becomes reactionary by confining man to the limits of character. Can we go beyond that to the next theatre, permanent change, permanent revolution: to Theatre of Joy (Nearness to God)? May we be alive to live it. And to do it.

Giving Notes

In giving notes during rehearsals, Living Theatre actors often preface their notes with: "Look, we are all musicians. . . ."

The Trouble with Rational Theatre

The Rational Theatre of intellectual discussion in which we all remain cool, unparticipating, cut off from real feeling and real experience, reinforces our own lifelessness, our feelinglessness, our state of cutoff.
We must fly. Eric Gutkind.

Fear of Chaos and Revolutionary Trust

The traditionalists accuse the revolutionary theatre of being no-form no-content antitheatre. At the same time they accuse it of a hodgepodge of ancient ritual, barbaric traditions, age-old festival and ceremonies.

Isn't that what it's about: to accept nothing and everything.

To assault the total culture totally is to be free to use all the fruits of mankind's wisdom and experience without the rotten structure in which these glories are encased and encrusted.

In breaking open this dead shell all the real works of man will emerge, useful, excellent, and if at first crude and haphazard, eventually finding their fundamental harmony, their subtlety and their real relationships.

The "disorder" is a wave of purity breaking down the painted scenery of the mind in the way that radical theatre of the 1920s broke down the painted scenery of the stage.

But the mind offers greater resistances to keep its neatly painted flats and papier-mâché gardens in order.

The new actors say, "Don't be afraid of chaos." The surface orderliness, like the pseudocleanliness of the existing culture is a lie protected by the partially hidden violence of the law enforcers, armies, jails, and psychiatric hospitals.

The natural order will emerge only if we let go of the fear of the disorder. If we trust each other.

During the Rite of Study in Paradise Now, *Bill Shari invented the mantra: "Trust is a Revolutionary Change."*

How can we fly?

How can we fly? Not by watching and observing. It will not happen to us. We have to do it.

Sure, by making the proper preparations, by figuring it out, by observing and then by taking the route that will bring on the MUTATION, by trying.

Why should we fly?

Because we have dreamed of it for so long that we have to. Because it is useful. Because once we are able to fly it will mean that we are capable of so much else.

And because, when we dream it, it is because we dream of being free. Since this yearning to be free is a fundamental component of the truth of everyman, the actor has always to be expressing this yearning, this yearning to fly, to be free.

The Actor's Reality

Steven Ben Israel, playing the Creature in Frankenstein, *fell from the top of the three-tier set during a rehearsal and broke his back. Michele Mareck was playing a scene from Ibsen's* When We Dead Awaken *on the bottom tier. As he fell she heard him say: "I don't believe this."*

Things to play:

The mutilation of cell structure by the diseases of life.
The recoiling of muscles at the onslaught of capitalism.
The causes of violence.
The crippling of character within the authoritarian class structure. (This is particularly important for the playing of all the roles in Shakespeare.)
The remembrance of Eden. Of the ocean.
The Impatience.
The Creative.
The Lusts of the Flesh which win every battle.
The joy of still being alive.
The changes.
The Other.
The interior conflict between the Superior-Man-Within and Things As They Are.
The electrochemical transmissions.
The automatic responses to any impetus.
The voice attached to the nerves, the muscles, the organs, as opposed to the voice as slave of the brain.
The Natural Man.
Et Cetera.
How do you play these things?
What exercises do you do?
This is the work that the actor is engaged in.

Working on the Brink of Breakthrough

We work as if every moment we are about to make the Great Discovery.
How to suffuse everything with joyous utility.
How to speak so that we are believed.
How to dissolve the barrier between art and life.
(The Wall: it must be torn down.)
How to destroy the false imprisoning structure so that it shall fall without injuring anyone or burying any human heart in the rubble.

Beauty and the Beast

There is no reason why the consciously aware actor should continue to exemplify the criteria of beauty created by the Ruling Clawss. That is, the esthetics of, for instance, the Troubadour poets, or of the Ancient World, which still dominate

[657]

our cultural perceptions, might simply be false definitions of what is beautiful. The beauty created for the critical approbation, and admiration, of the Masters (certainly not the Slaves) might be just as corrupt as the beauty created by Modern Advertisers. Both keep the People in thrall.

The new definition of beauty cannot be found in The Theatre of Fiction, in which established esthetics and ethics are portrayed, but in a theatre in which acting is the process of entering into a state of being, the very process of which would be a state of discovery. In which even the perception of the actor changes.

Are you a Messenger or a Beauty Queen?

To stand up on the stage is to say to many people: "Look at me." How can you do that without speaking the only truth you know? There is no such thing as an uncommitted actor.

Mottoes

Don't enact. Act.
Don't re-create. Create.
Don't imitate life. Live.
Don't make graven images. Be.

Motto:

The best motto is: If you don't like it, change it.

The body, the brain, and history

The Historic Process. Marx. That's what we're in.

To find out where you're at in the midst of the Historic Process. To observe it. Then to decide what to do about it. This is the virtue and work of the intellectual process, the brain in history.

But Intellectual Awareness is not enough. It is necessary to decide what to do *guided and impelled by feeling.* That is, observation has to be perceived not only by the brain (spirit created by biology) but by the rest of the body. The body has something at stake.

Not Spitting

"I am not spitting on you," said the signaling actor, "I am covering you with the love of my body fluids."

How to Act

As if your life depended on it. Acting is earnest communication of everything you are with the people who have earnestly assembled to be guided through the mysteries. Whatever you know of the mysteries must be transmitted. The actor, whatever school he derives from, must be engaged in this, no? In communicating what he has learned from his experience during his psychic voyages into the recesses, his physical voyages into the anatomy of life and space, his voyages into the unknown. Your life depends on charging and being charged by the contacts of your life. The actor lives his most intense hours during the performance. When he is invoking the creative forces, drawing out of himself the creative event. The creative extends life. The creative as communal art surpasses the individual act because we are men, and our existence and well-being depend on one another. The classical theatre, which has survived until our time, is a product of capitalist and authoritarian culture, and therefore emphasizes the accomplishment of the individual, as if only the individual can find salvation.

To create love in the community means establishing relationship with the life around you. Just as the actor depends on the farmer for nourishment and on the day laborer for streets to walk on and on the factory worker for cloth to clothe him, so the public depends on the artist to guide him toward comprehension of the nature of things. The nature of things is rooted in the interdependence of all men. Therefore the dependence of the public on the actor and of the actor on the public has to be reestablished and reinforced. To do this, a creative relationship between the actor and the public has to be invented and then explored. Then the two, creating together, create not the representation of life, but life itself. The exhilaration and importance of this are irresistible.

Fear of the Holy

The Chassidim say: "Act each moment as if the whole universe were in perfect balance between the forces of good and evil: and it is your next action that is the final straw that will sway the whole of creation to one side or the other."
That's why actors have stagefright. They feel this balance and their role in it. When, after years of acting, stagefright subsides, it is because we have forgotten the enormous responsibility of our next action.
Tremble: your whole life is a rehearsal for the moment you are in now.

I THOU

The heroic struggle of the actor
is to establish a relationship with the audience
an I THOU
filling in the space
finding the real
the real feeling between us
so that we all feel it
know it
have it
exorcise and celebrate it.
The theatre becomes life, not an image of it.
The actor lives, instead of imitating life.
The public lives, instead of watching life.
What comes after that?
We will find out later.
May we be alive to see it.

Read the Talmud

When an actor asks a question there are always 2 (two) answers:
1. *Specific details as to immediate action and motivation.*
2. *A discussion of "what is the meaning of this play."*

How is this different from Stanislavsky's beats and superobjectives? Not at all. We have different vocabularies. My grandfather said: "Es ist schon Alles dagewesen, nur ordentlich in dem Talmud lesen." *(Everything has always been there. Just read in the Talmud carefully.)*

Collective Acting

The Capitalist/Authoritarian Culture, by reinforcing the position of the public (in the theatre, for instance) as passive observer of high and mighty events, reinforces the subservience of the public. The public becomes more and more habituated to doing nothing but watching. That is why The Theatre of the Revolution seeks to find ways to help the public learn to take action, to find out how it feels to take action, to jump or tiptoe, creep or fall into the unknown, that the public (The People) may get accustomed to taking action. So that the awakened man, yea even the awakened Bourgeois, may soon take the action we all need.

Also that we may get accustomed to taking action together, that the dependence on leaders wither away, that we learn to do for ourselves, which is easy when you do it collectively. That's why we have to get together.

The controlling powers of State and Money would have us separated, unable to unify, unable to act together. We have to do something about this.

"The problem of the artists," said Berdyaev somewhere, "is to make good as interesting as evil."

When the police surround the theatre they are always more dramatic than the play. Especially the French C.R.S. with their black helmets. Their theatrical presence charges the air—their shining formation, their exquisite costuming as the forces of hell, their weapons, their tensions. Their presence eclipses Paradise. I am impressed by their theatre. We have to make good a lot more interesting.

Work on What Has Been Spoiled

In the process of civilization, in our retreat from barbarism, in our unaware states, colossal errors have been made. To undo these errors is the work of the revolutionary artist. It is the work at hand.

The Dean says that the audience should not act because they are not "sublime artists."

The art has to become so great that everyone can be the sublime artist. Why shouldn't he? Isn't it so in love? Are the famous seducers "greater" lovers than the humble men sweaty and hungry home from the fields? They are not! They are not more (nor for that matter less) ardent than the lusty fisherman's boy. And it is because the art is such a great art that anyone can rise to its greatest moments because he is moved. This is the art we will make of the theatre—and listen!—Those who tell everyman that he is not *a sublime artist are lying to him—oppressing him—repressing him. Listen! We are making a theatre where we will be sublime artists together— Trust us, help us, and we will, together, shake the foundations of the earth into a place of joy and usefulness.*

The Physical Body

The body is the enterprise of accumulated culture, of character, of spirit. It has the shape of all this. It has directed itself during the evolutionary process to the physical manifestation of what the uppermost class has alway found the most commanding physical manifestation. And the most available to itself. Therefore the body strives toward Greek/Nordic imperiousness, the spine rigid, the head held uncomfortably up, the rib cage puffed up to exhibit Power (corrupting the natural breathing process to achieve this), composed physical movement (to hide the uncomposed anguish and the claws of the militant parasitism within). It is a good exercise for the actor to continue this examination of physical manifestation of the corruption of civilization.

Now, in addition to this, and this is the important part, now that the actor is not so much interested in representing the debris of the human condition but in creating a state of being that is a change, we need to extend human expression. This should happen if the actor, as human being, extends his feeling and empathy.

Breaking the Form

During a rehearsal one of the actors in the Breathing Scene in Mysteries *broke the form. Instead of finishing the breathing as directed, he fell backward, his body in a strange rigid knot until the end of the scene. He said to me afterward: "I found the Universal Lock." He had until then been a hip, easygoing, smiling person. Thereafter he became studious and serious. He went on a long trip into himself— for a long time he hardly spoke—for weeks he said no words, but looked at us carefully from a distance. Now, years later, he is seriously studying the political situation.*

In such a case it is useful to break the form of a scene.

Violence and Cruelty, Part I

Passion is not violence. And anger is there to be felt and there is a lot to be angry about. Cruelty exists. The Ultimate Theatre transforms cruelty. But the display of it and the actual sensing of it have to be part of that process. And over and above this: Cruelty will not stop until the causes are eliminated. Nor violence.

Robert's Rules of Order

Some of the actors of The Living Theatre *(Rufus Collins, Steven Ben Israel, Henry Howard, Jenny Hecht, Steve Thompson, Echnaton, Jimmy Tiroff) burst into a spontaneous theatrical performance during a discussion of Theatre & Therapy at a forum of New York intellectuals.*

Two theatre directors, one the widow of a German radical writer, one far-out scene-maker, and a few others appreciated the actors' beautiful spectacle and gorgeous ravings.

Most of the intellectuals were offended. They cried "Fascism, Fascism" and wrote letters to The Times *suggesting that the management should have called the police. A famous critic shouted: "This is a rehearsed performance." High-class minds insisted it had to be the work of the directors because critics believe that actors can't create anything by themselves. Some spectators in the balcony shouted "Sieg Heil!" in chorus.*

The actors came away with a glowing sense of breakthrough and joyousness.

Later, some one smart (Victor Herbert) said: "The New York intellectuals better learn that Robert's Rules of Order is not the only thing that stands between them and Adolf Hitler."

The Theatre and Violence

You want to feed all the starving. You want to free the exploited. You want to end forever Racism, forever. You want to stop the suffering. You can't imagine how it can be done without violence, how those who hold power will ever let go without a fight to the death. Lenin and Mao say that's how it has to be done.

Now then, could it give you pleasure to go out and put a bullet through that policeman's heart, through that Marine's brain, would it personally give you physical pleasure to choke some banker or manufacturer to death? If not, don't do it, don't encourage others to do it for you, don't imagine doing it. Don't rely on violence. Find another way.

If it would give you satisfaction to do so if the policeman or Marine were directly attacking you; that is, if, even then, it would *not* make you feel sick and poisoned, then there is something wrong with you physically.

Consider, even if you were personally attacked, and found that terrible circumstances forced you to make the choice to be violent, to kill: would it give you physical pleasure?

Perhaps yes, to the degree that you would have the pleasure of being alive for the rest of your life. Because the moral choice at the moment of the action came when it was too late, perhaps, to have acted otherwise. Because we have been copping out for 10,000 years. Find a way to reverse history. If there are those among us who believe they would get an actual sensation of physical pleasure from the act of killing, then the magnitude of our work becomes clearer. And the Actor of the Revolution needs to investigate this avowal, find out where in the body it feels good, find the causes. What a research! The results could change the world.

In The Theatre of Creative Joy, of Healing, The Theatre of Life, The Theatre of the Street, which is The Theatre of the Future, and which begins *now,* everything must be based on how it affects the Body. If it feels good, do it. The research will prove that it does not give physical pleasure to kill. Thus, if it feels good, do it. If it doesn't, let it rot among the debris of actions and emotions of the civilization we are helping to wither away.

Sic Transit Gloria Mundi

Twenty years ago the young actor was entering an environment in which he strove to rise to the heights of those who were his masters.

He admired the great actors and worked to become like them. He was humble before them and proudly served his apprenticeship under them.

Today the young actors regard their environment with rage and disgust. They regard their Master not as disciples regard their Master, but as slaves regard their Master.

Violence and Cruelty, Part II

Now the causes of violence are partly sexual, partly economic. Out of our sexual hangups comes much of the anger that expresses itself in violence. And out of the pain of wasting one's life at hated labor, working only for money, whether it's a few sous per hour or a thousand dollars a day, comes the same self-disrespect that makes one lose respect for all life.

So The Ultimate Theatre, which transforms cruelty, will participate in hastening the Sexual Revolution and the revolution that brings about the end of the use of money and the end of the authority of the state and the police and racism and all the antiman antifreedom things.

That is, it will be the theatre that aids in precipitating The Beautiful Nonviolent Anarchist Revolution.

Actors: We need these revolutions ourselves as much as the people we address. The creative periods of our unique lives pass largely in the theatre. That is the time to push these revolutions, turnings, further within ourselves. This is the Interior Revolution. The Interior Revolution and the Exterior Revolution must happen simultaneously. In the theatre the Interior Revolution begins with the actor.

The Theatre of Sexual Revolution is The Theatre That Diminishes Violence. The theatre in which passion and anger, real feeling, depose the cold reign of the logic (illogic) of the all-destroying Economic and Power Structures is also The Theatre That Diminishes Violence. And increases life.

Love and gentleness, all the rest is treason. Patchen.

To make good more interesting than evil. Berdyaev.

All the rest is the theatre of the confounded past.

Use of the Stage

Today the contestataires *are shouting: "No more theatre, no more theatre!" Yesterday they said: "The theatre is not in the theatre, it is in the streets!" What does this mean?*

When the Action Committee of Artists met in May 1968 in Paris to discuss how the radical artists could support the students, the first suggestions were to perform plays at the barricades.

It was later decided that to support the students' occupation of the schools and to encourage the workers to occupy the factories, the artists would take the theatres of Paris.

When the Ex-Theatre of France (The Odéon) *was occupied no one was sure what use would be made of the stage.*

There was talk of plays/movies/dances, but when the occupation took place the microphone was kept busy for weeks—there was that much to say—

Fools and philosophers, activists and creeps and students and planners and complainers all talked. Where was The Theatre of Action?

At the next street battle, the stalls were used for treating the wounded.

On the night of the occupation the American performer who was scheduled to play the next night was asked if he would give his performance free for the occupants (if they decided they wanted him) but he said: "I saw them—they are dirty, they are stupid, and they don't know what they want!"

Today they are shouting: "No more theatre!"

Audience Participation

When the audience cries out: "You're hung up!" we shout: "Set us free!"

JOSEPH CHAIKIN

(b. 1935)

Joseph Chaikin's quality as a theatre artist is neatly summed up in the title of an article about him in *The New York Times*, "He Doesn't Aim to Please." This reticent explorer in the uncharted territories of acting derives his undogmatic approach from his training in the Stanislavsky Method, his apprenticeship with the Becks in the Living Theatre, and his devotion to Brecht and to Artaud.

Brooklyn born, but brought up in Des Moines, Iowa, he was graduated from Drake University. He then studied acting at the Berghof Studio, with Mira Rostova and Peter Kass. In 1959 he became a member of the Living Theatre, for which he played roles in Gelber's *The Connection* and the Brecht plays, *In the Jungle of Cities* and *Man is Man*. For his performance as Galy Gay in the latter play, he won the off-Broadway *Village Voice* award, an Obie, and later won a second Obie for roles in Brecht's *The Exception and the Rule* and Ionesco's *Victims of Duty*.

His work on the Brecht plays marked an important change for him since it made him feel the inadequacy of Method acting. While with the Becks, he organized a study group to explore acting and the problem posed by the different approaches to it. Although there was interest in such study, political and organizational activities by the other members of the Living Theatre left him the only member of his group, out of which he started his Open Theatre in 1963. He did not follow the Becks into exile. He has stated that he lacks "the political fanatacism of the Becks," although during their years of exile he continued to feel like a member of their company.

The goals of his Open Theatre are "to redefine the limits of the stage experience, or unfix them. To find ways of reaching each other and the audience. To encourage and inspire playwrights who work with us. To find ways of presenting plays and improvisational programs without the pressures of money, real estate, and other commercial considerations which usurp creative energy. To develop the ensemble." The key words in his work are "explore" and "problems," for one of his motivations is to avoid the "smugness of all my teachers" who "accepted a predefined, but rarely stated limitation on the art," and "who never think of moving towards something new." For his workshop, which includes playwrights and critics as well as actors, talent and preliminary training are necessary. He uses "Method" actors who are not content to stop with the "Method." Working collectively, the group members explore all aspects of theatre through exercises, improvisations and extensions of the audience-performer relationship. Under Chaikin's guidance they move away from the purely logical to "behavior's irrational and more fragile qualities." Their "visceral explorations" have led to the creation of plays that come not out of the playwright's head but out of group improvisations. Megan Terry's *Viet Rock,* for example, came out of the exploration of aggression by the workshop. Jean-Claude van Itallie's *America Hurrah,* three one-act plays, and his *The Serpent* also grew out of participation in the workshop. The title page of *The Serpent* indicates the experience out of which it grew. "*The Serpent,* a ceremony created by the Open Theatre under the direction of Joseph Chaikin, assisted by Roberta Sklar, words and structure by Jean-Claude van Itallie."

Chaikin contrasts his view of the actor's contribution with that commonly found. "Within the theatre it is often believed that except for the concerns of the particular character he is playing, the less an actor knows about the implications of a work, the better. In a work like *The Serpent* the actor must understand as much as can be understood. Here the ideas in the piece are as important to the actor's understanding as are his individual character motivations."

Despite successes—both *America Hurrah* and *The Serpent* won critical acclaim —Mr. Chaikin remains aloof from the "wish to please." He looks upon his efforts as "just beginning." "We have much to learn—we still need to define ourselves." Part of this ongoing exploration and definition is contained in the following essay written in 1969.

The Context of Performance

Art creates another universe of thought and practice against and within the existing one. But in contrast to the technical universe, the artistic universe is one of illusion, semblance, *Schein*. However, this semblance is resemblance to a reality, which exists as the threat and promise of the established one.

—MARCUSE

Assumptions on Acting

The context of performance—that world which the play embraces and the mode of playing which is the entrance into that world—is different from one play to another. Each writer posits another world (realm) and even within the works of one writer, the worlds may be quite different. An actor, no matter how he is prepared in one realm (world) may be quite unprepared when he approaches another. He must enter into it with no previous knowledge so as to discover it. An actor prepared to play in Shaw's *Saint Joan* is hardly closer to playing in Brecht's *Saint Joan of the Stockyards* than one not prepared for Shaw's work. It requires a whole new start, not only into Brecht's world, but into an empathy with his intentions in that particular work. An actor can no more proceed without empathy with the writer's struggle than with the struggle of the character whom he is to play.

Questions come up for the actor which involve a total reassessment of everything as he moves from one play to another. What is his relationship to the character he is playing? Is it a merging, so that the audience will believe he is the character, or is the actor to impersonate, or is it some other relationship between actor and character?

One of the most confusing of all questions to the actor is "Who is the audience?" Is the audience like that of a film?—A group of individual spectators, each dreaming the action in a dark room? Is the audience a number of people who are each potential rescuers of the action which is of a drowning civilization? Is the audience anonymous intimates who are being signaled about their own fate by a spy who's been with the enemy? Or is the audience a group of people wanting the relaxation of an entertainment—to be comfortably purged, fascinated, or amused? Is the audience to be addressed as fools or saints? Every performer makes some decision about the audience in his own mind: personalizing, making specific the anonymous. He makes a secret choice, in the course of events, as to "who" the audience is. When that choice is controlled, the result is entirely different. In attributing a particular quality to the audience, one invites the participation of that quality. Whom is he secretly addressing? The casting agent present in the audience? The critic who could advance his career? His parents? The ghost of Gandhi? His greatest love? Himself? The same action performed addressing each of these has in it very different messages. In other words, to whom does the actor personally dedicate his performance?

"The Context of Performance" was written especially for this volume.

What is the reality of one actor to another while they are together on the stage? The relationship of actor to actor is inseparable from the relationship of actor to audience, and both of these questions need to be answered by the particular text performed and by decisions taken on the text by the actors. These problems must be consciously considered by the actor in order to avoid letting these relationships fall into an unexamined pattern.

The theatre is different from the film in that those who attend and those who perform are all present. This is the single most important distinction. It is with this distinction that the actor needs to come to terms.

A List of Assumptions

"Does it require deep intuition to comprehend that man's ideas, views and conception, in one word, man's consciousness, changes with every change in the conditions of his material existence in his social relations and his social life?"

Marx & Engels, 1848

All entertainment becomes instructive. It instructs the sensibility. It needn't give information in order to instruct. In fact, the information can more easily be neglected than the ambiance of the entertainment.

All acting is an example of human action, including that which takes place on the stage. The modes of expression in behavior give us examples of human realms.

The ultimate value in acting on a stage is to see heroism. The ultimate value of even a temporary community of people—that of the audience and actors—*is to confront our own morality.*

Technique is a means to free the artist. The technique which frees the artist for one realm of reality may draw him no closer to another than an artist who has never been free for any. The accomplishment of the set of tasks for the playing of a family comedy is of no use to the actors whose tasks are performing political theatre or theatre of dream. The actor must be able to play the material with full understanding—not just play himself. Of course an actor's tool is himself, but his use of himself is informed by all the same things that inform his mind and body—his observations, his struggles, his nightmares, his prison, his clichés—him as a citizen of his times and society.

Just as good manners very often keep in check the violence in a situation, confining behavior on the stage to the simple social reality keeps concealed all that which is bewildering. Bewilderment is one of the fundamental common denominators.

Shock: We live in a constant state of astonishment which we must ward off by screening out much of what bombards us and focusing on a negotiable position. An actor must in some sense be in contact with his own sense of astonishment. Reality is not a fixed state. The word "reality" comes from the Latin *"RAS"* which means —that which we can fathom.

Process

When beginning work in a particular realm, the first problem is to be able to mark off the area of belief that the company is projecting itself into. Even when it is clear and agreed on by the company involved, it is easier to imagine than to act. One way an actor can find to play that which he understands, but which isn't in the field of immediate social behavior, is to play through the cliché. This may very well come out first for an actor, but if he censors it, he may always stay behind it. If he plays the cliché out, it's more possible that he will go beyond it.

With the inundation of advertising and platitudes, an actor must be able to discern the authentic from the popular. What we know takes on a more and more separate life in the imagination, and what we act takes on a smaller and smaller repertoire of responses. In order to release action which is in the imagination, but cut off from the behavior, one has to go through a process. That process must be discovered by each actor for himself. For example, Stanislavsky developed a process through which the actor would have a reliable technique for the use of himself in relation to a role. However, according to the actor's vision, the process is altered. The aesthetic remakes the process. One can learn steps which have been taken by other people, but they apply to the other people, and the steps must be completely reexamined for each company and each actor. We can get clues from others, but our own culture and sensibility and aesthetic will lead us into a totally new kind of expression, unless we simply imitate both the process and the findings of another.

As for the disciplines of movement and voice, the actor must carefully choose. Particular mannerisms go along with the particular kind of movement discipline. Modern dance, acrobatics, yoga, etc.—each have associations that are not separated from the particular discipline. The same is true of the voice. The actor must discern what kinds of expressions he wants to release. The focus is acting with all the implications of behavior and "real life" and the formalizing of this rather than the borrowing of an already developed formalized process that is unrelated. Acting is the expression using the personality in all its manifestations. If it doesn't seem possible to develop one's own system of related disciplines, an actor should study another only to the point where he can still depart from it.

The Situation

Most of the time when we learn about acting, it is in relation to naturalistic situations. In our lives we are all involved in situations and we often identify ourselves to ourselves in terms of the situation we are in. Yet, if you move to a foreign town where, as a stranger, you have no particular interest in the existing circumstances, it isn't long before you become quite involved with the currents and stakes with which the townspeople are involved. The same is true of a new job, new friends, etc. Situations enclose us like caves and become the walls and ceilings of our concerns. When we first learn about acting, we learn how to find out what really matters to the character we are playing. We say, "If I have been starving for one week without a morsel of food while lost in the woods and I suddenly come upon an apple tree full of ripe apples, how would that be?" Then the actor imagines for himself this set of circumstances and comes to experience the kinds of sensations that might follow. He puts himself in the shoes of the starving man. Where he has no particular empathy with the man, he substitutes imaginary circumstances of his own that would bring the part alive for him.

In the work of Brecht, the ordinary is set against the strange: and an actor giving a sensitive account of the starving man's plight, without being sensitive to Brecht's plight as a particular poet rather than a reporter, would tilt the emphasis and obscure his intentions. Here, the event of the playing and of the actor-audience relationship forms its own situation for the actor to respond to and play within. For situations of the mind, which deal not with the actual but with the imaginary, the actor would have to know the circumstances of the dream (which I will call the situations of the mind). He must ask himself of his relationship to the dreamer, without narrowing the circumstances to that same kind of logic which limits the perception of actual "reality." Only when he is awake to the whole event of the piece, rather than just his part, and his interest in what is told in the piece is immediate, rather than substituted, can his work be organized to each performing situation. What he learns is how to live through the situation each time, instead of simply repeating the results. If he simply repeats his findings and plays the result, his performance is without the most essential acting dimension—that of being there and inhabiting the play as it's performed.

The actor is a collaborative artist informed and influenced by all those people whose efforts are also involved in the event which he performs. In rehearsal, he exposes himself to the elements which together form the event. In performance he is awake after a process of discovery. The situation, if it is a dream, requires different responses by the actor than the kind of rage and delight of the actual, even when the dream may be a retelling of an experience that has also been actual. But always to limit responses to those which are understandable in the realm of the actual is to diminish the actor's possible choices to the same few which he permits himself at other times, and to limit the possible stage behavior to the existing laws of society.

The actor must come to a connection with the material as a person is connected with his environment. When he performs, he plays the material rather than himself. He should be like a singer who sings the song, rather than singing his voice, which one often hears.

There is that theatre which concerns itself with what we already know and that theatre which explores what we don't clearly know. The choice an acting company and the actors within it make is whether they will follow the interpretations of human action which the times and society give or follow a kind of inner speculation.

I have a notion that what attracts people to the theatre is a kind of despair. We despair with life as it is lived, so we try to alter it through a model form. We present what we think is possible according to what is possible in the imagination rather than what is socially possible.

Perhaps the ultimate in acting through an exploration of behavior is to show not so much another kind of society, but rather another kind of man.

The teacher of the actor is like the teacher of small children who looks for the right steps for the particular student, and when the student is about to make his discovery, the teacher must disappear. If the teacher looks for his own satisfaction of having brought the student to the point of discovery, the student does not fully discover.

My own studies as an actor have introduced me to many teachers and their techniques, and I have sought to learn about all those teachers I couldn't study with personally whose work grabbed me. Peter Brook said once, of improvisation, that it opens a door which, until that point, has been shut, and once it is opened, one finds oneself in a vast place where all there is to do is waltz around and around the same space. I think there is much improvisation which does that. Among those teachers with whom I studied I found the Theatre Games of Viola Spolin, with whom I took four classes and had two conversations, to be the most initially freeing but ultimately confining. The exercises of Nola Chilton, who was an early teacher of mine, opened an enormous area within a psychological approach. From Mira Rostova I found the subtlety of invisible intentions which criss-cross each other all the time made visible. But beyond that invaluable perception I found her system to be a very narrow study. I have studied and been exposed to many other influences which I've repudiated or incorporated. There has been no single influence which was greater than the dialogues I had with Judith Malina and Julian Beck. None of this involved exercises, acting, specific techniques—because for the time that I was a member of the Living Theatre they did not inquire into real stage behavior or ritual. But they were free of all the aspirations and assumptions of established theatre, and therefore did not need to structure their inquiry according to the banal goals. Most recently, the biggest influence on me has been the company of people with whom I've been working, and their ideas and gestalts.

I think that each step of the acting requires the actor to return to a conscious awareness of what he is doing. Still, most of the creative work is done in that dream life between thinking and fantasy, and requires sometimes that the actor rest, and let the image move itself in his mind.

The realm of a situation dictates the kind of responses, and because at this time we have so much separated our actions from our impulses, renamed our acts and committed ourselves to a servitude of denial, replacing what we feel we need with what is recommended, we must not close the possibilities of behavior in the theatre to correspond with the international office etiquette. We should keep it open to the vast range of understanding. One has to be able to imagine an alternative realm of behavior expression in order to play it. The spectator will feel that what is true on the stage is what most represents himself—that realm which he most identifies with as his "real life" and perhaps that one which he most inhabits. But at the same time, the realm played recommends a "reality" that he may adapt.

Everything we do changes us a little, even when we purport to be indifferent to what we've done. And what we witness, we also do.

The mask which an actor wears is apt to become his face.—PLATO

BIBLIOGRAPHY

The following bibliography includes the books and periodicals used in the prepara-tion of this volume and those additional publications which may be useful to the student of acting. Only entries which contribute specifically to the history, theory, and practice of acting were listed. Although the bibliography is extensive, it is not exhaustive, but represents those works encountered in American libraries. The first section of the bibli-ography contains the indispensable general histories and surveys of acting. Books by and about individual actors and studies of each period will be found in the succeeding sections which correspond to the national and chronological organization of this book. General theatre histories and periodicals complete the bibliography.

ACTING HISTORIES AND SURVEYS

ALPERS, BORIS V. *Aktiorskoe Iskusstvo v Rossii* [The Actor's Art in Russia]. Moscow: Isskustvo, 1945.

AMERICAN EDUCATIONAL THEATRE ASSOCIATION. *A Selected Bibliography and Critical Comment on the Art, Theory and Technique of Acting.* Compiled and edited by the Committee on Re-search, John H. McDowell, Chairman, and others. Ann Arbor: 1948.

ARCHER, WILLIAM. "Masks or Faces," in Denis Diderot, *The Paradox of Acting,* and William Archer, *Masks of Faces.* New York: Hill & Wang, 1957.

AUBERT, CHARLES. *The Art of Pantomime* (1927). New York: Benjamin Blom, 1969.

AUGER-DUVIGNAUD, JEAN. *L'acteur: esquisse d'une sociologie du comédien.* Paris: Gallimard, 1965.

BALL, ROBERT HAMILTON. *The Amazing Career of Sir Giles Overreach.* Princeton University Press, 1939.

BROADBENT, R. J. *A History of Pantomime* (1901). New York: Benjamin Blom, 1965.

CALENDOLI, GIOVANNI. *L'attore; storia di un'arte.* Rome: Edizione dell Ateneo, 1959.

CHIARINI, LUIGI. *L'arte dell' attore.* Rome: Bianco e Nero, 1950.

CRAUFORD, LANE. *Acting: Its Theory and Prac-tice, with Illustrative Examples of Players Past and Present* (1930). New York: Benjamin Blom, 1969.

DARLINGTON, W. A. *The Actor and His Audience.* London: Phoenix House, 1949.

DISHER, MAURICE WILLSON. *Clowns and Panto-mimes* (1925). New York: Benjamin Blom, 1968.

DOLMAN, JOHN. *Art of Acting.* New York: Harper, 1949.

DOWNER, ALAN S. "In Defense of Roscius." *Play-ers Magazine,* XIX, February, 1943.

———. "The Natural History of Acting." *Players Magazine,* XXI, November, 1944.

———. "The Private Papers of George Spelvin: A Series on the Development of the Actor's Art." *Players Magazine,* XIX, May, 1943; XX, Octo-ber, 1943; November, 1943; December, 1943; January, 1944; February, 1944.

DRAMATIC MUSEUM OF COLUMBIA UNIVERSITY SERIES II & V. *Papers on Acting* (See entries under Boucicault, Coquelin, Gillette, Frances Anne Kemble, Irving, Sarcey, Mrs. Siddons, Talma.)

DUERR, EDWIN. *The Length and Depth of Acting.* New York: Holt, Rinehart & Winston, 1962.

EATON, WALTER PRICHARD. *The Actor's Heritage.* Boston: Atlantic Monthly Press, 1924.

EUSTIS, MORTON. *Players at Work: Acting Accord-ing to the Actors* (1937). New York: Benjamin Blom, 1969.

FITZGERALD, PERCY H. *The Art of Acting; in Connection with the Study of Character, the Spirit of Comedy and Stage Illusion.* New York: Macmillan, 1892.

FUNKE, LEWIS and BOOTH, JOHN E. *Actors Talk About Acting.* New York: Random House, 1961. (Vivien Leigh, John Gielgud, Lynn Fon-tanne, Alfred Lunt, Shelley Winters, Katharine Cornell, Maureen Stapleton, Morris Carnovsky, Anne Bancroft, Sidney Poitier, Helen Hayes, Jose Ferrer, Paul Muni, Bert Lahr.)

GILDER, ROSAMUND. *Enter the Actress: The First Women in the Theatre.* New York: Theatre Arts Books, 1960.

GIONETTI, CARLO A. *L'attore.* Florence: Valecchi, 1959.

Great Acting: Olivier, Thorndike, Richardson, Ashcroft, Redgrave, Evans, Gielgud, Coward. Edited by Hal Burton. New York: Hill & Wang, 1968.

HAMMERTON, J. A., ed. *The Actor's Art: Theatri-cal Reminiscences. Methods of Study and Ad-vice to Aspirants Specially Contributed by Leading Actors of the Day* (1897). New York: Benjamin Blom, 1969.

JAMES, HENRY. *The Scenic Art: Notes on Acting and the Drama, 1872-1901.* Rutgers University Press, 1948.

JOSEPH, BERTRAM. *The Tragic Actor: A Survey of Tragic Acting in England from Burbage and Alleyn to Forbes-Robertson and Irving.* New York: Theatre Arts Books, 1959.

LEWES, GEORGE HENRY. *On Actors and the Art of Acting.* New York: Holt, 1878.

LVOV, NIKOLAI I. and MAKSIMOV, I. *Masterstvo Aktiora: Khrestomatiya* [*The Actor's Craft: An Anthology*]. Moscow: Gosizdat, 1935.

MANTZIUS, KARL. *A History of Theatrical Art in Ancient and Modern Times.* 6 vols. Translated

[670]

by Louise von Cossel, with an introduction by William Archer. New York: Peter Smith, 1937.

MATTHEWS, BRANDER, and HUTTON, LAURENCE. *Actors and Actresses of Great Britain and the United States: From the Days of David Garrick to the Present Time* (1886). 5 vols. New York: Benjamin Blom, 1969.

ODELL, GEORGE C. D. *Shakespeare from Betterton to Irving* (1920). 2 vols. New York: Benjamin Blom, 1963, and Dover, 1966 (the latter with a new introduction by Robert H. Ball).

ORMSBEE, HELEN. *Backstage with Actors: From the Time of Shakespeare to the Present Day* (1938). New York: Benjamin Blom, 1969.

PANDOLFI, VITO, ed. *Antologia del grande attore: raccolta di memorie e di saggi dei grandi attori italiani dalla riforma goldoniana ad oggi, preceduti da scritti dei maggiori studiosi dell'epoca e da una introduzione storica.* Bari: Editore Laterza, 1954.

POLLOCK, ARTHUR. "Evolution of the Actor." *Drama*, V, August, 1915, November, 1915; VI, November, 1916.

"Realism and the Actor; An International Symposium." Florence: *Mask*, I, 1908-1909.

RIDENTI, LUCIO, ed. *L'attore.* Turin: Edizioni di Il Dramma, 1947.

Rôle de l'improvisation dans l'enseignement de l'art dramatique, Le. Bucharest: Centre Roumain de l'IIT. (International Theatre Institute) 1965.

ROSS, LILLIAN and HELEN. *The Player.* New York: Simon and Schuster, 1961.

SCHYBERG, FREDERICK. "The Art of Acting: What Is an Actor." Translated by Harry G. Carlson. *Tulane Drama Review*, V, Summer, 1961.

———. "The Art of Acting: What's Hecuba to Him?" Translated by Harry G. Carlson. *Tulane Drama Review*, VI, Spring, 1962.

———. "The Art of Acting: The Actor as Phenomenon." Translated by Harry G. Carlson. *Tulane Drama Review*, VI, Summer, 1962.

SPEAIGHT, ROBERT. *Acting: Its Idea and Tradition.* London: Cassell, 1939.

SPRAGUE, ARTHUR COLBY. *Shakespeare and the Actors; the Stage Business in His Plays* (1660-1905). Harvard University Press, 1944.

Theatre Arts Monthly, Special Issue. "On Actors and Acting," XV, September, 1931.

Theatre Workshop "Art of Acting Issue." Vol. 1, No. 1, October-December, 1936.

World Theatre. "The Actor." Vol. IV, No. 1, October, 1954.

YOUNG, STARK. "The Actor" in *The Theatre.* New York: Hill & Wang, 1954.

GREECE AND ROME

ALLEN, JAMES TURNEY. "Greek Acting in the Fifth Century." *University of California Publications in Classical Philology*, II, Number 15, March 3, 1916, pp. 279-289.

———. *Stage Antiquities of the Greeks and Romans and Their Influence.* New York, Longmans, Green, 1927.

ARISTOTLE. *Poetics.* Translated by Thomas Twining. London: Everyman's Library, J. M. Dent, 1941.

———. "Rhetoric." Translated by W. Rhys Roberts. *Basic Works of Aristotle.* New York: Random House, 1941.

BIEBER, MARGARETE. *The History of the Greek and Roman Theatre.* Princeton University Press, 1961.

BROWN, IVOR. *First Player: The Origin of Drama.* New York: William Morrow, 1928.

CICERO. "For Quintus Roscius Comedian." *The Speeches.* Translated by John Henry Freese. London: Loeb Classical Library, William Heinemann, 1945.

———. "On Oratory and Orators." Translated by J. S. Watson. London: George Bell, 1876.

DEMOSTHENES. *On the Crown.* Translated by C. Rann-Kennedy. New York: E. P. Dutton, 1911.

FLICKINGER, ROY C. *The Greek Theatre and Its Drama.* University of Chicago Press, 1939.

FRANK, T. "On T. Publilius Pellio, the Plautine Actor." *American Journal of Philology*, LIII, July-September, 1932.

GELLIUS, AULUS. *Attic Nights.* Translated by John C. Rolf. London: Loeb Classical Library, William Heinemann, 1927.

GREEN, WILLIAM M. "Status of Actors at Rome." *Classical Philology*, XXVIII, October, 1933.

HAIGH, A. E. *The Attic Theatre.* Oxford at the Clarendon Press, 1907.

HENRY, G. K. G. "Roman Actors." *Studies in Philology*, XVI, October, 1919.

KNAPP, CHARLES. "References in Plautus and Terrence to Plays, Players and Playwrights." *Classical Philology*, XIV, January, 1919.

LUCIAN. "Of Pantomime." *The Works of Lucian of Samosata.* Translated by H. W. Fowler and F. G. Fowler. London: Oxford at the Clarendon Press, 1905.

NICOLL, ALLARDYCE. *Masks, Mimes and Miracles: Studies in the Popular Theatre.* New York: Harcourt Brace, 1931.

NORWOOD, GILBERT. *Greek Comedy.* New York: Hill & Wang, 1963.

———. *Greek Tragedy.* New York: Hill & Wang, 1960.

O'CONNOR, JOHN BARTHOLOMEW. *Chapters in the History of Actors and Acting in Ancient Greece.* University of Chicago Press, 1908.

PICKARD, JOHN. *The Relative Position of Actors and Chorus in the Greek Theatre of the Fifth Century.* Baltimore: Press of the Friedenwald Co., 1893.

PICKARD-CAMBRIDGE, A. W. *The Dramatic Festivals of Athens.* Oxford University Press, 1953.

PLATO. "Ion." *The Dialogues.* Translated by Benjamin Jowett. New York: Oxford University Press, 1892.

———. *The Republic.* Translated by Benjamin Jowett. New York: Modern Library, Random House.

BIBLIOGRAPHY

PLUTARCH. *The Lives of the Noble Grecians and Romans*. Translated by John Dryden and revised by Arthur H. Clough. New York: Modern Library, Random House.

——. *Miscellanies and Essays*. Edited by William W. Goodwin. Boston: Little, Brown, 1888.

POLLUX, JULIUS. "Extracts Concerning the Greek Theatre and Masks." *Aristotle's Poetics*. London: Dodsley, Richardson and Urquhart, 1775.

PRESCOTT, HENRY W. "Silent Roles in Roman Comedy." *Classical Philology*, XXXI, April, 1936.

QUINTILIAN, MARCUS FABIUS. *Institutes of Oratory*. Translated by Rev. John Selby Watson. London: George Bell, 1913.

REICH, HERMANN. *Der Mimus*. 2 vols. New York: Benjamin Blom, 1969.

REQUENO, ABATE VINCENZO. *Scoperta della chironomia ossia dell'arte di gestire con le mani*. Parma, 1794.

SHISLER, F. L. *The Technique of the Portrayal of Emotion in Greek Tragedy*. University of Michigan. Dissertation, April, 1942.

——. "The Use of Stage Business to Portray Emotion in Greek Tragedy." *American Journal of Philology*, LXVI, October, 1945.

WRIGHT, WARREN F. "Cicero and the Theatre." *Smith College Classical Studies*, Number 11, March, 1931, Northampton, Massachusetts, 1931.

THE MIDDLE AGES

ADAMS, JOSEPH QUINCY. *Chief Pre-Shakespearean Dramas*. New York: Houghton Mifflin, 1924.

CHAMBERS, E. K. *The Medieval Stage*. 2 vols. New York: Oxford University Press, 1903.

COHEN, GUSTAVE. *Histoire de la mise en scène dans le théâtre religieux français du Moyen Age*. Paris: Champion, 1951.

——. *Le Théâtre en France au Moyen Age*. 2 vols. Paris: Rieder, 1928.

MEADE, ANNA MCCLYMONDS. *The Actor in the Middle Ages*. Columbia University Master's Thesis, May, 1927.

NICOLL, ALLARDYCE. *Masks, Mimes and Miracles*. New York: Cooper Square, 1963.

PETIT DE JULLEVILLE, LOUIS. *Les Comédiens en France au moyen age*. Paris: Léopold Cerf, 1855.

——. *Les Mystères*. 2 vols. Paris: Librairie Hachette, 1880.

SMITH, LUCY TOULMIN, ed. *York Plays*. Oxford at the Clarendon Press, 1885.

YOUNG, KARL. *The Drama of the Medieval Church*. 2 vols. Oxford at the Clarendon Press, 1933.

ITALY: COMMEDIA DELL' ARTE

BASCHET, ARMAND. *Les Comédiens Italiens à la cour de France sous Charles IX, Henri III, Henri IV et Louis XIII*. Paris: 1882.

BEAUMONT, CYRIL V. *The History of Harlequinade* (1926). New York: Benjamin Blom, 1967.

CONSTANTINI, ANGELO. *The Birth, Life and Death of Scaramouch*. Translated by Cyril Beaumont. London: C. W. Beaumont, 1924.

COURVILLE, XAVIER DE. *Luigi Riccoboni dit Lelio: un apôtre de l'art du théâtre au xviiie siècle*. 2 vols. Paris: E. Droz, 1943.

DUCHARTRE, PIERRE LOUIS. *The Italian Comedy: The Improvisations, Scenarios, Lives, Attributes, Portraits and Masks of the Illustrious Characters of the commedia dell' arte*. Translated by Randolph T. Weaver. New York: John Day, 1928.

GHERARDI, EVARISTO. "On the Art of Italian Comedians." *Theatre Arts Monthly*, X, February, 1929.

——. *Le Théâtre Italien de Gherardi*. 6 vols. Paris: P. Witte, 1700.

HERRICK, MARVIN T. *Italian Comedy in the Renaissance*. Urbana: University of Illinois Press, 1960.

KENNARD, JOSEPH SPENCER. *Masks and Marionettes*. New York: Cooper Square, 1968.

LEA, KATHLEEN M. *Italian Popular Comedy: A Study of the Commedia dell' arte, 1560-1620 with Special Reference to the English Stage* (1934). 2 vols. New York: Russell and Russell, 1962.

The Myth of Commedia dell' arte, by D'Amico, Cecchini, Barbieri, Perrucci, Gherardi, Riccoboni, Goldoni, Gozzi, Meyerhold, Evreinov, Vakhtangov, Strehler, Fo (in Danish, Swedish and Norwegian). Odin Teatrets Forlag, Denmark, 1968.

NICOLL, ALLARDYCE. *The World of Harlequin*. Cambridge University Press, 1963.

NIKLAUS, THELMA. *Harlequin, or the Rise and Fall of a Bergamask Rogue*. New York: George Braziller, 1956.

OREGLIA, GIACOMO. *The Commedia dell' arte*. New York: Hill & Wang, 1968.

PETRACCONE, ENZO, ed. *La Commedia dell' arte: storia, tecnica, scenari*. Naples: Riccardo Ricciardi, 1927.

RICCOBONI, FRANCESCO ANTONIO. *L'art du théâtre*. Paris: Simon et Giffart, 1750.

RICCOBONI, LUIGI. *An Historical Account of the Theatres in Europe . . . Together with . . . An Essay on Action* (1738). New York: Benjamin Blom, 1969.

——. "Riccoboni's Advice to Actors." Translated by Pierre Rames. *Mask*, III, April, 1911.

SAND, MAURICE. *The History of the Harlequinade* (1915). 2 vols. New York: Benjamin Blom, 1968.

SCHWARTZ, ISIDORE A. *The Commedia dell' arte and Its Influence on French Comedy in the Seventeenth Century*. Paris: H. Samuel, 1933.

SMITH, WINIFRED. *The Commedia dell' arte: A Study in Italian Popular Comedy*. New York: Benjamin Blom, 1965.

——. *Italian Actors of the Renaissance* (1930). New York: Benjamin Blom, 1968.

SOMI, LEONE DI. "Dialogues on Stage Affairs." *The Development of the Theatre* by Allardyce Nicoll. New York: Harcourt Brace, 1937.

BIBLIOGRAPHY

SPAIN

FITZMAURICE-KELLY, JAMES. *Lope de Vega and the Spanish Drama*. London: R. Brimley Johnson, 1902.

"Lope de Vega: Three Hundred Years After." *Theatre Arts Monthly*, A Special Memorial Issue, XIX, September, 1935.

RENNERT, HUGO ALBERT. *The Life of Lope de Vega* (1904). New York: Benjamin Blom, 1968.

———. *The Spanish Stage in the Time of Lope de Vega*. New York: Dover, 1964.

ELIZABETHAN ENGLAND

ARMIN, ROBERT. *Fools and Jesters*. London: The Shakespeare Society, 1842.

BALDWIN, THOMAS WHITFIELD. *The Organization and Personnel of the Shakespearean Company*. Princeton University Press, 1927.

BENTLEY, GERALD EADES. *The Jacobean and Caroline Stage*. 2 vols. Oxford: The Clarendon Press, 1941.

———. *Shakespeare and His Theatre*. Lincoln: University of Nebraska Press, 1964.

BRADBROOK, MURIEL CLARA. *Elizabethan Stage Conditions*. Cambridge at the University Press, 1932.

———. *The Rise of the Common Player: A Study of Actor and Society in Shakespeare's England*. Harvard University Press, 1962.

BROWN, JOHN RUSSELL. "Marlowe and the Actors." *Tulane Drama Review*, VIII, Summer, 1964.

CAMPBELL, LILY B.: *Scenes and Machines of the English Stage During the Renaissance*. New York: Barnes & Noble, 1960.

CHAMBERS, E. K. *The Elizabethan Stage*. 4 vols. New York: Oxford University Press, 1923.

COLLIER, JOHN PAYNE. *Memoirs of Edward Alleyn*. London: Shakespeare Society, 1841.

———. *Memoirs of the Principal Actors in the Plays of Shakespeare*. London: Shakespeare Society, 1846.

Cyprian Conqueror, or, The Faithless Relict (c. 1633). British Museum M.S. Sloane 3709-P7320.

DAVIES, ROBERTSON. *Shakespeare's Boy Actors*. London: Russell & Russell, 1964.

FLECKNOE, RICHARD. "A Short Discourse of the English Stage." *Critical Essays of the Seventeenth Century*, 1650-1685. Edited by J. E. Spingarn. Oxford at the Clarendon Press, 1908.

HACKETT, JAMES HENRY. *Notes, Criticisms, and Correspondence upon Shakespeare's Plays and Actors* (1863). New York: Benjamin Blom, 1968.

HARBAGE, ALFRED. "Elizabethan Acting." *Publications of the Modern Language Association*, LIV, September, 1939.

HARRISON, G. B. *Elizabethan Plays and Players*. London: Routledge, 1940.

Henslowe's Diary. Edited by Walter W. Greg. London: A. H. Bullen, 1904.

HEYWOOD, THOMAS. *An Apology for Actors, and a Refutation of the Apology for Actors* (1615). New York: Scholars' Facsimilies and Reprints, 1941.

HILLEBRAND, HAROLD NEWCOMB. *The Child Actors: A Chapter in Elizabethan Stage History*. London: Russell & Russell, 1964.

HOSKING, G. L. *The Life and Times of Edward Alleyn*. London: Jonathan Cape, 1952.

ISAACS, J. "Shakespeare as Man of the Theatre." *Shakespeare Criticism*, 1919-1935. London: Humphrey Milford, 1937.

JONSON, BEN. *Works*. VIII. Edited by W. Gifford. London: Bickers, 1875.

JOSEPH, B. L. *Elizabethan Acting*. London: Oxford University Press, 1951.

KERNODLE, GEORGE R. *From Art to Theatre: Form and Convention in the Renaissance*. Chicago University Press, 1944.

LAWRENCE, W. J. *The Physical Conditions of the Elizabethan Public Playhouse*. Cambridge: Harvard University Press, 1927.

———. *Pre-Restoration Stage Studies*. Cambridge: Harvard University Press, 1927.

McNEIR, W. F. "Gayton on Elizabethan Acting." *Publications of the Modern Language Association*, LVI, June, 1941.

MURRAY, JOHN TUCKER. *English Dramatic Companies*, 1558-1642. 2 vols. London: Constable, 1910.

NUNGEZER, EDWIN. *A Dictionary of Actors and of Other Persons Associated with the Public Presentation of Plays in England Before 1642*. Yale University Press, 1929.

PRYNNE, WILLIAM. *Histrio-Mastix. The Player's Scourge or, Actors Tragedie.* . . . London: 1633.

"Return from Parnassus, The." (c. 1601-1603). *Dodsley's Old English Plays, IX.* London: 1874.

REYNOLDS, GEORGE FULLMER. *The Staging of Elizabethan Plays; At the Red Bull Theatre, 1605-1625*. New York: Modern Language Association of America, 1940.

SHAKESPEARE, WILLIAM. *The Complete Works*. Edited by George Lyman Kittredge. Boston: Ginn, 1936.

SIMPSON, PERCY. "Actors and Acting." *Shakespeare's England: An Account of the Life and Manners of His Age, I.* Oxford at the Clarendon Press, 1932.

STOPES, CHARLOTTE C. *Burbage and Shakespeare's Stage*. London: A. Moring, 1913.

TARLTON, RICHARD. *Tarlton's Jests, and News out of Purgatory*. With Notes and Some Account of the Life of Tarlton by James Orchard Halliwell. London: The Shakespeare Society, 1844.

THALER, ALWIN. *Shakespeare to Sheridan* (1922). New York: Benjamin Blom, 1965.

THORNDIKE, ASHLEY H. *Shakespeare's Theatre*. New York: Macmillan, 1916.

WEBSTER, JOHN. "An Excellent Actor" (1615), *The Miscellaneous Works in Prose and Verse of Sir Thomas Overbury*. London: John Russell Smith, 1856.

BIBLIOGRAPHY

ENGLAND—17th AND 18th CENTURIES

ABINGTON, FRANCES. *The Life of Mrs. Abington Celebrated Comic Actress with Full Accounts of Her Various Performances in the Theatres of London and Dublin* (1888). By the Editor of the "Life of Quin." New York: Benjamin Blom, 1969.

The Actor's Remonstrance, or Complaint, for the Silencing of Their Profession, and Banishment from Their Several Playhouses. . . . As It was Presented in the Names and the Behalfs of All Our London Comedians. 1643.

BELLAMY, GEORGE ANNE. *An Apology for the Life of George Anne Bellamy.* 6 vols. London: 1785.

BELLAMY, THOMAS. *The Life of Mr. William Parsons, Comedian.* London: 1795.

BETTERTON, THOMAS. *The History of the English Stage, From the Restauration to the Present Time. . . . With Instructions for Public Speaking, Wherein the Action and Utterance of the Bar, Stage, and Pulpit Are Distinctly Considered.* London: E. Curll, 1741.

GILDON, CHARLES. *The Life of Mr. Thomas Betterton, the Late-Eminent Tragedian. Wherein the Action and Utterance of the Stage, Bar, and Pulpit Are Distinctly Considered.* London: Robert Gosling, 1710.

LOWE, ROBERT. *Thomas Betterton* (1891). New York: Benjamin Blom, 1969.

SPRAGUE, ARTHUR COLBY. "Did Betterton Chant?" *Theatre Notebook,* I, October, 1946.

BOOTH, BARTON

CIBBER, THEOPHILUS. *The Life and Character of That Excellent Actor Barton Booth, Esq.* . . . London: 1753.

BOSWELL, JAMES. *Life of Samuel Johnson, The.* New York: Modern Library, Random House.

———. *On the Profession of a Player; Three Essays, Reprinted from the London Magazine for August, September and October,* 1770. London: Elkin, Mathews and Marrot, 1929.

CAMPBELL, LILY B. "The Rise of a Theory of Stage Presentation During the Eighteenth Century." *Publications of the Modern Language Association,* XXXII (New Series XXV), June, 1917.

CHETWOOD, WILLIAM RUFUS. *A General History of the Stage. . . . With the Memoirs of Most of the Principal Performers That Have Appeared on the English and Irish Stage for the Last Fifty Years.* London: W. Owen, 1749.

CHURCHILL, CHARLES. *The Rosciad and the Apology* (1761). Edited by Robert Lowe, 1891. New York: Benjamin Blom, 1969.

Colley Cibber's Apology for His Life. With an Appreciation by William Hazlitt. New York: Dutton.

ASHLEY, LEONARD. *Colley Cibber.* New York: Twayne, 1965.

ASTON, ANTHONY. "A Brief Supplement to Colley Cibber, Esq.: His Lives of the Late Famous Actors and Actresses." *Anthony Aston, Stroller and Adventurer,* by Watson

Nicholson. South Haven, Michigan: The Author, 1920.

BARKER, RICHARD HINDRY. *Mr. Cibber of Drury Lane.* Columbia University Press, 1939.

SENIOR, F. DOROTHY. *The Life and Times of Colley Cibber.* New York: R. D. Henkle, 1927.

CIBBER, SUSANNA MARIA

An Account of the Life of That Celebrated Actress, Mrs. Susanna Maria Cibber. . . . London: Reader, 1887.

CIBBER, THEOPHILUS. *To David Garrick, Esq.: With Dissertations on Theatrical Subjects.* London: W. Reeves, 1759.

CLIVE, CATHERINE

FITZGERALD, PERCY H. *The Life of Mrs. Catherine Clive* (1888). New York: Benjamin Blom, 1969.

COLLIER, JEREMY. *A Defence of the Short View of the Profaneness and Immorality of the English Stage.* London: 1699.

———. *A Short View of the Immorality and Profaneness of the English Stage. Together with the Sense of Antiquity upon This Argument.* London: 1698.

COOKE, GEORGE FREDERICK

DUNLAP, WILLIAM. *Life and Memoirs of George Frederick Cooke* (1815). 2 vols. New York: Benjamin Blom, 1969.

COOKE, WILLIAM. *The Elements of Dramatic Criticism; . . . With a Sketch of the Education of the Greek and Roman Actors; Concluding with Some General Instructions for Succeeding in the Art of Acting.* London: G. Kearsley, 1775.

CUMBERLAND, RICHARD. *Memoirs* (1807). 2 vols. New York: Benjamin Blom, 1969.

DECASTRO, J. *The Memoirs of J. Decastro, Comedian . . . Ancedotes of . . . Dr. Johnson, Garrick, Foote.* London: Sherwood, Jones, 1824.

DOWNER, ALAN S. "Nature to Advantage Dressed; Eighteenth Century Acting." *Publications of the Modern Language Association,* LVIII, December, 1943.

DOWNES, JOHN. *Roscius Anglicanus.* Edited by Montague Summers (1929). New York: Benjamin Blom, 1968.

ELLISTON, ROBERT WILLIAM

RAYMOND, GEORGE. *Memoirs of Robert William Elliston, Comedian* (1846). New York: Benjamin Blom, 1969.

FOOTE, SAMUEL. *A Treatise on the Passions So Far as They Regard to the Stage; With a Critical Inquiry into the Theatrical Merit of Mr. G-K, Mr. Q-N, and Mr. B-Y. The First Considered in the Part of Lear, the Last Two Opposed in Othello* (1747). New York: Benjamin Blom, 1969.

FITZGERALD, PERCY. *Samuel Foote: A Biography* (1910). New York: Benjamin Blom, 1969.

FYVIE, JOHN. *Tragedy Queens of the Georgian Era* (1909). New York: Benjamin Blom, 1969.

GARRICK, DAVID. *An Essay on Acting: In Which Will Be Considered the Mimical Behavior of a*

Certain Fashionable Faulty Actor.... To Which Will Be Added a Short Criticism on His Acting Macbeth. London: W. Bickerton, 1744.

————. *The Private Correspondence of David Garrick with the Most Celebrated Persons of His Time.* 2 vols. London: Henry Colburn and Richard Bentley, 1831.

ANGUS, WILLIAM. "An Appraisal of David Garrick: Based Mainly upon Contemporary Sources." *The Quarterly Journal of Speech.* XXV, 1939.

BARTON, MARGARET. *Garrick.* New York: Macmillan, 1949.

BURNIM, KALMAN A. *David Garrick Director.* University of Pittsburgh Press, 1961.

DAVIES, THOMAS. *Dramatic Miscellanies: Consisting of Critical Observations on Several Plays of Shakespeare . . . As Represented by Mr. Garrick, and Other Celebrated Comedians* (1784). 3 vols. New York: Benjamin Blom, 1969.

————. *Memoirs of the Life of David Garrick* (1808). New York: Benjamin Blom, 1969.

ENGLAND, MARTHA WINBURN. *Garrick's Jubilee.* Columbus: Ohio State University Press, 1964.

FITZGERALD, PERCY. *The Life of David Garrick; from Original Family Papers.* 2 vols. London: Tinsley Brothers, 1868.

HEDGCOCK, FRANK A. *David Garrick and His French Friends* (1912). New York: Benjamin Blom, 1969.

KNIGHT, JOSEPH. *David Garrick* (1894). New York: Benjamin Blom, 1969.

Lichtenberg's Visits to England: As Described in His Letters and Diaries. Translated and annotated by Margaret L. Mare and W. H. Quarrell (1938). New York: Benjamin Blom, 1969.

MURPHY, ARTHUR. *The Life of Garrick* (1801). New York: Benjamin Blom, 1969.

OMAN, CAROLA. *David Garrick.* London: Hodder & Stoughton, 1958.

PARSONS, MRS. CLEMENT. *Garrick and His Circle* (1906). New York: Benjamin Blom, 1969.

GRAY, CHARLES H. *Theatrical Criticism in London to 1795* (1931). New York: Benjamin Blom, 1966.

GRIMALDI, JOSEPH. *Life of Joseph Grimaldi: the Noted English Clown. Written Out from Grimaldi's Own Manuscript . . . Left at the Time of His Death* (1854). Edited by Charles Dickens. New York: Benjamin Blom, 1969.

GWYNN, NELL

BAX, CLIFFORD. *Pretty Witty Nell* (1932). New York: Benjamin Blom, 1969.

DASENT, ARTHUR IRWIN. *Nell Gwynne 1650-1687* (1924). New York: Benjamin Blom, 1969.

HARBAGE, ALFRED. *Sir William Davenant, Poet Venturer, 1606-1668.* Philadelphia: University of Pennsylvania Press, 1935.

HENDERSON, JOHN

DAVIES, THOMAS. *A Genuine Narrative of the Life and Theatrical Transactions of Mr. John Henderson, Commonly Called the Bath Roscius.* London: T. Evans, 1777.

HILL, AARON. *The Actor, or Guide to the Stage; Exemplifying the Whole Art of Acting; in Which The Dramatic Passions Are Defined, Analyzed, and Made Easy of Acquirement.* London: J. Lowndes, 1821.

————. *The Art of Acting. Deriving Rules from a New Principle, for Touching the Passions in a Natural Manner . . . with View to Quicken the Delight of Audiences, and Form a Judgement of the Actors, in Their Good, or Bad, Performances. A Poem.* London: J. Osborn, 1746.

————. *The Prompter* (1734-1736). Selected, edited, with Notes and Introductions by William W. Appleton and Kalman A. Burnim. New York: Benjamin Blom, 1966.

————. *The Works of the Late Aaron Hill, Esq.; . . . Consisting of Letters on Various Subjects, and of Original Poems, Moral and Facetious, with an Essay on the Art of Acting,* vol. IV. London: 1754.

BREWSTER, DOROTHY. *Aaron Hill, Poet, Dramatist, Projector.* Columbia University Press, 1913.

HILL, JOHN. *The Actor; or, A Treatise on the Art of Playing* (1750). New York: Benjamin Blom, 1969.

————. *The Actor; or, A Treatise on the Art of Playing. A New Work, Written by the Author of the Former, and Adapted to the Present State of the Theatre . . .* (1755). New York: Benjamin Blom, 1969.

JOSEPH, B. L. "Acting and Rhetoric." *Theatre Notebook,* 1, July, 1946.

KEMBLE, JOHN PHILIP. *Macbeth, and King Richard III: an Essay.* London: John Murray, 1817.

BAKER, HERSCHEL C. *John Philip Kemble: The Actor in His Theatre.* Harvard University Press, 1942.

BOADEN, JAMES. *Memoirs of the Life of John Philip Kemble, Esq.* (1825). 2 vols. New York: Benjamin Blom, 1969.

FITZGERALD, PERCY H. *The Kembles: An Account of the Kemble Family, Including the Lives of Mrs. Siddons, and Her Brother John Philip Kemble* (1871). 2 vols. New York: Benjamin Blom, 1969.

LANIER, HENRY WYSHAM. *The First English Actresses, from the Initial Appearance of Women on the Stage in 1660 till 1700* (1930). New York: Benjamin Blom, 1969.

LLOYD, ROBERT. *The Actor. A Poetical Epistle.* London: Dodsley, 1760.

MACKLIN, CHARLES

APPLETON, WILLIAM W. *Charles Macklin: An Actor's Life.* Harvard University Press, 1960.

COOKE, WILLIAM. *Memoirs of Charles Macklin* (1804). New York: Benjamin Blom, 1969.

KIRKMAN, JAMES THOMAS. *Memoirs of the Life of Charles Macklin, Esq. . . . Together with His Valuable Observations on the Drama, on the Science of Acting, and on Various Other Subjects . . .* (1799). 2 vols. New York: Benjamin Blom, 1969.

MATTHEWS, BRANDER and HUTTON, LAURENCE. *Actors and Actresses of Great Britain and the United States; From the Days of David Garrick to the Present Time.* Volume I: *Garrick and His Contemporaries.* Volume II: *The Kembles and Their Contemporaries.* New York: Cassell & Co., 1886.

MELVILLE, LEWIS. *Stage Favorites of the Eighteenth Century* (1928). New York: Benjamin Blom, 1969.

———. *More Stage Favorites of the Eighteenth Century* (1929). New York: Benjamin Blom, 1969.

MOUNTFORT, WILLIAM
BORGMAN, ALBERT S. *The Life and Death of William Mountfort.* Harvard University Press, 1935.

NETHERCOT, ARTHUR HOBART. *Sir William D'Avenant: Poet Laureate and Playwright-Manager.* University of Chicago Press, 1938.

OLDFIELD, ANNE
EGERTON, WILLIAM. *Faithful Memoirs of the Life, Amours and Performances of . . . Mrs. Anne Oldfield.* Introduction by Colley Cibber. London: 1731.

ROBINS, EDWARD. *The Palmy Days of Nance Oldfield* (1898). New York: Benjamin Blom, 1969.

Oxberry's Dramatic Biography and Histrionic Anecdotes. London: G. Virtue, 1826.

PEPYS, SAMUEL. *Diary.* 2 vols. London: J. M. Dent, 1933.

QUIN, JAMES
Life of Mr. James Quin, Comedian, The (1766). New York: Benjamin Blom, 1969.

ROSENFELD, SYBIL. *Strolling Players and Drama in the Provinces, 1660-1765* (1939). New York: Benjamin Blom, 1969.

———. *The Theatre of the London Fairs in the Eighteenth Century.* Cambridge University Press, 1960.

SIDDONS, HENRY. *Practical Illustrations of Rhetorical Gesture and Action* (1822). New York: Benjamin Blom, 1968.

SIDDONS, SARAH. *The Reminiscences of Sarah Kemble Siddons, 1773-1783.* Edited by William Van Lennep. Harvard University Department of Printing and Graphic Arts, 1942.

BOADEN, JAMES. *Memoirs of Mrs. Siddons* (1827). 2 vols. New York: Benjamin Blom, 1969.

CAMPBELL, THOMAS. *Life of Mrs. Siddons* (1834). 2 vols. New York: Benjamin Blom, 1969.

JENKINS, H. C. FLEEMING. *Mrs. Siddons as Lady Macbeth and as Queen Katherine.* Papers on Acting, 2nd Series, III, Published for the Dramatic Museum of Columbia University, New York, 1915.

PARSONS, MRS. CLEMENT. *The Incomparable Siddons* (1909). New York: Benjamin Blom, 1969.

SIMPSON, HAROLD and BRAUN, MRS. CHARLES. *A Century of Famous Actresses, 1750-1850* (1913). New York: Benjamin Blom, 1969.

The Thespiad. A Poem. London: Stockdale, 1809.

The Thespian Dictionary, or, Dramatic Biography of the Eighteenth Century, Forming a Concise History of the English Stage (1805). New York: Benjamin Blom, 1969.

The Thespian Oracle . . . and an Introduction on Oratory and Acting, with Rules for Acquiring the Same. London: 1791.

The Thespian Preceptor; or, a Full Display of the Scenic Art: Including Ample and Easy Instructions for Treading the Stage.... Boston: Joshua Belcher, 1810.

WASSERMAN, EARL R. "The Sympathetic Imagination in Eighteenth Century Theories of Acting." *The Journal of English and Germanic Philology,* XLVI, July, 1947.

WILKES, THOMAS. *A General View of the Stage.* London: J. Coote, 1759.

WILKS, ROBERT
The Life of That Eminent Comedian Robert Wilks, Esq. London: E. Curll, 1733.

WILSON, JOHN HAROLD. *All the King's Ladies; Actresses of the Restoration.* University of Chicago Press, 1958.

WOFFINGTON, PEG
DALY, JOHN AUGUSTIN. *Woffington* (1888). New York: Benjamin Blom, 1969.

MOLLOY, JOSEPH F. *The Life and Adventures of Peg Woffington* (1897). New York: Benjamin Blom, 1969.

YOUNG, JULIAN CHARLES. *A Memoir of Charles Mayne Young, Tragedian* (1871). 2 vols. New York: Benjamin Blom, 1969.

FRANCE

ANTOINE, ANDRÉ. *Memories of the Théâtre Libre.* Translated by Marvin Carlson. University of Miami Press, 1964.

———. *Mes Souvenirs sur le Théâtre Antoine et sur l'Odéon.* Paris: Bernard Grosset, 1928.

———. *Mes Souvenirs sur le Théâtre-Libre.* Paris: Arthème Fayard, 1921.

———. *Le Théâtre.* 2 vols. Paris: Les Editions de France, 1932.

———. *Le Théâtre Libre.* Paris: May, 1890.

THALASSO, A. *Le Théâtre Libre.* Paris: Mercure de France, 1909.

WAXMAN, SAMUEL M. *Antoine and the Théâtre-Libre* (1926). New York: Benjamin Blom, 1965.

ARTAUD, ANTONIN. *Lettres d'Antonin Artaud à Jean-Louis Barrault.* Boreas, 1952.

———. *The Theatre and Its Double.* Translated by Mary Caroline Richard. New York: Grove Press, 1958.

Tulane Drama Review. Issue on Artaud. Vol. VIII. Winter, 1963.

AUBIGNAC, L'ABBE D'. *La Pratique du théâtre* (1657). New Edition by Pierre Martino. Paris: Édouard Champion, 1927.

BARON, MICHEL
YOUNG, BERT-EDWARD. *Michel Baron; Acteur et auteur dramatique; la vie et les oeuvres de*

l'élève de Molière. Paris: Albert Fontemoing, 1905.

BARRAULT, JEAN-LOUIS. *Je suis homme de théâtre.* Paris: Editions du Conquistador, 1955.

———. *Reflections on the Theatre.* Translated by Barbara Wall. New York: Macmillan, 1952.

———. *The Theatre of Jean-Louis Barrault.* Translated by Joseph Chiari. New York: Hill & Wang, 1962.

BARRIÉRE, M. F., ED. *Mémoires de Mlle. Clairon, de Lekain, de Preville, de Dazincourt, de Molé, de Garrick, de Goldoni.* Paris: Fermin Didot Frères, 1846.

BATY, GASTON. *Lettre à une jeune comédienne.* Paris: Presses Littéraires de France, 1953.

———. *Théâtre nouveau; notes et documents.* Paris: A la Société des spectacles, 1927.

BERGSON, HENRI. *Laughter—An Essay on the Meaning of the Comic.* Translated by C. Brereton and F. Rothwell. New York: Macmillan, 1921.

BERNHARDT, SARAH. *The Art of the Theatre* (1924). Translated by H. J. Stenning. New York: Benjamin Blom, 1969.

———. *Memories of My Life* (1908). New York: Benjamin Blom, 1969.

AGATE, MAY. *Madame Sarah.* New York: Benjamin Blom, 1969.

BARING, MAURICE. *Sarah Bernhardt* (1933). New York: Benjamin Blom, 1969.

HAHN, REYNALDO. *Sarah Bernhardt* (1932). New York: Benjamin Blom, 1969.

SHAW, GEORGE BERNARD. "Duse and Bernhardt," in *Shaw's Dramatic Criticism,* 1895-1898. Selected by John F. Matthews. New York: Hill & Wang, 1959.

SKINNER, CORNELIA OTIS. *Madame Sarah.* Boston: Houghton, Mifflin, 1967.

VERNEUIL, LOUIS. *The Fabulous Life of Sarah Bernhardt.* Translated by Ernest Boyd. New York: Harper, 1942.

BRASILLACH, ROBERT. *Animateurs de théâtre.* Paris: Correa, 1936.

CAMPARDON, EMILE. *Les Comédiens du roi de la troupe française pendant les deux derniers siècles.* Paris: H. Champion, 1879.

———. *Nouvelles pièces sur Molière et sur quelques comédiens de sa troupe.* Paris: Berger-Lerault, 1876.

CHAMPMESLÉ, MARIE

MAS, EMILE. *La Champmeslé.* Paris: Alcan, 1927.

CLAIRON, HYPPOLITE. *Memoirs of Hyppolite Clairon, the Celebrated French Actress: With Reflections upon the Dramatic Art* (1800). 2 vols. New York: Benjamin Blom, 1969.

GONCOURT, EDMOND DE. *Mademoiselle Clairon, d'après ses correspondances et les rapports de police du temps.* Paris: Charpentier, 1890.

COPEAU, JACQUES. *Etudes d'art dramatique, critiques d'un autre temps.* Paris: Editions de la Nouvelle Revue Française, 1923.

———. *Impromptu du Vieux Colombier.* Paris: Collection du Vieux Colombier, 1917.

———. *Notes sur le métier de comédien.* Paris: Michael Brient, 1955.

———. *Souvenirs du Vieux-Colombier.* Paris: La Compagne des Quinze, Nouvelle Editions Latines, 1931.

ANDERS, FRANCE. *Jacques Copeau et le Cartel des Quatre.* Paris: A. G. Nizet, 1959.

BORGAL, CLEMENT. *Jacques Copeau.* Paris: L'Arche, 1960.

DOISY, MARCEL. *Jacques Copeau; ou, l'absolu dans l'art.* Paris: Le Cercle du Livre, 1954.

ELDER, JUDITH. "The Cartel of Four." Cleveland: *Theatre Annual.* XVIII, 1961.

FRANK, WALDO. *The Art of the Vieux Colombier; A Contribution of France to the Contemporary Stage.* Paris, Editions de la Nouvelle Revue Française, 1918.

COQUELIN, CONSTANT. *Art and the Actor.* Translated by Abby Langdon Alger, with an introduction by Henry James. Papers on Acting, Second Series, II, Published for the Dramatic Museum of Columbia University, New York, 1915.

———. *The Art of the Actor.* Translated, with an Introduction by Elsie Fogerty, with an Appendix Containing an Interview with Dame Madge Kendal. London: Allen and Unwin, 1932.

COQUELIN, CONSTANT; IRVING, HENRY; and BOUCICAULT, DION. *The Art of Acting.* Papers on Acting, Fifth Series, II, published for the Dramatic Museum of Columbia University, 1926.

COQUELIN, ERNEST ALEXANDRE HONORÉ, and CONSTANT. *Coquelin, L'Art de dire le monologue.* Paris: P. Ollendorff, 1904.

DEBURAU, JEAN-BAPTISTE GASPARD

JANIN, JULES. *Deburau* (1928). Translated by Winifred Katzin. New York: Benjamin Blom, 1969.

DELSARTE, FRANCOIS ALEXANDRE. *Delsarte's Own Words, Being His Posthumous Writings.* Translated by Abby L. Alger. New York: Werner, 1892.

Delsarte System of Oratory. New York: Werner, 1884.

DELAUMOSNE, ABBÉ, and ARNAUD, ANGÉLIQUE. *The Art of Oratory, System of Delsarte.* New York: Werner, 1884.

MORGAN, ANNA. *An Hour with Delsarte: A Study of Expression.* Boston: Lee and Shepard, 1889.

NEELY, GEORGE ALBERT. *The School of Delsarte: Based on an Original Notebook.* Louisiana State University Thesis, 1942.

DIDEROT, DENIS. *Paradoxe sur le comédien.* Recueillies et présentées par M. Blanquet. Opinions de: Marcel Achard, J.-P. Aumont, J.-P. Barrault, Pierre Blanchar, Bernard Blier, Pierre Brasseur, Beatrice Bretty, Jacques Copeau, Claude Dauphin, Charles Dullin, Edwige Feuillere, Pierre Fresnay, Denis d'Ines, Louis Jouvet, François Perier, Ludmilla Pitoëff, Pierre Renoir, Henri Rollan, Réné Simon, Pierre Valde. Paris: Editions Nord-Sud, 1949.

———. "The Paradox of Acting" (c. 1773) in Denis Diderot, *The Paradox of Acting,* and William Archer, *Masks or Faces.* New York: Hill & Wang, 1957.

———. *Writings on the Theatre.* Edited by F. C. Green. Cambridge at The University Press, 1936.

DULLIN, CHARLES. *Souvenirs et notes de travail d'un acteur.* Paris: Odette Lieutier, 1946.

CROZIER, ERIC. "Charles Dullin and the Atelier." Theatre Arts Monthly, XX, 1936.

DUMESNIL, MARIE-FRANÇOISE. *Memoires de Marie-Françoise Dumesnil, en réponse aux mémoires d'Hyppolite Clairon; suivis d'une lettre de célèbre Lekain.* Paris: Dentu, 1800.

FRESNAY, PIERRE. *Je suis comédien.* Paris: Editions du Conquistador, 1954.

FUCHS, MAX. *Lexique des troupes des comédiens au xviiiᵉ siècle.* Paris: E. Droz, 1944.

GALLOIS, N. *Biographe contemporaine des artistes du Théâtre-Français: Précédée d'une notice historique sur la Comédie-Française.* Paris: Tresse, 1867.

Gaultier-Garguille Comédien de l'Hôtel de Bourgogne. Paris: Michaud, 1911.

GEMIER, FIRMIN

MARX, MAGDELEINE. "France's Greatest Actor." *Theatre Guild Magazine,* VIII, September, 1931.

GOT, EDMOND. *Journal de Edmond Got, sociétaire de la Comédie-Française.* 2 vols. Paris: Plon-Nourret, 1910.

GUITRY, LUCIEN. "Souvenirs: pages inédites." *Les Oeuves Libres,* June, 1923.

GUITRY, SACHA. *Lucien Guitry, sa carrière et sa vie.* Paris: C. Gerschel, 1930.

GUITRY, SACHA. *If Memory Serves: Memoirs.* Translated by Lewis Galantière. New York: Doubleday, Doran, 1935.

———. "Le Manuel du comédien." *Les Annales Politiques et Littéraires,* LXXXIII, July 13, 1924.

———. *Théâtre je t'adore.* Paris: Hachette, 1958.

HILLEMACHER, FRÉDÉRIC. *Galerie historique des portraits des comédiens de la troupe de Molière.* Lyon: Scheuring, 1869.

HOUSSAYE, ARSÉNE. *Behind the Scenes at the Comédie Française* (1889). Translated and edited by Albert D. Vandam. New York: Benjamin Blom, 1969.

———. *La Comédie Française, 1680-1880.* Paris: L. Baschet, 1880.

———. *Les Comédiennes d'autrefois.* Paris: Levy & Blanchard, 1855.

———. *Les Comédiennes de Molière.* Paris: Dentu, 1879.

JOUVET, LOUIS. *Molière et la comédie classique: extraits des cours de Louis Jouvet au Conservatoire* (1939-40). Paris: Gallimard, 1965.

———. *Réflexions du comédien.* Paris: Editions de la Nouvelle Revue Critique, 1938.

CEZAN, CLAUDE. *Louis Jouvet et le théâtre d'aujourd'hui.* Introduction by Jean Giraudoux. Paris: Editions Emile-Paul Frères. 1938.

KNAPP, BETTINA LIEBOWITZ. *Louis Jouvet, Man of the Theatre.* New York: Columbia University Press, 1958.

LA GRANGE, CHARLES VARLET. *Registre de la Grange, 1658-1685.* Edited by Edouard Thierry. Paris: J. Calye, 1876.

LECOUVREUR, ADRIENNE. *Lettres de Adrienne Le Couvreur.* Paris: Librairie Plon, 1892.

LEKAIN.

Memoires de Lekain précédés de reflexions sur cet acteur, et sur l'art théatral par F. Talma. Paris: Ponthieu, 1825.

LEMAÎTRE, FRÉDÉRIC.

BALDICK, ROBERT. *The Life and Times of Frédéric Lemaître.* Fair Lawn, New Jersey: Essential Books, 1959.

DUVAL, GEORGES. *Frédéric Lemaître et son temps, 1800-1876.* Paris: Tresse, 1876.

SILVAIN, EUGENE. *Frédéric Lemaître.* Paris: Alcan, 1926.

LEMAITRE, JULES. *Theatrical Impressions* (1924). Selected and Translated by Frederic Whyte. New York: Benjamin Blom, 1969.

LUGNÉ-POE, AURELIE. *Sous les étoiles, souvenirs de théâtre, 1902-1912.* Paris: Gallimard, 1933.

LYONNET, HENRI. *Dictionnaire des comédiens français* (1902-1908). 2 vols. New York: Benjamin Blom, 1969.

MANNE, E. D. DE, et FREDERIC HILLEMACHER. *Galerie historique des comédiens de la troupe de Talma.* Lyon: Scheuring, 1866.

———. *Galerie historique des portraits de comédiens de la troupe de Voltaire.* Lyon: Scheuring, 1861.

MANNE, E. D. DE, and MENETRIER, C. *Galerie historique de la Comédie Française pour servir de complément à la troupe de Talma.* Lyon: Scheuring, 1877.

———. *Galerie historique des acteurs français, depuis 1760 jusqu'à nos jours.* Lyon: Scheuring, 1877.

MOLIÈRE. *The Dramatic Works.* 6 vols. Translated by Henri Van Laun. Edinburgh: William Paterson, 1875-1876.

GRIMAREST, DE. *La Vie de Molière.* Edited by A. P. Malossis from the Paris, 1705 edition. Paris: Isidore Liseux, 1877.

MATTHEWS, BRANDER. *Molière: His Life and His Works.* New York: Scribner's, 1910.

PALMER, JOHN. *Molière.* New York: Brewer and Warren, 1930.

MOUNET-SULLY, JEAN. *Souvenirs d'un tragedien.* Paris: Pierre Lafitte, 1917.

OLIVIER, JEAN JACQUES. *Voltaire et les comédiens interprètes de son théâtre.* Paris: Lecène, Oudin, 1900.

PERICAUD, LOUIS. *Le Théâtre des Funambules* (1897). New York: Benjamin Blom, 1969.

PHILIPE, GERARD

PHILIPE, ANNE et ROY, CLAUDE. *Gerard Philipe.* Paris: Librairie Gallimard, 1960.

PITOËFF, GEORGES. *Notre théâtre, textes et documents*. Paris: Messages, 1949.

LENORMAND, HENRI RENÉ. *Les Pitoëffs, souvenirs*. Paris: O. Lieutier, 1943.

MARX, MAGDELEINE. "The Pitoëffs." *Theatre Guild Magazine*, VII, May, 1930.

RACHEL

AGATE, JAMES. *Rachel*. New York: Benjamin Blom, 1969.

BEAUVALLET, LEON. *Rachel and the New World*. Translated and edited by Colin Clair. New York: Abelard-Schuman, 1967.

CHAMBRUN, CHARLES ADOLPHE DE. *Mlle. Rachel, ses succès, ses défauts, quelques réflexions sur l'art dramatique*. Paris: Garnier Frères, 1853.

FALK, BERNARD. *Rachel the Immortal* (1935). New York: Benjamin Blom, 1969.

GRIBBLE, FRANCIS HENRY. *Rachel* (1911). New York: Benjamin Blom, 1969.

JANIN, JULES. *Rachel et la tragédie*. Paris: Amyot, 1859.

LYNN, GRACE. "Mme. Rachel in America." *Theatre Guild Magazine*, VII, February, 1930.

REGNIER, P. *Souvenirs et études de théâtre*. Paris: P. Ollendorff, 1887.

SAINT-DENIS, MICHEL. *Theatre: The Rediscovery of Style*. New York: Theatre Arts Books, 1960.

————. "L'improvisation en tant que moyen de développement des aptitudes physiques et psychiques de l'acteur," in *Le Rôle de l'improvisation dans l'enseignement de l'art dramatique*. Bucharest: Centre Roumain de L'IIT (International Theatre Institute) 1965.

SAINTE-ALBINE, PIERRE REMOND DE. *Le Comédien*. Paris: Desaint and Saillont, 1747.

SAMSON, JOSEPH ISIDORE. *L'art théâtral*. Paris: Dentu, 1863.

————. *Memoires de Samson de la Comédie Française*. Paris: P. Ollendorff, 1882.

LEGOUVE, E. *M. Samson et ses élèves*. Paris: Hetzel, n.d.

SARCEY, FRANCISQUE. *Comédiens et comédiennes de la Comédie Française*. 2 vols. Paris: Librairie des Bibliophiles, 1876, 1884.

————. *A Company of Actors* (The *Comédie Française*), with an introduction by Brander Matthews. Papers on Acting, 5th Series, IV, published for the Dramatic Museum of Columbia University, New York, 1926.

SERVANDONI, D'HANNETAIRE. *Observations sur l'art du comédien et sur d'autres objets concernant cette profession en général: avec quelques extraits de différents auteurs et des remarques analogues au même sujet* (1774). New York: Benjamin Blom, 1969.

TALMA, FRANÇOIS JOSEPH. *Reflections on the Actor's Art, With an Introduction by Sir Henry Irving and a Review by H. C. Fleeming Jenkin*. Papers on Acting, 2nd Series, Number 4. Printed for the Dramatic Museum of Columbia University, 1915.

COLLINS, HERBERT F. *Talma: A Biography of an Actor*. New York: Hill & Wang, 1964.

KIEM, ALBERT. *Talma*. Paris: Pierre Lafitte, 1914.

TALMA, MME F. J. *Etudes sur l'art théâtral, suivies d'anecdotes inedites sur Talma et de la correspondance de Ducis avec cet artiste depuis 1792 jusqu'en 1815*. Paris: Feret, 1836.

Theatre Arts Monthly Special Issue on French Theatre, XXI, September, 1937.

VAN TIEGHEM, PHILIPPE. *Les grands acteurs contemporain, 1900-1960*. Paris: Presses Universitaries de France, 1960.

VILAR, JEAN. *De la tradition théâtrale*. Paris: Gallimard, 1955.

WILSON, GEORGES. "Redescendre en soi." *Paris Théâtre*, année 13, February, 1960.

ZOLA, EMILE. *Le Naturalisme au théâtre*. Paris: E. Fasquelle, 1912.

GERMANY

APPIA, ADOLPHE. "Living Art or Frozen Nature." Translated by Marvin Carlson. *Players Magazine*, XXXIII, January, 1962.

————. *Music and the Art of the Theatre*. Translated by Robert W. Corrigan and Mary Douglas Dirks, and edited by Barnard Hewitt. University of Miami Press, 1962.

————. *The Work of Living Art: A Theory of Theatre*. Translated and edited by Barnard Hewitt. University of Miami Press, 1960.

"ADOLPHE APPIA: A Memorial." *Theatre Arts Monthly*, XVI, August, 1932.

BAB, JULIUS. *Schauspieler und Schauspielkunst*. Berlin: Oesterheld, 1926.

————. *Das Theater der Gegenwart*. Leipzig: Weber, 1928.

BAHR, HERMANN. *Schauspielkunst*. Leipzig: Duerr & Weber, 1923.

BASSERMANN, ALBERT

BAB, JULIUS. *Albert Bassermann, Weg und Werk*. Leipzig: Erich Weibezahl, 1929.

BRAHM, OTTO. *Kritische Schriften über Drama und Theater*. Berlin: S. Fischer, 1913.

————. *Theater. Dramatiker. Schauspieler*. Berlin: Henschelverlag, 1961.

NEWMARK, MAXIM. *Otto Brahm, the Man and the Critic*. New York: Stechert, 1938.

BRECHT, BERTOLT. *Aufbau einer Rolle: Buschs Galilei*. Berlin: Henschelverlag, 1962. Ernst Busch.

————. *Brecht on Theatre*. Edited and translated by John Willett. New York: Hill & Wang, 1964.

————. "Chinese Acting," translated by Eric Bentley, pp. 68-77, *Furioso*, Vol. IV, No. 4, Fall, 1949, and *Tulane Drama Review*, Vol. VI, No. 1, September, 1961, pp. 130-136.

————. "A Model for Epic Theater." Translated by Eric Bentley. *The Sewanee Review*, LVII, Summer, 1949.

————. "A New Technique of Acting." Translated by Eric Bentley. *Theatre Arts*, XXXIII, January, 1949.

BIBLIOGRAPHY

————. "Notes on Stanislavsky." Translated by Carl R. Mueller. *Tulane Drama Review*, IX, Winter, 1964.

Schriften zum Theater. 7 vols. Frankfurt: Suhrkamp Verlag, 1963-1964.

BRECHT, BERTOLT, and others: *Theaterarbeit.* Dresden: VVV Dresdner Verlag, 1952.

ESSLIN, MARTIN. *Brecht: The Man and His Work.* New York: Doubleday, 1960.

The Tulane Drama Review, "The Theatre of Bertolt Brecht" (entire issue), Vol. VI, September, 1961.

WILLET, JOHN. *The Theatre of Bertolt Brecht.* New York: New Directions, 1959.

World Theatre, Brecht, 1956-1966. Combined issues 3 and 4. Vol. XV, 1966.

BRUFORD, W. H. *Theatre Drama and Audience in Goethe's Germany.* London: Routledge and Kegan Paul, 1957.

DEVRIENT, EDUARD. *Geschichte Der Deutschen Schauspielkunst.* 5 vols. Leipzig: Weber, 1848-1874.

————. *Geschichte der Deutschen Schauspielkunst.* Newly revised and brought up to the present by Willy Stuhlfeld. Berlin: Eigenbrödler, 1929.

GOLDSCHMIT, RUDOLF KARL. *Eduard Devrient's Bühnenreform am Karlsruher Hoftheater.* Leipzig: L. Voss, 1921.

REIN, FERDINAND. *Eduard Devrient als Oberregisseur in Dresden von 1844-1846.* Altenburg: Stephan Geibel, 1931.

DEVRIENT, LUDWIG

ALTMAN, GEORG. *Ludwig Devrient; Leben und Werke eines Schauspielers.* Berlin: Ullstein, 1926.

BAB, JULIUS. *Die Devrients.* Berlin: George Stilke, 1932.

FUNCK, Z. *Aus dem Leben Zweier Schauspieler; Iffland und Ludwig Devrient.* Leipzig: Brockhaus, 1839.

FLECK, JOHANN FRIEDRICH FERDINAND

GROSS, EDGAR. *Johann Friedrich Ferdinand Fleck.* Berlin: Gesellschaft für Theater-Geschichte, 1914.

Goethe on the Theatre: Selections from Conversations with Eckermann. Translated by John Oxenford. New York: Ungar, 1964.

"Goethe's Rules for Actors" (1803). Translated with an Introduction by Arthur Woehl. *Quarterly Journal of Speech Education,* XIII, June, 1927.

BRANDES, GEORG. *Wolfgang Goethe.* 2 vols. Translated by Allen W. Porterfield. New York: Brown, 1924.

ECKERMANN, J. P. *Conversations with Goethe.* Translated by Gisela C. O'Brien. New York: Frederick Ungar, 1964.

STEIN, PHILIPP. *Goethe als Theater-Leiter.* Berlin: Schuster & Loeffler.

GRUBE, MAX. *Am Hofe der Kunst.* Leipzig: Grethlein, 1918.

HURWICZ, ANGELIKA. *Inszeniert der Kaukasische Kreidekreis.* Hanover: Friedrich Verlag, 1964.

IFFLAND, AUGUST WILHELM. *Über Meine Theatralische Laufbahn.* Heilbronn: Holstein, 1886.

————. *Über Schauspieler und Schauspielkunst.* Berlin: Ministerium für Kultur, 1954.

HARLE, HEINRICH. *Iffland's Schauspielkunst; Ein Rekonstrucktionsversuch auf Grund der etwa 500 Zeichnungen und Kupferstiche.* Berlin: Wilhelm Henschels.

KLIEWER, DR. ERWIN. *A. W. Iffland; Ein Wegbereiter in der Deutschen Schauspielkunst.* Berlin: Emil Ebering, 1937.

KOFFKA, WILHELM. *Iffland und Dalberg: Geschichte der Classischen Theaterzeit Mannheims.* Leipzig: Weber, 1865.

REIMAN, VIKTOR. *Der Iffland Ring: Legende und Geschichte.* Vienna: H. Deutsch, 196-.

IHERING, HERBERT. *Schauspieler in der Entwicklung.* Berlin: Aufbau-Verlag, 1956.

IMMERMAN, KARL LEBERECHT. *Theater-Briefe.* Berlin: Dunder, 1851.

JACOBS, MONTAGUE. *Deutsches Schauspielkunst.* Berlin: Henschel Verlag, 1954.

KAINZ, JOSEPH. *Briefe.* Berlin: Ricola, 1921.

BAB, JULIUS. *Kainz und Matkowsky.* Berlin: Oesterheld, 1912.

BRAHM, OTTO. *Kainz, Gesehnes und Gelebtes.* Berlin: Egon Fleischel, 1910.

KERR, ALFRED. *Schauspielkunst.* Berlin: Bard, Marquardt, 1904.

KJERBUHL-PETERSEN, LORENZ. *Psychology of Acting: A Consideration of Its Principles as an Art.* Translated from the German by Sarah T. Barrows. Boston: Expression Company, 1935.

KORNFELD, PAUL. "Nachwort an der Schauspieler." *Die Verführung.* Berlin: S. Fischer, 1921.

KORTNER, FRITZ. *Aller Tage Abend.* Munich: Kindler, 1959.

KRAUSS, WERNER. *Das Schauspiel Meines Lebens.* Stuttgart: Henry Goverts Verlag, 1956.

LEMMER, KLAUS J. *Deutsche Schauspieler der Gegenwart.* Berlin: Rembrandt Verlag, 1955.

LESSING, GOTTHOLD EPHRAIM. *Hamburg Dramaturgy.* With a New Introduction by Victor Lange. New York: Dover, 1962.

————. *Selected Prose Works.* Translated by E. C. Beasley and Helen Zimmern, edited by Edward Bell. London: George Bell and Sons, 1879.

ROBERTSON, G. J. *Lessing's Dramatic Theory; Being an Introduction to and Commentary on his Hamburgische Dramaturgie.* Cambridge at the University Press, 1939.

LEWINSKY, JOSEF. *Vor den Coulissen: Originalblätter von Celebritäten des Deutschen Theaters.* Berlin: A. Hofman, 1881.

RICHTER, HELENE. *Josef Lewinsky: Fünfzig Jahre Wiener Kunst und Kultur.* Vienna: Jugent und Volk.

LINGEN, THEO. *Ich über mich: Interview eines Schauspielers mit sich selbst.* Hanover: E. Friedrich, 1963.

MARTERSTEIG, MAX. *Der Schauspieler, ein Kunstlerisches Problem.* Leipzig: 1900.

BIBLIOGRAPHY

MATKOWSKY, ADALBERT
BAB, JULIUS. *Adalbert Matkowsky.* Berlin: Oesterheld, 1932.
MELCHINGER, SIEGFRIED. *Schauspieler.* Frankfürt: Buchengild Gutenberg, 1966.
MINOR, JACOB. *Aus dem Alten und Neuen Burgtheater.* Vienna: Amalthea, 1920.
MOISSI, ALEXANDER
BOHM, HANSÖ, ed. *Moissi.* Berlin: Eigenbrödler, 1927.
NEUBER, FRIEDERIKE CAROLINA
REDEN-ESBEK, F. J. VON. *Carolina Neuber und ihre Zeitgenossen.* Leipzig: Barth, 1881.
SASSE, HANNAH. *Friederike Caroline Neuber.* Berlin: Emil Wild, 1937.
PISCATOR, ERWIN. *Das Politische Theater.* Berlin: Adalbert Schultz, 1929.
LEY-PISCATOR, MARIA. *The Epic Theatre: Rebels, Guardians and Battles.* New York: James H. Heineman, 1966.
————. *The Piscator Experiment: The Political Theatre.* New York: Heineman, 1967.
REINHARDT, MAX. "The Actor." *Encyclopaedia Britannica,* THEATRE, XXII, 1929.
CARTER, HUNTLY. *The Theatre of Max Reinhardt* (1914). New York: Benjamin Blom, 1966.
ROTHE, HANS. *Max Reinhardt: 25 Jahre des Deutsches Theatre.* New York: Benjamin Blom, 1969.
SAYLER, OLIVER M., ed. *Max Reinhardt and His Theatre* (1924). New York: Benjamin Blom, 1969.
SAXE-MEININGEN, GEORGE II, DUKE OF
GRUBE, MAX. *Geschicht der Meininger.* Berlin: Deutsche Verlags-Anstalt, 1926.
————. *The Story of the Meininger.* Translated by Ann Marie Koller. University of Miami Press, 1963.
SCHLEGEL, AUGUST WILHELM. *Lectures on Dramatic Art and Literature.* Translated by John Black. London: George Bell, 1892.
SCHROEDER, FRIEDRICH LUDWIG
BRUNIER, LUDWIG. *Friedrich Ludwig Schroeder: Ein Kunstler und Lebensbild.* Leipzig: Weber, 1864.
LITZMAN, BERTHOLD. *Friedrich Ludwig Schroeder; Ein Beitrag zur Deutschen Litterature—und Theater Geschichte.* 2 vols. Leipzig: Leopold Zorp, 1890.
MEYER, F. L. *Friedrich Ludwig Schroeder.* 2 vols. Hamburg: 1819.
SMEKAL, RICHARD. *Das alte Burgtheater, 1776-1888.* Vienna: Anton Schroll, 1916.
SORMA, AGNES
AGNES SORMA: *Ein Gedenkbuch: Zeugnisse ihres Lebens und ihrer Kunst.* Collected by Julius Bab. Heidelberg: Niels Kampmann, 1927.
STEIN, PHILIPP. *Deutsche Schauspieler.* 2 vols. Berlin: Gesellschaft für Theater-Geschichte, 1907.
THIMIG FAMILY
DARNTON, MAIDA. "The Four Thimigs—the

Royal Family of the German-Speaking Stage." *Theatre Guild Magazine,* VIII, April, 1931.
TIECK, LUDWIG. *Kritische Schriften,* 2 vols. Leipzig: Brochaus, 1848.
WAGNER, RICHARD. *Über Schauspeiler und Sänger.* Leipzig: Fritzsch, 1872.
WEIGEL, HELENE
BRECHT, BERTOLT. *Helene Weigel: Actress.* Translated by John Berger and Anna Bostock. Leipzig: VEB Editore, 1961.

ENGLAND—19th AND 20th CENTURIES

ADAMS, WILLIAM DAVENPORT. *A Dictionary of the Drama: A Guide to the Plays, Playwrights, Players . . . of the United Kingdom and America from the Earliest Times to the Present.* Only Vol. 1 (A-G) published. London: Chatto and Windus, 1904.
AGATE, JAMES. *The English Dramatic Critics; An Anthology, 1660-1932.* London: Arthur Barker, n.d.
ARCHER, WILLIAM. *About the Theatre.* New York: Benjamin Blom, 1969.
————. *The Old Drama and the New.* New York: Benjamin Blom, 1969.
————. "Masks or Faces," in Denis Diderot, *The Paradox of Acting,* and William Archer, *Masks or Faces.* New York: Hill and Wang, 1957.
ARLISS, GEORGE. *Up the Years from Bloomsbury.* Boston: Little Brown, 1927.
ARTHUR, SIR GEORGE. *From Phelps to Gielgud* (1936). New York: Benjamin Blom, 1969.
ASHCROFT, PEGGY
KEOWN, ERIC. *Peggy Ashcroft.* London: Rockliff, 1955.
BAKER, HENRY BARTON. *History of the London Stage and Its Famous Players* (1576-1903). New York: Dutton, 1904.
BANCROFT, MARIE and SQUIRE. *The Bancrofts: Recollections of Sixty Years* (1909). New York: Benjamin Blom, 1969.
————. *Mr. and Mrs. Bancroft On and Off the Stage.* 2 vols. London: Richard Bentley, 1888.
BENSON, FRANK. *I Want to Go on the Stage.* London: Ernest Benn, 1931.
BETTY, WILLIAM HENRY WEST
MERRITT, J. *Memoirs of the Life of William Henry West Betty, Known by the Name of the Young Roscius.* Liverpool: J. Wright, 1804.
BISHOP, G. W. *Barry Jackson and the London Theatre* (1933). New York: Benjamin Blom, 1969.
BRERETON, AUSTIN. *Some Famous Hamlets from Burbage to Fechter.* London: David Bogue, 1884.
BROOK, DONALD. *A Pageant of English Actors.* London: Rockliff, 1950.
BROOK, PETER. *The Empty Space.* New York: Atheneum, 1969.
BROOKE, GUSTAVUS VAUGHAN
LAWRENCE, W. J. *The Life of Gustavus Vaughan Brooke, Tragedian.* Belfast: Baird, 1892.

CAMPBELL, MRS. PATRICK. *My Life and Some Letters* (1922). New York: Benjamin Blom, 1969.

DENT, ALAN. *Mrs. Patrick Campbell.* London: Museum Press, 1961.

CLUNES, ALEC
TREWIN, J. C. *Alec Clunes.* London: Rockliff, 1958.

COOK, DUTTON. *Hours With the Players* (1883). 2 vols. New York: Benjamin Blom, 1969.

——. *On the Stage: Studies of Theatrical History and the Actor's Art.* 2 vols. London: Low, Marston, Searle & Rivington, 1883.

COOPER, GLADYS. "Acting in Tragedy." Edited by Harold Downs. *Theatre and Stage,* I, London: Sir Isaac Pitman, 1934.

CRAIG, EDWARD GORDON. "Hamlet in Moscow; Notes for a Short Address to the Actors of the Moscow Art Theatre." *Mask,* I, May, 1915.

——. *Index to the Story of My Days.* New York: Viking, 1957.

——. "A Letter to Ellen Terry from Her Son." *Mask,* I, August, 1908.

——, ed. *The Mask* (facsimile edition in 15 vols.) New York: Benjamin Blom, 1966.

——. *On The Art of the Theatre.* New York: Theatre Arts Books, 1961.

——. *The Theatre Advancing* (1919). New York: Benjamin Blom, 1965.

——. *Toward a New Theatre* (1913). New York: Benjamin Blom, 1969.

BABLET, DENIS. *Edward Gordon Craig.* Translated by Daphne Woodward. New York: Theatre Arts Books, 1966.

BARSHAY, BERNARD. "Gordon Craig's Theories of Acting." *Theatre Annual,* 1947.

CRAIG, EDWARD. *Gordon Craig.* New York: Knopf, 1969.

"How Stanislavsky and Gordon Craig Produced Hamlet." Translated by Eugene Ilyin. *Plays and Players,* IV, March, 1957.

DARBYSHIRE, ALFRED. *The Art of the Victorian Stage* (1907). New York: Benjamin Blom, 1969.

DARLINGTON, WILLIAM A. *Six Thousand and One Nights: Forty Years a Critic.* London: Harrap, 1960.

DARWIN, CHARLES R. *Expression of the Emotions in Man and Animals.* London: John Murray, 1873.

DORAN, JOHN. *Annals of the English Stage from Thomas Betterton to Edmund Kean.* 3 vols. Edited and revised by Robert W. Lowe. London: Nimmo, 1888.

DOWNER, ALAN S. "Players and Painted Stage—Nineteenth-Century Acting." *Publications of the Modern Language Association,* LXI, June, 1946.

DOWNS, HAROLD, ed. *Theatre and Stage; a Modern Guide to the Performance of All Classes of Amateur Dramatic, Operatic, and Theatrical Work.* 2 vols. London: Sir I. Pitman, 1934.

DU MAURIER, GERALD
DU MAURIER, DAPHNE. *Gerald.* London: Gollancz, 1936.

EVANS, EDITH
TREWIN, JOHN. *Edith Evans.* London: Rockliff, 1954.

FAUCIT, HELENA. *On Some of Shakespeare's Female Characters.* London: William Blackwood, 1904.

MARTIN, THEODORE. *Helena Faucit.* London: William Blackwood, 1900.

FAY, WILLIAM GEORGE and CARSWELL, CATHERINE. *The Fays of the Abbey Theatre* (1935). New York: Benjamin Blom, 1969.

FAY, WILLIAM GEORGE. *Merely Players.* London: Rich & Cowan, 1932.

FECHTER, CHARLES
DICKENS, CHARLES. "On Mr. Fechter's Acting." *Atlantic Monthly,* XXIV, August, 1869.

FIELD, KATE. *Charles Albert Fechter* (1882). New York: Benjamin Blom, 1969.

FOGERTY, ELSIE. "Speech in the Theatre." *Theatre Arts Monthly,* XV, July, 1931.

FORBES-ROBERTSON, SIR JOHNSTON. *A Player Under Three Reigns* (1925). New York: Benjamin Blom, 1969.

FORSTER, JOHN and LEWES, GEORGE HENRY. *Dramatic Essays* (1896). New York: Benjamin Blom, 1969.

GIELGUD, JOHN. *Early Stages.* New York: Macmillan, 1939.

——. *Stage Directions.* New York: Random House, 1963.

GILDER, ROSAMUND. *John Gielgud's Hamlet; a Record of Performance.* With Notes on Costume, Scenery and Stage Business by John Gielgud. New York: Oxford University Press, 1937.

STERNE, RICHARD L. *John Gielgud Directs Richard Burton as Hamlet: A Journal of Rehearsals.* New York: Random House, 1967.

GILLILAND, THOMAS. *The Dramatic Mirror: Containing the History of the Stage . . . Including a Biographical and Critical Account . . . of the Most Distinguished Performers.* 2 vols. London: C. Chapple, 1808.

GODDARD, ARTHUR. *Players of the Period: A Series of Anecdotal, Biographical and Critical Monographs of the Leading English Actors of the Day* (1891). New York: Benjamin Blom, 1969.

GOODWIN, JOHN, ed. *Royal Shakespeare Theatre Company 1960-63.* New York: Theatre Arts Books, 1964.

GRANT, GEORGE. *An Essay on the Science of Acting.* London: Cowie and Strange, 1828.

GRANVILLE-BARKER, HARLEY. *The Exemplary Theatre.* New York: Benjamin Blom, 1969.

——. "The Heritage of the Actor." *The Quarterly Review,* CCXXXIX, July, 1923.

Great Acting: Olivier, Thorndike, Richardson, Ashcroft, Redgrave, Evans, Gielgud, Coward. Edited by Hal Burton. New York: Hill & Wang, 1968.

GREGORY, LADY AUGUSTA. *Lady Gregory's Journals, 1916-1930.* Edited by Lennox Robinson. New York: Macmillan, 1947.

——. *Our Irish Theatre.* New York: G. P. Putman's, 1913.

BIBLIOGRAPHY

GREIN, J. T. *Dramatic Criticism* (1899-1905). 5 vols. New York: Benjamin Blom, 1969.

GUINNESS, ALEC

TYNAN, KENNETH. *Alec Guinness.* London: Barrie & Rockliff, 1961.

GUTHRIE, TYRONE. *A Life in the Theatre.* New York: McGraw-Hill, 1959.

HAMILTON, CECILY, and BAYLIS, LILIAN. *The Old Vic.* New York: George H. Doran, n.d.

HARDWICKE, CEDRIC. *Let's Pretend; Recollections and Reflections of a Lucky Actor.* London: Grayson and Grayson, 1932.

——. "The Moribund Craft of Acting." *Theatre Arts Monthly*, XXXIII, February, 1939.

HARE, JOHN

PEMBERTON, T. EDGAR. *John Hare, Comedian, 1865-1895.* London: George Routledge, 1895.

HARVEY, JOHN MARTIN. *Autobiography* (1933). New York: Benjamin Blom, 1969.

——. *The Book of Martin Harvey* (1928). New York: Benjamin Blom, 1969.

HAZLITT, WILLIAM. *Criticism and Dramatic Essays of the English Stage.* London: George Routledge, 1851.

——. *Hazlitt on Theatre.* Edited by William Archer and Robert Lowe. New York: Hill & Wang, 1957.

HUNT, LEIGH. *Dramatic Essays.* Edited by William Archer and Robert Lowe. London: W. Scott, Ltd., 1894.

IRVING, HENRY; COQUELIN, CONSTANT; and BOUCICAULT, DION. *The Art of Acting.* Papers on Acting, 5th Series, II, Published for the Dramatic Museum of Columbia University, 1926.

——. *The Drama; Addresses* (1893). New York: Benjamin Blom, 1969.

——. *English Actors: Their Characteristics, and Their Methods; A Discourse, Delivered in the University Schools at Oxford . . . June 26, 1886.* Oxford: the Clarendon Press, 1886.

BRERETON, AUSTIN. *The Life of Henry Irving* (1908). New York: Benjamin Blom, 1969.

——. *The Lyceum and Henry Irving* (1903). New York: Benjamin Blom, 1969.

CRAIG, EDWARD GORDON. *Henry Irving* (1930). New York: Benjamin Blom, 1969.

IRVING, LAURENCE. *Henry Irving: The Actor and His World.* New York: Macmillan, 1952.

JONES, HENRY ARTHUR. *Shadow of Henry Irving* (1931). New York: Benjamin Blom, 1969.

POLLOCK, WALTER HERRIES. *Impressions of Henry Irving* (1908). New York: Benjamin Blom, 1969.

SAINTSBURY, HARRY ARTHUR and PALMER, CECIL, eds. *We Saw Him Act: A Symposium on the Art of Sir Henry Irving* (1939). New York: Benjamin Blom, 1969.

STOKER, BRAM. *Personal Reminiscences of Henry Irving* (1906). 2 vols. New York: Benjamin Blom, 1969.

JONES, STANLEY. *The Actor and His Art: Some Considerations of the Present Condition of the Stage.* London: Downey, 1899.

KEAN, CHARLES

COLE, JOHN WILLIAM. *The Life and Theatrical Times of Charles Kean* (1859). 2 vols. New York: Benjamin Blom, 1969.

KEAN, EDMUND

DISHER, M. W. *Mad Genius: A Biography of Edmund Kean.* London: 1950.

HAWKINS, FREDERICK WILLIAM. *Life of Edmund Kean* (1869). 2 vols. New York: Benjamin Blom, 1969.

HILLEBRAND, HAROLD NEWCOMB. *Edmund Kean.* Columbia University Press, 1933.

MOLLOY, J. FITZGERALD. *The Life and Adventures of Edmund Kean, Tragedian, 1787-1833.* London: Downey, 1897.

PLAYFAIR, GILES. *Kean.* New York: Dutton, 1939.

PROCTER, BRYAN WALLER. *The Life of Edmund Kean* (1855). 2 vols. New York: Benjamin Blom, 1969.

KEMBLE, FRANCES ANNE. "On the Stage." Papers on Acting, Fifth Series, Number 3, Published for the Dramatic Museum of Columbia University, 1926.

——. *Records of Later Life* (1882). New York: Benjamin Blom, 1969.

ARMSTRONG, MARGARET. *Fanny Kemble, a Passionate Victorian.* New York: Macmillan, 1938.

BOBBE, DOROTHIE. *Fanny Kemble* (1932). New York: Benjamin Blom, 1969.

DRIVER, LEOTA STULTZ. *Fanny Kemble* (1933). New York: Benjamin Blom, 1969.

KENDAL, MADGE. *Dame Madge Kendal: By Herself.* London: John Murray, 1933.

——. *Dramatic Opinions.* Boston: Little, Brown, 1890.

COQUELIN, CONSTANT. "An Interview." *The Art of the Actor.* London: Allen & Unwin, 1932.

PEMBERTON, T. EDGAR. *The Kendals.* New York: Dodd, Mead, 1900.

LAMB, CHARLES. *The Dramatic Essays of Charles Lamb.* Edited with an Introduction and Notes by Brander Matthews. New York: Dodd, Mead, 1892.

LOWE, ROBERT W. *A Bibliographical Account of English Theatrical Literature; from the Earliest Times to the Present Day.* London: John C. Nimmo, 1888.

MACLIAMMOIR, MICHEAL. *All for Hecuba; an Irish Theatrical Autobiography.* London: Methuen, 1946.

MACQUEEN-POPE, W. *Haymarket: Theatre of Perfection.* London: W. H. Allen, 1948.

MACREADY, WILLIAM CHARLES. *The Diaries of William Charles Macready 1833-1851* (1912). 2 vols. Edited by William C. Toynbee. New York: Benjamin Blom, 1969.

The Journal of William Charles Macready, 1832-1851. Abridged and Edited by J. C. Trewin. London: Longman's, 1967.

——. *Macready's Reminiscences, and Selections from His Diaries and Letters* (1875). Edited by Sir Frederick Pollock. New York: Benjamin Blom, 1969.

BIBLIOGRAPHY

ARCHER, WILLIAM. *William Charles Macready.* New York: Benjamin Blom, 1969.

DOWNER, ALAN S. *The Eminent Tragedian, William Charles Macready.* Cambridge, Harvard University Press, 1966.

POLLOCK, JULIET. *Macready as I Knew Him* (1884). New York: Benjamin Blom, 1969.

MAROWITZ, CHARLES. "*Lear* Log," in *Theatre at Work.* Edited by Charles Marowitz and Simon Trussler. New York: Hill & Wang, 1968.

————. "Notes on the Theatre of Cruelty," in *Theatre at Work.* Edited by Charles Marowitz and Simon Trussler. New York: Hill & Wang, 1968.

MAROWITZ, CHARLES, MILNE, TOM and HALE, OWEN, eds. *The Encore Reader: A Chronicle of the New Drama.* London: Methuen, 1965.

MAROWITZ, CHARLES and TRUSSLER, SIMON, eds. *Theatre at Work: Playwrights and Productions in the Modern British Theatre.* New York: Hill & Wang. 1967.

MATHEWS, CHARLES. *The Life and Correspondence of Charles Mathews the Elder* (1860). Edited by Edmund Hodgson Yates. New York: Benjamin Blom, 1969.

MATHEW, MRS. ANNE. *Memoirs of Charles Mathews, Comedian.* 4 vols. London: Richard Bentley, 1838.

MATHEWS, CHARLES JAMES. *The Life of Charles James Mathews* (1879). Edited by Charles Dickens. New York: Benjamin Blom, 1969.

MATTHEWS, BRANDER, and HUTTON, LAURENCE. *Actors and Actresses of Great Britain and the United States; From the Days of David Garrick to the Present Time.* Vol. 3: *Kean and Booth; And Their Contemporaries.* Vol. 4: *Macready and Forrest; And Their Contemporaries.* Vol. 5: *The Present Time.* New York: Cassell & Co., 1886.

NEVILLE, JOHN
TREWIN, JOHN C. *John Neville.* London: Barrie & Rockliff, 1961.

OLIVIER, LAURENCE. "The Great Sir Laurence: Our Finest Shakespearean: Olivier Takes on Othello and Talks Uniquely About Himself." *Life,* May 18, 1964.

————. "The Olivier Method." Interview. New York Sunday *Times,* February 7, 1960, X, 1-3.

BARKER, FELIX. *The Oliviers.* London: Hamish Hamilton, 1953.

DARLINGTON, W. A. *Laurence Olivier.* London: Morgan Grampian Books Ltd., 1968.

DENT, ALAN. *Hamlet: The Film and the Play.* Foreword by Sir Laurence Olivier. London: World Film Publications, 1948.

HARRIS, KENNETH. "All the Stage Is His World: A Talk with Laurence Olivier." *New York Post,* February 22, 1969.

TYNAN, KENNETH, Ed. *Othello: The National Theatre Production.* London: Hart-Davis, 1966.

O'NEILL, ELIZA
JONES, CHARLES INIGO. *Memoirs of Miss O'Neill.* London: D. Cox, 1816.

PASCOE, CHARLES EYRE, Ed. *The Dramatic List;* a Record of the Performances of Living Actors and Actresses of the British Stage: with Criticisms from Contemporary Journals* (1880). New York: Benjamin Blom, 1969.

PEARSON, HESKETH. *The Last Actor-Managers.* New York: Harper, 1950.

PHELPS, SAMUEL
COLEMAN, JOHN and EDWARD. *Memoirs of Samuel Phelps* (1886). New York: Benjamin Blom, 1969.

PHELPS, W. MAY and FORBES-ROBERTSON, JOHN. *The Life and Life-Work of Samuel Phelps* (1886). New York: Benjamin Blom, 1969.

WEST, E. J. "The Victorian Voice on the Stage: Samuel Phelps." *The Quarterly Journal of Speech,* XXXI, February, 1945.

PLAYFAIR, SIR NIGEL ROSS. *The Story of the Lyric Theatre, Hammersmith* (1925). New York: Benjamin Blom, 1969.

POEL, WILLIAM. *Monthly Letters* (1929). New York: Benjamin Blom, 1969.

————. *Shakespeare in the Theatre.* London: Sidgwick and Jackson, 1913.

SPEAIGHT, ROBERT. *William Poel and the Elizabethan Revival.* London: William Heinemann, 1954.

REDGRAVE, MICHAEL. *The Actor's Ways and Means.* New York: Theatre Arts Books, 1954.

————. *Mask or Face: Reflections in an Actor's Mirror.* New York: Theatre Arts Books, 1958.

————. "The Stanislavsky Myth." *New Theatre,* London, III, June, 1946.

FINDLATER, R. *Michael Redgrave: Actor.* New York: Theatre Arts Book, 1956.

RICHARDSON, RALPH. "Acting in Romantic Drama." *Theatre and Stage,* 11, Edited by Harold Downs. London: Sir Isaac Pitman, 1934.

HOBSON, HAROLD. *Ralph Richardson.* London: Rockliff, 1958.

ROBINSON, LENNOX, Ed. *The Irish Theatre.* New York: Macmillan, 1939.

ROBSON, FLORA. "Acting in Naturalistic Drama." *Theatre and Stage,* I. Edited by Harold Downs. London: Sir Isaac Pitman, 1934.

————. "What Is Acting? Illusions I Would Like to Dispel." *Theatre World,* XX, August, 1933.

DUNBAR, JANET. *Flora Robson.* London: Harrap, 1960.

ROGERS, PAUL
WILLIAMSON, AUDREY. *Paul Rogers.* London: Rockliff, 1956.

RUSSELL, WILLIAM CLARK. *Representative Actors, a Collection of Criticism, Anecdotes, Personal Descriptions, Referring to Many Celebrated British Actors from the Sixteenth to the Present Century . . . and a Short Account of English Acting.* New York: Scribner, n.d.

SCOFIELD, PAUL
ROSS, LILLIAN and HELEN. "Paul Scofield," in *The Player.* New York: Simon and Schuster, 1961.

TREWIN, JOHN C. *Paul Scofield.* London: Rockliff, 1956.

SCOTT, CLEMENT. *The Drama of Yesterday and Today.* 2 vols. New York: Macmillan, 1899.

———. *Some Notable Hamlets of the Present Time* (1900). (*Sarah Bernhardt, Henry Irving, Wilson Barrett, Beerbohm Tree, Forbes Robertson.*) New York: Benjamin Blom, 1969.

SEYLER, ATHENE. "A Series of Letters on the Art of Period Acting." *Theatre Arts,* XXXI, November, 1947.

SEYLER, ATHENE and STEPHEN HAGGARD. *The Craft of Comedy.* New York: Theatre Arts, 1946.

SHAW, GEORGE BERNARD. *The Art of Rehearsal; A Private Letter to an Irish Colleague in Response to a Request for Advice and Information.* New York: Samuel French, 1928.

———. *Dramatic Opinions and Essays.* 2 vols. New York: Brentano's, 1928.

———. "From the Point of View of a Playwright." *Herbert Beerbohm Tree: Some Memories of Him and of His Art.* London: Hutchinson, n.d.

———. *Our Theatres in the Nineties.* 3 vols. London: Constable, 1932.

———. *Plays and Players: Essays on the Theatre.* Selected by A. C. Ward. London: Oxford University Press, 1952.

Shaw's Dramatic Criticism (1895-1898). A selection by John F. Matthews. New York: Hill & Wang, 1959.

SULLIVAN, BARRY

SILLARD, ROBERT M. *Barry Sullivan and His Contemporaries: A Histrionic Record* (1901). 2 vols. New York: Benjamin Blom, 1969.

SYMONS, ARTHUR. *Plays, Acting, and Music* (1903). New York: Benjamin Blom, 1969.

TERRISS, WILLIAM

SMYTHE, ARTHUR J. *The Life of William Terriss, Actor.* Westminster: Constable & Co., 1898.

TERRY, ELLEN. *Ellen Terry and Bernard Shaw: A Correspondence.* Edited by Christopher St. John. New York: Theatre Arts Books, 1949.

———. *Ellen Terry's Memoirs.* Edited by Christopher St. John and Edith Craig. New York: Benjamin Blom, 1969.

———. *Four Lectures on Shakespeare* (1932). New York: Benjamin Blom, 1969.

———. *The Story of My Life.* New York: McClure, 1908.

CRAIG, EDWARD GORDON. *Ellen Terry and Her Secret Self* (1932). New York: Benjamin Blom, 1969.

HIATT, CHARLES. *Ellen Terry and Her Impersonations* (1898). New York: Benjamin Blom, 1969.

MANVELL, ROGER. *Ellen Terry.* New York: G. P. Putnam's, 1968.

SCOTT, CLEMENT. *Ellen Terry.* New York: Frederick A. Stokes, 1900.

THORNDIKE, SYBIL and RUSSELL. *Lilian Baylis.* London: Chapman and Hall, 1938.

TREWIN, JOHN C. *Sybil Thorndike.* London: Rockliff, 1955.

TREE, HERBERT BEERBOHM. *The Imaginative Faculty.* London: Mathews and Lane, 1893.

———. *Thoughts and Afterthoughts* (1913). New York: Benjamin Blom, 1969.

Herbert Beerbohm Tree: Some Memories of Him and of His Art. Edited by Max Beerbohm. London: Hutchinson.

TREWIN, JOHN C. *The Birmingham Repertory Theatre,* 1913-1963. London: Barrie & Rockliff, 1963.

TYNAN, KENNETH. *Curtains.* New York: Atheneum, 1961.

———. *He That Plays the King.* London: 1950.

VESTRIS, ELIZA LUCY

PEARCE, CHARLES E. *Madame Vestris and Her Times* (1923). New York: Benjamin Blom, 1969.

WATSON, ERNEST BRADLEE. *Sheridan to Robertson; A Study of the Nineteenth Century London Stage.* Harvard University Press, 1926.

WESTWOOD, DORIS. *These Players: A Diary of the Old Vic.* London: Heath Cranton, 1926.

WILLIAMS, EMLYN

FINDLATER, RICHARD. *Emlyn Williams.* London: Rockliff, 1956.

WILLIAMS, HARCOURT, Ed. *Vic-Wells: the Work of Lilian Baylis.* London: Cobden-Sanderson, 1938.

WILLIAMS, P. C. *English Shakespearian Actors: A Review.* London: Regency Press, 1966.

WILLIAMSON, AUDREY. *Old Vic Drama: A Twelve Years' Study of Plays and Players.* New York: Macmillan, 1949.

YEATS, WILLIAM BUTLER. *Autobiography.* New York: Macmillan, 1938.

———. *Plays and Controversies.* New York: Macmillan, 1924.

WATSON, ERNEST BRADLEE. *Sheridan to Robertson: A Study of the Nineteenth-Century London Stage* (1926). New York: Benjamin Blom, 1965.

ITALY

APOLLONIO, MARIO. *Storia del teatro italiano.* 2 vols. Firenze: Sansoni, 1958.

BELLOTTI-BON, LUIGI. "Scritti," in *Antologia del grande attore.* By Vito Pandolfi. Bari: Editore Laterza, 1954.

BRACCO, ROBERTO. "A Century of Italian Acting." *Theatre Guild Magazine,* VII, September and October, 1930.

CALENDOLI, GIOVANNI. *L'attore; storia di un'arte.* Rome: Editizione dell' Ateneo, 1959.

CERVI, ANTONIO. *Tre artisti-Emanuel-Zacconi-Novelli.* Bologna: L. Beltrami, 1900.

CHIARINI, LUIGI. *L'arte dell' attore.* Rome: Bianco e Nero, 1950.

DE FILIPPO, EDUARDO. *Eduardo De Filippo e il Teatro San Ferdinando,* 1790-1954. Naples, 1954.

MAGLIULO, GENNARO. *Eduardo De Filippo.* Bologna: Cappelli editore, n.d.

DUSE, ELEONORA. *Confessioni di Eleonora Duse; memoire e documenti,* 3 vols. Edited by Luciano Nicastro. Milan: Gentile, 1945.

———. "Lettere di Eleonora Duse," in *Antologia del grande attore.* By Vito Pandolfi. Bari: Editore Laterza, 1954.

———. *Memorie e Relique.* Milan: 1925.

BOGLIONE, GIUSEPPE. *L'arte della Duse.* Rome: 1960.

BORDEUX, JEANNE. *Eleonora Duse* (1924). New York: Benjamin Blom, 1969.

LE GALLIENNE, EVA. *The Mystic in the Theatre: Eleonora Duse.* New York: Farrar, 1966.

MAPES, VICTOR. *Duse and the French* (1898). New York: Benjamin Blom, 1969.

NORMAN, GERTRUDE. "An Interview with Eleonora Duse." *Theatre,* (New York), VI, April, 1906.

RHEINHARDT, E. A. *The Life of Eleonora Duse* (1930). New York: Benjamin Blom, 1969.

SCHNEIDER, EDOUARD. *Eleonora Duse, souvenirs, notes et documents.* Paris: B. Grasset, 1925.

SHAW, GEORGE BERNARD. "Duse and Bernhardt," in *Shaw's Dramatic Criticism,* 1895-1898. Selected by John F. Matthews. New York: Hill & Wang, 1959.

SIGNORELLI, OLGA. *Eleonora Duse.* Rome: Gherardo Casini Editore, 1955.

SYMONS, ARTHUR. *Eleanora Duse* (1927). New York: Benjamin Blom, 1969.

VIRGANI, LEONARDO, ed. *Eleonora Duse.* Milan: A Martello, 1958.

EMANUEL, GIOVANNI. "Scritti," in *Antologia del grande attore* by Vito Pandolfi. Bari: Editore Laterza, 1954.

FERRAVILLA, EDOARDO. *Ferravilla parla della sua vita, della sua arte, del suo teatro.* Milan: 1912.

GASSMAN, VITTORIO. "L'attore italiano e la tradizione," in *L'attore: storia di un'arte,* by Giovanni Calendoli. Rome: Edizione dell Ateneo, 1959.

GAMBETTI, GIACOMO. *Vittorio Gassman.* Bologna: Cappelli editore, n.d.

GIONETTI, CARLO A. *L'attore.* Florence: Valecchi, 1959.

GOLDONI, CARLO. *Memoirs.* Translated by John Black. New York: Alfred A. Knopf, 1926.

GRASSO, GIOVANNI. "Storia del Teatro Machiavelli a Catania," in *Antologia del grande attore,* by Vito Pandolfi. Bari: Editore Laterza, 1954.

KENNARD, JOSEPH SPENCER. *The Italian Theatre* (1932). 2 vols. New York: Benjamin Blom, 1967.

McLEOD, ADDISON. *Plays and Players of Modern Italy.* London: Smith, Elder, 1912.

MODENA, GUSTAVO. "Scritti," in *Antologia del grande attore,* by Vito Pandolfi. Bari: Editore Laterza, 1954.

MORROCCHESI, ANTONIO. *Lezioni di declamazione d'arte teatrale.* Firenze: 1832.

MUSCO, ANGELO. "Scritti," in *Antologia del grande attore,* by Vito Pandolfi. Bari: Editore Laterza, 1954.

NOVELLI, ERMETE. *Foglietti sparsi narranti la mia vita.* Rome: 1919.

———. "La mia vita," in *Antologia del grande attore,* by Vito Pandolfi. Bari: Editore Laterza, 1954.

CASSERES, BENJAMIN DE. "Ermete Novelli Coming to America." *Theatre,* V, March, 1907.

PANDOLFI, VITO, ed. *Antologia del grande attore: raccolta di memorie e di saggi dei grandi attori italiani dalla reiforma goldoniana ad oggi, preceduti da scritti dei maggiori studiosi dell'-epoca e da una introduzione storica.* Bari: Editore Laterza, 1954.

PETITO, ANTONIO. *Autobiografia di Antonio Petito.* Edited by A. G. Bragaglia. Rome: 1944.

PETROLINI, ETTORE. "Scritti," in *Antologia del grande attore,* by Vito Pandolfi. Bari. Editore Laterza, 1954.

Piccolo teatro, 1947-1958. Milan: Nicola Moneta, 1958.

RASI, LUIGI. *L'art del comico.* Milan: Reno Sandron, 1923.

———. *I Comici italiani; biografia, bibliografia, Iconografia,* 1897-1910. 2 vols. New York: Benjamin Blom, 1969.

RIDENTI, LUCIO, ed. *L'ittore.* Turin: Edizioni di Il Dramma, 1947.

RISTORI, ADELAIDE. *Memoirs and Artistic Studies* (1907). Translated by G. Mantellini. New York: Benjamin Blom, 1969.

———. *Studies and Memoirs.* London: W. H. Allen and Co., 1888.

FIELD, KATE. *Adelaide Ristori* (1867). New York: Benjamin Blom, 1969.

ROSSI, ERNESTO. *Quarant anni di vita artistica.* 3 vols. Firenze: L. Niccolai, 1887-1889. Several selections reprinted in *Antologia del grande attore.* By Vito Pandolfi. Bari: Editore Laterza, 1954.

———. *Studii drammatici e lettere autobiografiche.* Firenze: Successori LeMonnier, 1901.

50 let artisticheskoi deiatel'nosti Ernesto Rossi (50 years of the Artistic Activity of Ernesto Rossi). Compiled from the memoirs of E. Rossi by S. I. Lavrenteva, St. Petersburg: A. M. Lesman, 1896.

RUGGERI, RUGGERO. "Scritti," in *Antologia del grande attore.* By Vito Pandolfi. Bari: Editore Laterza, 1954.

SALVINI, TOMMASO. "Impressions of Some Shakespearean Characters." *Century Magazine,* XXIII, November, 1881.

———. *Leaves from the Autobiography of Tommaso Salvini* (1893). New York: Benjamin Blom, 1969.

———. *Ricordi, anedotti e impressioni.* Milan: Fratelli Dumolord, 1895.

———. "Some Views on Acting." *Theatre Workshop,* I, October, 1936.

LAZURUS, EMMA. "Tommaso Salvini." *Century Magazine,* XXIII, November, 1881.

MASON, EDWARD TUCKERMAN. *The Othello of Tommaso Salvini.* New York: Putman's, 1890.

SALVINI, CELSO. *Tommaso Salvini, nella storia del teatro italiano e nella vita del suo tempo.* Rocca San Casciano: Cappelli, 1955.

SCARPETTA, EDOARDO. "Il mio teatro," in *Antologia del grande attore.* By Vito Pandolfi. Bari: Editore Laterza, 1954.

TALLI, VIRGILIO. "Scritti," in *Antologia del grande attore*, by Vito Pandolfi. Bari: Editore Laterza, 1954.

VIVIANI, RAFFAELE. *Dalla vita alla scena*. Bologna: 1928.

SPAINI, ALBERTO. *L'arte di Raffaele Viviani, scritti di varii*. Turin: 1926.

ZACCONI, ERMETE. *Ricordi e battaglie*. Milan: Garzanti, 1946.

THE SOVIET UNION AND POLAND

ALPERS, BORIS V. *Aktiorskoe Iskusstvo v Rossii* [The Actor's Art in Russia]. Moscow: Isskustvo, 1945.

BAKSHY, ALEXANDER. *The Path of the Modern Russian Stage*. London: Palmer and Hayward, 1916.

BEN-ARI, R. "Four Directors and the Actor." *Theatre Workshop*, I, January-March, 1937.

BIRMAN, SERAFIMA. *Trud Aktiora* [Work of the Actor]. Moscow, 1939.

BOLESLAVSKY, RICHARD. *Acting: the First Six Lessons*. New York: Theatre Arts Books, 1949.

———. *The Creative Theatre* 1923 (Manuscript). Organized and Translated by Michel Barroy. Available at the Theatre Collection, New York Public Library.

BOWERS, FAUBION. *Broadway, U.S.S.R.: Theatre, Ballet, and Entertainment in Russia Today*. New York: Thomas Nelson & Sons, 1959.

CARTER, HUNTLY. *The New Spirit in the Russian Theatre, 1917-1928* (1929). New York: Benjamin Blom, 1969.

CHALIAPIN, FEDOR. *Man and Mask: Forty Years in the Life of a Singer*. Translated by Phyllis Mégroz. London: Victor Gollancz, 1932.

CHEKHOV, ANTON. *The Personal Papers of Anton Chekhov*. New York: Lear Publishers, 1948.

CHEKHOV, MICHAEL. *The Problem of the Actor: Memoirs*. New York: The Group Theatre.

———. *Put Aktiora* (Path of the Actor). Leningrad: Academia, 1928.

———. *To The Actor: On the Technique of Acting*. New York: Harper & Brothers, 1953.

CHERKASOV, N. *Notes of a Soviet Actor*. Moscow: Foreign Languages Publishing House, n.d.

ZUBKOV, YURI. *Tvortchestvo N. K. Cherkasova —Problema Perevoplochtchenia v Iskusstve Aktioia* [The Life Work of N. K. Cherkassov —Problems of Assimilation in the Art of Acting]. Moscow: Ob-vo, 1964.

DANA, H. W. L. *A Handbook on Soviet Drama*. New York: The American Russian Institute, 1938.

FÜLOP-MILLER, RENÉ, and GREGOR, JOSEPH. *The Russian Theatre* (1930). New York: Benjamin Blom, 1968.

GORCHAKOV, NIKOLAI A. *The Theatre in Soviet Russia*. Translated by Edgar Lehrman. New York: Columbia University Press, 1957.

GROTOWSKI, JERZY. *Theatre Laboratorie* (in French). Wroclaw, 1967.

———. *Towards a Poor Theatre*. New York: Simon and Schuster, 1969.

GYSEGHEM, ANDRE VAN. *Theatre in Soviet Russia*. London: Faber and Faber, 1943.

HOUGHTON, NORRIS. *Moscow Rehearsals: An Account of Methods of Production in the Soviet Theatre* (1936). New York: Grove Press, 1962.

ILINSKY, IGOR. *Sam o sebe* [I About Myself]. Moscow: Teatralnoe Ob-vo, 1961.

KACHALOV, V. I.

VILENKIN, V. *Vasily Ivanovich Kachalov; sbornik stati, vospominanii, pisem* [Kachalov; Collection of Articles, Recollections, Letters]. Moscow: Isskustvo, 1954.

KHMELYOV, NIKOLAI P. "My Karenin." *Theatre Workshop*, I, September-October, 1937.

KOMISARJEVSKAYA, VERA

Sbornik Pamiati V. F. Kommissarzhevskoi [In Commemoration of Vera F. Komisarjevska]. St. Petersburg: 1911.

KOMISARJEVSKY, THEODORE. *The Costume of the Theatre* (1931). New York: Benjamin Blom, 1968.

———. *Myself and the Theatre* (1930). New York: Benjamin Blom, 1969.

LENSKI, ALEKSANDR P. *Stati, Pisma, Zapiski* [Notes, Letters, Articles]. Moscow: Iskusstvo, 1950.

LVOV, NIKOLAI I. and MAKSIMOV, I., *Masterstvo Aktiora* [The Actor's Craft]. Moscow: Gosizdat, 1935.

MACLEOD, JOSEPH. *Actors Cross the Volga; a Study of the Nineteenth-Century Russian Theatre and of Soviet Theatres in War*. London: Allen and Unwin, 1946.

———. *The New Soviet Theatre*. London, Allen and Unwin, 1943.

MARKOV, PAVEL A. *The First Studio—Sulerzhitsky, Vakhtangov, Chekhov*. Translated by Mark Schmidt. New York: Group Theatre, 1934.

———. *The Soviet Theatre* (1934). New York: Benjamin Blom, 1969.

Meyerhold on Theatre. Edited by Edward Braun. New York: Hill and Wang, 1969.

MEYERHOLD, VSEVOLOD. "From *On the Theatre*." Translated by Nora Beeson. *Tulane Drama Review*, IV, May, 1960.

———. *Meyerhold on Theatre*. Edited and translated by Meyer Braun. New York: Hill & Wang, 1969.

———. "Farce." Translated by Nora Beeson. *Tulane Drama Review*, IV, September, 1959.

———. *Stati, Pisma, Rechi, Besedi* [Articles, Letters, Speeches, Conversations]. 2 vols. Moscow: Iskusstov, 1968.

———. *Le Théâtre théâtral*. Traduction et présentation de Nina Gourfinkel. Paris: Gallimard, 1963.

ALPERS, B. *The Theatre of the Social Mask*. Translated by Mark Schmidt. New York: Group Theatre, 1934.

ANNENKOV, YURI P. "Meierkhold." *Novyi Zhurnal* (New York) 72, 1963.

BIBERMAN, HERBERT. "Meyerhold at Work." *Theatre Guild Magazine*, VI, January, 1929.

FAGIN, B. "Meyerhold Rehearses a Scene." *Theatre Arts*, XVI, October, 1932.

GVOZDEV, A. A. *Teatr imeni Vs. Meierkholda* [The Theatre of Vsevolod Meyerhold]. Leningrad: Academia, 1927.

ILINSKY, IGOR. *Sam o sebe* [I About Myself]. Moscow: Teatralnoe Ob-vo, 1961.

LOZOWICK, LOUIS. "V. E. Meyerhold and His Theatre." *Hound and Horn,* IV, October-December, 1930.

MARTIN, JOHN. "How Meyerhold Trains His Actors." *Theatre Guild Magazine,* VII, November, 1930.

STRASBERG, LEE. "The Magic of Meyerhold." *New Theatre,* I, September, 1934.

VOLKOV, NIKOLAI. *Meyerhold.* 2 vols. Moscow: Academia, 1929. (The most definitive biography, to 1917; the volume dealing with the Soviet period was never published and eventually lost).

MIKHOELS, SOLOMON

GRINVALDI, Y. *Mikhoels.* Moscow: Ogiz, 1948. *Moskovskii Khudoshetvennii Teatr v Illustrastiiach i Dokumenti,* 1898-1938. [The Moscow Art Theatre in Illustrations and Documents, 1898-1938]. Moscow: The Moscow Art Theatre, 1938.

MOSKVIN, IVAN. *The Soviet Theatre.* Moscow: Foreign Languages Publishing House, 1939.

———. *Stati i Materiali* [Articles and Materials]. Moscow: Teatralnoe Ob-vo, 1948.

Dzyubinskaya, Olga S. *I. M. Moskvin: Tvorcheskii Put Aktiora, Stenogramma Publichnoi Lektsii* [Creative Path of an Actor]. Moscow: Znanie, 1955.

VILENKIN, V. Y. *I. M. Moskvin na Stsena Mkhat* [Moskvin on the Stage of the Moscow Art Theatre]. Moscow: Moscow Art Theatre, 1946.

NEMIROVICH-DANCHENKO, VLADIMIR. *My Life in the Russian Theatre.* Translated by John Cournos. New York: Theatre Arts Books, 1968.

———. "Simplicity in Acting." *The Moscow Art Theatre Yearbook for 1944.* Moscow: Museum of the Moscow Art Theatre, 1946.

FREIDKINA, L. *Dni i Godi Vladimir I. Nemirovich-Danchenko: Letopis o Zhisn i Tvorchestva* [Chronicle of the Life and Creative Work of Nemirovich-Danchenko]. Moscow: Teatralnoe Ob-vo, 1962.

New Theatre. Soviet Issue, II, January, 1935.

RAPOPORT, I. *Rabota Aktiora* [The Work of the Actor.] Moscow: Krestinskaya Gazeta, 1937. Excerpt in English in *Acting: A Handbook of the Stanislavski Method.* Compiled by Toby Cole. New York: Crown, 1947.

SAYLER, OLIVER M. *Inside the Moscow Art Theatre.* New York: Brentano's, 1925.

———. *The Russian Theatre Under the Revolution.* Boston: Little, Brown, 1920.

SHCHEPKIN, MICHAEL. *Zapiski Aktiora Shchepkina* [Memoirs of the Actor Shchepkin]. Moscow: Academia, 1933.

SLONIM, MARC. *Russian Theatre: From the Empire to the Soviets.* New York: World, 1961.

STANISLAVSKI, KONSTANTIN S. *An Actor Prepares.*

Translated by Elizabeth Reynolds Hapgood. New York: Theatre Arts Books, 1936.

———. *An Actor's Handbook: An Alphabetical Arrangement of Concise Statements on Aspects of Acting.* Edited and translated by Elizabeth Reynolds Hapgood. New York: Theatre Arts Books, 1963.

———. "Art Notes; 1877-1892." *International Literature,* Numbers 11-12, November-December, 1940.

———. *Besedi v Studii Bolshovo Teatra, v 1918-1922* [Chats with the Students of the Bolshoi Theatre, 1918-1922]. Moscow: Teatralnoe Ob-vo, 1947.

———. *Building a Character.* Translated by Elizabeth Reynolds Hapgood. New York: Theatre Arts Books, 1949.

———. *Creating a Role.* Translated by Elizabeth Reynolds Hapgood. New York: Theatre Arts Books, 1961.

———. *Masterstvo Aktiora v Terminach i Opredeleniach Konstantin Stanislavsky* [A Dictionary of Stanislavsky's Terms and Definitions of the Actor's Craft]. Moscow: Sovetskaya Rossia, 1961.

———. *My Life in Art.* Translated by J. J. Robbins. New York: Theatre Arts Books, 1948.

———. *Sobraniye Sochinenii* [Collected Works]. 7 vols. Moscow: Iskusstvo, 1954-1960.

———. *Stanislavsky on the Art of the Stage.* Introduced and translated by David Magarshack. New York: Hill & Wang, 1961.

———. *Stanislavski's Legacy: A Collection of Comments on a Variety of Aspects of an Actor's Art and Life.* Edited and translated by Elizabeth Hapgood Reynolds. New York: Theatre Arts Books, 1958.

———. *Stati, Rechi, Besedi, Pisma* [Articles, Speeches, Talks, Letters]. Moscow: Iskusstvo, 1953.

ABOLKIN, N. *Sistema Stanislavskovo i Sovetskii Teatr.* Moscow: Iskusstvo, 1950.

Acting: a Handbook of the Stanislavski Method. Compiled by Toby Cole, with an Introduction by Lee Strasberg. New York: Crown, 1947.

BENTLEY, ERIC. "Are Stanislavsky and Brecht Commensurable?" *Tulane Drama Review,* IX, Fall, 1964.

BLOK, VLADIMIR B. *Sistema Stanislavskovo i Problemi Dramaturgi.* Moscow: Teatralnoe Ob-vo, 1963.

DAYKARHANOVA, TAMARA. "The Art of Acting: Much Ado About the Method." *Theatre,* II, October, 1960.

EDWARDS, CHRISTINE. *The Stanislavsky Heritage: Its Contribution to the Russian and American Theatre.* New York: New York University Press, 1965.

FREED, DONALD. *Freud and Stanislavsky: New Directions in the Performing Arts.* New York: Vantage Press, 1964.

GORCHAKOV, NIKOLAI M. *Stanislavsky Directs.* Translated by Miriam Goldina. New York: Funk & Wagnalls, 1954.

BIBLIOGRAPHY

GRAY, PAUL. "Stanislavski and America: A Critical Chronology." *Tulane Drama Review,* IX, Winter, 1964.

HOFFMAN, THEODORE. "At the Grave of Stanislavsky, or, How to Dig The Method." *Columbia University Forum,* III, Winter, 1960.

MAGARSHACK, DAVID. *Stanislavsky: A Life.* New York: Chanticleer Press, 1951.

MAROWITZ, CHARLES. *Stanislavsky and the Method.* New York: Citadel, 1964.

MOORE, SONIA. *Training an Actor: The Stanislavski System in Class.* New York: Viking, 1968.

MUNK, ERIKA, Ed. *Stanislavski and America.* New York: Hill & Wang, 1966.

O Stanislavskom: Sbornik Vospominanii [Anthology of Remembrances]. Moscow: Teatralnoe Ob-vo, 1948.

PROKOFIEF, VLADIMIR. *V Sporach o Stanislavskom* [Discussion About Stanislavsky]. Moscow: Iskusstvo, 1962.

World Theatre: "The Actor and Stanislavski." Vol. VIII, Spring, 1959.

TAIROV, ALEKSANDER Y. *Das Entfesselte Theater; Aufzeichnungen Eines Regisseurs.* Cologne: Kiepenheuer & Witsch, 1964.

―――. *Notes of a Director.* University of Miami Press, 1969.

LOZOWICK, LOUIS. "The Theatre is for the Actor; An Iconoclast's Methods in Moscow." *Theatre Guild Magazine,* VII, October, 1929.

Theatre Arts Magazine Special Issue: The Moscow Art Theatre, IV, October, 1920.

Theatre Arts Monthly Special Issue: The Soviet Theatre Speaks for Itself, XX, September, 1936. Edited by Jay Leyda.

TOPORKOV, V. O. "Le Rôle de l'improvisation dans l'incarnation du personnage scénique," in *Le Rôle de l'improvisation dans l'enseignement de l'art dramatique.* Bucharest: Centre Roumain de L'IIT (International Theatre Institute) 1965.

VAKHTANGOV, EUGENE. *Materiali i Stati.* Moscow: Teatralnoe Ob-vo, 1959.

―――. "Preparing for the Role; From the Diary of E. Vakhtangov" in *Acting: A Handbook of the Stanislavski Method.* Compiled by Toby Cole. New York: Crown, 1947.

―――. *Zapiski, Pisma, Stati* [Notes, Letters, Articles]. Moscow: Iskusstvo, 1939.

GORCHAKOV, NIKOLAI M. *Rezhisserskie uroki Vakhtangova.* Moscow: Isskustvo, 1957.

―――. *The Vakhtangov School of Stage Art.* Moscow: Foreign Languages Publishing House, 1961.

VARNEKE, B. V. *History of the Russian Theatre, 17th to 19th Centuries.* Translated by B. Brasol and Belle Martin. New York: Macmillan, 1950.

YERMOLOVA, MARIA N. *Pisma* [Letters]. Moscow: Iskusstvo, 1955.

YERSHOV, P. *Tekhologia Aktiorskovo Iskusstva* [The Technique of the Actor's Art]. Moscow: Teatralnoe Ob-vo, 1959.

AMERICA

ADAMS, MAUDE
PATTERSON, ADA. *Maude Adams* (1907). New York: Benjamin Blom, 1969.
ROBBINS, PHYLLIS. *Maude Adams.* New York: G. P. Putnam's, 1956.

ADAMS, W. DAVENPORT. *A Dictionary of the Drama: A Guide to the Plays, Playwrights, Players and Playhouses of the United Kingdom and America, from the Earliest Times to the Present.* Only Vol. I (A-G) published. Philadelphia: Lippincott, 1904.

ALDRIDGE, IRA
DURYLIN, S. *Ira Aldridge.* (In Russian). Moscow: Iskusstvo, 1940.
DURYLIN, S. *Ira Aldridge.* A translation of an excerpt by E. Blum. *The Shakespeare Association Bulletin,* XVII, No. 1, January, 1942.
MARSHALL, HERBERT and STOCK, MILDRED. *Ira Aldridge: The Negro Tragedian.* Carbondale: Southern Illinois University Press, 1968.

ANDERSON, JUDITH. "A Stage Vamp on Women." *Theatre Magazine,* XL, October, 1924.

ANDERSON, MARY. *A Few Memories.* New York: Harper, 1896.
WINTER, WILLIAM. *The Stage Life of Mary Anderson.* New York: George J. Coombes, 1886.

ATKINSON, BROOKS. *Broadway Scrapbook.* New York: Theatre Arts Books, 1947.

AYRES, ALFRED. *Acting and Actors, Elocution and Elocutionists: A Book about Theatre Folks and Theatre Art.* New York: D. Appleton, 1894.

BARRYMORE, ETHEL. *Memories: An Autobiography.* New York: Harper, 1955.

BARRYMORE, JOHN. *Confessions of an Actor* (1926). New York: Benjamin Blom, 1969.
FOWLER, GENE. *Good Night Sweet Prince.* New York: Viking Press, 1944.
STEVENS, ASHTON. "John Barrymore." *Actorviews: Intimate Portraits.* Chicago: Covici-McGee, 1923.
TEN BROECK, HELEN. "From Comedy to Tragedy: An Interview with John Barrymore." *Theatre Magazine,* XXIV, July, 1916.

BARRYMORE, LIONEL. *We Barrymores.* New York: Appleton Century Crofts, 1951.
ALPERT, HOLLIS. *The Barrymores.* New York: Dial Press, 1964.

BAYES, NORA. "Holding My Audience." *Theatre Magazine,* XXVI, September, 1917.

BELASCO, DAVID. *The Theatre Through Its Stage Door* (1919). Edited by Louis V. Defoe. New York: Benjamin Blom, 1969.
WINTER, WILLIAM. *The Life of David Belasco* (1925). 2 vols. New York: Benjamin Blom, 1969.

Biographical Encyclopaedia and Who's Who of the American Theatre, The. Edited by Walter Rigdon. New York: James H. Heineman, 1966.

BOOTH, EDWIN. "Edwin Booth's Opinion of the Players of His Day." *Theatre,* XI, May, 1910.
―――. "A Few Words About Edmund Kean." *Actors and Actresses of Great Britain and the*

BIBLIOGRAPHY

United States, III. Edited by Brander Matthews and Laurence Hutton. New York: Cassell & Co., 1886.

————. "Some Words About My Father." *Actors and Actresses of Great Britain and the United States, III.* Edited by Brander Matthews and Laurence Hutton. New York: Cassell & Co., 1886.

CLARK, ASIA BOOTH. *The Elder and the Younger Booth.* Boston: James R. Osgood, 1882.

GOODALE, KATHERINE. *Behind the Scenes with Edwin Booth* (1931). New York: Benjamin Blom, 1969.

GROSSMAN, EDWINA BOOTH. *Edwin Booth: Recollections by His Daughter* (1894). New York: Benjamin Blom, 1969.

LOCKRIDGE, RICHARD. *Darling of Misfortune: Edwin Booth* (1932). New York: Benjamin Blom, 1969.

RUGGLES, ELEANOR. *Prince of Players.* New York: W. W. Norton, 1953.

SKINNER, OTIS. *The Last Tragedian; Booth Tells His Own Story.* New York: Dodd, Mead, 1939.

SPRAGUE, ARTHUR COLBY. "Edwin Booth's Iago: A Study of a Great Shakespearean Actor." *Theatre Annual,* 1947.

WINTER, WILLIAM. *The Life and Art of Edwin Booth* (1894). New York: Benjamin Blom, 1969.

BOOTH, JUNIUS BRUTUS. *Memoirs of Junius Brutus Booth, From His Birth to the Present Time . . . Containing Original Letters . . . and Copious Extracts from the Journal Kept During His Theatrical Tour on the Continent.* London: Chapple, 1817.

CLARKE, ASIA BOOTH. *Passages, Incidents, and Anecdotes in the Life of Junius Brutus Booth.* New York: Carleton Publishers, 1886.

GOULD, T. R. *The Tragedian: An Essay on . . . Junius Brutus Booth* (1868). New York: Benjamin Blom, 1969.

BOUCICAULT, DION. *The Art of Acting.* Papers on Acting, 5th Series, I, Published for the Dramatic Museum of Columbia University, New York, 1926.

BOUCICAULT, DION; IRVING, HENRY; and COQUELIN, CONSTANT. *The Art of Acting.* Papers on Acting 5th Series, II, published for the Dramatic Museum of Columbia University, 1926.

WALSH, TOWNSEND. *The Career of Dion Boucicault.* New York: The Dunlap Society, 1915.

BRADY, ALICE. "The Problem of Casting by Type." *Theatre Magazine,* L, December, 1929.

BROWN, JOHN MASON. *Two on the Aisle: Ten Years of the American Theatre in Performance.* New York: W. W. Norton, 1938.

BROWN, THOMAS ALLSTON. *History of the American Stage: Containing Biographical Sketches of Nearly Every Member of the Profession . . . from 1733 to 1870.* New York: Dick and Fitzgerald, 1870.

CARNOVSKY, MORRIS. "Design for Acting: The Quest of Technique." *Tulane Drama Review,* V, Spring, 1961.

————. "Mirror of Shylock." *Tulane Drama Review,* III, October, 1958.

CHAIKIN, JOSEPH. "The Actor's Involvement: Notes on Brecht," *Drama Review,* Vol. XII, No. 2, Winter, 1968, pp. 147-151.

————. "The Open Theatre." *Tulane Drama Review,* IX, Winter, 1964.

CHAPLIN, CHARLES. *My Autobiography.* New York: Simon and Schuster, 1964.

CLAPP, JOHN, and EDGETT, EDWIN F. *Players of the Present* (1899-1901). New York: Benjamin Blom, 1969.

CLURMAN, HAROLD. *The Fervent Years: The Story of the Group Theatre and the Thirties.* New York: Alfred A. Knopf, 1945.

COHAN, GEORGE M. *Twenty Years on Broadway.* New York: Harper, 1925.

COLLIER, CONSTANCE. *Harlequinade: The Story of My Life.* London: John Lane, 1929.

COOPER, THOMAS ABTHORPE

  IRELAND, JOSEPH N. *A Memoir of the Professional Life of Thomas Abthorpe Cooper* (1888). New York: Benjamin Blom, 1969.

  HEWITT, BARNARD, Ed. "Four Hamlets of the 19th-Century American Stage. Part I: Thomas Abthorpe Cooper and J. B. Booth, *Tulane Drama Review,* VI, Spring, 1962, Part II: Edwin Forrest and Edwin Booth, VI, Summer, 1962.

CORNELL, KATHARINE. *I Wanted to Be an Actress.* New York: Random House, 1939.

COWL, JANE. "Is Stage Emotion Real?" *Theatre,* XXII, March, 1916.

CROWLEY, ALICE LEWISOHN. *The Neighborhood Playhouse, Leaves from a Theatre Scrapbook.* New York: Theatre Arts Books, 1959.

CUSHMAN, CHARLOTTE. *Charlotte Cushman: Her Letters and Memories of Her Life* (1879). Edited by Emma Stebbins. New York: Benjamin Blom, 1969.

  BARRETT, LAWRENCE. *Charlotte Cushman.* New York: The Dunlap Society, 1889.

  WATERS, MRS. CLARA CLEMENT. *Charlotte Cushman* (1882). New York: Benjamin Blom, 1969.

DALY, JOSEPH FRANCIS. *The Life of Augustin Daly* (1917). New York: Benjamin Blom, 1969.

FELHEIM, MARVIN. *The Theatre of Augustin Daly.* Cambridge: Harvard University Press, 1956.

DAVENPORT, EDWARD LOOMIS

  EDGETT, EDWIN FRANCIS. *Edward Loomis Davenport.* New York: The Dunlap Society, 1901.

DAVIS, RONALD G. "Method in Mime." *Tulane Drama Review,* VI, Summer, 1962.

DAYKARHANOVA, TAMARA. "Actor Faces the Footlights." *Theatre Arts Monthly,* XVI, July, 1932.

DEUTSCH, HELEN, and HANAU, STELLA. *The Provincetown,* 1931.

DREW, JOHN. *My Years on the Stage.* New York: Dutton, 1922.

DREW, LOUISA LANE. *Autobiographical Sketch of Mrs. John Drew.* New York: Scribner's, 1899.

DUNLAP, WILLIAM. *History of the American Theatre.* 2 vols. London: Richard Bentley, 1833.

DURANG, JOHN. *The Memoirs of John Durang, American Actor,* 1785-1816. Edited by Alan S. Downer. University of Pittsburgh Press, 1966.

EAGELS, JEANNE. "The Actor Is More Important Than the Play." *Theatre,* XLVII, January, 1928.

EAMES, CLAIRE. "None of My Best Friends Are Critics." *Theatre,* XLV, January, 1927.

EATON, WALTER PRICHARD. *Plays and Players.* Cincinnati: Stewart and Kidd, 1916.

————. Ed. *The Theatre Guild—The First Ten Years.* New York: Brentano's, 1929.

ELLIOTT, MAXINE. "Beautiful Maxine Elliott: an interview." *Theatre Magazine,* III, November, 1903.

FORBES-ROBERTSON, DIANA. *My Aunt Maxine.* New York: Viking, 1964.

EUSTIS, MORTON. *Players at Work; Acting According to the Actors.* New York: Theatre Arts, 1937.

EVANS, MAURICE. *Maurice Evans' G.I. Production of Hamlet.* New York: Doubleday, 1947.

FENNELL, JAMES. *An Apology for the Life of James Fennell* (1814). New York: Benjamin Blom, 1969.

FISKE, MRS. MINNIE MADDERN. *Mrs. Fiske, Her Views on Actors, Acting and the Problems of Production.* As told to Alexander Woollcott (1917). New York: Benjamin Blom, 1968.

BINNS, ARCHIE and KOOKEN, OLIVE. *Mrs. Fiske and the American Theatre.* New York: Crown, 1955.

GRIFFITH, FRANK CARLOS. *Mrs. Fiske* (1912). New York: Benjamin Blom, 1969.

FLANAGAN, HALLIE. *Arena: The History of the Federal Theatre.* New York: Benjamin Blom, 1965.

FORREST, EDWIN

ALGER, WILLIAM ROUNSEVILLE, *Life of Edwin Forrest* (1877). 2 vols. New York: Benjamin Blom, 1969.

BARRETT, LAWRENCE. *Edwin Forrest* (1881). New York: Benjamin Blom, 1969.

HARRISON, GABRIEL. *Edwin Forrest* (1889). New York: Benjamin Blom, 1969.

MOODY, RICHARD. *Edwin Forrest: First Star of the American Stage.* New York: Knopf, 1960.

MOSES, MONTROSE J. *Fabulous Forrest* (1929). New York: Benjamin Blom, 1969.

REES, JAMES. *The Life of Edwin Forrest, with Reminiscences and Personal Recollections* (1874). New York: Benjamin Blom, 1969.

FROHMAN, DANIEL. *Memories of a Manager* (1911). New York: Benjamin Blom, 1969.

FUNKE, LEWIS and BOOTH, JOHN E. *Actors Talk About Acting.* New York: Random House, 1961.

GILLETTE, WILLIAM HOOKER. *The Illusion of the First Time in Acting.* Papers on Acting, 2d Series, I. Printed for the Dramatic Museum of Columbia University, 1915.

HARDING, ALFRED. *Revolt of the Actors.* New York: William Morrow, 1929.

HAYES, HELEN. *A Gift of Joy.* Philadelphia: Lippincott, 1965.

HEWITT, BARNARD. *Theatre U.S.A.:* 1668-1957. New York: McGraw-Hill, 1958.

HOPKINS, ARTHUR. *To a Lonely Boy.* New York: Doubleday, Doran, 1937.

HORNBLOW, ARTHUR. *Training for the Stage: An Exposition of the Practical Side of Acting Drawn from the Opinions of Successful Actors.* Philadelphia: Lippincott, 1916.

HUSTON, WALTER. "In and Out of the Bag: Othello Sits Up in Bed the Morning After and Takes Notice." *Stage* XIV, March, 1937.

ISAACS, EDITH J. R. *The Negro in the American Theatre.* New York: Theatre Arts, 1947.

————. (Ed.). *Theatre: Essays on the Arts of the Theatre.* Boston: Little Brown, 1927.

JEFFERSON, JOSEPH. *The Autobiography of Joseph Jefferson.* Edited by Alan S. Downer. Cambridge, Mass.: Belknap Press, 1964.

JEFFERSON, EUGENIE PAUL. *Intimate Recollections of Joseph Jefferson* (1909). New York: Benjamin Blom, 1969.

WILSON, FRANCIS. *Joseph Jefferson* (1906). New York: Benjamin Blom, 1969.

WINTER, WILLIAM. *Life and Art of Joseph Jefferson: Together with Some Account of His Ancestry and of the Jefferson Family of Actors* (1894). New York: Benjamin Blom, 1969.

KEENE, LAURA

CREAHAN, JOHN. *The Life of Laura Keene. Actress, Artist, Manager and Scholar.* Philadelphia: Rodgers Publishing Co., 1922.

KIRBY, MICHAEL, Ed. *Happenings.* New York: Dutton, 1965.

Tulane Drama Review, Happenings Issue, X, Winter, 1965.

LANCHESTER, ELSA. *Charles Laughton and I.* New York: Harcourt, Brace, 1938.

LE GALLIENNE, EVA. *At 33.* New York: Longmans, Green, 1934.

LEWIS, ROBERT. "Emotional Memory." *Tulane Drama Review,* VI, Summer, 1962.

————. *Method or Madness?* New York: Samuel French, 1958.

LIVING THEATRE, THE

BECK, JULIAN. "How to Close a Theatre," and "The Living Theatre and Larger Issues." *Tulane Drama Review,* VIII, Spring, 1964.

BINER, PIERRE. *Le Living Theatre.* Lausanne: La Cité, 1968.

DRAMA REVIEW, THE. "The Return of the Living Theatre," Vol. XIII, No. 3, Spring, 1969.

GOTTLIEB, SAUL. "The Living Theatre in Exile." *Tulane Drama Review,* X, Summer, 1966.

SCHECHNER, RICHARD. "Interviews with Judith Malina and Kenneth M. Brown." *Tulane Drama Review,* VIII, Spring, 1964.

BIBLIOGRAPHY

Yale/Theatre, "The Living Theatre," Vol. II, No. 1, Spring, 1969.

LUNT, ALFRED, and FONTANNE, LYNN

LUNT, ALFRED. "Working Together on *The Visit,*" in *Drama on Stage.* Edited by Randolph Goodman. New York: Holt, Rinehart and Winston, 1961.

FREEDLEY, GEORGE. *The Lunts.* London: Rockliffe, 1957.

ZOLOTOW, MAURICE. *Stagestruck: The Romance of Alfred Lunt and Lynn Fontanne.* New York: Harcourt Brace, 1965.

MACKAYE, PERCY. *Epoch; the Life of Steele Mac-Kaye.* 2 vols. New York: Boni and Liveright, 1927.

MANSFIELD, RICHARD. "Concerning Acting." *North American Review,* CLIX, September, 1894.

WILSTACH, PAUL. *Richard Mansfield* (1908). New York: Benjamin Blom, 1969.

WINTER, WILLIAM. *Life and Art of Richard Mansfield.* 2 vols. New York: Moffat, Yard, 1910.

MARLOWE, JULIA. "Eloquence of Silence." *Green Book Magazine,* IX, March, 1913.

RUSSELL, CHARLES EDWARD. *Julia Marlowe, Her Life and Art* (1926). New York: Benjamin Blom, 1969.

SOTHERN, E. H. *Julia Marlowe's Story.* New York: Rinehart, 1954.

MATTHEWS, BRANDER. *On Acting.* New York: Scribner's, 1914.

———. *Rip Van Winkle Goes to the Play.* New York: Scribner's, 1926.

MATTHEWS, BRANDER, and HUTTON, LAURENCE. *Actors and Actresses of Great Britain and the United States: From the Days of David Garrick to the Present Time.* Vol. III: *Kean and Booth: And Their Contemporaries.* Vol. IV: *Macready and Forrest: And Their Contemporaries.* Vol. V: *The Present Time.* New York: Cassell & Co., 1886.

MODJESKA, HELENA. *Memories and Impressions* (1910). New York: Benjamin Blom, 1969.

ALTEMUS, JAMESON TORR. *Helena Modjeska* (1883). New York: Benjamin Blom, 1969.

COLEMAN, MARION MOORE. *Fair Rosalind: The American Career of Helena Modjeska.* Connecticut: Cherry Hill Books, 1969.

MORRIS, CLARA. *Stage Confidences; Talks About Players and Play Acting.* Boston: Lothrop, 1902.

MOSES, MONTROSE J. *Famous Actor-Families in America.* New York: Crowell, 1906.

MOSES, MONTROSE J., and BROWN, JOHN MASON, Eds. *The American Theatre as Seen by Its Critics* (1934). New York: Cooper Square, 1967.

MOWATT, ANNA CORA. *Autobiography of an Actress* (1854). New York: Benjamin Blom, 1969.

NAZIMOVA, ALLA. "I Come Full Circle." *Theatre Magazine,* XLIX, April, 1929.

BARNES, DJUNA. "Alla Nazimova, One of the Greatest of Living Actresses Talks of Her Art." *Theatre Guild Magazine,* VII, June, 1930.

EUSTIS, MORTON. "Alla Nazimova." *Players at Work.* New York: Theatre Arts, 1937.

NEILSON, ADELAIDE

HOLLOWAY, LAURA C. *Adelaide Neilson.* New York: Funk & Wagnalls, 1885.

ODELL, GEORGE C. D.: *Annals of the New York Stage.* 15 vols. Columbia University Press, 1927-1949.

PAGE, GERALDINE. "The Bottomless Cup." Interview by Richard Schechner, ed. by Charles Mee, Jr. *Tulane Drama Review,* IX, Winter, 1964.

PAYNE, JOHN HOWARD

Memoirs of John Howard Payne, the American Roscius. London: J. Miller, 1815.

HANSON, W. T. *The Early Life of John Howard Payne* (1913). New York: Benjamin Blom, 1969.

POWER, TYRONE

WINTER, WILLIAM. *Tyrone Power* (1913). New York: Benjamin Blom, 1969.

REDFIELD, WILLIAM. *Letters From an Actor.* New York: Viking, 1967.

REHAN, ADA

WINTER, WILLIAM. *Ada Rehan* (1891). New York: Benjamin Blom, 1969.

ROBESON, PAUL. "Reflections on O'Neill's Plays." *Opportunity,* December, 1924.

ROGOFF, GORDON. "The Actor as Private Man." *Tulane Drama Review,* VII, Summer, 1963.

SCHILDKRAUT, RUDOLF

CLURMAN, HAROLD. "Rudolf Schildkraut." *Theatre Guild Magazine,* VIII, November, 1930.

SCHILDKRAUT, J. *My Father and I.* New York: Viking, 1959.

SHAVER, CLAUDE L. "Steele MacKaye and the Delsartian Tradition" in Karl R. Wallace, Ed., *History of Speech Education in America.* New York: Appleton-Century-Crofts, 1954.

SILLS, PAUL. "The Celebratory Occasion." *Tulane Drama Review,* IX, Winter, 1964.

SKINNER, OTIS. "The Art of Acting After Booth." *Theatre Arts Monthly,* X, July, 1926.

———. *Footlights and Spotlights; Recollections of My Life on the Stage.* Indianapolis: Bobbs-Merrill, 1924.

———. "Good Diction on the Stage." *Emerson Quarterly,* IX, March, 1929.

SOTHERN, EDWARD ASKEW. *Birds of a Feather Flock Together, or, Talks with Sothern.* Edited by F. G. DeFontaine. New York: G. W. Carleton, 1878.

SOTHERN, EDWARD HUGH. *The Melancholy Tale of "Me"; My Remembrances.* New York: Scribner's, 1916.

SPOLIN, VIOLA. *Improvisation for the Theatre.* Northwestern University Press, 1963.

STARR, FRANCES. "How I Prepare a Role." *Delineator,* XCVI, June, 1920.

STRASBERG, LEE. "Acting and the Training of the Actor." *Producing the Play.* Edited by John Gassner. New York: The Dryden Press, 1941.

——. "Actors Studio Is Not a School." *Plays and Players,* IV, February, 1957.

——. *Strasberg at the Actors Studio.* Edited by Robert E. Hethman. New York: Viking, 1965.

——. "Working with Live Material." *Tulane Drama Review,* IX, Fall, 1964.

RICHARDSON, TONY. "An Account of the Actors Studio: The Method and Why." *Sight and Sound,* XXVI, Winter, 1956/1957.

STRANG, LEWIS C. *Famous Actors of the Day in America* (1900-1902). 2 vols. New York: Benjamin Blom, 1969.

——. *Famous Actresses of the Day in America* (1899-1902). 2 vols. New York: Benjamin Blom, 1969.

TAYLOR, LAURETTE. "The Quality Most Needed." *Green Book Magazine,* XI, April, 1914.

——. "Versatility." *Theatre,* XXVII, January, 1918.

COURTNEY, MARGUERITE. *Laurette.* New York: Rinehart & Co., 1955.

WAGENKNECHT, EDWARD C. *Merely Players.* Norman: University of Oklahoma Press, 1966.

WALLACK, JAMES WILLIAM. *A Sketch of the Life of the Late Actor and Manager James William Wallack.* New York: Morrell, 1865.

WALLACK, JOHN LESTER. *Memories of Fifty Years* (1889). New York: Benjamin Blom, 1969.

WARFIELD, DAVID. "How I Created Simon Levi." *Theatre,* II, 1902.

WEMYSS, FRANCIS COURTNEY. *Theatrical Biography, or The Life of an Actor and Manager.* Glasgow: R. Griffin, 1848.

Who's Who on the Stage; The Dramatic Reference Book and Biographical Dictionary of the Theatre Containing Records of the Careers of Actors, Actresses, Managers, and Playwrights of the American Stage. New York: Walter Browne and F. A. Austin, Editors and Publishers, 1906; Dodge & Co., 1908.

WILSON, GARFF B. *A History of American Acting.* Bloomington: Indiana University Press, 1966.

WINTER, WILLIAM. *The Actor and Other Speeches Chiefly on Theatrical Subjects.* New York: Dunlap Society, 1891.

——. *Shakespeare on the Stage.* 3 vols. New York: Moffat, Yard, 1911.

——. *The Wallet of Time* (1913). New York: Benjamin Blom, 1969.

YOUNG, STARK. "Billets Doux: Letters to Actors on the Technique of Acting." *Theatre Arts Monthly,* XIII, October, 1929; XIV, May, 1930; XV, May, 1931; XVI, April, 1932.

YURKA, BLANCHE. *Dear Audience.* Englewood Cliffs, N. J.: Prentice Hall, 1959.

THEATRE HISTORIES AND CRITICISM

BENTLEY, ERIC. *The Dramatic Event.* Boston: Beacon Press, 1957.

——. *In Search of Theatre.* New York: Knopf, 1963.

——. *The Life of the Drama.* New York: Atheneum, 1964.

——. *The Playwright as Thinker: A Study of Drama in Modern Times.* New York: Reynal and Hitchcock, 1946.

——, Ed. *The Theory of the Modern Stage: An Introduction to Modern Theatre and Drama.* London: Penguin Books, 1948.

——. *What Is Theatre?* Boston: Beacon Press, 1957.

BROWN, JOHN MASON. *The Modern Theatre in Revolt.* New York: W. W. Norton, 1929.

BRUSTEIN, ROBERT. *Seasons of Discontent: Dramatic Opinions 1959-1965.* New York: Simon and Schuster, 1965.

——. *The Third Theatre.* New York: Knopf, 1969.

CHENEY, SHELDON. *The Art Theatre* (1925). New York: Benjamin Blom, 1969.

——. *The New Movement in the Theatre.* New York: Benjamin Blom, 1969.

——. *The Theatre: Three Thousand Years of Drama, Acting and Stagecraft.* New York: Longmans, Green, 1929.

CLARK, BARRETT H. *European Theories of the Drama.* Revised and edited by Henry Popkin. New York: Crown Publishers, 1965.

CLURMAN, HAROLD. "Actors—The Image of Their Era." *Tulane Drama Review,* IV, Spring, 1960.

——. *Lies Like Truth.* New York: Macmillan, 1958.

——. *The Naked Image.* New York: Macmillan, 1966.

COLE, TOBY and CHINOY, HELEN KRICH, Eds. *Directors on Directing: A Source Book of the Modern Theater.* With an Illustrated History of Directing by Helen Krich Chinoy. Indianapolis: Bobbs-Merrill, 1963.

DICKINSON, THOMAS H., Ed. *The Theatre in a Changing Europe.* New York: Henry Holt, 1937.

DUBECH, LUCIEN; MONTBRIAL, JACQUES DE; and HORN-MONVAL, MADELEINE. *Histoire générale illustrée du théâtre.* 5 vols. Paris: Librairie de France, 1931-1934.

FERGUSSON, FRANCIS. *The Idea of a Theatre.* Princeton University Press, 1949.

FLANAGAN, HALLIE. *Shifting Scenes of the Modern European Theatre* (1928). New York: Benjamin Blom, 1969.

FREEDLEY, GEORGE and REEVES, JOHN A. *A History of the Theatre.* New York: Crown Publishers: rev. ed. 1968.

GORELIK, MORDECAI. *New Theatres for Old.* New York: E. P. Dutton, 1962.

MACGOWAN, KENNETH and JONES, ROBERT EDMOND. *Continental Stagecraft* (1922). New York: Benjamin Blom, 1964.

MILLER, ANNA IRENE. *The Independent Theatre in Europe: 1887 to the Present.* New York: Long & Smith, 1931.

NAGLER, A. M., Ed. *A Source Book in Theatrical History.* New York: Dover Books, 1959.

SIMONSON, LEE. *The Stage Is Set.* New York: Harcourt, Brace, 1932.

VARDAC, A. NICHOLAS. *Stage to Screen: Theatrical*

Method from Garrick to Griffith. New York: Benjamin Blom, 1969.

YOUNG, STARK. *The Flower in Drama; a Book of Papers on the Theatre.* New York: Scribner's, 1923.

———. *Glamour, Essays on the Art of the Theatre.* New York: Scribner's, 1925.

———. *Immortal Shadows: A Book of Dramatic Criticism.* New York: Scribner's, 1948.

———. *The Theatre* (1927). New York: Hill & Wang, 1963.

———. *Theatre Practice.* New York: Scribner's, 1926.

PERIODICALS

Drama (Chicago)
Drama Review (formerly *Tulane Drama Review*, New York)
Educational Theatre Journal (Organ of the American Educational Theatre Association)
Encore (London)
Freie Bühne für Modernes Leben (Berlin)
Gesellschaft für Theater Geschichte (Berlin)
International Theatre (Moscow)
International Theatre Annual (London)
Mask (Florence)
Moscow Art Theatre Yearbook (Moscow)
New Theatre (London)

New Theatre Magazine (New York)
New York Dramatic News
New York Mirror
Players Magazine (Racine, Wisconsin)
Plays and Players (London)
Quarterly Journal of Speech (Columbia, Missouri)
Revue d'Art Dramatique (Paris)
Revue d'Histoire du Théâtre (Paris)
Scene, Die (Berlin)
Shakespeare Survey: An Annual Survey of Shakespearian Study and Production.
Sovetskoe Iskusstvo (Moscow)
Stage (New York)
Teatr (Moscow)
Theatre (New York)
Theatre Annual. A Publication of Information and Research in the Arts and History of the Theatre (New York)
Theatre Arts Monthly & *Theatre Arts* (New York)
Theatre Guild Magazine (New York)
Theatre Notebook (London)
Theatre Workshop (New York)
Theatre World (London)
Tulane Drama Review (New Orleans)
Voks (Moscow)
World Theatre (International Theatre Institute, UNESCO—Brussels)
Yale/Theatre (New Haven, Conn.)

GENERAL INDEX

Actors, major roles, plays, films, companies, theatres, movements, and other subjects pertinent to the history of acting.

Aaron (*Titus Andronicus*), 413
Abba, Marta, 443
Abbey Theatre, 325, 386, 387, 388, 404, 541
Abel Drugger (*The Alchemist*), 95, 134
Abel, Raymond, 432
Abington, Frances, 95, 574
Abraham Lincoln (film), 599
Accesi, 43, 49
Achard, Marcel, 226
Achilles, 16, 61, 79, 100, 177
Achurch, Janet, 324, 367, 371
Ackermann, Charlotte, 277
Ackermann, Konrad, 255, 276, 277
Actes des Apôtres, Les (Anon.), 35
Actors Equity Association, 539
Actors Laboratory Theatre, Hollywood, 613
Actors Studio, New York, 411, 542, 622, 623, 629, 635, 637, 638
Actresses, earliest appearances of, 20, 44, 66, 73, 92, 138
Adam (*As You Like It*), 78
Adams, Maude, 539, 598
Addison, Joseph, 335, 357
Adler, Jacob, 601
Adler, Luther, 404, 541
Adler, Sarah, 601
Adler, Stella, 510, 541, 601–602, 622
Adriano, 56
Adrienne Lecouvreur (Scribe, Legouvé), 150
Adventure Story (Rattigan), 420
Aegisthus, 32
Aërope, 29, 32
Aeschines, 4, 14, 28
Aeschylus, 3, 4, 5, 166, 294, 472, 497, 618
Aesop, Clodius, 14, 19, 20, 21, 29, 77, 83, 102
African Company, 540
After the Fall (Miller), 649
Agamemnon, 5, 168, 472
Agate, James, 541
Agrippina, 163, 166, 250, 251
Aiglon, L' (Rostand), 191, 203
Ajax, 5, 29, 33
Alarcón, Juan Ruiz de, 66
Albani, Elsa, 443
Albee, Edward, 397
Albertazzi, Giorgio, 443
Albufar, 187

Alchemist, The (Jonson), 95, 134
Aldridge, Ira, 328, 476, 540
Aldwych Theatre, London, 326, 423
Alexander (*Adventure Story*), 420
Alexander, George, 324
Alexander the Great, 100, 108, 114, 115
Alexandrinsky Theatre, Leningrad, 477, 527
Alfieri, Count Vittorio, 440, 454, 459, 460, 461, 472, 473, 474
Alias Jimmy Valentine (Paul Armstrong, O. Henry), 595
"Alienation effect," see *Verfremdungseffekt*
Allen, James Turney, 30
Allen, Viola, 582
Alleyn, Edward, 76, 77, 78, 83, 86, 87
Allgood, Sara, 388
Alma (*Summer and Smoke*), 635, 639
Almenas de toro, Las (Vega), 65
Alonzo (*The Mourning Bride*), 115
Amanda Wingfield (*The Glass Menagerie*), 595
Amateur actors, 35, 36, 39–40, 42
Ambigu-Comique, 150
Ambivius, L. Turpio, 20
Amenaide, 172
America Hurrah (van Itallie), 664
American Company, 536, 537
American Laboratory Theatre, 510, 602, 622, 631
American Moon, The (Happening), 650, 651
American Shakespeare Festival and Academy, Stratford, Connecticut, 613
American Theatre Wing, 622
Ames, Winthrop, 540
Ami Fritz, L' (Erckmann-Chatrian), 215
Amigos trocados, Los (Anon.), 71
Amour et étourderie (Taylor, Nodier), 201
Amphitryon (Dryden), 106
Amphitryon 38 (Giraudoux), 607

Andersen, Hans Christian, 568
Anderson, Judith, 540, 636
Anderson, Mary, 367, 566, 587
Anderson, Maxwell, 540
Ando, Flavio, 442
Andreini, Francesco, 43
Andreini, Giovan Battista, 42, 43, 49, 50, 52
Andreini, Isabella, 42, 43, 44, 52, 159
Andreini, Virginia, 43, 44, 49, 50, 66
Andreyev, Leonid, 152, 496, 501
Andromache, 30
Andromaque, 209
Andromaque (Racine), 205
Andronicus, Livius, 14, 19, 20, 28
Anna Christie (O'Neill), 523, 543
Anna Onoshenkova (*The Mother*), 319
Anouilh, Jean, 226, 420
Anthony (Dumas), 201
Antigone (Brecht/Living Theatre Production), 653
Antiworlds (Voznesensky/Lyubimov Production), 481
Antoine, André, 151, 152, 209–210, 217, 228, 229, 231, 258, 284, 324, 386, 463, 475, 479
Anton Schill (*The Visit*), 608, 610
Antonio (*The Merchant of Venice*), 397
Antonio Barracano (*Il Sindaco del Rione Sanità*), 471
Antony and Cleopatra (Shakespeare), 409, 540
Anzengruber, Ludwig, 257, 258, 259
Aphrodite, 32
Appia, Adolphe, 258, 324, 540, 577, 615
Arch Street Theatre, Philadelphia, 538
Archer (*The Beaux' Stratagem*), 127
Archer, William, 123, 161, 191, 325, 353, 363, 370, 371
Archie Rice (*The Entertainer*), 409, 415
Arden, John, 325
Ares, 32
Aretino, Pietro, 41
Ariel (*The Tempest*), 616, 618
Ariosto, Lodovico, 41, 64

Aristocrats (Pogodin), 507
Aristodemus, 4, 5, 14
Aristophanes, 5, 497
Aristotle, 5, 6, 11, 51, 261, 396, 432
Arkin, Alan, 641
Arlecchino see Harlequin
Arliss, George, 338, 363
Armand Duval (*Camille*), 461
Armin, Robert, 77
Armonici di San Bartolomeo, 55
Arms and the Man (Shaw), 397, 409, 411, 567, 606
Arnould, Sophie, 574
Arrah-na-Pogue (Boucicault), 546
Art and Literary Society, Moscow, 484, 485 n., 486 n., 487 n., 488, 489 n.
Artaud, Antonin, 152, 226, 234–235, 423, 428, 430, 431, 434–435, 437, 438, 481, 530–531, 543, 653, 655, 664
Artists of Dionysus, 4
Arturo Ui (Brecht/Tovstanogov Production), 481
As I Lay Dying (Barrault, Faulkner), 245
As You Like It (Shakespeare), 78, 260, 403, 472
Ashcroft, Peggy, 326, 397, 403
Aston, Anthony, 93, 113–114, 536, 576
Astor Place Opera House Riot, 334, 544
Astrov (*Uncle Vanya*), 485
At Mrs. Beam's (Munro), 606
Atelier, L' (Dullin), 152, 226
Atellanae, 20, 42
Athalie, 176
Athalie (Racine), 176, 201, 203, 205
Athenodorus, 4
Atkinson, Brooks, 600
Atlas-Hôtel (Salacrou), 230
Atreus, 14, 20, 32
Auberge des Adrets, L' (Antier), 150
Aubrey, John, 82
Augier, Emile, 151, 191, 440
Auguste (*Atlas-Hôtel*), 230
Augustus, 19, 162, 205
Auric, Georges, 226
Autobodys (Happening), 650, 651
Autocrats (Pisemsky), 488
Autor de comedias, 64, 65, 67, 71
Autos sacramentales, 36, 64, 65, 67, 70
Avare, L' (Molière), 155, 225
Awake and Sing (Odets), 602, 613
Axer, Erwin, 481

Baal (Brecht), 307
Bab, Julius, 260, 282, 294, 295
Bablet, Denis, 530 n.
Bacchae (Euripides), 472
Badly Loved, The (Mauriac), 246
Baggesen, Jens, 277
Bainter, Fay, 599
Bajazet, 116
Bajazet (Racine), 205
Baker, George Pierce, 540
Balbus, Cornelius, 19
Balcony, The (Genet), 422, 425
Baldovino (*The Pleasure of Honesty*), 230
Bancroft, Anne, 543, 622
Bancroft, Marie Wilton, 323, 324, 353, 360, 367, 558
Bancroft, Squire, 323, 324, 353, 360, 367, 548, 558, 570
Bannister, John, 357
Baptiste (Barrault), 246
Barbier, Jules, 203
Barbieri, Nicolo, 43, 52–53
Barker, The (Nicholson), 599
Barnum, P. T., 587
Baron (*The Lower Depths*), 479
Baron (*The Miser-Knight*), 485 n., 488
Baron Chevrial (*A Parisian Romance*), 567
Baron, Michel, 136, 146, 147, 148, 158–160, 180
Barrault, Jean-Louis, 152, 245–246, 306, 481
Barrett, Lawrence, 539, 558, 574, 587
Barrett, Wilson, 367, 548
Barrie, James, 360
Barry, Elizabeth, 94, 98, 101, 103, 111-112, 114, 115, 138, 367, 575
Barry, Philip, 540
Barry, Spranger, 95, 559
Barrymore, Ethel, 538, 591
Barrymore, Georgiana Drew, 538, 591
Barrymore, John, 415, 538, 543, 591–593, 594
Barrymore, Lionel, 538, 591, 593, 594
Barrymore, Maurice, 538, 539, 591
Bartholomew Fair (Jonson), 90
Bartley (*Riders to the Sea*), 388
Basochians, 36
Bassanio (*Merchant of Venice*), 419
Basserman, Albert, 258, 259, 279, 295
Bateman, H. L., 353
Bateman, Isabel, 367
Bates, Blanche, 539, 577

Bathhouse, The (Mayakovsky), 481
Bathyllus, 21
Baty, Gaston, 152
Baumert (*The Weavers*), 294
Bayes (*The Rehearsal*), 112
Baylis, Lilian, 325
Beatrice (*Much Ado About Nothing*), 138, 489
Beau Brummel (Fitch), 539, 567
Beau Geste, 408
Beaubourg, Pierre Trochon de, 148, 159
Beauchâteau, Madame de, 157
Beaumarchais, Pierre-Augustin, 149, 151, 191, 460
Beaumont, Hugh, 607
Beaux Jours, Les (film), 245
Beaux' Stratagem, The (Farquhar), 127
Beck, Heinrich, 256, 278
Beck, Julian, 235, 543, 641, 652–653, 664, 669
Becket (Tennyson), 579
Beckett, Samuel, 418, 423, 542
Becque, Henri François, 258
Bedbug, The (Mayakovsky), 481
Beerbohm, Max, 354, 371
Beer-Hofmann, Richard, 294
Beggar's Opera, The (Gay), 403
Behrman, S. N., 613
Beil, Johann David, 256, 278, 290
Béjart family, 147, 154
Béjart, Armande (Mme. Molière), 147, 155, 156, 158
Béjart, Geneviève, see Hervé, Mlle.
Béjart, Madeleine, 147, 155
Belasco, David, 539, 576–577
Belasco Theatre, New York, 577
Bell, G. J., 141, 445, 446
Bellamy, George Ann, 138
Bellerose, 147
Belleville, 153
Bells, The (Lewis Erckmann-Chatrian), 353, 391, 392
Beltrame, 52
Belvidera (*Venice Preserved*), 112, 141
Ben (*Love for Love*), 103, 134, 135
Ben-Ami, Jacob, 629
Ben Ari, R., 295, 507
Benchley, Robert, 590
Benedick (*Much Ado About Nothing*), 138, 337, 360, 489
Benini, 460
Benson, Frank, 324, 360
Bentley, Eric, 246, 260, 307, 314, 470
Bentley, John, 87
Berdyaev, Nicholas, 660, 663
Berenger (*Rhinoceros*), 409

Berghof, Herbert, 630, 664
Bergner, Elisabeth, 259, 260, 295
Berliner Ensemble, 260, 308, 312 n., 313, 314, 634
Bernhardt, Sarah, 151, 191, 202–204, 247, 367, 370, 371, 441, 465–466, 595, 596
Bernstein, Henri, 575
Bertens, Rose, 289
"Betterton," 328
Betterton, Thomas, 66, 91, 93, 94, 96, 97, 98, 103, 104–107, 108, 113, 114, 115, 116, 326, 358, 559, 561, 574, 575, 576
Betterton, Mrs. Thomas (Mary Saunderson), 94, 103, 112, 138
Betti, Ugo, 443
Betty, William Henry West, 326
Beyond Human Power (Bjørnson), 204
Beys, Denys, 154
Bibbiena, Cardinal, 41
Bibiena family, 440
Big Knife, The (Odets), 622
Big Lake, The (Riggs), 602
Biomechanics, 479, 480, 501–502, 504–506
Bird of Paradise, The (Tully), 595, 598
Birmingham Repertory Theatre, 325, 388, 408, 417, 419, 422
Birthday Party, The (Pinter), 429
Bjørnson, Bjørnstjerne, 204
Blackfriars Theatre, London, 78, 90
Blakely, Colin, 326
Blanchette (Brieux), 231
Blin, Roger, 429
Blitzstein, Marc, 542
Blok, Alexander, 501
Bloom, Claire, 419, 420
Blumenthal, Oscar, 289
Bob Acres (*The Rivals*), 551
Bocage, 150
Boccaccio, 438
Boddington, Diana, 412
Bogart, Humphrey, 599
Boileau, Nicolas, 285
Boker, George Henry, 539
Boleslavsky, Richard, 480, 509–510, 518, 602, 604, 622, 631
Bolingbroke (*King Richard II*), 374, 403
Bolt, Robert, 418, 421
Bon, Louis Belloti, 440, 441, 442
Bond, Edward, 325
Booth, Barton, 94, 95, 103, 113, 120, 322, 559, 561
Booth, Edwin, 323, 353, 358, 444, 454, 536, 538, 539, 557–559, 566, 574, 576, 577, 579–580, 587, 593, 625
Booth, John Wilkes, 558
Booth, Junius Brutus, 322, 328, 537, 557, 561
Booth, Mary Devlin, 558
Booth Theatre, New York, 558
Bost, Pierre, 420
Bottom (*A Midsummer Night's Dream*), 36, 77, 78, 80, 81
Boucicault, Dion, 323, 353, 538, 546–547, 551, 576–577
Bouhélier, Saint-Georges de, 228
Boule-Rouge, Paris, 176
Bourgeois Gentilhomme, Le (Molière), 206
Bowery Theatre, New York, 537, 544
Boy Players, 36, 66, 75, 83, 94, 138
Boyd, Neva, 641
Braccao, 461
Bracco, Roberto, 441, 442, 459
Bracegirdle, Anne, 94, 103, 113, 115, 138
Bradshaw, Lucretia, 97, 101, 115
Brady, Alice, 540
Brahm, Otto, 258, 259, 268, 288–289, 294, 377, 386, 475, 479
Brand, Phoebe, 541
Brando, Marlon, 543, 614, 622, 630
Brecht, Bertolt, 260, 301, 304, 307–308, 314, 320, 423, 427, 471, 481, 505, 530, 542, 543, 634, 650, 652, 653, 664, 665, 667
Brécourt, 158
Bressant, Jean Baptiste Prospère, 193, 348
Brieux, Eugène, 151, 210, 231, 372
Brig, The (Brown), 652, 653
Brigadoon (Lerner, Loewe) 629
Brighella, 43, 440
Briusov, Valery Y., 499, 500
Brockmann, Johann Franz Hieronymus, 256
Bromberg, J. Edward, 541
Brook, Peter, 235, 260, 326, 397, 417, 418, 420, 422–423, 430, 432, 437 n., 530, 607, 608, 610, 668
Brooke, Gustavus V., 327
Brothers Karamazov, The (Copeau Production), see *Frères Karamazov, Les*
Brothers Karamazov, The (Moscow Art Theatre Production), 479
Brothers Karamazov, The (Theatre Guild Production), 606
Brough, Fanny, 571
Brough, Lionel, 367
Brown, John Mason, 510, 587
Brown, Kenneth, 652
Brown, Pamela, 420
Bruehl, Count, 257
Brustein, Robert, 653
Brutus, 104, 105, 116, 207
Brutus (Voltaire), 178
Büchner, Georg, 314
Buckstone, John Baldwin, 323
Buffoons, 52–55, 260
Bulgakov, Leo, 480
Bullins, Ed, 541
Bulwer-Lytton, Edward, 321, 334, 342
Burbage, Cuthbert, 90
Burbage, James, 64, 76, 90
Burbage, Richard, 76, 77, 78, 84, 85, 86, 88, 90–91, 93, 97, 559, 561, 562
Burgtheater, Vienna, 256, 257, 277, 318
Buridan (*Blanchette*), 231
Burke, Billie, 539
Burke, Charles, 551
Burke, Edmund, 131
Burrell, John, 411
Bury the Dead (Shaw), 542
Busch, Ernst, 314, 634
Butler, Mrs., 103
Byron, George Noel Gordon, Lord, 327, 343

Cabinet of Dr. Caligari, The (film), 259
Caesar, Julius, 19
Caesar and Cleopatra (Shaw), 409
Café Crown, 613
Cafe LaMama, 543
Cage, John, 543, 648, 653
Cain, Henri Louis, see Lekain
Calandria (Bibbiena), 41
Calderón, Maria, 66
Calderón de la Barca, Pedro, 66, 67, 271 n.
Caleb Plummer (*Cricket on the Hearth*), 546, 551
Callipides, 12
Camden, William, 82
Cameron, Beatrice, 539
Camilla (*Les Horaces*), 157
Camille, 465
Camille (Dumas *fils*), 466, 538
Camille (film), 590
Campbell, Lily B., 96
Campbell, Mrs. Patrick, 371, 373, 611
Campbell, Thomas, 141
Camus, Albert, 246
Candide (Hellman, Bernstein), 629

Cannan, Dennis, 420
Capek, Karel, 602
Capitano, 43
Caprice (Sil-Vara, Moeller), 415, 584, 606, 609
Captain Thorne (*Secret Service*), 563
Caramuel, J., 66
Careless Husband, The (Cibber), 103
Carey, Mother, 562
Carnaval des Enfants (Saint-Georges de Bouhélier), 228
Carnovsky, Morris, 404, 541, 606, 613
Carradine, John, 240
Carrington, Margaret, 592
Carson, Murray, 375
Carswell, Katherine, 388
Cartel des Quatre, 152
Carter, Mrs. Leslie, 539, 577
Carton, Richard Claude, 372
Casa di Goldoni, La, 442
Case of J. Robert Oppenheimer, The (Kipphardt), 301
Casket, The (Plautus), 19
Cassius (*Julius Caesar*), 105, 116
Castalio (*The Orphan*), 101, 107
Castle Square Theatre, Boston, 606
Cato (Addison), 337, 357
Caucasian Chalk Circle, The (Brecht), 308, 314, 505
Cecchini, Orsola, 43, 44, 49, 50
Cecchini, Pietro Maria, 43, 49
Cenci, Les (Artaud Production), 235
Cercle Gaulois, 210
Cervantes, Miguel de, 66, 67, 195, 514
Chaikin, Joseph, 235, 543, 663–665
Chairs, The (Ionesco), 529
Chaliapin, Fyodor, 374, 493, 617, 634
Chambers, E. K., 88
Champsmeslé, Marie, 147, 148, 159, 367
Chantecler (Rostand), 191, 598
Chaplin, Charles, 44
Charington, Charles, 324
Charles I (Wills), 353
Charles IX, 177, 179
Charles IX (Chénier), 149, 177 n., 178
Charles Surface (*The School for Scandal*), 345, 377, 403
Charley's Aunt (Thomas), 397
Chekhov, Anton, 304, 398, 399, 421, 477, 484, 490, 491, 496, 507, 518, 523, 529, 541, 591, 649
Chekhov, Michael, 404, 416,

480, 506, 518–519, 527, 617, 618, 620, 621, 622
Chekhov Theatre Studio, 519
Chénier, Marie-Joseph, 149, 177, 178
Cherry Orchard, The (Chekhov) 478, 485, 523, 590
Chester plays, 35, 39
Chicago Little Theatre, 540
Chichester Festival Theatre, 409
Chichikov (*Dead Souls*), 523, 525–527
Children of Paradise (film), 246
Chilton, Nola, 668
Chirikov, Eugene N., 589
Chironomia, 27, 264
Chosen People, The (Chirikov), 589
Chris Christopherson (*Anna Christie*), 523
Christine Mannon (*Mourning Becomes Electra*), 590
Christopher Mahon (*The Playboy of the Western World*), 388
Chronegk, Ludwig, 284
Churchill, Charles, 96, 332, 333
Cibber, Colley, 93, 94, 95, 96, 102–103, 114, 138, 536, 559, 574
Cibber, Susanna Maria, 95, 116, 131, 138, 367, 576
Cibber, Theophilus, 138
Cicero, Marcus Tullius, 19, 20, 21, 26, 27, 55, 83, 89, 358, 366
Cid, Le (Corneille), 146, 157, 205, 453
Cieslak, Ryszard, 529, 535
Circle-in-the-Square, New York, 635
Citta morta, La (D'Annunzio), 466
City Dionysia, 3, 4
Civic Repertory Theatre, New York, 541, 629
Claire (*The Visit*), 608
Clairon, Hyppolite, 132, 136–137, 148, 149, 152, 161, 162, 163, 166, 170, 174, 175, 177, 178, 214
Claramonte, Andrés de, 65
Clarence (Tarkington), 606
Claudel, Paul, 152, 216, 243, 246
Clayton, John, 367
Cleander, 4
Cleante (*The Imaginary Invalid*), 397
Cleidemides, 4
Cleomenes (Dryden), 111
Cleopatra, 166, 197
Cléopâtre (Moreau), 203
Cléopâtre captive (Jodelle), 146

Clift, Montgomery, 622, 630
Clive, Catherine, 95, 131, 138, 139
Cloten (*Cymbeline*), 417, 418
Clough, Inez, 540
Clurman, Harold, 510, 518, 541, 602, 617, 622
Clytemnestra, 174, 177, 590, 637
Clytemnestra, 19
Cobb, Lee J., 541, 543
Cocteau, Jean, 152
Cold Wind and the Warm, The (Behrman), 613
Coleman, Mrs., 92
Coleridge, Samuel Taylor, 327
Collage Hamlet (Marowitz), 432–433
Collé, Charles, 159, 174
Collier, Constance, 592
Collier, Jeremy, 93, 99
Collier, William, 592
Collins, Rufus, 654, 655, 661
Comedias, 55, 64, 65, 67, 68, 70, 71, 72, 73, 74
Comedias de capa y espada (cloak and sword dramas), 65
Comédie des Champs-Elysées, 152, 240
Comédie Française, see Théâtre Français
Comédie Italienne, see Théâtre Italien
Comic servants, 52, 151, 153, 191, 243
Commedia dell' arte, 20, 41–44, 50, 56, 58, 59, 64, 65, 76, 152, 153, 154, 226, 240, 242, 243, 246, 277, 377, 391, 439–440, 442, 470, 471, 479, 497, 651
Compagnia Teatro Nuovo, 470
Compass, The, Chicago, 641
Condell, Henry, 78
Confidenti, 43
Confrérie de la Passion, 35, 146
Congreve, William, 93, 94, 103, 115, 336, 420, 536
Connection, The (Gelber), 649, 652, 664
Connelly, Marc, 541, 606
Cons, Emma, 325
Conservatoire, 149, 150, 178, 179, 187, 190, 203, 210, 212, 213, 215
Constance (*King John*), 141
Constant Nymph, The (Kennedy, Dean), 397, 399
Constant Prince, The (Calderon), 271 n., 534, 535
Contrast, The (Tyler), 536
Cook, George Frederick, 322, 327, 537, 544, 559, 561, 562
Cooper, Thomas Abthorpe, 537

Copeau, Jacques, 152, 216–217, 225, 226, 228, 229, 230, 231, 240, 615, 624, 634
Coppée, François, 151
Coquelin, Benoit Constant, 123, 151, 152, 161, 190–192, 196, 209, 354, 363, 367, 392, 456, 457, 458, 459, 552, 554 n.
Coquelin, Ernest Alexandre Honoré, 191
Corcoran, Katherine, 538
Cordelia (*King Lear*), 116
Coriolanus, 96, 334, 336, 409, 414, 451
Coriolanus (Shakespeare), 140, 314, 322
Coriolanus (Berliner Ensemble Production), 314
Corley (*Glad of It*), 591
Corneille, Pierre, 146, 147, 157, 165, 166, 173, 174, 175, 186
Cornell, Katharine, 542, 636
Corpus Christi Festival, 36, 39, 64
Corrado, Gregorio, 41
Corral de la Cruz, 64, 65, 66
Corral del Principe, 65
Corrales, 64
Costard (*Love's Labour's Lost*), 76
Costume, 30, 36, 39, 52, 67, 68–69, 71, 72, 74
Cottin, 468
Counsellor-at-Law (Rice), 403
Counterattack (Stevenson), 613
Country Wife, The (Wycherley), 109
Court Theatre, Dresden, 282
Court Theatre, Gotha, 256, 278
Covent Garden, 96, 120, 122, 131, 321, 322, 323, 333, 337, 422, 546
Coventry plays, 35
Coward, Noel, 408, 415, 607, 610
Cracow Theatre School, 529
Cradle Will Rock, The (Blitzstein), 542
Craig, Edward Gordon, 246, 324, 325, 353, 360, 376–377, 386, 479, 509, 540, 577, 615
Crawford, Cheryl, 541, 542, 622, 629
Cricket on the Hearth, The (Boucicault, Dickens), 546, 551
Cricket on the Hearth, The (Sulerzhitsky Production), 518
Crime and Punishment (Gielgud Production), 397
Crime and Punishment (Orleneff Production), 575

Critic; or, a Tragedy Rehearsed, The (Sheridan), 409, 553
Critique de l'école des femmes (Molière), 155, 157, 158
Crommelynck, F., 504
Cromwell (Hugo), 179
Crosse, Samuel, 87
Crossings (De la Mare), 360
Croué, 228
Croyden Repertory Theatre School, 417
Cumberland, Richard, 94
Curel, François de, 151, 210, 442, 459
Curiatius (*Les Horaces*), 157, 160
Cushman, Charlotte, 323, 353, 359, 367, 451, 536, 537, 538, 589
Cymbeline (Shakespeare), 417, 418
Cyprian Conqueror, or, The Faithless Relict, The (Anon.), 89, 97
Cyrano de Bergerac, 151, 154, 191, 539, 567
Cyrano de Bergerac (Rostand), 147, 541, 592
Cytheris, 20

Dalberg, Baron Wolfgang Heribert von, 256, 278
Dalcroze, Emile Jacques, 220
Daly, Augustin, 536, 538, 562, 587
D'Amico, Silvio, 442
Dame aux camélias, La (Dumas fils), see *Camille*
Dangeville, Marie Anne Botot, 149
D'Annunzio, Gabriele, 151, 362, 441, 442, 459, 466
Dante Alighieri, 59, 451
Darbes, 439, 440
Darnton, Maida, 257
Darwin, Charles, 369
Daudet, Alphonse, 192, 210
d'Aulnoy, Comtesse, 72
Davenant, Sir William, 92, 93, 97, 98, 133
Davenport, Edward Loomis, 323, 538, 584
Davenport, Fanny, 538
Davey, Thomas, 584
David, Jacques Louis, 178
Davidov, Vladimir N., 503
Davies, Thomas, 102, 120, 121, 132
Davis, Ossie, 541
Davis, Richard Harding, 592
Daykarhanova, Tamara, 480
Dead Souls (Gogol), 523, 525–526
Dean, James, 622

Death of a Salesman (Miller), 543, 607
Debrie, Mlle., 156, 157, 158
Debt of Honor, A (Grundy), 488
Deburau, Jean-Baptiste Gaspard, 150, 246, 580
Decroux, Etienne, 246
Dee, Ruby, 541
Deirdre (Russell), 387
Dekker, Thomas, 82
De la Mare, Walter, 360
Delaunay, Louis-Arsène, 197, 198, 212
Delsarte, François, 187, 530, 539
Demetrius, 21, 31, 32
Democritus, 22
Demosthenes, 4, 5, 14, 21, 28, 102, 331
Denise (Dumas fils), 196, 468
Dent, Alan, 398
Dépit amoureux, Le (Molière), 191
Deputy, The (Hochhuth), 301
Desdemona, 489, 506, 524–525, 582
Design for Living (Coward), 607
Desire Under the Elms (O'Neill), 496, 599
Despiau, Charles, 252
Destouches, Philippe, 255
Detective Story (Kingsley), 472
Deuteragonist, 4
Deutsches Theater, Berlin, 258, 259, 289, 294, 314
Devine, George, 325
Devrient, Eduard, 150, 282, 290
Devrient, Gustave Emil, 282, 560
Devrient, Karl August, 282
Devrient, Ludwig, 257, 279, 282, 560
Devrient, Otto, 282
Dexter, John, 409
D'Holbach, Baron, 131
Dickens, Charles, 341, 342, 514, 518, 546
Dictator, The (Davis), 592
Diderot, Denis, 123, 131, 132, 153, 161, 191, 201, 223, 224, 225, 233, 244, 354, 357, 363, 366, 368, 369, 462, 463
Dido, 177
Dido (Jean-Jacques Le Franc, Marquis de Pompignan), 177
Dido and Aeneas (Purcell), 376
Digges, Dudley, 387, 388, 540, 606
Dillingham, C. B., 571
Dionysus, 3, 5
Dionysus '69, (The Performance Group), 235

Diotti, 468
Disney, Walt, 410
Ditrichstein, Leo, 594
Divorce, Le (Regnard), 57
Divorçons (Sardou), 466
Dmitrevsky, Ivan, 475
Doctor Astrov (Uncle Vanya), 409
Dr. Faustus (Marlowe), 422, 534
Dr. Jekyll and Mr. Hyde (Forpaugh, Fiske), 539, 567
Doctor Knock (Romains), 240
Doctor Pangloss (The Heir-at-Law), 551
Doctor Stockman (An Enemy of the People), 485, 490–491, 493
Doctor's Dilemma, The (Shaw), 606
Dodsworth, 599
Dogberry (Much Ado About Nothing), 77
Doggett, Thomas, 94, 115, 135, 562
Doll's House, A (Ibsen), 371, 394, 539, 584, 590
Doll's House, A (film), 590
Don Adriano de Armado (Love's Labour's Lost), 418
Don César (D'Ennery), 197
Don Juan (Alarcón), 66
Don Juan (Molière), 155, 240, 501
Don Juan (Pushkin), 489–490
Don Quixote, 195
Doña Sol (Hernani), 203
Donne Curiose (Goldoni), 454
Doolittle, Alfred (Pygmalion), 611
Doolittle, Eliza (Pygmalion), 611
Dorante (L'Ecole des femmes), 155 n., 160
Dorsch, Käthe, 260
Dorset Gardens, London, 94
Dorval, Marie, 150, 367
Dostoyevsky, Fyodor, 216, 225, 228, 258, 519, 575
Dottore, 43, 51, 87
Douglas (Home), 140, 537, 543
Douglass, David, 536
Dovizio, Bernardo, see Bibbiena, Cardinal
Downer, Alan S., 328
Downes, John, 102
Drama of Life, The (Hamsun), 493
Dramatic Workshop, New York, see Piscator, Erwin
Dream Play (Strindberg), 235
Dreigroschenoper (Brecht, Weill), 260, 307

Drew, John, 538, 539, 562, 587, 591, 594
Drew, Georgiana, see Barrymore, Georgiana Drew
Drew, Louisa Lane, 538, 591
Dreyer, Carl, 234
Drums in the Night, see Trommeln in der Nacht
Drury Lane Theatre, London, 94, 95, 96, 102, 103, 111, 116, 120, 122, 131, 132, 139, 140, 323, 326, 333
Dryden, John, 93, 106, 108, 109, 111, 112, 345
Dublin Gate Theatre, 388
Duchenois, Mlle., 179
Duchess of Malfi, The (Webster), 88
Ducis, Jean François, 179, 186
Duclos, Mlle., 148
Du Croisy, Mlle., 158
Du Croisy, Philbert Gassot, 147, 157
Duerrenmatt, Friedrich, 607
Dugazon, Henri G., 177, 178, 179
Duhamel, Georges, 216
Duke in Darkness, The (Hamilton), 403
Duke Karl August, 256, 267, 274 n.
Duke of Saxe-Meiningen, see Saxe-Meiningen, George II, Duke of
Duke of York's Company, 93, 94, 97
Duke's Motto (McCarthy), 339
Dulcy (Connelly, Kaufman), 606
Dullin, Charles, 152, 216, 225–226, 229, 234, 240, 245, 530, 531
Dumas, Alexandre, 150, 548
Dumas, Alexandre fils, 151, 191, 440, 441, 459, 466
Dumb Kattrin (Mother Courage), 314, 315, 319
Dumesnil, Marie-Françoise, 149, 152, 163, 170, 174, 176, 177, 178
Dunlap, William, 537
Dunnock, Mildred, 630
Dunsany, Lord, 443
Du Parc, 154, 191
Du Parc, Mlle., 156, 157, 158
Dupuis, Adolphe, 214
Durec, 228 229,
D'Urfey Thomas, 112
Duse, Eleonora, 203, 224, 370, 371, 377, 381, 439, 441–442, 459, 465–466, 490, 493, 585, 586, 596, 617, 634
Duse, Luigi, 465
Dybbuk, The (Ansky), 480, 506

Eagels, Jeanne, 543, 614
Eames, Claire, 540, 606
Earl of Worcester's Men, 86
Eastcourt, Richard, 114
Eaton, Walter Prichard, 103
Echange, L' (Claudel), 216
Echnaton, 661
Eckermann, Johann Peter, 268
Ecole des femmes, L' (Molière), 147, 155
Edgar (King Lear), 116
Edwards, Christine, 622
Edwards, Hilton, 388
Egisto (Mérope), 454
Ekhof, Konrad, 255, 256, 258, 261, 262, 274 n., 276, 277, 278, 279, 290
Elder, Lonne, 541
Eldridge, Florence, 543
Electra, 4, 5, 15
Electra (Giraudoux), 637
Eliot, T. S., 403, 418, 420
Elizabeth the Queen (Anderson), 606, 613
Elizabethan Stage Society, 324, 390
Elliott, Madge, 419
Elliott, Maxine, 539
Elliston, Robert William, 376
Ellmenreich, Frau, 291
Elmhurst, Mr. and Mrs. Leonard, 518
Elvira (Pizarro), 140
Emanuel, Giovanni, 442, 460
Embezzlers, The (Katayev), 523
Emilia Galotti (Lessing), 262, 277
Emma (Herr Puntila and His Man Matti), 320
Emmet, J. K., 584
Enemy of the People, An (Ibsen), 204, 459, 485, 490, 541, 613, 629
Enemy of the People, An (Miller version), 613
Enfants de Famille, Les, 154
Enfants Sans Souci, 36
Engels, Friedrich, 666
English Stage Society, 325
Ennius, 19
Entertainer, The (Osborne), 325, 409, 412, 415
Entremeses, 68, 70
Ephraim Cabot (Desire Under the Elms), 599
Epic Theatre, 260, 301–307, 308–311, 314
Erckmann-Chatrian, 215, 392
Eric IV (Strindberg), 518
Eros, 25
Ervine, St. John, 388
Eternal Road, The (Werfel), 294

Ethelwold, Bishop of Winchester, 37
Etherage, George, 93, 103
Etourdi, L' (Molière), 215
Eufemia (Rueda), 67
Eunuch, The (Terence), 57
Euripides, 4, 5, 7, 16, 459, 472, 481, 497
Eustis, Morton, 590
Eva *(Herr Puntila and His Man Matti)*, 320
Evans, Edith, 325, 397
Evans, Jack, 114
Evans, Maurice, 325
Every Man in His Humour (Jonson), 78
Everyman (Reinhardt Production) see *Jedermann*
Evreinov, Nikolai, 443
Exception and the Rule, The (Brecht), 664
Expressionism, 259, 260, 299–301, 443
Eysoldt, Gertrude, 259

Fairbanks, Douglas, 415
Falk, Rossella, 443
Falstaff, 94, 114, 360, 522, 537, 551, 587
Family Reunion, The (Eliot), 403, 418, 420, 422
Farceurs, 41, 153
Farmer, Frances, 541
Farquhar, George, 94, 536
Farr, Florence, 371, 385
Farren, William, 349, 549
Fashion (Mowatt), 538
Father, The (Strindberg), 403
Faucit, Helen, 353
Faulkner, William, 245
Faust (Goethe), 318, 529
Fay, Frank, 386, 387, 388
Fay, William George, 386, 387–388
Fear and Misery of the Third Reich (Brecht), 314
Feast of the Boy Bishop, 35
Feast of the Ass, 35
Fèbvre, 214
Fechter, Charles, 323, 346, 353, 547, 558
Fedeli, 43, 52
Federal Theatre, 542
Fedora (Sardou), 468
Fedotov, A. F., 485 n., 488
Fedotova, Glikeria, 476, 486, 493
Fehling, Juergen, 259, 260
Felix, 186
Femmes savantes, Les (Molière), 155
Fennell, James, 537
Ferdinand *(Love's Labour's Lost)*, 403

Fergusson, Francis, 510
Fescennine Verses, 19
Feste *(Twelfth Night)*, 77
Feuerbach, Anselm, 293
Field, Nathan, 91
Field, Sid, 415
Fielding, Henry, 536
Fifth Column, The (Hemingway), 622
Figaro, 149, 151, 191, 193, 196
Filippo, Eduardo De, 443, 470
Filippo, Peppino De, 470
Filippo, Tina De, 470
Fils Louverne, Les (Schlumberger), 216
Filumena Marturano (De Filippo), 470
Finney, Albert, 325, 409
Fiorilli, Tiberio, 43, 154, 440
Fiske, Harrison Grey, 584
Fiske, Minnie Maddern, 539, 584, 587, 594, 614
Fitch Clyde, 536, 567
Fitzgerald, Barry, 388
Fitzmaurice-Kelly, James, 67
Flaminia, 43, 44, 48, 49, 50, 59
Flavio, 42
Flechelles, 153
Fleck, Johann Friedrich Ferdinand, 257, 290, 291
Flecknoe, Richard, 91
Fleetwood, Charles, 120, 131
Fletcher, John, 112
Florentine Theatre, 465
Floridor, 147, 157 n.
Florinda, 44
Fogerty, Elsie, 408
Foire Saint-Germain, La, 146
Foldal *(John Gabriel Borkman)*, 294
Fonda Theatre, Naples, 451
Fontanne, Lynn, 415, 540, 595, 606–607, 608, 609
Foote, Samuel, 96
Forbes-Robertson, Johnston, 324, 325, 371, 373
Forest, The (Ostrovsky), 476, 503
Forrest, Edwin, 322, 327, 334, 536, 537, 538, 543–545, 557, 558, 575, 589
Fort, Paul, 151
Fortune Hunter, The (Smith), 592
Fortune Theatre, London, 76
Fountain, The (O'Neill), 599
Fourberies de Scapin, Les (Molière), 215, 252
Fourberies de Scapin, Les (Jouvet Production), 251, 252
Fowler, Gene, 591
Francesca da Rimini (Boker), 539

Francesca da Rimini (Pellico), 454, 466
Frank, Waldo, 216, 240
Frankenstein (Living Theatre), 653, 657
Franz, Ellen, 284
Franz Moor *(The Robbers)*, 257
Freie Buehne, 258, 259, 288
Freie Volkebuehne, 259, 260, 289, 314
Frenzel, Karl, 290, 292, 293
Frères Karamazov, Les (Copeau Production), 216, 225, 228
Freud, Sigmund, 621
Frittellino, 49
Frohman, Charles, 388, 539
Frohman, Daniel, 570, 577
From Rags to Riches, 595
Fry, Christopher, 419, 420
Furness, Horace Howard, 559
Futurism, 443

Gabriel, 87
Galli-Bibiena, see Bibiena
Galsworthy, John, 390, 391
Galy Gay *(Man Is Man)*, 664
Ganassa, Alberto, 43, 64
Garden, Mary, 584
Garfield, John, 404, 541
Garibaldi Theatre, Padua, 465
Garland, Robert, 584
Garnier, Robert, 146
Garrick, David, 94, 95, 96, 103, 116, 120, 122, 127, 130, 131–133, 136, 137, 138, 140, 141, 148, 161, 168, 170 201, 241, 256, 321, 322, 326, 327, 331, 332, 333, 336, 339, 356, 367, 393, 475, 536, 537, 557, 559, 561, 574, 575, 576
Gary, 228
Gaskill, William, 409
Gassman, Vittorio, 443, 472–473
Gassner, John, 507
Gattinelli, Gaetano, 463
Gaultier-Garguille, 146, 153
Gaussin, Mlle., 149, 367
Gautier, Théophile, 150
Gayev *(The Cherry Orchard)*, 485
Gayley, Charles Milles, 36
Gazzara, Ben, 622
Gelber, Jack, 652, 664
Gellius, Aulus, 14
Gelosi, 43, 44, 52, 53, 146, 153
Gémier, Firmin, 152, 219
Genast, Anton, 271 n.
Genet, Jean, 425, 428, 429
Gentlemen of the Press (film), 599
Gentlewoman (Lawson), 602
Geoffroy, Jean-Marie-Joseph, 193
George, Mlle., 150

Georges Dandin (Molière), 485, 486, 487
Germanova, Maria, 479
Gershwin, George, 304
Gherardi, Evaristo, 43, 57–58
Ghost *(Hamlet)*, 78, 104, 256
Ghosts (Ibsen), 258, 324, 357, 400, 442, 459, 466, 590
Giacometti, Paolo, 441, 454
Gide, André, 152, 217, 246
Giehse, Therese, 314
Gielgud, John, 325, 326, 397–398, 403, 408, 409, 418, 420, 421, 424
Gilbert, William Schwenk, 548
Gilbert and Sullivan companies, 567, 571
Gildon, Charles, 97
Gillette, William, 538, 563, 624
Gillmore, Margalo, 540, 606
Gilpin, Charles, 541
Ginsberg, Allen, 655
Giraudoux, Jean, 152, 240, 252, 613, 637
Girl in Waiting (Manners), 595
Glad of It (Fitch), 591
Gladiator, The (Bird), 544
Glass Menagerie, The (Williams), 543, 595, 649
Gleeman, 34
Globe Theatre, London, 76, 90, 579
Goat Song, The (Werfel), 606
Godfrey, Thomas, 536
Godunovs, The (Fedotov), 485 n.
Goethe, Johann Wolfgang von, 256, 267–268, 269 n., 271 n., 274 n., 277, 282, 289, 290, 291, 292, 293, 318, 319, 341, 529, 580
Goetz von Berlichingen (Goethe), 256, 267, 277, 290
Gogol, Nikolai, 481, 502, 518, 523, 525, 526, 527
Gold-Eagle Guy (Levy), 602
Golden Boy (Odets), 404, 541, 602, 613
Goldoni, Carlo, 439–440, 441, 442, 454, 460, 466, 472, 485, 497, 523
Goldsmith, Oliver, 93, 131, 170
Golem, The (film), 259
Good Earth, The (Buck), 590 n.
Good Hope, The (Hejermans), 510, 512
Good Soldier Schweik, The (Piscator Production), 260, 301, 306
Goodman Theatre, Chicago, 635, 639, 640
Goodman's Fields, England, 131
Gorboduc (Sackville, Norton), 75

Gordin, Gene, 655
Gordon, Ruth, 636
Gorky, Maxim, 294, 315, 319, 477, 484, 485, 496, 507
Gorky Theatre, Moscow, 481
Gosse, Edmund William, 363
Gosson, Stephen, 92
Got, Edmond, 191, 212, 214, 244, 345
Gottsched, Johann Christoph, 254, 255, 261
Gozzi, Carlo, 440
Gozzi, Caspare, 440
Gramatica, Emma, 442
Gramatica, Irma, 442
Granville-Barker, Harley, 324, 325, 371, 390–391, 397
Grass Harp The (Capote), 629
Grasso, Giovanni, 442
Gray, Charles Harold, 96
Gray, Paul, 542, 622, 623
Greek Theatre of Syracuse, 472
Green, Paul, 541, 622
Green Goddess, The (Archer), 363
Greene, Graham, 418, 420
Greene, Robert, 84
Greet, Philip Ben, 324, 390
Gregor, Joseph, 257
Gregory, Lady Augusta, 386, 388, 597
Grein, Jacob Thomas, 324, 371, 475
Grillo, Marquis del, 444
Grillparzer, Franz, 257, 259
Grimaldi, Joseph, 371
Grimm, Friedrich Melchior, Baron von, 132, 161
Gringoire, 198
Gropius, Walter, 304
Gros-Guillaume, 146, 153
Gros-René, see Du Parc
Grosses Schauspielhaus, 294
Grotowski, Jerzy, 235, 423, 428, 481, 529–530, 543
Gurawski, Jerzy, 529
Group Theatre, 404, 507, 518, 541, 542, 543, 602–606, 613, 616, 621, 622, 629, 630, 631
Guardsman, The (Molnar), 606, 608
Guinness, Alec, 403, 411
Guitry, Lucien, 151, 463
Guthrie, Tyrone, 409, 413
Gutkind, Eric, 656
Guy Mannering (Scott), 359, 537
Gwyn, Nell, 66, 94
Gypsy Theatre, U.S.S.R., 480

Haak Company, 254
Habimah Theatre, 295, 480, 506, 507

Hackett, James Henry, 323, 537, 538, 551
Hagen, Uta, 543, 635, 640
Haigh, Kenneth, 325
Hall, Peter, 326, 437
Hallem, Lewis, 536
Hallem, Lewis, Jr., 536
Hamburg Dramaturgy, 255, 261
Hamburg National Theatre, 255, 261, 277, 291, 292
Hamlet, 36, 39, 76, 77, 79, 81–82, 86, 90, 93, 97, 100, 104, 113, 114, 115, 122, 138, 168, 203, 205, 209, 246, 252, 256, 282, 324, 331, 336, 346, 353, 354, 355, 357, 360, 362, 370, 371, 372, 376, 377, 378, 397, 400–401, 403, 409, 414, 418, 419, 421, 433, 441, 442, 451, 475, 479, 512, 522, 533, 537, 538, 550, 551, 557, 558, 559, 560, 566, 579, 580, 587, 592–593, 625
Hamlet (Shakespeare), 78, 79, 81, 167, 214, 246, 252, 266, 353, 400, 403, 409, 415, 418, 420, 422, 423, 432–433, 472, 481, 509, 518, 539, 541, 543, 558, 592–593
Hammersmith Lyric Theatre, London, 418, 420
Hammerstein II, Oscar, 304
Hampden, Walter, 541
Hanswurst, 254, 255
Hapgood, Elizabeth Reynolds, 485
Hapgood, Emilie, 540
Hapgood, Norman, 567, 601
Happenings, 648–651
Happy Time, The (Taylor), 543, 629
Harbage, Alfred, 77, 89
Harden, Maximilian, 258
Hardy, Alexandre, 146, 153
Hare, John, 323, 360, 548
Harlequin, 43, 57, 87, 391
Harp of Life, The (Manners), 595
Harpagon (*L'Avare*), 193, 195, 199, 226, 230, 527
Harper, John, 114
Harrigan, Edward, 538
Harris, Barbara, 641
Harris, Henry, 94
Harris, Jed, 410
Harris, Julie, 543, 622
Harrison, Rex, 416
Harrison, Richard, 541
Hart, Charles, 92, 94
Hartmann, Edward von, 368
Hasenclever, Walter, 259, 540
Hathaway, Anne, 78
Haupt-und-Staatsaktionen, 254

Hauptmann, Gerhart, 151, 204, 210, 258, 259, 289, 294, 442, 459, 601
Hauteroche, 157
Hayes, Helen, 540, 542, 611
Haymarket Theatre, London, 94, 116, 120, 122, 323, 360
Hazlitt, William, 139, 322, 327, 328, 332
Heart of Maryland, The (Belasco), 577
Hebbel, Christian Friedrich, 257
Hebertot, Jacques, 240
Hecht, Jenny, 655, 661
Hecuba, 30
Hedda Gabler, 470, 586, 590
Hedda Gabler (Ibsen), 589
Hegel, George W. F., 245
Heimat, see *Magda*
Heir-at-Law, The (Colman the Younger), 551
Hejermans, Hermann, 510, 512
Helburn, Theresa, 607
Held by the Enemy (Gillette), 563
Helpmann, Robert, 419
Hemminge, John, 78
Henderson, John, 137
Henry, John, 536, 537
Henry (Harry) Bertram (*Guy Mannering*), 359
Hensel, Sophie Friedericke, 261
Henslowe, Philip, 76, 77, 82, 85, 86
Henze, Herbert, 289
Hercules (Heracles), 29, 30
Herlie, Eileen, 420
Hermione, 209
Hernani (Hugo), 149, 203
Herne, James A., 538
Herod, 35, 36, 77, 82, 115, 147, 442
Heron, Matilda, 537
Herr Puntila and His Man Matti (Brecht), 320
Hervé, Mlle., 158
Hester Crewe (Fiske), 584
Hewlett, James, 540
Heywood, Dubose and Dorothy, 541
Heywood, Thomas, 77, 85–86
Hibner (*The Inspector General*), 503
Hieronimo, 82, 90
Higgins (*Pygmalion*), 376
Hill, Aaron, 95, 96, 116–117
Hill, John, 96, 120, 122–123, 133, 161
Hillebrand, Harold Newcomb, 328
Himmel und Hoelle (Kornfeld), 299
Hobson's Choice, 403
Hochhuth, Rolf, 301

Hodgkinson, John, 537
Hoffmann, Karl Ludwig, 254
Hofmannsthal, Hugo von, 259, 294
Hofmeister, Der (Lenz), 319
Hogarth, William, 265, 559
Holinshed, Raphael, 438
Home, John, 543
Home Sweet Home (Payne), 538
Homer, 7, 8, 10, 31, 202
Homolka, Oscar, 259, 314
Honte et remords (Taylor, Nordier), 201
Hooks, Robert, 541
Hopkins, Arthur, 592, 593
Horace, 21, 85, 96, 101, 137
Horaces, Les (Corneille), 157, 160
Hornimann, A. E. F., 386
Hôtel de Bourgogne, 57, 146, 147, 153, 155, 156 n., 157, 159
Hotspur, 104, 105, 108, 397, 403, 407, 409, 413, 537
Houghton, Norris, 405, 480, 595
Hour Glass, The (Yeats), 387
House of Connelly, The (Green), 602, 613, 622
Howard, Bronson, 536
Howard, Henry, 661
Howard, Leslie, 593
Howard, Sidney, 540, 599
Howells, William Dean, 539
Hugo, Victor, 149, 150, 151, 179, 441
Hull House, Chicago, 641
Humoresque (Hurst), 595
Hunt, Leigh, 322, 327, 334, 338
Hunt, Martita, 240
Hunter, Ian, 420
Hurok, Sol, 518
Hurst, Fannie, 595
Hurwicz, Angelika, 314
Huston, John, 599
Huston, Walter, 540, 598–599
Hylas, 21
Hyppolyte (*Phèdre*), 252

Iago (*Othello*), 103, 109, 115, 196, 257, 328, 353, 357, 358, 409, 413, 454, 472, 539, 559, 566, 574
Ibsen, Henrik, 151, 204, 210, 258, 259, 288, 294, 304, 324, 325, 353, 363, 370, 371, 376, 385, 388, 390, 392, 393, 395, 441, 442, 459, 463, 466, 469, 472, 485, 539, 584, 586, 590, 591, 601, 657
Idiot's Delight (Sherwood), 607
Iffland, August Wilhelm, 256, 257, 278–279, 290
Iffland's Ring, 279

Ilinsky, Igor, 502
Illustre Théâtre, L', 147, 155
Imaginary Invalid, The (Molière), see *Malade Imaginaire, Le*
Immerman, Karl, 257
Imperial Theatre, London, 360, 377
Importance of Being Earnest, The (Wilde), 397
Impromptu de l'Hôtel de Condé, L' (Montfleury), 155
Impromptu de Versailles, L' (Molière), 147, 152, 155–158
Improvisation, 435, 528–529, 637, 641, 651
Imshim (*The Autocrats*), 488–489
In Convict Stripes (Reid), 599
In-Stage, London, 432
In the Jungle of Cities (Brecht), 314, 652, 664
Inchbald, Elizabeth, 336
Incorporated Stage Society, London, 324, 390
Independent Theatre, London, 324, 371
Inge, William, 542
Ingram, Rex, 541
Innamorata, 42, 43
Innamorato, 42, 50
Inspector General, The (Gogol), 502–503, 518, 527
Institute for Research into Acting, Wroclaw, Poland, 481, 529
Intermezzi, 55
International Ladies Garment Workers Union, 541
Intervention (Slavin), 507
Investigation, The (Weiss), 301
Ion, 6, 7, 8, 48
Ionesco, Eugène, 152, 409, 415, 481, 529, 542, 613, 664
Iphigenia in Aulis (Racine), 174, 176, 203, 205
Irish Literary Theatre, 386, 388
Irish National Theatre, see Abbey Theatre
Irving, Henry, 123, 161, 191, 194, 201, 242, 321, 324, 325, 353–354, 360, 361, 362, 363, 367, 370, 371, 372, 373, 376, 377, 391, 392, 408, 410, 456, 547, 548, 552, 554 n., 558, 566, 572, 573, 579, 582, 585, 592, 601, 606
Irwin, May, 587
Isaacs, Edith, 540
Isabella, or The Fatal Marriage (Southerne), 140
Israel, Steven Ben, 657, 661
Itallie, Jean-Claude van, 664

Jack Tanner (*Man and Superman*), 422
Jackson, Barry, 325, 388, 408, 417, 418, 422
Jacob (*Awake and Sing*), 613
Jacobowsky and the Colonel (Werfel), 403
Jacques Damour (Zola), 210
Jagemann, Karoline, 268
James, Henry, 191, 441, 454
Janauschek, Fanny, 539, 566, 585
Jannings, Emil, 259
Jarry, Alfred, 152, 234
Jason (Jeffers' *Medea*), 397
Jeanne d'Arc (Barbier), 203
Jeans, Isabel, 420
Jedermann (Hofmannsthal), 259, 294
Jeffers, Robinson, 397
Jefferson, Joseph, 536, 538, 546, 551–552, 566, 567, 583, 584, 594
Jellicoe, Ann, 325
Jenkin, H. C. Fleeming, 141
Jenny Wren, 508
Jessner, Leopold, 259, 260, 307, 314, 615
Jest, The (Benelli), 592
Jet of Blood (Artaud), 235, 437
Jewish State Theatre, Moscow, 480
Joash (*Athalie*), 176
Jodelet, 146, 147
Jodelle, Etienne, 146
John Gabriel Borkman (Ibsen), 294, 459
John Worthing (*The Importance of Being Earnest*), 397
Johnson, Benjamin, 100
Johnson, James Weldon, 540
Johnson, Samuel, 131, 132, 138, 559
Johnny Johnson (Green), 613
Jones, Ernest, 409, 413
Jones, Henry Arthur, 324, 372
Jones, Inigo, 92
Jones, James Earl, 541
Jones, LeRoi, 541
Jones, Robert Edmond, 540, 593, 599
Jongleur, 34
Jonson, Ben, 75, 77, 78, 82–83, 85, 86, 90, 100
Joseph, B. L., 77
Joseph Surface (*The School for Scandal*), 377, 397
Jouassain, Mme., 197
Journey's End (Sherriff), 408
Jouvet, Louis, 152, 216, 240, 252, 306
Juarez and Maximilian (Werfel), 606

Judith Keith (*Fear and Misery of the Third Reich*), 314
Judson Poets' Theatre, New York, 543
Julian (*Tiny Alice*), 397
Juliet, 94, 132, 207, 209, 337, 338, 362, 379, 397, 417, 441, 465, 489, 558, 595
Julius Caesar, 207, 258
Julius Caesar (Shakespeare), 397, 539, 599
Junge Gelehrte, Der (Lessing), 261
Jupiter, 204
Justice (Galsworthy), 592
Justinian, 20
Juvenal, 21

Kachalov, Vasily, 476, 478, 496
Kainz, Josef, 259, 289, 318
Kaiser, Georg, 152, 259, 294, 540
Kamerny Theatre, Moscow, 479, 480
Kammerspiele, Berlin, 294
Kaprow, Allan, 648
Karlsruhe Theater, 282
Kass, Peter, 664
Katayev, Valentin, 523
Katherine (*The Taming of the Shrew*), 489, 595
Kaufman, George S., 606
Kayssler, Friedrich, 259
Kazan, Elia, 541, 542, 607, 622, 623, 629, 630, 635, 636, 639
Kean, Charles, 258, 321, 323, 353, 360, 537, 546, 558
Kean, Edmund, 149, 150, 207, 257, 322, 323, 324, 326–328, 329–333, 334, 337, 340, 341, 342, 343, 352, 355, 357, 381, 394, 416, 440, 537, 538, 544, 548, 550, 557, 559, 560–562, 573, 574, 575, 576, 579
Keene, Laura, 551, 584
Kemble, Charles, 322, 337, 343, 537
Kemble, Frances Anne, 322, 337–338, 367, 537
Kemble, John Philip, 96, 140, 321, 322, 323, 326, 327, 328, 334, 336–337, 357, 358, 550, 557, 559, 560, 574, 575
Kemble, Roger, 140
Kemp, William, 44, 76, 77, 84, 85, 87
Kendal, Madge, 367, 389
Kendal, William H., 367, 369, 548
Kerrigan, J. M., 388
Khlestakov (*The Inspector General*), 518, 527
Kiki, 583
Killigrew, Thomas, 93

King Henry IV, 107
King Henry IV (Shakespeare), 397
King Henry V, 409, 417, 567
King Henry V (Shakespeare), 412, 418, 567
King Henry V (film), 411
King Henry VIII (Shakespeare), 140
King John, 334
King John (Shakespeare), 141, 339, 360, 419, 613
King Lear, 77, 90, 95, 122, 132, 257, 277, 282, 326, 371, 372, 377, 397, 403, 414, 417, 418, 441, 442, 451, 454, 460, 559, 613
King Lear (Shakespeare), 116, 133, 256, 418, 422–423, 430, 537
King Richard II, 79, 374, 397, 400, 403, 413, 559
King Richard II (Shakespeare), 403, 418, 420, 539, 559, 592
King Richard III, 77, 122, 130, 131, 132, 193, 226, 230, 325, 327, 331, 332, 334, 382, 407, 410, 413, 451, 472, 539, 557, 558, 592
King Richard III (Shakespeare), 131, 409, 413, 558, 567, 592
King's Company, 93, 94
King's Men, France, 146
Kippardt, Heimar, 301
Kirby, Michael, 648
Kirkland, Alexander, 541
Kirkman, James Thomas, 121
Kleines Theater, Berlin, 294
Kleist prize, 307
Kloepfer, Eugen, 260
Knell, William, 87
Knipper-Chekhova, Olga, 478, 496, 501
Knowles, Sheridan, 321, 334
Koch, Gottfried Heinrich, 254, 255
Kohlhardt, Friedrich, 254
Kokoschka, Oscar, 259
Komisarjevskaya, Vera, 488 n., 501
Komisarjevsky, Fyodor, 284, 488 n.
Komisarjevsky, Theodore, 397, 399, 482, 488 n., 501
Kongo, 599
Koonen, Alice, 479
Korneichuk, A., 523
Kornfeld, Paul, 259, 299
Korsh Theatre, 486, 503, 523
Kortner, Fritz, 259, 260, 314
Kotzebue, August von, 140, 141
Krauss, Henry, 228
Krauss, Werner, 259, 260

Kreutzer Sonata, The (Gordin/ Tolstoy), 575
Kurz, Joseph von, 277
Kyd, Thomas, 438
Kynaston, Edward, 94, 103, 107–108

Labor Stage, 541
La Chaussée, Pierre, 149, 174, 255
Lacy, John, 94
Ladies of the Jury (Ballard), 584
Lady Capulet (*Romeo and Juliet*), 337, 638
Lady Macbeth, 96, 112, 138, 140, 141, 142–145, 207, 314, 340, 403, 444–450, 537, 539, 626, 638
Lady of Lyons, The (Bulwer-Lytton), 361
Lady Randolph (*Douglas*), 140
Lady Teazle (*The School for Scandal*), 345
Laertes (*Hamlet*), 322, 337, 403
Lafleur, 153
La Grange, Charles Varlet, 147, 158, 159
Lahr, Bert, 649
Lamb, Charles, 86, 141, 376
Lamda (London Academy of Music and Dramatic Art), 430, 432, 437
Lanehan, John, 87
Langner, Lawrence, 540
Lansdowne, Lord, 562
Larimore, Earle, 606
Larive, 177
L'Arronge, Adolphe, 258, 289, 294
Laube, Heinrich, 257, 291, 292
Laughton, Charles, 423
Launce (*Two Gentlemen of Verona*), 77
Lawrence, Thomas, 336
Lawson, John Howard, 541
Lazarus, 71
Lazzi, 42, 76
Lecomte, Valleran, 146, 153
Lecouvreur, Adrienne, 148, 159, 174
Lee, Canada, 541
Lee, Nathaniel, 93, 106, 112
Le Gallienne, Eva, 541, 629
Legouvé, Gabriel, 444
Lehmann, Else, 258
Lehrstücke (Brecht), 307
Leigh, Mrs. Tony, 103
Leigh, Tony, 103
Leigh, Vivien, 409, 437 n.
Leigheb, Claudio, 460
Leipzig Theatre, 292
Lekain, 149, 180–187, 242, 331, 358

Lelio, 42, 59
Lemaître, Frédéric, 150, 151, 196, 197, 200, 202, 341, 352, 367, 371 n.
Lemaître, Jules, 203
Lenaea, 5
Lenin, Vladimir I., 662
Lensky, Alexander P., 476
Lentulus, 21
Leonardo da Vinci, 519, 621
Lermontov, Mikhail Y., 475
Leshkovskaya, Elena K., 499
Lessing, Gotthold Ephraim, 255, 256, 257, 261–262, 277, 291, 292, 294
Lessing Theatre, Berlin, 258, 289
Lesueur, François Louis, 195, 196
Lewes, Charles Lee, 341
Lewes, George Henry, 150, 341–342, 556, 560, 572
Lewinsky, Josef, 194, 257
Lewis, Robert, 542, 622, 629–630
Lewis, Sinclair, 599
Lichtenberg, Georg Christoph, 132
Life of St. Anthony, The (Anon.), 72
Lifeline, 403
Lilina, Maria Petrovna, 479, 487 n.
Liliom (Molnar), 592
Lillo, George, 94
Lincoln Center Repertory Theater, 623, 630
Lincoln's Inn Fields, 94
Lind, Jenny, 342
Liston, John, 350, 352
Little Actors of the Dauphin, 158
Little Eyolf (Ibsen), 590
Little Something for the Maid, A (Abel), 432
Littlewood, Joan, 325
Living Corpse, The (Tolstoy), 509
Living Newspaper, 542
Living Theatre, 235, 543, 641, 652, 653, 656, 661, 664, 669
Lloyd, Robert, 94, 96
Locandiéra, La, see *Mistress of the Inn, The*
Lockridge, Richard, 558
Loeb, Philip, 541, 606
Loewe, Ludwig, 257
Logician (*Rhinoceros*), 613
London Assurance (Boucicault), 546
London Central School of Drama and Speech, 408
Long Day's Journey into Night (O'Neill), 543

Look Back in Anger (Osborne), 481
Lopez Pinciano, Alonzo, 68
Lord Admiral's Company, 76, 77
Lord Chamberlain's Company, 76, 77, 78, 79
Lord Dundreary (*Our American Cousin*), 323, 371, 551, 570
Lord Foppington (*The Relapse*), 103
Lord, Pauline, 540, 543
Lorenzo the Magnificent, 41
Lorenzo, Tina di, 442
Lorre, Peter, 307, 314
Louis XI (Delavigne, Boucicault), 353
Love for Love (Congreve), 94, 103, 135, 397
Love in a Hurry (Aston), 113
Love's Kingdom (Flecknoe), 91
Love's Labour's Lost (Shakespeare), 403, 418, 422
Love's Last Shift (Cibber), 103
Lower Depths, The (Gorky), 294, 478, 479, 485, 496
Lowin, John, 78
Lubitsch, Ernst, 259
Lucian, 20, 21, 30
Lucio (*Measure for Measure*), 417
Lucrèce Borgia (Hugo), 201
Lugne-Pöe, Aurélie François, 151, 234, 324
Luka (*The Lower Depths*), 478
Lullo, Giorgi de, 443
Lunt, Alfred, 415, 427, 540, 606–607, 612
Lunts, the, 542, 606, 608, 613
Lutz, Regine, 312 n.
Luzhsky, Vasily, 479
Lyceum Theatre, London, 324, 353, 360, 547, 570
Lyceum Theatre, New York, 539, 577
Lycurgus, 4
Lyly, John, 75
Lyonard, 36
Lyric Theatre, Hammersmith, London, 360
Lyubimov, Yuri, 481

Macaulay, Thomas Babington, 367
Macbeth, 94, 104, 120, 132, 133, 134, 135, 138, 142–145, 168 n., 209, 325, 334, 377, 397, 398, 400, 403, 407, 409, 413, 414, 419, 444, 445, 446, 447, 448, 450, 451, 454, 539, 559, 587
Macbeth (Shakespeare), 133, 138, 167 n., 337, 339, 360, 444, 537, 539, 626, 638
Macbeth Robert, 541

Machiavelli, Niccolo, 41, 473
McClendon, Rose, 541
McCullough, John, 539, 577, 584
Macgowan, Kenneth, 540, 599
MacKaye, Percy, 540, 599
MacKaye, Steele, 539, 577
Macklin, Charles, 95, 96, 120–121, 131, 148, 321, 322, 332, 333, 537, 559, 561, 562
MacLiammoir, Micheál, 388
Macready, William Charles, 321, 322, 323, 324, 333–334, 337, 341, 342, 343, 350, 352, 353, 354, 357, 416, 537, 538, 544, 555, 562, 589, 632
McVicker, Mary, 558
Madame Ranevsky (*The Cherry Orchard*), 590
Maddermarket Theatre, Norwich, 388
Maddern, Lizzie, 584
Madison Square Garden Theatre, New York, 539, 546, 577
Madonna of the Streets, The (film), 590
Madras House, The (Granville-Barker), 390
Madwoman of Chaillot, The (Giraudoux), 240
Maeterlinck, Maurice, 151, 259, 294, 470, 485, 490, 501
Maffei, Marchese Francesco Scipioni di, 440
Magda (Sudermann), 203, 466
Magee, Patrick, 429
Magnani, Anna, 443
Magnificent Cuckold, The (Crommelynck/Meyerhold Production), 504
Mahomet, 171, 178
Mahomet (Voltaire), 177
Maieroni, Achille, 463
Maître Pierre Pathelin (Anon.), 36, 146
Maksheyev, 503
Malade imaginaire, Le (Molière), 155, 397
Malcontent, The (Marston), 90
Malden, Karl, 622, 630
Malina Judith, 235, 543, 652–653, 669
Mallarmé, Stéphane, 151
Maltz, Albert, 541
Malvern Festival, 325
Malvolio (*Twelfth Night*), 374, 375, 409, 522, 614
Maly Theatre, Moscow, 476, 480, 481, 486, 489 n., 499 n., 506
Man and Superman (Shaw), 422
Man for All Seasons, A, (Bolt), 418, 421

Man Is Man (Brecht), 652, 664
Man of Destiny, The (Shaw), 370
Man of Mode, The (Etherege), 103
Man of the World, The (Macklin), 120
Manhattan Theatre, New York, 584
Mankind (Anon.), 35
Mann Ist Mann (Brecht), 307, 314
Manners, J. Hartley, 595
Mannheim National Theatre, 256, 278, 279
Mansfield, Richard, 539, 567–568, 599
Mantle, Burns, 600
Mantzius, Karl, 36, 141, 155, 174, 277
Mao Tse Tung, 662
Marat/Sade (Weiss), 326, 423, 430, 437
Marceau, Marcel, 44, 425
March, Fredric, 543
Marco Millions (O'Neill), 606, 613
Marcuse, Theodore, 665
Mareck, Michele, 657
Marenco, 461
Margel, 228
Marie Antoinette (Giacometti), 444
Marinetti, Filippo Tomasso, 443
Marini, De, 463
Marius, 179
Marivaux, Pierre Carlet de Chamberlain de, 152
Mark Antony (*Julius Caesar*), 397, 403
Marlowe, Christopher, 41, 75, 76, 77, 84, 422, 438
Marlowe, Julia, 539, 540, 570–571
Marmontel, Jean-François, 161, 170
Marowitz, Charles, 235, 418, 422, 423, 429–430
Mars, Mlle., 149
Marston, John, 90
Martin, Karlheinz, 260
Martin-Harvey, John, 324
Martinelli, Drusiano, 49
Martinelli, Tristano, 43, 49
Martyn, Edward, 386
Mary Mary, 655
Mary Stuart, 441, 444
Marx, Karl, 654, 658, 666
Masha (*The Three Sisters*), 636
Masks, 3, 4, 5, 15–18, 20, 24, 29, 30, 31, 32, 46, 54, 439
Masse Mensch (Toller), 259
Massinger, Philip, 78
Massnahme, Die (Brecht), 307

Master Builder, The (Ibsen), 403, 590
Master of the Revels, 75
Mathews, Charles, 323, 341, 358, 537, 546
Mathias (*The Bells*), 353, 392
Matkowsky, Adalbert, 259
Matthews, Brander, 540, 599
Maubant, 212
Mauriac, François, 246
Mayakovsky, Vladimir, 481
Mayor (*The Inspector General*), 502–503
Measure for Measure (Shakespeare), 417, 422
Measures Taken, The, see *Die Massnahme*
Mecour, Susanna, 261
Medea, 29, 126
Medea (Euripides), 420, 481
Medea (Jeffers), 397
Medea (Legouvé), 444
Médecin amoureux, Le (Molière), 154
Medici, Catherine de, 43
Medici, Maria de, 43
Medvedeva, Nadezhda, 486
Meg Merrilies (*Guy Mannering*), 359, 537
Meiningen Company, see Saxe-Meiningen
Meisner, Sanford, 541, 602
Melmouth, ou l'homme errant (Taylor, Nodier), 201
Melpomene, 559
Member of the Wedding, A (McCullers), 543
Menaechmi (Plautus), 41
Menander, 6
Menzel, Adolf, 293
Mephistopheles (*Faust*), 194, 257
Merchant of Venice, The (Shakespeare), 120, 209, 329, 353, 397, 419, 539, 559, 567, 601
Mercutio (*Romeo and Juliet*), 322, 337, 360, 394, 397, 408, 409, 417, 419, 593
Mérope 166, 171, 174, 176
Mérope (Alfieri), 453, 454
Mérope (Voltaire), 173
Merry, Anne, 537
Metamora (Stone), 544
Meteor (Behrman), 606
"Method" acting, 403–408, 411, 425, 433, 434–435, 477–478, 485–495, 504, 507–509, 510, 602, 604–605, 617–618, 621, 622–623, 629, 630, 631, 639, 651, 664
Method of Physical Actions, 478, 504, 506, 523–529
Meyerhold, Vsevolod, 226, 259, 479, 480, 481, 490 n., 496,

501–502, 504, 505, 506, 518, 523, 524, 530, 532

Meynardier Company, 440

Midsummer Night's Dream, A (Shakespeare), 36, 78, 80–81, 294

Miles Company, 571

Milhaud, Darius, 226

Miller, Arthur, 542, 613, 629

Miller, Henry, 539

Millionairess, The (Shaw), 628

Mils, Tobias, 87

Mimes and miming, 20, 21, 34, 37, 42, 44, 152, 246, 248

Minna von Barnhelm (Lessing), 261

Miracle, The (Vollmoeller), 294

Miracle Worker, The (Gibson), 543

Mirra (Alfieri), 453

Misanthrope, Le (Molière), 155

Miser-Knight, The (Pushkin), 485, 486

Miss Sara Sampson (Lessing), 261

Mister Puff (*The Critic*), 409, 553, 554

Mistress of the Inn, The (Goldoni), 440, 466

Mitchell, Abbie, 540

Mitchell, Langdon, 584

Mithridate, 160

Mnemosyne, 31

Mochalov, Pavel, 475

Modena, Giacomo, 463

Modena, Gustavo, 440, 441, 451, 453, 454, 463

Modjeska, Helena, 539, 558, 566, 587

Moeller, Philip, 540, 606

Mohun, Michael, 92, 94, 106

Moissi, Alexander, 259, 279, 294, 295

Molé, François René, 149, 350

Molière, 43, 44, 59, 122, 147, 152, 154–158, 159, 175, 191, 193, 202, 204, 206, 207, 214, 216, 225, 243, 252, 255, 277, 306, 375, 397, 439, 442, 459, 485 n., 486, 497, 501, 523, 528, 542, 618, 634, 649

Molnar, Ferenc, 459, 606

Moncalvo Company, 443

Monck, Nugent, 388

Mondory, 146, 147, 148, 158

Monimia (*The Orphan*), 112

Monnier, Henry, 197

Monroe, Marilyn, 622

M. Poirier, 195

M. Prudhomme, 197

Montefalco, 48

Montfleury, 147, 148, 155, 157

Month in the Country, A (Turgenev), 403, 485, 509

Monti, Luigi, 460, 461

Monval, Georges, 159

Moody, William Vaughan, 540

Moore, Douglas, 510

Moore, George, 386

Mordkin, Mikhail, 510

Moreau, Emile, 203

Morelli, Alemanno, 463

Moreno, Marguerite, 240

Morozov, Savva Timofeyevich, 490

Morris, Clara, 367, 538

Morta civile, La (Giacometti), 441, 454

Moscow Art Theatre, 284, 294, 377, 404, 417, 475, 476, 477, 478, 479, 480, 482, 484, 485 n., 487 n., 490, 496, 500, 501, 509, 510, 518, 541, 589, 604, 621, 622, 631

Moscow Art Theatre First Studio (Second Moscow Art Theatre), 480, 501, 506, 509, 510, 518, 523, 527, 528, 541

Moscow Art Theatre Third Studio, 506

Moscow Art Theatre Musical Studio, 496

Moses, Montrose, 544, 577

Moskvin, Ivan, 476, 478, 496, 501

Mossoviet Theatre, Moscow, 481

Mother, The (Gorky, Brecht), 314, 315, 316

Mother Blitzer (*Der Hofmeister*), 319, 320

Mother Courage (*Mother Courage and Her Children*), 260, 308, 314, 315, 319, 634

Mother Courage and Her Children (Brecht), 314, 481

Mother-in-Law, The (Terence), 19, 57

Mounet-Sully, Jean, 151, 194, 214, 242, 244

Mountebanks, 42, 52, 56

Mountfort, William, 103, 108–109, 113

Mountfort, Mrs. William, 103, 112, 114, 116

Mourning Becomes Electra (O'Neill), 590, 635, 640

Mourning Bride, The (Congreve), 115, 140, 336

Mowatt, Anna Cora, 323, 538

Mrs. Haller (*The Stranger*), 140, 141, 537

Mrs. Midget (*Outward Bound*), 595

Much Ado About Nothing (Shakespeare), 353

Müller, Gerda, 260

Murray, Alma, 367

Musco, Angelo, 442

Musset, Alfred de, 150

My Dear Children (Turney, Horwin), 593

My Heart's in the Highlands (Saroyan), 629

My Sister Eileen (Fields, Chodorov), 613

Myniscus, 4, 11

Mystère du Nouveau Testament (Anon.), 35

Mystère du Viel Testament (Anon.), 35

Mysteries (Living Theatre), 653, 661

Mysteries of Love, The (Vitrac), 235

Naevius, 19

Naharro, Bartolemé de Torres, 67, 68

Nancy Sykes (*Oliver Twist*), 537

Napoli milionaria! (De Filippo), 470

Narcissus, 186

Nashe, Thomas, 77, 84

Nat Duncan (*The Fortune Hunter*), 592

Natasha (*The Three Sisters*), 636

Natella (*The Caucasian Chalk Circle*), 314

Nathan der Weise (Lessing), 257, 262

Nathan, George Jean, 192

National Theatre of Great Britain, 326, 403, 408, 409, 412, 481

Naturalism, 151, 201, 207–208, 214, 258, 288, 289–293, 344–346

Nazimova, Alla, 480, 496, 540, 589–590

Ned McCobb's Daughter (Howard), 606

Neher, Carola, 314

Neighborhood Playhouse, New York, 540

Neilson, Adelaide, 367, 539

Nemirovich-Danchenko, Vladimir I., 404, 407, 475, 476, 477, 484, 491, 495–496, 589

Neoptolemus, 4, 5, 14

Nero, 186, 250, 251

Neuber, Carolina, 254, 255, 261

Neuber, Johann, 254, 255, 261

Neues Theater, 294

New Queen's Theatre, London, 360

New Theatre, New York, 540

New Theatre League, 541

New Way to Pay Old Debts, A (Massinger), 328

New York Idea, The (Mitchell), 584
Newman, Paul, 622
Niccolini, Giovanni Battista, 441, 461
Nicoll, Allardyce, 42, 45
Nicomède (Corneille), 157
NicShuibhlaigh, Maire, 388
Nifty Miller (The Barker), 599
Night Music (Odets), 613
Night Over Taos (Anderson), 602, 613
Nikita (The Power of Darkness), 442, 459
Nikulina, Nadezhda A., 499
Nimrod Wildfire (Lion of the West), 537
Nina Leeds (Strange Interlude), 635
Noah (Obey), 397
Noah and the Flood (Anon.), 35, 36
Noble Heart, The (Lewes), 341
Nodier, Charles, 201
Nokes, James, 103, 110–111
Nora (A Doll's House), 470, 590
Northbrooke, John, 92
Norval (Douglas), 543
Novelli, Ermete, 442
Nurse (Romeo and Juliet), 397

O Mistress Mine (Rattigan), 608
Obey, André, 226
Obie Award, 664
Obnovlensky (The Ruble), 488
O'Casey, Sean, 325
Octoroon, The (Boucicault), 546, 551
Odéon, Paris, 150, 151, 152, 203, 210, 211, 228, 246, 653, 663
Odets, Clifford, 404, 541, 634
Odysseus, 33
Oedipus, 4, 5, 100, 314, 391, 409
Oedipus (Niccolini), 454
Oedipus (Seneca), 423
Oedipus at Colonus (Jessner production), 314
Oedipus Rex (Jessner production), 314
Oedipus Rex (Sophocles), 294, 412
Off-Broadway, 542, 664
Off-Off-Broadway, 542
Okhlopkov, Nikolai, 480
O-Lan (The Good Earth), 590
Old Vic Theatre, London, 325, 326, 397, 400, 403, 409, 410, 417
Oldenburg, Claes, 650
Oldfield, Anne, 94, 103, 111, 138, 575

Olga (The Three Sisters), 636, 638
Olivia, 360
Oliver Twist, 537
Olivier, Laurence, 305, 306, 325, 326, 397, 398, 403, 407, 408–409, 418, 420, 423, 542, 607
Olivo, 48
Olympic Theatre, London, 376
O'Neill, Eliza, 184, 322, 367
O'Neill, Eugene, 496, 523, 540, 541, 542, 590, 599
O'Neill, Maire, 388
Open Space, London, 430
Open Theatre, New York, 235, 543, 664
Opéra, Paris, 170
Ophelia, 114, 252, 339, 355, 360, 362, 419, 625
Oreste (Alfieri), 454, 472, 473
Oreste (Rucellai), 41
Oresteia (Aeschylus), 294
Orestes, 15, 179
Orgon (Tartuffe), 523, 528
Orlando (As You Like It), 403, 472
Orleneff, Paul, 575
Oroonoko, 116
O'Rourke, J. A., 388
Orphan, The (Otway), 101
Orpheus (John Hill), 122
Osborne, John, 325, 409, 415, 481
Osiris Passion Play, 3
Ostrovsky, Alexander, 475, 476, 484
Oswald (Ghosts), 442, 459
Oswyn (The Mourning Bride), 336
Othello, 77, 90, 104, 107, 113, 208, 329, 330, 331, 334, 353, 358, 366, 377, 398, 409, 413–414, 441, 442, 451, 454, 460, 472, 476, 489, 506, 516, 524–525, 537, 539, 550, 559, 560, 566, 567, 574, 579, 582, 599–601
Othello (Shakespeare), 206, 209, 328, 353, 357, 413, 415, 524, 536, 537, 541, 559, 574, 599–601, 632
O'Toole, Peter, 409
Otway, Thomas, 93, 112, 420
Our American Cousin (Taylor), 323, 360, 551, 570
Our Town (Wilder), 649
Ouspenskaya, Maria, 480, 510, 602, 604, 622
Outward Bound (Vane), 595
Overbury, Sir Thomas, 88
Ovid, 85

Pacuvius, 19, 22
Paderewski, 585

Padilla, 489
Paganini, 514
Page, Geraldine, 543, 622, 635
Pailleron, Edouard, 191
Painter's Portrait, The, or Counter-critique of the School for Wives, 155, 156
Palais Royal, Paris, 147, 155, 158
Pallenberg, Max, 260, 279, 295
Palme oder der Gekraenkte (Kornfeld), 299
Pantalone, 43, 51, 59, 87, 439, 440, 587
Panurgus, 21, 25, 26
Paolo (Francesca da Rimini), 454
Paradise Lost (Odets), 602
Paradise Now (Living Theatre), 653, 656
Paredes oyen, Las (Alarcón), 66
Paris, 21
Parisian Romance, A (Cazauran, Feuillet), 567
Parisienne, La (Becque), 403
Park Theatre, New York, 537, 544, 570
Parker, Joy, 418
Parmenon, 5, 13
Parnassus Plays (Anon.), 84
Parsons, Mrs. Clement, 141
Partage de Midi (Claudel), 246
Pasos, 64
Passion de Jeanne d'Arc (film), 234
Pasta, Mme., 340
Patchen, Kenneth, 663
Paulsen, Carl Andreas, 254
Pauvre Jacques, 199
Pavlov, Ivan, 425, 501, 632
Pavlova, 585
Payne, John Howard, 538
Peele, George, 75, 84
Peer Gynt (Ibsen), 409, 411, 472, 567, 622
Peg o' My Heart (Manners), 595
Pelagea Vlassova (The Mother), 315
Pelagia, 20
Pellico, Silvo, 454, 461, 466
Pellio, 20
Peñafiel, Damian Arias de, 66
Pepys, Samuel, 94, 97
Performance Group, The, New York, 235, 543
Pericles, 417
Pericles (Shakespeare), 419, 420
Perrucci, Andrea, 55
Persians, The (Aeschylus), 472
Peter Grimm, 583
Peter Ibbetson, 594
Peter Ibbetson (Du Maurier/Raphael), 592
Peters, Paul, 541

Petit-Bourbon, Paris, 43, 147, 155
Petito, Antonio, 470
Petrolini, Ettore, 442
Petruchio (*The Taming of the Shrew*), 489
Pezzana, Giacinta, 460
Phèdre, 170, 209, 252
Phèdre (Racine), 203, 247–248, 453
Phelps, Samuel, 323, 353, 367, 373
Philip, King of France (*King John*), 419
Philipe, Gérard, 152
Philipov, 486
Phillips, Augustine, 87
Philogenia (Pisani), 41
Phocas, 186
Phoenix Theatre, London, 324, 403, 418, 420
Phoenix Too Frequent, A (Fry), 419
Picasso, Pablo, 652
Piccolo Teatro, Milan, 443
Pierre (*Venice Preserved*), 130
Pierrot, 44, 150, 228, 246, 580
Pilgrimage to Parnassus (Anon.), 84
Pinciano, Alonzo Lopez, 68
Pinero, Arthur Wing, 324, 372, 470, 584
Pinter, Harold, 429
Pioneer Company, London, 324
Pirandello, Luigi, 152, 226, 230, 442, 443, 472, 473, 652
Pisani, Ugolino, 41
Piscator, Erwin, 260, 301, 307, 652, 653
Piscatorbuehne, Berlin, 260
Pisemsky, Alexander F., 488
Pisistratus, 3
Pitoëff, Georges, 152, 234, 240, 246
Pizarro (Sheridan), 140
Plague, The (Camus), see *State of Siege, The*
Planché, James Robinson, 337
Plato, 6, 11, 22, 27, 48, 96, 380 n., 557, 669
Platon Krechet (Korneichuk), 523
Plautus, 19, 20, 41, 42, 55, 390, 497
Plavilshchikov, Peter, 475
Play Actors Society, London, 324
Playboy of the Western World, The (Synge), 388
Players of the Prince of Orange, 146
Playhouse, Liverpool, 403
Pleasure of Honesty, The (Pirandello), 230
Pléiade, 146

Plessis, Mme., 484
Pliny, 336 n.
Plowright, Joan, 325, 326, 409
Pluchek, Valentin, 481
Plutarch, 5, 6, 12, 20, 21
Poder en el discreto, El (Vega), 66
Poel, William, 324
Pogodin, Nikolai, 507
Point Valaine (Coward), 607
Pollock, Frederick, 343
Pollux, Julius, 5, 6, 15, 89, 97
Polonius (*Hamlet*), 81, 400
Polus, 4, 5, 14, 15
Polyeucte (Corneille), 160, 200, 205
Polyhymnia, 31
Pompey, 19
Pompignan, Jean Jacques de, 177
Poor of New York, The (Boucicault), 546
Pope, Alexander, 103, 120
Pope, Thomas, 87
Porte-Saint-Martin, 150, 191
Porter, Mary, 115
Portia (*Merchant of Venice*), 95, 140, 360, 595
Portman, Eric, 639
Possessed, The (Dostoyevsky/Boleslavsky), 519
Powell, George, 115
Powell, Mrs., 338
Powell, William, 136
Power and the Glory, The (Greene), 418, 420, 422
Power of Darkness, The (Tolstoy), 211, 442, 459
Précieuses ridicules, Les (Molière), 155, 215
Premise, The, 651
Préville, 149
Priam (*Tiger at the Gates*), 613
Prince de Conti, 154
Prince Karl (Gunter), 567
Prince of Parthia, The (Godfrey), 536
Prince of Wales Theatre, London, 323
Princess Pazmezoglu (*Sweet Bird of Youth*), 635, 639
Princess Theatre, London, 323, 353, 360, 546, 558
Princess Turandot (Vakhtangov production), 480, 507
Prioress (*Herr Puntila and His Man Matti*), 320
Prisoner of Zenda, The (Hope), 570
Pritchard, Mrs. Hannah, 95, 138, 367, 576
Private Life of the Master Race, The, see *Fear and Misery of the Third Reich*
Private Lives (Coward), 408

Proclemer, Anna, 443
Proculus (*Brutus*), 178
Progne (Corrado), 41
Prometheus, 204, 472
Prompter, The, 95, 116–117
Prospero (*The Tempest*), 397, 403
Protagonist, 4
Proust, Marcel, 247
Provincetown Playhouse, 540
Prynne, William, 89, 92
Puck (*A Midsummer Night's Dream*), 360
Pulcinella, 43, 466, 470
Puntilla, see *Herr Puntilla and His Man Matti*
Purcell, Henry, 376
Purgatory (Yeats), 652
Pushkin, Alexander, 475, 485 n., 489 n.
Pygmalion (Shaw), 373, 422, 606, 611
Pylades, 21

Quayle, Anthony, 413
Queen (*King Richard II*), 420
Queen Constance (*King John*), 141, 340
Queen Elizabeth (Giacometti), 444
Queen Gertrude (*Hamlet*), 138
Queen Katherine (*King Henry VIII*), 140, 141
Queen of Carthage, 177
Queen's Men, 86
Queen's Theatre, Dublin, 387
Queen's Theatre, London, 403
Quem Quaeritis (Anon.), 34, 35
Quentin (*After the Fall*), 649
Questi Fantaami (De Filippo), 470
Quin, James, 94, 120, 131, 322, 327, 332, 559, 561
Quinault-Dufresne, Abraham Alexis, 148, 159, 367
Quinn, Arthur Hobson, 563
Quintilian, Marcus Fabius, 20, 21, 26, 89, 96, 97, 366
Quintero, Jose, 635, 639

Rabelais (Barrault), 246
Rachel, 150, 187, 207, 340, 341, 352, 381, 441, 444, 453, 484, 560
Racine, Jean, 147, 152, 159, 165, 166, 174, 175, 177, 201, 203, 205, 214, 248, 652
Rain (Colton/Randolph), 543
Rain (film), 599
Rainmaker, The (Nash), 638
Rains, Claude, 606
Raisin, 158
Rakitin (*A Month in the Country*), 403, 485

Ralph Roister Doister (Udall), 75
Ramirez, Miguel, 69
Randford, Maud, 387
Rapoport, I., 507
Raskolnikoff (*Crime and Punishment*), 397
Rasputin (Piscator production), 305
Rats, The (Hauptmann), 289
Rattigan, Terence, 415, 420
Raucourt, Mlle., 179
Reade, Charles, 360, 361
Realistic Theatre, Moscow, 480
Redemption (Tolstoy), 592
Redgrave, Colin, 492
Redgrave, Lynn, 402
Redgrave, Michael, 326, 402–403, 413
Redgrave, Vanessa, 402
Reed, John, 481
Regent's Company, 43, 59
Régnard, Jean-François, 57, 191
Régnier, François Joseph, 150, 190, 191, 196, 198
Regularis Concordia, 37–39
Rehan, Ada, 539, 587
Rehearsal, The (Duke of Buckingham), 112
Reicher, Emanuel, 258, 288
Reid, Hal, 599
Reinhardt, Max, 258, 259, 294–295, 307, 377, 615
Réjane, Gabrielle, 151, 214, 463, 585
Relapse, The, or, Virtue in Danger (Vanbrugh), 103, 419
Relph, George, 412
Renaud-Barrault Company, 246
Rennert, Hugo Albert, 66
Representation of Adam, The (Anon.), 39
Resurrection of Lazarus, The (Anon.), 71
Return from Parnassus, The (Anon.), 84–85
Reunion in Vienna (Sherwood), 606
Revolutionary Theatre, Moscow, 480
Reynolds, Joshua, 140, 336, 559
Rhapsodes, 6–8, 9
Rhinoceros (Ionesco), 409, 415, 481, 613
Rhodes, John, 97
Ribot, Théodule, 511
Ricci, Teodora, 440
Riccoboni, Antonio, 43, 59
Riccoboni, Antonio Francesco, 43, 59, 161, 261
Riccoboni, Elena, 59, 159
Riccoboni, Luigi, 43, 59, 60, 62, 63, 159, 440
Rice, Elmer, 540

Rich, Christopher, 94
Richardson, Ralph, 325, 326, 411, 413, 416, 417, 418
Richelieu, 146, 147, 155, 566
Richelieu (Bulwer-Lytton), 334
Riders to the Sea (Synge), 388
Riggs, Lynn, 602
Right to Live, The (Bracco), 459
Rimbaud, Arthur, 654
Ring Round the Moon (Anouilh), 418, 420
Rios, Nicolas de los, 65, 69
Rip Van Winkle, 537, 538, 551, 566, 583, 594
Rip Van Winkle (Boucicault), 546, 557, 571
Ristori, Adelaide, 199, 439, 441, 443–444, 451, 453, 454, 458, 465, 558
Ritchard, Cyril, 419
Rittner, Rudolf, 258, 289
Rivals, The (Sheridan), 538, 551
Robbers, The (Schiller), 257, 301
Robbins, Jerome, 630
Robert Macaire (*L'Auberge des Adrets*), 150, 196, 197, 200, 371
Robertson, Agnes, 538, 546
Robertson, Thomas William, 322, 323, 548
Robeson, Paul, 540, 541
Robins, Elizabeth, 324
Robinson, Edward G., 540, 606
Robinson, Lennox, 388
Robson, Flora, 325, 403
Rocket to the Moon (Odets), 613
Rodgers, Richard, 304
Rois, Les (Lemaître), 203
Rojas, Agustin de, 65, 69, 71 n.
Rolla (*Pizarro*), 336
Romains, Jules, 152, 240
Romanticism, 149, 150, 177, 204
Romeo, 94, 177, 193, 333, 345, 379, 394, 397, 398, 400, 408, 409, 451, 484, 489, 550
Romeo and Juliet (Shakespeare), 397, 408, 417, 419, 422, 430, 472, 558, 571, 638
Romeo and Juliet (film), 593
Roots (Wesker), 325
Rosalind (*As You Like It*), 260, 345, 417
Roscius (Quintus Roscius Gallus), 19, 20, 21, 23, 24, 25, 29, 42, 77, 83, 91, 100, 102, 137 n., 150, 439, 559
Rosencrantz and Guildenstern Are Dead (Stoppard), 472
Ross, David, 636

Rossi, Cesare, 441, 442, 459, 465
Rossi, Ernesto, 441, 451, 484, 493, 617
Rostand, Edmond, 151, 191, 203
Rostova, Mira, 664, 668
Rouché, Jacques, 225, 228, 231
Rout, The (John Hill), 122
Rover, The (Behn), 109, 116
Rovetta, Gerolamo, 442
Rowe, Nicholas, 536
Roxane, 172
Royal Court Theatre, Berlin, 256, 257, 279
Royal Court Theatre, London, 324, 325, 360, 390, 409, 412, 421, 436
Royal Sardinian Company, 444, 451
Royal Shakespeare Theatre Company, London, 326, 422, 423, 430, 432, 481
Royal Theatre Copenhagen, 377
Ruble, The (Fedotov), 488
Rucellai, Giovanni, 41
Rudersdorff, Erminia, 567
Rudolf (*The Prisoner of Zenda*), 570
Rueda, Lope de, 64, 66, 67, 68
Rueda, Mariana de, 66
Ruggeri, Ruggero, 442
Russell, George (A. E.), 387, 388
Rutherford, Margaret, 420
Rutland House, 92
Ruy Blas, 196, 197
Ruy Blas (Hugo), 196
Ruzzante, 42
Ryabov, P. Y., 489

Sacchi company, 440
Sachs, Hans, 36, 254
Sacre rappresentazioni, 36
Sadler's Wells, London, 323, 353
Sadovsky, 484
Saint-Denis, Michel, 397, 403
Saint-Germain, François-Victor de, 214
Saint Joan (Shaw), 613, 665
Saint Joan of the Stockyards (Brecht), 665
Sainte-Albine, Pierre Rémond de, 96, 122–123, 153, 161, 175, 261
Salacrou, Armand, 226, 230
Salathiel Pavy, 82, 83
Salem Scudder (*The Octoroon*), 551
Salome (Wilde), 442
Salome (film), 590
Salvation Nell (Sheldon), 584
Salvini, Tommaso, 214, 366, 367, 381, 439, 441, 444, 453, 454, 463, 465, 489, 490, 493,

539, 558, 566, 567, 579, 582, 617
Samaras, Lucas, 650
Samarin, I. V., 489, 499 n.
Samson, Joseph Isidore, 150, 191, 195, 196
San Francisco Mime Troupe, 44
Sandford, Samuel, 103, 109, 115
Sant'Angelo Theatre, 440
Sarcey, Francisque, 203, 284
Sardou, Victorien, 151, 466, 470, 548
Saroyan, William, 541, 629
Sartre, Jean-Paul, 226
Satin (*The Lower Depths*), 485
Satin Slipper, The (Claudel), 246
Satiromastix (Dekker), 82
Satonville (*Georges Dandin*), 485 n., 486, 487 n.
Saturae, 19
Satyr play, 3
Satyrus, 5
Sauer, Oscar, 258
Saul (Alfieri), 440, 453, 454
Saunderson, Mary, see Mrs. Thomas Betterson
Savina, Maria, 484, 493
Savoy Theatre, London, 324
Saxe-Meiningen, George II, Duke of, 151, 210, 257, 258, 259, 284–285, 287, 292, 353, 476
Scala, Flaminio, 42, 43, 52
Scapin (*Fourberies de Scapin, Les*), 250, 251, 252
Scapino, 43
Scaramouche, 43, 154, 330
Schall und Rauch, 294
Schechner, Richard, 235, 635
Schildkraut, Joseph, 259
Schildkraut, Rudolf, 259
Schiller, Friedrich, 255, 256, 257, 259, 268, 269 n., 278, 289, 290, 292, 293, 294, 301, 318, 441, 444
Schlegel, August Wilhelm, 257
Schlumberger, Jean, 216
Schoenemann, Johann Friedrich, 254, 255
School for the Art of the Theatre, Florence, 377
School for Scandal, The (Goldsmith), 377, 397, 403
School for Wives Criticized, see *Critique de l'école des femmes*
School of Elocution, see *Conservatoire*
Schopenhauer, Arthur, 305
Schreyvogel, Joseph, 257
Schroeder, Friedrich Ludwig, 255, 256, 258, 276–277, 279, 290, 291, 292
Schroeder, Sophie, 255, 276

Schweik (*Good Soldier Schweik, The*), 260
Scofield, Paul, 326, 417–418, 422, 424, 430, 542
Scop, 34
Scott, Clement, 353
Screens, The (Genet), 429, 437
Scribe, Eugène, 150
Sea Beast, The (film), 593
Sea Gull, The (Chekhov), 418, 420, 477, 479, 496, 607
Second City, Chicago, 641, 651
Second Man, The (Behrman), 606
Secret Service (Gillette), 563
Seide (*Mahomet*), 178
Seige of Rhodes, The (Davenant), 92
Sejanus (Jonson), 78
Semi-detached (Turner), 415
Semiramis, 176
Seneca, 19, 20, 41, 75, 423, 472, 473
Senora Carrar's Rifles (Brecht), 314
Sentimental Journey (film), 422
Sergius Saranoff (*Arms and the Man*), 397
Serpent, The (van Itallie), 664
Servant of Two Masters, A (Goldoni), 523
Seven Sisters, 595
Seydelmann, Karl, 257
Shakespeare Memorial Theatre, Stratford, England, 325, 403, 409, 413, 417, 418, 419, 420, 422, 423, 430
Shakespeare, William, 36, 41, 45, 65, 75, 76, 77, 78–79, 82, 85, 86, 93, 94, 96, 104, 105, 107, 112, 119, 120, 121, 122, 131, 133, 134, 135, 136, 140, 149, 165, 178, 179, 202, 204, 207, 209, 216, 243, 246, 255, 256, 259, 265, 267, 277, 278, 282, 294, 298, 299, 306, 318, 321, 323, 324, 325, 326, 327, 328, 337, 343, 346, 348, 355, 356, 357, 358, 360, 361, 366, 370, 371, 372, 373, 374, 375, 376, 382, 390, 395, 397, 398, 400, 403, 409, 411, 413, 414, 415, 416, 418, 419, 421, 426, 432, 433, 438, 441, 442, 444, 445, 447, 451, 459, 460, 463, 469, 472, 475, 497, 498, 532, 536, 538, 539, 542, 547, 557, 558, 561, 562, 563, 568, 570, 571, 572, 573, 579, 586, 587, 589, 592, 595, 600, 601, 609, 613, 616, 618, 624, 626, 634, 649, 657
Shanghai Gesture, The (film), 599

Shari, Bill, 654, 656
Shaughraun, The (Boucicault), 546, 549
Shaw, George Bernard, 152, 203, 216, 259, 324, 325, 353, 360, 370–371, 372, 390, 391, 421, 442, 466, 540, 567, 584, 606, 611, 618, 665
Shaw, Irwin, 541
Shchepkin, Michael, 476, 481–482, 499 n., 525
Shearer, Norma, 593
Sheldon, Edward, 584, 592, 599
Shelley, Percy Bysshe, 327, 385
Sheridan, Richard Brinsley, 93, 94, 409, 553
Sherlock Holmes (Gillette), 563
Shields, Arthur, 388
Shilovsky, K. S., 486
Shubert brothers, 539
Shumsky, S. V., 482, 489
Shylock (*The Merchant of Venice*), 95, 120, 257, 326, 329, 331, 341, 361, 371, 403, 451, 559, 562–563, 587, 613
Siddons, Sally, 141
Siddons, Sarah, 66, 93, 95–96, 139–141, 322, 326, 327, 333, 336, 337, 338, 339, 340, 367, 443, 445, 446, 537, 557, 559, 560, 589, 626
Siddons, William, 140
Sign of the Cross, The (Barrett), 599
Sills, Paul, 641
Simonov, Reuben, 481
Simonson, Lee, 540
Simpson, N. F., 325
Sinclair, Arthur, 388
Sindaco del Rione Sanità, Il (De Filippo), 471
Singer, John, 87
Sir Courtly Nice, 109
Sir Fopling Flutter (*The Man of Mode*), 103
Sir Giles Overreach (*A New Way to Pay Old Debts*), 328, 331, 558, 562
Sir Harcourt Courtley (*London Assurance*), 549
Sir Martin Marr-all, 110
Sir Oliver Surface (*The School for Scandal*), 377
Sir Peter Teazle (*The School for Scandal*), 377
Sir Thomas More (*A Man for All Seasons*), 418, 421–422
Sir Toby Belch (*Twelfth Night*), 409
Six Characters in Search of an Author (Pirandello), 649
Skinner, Cornelia Otis, 587
Skinner, Otis, 539, 587, 614
Sklar, George, 541

Sklar, Roberta, 664
Slavin, Lev, 507
Sleeping Prince, The (Rattigan), 415
Sly, William, 87
Smerdiakov (Les Frères Karamazov), 216, 225, 228, 229, 232
Smith, Art, 541
Smith, Maggie, 326, 409
Smith, Winifred, 42, 44
Sociétaires, 147, 149, 178, 191, 245
Socrates, 6, 7, 8, 27
Sofonisba (Trissino), 41
Sokoloff, Vladimir, 259
Solano, Agustin, 69, 70, 71, 72
Sollogub, Fyodor, 486
Solon, 3
Soloviova, Vera, 518
Somi, Leone di, 44
Sonnenthal, Adolph, 257
Sophocles, 3, 4, 5, 15, 16, 459, 542
Sordi, Alberto, 443
Sorex, 21
Sorge, Reinhard, 259
Sorma, Agnes, 259
Sothern, Edward Askew, 323, 371 n., 551, 570
Sothern, Edward Hugh, 539, 540, 570–571
Sotties, 36, 153
Southerne, Thomas, 140
Sparkish (The Country Wife), 109
Spiegelberg, Christian, 254
Spolin, Viola, 641, 668
Spring Happening, A (Happening), 651
Springtime for Henry (Levy), 403
Spurt of Blood, see Jet of Blood
Squarzina, Luigi, 443, 472
Stage Manager (Our Town), 649
Standing, Guy, 597
Stanislavsky, Konstantin S., 243, 246, 251, 258, 284, 295, 302, 304, 308, 318, 403–408, 426, 428, 434–435, 451, 454, 471, 475, 476, 477–478, 479, 480, 481, 484–485, 487 n., 488, 493, 495, 496, 498, 499, 500, 501, 504, 505, 506, 507, 508, 509, 510, 512, 518, 519, 523, 524, 525, 526, 527, 528, 529, 530, 531, 532, 534, 541, 543, 602, 604, 613, 615, 617, 618, 620, 622, 624, 627, 628, 629, 630, 631, 632, 640, 650, 651, 660, 664, 667
Stanley, Kim, 543, 622, 623, 636

Stanley Kowalski (A Streetcar Named Desire), 472
Stapleton, Maureen, 630
Starr, Frances, 539, 577
State of Siege, The (Barrault production), 246
Statilius, 25
Steele, Sir Richard, 97
Stein, Gertrude, 652
Stella Adler Theatre School, New York, 602
Stendhal, Henri, 215
Stephens, Robert, 326, 409
Stevens, Ashton, 593
Stevens, Emily, 614
Stevens, Roger, 607
Stevenson, Robert Louis, 572
Sticotti, Antonio Fabio, 123, 162 n.
Stoddart, James Henry, 567
Stone Guest (Pushkin), 489 n.
Stoppard, Tom, 472
Straight, Beatrice, 519
Strange Interlude (O'Neill), 606, 635
Stranger, The (Kotzebue), 140, 141, 537
Strasberg, Lee, 187, 485, 510, 541, 542, 607, 621–623, 635, 636, 637, 638, 639, 640
Stratford Jubilee, 131
Strato, 13
Stratocles, 21
Straub, Agnes, 260
Strauss, Richard, 294
Streetcar Named Desire, A (Williams), 472, 543
Strehler, Giorgio, 443
Strindberg, August, 235, 258, 259, 292, 518, 540
Stubbes, Philip, 92
Sturm und Drang, 256
Sturz, Helferich Peter, 136
Success Story (Lawson), 602
Sudermann, Hermann, 203, 441, 466
Sulerzhitsky, Leopold, 506, 518
Sullivan, Barry, 341, 370
Summer and Smoke (Williams), 635, 639, 640
Swan Theatre, London, 76
Sweet Bird of Youth (Williams), 543, 635, 639
Symbolism, 151, 507
Symons, Arthur, 570
Synge, John Millington, 152, 325, 386, 388

Taganka Theatre, 481
Tairov, Alexander, 259, 479
Talma, François-Joseph, 149, 150, 152, 159, 177, 178–179, 200, 201, 209, 274 n., 292,

335, 337, 350, 351, 352, 354, 357, 406, 441, 451, 453, 548, 624
Taming of the Shrew, The (Shakespeare), 78, 79–80, 607, 613
Tamiroff, Akim, 404, 480
Tandy, Jessica, 543
Tarasova, Alla, 479
Tarkington, Booth, 606
Tarleton, Richard, 76, 87
Tartaglia, 440
Tartuffe, 147, 193, 196, 348, 528
Tartuffe (Molière), 155, 205, 478, 523, 528
Taubman, Howard, 542
Tauriscus, 25
Taylor, Baron, 201
Taylor, Joseph, 78, 97
Taylor, Laurette, 543, 595, 606, 610
Taylor, Tom, 360, 361
Teahouse of the August Moon, The (Patrick), 629
Tearle, Godfrey, 418
Teatr Polski, Poznan, 529
Teatr Stary, Cracow, 529
Teatr 13 Rzedow, Opole, see Theatre Laboratory, Wroclaw
Teatro San Ferdinando, Naples, 470
Teatro Stablile, Genoa, 443
Teatro Umoristico I de Filippo, Il, 470
Teatro Valle, Rome, 454
Tegeus-Chromis (A Phoenix Too Frequent), 419
Tempest, The (Shakespeare), 423, 568
Ten Days That Shook the World (Lyubimov production), 481
Terence, 19, 20, 41, 57
Terriss, William, 324
Terry, Ellen, 324, 353, 360, 367, 370, 376, 397, 566, 585, 586, 596, 606, 612
Terry, Kate, 397
Terry, Marion, 398
Terry, Megan, 664
Tessero, Adelaide, 460
Thackeray, William Makepeace, 367
Thalia, 559
Thalia Theatre, New York, 444
Theater-am-Schiffbauerdamm, Berlin, 260
Theater in dem Redoutensaal, Vienna, 294
Theatralische Bibliotek, 261
Theatre, The, London, 64, 76
Théâtre Alfred Jarry, Paris, 234

Théâtre Antoine, Paris, 210
Théâtre Athénée, Paris, 152, 240
Théâtre d'Art, Paris, 151
Théâtre de France, 152, 246, 481
Théâtre de la Foire, 228
Théâtre de la Renaissance, Paris, 151
Théâtre de la République, Paris, 179
Théâtre de L'Oeuvre, Paris, 324
Théâtre des Arts, Paris, 151, 216, 225, 228, 231
Théâtre des Funambules, Paris, 150
Théâtre du Cartel, Paris, 231
Théâtre du Marais, Paris, 146, 147, 155, 158
Théâtre du Vieux Colombier, Paris, 152, 216, 217–218, 225, 226, 230, 231, 240, 541
Théâtre Français, Paris, 147, 148, 149, 150, 151, 152, 154, 169, 170, 174, 179, 191, 203, 210, 212, 215, 245, 246, 254, 431, 442, 589
Théâtre Français de la Rue de Richelieu, Le, see *Théâtre de la République*
Theatre Guild, New York, 540, 541, 590 n., 606, 607, 613, 622
Théâtre Italien, Paris, 170
Theatre Laboratory, Wroclaw, Poland, 529, 535
Théâtre Libre, Paris, 151, 210, 211, 213, 217, 258, 324
Théâtre Marigny, Paris, 152, 246
Théâtre National Populaire (*T.N.P.*) 152
Theatre of Cruelty, 152, 235, 326, 423, 425, 430–438
Theatre of Satire, Moscow, 481
Theatre Royal, Bristol, 360
Theatre Union, New York, 541, 542
Theatre Workshop (Littlewood), 436
Theobald, Lewis, 133
Theodora, 20
Theodora (Sardou), 466
Theodore, Luke, 655
Theodorus, 4, 5
Theophrastus, 24
There Shall Be No Night (Sherwood), 607, 608
Therese (Payne), 538
Thérèse Racquin (Zola), 465, 574
Thespis, 3, 4, 150, 559
Thettalus, 4
Thief, The (Bernstein), 575

Thimig, Hans, 257, 259
Thimig, Helen, 257, 259
Thimig, Hermann, 257, 259
Thimig, Hugo, 257, 259
Thompson, Steve, 661
Thorndike, Sybil, 325, 420
Thouvenin (*Denise*), 196
Thrasymachus, 12
Three Black Cloaks, 567
Three Musketeers, The, 234
Three-Penny Opera, see *Dreigroschenoper*
Three Plays for a Negro Theatre (Torrence), 540
Three Sisters, The (Chekhov), 397, 403, 479, 485, 496, 543, 623, 635, 636, 637
Thunder Rock (Ardrey), 403, 613
Thyestes, 14, 32
Thyestes (Seneca), 472, 473
Tieck, Ludwig, 272 n., 328
Tiger at the Gates (Giraudoux), 403, 613
Tiny Alice (Albee), 397
Tiroff, Jimmy, 661
Titus Andronicus, 409, 413
Titus Andronicus (Shakespeare), 413, 437 n.
Tlepolemus, 4
Toller, Ernst, 259, 540
Tolstoy, Alexei, 478, 485
Tolstoy, Leo, 151, 210, 211, 258, 442, 459, 463, 475, 485, 509, 592, 601
Tom (*The Glass Menagerie*), 649
Tone, Franchot, 541
Tonight We Improvise (Pirandello), 652
Toporkov, Vasili O., 478, 523
Torn, Rip, 638
Torrence, Ridgely, 540
Touchstone (*As You Like It*), 77
Tour de Nesle, La (Caligula), 201
Tovarich (Deval/Sherwood), 443
Tovstanogov, Georg, 481
Towneley plays, 35
Towse, John Ranken, 537
Toy Theatre, Boston, 540
Travers, Henry, 611
Treasure of the Sierra Madre (film), 599
Tree, Ellen, 537, 545
Tree, Herbert Beerbohm, 321, 324, 360, 367, 371–376, 592
Treplev (*The Sea Gull*), 420, 479
Tressel (*Richard III*), 557
Tribuene, Die, 260

Trissino, Giovanni Giorgio, 41
Tritagonist, 4
Triumph, The (Bracco), 459
Trofimov (*The Cherry Orchard*), 398
Troilus and Cressida (Shakespeare), 79
Trommeln in der Nacht (Brecht), 307
Tropes, 34, 38
Troupe de Monsieur, 155
True Light Among the Shadows (Perrucci), 55
Truffaldino (*A Servant of Two Masters*), 440, 523
Tsar Fyodor (Alexei Tolstoy), 478
Tully, 87
Turandot (Gozzi), 440
Turgenev, Ivan, 459, 475, 509
Turlupin, 146, 153
Tuzenbach (*The Three Sisters*), 403
Twelfth Night (Shakespeare), 403, 571
Tyler, Royall, 536
Tynan, Kenneth, 326, 409
Tyndarus, 12

Ubu Roi (Jarry), 152, 234
Ulric, Lenore, 577, 583
Uncle Harry (Job), 403
Uncle Tom's Cabin (Aiken), 323
Uncle Vanya (Chekhov), 403, 409, 485, 529, 613
Underhill, Cave, 103
Union Square Theatre, New York, 567
Unruh, Fritz von, 259
Unzelmann, Frau, 290
Ure, Mary, 419
Uriel Acosta (Gutzkow), 485
US (Peter Brook production), 423
Ustromskaya, Maria, 486

Vaca, Jusepa, 65
Vakhtangov, Eugene, 295, 440, 479–480, 506–507, 518, 527, 530, 541, 617, 618, 622, 650
Vakhtangov Theatre, Moscow, 481, 507
Valency, Maurice, 607
Valentin, Kurt, 307
Valentine (*Love for Love*), 397
Valentino, Rudolf, 415
Valets de Molière, see Comic servants
Valli, Romolo, 443
Vampires, Les (Taylor/Nodier), 201
Van Doren, 228
Van Gyseghem, André, 501
van Itallie, 664

Vanbrugh, Sir John, 94, 103, 419
Vanhove, 274 n.
Varaldo, Alessandro, 462, 463
Varlamov, 527
Vedrenne, J. E., 371, 390
Vega, Lope de, 41, 65, 66
Veidt, Conrad, 259
Velázquez, Elena Osorio, 65
Velázquez, Jerónimo, 65
Velten, Johannes, 254
Venice Preserved (Otway), 130, 141, 418, 420
Venus Observed (Fry), 409
Verbruggen, Jack, 95, 115–116
Verbruggen, Mrs. John, see Mountfort, Mrs. William
Verfremdungseffekt, 304, 308–311, 530, 634
Verfuehrung, Die (Kornfeld), 299
Verga, Giovanni, 472
Verlaine, Paul, 151
Verrato, 48
Vershinin (The Three Sisters), 397, 485
Vestri, Angelo, 463
Vestris, Eliza Lucy, 323, 546, 547
Vezin, Hermann, 367
Vicar of Wakefield, The (Wills), 360
Victims of Duty (Ionesco), 664
Viet Rock (Terry), 664
Vieux Colombier, see Théâtre du Vieux Colombier
Vikings, The (Ibsen), 376
Vilar, Jean, 152
Vildrac, Charles, 216
Villiers, de, 157
Villon, François, 225
Virginius (Knowles), 334, 357, 537
Viriate, 172
Visconti, Luchino, 443, 472
Vishnevsky, Alexander, 479
Visit, The (Dürrenmatt), 422, 607–608, 609
Vitalis, 37
Vitrac, Roger, 234, 235
Vitruvius, 42
Viviani, Raffaele, 442, 472
Volkis, Mme., 484
Volksbuehne, see Freie Volksbuehne
Volpone, 226, 231
Volpone (Jonson), 606, 613
Voltaire, 148, 149, 161, 165, 170, 174, 175, 176, 178, 186, 201, 255, 349
Volumnia (Coriolanus), 140, 314
Voysey Inheritance, The (Granville-Barker), 390

Voznesensky, Andrei, 481

Wagner, Richard, 151, 258, 324, 375
Wahle, Julius, 292
Waiting for Godot (Beckett), 649
Waiting for Lefty (Odets), 542, 613
Walker, George, 540
Wallach, Eli, 622, 630
Wallack, James William, 537, 538
Wallack, Lester, 546
Wallenstein (Schiller), 257, 282
Walpole, Horace, 576
Warbeck (The Witch of Edmonton), 403
Ward, Douglas Turner, 541
Ward, Sarah, 140
Warfield, David, 539, 577, 583, 593, 614
Warner, Mary, 555
Warren, William, 537
Washington Square Players, 540
Waters, Ethel, 541
Way of the World, The (Congreve), 418, 420
Wayne, David, 622
Weavers, The (Hauptmann), 204, 294
Webster, Benjamin, 323, 367
Webster, John, 88
Wedekind, Frank, 259
Wegener, Paul, 259
Weigel, Helene, 260, 307, 314, 634
Weill, Kurt, 304
Weimar Theatre, 256, 258, 271 n., 274 n., 282, 283, 289, 290, 291, 292, 293, 301, 326
Weiss, Peter, 423, 430
Weisse, Christian Felix, 255
Welles, Orson, 542
Werfel, Franz, 259, 294
Werner (Byron), 555
Wesker, Arnold, 325
Western Lass, The (D'Urfey), 112
Western, Lucille, 584
Westley, Helen, 540
Westminster Theatre, 417
When We Dead Awaken (Ibsen), 657
Whipper, Leigh, 541
White Devil, The (Webster), 88
Whitlock, Elizabeth, 537
Whitman, Walt, 388, 544, 545, 557
Who's Afraid of Virginia Woolf? (Albee), 543
Widow Begbick (A Man's a Man), 314

Widowers' Houses (Shaw), 324, 371
Wife, The (Overbury), 88
Wigan, Alfred, 353, 360
Wignell, Thomas, 537
Wild Rose, The (Nemirovich-Danchenko), 496
Wilde, Oscar, 397, 442, 584
Wilkes, Robert, 94, 95, 100, 103, 113
Wilkes, Thomas, 96
Wille, Bruno, 259, 289
William Tell (Knowles), 334
Williams, Bert, 540
Williams, Harcourt, 397
Williams, Tennessee, 542, 595, 635
Williams, William Carlos, 652
Williamson, Nicol, 325
Wills, W. G., 353, 360
Wilmore (The Rover), 116
Wilson, Georges, 152
Wilson, Robert, 87
Willy Loman (Death of a Salesman), 607
Wingless Victory, The (Anderson), 403
Winter Garden Theatre, New York, 546, 551, 558
Winter, William, 538, 580
Winters, Shelley, 622
Winter's Tale, The (Shakespeare), 360
Witch of Edmonton, The (Ford, Dekker, Rowley), 403
Witness for the Prosecution, 629
Witwoud (The Way of the World), 420
Woffington, Margaret, 95, 131, 138, 367, 574, 575
Wolff, Pius Alexander, 257, 291
Wolff, Theodor, 258
Wolfit, Donald, 410
Wolsey (King Richard II), 374
Wolter, Charlotte, 257, 291
Woman Killed with Kindness, A (Heywood), 86
Woollcott, Alexander, 606
Wordsworth, William, 327
World We Live In, The (Capek), 602
Worms, Hippolyte, 200, 212
Woyzek (Büchner), 314
WPA (Works Progress Administration), 641
Wycherley, William, 93, 109

Xerxes, 204

Yale Drama School, 602, 652, 653
Yeats, William Butler, 324, 325, 377, 385–386, 387, 388, 652

Yefremov, Oleg, 481
Yegor Bulychev (Gorky), 507
Yepikhodov (*The Cherry Or-
chard*), 478, 523
Yermolova, Maria, 476, 484,
490, 493, 617
Yorick (Howell), 539
York plays, 35, 39, 40
Young Actors Company, Holly-
wood, 641
Young, Charles Mayne, 322, 343
Young Fashion (*The Relapse*),
419

Young Germany movement,
257
Young, Stark, 441, 442, 540
Youngest Germany Movement,
258
Yurka, Blanche, 606
Yuzhin, A. I., 486
Yvette (*Mother Courage and
Her Children*), 315

Zabaleta, Juan de, 72, 73
Zacconi, Ermete, 442, 459–460

Zakhava, B. E., 507
Zanni, 43, 49, 87
Zanoni, 440
Zara (*The Mourning Bride*),
115, 140
Zarabanda, 66, 72
Zavadsky, Yuri, 481, 518
Zeffirelli, Franco, 409, 443
Zen, 431, 640
Zetterling, Mai, 420
Zola, Emile, 151, 202, 209, 210,
258, 293, 324, 574
Zoppino, 48